Documents of the
Coronado Expedition, 1539–1542

Published in cooperation with the
William P. Clements Center for Southwest Studies

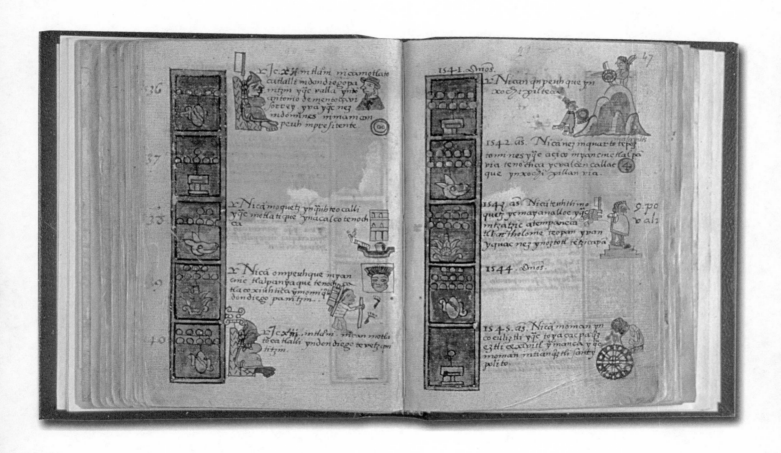

Documents of the
Coronado Expedition, 1539–1542

*"They Were Not Familiar with His Majesty,
nor Did They Wish to Be His Subjects"*

Edited, Translated, and Annotated by

RICHARD FLINT
and
SHIRLEY CUSHING FLINT

SOUTHERN METHODIST UNIVERSITY PRESS
Dallas

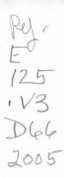
ALSO BY RICHARD FLINT:

Great Cruelties Have Been Reported: The 1544 Investigation of the Coronado Expedition

Library of Congress Cataloging-in-Publication Data

Documents of the Coronado expedition, 1539-1542 : "they were not familiar with His Majesty, nor did they wish to be his subjects" / edited, translated, and annotated by Richard Flint and Shirley Cushing Flint— 1st ed.
    p. cm.
   English translations and annotations, with complete transcriptions of the Spanish, Italian, and Nahuatl originals.
  Includes bibliographical references and index.
  ISBN 0-87074-496-8 (alk. paper)
  1. Coronado, Francisco Vâsquez de, 1510-1554. 2. Southwest, New—Discovery and exploration—Spanish—Sources. 3. Southwest, New—History—To 1848—Sources. I. Flint, Richard, 1946- II. Flint, Shirley Cushing.

E125.V3D66 2005
979'.01—dc22

                          2004062562

Jacket art: *Obsidian Mountain* by Douglas Johnson
Jacket and text design by Tom Dawson

Printed in the United States of America on acid-free paper
10 9 8 7 6 5 4 3 2 1

Frontispiece. Folios 46v and 47r of the *Codex Aubin*, "Chronicle of Mexican History to the year 1576, continued to 1607." Add MSS 31219. Reproduced with permission of the Library of the British Museum.

*A los escribanos, tanto conocidos como desconocidos, que
redactaron estos documents y otros innumerables, gracias,
mil gracias. Sin ellos no habría casi ninguna historia de
la conquista de las Américas ni otros muchos asuntos.*

A thousand thanks to the *escribanos,* both known and unknown,
who drafted these documents and countless others. Without them,
there would be nearly no history of the conquest of the
Americas or many other subjects.

Contents

Illustrations

Maps

Figures

Documents of the
Coronado Expedition, 1539–1542

General Introduction

ost of what is known about the Coronado expedition of 1539–42 derives from documents that were prepared prior to, in the course of, or within two decades or so immediately following the events of the *entrada* itself. There are about two hundred such documents that shed light on the expedition, its motivations, its outcomes, and its aftermath. The surviving documents do not speak with a single voice, though they often bear a "family resemblance." Not infrequently, the patchwork of documentary evidence about the expedition is confusing, ambiguous, and seemingly in conflict internally. Nevertheless, from a sufficient distance the contradictory details blur into each other, and a broad outline of the enterprise can be pieced together. That outline, though lacking the intricacy of detail necessary for deep understanding, can serve to organize the documentary sources from which it descends.

In an atmosphere already supercharged with expectations of future lives as overlords in the New World, the news brought to the Ciudad de México in 1536 by four survivors of the Pánfilo de Narváez expedition set anticipation ablaze for many Europeans. Álvar Núñez Cabeza de Vaca and his three companions had returned to the Spanish colonial world after six years among the Indians of what is now southern Texas and northern Mexico. Besides a stirring tale of captivity and escape, they reported having been told repeatedly about a land farther north of their travels where there were "*pueblos* with many people and very large houses," the inhabitants of which "wear cotton shirts" and where there were "many very fine turquoises" and "metalworking."[1]

That enticing prospect quickly led to intense competition for the right to mount a privately financed expedition to take control of the wealthy new land, or Tierra Nueva. Five powerful rivals vied for the Spanish king's permission to make the *entrada*: Viceroy Antonio de Mendoza; the conqueror of the Mexica capital of Tenochtitlan, Hernán Cortés; the former president of the *audiencia* in the Ciudad de México, Nuño Beltrán de Guzmán; the *adelantado* of Guatemala, Pedro de Alvarado; and one of the principal conquistadores of Peru, Hernando de Soto. Litigation over the issue was ongoing even after Mendoza launched his expedition to Tierra Nueva late in 1539 (see especially Documents 4, 7, 18, and 20).

Even before the king and the Consejo de Indias granted Mendoza formal license to organize an expedition, the viceroy was laying plans to send reconnaissance parties northward to verify the Cabeza de Vaca party's reports. After unsuccessful negotiations to engage Andrés Dorantes, one of the survivors, to lead such a reconnaissance (see Document 4), Mendoza settled on a Franciscan friar, Marcos de Niza, to be accompanied by Esteban de Dorantes, a black slave who was also one of the survivors.

Marcos and Esteban left the Ciudad de México late in 1538 in the company of the newly appointed governor of Nueva Galicia, Francisco Vázquez de Coronado, a favorite in the viceroy's court (for Vázquez de Coronado's earlier career, see Documents 1–5). By September of the following year, Marcos and Vázquez de Coronado were back in the viceregal capital with electrifying news (see Document 6). In effect, the friar's lengthy formal report confirmed that the place told about by the Narváez expedition survivors existed; it was a place called Cíbola. Its people had proven unreceptive to Spanish overtures, however, having killed the king's first messenger, Esteban.

Within days of making his report to the viceroy, Marcos's news and the many extrapolations and conjectures based on it were the hottest topics in Nueva España (see especially Document 8). In short order, the viceroy named Vázquez de Coronado to lead a full-fledged, armed expedition (see Documents 9 and 10). Arrangements for financing such a large enterprise and purchasing the necessary supplies and equipment began immediately (see Documents 11, 20, 31–33). Volunteers for the expedition, dominated by Mexican Indians, were dispatched in small groups late in 1539 to a rendezvous in Compostela, the capital of Nueva Galicia on the Pacific coast (see Documents 12 and 13).

Dodging complaints that his Cíbola *entrada* was depriving Nueva España of a vital defensive force, Mendoza formally launched both land and sea components of the expedition early in 1540 (see Documents 14–17). Although sea and land units were supposed to rendezvous in the vicinity of Cíbola, geographical reality made that impossible, so by early fall the land expedition was proceeding without the expected support of sea-borne supplies.

On July 7, 1540, according to the Julian calendar, an advance party of the large ground expedition arrived within sight of the first *ciudad* of Cíbola, probably the ancestral Zuni pueblo of Hawikku in what is now west-central New Mexico.[2] As required by royal ordinance, Captain General Francisco Vázquez de Coronado

> sent *maestre de campo* don García López, fray Daniel, fray Luis, and Fernando Bermejo some distance ahead with some horsemen, so that the Indians might see them. [I ordered them] to tell [the Indians] that [the purpose of] our coming was not to do them injury but to protect them in the name of the emperor, our lord.

The *requerimiento* was made intelligible to the natives of that land through an interpreter.[3]

The *requerimiento* was a formal demand that peoples of the New World submit to the rule of the Spanish king and accept missionaries to teach them the rudiments of the Roman Catholic faith. The exact wording of the summons was specified by royal *cédula*. The text concluded with this ultimatum:

> If, [however], you do not do [what I ask] or you maliciously delay [doing] it, I assure you that, with the help of God, I will attack you mightily. I will make war [against] you everywhere and in every way I can. And I will subject you to the yoke and obedience of the Church and His Majesty. I will take your wives and children, and I will make them slaves. As such, I will sell and dispose of them as His Majesty will order. I will take your property. I will do all the harm and damage to you that I can, [treating you] as vassals who do not obey and refuse to accept their lord and resist and oppose him.
>
> I declare that the deaths and injuries that occur as a result of this would be your fault and not His Majesty's, nor ours, nor that of these *caballeros* who have come with me.[4]

It is unimaginable that the people of Hawikku understood the specifics of the demands relayed to them by the interpreter. The text is replete with concepts and terms that lacked equivalents in the Zuni world of that day, which rendered it completely unintelligible in its details. The insistence of the strangers that they be allowed to enter the town must have been clear enough, though. As was the Cíbolans' reply: "they refused to come to peace, but instead showed themselves to be angry."[5] In their anger, "they wounded Hernando Bermejo's horse. And with an arrow they pinned together the skirts of the habit of Father fray Luis, who was an associate of the lord bishop of México."[6]

Recalling a similar confrontation that took place several months later in the valley of the Río de Tiguex in modern central New Mexico, Vázquez de Coronado, through his attorney, indicated that the Indians had replied "that they were not familiar with his majesty nor did they wish to be his subjects or serve him or any other Christian."[7] The apparent facility of communication is again incredible, though the native rejection of the demands of the *requerimiento* was unmistakable to the captain general.

These scenes and similar ones that took place during the course of the expedition reveal underlying attitudes and aspirations that made for recurrent conflict between conquistadores and native peoples of the Southwest. First and foremost, as is made apparent over and over again in the documents in this volume, what drew the expedition to the Southwest was principally the prospect of populous and wealthy native peoples from whom significant tribute likely could be extracted. More than raw precious metals, gemstones, or pearls, far more than geographical information, it was the indigenous people themselves who were the chief attractions of Cíbola, Quivira, and the rest of Tierra Nueva. Thus, when the expedition withdrew from Tierra Nueva in 1542 it was because "there was no settlement in what had been reconnoitered where *repartimientos* [*encomiendas*] could be made to the whole expedition."[8] Before that withdrawal took place in April 1542, the expedition, as a whole and in smaller units, made repeated and concerted efforts to locate population centers that would support the Europeans. But as expedition member Pedro de Castañeda de Nájera made clear in Part 2 of his lengthy *relación*, they found only small settlements of agricultural people and even smaller bands of seminomadic hunters.[9] And nearly everywhere the expedition stopped for longer than a few days, friction and often conflict with the natives eventually arose (see Documents 19, 22–26, 28–30).

When the expedition retreated southward, it left behind a hostile land in which were buried a score of European expeditionaries and dozens of their Mexican Indian allies (for one example, see Document 27). Other natives of central and western Mexico chose to throw in their lot with the Pueblos of what is now New Mexico rather than follow their European comrades in arms back south.

Though some modern historians have emphasized the increase in geographical knowledge that resulted from the expedition as a positive result, for the expeditionaries themselves, almost without exception, the *entrada* was a failure. Most were heavily in debt from outfitting and supplying themselves and their slaves and servants for the nearly three-year odyssey. Some were disabled from wounds inflicted in Tierra Nueva. Many never fully recovered. Others were eventually able to gain recompense from the king for some of the expense and hardship they had suffered (see Documents 31–34).

The expedition fell apart as it retreated southward. It was blamed for the outbreak of a major uprising of native people of Nueva Galicia that followed in its wake. Both the Audiencia de México and the Consejo de Indias concluded that it had been responsible for frequent abuses of American natives. It took late-nineteenth-century and twentieth-century North American writers to rehabilitate the *entrada* and turn it into a heroic adventure of exploration.

Despite the great divergence of opinion about the success or failure of the Coronado expedition, there is no doubt among modern scholars about the extraordinary value of the rich documentary record the expedition left. It provides the first written record of the peoples, environment, and flora and fauna of what was to become northwestern Mexico and the southwestern United States. It sheds light on events that shaped and still affect interethnic relations in the region; on motives, attitudes, and strategies of Spain's century of conquest; and on attempts to extend economic, religious, and political dominion in general. Further, in these documents is a baseline for assessing historical change in what is now the American Southwest and northwestern Mexico and a window onto the late prehistory of native peoples of the region.

A Squeezed Orange and the Legacy of the Cuarto Centennial

The rich documentary record of the Coronado expedition has been underexplored for decades. Notable exceptions exist, especially within the discipline of ethnohistory, but even there few attempts have been made to dig into the record any farther than those documents that have been available in print for 60 to 100 years. This situation can be explained by a widely held assumption that, in terms of historical research, the Coronado expedition is an orange that was squeezed dry long ago. In other words, virtually everything worth knowing about the expedition has already been extracted and can simply be looked up in modern books. The stories of the expedition are taken for granted as firmly and safely fixed.

The Coronado expedition is the episode from the Southwest's Spanish colonial past that has been, for a least a century, most indelibly imprinted on popular consciousness. It is memorialized and capitalized on across the landscape with Coronado Centers; Coronado Airport; Coronado Theaters; Coronado Roads, Lanes, Streets, Avenues, and Highways; Coronado Children's Center; Coronado Auto Recyclers; Coronado Boot and Shoe Repair; Coronado Heating and Air Conditioning; Coronado Restaurant; Coronado Self-Storage; Coronado Towing; Coronado Wrecking and Salvage; Coronado Motel; Coronado Baptist Church; Coronado Condominiums; Coronado Paint and Decorating; Coronado National Forest; Coronado National Memorial; Coronado State Monument; and Coronado-Quivira Museum—to mention only a sampling of the scores of places that bear part of the surname of the expedition's captain general.

Nearly everyone who has lived for any length of time in the Southwest is familiar with the name Coronado. Most know and can recount stories or fragments of stories about the expedition. Many people are passionate in their feelings about that long-ago event: some are enormously proud of the daring and nerve of the first conquistadores, some are angered or dismayed by the expedition's generally arrogant and brutal conduct, others are inspired by the expedition's role as the vanguard of European civilization, and still others revel in the ingenuity and resourcefulness of the native people of the Southwest in their responses to the uninvited *entrada*.

This spectrum of emotion, lore, and commemoration is nearly all founded on the small selection from the documentary record of the expedition that has been published in English translation. Hundreds of books, articles, poems, plays, movies, paintings, sculptures, and other representations and interpretations have offered a fairly standardized vision of the expedition to successive generations of Southwesterners and others interested in the region.

Perhaps the greatest and most enduring impact on public perception of the Coronado *entrada* in the last hundred years was made by the Coronado Cuarto Centennial, which was celebrated throughout the Southwest and in the United States more generally more than 60 years ago. Highlighted by the issuance of a commemorative postage stamp and the performance of a touring pageant, the celebration lasted throughout 1940. As Clinton P. Anderson, managing director of the United States Coronado Exposition Commission, wrote:

> In hundreds of communities folk festivals have been held, drawing upon the rich cultural background of the Southwest and emphasizing its Spanish, Indian and cowboy characteristics. Existing museums have been assisted financially and provisions have been made for the development of a new Coronado Museum near his winter camp at Bernalillo, New Mexico, and for a proposed international monument at the spot along the Arizona border where his expedition crossed into territory of what is now the United States.[10]

The legacy of the Cuarto Centennial has proved consistently heroic and romantic—the art, the speeches, the panegyrics to intrepid conquistadores, and above all, the pageant. The pageant's author, Thomas Wood Stevens, had previously written similar extravaganzas for Old Fort Niagara and Yorktown. A thousand elaborate costumes were created by a New York designer, and portable sets for 18 scenes were professionally prepared. The effect was to be "dramatic and beautiful." The script was to take cognizance of "new material and documents which historical research have [*sic*] brought to light." Yet it was understood that there would be "variations from the record as required by the exigencies of time and dramatic effect."[11] The tone of the production, which played in 17 towns in Arizona, New Mexico, and Texas between May and October 1940,[12] is apparent in the following modern poem Stevens put in the mouth of expedition member Pedro de Castañeda de Nájera:

They said that we had failed.
We thought so too.

But I remembered, and I wrote it down, that even in
    the tales of chivalry no hero so far rode, or fought
    so bravely as some of us.
No general kept the faith, or was so well beloved, and
    well obeyed, as our Francisco Vásquez [*sic*].
Little men with little wrongs, barked at his heals like
    hounds.
The bitter law hedged him and tortured him.
The Judge Tejada, who listened to his enemies, con-
    demned him.
He was already broken with his wounds, bewildered
    and uncomforted.
Two years they kept him on the rack before his sen-
    tence.
Then two more years his conscience and his honor
    fought to clear his name.
But now, in Mexico, the Viceroy Mendoza sits with
    the high court of final justice.
Justice! Justice for Coronado! Pray for him.[13]

And when, in the pageant, the final exoneration comes for the former captain general, the audience is expected to join in the general "cheers . . . and laughter, and . . . dancing."[14] There is no doubt that the crowd's sympathy and identification are assumed to lie fully with the expeditionaries. Describing his own biography of Francisco Vázquez de Coronado, published that same year, Professor A. Grove Day likewise characterized "the story of Coronado's journey" as "a brave adventure with which every American should be familiar."[15]

Certainly the national and state Cuarto Centennial commissions succeeded spectacularly in permanently adding a stirring enterprise of derring-do to the lore of the West and Southwest. Vázquez de Coronado and his expedition became "pioneers," "gold-rushers," and "explorers" to set alongside Daniel Boone, Lewis and Clark, Zebulon Pike, John C. Frémont, and Custis and Freeman.

Nor did the impact of the commemoration end with the Cuarto Centennial year. The state of New Mexico, for instance, through its own Cuarto Centennial Commission, authorized publication of a projected 11-volume Coronado Historical Series of books. Produced by the University of New Mexico Press, the series was planned to "promote and perpetuate a better knowledge of New Mexico's and the Southwest's illustrious history and to serve as a lasting literary monument to the courage and enterprise of its pioneers." Included in the Coronado Historical Series were to be George P. Hammond and Agapito Rey's *Narratives of the Coronado Expedition* (published in 1940) and Herbert E. Bolton's *Coronado on the Turquoise Trail: Knight of Pueblos and Plains* (published belatedly in 1949).[16]

Together, these two volumes, superseding and enlarging on George Parker Winship's 1896 *The Coronado Expedition, 1540–1542,* have constituted since their publication the authoritative basis for both scholarly study and popularization of the *entrada*.[17] Other volumes in the series have proved equally influential in the study and portrayal of other prominent episodes in the history of the Spanish colonial Southwest.[18] The two Coronado expedition volumes followed the highest academic standards of the day and provided much more detailed and comprehensive narrative accounts of the *entrada* than had previously been available to English-speaking readers.

A nearly inevitable consequence of the publication of such weighty and authoritative books was a stifling, for many decades, of reexamination of the primary sources on which they were founded. Thus, basic historical scholarship on the Coronado expedition has remained "frozen" at the level of the latest masterworks. While complementary fields such as archaeology, anthropology, geography, linguistics, and even the history of sixteenth-century Latin America more broadly have all grown and evolved markedly in the intervening years, the corpus of Coronado expedition documents used by scholars has remained all but static. The 1940s English translations are commonly substituted for the primary sources on which they were based. Now, however, after more than 60 years, the documentary base for understanding the Coronado expedition seems meager and unvaried and its interpretation long out-of-date.

Previous Editions

There have been three previous editions devoted exclusively to Coronado expedition documents, two in English and one in Spanish. In addition, a lengthy series of Spanish transcriptions of documents dealing with the New World, published in the late 1800s, includes many documents deriving from the expedition. Unfortunately, all four of these published sources are inadequate today for use by both English-speaking scholars and general readers, because they are replete with errors and misinterpretations, rely on obsolete research, and lack comparison of English translations and original-language versions.

Of the two previous English-language editions, principally of narrative documents, one was published just over 100 years ago and the other more than 60 years ago. The earlier of these, *The Coronado Expedition, 1540–1542,* edited and translated by George Parker Winship, makes up pages 329–613 in Part 1 of the *Fourteenth Annual Report of the Bureau of Ethnology* (Washington, DC: Government Printing Office, 1896). The more recent edition appeared as the second volume in the Coronado Cuarto Centennial Publications, 1540–1940: *Narratives of the Coronado Expedition, 1540–1542,* by George P. Hammond and Agapito Rey (Albuquerque: University of New Mexico Press, 1940). Winship published English translations of 10 documents and Spanish transcriptions of 2 of those. Hammond and Rey included English translations of 29 documents in their edition (including all of those that Winship had published), but no transcriptions. Neither volume is adequate as a research tool, and both are long out of print.[19] Both broadly tell the expeditionary story but cannot stand up to scrutiny on details. Furthermore, no matter how good a translation is, consultation with the original language is crucial for serious research.

With regard to the original language of the surviving Coronado expedition documents, nearly all of them, though not without exception, are in Spanish. Between 1864 and 1884 a team of Spanish paleographers headed by Joaquín Pacheco and Francisco de Cárdenas published a massive series of transcriptions of Spanish documents related to the New World, which includes a number of documents deriving from the Coronado expedition (the series is hereafter cited as *CDI,* for *Colección de documentos inéditos*). Sadly, the production-line method the team followed and the obvious lack of proofreading produced generally unreliable transcripts sprinkled with omissions and errors.[20]

In 1992 Carmen de Mora, a professor of Spanish American literature at the Universidad de Sevilla, published a volume called *Las Siete Ciudades de Cíbola: Textos y testimonios sobre la expedición de Vázquez Coronado* (Sevilla: Ediciones Alfar; hereafter cited as Mora). It contains her own transcriptions of four documents and six transcriptions of other documents done by the Pacheco and Cárdenas team (all of these were documents previously published by Winship and Hammond and Rey). For the most part, then, the transcripts in the volume simply repeat the errors of *CDI.* Further, Mora's light annotations are badly flawed, because they rely heavily on outdated information from nineteenth-century sources, especially Frederick W. Hodge and Adolph F. Bandelier.

Misdirection by the Previous Editions

Winship and Hammond and Rey provided countless instances of misdirection in their translations. One example recently had amusing repercussions for us. In the course of a field session during archaeological work at the Jimmy Owens Site, a Coronado expedition campsite in the Texas South Plains, we were asked, "What ever happened to the sea nets?" In explanation, we were shown a copy of the Winship translation of the following passage of the narrative of Pedro de Castañeda de Nájera, Document 28 in the present volume:

> While the army was resting in this ravine, as we have related, a tempest came up one afternoon with a very high wind and hail, and in a very short space of time a great quantity of hailstones, as big as bowls, or bigger, fell as thick as raindrops, so that in places they covered the ground two or three spans or more deep. And one hit the horse—or I should say, there was not a horse that did not break away, except two or three which the negroes protected by holding *large sea nets* over them [emphasis added].[21]

Unaccountably, Winship seems to have rendered the Spanish term *empavesados,* meaning "shielded," so that it implied the use of nets, a wholly gratuitous reading.[22]

A second example of misdirection by the existing documentary editions concerns the geographical context of the expedition. While on the Llano Estacado in present-day eastern New Mexico or western Texas in late May or early June 1541, Vázquez de Coronado dispatched a reconnaissance party toward the east under Captain Diego López. The Spanish text of the surviving copy of Castañeda de Nájera's *relación* says that scouts sent out later to seek the López party were to look "en las entradas o las salidas del rrio [the ingresses to and egresses from the river]"—that is, in muddy areas where hoofprints would be obvious.[23]

Hammond and Rey, in their 1940 translation, erroneously interpreted this passage as referring to the "source and mouth of the river."[24] The great historian Herbert Bolton, accepting that interpretation, concluded that

> If in a brief space of time the searching party could reconnoiter the whole length of the creek from source to mouth, it must have been a short one. Coronado was obviously still close to [the] Canadian River, most of whose branches here are short, run north and south, and would thus cut across the path of López returning from the east.[25]

Bolton's conclusion was based solely on Hammond and Rey's poor translation of the passage in Castañeda de Nájera and has no foundation in the actual document. Rather than the expedition's being in the Canadian River valley, documentary and archaeological evidence has shown that it was almost certainly atop the Llano Estacado at this time, more than 100 miles south of Bolton's location.[26] This more southerly location is consistent with the translation that appears in this volume.

Winship occasionally has been equally misleading on geographical issues. For instance, in his translation of Juan Jaramillo's description of the expedition's route through what is now southeastern Arizona, he wrote: "Crossing the mountains, we came to *a deep and reedy river*, where we found water and forage for the horses" (emphasis added).[27] This characterization of the water source as deep and reedy has supported various route reconstructions that identify the river as the modern Gila.

The original manuscript, however, refers to "un arroyo hondo y cañada [a deep arroyo and canyon]."[28] This implies a relatively small, perhaps even intermittent, watercourse deeply entrenched in a defile. The Gila River does not match Jaramillo's actual description at all, since it runs through a wide, flat valley in the vicinity of Bylas, Arizona (and for many miles upstream and down), the location for this encounter favored by Bolton and others.[29]

One final example. A muster of the expedition was conducted at Compostela in February 1540. In their 1940 translation of the resulting expeditionary roll, Hammond and Rey listed a Diego Gutiérrez, "captain of cavalry."[30] The Spanish document (Document 12 in this volume), on the other hand, has "Capitan diego gutierrez d*e* la caballeria." This is almost certainly the brother of Francisco Vázquez de Coronado's mother-in-law, Marina Gutiérrez de la Caballería, rather than a captain of cavalry named Gutiérrez.[31]

In the annotations to this volume, we have pointed out many other errors and instances of misinformation in the previous editions. We do not mean to imply by such examples that Winship and Hammond and Rey were deficient scholars. In fact, they produced remarkable works that represented the state of knowledge in their day, and they played major roles in adding the Spanish colonial period to the standard repertoire of American history. Indeed, our own interest in the Coronado *entrada* might never have been awakened had it not been for their work.

Nevertheless, in the last 60 years (100 years for Winship) an extraordinary amount has been learned about the Coronado expedition, the early Spanish colonial period in general, and the protohistoric peoples of what has become the American Southwest and northwest Mexico—information and paradigms that were unknown to Winship and Hammond and Rey. In addition, historians today have generally moved beyond the production of credulous narrative epics. Thus, the selection of documents published in 1896 and 1940 now seems narrow and impoverished. Furthermore, the work of Winship and Hammond and Rey is seriously diminished by the absence of Spanish transcriptions that would tend to compensate for any errors or oversights in translation.

This Edition

In order to remedy such inadequacy and inaccuracy, we have undertaken to provide new transcriptions and translations of the Coronado expedition sources, based on the manuscript documents themselves. The reliability of printed primary sources dealing with the expedition is substantially increased by making available accurate, semipaleographic transcriptions of the documents together with English translations informed by the latest relevant historical, archaeological, linguistic, and geographical research.

Our greatest efforts in preparing *Documents of the Coronado Expedition* have thus been fourfold:

1. To dispel the frequent misguidance of earlier editions, due to error, misinterpretation, and lack of information that has become available in the last 60 years and more, first by scrupulously providing the most accurate and complete translations possible;

2. In the conviction that a broader and fuller collection of sources will make deeper understanding possible, to make available a significantly larger and more varied suite of documents than has hitherto been available;

3. With the recognition that no translation can serve all purposes or convey all the content of the original documents, to provide those documents in a single volume in semipaleographic transcription and English translation, to permit ready assessment and modification, when necessary, of the translations (this has never before been available to students of the expedition to Tierra Nueva);

4. Because much contextual and background information about the period, people, and places that form the framework of the documents is not common knowledge or easily available, to provide extensive annotations to both transcripts and translations, along with concise introductions to the documents.

Thus, scholars and lay historians alike are offered here what we believe are the most accurate and up-to-date

English translations and explanatory notes and the opportunity to consult faithful and complete transcriptions of the Spanish, Italian, and Nahuatl originals. Presented in this annotated, dual-language edition are 34 documents derived from the Coronado expedition. Together with Richard Flint's *Great Cruelties Have Been Reported: The 1544 Investigation of the Coronado Expedition*, it makes available the most comprehensive collection of primary sources for study of the expedition that has been published.[32]

The original manuscript documents themselves reside in archives scattered throughout Europe and the Americas. In the past this has made consultation of the documents a major undertaking for scholars and all but impossible for lay historians. To facilitate location of the manuscripts by other researchers, in the introductions to the individual documents we identify the source archives as well as the catalog numbers or other filing designations assigned by those archives to the documents or, more often, to the bundles of documents in which the specific manuscripts are located.

Those who are familiar with the most complete earlier edition of Coronado expedition documents, the one edited by Hammond and Rey, may wonder why eight documents included in that 1940 edition do not appear in the table of contents for this volume. Four documents listed by Hammond and Rey as "Licenciate Tejada's Commission," "Coronado's testimony on the management of the expedition," "Charges against Coronado resulting from management of the expedition," and "Absolutory sentence of Coronado" are excerpts from documents recently published in full in *Great Cruelties;* the excerpts are therefore not republished here. Two other Hammond-and-Rey-edition documents, "Testimony of López de Cárdenas on charges of having committed excesses on the expedition" and "Sentences of López de Cárdenas," are short excerpts from a massive case file that is hundreds of folios long (AGI, Justicia, 1021, piezas 1, 2, 5, and 6). Both of them are summarized and discussed in *Great Cruelties* (pp. 336–39), but piezas 1, 2, 5, and 6 of Justicia 1021 are much too lengthy to permit full inclusion in either *Great Cruelties* or this volume. The two remaining documents from the Hammond and Rey edition, "Coronado's residencia, charges and testimony" and "Sentence of Coronado on residencia charges," are again very brief excerpts from a case file (AGI, Justicia, 339) that is much too long to be included here; it deserves separate publication. Both are mentioned and partially summarized in the introduction to Document 34 in this volume.

Previously Unpublished Documents

Our most important window onto the actions and attitudes of both the Coronado expeditionaries and the wary natives over whom they sought authority has been and remains the rich documentary record generated by and resulting from the expedition. In past generations, historians have been most concerned to develop strong narratives of the "epic adventure." As a consequence, sixteenth-century narrative documents concerning the Coronado *entrada* have received disproportionate attention from historians in comparison with more mundane records that are revelatory of social, economic, political, and cultural issues. The potential for understanding the conflicts that arose between the expeditionaries and Southwestern natives, for instance, has thus been severely limited. Furthermore, historical treatments have, by and large, mirrored the image presented in the sixteenth century by a handful of conquistadores of themselves and their own exploits. The result has been lopsided and extremely simplistic representations, involving little critical historical analysis. It is our goal to expand and enrich the available pool of source documents and provide generous explanatory notes to render the documents more meaningful to modern readers.

In this book we add to what for 60 years has been the canon of primary source documents relating to the Coronado expedition 14 relatively short documents that have never been available before in print in their original language, in English translation, or in both.[33] We selected these additional documents for any or all of the following reasons: (1) unlike most of the documents of the canon, they are not narratives and thus provide very different data and perspectives on the expedition; (2) they focus on individuals, groups, or topics little discussed in the documents of the canon; and (3) they are particularly rich sources of data about the expedition.

The "new" documents range from a group of instruments prepared in 1542 after the death of an expedition member in Tiguex (Document 27) to proofs of service of three little-known members of the expedition (Documents 31–33); from a contract dealing with the financing of the expedition (Document 20) to a recently revealed royal *cédula* confirming Francisco Vázquez de Coronado's appointment as captain general of the expedition (Document 10); and from a record in Nahuatl of the departure of Indian members of the expedition from Tenochtitlan, now the Ciudad de México (Document 13), to testimony of Vázquez de Coronado's purchasing agent regarding goods bought to supply the *entrada* (Document 11).

The result is a much richer and more rounded vision than has heretofore been available of the first recorded contacts between Europeans and Native Americans in what in the sixteenth century was known as Tierra Nueva. That is not to say that this edition of documents is exhaustive. There remain scores of other existing but unpublished documents that shed light on the expedition, its precursors, its aftermath, and the people who participated in it. For example, as pointed out in Document 31, note 2, there are at least 17 known proofs of service of expedition members besides the three published here.[34] Also, only small excerpts from the documents deriving from Vázquez de Coronado's *residencia* and his attempt to recover *encomiendas* have been published to date.[35] Nor has the entirety of the massive record of the investigation of García López de Cárdenas's role in the mistreatment of Indians during the expedition yet been published.[36] Countless archives, both in Spain and in Mexico, have yet to be searched for documents pertinent to study of the Coronado expedition. Michael Mathes, for example, recently pointed out that there are many documents concerning former expeditionaries in the district and municipal archives of Colima, Mexico.[37] These documents remain not only unpublished but also largely unstudied. Besides such sources, there are many others that scholars have consulted on this subject that have never been published.[38] Beyond this already long list, dozens of relevant documents are known to have existed in the sixteenth century but have disappeared over the centuries since.[39] Some of them may well still exist and may eventually be located.

Order of the Documents

In order to avoid as much as possible disorienting readers who are familiar with the earlier editions of Coronado expedition documents, we have in most cases retained the order of documents followed by Hammond and Rey. That order is generally chronological, according to the dates of the events described in the documents rather than the dates of preparation of the documents themselves.

In some cases, however, we find their order misleading. One case in particular comes to mind. In their 1940 edition, Hammond and Rey published the "Instructions to Alarcón, 1541" before the "Report of Alarcón's Expedition."[40] The unwary reader may thus imagine that the instructions applied to the voyage described in the "Report," whereas in fact they were provided to Alarcón in preparation for a second voyage, which in the end never took place.

In general, with the 14 "new" documents included in this volume we have adhered to the chronological principle followed by Hammond and Rey. That means they are interspersed, as appropriate, among the documents of the earlier canon. Sometimes, when the events recorded were of long duration, we placed them according to either the beginning or the end of that series, as seemed most suitable. For instance, the complaint of Hernán Cortés regarding injuries caused to him by the viceroy (Document 18) is placed according to the date of the decision in the case, June 1540.

Caveat Lector

In preparing introductions to the 34 documents, we have taken particular pains to provide information that could be useful in assessing the reliability and trustworthiness of the sources. Although this is a critical task for historians, as it must be for representatives of modern news media, it is often not made explicit in historical writing and, more often than one would wish, is slighted or ignored by historians themselves. Information especially relevant to the issue of reliability includes the intended purpose and audience of a document; the relation of author to audience; the presence of obvious partisan, sectarian, social, or cultural biases; the identity of the source or sources of reports made in a document, if not

the author; and the proximity (in both time and space) of the reporter to the events described. One aspect of an author's proximity is whether he or she was an eyewitness or recounts only hearsay. That is especially tricky to determine for sixteenth-century Spanish documents because, even in strictly legal proceedings of the day, hearsay was allowed much greater weight than we expect it to be given today.

Among the many factors that must be considered in judging trustworthiness, we point out that virtually all of the documents included in this volume were drafted by *escribanos* (see glossary), even when other persons are recorded as the nominal authors, placing at least one filter between the "authors" and modern readers. Furthermore, many of the surviving versions of the documents are second- and even third-generation copies, increasing the possibility of introduced copying errors and unnoted revisions made by the copyists.[41] Four documents in this edition, though originally written in Spanish, survive only in sixteenth-century Italian translations, setting yet another interpretive layer between author and reader. As with historical sources of all sorts—documentary, visual, audio—there is always the possibility of deliberate distortion or obfuscation on the part of the original author. And subtlest of all are the cultural assumptions of author and reader alike, which can frustrate comprehension. Our message is certainly not that the documents are to be discounted or distrusted but that they must not be used uncritically. Verification, contextualization, and cross checking are always necessary.

A single example among many is provided by the February 1540 muster roll of the Coronado expedition. It has been said to be a full and complete record of those who participated in the *entrada*, but it is very far from it, omitting at least three-fourths of the expedition members (see the introduction to Document 12).

We owe the existence of most sixteenth-century documents to the work of *escribanos*. Without the products of that most abundant group of sixteenth-century functionaries, the period would be hopelessly in the dark. Recognition of that fact is expressed in our dedication of this volume to the memory of the *escribanos* who prepared the documents. They do, however, stand between us and the people and events we would most like to understand. It is the *escribanos'* voices and their attitudes that are most readily manifest in the documents. Sometimes it is only with considerable effort that one can get "behind" the *escribano* to the ostensible author. Even in the case of records of legal testimony, *escribanos* of the period, as a matter of course, took down notes as testimony was given and then hours or days later prepared third-person renditions based on those notes. Consequently, the vocabulary and phraseology of a series of witnesses may read nearly identically, although the actual witnesses surely had varying educational backgrounds and personal experiences that would have colored their statements. So *escribanos*, for all their indispensability, tend to give their own flavor and homogeneity to people and events that were surely more varied than is conveyed by the documents.

Dates and Distances

Nearly all of the documents published here were prepared or copied before the revision of the calendar in the Catholic world under Pope Gregory XIII in 1582. There is one major exception. The surviving copy of Castañeda de Nájera's lengthy *relación* (Document 28) was made in 1596. Bartolomé Niño Velásquez, who prepared the copy, lived in a world ordered by the Gregorian calendar, under which 10 days had been dropped from the year 1582 in order to resynchronize dates and celestial events. Castañeda de Nájera naturally wrote his *relación* using dates in the Old Style, or Julian, calendar. Niño Velásquez, in order to "modernize or correct" Castañeda de Nájera's dates, evidently converted them all to the Gregorian calendar. Thus, they appear to be badly out of step with those provided in the other documents published here. To keep readers alert to this inconsistency, we refer to it from time to time in the annotations.

A number of the Coronado expedition documents supply information on distances between places that figure repeatedly in the events referred to in the texts. Sometimes those distances are measured in *jornadas*, or days of travel, but frequently they are given more precision and rendered in leagues. For comparison with modern geography, we frequently provide equivalent straight-line map mileages in the annotations. We have chosen to give straight-line rather than actual travel distances for two reasons. First, for most of the Coronado expedition's route the precise courses followed are unknown; they are subjects of considerable and significant scholarly debate. Second, the use of straight-line distances has proved in many cases to reflect closely the figures provided in the sixteenth-century documents.

Comparison of modern, straight-line map mileages and sixteenth-century league distances has revealed that the authors of these documents did not all use a single standard league. Most frequently the standard of choice was the old *legua legal*, but some authors, notably Juan Jaramillo, seem to have used the *legua común*. Meanwhile, the Coronado expedition contemporary Francisco de Ulloa, who is referred to in several of the documents, appears to have given measurements using the *legua geográfica*.[42] When league measurements are stated in the documents, we make every effort to identify in the annotations which sixteenth-century standard is used.

Translation and Transcription Protocols

Because the intended core readership of this volume is North Americans who are interested in the history of the American Southwest and northwest Mexico and whose principal language is English, the key component of the book is complete translations of primary source documents that are as accurate as possible, in keeping with current knowledge in the fields of history, anthropology, archaeology, geography, and linguistics. Some persons of extremely narrow academic vision reject the need for English translations at all, maintaining that any translation impoverishes and distorts the original. Such a radical doctrine would confine knowledge of a great portion of the history of the region to those of us fortunate enough to be literate in the languages of the original source documents. That view can have no place in a society that values the widest possible dissemination of information and knowledge to all its members. We reject it categorically. This book is not solely for specialists in Spanish colonial history but rather is intended to provide broad-spectrum access to a large suite of documents that form the basis for most understandings of a crucial period in what is now the United States–Mexican borderlands. During this span of two and a half years, heterogeneous groups from the Eastern and Western Hemispheres, with markedly disparate views of life and the world, met and interacted in that region for the first time.

As translators of the documents presented here, we acknowledge that we ourselves represent the most pervasive interpretive filter between exclusively English-speaking readers and the sixteenth-century authors. Countless choices of vocabulary, of grammatical construction, of rhetorical slant and emphasis, of identification of antecedents and referents, and of many other matters are inherent in translation. One result is that no two people could independently produce identical translations of any text longer than a handful of words. The thousands of such choices we have made in preparing *Documents of the Coronado Expedition* are informed by our nearly quarter-century of study of the Coronado expedition, sixteenth-century Spain and its activities in the New World, and the native peoples and environments of Tierra Nueva. We have also drawn on the work of a multitude of our predecessors and colleagues. Thus, we flatter ourselves to think the translations stay as close to the content, sense, and spirit of the originals as is currently possible, short of relying strictly on the original manuscripts themselves.

Nevertheless, readers and users of this volume, or any publication like it, need to remain aware that the translations are not equivalent to or interchangeable with the original documents for all purposes. The most important reason that we also provide transcripts of the originals here is to permit ready assessment of the translations and adaptation of them or any portion of them for other purposes or from other perspectives. Folio numbers are included in both transcripts and translations to facilitate navigation back and forth between the two, and even between them and the original manuscripts when that may seem advisable. Folio numbers, either recto [r] or verso [v], are shown in square brackets [ ].

While adherence to the original sources has been our foremost concern, close behind it has been to render them into fluid English of a complexity and range of vocabulary comparable to that of the originals. In the recent past, there has been a misguided fad of so-called literal translation, in which the word order and sentence structure of the original language are slavishly retained in the translation. The result has been a clumsy hybrid that is neither English nor the

original language and conveys the erroneous impression that speakers of the original language were linguistically inept. Unless there is compelling evidence to the contrary in a particular case, an author's practiced ability in his native language should be represented by fully competent English. That sometimes means, for instance, breaking up and shortening the incredibly long sentences many writers of Spanish still are fond of.

Many words that occur in the original manuscripts, including archaisms, technical terms, and obsolete usages of seemingly familiar words, are extremely cumbersome to render into English. Spanish words that fall into this category are *criado, caballero, encomendero, entrada, hidalgo, oidor, repartimiento, requerimiento,* and dozens of others. We have left such words untranslated throughout the documents but have provided a glossary at the end of the book that explains such terms. Whenever used in the English translations, such words are printed in italics. If such a term appears only once in the documents, an explanation is provided immediately adjacent to its occurrence. When common words are used in uncommon or obsolete ways, we usually provide a citation to an entry recording that usage in the Real Academia Española's *Diccionario de la lengua española,* Sebastián de Covarrubias Orozco's *Tesoro de la lengua castellana o española,* or another appropriate source.

The sixteenth-century usages of *ciudad, pueblo,* and *villa* deserve special note. Spanish society of the era was thoroughly hierarchical. Persons had their ranks and stations, but so did political and social entities. When people spoke of settlements, as they did frequently throughout the Coronado expedition documents, that hierarchy was never out of mind. Thus, to designate a place a *ciudad,* as fray Marcos did of Cíbola, was to recognize that community as being among the highest-ranking, most important, and largest settlements. In the Spanish world, in order to be called a *ciudad,* a place had to be so designated by the king. In all of the *provincia* of Nueva España at the time of the Coronado *entrada* there existed only two places meriting that title, the Ciudad de México and Puebla de los Ángeles. The much smaller Guadalajara and Compostela, the capital of Nueva Galicia, were the only *ciudades* in that *provincia.* Outside the Spanish sphere of control, a *ciudad* was a place of comparable status, importance, and, usually, size. In descending order of importance and size, *ciudad* was followed by *villa, lugar,* and *aldea* (hamlet). *Pueblo,* though less precise, referred to a place of minor importance. None of these names for political units was limited to dense nuclei of domestic, commercial, administrative, and ecclesiastical architecture; also included were their extensive hinterlands, often of indefinite extent but thought to be sufficient for the support of and under the control of the urban centers. The terms were not used lightly, indiscriminately, or interchangeably.

In this regard, the word *pueblo* presents special complications for modern Southwestern readers, for it has come into English as the designation of the permanent, compact, traditional settlements of the Pueblo peoples of New Mexico and Arizona. Because that sense of the word would have been unknown to the authors of the documents published here, we have chosen to render the word in italics wherever it is retained in the English translations, even when applied to communities now called by the assimilated English version of the word. In introductions and annotations, however, when we refer to those modern communities we use "pueblo" in roman type, signaling the modern, English sense of the word.

Readers will note some common elements of sixteenth-century Spanish rhetorical style that are preserved in the English. For example, it was common to use paired adjectives, nouns, or verbs, usually synonyms or near synonyms, to emphasize a description or characterization. To English ears this often sounds unnecessarily, even annoyingly repetitious. In the annotations we point out numerous cases of this usage throughout the documents, including Pedro de Castañeda de Nájera's statement that "the horses were wide and fat [*gordo y holgado*]" and Carlos V's "they are to give and must give you all the aid and assistance [*favor y ayuda*] which you request and have need of."[43]

Even today, Spanish uses the passive voice much more liberally than is generally considered proper in modern English. We have usually retained passive constructions in our translations, though occasionally we convert them to active voice to avoid extremely clumsy sentences.

Something that is again still frequently found in modern Spanish, which often frustrates English-speaking readers and

listeners, is the great distance between pronouns and their referents. Occasionally a referent is omitted altogether. Either of these practices can make for extreme uncertainty and ambiguity. When such uncertainty exists in the original document, we have sought to clarify it in the English by supplying the apparent referent in square brackets. In a few situations in the course of the hundreds of folios involved in this volume, we have been hopelessly unable to determine referents with certainty and have made only a suggestion or two.

Punctuation is almost totally lacking in sixteenth-century Spanish manuscript documents. Visually, and often syntactically as well, a flow of thought can run on for the better part of a folio without evident interruption. In the English translations we have supplied punctuation and paragraphing. Although modern Spanish is thoroughly punctuated, sentences still tend to be much longer than is usual in English, often including multiple modifying clauses and phrases. In the English translations we divide such lengthy thoughts into shorter, less convoluted sentences. The lack of punctuation in the original documents from time to time leads to ambiguity and possible alternative divisions into sentences. In several instances, our division of text into sentences has resulted in readings quite different from those of earlier scholars. These are noted in the annotations.

We have also occasionally inserted transitional words or phrases in order to ease the flow of particularly abrupt passages. All such insertions are identified by enclosure between square brackets. Archaic and variant spellings of non-Spanish proper names and toponyms are retained in the English translations. This is occasionally also true for Spanish names. "Pero," a common variant of Pedro, for instance, is kept in translation. Similarly, both Garci and García appear in the translations as the given name of the expedition's *maestre de campo.* Both Melchor and Melchior, its French equivalent, appear in the original documents as well, Melchior being the more frequent. Both are retained in the English. In both transcripts and translations, scribal marginalia, titles, addresses, and like matter are enclosed and designated by flourished brackets { }.

For persons whose names appear more than twice in this volume and for whom explanatory information is provided, the name is listed in Appendix 1, "Biographical Data."

Persons whose names appear twice or less are identified only in a note. Information about places that are named repeatedly throughout the documents is supplied in Appendix 2, "Geographical Data." Two Spanish terms in particular are used throughout the documents to refer to animals unknown in Spain. *Gallina,* unless clearly referring to an Asiatic-European chicken, is translated as "[turkey]," the only gallinaceous bird domesticated at the time in the Americas. Only after this period was the Amerindian-derived word *guajolote* adopted into some Western Hemisphere dialects of Spanish to refer to the turkey. The American bison was consistently called a *vaca,* or cow, during the sixteenth century. Except when *vaca* clearly refers to Old World domesticated cattle or to the female bison, we have translated it as "[bison]."

In preparing the original-language transcriptions, we have adhered to the following typographic conventions. All emendations, additions, and expansions, whether scribal or editorial, including interlineations, are rendered in italics, as are the infrequent Latin words and phrases present in the documents. In the case of scribal emendations, the characters or words in italics are preceded by a caret ^. Marginal notes, symbols, and marks appearing in the texts are rendered in roman type but are enclosed between flourished brackets { }. Letters that are superscribed in the documentary texts are lowered to the main text line in the transcriptions. Both scribal and editorial deletions are preserved in the transcripts but are identified as deletions by being enclosed between standard parentheses ( ). In the case of scribal deletions, a caret is also included within the parentheses (^). We have made editorial deletions in cases where modern orthography and sixteenth-century scribal spelling vary sufficiently to render words awkward, ambiguous, or difficult to identify for many modern readers. But even in cases of editorial deletion, all letters present in the documentary texts appear in the transcripts. Scribal use of majuscule characters is adhered to in the transcripts.

Throughout the transcriptions we have adhered to individual scribal practices when, as was often the case, an *escribano* included a catchword, a preview of the first word on the next folio, at the bottom of a folio.

For those unfamiliar with sixteenth-century spelling practices, a few remarks about the interchangeability of characters may be helpful in reading the Spanish transcriptions. First, spelling was less standardized and thus more variable in the 1500s and earlier than it is today. Different *escribanos* frequently used slightly different spellings. Even a single *escribano* might change spelling within a document, often even within a single line of text. For the most part, though, the differences in spelling conformed to a pattern of possibilities. For example, specific pairs or sets of consonants were regularly interchanged.

Perhaps the most common interchange was between *b* and *v.* Accordingly, throughout the transcriptions that follow, the Spanish equivalent of "to know" appears variously as *saber* and *saver,* with equal validity. Likewise, the equivalent of "to have" is spelled either *haber* or *haver.* In the original manuscripts themselves, the characters *b* and *v* are nearly indistinguishable. It is our practice to transcribe as *b* or majuscule *V* such a character whose left-hand member or leg is longer than its right-hand member. When the legs are of equal length the character has been transcribed as miniscule *v.*

Further complicating the transcription of *b* and *v* in sixteenth-century Spanish, the characters for *v* and *u* were orthographically interchangeable, in both minuscule and majuscule. Thus, in transcribing the characters *b*, *v*, and *u*, we have followed the protocols in the preceding paragraph when, phonetically, a consonant is clearly intended. When, on the other hand, a vowel is appropriate, the character is rendered as *u* or *U.* It has become habitual among many Spanish paleographers to transcribe *cibdad* rather than *ciudad,* even though the character that can be mistaken for a *b* had lost its consonantal value well before the sixteenth century.[44] Consequently, we have chosen to render the word as *ciUdad,* recognizing the character's status as a vowel at the time the documents were written.

Other common consonant interchanges in sixteenth-century Spanish included the following:

1. *c, ç, s,* and *z* for the soft or sibilant *c;* thus, one sees *decir, deçir, desir,* and *dezir* for the Spanish equivalent of "to speak" or "to say."

2. *c*, *q*, and occasionally *g* for the hard *c* or *k* sound, as in *descubrir*, *desgubrir*, and *desqubrir*.

3. *g*, *j*, and *x* for the fricative *h*, as in *elexir*, *elejir*, and *elegir*.

4. *m* and *n*, as in *campo* and *canpo*.

5. *t* and *th*, as in *tener* and *thener*.

A few vowels were also commonly interchanged, including the following:

1. *i* and *y*, as in *fin* and *fyn*.

2. *i* and *e*, as in *ningun* and *nengun*.

3. *o* and *u*, as in *descubrir* and *descobrir*.

In transcribing the documents, we have not modified such interchanges unless they render the words in which they occur particularly difficult to read. Ordinarily this is when the interchange occurs in the first or second syllable of the word or is compounded by other spelling irregularities.

Several archaic usages appear throughout the documents that would have been extremely clumsy and confusing to emend while retaining all the original text. Therefore, we mention them here and leave them unmodified in the transcripts. *Así* appears regularly in the archaic form *ansí*. Frequently, when an infinitive is followed by a pronoun that begins with *l*, the terminal *r* in the infinitive is also altered to *l*. For example, what would today be written *visitarla* appears as *visitalla*.[45] When the second-person future indicative is linked with a pronoun, the pronoun is routinely inserted between the infinitive and the future ending. Thus, what today would ordinarily be *lo entregaréis* appears in the sixteenth-century documents as *entregalloéis*.[46] Also, during the sixteenth century a change was under way in the future tense of verbs whose infinitives ended in *ner* and *nir*. Thus, for example, where one would today expect *tendrán*, one sometimes sees *ternán* in the documents included here.[47] Another verb form that was in transition during the sixteenth century is the third-person preterit indicative of *ver*, "to see." As a result, the archaic form *vido* sometimes appears in these documents instead of the modern *vio*. To facilitate intelligibility by modern readers, throughout the Spanish transcripts we have displayed *vido* as *vi(d)o*, indicating that the *d* is an archaic element not included in the modern spelling.[48]

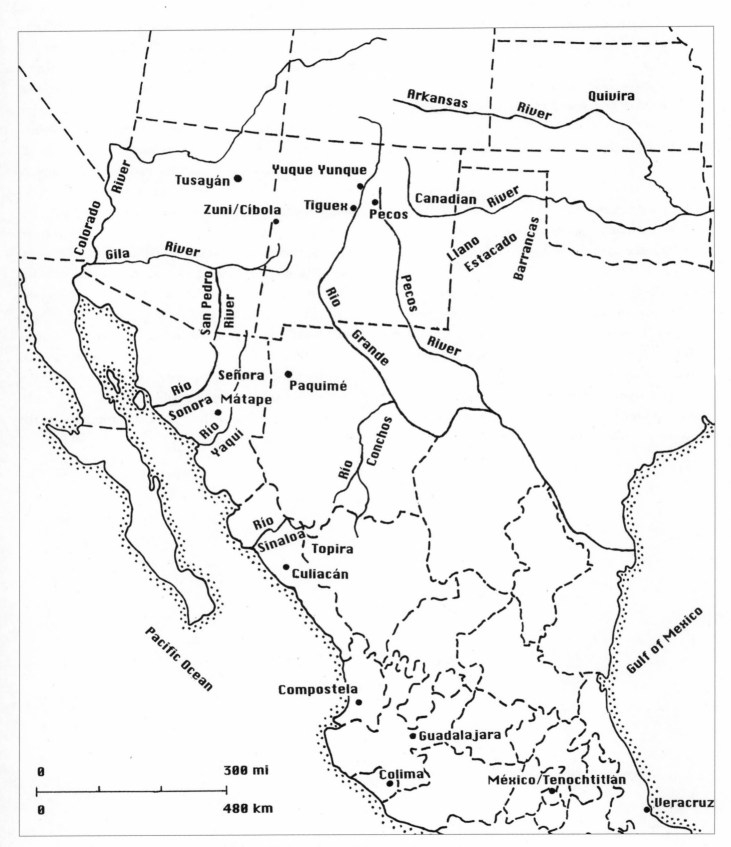

MAP 1. Northwestern Spanish America in the sixteenth century.

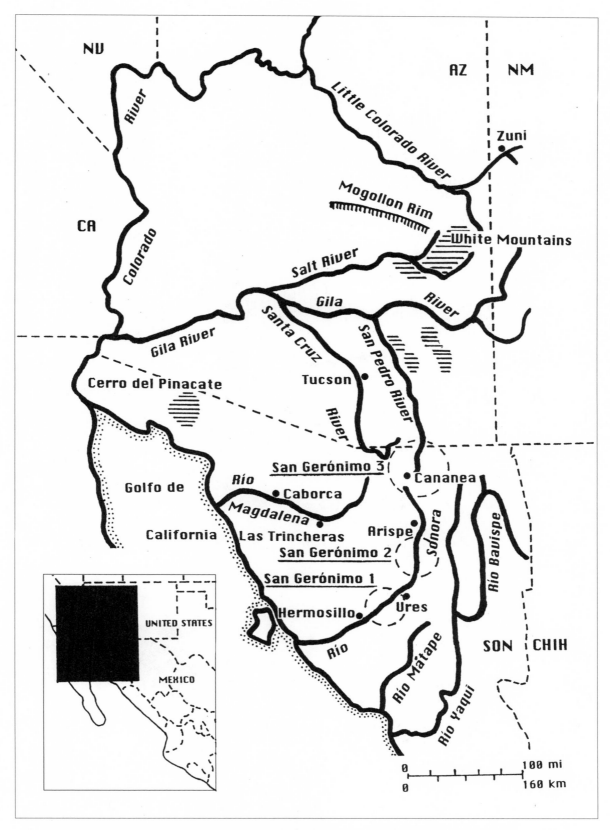

MAP 2. From the Río Yaqui to Zuni: Sonora, Arizona, and New Mexico. Areas enclosed by dashed lines indicate the probable locations of the three successive sites of the expedition's Sonoran base, San Gerónimo.

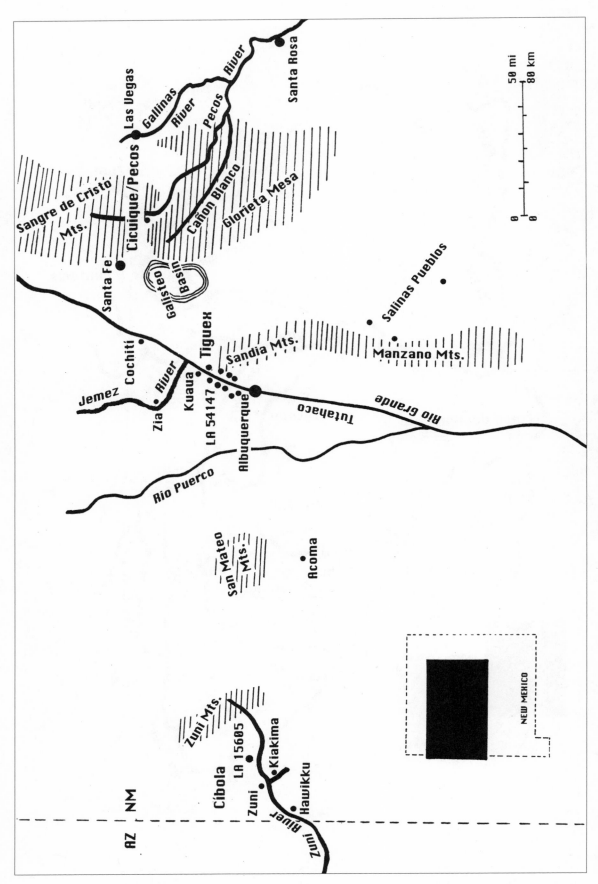

MAP 3. From Cíbola to Cicuique: New Mexico.

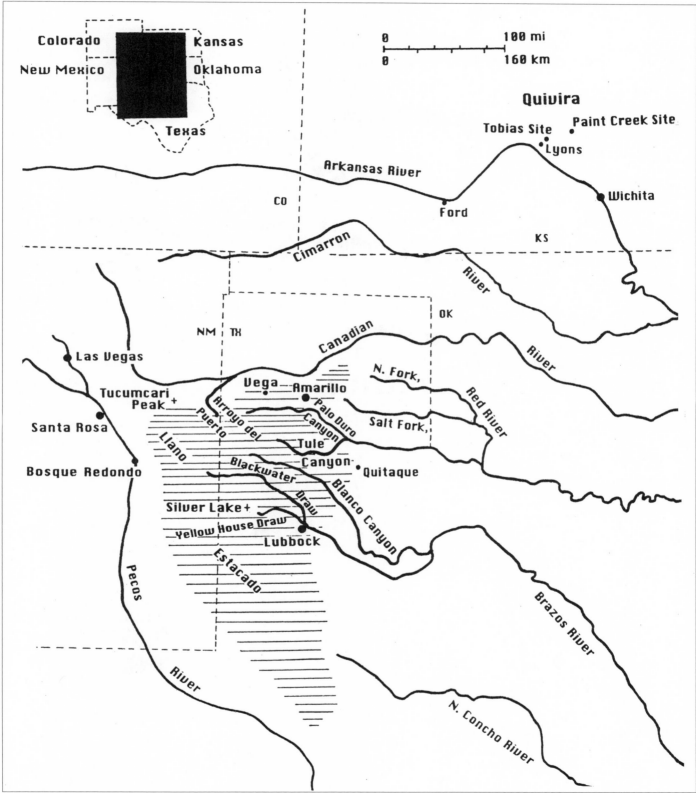

MAP 4. From the Pecos River to Quivira: New Mexico, Texas, Oklahoma, and Kansas.

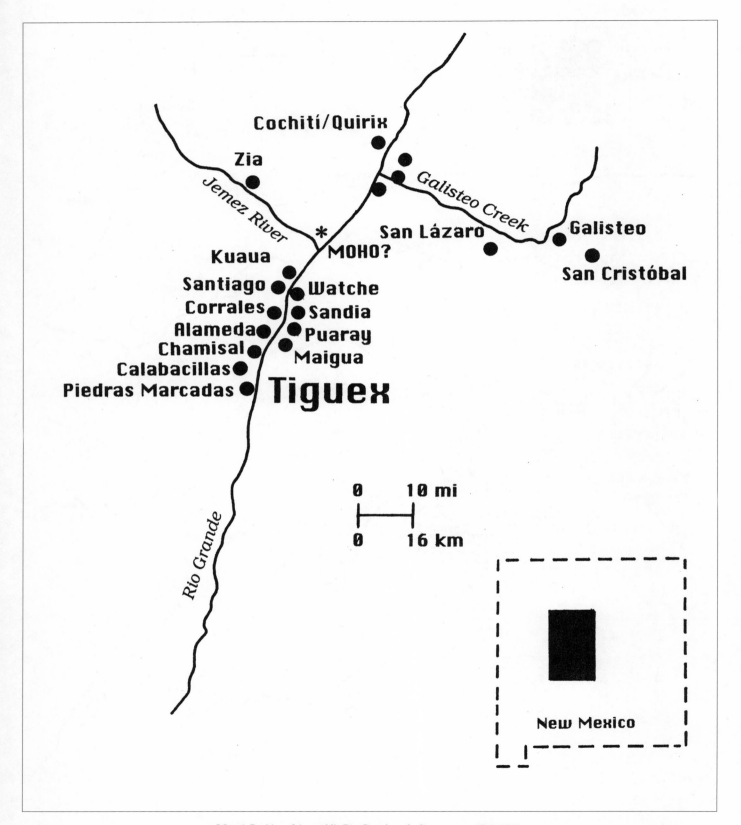

Cochití/Quirix

Zia

Jemez River

Galisteo Creek

*

MOHO?

San Lázaro

Galisteo

Kuaua

San Cristóbal

Santiago   Watche

Corrales   Sandia

Alameda   Puaray

Chamisal   Maigua

Calabacillas

Piedras Marcadas   **Tiguex**

0 ——— 10 mi

0 ——— 16 km

Rio Grande

New Mexico

MAP 5. Pueblos of the middle Rio Grande and adjacent areas, 1540–1542.

Document 1

Letter of Vázquez de Coronado to the King, December 15, 1538

AGI, Guadalajara, 5, R.1, N.5

INTRODUCTION

When he arrived in the New World in 1535 in the company of the newly appointed viceroy, Antonio de Mendoza, young Francisco Vázquez de Coronado was already a rising star. What led to Mendoza's patronage of the young native of Salamanca is not altogether clear. It seems likely that the service of Juan Vázquez de Coronado, Francisco's father, as *corregidor* in Granada during 1515 and 1516 and as *prefecto,* or chief administrator, there led to a close relationship with the Mendoza family, especially with Luis Hurtado de Mendoza, the Conde de Tendilla and Marqués de Mondéjar, the viceroy's older brother, who was captain general in Granada from 1512 until 1564, and perhaps also with Antonio de Mendoza himself.[1]

In 1537 Vázquez de Coronado received the first assignments on record from the viceroy. Mendoza sent him to investigate an uprising of black slaves and Indians at the mines of Amatepeque, southwest of the Ciudad de México. A group of Blacks confessed to fomenting the uprising; they were drawn and quartered in punishment. Mendoza was pleased with Vázquez de Coronado's discharge of the assignment and wrote as much to the king.[2] The same year, Vázquez de Coronado was sent as *visitador* to look into reported mistreatment of Indians working in the mines at Sultepec, in the same general area as Amatepeque.[3]

In 1536 Vázquez de Coronado had married Beatriz de Estrada, daughter of the deceased former royal treasurer in Nueva España, Alonso de Estrada, and Marina Gutiérrez Flores de la Caballería.[4] One of the significant consequences of that marriage was the bridegroom's receipt as dowry of one-half of the *encomienda* of Tlapa, the third largest *encomienda* in Nueva España, which provided financial leverage that he lacked as the second son of Juan Vázquez de Coronado, *comendador*[5] of Cubillas and former *corregidor* of Granada.[6] That resource permitted the couple two years later to invest in the expedition to Tierra Nueva.

The career of the viceroy's young *criado* surged ahead in 1538. In June he and his brother-in-law Juan Alonso de Sosa were both made *regidores* of the *cabildo* of the Ciudad de México, an office Vázquez de Coronado held until within three months of his death in September 1554, at about age 43.[7] The most momentous change in his political status within the viceroyalty came in August 1538, when the viceroy named him governor and *residencia* judge of Nueva Galicia, on the northwest fringe of Spain's dominion in North America.[8] By November he was on his way to take up his duties in that west coast *provincia.*[9]

Vázquez de Coronado did not travel alone. In his entourage were two Franciscans, fray Marcos de Niza and fray Onorato, as well as the slave Esteban de Dorantes. They had been dispatched by the viceroy to verify the 1536 reports of wealthy and populous places far to the north that had been made by the four sole survivors of the 1528 Narváez expedition to La Florida. The possibility of a subsequent major expedition toward the north was already in the air, though actual recruiting might not yet have begun.

Even with that prospect looming, the new governor's first priority was ongoing threats to the continued Spanish settlement of Nueva Galicia. The letter published here represents Vázquez de Coronado's first report to King Carlos I (Holy Roman Emperor Carlos V) on the state of affairs in Nueva Galicia. It exhibits his preoccupation with the safety of the *provincia*. In 1939 Arthur Aiton wrote of the letter: "It is an honest, straightforward description of the obvious deficiencies of the administration of a newly conquered region. Its author shows no unusual grasp of underlying causes, applies superficial routine remedies, and displays a lack of initiative."[10]

At Guadalajara Vázquez de Coronado found his predecessor dead from injuries suffered in a fall from a horse while on campaign against native people.[11] Advancing to the seat of his jurisdiction, Compostela, the governor found both that *ciudad* and the farthest outpost of Spanish control, Culiacán, threatened with abandonment.[12] He identified the principal leader of assaults on Spaniards by Indians as a man named Ayapín.[13]

The settlers of Nueva Galicia, where the natives had been overrun in the early 1530s by forces led by Nuño Beltrán de Guzmán, had a dismal reputation for their treatment of the resident Indians. Vázquez de Coronado, acting under the viceroy's directives, looked into charges of abuse of natives and the levels of tribute they were being assessed. The findings he reports here are generally favorable to the settlers.[14] In an effort to ameliorate some of the settlers' distress, the governor agrees that the *ciudad* of Compostela should be moved, which it subsequently was.[15]

These and other matters of administration are the subjects of the letter dated December 15 (Julian) from Compostela, two manuscript copies of which survive in the Archivo General de Indias in Sevilla under the *signatura*, or catalog number, AGI, Guadalajara, 5, R.1, N.5. Both are signed by Vázquez de Coronado, though they are written in the hand of an *escribano*, perhaps Hernando Martín Bermejo, the governor's secretary.[16] Hernando and his cousin Juan Martín Bermejo, like Vázquez de Coronado, had come to the New World in Viceroy Mendoza's entourage in 1535.[17] Both were also members of the Coronado expedition.[18] Hernando prepared the originals of the papers incident to the death of Juan Jiménez at Tiguex in 1542, which are published from a later copy as Document 27 in this volume. By the 1560s, with Vázquez de Coronado now dead, *licenciado* Hernando Bermejo was living in Guatemala, where he was associated with the viceroy's former secretary Juan de León.[19]

Numerous, mostly minor differences exist between the two extant copies of the December 1538 letter. One more significant difference exists as well, even though the two copies were prepared by the same *escribano*, probably within hours or days of each other. In this case, the word *pacíficos* is substituted for *conquistados*, considerably altering the meaning of the sentence in which the words appear.[20] Other differences between the two copies include the existence on Copy 1[21] of *postiles*, or marginal notes, probably added by an official of the Consejo de Indias in Spain, which is where a letter addressed to the king would have ended up.[22] The *postiles* include both verbal comments and organizational markers in the form of crosses {+}.

Arthur Aiton published the only previous transcription of this letter in 1939. George Hammond and Agapito Rey published the first (and only previous) English translation the following year.[23] In preparing and editing the new transcription and translation that follow, we relied on both of the manuscript copies in the AGI and consulted both previous printed editions. Significant differences between the current work and that of the earlier scholars are pointed out in the annotations.

TRANSLATION

[1r]

Holy Catholic Imperial Majesty

{1538 Nueva Galicia}[24]

The viceroy of Nueva España delivered to me a royal commission from Your Majesty by which Your Majesty orders me to come to this *provincia* of Nueva Galicia to assume authority over it and to take the *residencia* of *licenciado* [Diego Pérez] de la Torre,[25] who was *residencia* judge here.

In fulfillment of what Your Majesty orders me, as soon as Your Majesty's commission was given to me, I departed from the Ciudad de México.[26] When I arrived in this jurisdiction, I found that *licenciado* de la Torre (whose *residencia* Your Majesty orders me to take) [had] died in the *villa* of Guadalajara in this *provincia*,[27] where the *licenciado* lived and died. I publicly announced a *residencia* against the assets that remained to his heirs in that *villa*. I arranged a few things that were advantageous to Your Majesty's service.

The *procurador* of the *villa* of San Miguel in the *provincia* of Culiacán,[28] who wanted me to come to this *ciudad* of Compostela,[29] arrived and told me that the *vecinos* of that *villa* were on their way here and were leaving the [*villa*] depopulated, and that the whole *provincia* was about to be lost. He asked me, in Your Majesty's name, to go quickly to put it in order. [He] assured me that if I did not go within forty days, the *vecinos* would come [here] because of the many dangers they suffer and the injuries that Ayapín,[30] an Indian who has taken up arms, inflicts on them.

I asked him for a report, and he gave me one [that was] more adequate than I needed. [That is] because it is apparent from it [that only] with much work do the *vecinos* of the *villa* of San Miguel and the Indians who are there remain at peace.[31] With this [letter] I am sending Your Majesty the petition which was made to me and the report,[32] so that Your Majesty may order it to be reviewed, if that would be of service, to ascertain the condition [1v] that *provincia* is in.

I became convinced to go visit [the *villa* of San Miguel], having the authority to do it, since the viceroy of Nueva España so ordered me on Your Majesty's behalf. Knowing their needs, he [had] provided me with certain financial aid that I might take to the *vecinos* of that *villa* of San Miguel. Fearing what is now occurring (that is, that they might come [here] and leave that *villa* depopulated), I will leave here in eight days and would have left earlier had it not been for having arranged things here which are advantageous to Your Majesty's service. I will do everything possible to assist that *villa* and *provincia*, and I will find out whether it is advantageous to Your Majesty's service for it to be maintained. I will make a report to Your Majesty about everything.[33]

{+} Your Majesty probably already has a report concerning what this *provincia* of Nueva Galicia is [and] about those [persons] who have governed in it for Your Majesty. For this reason and because I have been in it for only a short time, at present I refrain from giving [a report] to Your Majesty, until I have examined it all thoroughly. Here I will give Your Majesty only a report about the condition in which I find it.[34]

Your Majesty is to be aware that most of the Indians of [the *provincia*] are at war. Some [are ones] who have not [yet] been subdued, and others [are ones] who have risen up in arms after having been subdued and placed under Your Majesty's dominion. Of those [Indians] who are at peace, Nuño de Guzmán[35] and three or four of his *criados* and friends hold the majority and the best [most profitable] ones [in *encomienda*].

For that reason and because there are so few peaceful Indians, many [individuals] who have served Your Majesty in the conquest of this place and others who have come to settle [it] are in great need. Being so, they take little interest in instructing the Indians in things pertaining to the faith. But [they] very diligently make use of [the Indians] in more ways than they should. Because the tribute they can render has not been assessed for the Indians of this *provincia,* [the Spaniards] avail themselves of them for personal services. [That is] because very few Indians of this *provincia* pay [tribute], unless it is those whom Nuño de Guzmán holds in *encomienda.* And those [Indians] pay him [only] a small amount, even though they are numerous.

The way the *vecinos* of this jurisdiction {/} who have Indians in *encomienda* support themselves is [from] the gold mines.[36] Most [Indian] towns supply their *encomenderos* [with] Indians who obtain the gold for them. Some [of these come] from among those who are traded, sold, and bought as slaves among the Indians, without being branded, and others are free. They have [followed] this way of life since the mines were discovered, which could be three years ago. This is a result of the lack of [Spanish-made] slaves in this *provincia.*[37] Although [slaves] were made in huge numbers in [this *provincia*], they were all taken to be sold [2r] outside [of it]. Because there exists this lack [of slaves], the mines are worked with Indian slaves and free Indians.

I came to the mines known as Nuestra Señora de la Concepción so as to establish order and learn how those [Indians] who work in them are treated.[38] I conducted an investigation, both in public and privately, among the Indians themselves. I found that they are well treated, both in that their work is moderate and in that they are well fed and clothed, according to their custom. They are taught matters of the faith; [this is] so much the case that I have not seen any Indian in this whole *provincia* who exhibits the slightest trace of Christianity, except those I saw at the mines. For this reason it seemed to me best to leave things as they stand,[39] ([which is] as those who have [previously] governed have done it), without stirring anything [up] until I give Your Majesty a report about it. [This is] so that Your Majesty may order what[ever] may be of service.

{+} The *vecinos* of this *provincia* were availing themselves of the Indians they have in *encomienda* in another way before I came to [the *provincia*]. They rented them [out to go] to the Ciudad de México, and from there they brought them loaded with merchandise. This was completely without authorization, so that I encountered them when I came from [the Ciudad de] México, in forties and fifties, loaded. They came and went nearly dead from hunger because they were not even provided food for their work. In Your Majesty's name, under severe penalties I have forbidden anyone to remove a free Indian from the *provincia,*[40] because it did great harm to the natives of this *provincia* that some of them went loaded in this way [as much as] eighty leagues from their homes. The *vecinos* of this *provincia* have felt so aggrieved by [my action] that they say they must protest to Your Majesty.

{that he did well and for it he is considered to have been of service}[41] {/}

{+} By means of your royal commission Your Majesty directs me to make use of[42] the letters and decrees addressed to *licenciado* de la Torre from Your Majesty just as if they had been sent to me. Among them there is one in which Your Majesty orders *licenciado* de la Torre and the *protector* Cristóbal de Pedraza[43] to assess the tribute which the Indians of this jurisdiction are able to pay to the persons who hold them in *encomienda* on Your Majesty's behalf. Because the *protector* is not now present in this *provincia,* I will not put [that decree] into effect until I learn what Your Majesty orders be done. There is a great need that the Indians be assessed, because even though they will pay [only] a small amount of tribute, during the time they are not assessed they are employed by [the *encomenderos*] in [whatever] personal services they decide. For this [reason] Your Majesty is likely to ease your royal conscience by ordering that they be assessed.

When the decree in which Your Majesty orders that the Indians be assessed was issued, there [were] some [persons] who levied payments from the Indians they have in *encomienda.* Concerning this [the Indians] state that as a result they pay [the *encomenderos*] much more tribute [2v] than they should pay and are able to pay. [This was done] so that if [the officials] were to assess them, they would find [the Indians] paying at a high rate and would believe that from then on the assessment would have to be continued [at that level]. Although I see that [the *encomenderos*] are mistaken, it seems right to me to give Your Majesty information about it.

{to the lord viceroy: Send it to him blank in order that with the governor he [may] fill [it] in.}[44]

{+} Upon returning from Culiacán, which will be as soon as I can, I mean to put everything in order from then on. I will try to bring to peace the Indians of this *provincia* who have risen up in arms by treating them benevolently and doing good works and also with the ecclesiastics whom the viceroy of Nueva España told me he would send for this purpose. In the event that [the ecclesiastics] and I are not able to bring them to knowledge of the faith and into Your Majesty's service, I will work by all the means I can to place them under Your Majesty's dominion.

{Good}[45] {/}

{+} The *licenciado* de la Torre assigned many Indians in this *provincia* in *encomienda* who had not been subjugated or [even] seen. And he was giving to whoever asked him for them fifteen and twenty leagues of land with all the Indians who were on it. There was even a certain grant of more than fifty leagues. These [*encomenderos*] are guarding the *cédulas* until the land is pacified. May Your Majesty order what is of service. In this [case] may [what has been done] be preserved. [That is] because those who have served and may yet serve Your Majesty in the subjugation and pacification of this land would receive injury if others who had not done [service] were to get the benefit.

{That which in the lifetime of the *licenciado* was not carried out, will not be completed.}[46]

{+} In the environs of this *ciudad* of Compostela there are

thirty *repartimientos* granted to its *vecinos*. In this entire *ciudad*, however, there are only ten houses, because the *vecinos* have refused to reside [here], some saying that the Indians they have in *encomienda* are at war and others that [the Indians] do not yield them any profit. Their absence is one reason this region is not pacified and more than enough [reason] the Indians are not instructed in matters of the faith. Thus, I found there that it has been too much neglected, since, as I say to Your Majesty, in this entire *provincia* I have not seen [a single] Indian who shows any evidence of [being a] Christian, except those I saw in the mines and five or six boys whom the *protector* left here.

At this time the *vecinos* of this *ciudad* of Compostela have filed a petition [stating] that they would like to move [the *ciudad*] to a place which would be in greater proximity to the Indians who serve them. Seeing that the location of this place is not good and that the Indians would benefit because, in order to perform their services, they will not be going as far from their homes, a location to which they may go has been designated. And I have had it publicly [3r] announced that, within a specified time, all those who hold Indians [in *encomienda*] in this *ciudad* are to come [and] reside at [the new location],[47] along with [the] warning that, [if they do not], their Indians will be granted in Your Majesty's name to other persons who do reside [there] and would teach and instruct them in matters of the faith. May Your Majesty order that what is of service be done in this [matter]. [That is] because it is fitting for the pacification of this *provincia* and so that the Indians may be taught, that those [persons] who hold the [Indians] in *encomienda* reside among them.[48]

{Assure [him].}[49] {/}

{+} No one has raised questions about *licenciado* de la Torre during his *residencia*, except Nuño de Guzmán. He filed four complaints against him made by some of the Indians he holds in *encomienda*, whom the *licenciado* used. Nothing resulted from this during the closed investigation, which had to be charged against his heirs, although plenty [of charges] could have been lodged against him in person. [Since] he has now given an accounting to God concerning [the charges],

I am not sending it [the record of the closed investigation], [even though I ordinarily would] so that Your Majesty might order it reviewed. He did not have any lieutenants in this jurisdiction of whom *residencia* was taken, nor were there even *alcaldes* in the *villa* of Guadalajara when I arrived. In Your Majesty's name I installed and appointed the *regidores*.[50]

{He did well.}[51]

{+} *Licenciado* de la Torre examined the accounts of Your Majesty's officials who are in charge of Your Majesty's royal treasury in this *provincia*. When I arrived I found that Your Majesty's treasurer[52] had in his possession all the account records, balances due, and the [audit] decision[53] which had been rendered concerning them. [He had these documents] because since the death of the *licenciado* the treasurer [had] remained here as *justicia mayor*. Together with other files and decrees from Your Majesty, I am removing the account records.[54] [The treasurer] now says that the *licenciado* wronged him [in the audit decision] with regard to certain entries. He has requested that I provide him an authenticated copy of the account records, balance[s] due, decision, and proceedings. He has been given it. Even though I do not know that anything has been done in the account records that ought not to have been done, it seemed appropriate to me to make a report of it to Your Majesty.

{Review them.}[55]

{+} The commission by which Your Majesty orders me to come to take charge of this jurisdiction carries no designated salary. I beg Your Majesty to order that [3v] what may be of service be specified, with which I would be able to support myself in accordance with the high cost of this land. It is high, because it is very far away from the port and the Ciudad de México.[56]

{[It is] provided.}[57]

May Our Lord protect the Holy Catholic Imperial Majesty of Your Majesty and make [Your Majesty] prosper with an increase of more [and] greater kingdoms and dominions, as Your Majesty desires.

From this *ciudad* of Compostela in Nueva Galicia, the 15th of December of the year 1538.[58]

Holy Catholic Imperial Majesty

Your Majesty's humble vassal and servant, who kisses your royal feet and hands, Francisco Vázquez de Coronado [no rubric][59]

[4r] [blank]

[4v]
{[15]38 Nueva Galicia}

To the Holy Catholic Imperial Majesty of the Emperor and King of Spain, our lord

{[It has been] answered.}

To His Majesty from Francisco Vázquez de Coronado, 15 December 1538

{Reviewed}
{Completed}
{Nueva Galicia}[60]

TRANSCRIPTION

[fol. 1r]

Sacra Catolica Cesarea Magestad
{1538 Nueva galizia}

El Visorrey d*e* la nue*V*a españa me dio *U*na pro*V*ision rreal
de *V*u*est*ra mag*e*s*ttad* por la qu*al* / *V*u*estra* m*age*s*ttad* me
manda *V*enir a esta pro*V*inçia d*e* la nue*V*a galizia a tener
cargo d*e* *e*lla / y a tomar rresidençia al liçençiado d*e* la torre
Juez de rresidençia que aqui fue[61] y / en cumplimiento d*e* lo
que *V*u*est*ra mag*e*s*ttad* me manda luego que se me entrego la
pro*V*ision / de *V*u*est*ra mag*e*s*ttad* me parti de la çi*U*dad de
m*exic*o y quando llegue a esta gobernaçion halle / muerto al
liçençiado d*e* la torre a quien *V*u*est*ra mag*e*s*ttad* me manda
tomar rr*e*sidençia / en la *V*illa de guadalajara d*e* *e*sta
pro*V*inçia *A*donde el liçençiado rr*e*sidio y / murio pregone
rresidençia contra los bienes que quedaron a sus h*e*r*e*deros /
en aquella *V*i*lla*[62] pro*V*ey algunas cosas que con*V*enian al
ser*V*içio de *V*u*est*ra mag*e*s*ttad* / y queriendome *V*enir a esta
çi*U*dad de conpostela llego el procurador d*e* la *V*illa de san /
miguel de la pro*V*inçia de culiacan y me dixo que los *V*ezinos
de aquella *V*illa / se *V*enian y la dexaban despoblada y que
toda la pro*V*inçia estaba *A* punto de / se perder y me rre-
quirio de parte de *V*u*est*ra mag*e*s*ttad* que con bre*V*edad fuese
a poner / rremedio en ello çertificandome que si dentro de
quarenta dias no yba que / los *V*ezinos se *V*endrian a ca*U*sa
de muchas neçesidades[63] que padeçen y de los / daños que
ayapin *U*n yndio que anda[64] alçado les haze pedile ynformaçion / y diome la mas bastante de lo que yo la quisiera
porque pareçe por ella estar / los *V*ezinos d*e* la *V*ylla de san
miguel y los yndios que alli estan de paz con mu- / cho trabajo con esta en*V*io a *V*u*est*ra mag*e*s*ttad* el rrequirimiento
que se me hizo y la / ynformaçion para que *V*u*est*ra mag*e*s-
ttad lo mande *V*er si fuere ser*V*ido de s*a*ber el(l) est*a*do

[fol. 1v]

en que esta aquella pro*V*inçia yo traya[65] Determina*D*o de yr
a *V*isitalla en pu- / diendome[66] desocupar[67] porque ansi me
lo mando el *V*isorrey d*e* la nue*V*a españa / De parte de
*V*u*est*ra mag*e*s*ttad* y me dio çierta ayuda de costa que lle*V*ase
a los *V*ezinos de aqu*e*- / lla *V*illa de san miguel sabiendo sus
neçesidades temiendo lo que a*h*ora su- / çede que es *V*enirse
y dexar despoblada aquella *V*illa yo me partire de a- / qui a
ocho dias y antes me *h*obiera partido si no por dexar
pro*V*eydo en lo de aqui / lo que con*V*iene al ser*V*içio de
*V*u*est*ra mag*e*s*ttad* y hare todo lo posible por rreme- / diar
aquella *V*illa y pro*V*inçia y *V*ere si con*V*iene al ser*V*içio de
*V*u*est*ra mag*e*s*ttad* / sostenerse y de todo dare Relaçion a
*V*u*est*ra mag*e*s*ta*d

{+} ya tendra *V*u*est*ra mag*e*s*ta*d rrelaçion d*e* lo que es esta
pro*V*inçia d*e* la nue*V*a galizia d*e* los q*ue* / en ella *h*an gobernado por *V*u*est*ra mag*e*s*ta*d y de *e*sta ca*U*sa y de que a poco
que estoy en ella / dexo de dalla al presente a *V*u*est*ra mag*e*s-
ttad hasta tenello todo bien *V*isto sola- / mente dare aqui
cuenta[68] a *V*u*est*ra mag*e*s*ttad* del estado en que la hallo sepa
*V*u*est*ra / mag*e*s*ttad* que la mayor parte de los yndios d*e* *e*lla
estan de guerra *U*nos que no se / *h*an conquistado y otros que
despues de conquistados[69] y puestos deba- / xo d*e*l dominio
de *V*u*est*ra mag*e*s*ta*d se *h*an rrebelado y d*e* los que estan de
paz tienen / nuño de guzman y tres o quatro criados y amigos suyos lo mejor y mas de / Cuya c*a*Usa y de *h*aber tan
pocos yndios de paz muchos que *h*an ser*V*ido a / *V*u*est*ra
mag*e*s*ta*d *e*n la conquista de aqui y otros que *h*an *V*enido a
poblar padeçen / mucha n*e*çesidad y con ella tienen poco
cuydado de yndustryar los yn- / Dios e*n* las cosas d*e* la fe y
mucho de apro*V*echarse d*e* *e*llos en mas de lo que / Deben
que como los yndios de esta pro*V*inçia no estan tasados en el

/ tributo que pueden dar sirVense de *e*llos en serViçios personales porque / tributos muy pocos yndios de *e*sta proVinçia lo dan sino son los que tiene / encomendados nuño de guzman y estos le dan poco aUnque ellos son / muchos la manera como se sostienen los (yndios) *vezinos*[70] de *e*sta goberna- / {/} çion que tienen yndios en encomienda es que en las minas de oro dan / todos los mas pueblos A sus comenderos yndios que les saquen oro / algunos de los que entre los yndios se tratan Venden y conpran / por esclaVos sin tener hierro y otros que son libres y esta manera / de ViVir tienen despues qu*e* se desCubrieron las minas que puede *h*aber / tres años y esto es por la falta que en esta proVinçia *h*ay de esclaVos que / aUnque en ella se hizieron en harta cantidad todos se sacaron a Ve*n*der

[fol. 2r]
Fuera y por esta falta que *h*ay d*e e*llos las minas se labran con esclaVos de yn- / dios y con yndios libres yo Vine a las minas que llaman de n*uest*ra señora d*e* la / conçepçion para dar orden en esto y para saber como son tratados los que / sirVen en ellas y hize pesquisa publica y secreta entre los mismos yn- / dios y halle que son bien tratados asi en ser su trabajo moderado como en / dalles bien de comer y de Vestir a su Uso y son enseñadas en las Cosas d*e* la / fe tanto que no *h*e Visto yndio en toda esta proVinçia[71] q*ue* tenga señal De / *crist*iano sino son los que Vi en las minas y por esto me pareçio dexallo en / este estado sin menear nada como lo *h*an fecho los que *h*an gobernado has- / ta dar cuenta d*e e*llo[72] a V*uest*ra mag*est*ad para que V*uest*ra mag*est*ad mande en ello lo que / fuere servido

{+} {q*ue* hizo / bie*n* y se le / tiene *en* / *servy*cio} {/}
en otra manera se aproVechaban los Vezinos en esta proVincia antes / que yo Viniese a ella d*e* los yndios que tienen enComendados que los arrenda- / ban para la çiUdad de mexico y de alli los trayan cargados de m*er*caderi*a*s[73] y era / esto tan sin orden que yo los tope quando Vine de mexico de quarenta / en quarenta y de çincuenta en çincuenta cargados que yban y Venian / tan muertos de hanbre que aUn de comer no se les daba por su tra- / bajo *h*e pro*h*ybido en nonbre de V*uest*ra mag*est*ad que ninguno[74] saque yndio lybre / De la proVinçia so graVes penas porque era en gran detri-

mento de los / naturales de *e*sta proVinçia que algunos yban asi cargados ochenta / leguas de sus casas *h*an lo sintido tanto los Vezinos de *e*sta proVinçia / que dizen que sean de quexar a V*uest*ra mag*est*tad

{+} {al s*e*ñor / Visorey / y *en*Viese- / le *en* blan- / co porq*ue* / el jncha[75] / co*n e*l *gobernado*r}

V*uest*ra mag*est*ad ^*me* manda por su proVision rreal que Use de las Cartas y p*ro*visiones / de V*uest*ra mag*est*ad dirigidas al liçençiado de la torre como si a mi fueran dadas / y entre ellas *h*ay Una en que V*uest*ra mag*est*ad manda al licençiado De la torre y a / *e*l prote*c*tor *crist*obal de pedraza que tasen los tributos que los yndios / De *e*sta gobernaçion pueden dar A las personas que los tienen enComen- / dados por V*uest*ra mag*est*ad y porque el prote*c*tor no esta *en esta* proVinçia[76] no Usa- / re de *e*lla hasta saber que manda V*uest*ra mag*est*ad que se haga *h*ay mucha ne- / çesidad que los yndios se tasen porque aUnque dan poco tributo como / no estan tasados sirVense de *e*llos en serViçios personales como / quieren y por eso V*uest*ra mag*est*ad desCargara su rreal conçiençia[77] con man- / dar que se tasen como se publico esta proVision en que V*uest*ra mag*est*ad man- / da que se tasen los yndios *h*ay algunos que ynponen a los yndios que / tienen en Comendados en que digan[78] que les dan mucho mas *t*ributo

[fol. 2v]
d*e e*l que les dan y pueden dar[79] con fin de que si los tasaren los hallen / subidos en lo que dan creyendo que por alli sea de siguir la tasa y a*u*n- / que Veo que se engañan pareçeme dar aViso d*e e*llo a V*uest*ra mag*est*ad

{+} {/} {bien} en VolViendo De culiacan que sera lo mas presto que pueda quanto de or- / den en lo de alli procurare de traer de paz los yndios de *e*sta proVinçia q*ue* / estan rrebelados con hazelles buenos tratamientos y buenas obras y / con rreligiosos que el Visorrey d*e* la nueVa españa me dixo que enViaria / para esto y quando ellos y yo no pudieremos traellos al conosçimi*ent*o de / la fe y serViçio de V*uest*ra mag*est*ad trabaJare[80] por todas las Vias que pueda De / ponellos debaxo d*e*l domino de V*uest*ra mag*est*tad

{+} {que lo que en / vida del / licenciado no / se efectuo / no se / cumpla} {/}

el liçençiado de la torre rrepartio en esta proVinçia muchos yndios de los / que no se han conquistado ni Visto y dabalos a quien se los pedia a quin- / ze y a Veynte leguas de tierra con todos los yndios que estoViesen en ella / y aUn algun rrepartimiento hUbo de mas de çincuenta leguas y estos / tienen las çedulas guardadas hasta que la tierra se paçifique Vuestra magestad / mande lo que es serVido que en esto se guarde porque rreçibiryan / agraVio los que han sirVido y sirVieren A Vuestra magestad en la conquysta / y paçificaçion de esta tierra si otros que no lo han fecho se lleVasen / el proVecho

{+} {/} {fiar}

En comarca De esta çiUdad de conpostela hay treynta rrepartymien- / tos encomendados a Vezinos de ella y solas diez Casas hay en toda / esta çiUdad porque los Vezinos no han querido rresidir diziendo los / Unos que los yndios que tienen de rrepartimientos estan de guerra / y los otros que no les dan ningun proVecho y su aUsençia es alguna caU- / sa de no estar paçificada esta comarca y harta de no estar los yn- / dios yndustriados en las cosas de la fe que en esto hallo que ha / habido demasiado DesCuydo porque como digo[81] a Vuestra magestad no he Visto / en toda esta proVinçia yndio que tenga señal de cristiano sino son / los que Vi en las minas y çinco o seys muchachos que dexo aqui el / protector Ahora hAn pedido los Vezinos de esta çiUdad de conpostela / que la quieren mudar Adonde este en mas comarca[82] de los yn- / dios que les sirVen y Viendo que el asiento de aqui no es bueno y que / los yndios rreçiben[83] benefiçio porque no saldran A syrVir / tan lejos de sus casas e señalado sitio do se pasen y hE hecho

[fol. 3r]

pregonar que todos los que tienen yndios en esta çiUdad Vengan / A rresidyr en ella[84] dentro de çierto tienpo con aperçibimiento que / en nombre de Vuestra magestad se enComendaran sus yndios A otras personas / que rresidan y los enseñen y yndustrien en las cosas de la fe e Vuestra / magestad mande en esto lo que es sirVido que se haga porque para la / paçificaçion de esta proVinçia y para que los

yndios sean enseña- / dos conViene que los que los tienen en enComienda rresidan / en ellos

{+} {hizo / bien} {/}

al liçençiado de la torre no le ha pedi(di)do en su rresiDençia sino nuño / De guzman que le puso quatro demandas de çiertos yndios de los / que tiene encomen(^q)dados de que el liçençiado se sirVio y por / que de la pesquisa secreta no rresulta ninguna cosa de que se le / haya de hazer cargo a sus herederos aUnque a su persona se pudieran / hazer hartos y tiene ya dado cuenta A dios de ellos no la ynVio / para que Vuestra magestad la mande Ver no tuVo tenientes ningunos / en esta gobernaçion a quien se tomase rresidençia ni aUn alcal- / Des no habia en la Villa de guadalajara quando a ella llegue que yo / los puse y proVey los rregidores en nombre de Vuestra magesttad

{+} {que las / ReVea} {/}

El liçençiado de la torre tomo cuenta a los ofiçiales de (sta) Vuestra / magestad que tienen cargo en esta proVinçia de la rreal hazienda de Vuestra magestad[85] / y quando yo Vine a ella halle que el tesorero de Vuestra magestad tenia en / su poder todas las Cuentas alcançes[86] y sentençia que en ellas se ha- / bia dado porque como por muerte del liçençiado el tesorero quedo / por Justyçia mayor aqui y con otros proçesos y proVisiones / de Vuestra magestad saco las cuentas y agora dize que el liçençiado le a- / GraVio en çiertas partidas hA pedido que le de Un traslado aUto- / rizado de las cuentas alcançe y sentençia y aUtos ha se le dado y aUn- / que no se que en las cuentas se haya hecho cosa que no se deba hazer / pareçiome dar rrelaçion de ello a Vuestra magestad

{+} {proveydo} {/}

La proVision por que Vuestra magestad me manda Venir al cargo de esta goberna- / çion no trae señalado salario suplico a Vuestra magestad mande señalar

[fol. 3v]

el que fuere serVido con que yo me Pueda sustentar conforme a la / careza de esta tierra que es grande por estar muy[87] desViada de / puerto y de la çiUdad de mexico nuestro señor la Sacra Catolica Cesarea Magestad de Vuestra / magesttad

guarde y prospere[88] con acrecentamiento de otros mayores /
rreynos y señorios como V*uest*ra m*agestad* desea de *e*sta
çiUdad de conpos- / tela de la nueVa Galizia A 15 dias d*el*
mes de diZienbre de 1538 años

S*acra* C*atolica* C*esarea* M*agestad*

humyl Vasallo y criado de V*uest*ra m*agestad* / q*ue* sus rreales
pies y manos besa
Fran*cis*co Vazq*ue*z / de coronado {rúbrica}

[fol. 4r] [blank]

[fol. 4v]
{38 N*ue*va G*alici*a}

A la S*acra* C*atolica* C*esarea* M*agestad* d*e*L enperador / y
rrey de españa n*uest*ro señor

{R*espond*ida}

a su m*agestad* / de Fran*cis*co Vazquez de coronado de xV de
diz*iembr*e de 1538

{Vista}
{f*e*cha}
{nu*e*va Galizia}

Document 2

Letter of Vázquez de Coronado to Viceroy Mendoza, March 8, 1539

History Library, Museum of New Mexico, Santa Fe

Ramusio, *Terzo volume delle navigationi et viaggi*, 1556, fols. 354v–355r

INTRODUCTION

Francisco Vázquez de Coronado, a *regidor* of the *cabildo* of the Ciudad de México and the newly appointed governor of Nueva Galicia, was dispatched by Viceroy Mendoza in late 1538 to take up his post at Compostela.[1] With him went the Franciscan fray Marcos de Niza and the black slave Esteban de Dorantes, whom the viceroy had recently purchased.[2] The governor escorted the friar and the slave, who was to serve as Marcos's guide, to the farthest outpost of his jurisdiction, San Miguel de Culiacán. There, he turned over written instructions from the viceroy to Marcos regarding the reconnaissance he was to make in an attempt to verify the reports of Álvar Núñez Cabeza de Vaca and his associates. Their stories promised large, sophisticated populations living in luxury far to the north.

But as Vázquez de Coronado makes clear in the following excerpt from his letter of March 8, 1539, the affluent and populous places made known by Cabeza de Vaca were not the only lure toward the north. Local Indians had told the governor about a group of at least 50 settlements known collectively as Topira. Either there or in another, even larger, unnamed land beyond lived people who were said to "wear gold, emeralds, and other precious stones," eat from gold and silver dishes, and even decorate their houses with gold.[3] After touting the possibilities for profit at Topira and the more distant, nameless population

center in its direction and telling of Marcos and Esteban's departure for what was soon to become known as Cíbola, Vázquez de Coronado closed the extant fragment of his letter glowingly. He told Mendoza, "I trust in God that in the one area or the other we are about to find something excellent."[4]

How much more there was to the governor's original letter we may never know, for it disappeared centuries ago. All that survives is an Italian translation of the Topira-Cíbola excerpt. Evidently that was all that was titillating enough to suit the taste or match the book concept of its publisher, Giovanni Battista Ramusio. Though we can lament his choice not to publish the letter in full, at the same time we must be grateful for his preserving an important part of it, as well as three other documents included in the present edition.[5]

Ramusio was secretary of the Venetian senate and an avid collector and publisher of manuscripts. Among his sources for manuscripts dealing with the New World were Diego Hurtado de Mendoza, brother of Viceroy Antonio de Mendoza and Spain's ambassador to Venice from 1539 to 1546,[6] and Gonzalo Fernández de Oviedo y Valdés, Carlos V's official chronicler of the Indies beginning in 1532.[7] It was probably from one of these men that Ramusio received a copy of the Vázquez de Coronado letter that he later excerpted and published in 1556 in the first edition of the *Terzo volume* of his *Navigationi et viaggi*, which is the version used in this volume. Both men passed documents on to Ramusio in other instances. Oviedo was particularly assiduous in supplying documents to Ramusio because, from 1538 to 1543, he and the Venetian were business partners in a commercial trading enterprise between Europe and the Indies.[8]

However Ramusio came by a copy of the 1539 letter, he subsequently translated it (or had it translated) into Italian for publication. It is unknown what happened to the Spanish-language copy from which the translation derived. We point out elsewhere in this volume that the translator may have been more comfortable in Spanish than in Italian; his Italian renditions are peppered with hispanisms.[9] As is evident from Ramusio's unannounced and gratuitous embellishment of the original text of fray Marcos's *relación,* the fidelity of the translations he published must always remain in doubt in cases such as this one, in which the original-language text is no longer available for comparison.[10] Ramusio or his translator was the author of the title and heading that open the excerpt, but there are no other blatant intrusions by the publisher. To indicate that the heading and title were not part of the original manuscript, in the transcript and translation that follow they are enclosed in flourished brackets { }.

Serious questions exist, however, about the authenticity of the item that immediately precedes Vázquez de Coronado's letter to the viceroy in the *Terzo volume.* It purports to be the synopsis of another letter written by Vázquez de Coronado on the same day, March 8, but to the viceroy's secretary rather than to the viceroy himself. In fact, it is a fanciful concoction that combines many elements, both real and imagined, from numerous locales, ascribing them all to Topira and a neighboring community. Here are some of the more florid and fantastic portions of the "synopsis," provided in Hakluyt's translation of 1600:

They have great store of gold, which is as it were lost, because they know not what use to put it to. . . . [They have] very strong armour made of silver, fashioned after

divers shapes of beasts. . . . they seeke no other riches but to feede cattel. . . . before their temple is a great round ditch, the brim of which is compassed with the figure of a serpent made of gold and silver, and with a mixture of unknown metals.[11]

None of these descriptions was ever confirmed. For instance, there is no evidence whatsoever for the domestication of bison by preconquest indigenous people of North America. The "synopsis" further makes the claim that fray Marcos had visited Topira before March 8, even though Vázquez de Coronado mentions nothing about such a trip in the excerpt from his letter to Mendoza. Indeed, he explains that the trip to Topira would be risky and arduous until April, when he himself plans to go there, many days after Marcos departed for Cíbola.[12] Nor does the friar himself tell in his *relación* of having made a journey to Topira.[13] Yet all the descriptions in the "synopsis" are ascribed to Marcos. The document appears to be an outright fabrication, but whether Ramusio was victim or perpetrator remains a mystery.

Ramusio's translation of the fragment of Vázquez de Coronado's March 1539 letter to Mendoza was translated into English and French and published in those languages in the seventeenth, nineteenth, and twentieth centuries. In 1600 Richard Hakluyt published an English translation in the third and final part of his *Principal Navigations, Voyages, Traffiques, and Discoveries of the English Nation.*[14] Henri Ternaux-Compans's French translation appeared in 1838 in the ninth volume of his *Voyages, relations et memoires originaux pour servir a l'histoire de la decouverte de l'Amerique.*[15] And a century later, in 1940, George Hammond and Agapito Rey published their modern English translation.[16] In editing the translation we publish here, we have consulted all three of these earlier translations. In both translation and transcription, folio numeration conforms to the published 1556 Italian edition.

TRANSLATION

[354v]

{Copy of the letter from Francisco Vázquez de Coronado, governor of Nueva Galicia, to the lord Antonio de Mendoza, viceroy of Nueva España, dated at San Miguel de Culiacán, the eighth of March 1539.}

{Concerning the difficult sea voyage[17] from San Miguel de Culiacán to Topira; a description of that *provincia* and another one near it [that is] very rich in gold and precious stones; the number of persons Vázquez is taking in order to go there; and how fray Marcos de Niza is looked up to by the Indians of Petatlán.}[18]

With Lord God's help, I will depart for Topira from this land of San Miguel de Culiacán on the tenth of April. It cannot be earlier because [not] until then will the gunpowder and fuse cord Your Lordship is sending me have arrived.[19] I think they are already at Compostela. Besides this, [in order to go there] at this time I [would] have to travel many leagues to go around very high mountains that rise to the heavens and a river that is so large and swollen there is no place where I can ford it. If I leave at the aforesaid time, [the Indians] say it will be possible to wade across. [Previously] they were telling me that from here to Topira it was not more than fifty leagues, [but] I have learned that it is more than eighty.

I do not remember whether I have written to Your Lordship yet [concerning] the information I have obtained about Topira.[20] But I must do so anyway because later they told me about some more things. It seems appropriate to me to write them to Your Lordship in this [letter] of mine. You may, therefore, [already] know what they are telling me, [namely] that Topira is a very populous *provincia* situated between two rivers and that there are more than fifty inhabited places there.

{The Indians cover their houses with gold and silver.}[21] And [they say] that farther on there is another, larger *provincia*, the name of which the Indians did not know so they could tell me. In that place there are many types of food: corn, beans, chile, melons, and squash, and a great abundance of native fowls. In addition, the inhabitants wear gold, emeralds, and other precious stones and ordinarily serve [their meals] on silver and gold, with which they cover their houses [also]. The *principales* wear heavy, well-worked chains of gold around their necks. And they go about dressed in painted *mantas*. There are many cattle there, but not domesticated.[22]

They told me not to go visit [that land], because I have [only] a few people from this land and the Indians [of the other land] are numerous and skillful men. What I am saying is [what was] learned from two earlier reports from Indians [who are] neighbors of those [people].

I will leave at the time I have stated with at least 150 horsemen, with twelve horses being led, and 200 footmen, comprising crossbowmen and arquebusiers.[23] I will take hogs,[24] wethers, and everything [in the nature of supplies] I have been able to find to buy.

Your Lordship may be certain I will not return to [the Ciudad de] México until I can speak about what is likely there with greater certainty. Further, if I find anything from which profit can be derived, I will remain there until I notify Your Lordship, so that you may order what must be done. If, unfortunately, nothing [of value] is there, I will attempt to give a report of the 100 leagues immediately beyond [there]. I trust in God that in that place there will be something in which Your Lordship can be served by all these *caballeros* and those who may come afterward. I think I will not be able to do anything besides stay put. The rains, the weather, and the character of the land, as well as whatever I find, will dictate what I have to do.

Fray Marcos went [355r] farther into the interior of that land on the seventh of last month (February).[25] With him [was] Esteban.[26] When I parted from them I left them in the hands of more than a hundred Indians from Petatlán and the leader who had come [from there]. They held the father in the highest esteem, doing everything possible to please him.[27] It would not be possible to set down or depict his entry [into the land] better than was done in all the reports made in my letters from Compostela and San Miguel [de Culiacán].[28] I wrote ones as lengthy as they could be; even so, they may be [only] the tenth part since it is [such] a large subject.

With this [message] I am sending Your Lordship a letter I have received from the aforementioned father.[29] The Indians tell me that everyone there esteems him, and thus I believe he could go on for two thousand leagues.[30] He says that if he finds an excellent land, he will write me. I will not go there [myself] without [first] informing Your Lordship.

I trust in God that in the one area or the other we are about to find something excellent.

TRANSCRIPTION

[fol. 354v]

{COPIA DELLE LETTERE DI FRANCESCO / Vazquez di Coronado, governatore della nuova Galitia, al Signore An- / tonio di Mendozza, Vicere della nuova Spagna, date in san / Michiel di Cul(n)uacan, alli otto di Marzo. M D XXXIX}

{Della difficile naviga(t)zione da san Michiel di Cul(n)uacan a Topira; descrittione di quella provincia, & di / Un'altra allei Vicina molto ricc(h)a d'oro, et pietre pre(t)ziose: numero delle genti che seco conduce il / Vazquez per andarvi, et qua*n*to sia (h)onorato fra Marco da Nizza dall'Indiani di Petatlan.}

COn l'aiuto del Signor Iddio io partiro da q*u*esta terra di san Michiel di Culnacan per To- / pira, alli dieci di Aprile, & non potra essere avanti, perche all'(h)ora sara venuta la polve- / re, & la corda che mi manda V*ostra* S*ignoria* & penso che debbi esser gia in Co*m*postella, & oltra di que- / sto ho da caminare tante leghe all'intorno di montagne altissime che vanno in cielo, & un / fiume ch'è al presente cosi grosso & gonfio, che no*n* v'è luogo dove si possi guadarlo, & par- / tendo al te*m*po sopradetto, dicono che si potra guazzare: mi (h)avevano detto che di qui à To- / pira non vi erano piu di cinquanta leghe, & ho saputo che ve ne sono piu di ottanta, non mi / ricordo se ho scritto à V*ostra* S*ignoria* la relation che tengo di Topira, nondimeno anc(h)or*a* che l'(h)abbi / fatto, perche da*p*poi qui mi sono informato d'alcune cose di piu, mi par*e* di scriverle à V*ostra* S*ignoria* in / q*u*este mie. Sappia du*n*que quella, che mi dicono, che Topira è una provincia molto popolata, / posta fra duoi fiumi, & che vi son piu di cinquanta luoghi (h)abitati, et che piu avanti di lei v'è / {Gl'indiani / c(u)oprono / le lor case / di oro & d' / argento.} un'altra provincia maggiore, & non mi seppero dir*e* gl'Indiani il nome di quella, dove vi so- / no molte vettovaglie di Maiz, fasoli & axi,[31] melloni, & zucche,

& copia grande di galline del / paese: portano a dosso[32] gli (h)abitatori, oro, smeraldi, & altre pietre pre(t)ziose, & si ser- / vono ordi- / nariamente con oro & argento, colqual c(u)oprono le case, & li principali portano a torno al / collo catene d'oro grosse & ben lavorate, & vanno vestiti con coperte dipinte, & vi sono / molte vacche, ma non domestiche, & mi dicono che non va di à trovargli per (h)aver poche / genti di quelle di questo paese, perche gl'Indiani sono molti & valenti (h)uomi- / ni. questo che / io dico lo inteso per due altre relationi d'Indiani vicini à quelli. Io mi partiro al tempo che / ho detto, & meno meco. 150. (h)uomini à cavallo, & dodici cavalli à mano, &. 200. fanti à pie / di balestrieri & schioppetieri: con- / duco porci, castrati, & tutto quello che ho potuto trovar*e* da / comperare, V*ostra* S*ignoria* sia certa ch'io non ritornero al Messico fin tanto che no*n* possi dire à quella / quel che vi sarà co*n* maggior certezza. & se trovero cosa sopra la qual si possi far*e* frutto,[33] mi fer- / mero fino che avisi V*ostra* S*ignoria* accio che comandi quello che si (h)abbi*a* da fare: & se per disgra(t)zia no*n* / vi sarà cosa alcuna, procurero di dar conto di altre. 100. leghe avanti, dove spero in Dio che / ivi sarà cosa per la qual V*ostra* S*ignoria* potra adoperar*e* tutti questi caval- / lieri & quelli che sopra venisse- / ro. Io penso che non potro far che non mi fermi li, & le acque, i tempi & la disposi(t)zione del / paese, & quello che trovero mi dira quel- / lo che (h)avero da fare. Fra Marco entrò nella terra / piu

[fol. 355r]

355

piu dentro, & con lui Stephano à sette del mese passato di Febraro, quando mi parti da loro / gli lasciai in poter*e* di piu di cento Indiani di Petatlan, & da quel capo che erano venu- / ti, por- / tavano il Padre in palma di mano, facendoli tutti i piaceri che possibili fosse: no*n* si potria di / mandar*e* ne dipingere la sua (i)entra(d)ta meglio di quello che stato fatto in tutte le relationi fatte / per mie lettere in compostella & in san Michiele le scrissi le maggiore che potessero essere. & / anc(h)ora che siano la decima parte è gran cosa. con questa mando a Vostra Signoria una lettera che ho rice- / vuto da detto padre, mi dicono gl'Indiani, che tutti ivi l'adorano, & cosi credo che'l porria / andare due mila leghe avanti, dice che trovando buon paese mi scrivera, non vi andero senza / farlo sapere à vostra Signoria: spero in Dio che per una parte ò per l'altra siamo per trovar alcu- / na buono cosa.

Document 3

Letter of Vázquez de Coronado to the King, July 15, 1539

AGI, Guadalajara, 5, R.1, N.6

INTRODUCTION

In mid-July 1539, Francisco Vázquez de Coronado, in his capacity as governor of Nueva Galicia, wrote an administrative report to Carlos V. Although he was not yet back, Marcos de Niza's northern trek was just about to end. On the strength of interim reports the friar had dispatched during the course of his reconnaissance, the governor permitted himself some enthusiasm about Cíbola. He wrote, in the second longest section of his letter, "God and Your Majesty must be well pleased . . . by the magnificence of the land which fray Marcos reports." He praised "the excellent method and skill the viceroy has employed" in sending priests to perform reconnaissance.[1]

Within days, though, Vázquez de Coronado would learn from fray Marcos himself that all was not quite so auspicious in the north. After a breathless retracing of his steps from Cíbola, the friar would make known the killing of Esteban de Dorantes by people of Cíbola and the fear and anger this inspired in Marcos's companions and guides from Sonora. Nevertheless, the tenor of his report would be upbeat, and Cíbola would remain an enticing, if now somewhat menacing, destination.

In the absence of a full report from fray Marcos, the topic of greatest moment in Vázquez de Coronado's letter is his claim to have restored apparent tranquillity between the Indians and European newcomers in the *provincia* of Culiacán. Since 1536, warfare in response to Spanish slaving activities in the *provincia* had threatened the viability of Spanish presence there.[2] By 1539, the Spaniards of Culiacán had identified the chief war leader of the native people of the vicinity as a man called Ayapín. With the large expeditionary force with which the governor had intended to reconnoiter Topira, he instead waged a campaign against Tahue-speaking warriors.[3] The quasi-military force tracked down and captured Ayapín, who was subsequently executed and quartered. In the immediate wake of such repressive measures, the Spanish population seemed in far less danger, which Vázquez de Coronado proudly reported in his July 1539 letter.[4]

The remainder of the letter is a routine administrative report that includes an assessment of the modest success in religious conversion of native people and a restatement of the need for more ecclesiastics to accomplish that task. The tone of the letter, however, is insistently optimistic and self-congratulatory. Vázquez de Coronado portrays himself as a responsive and capable governor who is dealing with serious threats to royal dominion while pursuing opportunities to extend that dominion.

The surviving copy of the letter, which bears Vázquez de Coronado's signature (though the body is in a scribal hand), is likely the original that was dispatched to the emperor through his Consejo de Indias. The *escribano*, who composed the letter for the governor's signature, was probably not Hernando Martín Bermejo, Vázquez de Coronado's secretary at the time. The hand of the letter is different than than of the text of Document 1 in this volume, which was prepared seven months earlier, and Document 26, written 27 months later.[5] Both of these were also signed by the governor and captain general.

The letter is published here in Spanish in its entirety for the first time. One earlier translation into English has been published, that by George Hammond and Agapito Rey in 1940.[6] In editing our translation, which follows, we have collated it with Hammond and Rey's version and have noted the inevitable differences between the two.

TRANSLATION

[1r]

Holy Catholic Imperial Majesty

{Nueva Galicia}

{Francisco Vázquez Coronado}

{*Audiencia*}⁷

As soon as I reached this *provincia* of Nueva Galicia by Your Majesty's order, I made a report to Your Majesty by means of my letters regarding the state in which I found things in this *provincia* and how [the *procurador*] petitioned me, on behalf of the *villa* of San Miguel in the *provincia* of Culiacán, to go [there] to remedy the difficulty it is in. The *vecinos* of that *villa* were leaving because the natives of that *provincia*, or most of them, had risen up in arms with a *cacique* who was called Ayapín,⁸ whom they made their leader and captain in the uprising.

Since it seemed to me that I had to serve Your Majesty in [pursuing this] journey with the greatest speed I was capable of,⁹ I immediately left for that *provincia*. When I had arrived there, I found that all the *vecinos* were already about to come [here] and leave the *villa* uninhabited,¹⁰ both on account of the straits in which Ayapín had them and because they were very poor and received no profit from the land since the Indians they hold by *repartimiento* did not work for them.

With my arrival [1v] and the financial assistance that the viceroy of Nueva España sent the *vecinos* in Your Majesty's name, they calmed down again. So I divided among them certain small villages which Nuño de Guzmán held there by *repartimiento*. I distributed those [villages] to them with the consultation and willingness of Nuño de Guzmán, since he considered it a good thing, understanding

that, until such time as Your Majesty orders something else, it is advantageous to Your Majesty's service and that those *vecinos* were not able to support themselves without them.

This done, I went out through the *provincia* in order to prevent the deaths of men by all the ways and means I could. I was pacifying [the natives] and attracting them to Your Majesty's service little by little, making them understand that they are Your Majesty's vassals. And that Your Majesty's royal will is that they be Christians and be treated benevolently. When I understood that their uprising had been caused more by ignorance and abuse than by malice, I promised them forgiveness, in Your Majesty's name, for what had occurred, if by their [own] volition they came to the service of Your Majesty, so [that] henceforth they would not do disservice whereby they would deserve to be punished.

When they had been made to understand [this] through interpreters who understood them well,¹¹ most of those who were up in arms came to peace, without any death or punishment occurring. When it was understood by Ayapín that all or most of his people were abandoning him and coming to me in peace, he left, withdrawing and fleeing until he went up into some very rugged mountains. Traveling always in his pursuit, [2r] I apprehended him there. When he had been taken prisoner I instituted a proceeding against him. By this [procedure] I found [him] deserving of death, and I had him quartered. With this administration of justice that whole land has just [now] settled and calmed down.¹²

Since up to that point all the natives [had been] going about in the mountain ranges because of their uprising, they had no houses nor did they plant [anything]. They are already beginning to build houses and prepare fields. They have returned to the locations where they were accustomed to have [their] settlement[s], even though many people are missing from among those there used to be in that *provincia*. [That is] because of the fighting men and the death toll there has been in [the *provincia*]. But since [the land] is very fertile and productive of all [sorts of] food, I trust in God that it will again recover and that the Spanish *vecinos* of that *villa* will calm down. [That is] because the land is very excellent and there are many signs of gold and silver. From these they will be able to obtain more profit than [they have] until now.

{Item} I took with me to this *provincia* of Culiacán an ecclesiastic of the Franciscan Order who is called fray Marcos de Niza.[13] The viceroy of Nueva España directed me[14] to convey him to the land toward the interior. [That is] because he was going [there] by [the viceroy's] order in Your Majesty's name to reconnoiter the coast of this Nueva España by land. [This was] in order to learn what secrets, lands, and people there are in it which have not [previously] been seen.

So that [fray Marcos] might penetrate [the land] in greater security, I sent to the towns of Petatlán[15] and Cuchillo (which [are] nearly sixty leagues beyond Culiacán) some of the Indians [2v] whom the viceroy [had] set free from [among] the slaves that had been taken in this *provincia* of [Nueva] Galicia. I told those [Indians] to summon some native Indians from those towns and tell them not to be afraid because Your Majesty has ordered that war not be waged against them. Nor were they to be abused or enslaved.

As a result of this [message] and seeing that the messengers who were going to summon them had been freed (they were not a little amazed by their freedom), more than eighty men came to me.[16] After having made those [Indians] understand very thoroughly Your Majesty's royal will (which is that at present Your Majesty does not desire anything from them except that they become Christians and come to know God and Your Majesty, as their lord), I directed them to take fray Marcos and Esteban to the interior of the land in complete safety. A Black whom the viceroy bought for this purpose from one of those who escaped from La Florida is called Esteban.[17]

[The Indians from Petatlán and Cuchillo] performed it just as I [had] asked, treating them most excellently and traveling by their daily journeys. I pray to God[18] that they [have] come upon a land as excellent as [what] Your Majesty will perceive from the report of fray Marcos[19] and from what the viceroy is writing to Your Majesty. Since [the viceroy] is doing that, I will not make [a report].

From this vantage I believe that God and Your Majesty must be well pleased both by the magnificence of the land which fray Marcos reports and by the excellent method[20] and skill the viceroy has employed in reconnoitering it and will employ in its pacification and placing it under Your Majesty's dominion.

{Item} I [have] already made a report to Your Majesty regarding the need there is in this *provincia* of [3r] [Nueva] Galicia for ecclesiastics who would instruct its natives in [Christianity]. Because of this [lack] there is scarcely a man in the whole [*provincia*] who exhibits any sign of [being] Christian unless it is those who labor in and have dealings with the Spaniards at the mines.[21] I have tried in every way possible to have the ecclesiastics come, [and] they have written to me that they will come very soon. I trust in God that with their teaching and good example many positive results will be produced in this *provincia*. In addition to this, I have arranged that they build churches in all the towns, where the natives are to come together for instruction. Some of the towns which were up in arms have come to peace, although many others remain that are still in revolt. I will try with good deeds to bring them [to peace] voluntarily. And if I cannot, I will try [to do] it in the way which is most advantageous to the service of God and Your Majesty.

{Item} I received a decree from Your Majesty in which you command that all Spaniards who live in that *provincia* [Nueva Galicia] are to build [their] houses with stone or mud walls.[22] [I received] a letter from Your Majesty in which you command that [the decree regarding house construction] be put into effect. As soon as I received the [letter] I put what Your Majesty commands me [to do] into effect, and it was publicly announced in this *ciudad* of Compostela and in the rest of the *villa*s of this *provincia*. And [it was proclaimed] that it was to be done as Your Majesty commands without inconvenience to the *vecinos*. [That is] because with the gold they are extracting they are beginning to have the means available for building houses.

{Item} By one of Your Majesty's decrees it is ordered that an accounting be taken of the custodians of the [goods of the] deceased and that any balance that may be due be sent to the Casa de la Contratación of the Indies, to Your Majesty's officials [3v] who occupy it.[23] As soon as I arrived in this *provincia*, I began auditing the accounts of the custodians. Most all of the goods of the deceased [that the custodians] hold consist of documents [records of indebtedness]. These belonged to people who have gone away and [then] died without having left [anything] from which to pay [them]. These documents, [from] six or seven years ago, pass from custodian to custodian because the goods of the deceased were customarily sold on credit at public auctions.[24] The reason for this was that at that time there was no gold in this *provincia*, and the governor, Nuño de Guzmán, therefore ordered that the custodians provide accounting to each other of those instruments regarding what could not be collected. May Your Majesty be pleased to send [a letter] to order what should be done about this. [That is] because those who at present hold the goods of the deceased do not appraise their estates at more than two hundred *castellanos*. The balance owed from the instruments amounts to more than one thousand three hundred [*castellanos*].

May Our Lord preserve the Holy Catholic Imperial person of Your Majesty, and may he glorify [you] with an increase of grander kingdoms and dominions, as we, your servants, desire.

From [Nueva] Galicia in Nueva España; in Compostela, 15th of July in the year 1539.

Holy Catholic Imperial Majesty

Your Majesty's humble servant who kisses your royal feet, Francisco Vázquez de Coronado [no rubric][25]

[4r] [blank]

[4v]
To the Holy Catholic Imperial Majesty of the most triumphant Emperor and Lord

{Nueva Galicia}[26]
{Answered}
{Reviewed}

{To His Majesty from Francisco Vázquez de Coronado, 15 July 1539}[27]

{Response being made to the viceroy: that in the absence of Francisco Vázquez, he is to look after this *provincia*; response to Francisco Vázquez: thank him for the attention he is paying to it}[28]

{1539}
{Guadalajara}
{[15]39 Nueva Galicia}

TRANSCRIPTION

[fol. 1r]
Sacra Catolica Cesarea Magestad
{Nueva galizia 1539}
{Francisco Vazquez coronado}
{audiencia}

Luego como llegue por mandado de Vuestra magestad a esta pro- / vinçia de la nueva Galizia hize rrelaçion a vuestra magestad por mis / Cartas del estado en que halle las cosas de aquesta proVin- / çia y de como me rrequirieron por parte de la Villa de san / miGuel de la proVinçia de Culiacan que fuese a rreme- / diar el aprieto en que esta van los Vezinos de aquella Villa / a CaUsa de que las naturales de aquella pro- Vinçia o la / mayor parte de ellos andaban leVantados con Un caçique que / se dezia *ayapin* que trayan por su caUdillo y capitan / en el levantamiento pareçiendome que en la jornada / habia de serVyr a Vuestra magestad con la mayor priesa que pude / me parti luego a aquella proVinçia adonde llegado halle / que todos los Vezinos estaban ya para venyrse y dexar la / Villa despoblada asi por el aprieto en que ayapin los te- / nya como por estar muy p(r)obres y sin tener ningun / aproVechamiento de la tierra a caUsa de no syrVilles los / yndios que tienen de rrepartimiento y con mi llegada

[fol. 1 v]
y con el ayuda de costa que el visorrey de la nueVa españa / en nombre de vuestra magestad les enVio los Vezinos tornaron a so- / segarse y conque les rreparti çiertos poblezuelos que / tenia nuño de guzman alli de rrepar- timiento los quales / les Reparti con pareçer y Voluntad De nuño de guzman / porque viendo que conVenia al serViçio de Vuestra magestad y que a- / quellos Vezinos no se podian

sostener sin ellos lo *hobo*[29] por bien / hasta tanto que Vuestra magestad otra cosa mandase y hecho esto / sali por la pro- Vinçia por todas las Vias y formas que pude / por esCusar muertes de honbres los fuy poco a poco / paçificando y atrayendo al serViçio de Vuestra magestad dandoles / a entender como son Vasallos de Vuestra magestad y que su rreal / Voluntad de Vuestra magestad es que sean *cristianos* y que sean / bien tratados y Visto que su alçamiento habia sido mas / por ygnorançia y malostratamientos que no por maliçia / en nonbre de Vuestra magestad les prometi perdon de lo pasado si de / su Voluntad Viniesen al serViçio de Vuestra magestad conque de ahy / adelante no hiziesen De(s)serViçio por donde mereçiesen / ser castigados y habiendoselo dado a entender con yn- / Terpret(r)es que los entendian bien Vinieron de paz la ma- / yor parte de los que andaban leVan- tados sin ynterVe- / nia muerte ni ningun castigo y Visto por el aya- / pin que toda la mas gente le dexaban y me Venian de paz / se fue rretrayendo y huyendo hasta subirse en Unas / sierras muy agras adonde yendo sienpre en su siGui-

[fol. 2r]
miento le prendi y preso hize proçeso Contra el por / el qual aVeriGue ser digno De muerte y le hize hazer / quatro quartos con la qual justiçia se acabo de asentar / y apaziGuar toda aquella tierra y como hasta en(s)- / Tonçes todos los naturales andaban por las sierras / a caUsa de su levan- tamiento no tenian casas ni senbra- / ban las quales casas y sementeras comiençan ya / a hazer y se han Vuelto a los sitios do solian tener po- / blado aUnque falta mucha gente de la que en aquella pro- / Vynçia solia haber a caUsa de l(a)os honbres de Guerra y mor- / Tandades que en ella ha habido mas como es muy fertyL / y abundosa de todos manten-

imientos espero en dios que / se tornara a Rehazer y que los españoles Vezinos de aque- / lla Villa asentaran por ser la tierra muy buena y haber / en ella muchas muestras de oro y de plata de que podran / Tener aproVechamiento mas que hasta aqui

{ytem} yo lleVe conmigo a esta proVynçia de Culiacan Un rre- / ligioso de la (h)orden de san francisco que se dize fray marcos / de nisa el qual me encomendo el Visorrey de la nueVa españa / que metiese[30] la tierra adentro porque yba por su man- / dado en nombre de Vuestra magestad a descubryr por tierra la costa / De esta nueVa españa para saber los secretos tierras / y Gente que hay en aquello que no se ha Visto y para / que entrase Con mas siguridades enVie çiertos yndios

[fol. 2v]
de los que el visorrey liberto de los esclaVos que se hizieron / en esta proVinçia de Galizia a los pueblos de petatlan / y del cuchillo que es çerca de sesenta leguas adelante de Cu- / liacan a los quales dixe que llamasen algunos yndios na- / Turales de aquellos pueblos y que les dixesen no toViesen / Temor porque vuestra magestad tiene mandado que no se les haga / Guerra ni maltratamiento ni sean hechos esclaVos y / con esto y con Ver libres los mensaJeros que los yban a llamar / de que no poco se espantaron de su libertad me Vinieron mas / de ochenta honbres a los quales despues de habelles dado muy / partiCularmente a entender la rreal Voluntad de / Vuestra magestad que es que Vuestra magestad al presente no quiere de ellos otra / cosa sino que sean cristianos y conoçan a dios y a Vuestra magestad por / señor les encomende lleVasen con toda siguridad la / Tierra adentro al fray marcos y a esteban Un negro que el / Visorrey conpro para este efecto de Uno de los que escapa- / ron de la florida que se dize esteban y ellos lo hizieron asy / haziendoles todo bien tratamiento y yendo por sus jor- / nadas pliego a dios que toparon con Una tan buena tierra / como Vuestra magestad Vera por la rrelaçion de fray marcos y por / lo que el Visorrey escribe a Vuestra magestad que por hazello el no lo / hago yo aqui espero[31] que dios y vuestra magestad han de ser muy ser- / Vidos asi por la grandeza que fray marcos cuenta de la / Tierra como por la

buena (h)orden e yndustria que el Vyso- / rrey ha tenido en desCubrilla y tendra en paçificalla y / ponella debaxo del dominio de Vuestra magestad

{ytem} ya hize rrelaçion a Vuestra magestad de la neçesidad que en esta proVynçia de

[fol. 3r]
Galizia hay de rreligiosos que yndustrien los naturales[32] de ella a caUsa / de que apenas hay honbre en toda ella que tenga señal de cristiano syno / son los que andan[33] y conVersan con los españoles en las minas yo / he procurado lo muy posible que Vengan rreligiosos escritome / han que Vendran muy presto espero en dios que con su doctrina[34] / y buen e(n)xemplo se hara mucho fruto en esta proVynçia / de mas de que yo tengo proveydo que en todos los pueblos hagan / yGlesias donde se junten los naturales a la doctrina al- / Gunos de los pueblos que andaban alçados han Venido de paz aUn- / que quedan otros muchos que todaVia estan rrebelados pro- / curare con buenas obras de traellos por bien[35] y si no pu- / diere procurallo (h)e de la manera que mas conVenga al ser- / Viçio de dios y de vuestra magestad

{ytem} Reçibi Una proVision de Vuestra magestad en que manda que todos los / españoles que en aquella proVinçia ViVen hagan casas de pie- / dra o de tapias y una carta de Vuestra magestad en que me manda / el cumplimiento de ella y luego como la rreçibi puse en efecto / lo que vuestra magestad manda y se pregono en esta çiUdad de conpos- / Tela y en las demas Villas de aquesta proVinçia y hazer sea / como Vuestra magestad lo manda sin Vexaçion de los Vezinos porque / con el oro que sacan comiençan a tener posibilidad[36] para / hazer casas

{ytem} por Una proVision de Vuestra magestad esta mandado que se tome Cuenta / a los tenedores de los difuntos y que el alcançe que se hiziere se / enVie a la casa de la contrataçion de las yndias a los ofiçiales de

[fol. 3v]
Vuestra magestad que en ella rresiDen y luego como llegue a

esta proVinçia / començe a tomar Cuenta a los tenedores los quales todos los mas bienes / de difuntos que tienen son (son) escrituras y estas de personas / que se *h*an ydo y muerto sin dexar De que pagar y andan estas escry- / Turas De tenedores en tenedores mas ha de seys o siete años por- / que los bienes d*e* los difuntos se Vendian en las almonedas fiados / *l*a caUsa de que *fue* en aquel tienpo no *h*abia oro en esta proVinçia y eL / Governador nuño de guzman mandaba que asi los tenedores Unos / a otros Diesen Cuenta en aquellas escrituras d*e* lo que no se podia / cobrar V*uest*ra m*a*g*estad* sea serVido de enViar a mandar lo que en esto se / debe hazer porque los que al presente tienen los bienes de difun- / Tos no Valen sus haziendas dozientos castellanos y el alcançe d*e* las es- / crituras es mas de myll y trezientos n*uest*ro señor la S*acra* C*atolica* C*esarea* per- / sona de V*uest*ra m*a*g*estad* Guarde y ensalçe con acrecentamiento de ma- / yores rreynos y señorios como sus criados deseamos de galizia / d*e* la nueVa españa en conpostela a 15 de Jullio de 1539 años

S*acra* C*atolica* C*esarea* M*a*g*estad*

humyl criado de V*uest*ra m*a*g*estad* / q*ue* sus Reales piez besa Fran*cis*co Vazqu*ez* de / coronado {rúbrica}

[fol. 4r] [blank]

[fol. 4v]
A la S*acra* C*atolica* C*esarea* M*a*g*estad* del ynVi*c*tisim*o* / enperador y / señor

{nu*ev*a Galiçia}
{R*esp*o*ndid*a}
{Vista}

{a su m*a*g*estad* / de Fran*cis*co Vazquez de coronado a 15 de Jullio de 1539}

{R*esp*u*est*a al Virrey q*ue* en ausençia de Fran*cis*co / Vazqu*ez* tenga cuydado de esta p*r*ov*y*n*cia* / y R*esp*uesta a Fran*cis*co Vazqu*ez* agradeçell*e* / el cuydado q*ue* tiene de *e*lla}

{1539}
{Guadalajara}
{39 N*uev*a G*alici*a}

Document 4

Letter of the Viceroy to the King, 1539

History Library, Museum of New Mexico, Santa Fe

Ramusio, *Terzo volume delle navigationi et viaggi*, 1556, fols. 355r–355v

INTRODUCTION

Preserved only in an Italian translation made in the 1540s or early 1550s is an excerpt from a letter from Viceroy Antonio de Mendoza to Emperor Carlos V reporting on the apparent success of the trek north made by fray Marcos de Niza. Although the letter fragment is undated, its final line indicates that it was written after the end of Marcos's trip, perhaps in September 1539. It may, in fact, have accompanied the transmittal to Spain of the friar's official report.[1]

In addition to recounting the antecedents of fray Marcos's trip, the excerpt seems intended to support the policy then current in the imperial court that incorporation of new peoples into the imperial dominion should be brought about under the guidance of ecclesiastics. A powerful voice for such a policy at the time was that of fray Bartolomé de las Casas. He had even advocated, in 1536 or 1537, that "conquest" be undertaken without any force whatsoever, by mendicant friars alone.[2] Going even farther, he obtained imperial permission to demonstrate the feasibility of such "conquest" in the *provincia* of Tuzutlán in what is now Guatemala. The attempt began in the fall of 1537 and was still under way—and generating glowing reports of success from las Casas—when Marcos made his journey north in 1539. Even the governor of Guatemala, Pedro de Alvarado, was enthusiastic about las Casas's results, at least in official correspondence.

The king and emperor himself, in a *cédula* addressed to the viceroy in November 1538, spelled out the royal position. "I have been informed," he wrote, 'that there are in that land some ecclesiastics of virtuous and exemplary life and high purpose who desire to travel to newly discovered lands that have not been conquered or entered by Spaniards in order to bring their native people into knowledge of our Holy Catholic Faith, this in the service of Our Lord God and also in our [royal] service." King Carlos then concluded that "since [those ecclesiastics] have confidence that by this means [the native peoples] will come more quickly to peace and under our dominion, . . . you [Mendoza] are to grant them license for this [purpose]."[3]

Consequently, when the Coronado expedition was launched only months after Marcos's return, the event took place in the midst of a flurry of *cédulas* and royal directives supporting las Casas's work and peaceful conversion of the Indians in general. Just a little more than four years later las Casas was consecrated bishop of Chiapa, by which time the ecclesiastical enterprise in Vera Paz, as Tuzutlán had been renamed, was unraveling.[4]

But it was in the spirit of optimistic times that Mendoza could inform his sovereign in 1539 that conquistadores were being thwarted left and right by what seemed the hand of God. Of Cortés the viceroy wrote, "it seemed God was keeping [success] away from him by divine power."[5] In summarizing the singular lack of success of Nuño de Guzmán and Francisco Vázquez de Coronado, at least to that point, he said it seemed as if "Our Lord God wants to block the door to all those who, by the force of [mere] human strength, have sought to attempt this enterprise."[6] In contrast, the deity chose "to reveal it to a barefoot, mendicant friar."[7] Thus, the policy of peaceful conversion seemed to be ratified from heaven.

Despite the viceroy's seeming enthusiasm for the extension of political and religious sovereignty by ecclesiastics alone, the expedition he himself was about to raise would not conform to that ideal. Instead, it was to be a massive armed force accompanied by only five ecclesiastics with their small retinues.[8] To inspire adherence to the various royal directives regarding benevolent treatment of American natives, Mendoza would rely on a set of written instructions and the skill at governance of his 29-year-old protégé, Francisco Vázquez de Coronado, who was to be in command.

Part of the viceroy's disappointment when the expedition returned from Tierra Nueva in 1542 must have stemmed from the sad inability of the captain general to hold the expeditionaries strictly to the standards Mendoza had laid out. Not only did the expedition prove less than exemplary in its behavior toward Indians, but weighty charges of abuse were leveled against its leader and his subordinates. Those charges included the setting of dogs on Indians, burning Indian prisoners alive, raping Indian women, and cutting off Indians' hands, noses, and ears.[9]

At the time of Mendoza's 1539 letter, though, such charges were unforeseeable, and it brims with optimism. Presumably it was the viceroy's confidence in the possibility of peaceful assimilation and conversion and the enticing prospect of affluent Cíbola and Topira that induced Giovanni Battista Ramusio to include an excerpt from the letter in the first edition of the *Terzo volume delle navigationi et viaggi* in 1556.[10] The transcription and translation of that excerpt that follow were prepared on the basis of Ramusio's Italian text, because the Spanish original disappeared centuries ago.

As with all of Ramusio's published documents, readers need to be alert to the Italian collector's penchant for altering and embellishing the original texts in the process of translation. Such emendations are seldom so identified in the published versions. This is particularly troublesome when, as in this case, the original document is no longer known to exist and is therefore unavailable for comparison with the Italian translation.[11] Many of the statements included in Ramusio's text of Mendoza's letter, however, can be cross-checked and compared with parallel information from other documents such as Marcos de Niza's *relación* (Document 6) and Vázquez de Coronado's July 1539 letter to the king (Document 3). We can say with certainty that Ramusio or his translator is the author of the title and heading that open the excerpt and that there are no other blatant intrusions by the publisher. To indicate that the heading and title were not part of the original manuscript, in the transcript and translation they are enclosed in flourished brackets { }.

Like a number of other documents translated by Ramusio, this one was subsequently retranslated into English in 1600 by Richard Hakluyt and into French in 1838 by Henri Ternaux-Compans.[12] In 1940 it was translated anew into English by George Hammond and Agapito Rey.[13] We consulted all three of these previous translations in editing our own English translation. In both the translation and the transcription that follow, folio numeration conforms to the published 1556 Italian edition.

TRANSLATION

[355r] 355
{A letter written by the most illustrious lord don Antonio de Mendoza, viceroy of Nueva España, to His Majesty, the Emperor.}

{Concerning the *caballeros* who with great harm to themselves have worn themselves out in reconnaissance of the farthest extremity of the continent from Nueva España toward the north; the arrival of Vázquez [de Coronado] with fray Marcos [de Niza] at San Miguel de Culiacán,[14] with a charge [from] those monarchs[15] to protect the Indians and not to make [them] slaves any more.}

With the most recent *navíos*, in which Miguel de Usnago[16] traveled, I wrote to Your Majesty that I had sent two ecclesiastics of the Order of San Francisco[17] to reconnoiter the farthest extremity of this continent, which stretches to the north.[18] Because their journey has succeeded even more than was expected, I will recount this matter from its beginning.

Your Majesty must remember how many times I have written that I was eager to find out where this *provincia* of Nueva España ended. [That was] because it is such a large extent of land and there has not been any information about that. Nor have I been alone in harboring this desire, since Nuño de Guzmán left this *ciudad* with four hundred horsemen and fourteen thousand footmen [who were] natives of these Indies.[19] [They were] the best and most orderly company of people that has been seen in this part of the world. [But] he accomplished so little with them because they nearly all perished during the undertaking.[20] And he was [thus] unable to penetrate [farther] or learn about more than [was known] in the past. Afterward, as governor of Nueva

Galicia,[21] on several occasions he dispatched captains with horsemen, who had no better result than he [himself] had.

Similarly, the Marqués del Valle, Hernán Cortés, sent out a captain with two *navíos* to reconnoiter the coast.[22] [The captain] and the *navíos* all were lost. Later he dispatched two other *navíos*. One of them was separated from the other, and the pilot, with some sailors, seized the *navío* and killed the captain.[23] After this was done, they arrived at an island where, when the pilot disembarked with some sailors, the Indians of that land killed them and took the *barca*. The *navío* returned with those who remained in it along the coast of Nueva Galicia, where it struck on [its] beam. From the men who came in this *navío*, the *marqués* obtained information about the land they had reconnoitered.

At that time, either because of friction he was having with the bishop of Santo Domingo[24] and the *oidores* of this royal *audiencia*, or simply because everything had gone so well for him in Nueva España, without waiting for full verification of what was on that island, he committed himself to that journey with three *navíos* and some footmen and horsemen.[25] [They were] poorly provisioned with the necessities. This turned out so much to the contrary of what he had expected that the majority of men he had with him died of hunger. Although he had *navíos* and land [was] very near, with an abundance of foodstuffs, he was never able find a way to conquer it. On the contrary, it seemed God was keeping it away from him by divine power. Without doing anything further, he returned home.

After this, since I had Andrés Dorantes, one of those who went with the expeditionary force of Pánfilo de Narváez, here with me, I spoke with him many times because it seemed to me that it could be of much service to Your Majesty to send him with forty or fifty horse[men] to learn the secret of those regions.[26] When I had arranged what was necessary for his journey and had spent a great deal of money for this purpose, the [agreement] came apart, I do not know how, and such an enterprise was not undertaken.

[355v] Among the things that had been readied for accomplishing this purpose, a Black who came with Dorantes remained with me, [as well as] some slaves I had bought and some Indians I had recruited [who were] natives of those regions. These [people] I sent with fray Marcos de Niza and a companion of his, an ecclesiastic of the Order of San Francisco. [I sent these two] because they are men who have been in this part of the world a long while, [are] accustomed to labor, and [have] experience with matters in the Indies. And [because they are] persons of virtuous life and good conscience, I requested them from their provincial.[27]

For these reasons they traveled with Francisco Vázquez de Coronado, governor of Nueva Galicia, as far as the *villa* of San Miguel de Culiacán, which is the place farthest in that direction secured by Spaniards, two hundred leagues from this *ciudad*.[28]

When the governor had arrived at that place with the ecclesiastics, he dispatched some of the Indians I had provided to him.[29] [They] were to be teachers in their land and tell the people there that they should know that Your Majesty had ordered that they not be enslaved anymore. And, [further,] that they were not to be afraid any longer, and were to return to their houses and live peacefully in them. [In addition,] that since they had been greatly oppressed by the [ill] treatment they had been afforded in the past, Your Majesty would see that those who had caused this were punished.

After twenty days, about four hundred men came back with these Indians. When they had come before the governor, they told him they were coming on behalf of all the inhabitants, in order to tell him they desired to see him and to be acquainted with those who were doing them so much good, such as [he who] was allowing them to return to their home[s]. And they would be planting corn in order to be able to eat. [That was a great thing] because they had been in flight among the mountains for many years, hiding like wild beasts out of fear that they might be made slaves. And [they told the governor] that they and all [their people] were ready to do as they would be directed.

[Thereupon] the governor comforted them with kind words and had them fed. And he kept [them] there with him for three or four days. During those days the religious brothers taught them to make [the sign of] the cross and to say the name of Our Lord Jesus Christ. And applying themselves earnestly, they sought to learn this. When these days had passed, [the governor] sent them back to their home, telling them they should not be afraid, but rather they were to remain calm. He gave them clothing, rosary beads, knives, and other similar things, which I had previously given him for such purposes.[30] The aforesaid [people] went away from there very satisfied. They said that whenever [the governor] sent [someone] to summon them, they and many others will come to do what I might direct them [to do].

When the groundwork for the *entrada* had thus been laid and fray Marcos and his companion had spent ten or twelve days with the Black and the other slaves and Indians whom I had given them, they [all] departed.

Because I also had received information about a *provincia* located among mountains known as Topira, I had arranged with the governor that he was to pursue some way of finding out what it was.[31] Considering this a most important matter, he resolved to go see it in person. He had arranged with the aforesaid ecclesiastic [fray Marcos] that he would return from that place in the mountains to meet [the friar] at a *villa* called Los Corazones, 120 leagues from Culiacán.[32]

When [the governor] had traveled about in this *provincia*, he found that there was, as I have written in another one of my letters, a great scarcity of foodstuffs. And the mountain range [was] so rugged that he found no route by which he could go on. [Therefore] he was forced to return to San Miguel.

Thus [it transpired] in such a way (in choosing to go but not being able to find a route) that it seems to everyone that Our Lord God wants to block the door to all those who, by the force of [mere] human strength, have sought to attempt this enterprise and [instead,] to reveal it to a barefoot, mendicant friar.[33] Thus [fray Marcos] began to penetrate the interior of that land. He was thoroughly welcomed, because he found his entrance had been so well prepared. Because, in accordance with the instructions I gave him for making this trip, [fray Marcos] has written [directly] to you what has happened to him on the entire journey, I will not elaborate further.[34] Instead, I will transcribe for Your Majesty as much as he has recorded.

TRANSCRIPTION

[fol. 355r]

355

{LETTERE SCRITTE DAL ILLUSTRISSIMO / Signor don Antonio di Mendozza, ViceRe della nuova Spagna, / alla Maesta dell'Imperadore

Delli Cavallieri quali con lor gran danno si sono affaticati per scoprire il capo della terra ferma / della nuova Spagna Verso tramontana, il gi(o)*ungere* del Vazquez con fra Marco à san / Michiel di Cul(n)*ua*can con commissione à quelli Reggenti di assicurare & non / far*e* piu schiavi gli Indiani.}

NElle navi passate nelle quali fu Michiel di Usnago, scrissi alla Maesta vostra, come (h)a- / veva ma*n*dato duoi religiosi dell'ordine di san Francesco à discoprir*e* il capo di q*ue*sta terra / ferma che corre alla parte della Tramontana, & p*er*che la sua andata è success(a)*o* di maggior qua- / lita di quel che si pensava, dirò q*ue*sta materia dal suo principio. Vostra Maesta debbe (h)aver / memoria quante volte le ho scritto ch'io desiderava saper*e* dove finisse questa provincia del- / la nuova Spagna per esser*e* cosi gran pezzo di terra, & non (h)aversi notitia di quella, & non / son*o* stato io solamente che ho (h)auvto q*ue*sto desiderio, perche Nugno di Gusman usci di q*ue*sta / citta con quattrocento (h)uomini à cavallo, et quatordici mila (h)uomini da pie delli naturali di / queste Indie, la miglior*e* gente & meglio ad ordine che si (h)abbia visto in queste parti, & fece / tanto poco con loro che quasi tutti si consumorono nella impresa, & non pote penetrar*e* ne / saper*e* piu del passato: dopo questo stando il detto gover- / nator nella nuova Galitia mando al- / cune volte Capitani con genti da cavallo, li quali no*n* fecero maggior frutto di quello che egli / (h)aveva fatto. Similmente il Marchese de Valle, Hernando Cortese, ma*n*dò con un Capitano / due

navi per scoprir la costa, la quale nave & lui insieme si perdettero. dipoi tornò à mandar / altre due navi, una delle quali si separo dall'altra, & il Piloto con alcuni marinari s'im-patroni- / rono della nave, et ammazzorono il Capitano: fatto q*ue*sto arrivorono ad una Isola, nella qual / dismontando il Piloto con alcuni marinari, gl'Indiani della terra gli ammazzorono, et prese- / ro la barca, & la nave ritorno con quelli ch'erano rimas*ti* in essa alla costa della nuova Galitia, / dove dette[35] al traverso. De gli (h)uomini che vennero in questa nave, (h)ebbe notitia il Marche- / se della terra che (h)avevan discoperto, & all'(h)ora ò per (di)scontento[36] che l'(h)aveva col Vesco- / vo di san Dominigho, & degli auditori di questa real audientia, ò veramente p*er* esserli succes- / so tanto prosperamente tutte le cose in questa nuova Spagna senza guardar di (h)aver mag- / gior certificatione di quello ch'era in quella Isola con tre navi, & con alcune genti da pie & / da cavallo non molto ben provisto delle cose necessarie, se (n)*m*ando à quel cammino, il qual gli / successe tanto à rove(r)*s*cio da quello che pensava, che la maggior parte della ge*n*te che gl'(h)ave- / va seco li morisse di fame, & anc(h)or*a* che gl'(h)avess(i)*e* navi, & la terra molto propinqua con ab- / bondan(ti)*z*a di vettovaglie, mai pero pote trovar*e* modo di poterla conquistare, anzi pareva / che Dio miracolosamente glela levasse davanti, & senza far*e* altro se ne ritornò à casa. Dopo / questo (h)avendo qui in mia compagnia Andrea Dorantes che è uno di quelli che furono / con l'essercito di Pamphilo Narbaez, praticai[37] con lui molte volte, pare*n*domi che poteva far*e* / gran servitio à vostra Maesta, mandandolo con quaranta ov*v*ero cinquanta cavalli per saper*e* il / se(c)greto[38] di quelle parti, & (h)avendo à ordine quel ch'era necessario per il suo cammino, & / spesi molti danari[39] per questa causa, non so come la cosa si disfece, & cessò di farsi tal impresa, / & delle

[fol. 355v]

& delle cose ch'erano apparecchiate per far*e* questo effetto, mi restò un negro che venne con / Dorante*s*, & certi schiavi che (h)avevo comprato, & alcuni Indiani c'(h)avevo raccolt(i)*o* naturali / di quelle parti, li quali mandai con fra Marco da Nizza, & un suo compagno religioso del- / l'ordine di san Francesco, per essere (h)uomini che gia gran tempo stavano in queste parti es- / (s)ercitati nella fatica, & con esperien(ti)*z*a delle cose dell'Indie, & persone di bona vita, & co(n)- / scien(ti)*z*a:[40] li doman*d*ai al suo provinciale, & cosi se n'and(o)*a*rono con Francesco Vazquez di Co- / ronado governatore della nuova Galitia fin alla villa di san Michiel di Culiacan ch'è l'ulti- / mo r(e)*id*(u)*o*tto di Spagnuoli verso quella parte ducento leghe di questa Città. Arrivato che fu / il Governator in quel luogo con li religiosi mandò certi Indiani di quelli ch'io gli (h)avevo da- / to, che am*m*aestrassero nelle sue terre, & dicessero alle genti di quelle che dovessero saper*e*, che / V*ostra* M*aesta* (h)aveva ordinato che non si facessero piu schiavi, & che no*n* (h)avessero piu paura, & ri- / tornassero alle case sue, & vivessero pacificamente in quelle, perche per il passato erano stati / molto travagliati per li trattamenti che gli erano stati fatti, & che V*ostra* M*aesta* faria castigare quelli / ch'erano stati causa di questo. Con questi Indiani in capo di ve*n*ti di ritornorono da circa quat- / trocento (h)uomini, quali venuti avanti il Governatore li dissero, che loro venivano da parte / di tutti gli (h)abitatori à dirli che desideravano vedere, & conoscere quelli che li facevano tan- / to bene, come è lasciarli ritornar à casa sua, & che seminassero Maiz per poter mangiare, per- / che erano molti anni che andavano fuggendo per li monti, nascondendosi come fiere s(a)*e*lva- / tiche per paura che no*n* li facessero schiavi, & loro & tutti erano apparecchiati di far*e* quel che / li fosse coman*d*ato: li quali il Governator co*n*solò con buone parole, & feceli dar*e* da ma*n*giare, & / ci te*n*ne seco tre ò quattro di, & in qu*e*lli giorni i religiosi frati gl'insegnorono à

farsi la croce, & no- / minare il nome di Iesu Christo nostro Signore, & essi con grande efficacia procurando di sa- / perlo. Passati questi giorni li rimandò à casa sua, dicendoli che non (h)avessero paura, ma che / stessero cheti, donandoli veste, paternostri, coltelli, & altre cose simili, le quali io gli (h)avevo / date p*er* simili effetti. Li detti se n'andarono molto co*n*tenti, & dissero, che ogni volta che li man- / dasse à chiamare, loro & molti altri verr(i)an*n*o à far*e* quello che li coman*d*assi. Preparata l'entra- / ta di questa maniera, fra Marco col suo compagno passati dieci ò dodici giorni col negro, & / con gli altri schiavi, & Indiani che io gli (h)avevo dat(i)*o* si partirono: & perche io similmente (h)a- / vevo notitia di una provincia che si chiama Topira situata tra montagne, & (h)avevo ordina- / to col Governatore, che tenessi modo di saper quel che la era, tenendo questo per cosa prin- / cipale, determinò d'andar*e* in persona à vederla, (h)avendo posto ordine col detto religioso che / per quel luogo della montagna daria[41] la volta à congiungersi con lui à una villa dimandata / De loz Corazones. 120. leghe da Culia- / can, & andato lui in questa provincia, trovò esser co- / me ho scritto in altre mie lettere, gran mancamento di vettovaglie, & tanto aspra la monta- / gna che per niuna via trovò camino per poter*e* andar*e* avanti, & fu forzato ritornarsene à san / Michiel, di maniera che cosi nell'el(l)eggere l'*a*ndata, come di non poter trovar strada, par*e* à tut- / ti ch'el nostro Signor Dio voglia serrar*e* la porta a tutti quelli che hanno per vigor*e* di forze (h)u- / mane voluto tentar questa impresa, & mostrarla à un frate povero & scalzo, & cosi comin- / ciò à entrar nella terra dentro, il quale per trovar*e* l'entrata tanto ben*e* preparata fu mol- / to ben*e* ricevuto, & perche quello che glè successo in tutto il viaggio eglielo scris- / se sotto la instruttione che io li detti per far*e* questo cam*m*ino: non mi estende- / ro piu avanti, ma trascrivero à Vostra Maesta, qua*n*to per lui fu notato.

Document 5

Decree of the King Appointing Vázquez de Coronado Governor of Nueva Galicia, April 18, 1539

John Carter Brown Library, Brown University

Tello, *Crónica miscelánea de la sancta provincia de Xalisco, libro segundo*, fols. 406r–407v

INTRODUCTION

Upon the death of Diego Pérez de la Torre in 1538, the eight-year-old *provincia* of Nueva Galicia was left without a royal administrator. Two years earlier Pérez de la Torre had been dispatched from Spain to Nueva Galicia to arrest the *provincia*'s founding governor, Nuño Beltrán de Guzmán, and take over leadership of the government there.[1] He made the arrest as ordered upon his arrival in the Ciudad de México, where he found Guzmán, and departed for Compostela, the seat of his jurisdiction. But his tenure was to last only two years.

Perhaps designated as early as August 1538 by Viceroy Antonio de Mendoza to succeed Pérez de la Torre and conduct a *residencia,* or judicial review, of his administration was Francisco Vázquez de Coronado, then about 28 years old.[2] When the viceroy's young subordinate reached Nueva Galicia he found that Pérez had died from injuries suffered in a fall from a horse while in battle with natives of the *provincia.*[3] Consequently, he immediately assumed office and determined that a *residencia* of his predecessor's performance was unnecessary. So it was that Vázquez de Coronado was already in possession of the office of governor of Nueva Galicia and exercising its duties when the king's confirmation of his appointment arrived sometime during the second half of 1539, in the form of the royal *cédula* published here.

The steps that would lead to the launching of an expedition to Tierra Nueva were already well under way. Marcos de

Niza was even then making his hurried return trip from the north. Participants in the expedition were being recruited, many of them already preparing to depart for Compostela later in the year. Vázquez de Coronado may well have received the king's *cédula* while in the Ciudad de México after escorting fray Marcos to the viceregal court so that he could make a formal report of his reconnaissance to Cíbola.

With the exception of the opening lines of the body of the royal *cédula*, the appointment letter is a formulaic text varying only slightly from other commissions of royal officials of this period.[4] For example, the grant of authority to summon residents and *vecinos* into the governor's presence and caution them about the penalty of banishment is a standard element in such *cédulas* and should not be taken as implying special royal concern about or provision for Nueva Galicia or Vázquez de Coronado. The *cédula* grants no extraordinary powers and refers only to customary procedures. There were at this time hundreds of *oidores,* governors, *alcaldes,* and lesser officials serving the Spanish monarch in the New World. The appointment of Francisco Vázquez de Coronado was looked upon as nothing out of the ordinary.

Despite its status as a set form, the *cédula* lays out in brief outline the institutional framework within which the young governor was required to work. That framework included a preexisting hierarchical bureaucracy of appointed functionaries within a matrix of Spanish and Indian communities. Although Nueva Galicia at the time can rightly be considered a frontier with regard to Spanish occupation, its administrators adhered to the same formalities and the same code of institutional behavior that were then being observed in the peripatetic royal court in Valladolid, Madrid, Sevilla, or Toledo.

The only surviving copy of the *cédula* addressed to Vázquez de Coronado has been preserved thanks to an assiduous seventeenth-century Franciscan chronicler, fray Antonio Tello. Born about 1567 in Galicia in the humid northwest of Spain, Tello studied at the university and entered the Order of Friars Minor (the Franciscans) in Salamanca.[5] When he heeded the missionary call and was assigned to the Franciscan province of Santiago de Jalisco in Nueva España is not known. But his duties in the province led to extensive travel over many years while he served as *guardián* at several *conventos* throughout Jalisco.[6]

As the province's first official chronicler, fray Antonio read copiously in books written about the New World and amassed a sizable collection of documents relating to Franciscan activities in Nueva Galicia and to the history of the region more generally.[7] Begun while he was at Zacoalco, west of Lake Chapala, Tello's major historical writing, *Crónica miscelánea en que se trata de la conquista espiritual y temporal de la sancta provincia de Xalisco en el nuevo reino de la Galicia y Nueva Vizcaya y descubrimiento del Nuevo México,* was finished at the Convento de San Francisco de Guadalajara just two months before his death at age 86 in 1653.[8]

The manuscript was divided into six books dealing with the reconnaissance, conquest, and settlement of Nueva España and Nueva Galicia; biographies of friars who served in the province of Santiago de Jalisco; the conventos established by them; and the contributions of Franciscan friars to the life and well-being of Jalisco. Surprisingly modern in his attitude toward historical source material, fray Antonio scrupulously cited the names and authors of books and documents that served as the basis for his statements about events he had not personally witnessed. And he surpassed his modern counterparts by frequently inserting full transcripts of documents into the text of his history. An entry from the minutes of the *cabildo* of Guadalajara for January

1540,[9] which includes a copy of the *cédula* of April 18, 1539, addressed to Francisco Vázquez de Coronado, is one of those.

All indications are that Tello was an excellent copyist, comfortable with the sixteenth-century hand in which the *cédula* was written, though he did make a few obvious errors. Several such errors he corrected himself. Tello's copy is, however, a third-generation rendering, being at least a copy of a copy of the original *cédula*. The manuscript of the *Libro segundo* of *Crónica miscelánea,* in which Tello's transcript of the *cédula* appears, was bound at some later time. As a result, the ends of words along the right-hand margins of verso sides of folios were very difficult to read in the microfilm version to which we had access, being obscured by the binding gutter. The unreadable letters could, though, nearly always be easily inferred.

It is presumed that the chronicler once had the original *cabildo* minutes in his possession. But sometime after the mid-eighteenth century they disappeared, as did many other documents fray Antonio had collected and used, including, for instance, a group of papers belonging to and perhaps written by Pedro de Tovar, one of the captains of the Coronado expedition and a prominent *vecino* of Culiacán.[10]

Over the centuries, Tello's *Crónica* was cited from time to time by authors writing about Jalisco, but the voluminous manuscript itself went unpublished and, in its entirety, is still unpublished, even in Spanish. Book 1 was stolen from the library of the convento in Guadalajara and is missing to this day. Books 2 and 3 (*Libros segundo y tercero*) were sold to a collector and eventually found their way to the John Carter Brown Library at Brown University in Providence, Rhode Island. In preparing the transcription and translation we publish here, we used a microfilm copy of the *Libro segundo, capítulo 94,* prepared at the John Carter Brown Library. At least two Spanish-language editions of the *Libro segundo* have been published over the last 110 years, but none of the *Crónica* is available to English speakers.[11] Books 4, 5, and 6 of the *Crónica* remained at the *convento* and were finally transferred to the Biblioteca Pública de Jalisco.

TRANSLATION

[406r]
{the year 1539 [1540]}[12]

Chapter 94
Herein what concerns the governorship of
Francisco Vázquez Coronado and the *villa* of
Guadalajara is continued.

On the ninth day of the month of January in the year one thousand five hundred and thirty-nine [1540][13] the *alcaldes* and *regidores* of the *villa* of Guadalajara, meeting as the *cabildo*, admitted Benito Monester, Francisco Iñigo, and Diego Sánchez as *vecinos*. On the twenty-fifth of January Santiago de Aguirre[14] was named *procurador* in order to travel to Castilla concerning things pertaining to the *villa*. They granted him power of attorney in the form [required by law].

This same [month and] year, the *alcaldes* Diego de Proaño and Toribio de Bolaños and the *regidores* Juan del Camino, Pedro de Plasencia, Miguel de Ybarra, Hernán Flores, and Francisco de la Mota[15] meeting as the *cabildo*, Francisco Vázquez Coronado presented a royal decree and *cédula* in which the emperor confirms and appoints him governor of [Nueva] Galicia, which is what follows:

Cédula and decree from the emperor to Francisco
Vázquez Coronado in which he appoints him governor
of [Nueva] Galicia

[406v]
Don Carlos, by divine mercy, Emperor, *semper augustus* [always venerable], king of Germany. Doña Juana, his mother, and the same don Carlos, by the same [divine] grace, sover-eign[s] and lord[s] of Castilla, León, Aragón, the two Sicilys, Jerusalem, Navarra, Granada, Toledo, Valencia, Galicia, the Mallorcas, Sevilla, Sardinia, Córdoba, Corsica, Murcia, Jaén, the Algarves, Algeciras, Gibraltar, the Canary Islands, the Indies (the islands and continent of the Ocean Sea); counts of Barcelona; lords of Vizcaya and Molina; dukes of Athens and Neopatria; counts of Flanders, Tyrol, etc.[16]

Inasmuch as we, by another decree of ours, ordered you, Francisco Vázquez Coronado, to go to the *provincia* of [Nueva] Galicia in Nueva España and to take the *residencia* of *licenciado* [Diego] de la Torre, who was our *residencia* judge for [the *provincia* but is] now deceased, and its officials, in accordance with what is contained at length in the aforesaid decree;

And because the time limit for the *residencia* has already passed; and at present no governor of the *provincia* (who might perform the duties and serve as our *justicia*) has been appointed by us;

Therefore, taking notice of your competence and ability, and because we understand that in this manner you are performing our service, [the] good governance of the afore-said *provincia* and the administration and execution of our laws, it is our will and desire that now and henceforth (for as long as it may be our will and desire) you are to be our governor and captain general of the *provincia* of Nueva Galicia. You are to administer and uphold our law, [both] civil and criminal, in the *ciudades, villas,* and *lugares* which are settled and may be settled in the future in the aforemen-tioned *provincia*. [You are to do this] with the judicial posts which may exist in it.

By this our writ, we order that the *consejos, justicias, regi-dores, caballeros, escuderos,* and *hombres buenos* of all the *ciudades, villas,* and *lugares* there are and will be or may be settled in that *provincia*, and our officials and other persons who may reside in it, and each one of them individually, are to accept and admit you, Francisco Vázquez Coronado, and your lieutenants, as soon as they are notified.[17] [This they must do] without any procrastination or other delay,[18] without requiring more from us, [without] consulting or hoping or expecting another writ from us (or a second or third directive). Each of those [lieutenants] you may appoint, remove, or dismiss as you see fit. Without contradiction, you are to take [whatever] oath and solemn statement [from the *vecinos* and officials] which may be required in such a case; and you should do it.

When that has been done in that way, they are to accept, admit, and consider you our governor, captain general, and *justicia* of the *provincia* for the time it is our will and desire, as is stated [above]. They are to allow and permit you to use and exercise freely the aforesaid offices and to perform the duties of and serve as our *justicia* in [the *provincia*]. [This is to be done either] by yourself or by your lieutenants who occupy the posts of governor, captain general, *alguacil*, and other offices associated with and pertaining to the aforementioned governorship. And [the *vecinos* and officials are to permit you] to conduct whatever investigations [are necessary] in legal cases and [also] preliminary [investigations] and all the other things associated with and pertaining to the aforesaid offices.

You and your lieutenants are to have authority to determine what is conducive to our service, to the administration of our laws, and to the settlement and government of the aforesaid lands and *provincias*. In order [for you] to perform the duties of and discharge the aforementioned office, to execute and administer our laws, everyone is to be subject to you, both themselves and their households. They are to give and must give you all the aid and assistance which you request and have need of. They are to obey and conform to you in everything and comply with your [407r] orders and [those] of your lieutenants. They are not to place or allow to be placed any impediment or obstruction to your [orders] or any portion of [them].

By the present [instrument], we accept you and consider you accepted in the aforementioned offices and in their performance and discharge. In the event you are not accepted by [the *vecinos* and officials] or [by] any one of them, by this our writ, we order whatever person or persons who possess or may possess the *varas* of our *justicia* in the *provincia* to give and deliver them immediately to you, Francisco Vázquez Coronado. They are not to employ them any longer without our permission and special mandate (under the penalties which apply to and are incurred by private persons who perform the duties of royal and public offices). [That is] because they do not have the power or authority. By the present [instrument], we temporarily remove them and consider them suspended [from office].

Furthermore, concerning matters pertaining to our treasury, when you and your lieutenants and *alcaldes* impose fines to be paid to our treasury, you are to carry [them] out and must carry [them] out and turn [them] over and deliver [them] to our treasurer of the aforementioned *provincia*.[19]

Moreover, it is our will that if you, the aforesaid Francisco Vázquez Coronado, determine, in performing our service and in applying our laws, that any persons whatsoever are to come and present themselves before you, you are empowered to order that on our behalf. [This applies equally to persons] who are now present or may be present in the aforesaid *provincia* or [who] may leave and are not in it. And you may compel [them] to leave [the *provincia*], explaining to those persons who are thus banished why you are banishing them, in conformance with the *pragmatica* which deals with this.[20] If it seems appropriate to you that [the reason] be confidential, [then] you will provide it to them sealed and in private. On the other hand, you are to send us another such [statement] by means of which we may be informed about [the banishment]. You must be warned, however, that when you have to banish someone, it is not to be [done] without a very good reason.

For everything that is stated [herein], and so that you may discharge the duties of our governor and captain general of the aforesaid *provincias* and execute and administer our laws in them, we concede to you complete power with all its concomitants, adjuncts, and additional authority and rights.

It is our will and desire that each year you are to obtain and receive one thousand five hundred *ducados*, which amount to five hundred seventy-two thousand *maravedís*.[21] They must be paid to you from the revenues and profits we may receive in the aforesaid *provincia*. [In the event] we do not have [the money] in [the *provincia*], we are not obligated to order that you be paid any portion of the aforesaid salary. So that you may enjoy [the salary] we order that [you be paid] from this day (the date of this our writ) forward. [For the time] up to the aforesaid day you are to receive the one thousand *ducados* as salary which is designated for you. [We order] that you are to enjoy the aforesaid salary which we now designate for you for all the time you occupy and serve [in] the office and position of our governor and captain general of the aforesaid *provincia*. We order our treasurer of [the *provincia*] to deliver it and pay it to you each year, and he is to accept your receipt for payment. We order that [the receipt] be accepted by [the treasury officials], along with a signed copy of this our decree. When the one thousand five hundred *ducados* have been paid, [neither] party [Vázquez de Coronado nor the officials] is to engage in any [legal action about the payment] whatsoever from that point on. [This] under the penalty [which is] our will, plus ten thousand *maravedís* for our treasury, [imposed on] each one who may do the contrary.

Issued in the *ciudad* of Toledo, on the eighteenth day of the month of April in the year one thousand five hundred and thirty-nine.[22]

I, the King

I, Juan de Sámano, secretary of His Imperial and Royal Majesty, had [this] drafted by his order.[23]

When the *alcaldes* and *regidores* of the aforesaid *villa* had seen and heard [the *cédula*], they stated that they would obey it as a writ from their king [407v] and natural lord and [would obey] the lord Francisco Vázquez as their governor. [This is] as specified in [the *cédula*]. Having sworn the oath with the ceremony required in accordance with the law in such [matters], they delivered to him their *varas*. And they signed it.

Francisco Vázquez Coronado
Diego de Proaño [and] Toribio de Bolaños, *alcaldes*
Juan del Camino, Miguel de Ybarra, Hernando López, Pedro de Plasencia, and Francisco de la Mota

TRANSCRIPTION

[fol. 406r]

{*Añ*o de / *1539*}

Capitulo 94

En que se prosigue Lo tocante al go- / vierno de Francisco Basquez Coronado / Y Villa de Guadalaxara

En nueVe dias del mes de Henero de mill y quinientos Y treynta y nueVe años estan- / do en cavildo loS Alcaldes Y Regidores de la Villa de Guadalaxara reSivieron / por Vezinos a Benito Monester y a Françisco Iñigo y a Diego Sanchez Y en / Veynte y çinco de Henero Se nombro por procurador para ir a Castilla a cossas / tocantes a la Villa a Santiago de Aguirre y le dieron poder en forma / y este mismo Año estando en Cavildo Diego de Proaño Y Toribio / de Bolaños Alcaldes Y Juan del Camino Pedro de (Plaza) *Plasençia* Miguel de Yba- / rra Hernan flores Y Françisco de la Mota Regidores el Governador Fran- / çisco Basquez Coronado present(e)*o* Una Real provission y Cedula / En que el Emperador le conFirma y haçe Governador de la Galiçia / que es La que se sigue

Cedula y Provission del Emperador para Françis- / Co Basquez Coronado en que Le haçe / Governador de la Galiçia / Don

[fol. 406v]

Don Carlos por la divina clemençia Emperador Semper August*o* / Rey de Alemañia doña Juana Su Madre y el mismo Don Car*los* / por la misma graçia Rey Y señor de castilla de Leon de Aragon de / las dos Seçilias de JeruSalen de Navarra de Granada de Toledo de Va- / Lençia de Galiçia de Mallorcas de Sevilla de Serdeña de Cordova (^d)y cor*cega* / de Murçia de Jaen de los Algarves de A*l*gesira de Gibraltar de las Y(^ndi)slas de *ca-* / naria de las Yndias y Yslas y tierra firme del mar occeano Condes de Bar*ce-* / lona Señores de Viscaya de Molina Duques de Athenas y de Neop*a* - / tria Condes de flandes de Tirolo *etceter*a

Por quanto nos por otra nuestra provission mandamos / A Vos françisco BaSquez Coronado que fuessedes a la Pro- / vinçia de Galiç*ia* / de la nueva España y tomassedes ReSidençia al Liçenciado de la Torre / nuestro Juez de ReSidençia que fue de ella Ya deFun(c)to y a Sus offiç*iales* / Segun mas largemente Se contiene en la dicha provission e porque el ter*mino* / de la dicha Residençia es ya paSsado e al preSente no esta por nos provei*do* / EN ella Governador que *us*e y exerssa la nuestra Justiçia por ende *aca*- / tando Vuestra SuFiçiençia e habilidad e porque entendemos que asi cumple *a* / nuestro Serviçio Y buena governaçion de la dicha Pro- / vinçia y administra*cion* / y execusion de la nuestra Justiçia es nuestra mersed y Voluntad qu*e* / agora y de aqui adelante qu*an*to a nuestra merSed y Voluntad Fuere / Seays nuestro Governador y Capitan General de la dicha Provinçia d*e la* / nueva Galiçia e que *h*ayades y tengades la nuestra Justiçia SiVil y cr*i*- / minal en las Ciudades Villas y lugares que en la dicha Provinçia *h*ay / pobladas Y se poblaren de aqui delante con los offiçios de Justiçia que / en ella hubiere E por esta nuestra carta mandamos a los conçejos *jus*- / tiçias Y Regidores cavalleros escuderos Y hom*b*res buenos de Toda*s* / las ciudades Villas y lugares que en la dicha Proviniçia *h*ay e hubi*ere* / Y Se poblaren e a los nuestros offiçiales e otras personas que en ella reSidi*e*- / ren e a cada Uno de ellos que luego que Fueren requeridos sin otra larga / Ni dilaçion alguna Sin nos mas requerir ni conSultar ni esperar ni / atender otra nuestra carta ni mandamiento Segunda ni terçera se / tomen y reSivan[24] de Vos el dicho Françisco Basquez Coronado y de / Vuestros lugartenientes los quales podays poner y los quitar e amo- / ver cada que quisieredes Y por bien[25] tuVieredes el Juramento Y so- / lemnidad que en tal casso se requiere y deveys haçer el qual / asi hecho vos *h*ayan y resiban y tengan por nuestro Governado*r* / Y Capitan General E Justiçia de la dicha Provinçia por el tiempo qu*e* / nuestra mersed y Voluntad Fuere como dicho es e Vos dexen y consient*an* / libremente Ussar y exerçer los dichos offiçios y cumplir y executar / la nuestra Justiçia en ella por Vos o por los dichos Vuestros lugartenien*tes* / que en los dichos offiçios de Governador E capitan general e al- / guaçiladg*os*[26] y otros offiçios a la dicha governaçion anexos Y perte- / neçientes y haçer qualesquier pesquisas en los cassos de derecho pr*e*- / missas e todas las otras cossas a los dichos offiçios anexas y conçerni*en*- / tes e que vos e Vuestros tenientes entendays[27] en lo que a nue*stro* / Serviçio y exicuçion de la nuestra Justiçia e poblaçion e governaçio*n* / de las dichas tierras e Provinçias convengan Y para Ussar y exer- / Ser el dicho offiçio cumplir y executar la nuestra Justicia todos *se* / Conformen con Vos con sus personas y gentes Y Vos den y hag*an* / dar todo el Favor y ayuda[28] quales pidieredes e menester hu*bie*- / redes Y en todo Vos ovedescan e acaten y cumplan Vuestros ma*n*- / damientos

[fol. 407r]

(Man)damientos Y de Vuestros Lugartenientes e que en ello ni en parte de ello enbargo[29] / ni contrario alguno Vos no pongan ni consientan poner e a vos por la preSente / Vos resevimos e havemos por reSevidos a los dichos offiçios Y al Usso de exer- / Siçio de ellos caSo que por ellos o por alguno de ellos no seays resevido e por esta nuestra / Carta mandamos a qualquier persona o personas que tienen o tuVieren las Varas / de la nuestra Justiçia en la dicha Pro- vinçia que luego que por Vos el dicho françis- / co Basquez Coronado Vos las den y entreguen e no Ussen mas de ellas sin / nuestra Liçençia y espeçial mandado So las penas en que caen e incurren las / personas privadas que ussan de

offiçios publicos y Reales para que no tienen poder / ni Facultad y a nos por la preSente les suspendemos y damos por suspensos E o- / trosi que las (^p)cossas perteneçientes a nuestra Camara y Fisco en que vos Y Vuestros / lugarte- nientes e Alcaldes condenaredes para la dicha nuestra Camara e Fisco / Executeys e hagays executar y dar y entregar a nuestro TheSorero de la di- / cha Provinçia e otrosi es nuestra mersed que si voS el dicho Françisco Basquez / Coronado entendieredes ser cumplido nuestro Serviçio y a la execuçion de la / nuestra Justiçia y a qualesquier personas que agora estan o estuVieren en la dicha / Provinçia salgan y no esten en ella y se Vengan a presentar ante Vos que Vos lo / podays mandar de nuestra parte Y lo hagays de ella Salir conForme la prag- / matica que sobre esto habla dando a las personas que asi desterra- dedes por que / los desterrays Y si os paresiere que conViene que Sea secreta darsela eis secreta / Y Sellada Y por otra parte emViarnos eys otra tal por manera que seamos in- / Formados de ello pero *h*aveys de estar advertido que quando hubieredes de desterrar / A alguno no Sea sin muy gran caussa para lo qual todo lo que dicho es o para / Ussar los dichos offiçios de nuestro Governador y Capitan General de las / dichas Provinçias Y cumplir y executar la nuestra Justiçia en ellos Vos / damos poder cumplido con todas sus inçi- dençias y dependençias anexidades / Y Conexidades Y es nuestra mersed Y Voluntad que *h*ayays Y llevays en / Cada Un año mill y quinientos ducados que montan quinientos y se- / Senta y dos mil maravediz los quales Vos han de pagar de las Rentas y / provechos que tuVieremos EN la dicha Provinçia y no los *h*aviendo / En ella No seamos obligados a vos mandar pagar cossa alguna de / dicho Salario del qual que gozeys mandamos desde el dia de la data de / esta nuestra Carta en adelante Y hasta el dicho dia lleveys los mill / ducados de Salario que vos estan señalados Y que de este dicho salario / que agora Vos señalmos gozeys todo el tiempo que tuVieredes y sir- / vieredes el dicho offiçio e cargo de nuestro Governador e Capitan Gene- / ral de la dicha Pro- vinçia lo qual (^a)mandamos a nuestro TheSorero de / ella que Vos de y os pague en cada Un Año Y que tome Vuestra carta de / pago con la qual y con el traslado signado de esta nuestra ProviSsion / mandamos que les sean[30] resividos y

pa(S)gados los dichos mill y quinientos / ducados e los Unos
ni los otros no Fagades ne Fagan ende a *e*l por alguna /
manera y so pena de nuestra mersed e de dies mill maravediz
para la nuestra camara / Cada Un^o que lo contrario hiçiere
dada en la Ciudad de Toledo a dies y ocho dias del mes de
Abril de mill y quinientos y treynta Y nueVe años Yo / El
Rey Yo Juan de Samano Secretario de su CeSarea Y Real /
Magestad la fiçe escrevir por su mandado

Y *h*aviendola visto y oydo los Alcaldes Y Regidores / de la
dicha villa dixeron qu*e* l(o)*a* ovedeçian como a Carta de Su
Rey / Y Señor

[fol. 407v]

Y Señor natural Y al dicho señor Françisco Basquez por su
Go*ver*- / nador como en ella Se contiene Y *h*aviendo hecho
haçer el Juramen*to* / con la Solemnidad que segun derecho
en tal Se requiere le entregaron *las* / Baras Y lo Firmaron
Françisco Basquez Coronado Diego de Proaño / Toribio de
Bolaños Alcaldes Juan del Camino Miguel De Yb*a*- / rra
Hernando Lopez Pedro de PlaSençia Françisco de La Mota

Document 6

The Viceroy's Instructions to Fray Marcos de Niza, November 1538
Narrative Account by Fray Marcos de Niza, August 26, 1539

AGI, Patronato, 20, N.5, R.10

INTRODUCTION

Late in July 1536 four survivors of the Pánfilo de Narváez expedition reached the Ciudad de México with news of wealthy and populous places to the north of Nueva España. Within months Viceroy Antonio Mendoza had decided to send an expedition north to investigate. His first choice to lead the expedition was Andrés Dorantes, one of the survivors. As late as December 1537 that was still his plan.[1] For unknown reasons the arrangement fell apart, even though outfitting for such an expedition had already begun.

In June of the same year Pope Paul III had proclaimed in his bull *Sublimus Deus* that "Indians and other peoples should be converted to the faith of Jesus Christ by preaching the word of God and by the example of good and holy living."[2] In Guatemala, fray Bartolomé de las Casas had anticipated the papal bull with a lengthy treatise titled "The Only Method of Attracting All People to the True Faith," in which he asserted that "those who wage war saying that they are not forcing the infidels to accept the faith . . . are making . . . absurd and foolish claims."[3] And in that very year of 1537 Las Casas launched his attempt to demonstrate the practicality of conversion without arms in Vera Paz, Guatemala.

Thus, in the spirit of the times, when Dorantes withdrew from leadership of the viceroy's reconnaissance, Mendoza decided to entrust the enterprise to a Franciscan friar, Marcos de Niza, who would travel ostensibly without armed

support,[4] guided by Dorantes's former slave, Esteban. Marcos, a French-speaking Savoyard, probably in his early to middle forties, was a correspondent of Las Casas's.[5] Indeed, a version, probably edited, of his account of conquistador abuse of Peruvian natives was appended several years later to the great Dominican's famous indictment of common conquistador practices, *Brevissima relación de la destrucción de las Indias* (A brief account of the devastation of the Indies).[6]

Marcos went to Spain from Savoy around 1530 and was in Peru about the time of or shortly after the conquest of Cajamarca, led by Francisco Pizarro in late 1532.[7] Fray Marcos himself testified that he made a voyage to Peru with Pedro de Alvarado in January 1534.[8] It is possible, therefore, that he made two different trips to Peru. During his time in Peru and Ecuador, which may have lasted about three years, Marcos was selected as *custodio,* or superior, of the small contingent of Franciscans there.[9] According to the late-eighteenth-century Jesuit priest and historian Juan de Velasco, during his tenure in Peru Marcos wrote a series of manuscripts outlining the prehistory and conquest of Peru and Ecuador. The existence of those manuscripts has not generally been credited by historians, because no researcher either before or after Velasco's time is known to have seen them.[10]

Having left Peru, Marcos was present in September 1536 in the town of Santiago de Guatemala, testifying on behalf of Pedro de Alvarado.[11] It is possible that during the Franciscan's stay in Guatemala he met Las Casas there, for the great apostle to the Indians was in Guatemala from 1535 to 1540. But Marcos's time in Guatemala was short. By April 1537 he had already been in the Ciudad de México for some time, staying with the bishop, fray Juan de Zumárraga.[12] Less than 12 months later the head of the Franciscan Provincia del Santo Evangelio (Province of the Holy Gospel), fray Antonio de Ciudad Rodrigo, and Viceroy Mendoza were agreed that Marcos was the person to perform the reconnaissance to verify the reports of Dorantes and the others.[13]

Departing from the Ciudad de México late in 1538 with fray Onorato, another Franciscan, and Francisco Vázquez de Coronado, who was to take the *residencia* of the late governor of Nueva Galicia, Marcos was back from the north by the end of August 1539. On or about August 26 of that year he seems to have dictated the *relación* that is published here. What was said in Nueva España about Marcos's statements regarding what he had seen and heard, both written and oral, created a sensation. As a consequence, "in a few days more than three hundred Spaniards were assembled and about eight hundred Indians native to Nueva España" for an expedition to the newly discovered land.[14] In essence, what Marcos wrote in his official report was, "Yes, Cíbola exists, and it is said by people who have been there to be a wealthy and populous place." Adding to such intriguing hearsay evidence, Marcos stated further that he himself had glimpsed the first of the seven *ciudades* of Cíbola from a distance.

Apparently, in private conversation Marcos amplified his generally sober written statements. His barber, for instance, is said to have been told directly by the friar that the people of Cíbola were "very wealthy, and there were silversmiths. The women were accustomed to wear golden necklaces, and the men, belts made of gold."[15] Conversations with Marcos persuaded the viceroy personally to invest about 85,000 silver *pesos* in mounting an expedition. Vázquez de Coronado and his wife, Beatriz de Estrada, invested a comparable amount. Hundreds of other people, influenced by the organizers' confidence as well as the rumors that magnified even the most sanguine private reports, spent lesser though sizable sums to outfit themselves and their companions for the enterprise. Estimated investments totaled nearly 600,000 *pesos.*[16]

It is impossible to imagine seriously that Vázquez de Coronado and Viceroy Mendoza, each of whom invested a considerable fortune in the expedition, would have made such substantial outlays without strong indications from fray Marcos that those monies were likely to be recouped at Cíbola. The theory that Mendoza colluded with Marcos in mounting an expedition to a place he already knew would disappoint the participants' aspirations is hardly credible, for he himself was to suffer the greatest financial loss in that event.[17] Both of the principal underwriters of the expedition must have had extensive face-to-face conversations with Marcos before launching the enterprise and thus had access to details not included in the written report. Further, the captain general had additional months to talk with the friar about what he had seen and been told, both en route from Culiacán to the Ciudad de México immediately following Marcos's return from the north in the summer of 1539 and again from November 1539 to July 1540 as Marcos accompanied the full-fledged expedition back toward the Seven Cities. During the interval between his reconnaissance with Esteban and the launch of the expedition, Marcos was selected as *ministro provincial,* or superior, of the entire Franciscan province of Santo Evangelio. Perhaps this was in anticipation of the addition to the province of such an extensive and "civilized" missionary field as Cíbola looked to be.[18]

In mid-July 1540, when the advance guard of the Coronado expedition came within sight of the first *ciudad* of Cíbola,[19] "such were the curses that some of them hurled at fray Marcos, that may God not allow them to reach [his ears]."[20] The captain general, writing to the viceroy shortly after the advance guard captured the *ciudad,* elaborated on his own anger at Marcos: "So as not to beat around the bush, I can say truthfully that he has not spoken the truth in anything he said. Instead, everything has been quite contrary, except the name of the *ciudad* and the large, stone houses."[21] In the same letter Vázquez de Coronado, annoyed by what he saw as the friar's exaggerations, wrote, "This distressed the men-at-arms not a little, [especially] when they saw that everything the friar had said was found [to be] the opposite."[22]

To what extent did fray Marcos knowingly misrepresent what he had seen and been told about during his reconnaissance to Cíbola? Much thought and considerable ink have been expended over the last 70 years in efforts to settle that question. Arguments over whether or not Marcos actually completed his trek to Cíbola have hinged on claims and counterclaims about whether sufficient time lapsed for the friar to have covered the distance between Culiacán and Cíbola. Those claims, in turn, depend largely on reconstructions of Marcos's route and the length of time he took to cover it. Because his *relación* is vague at many points, it has proved nearly impossible for scholars to reach agreement on these points. In the 1930s and 1940s three prominent scholars, Henry Raup Wagner, Carl O. Sauer, and Cleve Hallenbeck, on the basis of their reconstructed routes and presumed calendar of the friar's trip, all concluded that Marcos simply had too little time to have made the round-trip to Cíbola.[23]

More recently, William K. Hartmann reexamined the *relación*, looking specifically at distances and rates of travel. His most significant contribution was the recognition that Marcos sent native messengers back to Vázquez de Coronado, so that the governor had news of the friar's progress ahead of Marcos's own return. This added two to three weeks to what has been commonly assumed to have been his period of travel. Hartmann concluded that Marcos traveled some 1,029 road miles from Culiacán to Cíbola, taking 45 to 54 days to do so, for an average rate of travel of 19 to 23 miles a day. Then, according to Hartmann, he retraced his route in 43 days, averaging 24 miles a day. Though strenuous as a daily regimen, these rates are easily within human capacity.[24]

Although Hartmann's argument is persuasive in regard to the length of time available to fray Marcos during his reconnaissance, and his reconstructed itinerary could conceivably have transpired, we are convinced that it did not. To begin with, there is the unanimous conviction of Marcos's contemporaries for whom we have documentary evidence that he had not in fact seen Cíbola or the long approach to it through unsettled land before he arrived there with the advance unit of the expedition in July 1540. See, for instance, the introduction to Document 19 and the document itself for Vázquez de Coronado's own bitter and unqualified denunciation of the friar's untruthfulness.

As early as the spring of 1540, when another reconnaissance party returned to the expedition after having reached Chichilticale, the news was grim. Melchior Díaz and Juan de Zaldívar had been unable to confirm Marcos's report.[25] In 1544 Captain Diego López stated under oath that "it was publicly known and widely held that fray Marcos had not seen things previously that he had pretended to."[26] Similarly, Lorenzo Álvarez testified in 1544, with evident annoyance, that Marcos's reports about Acuco/Acoma and Totonteac were found to be greatly exaggerated.[27] Some members of the expedition were so angry "because the *reinos* he [Marcos] had told about had not been found, nor [had the] populous *ciudades* or wealth of gold or rich jewels that had been publicized, nor [the] brocades or other things that had been told about from the pulpits,"[28] that Marcos "did not consider himself safe staying in Cíbola"[29] and escaped reprisal by immediately leaving the expedition and returning southward with Captain Juan Gallego.

As far as evidence from the time reveals, after July 7, 1540, no members of the expedition credited the friar's claim that he had previously seen Cíbola.[30] Marcos's behavior after reaching Cíbola with the advance guard in July 1540 also strongly suggests that he had lied about having seen Cíbola before. Most tellingly, there is no evidence that he defended himself against the charge of lying. He did nothing to rebut the recriminations heaped upon him by members of the expedition, nothing to calm the ire of those men as he had done earlier after Díaz's disappointing report. Evidently, neither in July 1540 nor later did he deny the charge of having lied about reaching Cíbola in 1539. Instead, his only protection, as we have seen, was to flee from the expedition, which he promptly did, all but confessing his guilt. The friar's life of seclusion and silence after his hasty retreat from Cíbola until his death in 1558 suggests that he suffered an enduring ostracism owing to his reputation for having misled so many aspiring conquistadores.[31] That Marcos, seemingly a prime witness, did not testify during the 1544 investigation of the expedition's treatment of natives of Tierra Nueva may indicate that he was disqualified as a person who had broken his word.[32]

Internal evidence from Marcos's written *relación* of the 1539 reconnaissance also tends to support the unequivocal verdict of his fellow expeditionaries. Following receipt of the news of Esteban's death, reported in minute detail from folio 6r to folio 7r, the friar's narration of the final leg of his trek to Cíbola is bereft of specifics. He dispenses with the crossing to Cíbola itself, for instance, in a single sentence: "With those [*principales*] and with my own Indians and interpreters, I continued on my way until [I was] within sight of Cíbola."[33] Then he describes Cíbola, supposedly viewed from a distance, in just four brief sentences—incredibly, all the space he devotes to the place that was the object of his journey. The only new information provided in those sentences is that Cíbola "is situated in a plain, on the lower slope of a round hill."[34] Even these scanty details could easily have been learned from the Indians who had accompanied Esteban— and had thus seen Cíbola—and who were now fleeing southward. More than 50 years ago Hallenbeck made a similar observation about this portion of the *relación*, commenting on "the absolute barrenness of [Marcos's] narrative as regards anything seen above the Sonora valley."[35] Particularly telling is his failure to comment on the number of columns of smoke rising from the hearths at Cíbola, as he did when recounting his observation of towns in a valley farther south some days later during his flight back to Culiacán.[36]

Also missing, for example, is any reference to the extreme caution and stealth that would have been necessary for Marcos and his companions to get within sight of Cíbola so recently after the fracas with Esteban there. Even under normal circumstances it would have been all but impossible for Marcos to get as far as he says he did without being detected and apprehended.[37] And given that Esteban had alerted the Cíbolans that others were coming behind him, it strains credulity to suppose that the friar could have gotten within sight of the town with such apparent ease. It thus seems improbable that Marcos crossed the last *despoblado* (unsettled area) to Cíbola before doing so in company with the captain general.[38]

There have, nevertheless, been several modern defenders of Marcos's veracity on this point.[39] Lansing Bloom, for instance, responded to Carl Sauer's assertion that Marcos had lied about or misrepresented 10 separate points by insisting that the friar should be considered innocent until proven guilty.[40] In 1947 George Undreiner, arguing that Hawikku

and the Ciudad de México might have been of comparable size at that time, concluded that "the charge of mendacity [regarding the size of Cíbola] falls necessarily."[41] More than 40 years later Daniel Reff weighed in on the argument, offering plausible explanations for what appeared to Sauer and Hallenbeck to be irregularities in the friar's report.[42]

In an even more recent study, however, William Hartmann and Richard Flint offered the following summary regarding Marcos de Niza's credibility: "[Marcos] was not lying, in that he probably really believed that Cíbola was wealthy in a European sense. But to say he was not lying— that is, intentionally telling untruths—does not mean he was producing an accurate and unbiased picture of Cíbola."[43] We now go one step farther by saying that Marcos might well have lied in reporting that he had seen Cíbola, but he was also probably confident that the information he provided about the Seven Cities was accurate, based as it was on reports from informants he thought were reliable.

Angélico Chávez claimed that Marcos's facility with Castellano (Castilian Spanish) was none too great and that his *relación* was edited and embellished by someone else.[44] It is true that neither of the extant copies of the *relación* is in Marcos's hand, which may indicate that the friar dictated his report to a scribe. This would not have been unusual at the time, even for a native speaker of Spanish of relatively high status. It certainly does not prove the friar's lack of skill in the language. Nevertheless, as in most scribally written documents of the day, the selection of vocabulary and phrasing is frequently the *escribano*'s rather than the nominal author's. A scribally written document such as this one therefore interposes a largely invisible filter, the *escribano*, between sixteenth-century author and readers.

Fray Marcos's *relación* survives in two contemporaneous copies bearing his signature, curated together at the Archivo General de Indias in Sevilla as AGI, Patronato, 20, N.5, R.10.[45] Both bear the same date—the date of certification of the report in the Ciudad de México—and were prepared by the same *escribano*. We have chosen to transcribe and translate here the first of those two copies, designated B1 by the philologist Jerry Craddock. Erosion of the right corners of recto folios of B1, which Craddock mentions but ignores as insignificant, indicates that this copy has been the one most consulted over the years and may, therefore, have been considered the more authoritative copy. Contrary to Craddock's statement, B1 also includes marginalia, in the form of scribal or official highlighting of certain passages with virgules (/).[46] Such highlighting occurs 11 times in B1 and marks passages that would have been particularly important for someone planning an expedition. For instance, that person has called attention to the passages in which Marcos reports natives of Sonora referring to cloth made at Totonteac but similar to a European cloth called "Zaragoza," their opinion that "no one is a match for the might of Cíbola," and the stationing of shelters and supplies of food across one of the *despoblados*.[47] This highlighting may have been added by viceregal staff, perhaps even by Viceroy Mendoza himself. For these reasons B1 is likely the historically more significant of the two copies. Although they may have been drafted within hours or days of each other, there are many, mostly minor textual differences between the two copies, which we point out in the notes.

Craddock himself recently published a philological, annotated transcription of the second AGI copy, which he has designated B2.[48] Copy B2 utilizes more scribal abbreviations than does B1, which suggests that B2 is the later of the two copies, destined for a less important recipient or repository. For ease in comparing the two editions in the notes, we follow Craddock's numbering system.

There exists, in addition, a later copy of the *relación* in Spanish, probably from the seventeenth century, judging by its more modern script. It is owned by the Haus-, Hof-, und Staatarchiv in Vienna, Austria, where it has been assigned the number Hs. B 192 (Böhm 682). The Vienna copy seems to be more closely related to B2 than to B1. In vetting our transcription of B1, we consulted this more modern copy along with the others, because it provides an independent reading of the scribal hand.

Joaquín F. Pacheco and Francisco de Cárdenas included a hasty transcription of B2 in their monumental, 42-volume *Colección de documentos inéditos relativos al descubrimiento, conquista y organización de las antiguas posesiones españolas de América y Oceania*.[49] Their transcription has recently been reprinted with Southern Methodist University Press's republication of Cleve Hallenbeck's *The Journey of Fray Marcos de Niza*.[50]

A sixteenth-century printed translation of the *relación* also exists. It was prepared in Italian and published by Giovanni Battista Ramusio in 1556.[51] Although for the most part it conforms to the two 1539 Spanish copies, a number of significant differences exist between them and it. The Ramusio translation inserts several references to precious metals that are absent from the Spanish texts. One instance in particular drastically alters the content of the friar's report. The Spanish texts use the words *rica* (wealthy) and *riquezas* (wealth) in relation to Cíbola and Totonteac.[52] Although European-style wealth—precious metals and gems—are likely implied in these terms, the Spanish *relación* makes no explicit and unequivocal reference to gold, silver, pearls, or other jewels when speaking of Cíbola and the other communities in its region. Ramusio's version, on the other hand, adds a lengthy section to Marcos's surprisingly brief description of Cíbola, discussed earlier. The addition reads as follows:

la qual passa venti mila case, le genti sono quasi bianche, vanno vestiti, & dormono in letti, tengono archi per arme, hanno molti smeraldi, & altre gioie, anchor che non prezzino se no turchese, con le qual adornano li pareti delli portali delle case, & le vesti, & li vasi, & si spende some moneta in tutto quel paese. Vestono di cotone, & di cuoi di vacca: & questo e il piu apprezzato, & (h)onorevole vestire: usano vasi d'oro, & d'argento, perche non hanno altro metallo, del quale vi e maggior uso, & maggior abbondanza che nel Peru, &questo comprano per turchese nella provincia delli Pintadi, dove si dice che vi sono le minere in grande abbodanza.[53]

[Cíbola] exceeds twenty thousand households. The people are nearly white. They go about clothed and sleep on beds. They have bows as weapons. They possess many emeralds and other jewels, though they do not prize them, but rather only turquoise. With this [stone] they decorate the walls at the doors to their houses, their clothing, and their drinking cups. It is spent like money in all that country. They dress in cotton and [bison] hides. This [cotton] is more valued and desirable to wear. They use drinking cups made of gold and silver, because they have no other metal. They employ [these metals] more often and in greater quantity than [they do] in Peru. They buy [the precious metals] from the *provincia* of the tattooed people, with turquoise. They know [the metals] are mined there in great quantity.[54]

Because neither of the extant Spanish copies of the *relación* contains this passage, we and other researchers assume that Ramusio himself or his translator added it, perhaps on the basis of rumors or other written reports.[55] Certainly the amount of detail the passage contains is closer to what one might expect if Marcos had actually reached Cíbola; the sort of information included could not have been obtained by viewing the town from a distance. While not an accurate rendering of the friar's *relación*, therefore, Ramusio's translation suggests the sort of hearsay that might have derived from Marcos's private statements.

Ramusio's version of the *relación* was rendered into French and published by Henri Ternaux-Compans in 1838.[56] In addition to the defects of the Ramusio edition, this French rendition suffers from being one step farther removed from the original Spanish document.

Six previous English translations of the *relación* have been published. The earliest was Richard Hakluyt's of 1600.[57] Because Hakluyt used Ramusio's Italian translation as his source document, his English translation contains all the defects of the Italian's work and is, of course, twice removed from the original Spanish *relación*. Nevertheless, Hakluyt's version stood as the authoritative English translation for over 300 years. In 1905 Adolph F. and Fanny R. Bandelier reprinted Hakluyt's translation, calling it "quite indifferent."[58] Twenty-one years later Percy M. Baldwin published a new English translation, along with a trancrip-

tion of the Spanish text.[59] Then, in close succession, Bonaventure Oblasser (1939)[60] and the team of George Hammond and Agapito Rey (1940)[61] each published their own translations. Finally, in 1949 Cleve Hallenbeck published yet another translation.[62] Although we have found each of these previous translations unsatisfactory in some respects, we have consulted them all and considered their readings in editing the translation we offer here.

One question that has arisen for all translators of the *relación* deserves special attention, because it bears heavily on the character of the friar's report. That is whether words such as *grande, mayor,* and *razonable,* as used in this document, refer to size or quality, since they all can refer to either. It has been usual in past translations to assume that such words refer to the sizes of places. That assumption has led many historians to conclude that Marcos claimed, for instance, that Cíbola was larger than Tenochtitlan/México, which was clearly not the case. We have, instead, consistently translated such terms as referring to quality; see, for example, folio 3r, "que fuese cosa grande" (which would be a grand thing) and "si la cosa fuese razonable" (if what was reported was of moderate importance). Thus, in the instance just cited, Marcos claimed that Cíbola was grander or more excellent than Tenochtitlán/México, a judgment based on its reported wealth. Quality rather than mere size was what was certainly of most interest to lay conquistadores and often also to ecclesiastics (if we are to judge by the places they first missionized heavily). Marcos's use of *grande* and similar words as adjectives of quality is rendered all the more probable by his first language's having been French, in which qualitative usage of the corresponding word *grand* is perhaps even more common than in Spanish.

TRANSLATION

[1r]
{Nueva España}
{Excellent Report}
{1539}

{Item} Father fray Marcos de Niza, what you must do during the journey which you are going on (for the honor and glory of the most Holy Trinity and the exaltation of our Holy Catholic Faith) is the following:

{Item} First, as soon as you arrive in the *provincia* of Culiacán, you will exhort and encourage the Spaniards who live in the *villa* of San Miguel to treat the Indians who are at peace benevolently.[63] [The Spaniards] are not to use the labor of [Indians] in excessive undertakings. You are to make it clear to them that if they act in this way, grants will be made to them and they will be recompensed by His Majesty [for] the hardships they have suffered there. To that end, they will have in me an excellent benefactor. If [however], in the remote possibility[64] that they do the contrary, they will be punished and will fail to be assisted.

{Item} You will make the Indians understand that I am sending you (in His Majesty's name) in order that you may tell the [Spaniards] to treat the [Indians] benevolently and to be aware that [the King] has been weighed down by the injuries and abuses [the Indians] have received and that from now on they will be treated benevolently.[65] Further, those who may possibly abuse them will be punished.

{Item} Likewise, you will make it clear to [the Indians] that they will no longer be made slaves by [the Spaniards]. Nor will they be taken from their lands; rather, [the Spaniards] will allow them to live on [their lands] without doing them harm or hurt. [This is] so that they may lose their fear and may come to know God, Our Lord, who is in heaven, and the emperor, who is placed on Earth by his hand to rule and govern it.

{Item} Since Francisco Vázquez de Coronado, whom His Majesty has appointed as governor of that *provincia*, will travel with you as far as the *villa* of San Miguel de Culiacán, you will advise me as to how he arranges things in that *villa* insofar as they pertain to the service of God, Our Lord, and [to] the conversion and benevolent treatment of the natives of that *provincia*.

{Item} If, with the help of God, Our Lord, and the grace of the Holy Spirit, you find a route by which to travel on and penetrate the interior, you will take with you as guide Esteban de Dorantes (whom I ordered to obey you completely, as [he would obey] me myself, in whatever you might order him).[66] If he does not do that, he would bring disapproval upon himself and incur the penalties that befall those who do not obey the persons who are authorized by His Majesty as empowered to direct them.

{Item} Furthermore, Governor Francisco Vázquez is taking [with him] the Indians who came with Dorantes, as well as others whom he has been able to gather from those places [in Nueva Galicia]. [This is] so that if it happens to seem [appropriate] to him and to you that you take some [of them] in your company, you may do so and make use of them, if you see that it is conducive to the service of God, Our Lord.

{Item} You will always strive to travel by the safest way possible, first inquiring whether some of the Indians are at peace or at war with others. [This is] so that you do not present an opportunity for [the Indians] to do something rash against your person, which would result in taking legal action against them [1v] and inflicting punishment [on them]. [That would not be desirable] because in this case, instead of benefiting and enlightening them, [the result] would be the opposite.

{Item} You will take great care to observe the people who are there. [In particular] whether they are numerous or few and whether they are scattered or live together.[67]

{Item} [You will take great care to observe] the quality and fertility of [the land], its temperateness, the trees, plants, and domestic and wild animals there may be; the type of land, whether it is broken or level; the rivers, whether they are large or small; [and] the rocks and metals which are in it. {scribal highlighting}[68] Concerning the things of which samples could possibly be sent or brought, [you will take great care] to bring or send them, so that His Majesty can be informed about everything.[69]

{Item} [You will take great care] always to ascertain whether there is knowledge of the seacoast, both in the northern direction and in the southern. [This is] because it may be that the land narrows or some arm of the sea penetrates the interior of the landmass. If you reach the coast of the Mar del Sur,[70] on the points [of land] which [extend into the sea], at the foot of some tree notable for its great size [you will take great care] to leave letters buried concerning what[ever] may seem appropriate for you to provide information about. On such a tree where the letter would be, make some sort of cross, so that it may be distinguished. Likewise, [you will take great care] to make the same sign of the cross on the most conspicuous trees next to the water and to leave letters at the mouths of rivers and at locations suitable for ports.[71] [This is] because if ships are sent, they will be advised to look for this sign.

{Item} You will always make an effort to send information via Indians about how things are going for you, how you are being received, and most especially what you are finding.[72]

{Item} If God be pleased that you find some grand settlement where it may seem to you there are probably good materials so that a monastery could be erected and religious could be sent who are knowledgeable about conversion, you will inform [me] via Indians or you will return yourself to Culiacán in complete secrecy. Then you will inform [me], so that what is appropriate may be arranged without [any] disturbance. [This is] so that in the pacification of what will be found, the service of Our Lord and the good of the people of the land may be looked after.

{Item} Even though all the land belongs to our lord the emperor, you will take possession of it on behalf of His Majesty in my name. You will make the signs and ceremonies that may seem to you required in such a case. You will make the natives of the land aware that there is one God in heaven and [there is] the emperor who is on Earth in order to command and govern it. [And that] everyone must be his subjects and serve him.

don Antonio de Mendoza[73]

{Item} I, fray Marcos de Niza, [one] of those who strictly observe the rule of San Francisco,[74] state that I received a copy of this directive, signed by the illustrious lord don Antonio de Mendoza, viceroy and governor of this Nueva España. It was delivered to me by order of His Lordship and in his name by Francisco Vázquez de Coronado, governor of this Nueva Galicia. The copy [included here] is taken verbatim from this directive and [has been] corrected and reconciled [with it]. I promise to comply faithfully with the directive [2r] and not to exceed or act against it, or against anything that is contained in it, either now or at any time. In order [to certify that] I will thus keep and fulfill it, I sign my name here. In Tonalá (which is in this *provincia* of Nueva Galicia), the twentieth day of November in the year one thousand five hundred and thirty-eight, where [Francisco Vázquez de Coronado], in the name of the aforesaid, presented and delivered the aforesaid directive to me.[75]

fray Marcos de Niza[76]

{Item} I, fray Antonio de Ciudad Rodrigo, friar of the Order of [Friars] Minor and minister provincial of the province of the Santo Evangelio of this Nueva España (which I am at this time), state that it is true that I dispatched fray Marcos de Niza, a priest, professed friar, and religious, wholly virtuous and fully observant.[77] [He is] such that he was approved and considered suitable and competent to make this journey and reconnaissance by me and my brothers the *definidores* [members of the advisory council] ([who are] designated to be consulted about difficult and perplexing topics). [He was approved] both because of the fitness of his person mentioned earlier and because he is learned not only in theology but also in cosmography and in the art of sea [navigation].[78]

When the consultation and determination had been made, he went with another companion, a lay friar named fray Onorato, by order of lord don Antonio de Mendoza, viceroy of this Nueva España.[79] His Lordship gave him all the gear and gifts that were needed for the aforesaid trip and journey, also this directive which is recorded here and which I saw. His Lordship communicated with me about [the directive], asking me what I thought about it. Since it appeared excellent to me, it was delivered to fray Marcos personally by Francisco Vázquez de Coronado.[80] [Fray Marcos] received it without omission and faithfully carried [it] out, as is evident in truth.

Because what is stated above is thus the truth and contains no error, I have set down in writing this certification and affidavit and signed it with my name.

Executed in [the Ciudad de] México the twenty-sixth of August in the year one thousand five hundred and thirty-nine.

fray Antonio de Ciudad Rodrigo, Minister Provincial[81]

Relación

{Item} With the aid and patronage of the Most Holy Virgin María, Our Lady, and of our seraphic Father, San Francisco, I, fray Marcos de Niza, a professed friar of the Order of San Francisco, in fulfillment of the directive (included above) from the most illustrious lord don Antonio de Mendoza,

viceroy and His Majesty's governor of Nueva España, departed from the *villa* of San Miguel in the *provincia* of Culiacán on Friday, the seventh day of March in the year one thousand five hundred and thirty-nine. I took as companion Father fray Onorato, taking with me also Esteban de Dorantes, the Black, and certain Indians from among those whom the aforesaid lord viceroy bought and set free for this purpose. Francisco Vázquez de Coronado, governor of Nueva Galicia, delivered them to me. [I also left] with an additional great multitude of Indians from Petatlán and from the *pueblo* they call Cuchillo, which is probably fifty leagues from the aforementioned *villa* [San Miguel].[82] [The Indians from Petatlán, etc.] came to the valley of Culiacán expressing great happiness because the emancipated Indians (whom the governor had sent ahead to make them aware of their freedom) attested to them that they could [no longer] be made slaves by [the Spaniards] nor could [the Spaniards] make war on them or abuse them at all, telling them that His Majesty wishes and orders it thus.

With this company that I mention, I made my way until I arrived at the *pueblo* of Petatlán, finding along the route grand receptions [2v] and presents of food, roses, and other things of this character, also buildings they put up for me made from mats and boughs in all the places that were not settled. In this *pueblo* of Petatlán I rested for three days because my companion fray Onorato suffered from a sickness.[83] Because of that, it was advisable for me to leave him there.

In accordance with the aforementioned directive, I continued my journey by the way the Holy Spirit led me, without [myself] deserving it. I [continued my journey], Esteban Dorantes, the Black, being with me, and some of the emancipated [Indians], and a lot of the people from that land. In all the places I reached [the natives] made grand receptions for me [with] merrymaking and triumphal arches. They gave me [some] of the food they had, even though [only] a little. [That is] because they say that it had not rained in three years and because the Indians of that region are more skillful in hiding themselves {scribal highlighting} than in planting. [This latter is] for fear of the Christians from the *villa* of San Miguel, who until then customarily came to make war against them and [to make them] slaves.

Along this entire route (which would be twenty-five or thirty leagues from the area of Petatlán) I did not see anything worthy of setting down here, except that Indians came to me from the island where the Marqués del Valle had been. From those [Indians] I assured myself that it is an island and not, as some have tried to say, continental land.[84] I understood that they traveled from [the island] to the continent and from the continent to it on rafts.[85] The distance from the island to the continent {scribal high-lighting} could be half a league by sea, more or less.[86]

{scribal highlighting} Likewise, Indians came to see me from another island, larger than this [one], which is farther on.[87] From them I had a report that there are thirty other small islands settled by people and lacking food, except two which they say have corn.[88] These Indians wore many shells hung from their necks. In [these shells] there customarily are pearls. I showed them a pearl which I brought along as a sample, and they told me that there were [some] of those on the islands, but I did not see any of them.[89]

I continued my trip through an unsettled area of four days' duration. Indians, both from the islands that I mention[ed] and from the *pueblos* I left behind, went with me. At the end of the unsettled area I found other Indians who marveled to see me because they had heard nothing about Christians, on account of not having dealings with those back across the unsettled area.[90] These [Indians] put on a grand reception for me and gave me much food. They tried to touch me on my clothes and called me "Sayota," by which they mean in their language, "man from the sky."[91] I made them understand the best I could, through interpreters, what is included in the directive. That is, the knowledge of Our Lord in heaven and His Majesty on earth.

In every way I could, I always sought to learn about [any] land with many settlements and people [who were] more civilized and intelligent than [was the case] among those whom I was encountering.[92] I had no [such] news other than that [the natives along the route] told me that the land four or five days' journey inland (where the mountain chain comes to an end) forms a wide, level valley with much tillable land.[93] In [the valley], they told me, are many very

grand settlements in which there are people who wear cotton clothing.

Having shown them some pieces of metal which I carried,[94] so that I could make a record of the metals in the land, [the native informants] picked up the gold metal and told me that there are jars made of that among those people of the valley and that they wear certain round objects made from that [same] gold hanging from their noses and ears. [They also told me] that [the people of the valley] have a few small spatulas made of [gold], with which they scrape away and remove their sweat. Since this valley deviates from the coast and my instruction was not to distance myself from it,[95] I decided [3r] to leave [the valley] for the return [trip] because then it could be examined more thoroughly.

Thus I traveled for three days, [the land being] popu-lated by those same people.[96] I was received by those [people] [in the same way I had been] by those farther back. I arrived at a fairly grand settlement called Vacapa where they gave me a grand welcome and presented me much food.[97] This they had in abundance since it is all irrigated land. It is forty leagues from this settlement to the sea. Finding myself so far removed from the sea and since it was two days before Dominica de Pasión,[98] I decided to remain there until Pascua in order to assure myself regarding the islands which I mention[ed] above (which I had received word [of]). And so I sent Indian messengers to the sea by three routes. I asked them to bring me Indians from the coast and from some of those islands, so I could find out about them.

In another direction I sent Esteban Dorantes, the Black, whom I told to travel along the northern route for fifty or sixty leagues in order to see whether, in that way, a report of some of the great things we were seeking could be obtained. I arranged with him that if he received word of a settled and rich land (which would be a grand thing), he was not to travel farther but to return in person or send me Indians with this sign which we agreed on. If what [was reported] was of moderate importance, he would send me a white cross [the size] of one *palmo;* if it was grand, he would send one two *palmos* [in size]; and if it was something grander and better than Nueva España, he would send me a large cross {scribal highlighting}.[99]

Thus Esteban, the Black, left me on Dominica de

Pasión after eating; I myself remaining in this settlement, which I say is called Vacapa. {scribal highlighting} In four days the messengers came from there from Esteban with a very large cross the height of a man. They told me on behalf of Esteban to depart myself at that very hour in pursuit of him, because he had come across people who gave him a report of the greatest thing in the world. He had [with him] Indians who had been in [that place]. He sent me one of the Indians who had been in the land. He told me so many magnificent things about it, that I stopped believing them until later [when] I might see them [myself] or might obtain further assurance about the thing.

He told me that it was thirty days' journey from where Esteban was to the first *ciudad* of the land, which is called Cíbola.[100] Because it seems to me worth setting down in this document what the Indian whom Esteban sent me said about the land, I want to do it. He said and affirmed that in this first *provincia* there are seven very great *ciudades,* all under one lord. [These *cuidades* consist] of grand houses made from stone and lime. The smallest [are] one story with a flat roof on top, and others [are] two and three stories.[101] [The house] of the lord [has] four stories all together at his disposal. On the facades of the principal houses [there are] many ornaments made of turquoise stones. He said there was a great abundance of this [turquoise]. [He said] that the people of these *ciudades* go about very well dressed. And he told me many other details, both about these seven *ciudades* and [about] other *provincia*s farther on. Each one of them, he says, is much more [excellent] than these seven *ciudades.*

In order to learn from him how he knew about this, we had much discussion,[102] and I found him [to have] a very keen intellect. I gave thanks to Our Lord. I deferred my departure in pursuit of Esteban de Dorantes, believing that he would wait for me as I [had] arranged with him and because I [had] promised the messengers I sent to the sea that I would wait for them. [3v] [I did this] because I [had] determined to behave at all times very truthfully toward the people [with] whom I was dealing.

The messengers arrived on the day of Pascua Florida.[103] With them [came] people from the coast and from two islands. From them I learned [that] the islands which I mention[ed] above lacked food, as I had found out earlier.

Also that they [were] occupied by people [who] wore shells on their foreheads.[104] They said [those same people] have pearls. They gave me assurance of [the existence of] thirty-four islands close to one another. Their names I set down in another document where I [was] record[ing] the name[s] of the islands and settlements.[105] The people from the coast say they [also] have little food and that they trade with each other by raft.[106] Here the coast bears northerly as nearly as possible.

These coastal Indians brought me shields made of [bison] hide. [They are] very well worked [and] large enough that they covered them from head to foot, with some holes above the handle so they can see [from] behind [the shields]. They are so strong that I believe a crossbow [dart] probably will not pass through them.

On this day three Indians came to me from among those they call *pintados.*[107] [They have] their faces, chests, and arms decorated [in this way]. These [Indians] inhabit an arc [of territory] toward the east.[108] [Some] people among them reach [far enough] to nearly border the seven *ciudades.* They said that they were coming to see me because they [had] received information about me. Along with other things, they gave me much information about the seven *ciudades* and *provincias* which the Indian [who came] from Esteban told me about, [and] in almost the same way Esteban [had] sent him to say it to me.

Thus, I took my leave from the people from the coast, but the two Indians from the islands said they wanted to travel with me for seven or eight days. With them and the three *pintados* which I mention[ed], I departed from Vacapa on the second day of Pascua Florida, [going] along the route and course which Esteban took. I had received other messengers from him with another cross the size of the first. He sent it to me, urging me to hurry and assuring me that the land I was going in search of was the best and greatest thing that was ever heard of. The messengers spoke with me in detail without omitting the slightest thing from what the first [Indian] had said. Rather, they said much more and gave me a very clear report.

Consequently,[109] I traveled that day (the second day of Pascua)[110] and the next two days by the same daily stages which Esteban had taken. At the end of which I came across the people who had given [Esteban] news of the seven *ciudades* and the land farther on.[111] They told me that from that place they were accustomed to travel to the *ciudad* of Cíbola in thirty days of travel. That is the first of the seven [*ciudades*]. Not just one [person] told me this, but many. And they told me in great detail about the grandness of the houses and their form, just as the first [messengers had] told it to me. They told me that besides these seven *ciudades*, there are three other *reinos*, which are called Maratta, Acus, and Totonteac.[112]

I tried to learn why they traveled so far from their homes. They told me that they went for turquoises, [bison] hides, and other things and that [the people of Cíbola] have a great quantity of each of those in their *pueblo*. Likewise, I wanted to know the trade item for which they obtained [those things]. They told me that [they traded] for their sweat and their personal service.[113] They told me that they went to the first *ciudad*, which is called Cíbola, and labored there tilling the land and in other services. For their labor [the people of Cíbola] give them [bison] hides from among those they have there, and turquoises.

The [people] of this *pueblo* [in the south] all wear [4r] fine and excellent turquoises hanging from their ears and noses. They say that there are decorations on the main doors of the buildings in Cíbola which are made from [turquoises]. They told me that the form of dress of the [people] from Cíbola is some long cotton shirts [which reach] to the instep, with a button at the throat and a long cord which hangs from [the button].[114] The sleeves of these shirts [are] as wide at the top as at the bottom. To my way of thinking it is like a Bohemian outfit. They say that they go about girded with turquoise belts. On top of these shirts some wear very good *mantas* and others [wear] very finely worked [bison] hides, which they consider to be the best clothing. They say there is a great quantity of these [hides] in that land. In like manner, the women go about dressed and covered down to their feet in the same way.

These Indians received me very well and took great care to learn on what day I [had] left Vacapa in order to have food and lodgings for me along the route. They brought their sick to me so that I might cure them.[115] They tried to touch my clothing. I recited the Gospel over them. They gave me a few

[bison] hides so well dressed and worked that, judging from them, it appeared that they had been made by highly civilized men. They all said that [the hides] came from Cíbola.

On the next day I continued my travel, taking the *pintados* with me because they did not want to leave me. I reached another settlement where I was well received by the people.[116] In the same way as before, {scribal highlighting} they tried to touch my clothing. And they gave me information about the land I was pursuing in as much detail as those from farther back. They told me that people from that place had traveled with Esteban de Dorantes for four or five days' journey. Here I came upon a large cross which Esteban had left for me as an indication that information about the excellent land [of Cíbola] was growing more favorable.[117] And he left word that they were to tell me to hurry along, since he would be waiting for me at the end of the first uninhabited stretch.[118]

Here I erected two crosses and took possession in accordance with the [viceroy's] directive, because it seemed to me that [this land] was better than what I was leaving behind and that from there on it was appropriate to prepare records of possession.[119]

In this way I traveled for five days, always finding [the land] settled and [finding] excellent lodging and grand reception[s], many turquoises and [bison] hides, {scribal highlighting} as well as the same report of the land [of Cíbola]. Immediately they all told me about Cíbola and that *provincia*, like people who knew that I was going in search of it. They told me how Esteban was traveling ahead. There I received messengers from him [who were] among the *vecinos* of that *pueblo* who had gone with him. They persisted in telling me[120] about the magnificence of the land [of Cíbola] and that I should hurry.

At this place I learned that two days' journey from there I would come across an unsettled area of four days' journey [in expanse], in which there [was] no food.[121] But it was already arranged that [they] would erect buildings and carry food for me. I hurried on, thinking I would finally run into Esteban, since [it was] there that he [had] sent [the messengers] to tell me that he would wait for me.

Before arriving at the uninhabited region, I came upon a recently irrigated *pueblo*.[122] Here an inordinate number of people came out to receive me, men and women, dressed in cotton and some cloaked in [bison] hides. In general, they consider this to be better clothing than that made of cotton. All of the [people] from this *pueblo* went about with turquoise ornaments which hang from their noses and ears. This [sort of ornament] they call *cacona*.[123]

Among them came the lord of this *pueblo* and his two brothers, excellently [4v] dressed in cotton [clothing], wearing turquoise ornaments from their ears and noses, each with turquoise necklaces around their throats. They brought me much game (deer, rabbits, and quail) and corn and *pinole*,[124] all in great abundance. They offered me many turquoises, [bison] hides, very lovely gourd bowls,[125] and other things. I took none of this because I had made it a habit of behaving this way once I entered the land where [the natives] had not heard of us [Europeans].

Here I received the same report as before about the seven *ciudades, reinos,* and *provincias,* which I have told about earlier. I was wearing a habit made of gray, closely woven woolen cloth (which they call Zaragoza), which Francisco Vázquez de Coronado, governor of Nueva Galicia, had me wear.[126] The aforesaid lord of this *pueblo* and other Indians examined the habit with their hands and told me that there was much of this [material] in Totonteac and that the natives of that place [Totonteac] wore clothes made of it. I laughed about that and said that it was not [Zaragoza] but rather those cotton *mantas* which they wear. They replied to me, "Do you think that we do not know that what you wear and what we wear [are] different? You must understand that in Cíbola all the houses are full of the clothing which we wear. But in Totonteac there are some small animals from which they remove [the fur], with which this [material] you are wearing is made."

{scribal highlighting} I was surprised because I had not heard of such a thing until I arrived here. I sought to inquire in detail about this matter of the woolen cloth. And they told me that the animals are the size of [the] two Castilian greyhounds which Esteban had [with him].[127] They say there are many [of them] in Totonteac. I could not ascertain what sort of animal it might be.

The next day I entered the unsettled region. {scribal highlighting} Where I had to go to eat, I found shelters and

more than enough food. [This was] next to a stream. At night I found buildings and food in the same way. In this way I spent [the] four days the unsettled region lasted. At the end of those [four days] I entered a valley very heavily settled by people.[128] There, at the first *pueblo,* many men and women came out to me with food. All of them were wearing many turquoises which hung from their noses and ears. Some wore turquoise necklaces. [These were the same as] those which I [have] said the lord of the *pueblo* before the unsettled region and his brothers wore, except that [the people before the unsettled region] wore only one strand and these [later people] wear three and four strands. [They wear] very excellent *mantas* and [bison] hides. The women [wear] the same turquoises in their noses and ears [and] very fine skirts and long-sleeved blouses.

Here there was as much information about Cíbola as [there is] in Nueva España about [the Ciudad de] México and in Peru about Cuzco. They told in great detail about the style of houses, about the settlement, the streets, and its plazas, like persons who had been there many times. They brought from there the things of civilization which they had obtained by means of their labor, just as did those [people] farther back.[129]

I told them that it was not possible that the houses were made in the way they told me. In order to make me understand it, they took earth and ashes, mixed [them] with water, and showed me how [the people of Cíbola] laid the stone and made the building higher. [They] laid down that [mixture] and then stone until they laid them up to the height [they wanted]. I asked them whether the men of that land [Cíbola] had wings so they could climb to those upper stories. They laughed and pantomimed a ladder to me, as well as I could have indicated it [in gestures]. They took a stick, put it over their head, and said that is the height there is between floors.

Here I received another report [5r] about the woolen cloth of Totonteac. They say that the houses there are like those of Cíbola, [though they are] better and much more numerous. [They say] it is a marvelous thing and has no end.

Here I learned [for the first time] that the coast turns very sharply to the west, because as far as the beginning of this first uninhabited region I crossed, the coast had been penetrating the land[130] toward the north. Because the coast turning is something very important, I went in search of it, so this could be learned [with certainty] and understood. I understood clearly that at thirty-five degrees [latitude the coast] turns to the west.[131] From this [fact] I had no less happiness than from the good news about the land [of Cíbola].[132] Thus, I again continued my journey.

I traveled through that valley for five days. It is so heavily settled by splendid people and so well supplied with food that more than three hundred horsemen could be provisioned there. It is all irrigated and is like an evergreen garden.[133] The clusters of houses are half a league and a quarter of a league apart. In each of these *pueblos* I discovered [people who gave] very lengthy report[s] about Cíbola. They told me about it in as much detail as people who go there each year to earn their livelihood.[134]

Here I found a man, a native of Cíbola, who said [that] he had come [there] fleeing from the governor or from the person [administrator] who is placed there by the lord. [That was possible] because the lord of these seven *ciudades* lives and has his seat [of government] in one of them, which is called Ahacus, and in the others he has appointed persons who are in charge on his behalf.[135] This *vecino* of Cíbola is a man of good character, somewhat elderly, and much more intelligent than the natives of this valley and those farther back. He told me that he would like to go with me [to Cíbola] so that I might obtain a pardon for him.

I got detailed information from him. He told me that Cíbola is a great *ciudad* in which there are many people, streets, and plazas and that in some parts of the *ciudad* there are a few very large buildings which have ten stories.[136] In these [buildings] the *principales* assemble on certain days of the year. He says that the houses are made of stone and lime in the [same] way that those farther back told it. The facades and front parts of the most important buildings are [decorated] with turquoise.[137] He told me that the other seven *ciudades* are like this [one]. Some [are] larger, and the most important of them is Ahacus.

He says that to the southeast there is a *reino* called Maratta, in which there used to be many very grand settlements. They all have these [same] multistoried houses made

of stone. These [people] have been and are at war with the lord of these seven *ciudades*. Because of this war the *reino* of Maratta has shrunk to a great extent. It still rules itself,[138] however, and is at war with these other [*reinos*].

He also says that to the west is the *reino* they call Totonteac.[139] He says that it is a [great] thing, the grandest in the world, [with] the most people and greatest wealth. Here [at Totonteac] they wear [the same] woolen cloth as what I wear is made from, as well as others even finer. [The fleeces] are obtained from the animals which they indicated to me farther back. They are a very civilized people and different from the people whom I have seen [so far].

He also says that there is another very grand *provincia* and *reino* which is called Acus. [That is confusing] because there is Ahacus and Acus. [The one] with aspiration [Ahacus] is one of the seven *ciudades,* the most important. [The one] without aspiration, Acus, is a *reino* and *provincia* by itself.[140]

He told me that the clothing they wear in Cíbola is of the type they had told me about farther back. He says that everyone from that *ciudad* sleeps on beds high off the floor, with bedclothes and canopies above, which cover the beds. He told me he would travel with me as far as Cíbola and beyond if I wanted to take him [along]. Many other people gave me the same report in this *pueblo,* although not in as much detail.

[5v] I traveled through this valley [for] three days. Its natives made all the celebrations and demonstrations of joy they could for me. Here in this valley I saw more than two thousand extremely well dressed [bison] hides. I saw a much greater quantity of turquoises and [turquoise] necklaces in this valley than in all the places I had left behind. Everyone says that it comes from the *ciudad* of Cíbola. They have as much information about [Cíbola] as I [have] of that which I hold in my hands. They also have [information] about the *reinos* of Maratta, Acus, and Totonteac.

Here in this valley they brought me a hide half again as big as [one] from a large cow. They told me it is from an animal which has only one horn on its forehead.[141] This horn is curved in the direction of its breast and from there a straight point projects. Regarding this [point], they say it is so strong that, if [something] runs into it, nothing can keep from [being] pierced (no matter how stout it might be). They say there are many of these animals in that land. The color of its hide is like [that of a] goat and the hair [is] as long as a finger.

Here I received messengers from Esteban. They told me, on his behalf, that he was already traveling in the final unsettled region. And [he was] very happy, because he was more assured [than ever] of the magnificence of the land. He sent [them] to tell me that since he had separated from me he had never caught the Indians in the least lie. [He said this] because up to that point he had found everything [to be] the same as they had told him and supposed that he would find the rest [to be] that way. Thus, I hold [what Esteban says] as certain, for it is true that from the [very] first day I received news about the *ciudad* of Cíbola, the Indians have told me [accurately beforehand about] everything I have seen until now.[142] [They] always told me [about] the *pueblos* I would of necessity find along the trail, and their names.[143] In the places where there was no settlement, they indicated to me where it would be necessary to eat and sleep, without being mistaken on a single point. Having until today traveled a hundred and twelve leagues since receiving the first news of the land [of Cíbola], it seems not a little worth writing down the great veracity of this people.

Here, in this valley, as in the rest of the *pueblos* [encountered] before, I erected crosses and prepared the appropriate records and evidentiary documents,[144] in accordance with the [viceroy's] directive. The natives of this valley begged me to rest here three or four days because the uninhabited region was four days' journey from here. From its beginning until arrival at the *ciudad* of Cíbola there are fifteen long days of travel. They wanted to prepare food for me and get the essentials ready for [crossing the uninhabited area]. They told me that more than three hundred men from here had gone with Esteban, the Black, accompanying him and carrying food for him. Many [of them] also wanted to go with me to serve me, because they thought they would return as wealthy people.

I thanked them for [their offer] and told them to get ready immediately, for each day seems like a year to me

because of my desire to see Cíbola. Thus I halted three days without traveling farther. In these [three days] I continually inquired about Cíbola and about all the rest. I did nothing but employ Indians and question them separately, each one by himself. They all agreed on the same thing.[145] They told me [about] the multitude of people, the regular arrangement of the streets, the grandness of the houses, and the style of their doorways; everything just as those farther back had told it to me.

When the three days had passed, many people assembled in order to go with me. From among them I took as many as thirty *principales*, [who were] very well dressed, with the same turquoise necklaces (some of which had five and six strands). Along with them I took the necessary people who would transport the food for themselves and for me. And I set myself on the trail.

As for my daily journeys, I entered the unsettled region on the ninth day of May.[146] In this way we traveled the first day via a very wide and well-used road. We reached a water source at which to eat, which the Indians had indicated to me. And [we reached] another source of water at which to sleep. There I found a building which they had just finished putting up for me [6r] and another which had been built [earlier], where Esteban had slept when he passed [through]. [There were] old shelters and many signs of fires from the people who traveled to Cíbola along this trail.[147]

Under this same system I traveled for twelve days, always well provisioned with food from deer, jackrabbits, and partridges the same color and flavor as those in Spain, although not as large but a little smaller.[148]

An Indian arrived at this place, the son of one of the *principales* who were traveling with me. He had gone in the company of Esteban, the Black. He arrived exhausted [with his] face and body covered with sweat.[149] In his person [he] exhibited a profound sadness. He told me that one day's journey before reaching Cíbola, Esteban sent his gourd [ahead] with messengers in the same way he was always accustomed to send it in advance, in order that [the natives] might know he was coming. The gourd had some rows of bells and two feathers on it; one [feather was] white and one red.[150]

When [the messengers] arrived at Cíbola before the person whom the lord has placed there as *principal*, they gave him the gourd.[151] When [the *principal*] took it in his hands and saw the bells, he flung it to the ground with much wrath and anger. And he told the messengers that they must leave immediately. [He said] that he was acquainted with who those people were. [He told] the [messengers] to tell them not to enter the *ciudad*. [He said] instead that [if they tried to enter, the people of Cíbola] would kill them all.

The messengers returned and told Esteban what had transpired. [Esteban] told them that was nothing [to worry about], that those who exhibited anger customarily welcomed him best. Thus he continued his travel until he reached the *ciudad* of Cíbola. There he found a group of people who did not permit him to go inside. They put him in a large building which is outside the *ciudad*.[152] They immediately took away from him all the trade goods and turquoises and other things he was carrying. [These] he had obtained from the Indians along the trail.

He was there that night without [their] giving him or those who were traveling with him anything to eat or drink. In the morning the next day this Indian [who is telling the story] was thirsty and left the building to drink from a river which was nearby.[153] From [that place] in a very little while he saw Esteban begin to flee. And the people of the *ciudad* went after him. They were killing some of those who traveled with him. Because he saw this, this Indian hid himself upriver. Later he crossed the unsettled area on the trail.

With this news some of the Indians who were traveling with me began to cry. Because of this ugly news I feared I would die. I did not fear losing my life as much as not being able to return [to the Ciudad de México] to give information about the grandness of the land where God, Our Lord, could be served so much, his Holy Faith [could be] glorified, and His Majesty's royal patrimony [could be] increased. Given all this, I consoled them the best I could. I told them that that Indian ought not to be given complete credence. They replied to me with many tears, saying that the Indian would not say [anything] except what he had seen.

So I withdrew from the Indians to commend myself to Our Lord and to beg him to guide this [event] in the way he would best be served and to enlighten my heart. When this

was done I returned to the Indians, and with a knife I cut the cords on the leather trunks of clothing and trade items I was taking along, which until then I had not touched or given anything of to anyone. I distributed [the things] I was taking among all those *principales*. And I told them not to be afraid and to travel [on] with me. And they did so.

Traveling along our trail, one day's journey from Cíbola we came across two more of those Indians who had gone with Esteban.[154] They came [6v] stained with blood and with many wounds. When they arrived, they and those who were traveling with me began weeping so much that because of compassion and fear they made me cry, too. There was so much crying that they did not allow me to ask them about Esteban or what had happened to them. I begged them to be quiet [so that] we might learn what was happening.

They responded [by asking] how they could remain silent when they knew that from among their fathers, sons, and brothers more than three hundred men were dead.[155] [These had been] among the [men] who went with Esteban. [They] also [said] that they no longer dared go to Cíbola as they were in the habit [of doing]. Still, I tried as best I could to calm them and take away their fear, even though I myself was not without need of someone to take mine away.

I questioned the Indians who had been wounded about Esteban and what had happened. For a while they did not speak a word to me, crying [instead] with the [others] from their *pueblos*. Finally, they told me that when Esteban had arrived one day's journey from the *ciudad* of Cíbola, he sent his messengers to Cíbola with his gourd. [He sent them] to the lord, making him aware of his arrival and that he was coming in order to make peace and heal them. When they gave [the lord] the gourd and he saw the bells, he flung the gourd to the ground very angry. He said, "I recognize these people because these bells are not made like ours. Tell them they must go back immediately or else not a man of them will remain [alive]."[156] He was thus very angry.

The messengers [were] melancholy[157] [when] they returned and [at first] did not dare tell Esteban what had happened to them, although they still told him. [Esteban] told them not to be afraid [and] that he was intent on going there,[158] because even though [the people of Cíbola] had answered him in a bad way, they would receive him well.[159]

Thus he left [there] and reached the *ciudad* of Cíbola with all the people he took [with him], who comprised more than three hundred men, without [counting] many women besides. The sun was already about to set.

[The people of Cíbola] did not allow them to enter the *ciudad* but instead [conducted them to] a large building which is outside the *ciudad* (which provided good lodging).[160] Right away they took everything Esteban was carrying from him, saying that the lord ordered it thus.

"During this whole night they did not give us [anything] to eat or drink.[161] The next day, [when] the sun was one lance [high], Esteban left the building, and some of the *principales* with him. Immediately many people came from the *ciudad*. When [Esteban] saw them, he started to flee, and we [did], too. Right away they gave us these arrow wounds and injuries. We fell down and other dead people fell on top of us. We stayed that way until night without daring to stir. We heard great shouts in the *ciudad* and saw many men and women who were on the lookout on the roofs. We saw no more of Esteban; rather we believe they shot him with arrows as they did the rest who were traveling with him. And [we believe no one] escaped except us."

When I understood what the Indians were saying and saw the poor state of the gear I had for pursuing my journey as I desired, I did not fail to foresee his death and my own. God is witness to how much I wished I had someone from whom to seek counsel and opinion, since I confess I myself was lacking it.[162] I told [my native companions] Our Lord would punish Cíbola and that when the emperor knew what had happened, he would send many Christians to punish them. {scribal highlighting} They did not believe me because they say that no one is a match against the might of Cíbola.

I asked them to console themselves and not to cry. And I comforted them myself with the best words I could. These would be [too] long to set down here. With this [said], I left them and withdrew one or two stones' throw to commend myself to God. In this I probably spent an hour and a half.

When I returned to them I found an Indian of mine crying.[163] [7r] I had brought him from [the Ciudad de] México. He is called Marcos. He said to me, "Father, these [people who have come with us] have agreed to kill you, since they are saying that because of you and Esteban their

relatives have died. [And they are saying] it is certain that not a man or woman among them all [those still with you] will remain alive."[164] Once again I distributed what remained to me of the clothing and trade items among them, in order to calm them. I told them they would see that if they killed me, they would be doing me no ill, because I would die a Christian and would go to heaven. [I told them] further that those who might kill me would suffer for it, because Christians would come in search of me and would kill them all against my will.

With these and many other words I said to them they were calmed, even though they were still in deep sorrow because of the people whom [the natives of Cíbola] had killed. I begged that some of them consent to go to Cíbola to find out whether any other Indian had escaped and so that they might obtain some information about Esteban. This [their consent] I was unable to obtain from them. When I saw this, I told them that in any case I had to see the *ciudad* of Cíbola. They replied to me that no one would go with me. But finally, seeing me resolved [to go myself], two *principales* said they would go with me.

With those [*principales*] and with my own Indians and interpreters, I continued on my way until [I was] within sight of Cíbola. It is situated in a plain, on the lower slope of a round hill. As a town it has a very handsome appearance, the best I have seen in this region. As it appeared to me from a hill where I positioned myself in order to view it, the houses are arranged in the way the Indians told me, all made of stone with their upper stories and flat roofs. The settlement is grander than the Ciudad de México.[165] A few times I was tempted to go there myself, for I knew I was risking only my life, and I had rendered[166] that to God.

Considering my danger, from the day I began my journey until its end, I had feared that if I were to die, no report about this land could be obtained. In my view, this [land] is the grandest and best of all [those which have been] discovered. When I told the *principales* I had with me how excellent Cíbola seemed to me, they told me that it was the least of the seven *ciudades* and that Totonteac is much grander and better than all the seven *ciudades*. And [they said] that [Totonteac] comprises so many buildings and people that it has no end. Considering the excellence[167] of the *ciudad*, it seemed [appropriate] to me to call that land the Nuevo Reino de San Francisco.[168]

I erected a large mound of stones there with the help of the Indians. On top of it I set a small, thin cross, since I did not have the equipment to make it bigger. I declared that the cross and mound were being erected in token of possession in the name of don Antonio de Mendoza, viceroy and governor of Nueva España, [and] on behalf of the emperor, our lord, in accordance with the [viceroy's] directive. I declared [further] that [by] that act I was there taking possession of all the seven *ciudades* and the *reinos* of Totonteac, Acus, and Maratta. [I stated] that I was not going on to them [Totonteac, etc.] in order to return to give a report of what had been seen and done.

So I turned around with very much more fear than food. I traveled as quickly as I could across the whole [distance] until I came across the people who remained to me. I reached those [people] after two days' travel. I returned with them until we had crossed the unsettled area. At that place I was not received as well as [at] first.[169] [I say that] because both men and women raised a great lament on account of the people whom the [natives] in Cíbola had killed.

With trepidation I immediately said farewell to the people of that valley. The first day I traveled ten leagues. Then I traveled at a rate of eight or ten leagues [per day] without stopping until I returned across the second uninhabited region. Even though I had no shortage of [7v] fear, I resolved to reach the wide, level valley[170] where the mountain ranges come to an end (about which I stated before I had received a report). There I obtained a report that the valley is settled for many days' travel toward the east.

I did not dare enter [the valley] because it seemed to me that it was necessary [first] to come settle this other land of the seven *ciudades* and *reinos* which I am telling about. Then it would be possible to examine [the valley] better without putting my person at risk and, as a result, failing to give a report of what was seen.[171] Looking only from the mouth of the valley, I saw seven fair-sized settlements somewhat in the distance [and] a valley downstream, very verdant and with very excellent land.[172] From there [the settlements], many columns of smoke rose.[173] I obtained a report that in [the valley] there is much gold and that the natives of [the valley]

maintain a commerce in jars made from it, and in jewelry[174] for their ears and spatulas with which they scrape themselves and remove their sweat. They are people who do not permit those [people] from the other part of the valley to trade with them. They did not know how to tell me the reason [for this]. In accordance with the [viceroy's] directive, I erected two crosses here and took possession of this entire valley and the wide pass in the [same] manner and [by the same] means as in the earlier acts of possession.

From there I continued my return trip with all the speed I could until I reached the *villa* of San Miguel in the *provincia* of Culiacán, thinking I would find [the] governor of Nueva Galicia, Francisco Vázquez de Coronado, there. Since I did not find him, I continued my journey as far as the *ciudad* of Compostela, where I did find him. From there I immediately notified the illustrious lord viceroy of Nueva España of my arrival in writing, and our Father, fray Antonio de Ciudad Rodrigo, [the] provincial, because they had sent me. [I asked them] to direct [me] as to what was to be done [next].

I am not setting down many details here since they have no bearing on this matter. I state only what I saw and what [the natives] told me about the lands through which I traveled and about those of which I obtained report[s]. [I do this] in order to give the [report] to our Father Provincial, so that he may show what may possibly seem to him [appropriate from] it to the fathers of our order or [the fathers] in the chapter by whose direction I went, so that they [in turn] may present it to the illustrious lord viceroy of Nueva España, at whose request they sent me [on] this journey.

{Franciscan *comisario* seal}

fray Marcos de Niza, *vice comisario*[175]

In the great *ciudad* of Temistitán-México, in Nueva España, on the second day of September[176] in the year one thousand five hundred and thirty-nine since the birth of Our Lord Jesus Christ, the most reverend Father fray Marcos de Niza, *vice comisario* in this part of the Indies of the Mar Oceano[177] [and a member] of the order of San Francisco appeared before the most illustrious lord don Antonio de Mendoza, viceroy and governor for His Majesty in this Nueva España and president of the *audiencia* and the royal *chancillería* (which has its seat in [the *ciudad*]). Also present were the most [8r] excellent lords *licenciado* Francisco de Ceynos,[178] judge for His Majesty in the aforesaid royal *audiencia*, and Francisco Vázquez de Coronado, governor for His Majesty in the *provincia* of Nueva Galicia. [This was done] in the presence of ourselves, Juan Baeza de Herrera, chief *escribano* of the royal *audiencia* and government of Nueva España, and Antonio de Turcios, Their Majesties' *escribano* and [*escribano* in] the aforesaid royal *audiencia*.[179]

[Fray Marcos] presented before His Lordship and before us, the aforementioned *escribanos* and witnesses recorded above, this [viceregal] directive and report signed with his name and sealed with the general seal of the [Franciscan *comisaría*[180] of the] Indies. It comprises seven sheets, excluding this [one] on which our signs appear.

[Fray Marcos] stated, affirmed, and certified that what is contained in the aforesaid directive and report is the truth and that what is included in it did transpire, so that His Majesty may be informed of the truth of what is stated in it.

His Lordship ordered us, the aforesaid *escribanos*, when the *vice comisario* had presented and stated it as he did, to confirm and certify [what he said] at the end of [this report] by means of a formal certification authenticated with our registered signs.[181] Witnesses who were present at [the certification] [were] the aforementioned, as well as Antonio de Almaguer and fray Martín de Ojacastro, a friar in the aforesaid order.[182]

In certification of which I, Juan Baeza de Herrera, the aforesaid *escribano*, affixed here my sign [which is] such {sign} in testimony of the truth.
Juan Baeza de Herrera {rubric}

And I, the aforesaid Antonio de Turcios, the aforementioned *escribano*, who was present at what is stated, affixed here my sign which is thus {sign} in testimony of the truth.
Antonio de Turcios {rubric}

[8v]
{Report of the friar to His Majesty}

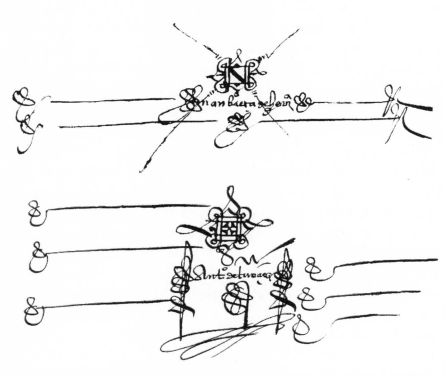

FIGURE 6.1. The signatures and registered signs (*signos*) of Juan Baeza de Herrera and Antonio de Turcios. AGI, Patronato, 20, N.5, R.10\15, 34.
Reproduced courtesy of Spain's Ministerio de Educación, Cultura y Deporte.

TRANSCRIPTION

[fol. 1r]

{nueva españa}

{buena relacion}

{1539}¹⁸³

{*ytem*} Lo que Vos EL padre fray marcos de niça *h*abeis de hazer en la jornada q*ue ys*¹⁸⁴ *a* / honrra y gloria de la santisima trenidad y ensalçamiento de n*uest*ra Santta *fe* / catholica es lo sig*uient*e

{*ytem*} Primeramentte Luego como llegaredes a la provinçia de culuacan ex*hor*- / tareis y animareis a los esPañoles que rresiden en la Villa de san miguel / (a) que¹⁸⁵ traten bien los yndios que estan de paz y no se *sir*van de *e*llos en cosas / eçesivas çertificandoles q*ue* haziendolo asi que les seran hechas m*erced*es y rre- / munerados por su mag*esta*d los trabajos q*ue* alli *h*an padesçido y En mi te(r)n*d*ran / buen ayudador para ello y si hizieren al contrario q*ue* seran Casti-gados / y desfavoresçidos

{*ytem*} Dareys a entender a los yndios que yo os enVio en nonbre de su mag*esta*d p*ar*a / que digais q*ue* los traten bien y que sepan que le *h*a pesado de los agravios y / males q*ue* han Resçibido y que de aqui adelant(r)e seran bien tratados y los / q*ue* mal les hizieren seran castigados

{*ytem*} Asimismo les çertificareis q*ue* no se haran mas esclavos de *e*llos ni los sa- / caran de sus t*ie*rras sino que los dexaran Vivir¹⁸⁶ en ellas sin haze*r*les mal ny / daño q*ue* pierdan El temor y conozcan a dios n*uest*ro señor que esta en el çielo / y al emp*erad*or q*ue e*sta puesto de su mano En la t*ie*rra para Regilla y governalla

{*ytem*} Y porque fran*cis*co Vazquez de coronado A quien su magestad tiene proveydo por / gover*nad*or de *e*sa provynçia yra con Vos hasta la Villa de san miguel de CuluaCan a- / Visarme ys Como provee las cosas de aquella Villa en lo que toca al serviçio de / dios n*uest*ro señor y conVersion y buen tratamiento de los naturales de a- / quella provinçia

{*ytem*} Y si con el ayuda de dios n*uest*ro señor y graçia del espiritu Santto hallaredes / Camino para pasar Adelant(r)e y entrar por la t*ie*rra adentro llevareis con / Vos a esteban de dorantes por guia al qual mando que os obedesCa en todo / y por todo lo q*ue* Vos le mandared*e*s como A mi misma p*er*sona y no haziendolo / asi que yncurra en mal caso y en las penas que Caen los que no obedesçen / a las personas que tienen poder de su mag*esta*d para poderles mandar

{*ytem*} Asimismo lleva El d*ic*ho gover*nad*or fran*cis*co Vazquez los yndios q*ue* Vinieron con / dorantes y otros que se *h*an podido Recoger de aquellas partes para q*ue* si a el / y a Vos os paresçiere que lleveys en V*uest*ra conpañia algunos lo hagays y Useys / de *e*llos como Vieredes que conViene al serviçio de dios n*uest*ro señor

{*ytem*} Sienpre procurareis de yr lo mas seguramentte q*ue* fuere posible E ynf*or*- / mando *o*s primero Si estan d*e* paz o de guerra los Unos yndios con los o- / tros porque no deis ocasion a que hagan Algun(d) desConçierto contra *vuestra* / persona El qual sera causa para que contra ellos se *h*aya de proçe*der*¹⁸⁷ / {rúbricas}

[fol. 1v]

y Hazer castigo porque de *es*Ta man*er*a en lugar de yr a haze*r*les bien y darles / lunbre seria al contrario {*ytem*} llevareis mucho aViso[188] de mirar La gentte que *h*ay si es mucha o poca y / si estan Derramados o Viven juntos

{*ytem*} la calidad y fertelidad de *e*lla la tenplança de la ti*e*rra los arboles y planta*s* / y animales domesticos y salvajes q*ue* huviere la man*e*ra de la ti*e*rra si es aspera / o llana los rrios si son grandes o pequeños y las piedras y metales q*ue h*ay *en e*lla / {scribal mark} y de las cosas q*ue* se pudieren EnViar o traer muestra traellas o enViallas / para q*ue* de todo pueda su magestad ser aVisado(^s)

{*ytem*} Saber sienpre si *h*ay notiçia de la costa de la mar asi de la partte del nortte como / a la del sur porque podria ser estrecharse la ti*e*rra o entrar algun(d) braço de / mar la ti*e*rra adentro y si llegared*e*s a la costa de la mar del sur en las puntas / q*ue* entran al pie de algun(d) arbol señalado de grande dexar enterradas Car*tas* / de lo que os Paresçiere que conViene aVisar y al tal arbol donde quedare / la Cartta haze(l)d*le* alguna cruz porq*ue* sea conosçido asimismo En las boCas / de los rrios y en las disPusiçiones de puertos en los arboles mas señalados / junto al agua hazer[189] la misma Señal de la cruz y dexar las Carttas porque / si se enViaren naVios yran adVertidos de buscar esta señal

{*ytem*} Sienpre procurareis de enViar aViso con yndios de como os Va y como sois / Resçibido y lo que hallared*e*s muy particularmentte[190]

{*ytem*} Y si dios fuere servido q*ue* hallaredes alguna poblaçion grande donde os Paresçiere / q*ue h*abra buen aparejo para q*ue* se pudiese[191] hazer monesterio y enViar Religiosas q*ue* / entendiesen En la conVersion aVisareis con yndios o Volvereys Vos a CuluaCa*n* / con todo secretto y dareis aViso para que se provea lo que conVenga sin / alteraçion porq*ue* En la paçiffi*ca*çion de lo que se hallare Se mire el serviçio De / n*uest*ro señor y bien de la gentte de la ti*e*rra

{*ytem*} y aUnque toda la ti*e*rra es del emp*erad*or n*uest*ro s*eñ*or Vos en mi nonbre tomareis Pose- / sion de *e*lla por su magestad y hareis las señales y autos[192] que os Paresçieren / q*ue* para tal Caso se rrequieren y dareis A entender a los

naturales de la / ti*e*rra q*ue h*ay Un dios en el çielo y el emp*e*rad*or* en la ti*e*rra q*ue e*sta para mandalla y gover- / nalla a quien todos *h*an de ser su(b)jettos y servyr don antonyo de mendoça

{*ytem*} Digo yo fray marcos de niça de los *ob*servantes de san franci*sc*o que rresçibi U*n* / treslado de *e*sta ynstruçion firmada del Yll*ustr*isi*m*o s*eñ*or don antonyo de mendoça / ViSorrey y gover*nad*or de *e*sta nueVa españa la qual me Entrego por m*a*nd*a*do de su *señoria* / y en su nonbre fran*cisc*o Vazquez de coronado gover*nad*or de *e*sta nueVa galizia EL / qual treslado es sacado de *e*sta ynstruçion de Verbo ad Verbun y Con ella corre- / gida y Conçertada la qual d*i*c*h*a ynstruçion prometto de la Cunplir fielmen*te* / {rúbricas}

[fol. 2r]
{11}
y de no yr ni passar contra ella ni contra cossa de lo en ella conten*ido ahora* / ni en nugun(d) *tie*mpo y por q*ue* a(n)si lo guardare E Cunplire firme aqui mi no*mbre* / En tonala a Veyntte dias del mes de noVienbre de mill y q*uinyentos* e treinta *e ocho* / años adonde me dio y entrego en el d*i*c*h*o nonbre la d*i*c*h*a ynstruçion que es en *la* / provy*nci*a de *e*sta nueVa galizia fray marcos de niça

{*ytem*} Digo yo frai antonio de çiudad Rodrigo frayle de la (h)orden de los menores y / ministro provinçial que a la sazon soy de la provy*nci*a del santo eVangelio de *e*sta / nueVa españa que es Verdad que yo enVie a fray marcos de niça saçerdotte / frayle profeso y rreligioso y en toda Virtud y Religion tal que de mi E de mis / hermanos los difinidores diputados para de *e*llos tomar consejo en las cosas / arduas y dificultosas fue aprovado y *h*abido por ydonio y sufiçientte para hazer / esta jornada y descubrimientto asi por la sufi(e)siençia arriba d*i*c*h*a de su persona / como por ser do*c*tto no solamente en la teologia pero en la cosmografia y en el / artte de la mar y a(n)si consultado y difinido q*ue* fuese El fue con otro conpañero / fraile lego q*ue* se llama fray onoratto por m*a*nd*a*do del señor don antonyo de mendoça / ViSorrey de *e*sta d*i*c*h*a nueVa españa y su señoria le dio todo el aparejo y rreCa(U)do[193] / q*ue* fue menester para El d*i*c*h*o Camino y jornada y esta ynstruçion que aquy esta / escri(p)ta la qual yo Vi y su señoria la comunico comigo preguntandome lo que / de ella me paresçia y paresçiendome bien se dio al dicho fray marCos por mano de / Francisco Vazquez de coronado la qual El rresçibio Sin falta y esecutto[194] fielmentte / como en efectto hA paresçido y porque lo sobredicho es a(n)si Verdad y en ello no ha / Falençia ninguna he escrito esta fee y testimonyo y lo firme de mi nonbre / Fecha en mexico a Veinte y seis de agosto año de myll y quinyentos E treinta E nueVe / Fray antonyo de çiUdad Rodrigo ministro provinçial

Relaçion[195]

{ytem} Con el ayuda y favor de la sacratisima Virgen maria nuestra señora y deL / serafico nuestro padre san francisco yo fray marcos de niça frayle profeso de la (h)orden / de san francisco en Cumplimiento de la ynstruçion arriba contenyda del Yllustrisimo señor don / antonio de mendoça Visorrey E governador por su magestad de la nueVa españa party / de la Villa de san miguel de la provyncia de CuluaCan Viernes siette dias del mes / de março de mill y quinyentos e treinta y nueVe años lleVando por conpañero / al padre fray onoratto y lleVando conmigo a esteban de dorantes negro y a / çiertos yndios de los que el dicho señor Visorrey libertto y Conpro para este efectto / los quales me entrego francisco Vazquez de Coronado governador de la nueVa galizia / y Con otra mucha cantidad De yndios de petatlan y del pueblo que llaman del / Cuchillo que seran çinquenta leguas de la dicha Villa los quales Vinyeron al VaIle / de culuaCan signyfiCando gran alegria por havelles certificado los yndios liber- / tados que el dicho governador enVio delant(r)e a hazelles saber su libertad y que no se habian / de hazer esclavos de ellos ni hazerles guerra ni maltratamyento ninguno diziendoles que / asi lo quiere y manda Su magestad y con esta conpañia que digo tome my camino / hasta llegar al pueblo de petatlan hallando En el Camino grandes Rescibimientos[196] / {rúbricas}

[fol. 2v]

Y presentes de comida Rosas y otras cosas de esta calidad y casas que me / hazian de petates y Ramas en todas las partes donde no habia poblado en este / pueblo de petatlan holgue

tres dias porque mi conpañero fray onoratto / adolesçio de enfermedad que me conVino dexallo alli y conforme a la / dicha ynstruçion segui mi Viage por donde me guio El espiritu santto sin / meresçello yo E yendo comigo el dicho esteban dorantes negro y algunos / de los libertados y mucha gentte de la tierra haziendome En todas las partes / que llegava muchos Resçibimyentos y rregozijos y arcos triunfales y dandome / de la comida que Tenian aUnque poca porque dizen haber tres años que no lloVia / y porque los yndios de aquella Comarca mas entendian En esCondersse / {//} que en senbrar por temor de los cristianos de la Villa de san miguel que hasta / alli solian llegar a les hazer guerra y esclavos en todo este Camino que Se- / rian Veyntte y çinco o treinta leguas de aquella partte de petatlan no / Vi cosa digna de poner aqui eçebto que Vinyeron a mi yndios de la ysla donde / estuvo El marques del Valle de los quales me çertifique ser ysla y no como / algunos queryan dezir ser[197] tierra firme y Vi que de ella pasaban a la tierra Firme / en balsas y de la tierra firme a ella y el espaçio que hay de la ysla a la tierra firme / {//} puede ser media legua de mar poco mas o menos asimismo me Vinieron / {//} a Ver yndios de otra ysla mayor que ella que esta mas adelant(r)e de los quales tuve / Relaçion haver otras treinta yslas pequeñas pobladas de gente y pobres de Comyda / eçebto dos que dizen que tienen mayz estos yndios trayan colgadas de la gar- / gantta muchas conchas en las quales suele haber perlas yo les mostre / Una perla que llevava para muestra y me dixeron que de aquellas habia en las / yslas pero yo no les Vi ninguna segui my Camino por Un desPoblado de / quatro dias yendo comigo yndios asi de las yslas que digo como de los pueblos / que dexava atras y al cabo del despoblado halle otros yndios que se admiraron / de me ver porque ninguna notiçia tenyan de cristianos a causa de no contratarse / con los de atras por el despoblado estos me hizieron mucho Resçibimyento / y me dieron mucha Comida y procuraban de tocarme en la rropa y me / llamaban sayota que quieren dezir en su lengua honbre del çielo a los / quales lo mejor que yo pude hize entender por las lenguas lo contenydo / en la ynstruçion que es el conosçimiento de nuestro señor en el çielo y de / su magestad en la tierra y sienpre por todas las Vias que podia proCuraba / de saber tierra de muchas poblaçiones y de

gentte de mas polesçia y rra- / zon que con los que Topava y
no tuve nueVa mas de que me dixeron que la tierra / Adentro
quatro o çinco jornadas do se rrematan las Cordilleras de las
sie- / rras se haze Una abra llana y de mucha tierra en la qual
me dixeron / haber muchas y muy grandes poblaçiones en
que hay gentte Vestida de algo- / don y mostrandoles yo
algunos metales que lleVaba para tomar / Razon De los
metales de la tierra tomaron el metal de oro y me dixeron /
que de aquel hay Vasijas entre aquella gente de la abra y que
traen colgadas de las / narizes y orejas çiertas cosas Redondas
de aquel oro y que tienen Unas / paletillas de el con que Raen
y se quitan El sudor y Como esta abra se des- / Via de la
costa y mi ynstruçion (h)era no apartarme de ella determine
De / {rúbricas}

[fol. 3r]
{12}
Dexalla para la Vuelta porque e(s)nTonçes se poDria Ver
mejor y asi anduve tres / dias poblados de aquella misma
gentte de los quales fuy Resçibido como de los de / atras llegue
a Una Razonable poblaçion que se llama Vacapa donde me
hicieron / gran rresçibimientto y me dieron mucha comida de
la qual tenian en abun- / dançia por ser toda tierra que se
rriega hay de esta poblacion a la mar quarenta le- / guas y por
hallarme tan apartado de la mar y por ser dos dias antes de
la / dominica de pasion determine de me estar alli hasta
pasCua por çertifi- / carme de las yslas de que arriba digo que
tuve notiçia y asi enVia mensajeros / yndios a la mar por tres
Vias a los quales Encargue que me truxesen yndios[198] / de la
costa y de algunas de aquellas yslas para ynformarme de ellos
y por o- / tra partte enVie a esteban dorantes negro al qual
dixe que fuese por la de- / rro(c)ta del nortte cinquentta o
sesenta leguas para Ver si por aquella / Via se podria tener
Relaçion de alguna cosa grande de las que busCabamos / y
conçerte con el que si tuviesse notiçia de tierra poblada y rrica
que fuese / cosa grande que no pasase adelant(r)e sino que
Volviesse En persona o me enVia- / se yndios con esta señal
que Conçertamos que si la cosa fuese rrazonable me en- /
Viasse Una cruz blanca de Un palmo[199] y si fuese grande la
enViase de dos palmos / Y si fuese cosa mayor y mejor que
la nueVa españa me enViase Una gran / {/} cruz y asi se

partio el dicho esteban negro de mi dominica de pasion des-
/ pues De comer quedando yo en esta poblaçion que digo que
se dize Vacapa y de / aya[200] a quatro dias Vinieron los
mensageros de esteban con Una cruz muy / {/} grande de
estatura de Un honbre y me dixeron de partte de esteban que
a la / hora me partiese en su seguimientto porque habia
topado gente que le dava Relacion / de la mayor cosa del
mundo y que tenya yndios que habian estado en ella / y me
enVio Uno de los yndios que habian estado en la tierra El
qual me dixo / tantas grandezas de ella que dexe de creellas
para despues de habellas Visto / o de tener mas çertificaçion
de la cosa y me dixo que habia treinta jornadas / desde donde
quedava esteban hasta la primera çiudad de la tierra que se
dize / Çivola y porque me paresçe Digno de poner en este
papel lo que este yndio / que esteban me enVio dize de la
tierra lo quiero hazer el qual afirma y dize / que en esta
primera provyncia hay siette Çiudades muy grandes todas
debaxo de / Un señor y de Casas de piedra y Cal grandes la
mas pequeña de Un sobrado / y açutea ençima y otras de dos
y de tres sobrados y la del señor de quatro / sobrados todas
juntas Por su (h)orden y en las portadas de las Casas prin- /
çipales muchas labores de piedras turquesas de las quales dixo
que habia en / granDe abundançia y que la gentte de estas
Çiudades anda muy bien / Vestida y otras muchas particularidades me dixo asi de estas siette çiUda- / des como de otras
provyncias mas adelant(r)e cada Una de las quales / dize ser
mucho mas que estas siette Çiudades y para saber del como /
lo sabia Tuvimos muchas demandas y Respuestas y hallele de
/ muy buena Razon di graçias A nuestro señor difiri my
partida en seguimiento / de esteban de dorantes creyendo que
me aguardaria como conçerte con el / y tanbien porque
prometti a los mensageros que enVie a la mar que los
aguardaria[201] / {rúbricas}

[fol. 3v]
porque sienpre propuse de tratar con la gentte que tratase
mucha Verdad los / mensageros Vinieron dia de pasCua
florida y con ellos gentte de la costa y / de dos yslas de los
quales supe ser las yslas que arriba digo pobres de Comida /
como lo habia sabido antes y que son pobladas de gentte
traian conchas en la / Frentte y dizen tener perlas çertifi-

caronme de treinta y quatro yslas / çerca las Unas de las otras
cuyos nonbres pongo en otro papel donde asy*ent*o / el nonbre
de las yslas y poblaçiones la gentte de la costa dize tener
poCa / comida asi ellos como los de las yslas y que se
contratan los Unos con / los otros por balsas aqui la costa se
va al nortte quanto mas Puede / estos yndios de la costa me
truxeron Rodelas de Cuero de Vacas muy bien / labradas
grandes q*ue* les cubrian de pies a Cabeça con Unos agujeros
en- / çima de la enpuñadura para poder Ver detras de *e*llas
son tan Rezias / q*ue* creo q*ue* no las pasara Una ballesta este
dia me Vinieron tress yndios de los / q*ue* llaman pintados
labrados los rrostros pechos y braços estos estan en arco a /
la partte del este y llegan a confinar gentte de *e*llos çerca de
las siette çiUda- / des los quales dixeron q*ue* me Venyan a Ver
porq*ue* tuvieron notiçia de my / y entre otras cosas me dieron
mucha notiçia de las siette çiUdad*es* y pro*v*yncias / que *e*l
yndio de esteban me dixo casi por la misma man*e*ra q*ue*
esteban me lo / *e*nVio a dezir y asi despedi la gente de la
costa y dos yndios de las yslas dixe- / ron q*ue* se querian
andar conmigo siette o ocho dias y Con ellos y Con los tress
/ pintados q*ue* digo me partti de Vacapa segundo dia de
pasCua florida por el / camino y derro(c)ta q*ue* lleVaba
esteban del qual *h*abia Resçibido otros / mensageros con otra
cruz del tamaño de la primera q*ue* me *e*nVio dandome /
priesa y afirmando ser la t*ie*rra en Cuya demanda yba la
mejor y mayor / cosa q*ue* Jamas se oyo los quales mensageros
particularmente me dixero*n* / sin faltar en cosa punto de lo
q*ue* dixo el primero ant*es* dixeron mucho / mas y me dieron
mas clara R*e*laci*o*n y asi Camine aquel dia segundo / dia de
pascua y otros dos dias por las mismas jornadas q*ue* lleVo
esteban / al cabo de los quales tope con la gentte q*ue* le dio
la notiçia de las siete çiUda- / d*es* y de la t*ie*rra de adelant(r)e
los quales me dixeron q*ue* de alli yban en / treinta Jornadas a
la çiudad de çivola que es la primera de las siette / y no me
lo dixo solo Uno sino muchos y muy p*a*rticularmente me dy-
/ Xeron la grandeza de las Casas y la man*e*ra de *e*llas como
me lo dixeron / los primeros y dixeronme²⁰² q*ue* demas de²⁰³
estas siette çiUdad*es* *h*ay otros / tress R*e*yn*o*s q*ue* se llaman
maratta y acus y totonteac q*ui*se sa- / ber a que yban tan lexos
de sus Casas y dixeronme q*ue* yban por / turq*ue*sas y por
cueros de Vacas y otras cosas y de lo Uno y de lo o- / tro

tienen *en e*ste pueblo Cantidad asimismo q*ui*se saber El
rresCatte / con que lo *h*abian y dixeronme q*ue* con el sudor y
servyçio de sus p*e*rsonas / q*ue* yban a la primera Çiudad q*ue*
se dize Çivola y q*ue* sirVen alli en CaVar / las t*ie*rras y en
otros Serviçios y que les dan Cueros de Vacas de aquellos /
q*ue* alli tienen y turquesas por su *s*ervyçi*o* y estos de *e*ste
pueblo traen todos / {rúbricas}

[fol. 4r]
{9}
Turquesas colgadas de las orejas y de las nariZes finas y
buenas *y dizen que de ellas* / *h*ay hechas lavores En las puertas
prinçipales de las casas de çivola *dixeronme* / q*ue* la man*e*ra
del Vestido de los de çivola es Unas camysas de algodon
largas *hasta el* / enpeyne del pie con Un boton a la gargantta
y Un torçal largo que cuelga *de el* / y las mangas de *e*stas
Camisas anchas tanto de arriba como de abaxo *a mi* /
paresçer es como Vestido bohemio dizen que andan
(^Vestidos) çeñidos con *cintas* / de turquesas y que ençima d*e*
*e*stas camysas los Unos traen muy buenas *man-* / tas y los
otros Cueros de Vaca muy bien labrados q*ue* tienen por
mejor Vestid*o* / de que en aquella t*ie*rra dizen q*ue h*ay mucha
Cantidad y asimismo las muge- / res Andan Vestidas y
Cubiertas hasta los pies de la misma man*e*ra Resçibie- /
ronme estos yndios muy bien y tuvieron mucho Cuydado de
saber el dia / q*ue* p*a*rti de Vacapa para tenerme en el Camino
comida y aposentos trayan- / me enfermos q*ue* les Curase y
procuraban de tocarme En la rropa sobre los / quales yo
dezia el *e*Vangelio dieronme algunos Cueros de Vaca tan
bien / adobados y labrados que en ellos paresçia ser hechos
de honbres de mucha / puliçia y todos dezian q*ue* Venian de
Çivola otro dia segui my Camino / llevando comigo los
pintados q*ue* no me querian dexar llegue a otra po- / blaçion
donde fuy bien rresçibido de la gentte de *e*lla los quales
asimis- / {/} mo procuraban de tocarme en la rropa y me
dieron notiçia de la t*ie*rra / q*ue* yo llevava tan particularmentte como los de atras y me dixero*n* / como de alli *h*abia
*i*do gentte con esteban de dorantes quatro o çinco jor- /
nadas y aqui tope Una cruz grande q*ue e*steban me *h*abia
dexado en señal / de que la nueVa de la buena t*ie*rra cresçia
y dexo d*i*cho q*ue* me dixessen q*ue* me diese / mucha priesa

que *e*l me aguardaria al cabo del primer despoblado aqui / puse dos cruzes y tome posesion conforme a la ynst*rucci*on porq*ue* me par*ecio* ser / aquella mejor T*ie*rra q*ue* la que quedava atras y q*ue* conVenya desde alli ha- / Zer autos de posesion y de *e*sta man*er*a anduve çinco dias hallando sien*pre*[204] / poblado y gran *h*ospedage y rresçibimy*ent*o y muchas turq*ue*sas y Cueros de Vac*a* / {/} y la misma R*elaci*on de la t*ie*rra y luego me dezian todos de çivola y de aquella / prov*y*n*ci*a como gentte q*ue* sabia que yba en demanda de *e*lla y me dezian Como es- / teban yba delant(r)e del qual tuve alli mensageros de los Vezinos de / aquel pueblo q*ue h*abian ydo con el y sienpre cargandome la mano en dezir / la grandeza de la t*ie*rra y q*ue* me diese priesa aqui supe q*ue* de(n)*s*de a doss jor- / nadas toparia con Un despoblado de quatro jornadas en que no *h*ay comyd*a* / mas q*ue* ya estava prevenydo p*ar*a hazerme Casas y lleVarme comyda y dy- / me priesa pensando de topar al fin de *e*l a esteban[205] porq*ue* alli me enVio a de*cir* / q*ue* me aguardaria antes de llegar al despoblado tope con Un pueblo fres*co* / de rregadio aqui me salio a rresçibir harta g*ent*e honbres y mugeres Ves*tidos* / de algodon y algunos Cubiertos con cueros de Vacas q*ue* en general ti*enen* / por mejor Vestido q*ue* el de algodon todos los de *e*ste pueblo andan enCaco*nado*s / con turquesas q*ue* les Cuelgan de las narizes y orejas y a esta llaman *Cacona* / entre los quales Venia el señor de *e*ste pueblo y dos hermanos suyos *muy bien*[206] / {rúbricas}

[fol. 4v]

Vestidos de algodon encaconados con sendos Collares De turq*ue*ssas aL / pescueço y me truxeron mucha Caça de Venados conejos y Codornyzes y / mayz y pinol todo en mucha abundançia y me ofresçieron muchas / turquesas y Cueros de Vaca y xicaras muy lindas y otras cosas de lo / qual no tome nada porq*ue* asi lo acostumbre a hazer despues q*ue* entre en la / t*ie*rra donde no tenyan notiçia De nosotros aqui tuve la misma R*elaci*on / q*ue* antes de las siete çiudad*e*s y Reyn*o*s y prov*y*n*ci*as q*ue* arriba digo E yo lleVaba / Vestido Un *h*abitto de paño pardo que llaman De çaragoça q*ue* me hizo traer / franc*isc*o Vazquez de coronado gover*nad*or de la nueVa galizia y el d*ic*ho señor / de *e*ste pueblo y otros yndios tentaron el *h*abito con las manos y me / dixeron q*ue* de

aquello *h*abia mucho en totonteac y que lo trayan Ves- / tido los naturales de alli de lo qual yo me rrey y dixe q*ue* no seria Sino / De aquellas mantas de algodon que *e*llos trayan dixeronme piensas q*ue* no sa- / bemos q*ue e*sso q*ue* tu traes y lo q*ue* nosotros traemos es diferentte sabe que en çivola to- / das las casas estan llenas de *e*sta rropa q*ue* nosotros traemos mas en totonteaCa / *h*ay Unos animales pequeños de los quales quytan lo con q*ue* se haze esto q*ue* tu traes / {/} yo me admire porq*ue* no *h*abia oydo tal cosa hasta que llegue Aqui quise me / ynformar muy particularmentte de *e*sto del paño[207] y dixeron me q*ue* los anima- / les son del tamaño de dos galgos de castilla que lleVaba esteban y dizen q*ue h*ay / muchos en totonteac no pude atinar q*ue* genero de animales fuese otro dia / entre En el despoblado y donde *h*abia de yr a comer hall(o)*e*[208] rranchos y comida / {//} bastante junto a Un arroyo y a la noche halle Casas y asimismo Comida y a- / si lo tuve quatro dias q*ue* turo[209] El despoblado al cabo de *e*llos entre en Un Valle / muy bien poblado de g*ent*e donde en el primer pueblo salieron A mi muchos hon- / bres y mugeres con comyda y todos trayan muchas turq*ue*ssas q*ue* les Colga- / ban de las narizes y de las orejas y algunos trayan collares de turq*ue*sas / de las q*ue* digo q*ue* trayan el señor y sus her*mano*s del pueblo Ant*e*s del despoblado E- / çebto que aquellos trayan sola Una Vuelta y estos traen tress y quatro Vuel- / tas y muy buenas mantas y Cueros de Vaca y las mugeres las mismas / turquesas en las narizes y orejas y muy buenas naguas y Camysas a- / qui *h*abia tanta notiçia de çivola como en la nueVa esp*añ*a de mexico y en eL / peru del cuzco y tan particularmentte contaban la man*er*a de las Casas / y de la poblaçion y Calles y plaças de *e*lla como personas q*ue h*abian estado en ella / muchas Vezes y q*ue* trayan de alla las cosas de puliçia q*ue* tenyan *h*abidas Por / su servycio como los de atras yo les dezia q*ue* no (h)era posible q*ue* las Casas fuesen / de la man*er*a q*ue* me dezian y para darmelo a entender tomaban t*ie*rra y / çeniza y echabanle agua y señalabanme como ponyan la piedra y su- / bian El (h)edifiçio arriba ponyendo aquello y piedra hasta ponello en lo alto / preguntabales los honbres de aquella t*ie*rra si tenyan alas para subir[210] / aquellos sobrados Reyanse y señalabanme El esCalera tan bien / como la podria yo señalar y tomaban Un palo y ponyanlo Sobre la Cabeça / y dezian q*ue* aquel altura *h*ay de sobrado a sobrado tanbien tuve Aqui R*elaci*on / {rúbricas}

[fol. 5r]
{10}
de*L* paño de lana de totonteac donde dizen que las casas *son como las de*[211] / çivola y mejores y muchas mas y que es cosa grande y q*ue* no tiene Cabo *aqui supe*[212] / q*ue* la costa se Vuel*V*e al pony*ent*e muy de rrezio porque hasta la entrada de *este primer*[213] / despoblado q*ue* pase sienpre la costa se Venya metiendo al norte y como cosa *que im-*[214] / portta mucho Volver la costa q*ue* se lo saber y ver y asi fuy en demanda de *ella y vi*[215] / claramentte q*ue* en los treinta y çinco grados Vuel*V*e al oeste de q*ue* no menos *alegria*[216] / tuve q*ue* de la buena nue*V*a de la t*ie*rra y asi me Volvi a proseguir my Camino y *fui*[217] / por aquel Valle çinco dias el qual es tan poblado de gente luçida y tan abastad*o* / de comida q*ue* basta p*ar*a dar de comer en el a mas de trezientos de Cavallo rriega- / se todo y es como Un Vergel estan los barrios a media legua y a quarto de legu*a* / y en cada pueblo de *e*stos hallava muy larga R*elaci*on de çivola y tan particularment*e* / me contaban de *e*lla como gentte q*ue* Cada año Van alli a ganar Su Vida aqui ha- / lle Un honbre natural de çivola el qual dixo *h*aberse Venydo huyendo del gover*nad*or / o de la persona q*ue* alli esta puesta por el señor[218] porque *e*l s*e*ñor de *e*stas siette Çiudad*e*s / Vive y tiene su asientto en la Una de *e*llas q*ue* se llama ahacus y en las otras / tiene puestas p*er*sonas q*ue* mandan por el este Vezino de çivola es honbre de / buena disp*o*sic*i*on algo Viejo y de mucha mas Razon que los naturales de *e*ste Valle / y que los de atras dixome q*ue* se queria yr comigo para q*ue* yo le alCançase p*er*don / ynformeme p*ar*ticularmentte de *e*l y dixome q*ue* çivola es Una gran çiudad en / q*ue* *h*ay mucha g*ent*e y Calles y plaças y q*ue* en algunas partes de la Çiudad *h*ay Unas Casas / muy grandes q*ue* tienen a diez sobrados y q*ue* en estas se juntan los prinçipales / çiertos dias del año dize que las casas son de piedra y Cal por la man*er*a q*ue* lo / dixeron los de atras y que las portadas y delanteras de las Casas prinçipa*le*s / son de turquesas dixome que de la man*er*a de *e*sta çiudad son las otras siette / y algunas mayores y que la mas prinçipa*L* de *e*llas es ahacus dize q*ue* / a la partte del sueste *h*ay Un Reyno q*ue* se llama maratta en q*ue* solia *h*aber / muchas y muy grandes poblaçiones y q*ue* todas tienen estas

Casas de piedra / y sobrados y que *e*stos *h*an tenydo y tienen guerra con el señor de *e*stas siette çiuda- / des por la qual guerra se *h*a diminuydo en gran Cantidad este Rey*n*o de maratta / aUnq*ue* todavia esta sobre sy y tiene guerra Con estotros y asimismo dize q*ue* a la / parte del ueste esta el rreyno q*ue* llaman totonteac y dize que es Una cosa la / mayor Del mundo y de mas gentte y rriquezas y que aqui Visten paños / de lo que es hecho lo que yo traygo y otros mas delicados y q*ue* se saCan de los a- / nimales q*ue* atras me señalaron y que es gentte de mucha puliçia y difer*ent*e / de la gentte que yo he Visto tanbien dixo q*ue* *h*ay otra pro*v*ynci*a* y rreyno muy gran*de* / q*ue* se dize acus porque *h*ay ahacus y acus con aspiraçion es Una de las / siette Çiudad*e*s la mas prinçipal y sin asPiraçion acus es Reyno y pro*v*yncia / por si dixome q*ue* los Vestidos q*ue* traen en çivola son de la man*er*a q*ue* atras *me*[219] / *h*abian d*ic*ho dize q*ue* todos los de aquella Çiudad duermen en Camas *altas*[220] / del suelo con rropas y toldos ençima q*ue* Cubren las Camas dixome *que iria*[221] / comigo hasta çivola y adelant(r)e si le quisiese llevar la mis*ma rela- cion*[222] / me dier*o*n en este pueblo otras muchas p*er*sonas aUnq*ue* no tan *particularmente*[223] / {rúbricas}

[fol. 5v]
por este Valle Camine tres dias HazienDome los naturales de *e*l todas Las fiestas / y rregozijos q*ue* podian aqui en este Valle Vi mas de doss myll cueros de Vacas es- / tremadamente bien adobados Vi mucha mas Cantidad de turq*ue*sas y Collares de las / en este Valle q*ue* en todo lo q*ue* *h*abia dexado atras y todo dizen q*ue* Viene de la Çiudad / De çivola de la qual tienen tanta notiçia como yo de lo q*ue* traygo entre las manos / y asimismo la tienen del rrey*n*o de maratta y de *e*l de acus y de *e*l de totonteac / aqui en este Valle me truxeron Un cuero tanto y medio mayor q*ue* de Una gran Vaca / y me dixeron q*ue* es de Un anymal q*ue* tiene solo Un cuerno en la frente y q*ue* este cuer- / no es corvo hazia los pechos y q*ue* de alli sale Una puntta d*erech*a en la qual dizen q*ue* t*ien*e / tanta fuerça q*ue* ninguna cosa por rrezia q*ue* sea dexa de rronper si topa con ella / dizen q*ue* *h*ay muchos animales de *e*stos en aquella t*ie*rra la color del Cuero es a man*er*a / de cabron y el pelo tan largo como el dedo aqui tuve mensageros de esteban los / quales De su partte me dixeron q*ue* yba ya en el postrer despoblado y muy alegre / por yr mas çertificado de las

grandeZas de la tierra y me enVio a dezir que desde / que se apartto de mi nunca habia tomado a los yndios en nynguna mentira por- / que hasta alli²²⁴ todo lo habia hallado de la manera que le habian dicho y que a(n)si penssaba hallar / lo demas y asi lo tengo por çierto porque es Verdad que desde el primer dia que yo / tuve notiçia de la çiudad de çivola los yndios me dixeron todo lo que hasta hoy he / Visto diziendome sienpre los pueblos que habia de hallar en el Camino y los nonbres / de ellos y en las parttes donde no habia poblado me señalaban donde habia de Comer / y dormyr sin haber (h)errado en Un puntto con haber andado desde la primera nueVa / que tuve De la tierra hasta hoy çiento y doze leguas que no pareçe poco digna de escre- / bir la mucha Verdad de esta gentte aqui en este Valle como en los demas pueblos / de atras puse cruzes y haze los autos y diligençias que ConVenyan conforme a la / ynstruccion los naturales de este Valle²²⁵ me rrogaron que desCansase aqui tress o quatro / dias porque estava el despoblado quatro jornadas de aqui y desde el prinçipio de eL / hasta llegar a la Çiudad de çivola hay largos quinze dias de Camino y que me querian / hazer comida y adereçar lo nesçesario para el y me dixeron que Con esteban / negro habian ydo de aqui mas de trezientos honbres aconpañandole y lleVan- / dole Comida y que Comygo tanbien querian yr muchos por servirme y porque / pensaban Volver Ricos yo se lo agradesçi y les dixe que adereçasen presto por- / que Cada dia se me haze Un año con desseo de Ver a çivola y asi me detuve tress / dias sin pasar Adelant(r)e en los quales sienpre me ynforme de çivola y de / todo lo demas y no hazia sino tomar yndios y pregun- talles apartte a Cada / Uno por si y todos se conformaban en Una misma Cossa y me dezian la muche- / dunbre de gentte y la (h)orden de las Calles y grandeza de las Cassas y la manera / de las portadas todo como me lo dixeron los de atras pasados los tress dias se / junto mucha gente para yr comigo de los quales tome hasta treinta prinçipales / muy bien Vestidos y Con aquellos collares de turquesas que algunos de ellos tenyan / a çinco y a seys Vueltas y Con estos tome la gente nesçesaria que lleVase comida para / ellos y para mi y me puse en camino por mis jornadas entre en el despoblado / a nueVe dias de mayo y asi fuymos el primero dia por Un Camino muy / ancho y Usado llegamos a comer a Una agua donde los yndios me habian señala- / do y a

dormir A otra agua donde halle Casa que habian acabado de hazer para my / {rúbricas}

[fol. 6r]
{12}

Y otra que estaba hecha donde durmio esteban quando paso y ranchos viejos²²⁶ / y muchas señales de fuegos de la gentte que passaba a çivola por este camino y por²²⁷ / esta misma (h)orden camine doze dias sienpre muy abastado de Comida de vena-²²⁸ / dos liebres y perdizes del mismo color y sabor que las de españa aUnque no tan²²⁹ / grandes pero poco menos aqui llego Un yndio hijo de Un prinçipal de los que venian²³⁰ / Comigo el qual habia ydo en conpañia de esteban negro y Venia aquexado el²³¹ / Rostro y Cuerpo Cubiertto de sudor el qual mostrava harta tristeza En su persona²³² / y me dixo que Una jornada Antes de allegar²³³ a çivola esteban enVio su Cala- / baço con mensageros como sienpre acostunbrava enViallo delant(r)e para / que supiesen Como yba el calabaço llevava Unas hyleras de Caxcaveles y doss / plumas la Una blanca y la otra colorada y como llegaron a çivola Ante la per- / sona que el señor tiene alli puesta por prinçipal y le dieron el CalabaÇo / como le tomo en las manos y Vi(d)o los caxcaveles con mucha yra y enojo a- / Rojo el Calabaço en el suelo y dixo a los mensageros que luego se fuesen que EL / conoscia que gentte (h)era aquella que les dixesen que no entrasen en la Çiudad / sino que a todos los matarian los mensageros se Volvieron y dixeron a esteban / lo que passava el qual les dixo que aquello no (h)era nada que los que se mostraban / Enojados le rresçibian mejor y asi prosiguio su Viage hasta llegar²³⁴ a la / Çiudad de çivola donde hallo gentte que no le consintio entrar dentro y le me- / tieron en Una casa grande que esta fuera de la Çiudad y le quitaron luego todo / lo que lleVaba de rrescattes y turquesas y otras cosas que habia habido en el Ca- / mino de los yndios y que alli estuvo Aquella noche sin darle de Comer ny de / bever a el ni a los que con el yban y que otro dia de manaña este yndio huvo sed y / salio de la casa a bever en Un rrio que estava çerca y de ahy a poco rratto Vi(d)o yr / huyendo a esteban y que tras el yba gentte de la çiudad y que mataban algunos / de los que yban con el y que como esto vio este yndio se fue esCondido El rrio a- / rriba y despues atraVeso al Camino del despoblado con las quales nueVas / Algunos de los yndios q*ue* yban comigo començaron a llorar yo con las / Ruynas nueVas temi perderme y no temi tanto perder la Vida como no / poder Volver a dar aViso de la grandeza de la t*ie*rra donde dios n*uest*ro señor pue- / de ser tan *ser*vido y su santta fee ensalçada y acresçentado El patrimony*o* / Real de su mag*esta*d y con todo esto lo mejor q*ue* pude los Console y les dixe q*ue* no se debia / dar entero creditto aquel yndio y ellos con muchas lagrimas me dixeron / que el yndio no diria sino lo q*ue h*abia Visto y asi me apartte de los yndios a en- / comendarme A n*uest*ro señor y a suplicalle guiase esta cosa como mas fues*e* / *ser*vido y alunbrase my Coraçon y esto hecho me Volvio a los yndios y Con Un cuchi- / llo cortte los Cordeles de las petacas q*ue* lleVaba de rropa y rresCattes q*ue* / hasta e(s)*n*tonçes no *h*abia llegado a ello ni dado nada a nadie y rrep*a*rti de lo q*ue* lle-[235] / Vava por todos aquellos prinçipales y les dixe q*ue* no temiesen y q*ue* se *fuesen*[236] / comigo y asi lo hizieron E yendo por n*uest*ro Camino Una jornada de *Cibola*[237] / topamos otros dos yndios de los q*ue h*abian ydo Con esteban los qu*ales venian*[238] / {rúbricas}

[fol. 6v]

Ensangrentados y Con muchas heridas y como llegaron ellos y los q*ue* Venyan / comigo Començaron tanto llanto que de lastima y temor tanbien a mi me / hizieron llorar y eran tantas las Vozes q*ue* no me dexaban preguntalles / por esteban ny lo que les *h*abia su(b)çedido y rrogueles q*ue* Callasen y supiese*mos* / lo q*ue* pasava y dixeron q*ue* Como callarian pues sabian q*ue* de sus padres hijos / y hermanos (h)eran muertos mas de trezientos *h*onbres de los q*ue* fueron con / esteban y que ya no osarian yr a çivola como solian todavia lo mejor q*ue* / pude proCure de amansallos y quit*a*rles el temor aUnq*ue* no estava yo Sin / nesçesidad de qu*i*en a mi me lo qu*i*taSe preguntte a los yndios q*ue* Venyan heridos / por esteban y lo q*ue h*abia pasado y estuvieron Un rratto Sin me hablar pala- / bra llorando con los de sus pueblos y al cabo me dixeron q*ue* como esteban / llego Una jornada de la çiudad de çivola enVio sus mensageros Con su Cala- / baço a çivola al señor haziendole saber su yda y Como Venya a hazer pazes / y a curallos y como le dieron El calabaço y Vi(d)o los caxcaveles muy enojado / arrojo en el suelo El calabaço y dixo yo conozCo esta gentte porque estos caxca- / Veles no son de la hechura de los n*uest*ros dezi(l)d*l*es

q*ue* luego se VuelVan sino q*ue* no que- / dara honbre de *e*llos y asi se q*ue*do muy enojado y los mensajeros Volvieron trist*es* / y no osaban dezir a esteban lo que les acaesçio aUnque todaVia se lo dixero*n* / y el les dixo q*ue* no temiesen que el queria yr alla porque aUnque le rres- / pondian mal le rresçib*i*r*ian*[239] bien y asi se fue y llego a la çiudad de çivola ya / q*ue* se queria poner el sol con toda la gentte que lleVaba que serian mas de / trezientos honbres sin otras muchas mugeres y no los consintieron / entrar en la Çiudad sino en Una casa grande y de buen aposento q*ue e*sta fuera / De la Çiudad y luego tomaron a esteban todo lo q*ue* lleVaba diziendo q*ue e*L / señor lo mando asy y en toda esta noche no nos dieron de Comer ni de beber / y otro dia El sol de Una lança fuera salio esteban de la casa y algunos / de los prinçipales con el y luego Vino mucha gentte de la Çiudad y Como / Ellos Vio (h)echo a huyr y nosotros tanbien y luego nos dieron estos flechazos / y heridas y Caymos y cayeron sobre nosotros otros muertos y asi estuv*imos* / hasta la noche sin osarnos menear y oymos grandes Vozes en la Çiudad y / Vimos sobre las açuteas muchos honbres y mugeres q*ue* miraban y no Vy- / mos mas a esteban sino q*ue* creemos q*ue* le flecharon como a los demas q*ue* yba*n* / con el q*ue* no esCaparon sino nosotros[240] yo Visto lo que los yndios dezian y eL / mal aparejo q*ue h*abia para proseguyr my jornada como deseava no dexe de sentir / su perdida y la mia y dios es testigo de quanto qu*i*siera tener A q*ui*en pedir conseJo / y paresçer porque confieso q*ue* a mi me faltava dixeles q*ue* n*uest*ro señor Castiga- / ria a çivola y que como El emp*erad*or supiese lo q*ue* pasava enViaria muchos / {/} *crist*ianos a que los Casti- gasen no me creyeron porq*ue* dizen q*ue* nadie basta / contra El poder de çivola pediles q*ue* se consolasen y no llorassen y Consolelos / con las mejores palabras q*ue* pude las quales seria largo de poner aqui y Con esto / los dexe y me apartte Un tiro o dos de piedra a enComendarme a dios en lo / qual tardaria *h*ora y media y quando Volvi a ellos halle llorando Un Yndio / {rúbricas}

[fol. 7r]
{14}

mio q*ue* traxe de mexico que se llama marcos y dixome padre estos Tie*nen* con[241] / çertado de te mattar porque dizen q*ue* por ti E por esteban *h*an muerto (a) s*us pa*-[242] / rientes y que no *h*a de quedar de todos ellos honbre ni muger q*ue* no muera*n* yo tor*ne*[243] / a rrepartir entre *e*llos lo q*ue* me quedava de rropa y rresCattes por aplaCallos / y dixeles q*ue* mirasen q*ue* si me mataban q*ue* a mi no me ha(z)*r*ian[244] ningun(d) ma*l* / porq*ue* moria *cristi*ano y me yria al çielo y q*ue* los que me matassen pen(y)ar*ian* / por ello porque los *cristi*anos Ve(r)n*d*ryan en mi busCa y Contra mi Voluntad los / matarian a todos con estas y otras muchas palabras q*ue* les dixe se aplaCaro*n* / algo aUnq*ue* todavia hazian gran sentimy*ento* por la *gent*e que les mataron rrogueles / q*ue* algunos d*e e*llos quisiesen yr a çivola a Ve*r*[245] si *h*abia escapado alguno otro yn- / dio y para q*ue* supiesen alguna nueVa de esteban lo qual no pude acabar con / ellos Visto esto yo les dixe q*ue* en todo caso *h*abia de Ver la çiudad de çivola y me / dixeron q*ue* ningu*n*o yria comigo y al cabo Viendome deter- / minado dos prin- / çipales dixeron q*ue* yrian comigo con los quales y Con mis yndios y lenguas / segui my Camino hasta la Vista de çivola la qual esta asentada en Un llano a la / falda de Un çerro Redondo tiene muy hermoso paresçer d*e* pueblo EL / mejor q*ue* en estas parttes yo he Visto son las casas por la (h)orden q*ue* los yndios / me dixeron todas de piedra con sus sobrados y açuteas a lo q*ue* me par*ecio* des- / de Un çerro donde me puse a Vella la poblaçion es mayor que la çiudad de mexico / Algunas Vezes fuy tentado de yrme a ella porq*ue* sabia q*ue* no aVenturaba sino la / Vida y esta ofresçi a dios el dia q*ue* Començe la jornada al cabo temi Considerando mi / peligro y que si yo moria no se podria *h*aber R*e*laci*o*n de *e*sta *ti*erra q*ue* a mi Ver es la mayor / y mejor de todas las desCubiertas diziendo yo a los prinçipales q*ue* tenia comigo / quan bien me par*eci*a çivola me dixeron q*ue* (h)era la menor de las siette Çiudades / y q*ue* totonteac es mucho mayor y mejor que todas las siette Çiudad*e*s y q*ue* es de / tantas Casas y gentte q*ue* no tiene cabo Vista la disPusiçion de la çiudad pares- / çiome llamar Aquella *ti*erra el nueVo R*e*yno de ssan francisco alli hize con ayuda / de los yndios Un gran monton de piedra y ençima de *e*l puse Una cruz delgada y / pequeña porque no tenya aparejo para hazella mayor y dixe que aquella / cruz y mojon ponia En nonbre de don antonyo de mendoça Visorrey y *gobernad*or de la / nueVa españa por el emp*erad*or n*uest*ro señor En señal de posesion conforme a la yn*s* - / truçion la qual posesion dixe q*ue* tomava alli de todas las siette Çiudad*e*s y de lo*s* / Rey*n*os de totonteac y de acus y de maratta y q*ue* no passava a ellos por Vol - / Ver a dar R*e*laci*o*n de lo hecho e Visto y asi me Volvi con hartto mas temor q*ue* Comyd*a* / y anduve hasta topar la gentte q*ue* se me *h*abia quedado todo lo mas apriesa / q*ue* pude los quales Alcançe a dos dias de jornada y Con ellos Vine hasta pasa*r* / el despoblado donde no se me hizo tan buen acogimy*ento* Como primero por- / q*ue* asi los honbres como las mugeres hazian Gran llantto por la *gent*e q*ue* les ma*ta*- / ron En çivola y Con el temor despedime luego de aquellas *gent*e de aquel Valle / y anduve El primer dia diez leguas y a(n)si anduve a ocho y a diez le*guas*[246] / sin parar hasta pasar El segundo despoblado Volviendo y aUnq*ue* no me *fal*-[247] / {rúbricas}

[fol. 7v]

Tava temor determine De allegar A la abra de q*ue* arriba digo q*ue* tenya / R*e*laci*o*n donde se rrematan las sierras y alli tuve R*e*laci*o*n q*ue* aquella abra Va po- / blada muchas jornadas a la partte del este no *o*se entrar en ella porque / como me par*ecio* q*ue* se *h*abia de Venyr A poblar estotra[248] *ti*erra de las siette Çiudad*e*s / y rrey*n*os q*ue* digo q*ue* entonçes se podria mejor Ver sin poner en aVentura my / persona y dexar por ello de dar R*e*laci*o*n de lo Visto solamentte Vi desde la boca / de la abra siette poblaçiones Razonables algo lejos Un Valle abajo muy / Fresco y de muy buena *ti*erra de donde salian muchos humos tuve R*e*laci*o*n q*ue* *h*ay / en ella mucho oro y q*ue* lo tratan los naturales d*e* ella en Vasijas E joyas / para las orejas y paletillas Con que se rraen y quitan El sudor y que es / *gent*e q*ue* no consiente q*ue* los d*e e*sta otra partte de la abra contraten con ellos no / me supieron dezir la causa aqui puse dos cruzes y tome posesion de / toda esta abra y Valle por la man*e*ra y (h)orden de las posesiones de arriba con- / Forme a la ynst*rucci*on de alli prosegui a la Vuelta de mi Viage con toda la priesa / q*ue* pude hasta llegar a la Villa de san miguel de la provy*nci*a de CuluaCan cre- / yendo hallar alli a franc*is*co Vazquez de coronado gover*nad*or de la nueVa galizia / y como no le halle prosegui mi jornada hasta la Çiudad de conpostela donde / le halle y de alli luego escrevi mi Venida al Yll*ustrisi*mo señor Visorrey de la nueVa / españa y a n*uest*ro padre fray ant*oni*o de Çiudad R*o*drig*o* provy*nci*al q*ue* me enViassen a / mandar lo q*ue* haria no pongo aqui muchas particularidad*e*s porq*ue* no ha- / zen a este caso solamentte digo lo que Vi y me dixeron de las tierras por / donde anduve y de las que tuve Relacion para dalla a nuestro padre provynciaL para / que el la muestre a los padres de nuestra (h)orden que le pareciere o en el Capitulo por / Cuyo mandado yo fuy para que la den al Yllustrisimo señor Visorrey de la / nueVa esPaña a cuyo pedimyento me enViaron esta jornada

{seal}

Fray Marcos de niza / Vice comissario {rúbrica}

En la gran(d) çiudad de temixtitan mexico de La nueVa España doss dias deL / mes de septienbre Ano del nasçimyento de nuestro senor Jesu cristo de myll E / quinyentos e treynta e nueVe años Ante el muy Yllustre senor don antonio de mendoça / ViSorrey E governador por su magestad en esta nueVa EsPaña e presidente del aUdiencia E / Chançilleria rreal que en ella rreside y estando presentes los muy / {rúbrica}

[fol. 8r]
{15}
magnificos señores Liçenciado(s) francisco de çeyños oydor por su magestad en La dicha Real / aUdiencia y francisco Vasques de coronado governador por su magestad en la proVinçia de la / nueVa galizia y en presençia de nos Juan baeça de herrera escribano mayor / de la dicha rreal aUdiencia e de la governaçion de la dicha nueVa españa y Antonyo / de turçios escribano de sus magestades y de la dicha rreal

aUdiencia paresçio el muy Reverendo / padre frai marcos de nyza Viçe comysario en estas partes de las yndias deL / mar oÇeano de la (h)orden de señor san francisco y presento Ante su señoria / E ante nos los dichos escribanos e testigos yuso escri(p)tos esta ynstruçion y rrelaçion firmada / De su nonbre y sellada con el sello general de las yndias la qual tiene / siete hojas sin esta en que Van nuestros signos y dixo afirmo y çertefico / ser Verdad lo contenydo en la dicha ynstruçion e rrelaçion E pasarlo en ella / Contenydo para que su magestad sea ynformado de la Verdad de lo que en ella se haze / mençion y su señoria mando a nos los dichos escribanos de como asy la presentaba e de- / claraba el dicho Viçe comysario lo asentasemos Al pie de ella E lo diese- / mos por fee signado(^s) con nuestros signos testigos que a ello fueron presentes los suso- / Dichos e antonio de almaguer y fray martin de oJacastro fraile de la / Dicha (h)orden[249]

En fee de lo qual Yo el dicho Juan baeça de herrera escribano susodicho Fize aqui este myo signo / (A)tal [signo] en testimonyo de Verdad / Juan baeça de herrera {rúbrica}

E Yo el dicho antonio de turçios escribano suSodicho que A lo que dicho es PresentE Fuy fize Aqui este myo signo que eS (A)tal / [signo] en TeStimonyo de verdad / Antonio de turçios / {rúbrica}

[fol. 8v]
{Relaçion del Frayle / para su magestad}

Document 7

Letters from Antonio de Mendoza and Rodrigo de Albornoz, October 1539

Biblioteca Real, Madrid, II/3042

Gonzalo Fernández de Oviedo y Valdés, *Historia general y natural de las Indias*,
Tercera Parte, Libro XL, Capítulo I, 1547, fols. 22r–23v

INTRODUCTION

Antonio de Mendoza and Rodrigo de Albornoz were acquaintances in Spain, where both served King Carlos I during the Comunero Revolt of 1520–21.[1] Before being posted to Nueva España as the royal *contador* in 1522, Albornoz served as the king's secretary.[2] He arrived in the new Ciudad de México in the company of Alonso de Estrada (royal treasurer and future father-in-law of Francisco Vázquez de Coronado) in 1523. He twice held the governorship of Nueva España jointly with Estrada and other officials during 1525 and 1526.[3] During his tenure of more than 20 years as *contador*, Albornoz returned twice to Spain, in 1534 carrying gold to support the king's campaign against Tunis.[4] When he returned to Nueva España after that trip in 1538, he brought with him an *escribano* named García Rodríguez, who worked in the royal accountancy office under Albornoz until joining the Coronado expedition in 1539.[5] Meanwhile, Mendoza had served the king in embassies to Flanders and Hungary before being appointed the first viceroy of Nueva España in 1535.[6]

In October 1539, just over a month after fray Marcos de Niza's return from his reconnaissance to the north, both men wrote letters to Alonso de la Torre, royal treasurer in Santo Domingo, a functionary with status generally similar to their own.[7]

Whether news of Tierra Nueva made up the bulk of their letters we do not know, but Albornoz at least devoted considerable space to what the friar had to say. The *contador* relayed the report that there were "very wealthy" and "populous" settlements in this newly discovered land, settlements large and important enough to merit the Spanish appellation *ciudades*.[8] Albornoz especially emphasized the production of turquoise and fine cloth in these places, as well as the presence of Old World animals, indicative perhaps of the proximity of the wealthy Orient.[9] Mendoza, on the other hand, was much more circumspect in his letter, revealing only "news of a very excellent and great land, comprising many settlements" and announcing the impending departure of a sizable expedition to go there.[10]

Also in residence in Santo Domingo at the time was Gonzalo Fernández de Oviedo y Valdés, who since 1532 had been the royal *cronista*, or chronicler, for the Indies.[11] In pursuance of what he saw as his duties as chronicler, Oviedo (as he is frequently called) was insistent that communications with the royal court and its constituent councils from officials throughout the Indies be routed through him. At times he badgered and pestered functionaries for information. Such was evidently what prompted Viceroy Mendoza's bristling, though diplomatic, response in October 1541 to a complaining letter from Oviedo.[12]

As exasperating as the chronicler could be for royal administrators, modern researchers seeking to understand the events of Oviedo's times owe him a considerable debt. The massive *Historia general y natural de las Indias* he eventually wrote incorporates the chronicler's own transcriptions of innumerable letters, reports, and other documents that passed through his office but have since disappeared. Among the documents he thus preserved are the excerpts from Albornoz's and Mendoza's letters, published here for the first time in English.

Born in Madrid in 1478, Oviedo had entered the profession of *notario*, a paralegal functionary authorized to certify contracts, wills, and other extrajudicial acts, in 1506. Practice as a *notario* led him to Italy as secretary to the "Gran Capitán" Gonzalo Fernández de Córdoba and to Castilla del Oro with Pedrarias Dávila. Appointment by the king as *veedor* on several occasions brought him eventually to residence at Santo Domingo in 1532. There he took up the post of chronicler and was drafted into the additional responsibility of *alcaide* of the city's fortress.[13]

By 1540 he had begun to write and assemble the *Historia*, which he did not complete until early 1549, after returning to Spain. While preparing the lengthy manuscript in Madrid and elsewhere, he interviewed persons who had been prominent in the Indies, including Álvar Núñez Cabeza de Vaca. Information gleaned during those interviews he then added to the burgeoning opus. Part 1 of the *Historia*, Books 1–19 of the eventual 50 books, covering the early years of Spanish presence in the New World up to the voyage of Magellan in 1519, was published in Salamanca in 1547.[14] That was to be all that was published during the chronicler's lifetime. Oviedo died in 1558, leaving the final two parts of the *Historia* unpublished until the mid-nineteenth century.[15]

On several occasions modern scholars have assessed the reliability of Oviedo's work, particularly of what he claims are verbatim transcriptions, such as the two published here. Some have taken the chronicler to task for intruding his own opinions and observations into material labeled as someone else's words. The most thorough recent reviewers of the issue, Demetrio Ramos in 1972 and Rolena Adorno and Patrick Pautz in 1999, have found, however, that Oviedo almost always made "it possible to clearly distinguish his personal interpolations from his source material."[16] In the case of the 1539 Albornoz and Mendoza letters, the royal chronicler takes great pains to segregate his own introductory material from the letter transcripts, which he insists several times are "verbatim" (*a la letra*) and in "exactly these words" (*estas palabras puntualmente*).[17]

In preparing our own verbatim transcription of Oviedo's transcripts of the Albornoz and Mendoza letter excerpts, we used the only extant manuscript copy. It may be in the chronicler's own hand and is preserved in the Biblioteca Real in the Palacio Real in Madrid. There it is cataloged as Biblioteca Real, II/3042, fols. 22r–23v.[18] This comprises Capítulo Primero of Libro XL, the second book of Part 3 of the *Historia*, as Oviedo designated it.[19] Folio numbers from the Biblioteca Real document have been retained in the transcription and translation that follow, in order to facilitate location of the passages in the original document. The English translation provided here is the first available in print.

TRANSLATION

[22r]

[. . .]

First Chapter

In which a brief report is dealt with concerning the new land discovered from Nueva España and concerning the travel of the Marqués del Valle to Castilla regarding the dispute about that discovery between himself and the lord viceroy don Antonio de Mendoza.[20]

In a section of a letter he wrote to Alonso de la Torre, Their Majesties' treasurer in this land, [the] island of Española, from the great *ciudad* of Temistitán,[21] which was drafted on the sixteenth of October of last year, one thousand five hundred and thirty-nine, the lord viceroy don Antonio de Mendoza wrote exactly these words:[22]

> What I can say further from here is that I am well [and] that this land is also, and is very far along in the service of God and His Majesty. And [I can say] that I dispatched two religious of the Franciscan Order to reconnoiter along the region of the coast of [the Mar del] Sur.[23] They have returned with news of a very excellent and great land, comprising many settlements.[24] What I have decided at present regarding this is to send as many as two hundred horsemen by land and two *navíos* by sea with as many as a hundred arquebusiers and crossbowmen, and these [*navíos*] also with some [22v] religious.[25] [I am doing this] only to see how they will be received by those natives. May God guide them as it may best serve him.

With this letter came another one to the same treasurer from the *contador* of Nueva España, Rodrigo de Albornoz, dated the eighteenth of October of the aforesaid year one thousand five hundred and thirty-nine, in which another section says, in exactly this way:[26]

I do not know whether when this [letter] arrives Your Grace will [already] have heard news about the new land that has been discovered in this Nueva España in the direction of the jurisdiction Nuño de Guzmán held along the Mar del Sur.[27] [That land is] adjacent to the island the Marqués del Valle most recently discovered [and] to which he has sent three or four fleets.[28] [Or whether you will have heard] that when he received news and obtained word of this [new] land the lord viceroy dispatched a friar and a Black who had come from La Florida with the others who came from there.[29] [He is one] of those, among the people whom Pánfilo de Narváez took there, who escaped [death]. According to the information the Black had obtained, these [individuals] were going to travel until[30] they reached an exceedingly wealthy land.

According to [what] he [the friar] says, the friar (who has already returned) has said there are seven very populous *ciudades*, with grand buildings.[31] He provides an eyewitness account about one of them, and about the rest farther on [he speaks] from hearsay.[32] This [land] where he has been has the name Cíbola, and the other, the reino of Marate.[33] And [there is] another very populous land about which he gives very marvelous news both in regard to its wealth and with regard to the harmony, excellent conduct, and orderliness that its people maintain among themselves. [This is] with respect both to their buildings and to all the rest, since they have houses made of lime [mortar] and stone of two or three stories. And at the doors and windows [they have] a great quantity of turquoises.

[23r] There are animals including camels, elephants, and cattle ([both ones] like ours and undomesticated [ones]) which the people of [that land] hunt in the woodlands.[34] [There are] a great many sheep like those of Peru and other animals that have only one horn which extends down to their feet, for which reason [the friar] says it eats lying on its side.[35] [The friar] says they are not unicorns but another kind of animal.

He says that the people go about dressed in some long articles of clothing made of camlet [which reach] to the ground and [are] girded around the waist and are in Moorish style.[36] Finally, it has been concluded that the people are intelligent and not like those of this land.

Concerning the subjugation of [the new land], there is a dispute between the lord viceroy, [who] says it pertains to him[37] because he has discovered it, and the *marqués*, [who] alleges and declares that he discovered it much earlier. [The *marqués* also says he has] spent a great sum of gold pesos in locating it. Concerning that, there have been many stipulations and responses [sent] from the one party to the other. Finally, it is considered certain that the marqués is going to Spain on the first ships that leave.

The viceroy is sending Francisco Vázquez de Coronado there [to the new land] with three hundred men (two hundred horsemen and one hundred footmen), who are to make an extensive report and provide information about the land.[38] And they are to do what they can easily. [These three hundred are going] together with twelve religious of the Order of Saint Francis, who are going with them in order to bring the [natives] to the knowledge of the true road to our Holy Catholic Faith.[39] Their departure from here [the Ciudad de México] will be in a month and a half.[40]

What is stated [here] I extracted verbatim from the viceroy's and *contador*'s original letters themselves. Afterward, when the *marqués* was continuing his journey to Spain, he wrote to me from the island of Cuba, from the port of Habana, on the fifth of February in the year one thousand five hundred and forty, informing me that he was going to Castilla [23v] and about other things that are not apropos of this history.[41] This is not said except to better understand that he went [to Castilla] in pursuit of the right he claims to this enterprise. What may result will be spoken of in its place.

[fol. 22r]

22

Libro segundo

tercera p*ar*te

libro xL

[…]

Capitulo primero en que se trata Una breve Rel*aci*on / de la
nueva ti*e*rra desCubrierta desde la nueva españa / e de la yda
del marq*ue*s del Valle a Castilla sobre la / contempÇion de
entre el e el *señ*or VisoRey don an- / Tonyo de mendoça
sobre aqueste descubrimyento

Dize el señor VisoRey don Antonyo de mendoça / en un
capitulo de Una carta que escribio desde la / Gran ÇiUdad de
temistitan a alonso de la toRe t(h)eso- / rero De Sus mag*es*-
tt*ade*s en aquesta ti*e*rra ysla[42] (h)espa- / ñola que fue fe*c*ha a 16
d*ia*s de otubre del año / que paso de myll e quinyentos E
treynta E / nueve a*ñ*os estas palabras puntualmente

lo que de aca puedo deCir es demas q*ue* yo / estoy bueno que
esta ti*e*rra a(n)simysmo lo esta / E muy Adelante en el
serVi*ci*o de dios y de Su / mag*es*tad e como *en*Vie a descubrir
por la p*ar*te de la / costa del Sur A dos Religiosos de la
(h)orden / de San(t) Fra*n*cisco e son Vueltos con nueVa / de
muy buena Ti*e*rra Grande Y de muchas / PoblaÇiones y lo
que al *pr*esente yo *pr*oVeo / En ello es *en*Viar hasta dozcientos
de caballo / por ti*e*rra e dos naVios por mar con hasta çien(t)
/ arcabuzeros e ballesteros: y aun[43] estos con alg*u*nos

[fol. 22v]

tercera p*ar*te

Religiosos a solamente Ver como seran / Resçebidos de
aquellos naturales dios les / Encamine como mas se sirVa {¶}
con esta / carta le Vino otra al mismo t(h)esorero / fe*c*ha a 18
de octubre del d*ic*ho año de 1539 / del contador de la nueVa
(h)españa Ro- / drigo de albornoz En la qual otro capit*ul*o /
dize a la letra de esta manera. no se si quando / esta llegue
sabra V*uestra* m*erced* nueVas de la ti*e*rra / nueva que se ha
descubierto en esta nueVa (h)es- / Paña hazia la p*ar*te de la
gobernaÇion que tenia / nuño de guzman a la mar del sur
Junto a la ysla que / aGora Ultimamente descubrio el
marques del Valle / Adonde ha enViado tres o quatro
armadas: que sabido[44] / nuevas E teniendo notiçia de esta
ti*e*rra el *señ*or Viso- / Rey enVio Un frayle y un negro q*ue*
Vino de la florida / con otros que de alli Vinieron de los que
escaparon de la Gente que alla lleVo panphilo de narvaeZ /
los quales fueron a parar con la notiÇia que tenia / el negro
a una ti*e*rra muy Riquissima segun dize / donde ha d*ic*ho el
fraYle (que es ya Vuelto) *h*aber siete / ÇiUdades muy populosas e de Grandes EdiffiÇios de la / Una de las quales da
nueVas[45] de Vista y de las demas / adelante por oydas que ha
nonbre esta donde ha es- / Tado çibola y la otra el Reyno de
marate e otra / {y*tem* Cibola ciudad / y*tem* Reyno de marate}
Ti*e*rra muy poblada de que da muy grandes nueVas asi / de
la Riqueza de *e*lla como del conçierto E buena man*er*a / E
(h)orden que entre si tienen la gente de *e*lla a(n)si de / EdiffiÇios como de todo lo demas porque tienen casas / de cal
e canto de dos o tres sobrados y en las puertas / E ventanas
mucha cantidad de turquesas

[fol. 23r]

23

libro xL

E *h*Ay animales de camellos y elephantes y / (y) vacas de las
nuestras e montesinas que las caçan / Por los montes la gente
de *e*lla y mu(n)cha cantidad de / oVejas como las del peru E
otros animales / {No*ta* / Este animal / Gente Vestida de /
chamelote} Que tienen Un cuerno solamente que le allega
hasta / los pies a cuYa causa dizque[46] come (h)echado de lado
/ dize que no son U(i)n*i*cornios[47] sino otra manera de
animales / la gente dizque anda vestida de Unas rropas
larGas / Hasta el Suelo[48] de chamelote e çeñidas e que tiene*n*
ma- / nera de moros en Fin se concluye[49] que es gente de
Razon / E no de la manera de los De *e*sta ti*e*rra. {¶} sobre la
conquis- / Ta de *e*lla *h*aY differençia entre el señor VisoRey
/ dize p*e*rtenezÇerle a el por *h*Abella el descubierto / E el
marqu*e*s alega e dize *h*aberla el descubierto mu(n)- / chos
{X} años ha E gastado En descubrilla mu(n)cha suma de /
pesos de oro e sobre *e*llo ha *h*abido de la Una p*ar*te a la otra
mu(n)- / chos RequerimienTos E Respuestas e *en* Fin / El
marques Se tiene por muy çierto yra a (h)españa / En los
primeros navios que fueren y el Visorrey enVia / {Francisco
Vazquez de / coronado capitan} a Fran*cis*co Vazquez de
coronado con treszientos hombres / los doszientos de caballo

y çien peones a que tomen larga / Relaçion e notiçia de la
ti*e*rra e hagan lo que buenamente / pudieren Juntamente con
doze Religiosos de la (h)orden / De s*an*t fran*cis*co que van
con ellos para tra(h)ellos en co- / nozçimyento del camino
*ver*dadero a nuestra san(c)ta fee / cat(h)olica Su partida sera
de aqui A mes E medio. {¶} esto / Que esta d*ic*ho saque yo
a la letra de las mysmas c*art*as / originales del visoRey e
contador E despues / Prosiguiendo el marqu*e*s su camino
p*ar*a (h)españa me / escribio desde la ysla de Cuba desde el
puerto de la / Havana a Çinco de hebrero de myll e
quiny*ent*os e qua- / renta años haziendome Saber como Yba
a castilla

[fol. 23v]
Tercera p*art*e

E otras cosas que no son al p*r*oposito de la historia / ni esto
se dize p*ar*a mas de *en*tender que el Fue / En continuaÇion
del d*e*r*ech*o que pretende al esta enpresa / lo que su(b)çediere
se dira en su lugar.
[. . .]

Document 8

Testimony of Witnesses in Habana regarding Fray Marcos's Discoveries, November 1539

AGI, Patronato, 21, N.2, R.4, fols. 66r–70v

INTRODUCTION

A persistent background or subtext to Spain's century of conquest in the Americas was fierce, sometimes violent, competition among potential conquistadores. One instance of this widespread and recurrent phenomenon arose in the late 1530s and early 1540s, a complex rivalry over the right to mount an expedition to seek out and subjugate numerous and affluent peoples said to inhabit the interior of North America. In total, five powerful individuals sought the king's license to organize such *entradas* northward from Nueva España: Hernán Cortés, Pedro de Alvarado, Nuño Beltrán de Guzmán, Hernando de Soto, and Antonio de Mendoza. The document published here for the first time in English and several others in this volume had their origins in the resulting dispute.[1] In addition, the dispute and its consequences are touched on frequently among the remaining documents deriving from the Coronado expedition.

In the end, the Consejo de Indias, on the king's behalf, dismissed the claims of Cortés and Guzmán and granted permission to both Soto, a veteran of the conquest of Peru, and Mendoza to launch separate expeditions. The final piece of the puzzle was to order Mendoza and Alvarado to cooperate jointly in seaborne enterprises coordinated with a land expedition directed at seeking Cíbola.[2]

Ignorance of and uncertainty about the size and geography of North America led to friction between Soto and Mendoza both before and after their receipt of formal grants of authority from the king.[3] As Juan de Barrutia, Soto's advocate before the Consejo, put it in 1540, "Your Majesty conceded [to Soto] a royal decree under which neither the viceroy of Nueva España [Mendoza] nor the Marqués del Valle [Cortés] nor any other persons whatsoever, nor any agent [of theirs] may intrude into the territory about which the Adelantado [Soto] has concluded a formal agreement with Your Majesty with the intention of reconnoitering or conquering it."[4]

The April 1537 *capitulación*, or concession, to Soto stipulated that he had the right to "conquer, pacify, and populate" "the Province of Rio de las Palmas to Florida . . . and the Provinces of Tierra-Nueva."[5] Tierra Nueva, in this case, referred to a large but ill-defined territory along the east coast of what is now the United States that had previously been assigned for conquest to Lucas Vázquez de Ayllón in 1523.[6] La Florida, too, was an extensive, indistinct region stretching along and inland from the Gulf of Mexico coast for an indeterminate distance. It extended from at least the Atlantic coast of the modern states of Florida and Georgia westward as far as the Río de las Palmas.[7] Only after the Soto and Coronado expeditions was it clear that at that latitude the continent was many hundreds of leagues wide and that Cíbola lay outside Soto's jurisdiction. In 1539 and 1540, it was not unreasonable for Soto to fear that Mendoza's attempt to reach Cíbola would necessarily infringe on the *adelantado*'s prerogatives.

Thus, both viceroy and *adelantado* tried to keep their

own actions secret while ferreting out every available bit of information about what the opposite party was up to. In the fall of 1539, when fray Marcos de Niza returned to the Ciudad de México with word of the *reinos* of Cíbola, Marata, and Totonteac, Viceroy Mendoza dispatched reports to the king in Spain but attempted to do so surreptitiously. Of primary concern was to keep details of Marcos's discoveries away from Soto's lieutenants in Cuba, then known as Fernandina, where he was governor.[8] Thus, according to the 1539 Habana witness Pero Núñez, "the viceroy has ordered that no *navío* is to call here [Cuba]."[9] Other witnesses testifying in Habana had much the same to report. Andrés García, for instance, declared that the viceroy had even prohibited people from leaving the Ciudad de México without license.[10] On August 26, 1539, Mendoza had, in fact, issued a directive forbidding anyone to leave Nueva España without his express permission.[11]

That permission was granted on occasion, and necessary sea traffic continued. Among the ships granted license to sail during this time was one of unknown name under the command of one Francisco de Leyba. As Leyba told the story in Habana, the ship, bound from Veracruz to Spain in October and November 1539 and suffering illness on board and the need for drinking water and food, was forced to land at Habana.[12] There may have been some collusion in this flouting of the viceroy's order. Certainly one of the passengers, Andrés García, was carrying messages for Governor Soto and therefore may have wanted to make sure the ship touched Cuba.[13]

At the time, November 1539, Soto himself was in Anhaica, the principal indigenous settlement of Apalachee, in the vicinity of modern Tallahassee, Florida, staying put there for the winter. His expedition had already been under way since May.[14] Back in Cuba, Soto's *mayordomo*, Alonso de Ayala, perhaps alerted by the letters delivered by Andrés García, called for formal testimony from García and others who had just arrived from Nueva España on Francisco de Leyba's ship. Dutifully, Soto's lieutenant governor in Habana, Juan de Rojas, ordered that such an examination be made, and the *escribano* Hernando Florencio recorded the testimony of seven witnesses.

Florencio's signed original summary of that testimony is preserved today in the Archivo General de Indias in Sevilla, under the *signatura* (catalog number) AGI, Patronato, 21, N.2, R.4, fols. 66r–70v. The list of questions that were asked of the witnesses, the *interrogatorio*, is not included in the manuscript. And the summary of testimony, as was typical of the time, is not a verbatim record but rather an abbreviated third-person rendition prepared by Florencio from notes taken during the actual inquiry. Hence the occasional disquieting similarity or even identity of statements made by the various witnesses.

Rojas's questions evidently concentrated on two points: what Marcos de Niza had to say about Cíbola and what actions Viceroy Mendoza was undertaking as a result. On the first point, all seven witnesses agreed that, according to what they had heard in Nueva España, Tierra Nueva was very wealthy and populous. By the term *rica*, or "wealthy," the witnesses certainly referred to wealth by European standards, particularly precious metals "and other items of trade."[15] In the latter category, Spaniards of Nueva España of that time would probably have expected fine fabrics, dyestuffs, gems, and condiments, commodities with high value in Europe.

Only one witness, Andrés García, claims that his information can be traced directly to fray Marcos. García's is also the most detailed of the testimonies with regard to Cíbola and its products. His statement concerning gold and silver at Cíbola certainly bears on the issue of whether the friar exaggerated or even lied about Tierra Nueva, as discussed in the introduction to Document 6. "It is difficult to dismiss the barber's [García's son-in-law's] story, for in all details other than gold it jibes nearly word for word with Marcos's written report."[16] It strongly suggests that in fact the friar did embellish what he saw and heard about while in the north in 1539. That was certainly the unanimous opinion of his contemporaries who had anything to say about the friar's veracity.[17]

On the matter of steps taken by the viceroy after Marcos's return from the north, again all seven witnesses are in essential agreement. Six of them refer to an expedition's having been organized by early October 1539, and five mention restrictions on travel outside Nueva España imposed by Mendoza.

Herbert Bolton made the statement that "[Viceroy] Mendoza planned at first to lead the Cíbola venture himself."[18] If that is true, then the idea must have been extremely short-lived. The November 1539 testimony in Habana shows that within a month of so of fray Marcos's return to the Ciudad de México it was public knowledge that Vázquez de Coronado would lead the expedition to Cíbola as captain general.[19] That decision must have been made very early, even though the documents officially certifying his appointment were not issued until January and June of the following year.[20] As a practical matter, it seems unlikely that Mendoza would seriously have considered leaving his seat of government for the period of at least two years required to make the expedition. Nueva España was still extremely fractious from a political standpoint. Its vulnerability to civil strife was patent to all and had earlier been manifested in a coup in the 1520s when Hernán Cortés had left the capital to pursue an expedition of conquest. Late 1539 was no time for the viceroy to leave a void in the structure of royal authority.

Because Soto's lieutenant governor viewed the testimony of the Habana witnesses as demonstrating that the viceroy was engaged in activities prejudicial to the *adelantado*'s interests, he forwarded the summary report to Barrutia in Spain for him to present before the Consejo. Soto's legal representative did just that, but to no avail. Ultimately, the Consejo concurred with the findings of its *fiscal*, Juan de Villalobos,

that "this discovery [of Cíbola] was made by your viceroy's order in Your Highness' name and at your expense and not by any of them [the contending parties, including Soto]. . . . it is necessary that Your Highness not permit any of the aforementioned [contenders] to go or send [anyone else on their behalf] on the aforesaid reconnaissance [of Cíbola].[21]

Soto was effectively debarred from entering the region of Cíbola by the Consejo's decision, but he died in May 1542 along the Mississippi River without ever knowing of the prohibition. The remnants of his expedition, after more than three years of almost continuous conflict with indigenous people of the American Southeast, managed to reach Nueva España on makeshift boats in September 1543.[22] The nearest they had approached to Cíbola was along one of two rivers in modern south-central Texas known today as the Brazos and the Colorado.[23]

In transcribing and translating the Habana testimony, we used the AGI manuscript described earlier. A Spanish transcript of it and the remainder of AGI, Patronato, 21, N.2, R.4, was published in 1871 in *Colección de documentos inéditos*, 15:300–408. Twenty-five years later, excerpts from the Pacheco and Cárdenas transcript were published in Winship, 44 n. 1. In vetting our transcription we made comparisons with the earlier transcript, and we remark on differences between our work and that of Pacheco and Cárdenas in the notes. Folio numbering in the transcript and translation corresponds to that in the original manuscript.

TRANSLATION

[66r]
Very Magnificent Lords,

In the name of the *adelantado* [Hernando de] Soto, in the lawsuit that dealt with what has been recently discovered,[24] I, Juan de Barrutia, present this record of an inquiry conducted before the *justicia* of the *villa* of San Cristóbal de Habana,[25] in which it is recorded [that] the viceroy [Antonio de Mendoza] had issued an order[26] and made a public announcement to the effect that should some of the *navíos* he was sending [to Spain][27] call at the *villa* of Habana, they were not to provide information about the new discovery to the *adelantado*, [my] party. I request and petition Your Highness that it be ordered that the report be filed with the file for the case so that, etc. {rubric}

[66v]
Adelantado Soto
It is to be placed in the file for the case.[28]
In Madrid, the 23rd of December 1540[29]

[67r]
{In Madrid on the 23rd of December in the year 1540, Juan de Barrutia presented the [record of inquiry] at the Consejo Real de las Indias, in the name of Adelantado Soto. The lords of the Consejo ordered that it be placed in the file for the case. {rubric}}

In the town of San Cristóbal de Habana, which is on the island of Fernandina[30] de las Indias del Mar Océano, on the twelfth day of the month of November in the year one thousand five hundred and thirty-nine after the birth of Our

Lord, Jesus Christ,[31] Alonso de Ayala, his lordship's [the *adelantado's*] *mayordomo*,[32] appeared here in [the *adelantado's*] name before the most noble lord Juan de Rojas[33] (lieutenant governor in this *villa* for the illustrious and very magnificent lord don Hernando de Soto, *adelantado* and governor of the *provincia* of Florida, governor and His Majesty's *justicia mayor* of this island) and in the presence of me, Hernando Florencio, His Majesty's *escribano*, a public *escribano*, and [an *escribano*] of the *consejo* of this *villa*. [Ayala] presented a written petition. In conformity with how it appeared, its sum and substance is the following:

{Item} Magnificent Lord:[34]
I, Alonso de Ayala, in the name of the illustrious lord *adelantado*, don Hernando de Soto, governor of Cuba, *adelantado* of La Florida, [and] my lord, appear before Your Grace and state that it has come to my notice that since the illustrious lord don Antonio de Mendoza, viceroy of Nueva España, has been informed of the wealth there is in the *provincia* of La Florida by certain persons whom the lord viceroy had sent to that *provincia* to trade for gold,[35] he is assembling a great expedition to send out to subjugate the aforementioned land. Concerning [the sending of an armed force], there have been great disputes between the Marqués del Valle and the lord viceroy from which great harm is expected.[36] [The sending of an armed force] is to the detriment of my lord the *adelantado*, and [it is] contrary to the covenant and contract he has made with His Majesty.

In order that what concerns this [case] may be clear to His Majesty, I request that Your Grace order an inquiry made into everything stated above. [I further request that] when it has been closed and sealed in a public manner, you order that it be delivered to me, so that I can present it before His Majesty or before the lords, president, and *oidores* [67v] of his most exalted Consejo de las Indias.

When the petition had been presented in the aforesaid manner, the lieutenant [governor] immediately declared that [Ayala] was to present the witnesses of whom he wanted to avail himself and that what they stated and declared was ordered delivered [to him] in accordance with what he requested.

{Witness} Pero Núñez, accepted as a witness for this purpose, swore his oath in accordance with the law. This witness declared that what he knows that pertains to the petition is that when this witness was in the Ciudad de México ([which] may have been three months ago, more or less), he heard it said publicly that a Franciscan friar had arrived [there].[37] He is called fray Marcos. [The witness had heard] that he came from the interior and that the aforesaid friar declared that he had discovered a very wealthy and populous land and that it was four hundred leagues from [the Ciudad de] México to there.[38]

[The people in the *ciudad*] say that it is certain they must travel there by way of the Río de Palmas.[39] [They also say] that the *marqués* Hernando Cortés has sent *navíos* to reconnoiter.[40] [Núñez] has heard it said that there is a dispute between the *marqués* and the viceroy concerning the subjugation of the aforementioned land. He has heard it said that in Nueva España the viceroy has ordered that no *navío* is to call here [Cuba]. This witness believes that it is probably so that [persons traveling on *navíos*] would not provide information about the [newly discovered] land.

[He declared] that this is the truth by the oath he swore. He signed it with his name. Pero Núñez

{Witness} García Navarro was accepted as a witness for this purpose and swore his oath in the form required by law. Concerning the content of the petition, he declared that it is true that when this witness was in [the Ciudad de] México ([which] may have been one month or a month and a half ago,[41] more or less), he heard it said publicly that a friar had recently arrived from a newly discovered land. [The people

in the *ciudad*] say that it is in the land of La Florida, five hundred leagues from México. They say it is toward the north of that land. He says it is a land wealthy in gold, silver, and other items of trade and [has an abundance of] grand towns. The buildings [68r] are made of stone and [have] flat roofs in the style of [the Ciudad de] México.[42] [The people there] have weights and measures[43] and [are] intelligent people. They do not marry more than once. They wear hooded cloaks and travel about mounted on animals (what they are called he does not know).[44]

[The witness declared] that the viceroy was openly mounting an expedition to that land, and that placards [had been] put up in order to raise a troop.[45] Pedro de Tovar and Hernando Alarcón [were to be] captains, and Francisco Coronado [would be going] as general.[46] The people were being assembled openly.

[Navarro] knows that the master [of the ship][47] did not want to call here, but in Matanzas instead.[48] He does not know the reason for that.

[He declared] that this is the truth by the oath he swore. He signed it with his name, García Navarro.

{Item} Francisco Serrano, accepted as a witness for this purpose, swore his oath in accordance with the law. He declared that what he knows is that when this witness was in [the Ciudad de] México (which may have been a month and a half ago, more or less),[49] he heard it said, and it was said publicly, that a Franciscan friar was coming from a newly discovered land, which by land is four hundred leagues from [the Ciudad de] México by way of Jalisco. It is very wealthy and very populous, and [there are] great, walled *ciudades*. The lords of [the *ciudades*] are called kings.[50] The buildings are multistoried. The people are very intelligent and their language is Mexican.[51]

[Serrano heard it said] that the viceroy is raising people for [the land expedition] and that the captains are Francisco Vázquez de Coronado [as] general, and other captains. He knows that much effort was being expended on it. And he knows that it was decreed by the viceroy that [the ships] were not to call at this island; instead they were to go directly to Spain.

[He declared] that this is the truth by the oath he swore. He signed it. Francisco Serrano

{Item} Pero Sánchez, a dyer, accepted as a witness for this purpose, [68v] swore his oath in accordance with the law. He declared that when this witness was in México (which may have been a month and a half ago, more or less), he heard it said publicly that a friar had arrived from a new land. [It was] very wealthy and heavily settled with *ciudades* and *villas*. It is four hundred or four hundred and fifty leagues by way of Jalisco. It was said that it was toward the middle of the land.[52] The viceroy was mounting an expedition in order to [reconnoiter] it, and he already had captains and was raising people for it.

[He declared] that this is the truth by the oath he swore. He did not sign because he said he did not know how to write.

{Item} Francisco de Leyba, accepted as a witness for this purpose, swore his oath in accordance with the law. He declared that what he knows is that when this witness was in Veracruz, [he] heard it said that a friar had arrived from a new land.[53] [It was] very wealthy and heavily settled with *ciudades* and *villas*. It is on the coast of the [Mar] del Sur about four hundred leagues from [the Ciudad de] México.[54] He heard it said publicly that the viceroy was raising people and assembling an expedition in His Majesty's name, and he had named captains to go to that land. He was ordered by the viceroy not to call either at Puerto Rico[55] or at any other place; instead his route was to be directly to Spain.

[He declared] that this is the truth by the oath he swore. He signed it. Furthermore, he declared it is the truth that, in calling at this port, he was not in any case abandoning the continuation of his voyage but had entered this port by necessity, because he was taking on water and other provisions and because of certain persons who were becoming very ill. Francisco de Leyba

{Item} Hernando de Sotomayor,[56] accepted as a witness for this purpose, swore his oath in accordance with the law. He declared that what he knows concerning the petition is that when this witness was in Puebla de los Ángeles[57] (which may

be a month and a half ago), [he] heard it said [69r] and it was said publicly that a friar had arrived from a new land. [It was] very wealthy and heavily settled with *ciudades* and *villas*. The buildings are made of stone [and are] multistoried. The *ciudades* [are] walled. The people are intelligent. It was four hundred leagues, more or less, from [the Ciudad de] México to there.

People were openly being raised on the viceroy's behalf and he had [appointed] captains. The expedition was formally announced in [the Ciudad de] México. The land [being talked about] is the place from where [Andrés] Dorantes and [Álvar Núñez] Cabeza de Vaca came. Those [men] escaped [death] after the expedition of [Pánfilo de] Narváez.[58] This witness knows and understood that the master [of the ship] was commanded by the viceroy's order and his formal directive not to call at any place, but rather to go directly to Spain with the *nao*. The viceroy's secretary[59] enjoined the master, going by sea, not to call either at this port or at any other place in these islands.

[He declared] that this is the truth by the oath he swore. He signed it. Hernando de Sotomayor

{Item} Andrés García, accepted as a witness for this purpose, swore his oath in accordance with the law. He declared that what he knows is that when this witness was in the Ciudad de México, a Francisco de Villegas[60] gave him letters to deliver in this *villa*, to give to the *adelantado*, don Hernando de Soto. If he did not find him, he was to take them to Spain and deliver them to his estate administrator.[61]

This witness [declared that] he has a son-in-law [who is] a barber, who customarily shaved the friar who had come from the aforementioned land. This son-in-law of his told this witness that while he was shaving the friar, [Marcos] told him that before they reached that land there was a mountain range. When that mountain range had been traversed, he crossed a river. There were many settlements, *ciudades* and *villas*. The *ciudades* are surrounded by walls and guarded at their gates. [They are] very wealthy, and there were silversmiths. The women were accustomed to wear golden necklaces, and the men, belts made of gold.[62] There were hooded cloaks, sheep, cattle, partridges, a meat market, [69v] a blacksmith's forge,[63] and weights and measures.

[García declared] that a [man named] Bocanegra told this witness to remain [in Nueva España] because a new world had been discovered. This witness heard it said that the viceroy was raising people for [an expedition to] the aforementioned land. It was publicly proclaimed and ordered that no one was to leave [the Ciudad de] México without [the viceroy's] express permission. [This was ordered] so that he would find out the truth [about] where they were going.

[This witness declared] that he heard it said in Veracruz that this *nao* must not make landfall until [it reached] Spain. The viceroy's secretary enjoined the master, going by sea, not to enter this port.

[He declared] that this is the truth by the oath he swore. He signed it. Andrés García

Juan de Rojas {rubric}[64]

I, Hernando Florencio, Their Majesties *escribano,* a public *escribano,* and [an *escribano*] of the *consejo* of this *villa* of San Cristóbal de la Habana, by order of the aforesaid lord lieutenant [governor] Juan de Rojas (who signed his name here) and because of the petition of Alonso de Ayala, had [this record of inquiry] set down in writing in accordance with what transpired before me. In certification and testimony of the truth I affix here this sign of mine which is thus. [The record of inquiry] is written on three sheets comprising full folios, including this [one], on which my sign appears. {sign}

{rubric} Fernando Florencio {rubric}
public *escribano* and [*escribano*] of the *consejo*

[70r] [blank]

[70v]
{Item} *Probanza* prepared in the villa of San Cristóbal de la Habana, *ad perpetuam rei memoriam,*[65] in accordance with the petition of Alonso de Ayala, in the name of the illustrious and very magnificent lord *adelantado* don Hernando de Soto {rubric}[66]

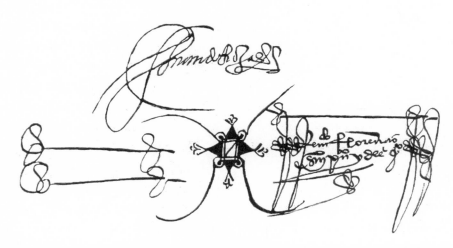

FIGURE 8.1. The signature and registered sign (*signo*) of Hernando Florencio and the signature of Juan de Rojas. AGI, Patronato, 21, N.2, R.4\144.
Reproduced courtesy of Spain's Ministerio de Educación, Cultura y Deporte.

TRANSCRIPTION

[fol. 66r]
Lxvj
muy Poderosos SeñoreS

Juan de baRutya en nombre del adelantado soto en el pleyto / que trato sobre el nueVo desCubrymyento hago presentaÇion / de esta ynformaçion habyda ante la JustiÇia de la Villa / de san cristoval de la habaña por do consta el dicho / VisoRey haber mandado e pregonado que naVyos algunos de los / que el enViaba Tocasen en la dicha Villa de la habaña a fin e caUsa / que no diesen notiÇia del dicho nueVo desCubrymyento al dicho ade- / lantado su parte⁶⁷ pido e suplico a Vuestra alteza se mande poner / la dicha ynformaçion con el dicho proçesso para lo qual etsetera
{rúbrica}

[fol. 66v]
el Adelantado soto
que se ponga en eL pro- / çeso
en madrid
A xxiij de diziembre de jUdxL

[fol. 67r]
LxVij
{en madrid A xxiij de diziembre de jUdxl años La presento en eL conseJo / Real de las yndias Juan de barrutia en nombre del Adelantado / soto los señores del conseJo mandaron que se ponga en el proÇesso {rúbrica}}

En la Villa de San cristobal de la habana que es en la ysla Fernandyna / de las yndias del mar oçeano en doze dyas del mes de / noVyenbre año del nasÇimyento de nuestro señor jesu cristo de myll / e quinyentos e treynta e nueVe años ante el muy noble señor Juan de / Rojas tenyente de governador en esta dicha Villa por el yllustre / y muy magnifico Señor don hernando de soto adelantado y governador / de la proVynçia florida governador y justicia mayor / de esta dicha ysla por su magestad y en presencia De my hernando / florencio escribano de Su magestad y escribano publico y del conÇeJo / de esta dicha Villa paresçio presente alonso de ayala / mayordomo de Su Señoria y en su nonbre y presento Un / escripto de pedimyento segun por el paresçia su thenor / del qual es este que Se sigue

{ytem} magnifico señor alonso de ayala en nonbre del yllustre señor / el adelantado don hernando de soto governador de Cuba a- / delantado de la florida my señor parezco ante Vuestra merced y / digo que a mi notiçia es Venido que ynformado / El Yllustre señor don antonyo De mendoça Virrey de la / nueVa españa de la Riqueza que en la dicha proVyn- / çia Florida hay de çiertas personas que el dicho Señor / Virrey habia enViado a Rescatar a la dicha proVyn- / Çia haze gran (h)armada para enVyar a conquistar la / Dicha tierra y sobre ello entre el marques del Valle y el / dicho señor Virrey ha habido grandes diFerençias de lo / qual se espera grandes daños y es en perJuyzio del dicho / Adelantado my señor y Contra la Capitulaçion y asyento / que con su magestad tiene hecho y para que de ello conste / A Su magestad pido a Vuestra merced mande haber ynFFormaçion / de todo lo Susodicho y habida Çerrada y sellada / en publica Forma me la mande dar para la presentar ante / su magestad o ante los Señores presidente e oydores / {rúbrica}

[fol. 67v]

de su muy alto consejo de las yndias

E presentado el di*ch*o es*crip*to en la manera que di*ch*a es /
luego el di*ch*o señor teniente dixo que prese*n*te los / T*e*stigos
de que se *en*tiende aproVechar e lo que di- / xeren e depu-
syeren se lo mande dar segu*n* que lo pide

{tt*estigo*} Pero nuñez T*e*stigo ResÇibido *en* la di*ch*a Razon /
Juro Segun d*e*rech*o* e dixo que lo q*ue* sabe *en* Razon del di*ch*o
pedimy*ento* / es que estando este t*e*stigo *en* la ÇiUdad de
mexico puede ha*ber* / tr*e*s meses poco mas o menos oyo d*e*cir
este t*e*stigo pu*bl*icame*n*te / que habia Venido Un Frayle
Fra*n*cisco q*ue* se dize Fray marcos / que Venia *de* la ti*e*rra
ade*n*tro e que dezia el di*ch*o Frayle / q*ue* se habia desCubierto Una ti*e*rra muy Rica e muy poblada / e que habia
quatroçientas leguas dende mexico alla / e que dizen que *h*an
de yr alla por çierta del Rio de / Palmas e que *e*l marq*ue*s
her*n*ando cortes ha enViado / naVyos a desCubrir e que
entre el di*ch*o marq*ue*s e el ViSorrey / *h*a oydo d*e*cir que *h*ay
diFerençia Sobre la conquista de la di*ch*a / ti*e*rra que *h*a oydo
dezir que en la nueVa españa el Virrey / *h*A mandado que
ningu*n* naVio toque aqui e que cree / este t*e*stigo q*ue* sera
porque no de aViso de la ti*e*rra e que / esta es la Verdad p*a*ra
el jurame*n*to que hizo e Firmolo / de su nonbre p*er*o nuñez

{tt*estigo*} Garçia naVarro t*e*stigo ResÇibido en la di*ch*a
Razon / habiendo Jurado en forma de d*e*rech*o* por el tenor
del di*ch*o pedy- / my*ento* dixo q*ue e*s v*er*dad que *e*stando este
t*e*stigo en mexico oyo / d*e*cir pu*bl*iCame*n*te puede haber un
mes o mes y medio / poco mas o menos que habia Venido
Un Frayle nueVame*n*te / de una ti*e*rra nueVame*n*te desCubierta que dizen q*ue e*s / quinientas leguas de mexico en la
ti*e*rra de la Florida / que dizen q*ue e*s hazia la p*a*rte del norte
de la di*ch*a ti*e*rra / la qual diz*e* que (e)es tierra Rica de oro e
plata e otros / Resgates e grandes pueblos que las caSas /
{rúbrica}

[fol. 68r]

LxViij

son de piedra e terrados a la manera de mexico e que /

Tienen peso e medida e ge*n*te de Razon e que no CaSan /
mas de Una Vez e que Visten albornozes e que an- / Dan
Cabalgando en Unos animales que no Sabe / como se llaman
e que publiCamente armaba p*a*ra / la di*ch*a ti*e*rra el VisoRey
e Carteles puestos p*a*ra / hazer ge*n*te e Capitanes pedro de
toVar e hernando / AlarCon e Fra*n*cisco coronado por
general e que / Pu*bl*icamente se Hazia ge*n*te e q*ue* sabe que
*e*l maestre / no quisiera toCar aqui syno en matanças e que
la / CaUsa de *e*llo que la no Sabe e q*ue e*sta es la Verdad /
p*a*ra el jurame*n*to que hizo e Firmolo de su nonbre gar- / cia
na(r)Varro

{y*tem*} Fra*n*cisco Serrano t*e*stigo ResÇibido en la di*ch*a
Razon Juro Segu*n* / d*e*rech*o* e dixo que lo q*ue* sabe es que
*e*stando este t*e*stigo en me- / xico puede ha*ber* mes e medyo
poco mas o menos oyo / dezir e publiCame*n*te se dezia que
Un Frayle Fra*n*cisco / Venya de Una ti*e*rra nueVamente
desCubierta / q*ue e*s quatroçientas leguas de mexico por
ti*e*rra por la / Via de xalisCo e q*ue e*s muy Rica e muy
poblada e gran- / des ÇiUdades çercadas e que los Señores
de *e*llas Se nom- / bran Reyes e que las Casas Son
Sobradadas e q*ue e*s / ge*n*te de mucha Razon e que la lengua
es mexicana / e que *e*l Visorrey haze gente p*a*ra ella e q*ue* son
Ca- / pitanes Fra*n*cisco Vazquez de coronado general e
(^que) / otros Capitanes e q*ue* sabe que en ello Se ponia
mucha / diligençia e q*ue* sabe que *e*staba proVeydo del ViSo-
/ Rey que no toCase*n* en esta ysla SalVo q*ue* Fuese*n* d*e*recha-
/ mente a españa e que *e*sta es la v*er*dad p*a*ra el Jurame*n*to
q*ue* / hizo e Firmolo Fra*n*cisco serrano

{y*tem*} Pero sanchez tinturero t*e*stigo ResÇibido *en* la di*ch*a
Razo*n* / {rúbrica}

[fol. 68v]

Juro segu*n* d*e*rech*o* e dixo que puede ha*ber* mes e medyo poco
/ mas o menos estando este t*e*stigo en mexico oyo d*e*cir /
pu*bl*icamente que habia Venido Un Frayle de Una ti*e*rra
nueVa / muy Rica e muy poblada de ÇiUdades e Villas e q*ue*
*e*s / quatroçientas o quatroçientas e çinq*ue*nta leguas por la /
Via de xalisCo e que se dezia que (h)era hazia en me- / dio
de la ti*e*rra e que *e*l Visorrey armaba p*a*ra ella e / que ya tenia

Capitanes e hazia gente para ella / e que esta es la verdad
para el Juramento que hizo e / no firm(a)(^r)o porque dixo
que no Sabia escrebir

{ytem} Francisco de leyba testigo ResÇibido en la dicha
Razon Juro segun / derecho e dixo que lo que sabe es que
estando este testigo en la / Veracruz oyo decir este testigo que
habia Venido Un / Frayle de Una tierra nueVa muy Rica e
muy poblada de / ÇiUdades e Vyllas e que es a la banda del
Sur obra / de quatroçientas leguas De mexico e que oyo decir
/ publicamente que el Virrey hazia gente e (h)armada en
nombre / de su magestad e que tenia nonbrados Capitanes
para yr / a la dicha tierra e que le Fue mandado por el Virrey
/ que no toCase en puerto Rico ny en otra parte SalVo que
Fuese / derechamente Su Camyno a españa e que esta es la
verdad / Para el Juramento que hizo e Firmolo de Su nonbre
/ e otrosi dixo que es verdad que no enbargante que en
toCar⁶⁸ / en este puerto dexaba de Seguyr Su Vyaje pero que
/ entro en este puerto por neÇeSidad que lleVaba de agua /
e otros bastimentos e de çiertas personas que Venyan / muy
enfermos Francisco de leyba

{ytem} hernando de sotomayor testigo ResÇibido en la dicha
/ Razon Juro segun derecho e dixo que lo que sabe en Razon
del dicho / pedimyento es que puede hazer mes e medio que
estando este / testigo en la puebla de los Angeles oyo decir
este testigo / {rúbrica}

[fol. 69r]
Lxjx
E publicamente se dezia que habia Venido Un Frayle de Una
tierra / nueVa muy Rica e muy poblada de ÇiUdades e Vyllas
/ e que las casas son de piedra sobradadas e las ÇiUdades /
çercadas e gente de Razon e que habia de meXyco alla /
quatroçientas leguas poco mas o menos e publicamente / se
hazia gente por parte del Virrey e que habia Capitanes / e Se
pregono la dicha armada en mexico e que esta dicha tierra /
es la parte donde Vyno dorantes e Cabeça de Vaca los qua-
/ les esCaparon de la armada de narVaez e que sabe e Vi(d)o
este / testigo que Fue mandado al maestre por mandado del
Virrey / e Con su mandamyento que no ToCase en parte

nynguna SalVo que fuese / derechamente a españa con la
dicha nao e que el Secretario / del Virrey hizo un Requerimyento al dicho maestre Viniendo / por la mar que no
toCase en este puerto ny en otra parte de estas / yslas e que
esta es la Verdad Para el Juramento que hizo e / Firmolo de
Su nonbre hernando de sotomayor

{ytem} Andres garçia testigo ResÇibido en la dicha Razon
Juro segun / derecho e dixo que lo que sabe es que estando este
testigo en la ÇiUdad / de mexico Un Francisco de Vyllegas le
dio Cartas para dar en esta (^ysla) ^Vylla / para dar al adelantado don hernando de soto e sy no lo hallaSe que las / lleVase
a españa e las diese al hazedor suyo e que este / testigo tiene
Un yerno barbero que afeytaba al Frayle / que Vyno de la
dicha tierra e que el dicho su yerno le dixo a / este testigo que
estando afeytando al dicho Frayle le / dixo como antes que
llegasen a la dicha tierra / estaba Una sierra e que pasando la
dicha syerra / pasaba⁶⁹ Un Rio e que habya muchas poblazones de / ÇiUdades e Villas e que las ÇiUdades Son /
ÇerCadas e guardas a las puertas e muy Ricas e que / habia
plateros e que las mugeres trayan Sartas / de oro e los
honbres çintos de oro e que habia alvor- / nyos⁷⁰ e oVeJas e
VaCas e perdizes e Carniçeria / {rúbrica}

[fol. 69v]
e herreria e peso e medyda e que Un boCanegra / dixo a este
testigo que se quedaSe que se habia des- / Cubierto un
nueVo mundo e que oyo decir este testigo / que el Virrey
hazia gente para la dicha tierra e que se a- / pregono e mando
que no Saliese nynguno de mexico / sin su licencia para Saber
la verdad donde yban e que oyo / decir este testigo en la
Veracruz que esta nao no habia de tomar / tierra hasta españa
e que Vyniendo por la mar el se- / cretario del Virrey hizo un
Requerimyento al maestre / que no entrase en este puerto e
que esta es la verdad para / El Juramento que hizo e Firmolo
de Su nonbre andres garcia / Juan de RoJas {rúbrica}

E yo el dicho hernando florençio escrybano de sus magestades e escrybano / Publico y del consejo de esta Villa de San
cristobal de la / habaña de mandado del dicho señor tenyente
Juan de Rojas y a- / quy firmo su nombre e de Pedimyento

del / dicho Alonso de ayala lo fize escrevyr / seGun(d) que
ante my Paso e en fe e testimonio de verdad Fize aquy / este
myo sygno que es (a)Tal lo qual Va escrito en tres hojas de
pliego / entero con esta en que Va myo sygno
{signo}
{rúbrica} Fernando florençio {rúbrica}
escrybano publico y del consejo

[fol. 70r] [blank]

[fol. 70v]
{ytem} probanca hecha en la Villa de / san(t) cristobal de la
habaña ad / Perpetuam Rey memoryam A / Pedimyento de
alonso de ayala en nombre / del yllustre e muy magnifico señor
el / adelantado don Fernando de soto / {rúbrica}

Document 9

The Viceroy's Appointment of Vázquez de Coronado to Lead the Expedition, January 6, 1540

AGI, Justicia, 336, N.1, "Francisco Vazquez Coronado, vecino y regidor de la Ciudad de Mexico con el fiscal de su magestad sobre ciertos yndios, Guadalajara, 1553," fols. 22right–26right

INTRODUCTION

Acting under authority conferred on him not quite five years earlier by means of a royal *cédula*,[1] Viceroy Mendoza, in January 1540, formally named Francisco Vázquez de Coronado "captain general of the company which is now on its way" to Tierra Nueva.[2] Issuance of the formal letter of appointment, however, constituted only one step in a process that had begun nearly a year and a half earlier. There seems little doubt that as early as the fall of 1538, when the decision was reached to dispatch fray Marcos de Niza on his northward reconnaissance, the viceroy already intended to place his protégé Vázquez de Coronado in charge of any expedition that might result.

For fiscal reasons, if no other, the formal appointment had to await departure of the expedition. The 1540 appointment letter provides that "you may receive and draw the same salary [as you receive as governor]."[3] This provision had to be executed in order not to result in double payment to Vázquez de Coronado while he remained governor of Nueva Galicia. And Mendoza clearly wanted Vázquez de Coronado in charge in Nueva Galicia until the last possible moment. Moreover, even after delivery of the letter on Epiphany, January 6, the appointment was not fully official. It still required written ratification by the king and his councilors, which was not forthcoming until June 1540, months after the expedition itself got under way.[4]

As is clear from testimony given in Habana during the fall of 1539, it was already then public knowledge that Vázquez de Coronado was to lead the expedition being organized.[5] Fray Antonio Tello maintained in the seventeenth century that Mendoza himself planned at first to lead the expedition to Tierra Nueva, but that seems highly improbable.[6] In the first place, no known sixteenth-century source supports Tello's assertion. But beyond that, Mendoza's political astuteness would certainly have argued against his abandoning the capital for two years or more.

That was because the political stability of Nueva España was not at all assured. Arthur Aiton has aptly described Nueva España when Mendoza arrived in 1535 as "in a very unsettled condition."[7] The Marqués del Valle, Hernán Cortés, and his partisans continued to mount challenges to viceregal authority, as did the *criados* and supporters of Nuño Beltrán de Guzmán and Pedro de Alvarado. As we discuss in more detail in the introduction to Document 20, at the time the Coronado expedition departed from Compostela in February 1540, serious rivalries within the viceroyalty of Nueva España threatened to spiral into civil war.[8]

The January 1540 appointment of Vázquez de Coronado as captain general was drafted as a royal letter of privilege, written as though by the king himself or a functionary in his royal court. In fact, it was prepared in Nueva España for Viceroy Mendoza acting as the king's proxy.[9] Arthur Aiton called the document "unusual" because of this. The viceroy, however, had broad authority to act on the king's behalf, and often did so. There is certainly no indication that he overstepped his royal charge or that the king was in any way displeased with Mendoza's action in this case. The 1540 letter is very similar in tone, structure, and content to the *cédula* that in 1539 had conferred the office of governor of Nueva Galicia on Vázquez de Coronado.[10] The earlier *cédula* was prepared in Spain by the king's secretary, Juan de Sámano, and ratified an earlier appointment made by the viceroy. This appears to be exactly parallel to the procedure followed with the 1540 appointment. The process followed in the two appointments was all but identical: a written assignment to the post prepared by the viceroy's staff on the king's behalf was followed months later by a formal royal appointment.

With the rising influence of advocates for Indian rights in Spain at the time, it is hardly unexpected that the 1540 letter stresses the captain general's responsibility to assure that native people he might encounter and subjugate not be abused.[11] Otherwise, the letter is highly formulaic, delineating the various prerogatives of and compensations owed to the captain general. One of these provisions specifies that "the Indians who are given to you in *encomienda* and placed in your keeping by us in our royal name are not to be removed from you or taken away at any time."[12] Despite this explicit prohibition, *oidor* Lorenzo de Tejada subsequently ordered Vázquez de Coronado stripped of several *encomiendas*. As part of a suit filed by the former governor and captain general in the early 1550s to recover those lost *encomiendas*,[13] Hernando de Balbuena made the copy of the 1540 appointment letter that is published here.

The original of the 1540 letter disappeared long ago. Preserved in the Archivo General de Indias in Sevilla, though, are four later, third-generation copies, all prepared for submission in connection with legal cases brought by Vázquez de Coronado and García López de Cárdenas in the 1540s and 1550s. The four extant copies are filed under the *signaturas* (catalog numbers) AGI, Justicia, 336, N.1, fols. 22right–26right; AGI, Justicia, 339, N.1, R.1, fols. 169r–171v; AGI, Justicia, 339, N.1, R.2; and AGI, Justicia, 1021, pieza 1.[14] The now-lost original of the 1540 letter was drafted by Diego de Almaguer, a secretary to the viceroy.[15] Several different *escribanos* had a hand in preparing the surviving copies. The copy from AGI, Justicia, 336, N.1, which is transcribed and translated here, was made in 1552 by *licenciado* Hernando de Balbuena, secretary of the Audiencia de Nueva Galicia (Guadalajara),[16] from a 1541 copy that had been prepared by Antonio de Turcios, chief *escribano* of the Audiencia de México.[17] In the transcription and translation that follow, the original folio numbers are retained.

In February 1940 Arthur Aiton published a Spanish transcription of the copy of the 1540 letter included in AGI, Justicia, 339, N.1, R.1.[18] Later that same year George Hammond and Agapito Rey published an incomplete English translation of the same copy.[19] After the lapse of another three years, Rey, at the behest of Herbert Bolton, transcribed the copy of the letter that appears in AGI, Justicia, 1021.[20] In preparing the transcription and translation that follow, we used the copy embedded in AGI, Justicia, 336, N.1, because it appears to contain fewer scribal errors than any of the other copies.[21] In the process, we consulted the earlier transcripts and translation just listed. This is the first time the letter has been published in full in English translation.

TRANSLATION

[22 right]²²

[...]

{Item} Don Carlos, by divine mercy emperor, *semper augustus* [always venerable]. Doña Juana, his mother, and the same don Carlos, by the grace of God, sovereigns of Castilla, León, Aragón, the two Sicilys, Jerusalem, Navarra, Granada, Toledo, Valencia, Galicia, the Mallorcas, Sevilla, Córdoba, Corsica, Murcia, Jaén, the Algarves, Algeciras, Gibraltar, the Canary Islands, the Indies (the islands and continent of the Ocean Sea); counts of Flanders, Tyrol, etc.²³

Inasmuch as [he] received information that beyond the *provincia* of Culiacán,²⁴ [traveling] by land, it would probably be possible to locate and discover towns and *provincia*s populated by native peoples of these regions who would likely be of service²⁵ to God, Our Lord, and ourselves, don Antonio de Mendoza, our viceroy and governor of Nueva España and president of our *audiencia* and royal *chancillería* which has its seat there, decided to dispatch, in our name, the reverend father fray Marcos de Niza, provincial of the Order of San Francisco in the province of the Santo Evangelio in Nueva España, [23 left] so that he might go to reconnoiter and learn about the aforesaid lands and *provincias*.²⁶

For that, [Mendoza] provided him with companions suitable for this purpose and the directive and commission that was appropriate for him to go on the expedition. God, Our Lord, was served in that [fray Marcos], traveling in pursuit of what had been decided, obtained information of grand and very populous *ciudades, provincias,* and even *reinos.*²⁷ With his own eyes he saw a great part of it. He came [back] in person to make a report about it to our viceroy.²⁸

The aforesaid [viceroy] sent to our Royal Person [the report], signed by our provincial, informing us that God, Our Lord, had been pleased that there be discovered, in our

times, such great lands where His Holy Name might be known and worshipped and His Holy Faith and Catholic Church [might be] enlarged and our royal patrimony increased. [He said further] that [any] delay caused by not obtaining [information] and learning fully what there is in those lands would likely result in harm.²⁹ [Additionally, the viceroy said] that in the meantime, we were being served by [his] preparing what ought to be done in pursuit of this aim. He would send ecclesiastics from the Order [of San Francisco], persons of knowledge and integrity, with the aforementioned provincial to go to the aforesaid lands to preach and proclaim [23 right] the Holy Gospel and to attract and convert³⁰ the natives of that [land] to the brotherhood of the Catholic Church. And then they would recognize and take us as their king and natural lord.

For the safety and protection of the ecclesiastics,³¹ he would send people whom he sees are suitable, with a captain, a person of status [such] as the enterprise and undertaking would require. Since the provincial and ecclesiastics are now going, both by sea and by land,³² to carry out and pursue the aforementioned expedition with the company which our viceroy assembled for it, he holds the authority from us, by virtue of our royal *cédula*, to be able to designate a person to fulfill and perform what is fitting for our service in these places. [The *cédula* is] issued in this manner.

The King

Don Antonio de Mendoza, our viceroy, governor of Nueva España and president of our *audiencia* and royal *chancillería* which has its seat there,

As you have been aware, don Hernando Cortés, Marqués del Valle, possesses a commission from us as our captain general of Nueva España.³³ However, with the interpretations and restrictions which afterwards were issued to him, he cannot exercise the office except when he is [so] ordered by our president and *oidores* [of the *audiencia*]. And [even] in that case [he may do so only] while adhering to [any] directive which they might give him. But because it could be that some things might arise, [24 left] the performance of which might suitably be entrusted to other persons, by the present [*cédula*] I order [and] confer on you the power and authority, so that when things present themselves, the completion and fulfillment of which might seem suitable to us to entrust to another person and not to the *marqués*, you may do it and are to do [it], as president, viceroy, and governor. Executed in Barcelona, on the seventeenth day of April of the year one thousand five hundred and thirty-five.[34] I, the King.[35]

by the order of His Majesty. Cobos, *comendador mayor*[36]

Seeing, thus, that it is conducive to the service of God, Our Lord, and ourselves that the aforementioned expedition be carried out in our name, since we have faith that you, Francisco Vázquez de Coronado, our governor and captain general in Nueva Galicia, are such a person who will well and loyally execute and fulfill what is entrusted and assigned to you by us, that you will pay special attention to the protection and defense of the aforementioned lands and their natives, by the present [*cédula*] we ratify and confirm the appointment of yourself, Francisco Vázquez de Coronado, by don Antonio de Mendoza, our viceroy in Nueva España. And we name you once again as captain [24 right] general of the company which is now on its way and [of any company which] may go later; of whatever [people] you may find there; of the lands and *provincias* of Acus, Cíbula, the Seven Ciudades, the *reinos* and *provincias* of Matata and Totinteac and all their dependencies and satellites;[37] of the rest of the lands and *provincias* that you may discover and may be discovered because of your effort.[38]

We order all the persons who are going there (of whatever class and social status they may be) to recognize and hold you, Francisco Vázquez de Coronado, as[39] our captain general. And they are to obey you and execute and fulfill your orders. They are to come and appear before you at your summons at those

intervals and under [pain of] the penalties you may impose on them or may order to be imposed on our behalf. By the present [*cédula*] we impose those [penalties] on them. We grant you the power and authority to carry out [such penalties] on those who may be rebellious and disobedient.

Furthermore, we grant you authority so that you can appoint and might appoint the captain or captains who are suitable and then dismiss and remove them.[40] And [also the authority] to install others, however many you may want and may be approved by you.[41]

Likewise, [we grant you authority] so that you can judge and may judge[42] all the civil and criminal cases which may come about and take place among the people [of the company], between the natives of the lands [25 left] through which you may travel and [where you may] be, and between them and the Spaniards. For judgment and resolution of the aforementioned cases you can promote and might promote a deputy or two, or more, whom you may find to be appropriate and necessary. And you can remove those and install others anew.

In regard to treatment of the native Indians of the lands through which you may travel and [where you may] be, and in regard to what you may have to do and [what agreements you may have] to conclude in [those lands], we order you to observe and fulfill the directive[43] which we have ordered given to the persons who go, as you are going, to reconnoiter and pacify lands and new *provincias* and which you are taking (signed by our viceroy and the secretary, [who have] signed at the end of the document). [You are to adhere to this] word for word,[44] without exceeding or running counter to its substance and form, under [pain of] the penalties referred to in the directive.

Further, we order that no hindrance or impediment whatsoever is to be put in your way in the discharge and exercise of the office of captain general of the aforesaid lands and that everyone is willingly to be subject to you. They are to provide and see that you are provided the fullest assistance and aid you may request from them and have need of, without offering any excuse or other delay.

[25 right] [We state] that we grant you complete power to discharge and exercise the aforesaid office and the rest of what is stated by this instrument, depending on what may be required in such a case, with all its subsidiary powers, limitations, and additional rights and authority.[45]

Inasmuch as you, the aforesaid Francisco Vázquez de Coronado, are our governor and captain general of the *provincia* of Nueva Galicia, and you are going by our order and in our service on the reconnaissance and pacification of Tierra Nueva[46] and to attract its natives to the knowledge of our Holy Catholic Faith and to place it under our royal crown, by the present [*cédula*] we grant you authority and power so that, during your absence, you can leave and might leave in your stead in the aforesaid *provincia* your lieutenant and deputies in the place or places which seem [fitting] to you and [are] persons who may be suitable for [those places]. We order the persons whom you thus leave and name in Nueva Galicia to be [recognized], held to be, and obeyed as such deputies of its governor.

[We decree that] you may receive and draw the same salary in the aforesaid office which is designated by us for you by the commission which was given according to custom.[47] [The salary] is to be delivered and paid to you notwithstanding your absence, just as it has been delivered and paid to you until now. Since you are going in our service (as you are), [we order that] the Indians who are given to you in *encomienda* and placed in your keeping by us in our royal name are not to be removed from you or taken away at any time, [26 left] neither [those] in Nueva España nor [those] outside it.

Furthermore, it is our will and we order that the aforementioned lands and those additional ones you may pacify and bring to our service as our captain general you may hold until such time as something else is arranged and ordered by us or our viceroy of Nueva España. You may protect and defend those [lands] in our royal name, and their natives so that harm is not done to them, nor any other abuse. Nor are any persons to enter [those lands], nor are they to seize or occupy them. You are to inform [such interlopers] [that] the government of Tierra Nueva has jurisdiction[48] over them until such time as it may be decided what is conducive to our service concerning it (as [has been] stated).

Delivered in the *ciudad* of Michoacán, on the sixth of January in the year one thousand five hundred and forty since the birth of Our Savior Jesus Christ.

Don Antonio de Mendoza
I, the secretary, Antonio de Almaguer, had it drafted by [the king's] order with the consent of his viceroy of Nueva España.[49]
Registered. Diego Agundes for *chanciller* Gaspar de Castilla.[50]

{Item} This copy of the original commission included above was made and extracted in the Ciudad de México on the first day of December in the year one thousand five hundred and forty-one since the birth of Our Savior [26 right] Jesus Christ. I, Antonio de Turcios, chief *escribano* of the Real Audiencia de Nueva España and its government for His Majesty,[51] have extracted the aforementioned copy from the petition of Governor Francisco Vázquez de Coronado and from the petition of the lords president and *oidores* of the aforesaid royal *audiencia*, inasmuch as they stated that a need for such a copy [existed], in keeping with their right.

Witnesses who saw it corrected and reconciled: Agustín Pinto and Andrés Péres, *estantes* in this *ciudad*.

In confirmation of this I affixed here my [registered] mark [which is made] in this way, in proof of its truth.
Antonio de Turcios

{Item} This copy was extracted from the authorized copy of the aforesaid commission from His Majesty on the twentieth day of the month of February in the year one thousand five hundred and fifty-two, in Compostela, in order to return the original from which it was taken to the party Francisco Vázquez de Coronado. Witnesses who were present when it was corrected and reconciled on this day: Blas de Molina, Antonio de Peñalosa, and Simón de Coca,[52] *estantes* in this *ciudad*, and *licenciado* Balbuena, His Majesty's *escribano* and secretary of the royal *audiencia* which has its seat in this *ciudad* of Compostela.

I was present at the aforementioned. In testimony of the truth I here affixed my [registered] mark.
licenciado de Balbuena, His Majesty's *escribano*

[fol. 22 right]

[...]

{*ytem*} Don Carlos por la diVina clemenÇia enperador / senper augusto dona Juana su madre y el / mysmo don Carlos por la graÇia de dios rreyes / de Castilla de leon de aragon de las dos çeçilias / de Jerusalen de naVarra de granada de toledo de Va- / lenÇia de galizia de mallorcas de seVilla de Cor- / doba de Corçega de murÇia de Jaen de los algarVes / de alg*er*zira de gibraltar de las yslas de Cana- / ria y de las yndias yslas y t*ie*rra firme / del mar oÇeano condes de Flandes Y de tiroL / *etcetera* por quanto tenyendo notiÇa don an- / tonyo de mendoÇa n*uest*ro⁵³ VisoRey y goVernador / de la nueVa espana y presidente de la / n*uest*ra aUdienÇia y chanÇilleria Real que en / ella Reside que adelante de la proVin- / Çia de CuluaCan por tieRa se podra hallar / y descubrir pueblos y proVinÇias po- / bladas de gentes naturales de *e*stas partes / de que dios n*uest*ro señor y nos seriamos servidos / determyno de enViar en ^n*uest*ro nonbre al ReVe- / rendo padre Fray marcos de nyÇa proVinçiaL / de la orden de san F*ranc*isco *en* la proVin- / Çia de la nueVa espana del santo eVan- / {rúbricas} / xxij

[fol. 23 left]

gelio para q*ue* Fuese⁵⁴ a descubrir y saber las / d*ic*has tieRas y proVinçias e para / ello le dio la conpanya conVinyente a es- / te proposito y la ynstru(y)Çion y or- / den q*ue* ConVenya q*ue* Fuese *en* la d*ic*ha Jornada / Yendo en proseCuçion de la d*ic*ha d*e*ter- / mynaçion⁵⁵ Fue dios n*uest*ro señor serVido q*ue* / tuViese notiÇia de grandes Y muy pobla- / das ÇiUdades proVinçias e aUn / {/} Reynos y por Vista de ojos Vio mucha(^s) par- / te de *e*llo de lo qual en persona Vino / A hazer Relaçion al d*ic*ho n*uest*ro VisoRey / la qual el d*ic*ho⁵⁶ enVio A n*uest*ra persona ReaL / Firmada del d*ic*ho n*uest*ro

proVinçial dandonos no- / tiÇia q*ue* pues en n*uest*ros dias dios / n*uest*ro señor *h*abia sido serVido de descubrir tan / grandes tierras donde su santo nonbre Fuese / conoÇido y adorado y su santa Fee y y- / Glesia catholica dilatada y n*uest*ro pa- / trimonyo Real aUmentado que por⁵⁷ *en* la / dilaÇion de no se Conseguyr y saber / ent*er*ramente lo que *en* las d*ic*has tierras / *h*Ay podria*n* suçeder ynconVinyentes⁵⁸ / que *en* el entretanto q*ue* eramos serVi- / dos de Proveer lo que *en* la proseCuÇion / de *e*ste proposito se debia hazer eL / EnViaria Religiosos de la d*ic*ha orden / personas de çiençia y Con(^oÇimy*ent*o)çiençia / con el d*ic*ho proVinçial porq*ue* Fuesen a / las d*ic*has tieRas a p*re*d(r)iCar y publicar / {rúbricas} / xxiij

[fol. 23 right]

el santo eVangelio y atraer y Reduzyr los / naturales de *e*lla al gremyo de la ygles*i*a / catolica e aqu(*e*)í⁵⁹ nos conoÇiesen Y tuViesen / por su Rey y señor natural Y para la / seguridad y anparo de los d*ic*hos Religiosos / enViaria a la gente que Viese q*ue* ConVenya con / capitan persona de Calidad como / el Caso Y negoÇio lo rrequerya e porque agora / el d*ic*ho proVinçial e Religiosos en prose- / cuçion y siguymy*ent*o de la d*ic*ha jornada Van con / la gent*e* q*ue* para ello el d*ic*ho n*uest*ro VisoRey hizo / Ansi por mar como por tieRa y por- / q*ue* *e*l tiene de nos FaCultad para poder / proVeer persona q*ue* Cunpla y execute lo q*ue* / A n*uest*ro serViÇio en estas partes conVen- / ga por Virtud de Una n*uest*ra Real çedula / F*ec*ha en esta g*ui*sa El Rey don antonyo de men- / doÇa n*uest*ro VisoRey goVernador d*e* la / nueVa espana y presidente de la n*uest*ra a- / UdienÇia e chançilleria Real que en ella / Reside porq*ue* Como *h*abeys sabido don hernan- / do⁶⁰ cortes marques del Valle tiene de nos / proVision de n*uest*ro capitan general de la / d*ic*ha nueVa espana y Como quyera

que Con / las declaraÇiones y limytaçiones que des- / pues
se hizieron el no puede Usar de el / dicho oFicio syno quando
por el nuestro presiden- / te e oydores le fuere mandado y
e(s)ntonçes guar- / dando la orden que ellos le dier(o)en[61]
pero por que / podria ser que nascan algunas cosas[62] /
{rúbricas} / xxiij

[fol. 24 left]
que con(^V)Vengan cometerse la execuÇion / de ellas A
otras personas por la / presente os mando doy poder y facul-
/ tad para que quando se ofreçieren co- / sas que nos
paresca[63] que sea conVenyente / cometerse la execuçion y
CunplimYento de ella / A otra persona y no al dicho marques
lo po- / days hazer y hagays como presidente / VisoRey y
gobernaDor fecha en barçelona / A diez y siete dias del mes
de abril de mill / Y quynientos Y treynta y ÇinCo anos[64] yo
el Rey / por mandado de su magestad cobos comenDaDor /
mayor Viendo que Ansi conVenya al / serViçio de (^su
magestad) dios nuestro señor y nuestro / que la dicha jornada
hAya efecto en nuestro nonbre / conFiando de Vos Francisco
Vazques de Co- / ronado nuestro gobernador y Capitan
general / de la nueVa galizia que soys tal persona / que bien
y Fielmente hareys y Cumplireys / lo que por nos os Fuere
enComendado y Come- / tido[65] que (^d) te(r)ndreys espeçial
cuydado en el anparo y deFendimYento de las / dichas tierras
y de los naturales / de ellas por la presente aprobamos / y
ConFirmamos el dicho nonbramYento hecho de / Vos el
dicho francisco Vazques de Coronado / por el dicho don
Antonyo de mendoÇa nuestro / VisoRey de la nueVa espana
y / de nueVo os nonbramos por tal capitan / {rúbricas} / xxiiij

[fol. 24 right]
general de la gente que agora Va y Fuere des- / pues y de otra
qualquyera que alla halla- / redes[66] y de las tierras y pro-
Vinçias[67] de Acus / y Çibula y las siette ÇiUdades y los
Reynos / y proVinÇias de matata y totinteac y todos / sus
su(b)jetos y a(V)nexos y de las demas tie- / Ras e proVinçias
que Vos descubrieredes y por / Vuestra yndustria se descubrieren y mandamos / a todas las personas que alla Fueren de /
qualquier estado y Condiçion que sean que ha- / yan y
tengan a Vos el dicho Francisco VazqueS / de Coronado por
tal nuestro capitan generaL / y os obedescan y hagan y

Cumplan Vuestros man- / damYentos Vengan e parescan
ante Vos A Vuestros / Ñamamyentos a los plazos y so las
penas que / Vos de nuestra parte[68] les pusieredes o man- /
daredes poner las quales nos por la / presente les ponemos y
Vos damos po- / der y faCultad para las exeCutar en los / que
Rebeldes e ynobidientes Fueren otro- / si Vos damos
faCultad para (para) que podays / proVeer[69] ^y proveays del
capitan o Capitanes / que ConVengan y aquellos RemoVer y
/ quytar y otros de nueVo poner qu- / Anto quysieredes y
bien Visto Vos / Fuere e para que ansimysmo podays /
conoçer y Conozcays de todas las caUsas / ÇeViles y cremy-
nales que entre la dicha / gente se oFreÇiere y aCaesçiere y
en- / tre los naturales de las dichas tieRas / {rúbricas} / xxiiij

[fol. 25 left]
por donde pasaredes y estuVieredes y en- / tre los dichos
espanoles y ellos y para el / conoçimyento y determynaçion
de las / dichas caUsas podays criar y crieys Un / tenyente dos
o mas los que Viere / des que ConVengan y sean neçesarios
/ y aquellos AmoVer y aponer[70] otros de nueVo / y en
quanto[71] al tratamyento de los yndios na- / turales de las
dichas tierras por donde pa- / saredes y estuVieredes y en lo
que en ellas / hAbeys de hazer y Contratar os manda- / mos
que guardeys y Cumplays en quanto / A lo susodicho al pie
de la letra la ynstruyçion / que nos tenemos mandado dar y
dada[72] / A las personas que Van a descubrir y / paÇiFiCar
tierras e proVinçias nueVas / como Vos Vays la qual lleVays
firma- / da del dicho nuestro VisoRey y del se- / cretario
ynFraescritos sin pasar / ny exçeder contra el tenor y Forma
/ de ella so las penas en la dicha ynstruyçion[73] / contenydas y
mandamos que en el Uso / y exerçicio del dicho cargo de
Capitan / general de las dichas tierras no os sea pues- / to
enbargo ny enpedimyento alguno y que / todos se
conFormen con Vos (^den) y os den / y hagan dar[74] todo el
FaVor y ayuda que les / pidieredes y menester hobieredes /
syn poner escusa ny otra dilaÇion alguna / {rúbricas} / xxV

[fol. 25 right]
que para el Uso y exerçiçio del dicho cargo y para / lo demas
que dicho es por esta Cartta / os damos poder Cumplido
segun que en taL / caso se rrequyere con todas sus ynçiden- /
Çias e dependençias anexidades y Conexi- / dades e por

quanto Vos el d*ich*o Fr*ancis*co Vaz- / ques de Coronado soys n*uest*ro gobernador y Ca- / pitan general de la d*ich*a Pro- / Vin*Ç*ia de la / nue*V*a galizia y Vays[75] por n*uest*ro mandado y en / n*uest*ro ser*V*i*Ç*io al descubrim*Y*ento y pa*Ç*i*F*i*Ç*a*ç*ion / de la d*ich*a tierra nue*V*a y atraer a los / naturales de *e*lla A Cono*Ç*im*Y*en*t*o de n*uest*ra / santa *F*ee catolica y a ponerla debaxo de n*uest*ra / corona Real por la presente Vos damos / pod*e*r y *F*aCultad para que durante *V*ues*t*ra / AUsen*Ç*ia *en* la d*ich*a pro*V*in*Ç*ia podays / dexar y dexeys en *V*uest*r*o lugar tenyente y ti- / nyentes en la parte e partes que os pa- / re*Ç*iere[76] y personas q*ue* les con*V*engan / Y mandamos que a las personas q*ue* / Ansi dexaredes y nonbraredes *en* la d*ich*a / nue*V*a galizia sean *h*abidos[77] y tenydos y o- / bede*ç*idos por tales tenyentes de go- / bernador en ella e que *h*ayays y lle*V*eys / el mysmo salario q*ue* por nos os esta ^se*n*ala- / do con el d*ich*o cargo por la pro*V*i*Ç*ion que / del Uso[78] *F*ue dada y que os sea librado y paga- / do no enbargante *V*ues*t*ra aUsen*Ç*ia como has- / ta aquy os *h*a librado e pagado y por yr como / *V*ays en n*uest*ro ser*V*i*Ç*io que no os sean quyta- / dos ny Remo*V*idos los yndios q*ue* por nos en n*uest*ro / {rúbricas} / xx*V*

[fol. 26 left]

Real nonbre os estan encomendados y deposi- / tados Ansi en esta nue*V*a espana co- / {scribal mark} mo *F*uera de *e*l^*l*a en tyenpo alguno[79] otrosi es / n*uest*ra m*e*r*c*ed y mandamos que las d*ich*as tie- / Ras y las que mas pa*Ç*i*F*iCaredes / y traxeredes A n*uest*ro ser*V*i*Ç*io como tal n*uest*ro / capitan general la*s* tengays hasta en tan- / to q*ue* por nos o por el d*ich*o n*uest*ro Viso*R*ey de la / nue*V*a espana se pro*V*ea y mande otra / cosa y las anpareys y defendays en n*uest*ro / Real nonbre A ellas e a los naturales de *e*llas / para que no les sean hechos agra*V*ios ny otros / malostratamy*ent*os algunos ny nengunas per- / sonas se entren en ellas ny las tomen ny oCupen / diziendoles perteneçerles la governa*Ç*ion / de la d*ich*a tierra nue*V*a hasta tanto q*ue* Como / d*ich*o es sea pro*V*eydo sobre ello lo que a n*uest*ro / ser*V*i*Ç*io con*V*enga dada *en* la *Ç*i*U*dad de / mechuaCan A seys de enero año del na*Ç*i- / m*Y*en*t*o de n*uest*ro sal*V*ador *jesu cris*to de mill y

quy*nient*os / y quarenta años don antonyo de men- / do*Ç*a yo el secretario antonyo de almaguer / lo *F*iz escrebir por su mandado con aquer- / do de su Vi*R*ey de la nue*V*a espana[80] / Registrada diego agurdes por chan*Ç*iller / gaspar del castill(o)*a*

{*ytem*} *F*e*ch*o y sa*C*ado *F*ue este d*ich*o traslado de la d*ich*a / pro*V*ision oreginal[81] de suso *en*Corporada / *en* la *Ç*i*U*dad de mexico A primero dia del / mes de dizienbre Año del na*Ç*imy*ent*o de n*uest*ro sa*L*- / {rúbricas} / *xxvi*

[fol. 26 right]

Vador *jesu cris*to de mill y quy*nient*os y *Ç*inCuenta y Un / Años el qual d*ich*o traslado yo antonyo / de tur*Ç*ios es*c*riba*n*o mayor del a*U*den*Ç*ia Rea*L* / de *e*sta nue*V*a españa y gober- / na*Ç*ion / de *e*lla por su m*a*gestad haze sa*C*ar de pedimy*ent*o del / d*ich*o gobernador Fr*ancis*co Vazques de Coronado / e de *pedi*my*ent*o de los senores presidente y oydores / de la d*ich*a Real a*U*dien*Ç*ia por quanto / dixero*n* tan la neçesidad del d*ich*o traslado para / en guarda de su d*erech*o testigos q*ue* lo Vieron corre- / gir y Con*ç*ertar agustin pinto y andres peres / y (andres peres) estantes en esta *Ç*i*U*dad / *en* *F*e del qual *F*iz[82] Aquy este myo signo[83] (A)ta*L* / en testimonyo de Verdad antonyo de tur- / *Ç*ios

{*ytem*} sa*C*ose este traslado del d*ich*o traslado aU- / torizado de la d*ich*a pro*V*ision de su m*a*gestad en con- / postela en Veynta dias del mes de hebrero / de myll y quy*nient*os e *Ç*inCuenta e dos anos para / dar el original de donde se sa*C*o a la parte del / d*ich*o Fr*ancis*co Vazques de Coronado e Co*R*egirse E / con*ç*ertarse esto d*ich*o dia testigos q*ue* *F*ueron / presentes de *e*llo blas de molina e antonyo / de peñalosa y simon de Coca estantes en es- / ta d*ich*a *Ç*i*U*dad y li*cencia*do de balbuena es*c*ryb*an*o d*e* su / m*a*gestad secretario del au- / dien*Ç*ia Real que / Reside en esta *Ç*i*U*dad de Conpostela / Fuy presente a lo susod*ich*o y en testi- / monyo de Verdad *F*iz Aqui este myo signo / li*cencia*do de balbuena es*c*ryb*an*o d*e* su m*a*gestad / {rúbricas} / xx*V*j

Document 10

The King's Confirmation of Vázquez de Coronado's Appointment, June 11, 1540

Private Collection

INTRODUCTION

When Herbert Bolton published his classic narrative history of the Coronado expedition in 1949, he included in it a list of "lost documents" relating to the expedition. These were documents known, on the basis of references to them in other surviving documents, to have been written but not known to have been preserved.[1] Included among the nearly 70 documents on Bolton's list were two described as "King's letter to Coronado," one supposedly dated June 11, 1540, and the other, June 21 of the same year. In his brief comments in the entries for these documents, Bolton conjectured that the two might actually represent only a single manuscript.[2]

Nearly 50 years later, in the catalog for the December 1995 auction at Christie's in New York, there appeared a stunning announcement. Item 58 among the many offerings was described as a "manuscript letter signed on behalf of King Charles V by Francisco de Loyasa [sic], president of the Council of the Indies to Francisco Vasquez [sic] de Coronado, Madrid: 21 June 1540."[3] In response to the catalog announcement, a Santa Fe, New Mexico, textile dealer, Mark Winter, put together a group that hoped to make the winning offer at the auction. When bids for the letter soared far beyond the auction house's estimated sale price, Winter and his group dropped out, leaving the document to another private collector.

Not long after the conclusion of the auction, however, Winter was contacted by the document's former owner. His message to the disappointed bidder was that he still owned a second manuscript, thought at the time to be a draft of the letter that had sold at auction. And he wanted to sell, this time for a fixed price, no bidding or haggling. Winter and his partners were interested. In an effort to confirm for themselves the manuscript's authenticity, they asked us to look the document over. We said we would, and a few days later it arrived by delivery service.

We then transcribed and translated the document, compared it with a photograph of its former companion document, which had sold during the auction, and noted any oddities or apparent discrepancies between the two. There had been little reason to suspect the genuineness of the manuscript, and our study of the text and scribal usage (our area of particular competence) raised no doubts about the document as a sixteenth-century artifact. In the end, our principal concern was over the document's provenance and how it had come to be for sale at all, since all the rest of the surviving documentary record of the Coronado expedition resides in public institutions. Specifically, we worried that it had been stolen. Although our curiosity about its origin was never fully satisfied, we were convinced that the document had probably never been in the possession of a public archive or other such institution.

The Winter partnership did subsequently purchase the document, and it is lodged in Santa Fe, with some hope that eventually it will be added to the permanent collection of the

Museum of New Mexico. Its text and translation are published here for the first time.

Our initial examination and continuing study of the single-folio manuscript have revealed a number of significant facts about it. As is clear both from the handwriting and the signature at the bottom right corner of folio 1r, it was prepared in the Ciudad de México by Antonio de Turcios, chief *escribano* of the royal *audiencia* there. Rather than being a draft of the auctioned letter, it is a copy of it, made once the original had reached Nueva España from Spain, likely in the fall of 1540. That means that the expedition, having departed from the Ciudad de México ten months or more before the arrival of the letter, had not awaited receipt of the king's confirmation of Vázquez de Coronado's appointment as captain general.

This procedure was neither particularly unusual nor an overstepping of authority; the resident viceroy had full power of the monarch in most matters, including an appointment such as this one. Even the viceroy, though, was constrained to obtain license from the king before launching a major expedition of conquest and reconnaissance. Following a lengthy legal wrangle with other contenders for the same right (Hernán Cortés, Hernando de Soto, Álvar Núñez Cabeza de Vaca, and Pedro de Alvarado), Antonio de Mendoza's claim that he held the right to mount an expedition prevailed.[4]

Although Christie's staff had identified the date of the original letter prepared in Madrid as June 21, that is an error. What in the date looks at first glance like the Roman numeral *xxi* is in fact "*A xi.*" In certain sixteenth-century hands, majuscule *A* is easily mistaken for *x*. Not only was the auction house misled in this regard, but so was the *escribano* who prepared a 1605 petition to which Bolton referred in his entry about the presumed June 21 letter. The actual date of the Madrid original is June 11, 1540, the date that Turcios correctly read and entered in his Ciudad de México copy. Therefore, as Bolton suspected, only a single letter was sent under the king's name to Vázquez de Coronado in June 1540.

In the letter, addressed to Vázquez de Coronado, the president of the Consejo de Indias, García de Loaysa, on the king's behalf, and through the medium of the *consejo*'s chief *escribano*, Juan de Sámano, acknowledges that Viceroy Mendoza "sent you as captain general." Further, he expresses approval of that action, writing, "this pleases us," and confirms the viceroy's choice with the words "we commission you."[5] This confirmation and commission were the ultimate statement of Vázquez de Coronado's authority to exercise the office of captain general.

As such, it was crucial that the letter be forwarded to the appointee as soon as possible, so that it could be employed in diplomatic encounters or in case of any challenge to his jurisdictional authority during the course of the expedition. Thus, shortly after it arrived in the Ciudad de México, Turcios made several copies, including the one now in Santa Fe. One or more of those was then dispatched with the next courier headed toward Cíbola.[6] Meanwhile, the original was either sent on to doña Beatriz de Estrada, the captain general's wife, who was residing in Compostela at the time, or was held in the *audiencia*'s archive for later delivery.

It seems likely that at least one copy reached Vázquez de Coronado along the Rio Grande, probably no later than the fall of 1541. It may even be the Santa Fe copy. That possibility is suggested by the fact that for some time until the sale of the Madrid original in 1995, the two versions of the letter were together. The most likely explanation for that unusual circumstance is that both were once in the possession of Vázquez de Coronado himself. He would have received the copy during the expedition and would have been given the original upon his return to the Ciudad de México in 1542. It is otherwise difficult to explain how the two versions of the document came to be together.[7]

For future research on the Coronado expedition, it is worth noting that the Santa Fe copy of the letter bears two numbers in the upper right-hand corner of folio 1r: 4 and 40. The 40 has been struck out and indicates that at some time this copy was in a *legajo*, or bundle, with at least 39 other folios. The 4, on the other hand, shows that slightly more recently it was in a *legajo* of at least three other folios.[8] Either way, there once existed with this letter other folios possibly pertaining to the expedition. They, too, may have been dispersed or may still be together somewhere.

TRANSLATION

[1r]
4 (^40)
The King

Francisco Vázquez de Coronado, our governor and captain general of the *provincia* of Nueva Galicia in Nueva España:[9]

We have seen your letter of the 15th of July of last year, 1539,[10] in which you have given us an account of the state of affairs in that *provincia* and of the work you have done to bring to peace its natives, who have revolted. For this I thank you and hold it as a service [to us], as well as the care you have taken and are taking in the pacification and peopling of the *provincia*. And also your benevolent treatment of the natives who live there, thus we enjoin you to continue.

{+} By means of letters from don Antonio de Mendoza, our viceroy in Nueva España, I have been aware that, in our name, he sent you as captain general of certain people for the conquest and settlement of the land discovered by fray Marcos de Niza.[11] This pleases us because we expect that with your going Our Lord will be highly served and our royal kingdom augmented. And also that through your excellent efforts you will place the natives of that *provincia* under our

sway and dominion and will bring them into knowledge of our Holy Catholic Faith. Thus, we commission you to bend your efforts toward that, with sound judgment and good order, in the process adhering to the laws and decrees we have issued and any directive our viceroy may have given you. You are to inform us of what you accomplish.

We have sent [a dispatch] ordering our viceroy to look assiduously after your jurisdiction during your absence and to provide what in his view suits the service of God, Our Lord, and of ourselves.[12]

In Madrid, the 11th day of June one thousand five hundred and forty. Fray García, Cardinal of Spain, by order of His Majesty, governor in his name, Juan de Sámano[13] Reconciled with the original[14]
{rubric} Antonio de Turcios {rubric}

[1v–2r] [blank]

[2v]
Francisco Vasquez Coronado
Letter from His Majesty for the general
Copy of a letter from His Majesty for the governor Francisco Vázquez de Coronado, my lord.

TRANSCRIPTION

[fol. 1r]
4 (^40)
El ReY

Francisco Vazquez de coronado nuestro governador e capitan
general de la proVincia de la nueVa galicia de la nueva españa
/ Vimos Vuestra letra de xV de Jullyo del año pasado de
UdxxxJx / en que nos hazieredes Relacion del estado de las
coSas de aquella proVinÇia / E de lo que habeys TrabaJado
en (^o) traer de paz a los naturales de ella / que andavan
alçados lo qual os agradezco e tengo en servycio e eL /
cuydado que habeys tenydo e Teneys en la paÇificaÇion e
poblacion / de ella del buen tratamyento de los naturales que
en ella Residen y asy / os enCargamos lo continueys

{+} por cartas de don antonio de mendoÇa nuestro ViSorey
de la nueVa españa / he Sabido como en nuestro nombre os
ymVio por capitan general de Çierta / gente a la conquista e
poblaÇion de la tierra que descubrio Fray marcos / de nyça
de que hemos Holgado porque esperamos que con Vuestra
yda / nuestro señor sera muy servydo e nuestra corona Real
acresÇentada e que / con Vuestra buena yndustria
po(r)ndreis debaxo de nuestro yugo / e señorio real aquella
Tierra e Traereis a los naturales / de ella en conosÇimyento
de nuestra santa Fee catholica y asy os encargamos / que Con

toda prudençia e buena orden trabaJeys de lo hazer asy /
guardando açerca de ello las ordenanças y proVisiones que
por / nos estan dadas e la orden que el dicho nuestro ViSorey
os hovyere dado y / aVisarnoseys de lo que en ello hazieredes
que durante Vuestra aUsenÇia / hemos ymViado a mandar
al dicho nuestro ViSorey que tenga cuydado / de mirar por
Vuestra governaÇion e proVeer en ella lo que Viere / que
ConViene (^e) al servycio de dios nuestro señor e nuestro de
madrid / A (h)onze dias del mes de Junyo de myll e
quinientos e quarenta años / Frai garcia cardinalisS
hispalensys por mandado de su magestad el governador / en
su nombre Juan de Samano

Corregido con el originaL / {rúbrica} antonio de turçios
{rúbrica}

[fols. 1v–2r] [blank]

[fol. 2v]
{Francisco Vasquez Coronado}
{carta de su magestad para El / GeneraL}
{scribal mark}
{treslado De Una Carta de / Su magestad Para el ggover-
nador Francisco Vaz- /quez de coronado mi señor}

Document 11

Testimony of Juan Bermejo and of Vázquez de Coronado's Purchasing Agent, Juan Fernández Verdejo, 1552

AGI, Justicia, 336, N.1, "Probança de Francisco Vázquez hecha en Compostela, May 2, 1552, and March 23, 1553," fols. 65v–68r, 41r–43v, and 71r–73r

INTRODUCTION

The major investors in the expedition to Tierra Nueva were Viceroy Antonio de Mendoza, Francisco Vázquez de Coronado and his wife, Beatriz de Estrada, and Pedro de Alvarado. Mendoza claimed to have spent the equivalent of 85,000 silver pesos in outfitting and provisioning the expedition. Meanwhile, the captain general maintained that he had expended the equivalent of 71,000 silver pesos. And Alvarado's belated investment has been estimated to have equaled at least 90,000 silver pesos.[1] No complete and itemized enumeration of the expenditures made by each of the investors is known to exist. Indeed, very few details of the cost of the expedition and the specific goods purchased for it are found in the surviving documents. If pertinent bills of sale or purchase contracts still exist, they have yet to be located.

In the midst of this dearth of information, the 1552 testimonies of Juan Bermejo and Juan Fernández Verdejo stand as exceptions. The evidence the two men provide is not copious, but it is important in supplying some of the rare extant details on the subject of provisioning. Fernández Verdejo, for instance, reports that he himself "bought and supplied many things for Francisco Vázquez," who "spent more than thirty thousand pesos."[2] He probably could have told much more, because he was Vázquez de Coronado's *mayordomo*, the manager of his household, at the time.[3] But he evidently confined his responses to the *interrogatorio*

strictly to the questions at hand. At least, the *escribano* recorded his testimony that way.

Fernández Verdejo had been in Nueva España since about 1529 and would have been 23 or so at the time of the expedition to Tierra Nueva. He was then a *vecino* of the Ciudad de México, where he later served as lieutenant to the *alguacil* of the *audiencia*. By 1552 he had become a *vecino* of Compostela, where he gave the testimony that is published here.[4]

In addition, expedition member Juan Bermejo lists some of the items that he saw the captain general taking with him: "much livestock (cattle, sheep, and pigs), hardtack, wheat, and the whole supply of oil and vinegar, plus medicines."[5] Bermejo must have been fairly close to Vázquez de Coronado or members of his household or entourage, given his detailed knowledge of the captain general's retinue and supply train.[6] Seven years before giving the testimony that is published here, he provided further details. At that time he stated that Vázquez de Coronado took 7 very good horses, plus another 12 or 15 horses "which he provided to his *criados,*"[7] and 15 mules, as well as four black men and three black women. He also made it clear that the captain general distributed many items to members of the expedition who were in need. His estimate of Vázquez de Coronado's total expenditures was lower than the few others that have survived: 20,000 *pesos de oro de minas.*[8]

Both Juan Bermejo and Fernández Verdejo were *de parte* witnesses in the 1552 case the former captain general brought in an effort to recover *encomiendas* that had been taken from him.[9] That is, they were called to testify on behalf of Vázquez de Coronado on the assumption that they would support his claims. Four other *de parte* witnesses testified in the case (Hernando del Valle, Juan Galeas, Juan Pastor, and Froylano Bermúdez), as well as four *de oficio* witnesses (Melchior Pérez, Pedro de Ledesma, Pedro de Castro, and Juan Ruiz).[10]

From this group of testimonies we have selected those of Bermejo and Fernández Verdejo specifically because of the information they provide about procurement for the expedition. Nevertheless, both men also supply other information of interest. For example, Bermejo repeats the judgment made frequently by the expeditionaries that Tierra Nueva was "not suitable for settlement" and was "such an inferior land." He even suggests that because of their disappointment, some expeditionaries threatened mutiny.[11]

The original record of the testimony is no longer known to exist. What survives is a copy that was probably made in May 1552, within days of conclusion of the examination of witnesses, and forwarded to the Consejo de Indias in Spain.

More than two centuries later, that copy of the court record was incorporated into the collection of the Archivo General de Indias in Sevilla. It still resides there under the *signatura* (catalog number) AGI, Justicia, 336, N.1, "Probança de Francisco Vázquez hecha en Compostela." Three excerpts from that *legajo*, or bundle, of documents are published in this volume.[12]

The 1552 witnesses were examined in three groups. In March, two *de parte* witnesses testified, followed by the four *de oficio* witnesses. The four remaining *de parte* witnesses were presented in April. The record of the testimony of each group of *de parte* witnesses is preceded by a copy of the *interrogatorio* that had been presented by Vázquez de Coronado's attorney. We include here a transcript and translation of the second copy of the *interrogatorio* (which was presented in April). For publication, the March testimony of Juan Bermejo has been moved from its actual location in the *legajo*, where it precedes the second copy of the *interrogatorio*. We retain the original foliation, however, in both transcript and translation. This is the first publication of this excerpt in either English or Spanish.

TRANSLATION

[65v]

[. . .]

{1} First, [the witnesses] are to be asked whether they are familiar with the aforementioned [persons] and for how long a time before now and whether they have knowledge of the aforesaid *pueblos* and the subject of this legal action.[13]

{2} Item. Whether they know that Francisco Vázquez de Coronado is commonly recognized as a *caballero hidalgo* and has been and is in possession of such [*encomiendas*]. And [do they know that] His Majesty made him the concession of appointing him governor and captain general of the *provincia* of Nueva Galicia[14] because he has such status and is wise and prudent, and also in consideration of the service [Vázquez de Coronado] has done and is doing him in this Nueva España. They are to state what they know.

{3} Item. Whether they know that Francisco Vázquez de Coronado has served His Majesty in the aforesaid offices loyally [and] with complete correctness and diligence, just as he should and was obligated [to do] in similar offices. They are to state what they know.

{4} Item. Whether they know that because the *provincia* of Nueva Galicia is so distant and remote from the Ciudad de México and the ports of the Mar del Norte,[15] all things necessary for maintenance [66r] were and continue to be available [only] at exorbitant prices. And for this reason Francisco Vázquez de Coronado would [naturally] expend and did expend not only the salary he received as governor[16] but also the greater part of his assets. The aforementioned [salary] was not adequate or sufficient to maintain himself in accordance with the status of his person and of the aforesaid office. Because of this it was necessary for him to entrust and assign *pueblos* of Indians to himself in *encomienda* as he did, in order to be better able to serve His Majesty. They are to state what they know.

{5} Item. Whether they know, etc., that the governors who have been in this part of the world on His Majesty's behalf have customarily assigned *pueblos* of Indians to themselves in *encomienda* and in [their] care and themselves have taken charge[17] of the [Indians] in *encomienda*. This came to His Majesty's notice [previously], and he has not opposed it before the New Laws [were issued].[18] He [has in fact] permitted it and in some [instances] has approved it, as was the case for the Marqués del Valle, don Hernando de Cortés, and for Nuño de Guzmán,[19] former governor in the aforesaid *provincia*. They are to state what they know.

{6} {Item} Item. Whether they know, etc., that because of what is referred to in the previous questions, Francisco Vázquez de Coronado, in His Majesty's name, assigned to himself in *encomienda* the *pueblos* of Indians mentioned above. He provided himself formal documents of *encomienda* for them, which are signed with his name and countersigned by Hernando Bermejo, his secretary.[20] These are the ones which are being presented in this case [and] must be shown to the witnesses in order that they may declare what they know.

[66v]

{7} Item. Whether they know that on the basis of the *encomiendas* and the formal titles to them, Francisco

Vázquez de Coronado held and exercised authority over the aforementioned *pueblos* and *estancias*, obtaining their tributes, services, and profits, quietly and peacefully, without opposition from anyone. They are to state what they know.

{8} Item. Whether they know that while Francisco Vázquez de Coronado was governor and at ease in his house with his wife and children he was chosen and appointed captain general of Tierra Nueva by means of a royal commission.[21] [This was] in order that he go on reconnaissance and conquest of it. As such captain general, he was ordered to lead an armed force of footmen and horsemen under his command for the expedition and conquest, as is recorded in the royal commission (which he requested be shown to the witnesses). They are to state what they know.

{9} Item. Whether they know that Francisco Vázquez de Coronado accepted the aforesaid duty to go on the expedition, in order to serve His Majesty and with trust in the concessions which were promised to him by the royal commission that the Indians whom he held in *encomienda* and in trust in His Majesty's name in Nueva España and outside it would not be taken or seized from him at any time. [Thus he did] as the royal commission ordered him and in order to secure the grants which the Catholic Monarchs (of glorious memory)[22] and His Majesty were and are accustomed to make to those who faithfully, loyally, and diligently have served them, as Francisco Vázquez de Coronado intended to do and did. He requested that the royal commission [67r] be shown to the witnesses.

{10} Item. Whether they know that in fulfillment of what is referred to in the previous questions and in order to obtain the reward promised to him by the royal commission, he went [on] the expedition with the people in the armed force. Because the land to which he was ordered to go was so distant and remote from Nueva España (which [is to say] more than a thousand leagues from it, through many lands which [are] not suitable for permanent residence and [are] unsettled) and with so many people, he spent more than fifty thousand castellanos of his own assets on [the expedition]

and in order to accomplish it in His Majesty's service. [And that] the governor declared and made known, at the time that he made the expedition, that he was doing it to obtain the grants referred to in the previous questions. They are to state what they know.

{11} Item. Whether they know, etc., that the aforesaid governor Francisco Vázquez de Coronado led the expedition he was taking under his command in good order. [That] he led it very well arranged, managed, and governed. [That] he took special care that God, Our Lord, was served during it. That the natives of the lands through which he traveled and passed were aware of God, Our Lord, and some of them served His Majesty. [That] they were very well treated, managed, and governed. And that in every way what His Majesty had stipulated and ordered through his instructions was done and accomplished (as it was done and accomplished). They are to state what they know.

{12} Item. Whether they know that the aforesaid governor Francisco Vázquez de Coronado suffered much danger from hunger, cold, [and] heat during the expedition.[23] [That] he spilled [67v] his blood as a result of the many wounds the natives of those lands inflicted on him.[24] [That] because of them he was on the point of death. And [that] he subjected his person and life to very great risk and danger many times in His Majesty's service. They are to state what they know.

{13} Item. Whether they know that in the entire Tierra Nueva where Francisco Vázquez de Coronado traveled and was, both he and the captains, who by his order traveled through many places reconnoitering, took possession of the lands for His Majesty. And [that] in [those lands] they set up crosses at the sites of formal possession. They are to state what they know.

{14} {Item} Item. Whether they know that in the reconnaissance of Tierra Nueva and as a result of the governor's having conducted the expedition, His Majesty has been pleased because there is knowledge and information that has been obtained concerning that land about which there was ignorance and lack of understanding in other times. And [that] because of [the expedition] it is possible to travel to many other lands, and especially to La Florida, a land heavily settled by Indians, fertile, and productive, [a land] where His Majesty can be served. They are to state what they know.

{15} Item. Whether they know that the governor Francisco Vázquez de Coronado went to where the royal commission ordered him [to go]. [That] when he had reached [it] there was no place to increase the royal patrimony. [That] because he desired to best serve God, Our Lord, [and] His Majesty and to enlarge the royal patrimony, he dispatched captains and people through various areas to reconnoiter and look for lands and people [among which] to settle, so they might know God, Our Lord, and His Majesty might be served. [That] those captains and people traveled and journeyed through many regions and lands. When [the land] had been examined and traversed [68r], no means was found[25] by which it was possible to settle. And [that] the governor traveled five hundred leagues beyond Cíbola to Quivira.[26]

{16} Item. Whether they know that because of what is referred to in the previous questions, the captains and men-at-arms of the expeditionary force persuaded the governor to return them to Nueva España, whence he had brought them. [Namely,] that [this was] because there was no means by which it was possible to settle and to serve God, Our Lord, and His Majesty.[27] [And that] the expedition returned for this reason.

{17} Item. Whether they know that everything stated above is commonly and widely known.

licenciado Caballero[28]
Hernando de Balbuena, His Majesty's escribano[29]
[...]

[41r]
[...]
{Witness} {On the second of May [March][30] in the year one thousand five hundred and fifty-two, the aforementioned Pedro Ruiz de Haro presented Juan Bermejo as a witness

before the lord licenciado de la Marcha.[31] And in the form required by law, he gave his oath to state the truth. {rubric}}

{Witness} Juan Bermejo, a witness presented by the aforesaid Pero Ruiz de Haro in the name of Francisco Vázquez de Coronado, after having given his oath, when questioned concerning the substance and form of the interrogatorio declared the following:

{1} In response to the first question he stated that he knows the persons referred to in the question. He has known Francisco Vázquez de Coronado for more than fifteen years, and he has known Juan Rodríguez, the fiscal, for what may have been three or four months. He has knowledge of the aforementioned pueblos because he has been in them.

{Item} Questioned concerning personal data, this witness declared that he is thirty-two years old, more or less, and is neither a relative nor an enemy of any of the parties. [He said] that none of the questions concerning personal data affect him in such a way that he might answer contrary to the truth.

{2} To the second question he replied that he is aware of it, as stated in [the question]. Asked how he knows it, he said [it is] because he has always heard and considered Francisco Vázquez de Coronado [to be] a person such as is stated and declared in the question. All the time he has known [Vázquez de Coronado] in this place this witness has seen him to be such a person and to have such jurisdiction as the question states and declares.

[Bermejo stated] that it is true that because [Vázquez de Coronado is] a person of that sort His Majesty made him governor and captain general of this Nuevo Reino de Galicia. This witness also [41v] saw him govern and [saw him] esteemed as such a person in the way the question states and declares. He knows this [to be so] for this reason: because he saw it be and happen as the question states.

{3} To the third question he answered that he knows it [to be] as it is referred to in [the question]. Asked how he knows it, he said [it is] because he saw it be and happen exactly as the question states and declares. [The captain general] was considered to be such a person during the whole time he governed. He always did everything that was conducive to the service of God, Our Lord, and His Majesty.

This witness never heard or was aware that [Vázquez de Coronado] did anything to the contrary. And if he had done so, this witness would have been aware of it and [news of it] would have reached [him]. [This is because] this witness saw this and was in this jurisdiction during the time Francisco Vázquez governed.

{4} In response to the fourth question he declared that he knows it [to be] as it is referred to in [the question]. Asked how he knows it, he replied that [it is] because he saw it be and happen exactly as the question states and declares. [He said] that it is true that the aforesaid jurisdiction and Nuevo Reino is distant and remote from the Ciudad de México, and for this reason supplies are very expensive and offered for sale at very excessive prices. [He stated] that he knows [it] and it is thus the truth.

[Bermejo declared] that compared to Francisco Vázquez de Coronado's status and the excessive expenses that he had (for the reason that has been stated), the salary that he received is and was very small (compared to his great expenses). [He said] further that it is the truth that as governor, in His Majesty's name, [Vázquez de Coronado] distributed and assigned [42r] many *pueblos* in *encomienda* to individuals in this Nuevo Reino.

He is aware of everything else referred to in the question just as it is recorded in it.

{5} To the fifth question he replied that what he knows concerning it is that it is true that the governors who have been in Nueva España and [Nuevo] Reino de Galicia have distributed and did distribute many *pueblos* of Indians [in *encomienda*] to individuals, and they issued *cédulas* in His Majesty's name concerning them.

In the same way, they customarily designated [*encomiendas*] for themselves, as the Marqués del Valle, Nuño de Guzmán, and Francisco Vázquez de Coronado did. This witness saw that they had jurisdiction over the *pueblos* they thus assigned to themselves. To this day the

Marqués del Valle holds them [the *pueblos* he assigned himself].

This is the truth and it happen[ed] just as he has said because he has seen and [still] sees it exactly as he has stated.

{6} In reply to the sixth question he said that he knows it [to be] as it is referred to in [the question]. Asked how [he knows it], he answered that [it is] because this witness saw Francisco Vázquez de Coronado holding the aforementioned *pueblos* and [that] he held them in His Majesty's name. Further, he had a *cédula* relating to them, and [Bermejo] saw the *cédula*. [The witness stated] that it seems to him it was countersigned by Hernando Bermejo, [Vázquez de Coronado's] secretary. However, this witness does not know how to read. Nevertheless, he considers it to have been and occurred in this way. It is something very widely and commonly known. Thus, this witness believes it and considers it to be a certainty.

{7} To the seventh question he replied that he knows it [to be] as it is referred to in [the question] because he saw it be and happen [42v] just as the question states and declares it. And it is something widely and commonly known.

{8} To the eighth question he answered that he knows it [to be] as it is referred to in [the question]. Asked how [he knows it], he stated that [it is] because this witness saw Francisco Vázquez de Coronado go on the conquest of Tierra Nueva, and it was exactly as the question states and declares it.

[He said again that] it has happened and [continues to] happen as it is recorded in the question. The witness [knows this] because he [himself] traveled under His Majesty's banner [when] Francisco Vázquez went as captain general of the people in the expeditionary force who went there [to the seven *ciudades*]. And [Vázquez de Coronado] went with a commission from His Majesty, which [the king] gave him for [that purpose]. This witness saw it, and so it is the truth and transpire[d] just as recorded in the question.

{9} In response to the ninth question he stated that what he knows concerning this question is that this witness went on the expedition and has seen the aforementioned royal commission and what is referred to in the question. This witness says that when *licenciado* Tejada[32] came to take the *residencia* of [the officials of Nueva Galicia], he did not divest any person among those to whom Francisco Vázquez had granted Indians in *encomienda* in His Majesty's name. But he did take them [from the governor]. [As to] the rest [of what is] referred to in the question, he states that he has stated [previously].

{10} To the tenth question he said in answer that what he knows concerning this question is that this witness refers to His Majesty's commission. In regard to what the question states, it is a thousand leagues from Nueva España [to] where Governor Francisco Vázquez went. And [he declared] that it is true that it is as distant as the question says and that the land is not suitable for settlement and [is] unsettled. Also that it is true that this witness went [43r] on the aforesaid expedition and that he went with danger and much difficulty

[He also stated] that it is true that Francisco Vázquez spent a very large sum of gold pesos on the expedition since he took much livestock (cattle, sheep, and pigs),[33] hardtack, wheat, and the whole supply of oil and vinegar, plus medicines to treat those who might fall ill. In accordance with the quantity in which everything [was taken] (all at his own cost), what he spent, this witness said, would have been a great quantity.

This witness saw it thus with his own eyes in the way that he has stated, since he saw everything purchased, and it was a great quantity of gold pesos [which was expended]. This is [what] he knows about this question.

{11} To the eleventh question he replied that he knows it [to be] as it is referred to in [the question] because he saw it be and occur just as it is recorded in the question. [He declared] that it is true that the governor was [in the habit of] ordering and did issue orders to all those who were going with him on the expedition that no one was to mistreat the Indians [in the places] through which they were traveling. And it was carried out thus: they did not dare take [even] an ear of corn from them.[34]

[He stated] that [in the places] through which [the expedition] traveled they gave the Indians an understanding of the power of God, Our Lord, and attracted them to the Christian faith. In everything he took special care not to do them harm, [just] as he did not do them any. Instead, he gave the Indians trade goods so as to deal with them commercially and attract them to the Christian doctrine and to the dominion of His Majesty.

[He knows] this is so because he saw it with his own eyes.

{12} In reply to the twelfth question he declared that he knows it [to be] as it is referred to in [the question] because he saw it be and occur just as it is stated in the question. [This is] because this witness and all the rest [of the people], and the governor too, suffered much cold and hunger and much danger from the natives besides.

This witness saw the governor wounded [and] on the point of death and beyond hope of all those who went on the expedition. [This was] because during the expedition the Indians shot him with arrows in many parts of his body.[35] Everything happened as the question says.

{13} To the thirteenth question he answered that he knows it [to be] as it is referred to in [the question]. Asked how he knows it, he declared that [it is] because he saw it be and [43v] occur as the question states. He saw that crosses were erected in whatever places they reached, and they took possession in His Majesty's name. This witness knows everything referred to in the question because he saw it and it happened that way.

{14} To the fourteenth question he replied that he knows it [to be] as it is referred to in [the question] because it is happening in this way. And so it is true as the question states and declares that they can travel by way of Tierra Nueva to where the question states, as well as to many other places. [He said] that thus it is as the question states.

{15} In answer to the fifteenth question he said that he knows it [to be] as it is referred to in [the question]. Asked how he knows it, he declared that [it is] because this witness traveled on the aforesaid expedition throughout its duration. He saw it, and it occurred just as it is stated and declared in the question. Everything referred to in it is the truth.

{16} To the sixteenth question he answered that he knows it [to be] as it is referred to in [the question]. Asked how he knows it, he declared that [it is] because he saw it, and it happened just as the question states. [He declared] further that it is true that the men-at-arms who went with the governor may have persuaded him to leave the land, because they asked him [to do so] owing to its being such an inferior land. And [they said] that if the governor did not give it to them, they [would] take it from him.[36]

[He said] that what is referred to in the question is true and it occur[red][37] and is just as the question states.

{17} In reply to the seventeenth question he declared, by the oath he swore, that he knows what he has stated and nothing more. Among persons who have knowledge of [this matter], it is commonly held and accepted to be as stated.

He was confirming and did confirm what he has declared. He did not sign it because he said he did not know how.

Hernando de Aranda, His Majesty's *escribano*

[. . .]

[71r]

[. . .]

{Witness, Juan Fernández Verdejo}[38]

After what is stated above, on the eleventh day of the month of April in the aforementioned year [1552], before the lord *alcalde* and in the presence of me, the aforesaid public *escribano*, Francisco Vázquez de Coronado appeared in person and presented as a witness in this matter Juan Fernández Verdejo, a *vecino* of this *ciudad*. The oath was received from him to tell the truth about what he might know, by God, Our Lord, and the sign of the cross. Being questioned according to the substance of the *interrogatorio* he declared and asserted the following. Witnesses who saw him swear the oath: *bachiller* Salazar and Pero García.

{1} To the first question he replied that he knows Francisco Vázquez de Coronado but is not familiar with the *fiscal*.[39] He has knowledge of the aforementioned *pueblos* [71v] by hearsay and has seen them[40] referred to by name but has not been in them.

{Personal data} Questioned concerning personal data, he declared that he is more than thirty-five years old, is not a relative of any of the parties, and does not have a stake in this action. "May whoever has right [on his side] prevail."[41]

{2} To the second question he answered that he considers Francisco Vázquez de Coronado to be a *caballero*. That it is so is well known in Nueva España, [being] known and considered [as true] by everyone. Because he is such a person His Majesty made him the concession of appointing him governor of Nueva Galicia. [This the king did] both for this reason and because Francisco Vázquez de Coronado has served His Majesty in Nueva España in whatever has presented itself and because he is a prudent, wise, and experienced man. This is what he knows concerning this question.

{3} To the third question [the witness] replied that what is referred to in the question he has heard stated publicly and commonly in this *ciudad* among persons who observed [Vázquez de Coronado's diligence in office], and it has been understood that [Vázquez de Coronado] performed [his duties] just so.

{4} In response to the fourth question he declared that what he knows concerning the question is that at the time Francisco Vázquez de Coronado departed for the *provincia* of [Nueva] Galicia from this *ciudad* with the office of governor, he took his whole household. And he spent a great sum of gold pesos (because this witness saw it). [He spent so much] because they say that in [Nueva] Galicia Castilian goods are offered for sale at excessive prices and [that] individuals are unable to maintain themselves except with great difficulty.

[72r] [He knows that Vázquez de Coronado] made expenditures from his own assets because this witness, having been in the aforesaid jurisdiction, has seen exactly

what the question states. Because [Nueva Galicia] is separated[42] by many leagues from this Ciudad de México and [is] much more distant from the ports on the Mar del Norte, he considers it certain that Francisco Vázquez spent much more than his salary. [That is] because he could not maintain himself in accordance with the status of his person and the office, not even with two additional salaries, since Castilian goods are exceedingly expensive in that jurisdiction.

He also knows that [Vázquez de Coronado] had need of granting *pueblos* to himself in *encomienda* in His Majesty's name in order to better maintain himself and discharge the office of governor. [This is] because, with the need to be liked, if what is stated above is not done in this part of the world, such governors [would] not be held in such high regard. [And he knows] that so the people may be at peace and tranquil, [the governors] have spent from their own assets and provide food for the individuals who want to come and eat. It has been and is done this way. This is what he knows concerning the question.

{5} To the fifth question he replied that what is referred to in the question is very widely known in Nueva España, in Tierra Firme,[43] and [in] other places. [Namely] that such governors entrust *pueblos* to themselves in *encomienda*. What is stated above has not been opposed by His Majesty or the Real Consejo.[44] He has seen that [this practice] was not hindered in the past, but [it] has been by the New Laws. And it is publicly and widely known [to be] this way, since without doing so they could not maintain themselves in any way. This is what he knows concerning the question.

{6} To the sixth question he answered that he has heard what is referred to in the question said by persons in the [72v] jurisdiction of Jalisco.[45] Further, he refers to the *cédulas* of *encomienda* because what the question states is evident from them.

{7} In response to the seventh question this witness stated that when he was in the aforementioned jurisdiction [of Jalisco] he saw that Francisco Vázquez de Coronado was provided service by the Indians of the *pueblos* referred to in the first question. [He knows this] because the very Indians [who] were named are natives of the aforesaid *pueblos*. They rendered all their tributes, services, and profits [to Vázquez de Coronado] quietly and peacefully without opposition from any person. This is publicly and widely known among persons who are aware of it. This is what he knows concerning the question.

{8} To the eighth question he answered that he knows and saw that while Francisco Vázquez was quietly in his house His Majesty named him captain general of Tierra Nueva, as is evident [in] the aforementioned royal commission. This was shown to [the witness], and he declared that it was the same one which is referred to. As a result of [the commission], Francisco Vázquez, as captain general, took with him to Tierra Nueva all the footmen and horsemen. [The witness knows this] because he saw him leave with [them] in pursuance of the expedition in the *provincia* of Jalisco. This is publicly and widely known to be so in Nueva España among the persons who saw [the departure] and have information about it. That is what he knows concerning the question.

{9} To the ninth question he replied that what he knows concerning the question is that this witness saw [that] Francisco Vázquez de Coronado himself acquiesced to the order of His Majesty's commission. [And] he went [on the expedition] to secure what was promised to him in His Majesty's royal commission, namely that he would not be deprived or despoiled of the *pueblos* [73r] he held in *encomienda*. [He knows this is so] because Francisco Vázquez de Coronado told him so many times before he went on the aforesaid expedition. Because if this was not so, he would not have accepted [the commission], since he was tranquil and at rest in his house.

Thus this witness considers it certain that if it were not for the promises and the rest of the concessions he was expecting from His Majesty (as [His Majesty] has done it and is doing it with those who serve him well), [Vázquez de Coronado] would not have set out on the expedition. [That is] because, as he said, he has heard it talked about and said while discussing it with many of his friends. [This they knew] because when they asked [Vázquez de Coronado] why he was putting his person at such risk and trouble and [making] such expenditures from his assets and the dowry [the Estradas] had given him with doña Beatriz, his wife,[46] Francisco Vázquez stated and replied that [it was] in order to serve His Majesty and to secure the reward the aforesaid royal commission promised him. [And he said] that at no time were the *pueblos* he held in *encomienda* and in trust in His Majesty's name (in Nueva España and outside it) to be taken away and seized from him. Because of this assurance, [he said] he was glad to expend all of his assets and to place his person and life fully at risk and in danger and [expose himself to] the difficulties that might come to him. [This was so] even though they were telling him that there had to be very many [difficulties], because the journey is very long. [The witness] heard it said thus many different times. This is what he knows concerning this question.

{10} In response to the tenth question he replied that he says what he has said in the previous question. And [that] it is truly this way: that Francisco Vázquez de Coronado [73v] went on the expedition and took command of the armed force in fulfillment of what is referred to in the previous questions and in order to secure the reward which was promised to him by the royal commission.

In order to obtain the aforementioned grants and in order to serve His Majesty, Francisco Vázquez spent from his own assets a very large sum of gold pesos. This witness believes and considers it certain and established that [the captain general] spent more than thirty thousand pesos. [He knows this to be so] because at the time this witness bought and supplied many things for Francisco Vázquez. And [Verdejo] maintained an accounting and statement and gave it to [Vázquez de Coronado] (about the what and how [of his purchases]).[47] [He did this] because at the time he was in [Vázquez de Coronado's] household, and [the captain general] commissioned and charged him with helping him purchase and dispatch everything necessary for his departure.

He did it in this way and saw that he spent a large sum of money from his [own] assets. He had seen that [Vázquez de Coronado] went into debt and remained in debt. This is all publicly and commonly known in Nueva España. [This had to be so] because the expense was great for so many people and such a grand expedition. This is what he knows concerning the question.

Because this witness was not presented to [answer] more than these ten questions, he was not asked the remaining [ones]. [When his replies] were read to him, he declared that it is the truth about what he knows in the case. He certifies and did certify this and signed it with his name.

This witness also stated that because he has made his statement in this case another time, this [testimony] and the previous one are to be [taken as] a single [statement]. No harm has been seen in that, since everything he has declared is the truth and has been certified.

Juan Fernández [Verdejo]
Graviel de Aguilera[48]

Before me, Juan de Zaragosa, public *escribano*[49]
[. . .]

TRANSCRIPTION

[fol. 65v]

{j} Primeramente sean preguntados sy conosçen / A los dichos e de que tiempo A esta partE / y sy tienen notiçia de los dichos pueblos E / sobre que es este pleyto

{ij} {ytem} yten sy saben que el dicho francisco Vasquez de coronado / es caballero hijodalgo notorio y en tal po- / sesyon hA estado y esta y por ser de tal / calidad e ser sabio e prudente su magestad / le hizo merced de le proVeer por gobernador / y capitan general de la proVinçia de la / nueVa galizia t(h)eniendo rrespeto ansymismo / A lo que en esta nueVa españa le hAbia serVido / y sirVio digan lo que saben

{iij} yten sy saben que en los dichos cargos el dicho francisco / Vasquez de coronado sirVio a su magestad con toda / Rectitud y diligençia fielmente segun y como / Debia y (h)era obligado en semejantes cargos / Digan lo que saben

{iiij} yten sy saben que por estar la dicha pro- / Vinçia de la nueVa galizia tan distinta[50] / y apartada de la çiudad de mexico y de / los puertos de la mar del norte todas las / cosas nesçesarias para la sustentaçion / {rúbricas}

[fol. 66r]

Valian y Valen A (h)exçe(V)çiVos preçios por / cuya causa gastaria y gasto el dicho francisco Vasquez / De coronado no solamente el salario que / t(h)enia de gobernador pero la mayor parte de / su hazienda y lo dicho no bastaba ny basto / para se sustentar conforme a la calidad de su / persona y del dicho cargo por cuya causa / para mejor poder serVir a su magestad tuVo nesçe- / sidad de se encomendar y depositar pueblos / De yndios en rrepartimiento como lo hizo / Digan lo que saben

{V} Yten sy saben etcetera que los gobernadores que han sydo / por su magestad en estas partes han t(h)enido por / costumbre de rrepartir pueblos de yndios en / Deposito y en encomienda y encomendar- / los en sy y tomarlos para sy en la dicha en- / comienda lo qual Vino a notiçia de su magestad y / no lo ha contradicho antes de las nueVas leyes / y lo consintio y en algunos lo aprobo como fue / En el marques del Valle don hernando cortes / y en nuño de guzman gober- nador que fue / en la dicha proVinçia digan lo que saben

{Vj} {ytem} Yten sy saben etcetera que por rrazon de lo / contenido en las preguntas antes de esta / El dicho francisco Vasquez de coronado se enco- / mendo en nombre de su magestad en los pueblos[51] de / yndios de que de suso se haze minçion / y de ellos se dio titulos de encomienda que / estan firmados de su nombre y rrefrendados / de hernando bermejo su secretario los quales / son los[52] que en esta causa estan presentados / que se han de mostrar a los testigos para que digan / lo que supieren / {rúbricas} LxVj

[fol. 66v]

{Vij} Yten sy saben que por Razon de las dichas encomiendas / y titulos de ellas El dicho francisco Vasquez de coronado / tuVo y poseyo los dichos pueblos y estançias lle- / Vando los tributos serVicios y aproVechamientos / De ellos quyeta y paçificamente syn contra- / Diçion de persona alguna digan lo que saben

{Viij} Yten sy saben que Estando el dicho gobernador / francisco Vasquez de coronado en su casa e quye- / tud con su muger e hijos syendo gobernador / fue (h)elegido y nombrado por proVision ReaL / por capitan general de la tierra nueVa para que / fuese al descubrimiento y conquista de *e*lla y / se le mando como (a)tal capitan general / lleVase (h)exerçito de gente de pie y de a caballo / a su cargo que para la d*i*cha jornada y conquista / se hizo y emViaba como consta de la d*i*cha pro*Vi*syo*n* / R*e*aL que pido se muestre a los t*e*stigos y diga*n* lo q*ue* sabe*n*

{jx} Yten sy saben q*ue* *e*l d*i*cho gobernador fran*cis*co Vasquez de / coronado por serVir a su m*agestad* y en confiança de / las me*rced*es que por la d*i*cha proVision rreal se le p*ro*- / metiero*n* açerca de que no le serian quytados / ni rremoVidos en tiempo alguno los yndios q*ue* *e*l / En nombre de su m*agestad* tenia encomendados y depo- / sitados *e*n la nueVa españa y fuera de *e*lla açepto El / D*i*cho cargo de yr *a* la d*i*cha jornada[53] como por la / D*i*cha proVision Real se le mandaba e por / conseguir las me*rced*es que los rreyes catolicos / de glor*i*osa memoria y su m*agestad* acostum braron / y acostunbran hazer a los que fiel leal y / diligente- mente les *h*an serVido como el d*i*cho / fran*cis*co Vasquez de coronado lo penso hazer / e hizo e pido que la d*i*cha proVi- sion Real / {rúbricas}

[fol. 67r]
sea mostrada a los testigos

{x} Yten sy saben que en cumplimiento de lo / *conteni*do en las preguntas antes de *e*sta e por / conseguir el premio que se le prometyo por la d*i*cha / R*e*aL proVisio*n* fue la d*i*cha jornada con el d*i*cho (h)exerçito / De gente y en ella y para la hazer por ser / la tierra donde se le mando yr tan lexos / y apartada de la nueVa españa que fue mas / de mill leguas de *e*lla y por tierras muchas de / *e*llas yn*h*abitables y despobladas y con tanta / gente gasto en serVi*ci*o de su m*agestad* mas de çinq*uen*ta / mill castellanos de su propia hazienda lo q*ua*l / El d*i*cho gobernador dixo e publico que lo hazia / al tiempo que hizo la d*i*cha (p) jornada por con- / seguir las me*rced*es contenidas en las preguntas / antes de *e*sta digan lo que sabe*n*

{Xj} Yten sy saben *etcetera* q*ue* *e*l d*i*cho gobernador fran*cis*co Vas- / quez de coronado lleVo el d*i*cho Exerçito q*ue* lleVaba / a su cargo con muy buena orden y lo lleVaba muy bie*n* / conçertado rregido y gobernado y tuVo espe*cia*L / cuydado

q*ue* en *e*l dios n*uest*ro señor fuese serVido y q*ue* / los naturales de las tierras por donde anduVo es- / tuVo y pazo conosçiese*n* a dios n*uest*ro señor y los / Unos y los otros sirViesen a su m*agestad* y fuesen muy / bien tratados rregidos y gobernados y q*ue* / En todo se hiziese y cumpliese como se / hizo y cumplio lo que su m*agestad* por sus yns- / truçiones t(h)enia proVeydo y mandado diga*n* / lo que sabe*n*

{xij} Yten sy saben q*ue* *e*l d*i*cho gobernador fran*cis*co Vasq*ue*z / De coronado *en* la d*i*cha jornada paso muchas / nesçesi- dades de hambre y frio y calor y derramo / {rúbricas}

[fol. 67v]
su sangre con muchas heridas q*ue* le diero*n* los / naturales de aquellas tierras de que estuVo a punto / De muerte y muchas Vezes tuVo su persona y / Vida en muy gran rriesgo y peligro en serVi*ci*o de / su m*agestad* digan lo que sabe*n*

{xiij} Yten sy saben que en toda la tierra nueVa / Donde *e*l d*i*cho fran*cis*co Vasquez de coronado / anduVo y estuVo ansy el como los capitanes / que por su mandado por muchas partes fuero*n* / A descubrir tomaro*n* posesio*n* de las d*i*chas tierras / por su m*agestad* y en ellas *en* lugar de posesion pu- / syero*n* cruzes digan lo que sabe*n*

{xiiij} {*ytem*} yten sy saben que en se descubrir la d*i*cha tierra / nueVa y en *h*aber hecho la d*i*cha jornada el d*i*cho / gober- nador su m*agestad* *h*a sydo serVido porque se / sabe y tiene notiçia de aquella tierra no / sabida ny entendida en otro tiempo alguno / e porque por ella se puede yr a otras mu- / chas tierras *e* en espe*cia*l[54] a la florida tierra / muy poblada de yndios fertil y abundosa / Donde su m*agestad* puede ser serVido diga*n* lo q*ue* sabe*n*

{XV} Yten sy saben q*ue* *e*l d*i*cho gobernador fran*cis*co Vasq*ue*z / De coronado fue adonde por la d*i*cha proVision / R*e*aL se le mando y Viendo que alli no *h*abia adonde / ampliar el rreal patrimonyo deseando mejor / serVir a dios n*uest*ro señor a su m*agestad* y (cumplir) *ampliar*[55] el d*i*cho / Real patrimonyo *en*Vio capitanes y gentes por / DiVersas partes a descubrir y buscar tierras / y gente donde poblar para que conosçiesen / A dios n*uest*ro señor y su m*agestad* fuese serVido los quales / capitanes y gentes fueron y anduVieron por / muchas partes e tierras y Vista y andada / {rúbricas}

[fol. 68r]
no se hallo dispusiçion de poder poblar / y el dicho gober-nador paso quinientas leguas / Adelante de çibola hasta quiVira

{xVj} yten sy saben que por Razon de lo contenido / en las preguntas antes de esta los capitanes y solda- / dos del dicho (h)exerçito rrequirieron al dicho gober- / nador que pues no habia dispusiçion para poder / poblar y en que serVir a dios nuestro señor y a su magestad / que los VolViese a la nueVa españa donde los saco / por cuya causa VolVio el dicho (h)exerçito

{xVij} yten sy saben que todo lo susodicho sea publica Voz / y fama el liçenciado caballero hernando de balbuena / escribano de su magestad
[. . .]

[fol. 41r]
[. . .]
^{Testigo(s)} {En dos de mayo de myll e quinientos E çinquenta y dos anos el dicho pedro rruys de haro ante el dicho senor licen-ciado de la marcha presento por / testigo a juan bermeJo y juro en forma debida a de derecho decir verdad {rúbrica}

{Testigo} El dicho Juan bermeJo testigo presentado por El / dicho pero rruiz de haro en nombre del dicho francisco / Vasquez de coronado el qual despues de / haber Jurado e s(e)yendo preguntado por / El t(h)enor y forma del dicho ynterrogatorio dixo / lo seguyente

{j} A la primera Pregunta dixo que conosçe a las / personas en la pregunta contenidos al dicho / francisco Vazquez de coronado lo conosçe mas ha / de quynze años y al dicho Jhoan rrodriguez / Fizcal conosçe puede haber tres o quatro meses / y que tiene notiçia de los dichos pueblos / porque ha estado en ellos

{ytem} PreGuntado por las preguntas Generales dixo / Este testigo que es de (h)edad de treynta e dos / años poco mas o menos e que no es pariente / de ninguna de las dichas partes ny (h)enemigo / e que ninguna de las preguntas Generales / no le tocan para que diga en contrario de la / verdad

{ij} {ytem} A la segunda pregunta dixo que la sabe como en ella / se contiene preguntado como lo sabe dixo que / porque syempre hA oydo y t(h)enydo el / dicho francisco VasqueZ por tal persona como / la pregunta lo dize y declara y syenpre / lo Vi(d)o este testigo del tienpo que lo conosçe / aca ser tal persona y estar en tal po- / sesyon como la pregunta lo dize y declara / y que es verdad que por ser tal persona / su magestad lo hizo gobernador y capitan General / de este nueVo rreyno de galizia y este testigo / {rúbrica} / xLj

[fol. 41v]
lo Vi(d)o gobernar y (h)era tal persona y tan Estimado / como la pregunta lo dize y declara y por- / que lo Vi(d)o ser y pasar como la pregunta / lo dize y por esto lo sabe

{iij} {ytem} A la terçera pregunta dixo que la sabe como / En ella se contyene preguntado como lo / sabe dixo que porque lo Vi(d)o ser y pasar / segun y de la manera que la pregunta lo / Dize y declara por tal persona fuE / hAbido y t(h)enydo en todo el tiempo que / Goberno y siempre hizo todo aquello que / conVenia al serVicio de dios nuestro senor y de su / magestad y este testigo nunca oyo ny supo / que hiziese cosa al contrario y sy lo hi- / ziera este testigo lo supiera e alcança- / ra porque no pudiera ser menos porque este / Testigo lo Vi(d)o y estuVo este testigo en el dicho / Tiempo que goberno el dicho francisco Vasquez / En esta gobernaçion

{iiij} {ytem} A la quarta pregunta dixo que la sabe como en ella / se contiene preguntado que como lo sabe dixo / que porque lo Vi(d)o ser y pasar ansy / como la pregunta lo dize y declara y que es / verdad que la dicha gobernaçion y nueVo rreyno / Esta distinto⁵⁶ e apartado de la çiudad / de mexico por cuya causa los bastimentos / son muy caros y Valen a muy (h)exçe(V)çiVos / Preçios y que sabe y es ansy la verdad / que segun la calidad del dicho francisco VasqueZ / de coro-nado y segun los (h)exçe(V)çiVos gastos / que t(h)enya por rrazon de lo que dicho / Es y (h)era muy poco el salario que t(h)enya / segun los grandes gastos y que *es* Verdad / que *el* como Gobernador rrepartio y dyo A / {rúbrica}

[fol. 42r]
Personas particulares muchos pueblos / de *e*ste nueVo rreyno en encomienda en non- / bre de su m*agestad* y todo lo demas en la pregunta / contenydo sabe como en ella se contyene

{V} {y*tem*} A la quinta pregunta dixo que lo que sabe / de *e*lla es que *es* Verdad que los gobernadores / que *h*an sydo de *e*sta nueVa españa y rreyno / de galizia *h*an rrepartido y rrepartieron / muchos pueblos de yndios en personas / particulares y de *e*llos daban çedulas / en nombre de su m*agestad* y ansymysmo rrepartia*n* / para sy mesmos como hizo el d*ic*ho marques / del Valle y el d*ic*ho nuño de guzma*n* y el / d*ic*ho fran*cis*co Vasquez de coronado y este t*e*stigo / Vi(d)o como poseyan los pueblos que ansy / Repartian para sy e *h*oy dia los posee / El d*ic*ho marques del Valle y esta es la / *ve*rdad y pasa ansy como d*ic*ho tyene porque / lo Vi(d)o y Ve(e) segun y de la manera que d*ic*ho tyene

{Vj} {y*tem*} A la sesta pregunta dixo que la sabe como / En ella se contiene pregu*n*ado como dixo q*ue* / porque *e*ste t*e*stigo Vi(d)o al d*ic*ho fran*cis*co Vasquez / de coronado poseer los d*ic*hos pueblos y el / los t(h)enia en nombre de su m*agestad* y t(h)enya / Çedula de *e*llos y Vi(d)o la çedula y que le / paresçe que *e*staba rrefrendada de her- / nando bermeJo su secretario pero este / t*e*stigo no sabe lee(e)r mas de como lo tyene / por cosa çierta ser y pasar ansy y es / Cosa muy publica y notoria y este t*e*stigo / ansy lo cree y tyene por cosa çierta

{Vij} {y*tem*} A la setima pregunta dixo que la sabe como *en* / *e*lla / se contiene porque ansy lo Vi(d)o ser y pasar / {rúbrica} / xLij

[fol. 42v]
segun y como la pregunta lo dize y declara / y es cosa publica y notoria

{Viij} {y*tem*} A la octaVa pregunta dixo que la sabe como en / Ella se coniene preguntado como dixo que / {/} porque *e*ste testigo Vi(d)o yr al d*ic*ho fran*cis*co / {/} Vasquez de coronado

a la d*ic*ha conquysta de la d*ic*ha / tierra nueVa y fue segun y de la manera que la / pregunta lo dize y declara y pasa y paso / segun en la d*ic*ha pregunta se contiene porq*ue* *e*ste testigo fue debaxo de la bandera de su m*agestad* y el / d*ic*ho fran*cis*co Vasquez fue por capitan General / del (h)exerçito de la gente que fue alla y fue / con proVisyon de su m*agestad* que para ello le dyo / y este testigo lo Vi(d)o y es ansy Verdad y pasa / segun y como en la pregunta se contiene

{jx} {y*tem*} A la noVena pregunta dixo que lo que sabe de *e*sta / pregunta es *que este testigo* (que) fue en la d*ic*ha Jornada / y *h*a Visto la d*ic*ha proVision rreal y lo *conteni*do En / la d*ic*ha pregunta este testigo dize qu*E* / en el tiempo que Vino el liÇ*encia*do teJada A toma- / lle rresidençia no quyto a ninguna persona de / las que *e*l d*ic*ho fran*cis*co Vasquez *h*abia dado yndyos / En Encomienda en nombre de su m*agestad* se los / quyto y lo demas contenydo *en* la d*ic*ha preg*un*ta / dize lo que d*ic*ho tyene

{X} {y*tem*} A la deçima pregunta dixo que lo que sabe / De *e*sta pregunta es que *e*ste testigo se Re- / myte a la d*ic*ha proVisyon de su m*agestad* y En qua*n*to / A lo que dize la pregunta que son myll leguas / de la d*ic*ha nueVa espana donde *e*l d*ic*ho gobern*ado*r / fran*cis*co Vasquez fue que *es* Verdad que *es* tan lexos / como la pregunta dize y es tierra y(e)n*h*abitable / y despoblada y que *es* Verdad que *e*ste t*e*stig*o* fu*E* / {rúbrica}

[fol. 43r][57]
en la d*ic*ha Jornada y fue de mucho peligro y de gran trabaxo / y que *es* Verdad que *e*l d*ic*ho fran*cis*co Vazqu*ez* gasto mucha suma / de pesos de oro *e*n la d*ic*ha jornada porq*ue* saco muchos ganados / Vacas y Carneros y puercos y bizcocho y harina y to- / dos bastimentos de azeyte y Vinagre y botiCa p*ar*a Curar / a los q*ue* Cayesen malos segun todo *en* q*ue* Cantidad seria / lo que gasto dixo este testigo q*ue* mucha Cantidad / y todo a su Costa y este t*e*stigo ansy lo Vi(d)o por Vista de ojos / de la manera que tiene d*ic*ho porq*ue* lo Vi(d)o todo conprar / y (h)era mucha Cantidad de pesos de oro y esto sabe d*e* *e*sta / *p*regunta

{xj} {y*tem*} a las (h)onze p*r*eguntas dixo q*ue* la sabe como *en* *e*lla se *conti*e*ne* / porq*ue* lo Vi(d)o ser y pasar seg*un*(d) y

Como *en* la pregunta se *conti*ene / y que *es* ver*d*ad que *el* dicho gobernador mandaba y mando / a todos los q*ue* yban con el *en* la Jornada q*ue* nadie hiziese / maltratamy*ento* a los yndios por donde yban y ansy se hazia / y Una maçorca no les osaba tomar y que por donde / yba les daba a entender a los dichos yndios El / poderio de dios n*uest*ro senor y trayesen *en* la fe *cristi*ana / y en todo tuVo especial Cuydado de no hazelles / mal como no se les hizo antes les daba a los dichos yndios / ResCates p*ar*a Contratallos y traellos a la doctrina *crist*iana / y al domynyo *de* su m*a*g*estad* y esto es asy porq*ue* lo Vi(d)o por / Vista de ojos

{Xij} {y*tem*} a las doZe preguntas dixo que la sabe como *en* *e*lla / se *conti*ene porque lo Vi(d)o ser y pasar asy como la pregu*n*ta lo dize / porq*ue e*ste *te*stigo y todos los demas y el dicho gobernador / pasaron mucho frio y hanbre y mas mucho peligro de / los naturales y este *te*stigo Vi(d)o herido Al dicho gobernador / a punto de muerte y desahuziado de todos los q*ue en* la dicha / Jornada yban porq*ue* los dichos yndios de la dicha / Jornada lo flecharon *en* muchas partes y todo p*a*so / como la pregunta lo dize

{Xiij} {y*tem*} a las treze pregu*n*tas dixo que la sabe como *en* *e*lla se *conti*ene / pregunta*d*o (^dixo) como *la sabe* dixo que porq*ue* lo Vi(d)o ser y / {rúbrica} / xLiij

[fol. 43v]
pasar como la pregunta lo dize e Vi(d)o q*ue* se hazian cruzes / dondequ*y*era q*ue* llegaban y toma*ba*n posesyon *en* nonbre / *d*e su m*a*g*estad* y todo lo contenido *en* la dicha pregu*n*ta sabe este *te*stigo / porq*ue* lo Vi(d)o y p*a*so asy

{Xiiij} {y*tem*} a las catorze preguntas dixo q*ue* la sabe como *en e*lla se *conti*ene / porq*ue* pasa y es asy la Verdad de como la pregunta lo dize / y declara y que por la dicha tierra nueVa pueden yr / a do dize la pregunta y a otras muchas part*es* y que *es* asy / como la pregu*n*ta lo dize

{XV} {y*tem*} a las quynze preguntas dixo que la sabe como / *en e*lla se *conti*ene pregu*n*tado como la sabe dixo que / porq*ue e*ste *te*stigo anduVo *en* la dicha Jornada todo / el tienpo de *e*lla

y lo Vi(d)o y p*a*so asy como *en* la pregu*n*ta / lo dize y declara y es la ver*d*ad todo lo *en e*lla *conte*nido

{XVj} {y*tem*} a las diez y seys preguntas dixo q*ue* la sabe como / *en e*lla se *conti*ene preguntado como *la sabe* dixo que porq*ue* lo Vi(d)o y / p*a*so asy como la pregunta lo dize y que *es* ver*d*ad / que los soldados q*ue* Con el dicho gobernador / yban le Requir*i*eran q*ue* se saliese de la tierra por- / q*ue* se pe*d*ian por ser tan mala la tierra y q*ue* si / El dicho gobernador no se la daba que ellos se / la tomaron y que *es* ver*d*ad lo contenido *en* la dicha / pregunta y pasa y es ansy como la pregunta lo de- / clara

{XVij} {y*tem*} a las diez y syete preguntas dixo / que lo que dicho tiene sabe / y no otra cosa p*a*ra el Juramento q*ue* tiene hecho / y ansy es publica Voz y fama / *ent*re las personas que de *e*llo tienen no- / tiÇia y en lo que dicho tiene se Rectifi- caba / y rrectifico y no lo fyrmo porque / dixo que no sabia h*er*na*n*do de aranda es*cribano* *de* su m*a*g*estad* / {rúbrica} [. . .]

[fol. 71r][58]
[. . .]
{*te*stigo} / {ju*an* *fernand*es / VerdeJo}
E despues de lo susodicho en onze dias / del dicho mes de abril del dicho año ante *el* dicho / señor al*c*alde y en presençia de mi el dicho es*cribano* pu*blic*o / paresçio presente el dicho fran*c*isco Vasquez de / Coronado e presento por *te*stigo en la dicha / Razon a Juan fernandez VerdeJo V*ezin*o de *e*sta / dicha çiudad del qual fue rresçebido Juramento / por dios n*uest*ro señor e a la señal de la cruz + de / dezir Verdad de lo que supiese e siendo / preguntado por el t(h)enor del dicho ynterrog*atori*o / dixo e depuso lo seguiente *te*stig*o*s q*ue* lo Vieron / Jurar el bachiller salazar E pero garçia

{j} A la primera pregunta dixo que conosçe al dicho / fran*cis*co Vasquez de coronado e no conosçe al / dicho fizcal e que tiene notiçia de los dichos pueblos / {rúbricas} / lxx^*j*x(^j)

[fol. 71v]
De oydas q*ue* los *h*a Visto nombrar pero q*ue* / no *h*a estado en ellos

{*Generales*} Preguntado por las preguntas generales dixo / que *es* de (h)edad de mas de treinta e çinco años / e que no es pariente de ninguna de las partes / ni lleVa ynterese en esta causa que Vença quie*n* / tuViere Just*ici*a

{ij} A la segunda preg*un*ta dixo q*ue es*te *te*stigo tiene por caballero / Al d*ich*o fran*cis*co Vasquez de corondo lo quaL / es muy notorio en esta nueVa españa que lo es (es) tal / e sabido y t(h)enido entre todos e que por ser tal pe*r*sona / su m*ag*estad le hizo me*r*ce*d* de le proVeer de gobernador / de la nueVa galizia asy por esto como porq*ue* el / d*ich*o fran*cis*co Vasquez de coronado *h*a serVido / a su m*ag*estad En esta nueVa españa en lo que se *h*a o- / fresçido e por ser *h*onbre prudente e sabio / y Entendido e que *es*to es lo que sabe de la / d*ich*a pregunta

{iij} A la ter*ce*ra pregunta dixo que lo contenido en la p*regun*ta / este *te*stigo lo *h*a oydo dezir por publico e notorio en esta / Çiudad entre las personas q*ue* lo Viero*n* e asy se / tiene entendido que lo ha hecho

{iiij} A la quarta pregunta dixo que lo que sabe de la / d*ich*a pregunta es que al tiempo q*ue e*l d*ich*o fran*cis*co Vasqu*ez* / salio de *e*sta çiudad con el cargo de gobernador para / la d*ich*a proVinçia de galizia lleVo toda su casa / e gasto mucha suma de pesos de oro porque *es*te / *te*stigo lo Vio porque dezian que en la d*ich*a galizia / Valian las cosas de castilla A (h)ex̣çe(V)çiVos / Preçios e las personas no se podian / sustentar syno (h)era con gran trabaJo / {rúbricas}

[fol. 72r]
Gasto de sus haziendas porque *es*te *te*stigo *h*A *e*stado En la / d*ich*a gobernaçion e *h*a Visto que asy como la pregunta / lo dize por estar desViada muchas leguas de esta çiu- / dad de mexico e mucho mas lexos de los puertos de la / mar del norte e que (^p) tiene por çierto que *e*l d*ich*o fran*cis*co / Vasquez gasto mucho mas del d*ich*o salario porque / conforme a la calidad de su persona e del d*ich*o cargo / no pudo sustentarse ni aUn con otros dos salarios / ençima a causa de ser las cosas de castilla carisimas / En la d*ich*a gobernaçio*n* e que sabe q*ue* tuVo nesçesidad de / se

encomendar en nombre de su m*ag*estad pueblos de en- / comienda para meJor sustentarse e rrepresentar / El cargo de gobernador porque sy lo susod*ich*o no se / haze en estas partes no se tienen los tales gobernadores / en tanta estima e de nesçesidad para ser queridos / e que las gentes esten en paz e sosiego *h*an gastado de sus / haziendas e ponen mesa A las personas que quye- / ren yr a comer e asy se *h*a hecho y haze e que *es*to / es lo que sabe de la pregunta

{V} A la quinta pregunta dixo que lo contenido en la / pregunta es muy noTorio en esta nueVa españa / y En tierra firme e otras partes que los tales / gobernadores se depositan en sy pueblos de en- / Comienda e lo susod*ich*o no se *h*a contrad*ich*o / por su m*ag*estad ny el Real conseJo antes *h*a Visto / que no se *h*a Estorbado syno fue en las nueVas leyes / e que asy es publico y notorio porque no lo / haziendo ansy en ninguna manera se podrian / sustentar e que *es*to es lo que sabe de la d*ich*a preg*un*ta

{Vj} A la sesta pregunta dixo que *h*A oydo dezir / lo contenido en la pregunta a personas de la / {rúbricas} / lxxx(^ij)

[fol. 72v]
Gobernaçion de xelisco e que se rremite a las d*ich*as / çedulas de encomienda porque por ellas pa- / resçera lo que la pregunta dize

{Vij} A la setima pregunta dixo que *es*te *te*stigo estando *en* la d*ich*a / gobernaçion Veia que los yndios de los d*ich*os pueblos / contenidos en la primera Pregunta se serVia el d*ich*o / gobernador fran*cis*co Vasquez porque los mismos / yndios se nombraba*n* ser naturales de los d*ich*os / pueblos los quales acudian con todos los tributos / e serVic*i*os e aproVechamientos quyeta e paçifica- / mente syn contradiçion de persona alguna / e asy es publico y notorio entre las personas que / de *e*llo tienen notiçia e que *es*to es lo que sabe de la / d*ich*a pregunta

{Viij} A la o*ct*aVa pregunta dixo que sabe e Vio que / Estando el d*ich*o fran*cis*co Vasquez en su casa e quyetud / le nombro su m*ag*estad por capitan general de la d*ich*a / tierra nueVa como paresçe de la dicha proVision Real / la qual le fue mostrada e dixo ser la mesma a la qual / se rremite e que por rrazon de ella el dicho francisco Vas- / quez lleVo consigo toda la gente de pie y de A / caballo a la dicha tierra nueVa como tal capitan / general porque le Vio salir con ella en seguimiento / de la dicha Jornada en la dicha proVinçia de xelisco / lo qual es ansy publico y notorio en esta nueVa / españa entre las personas que lo Vieron e de ello / tienen notiçia e que esto es lo que sabe de la dicha pregunta

{jx} A la noVena pregunta dixo que lo que sabe / de la dicha pregunta es que este testigo Vio que sy / el dicho francisco Vasquez de coronado Açepto El / mando de la dicha proVision de su magestad fue por / Conseguyr lo que se le prometio en la dicha proVision / Real de su magestad en no le quytar ni rremoVer los pueblos / {rúbricas}

[fol. 73r]
De encomienda que t(h)enia porque asy se / lo dixo muchas Vezes el dicho francisco Vasquez de / coronado antes que fuese a la dicha Jornada por- / que sy asy no fuera no lo açep- tara a causa que el / Estaba paçifico e quyeto en su casa e descanso / e que ansy lo tiene por çierto este testigo que / sy no fuera por lo dichos prometimientos e de / las demas mercedes que de su magestad esperaba como / lo ha hecho y haze con los que bien le sirVen que / no fuera en seguimiento de la dicha Jornada por- / que como dicho tiene asy se lo oyo platicar e dezir / platicandolo con muchos amigos suyos porquE / diziendole que porque ponia su persona / A tantos peligros y trabaJos e tanto gasto / de su hazienda e dote que le habian dado con / doña beatriz su muger dezia e rrespondia el / dicho francisco Vasquez que por serVir a su magestad e / por conseguir el premio que por la dicha pro- / Vision rreal se le prometio que en ningun tiempo / le serian quytados ny rremoVidos los dichos / pueblos que en esta nueVa españa e fuera / de ella t(h)enia encomendados e deposi- / tados en nombre de su magestad e que por esta confiança / holgaba de gastar toda su hazienda e poner / su

persona e Vida a todo el rriesgo e peligro e / trabaJos que le Viniesen aUnque se le rrepresentaba / que habian de ser muchos por ser la Jornada muy / larga e que esto le oyo dezir diVersas e muchas / Vezes e es lo que sabe de esta pregunta

{x} A la dezima pregunta dixo que dize lo que / dicho tiene en la pregunta antes de esta e que es / asy verdad que el dicho francisco Vasquez de coronado / {rúbricas} / lxxxj(^iij)

[fol. 73v]
En cumplimiento de lo contenido en las preguntas / antes de esta e por conseguir el premio que / se le prometio por la dicha proVision Real fue / la dicha Jornada e lleVo a su cargo el dicho (h)e- / xerçito e por conseguir las dichas mercedes e por / serVir a su magestad gasto el dicho francisco Vasquez de su / hazienda muy gran suma de pesos de oro / tanto que cree este testigo e tiene por çierto e a- / Veriguado que gasto mas de treynta mill pesos / porque este testigo a la sazon compro e proVeyo / muchas cosas para el dicho francisco Vasquez / e tuvo de ello quenta E rrazon e se la dio en / que y como porque estaba a la dicha sazon en su / Casa e le encomendo y encargo le ayudase / A despachar y comprar todo lo nesçe- sario / para su yda e asy lo hizo e Vio que gasto mu- / cha suma de dinero de su hazienda e habia / Vido que se enpeño e quedo enpeñado e / que todo es publico y notorio en esta nueVa / españa porque el gasto fue mucho para tanta gente / e tan gran Jornada e que esto es lo que sabe de la / dicha pregunta e porque no fue presentado / este testigo para mas de estas diez preguntas / no se pregunto por las demas y sien- dole / leydas dixo que aquello es la Verdad de lo / que en el caso sabe en que se afirma e afirmo e / firmolo de su nombre e dixo que porque este / testigo ha dicho su dicho en este caso otra VeZ / que esto e lo otro sea todo Uno e no se ha Visto / para all(e)i perJuyZio porque todo lo que ha dicho / es la verdad y se rrectificaba en ello Juan fernandes / graViel de aguilera ante mi Jhoan de çaragoça escribano / publico
[. . .]
{rúbricas}

Document 12

Muster Roll of the Expedition, Compostela, February 22, 1540

AGI, Guadalajara, 5, R.1, N.7

INTRODUCTION

On February 22, 1540, at Compostela in the new Spanish *provincia* of Nueva Galicia,[1] the *escribano* Juan de Cuevas,[2] assisted by another *escribano*, prepared a list of 289 men bound for Cíbola as they passed in review before Viceroy Antonio de Mendoza.[3] Along with each man's name he recorded the number of horses each took with him on the expedition, if any, and a summary of what arms and armor he was equipped with. Such musters were a common, if not invariable, feature of preparations for launching an expedition of reconnaissance and conquest at this time.[4] About the list he drafted, Cuevas states: "the muster was conducted of all the people who are going to the land recently discovered by the Father Provincial fray Marcos de Niza."[5]

This muster roll, or *alarde*, has been published three times in the last 65 years, twice in Spanish and once in English. Arthur Aiton, the first researcher to locate the muster roll in the Archivo General de Indias in Sevilla, published a Spanish transcription in 1939.[6] He called the document "a nearly complete and authentic list of those who went on the expedition."[7] A year later, George Hammond and Agapito Rey published an English translation in their important *Narratives of the Coronado Expedition*.[8] Then, in 1992, Carmen de Mora published a new, modernized Spanish transcription in Spain.[9]

Despite assertions to the contrary, the *alarde* does not begin to list all the people who participated in the massive *entrada* to Cíbola and beyond. Most glaringly absent is any mention of the at least 1,300 natives of central and western Mexico, the so-called *indios amigos*, who made up the great bulk of the expedition, outnumbering the European members by at least three to one.[10] Joining the expedition primarily as warriors, Mexican Indians made possible the journey of Marcos de Niza and the establishment of a "Spanish" beachhead in Tierra Nueva. They preceded the advance guard of the expedition to Cíbola in an unsuccessful effort to pave the way for Spanish entrance.[11] They were present at and participated in the attack on Cíbola in July 1540. Indeed, their numbers probably explain the relative ease with which that fabled pueblo was overrun. They fought and died in the Tiguex War during the winter of 1540–41.[12] They made the trek onto the Great Plains the following summer, and some of them doubtless reached Quivira. Some even stayed in the Pueblo world when the expedition withdrew to Nueva España in spring 1542.[13] As was typical throughout Spanish America, native groups that had previously submitted to Spanish sovereignty made possible the extension of that control. It is no exaggeration to say that the conquest of the Americas during the sixteenth century was essentially the conquest of native groups by other American natives, at least nominally under the direction of Europeans. The Coronado expedition was no different.

Even many Europeans and other Old World natives who went on the expedition to the Tierra Nueva of Cíbola are missing from the muster roll. For instance, as Hammond and Rey mentioned, none of the five Franciscan friars who accompanied the expedition, nor at least three lay assistants, appear on the muster roll.[14] Nor do 67 more men-at-arms who are now known from other documentary sources to have gone on the expedition.[15] Some of these were simply not at Compostela at the time (for instance, Juan de Zaldívar and Melchior Díaz). Others, including a contingent from Culiacán, probably did not join the expedition until it moved north of Compostela. Juan de Cuevas himself tells us in the text that concludes the muster roll that some horsemen had gone ahead with the friars and some were "expected from [the Ciudad de] México to join the expedition."[16] Still others may purposely have stayed or been kept away from the review before the viceroy, perhaps to frustrate the simultaneous investigation that was being made into whether a significant number of established *vecinos* of the Ciudad de México was being drawn away by the lure of Cíbola.[17] Yet others do not appear on the muster because they were preoccupied by other preparations or were of status too humble to warrant counting.

Also participating in the expedition but not recorded in the official muster were many slaves and servants. Here, numbers can only be imagined. Surviving *probanzas de méritos y services,* or proofs of worthiness and service, of expedition members report that those men generally went to great expense to take servants and slaves with them. Typical was Juan de Zaldívar, whose claim that he had expended thousands of pesos to take with him an unspecified number of "criados y negros" and "servicio" (*criados,* black slaves, and servants) was corroborated by all the witnesses called in 1566 to support his petition for preferment by the king.[18] It would have been unheard of for the *hidalgos* and many persons of lesser rank on the expedition not to have been accompanied by servants and slaves. Francisco Vázquez de Coronado himself took on the expedition at least seven black slaves, four men and three women.[19] In all likelihood, the total number of slaves and servants equaled or exceeded the number of European men-at-arms in the expedition.

One final group not only is missing from the muster roll but is all but invisible in the documentary record as a whole: women. Only two women who accompanied their husbands on the expedition are known by name, María Maldonado

and Francisca de Hozes. Both were well remembered by former expedition members who later wrote chronicles of the undertaking. In addition, two men, Juan Troyano and Lope Caballero, had unnamed native wives with them on the expedition.[20] These four are surely not even the tip of the tip of the iceberg of women who traveled to Cíbola, performing tasks such as cooking and mending and nursing disdained by the conquistadores, not to mention serving as companions and lovers and the makers of field households.

Rather than just the 289 European men-at-arms listed on the *alarde,* the expedition probably included between 1,500 and 2,000 people of various ethnicities and nationalities. Pedro de Castañeda de Nájera gives a far closer estimate of the complete number than does the muster roll when he talks of "more than 1,500 persons among the allies and servants."[21] A list of the 358 persons of Old World origin or extraction and the 11 American natives who have so far been indentified by name as having participated in the Coronado expedition makes up Appendix 3. The list continues to grow as additional documents are located and studied.

As evidence of the size and composition of the expedition, then, the muster roll must be qualified and supplemented. On another matter, the original document tells us significantly more than its previous American editions do. Indeed, by failing to reproduce the format of the manuscript document, those editions have inadvertently but utterly suppressed rare information about the expedition's organization. No one consulting only Aiton's transcription or Hammond and Rey's translation of the muster roll would ever know, for instance, that Rodrigo Maldonado was captain of a company of horsemen that included at least nine men at the time Juan de Cuevas recorded the muster. Those men were Juan de Torquemada, Francisco Gutiérrez, Sancho Rodríguez, Alonso de Medina, Hernando de Barahona, Leonardo Sánchez, a man named Cepeda, Antón Miguel, Gaspar Guadalupe, and Hernando de Castroverde.[22] Probably more men were added to the six companies listed in the muster roll as the expedition traveled north. At least, we find that by later in the expedition's course, Juan Zaldívar's company, for example, comprised 17 horsemen, including the captain, and Hernando de Alvarado's comprised 21.[23] At the time of the muster itself, however, the great majority of the men listed were not yet assigned to any company. Altogether, 127 horsemen were listed in a large group following the six skeleton companies already mentioned.

This information about the composition of companies is available in the document itself because four folio sides of the manuscript are organized by companies. Each captain's name is set against the left margin, and the names of the men under his direction are indented below his. In this way, six companies of horsemen are delineated. Also shown is what appears to be the captain general's own company and retinue, which consists of those *caballeros* and men of lesser rank listed after Vázquez de Coronado's name and before the other company rosters, beginning with that of García López de Cárdenas.[24]

Because information about the Mexican Indian allies who accompanied the expedition was not included in the muster roll (and very little such information appears in any other document), we remain largely in the dark about how the contingent of allies was organized. It is likely, though, that the Mexican Indians adhered to their traditional organization for battle.[25] How or whether such native companies were associated with or mingled among the European companies is unknown.

The prevailing image of the appearance of the Coronado expedition is one of a troop of ironclad, medieval-looking knights. The manuscript muster roll offers abundant evidence to the contrary. Of course the Mexican Indians who made up the bulk of the expedition did not look like European

FIGURE 12.1. Sixteenth-century European and Native American arms and armor, after the *Lienzo de Tlaxcala*, sixteenth-century Mexico, fols. 10, 18, 32, 49, 53, 59, and 71. A, sallet (helmet with wide brim at the back); B, *adarga* (heart-shaped shield); C, rowel spur; D, broadsword; E, beaver (chin guard); F, *rodela* (round shield); G, *brida*-style tack (including Western-style saddle and long stirrups); H, gorget; I, jack plate armor; J, *lanza de encuentro* (double-tipped lance); K, gaff spur; L, pack frame; M, *alpargates* (hemp sandals); N, *macana* (obsidian-edged sword); O, quilted cotton armor; P, breastplate.

knights, but what about the European members? Of the 289 men recorded on the muster roll, only 61 declared that they had European-style body armor. In almost every case this amounted only to a coat of chain mail. No more than a handful of men had anything approaching a full suit of armor. Only 45 men possessed European-style helmets, and most of these were men who also had body armor. A few other pieces of European armor got carried along on the expedition—a stray sleeve of chain mail or a beaver (chin guard) here and there—but the majority of men listed on the muster roll had no European armor at all. In contrast, 90 percent of the men on the muster roll (260 out of 289) declared that they had "armas de la tierra," or native arms and armor, either solely or supplementing their meager compliment of European armor. The native arms and armor used by allies of the Coronado expedition undoubtedly included quilted cotton tunics, round shields, traditional feathered headgear, banners and other insignias; *macanas* (obsidian-edged swords), clubs, lances, slings, and bows and arrows.[26]

Much valuable information is available in or inferable from the muster roll, but the list should not be used uncritically. Besides its incompleteness, a further source of confusion and misinformation is the presence in the *alarde* of words that appear to be surnames but actually indicate only place of origin.[27] This occurs at least 11 times. Cristóbal Pérez from Ávila is the first such example on the list.[28] When he testified during Vázquez de Coronado's *residencia* in 1544, he signed his name "Cristóbal Pérez" and stated that

he was a native of Ávila. Thus, Hammond and Rey's rendering of his name as "Cristóbal Pérez Dávila" is mistaken.[29] There may be more cases of such usages on the muster than the 11 we have been able to identify positively. Variances such as these from Hammond and Rey's earlier translation and from Aiton's and Mora's transcriptions in the new transcription and translation that follow are noted in annotations to the document.

One other significant earlier misidentification should be highlighted. Captain Diego Gutiérrez de la Caballería,[30] brother of Marina Gutiérrez de la Caballería, mother of Vázquez de Coronado's wife, Beatriz de Estrada, was incorrectly identified by Hammond and Rey as "Diego Gutiérrez, captain of cavalry."[31] His participation in the expedition to Tierra Nueva can be seen as part of the Estrada-Gutiérrez-Coronado sponsorship of the venture. Information such as this helps to show that, like most other Spanish expeditions of the period, the Coronado expedition relied significantly for its makeup on people who were related to the organizers by birth, marriage, or place of origin or through habitual social or commercial contacts.

The numbers entered at the left margin of the document repeat the number of horses each man took with him. A running subtotal is entered at the bottom of each folio side. Several minor errors were made in this addition.

The original signed manuscript of the *alarde* is preserved in the Archivo General de Indias in Sevilla under the *signatura* (catalog number) AGI, Guadalajara, 5, R.1, N.7.

TRANSLATION

[1r][32]

I, Juan de Cuevas,[33] *escribano mayor* for mines and reports for His Majesty in this Nueva España, declare and attest that at the *ciudad* of Compostela in Nueva Galicia, in Nueva España, with the illustrious lord don Antonio de Mendoza present ([who is] viceroy and governor of this Nueva España for His Majesty), along with Gonzalo de Salazar (*factor*), Peralmindez Cherino (*veedor* of Nueva España), Cristóbal de Oñate (*veedor* of the aforesaid *provincia*), and many other people, the muster was conducted of all the people who are going to the land newly discovered by Father Provincial fray Marcos de Niza.[34] Francisco Vázquez de Coronado is going as captain general of this [expedition].

The muster[35] was conducted on the twenty-second day of the month of February in the year one thousand five hundred and forty in the following form and manner, the lord *licenciado* Maldonado being present:

{23}[36] Captain General Francisco Vázquez de Coronado swore that he is taking on this expedition in the service of His Majesty twenty-two or twenty-three horses and three or four sets of armored horse trappings for riding with long and short stirrups.[37]

{17} The *maestre del campo,* Lope de Samaniego, *alcaide,* swore that he is taking sixteen or seventeen horses, two elk hide jackets, a chain mail vest [with] its appurtenances, several breastplates, and native arms and armor, since the rest of what he was bringing was destroyed by fire.

{13} Don Pedro de Tovar, *alférez mayor* [chief lieutenant], swore that he was taking thirteen horses, a

[chain mail] vest, several breastplates and other appurtenances, and native arms and armor.

{5} Don Lope de Gurrea[38] [is taking] five horses, [1v] native arms and armor, Castilian armor, a helmet, and elk hide armor.

{4} Hernando de Alvarado, captain of artillery, [is taking] four horses, a [chain mail] vest with sleeves, native arms and armor, and other appurtenances, and native arms and armor.[39]

{3} Don Alonso Manrique [de Lara][40] [is taking] three horses, native arms and armor, Castilian arms and armor, head armor, and an elk hide jacket.

{7} Juan Gallego [is taking] a [chain mail] vest, [chain mail] breeches, an elk hide jacket, a crossbow, other native and Castilian arms and armor, and seven horses.

{3} Salinas, son of Andrés de Salinas, *estante* of [the Ciudad de] México, [is taking] three horses, a chain mail vest, native arms and armor, and head armor.

{3} Rodrigo de Frías [is taking] three horses, native arms and armor, and an elk hide jacket.

[2r]
{78}
{3} Francisco de Santillan[a][41] [is taking] two horses and a mare, an elk hide jacket, [and] native arms and armor.

{3}   Andrés de Campo[42] [is taking] three horses, native arms and armor, and an elk hide jacket.

{3}   Alonso de Velasco [is taking] three horses, native arms and armor, a [chain mail] vest, and a helmet.

{1}   Lope Gallego [is taking] one horse, an arquebus, [and] native arms and armor.

{2}   Antón Delgado [is taking] two horses, native arms and armor, and head armor.

{1}   Velasco [is taking] one horse, one [set of] harness, [and] native arms and armor.

{1}   Francisco de Simancas [is taking] one horse and native arms and armor.

{1}   Marco Romano [is taking] one horse and native arms and armor.

{1}   Juan Pérez, a native of Aragón, [is taking] one horse and native arms and armor.

{1}   Francisco Muñoz [is taking] one horse and native arms and armor.

{1}   Juan de Peña[s][43] [is taking] one horse and native arms and armor.

{1}   Martín de Estepa [is taking] one horse and native arms and armor.

{1}   Cristóbal de la Hoz [is taking] one horse and native arms and armor.

{1}   Andrés Berrugo [is taking] one horse and native arms and armor.

{1}   Gómez Román [is taking] one horse and native arms and armor.

{1}   Cristóbal Velasco [is taking] one horse [and] native arms and armor.

{1}   Pero Méndez de Sotomayor [is taking] one horse and two sets of native arms and armor.[44]

{4}   Gómez Suárez[45] de Figueroa [is taking] four horses, native arms and armor, a sallet, a beaver, and several breastplates.[46]

{4}   Juan Bautista de San Vitores [is taking] a [chain mail] vest, a sallet, a beaver, [an elk hide] jacket, native arms and armor, and four horses.

{110}[47]

[2v]

{5}   García del Castillo [is taking] five horses, an elk hide jacket, a chain mail vest, [and] a gauntlet.

{3}   Alonso de Canseco [is taking] three horses, a [chain mail] vest, an elk hide jacket, [and] native arms and armor.

{4}   Melchior Pérez [is taking] four horses, a chain mail jacket, an elk hide jacket, [and] native arms and armor.

{4}   Domingo Martín [is taking] four horses, a chain mail jacket, another of elk hide, a corselet,[48] [and] native arms and armor.

{2}   Lope de la Cadena [is taking] two horses [and] native arms and armor.

{2}   Melchior de Robles [is taking] two horses, a sallet, a beaver, native arms and armor, [and] an elk hide jacket.

{1}   Andrés Martín [is taking] one horse [and] native arms and armor.

{1}   Pedro de Écija [is taking] one horse, a helmet, a beaver, [and] native arms and armor.

{2} Pedro Linares [is taking] two horses and native arms and armor.

{2} Juan de Ramos [is taking] two horses and native arms and armor.

{5} Pedro de Ledesma [is taking] five horses, a [chain mail] vest, a beaver, a sallet, [and] native arms and armor.

{12} Captain don García López de Cárdenas [is taking] twelve horses, three sets of Castilian arms and armor, two pairs of breastplates,[49] [and] a chain mail vest.

{5} Juan Navarro [is taking] five horses, a chain mail vest, native arms and armor, a sallet, [and] a beaver.

{2} Alonso del Moral, *alférez* of this company, [is taking] two horses, a beaver, a sallet, [and] native arms and armor.

{155}[50]

[3r]

{5} Rodrigo de Ysla [is taking] five horses, native arms and armor, a [chain mail] vest, and other arms and armor.

{3} Juan López [is taking] three horses [and] native arms and armor.

{2} Francisco Gómez [is taking] two horses, native arms and armor, a crossbow, and a dagger.

{1} Hernando Botello [is taking] one horse [and] native arms and armor.

{3} maestre Miguel and his son [are taking] three horses, a chain mail vest, a chain mail doublet, [and] a helmet; and his son [is taking] native arms and armor, a beaver, and a sallet.

{6} Captain Diego Gutiérrez de la Caballeria[51] [is taking] six horses, a [chain mail] vest, some wide chain mail breeches,[52] an elk hide jacket, [and] three [sets] of native arms and armor.

{6} Juan de Villareal,[53] *alférez*, [is taking] six horses, a corselet, a sallet, a beaver, a chain mail jacket, [and] native arms and armor.

{4} Alonso López [is taking] four horses, a sallet, a beaver, [and] native arms and armor.

{2} Gerónimo de Estrada[54] [is taking] two horses, native arms and armor, a chain mail vest, [and] an elk hide jacket.

{2} Pero Boo [is taking] two horses, native arms and armor, [and] an elk hide jacket.

{1} Francisco de Parada [is taking] one horse, native arms and armor, [and] an elk hide jacket.

{2} Gonzalo[55] Hernández [is taking] two horses, an elk hide jacket, [and] native arms and armor.

{1} Baltasar de Acevedo [is taking] one horse [and] native arms and armor.

{2} Miguel Sánchez [is taking] one horse, one mare, [and] native arms and armor.

{1} Alonso Martín Parra [is taking] one horse and native arms and armor.

{5} Juan Gómez de Paradinas [is taking] five horses, a [chain mail] vest, a helmet, [and] native arms and armor.

{201}[56]

[3v]

{7} Captain Diego López, one of the 24 councilmen of Sevilla,[57] [is taking] seven horses, a chain mail jacket with its appurtenances, a beaver, [and] native arms and armor.

{2} Francisco de Castro [is taking] two horses, an elk hide jacket, [and] native arms and armor.

{1} Rodrigo de Escobar [is taking] one horse [and] native arms and armor.

{2} Diego de Morilla [is taking] two horses [and] native arms and armor.

{1} Nofre[58] Hernández [is taking] one horse [and] native arms and armor.

{1} Martín Hernández [is taking] one horse [and] native arms and armor.

{1} Pero Hernández [is taking] one horse [and] native arms and armor.

{1} Alonso de Aranda [is taking] one horse [and] native arms and armor.

{2} Graviel[59] López [is taking] two horses, native arms and armor, a beaver, and a sallet.

{3} Bartolomé Napolitano [is taking] three horses [and] native arms and armor.

{5} Captain don Rodrigo Maldonado [is taking] five horses, a chain mail vest with its appurtenances, wide [chain mail] breeches, a beaver, a sallet, [and] native arms and armor.

{5} Juan de Torquemada, *alférez*, [is taking] five horses, a [chain mail] vest, a helmet, and native arms and armor.

{2} Francisco Gutiérrez [is taking] two horses, native arms and armor, [and] a sallet.

{2} Sancho Rodríguez [is taking] two horses, native arms and armor, [and] an elk hide jacket.

{1} Alonso de Medina [is taking] one horse [and] native arms and armor.

{1} Hernando de Barahona [is taking] one horse [and] native arms and armor.

{1} Leonardo Sánchez [is taking] an elk hide jacket, a helmet, native arms and armor, [and] one horse.

{1} [Juan de] Cepeda[60] [is taking] one horse [and] native arms and armor.

{3} Antón Miguel [is taking] three horses [and] native arms and armor.

{1} Gaspar de Guadalupe [is taking] one horse [and] native arms and armor.

{2} Hernando de Castroverde [is taking] two horses, native arms and armor, an elk hide jacket, and a pack frame.[61]

{246}[62]

[4r]

{8} Captain don Tristán de Arellano [is taking] eight horses, a jacket, sleeves and wide breeches of mail, native arms and armor, some plate armor, a sallet, a beaver, an arquebus, two crossbows, a two-handed sword, three [other] swords, and other arms and armor for himself and his *criados*.[63]

{5} Alonso Pérez [de Bocanegra] [is taking] five horses, a chain mail vest and jacket, and native arms and armor.

{3} Juan de Solis Farfán [is taking] three horses [and] native arms and armor.

{1} Francisco Rodríguez [is taking] one horse, native arms and armor, [and] a sallet.

{2} Jorge Báez[64] [is taking] two horses [and] native arms and armor.

{1} Miguel de Castro [is taking] one horse [and] native arms and armor.

{2} Miguel Sánchez de Plasencia [is taking] two horses, an elk hide jacket, [and] native arms and armor.

{3} Pedro Nieto [is taking] three horses, a [chain mail] vest, [and] native arms and armor.

{5} Captain don Diego de Guevara [is taking] five horses, an elk hide jacket, a sallet, [and] native arms and armor.

{3} Diego Hernández, *alférez*, [is taking] three horses, a [chain mail] vest, [and] native arms and armor.

{4} Pedro Mayoral [is taking] four horses, a chain mail jacket with its skirts,[65] a beaver, a sallet, [and] native arms and armor.

{1} Francisco de Olivares [is taking] one horse [and] native arms and armor.

{1} Cristóbal Gutiérrez [is taking] one horse [and] native arms and armor.

{1} Andrés Pérez [is taking] one horse [and] native arms and armor.

{3} Gonzalo de Castilla [is taking] three horses and native arms and armor.

{2} Pedro de [Castañeda de] Nájera[66] [is taking] two horses, a chain mail jacket, [and] native arms and armor.

{2} Luis Hernández [is taking] two horses, a chain mail jacket, a gorget,[67] a beaver, [and] native arms and armor.

{293}[68]

[4v]

{5} Alonso González, *alférez*,[69] [is taking] five horses, a chain mail vest, an elk hide jacket, [and] native arms and armor.

{3} Alonso de Paradinas [is taking] three horses, a chain mail vest, an elk hide jacket, a beaver, a sallet, [and] native arms and armor.

{2} Cristóbal Caballero [is taking] two horses, several breastplates, a helmet, a beaver, [and] native arms and armor.

{2} Pero Hernández [is taking] two horses, native arms and armor, a sallet, [and] an elk hide jacket.

{3} Francisco de Pobares[70] [is taking] three horses, an elk hide jacket, a chain mail vest, [and] native arms and armor.

{2} Antón García [is taking] two horses [and] native arms and armor.

{2} Pedro Márquez [is taking] two horses and native arms and armor.

{1} Martín Hernández [is taking] one horse [and] an elk hide jacket.

{2} Alonso Maldonado [is taking] two horses [and] native arms and armor.

{2} Juan Paniagua[71] [is taking] two horses, native arms and armor, a [chain mail] vest, and a sallet.

{1} Pero González[72] [is taking] one horse [and] native arms and armor.

{1} Antonio Álvarez [is taking] one horse [and] native arms and armor.

{1} Fernánd González[73] [is taking] one horse [and] native arms and armor.

{1} Manuel Hernández [is taking] one horse and native arms and armor.

{1} Bartolomé del Campo [is taking] one horse and native arms and armor.

{2} Francisco González[74] [is taking] two horses and native arms and armor.

{2} Cristóbal Maldonado [is taking] two horses [and] native arms and armor.

{3} Juan de Contreras [is taking] three horses and native arms and armor.

{3} Juan Galeras [is taking] three horses, a [chain mail] vest, native arms and armor, [and] a beaver.

{4} Francisco Calderón [is taking] four horses, a [chain mail] vest, [and] native arms and armor.

{333}[75]

[5r][76]

{3} Velasco de Barrionuevo [is taking] three horses, a chain mail vest, an elk hide jacket, [and] native arms and armor.

{2} Rodrigo de Barrionuevo, his brother, [is taking] two horses, head armor,[77] and native [armor].

{5} Luis [Ramírez] de Vargas[78] [is taking] five horses, a chain mail vest, head armor, [and] native arms and armor.

{5} Francisco de Ovando[79] [is taking] five horses, a [chain mail] vest, head armor, [and] native arms and armor.

{1} Fernán González[80] with native arms and armor [and] one horse.

{2} Fernán Páez [is taking] two horses [and] native arms and armor.

{2} Gaspar de Saldaña [is taking] two horses and native armor.

{3} Juan Jaramillo[81] [is taking] three horses, native arms and armor, [and] a corselet.

{3} Juan de Villegas [is taking] three horses, a [chain mail] vest, an elk hide jacket, native armor, and bent head [armor].[82]

{2} Pedro de Vargas [is taking] two horses, an elk hide jacket, native armor, and head [armor].

{1} Rodrigo de Paz [Maldonado][83] [is taking] one horse, native arms and armor, [and] an elk hide jacket.

{2} Sebastián de Soto [is taking] two horses, an elk hide jacket, native arms and armor, and head [armor].

{2} Francisco Gorbalán [is taking] two horses and native arms and armor.

{2} Francisco de Caravajal [is taking] two horses [and] native arms and armor.

{3} Lope de la Cadena[84] [is taking] three horses and native arms and armor.

{3} Pedro de Benavides [is taking] three horses, native arms and armor, an elk hide jacket, head armor, and a chain mail vest.

{2} Cristóbal de Mayorga [is taking] two horses, an elk hide jacket, [and] native arms and armor.

{2} Juan de Benavides [is taking] two horses, an elk hide jacket, [and] native arms and armor.

{3} Luis de Escobedo [is taking] three horses, a chain mail vest, an elk hide jacket, and native head armor.

{2} Juan de Ribadeneyra [is taking] two horses, an elk hide jacket, [and] native arms and armor.

{383}[85]

[5v]

{2}   Hernando de Valle [is taking] two horses, an elk hide jacket, [and] native arms and armor.

{1}   Andrés de Miranda [is taking] one horse [and] native arms and armor.

{3}   Antonio de Riber[os][86] [is taking] three horses, native arms and armor, an elk hide jacket, and head armor.

{1}   García Rodríguez [is taking] one horse and native arms and armor.

{2}   Pedro [López] de Urrea[87] [is taking] two horses, native arms and armor, [and] an elk hide jacket.

{1}   Cristóbal Pérez[88] from Ávila [is taking] one horse and native arms and armor.

{1}   Luis de Pigredo [is taking] one horse and native arms and armor.

{7}   Juan Pérez de Vergara [is taking] seven horses, a mule, a jacket and breeches of chain mail, a beaver, a sallet, a gauntlet, native arms and armor, two arquebuses, and a crossbow.

{4}   Martín de Villarroya [is taking] four horses, a chain mail vest, [and] native arms and armor.

{1}   Juan de Beteta [is taking] one horse and native arms and armor.

{2}   Andrés de Covarrubias [is taking] two horses, native arms and armor, a chain mail vest, head armor, and a beaver.

{2}   Miguel de Entrambasaguas [is taking] two horses, chain mail sleeves, [and] native arms and armor.

{1}   Diego de Puelles [is taking] one horse [and] native arms and armor.

{1}   Juan de Bustamante [is taking] one horse and native arms and armor.

{1}   Juan Vaca [is taking] one horse and native arms and armor.

{3}   Gerónimo Ramos[89] [is taking] three horses and native arms and armor.

{2}   Florián Bermúdez [is taking] two horses and native arms and armor.

{1}   Pero Álvarez [is taking] one horse and native arms and armor.

{2}   Rodrigo de Vera [is taking] two horses and native arms and armor.

{2}   Diego de Cervatos[90] [is taking] two horses, a chain mail vest, wide [chain mail] breeches, and native arms and armor.

{1}   Rosele Vázquez de Garivel[91] [is taking] one horse and native arms and armor.

{3}   Juan Franco de Mentre [is taking] three horses, an elk hide jacket, wide [chain mail] breeches, and native arms and armor.

{427}[92]

[6r]

{2}   Juan Pastor [is taking] two horses, native arms and armor, head armor, and a beaver.

{3}   Rodrigo de Tamarán [is taking] three horses, native arms and armor, an elk hide jacket, and head armor.

{1}   Pascual Bernal de Molina [is taking] one horse and an elk hide jacket.

{1}   Juan Rodríguez from Alanje[93] [is taking] one horse, native arms, [and] an elk hide jacket.

{2}　　Francisco de Temiño [is taking] two horses and native arms and armor.

{1}　　Juan de Gastaca[94] [is taking] one horse, native arms and armor, and an elk hide jacket.

{1}　　Alonso Esteban de Mérida [is taking] one horse and native arms and armor.

{3}　　Cristóbal de Quesada [is taking] three horses, a chain mail vest, and native arms and armor.

{2}　　Lorenzo Álvarez [is taking] two horses, native arms and armor, [several pieces of] head armor, and an elk hide jacket.

{5}　　Domingo Alonso [is taking] five horses, an elk hide jacket, [and] native arms and armor.

{2}　　Cristóbal de Escobar [is taking] two horses, a chain mail vest, native armor, and head [armor].

{1}　　Florián de Mazuela [is taking] one horse and native arms and armor.

{1}　　Pero Sánchez from El Barco de Ávila[95] [is taking] one horse and native arms and armor.

{1}　　Francisco de Alcántara [is taking] one horse and native arms and armor.

{3}　　Juan López [de la Rosa] from Sayago[96] [is taking] three horses, native arms and armor, [and] an elk hide jacket.

{1}　　Francisco de Padilla [is taking] one horse and native arms and armor.

{2}　　Pero Martín Cano [is taking] two horses and native arms and armor.

{3}　　Diego de Madrid [Avendaño][97] [is taking] three horses and native arms and armor.

{1}　　Alonso de Sayavedra [is taking] one horse, an elk hide jacket, native arms and armor, and head [armor].

{2}　　Simón García [is taking] two horses, an elk hide jacket, and native arms and armor.

{1}　　Francisco Gómez [is taking] one horse and native arms and armor.

{1}　　Luis de la Chica [is taking] one horse and native arms and armor.

{1}　　Diego Núñez de Garveña[98] [is taking] one horse and native arms and armor.

{1}　　Hernando de Alba [is taking] one horse, an elk hide jacket, and native arms and armor.

{469}[99]

[6v]

{1}　　Cristóbal García [is taking] one horse and native arms and armor.

{1}　　Diego del Castillo [is taking] one horse and native arms and armor.

{1}　　Juan Rodríguez de Ávalos [is taking] one horse and native arms and armor.

{2}　　Pedro de Ortega [is taking] two horses, an elk hide jacket, [and] native arms and armor.

{2}　　Juan de Céspedes [is taking] two horses and native arms and armor.

{2}　　Martín Sánchez [is taking] two horses and native arms and armor.

{1}　　Francisco Martín [is taking] one horse and native arms and armor.

{2}   Juan Jiménez[100] [is taking] two horses, native arms and armor, [and] an elk hide jacket.

{1}   Pedro de Benavente [is taking] one horse, an elk hide jacket, and native arms and armor.

{1}   Rodrigo de Trujillo [is taking] one horse, an elk hide jacket, and native arms and armor.

{2}   Diego Sánchez from Fromista[101] [is taking] two horses and native arms and armor.

{1}   Alonso de Valencia [is taking] one horse and native arms and armor.

{2}   Bartolomé Serrano [is taking] two horses, native arms and armor, and an elk hide jacket.

{4}   Machín de Castañeda[102] [is taking] four horses, [several pieces of] head armor with their beaver[s], native arms and armor, a chain mail vest, [and] an elk hide jacket.

{2}   Francisco de Valdivieso [is taking] two horses, native arms and armor, and a helmet.

{7}   Alonso Sánchez and his son [are taking] seven horses, native arms and armor, and chain mail vests.

{2}   Juan Martín from Fuente de la Maestre[103] [is taking] two horses and native arms and armor.

{503}[104]

[7r]

{1}   Cristóbal Hernández Moreno [is taking] one horse and native arms.

{1}   Gonzalo Vázquez [is taking] one horse and native arms and armor.

{2}   Juan Cordero [is taking] two horses and native arms and armor.

{1}   Pero López from Ciudad Real[105] [is taking] one horse and native arms and armor.

{4}   Sancho Ordóñez [is taking] four horses, a chain mail jacket, [and] native arms and armor.

{2}   Julián de Sámano [is taking] two horses, a corselet, a chain mail jacket, two elk hide jackets, native arms and armor, and head armor.

{2}   Alonso González [is taking] two horses and native arms and armor.

{2}   Hernán Gómez de la Peña[106] [is taking] two horses, native arms and armor, and a strong doublet.

{1}   Pero Jerónimo[107] [is taking] one horse and a lance.

{1}   Pero Hernández Calvo [is taking] one horse and a lance.

{2}   Diego Núñez de Mirandilla [is taking] two horses and a chain mail vest.

{3}   Francisco Rojo Loro [is taking] three horses, native arms and armor, and head armor.

{1}   Andrés Hernández from Encinasola[108] [is taking] one horse and native arms and armor.

{2}   Miguel de Torres [is taking] two horses and native arms and armor.

{528}[109]

[7v][110]

{2}   Pedro Pascual [is taking] two horses, a chain mail vest, and native arms and armor.

{1}   [H]orta Homem,[111] a Portuguese, [is taking] one horse [and] native arms and armor.

{1}   Diego de Salamanca [is taking] one horse [and] native arms and armor.

{1}   Gaspar Álvarez, a Portuguese, [is taking] one horse [and] native arms and armor.

{1}   Cristóbal Gallego [is taking] one horse and native arms and armor.

{1}   Domingo Romero [is taking] one horse, an elk hide jacket, and native arms and armor.

{2}   Pedro Navarro [is taking] two horses, a chain mail jacket, [and] native arms and armor.

{2}   Gonzalo de Arjona [is taking] two horses and native arms and armor.

{1}   Juan Fioz, a trumpeter, [is taking] one horse, a corselet, an elk hide jacket, and native arms and armor.

{4}   Hernando [Martín] Bermejo[112] [is taking] four horses, native arms and armor, and an elk hide jacket.

Footmen

Captain Pablo de Melgosa [was] absent because he had not arrived from [the Ciudad de] México.

Lorenzo Genovés[113] [is taking] an arquebus and native arms and armor.
[{552}][114]

[8r]

Francisco de Espinosa [is taking] an arquebus and native arms and armor.

Alonso Jiménez [is taking] an arquebus [and] native arms and armor.

Juan de Salamanca [is taking] an arquebus and native arms and armor.

Francisco de Godoy [is taking] a round shield, sword, [and] native arms and armor.

Juan de Santovaya, a Galician, [is taking] an arquebus and native arms and armor.

Juan de Duero[115] [is taking] an arquebus, sword, dagger, and native arms and armor.

Domingo Ruiz [is taking] an arquebus, sword, [and] native arms and armor.

Juan Barbero [is taking] an arquebus, sword, dagger, and native arms and armor.

Diego Díaz from Santo Domingo[116] [is taking] a sword, round shield, [and] native arms and armor.

Francisco de Vargas [is taking] a sword, round shield, and native arms and armor.

Roque Álvarez [is taking] a crossbow, sword, and elk hide jacket.

Rodrigo de Gámez[117] [is taking] a sword and dagger.

Juan Francés [is taking] a sword and round shield.

Hernán García from Llerena [is taking] a crossbow, sword, dagger, and native arms and armor.

Juan Martín [Bermejo] from Fuente del Arco[118] [is taking] a crossbow, chain mail vest, and native arms and armor.

[8v]

Rodrigo Álvarez from Zafra[119] [is taking] a crossbow and a sword.

Alonso Millero, a Galician, [is taking] a crossbow, a sword, and native arms and armor.

Andrés Martín, a Portuguese, [is taking] a crossbow, a sword, and native arms and armor.

Juan de Vallarra [is taking] a sword, dagger, round shield, and native arms and armor.

Antonio de Laredo [is taking] a crossbow, a sword, [and] native arms and armor.

Juan Bermejo [is taking] a crossbow, sword, dagger, and native arms and armor.

{1}   Miguel Sánchez [is taking] a crossbow, sword, one horse, and native arms and armor.

Pero Martín de la Bermeja [is taking] a crossbow, sword, dagger, [and] native arms and armor.

{1}   Juan Morillo [is taking] one horse, a sword, round shield, [and] native arms and armor.

Alonso Vos from Ribadeo[120] [is taking] a sword, round shield, and native arms and armor.

Pedro de Talavera [is taking] a sword, round shield, chain mail sleeves, [and] native arms and armor.

Martín Alonso de Astorga [is taking] a sword and native arms and armor.

Pero Hernández de Guadalajara [is taking] an arquebus, sword, and dagger.

Martín Hernández Chillon [is taking] a elk hide jacket, sword, and native arms and armor.

Baltasar de Zamora [is taking] a sword, round shield, and native arms and armor.

[{554}][121]

[9r][122]

Antón Martín [is taking] a crossbow, sword, [and] native arms and armor.

Diego de Medina [is taking] a sword, round shield, crossbow, [and] native arms and armor.

Gulliver [is taking] an elk hide jacket, sword, and corselet.

Diego de Candía [is taking] an arquebus, sword, and round shield.

Miguel Hernández [is taking] a sword, round shield, and native arms and armor.

Jaco de Bruges [is taking] a sword, arquebus, and a round shield.

Esteban Martín [is taking] an arquebus, sword, [and] native arms and armor.

{2}   Miguel de Fuenterabia [is taking] two horses, three swords, and a round shield.

Francisco López [is taking] an elk hide jacket, a broadsword, [another] sword, and a dagger.

{1}   Francisco Górez[123] [is taking] one horse, a sword, and a round shield.

Gaspar Rodríguez [is taking] an arquebus, sword, and native arms and armor.

Bartolomé de [Cés]pedes [is taking] a sword, a dagger, a crossbow, and native arms and armor.

Juan Vizcaíno [Guernica] [is taking] a sword, a dagger, a sword, [and] native arms and armor.[124]

Pedro de Alcántara [is taking] a crossbow, a sword, [and] native arms and armor.

Gonzalo Yáñez [is taking] a round shield, sword, and native arms and armor.

{1} *Alférez* Pedro Ramos [is taking] an arquebus, sword, and one horse.

Lázaro, a drummer, [is taking] a sword and native arms and armor.

Antón Ruiz [is taking] an arquebus.

Juan de Celada [is taking] an arquebus.

Francisco de Villafranca [is taking] an arquebus [and] native arms and armor.

Juan de Plasencia [is taking] an arquebus [and] native arms and armor.

Francisco Gómez [is taking] an arquebus, a helmet, and native arms and armor.

Bartolomé Sánchez [is taking] a sword and a round shield.
[{558}][125]

[9v]

Alonso Hernández [is taking] native arms and armor, a round shield, and a sword.

Pedro de Trujillo [is taking] an arquebus [and] native arms and armor.

Miguel de Torrez [is taking] an arquebus, sword, [and] native arms and armor.

Alonso Álvarez [del Valle] [is taking] an arquebus, an elk hide jacket, [and] native arms and armor.

Francisco Martín [is taking] a crossbow, sword, [and] native arms and armor.

García de Perea [is taking] a round shield, sword, [and] native arms and armor.

Diego de Mata [is taking] a sword and a round shield.

Graviel Hernández[126] [is taking] a sword, a round shield, and native arms and armor.

552; [the] horses number five hundred and fifty-two [558].[127]

These horsemen were carrying their lances, swords, and other arms, in addition to the arms and armor declared [above]. The horsemen total two hundred and thirty-odd [226],[128] besides and in addition to those who are going ahead in the company of the religious[129] and those who are expected from [the Ciudad de] México, who are going on this trip and expedition.

The footmen number sixty-two [63] men,[130] [who are going] with the aforesaid arms and armor, in addition to the other native arms and armor which were given to them, plus the rest of the people whom the viceroy was sending [and] who are traveling by sea and by land.

[10r] When the people had been thus reviewed, inspected, and examined by his lordship, the captain general, *maestre de campo, alférez mayor,* captains, and *caballeros* named and declared above appeared before his lordship. And they declared that because they are motivated with proper zeal to go on this expedition in the service of God and His Majesty and to work and strive, in his royal name, during it to do what they ought to in his royal service, [and] since they were overflowing with this eagerness, they requested and petitioned his illustrious lordship [that] he allow and order them (like the rest of the people) to swear the formal oath which is required in such a case and [for such a] journey. [This was] so that they might do better and more truly what they ought as good vassals and servants of His Majesty, since thus it binds [them] to his royal service.

Immediately Captain General Francisco Vázquez de Coronado swore by Almighty God, by his Holy Mother, by a cross which was there, and by the words of the Holy Gospels (upon which he physically placed his right hand in a missal in the hands of Reverend Father fray Francisco de Vitoria,[131] a professed brother of the Order of the Lord San Francisco) that he will exercise the office of captain general (to which he has been appointed by his lordship in His Majesty's name for the aforementioned expedition and land) as a good Christian, vassal, and servant of His Majesty. And he will act in the service of God and His Majesty. As a good *caballero hidalgo* must do, he will, to the best of his knowledge and judgment, obey and fulfill [the king's] directives and [those] of the lord viceroy in his royal name.

Then the *maestre de campo, alférez mayor,* captains, *caballeros,* and the rest of the people gave their oaths, [10v] each one for himself [and] in the form required by law, exactly as described above, placing their right hands on the cross and book. Under this obligation they promised to be obedient to Francisco Vázquez de Coronado, their captain general, and to any other captain general whom His Majesty or the aforesaid lord viceroy, in his royal name, might commission. And [they pledged] not to abandon their captaincies and banners without his royal

order. And [further] that they will do everything they are obligated to do as good captains, people, [and] vassals of His Majesty.

This took place in the presence of his lordship, the aforementioned *caballeros,* and persons mentioned above, and in the presence of me, Juan de Cuevas, *escribano mayor* of Their Majesties' mines.

In confirmation of this and by order of the illustrious lord viceroy of Nueva España, I drew up the present muster roll in the *ciudad* of Compostela on the twenty-seventh day of the month of February in [the year] one thousand five hundred and forty. It is set down in writing on ten folios of paper in manuscript.

Juan de Cuevas {rubric}

[11r] [blank]

[11v]
{Muster; Compostela, 1540}
{The muster which was conducted of the people whom the viceroy sent to Cíbola}
{Cíbola men-at-arms}

TRANSCRIPTION

[fol. 1r]

Yo Juan de cueVas es*cri*vano m*a*yor de mynas ^*E relaçiones* de
*e*sta nueva *e*spaña por / su mag*esta*d digo e doy ffee que en la
çiudad de Compostella de la / nueVa galizia de la nueva
*e*spaña estando p*re*sent*e* El Yll*ustrisi*mo señor / don antonio
d*e* mendoca Visorrey e gover*nad*or d*e e*sta nueva *e*spaña por
su m*a*gestad / E gonçalo de salazar ffactor e peralmydez
cherino Veedor d*e* la d*i*cha / nueva *e*spana y *cristo*val d*e* oñate
Veedor d*e* la d*i*cha p*ro*Vinçia e otra / mucha gente se hizo El
alard*e* de toda la gente q*ue* Va a la ti*e*rra nuevame*n*te / d*e*scu-
bierta por el padre prov*y*nçi*a*l frai marcos d*e* nyça de que Va
por capi- / tan gen*e*rAl Fran*cis*co Vazqu*e*z d*e* coronado El
qual d*i*cho alarde se hizo / en veynt*e* e dos dias del mes de
hebre*r*o de myll E q*uiniento*s e quare*n*ta anos / siendo
p*re*sent*e* el s*e*ñor liç*enci*ado maldonado oidor *en* la forma e
manera sig*uient*e

{xxiij} Capitan general Fran*cis*co Vazquez de coronado /
Juro q*ue* lleva en esta dicha Jornada / en serv*y*çio de
su magestad Veynte e dos o / Veynt*e* e tres Cavallos
E tres o / quatro ad*e*reços de armas de la brida y d*e*
la gineta

{xvij} {+} El maestre de Campo lope de Samaniego al(l)*cay*de
/ Juro q*ue* lleva diez e seis o diez e siete Cavallos / e
dos cueras d*e* a(m)*n*ta e Una co(c)ta d*e* malla / sus
ad*e*reços y Unas coraças e armas d*e* la / Ti*e*rra porq*ue*
Lo demas q*ue* traia se le quemo

{xiij} {+} don pedro de toVar alferez mayor Juro / llevar Treze
Cavallos Una co(c)ta e Unas cora- / ças e otros
ad*e*reços e armas d*e* la ti*e*rra

{+} don lope de gurrea Çinco Cavallos y

[fol. 1v]

{V} armas d*e* la ti*e*rra e armaduras d*e* Castilla / E d*e*
Cabeca e d*e* cuera de anta

{iiij} {+} Hernando d*e* alvarado Capitan del arti- / lleria
quatro Cavallos Una co(c)ta e man- / gas y armas d*e*
la ti*e*rra e otros ad*e*reÇos / E armas d*e* la ti*e*rra

{iiij} {+} don alonsso manrrique Tres Cavallos / armas d*e* la
Ti*e*rra y armas de Castilla / e p*ar*a Cabeca y cuera
de anta

{Vij} {+} Juan gallego Una co(c)ta e calçones / E Una cuera
de anta e una ballesTa / E otras armas de Castilla e
d*e* la / Ti*e*rra e siet*e* Cavallos

{iiij} {+} SAlinas hijo de andres de Salinas / estant*e* en
mexico Tres Cavallos / Una co(c)ta de malla y armas
d*e* la ti*e*rra / E p*ar*a la Cabeça

{*iii*} {+} Rodrigo de Frias tres Cavallos / armas d*e* la ti*e*rra
e Una cuera de / anta

{rúbrica}

[fol. 2r]

{78}

{iiij} {+} Fran*cis*co de santillan dos caVallos e Una yegua
cuera d*e* anta / armas d*e* la Ti*e*rra

{iiij} {+} andres de campo tres caVallos Armas d*e* la / Tierra
y Una cuera de anta

{iij} {+} alonso d*e* Velasco tres caVallos E armas d*e* la / T*ie*rra co(c)ta e Un caxco

{j} {+} lope gallego Un cavallo Un arcabuz armas d*e* la t*ie*rra

{ij} {+} anton delgado dos CaVallos armas d*e* la t*ie*rra e para / la cab*e*za

{j} {+} Velasco Un cav*all*o y un arnes Armas d*e* la t*ie*rra

{j} {+} Fran*cis*co d*e* symancas Un cavallo y armas de la t*ie*rra

{j} {+} marco Romano Un cav*all*o y armas de la t*ie*rra

{j} {+} Juan perez aragones Un cavallo y armas de la t*ie*rra

{j} {+} Fran*cis*co munoz (^e) Un cav*all*o y armas de la T*ie*rra

{j} {+} Juan de pena Un cavallo e armas d*e* la t*ie*rra

{j} {+} m*art*yn d*e e*stepa Un cavallo y armas d*e* la t*ie*rra

{j} {+} *crist*oval de la hoz Un cav*all*o y armas de la T*ie*rra

{j} {+} andres berrugo Un cav*all*o e armas de la t*ie*rra

{j} {+} gomez Roman Un cavallo e armas d*e* la t*ie*rra

{j} {+} *crist*oval Velasco Un cav*all*o Armas d*e* la t*ie*rra

{j} {+} pero mendez de sotomayor Un cavallo e armas de la t*ie*rra dos p*are*s

{(^j)} {iiij} {+} gomez Xuarez de Figueroa q*u*atro caVallos armas / d*e* la T*ie*rra Çelada e barbote y Unas coraças

{iiij} {+} Juan (^p)^*ba*utista[132] de san Vitore(e)s Una co(c)ta e Una çelada e / Un barbote e Una cuera e armas d*e* la t*ie*rra e quatro caV*all*os

{110}

{rúbrica}

[fol. 2v]

{110}

{V} {+} garÇia del castillo Çinco Cavallos Una cuera d*e* anta Una / co(c)ta de malla Una manopla

{iiij} {+} alonso de Canseco Tres caVallos e Una co(c)ta e Una cuera / de anta armas d*e* la t*ie*rra

{iiij} {+} melchior perez q*u*atro caVallos Una cuera d*e* malla e cuera / d*e* a(m)*n*ta armas de la tierra

{iiij} {+} domingo m*art*yn quatro caVallos Una cuera d*e* malla / otra d*e* anta Un cos*ele*te[133] armas de la t*ie*rra

{ij} {+} Lope de la cAdena dos cavallos armas d*e* la t*ie*rra

{ij} {+} melchior de rrobles dos caVallos e Una çelada / Un barbotte armas d*e* la t*ie*rra Una cuera de anta

{j} {+} Andres m*art*yn Un cav*all*o armas d*e* la Tierra

{j} {+} pedro de *e*Çija Un cav*all*o e Un caxco barbote armas / d*e* la Tierra

{ij} {+} pedro lynarez dos caVallos y armas d*e* la Tierra

{ij} {+} Juan d*e* rramos dos caVallos E armas d*e* la t*ie*rra

{V} {+} pedro de ledesma Çinco Cavallos Una co(c)ta Un barbote / Çelada armas d*e* la T*ie*rra

{Xij} Capitan don garçia lopez de cardenAs doze cavallos Tres parez de / armas de Castilla e dos pares d*e* coraças Una co(c)ta / de malla

{V} {+} Juan navarro Çinco cavallos Una cuera d*e* malla armas / d*e* la Tierra Una çelada Un barbotE

{ij} {+} alonso d*e*l moral alferez de esta compañia dos / cavallos Un barbote Una çelada armas de la t*ie*rra

{155}

{rúbrica}

[fol. 3r]

{155}

{V} {+} R*odrig*o de ysla Çinco Cavallos armas d*e* la t*ie*rra / Una co(c)ta e otras armas

{iiij} {+} Juan lopez (^d)tres cavallos armas d*e* la t*ie*rra

{ij} {+} Fran*cisc*o gomez dos cavallos armas d*e* la t*ie*rra / Una ballesta e Un puñal

{j} {+} her*nand*o botello Un cavallo armas d*e* la t*ie*rra

{iiij} {+} mae(e)stre myguel e su hijo tres cavallos / Una co(c)ta d*e* malla e Un Jubon d*e* malla caxco / e su hijo armas d*e* la t*ie*rra barbote e Çelada

{Vj} Capitan diego gutierrez d*e* la cavalleria seis cavallos Una co(c)ta / Unos caraguelles d*e* malla Una cuera d*e* anta / Tres armas d*e* la t*ie*rra

{Vj} {+} Juan de Villareal alferez seys cavallos Un coselete / Una çelada Un barbote Una cuera d*e* malla armas / d*e* la t*ie*rra

{iiij} {+} alonso lopez quatro Cavallos e Una çelada / Un barbote armas d*e* la Tierra

{ij} {+} Ger*oni*mo de estrada dos cavallos armas d*e* la t*ie*rra Una cota / de malla Una cuera de anta

{ij} {+} pero boo dos cavallos armas d*e* la t*ie*rra Una cuera d*e* anta

{j} {+} Fran*cisc*o d*e* parada Un cav*all*o armas d*e* la Tierra / Una cuera de antta

{ij} {+} gonza*l*o hernandez dos cavallos Una cuera d*e* anta armas d*e* la t*ie*rra

{j} {+} baltasar d*e* azeVedo Un cav*all*o armas d*e* la tierra

{ij} {+} myguel *sanch*es Un caVallo e Una yegua armas d*e* la t*ie*rra

{j} {+} al*ons*o m*art*yn parra Un cav*all*o y armas d*e* la Tierra

{V} {+} Juan gomez de paradinas Çinco Cavallos Un*a* cota Un caxco / armas d*e* la t*ie*rra

{201}

{rúbrica}

[fol. 3v]

{201} (^6)

{Vij} Capitan diego Lopez Veynte e quatro de Sevylla siete Cavallos Una / cuera d*e* malla con sus adereços Un barbote armas d*e* la t*ie*rra

{ij} {+} Fran*cisc*o de caStro dos cavallos Una cuera d*e* anta armas / d*e* la T*ie*rra

{j} R*odrig*o d*e* *e*scobar Un cav*all*o A*r*mas d*e* la Tierra

{ij} {+} diego d*e* morilla dos cav*all*os armas d*e* la t*ie*rra

{j} {+} *o*nofre hernandez Un cav*all*o armas d*e* la t*ie*rra

{j} {+} martin hernandez Un cav*all*o armas d*e* la t*ie*rra

{j} {+} Pero hernandez Un cav*all*o armas d*e* la t*ie*rra

{j} {+} alonSo d*e* aranda Un cav*all*o armas d*e* la t*ie*rra

{ij} {+} Gravyel lopez dos cavallos armas d*e* la t*ie*rra / Un barbote e çelada

{iiij} {+} bAr*tolo*me napolitAno Tres Cav*all*os armas d*e* la t*ie*rra

{V} Capitan don R*odrig*o maldonado Çinco cavallos Una cota de malla con sus / adereços e çaragu*e*lles barbote e Çelada armas d*e* la t*ie*rra

{V} {+} Juan de torquemada alferez Çinco Cavallos Una cotta / caxco y armas de la tierra

{ij} {+} Francisco gutierrez dos cavallos armas de la tierra Una çelada

{ij} {+} sancho Rodrigues dos cavallos armas de la tierra Una cuera de anta

{j} {+} alonSo de medina Un cavallo armas de la tierra

{j} {+} hernando de barahona Un cavallo armas de la tierra

{j} {+} leonardo Sanchez UnA cuera de anta caxco armas de la tierra / Un Cavallo

{j} {+} çepeda Un Cavallo armas de la tierra

{iij} {+} anton myguel tres cavallos armas de la tierra

{j} {+} gaspar de guadalupe Un cavallo armas de la tierra

{ij} {+} hernando de CaSoVerde dos cavallos y armas de la tierra / Una cuera de anta e Un bastidor

{246}

{rúbrica}

[fol. 4r]

{246}

{+} {scribal mark}

{Viij} Capitan don tristan de arellano ocho Cavallos Una cuera mangas y çaraguelles / de malla armas de la tierra Unas platas[134] Una çelada Un barbote / Un arcabuz dos ballestAs Una espada de dos manos tres espadas / E otras armas para sy e para sus criados

{V} {+} alonSo perez Çinco Cavallos Una co(c)ta y cuera de malla / E armas de la tierra

{iij} {+} Juan de Solis Farfan tres cavallos armas de la tierra

{j} {+} Francisco Rodriguez Un cavallo armas de la tierra Una çelada

{ij} {+} Jorge baez dos cavallos armas de la tierra

{j} {+} miguel(l) de castro Un cavallo armas de la tierra

{ij} {+} miguel sanches de plazençia dos cavallos Una cuera de anta Armas / de la tierra

{iij} {+} pedro nyeto tres cavallos Una cotta armas de la tierra

{V} Capitan don diego de guevara Çinco Cavallos Una cuera de antta Una çelada / armas de la tierra

{iij} {+} diego hernandez alferez tres cavallos Una co(c)ta armas / de la tierra

{iiij} {+} pedro mayoral quatro Cavallos Una cuera de malla y con Sus / Faldas Un barbote e Çelada armas de la tierra

{j} {+} Francisco de olyvarez Un cavallo armas de la tierra

{j} {+} cristoval gutierrez Un cavallo armas de la tierra

{j} {+} andres perez Un Cavallo armas de la tierra

{iiij} {+} goncalo de caStilla tres (^armas e) cavallos e armas de la tierra

{ij} {+} pedro de naJera dos cavallos Una cuera de malla armas / de la tierra

{jj} {+} luys hernandez dos cavallos Una cuera de malla gorxal / Un barbote armas de la tierra

{293}

{rúbrica}

[fol. 4v]

{293}

{V} {+} alonSo gonzales alferez Çinco Cavallos Una co(c)ta de malla / Una cuera de anta armas de la tierra {iij} {+} alonSo de paradinas tres cavallos Una cota de malla / Una cuera de antA barbote e çelada armas de la tierra

{ij} {+} *crist*oval Cav*allero* dos cavallos Unas coraças caxco Un barbote / armas de la Tierra

{ij} {+} pero hernandez dos caVallos armas de la tierra Una çelada / Una cuera de anta

{iij} {+} Fran*cisco* de povares Tres cav*allo*s Una cuera de antta Una co(c)ta de / malla armas de la tierra

{ij} {+} anton g*arci*a dos caVallos armas de la tierra

{ij} {+} pedro marq*uez* dos caVallos e armas de la tierra

{j} {+} martin hernandez Un cav*allo* Una cuera de anta

{ij} {+} alonSo maldonado dos caV*allo*s arma*s* de la tierra

{ij} {+} Juan panyagua dos caVallos e armas de la tierra Una co(c)ta / e Una çelada

{j} {+} pero go*nzale*s Un cav*allo* armas de la tierra

{j} {+} (^V)antonio alvarez Un cav*allo* armas de la tierra

{j} {+} Fe*r*nand go*nzale*s Un cav*allo* armas de la tierra

{j} {+} manuel hernandez Un cav*allo* E arma*s* de la tierra

{j} {+} b*artolo*me d*e*l canpo Un cav*allo* y armas de la tierra

{ij} {+} Francisco go*nzale*s dos caVallos y armas de la tierra

{ij} {+} *crist*oval maldonado dos caVallos armas de la tierra

{iij} {+} Juan de contreras tres cav*allo*s e armas de la tierra

{iij} {+} Juan galeras tres cav*allo*s Una co(c)ta armas de la tierra Un barbote

{iiij} {+} Fran*cisco* calderon quatro caVallos Una co(c)ta armas de la tierra

{333}
{rúbrica}

[fol. 5r]
{333}

{iij} {+} VelasCo de barrionueVo tres cavallos Una cota de malla una cuera de anta armas / de la tierra

{ij} {+} RodriGo de barrionueVo Su he*rman*o dos cavallos armaduras de cabeça y de la tierra

{V} {+} luys de Vargas çinco cavallos una Cotta de malla armaduras de cabeça armas / de la tierra

{V} {+} Fran*cisco* de ovando çinco cavallos Una cotta armadura de cabeça armas de la tierra

{j} {+} Fernan go*nzale*s con armas de la Tierra Un cav*allo*

{ij} {+} Fernan paez doss cavallos armas de la Tierra

{ij} {+} gaspar de saldaña dos cavallos y armaduras de la tierra

{iij} {+} Juan Xaramy*llo* Tres cavallos Armas de la Tierra Un coselete

{iiij} {+} Juan de Villegas tres cavallos Una cotta Una cuera de anta armaduras de la / Tierra y de la cabeça dobladas

{ij} {+} Pedro de Vargas dos cavallos Una cuera de anta armaduras de la tierra y de la cabeza

{j} {+} R*odrig*o de paz Un cavallo armas de la Tierra cuera de anta

{ij} {+} sebastian de soto dos cavallos y Una cuera de anta e armas de la Tierra / y de la cabeça {ij} {+}   Fran*cis*co gorvalan dos cavallos E armas de la T*ie*rra

{ij} {+}   Fran*cis*co de carava*J*al dos cavallos armas de la t*ie*rra

{iij} {+}   lope de la Cadena tres cavallos y armas de la t*ie*rra

{iij} {+}   Pedro de bena*V*ides tres cavallos armas de la t*ie*rra Una cuera d*e* anta / armadura de Cabeça y Una co(c)ta de mal*l*a

{ij} {+}   *cris*toval de mayorga dos cavallos Una cuera d*e* anta armas de la t*ie*rra

{ij} {+}   Juan de bena*V*ides dos cavallos Una Cuera d*e* anta armas de la t*ie*rra

{iij} {+}   luys de *es*Cobedo tres cavallos Una Cota de malla y cuera d*e* anta E Ar- / mas de cabeça de la t*ie*rra

{ij} {+}   Ju*an* de Ribadeneyra dos cavallos y Una cuera d*e* anta armas / de la t*ie*rra
{383}

[fol. 5v]
{383}
{ij} {+}   h*er*n*and*o de Valle do*S* cavallos Una cuera d*e* anta armas de la T*ie*rra

{j} {+}   Andres de miranda Un cavallo armas de la t*ie*rra

{iij} {+}   antonio de Ribera tres cavallos y armas de la t*ie*rra cuera d*e* anta y / armas de cabeça

{j} {+}   g*ar*cia Ro*drigu*es Un cavallo y armas de la t*ie*rra

{ij} {+}   Pedro de Urre(e)*a* dos cavallos E armas de la t*ie*rra Una cuera d*e* anta

{j} {+}   *cris*toval perez d*e* aVila Un cavallo y armas de la tierra

{j} {+}   luis de pigredo Un cav*all*o y armas de la T*ie*rra

{vij} {+}   Juan PereZ de Ve*r*gara siete cavallos y Una açemila y Una cuera y / calças de malla e Un barbote y çelada y Una manopla armas de la / T*ie*rra dos arcabuzes y Una ballesta

{iiij} {+}   m*art*yn de Villarroya quatro cavallos Una cota de malla armas de la t*ie*rra

{j} {+}   Juan de beteta Un cavallo y armas de la t*ie*rra

{ij} {+}   andres de coVarrubias dos cavallos y armas de la t*ie*rra / y cota de malla armaduras de Cabeça E barbote

{ij} {+}   miguel de entrambasaguas dos cavallos y mangas de malla armas / de la Tierra

{j} {+}   diego de puelles Un cav*all*o armas de la T*ie*rra

{j} {+}   Ju*an* de bustamante Un cavallo y armas de la t*ie*rra

{j} {+}   Ju*an* Vaca un cav*all*o y armas de la t*ie*rra

{iiij} {+}   Geronimo Ramos tres cavallos y armas de la t*ie*rra

{ij} {+}   floria*n* bermudez dos cavallos y armas de la T*ie*rra

{j} {+}   Pero alvarez Un cav*all*o y armas de la T*ie*rra

{ij} {+}   R*odrig*o de Vera dos cavallos y armas de la t*ie*rra

{ij} {+}   diego de çerVatos dos caVallos y Una cota de malla y caraguelles / y armas de la t*ie*rra

{j} {+}   Rosele Vazquez de garivel Un cavallo y armas de la T*ie*rra

{iiij} {+}   Juan Franco de mentre tres cavallos Una cuera d*e* anta çara- / guelles y armas de la t*ie*rra
{427}

[fol. 6r]

{427}

{ij} {+} Juan pastor dos cavallos armas de la ti*e*rra y armaduras de cabeça(^s) y barbote

{iij} {+} R*odrig*o de tamaran tres cavallos y armas de la T*ie*rra y Una cuera / d*e* anta y armaduras de Cabeça

{j} {+} pasCual bernaL de molina Un cavallo y Una cuera d*e* anta

{j} {+} Ju*an* Ro*drigu*es de alanJe un cavallo y armas de la ti*e*rra Una Cuera d*e* antta

{ij} {+} Fran*ci*sco de temiño dos cavallos y armas de la ti*e*rra

{j} {+} Juan de gaztaca Un cav*all*o y armas de la T*ie*rra y Una cuera d*e* anta

{j} {+} Alonso estevan de merida Un cav*all*o y armas de la Tierra

{iij} {+} *crist*obal de quesada tres cavallos y Un*a* cota de malla y armas de la ti*e*rra

{ij} {+} lor*enz*o alvareZ dos cavallos armas de la ti*e*rra y armaduras de cabeça y / Una cuera d*e* anta

{V} {+} domingo alonso çinco cavallos Una cuera de anta armas de la ti*e*rra

{ij} {+} *crist*oval de *es*Cobar dos cavallos cota de malla armaduras de la ti*e*rra y de cabeça

{j} {+} Florian de maçuela Un cavallo y armas de la T*ie*rra

{j} {+} pero sanchez del barCo d*e* aVila Un cav*all*o y armas de la T*ie*rra

{j} {+} Fran*ci*sco de alcantara Un cav*all*o y armas de la ti*e*rra

{iij} {+} Juan lopez de sayago treS cavallos armas de la ti*e*rra(^s) Una cuera d*e* a*n*ta

{j} {+} Fran*ci*sco de Padilla un cavallo y armas de la T*ie*rra

{ij} {+} Pero m*art*yn cano dos cavallos y armas de la ti*e*rra

{iij} {+} di*e*go de madrid tres cavallos y armas de la T*ie*rra

{j} {+} alonso de sayavedra Un cav*all*o y Una Cuera d*e* anta y armas de la ti*e*rra y / de Cabeça

{ij} {+} Ximon g*arci*a dos cavallos Una cuera d*e* antta y armas de la T*ie*rra

{j} {+} Fran*ci*sco gomez Un cav*all*o y armas de la T*ie*rra

{j} {+} luis de la chica un cav*all*o y armas de la T*ie*rra

{j} {+} diego nunez de garveña Un cav*all*o y armas de la ti*e*rra

{j} {+} hernando de Alva Un cav*all*o E Una cuera d*e* anta y armas de la / Tierra

{469}

[fol. 6v]

{469}

{j} {+} *crist*oval g*arci*a Un cavallo y armas de la ti*e*rra

{j} {+} diego del castillo Un cavallo y armas de la ti*e*rra

{j} {+} Juan Ro*drigu*es de aValos Un cavallo y armas de la ti*e*rra

{ij} {+} Pedro de ortega dos cavallos y Una Cuera d*e* anta armas de la ti*e*rra

{ij} {+} Juan de çespedes dos cavallos y armas de la ti*e*rra

{ij} {+} m*art*in sanchez dos cavallos y armas de la ti*e*rra {j} {+} Francisco martyn Un cavallo y armas de la tierra

{ij} {+} Juan Ximenez dos cavallos y armas de la tierra Una cuera de anta

{j} {+} Pedro de benaVente un cavallo E cuera de anta y armas de la tierra

{j} {+} Rodrigo de trugillo Un cavallo cuera de anta y Armas de / la Tierra

{ij} {+} diego Sanchez de Fromista dos cavallos y armas de / la tierra

{j} {+} Alonso de Valençia Un cavallo y armas de la / Tierra

{ij} {+} bart(h)olome serrano dos cavallos y armas de la tierra y / Una cuera de anta

{iiij} {+} ma(^r)chin de castañeda quatro cavallos armaduras de cabeça / con su barbote y armas de la Tierra cota de malla cu- / era de anta

{ij} {+} Francisco de Valdivyeso dos cavallos y armas de la tierra / y Un caXco

{Vij} {+} Alonso Sanchez y Su hiJo syete cavallos y armas de / la Tierra y cottas de malla

{ij} {+} Juan martyn de la Fuente del maestre dos cavallos / E armas de la Tierra
{503}

[fol. 7r]
{503}
{j} {+} cristoval hernandez moreno Un cavallo y armas de la tierra

{i} {+} Gonçalo Vazquez un cavallo y armas de la tierra

{ij} {+} Juan cordero dos cavallos y armas de la Tierra

{j} {+} pero lopez de ÇiUdad Real Un cavallo y ar- / mas de la Tierra

{iiij} {+} Sancho ordoñez quatro Cavallos y Cuera de / malla Armas de la Tierra

{ij} {+} Julian de Samano dos cavallos Un coselete / y Cuera De malla y dos Cueras de anta ar- / mas de la Tierra y armaduras de cabeça(^s)

{ij} {+} Alonso gonçalez dos cavallos y armas de / la Tierra

{ij} {+} hernan gomeZ de la peña dos cavallos armas / de la Tierra y Un Jubon Fuerte

{j} {+} Pero geronimo Un cavallo y lança

{j} {+} Pero Hernandez calvo cavallo E lança

{ij} {+} diego nuñez de mirandilla dos cavallos y / Una cota de malla

{iiij} {+} Francisco RoXo loro Tres cavallos y armas de / la Tierra y armaduras de cabeça

{j} {+} andres HernandeZ de enzina(^s)sola Un cavallo / E armas de la Tierra

{ij} {+} miguel de torres dos cavallos y armas / de la Tierra
{528}

[fol. 7v]
{528}
{ij} {+} Pedro pasCual dos cavallos y cota de malla y armas de / la Tierra

{j} {+} Aorta home portugues Un cavallo Armas de la Tierra

{j} {+} diego de Salamanca Un cavallo Armas de la / Tierra

{j} {+}   Gaspar alvarez portugues Un cavallo Armas de / la t*i*erra

{j} {+}   *crist*oval gallego Un cavallo y armas De la Tierra

{j} {+}   domingo Romero Un cavallo y cuera d*e* anta y armas / de la T*i*erra

{ij} {+}   pedro navarro dos cavallos Cuera de malla Armas / de la t*i*erra

{ij} {+}   gonçalo de arJona dos cavallos y armas de la t*i*erra

{j} {+}   Juan Fioz Trompeta Un cavallo y Un coselete / y Una cuera d*e* anta y armas de la T*i*erra

{iiij} {+} hernando bermeJo quatro cavallos y armas de la T*i*erra / y Cuera d*e* anta

ynfanteria

{capitan} {+} pablo de melgossa AUsente porq*ue* no era allegado de mex*i*co

{+}   lorenço ginoves Un arcabuz y armas de la t*i*erra

[fol. 8r]

{+}   Fran*cis*co de espinosa Un arcabuz y armas de la t*i*erra

{+}   Alonso Ximenez Un arcabuz armas de la t*i*erra

{+}   Juan de Salamanca Un arcabuz y armas de la t*i*erra

{+}   Fran*cis*co de godoy Una Rodela y espada armas de la t*i*erra

{+}   Juan de santovaya galiçiano Un Arcabuz y armas / de la t*i*erra

{+}   Juan de duero Un arcabuz espada y puñal y armas / de la T*i*erra

{+}   domingo Ruiz arcabuz espada armas de la t*i*erra

{+}   Juan barvero Un arcabuz espada y puñaL y / armas de la Tierra

{+}   diego diaz de san(c)to domingo espada y Rodela / armas de la T*i*erra

{+}   Fran*cis*co de Vargas espada y Rodela y armas de / la t*i*erra

{+}   Roque alvarez ballesta espada y Cuera d*e* anta

{+}   R*odrig*o de gamez espada y puñaL

{+}   Juan frances espada y Rodela

{+}   Hernan g*arci*a de llerena Una ballesta espada / y puñaL y armas de la t*i*erra

{+}   Juan m*art*yn de la Fuente del arco Una ballesta / y Cuera d*e* anta y armas de la t*i*erra

[fol. 8v]

{+}   R*odrig*o alvarez de cafra Una ballesta y espada

{+}   Alonso millero Galiciano Una ballesta espada y / armas de la T*i*erra

{+}   Andres m*art*in portugues ballesta espada y armas de la / T*i*erra

{+}   Juan de Vallarra espada y puñaL y Rodela y armas / de la tierra

{+}   Antonio de laredo ballesta espada armas de la t*i*erra

        Juan bermeJo ballesta espada y puñaL y armas de la tierra

{j c*avall*o} {+}   miguel sanchez ballesta espada cav*all*o y armas de la t*i*erra

{+} pero m*art*yn de la bermeJa ballesta espada y puñaL / armas de la T*ie*rra

{j c*avall*o} {+} Juan morillo Un cavallo espada y Rodela armas de / la t*ie*rra

{+} Alonso Vos de Ribadeo espada y Rodela y armas de la / T*ie*rra

{+} Pedro de talaVera espada y Rodela mangas de / malla armas de la T*ie*rra

{+} m*art*yn alonso de *A*storga espada y armas de la T*ie*rra

{+} pero hernandez de guadalaJara Un arcabuz espada y puñaL

{+} m*art*yn Hernandez chillon Una cuera de anta espada y / armas de la t*ie*rra

{+} baltasar de çamora espada y Rodela y armas de la t*ie*rra

[fol. 9r]
{+} Anton m*art*yn Una ballesta Una espada Armas d*e* la t*ie*rra

{+} diego de medina Una espada e Una Rodela e Una ballesta / Armas d*e* la t*ie*rra

{+} galiVeer Una cuera de Anta espada e cos*e*lete

{+} diego de candia Un arcabuz espada E Rodela

{+} myguel hernandez espada e Rodela e armas d*e* la t*ie*rra

{+} Jaco de (^R) bruJas Una espada e arcabuz e Una Rodela

{+} estevan m*art*yn Una arcabuz espada Armas d*e* la t*ie*rra

{ij} {+} miguel de fuenteRabia dos caVallos tres espadas e Una rodela

{+} Fran*cis*co Lopez Una cuera d*e* anta Un montante epada e Un puñal

{j} {+} Fran*cis*co gorez Un cav*all*o Una espada e Una Rodela

{+} gaspar Ro*drigue*s Una ballesta espada e armas d*e* la t*ie*rra

{+} b*artolo*me de pedes Una espada e Un puñal Una ballesta e armaS / d*e* la T*ie*rra

{+} Juan Vizcayno Una espada Un puñal e Una espada armaS / d*e* la T*ie*rra

{+} pedro de alcantara Una ballesta e Una espada armas d*e* la t*ie*rra

{+} goncalo yañez Una Rodela espada e armas d*e* *la* T*ie*rra

{j} {+} alferez pedro Ramos Un arcabuz esp*a*da e Un cav*all*o

{+} Atambor Lazaro espada e armas d*e* la t*ie*rra

{+} anton rruiZ Un arcabuz

{+} Juan d*e* çelada Un arcabuz

{+} Fran*cis*co de VillaFranca arcabuz armas d*e* la t*ie*rra

{+} Juan de plazençia arcabuz armas d*e* la t*ie*rra

{+} Fran*cis*co gomez Un arcabuz e Un caxco e armas d*e* la t*ie*rra

{+}   bartolome sanches Una espada e Una Rodela

[fol. 9v]

{+}   alonso hernandez armas de la tierra Rodela e
        espada

{+}   pedro de trugillo Un arcabuz armas de la tierra

{+}   miguel de Torrez Un arcabuz espada armas de la
        tierra

{+}   alonso alvarez Un arcabuz e cuera de anta / armas de
        la tierra

{+}   Francisco martyn Una ballesta espada armas de la
        tierra

{+}   garcia de perea Una Rodela espada armas de la tierra

{+}   diego de mata espada e Una Rodela

{+}   graViel hernandez Una espada e Una Rodela e ar-
        / mas de la Tierra

D(^x)lij Y Son quinientos E çinquenta e dos caVallos

E esta dicha gente de Cavallo LLevavan sus lancas e espadas
/ de mas de las dichas armas declaradas e otras armas

Por suma que son dozientos e Treynta e tantos de Cavallo /
de mas y allende de los que Van adelante en conpanya / de los
Religiosos y de los que se esperan de meXico que Van / en
este dicho Viaje e Jornada

{+} e ynfanteria son sesenta e dos hombres con las dichas
armas / demas de otras Armas de la Tierra que Se les dio / e
(^d) la demas gente que Va por la mar e por la tierra que (^su
señoria) el ViSorey / ymVia / {rúbrica}

[fol. 10r]

E asy Vista mirada y eSaminada La dicha gentE / por su

señoria Los dichos Capitan general maestre / de Campo
alFerez mayor E capitanes y cavalleros / de susonombrados
e declarados Paresçieron ante su señoria / E dixeron que
porque ellos sean moVido co(m)n buen zelo A yr / en esta
Jornada en servyÇio de dios y de su magesTad y en su real /
nombre trabaJar e procurar en ella de hazer Lo que deven /
A su real servyçio como por manar de ellos esta Voluntad /
Pidieron y suplicaron A su senoria Yllustrisima permita y
mande / que asy Ellos como La demas gente hagan La
Solemnidad de / Juramento que en tal caSo e Viaje Se
requyere para que mejor / mas effectuoSamente hagan Lo
que deven como buenos Vasa- / llos y servidores de Su
magestad pues cunple asy a su real servycio / E luego el dicho
Capitan general Francisco Vazquez de coronado / Juro por
dios todo poderoSo y por su santa madre y por / Una cruz
que ally estava e palabras de los Santos Evangelios / donde
puso su mano derecha corporalmente en Un libro myssal /
en manos del Reverendo padre fray francisco de Vitoria
proffeSo / de la orden de Señor San francisco que Como
buen cristiano VaSallo / e servydor de Su magestad Usara el
dicho cargo de Capitan generaL / que por su señoria en
nombre de Su magestad es nombrado para la dicha Jornada e
tierra / E guardara el servycio de dios e de su magesTad y
obedesçera / y Cumplira sus mandamyentos e del dicho
senor ViSorey / en Su real nombre como buen Cavallero
hiJodalgo lo deve hazer / A todo Su saber y entender

E luego los dichos maestre de Canpo alferez mayor / E capitanes y Cavalleros e la demas gente / {rúbrica}

[fol. 10v]

Cada Uno por sy Juraron en forma de derecho segun(d) e
como de / suso se contiene (^su) poniendo sus manos derechas / en la dicha cruz e libro so cargo del qual prometieron
/ de Ser obidientes al dicho Francisco Vazquez de coronado
su capitan / General E a otro qualquier capitan general que
Su magesTad / o el dicho senor ViSorrey en su real nombre
mandare[135] e que no de- / Xaran sus capitañyas e banderas
syn su Real mandado / E haran todo aquello que Son obligados a hazer como buenos / capitanes e gente VaSsallos de
Su magestad lo qual paso en presencia / de su señoria e de los

dichos Cavalleros e *per*sonas arriba dichas y / *en* PresenÇia
de my El d*i*cho Juan d*e* CueVas esS*criba*no m*a*yor de my*n*as
d*e* sus / mag*estade*s / {rúbrica}

{+} *en* ffee d*e* lo q*ua*l y de mandamy*ent*o del d*i*cho (^señor)
YLL*ustris*imo ^*señor* Virrey / d*e* la nueva españa saq*ue* la
*pre*sent*e* nomyna del d*i*cho alard*e* en la / dicha Çiudad de
Compostella Veynte e siete dias del d*i*cho mes de / hebrero
de myll e q*uiniento*s e quarenta la q*ua*l va es*cri*(p)ta en diez /
foJas de papel es*cri*(p)tas
Juan de cueVas {rúbrica}

[fol. 11r] [blank]

[fol. 11v]
{Alarde}
{Compostela 1540}
{El alarde q*ue* se hizo d*e* la gente q*ue* *e*l virrey EnVio a çibola}
{cibola soldados}

Document 13

Record of Mexican Indians Participating in the Expedition, 1576

Codex Aubin, "Chronicle of Mexican History to 1576, continued to 1607,"
Add MSS 31219, Library of the British Museum, fols. 46v and 47r

INTRODUCTION

As we pointed out in the introduction to the February 1540 muster roll of the Coronado expedition (Document 12), the great majority of persons who participated in the *entrada* are missing from that official record. Most glaringly absent are the at least 1,300 natives of central and western Mexico, the so-called *indios amigos,* who made up the mass of the expedition and outnumbered the European contingent by about three to one.

This overwhelmingly Indian majority of members of the expedition is visible in the documentary record only rarely. Embedded in the documents of the Coronado expedition, though, is the story of a group of conquistadores far larger and much more diverse than the one that stands out in the narratives of the Old World participants themselves. This group was a huge and fearsome company of warriors, fully supported by slaves and servants, sometimes accompanied by wives and other female companions. It was not the small troop of Spaniards pitted against indigenous multitudes that much of the documentary record might suggest, but instead a legion of Spanish-led Mexican Indians accompanying a corps of Europeans with their servants and black slaves, supported by huge herds of livestock, overmatching native communities generally only a fraction of its size.[1]

In his *relación,* written in the 1560s, Pedro Castañeda de Nájera wrote about the recruiting of expedition members that took place in the Ciudad de México in 1539. In just a few days, he wrote, "more than 300 Spaniards were assembled, and about 800 Indians native to Nueva España."[2] The chronicler's figure for the European (mostly Spanish) members of the expedition is in approximate agreement with the 358 that is our own current count.[3] So the claim that 800 Indian allies from what is today central Mexico were also present on the *entrada* is perhaps generally accurate as well. Roughly another 500 Indian conquistadores evidently joined the expedition as it passed through the modern Mexican states of Michoacán, Jalisco, and Nayarit, bringing the total to the 1,300 reported by Vázquez de Coronado himself.[4]

Castañeda de Nájera had a considerable amount to say about the roles played by the *indios amigos* in the course of the two-year *entrada.* To begin with, he revealed that when Vázquez de Coronado selected "fifty horsemen and a few footmen" to travel as an advance guard to Cíbola, he also took along "most of the [native] allies."[5] Thus, when the advance guard arrived at Cíbola/Hawikku, it may have numbered 1,000 or more, principally Indians.

The expedition's former captain general testified in 1544 that when he had arrived near Cíbola, he had sent "two Nahua Indians" to the first pueblo, ahead of the advance guard, with a cross as a sign of peace. However, "when the accused [Vázquez de Coronado] had gotten three leagues from Cíbola, he found there the Nahuas whom he had sent and they told him that the pueblo and *provincia* were at war and refused to come to peace."[6] After subsequent demands that the Cíbolans surrender, which they rejected, Vázquez de Coronado ordered the pueblo attacked. The existence of the large corps of Mexican warriors in the Spanish-led force easily explains why it so quickly overran the pueblo.

Two months after the capture of Cíbola the captain general "sent don García López and some [Indian] allies, with Indians from Cíbola, to establish the camp and erect shelter where fray Juan [de Padilla] suggested."[7] In another of their fleeting appearances in the documents, a party of Indian allies is reported by Castañeda de Nájera as having accompanied Captain Melchior Díaz in what proved to be a long, unsuccessful attempt to rendezvous with the ships of Hernando de Alarcón.[8] The chronicler also repeats the information provided by earlier documents that some of the Indian allies served as guards for the expedition's horse herd. Indeed, after quarters for the winter of 1540–41 had been established at Tiguex on the Rio Grande, one or more of the allies were killed in a Pueblo raid on the remuda.[9]

In retaliation for this and other gestures of defiance by the Pueblos, one of the Tiguex towns was attacked and sacked, in the course of which, according to Castañeda de Nájera, "many allies from Nueva España" lit fires in the ground-floor rooms in an effort to smoke out the defenders.[10] This tactic proved decisive in the assault, and the residents of the pueblo quickly capitulated.

The sum of the fragmentary documentary information shows that Indian allies made up the overwhelming majority of the expedition as a whole and probably of each of its detachments, including the one taken by Vázquez de Coronado on the final leg of his march to Quivira. The *indios amigos* were, most importantly, part of the fighting force of the expedition; their involvement in combat helps explain the ease with which most of the indigenous communities met were subdued or overawed into pro forma submission. In addition, some of the Indian allies often traveled ahead of even the advance guard, serving as intermediaries and emissaries, as was the case at Cíbola. The *indios amigos* carried supplies, guarded livestock, and constructed shelter. Their active involvement in the expedition was essential to what success it had.

Regarding exactly where the Indian allies of the Coronado expedition came from, there is a small amount of docu-mentary evidence. As we have already seen, some 800 *indios amigos* were likely natives of Nueva España proper. Castañeda de Nájera qualified this region of origin by saying that "they were from Nueva España and most of them from hot climates," perhaps including today's *tierra caliente*, the hot lowlands.[11] As to the often repeated claim that Tlaxcaltecas, earlier allies of Hernán Cortés, were among those who made the trip to Cíbola, there is no documentary evidence whatsoever, though it is not unreasonable to suspect that some were present. Certainly Tlaxcaltecas had made up part of Beltrán Nuño de Guzmán's force that effected the initial conquest of Nueva Galicia in the early 1530s. Although they had suffered massive casualties during that *entrada*, primarily from sickness and starvation, some may have survived and remained in the Compostela and Culiacán areas. Survivors of those remnants might well have joined the Coronado expedition almost a decade later.[12]

With firm documentary support, however, we can say that at least some natives of the Valley of Mexico served during the *entrada*. The *Codex Aubin*, also known as the *Códice de 1576*, a small portion of the second part of which is reproduced, transcribed, and translated here, forms a key part of the evidence supporting that statement. The codex is a pictorial manuscript glossed in Nahuatl that was completed early in the seventeenth century. As Donald Robertson wrote more than 40 years ago, the second part of the *Codex Aubin* represents "a stage in the disintegration of the [precolumbian] native tradition" of annal writing.[13] It records events year by year from the history of Tenochtitlan, the Mexica capital that became the core of the Spanish Cuidad de México. The entry for the year 1539, when members of the Coronado expedition would have departed from the *ciudad* to rendezvous in Compostela, depicts Tenochca, or natives of Tenochtitlan, leaving for *yancuic tlalpan*, the lands newly discovered by fray Marcos de Niza. There can be little doubt that these Tenochca represent some of Vázquez de Coronado's *indios amigos*. The codex also documents the return of the survivors of this group from the north in 1542, having joined en route another contingent from Tenochtitlan that had been led to Nueva Galicia by Viceroy Mendoza to put down the native uprising known as the Mixtón War.[14]

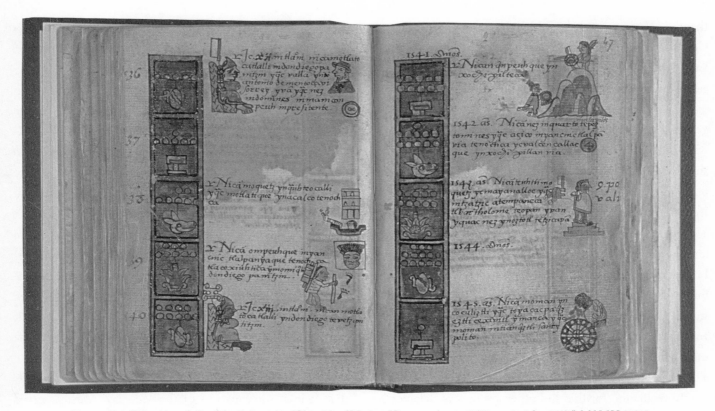

FIGURE 13.1. Folios 46v and 47r of the *Codex Aubin*, "Chronicle of Mexican History to the year 1576, continued to 1607," Add MSS 31219. Reproduced with permission of the Library of the British Museum.

From the neighboring island polity of Tlatelolco—which also became a barrio in the Cuidad de México—came at least two people, a man called Francisco Jiménez[15] and a don Luis de León, a *principal* at Santiago de Tlatlelolco.[16] Also from the immediate vicinity of Tenochtitlan was a man "called Andrés" from Coyoacán, who stayed in Quivira.[17]

Originating farther west in what is now Mexico, several expedition participants from the former Tarascan state are represented in the surviving documentary record. Importantly, an Indian honored by the name don Alonso, from Pátzcuaro, led a native contingent of unknown size from Michoacán.[18] From the same general area, a man named Lucas accompanied the ill-fated fray Juan de Padilla on his mission to Quivira and, after the friar's murder, returned south with Andrés de Campo.[19]

Incredibly, 40 years after the end of the Coronado expedition, the members of an *entrada* into New Mexico led by Antonio de Espejo found several *indios amigos* from a group that had stayed in the Zuni area as the expedition retreated southward. According to Diego Pérez de Luxán, a member

and chronicler of the Espejo *entrada*, they were "Mexican Indians [that is, from the Valley of Mexico], and also a number from Guadalajara, some of those that Coronado had brought."[20] The leader of the later *entrada* himself was more specific, providing the names of some of those found at Zuni: Andrés (from Coyoacán), Gaspar (from the Ciudad de México), and Antón (from Guadalajara).[21] Joining fray Juan de Padilla in his martyr's mission to Quivira when the Coronado expedition left Tierra Nueva were "two Indians I believe from Zapotlán and around there," one evidently known as Sebastián.[22]

One further Indian whose Christian name is known participated in the expedition, a woman named Luisa. A native of Culiacán, she evidently served as an interpreter but fled from Vázquez de Coronado during the force's return from Cíbola.[23]

This is the scant information available about the native members of the Coronado expedition. Despite the impressive size of the group they made up and their importance to the expedition, their presence in the surviving documentary record can easily be overlooked. Why the protagonists of nearly all the accounts of Spanish conquest of the time are European men of at least modest rank, even though they were frequently outnumbered by members of other groups, is easy enough to imagine. Most documents that have been used to study the Conquest are what might be called "bragging documents," manuscripts prepared principally to glorify the accomplishments of the conquistadores and portray them as worthy of recognition and reward, the achievement of prestigious position in the form of titles and authority being one of most conquistadores' principal aims. Thus, the failure to reveal the presence of a large body of Indian allies, or anyone else, heightened the apparent danger the men of the muster roll faced and increased their worthiness. Not that premeditated manipulation of the facts was necessary. It went without saying that a leader's company was an extension of himself; its accomplishments were his.

Therefore, the short excerpt from the *Codex Aubin* presented here is unique among documents of the Coronado expedition. Not only does it provide otherwise unavailable information about the expedition's *indios amigos*, but it provides information from an indigenous point of view, the rarest of rare evidence. It is published for the first time in English here.

Although the information contained in the codex, which spans the years 1168 to 1608, was clearly compiled by many individuals, the indigenous scribe who began the painting of the codex (and may have written the glosses as well) was likely from the barrio of San Juan near San José church west and south of the *zócalo*, or main square, near the modern Mercado de San Juan in the Ciudad de México.[24] This unnamed scribe, or perhaps his immediate predecessor, appears to have begun recording information from his own firsthand knowledge and observation with the year 1553, the year before Vázquez de Coronado's death.[25] From that point, the entries for each year are much more copious and detailed, even occasionally referring to *hoy,* or today, as though having been set down exactly contemporaneously with what was recorded. There is a lacuna in the record after 1591, resulting perhaps from the death or retirement of the first scribe. Another scribe picks up events for 1595 and is replaced in turn for recording the events of 1597 through

1607.[26] Although the glyph for 1608 has been entered, it is not accompanied by any alphabetic text. Eloise Quiñones Keber suggested that such gaps indicate either losses or that the codex as it exists today is "composite . . . incompletely stitched together."[27]

For the years prior to 1553—including 1539–42, the years of greatest interest to us here—for which the scribe was evidently not himself the recorder, entries are generally confined to only one of two major events. For 1539, for instance, the two events of note are the departure of Tenochca for Tierra Nueva (the Coronado expedition) and the death of Diego Panitzin, the indigenous ruler of the Tenochca.[28] In discussing indigenous *anales* (annals) in general, Ross Hassig has pointed out that in them "notable events of the year were recorded without explanation of their importance, cause, or consequence. Nevertheless, some notion of what the Aztecs/Mexica [including the Tenochca] thought was significant is revealed in what was recorded."[29] In that light, participation in the Coronado expedition must be seen as having been a significant undertaking for the Tenochca themselves. It was on a par with the death of the ruler or the onset of a serious epidemic recorded for 1545.[30]

The opening page of the codex bears the date September 27, 1576, in the Tenochca scribe's own hand; this must have been the date when the painting of the codex began.[31] It is assembled in the style of a European book, using European paper, rather than like a precolumbian accordian-folded book on *amate* paper or deerskin. It is organized according to the 365-day Mesoamerican calendar, the *xihuitl*. Each year is represented by a glyph in a column on the left side of the page. The glyph includes a number represented by dots and a day-name symbol determined by the day on which the year began. For instance, 1542 is signified by the glyph "11 *tochtli* [rabbit]."[32]

The number of the year in the Christian calendar is also included. For years before 1541, the final two digits in arabic numerals are crowded into the narrow left-hand margin of the page; beginning with the entry for 1541, the full arabic numeral heads the alphabetic text in Nahuatl, which occupies the right-hand portion of the page associated with each year glyph. Because the preconquest *xihuitl* did not coordinate exactly with the Christian calendar (each new annual cycle began between February 1 and March 1), it appears that by 1576 the two had been synchronized by some ad hoc method. Thus, 11-*tochtli* had been made to correspond exactly to 1542, rather than being part of 1542 and part of 1543. It is interesting that for a document as time-linked as the codex is, it makes no mention of the change from Julian to Gregorian calendars in the Spanish world in 1582, which would have required a corresponding adjustment in the traditional *xihuitl* to keep it in step. Evidently, the year glyphs had become mere conventional signs, and the process of actually calculating the year had been abandoned by the Tenochca by this time.[33]

The codex itself bears no title; the title used here refers to its late-nineteenth-century owner, Joseph-Marie Aubin, who acquired it along with a number of other manuscripts in Mexico.[34] It is now owned by the Library of the British Museum in London, which graciously permitted us to reproduce folios 46v and 47r. There the manuscript now bears the designation "Add MSS 31219, Chronicle of Mexican History to 1576, continued to 1607." Translations of the text have been published once in French and five times in Spanish. We consulted two of the Spanish translations, one by Robert Barlow in 1947 and the other by Charles Dibble in 1963, in preparing the English translation that appears here.[35] The translation as published is a collaboration between ourselves and Dr. John Frederick Schwaller, who undertook at our request to produce a draft translation. The final edited result, however, is our responsibilty. In writing the notes and introduction, we consulted a fine commentary and facsimile reproduction published 20 years ago in German.[36]

TRANSLATION

[46v]

5 *técpatl* [flint]

{1536} At this time don Diego Panitzin was inscribed as [the] twelfth ruler,[37] when Viceroy don Antonio de Mendoza arrived,[38] and when the *tomines* [first] appeared. At that time the president began [his term].

6 *calli* [house]

{1537} [no entry]

7 *tochtli* [rabbit]

{1538} [It was] at this time the wooden church was erected [and] when Tenochca hid in the [gun]boat.[39]

8 *ácatl* [reed]

{1539} [It was] at this time they departed for the new land; the Tenochca went.[40] At mid-year don Diego Panitzin died.

9 *técpatl* [flint]

{1540} At this time don Diego Teuetzquititzin was inscribed as the thirteenth ruler.[41]

[47r]

10 *calli* [house]

{1541} At this time [the Tenochca] conquered the people of Xochipillan.[42]

11 *tochtli* [rabbit]

{1542} At this time the four-*tomín* metal coins appeared when the Tenochca returned [from] the *villa* in the new land.[43] From there they came back together [with] those who had gone [to] the *villa* of Xochipillan.[44]

12 *ácatl* [reed]

{1543} At this time dust was raised by walking;[45] with it came hunger. At the same time Bartolomé, the loud voice[d man] from Atempan,[46] [came] to the church [as] *pregonero* [crier], when the Tetizacapan cave [came to light].

13 *técpatl* [flint]

{1544} [no entry]

1 *calli* [house]

{1545} [It was] at this time the pestilence[47] set in, when blood flowed from our noses. It lasted one year. [This was] when the San Hipólito market[48] was established.

TRANSCRIPTION

[fol. 46v]

{36} {*ytem*} Ic xii in tla*to*ani nica*n* motlato- / catlalli[49] in don diego pa- / nitzin yq*ua*c *h*ualla yn do*n* / antonio de mentoça vi- / sorrey yva*n* yq*ua*c nez / in domines nima*n* nican / peuh in presitente

{37} [no item]

{38} {*ytem*} Nica*n* moquetz yn q*ua*uh teocalli / yq*ua*c motla-tique[50] yn acalco[51] tenoch- / ca

{39} {*ytem*} Nica*n* ompeuhque[52] in yan- / cuic tlalpan yaque tenochca / tlacoxiuhtica[53] y*n* momiq*ui*lico[54] / don diego panitzin

{40} {*ytem*} Ic xiii in tla*to*ani nican motla- / tocatlalli yn don diego teuetzqui- / titzin

[fol. 47r]

1541 Años

{*ytem*} Nican q*ui*npeuhque yn / xochipilteca

1542 a*ñо*s Nica*n* nez in quarto tepoz- / tomines yq*ua*c açico in yancuic tlalpa*n* / vi*ll*a tenochca yc *h*ualcencallac- / que yn xochipillan vi*ll*a

1543 a*ñо*s Nica*n* teuhtli mo- / quetz yc mayanalloc[55] yq*ua*c/ in tzatzic[56] atempaneca- / tl bart(h)olome teopan yh*u*an / yq*ua*c nez yn oztotl tetzicapa*n* / {9 po- / vali}

1544 Años [no item]

1545 a*ñо*s Nica*n* moman yn / coculiztli yq*ua*c toyacacpa quiz- / eztli ce xiuitl y*n* manca yq*ua*c / moman in tianq*ui*ztli sant y- / polito

Document 14

Hearing on Depopulation Charges, February 26, 1540

AGI, Patronato, 21, N.2, R.3

INTRODUCTION

Fray Marcos de Niza's trip to Tierra Nueva reinforced earlier general expectations of wealthy peoples living to the north of Nueva España and seemed to confirm the grapevine intelligence brought by Cabeza de Vaca and his companions. As a result, in the fall of 1539, recruitment of an expedition bound for Cíbola was a simple matter. As Pedro de Castañeda de Nájera later remembered it, "in a few days more than three hundred Spaniards were assembled and about eight hundred Indians native to Nueva España."[1]

But the imminent departure from the Ciudad de México of such a large group raised fears and rekindled jealousies. Even nearly 20 years after the conquest of Tenochtitlan, central Mexico remained a land occupied and held largely by force. Resentments and animosities directed against the recent Old World usurpers ran deep and often flared into violence. Hostility was even more open and frequent in the recently subjugated *provincia* of Nueva Galicia.[2] Thus, the king, in approving the expedition, specifically admonished the viceroy "not to cause any deficiency in security or population of that Nueva España."[3] And it was only to be expected that when the Coronado expedition was mounted, some residents of the viceroyalty, including Hernán Cortés, argued that "if don Antonio [de Mendoza] pursues this exploration, he will not be able to do so without

leaving Nueva España unprotected and at great risk and danger. . . . And as a result [of the expedition], there would be the same problem in Nueva Galicia."[4]

Such misgivings were not idle imaginings. As Cortés was later only too ready to point out, "in confirmation of this, since I arrived in these kingdoms [Spain], letters have come from Nueva España in which is written news concerning these people sent by the viceroy [which] tells and affirms that those he sent first, which were twelve horsemen, are dead. Further, some native towns in Nueva Galicia in which Francisco Vázquez has been have risen in arms."[5]

One of the implications of Cortés's complaint is that not only was Nueva España rendered vulnerable by the expedition's departure, but the expedition's passage through native communities as it headed north actually provoked Indian attacks. Indeed, it hardly seems coincidental that the greatest threat to Spanish sovereignty to that point, the Mixtón War in Nueva Galicia, broke out within months of the Coronado expedition's departure. There were, certainly, powerful people in the New World who claimed a direct causal link between passage of the expedition and outbreak of the Mixtón War.[6] *Visitador general* Francisco Tello de Sandoval, for instance, lodged numerous charges against the viceroy, including one that "the native Indians of Jalisco had risen up and rebelled against His Majesty's service and had killed Spaniards, ecclesiastics, and lay brothers [events of the Mixtón War] because of the abuse they had suffered from the people [the viceroy] had sent in armed forces and for reconnaissance, especially those sent to the Tierra Nueva of Cíbola."[7]

In this matter Mendoza strenuously denied any negligence or malfeasance on his behalf, citing in his defense the testimony of 33 witnesses, including Vázquez de Coronado.[8] The captain general himself also took great pains to show that the expedition he led had not inflicted harm on native people north of Compostela. During the 1544 investigation of the expedition's treatment of Indians, Vázquez de Coronado and his attorney pointedly asked witnesses whether "the natives of all the lands and provinces through which the army passed, both men and women, were treated very benevolently" and whether "from the city of Compostela the aforesaid Francisco Vázquez de Coronado issued and ordered proclaimed ordinances very beneficial to the natives." As would be expected, the *de parte* witnesses of whom the questions were asked uniformly answered in the affirmative.[9]

Nor did such charges arise only after the expedition was under way. Rather, they were current and common during recruitment of the force. To parry those allegations, the captain general requested that, during the formal muster of the expedition, its participants be examined to demonstrate that the company was not made up of *vecinos* of the Ciudad de México or Nueva Galicia, who would have pledged to reside there and provide defense for a certain period as part of the condition for the grant of *vecino* status. Nor, he intended to show, was it composed of *encomenderos,* who were obligated to defend the native communities over which they held authority. At the same time, it was to be ascertained whether the expeditionaries were going voluntarily or had been coerced or tricked into joining the enterprise. Evidently, Cortés or others had complained on that score, too, although no direct documentary evidence of such accusations has come to light.

Preserved in Sevilla's Archivo General de Indias, under the *signatura* (catalog number) AGI, Patronato, 21, N.2, R.3, is a summary prepared on February 27, 1540, of the determination made by six witnesses about whether or not the men who appeared for muster were *vecinos* and whether they were willing participants in the expedition. The

witnesses were Hernán Pérez de Bocanegra, Antonio Serrano de Cardona, Gonzalo de Salazar, Pero Almíldez Cherino, Serván Béjarano, and Cristóbal de Oñate, all prominent *vecinos* of the Ciudad de México. Their testimony was recorded and then summarized by Juan de León, an *escribano* of the Audiencia de México. The surviving manuscript bears his signature and registered mark. According to Juan de León's preface to the testimony, there were to be three additional witnesses, Juan de Xaso/Jaso, Diego Ordóñez, and Juan Fernández, *vecinos* respectively of the Ciudad de México, Puebla de los Ángeles, and La Purificación in Nueva Galicia. Whether these last three actually testified is unknown, but even if they did, their testimonies were not included in Juan de León's summary.

The six summarized testimonies are in nearly unanimous agreement that only four *vecinos* of the Ciudad de México had been mustered into the Coronado expedition at Compostela on February 22. Those four were Alonso Sánchez, Domingo Martín, Lope de Samaniego, and the captain general himself. Cristóbal de Oñate added that two *vecinos* from Guadalajara also joined the expedition, but he provided neither of their names.[10] Further, the witnesses concurred that all were going "of their own volition."[11] Antonio Serrano de Cardona went so far as to say that the mustered expeditionaries were "the most contented [of] men he has seen go on conquests and *entradas* in this land."[12]

Certainly, on the subject of *vecinos* participating in the Coronado expedition the witnesses provided a substantial undercount. More than 30 additional expeditionaries of the 358 now known by name[13] were very likely *vecinos* of the Ciudad de México or of places in Nueva Galicia. We infer this on the basis of each individual's years of residence in Nueva España prior to the expedition, his evident elite status, and later reference to him as a *vecino*.[14] Probably even more of the expeditionaries were *vecinos,* but the documentary evidence now available does not permit making a strong case for any others. The decided undercount reported by the February 1540 witnesses suggests a slanting of their testimony in favor of the viceroy and captain general's claims that "[*vecinos*] are very few . . . and that they will not create a shortage."[15] That the witnesses deliberately ignored many *vecinos* cannot now be demonstrated beyond doubt, but it appears suspiciously as if they did. Such intentional orchestration of testimony taken during other investigations of the period was far from rare.[16] The motives behind the witnesses' apparently false testimony must have included their desire to further the viceroy's project, for they were all close associates of his. It is also possible, though unproven, that at least some of the witnesses were themselves investors in the enterprise and therefore had a stake in its going forward.

The questioning of witnesses in this case probably was scheduled deliberately to prevent the findings of the investigation from blocking or interferring with the expedition's departure; the witnesses were not examined until three days after the group left. As to whether expeditionaries were coerced or unscrupulously enticed into going to Cíbola, we have turned up no evidence to suggest that such was the case.

Juan de León's summary of the February 1540 testimony has been published twice before, once in Spanish and once in English, on the basis of the published Spanish transcript.[17] In preparing the new transcription and translation that follow, we have followed the AGI manuscript text. Major differences between the present renditions and the previously published versions are pointed out in the notes.

TRANSLATION

[1r]

In the *ciudad* of Compostela in Nueva Galicia[18] in this Nueva España on the twenty-first day of February in the one thousand five hundred and fortieth year[19] since the birth of Our Savior, Jesus Christ, before the very illustrious lord don Antonio de Mendoza,[20] viceroy and governor for His Majesty in this Nueva España and president of the *audiencia* and royal *chancillería* (which has its seat in the Ciudad de México), and in the presence of me, Juan de León,[21] *escribano* of Their Majesties' treasury and the royal *audiencia,* Francisco Vázquez de Coronado, governor and captain general of this *provincia* and captain general of the land newly discovered by the father provincial fray Marcos de Niza, presented a petition before His Lordship, the substance of which is what follows:[22]

Most Illustrious Lord,

I, Francisco Vázquez de Coronado, governor for His Majesty of this Nueva Galicia and named captain general for the newly discovered land by Your Lordship, state that it has come to my attention that several persons have declared[23] that many *vecinos* of the Ciudad de México, of the rest of the *ciudades* and *villas* of Nueva España, of this *ciudad* of Compostela, and of other *villas* of this *provincia* and jurisdiction are going on the expedition by my urging and inducement. For this reason, [they say,] the Ciudad de México and Nueva España [are] without aid and [have] few people. [And] because of this, injuries would ensue.[24] [They say this] because they disapprove of this expedition Your Lordship is ordering to be undertaken in His Majesty's name.

So that the truth may be learned concerning the *vecinos* of Nueva España and of this *provincia* who are going in my company, [namely] that they are very few, and [that] these

[few] are not going because of my enticement or inducement but of their own volition, and that they will not create a shortage in Nueva España because they are so few, I request and entreat Your Lordship to order that an inquiry about it [the matter] be conducted.

Since at present Gonzalo de Salazar and Pero Almildez Cherino, *factor* and *veedor* of Nueva España for His Majesty,[25] are here, as are other persons [who are] *vecinos* of [the Ciudad de] México, they will find out the truth about everything. [1v] Once the inquiry is conducted, may Your Lordship determine and order what is most conducive to His Majesty's service and the well-being and security of Nueva España.

Francisco Vázquez de Coronado

When the petition had been read, His Most Illustrious Lordship stated that the lord *licenciado* Maldonado, *oidor* of the Their Majesties' royal *audiencia,* who was present, is to conduct this inquiry and receive testimony. In order that it may be done better, it is to be arranged that the *factor, veedor, regidores,* and other persons who are thus here are present and are to be present at the inspection of the people at the muster. It is to be done this way.

Then on the aforesaid day, when the lord *licenciado* Maldonado had reviewed the petition and the decision made by the lord viceroy, he ordered that Gonzalo de Salazar and Pero Almíldez Cherino, His Majesty's *factor* and *veedor* of Nueva España, and Hernán Pérez de Bocanegra, Juan de Xaso, Antonio Serrano de Cardona, and Sebastián Béjarano, *vecinos* of the Ciudad de México, and Cristóbal de Oñate, *vecino* of this *ciudad* and His Majesty's *veedor* in this jurisdiction, and Diego Ordóñez, *vecino* of the *ciudad* of [Puebla de] los Ángeles, and Juan Fernández, *vecino* of La Purificación, who were then in this *ciudad* of Compostela and are [now] to be present at the muster that must be conducted tomorrow.[26] [This is] so that they may view and recognize the persons [who are] *vecinos* of [the Ciudad de] México and other places in this Nueva España, who are going on this expedition, in order that when [the people] have been viewed, [the witnesses] may testify under oath who they are. [The witnesses] were notified of [the order].

After what has been related, in accordance with a request from the captain general, on the twenty-sixth day of the month of February in the same year one thousand five hundred and forty, in the *ciudad* of Compostela, the lord *licenciado* Maldonado took the oath from Hernán Pérez de Bocanegra, the aforesaid Gonzalo de Salazar and Pero Almíldez Cherino (His Majesty's *factor* and *veedor* in this Nueva España), and Antonio Serrano de Cardona, *regidores* of the Ciudad de México. When they had sworn their oaths in the form required by law, they declared the following confidentially and in private, each one separately.

[2r] After what has been related, on the twenty-seventh day of the month of February in the same year one thousand five hundred and forty, in the *ciudad* of Compostela, the oath of Cristóbal de Oñate, *veedor* of this *provincia*, was taken and received in the form required by law. When he had sworn his oath in the [proper] manner, he stated the following, which comes afterward.

{Witness} Hernán Pérez de Bocanegra, a *vecino* of the Ciudad de México, a witness presented in the aforesaid matter for the aforementioned inquiry, having sworn his oath in accordance with the form required by law, when questioned according to the substance of the petition, declared the following:

[He was] asked if this witness was present last Sunday,[27] which was when the inspection was conducted of the people whom the very illustrious lord viceroy of this Nueva España [has] dispatched for the pacification of the land newly discovered by the father provincial fray Marcos de Niza (when the persons who are going on the expedition were screened and inspected). He replied that it is true that he was present during the entire inspection, at the screening and examination of the aforesaid people, and in the presence of His Lordship and many other *caballeros* and *vecinos* of Nueva

España. This took place before an *escribano,* and a list of them was made (which is enclosed).

This witness [was] asked to state and declare, as a *vecino* of the Ciudad de México, which *vecinos* of the Ciudad de México and of other places in Nueva España were at the inspection and review [and] are going to Tierra Nueva. This witness stated that, as he has said, he was present at the inspection and recognized and saw the persons who were present at it and are going on the pacification. As further verification, he requested that he be shown a copy [of] the list of those who passed before me, the *escribano*. It was shown to him, and he was read the [names of the] persons recorded on it.

He declared that among all those people he did not recognize any *vecino* of [the Ciudad de] México who is going, nor is any going, except Domingo Martín, who is a married man whom he has seen several times (residing in [the Ciudad de] México and providing couriers to him).[28] Further, one Alonso Sánchez is going with his wife and one son. This Alonso Sánchez used to be a shoemaker.[29] Also [there is] a young man, a son of *bachiller* Alonso Pérez, who arrived from Salamanca a few days ago.[30] His father was sending him to war because of [his] dissoluteness. [2v] And [there are] another two or three, [who are] journeymen[31] whom he saw working in [the Ciudad de] México, but he does not know whether they are *vecinos*.

This witness [declared], in accordance with the oath he swore, that he did not see [any other] person who might be a *vecino* of [the Ciudad de] México during the entire inspection which was conducted, except the aforementioned captain general Francisco Vázquez de Coronado and *alcaide* Lope de Samaniego, the *maestre de campo*.[32] [He knows this] because this witness has been a *vecino* and householder in [the Ciudad de] México for fourteen years, more or less.

He believes and holds [it] as certain that (those mentioned above) are going of their own volition, as are all the rest. [He declared] that this is the truth by the oath he swore. And he signed it with his name.
Fernán Pérez de Bocanegra

{Witness} {Item} Antonio Serrano de Cardona, a *vecino* and *regidor* of the Ciudad de México, a witness presented and accepted for the inquiry into the aforementioned, when questioned according to the substance of the petition, stated and declared the following:

This witness was asked whether he was present at the inspection and review which the lord viceroy ordered conducted and [which] was conducted this past Sunday. [That is, at the review] of the people he is sending (in His Majesty's name and in his royal service) for pacification of the land which fray Marcos de Niza, provincial of the Order of the Lord San Francisco, reconnoitered under His Lordship's direction. He answered that it is true that he was present during the entire inspection and review from beginning to end. He saw and observed everyone who passed there [in review] before the *escribano* of the royal *audiencia* and was enrolled.

As a *vecino* and *regidor* of the Ciudad de México, [he was] asked to state and declare which *vecinos* of the aforementioned *ciudad* and other places he saw were at the inspection and are going on this expedition with the captain general Francisco Vázquez de Coronado. This witness stated that he did not see other *vecinos* of [the Ciudad de] México who were at the inspection except Francisco Vázquez de Coronado, the captain general, and *alcaide* Lope de Samaniego, the *maestre* [3r] *de campo*. Also, one Alonso Sánchez, who used to be a *vecino* of [the Ciudad de] México, was going there [to Tierra Nueva]. But it [was] many days ago he saw him [at] home; afterward he left, seeking his livelihood as a merchant. Further, he saw one Domingo Martín who used to live in [the Ciudad de] México. But likewise for a long while he has had no knowledge of his [being at] home, nor does he believe that he has one, because he has not seen him residing in [the Ciudad de] México.

[He also stated] that no other *vecino* passed in review, nor does he believe that [any other] is going on this expedition, because if one was, this witness would be aware of it. He would recognize [any other *vecinos*], since he has resided in the [Ciudad de] México for twenty years, ever since that *ciudad* was captured and established by Christians. And also since he has been a *regidor* of it for fifteen years and [therefore] knows and is acquainted with its *vecinos*. With regard to the rest, [he declared] that everyone he has seen who is

going and was going [is] the most contented [of] men he has seen go on conquests and *entradas* in this land.

As to the others (those who are going), he is asked whether they are creating a shortage. The witness [declared] that it seems to him and he holds it to be certain that they are performing a useful service by going, rather than [causing] harm. [He stated] that they are not missed, since this witness left [the Ciudad de] México after the departure [of] the troop from the *ciudad* and saw it [still] full of people. There did not appear to be a shortage as a result of those who left and are going on this expedition. [He declared] that this is the truth by the oath he swore. And he signed it. Antonio Serrano de Cardona

{Witness} Gonzalo de Salazar, His Majesty's *factor* in this Nueva España, a *vecino* and *regidor* of the Ciudad de México, a witness presented and accepted for the aforesaid purpose, having given his oath in the manner required by law, when questioned according to the substance of the aforementioned petition, stated and declared the following:

This witness [was] asked whether he was present during the inspection and general review which was conducted this past Sunday. [That is, the review] of the people who are going in His Majesty's service to the newly discovered land. This witness stated that he was present at the aforesaid inspection and review.

As *factor* and a *vecino* of the *ciudad*, this witness was asked to state and declare [3v] which *vecinos* he saw who are going on this expedition. This witness declared that he is one of the persons who has most knowledge about all the individuals who are [present] in the land and [who], in it, is most familiar with them.

By the oath that he swore, [he stated] that he saw no person pass in the entire review who holds a benefice[33] or [has] a *repartimiento* in the whole land of Nueva España, except only the captain general Francisco Vázquez de Coronado. He recognized only one *vecino* of [the Ciudad de] México, [and] that one did not have a *repartimiento*. He did not recognize there any other *vecino* of [the Ciudad de] México or from the whole of Nueva España. Rather, one of the greatest benefits that had been done in this Nueva

España was to remove the unmarried and licentious people who were present in the *ciudad* and in the whole of Nueva España. [He declared] that he saw all of them go very much of their own volition. They importuned [Vázquez de Coronado] to go on the expedition rather than him talking them into it.

[He declared] that this is the truth by the oath he swore. And he signed it with his name.
Gonzalo de Salazar

{Witness} Pero Almildez Cherino, His Majesty's *veedor* in this Nueva España, a witness presented and accepted for this purpose, having given his oath in the manner required by law, when questioned, stated the following:

This witness was asked, in accordance with the substance of the petition, to state and declare whether he was present at the inspection and general review which was conducted this most recent Sunday. [That is, the review] of the people who are going in His Majesty's service on the pacification of the newly discovered land. He replied that it is true that he was present during the whole inspection and review, as he is asked.

As *veedor* and a *vecino* of the Ciudad de México, the witness [was] asked what *vecinos* of the Ciudad de México and of other places of this Nueva España he saw who were at the inspection and review in order to go on the expedition. [4r] This witness stated that he did not see any *vecino* who was at the inspection and [was going on the] journey except Francisco Vázquez de Coronado, the captain general; *alcaide* Lope de Samaniego, the *maestre de campo;* and one Alonso Sánchez, who is going with his wife and [about] whom he does not know [whether he] is a *vecino.*

This witness [declared] that he inspected and reviewed a great portion of the people and saw and observed all of them. [That is] because at the time of the inspection, so that it could be known, a written record was made of the horses and arms and armor they were taking. And [he stated] that all the rest of the people were single persons and [ones who] had very recently come to the land to seek a livelihood. [He stated] that he also saw one Domingo Martín, who for the better part of the year travels outside of [the Ciudad de]

México. In the opinion of this witness it has been a very beneficial thing that the people who were leaving were those who before had been doing harm to the *vecinos* in the *ciudad,* rather than being useful. [That is] because most of them were youthful and licentious *caballeros,* without [anything] they needed to do in the *ciudad* or their [own] land. From what he sensed from everyone, they are all going on the pacification of Tierra Nueva of their own volition and [are] very content.

In the opinion of this witness, if the aforesaid land were not being reconnoitered, most all of these people who are going there would return to Castilla or go to Peru or other places to seek a livelihood. [He stated] that this is the truth by the oath he swore. And he signed it.
Pero Almildez

{Witness} Serván Béjarano, a *vecino* of the Ciudad de México, a witness presented and accepted for this purpose, having sworn his oath in the manner required by law, when he was questioned according to the substance of the petition, stated the following:

This witness was asked whether he was present at the time the aforementioned inspection and general review was conducted. [That is, the review] of all the people [4v] who are going, in His Majesty's service, on the expedition for pacification of Tierra Nueva. This witness answered that he was present at the inspection from beginning to end and saw and recognized the people.

As a *vecino* of the *ciudad,* this witness was asked to state and declare what *vecinos* of the *ciudad* [or] of other *ciudades* and *villas* of this Nueva España he saw who [were] at the inspection. This witness stated that he has much knowledge about all the *vecinos* and householders of [the Ciudad de] México because he has resided in it since the *ciudad* was captured and has been raised among them. [He declared] that in the whole inspection he did not know [of] any other *vecino* [who is] going except the captain general Francisco Vázquez de Coronado, who is married in [the Ciudad de] México; Lope de Samaniego, the *maestre de campo,* who is unmarried and whom he believes to be a *vecino;* Domingo Martín, who is married; and one Alonso Sánchez, who is taking his wife. This witness knows [Alonso Sánchez] to be a small merchant, and because he is very short of funds[34] and does not have [anything] with which to sustain himself, he is going to the land to seek a livelihood. [Béjarano stated] that he did not see any other *vecino*.

[He declared] further that it seems to this witness and he holds it as most certain that it was and is a great benefit to the Ciudad de México and its *vecinos* that many single and licentious people are leaving, who did not have plans. Because a large portion of them are *caballeros* and individuals who did not have funds or *repartimientos* of Indians, except [enough] for eating and being idle, they were having to go to Peru and other places. [The witness declared] that all of these [individuals] were very content and going of their own volition. [He stated] that this is the truth by the oath he swore. And he signed it.

Serván Béjarano

Cristóbal de Oñate, a *vecino* of the Ciudad de México and His Majesty's *veedor* of this *provincia* of Nueva Galicia, a witness presented for this purpose, having sworn his oath in the form required by law, when he was questioned, stated the following:

This witness was asked whether he was present at the inspection and general review which was conducted [5r] this most recent Sunday. [That is, the review] of the people who are going in His Majesty's service on this expedition for pacification of Tierra Nueva. He replied that it is true that this witness was present during the inspection from beginning to end.

As a *vecino* of the Ciudad de México and *veedor* of this *provincia*, this witness was asked to state and declare what *vecinos* of the Ciudad de México and this *provincia* he saw were at the inspection and review. This witness declared that he has knowledge of and is familiar with the *vecinos* of the Ciudad de México and those of this jurisdiction because he has been present in the land for sixteen years, more or less. [He stated] that during the entire inspection and [among all the] people of those he saw he did not see that any other *vecinos* were going except the captain general Francisco Vázquez de Coronado and *alcaide* Lope de Samaniego. [He declared] also that Domingo Martín was a *vecino*, who is

leaving his wife in the aforesaid *ciudad*, and [also] one Alonso Sánchez, who is going on the expedition with his wife. [Oñate stated] that he has no knowledge of any other *vecino* of the Ciudad de México who is going. This witness believes that if there was, he would be aware of it.

By the oath he swore, [he stated] that he [did] not see any *vecino* of this *ciudad* of Compostela during [the review]. Two *vecinos* of Guadalajara are going; one [is] married to an Indian woman and the other [is] a single man.[35]

[He declared] that all the people whom this witness saw are going of their own volition without any coercion or compulsion. It seems to him that many *caballeros*, youths, and other persons who are going on the expedition and who were living in the *ciudad* and [were] from other parts of Nueva España produce more benefit than harm by leaving it. [That is] because they were licentious and had no [means] by which to sustain themselves.[36] [The witness stated] that this is the truth by the oath he swore. And he signed it with his name.

Cristóbal de Oñate

When the statements and testimonies of the aforementioned witnesses had been taken and accepted and reviewed by His Most Illustrious Lordship, he stated that he was ordering and did order that an authorized copy be extracted from the original, which remains in my possession. This is it, [prepared] in the required public form, in order that it can be sent [and presented] before His Majesty and the lords of his *consejo*, so that [they can] determine and order what may be of service.

[5v]

By His Lordship's order, I extracted the aforementioned report from the original today, Friday, the twenty-seventh of February in the year of Our Lord one thousand five hundred and forty. Witnesses: Secretary Antonio de Almaguer[37] and I, Juan de León, *escribano* of Their Majesties treasury and the royal *audiencia* of this Nueva España, which has its seat in the Ciudad de México.

I was present at what is related [above], during the observation, examination, and swearing of the aforementioned witnesses and during the inspection which was made mention of above. By order of His Most Illustrious Lordship, I prepared in writing and extracted it from the original, which remains in my possession. Thus I affixed here this my registered mark, [which is] such {sign} in testimony of the truth.

{rubric} Juan de León {rubric}

[6r] [blank]

[6v]

{[15]40 Nueva Galicia}

Report of an inquiry which the most illustrious lordship [the] viceroy of Nueva España sent to [be presented] before His Majesty. It concerns the people who are going to the newly discovered land in order to serve His Majesty.

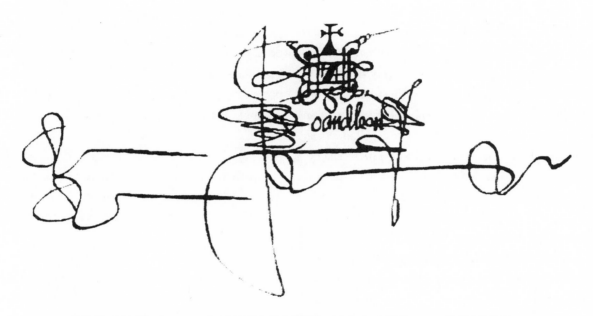

FIGURE 14.1. The signature and registered sign (*signo*) of Juan de León. AGI, Patronato, 21, N.2, R.3\10.
Reproduced courtesy of Spain's Ministerio de Educación, Cultura y Deporte.

TRANSCRIPTION

[fol. 1r]

En la çiudad de Compostella de la nueva / Galizia de esta nueva españa Veynte e Un dias / del mes de hebrero año del nasÇimiento de nuestro Salvador / *Jesu cristo* de myll y quinientos y quarenta años ante el / muy Illustre señor don antonio de mendoça Visorrei e governador / Por su magestad en esta nueva españa y presydente del audiençia e chancilleria / Real que Reside en la Çiudad de mexico e en presencia de my Juan / de leon escrivano de Camara de sus magestades y de la dicha real audiençia / Francisco Vazquez de coronado governador e capitan general de esta proVinÇia / E capitan general de la tierra nueVamente descubierta por el padre provynciaL / Fray marcos de nyca e presento ante su señoria Una petiçion el t(h)enor de la / qual es este que se sigue

Illustrisimo señor

Francisco Vazquez de coronado governador de esta nueva galizia por su magestAd E ca- / pitan general nombrado por Vuestra señoria para la tierra nuevamente descubierta / digo que a my notiÇia es Venido que algunas personas por no tener / buena Voluntad de esta Jornada que Vuestra señoria en nombre de su magestad / manda hazer han dicho que muchos Vecinos de la Çiudad de mexico e de las demas / Çiudades e Villas de la nueva españa e de esta Çiudad de compostella e de las / otras Villas de esta provynçia e gover-nacion por Ruego e yndu- / Zimyento myo Van en la dicha Jornada de Cuya causa la dicha Çiudad de mexico / E la nueva españa queda sola e con poca gente de lo qual se podrian / seguir ynconVinientes e por que se sepa la Verdad de los Vecinos de la / nueva españa e de esta provyncia que Van en my Companya que son muy pocos / y estos no Van por my atraemyento ny ynduzimiento syno de su Voluntad / E

no haran falta en la nueva españa A causa de ser tam pocos / pido y suplico a Vuestra señoria mande tomar ynformaÇion de ello / pues al presente (^p) estan aqui gonçalo de salazar e pero almidrez / cherino Facttor e Veedor de esta nueva españa por su magestad e otras / personas Vecinos de mexico que sabran la Verdad de todo y la dicha / {rúbrica}

[fol. 1v]

ynformacion habida Vuestra señoria provea e mande Lo que mas Convenga Al ser- / Viçio de su magestad e bien e seguridad de la dicha nueva españa francisco Vazquez / de coronado

E leida la dicha petiÇion su señoria Illustrisima dixo que el señor licenciado / maldonado oidor de la dicha rreal Au-diencia de sus magestades que pre- / sente estava tome e ResÇiba esta ymformaÇion e que para que mejor / se haga provea que los dichos factor e Veedor e Regidores e las / otras personas que estan aqui asy estan e esten presentes al esamen / de la dicha gente en el dicho alarde que asy se hiziere

E luego en este dicho dia el dicho senor licenciado maldonado Vista la dicha / PetiÇion e lo proVeido por el dicho senor Visorrey mando que / gonçalo de salazar e pero almidez cherino Factor e Veedor / de su magestad de esta nueva espana y hernand perez de bocanegra e Juan / de xaso y antonio serrano de cardona e sebastian bejarano Vecinos de / la çiudad de mexico e cristoval de oñate Vecino de esta Çiudad e Veedor de su magestad / en esta governacion e diego ordoñez vecino de la ÇiUdad de los Angeles / e Juan fernandez Vecino de la purificaÇion que estavan Al presente en esta / çiudad de compostella Asy estan e esten presentes al alarde / que se ha de hazer mañana para que Vean e conozcan las personas Vecinos de / mexico e de otras partes de esta nueva españa que Van en esta Jornada / para que Vistos con Juramento declaren las personas que son / lo qual les fue notificado[38]

E despues de lo susodicho en la dicha Çiudad de compostella de pe- / dimyento del dicho capitan general Veynte e seys dias del dicho mes de hebrero / E del dicho año de myll e quinientos e quarenta años el dicho señor licenciado mal- / donado ReÇibio Juramento de los dichos hernand perez de bocanegra / E de los (e de los) dichos gonçalo de salazar e pero almydez / cherino factor e Veedor de su magestad en esta nueVa espana e de / antonio serrano de cardoña Regidores de la dicha Çiudad de mexico / los quales habiendo Jurado en forma debida de derecho cada Uno por sy / dixeron lo syguyente secreta e apartadamente[39] / {rúbrica}

[fol. 2r]
2
E despues de lo susodicho en la dicha Çiudad de conpostella Veynte / e siete dias del dicho mes de hebrero del dicho año de myll e quinientos e quarenta / años fue tomado e Recibido Juramentos en forma de derecho de cristoval de onate / Veedor de esta proVinÇia el qual habiendo jurado en forma dixo lo siguiente / que esta Adelante

{Testigo} hernand perez de bocanegra Vezino de la ÇiUdad de mexico testigo presentado en la / dicha rrazon habiendo Jurado segun(d) forma de derecho para ynformacion de lo / susodicho preguntado por el tenor de la dicha petiÇion dixo lo syguiente

{+} preguntado sy estuvo este testigo presente el domyngo proXimo pasado / que fue quando se hizo el alarde de la gente que el muy yllustre / señor Visorrey de esta nueva espana ymVio A la paÇificaÇion de la / Tierra nueVamente descubierta por el padre proVinÇial fray / marcos de nyça e quando se contaron (y esaminaron) e exa- / minaron las personas que Van en la dicha Jornada dixo que es Verdad / que estuvo presente a todo el dicho Alarde e al contar e esaminar de la dicha / gente y en presenÇia de su señoria e de otros muchas Cavalleros e Vecinos de esta / nueVa espana el qual

paso por ante escrivano e se hizo nomyna de ellos / aqui se Remyte

{+} preguntado diga e declare este testigo como Vezino de la dicha çiudad de mexico / que Vecinos de la dicha Çiudad de mexico e de otras partes de esta nueva españa yban / en el dicho alarde e Resena que Van a la dicha tierra nueVa dixo este testigo / que como dicho tiene estuvo presente al dicho alarde e conosÇio e Vi(d)o[40] las / personas que en el yban e Van a la dicha paÇificaÇion e para mas JustificaÇion / pidyo le fuese mostrada la copia de nomyna de ellos que pasaron ante my / el dicho escrivano la qual le fue mostrada e leydo las personas en ella contenydo / e dixo que en toda la dicha gente no conosÇio yr ny Va otro Vezino / de mexico syno a domingo martyn que es Un hombre casado que le ha Visto algunos / Vezes Residir en mexico e proveelle de correos e Un alonso sanches / Va con su muger e Un hijo el qual dicho alonso sanches solia ser çapatero / e Un manÇebo hijo del bachiller alonso perez que ha pocos dias / que vino de salamanca que por traVieso le ymvia su padre a la guerra / {rúbrica}

[fol. 2v]
E otros dos o tres officiales que en mexico Veia trabaJar pero que no sabe / que sean Vecinos e que para el juramento que (^h) tiene hecho que este testigo no Vi(d)o en / Todo el dicho alarde que se hizo que fuese persona Vecino de mexico porque ha / catorze años poco mas o menos que este testigo es Vezino e mo- / rador en mexico syno es al dicho capitan general francisco vazquez de / (de) coronado e allcayde lope de samanyego maestre de Campo / e que cree e tiene por Çierto que Van los de arriba dichos / de su Voluntad como todos los demas e que esta es la verdad / para el Juramento que hizo e firmolo de su nombre fernand perez de boca- / negra

{Testigo} {ytem} Antonio serrano de cardona Vezino e Regidor de la dicha ÇiUdad / de mexico testigo presentado e Rescibido para ynformaÇion de lo / susodicho syendo preguntado por el tenor de la dicha petiÇion / dixo e depuso lo syguyente

{+} preguntado sy estuvo este testigo Al alarde e Reseña que el señor / Vissorrey mando hazer e se hizo el domingo proXimo pasado / de la gente que ymVia en nombre de su magestad y en su Real servycio / A la paÇificaÇion de la tierra que descubrio fray marcos / de nyÇa provyncial de la orden de senor San francisco con ynstruccion / de su señoria dixo que es Verdad que estuvo presente A todo el dicho / alarde e Reseña desde el prinÇipio hasta el cabo / e Vi(d)o e myro todos los que ally pasaron e se escrivyeron / ante el escrivano del audiencia real

{+} preguntado diga e declare como Vezino e Regidor de la / dicha Çiudad de mexico que Vezinos Vi(d)o que fuesen en el dicho alarde / e Van en esta Jornada de la dicha Çiudad (^con) e de otras partes / con el dicho capitan general francisco Vazquez de coronado dixo que este testigo / no Vi(d)o que fuese en el dicho alarde otros Vecinos de mexico syno el dicho francisco / Vazquez de coronado capitan general e allcayde lope de samanyego maestre / {rúbrica}

[fol. 3r]

3

de Canpo e que Un alonso sanches Asymysmo yba ally que solia ser Vecino de / mexico pero que ha muchos dias que le Vi(d)o en casa e despues se partio / syendo mercader e se fue a buscar de comer e que asymysmo / Vi(d)o a Un domingo martyn que solia Vivyr en mexico e que tanbien / hA muchos dias que no le conosÇe Cassa ny cree la tiene por- / que no le Veia Resydir en mexico e que otro nyngun(d) Vezino / paso en el dicho alarde ny cree que Va en esta Jornada porque si lo fuera / este testigo lo supiera e los conosÇiera porque ha Veynte años que ya que / se gano mexico que Resyde en la dicha ÇiUdad e desde que se fundo / de crisᵗianos e porque desde quinze anos a esta parte es Regidor / de ella e sabe e conosçe los Vecinos de ella e que en lo demas que el les / hA Vysto a todos yr e yban los mas contentos hombres que ha / Visto yr en esta tierra A conquystas e entradas e que en lo / demas que le es preguntado sy hazen falta los que Van que le parece / A este testigo e tiene por Çierto que antes hazen provecho en yr / que daño e que no fazen falta e porque despues de partida la gente / de mexico este testigo partio de la dicha Çiudad e la Vi(d)o llena de gente / e no parecio hAber falta la que salio e Va en la dicha Jornada e que / esta

es la verdad para el Juramento que hizo e firmolo Antonio serrano / de cardoña

{Testigo} gonçalo de salazar factor de su magestad en esta nueva espana / e Vecino e Regidor de la dicha ÇiUdad de mexico testigo presentado e Resçibido / en la dicha Rason habiendo Jurado en forma de derecho e s(e)yendo / preguntado por el tenor de la dicha petiÇion dixo e depuso los syguiente

{+} preguntado sy este testigo estuvo presente al alarde e Resena / general que se hizo el domyngo proXimo pasado de la gente / que Va en servycio de su magestad a la tierra nuevamente des- / cubierta dixo que este testigo estuvo presente al dicho alarde e resena / preguntado diga e declare que como tal factor e Vezino de la dicha / {rúbrica}

[fol. 3v]

ÇiUdad que Vezinos Vi(d)o que Van en esta Jornada dixo que / este testigo es Una de las personas que mas notiÇia tiene / de todas las personas que estan en la dicha tierra e de los que mas / conosÇe en ella

e que para el juramento que hecho tiene nynguna persona beneficiado / ny Con Repartimyento en la tierra de toda la nueVa españa no la Vi(d)o / pasar en todo el dicho alarde syno fue solo el Capitan generaL / Francisco Vazquez de coronado e que conosÇio Un Vezino solo / de mexico el qual no tiene Repartimyento e que otro Vecino no conosÇio / ally de mexico ny de toda la nueva españa antes Uno de los mayores / bienes que se han hecho en esta nueva españa fue sacar la gente moça / e Viçiosa que estava en la dicha Çiudad e en toda la nueva españa / e que A todos estos Vi(d)o yr de muy buena Voluntad e / ymportunado ellos antes por yr en la Jornada que persu- / adiendoles a ella e que esta es la verdad para el Juramento que hizo / e firmolo de su nombre gonçalo de salazar

{Testigo} pero almydez cherino Veedor de su magestad en esta nueva españa / Testigo presentado e Resçibido en la dicha rrazon habiendo Jurado en forma / de derecho e S(e)yendo preguntado dixo lo syguyente {ytem} preguntado por el tenor de la dicha petiÇion diga e declare sy estuvo / presente este testigo al alarde e Resena general que se hizo el / domingo proXimo pasado de la gente que Va en servycio de su magestad / A la paÇificaÇion de la tierra nuevamente descubierta dixo / que es verdad que estuvo presente a todo el dicho alarde e Reseña como / el es preguntado

{+} preguntado diga e declare este testigo como Veedor e Vezino / de la ÇiUdad de mexico que Vecinos Vi(d)o que fuesen en el dicho alarde / e Reseña para yr en la dicha Jornada de la dicha Çiudad de mexico / {rúbrica}

[fol. 4r]
4
E de otras partes de esta nueva españa dixo este testigo que no / Vi(d)o nyngun(d) Vezino que fuese en el dicho alarde e Viaje syno / a francisco Vazquez de coronado Capitan general e al allcayde lope / de samanyego maestre de Canpo e a Un alonso sanches que Va con / su muger e que no sabe que sea Vezino e que este testigo exsamyno / e Vi(d)o mucha parte de la dicha gente e la Vi(d)o e myro toda / porque al tiempo del dicho alarde se escrivyera para saber los Ca- / ballos e armas que llevavan e que toda la demas gente / era personas sueltas e de poco tiempo aca Venidas a la tierra / a buscar de comer e que asymysmo Vi(d)o a Un domingo martyn / que todo el mas tiempo del año anda fuera de mexico e que al / parecer de este testigo hA s(e)ydo cosa muy provechosa que saliese de mexico / la gente que f(a)ue que antes dañaban en la ÇiUdad de Vecinos de ella / que aprovechavan por ser los mas Cavalleros manÇebos e ViÇiosos / syn tener que hazer en la Çiudad ny en su tierra e a lo que syntio / de todos Van de su propia Voluntad e muy contentos a la dicha / paÇificaÇion de la dicha tierra nueVa e que al parecer / de este testigo sy la dicha tierra no se descubriera toda la mas / de esta gente que alla es yda se Volvyera A Castilla O / se fueran Al peru o a otras partes A buscar de comer / e que esta es la verdad para el juramento que hizo e firmolo pero / almydez

{Testigo} servan Vexarano Vezino de la ÇiUdad de mexico testigo presentado e rres- / Çibido en la dicha rrazon ha-

biendo Jurado en forma de derecho / e s(e)yendo preguntado por el tenor de la dicha petiÇion / dixo lo syguyente

{+} preguntado sy este testigo estuvo presente al tiempo que se hizo / el dicho alarde e Reseña general de toda la dicha gente / {rúbrica}

[fol. 4v]
que Va en esta Jornada en servycio de su magestad a la paÇificaÇion / de la dicha tierra nueva dixo que este testigo estuvo presente / al dicho alarde desde el prinçipio hasta al cabo e los Vi(d)o e / conosÇio la dicha gente

{+} preguntado diga e declare este testigo como Vezino de la dicha Çiudad / que Vezino Vi(d)o que fuese en el dicho alarde de la dicha Çiudad e de otras / ÇiUdades e Villas de esta nueva españa dixo que este testigo tiene / mucha notiÇia de todos los Vecinos e moradores de mexico / porque desde que se gano la dicha Çiudad hA estado en ella e se ha criado / entre los e que en todo el dicho alarde no conosÇio yr otro Vecino / alguno syno el Capitan general francisco Vazquez de coronado que es casado / en mexico e lope de samanyego maestre de campo que no es casado / e cree ser Vecino e a domyngo martyn que es casado e a Un alonso sanches que lleva A su / muger al qual este testigo conosçio ser tratante e por estar muy / Alcançado e no tener con que se sustentar se Va a la tierra / a buscar de comer e que no Vi(d)o otro nyngun(d) Vezino e que le paresçe / A este testigo e tiene por muy Çierto que fue e es mucho provecho / a la dicha Çiudad de mexico e Vecinos de ella salir mucha gente solteros / que no tenya en que entender e ViÇiosos e por ser mucha parte / de ellos Cavalleros e personas que no alcanÇavan ny tenyan / Repartimyentos de yndios syno comer e holgar e se habian de yr / al peru e a otras partes e que todos estos yban muy con- / Tentos e de buena Voluntad e que esta es la verdad para el / Juramento que hizo e firmolo servan Vexarano

{- +} cristoval de oñate Vecino de la ÇiUdad de mexico e Veedor por su magestad de esta proVincia / de la nueva galizia testigo presentado en la dicha rrazon habiendo Jurado en forma de derecho / e s(e)yendo preguntado dixo lo syguyente

preguntado sy este testigo estuvo presente al alarde e Resena general que se hizo / {rúbrica}

[fol. 5r]

5

el domingo ProXimo passado de la gente que Va en esta Jornada en / servycio de su magestad a la pacificaÇion de la tierra nueVa dixo que es / Verdad que este testigo estuvo presente al dicho alarde (^ha) desde el prinÇipio / hasta el Cabo

preguntado diga e declare este testigo como Vezino de la dicha Çiudad de mexico / e Veedor de esta provyncia que Vecinos Vi(d)o que fuesen en el dicho alarde e Re- / seña de la Çiudad de mexico e de esta provyncia dixo que este testigo tiene notiÇia / E conosçe los Vecinos de la Çiudad de mexico e los de esta governacion porque / ha diez e seys anos poco mas o menos que esta en la tierra e que en todo el / dicho alarde e gente no Vi(d)o que fuesen otros Vezinos a lo que este testigo Vi(d)o / syno el Capitan general francisco Vazquez de coronado e allcayde lope de / samanyego e tambien era Vezino domingo martyn que dexa su / muger en la dicha çiudad e Un alonso sanchez que Va con su muger en la dicha / Jornada e que no sabe otro Vezino (^d) que fuese de la dicha Çiudad de mexico / e que cree que si lo hoviera este testigo lo conosÇiera e que para el Juramento / que hizo de esta Çiudad de compostella Vecino de ella no Ve nynguno e de gua- / dalaJara Van dos Vezinos el Uno Cassado con Una yndia y el / otro soltero e que toda la dicha gente a lo que Vi(d)o este testigo Va de su Voluntad / syn premya ny fuerça ninguna e que antes le paresÇe que muchos / Cavalleros mançebos e otras personas que Van en la dicha Jornada que Residian / en la dicha Çiudad e de otras partes de esta nueva espana le pareÇe / que hazen mas proVecho que daño salir de

ella porque andavan ViÇiosos / e no tenyan con que se sustentar e que esta es la verdad para el Juramento que / hizo e firmolo de su nombre cristoval de onate

E asy tomados e ResÇibidos los dichos e depuseÇiones / de los dichos testigos e Vistos por su señoria Yllustrisima dixo que mandava / e mando saque del dicho oreginal que queda en my poder Un traslado / AUttorizado que es este en publica forma para lo ymViar Ante / su magestad e ante los señores de(l) su consejo para que provea E mande lo que sea servydo / {rúbrica}

[fol. 5v]

E por mandado de su señoria saque la dicha ynformacion del dicho oreginaL / hoy Viernes Veynte e siete de hebrero año del senor de myll e quinientos / E quarenta años testigos el secretario Antonio de almaguer E Yo / El dicho Juan de leon escrivano de camara de sus magestades y / del audiençia real de esta nueva espana que Reside en la dicha / Çiudad de mexico fuy presente a lo que dicho es al ver e exsaminar / e jurar los dichos testigos y al dicho alarde que de suso se / haze minÇion e por mandado de su senoria Illustrisima lo escrivy / e saque del dicho oreginal que queda en my poder e por ende / fize aquy este mio signo (A)tall

(A)tall [signo] En testimonio de verdad / {rúbrica} Joan de leon {rúbrica}

[fol. 6r] [blank]

[fol. 6v]

{40 Nueva Galicia}

Ynfformacion que ynVia el muy illustre señoria Visorrey / de la nueva espana para ante su magestad sobre la gente / que Va a servir A su magestad a la tierra nuevamente descubierta

Document 15

Narrative of Alarcón's Voyage, 1540

History Library, Museum of New Mexico, Santa Fe

Ramusio, *Terzo volume delle navigationi et viaggi*, 1556, fols. 363r–370v

INTRODUCTION

A great distance separated even the northernmost fringes of Nueva Galicia from the presumed affluent centers of population that came to be known as Cíbola. That much was apparent from the reports delivered by Álvar Núñez Cabeza de Vaca and his companions in 1536. Thus, for the expedition's organizers, keeping a large group bound for Cíbola supplied with food, clothing, armaments, and other materials without despoiling the native people along the way would be daunting. And doing so would be crucial if the viceroy was to adhere to his commitment "not [to] inflict injury on or [exercise] force against the Indians. . . . They are not to take anything they may possess from them against their will."[1]

The difficulty of supply could be greatly lessened, however, if the expedition could be reprovisioned by sea. Hence, when Mendoza dispatched fray Marcos de Niza northward late in 1538, it was not only to verify the existence of populous and prosperous settlements. He also instructed the friar "to ascertain whether there is knowledge of the seacoast."[2] The friar, for his part, as he trekked northward, dutifully sought to learn about the coast and to determine from time to time his distance from it. He was dismayed at one point to find himself "deviat[ing] from the coast and my instruction was not to distance myself from it."[3] At Eastertime 1539 Marcos was in Vacapa, as he reported, "forty leagues . . . to the sea," a distance that did not please him.[4]

Marcos's official report suggested that the route to Cíbola diverged increasingly from the Gulf of California as it proceeded north. Nevertheless, some persons, perhaps including the viceroy, got the impression that Cíbola itself might be near or even on the coast. For instance, a witness in Habana in 1539 stated that Cíbola "is on the coast of the [Mar] del Sur."[5] It was with such a possibility in mind that in 1540 Mendoza commissioned Hernando de Alarcón, a close associate and member of his personal guard, to rendezvous by sea with the Coronado expedition.[6]

As was made abundantly clear in instructions to him for a proposed second voyage the following year, Alarcón's principal mission was to carry goods and provisions to the expedition.[7] Many years later, Pedro de Castañeda de Nájera put it this way: "Alarcón was to depart with two *navíos* which were in the port of Navidad on the Costa del Sur and travel to the port of Jalisco, in order to carry the clothing the men-at-arms could not take [with them]."[8] According to Bernal Díaz del Castillo, writing during the same decade as Castañeda de Nájera, Alarcón also carried hardware, some artillery pieces, gunpowder, crossbows, and arms and armor of all sorts, as well as olive oil and hardtack.[9]

Although his first responsibility was to deliver such supplies, Alarcón seems, from his own report, to have been powerfully drawn to reconnaissance of the territory inland from the head of the Gulf of California. As we mention in regard to other narrative documents of the Coronado expedition, geographical and topographical descriptions are minor aspects of Alarcón's report. At center stage are the native people whom he and his party met as they ascended the Colorado River. The large, wealthy *reinos* of Cabeza de Vaca's and fray Marcos's *relaciones* were his goal. In the process of his search, however, Alarcón recorded detailed observations of the natives he encountered. Many of these are in harmony with reports of nineteenth- and twentieth-century ethnologists who worked among the Yuman peoples of the same area, likely descendants of those met by the Alarcón party.

Alarcón's report suggests that he had frequent and relatively easy communication with many of the native people he met. Given the common reliance on hand signs and the difficulty inherent in translating abstract words such as "God" from Castellano (Spanish) to the native languages, the completeness of this communication is highly suspect.

Among the many things revealed by the record of Alarcón's voyage are the rapid, long-distance communication and even intervisitation that were commonplace among the peoples of Tierra Nueva. About two months after the vanguard of the Coronado expedition arrived at Cíbola, for instance, linguistically unrelated people more than 350 miles away already had detailed and quite accurate descriptions of the Europeans. At least one man from the lower Gila River had been to Cíbola recently and had personally seen the foreigners.[10]

As captain, Alarcón had overall authority over the little fleet of three vessels, although technical management of the ships would have been left to the pilots, Nicolás Zamorano and Domingo del Castillo.[11] The latter pilot subsequently prepared a map of the Gulf of California on the basis of observations made during his service with Alarcón. The original map is not known to have survived, but an eighteenth-century copy of it, made by Francisco Antonio Lorenzana, does exist.[12]

Probably during the final, return leg of the trip Alarcón wrote an abbreviated summary report of his undertakings for the viceroy. The fate of that original manuscript is unknown, but an Italian translation of it was published within a matter of years by Giovanni Battista Ramusio.[13] Other records resulting from the Alarcón voyage, including a map painted by an indigenous elder, a lengthy and detailed logbook

prepared by Alarcón himself, and a register of latitudes measured during the voyage, have apparently disappeared.[14]

The Italian translation of the summary report was published in 1556 in the first edition of Ramusio's *Terzo volume delle navigationi et viaggi*.[15] The copy of that volume which we used to prepare the transcription and translation that follow is held by the History Library in the Museum of New Mexico, Santa Fe, New Mexico. Staff there graciously made the volume available to us for study. A draft English translation was made of the 1556 Ramusio text at our request by Larry Duncan Miller of the Spanish Colonial Research Center at the University of New Mexico. We then edited and revised that draft.

There are many obvious typographical errors in Ramusio's edition, even some that lead us to suspect the fluency of the sixteenth-century translator's Italian. He appears to have been more comfortable in Spanish than Italian and often lapses into Spanish forms, as we note repeatedly. In one case he even tries to Italianize the Spanish verb *ir* instead of using its Italian equivalent, *andare*. He frequently, though not always, drops the final *o* from third-person plural preterit indicative verbs. This yields forms that look more like Spanish than Italian—for instance, "-aron" instead of "-arono." Many of these errors were corrected in the book's second edition in 1565. Part of the explanation for this seemingly sloppy translation work is undoubtedly the heavy introduction of hispanisms into Italian during the sixteenth century, owing to Spain's dominant role in Europe throughout that period.[16]

As we pointed out in the introduction to Document 6, Ramusio has a deservedly poor reputation as a publisher of translations, because from time to time he introduced alterations and additions to the original texts without the slightest editorial acknowledgment. Fortunately, in the case of Alarcón's narrative, we have for comparison what is evidently a more abbreviated paraphrase of the Spanish original published by Antonio de Herrera y Tordesillos in the early 1600s.[17] There are no glaring inconsistencies between the Herrera and Ramusio versions. That said, there are obvious discontinuities in the Ramusio edition, as we later note several times. Whether these were introduced by Ramusio or reflect Alarcón's own composition of the document by excerpting passages and sections from his longer "book" cannot be answered.[18] It can be said with certainty, though, that Ramusio or his translator is the author of the headings for the chapters into which the report was divided for publication. To indicate that they were not part of Alarcón's original manuscript, in the transcript and translation that follow, the "chapter headings" are enclosed in flourished brackets { }.

All previously published editions of Alarcón's report are based directly or indirectly on the published Ramusio text. In the 1600s Richard Hakluyt issued an English translation, and in the 1830s Henri Ternaux-Compans published one in French. More recently, George Hammond and Agapito Rey included an English translation of the report in their 1940 *Narratives of the Coronado Expedition*.[19] We consulted all these editions in vetting the following translation. In both translation and transcription, folio numeration conforms to the published 1556 Italian edition.

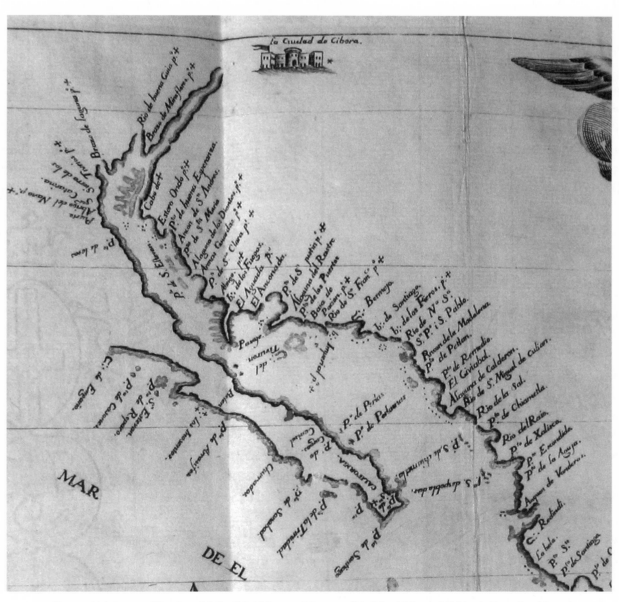

FIGURE 15.1. A copy of Domingo del Castillo's 1541 map of the coast of the Mar del Sur and California. Reproduced from *Historia de Nueva España*, by Francisco Antonio Lorenzana (1770). Courtesy DeGolyer Library, Southern Methodist University.

TRANSLATION

[363r]

{Report of the sea voyage and reconnaissance made by Captain Fernando [de] Alarcón by order of the most illustrious lord don Antonio de Mendoza, viceroy of Nueva España, provided at Colima, a port of Nueva España.}[20]

{Fernando [de] Alarcón, after having suffered a storm, joins the *armada* in the port of Santiago and risks great danger [going] from there to the port of Aguayaval and in attempting to reconnoiter a gulf. During this [journey] he discovers a river on the coast that has a strong current. Entering this [river] he discovers a great number of armed Indians, deals with them by means of sign language, and, fearing danger, returns to the *navío*.}[21]

On Sunday, the ninth of May 1540, I sailed with two *navíos*, the one named *San Pedro*, which was the flagship, and the other, *Santa Catarina*. We went in search of the port of Santiago de Buena Esperanza,[22] where, when we first arrived, we suffered a terrible storm. Those who were on the *navío Santa Catarina*, being more afraid of it than they should have been, threw overboard nine artillery pieces, two anchors and a cable, and many other things necessary for the enterprise in which they were engaged, as well as for the *navío* itself.

Once [we were] together [again], we traveled to the port of Santiago, where I repaired the damage [that had been] received, provided myself with the necessary things, and took onto the *navío* the men who were waiting for me. Then I set off on the route toward the port of Aguayaval.[23] When I had arrived there, I heard that the general, Francisco Vázquez de Coronado, had departed with all his men. I took over the *navío* called *San Gabriel*, which was traveling with

foodstuffs for the armed force, and conveyed it with me in fulfillment of Your Lordship's orders. Then I continued along the coast, without departing from it, in order to see whether I could find some sign or some Indian who could give me news of [the force the general was leading].

Traveling very close to the land, I happened to discover some other very good anchorages. [I say "discover"] because the *navíos* that Captain Francisco de Ulloa was leading for the Marqués del Valle did not see or locate [them].[24] When I had reached the shallows where the aforesaid *navíos* had turned back, it seemed to me, as well as to the others, that there was dry land in front of us and that it was a dangerous thing.

Those shallows frightened us; the bottom [363v] was something [that made us] consider whether we could enter there with *bateles* [*barcas*]. The pilots and other men wanted us to do the same as Captain Ulloa had done.[25] But because Your Lordship had commanded that I was to report to you concerning the secret of that gulf,[26] I determined that, even now that I had learned the *navíos* might be lost, by no means should I avoid seeing the head [of the gulf]. Therefore I commanded Nicolás Zamorano, the chief pilot, and Domingo del Castillo to each take a *batel* [*barca*] and, sounding line in hand, traverse the shallows to see whether they could find a channel through which the *navíos* could enter.[27] It seemed to them the *navíos* could [go] ahead, although there would be much work and danger.

In this manner, I, along with [the pilots],[28] started following the route they led [me on]. Shortly afterward, all three *navíos* were together, stuck in the sand, such that one could not aid the other. Nor were the *bateles* [*barcas*] able to give assistance, because the current was so great that [each] one was unable to approach the other. Because of this we ran great risk, since [part of] the deck of the flagship was under water many times. If a huge wave had not miraculously come, which righted the *navío* and allowed it to breathe [that is, to survive], we would have drowned there.[29] Similarly, the other two *navíos* were at very great risk. Yet because they were smaller and drew less water, their risk was not as great as ours. Now it was God's will that as the tide surged the *navíos* floated again, and with this we proceeded.

Although the men wanted to go back, I was still determined that we should go farther and continue the journey in that vicinity. We went on ahead with great effort, turning the bow now this way, now that way, to see if we could relocate the channel. Thanks be to God, by this means we came to the head of the gulf. There we found a very powerful river that flowed with a very furious current, because of which we could barely navigate. I determined to travel in this manner as well as I could [up] the river: with the twenty men and two *barcas*, leaving the other with the *navíos*. I began to ascend the river in a *barca* with Rodrigo Maldonado, treasurer of the *armada*,[30] and Gaspar de Castilleja, *contador*, and with some small pieces of artillery. I gave an order to all the men that no one should move or make any gesture that I did not order them to make, should we encounter Indians.

On the same day, which was Thursday, the twenty-sixth of August,[31] continuing our travel by boat by hauling on the towrope, we traveled as far as six leagues. The next day, which was Friday, at daybreak, continuing our way upriver, I saw some Indians who were going to certain rude shelters close to the water.[32] As soon as they saw us, some ten or twelve of them drew apart, disturbed. When they shouted loudly, others of their company came together there until there were fifty. This rapidly brought those within the rude shelters outside, and they took [the possessions] they had into some thickets. Many of them came running toward the place we were approaching, making broad gestures that we should turn back, making violent threats, and running from one side to the other.

Having seen matters so changed [from the way they had been when we were in midstream], I had the *barcas* form in the middle of the river, so that the Indians might be reassured. I went to ride at anchor and placed the men in the best order I could, ordering that no one speak or make a

gesture or any movement, or shift from his place, or show any emotion no matter what the Indians might do, or show any hostile intent. In this manner, the Indians came closer and closer to the river to see us, and little by little I went nearer to them where the river seemed to be deepest.

In the midst of this there were more than two hundred and fifty Indians with their bows and arrows and with some banners like [the Indians] of Nueva España use during war.[33] When they saw that I was going toward land, they came in our direction with loud cries [and] with their bows and arrows drawn and banners raised. I went to the prow[34] of the *barca* with the interpreter I was bringing with me [and] ordered him to speak to them. When he spoke, they did not understand him, nor he, them. Yet because they saw he was like them, they held back. When I saw this, I drew closer to the land, and they, with great cries, came to the edge of the river to engage me, making signs that I should not come any farther, placing stakes in the water and planting them on land.

The more I delayed, the more people continued to come together to see. At this, having made up my mind, I began to make signs of peace. Taking [my] sword and shield, I threw them into the *barca* [which was] beached, stepping my feet onto them, making them understand by this and other signs that I did not wish to make war with them, and that [364r] they should do the same. Having seized a banner, I lowered it and had the men I had with me also sit down. Taking the items I had brought with me for trade, I summoned them in order to give them [these things]. But with all that, not one of them moved to come to take anything from me.

[Instead] they gathered together and were talking. A great murmur rose up among them. Suddenly, one came out from among them with a rod that bore some shells. He entered the water to give it to me, and I took it. I made signs to him that he should approach me. When he had done so, I embraced him and gave him in exchange some beads and other things. Having returned with them to his people, he began to look at them and speak with them.Shortly afterward, many of them came toward me. I indicated to them that they should lower their banners and lay down their arms, which they did at once. Then I signaled to them that they should put them all in one place and withdraw from them, which they likewise did. With this, the Indians who had been there [before] began appearing again. [The other Indians] were making them abandon their arms and put them together with the others.

After this, I summoned them [all] to come to me. I gave everyone who came some of the trade goods, treating them with affection. There were so many [Indians] who were crowding around me that it seemed to me I was no longer safe there. I signaled to them to return and that they should all stay by a hill that was between a plain and the river and that no more than ten should approach me at a time.[35] Immediately, the oldest of them called to them in a loud voice, telling them they should do so. Some ten or twelve of them came to me from [among] them. Therefore I felt nearly safe.

I decided to go out onto the land in order to better assure them. And to make myself feel safer, I indicated to them that they should sit on the ground, which they did. But when they saw that ten or twelve of my men were coming after me onto the land, they became agitated. I signaled to them that among us there would be peace and they should not be afraid. With this they became calm, and they remained seated as they had been shortly before. I drew near them and embraced them, giving them some little things. I charged my interpreter to talk to them because I wished very much to understand the means of speaking with them and what they had been shouting to me.

In order to find out what kind of food they had, I indicated to them that we wanted to eat. They brought me some ears of corn and a bread made from mesquite.[36] They made signs to me that they wanted to see an arquebus fired, which I had fired. They were all frightened and marveled [at it], except two or three of their elders who made no movements at all. On the contrary, they yelled at the others, because they had showed fear.

As a result of what one of the elders said, they began to get up from the ground and pick up their arms again. Wishing to appease [the elder], I attempted to give him a multicolored silk cord. Very angrily he chewed his lower lip quite energetically, gave me a blow from his elbow in the chest, and again spoke to the people, [now] with greater

furor. Then, when I saw the banners being raised, I made my mind up to return quietly to my *barca*.

With a bit of wind, I made sail, and we were able to overcome the current, which was very strong, although it displeased my companions to have to go forward. Meanwhile, the Indians came following us along the bank of the river, indicating by signs that I was to land so that they might give us foodstuffs. Some [were] sucking their fingers and others entering the water with ears of corn in order to give them to me in the *barca*.

{Concerning the dress, arms and armor, and build of the Indians [who were] found. An account of the many others with whom trade was conducted by means of signs, [how] foodstuffs were obtained, and [how they were treated with] great courtesy.}

In this manner we went two leagues, and I arrived at a break in the mountains, within which there was a recently constructed arbor. There [Indians] beckoned to me, shouting that I was to go there, showing me where with their hands and telling me there was something to eat there. I saw that the place looked as though it could serve for an ambush. [So] I did not want to go there, but instead continued my journey onward. Shortly afterward, more than a thousand men armed with bows and arrows came out of there, and then many women and children appeared. I did not want to go nearer to them. But since the sun was about to set, I stayed in the middle of the river.

These [various] Indians came wearing different costumes; some had a mark that covered their faces from top to bottom; others covered half of [their faces], but all painted with charcoal and each as seemed best to him. Some wore loincloths[37] in front in the same color as the mark on the face. On their heads they wore a piece of buckskin two *palmos* long, like a helmet,[38] and [carried] some staffs with feathers on top. Their weapons were bows and arrows made of hard wood and two or three sorts of clubs made from fire-seasoned wood. These people were large, well-proportioned, and without any corpulence.

[364v] They have their noses pierced at the base, from where they attach some pendants. Others wear shells and

have their ears pierced with many holes, in which they fix beads and shells. Everyone, both large and small, wears a cord made of various colors at the level of the navel. In the middle of it is attached a round cluster of feathers, which hangs behind them like a tail. Likewise, on the flesh of the arm they have a narrow cord. This one they wrap so many times it attains the width of a hand. They wear some splints of deer bone tied to [one] arm, which they use to clean off sweat,[39] and on the other [arm], some cane tubes. Similarly, they have with them some long sacks the width of a hand, tied to the left arm. They are filled with seeds from which they make their [customary] drink.[40] These [bags] also serve them as an arm band when using the bow. The body is marked by fire. Their hair is cut in the front and in the back ends at the waist. The women go about naked and wear a covering[41] of painted and glued feathers in back and front.[42] And their hair [they wear] like the men. Among these Indians there were three or four men with the same clothing as the women.

Now, at a good hour on the next day, which was Saturday, I set out to continue the journey, going upriver, having removed two men from each *batel* [*barca*] to pull the towrope. At daybreak we heard very loud shouts from Indians from both banks of the river, with their arms but without any banner. It seemed best to me to wait for them, to see what they wanted, as well as to see if our interpreter could understand them. They approached together above us [and] from one bank and the other jumped into the river with their bows and arrows. When they spoke the interpreter did not understand them, whereupon I began to indicate to them with signs that they were to leave their weapons as the others had done [earlier]. Some did that and some did not. I had those who laid [their weapons] aside approach me and gave them some trade goods.[43] When the others saw this, in order to get their share, they also did likewise.

Judging it to be safe, I leapt onto the land with them and placed myself in their midst. When they understood that I did not want to do battle with them, they began to give me shells and beads. Some brought me well-dressed hides, and others, corn and a cake made of poorly ground [corn]. [It was] such that I did not see a single one who came without [some] item. Before they gave it to me, when they were [still]

a good ways off, they began to cry out loudly and make gestures with the body and arms. Then they hurried to give me what they had brought. Since the sun had already set, I drew myself away and went to the middle of the river.

It was not yet light the following day when we heard a great outcry from one side of the river and the other. [The Indians] seemed to be in greater numbers [than the previous day]. They threw themselves into the river, swimming. They were coming to bring me some ears of corn and the cake I have mentioned. I showed them wheat, fava beans, and other seeds to see whether they had any of those. But they indicated that they did not know about them and marveled over everything.

I came to understand by means of signs that what they had most reverence and esteem for was the sun. I made them understand I came from the sun,[44] about which they marveled. Now they set themselves to examining me from head to foot and showed me more affection than before. When I requested food from them, they brought so much that I was forced to lighten the *barcas* twice. From this time onward, they threw a part of everything they brought me toward the sun and then turned to me to give me the other part.

Thus, I was always well served and honored by them, both in pulling the towrope and in giving me food to eat. They showed me so much affection that when I was among them, they wanted to carry my weight in their arms to their houses. They did not go beyond what I told them in anything.[45] For my safety, I laid down the rule that they should not carry weapons in my presence. They were so vigilant in doing this that whenever someone new came there with [weapons], they immediately went to meet him to make him leave them far from me.

And I made it clear that I was very pleased with them. I gave capes and other little things to some of their *principales,* because if we had to give them to everyone in general, all the goods of Nueva España would not be enough. So much was the affection and good will they showed me that the time came when, if by chance new Indians came there with weapons and someone warned them to lay them aside and, by negligence or not having understood the warning at first, they did not leave them, [the local Indians] ran and took [the weapons] from them by force and broke them to pieces in my presence.

They took up the towrope with such willingness, competing with one another, that it was not necessary to command them to do so. Because the current of the river was very strong, if it had not been for this assistance and if [whoever] pulled the towrope had poor practice [at the job], it would have been impossible to go upriver, nearly against the [force of the] water.

When I saw that they understood me in every way [365r] and that I, likewise, understood them, it occurred to me to see whether by some means I could give a good beginning to a successful outcome of the hopes I had. With some sticks and paper I had some crosses made and, among those others [that is, the ordinary Indians], I made it clear to them that they were things I esteemed most. And I kissed them, suggesting to them they should honor and prize them greatly and wear them around their necks, making them understand that was the symbol of heaven. They took them and kissed them and raised them high. And they showed that they were very happy and glad when they did this. Sometimes I showed [the Indians] great affection by placing them in my *barca*. And at such times I presented them some of the small items I carried. The situation then developed that there was not enough paper or sticks with which to make crosses.

In this way I was thronged until, when night came, I distanced myself [from the Indians] in the river, again returning to the middle. The Indians came to request permission from me to leave, saying they would return with foodstuffs to see me the following day. And in small groups they left, so that no more than fifty remained there. These [who stayed] made fires at our meeting place and remained there all night, calling out to each other.

The day was not fully light when it came to pass that [they] jumped into the river, swimming and demanding the towrope. We gave it to them willingly, thanking God for the excellent provision he had made for being able to proceed upriver. [That is] because there were so many Indians that if they had wanted to impede our passage, they could have done so, even had we been many more than we were.

{One of the Indians, having understood the interpreter's language, asks him various questions about the origin of the Spaniards; [the interpreter] tells him that their captain is a son of the sun,[46] which directs [the captain] and [the rest of the Spaniards]. Further, [he tells the Indian that] they [all] are to accept [the sun] as their lord. [Alarcón's party] takes this Indian away in the vessel, and he provides much information to them about that country.}

Going upriver, we navigated this way until Tuesday afternoon, having my interpreter speak to the people to find out whether anyone might understand him. I was aware that one [Indian] had responded to him, and I had the *bateles* [*barcas*] stopped. I summoned the one who understood, enjoining my interpreter not to speak to him or say more than what I would tell him. I saw that when that Indian was [coming], he began to talk to those people with great fury. Then they all began to gather together. My interpreter understood that the one who was coming into the *barca* was telling them that he wanted to find out what people we were, where we came from, and whether I came from beneath the water or from the earth or had fallen from the sky. When he had said this, a multitude of people together joined him. They marveled at seeing me speak.

From time to time this Indian would revert to speaking to them in another language, which my interpreter did not understand. To the one who asked who we were, I responded that we were Christians and that we came from far away to see them.[47] Responding to the question about who sent me, I said I was sent by the sun, indicating [this to] him by means of [the same] signs as [I had] at first, so they might not catch me in a lie. He started over, asking me how the sun had sent me, since it traveled on high but did not stop. And since, [besides,] there had been many years and neither he nor the elders had seen any others like us and had never heard about such [people], nor had the sun, until that time, sent any other [person].

I replied to him that it was true that the sun started out [the day] on high, as he said, and that it never stopped, but they could see clearly that when it set and when morning arose, [the sun] customarily happened to draw near to the earth, where its home was. And [further,] they always saw it come out from a similar place. And [I said] that it had given birth to me in that land and country from which it came forth, as it had given birth to many others whom it sent to other places. And now it had sent me to visit and see that river and the people who lived along it, so that I might speak to them and bring them together in friendship and provide them what they did not have. And also so that I could tell them they should not make war among themselves.

To this [the Indian] responded that I should tell him the reason why the sun had not sent me earlier to stifle the wars there had been among them for a very long time, which had killed many [people]. I replied to him that they had continued because I had been a child. Then he asked the interpreter whether we were bringing him along by force [and] had seized him in war, or [whether] he was coming there by his own choice. He responded to him that he was with us by his own free will and was very satisfied with our company.

He again interrogated me as to why we were bringing with us only he who understood them and why we did not [ourselves] understand everyone else, since we were children of the sun. I answered him that the sun had created [the interpreter], too, and had given him a language which allowed him to understand [the Indian questioner] and me and all the others. [And I said] that the sun knew very well that [the Indians] were living there, but [365v] that because of having to do many other things, and since I was young, it had not sent me sooner.

Right away he again spoke to me, asking, "Therefore you are coming here in order to be our lord and we would have to serve you?" Thinking I would necessarily not please him by saying yes, I answered him, "Not as lord, but as a brother, and to give them [things] from among what I might have."

He demanded to know whether the sun had created me like the others and whether I was its relative or son. I responded by saying that I was its son. He followed this by asking to know whether the others who were with me were also children of the sun. I replied to him no, but that they were born as I was in the same land where I was raised.

At this point he cried out in a loud voice and then said, "Since you are doing so much good for us and you do not want us to make war, and [since you] are a son of the sun, we all desire to have you as our lord and to serve you always.[48] Therefore we beg you neither to go away nor depart from us."[49] Immediately he turned to the people and began to tell them how I was the son of the sun and that therefore they were all to choose me as [their] lord.

When the Indians had heard this, they must have been further amazed. They approached still closer to gaze at me. That Indian asked me still other questions, which, to avoid being too lengthy, I do not relate.

In this way we passed the day, and now that night was drawing near, I began to wear myself out over the best way to get that man into the *barca* with us. When he refused to do so, the interpreter told him we would leave him on the other side of the river. Under this condition, he entered the [*barca*]. I declared many endearments to him and treated him the best [way] I could, assuring him further.

When I deemed that he had abandoned all his suspicion, it seemed [appropriate] to me to ask him something about that land. Among the first things I asked him was whether he had previously seen any others like us around there, or had heard of them. He answered no, except that he had understood from the elders that very far from that land there were other white men with beards like ours, and that he knew nothing else.[50] I asked him whether he had heard of a place called Cíbola and a river called Totonteac,[51] and he answered no.

When I had seen that he could not give me news of Francisco Vázquez or his men, I decided to interrogate him about things concerning that land and about their way of life. I began by asking him whether [those people] believed there was one God, creator of heaven and earth, or some idol. He responded to me, saying no; rather, they held the sun in the greatest esteem and honor, before all other things, because it warmed them and caused their seeds to grow. And they threw a little of everything they ate into the air for it. Then I asked him whether they had a lord and he answered no, but that they were aware there was a very great lord, though they did not have any information about where he might have been. I told him that [God] abided in heaven and that he was called Jesus Christ. I was careful not to stretch myself farther into theology with him.

I asked him whether they were engaged in war and for what reasons. He responded by saying, "Yes, a very great [war] over trivialities." [That was] because at a time when they did not have a reason to make war, they assembled and someone from among them said, "Let us go make war at such a place." And then they all went off with their weapons.[52]

I asked him who among them gave orders to the men. He replied that [it was] the oldest and bravest, and when this man said they should fight no more, they withdrew from fighting. I asked him to tell me what they did with the men they killed in battle. He replied to me that they removed the hearts of some and ate them.[53] Others they burned. And he added that if it had not been for my assembly in that place, they would already be at war. [That was] because I was telling them that they should not do it and should lay aside their arms. Until and unless I were to tell them to take them up again, they would not be moved to make war against others. Among themselves, they were saying that since I had come to them[54] they had put aside the eagerness to make war and were completely willing to maintain peace.

[The native leader] complained about some [people] who resided on a mountain toward the interior who frequently made serious wars against them and killed many of their people. I replied to him that from then on they should not be afraid, because I had commanded [their enemies] to remain at peace. And whenever they did not do so, I would punish them and kill them. He responded to me in this manner: "How could you kill them, since we are so few, and they so many in number?"

Because it was now very late on this day, and I saw that it was bothering him to stay with me longer, I let him leave [the boat] and sent him away very content.

{From the interpreter[55] and other *principales* among those Indians they receive many foodstuffs. They have [the Indians] set up a cross in their land and show them how to venerate it. They receive reports of many peoples, of their diverse languages, [their] customs with regard to marriage, how they punish adultery, the opinions they hold about death, and the [principal] illness they suffer.}

Early the next day their *principal*, the aforesaid interpreter [different from Alarcón's own interpreter], came and told me that I was to come out [of the boat] [366r] onto the land because he had many items of food to give me. Accordingly, because I saw myself in a safe place, I did so without delay. Immediately an elder came with cakes made of corn and some small squash.[56] Calling to me loudly and making many gestures with his body and arms, he ended up approaching me. Having made me turn toward those people and similarly having turned toward them himself, he said, "Sagueyca." And all those people responded loudly, "Hu." And [they] made offerings to the sun from what [they] had,[57] a little from each item. Then [they offered] another small quantity to me, although they gave me the rest later.

They maintained the same procedure with all those who were with me. When the interpreter had come out [of the *barca*], I gave them thanks through him, telling them that because the *barcas* were so small I had not been able to bring many things with me to give them in exchange. But since I would be returning another time, I would do so [then]. Further, [I said] that if they wanted to come with me in those *barcas* to the *navíos* I had downriver, I would give them many things. They replied that they would be very happy to see it.

Then, by means of the interpreter, I wanted to make them understand what sort of symbol the cross is. [So] I ordered them to bring me a timber, from which I had a large cross made. [Then] I commanded all those who were with me to venerate it and beseech Our Lord to grant them his grace, so that such a large number of people might come to know his Holy Catholic Faith.

When this was done, I told them through the interpreter that I was leaving that symbol as an indication that I considered them brothers and that they were to take care of it diligently until I returned. Further, [I said] that each morning at sunrise they should all kneel down in front of it. They took it away immediately and carried it, without letting it touch the ground, to set it up in the midst of their houses, where they all could see it. I told them they should always venerate it because it would be what protected them from evil. They asked me how much of it they were to set into the ground, and I showed them. There were many people who went to accompany it. Those who remained there asked me how they were to join their hands and how they were to kneel to venerate it. They showed great concern about learning [this].

After this was done, I took the *principal* of the land and entered the *barcas* with him. And I set my course along the river. Everyone here [in the *barca*] and on the riverbank accompanied me with great good will. And [they] served me by pulling the towrope and pulling us from the gravel on which we often ran aground, because in many places we found the river so low that there was not enough water for the *barcas*. When we were traveling this way, the Indians I had left downstream came to ask me to show them how to properly join their hands for venerating the cross. Others demonstrated that they were well established in this custom, so that they did not let me rest.

Close to the other bank of the river, there was a larger number of people who, in great haste, called to me, [saying] that I should take the foodstuffs they were bringing me. Because I realized that the one [group] envied the other, in order not to leave these people unhappy, I did so. And there appeared another elder like the last one. He brought me some of the food with the same ceremony and offered [it to me].[58]

I wanted to learn something about him as I had about the other [elder]. In the same way this one said to the rest of the people, "This is our lord. You know how long ago we heard our ancestors say there were bearded, white people in the world. [And you know that] we made fun of them about this. I and others who are old have never seen any other people like these. If you [still] do not want to believe it, look at those who are on this river. Therefore, let us give them something to eat, and later they [will] give some of their food to us. Let us willingly serve this lord who shows good will, forbids that we make war, and embraces all of us. They have mouths, hands, and eyes, as we have, and they speak as we do."

I gave these [people] another cross like the one I had made for those downstream. And I made the same speeches to them. They listened to them most willingly. They employed more diligence in learning what I was telling them.

Then, going farther upstream, I found another people. The interpreter did not understand anything of [what they said].[59] Hence, I made them understand by signs the same ceremony of veneration of the cross, as [I had] the others. The principal man I had brought with me said that farther upstream I would have found people who would have understood my interpreter. Since it was already late, some of these people were summoning me to give me their food-stuffs. They acted the same as the others [had], making a celebration and engaging in games to give me pleasure.

I sought to know what people lived on the banks of this river. From that man I understood that it was inhabited by [speakers of] twenty-three languages.[60] These were close to the river [and] excluded others some small distance away. And [he said] that besides these twenty-three languages, there were more, also on the river, that he did not know. I asked him whether every [366v] group of inhabitants lived in only one settlement. He answered no; rather, there were more houses scattered throughout the countryside. And [he said] that each people had its own separate, well-known territory and that in every dwelling place there were many people.

He pointed out to me a village that was on a mountain, where he said there was a great multitude of people. [They were] of a bad sort, who constantly made war against the river people. Because they lived without any lord and inhabited that unsettled place, where little corn was harvested, they came down to the plains to get it through barter with deerskins. These they wore, along with long garments they cut out with very sharp blades and sewed with needles made from deer bone. They had large houses made of stone.[61] I asked him whether there was a person there from that land. I came across a woman who wore a garment like a small *manta* made of well-tanned deerskin that went from her waist to the ground.

I asked him whether the people who inhabited the banks of that river always remained there or whether they lived somewhere else at another time. He replied to me, saying that they always remained [there] and built their dwellings there and planted there. [But] once the harvest was in, they went to live in other houses they had on the foothills of the mountain, far from the river.[62] He indicated to me that the houses were made of wood, buried in the earth on the outside.[63] I found out that they were in the habit of building a circular room where they all, men and women, resided together.

I asked whether they shared women communally. He told me no, that if one married, he was allowed to have only one wife. I wanted to understand the formality they observed when they married. And he told me that if anyone had a [marriageable] daughter, he went to where the people were and stated, "I have a daughter to be married," and [asked,] "Does anyone here desire her?" If anyone there wanted her, he replied that he desired her, and the marriage was arranged. The father of the [man] who wanted her commonly took something to give to the young woman. From that time on, the marriage was understood to have been completed. They sang and danced, and when night had come, the parents took them and left them in a place where no one could see them.

I learned that brothers did not marry sisters or [close] relatives. Further, [I learned] that before being married the women were not familiar with and did not speak to men. Instead, they remained in their household[s] and among their goods to work. If it happened that one had had dealings with men before she married, the husband customarily left her and went to other villages.[64] And those who fell into that misconduct were considered to be wicked women. If, after they were married, a man was discovered in adultery with another woman, they customarily killed him. [I learned] that no one could have more than one wife, unless [it were] in secret.

They told me that they burned the dead.[65] Those [women] who were left widowed remained so for half a year, or a year, without remarrying. Then I wanted to find out what they believed about the dead. [The elder] responded to me, saying that they went to another world.[66] But they did not have [a place of] either suffering or felicity.

The principal infirmity from which those people die involves blood pouring from the mouth.[67] They have healers who treat them with words and by exhaling on them. The dress of these [people] is like that of those before. They carry

their tubes to incense themselves, as the Tavagi people of Nueva España [do].[68] I wanted to learn whether those people had a lord, and I found out they did not, but that each household designated its own lord for itself. In addition to corn, they had some squash and another seed similar to millet.[69] They have grinding stones and pots in which they cook the squash and very excellent fish they obtain from the river.

From here onward the interpreter could not come [with us], because he said that those whom we were certain to encounter farther ahead on the route were enemies of his.[70] Accordingly, I sent him back very satisfied.

[It was] not much later that I saw many Indians approaching, crying out loudly and running behind me. I stopped to find out what they wanted, and they told me they had set up the cross I had given them among their dwellings, as I had directed them. [They told me,] though, that I should be aware that when the river flooded, it usually reached [where the cross was]. On this account I should give them permission to move it and set it up in another place where the river could not touch it and carry it away. I granted them this.

{From an Indian on the bank they receive a report about the state of affairs at Cíbola, about the capacity and customs of those people, and about their lord. And the same [sort of report] about the lands near there, one [called] Quicama and the other, Coana. They receive ceremonious welcome from [the people] of Quicama and then from other Indians not far away.}

Traveling this way by boat, I reached [a place] where there were many Indians and another interpreter. I had him enter the *barca* with me. Because it was cold and the people [with me] had gotten wet, I leapt onto the land and ordered that a fire be made. When we were thus warming ourselves an Indian came and touched me on the arm, pointing out a woods to me with his finger. From it I saw two squadrons of men emerging [367r] with their arms and armor. He indicated they were coming to oppose us.

Because I did not want to engage anyone, I gathered my people into the *bateles* [*barcas*]. The Indians who were with [the Spaniards] and me threw themselves into the water and got themselves to safety on the other bank. In the meantime, I asked the Indian I had with me what people those were who had come out of the woods. He told me they were his enemies. Therefore these others [his people] took to the [river] on the arrival of [the armed group], without saying a word. They had done this because they wanted to turn back, since they were unarmed, having understood my commandment and wish, [namely,] that I did not want them to carry arms.

I wanted to ask this interpreter the same questions I had asked the other one concerning things about that land. [For one thing,] I had understood that among some peoples a man customarily had many wives, and among others, no more than one. Now I learned from him that he had been in Cíbola[71] [and] that it was a journey of one month from his land. [I learned from him] further that he customarily traveled from that place along a trail that followed the river, [and] it consumed forty days.

The reason that moved him to go there had been just to see Cíbola, because it was an extraordinary thing. It had very tall stone houses of three and four stories, with windows on each side. [They were] surrounded entirely by a wall one and a half times the height of a man. The upper and lower [floors] were occupied by people.

[The people of Cíbola] used the same arms and armor as the others I had seen used, namely, bows and arrows, maces, clubs, and round shields. They had one lord. And they went about dressed in mantas and with [bison] hides. Their *mantas* had painting all over. The lord wore a long shirtlike garment,[72] a very narrow belt, and several *mantas* over that. The women wore very long garments, which were white. And they all went about fully dressed. Each day many Indians were at the lord's door to serve him. They wore many blue stones which they dug from a stony ridge.

These [people of Cíbola] were not married to more than one wife. When the lords died, they buried all the belongings they owned with [them]. Also, when [the lord] ate there were many of his [people] there at the table to form his retinue and watch him eat. They ate with table cloths, and they had places for bathing.

Now, at daybreak on Thursday[73] the Indians came to the bank of the river with the same shouts and with greater will-

ingness to serve us. They brought [food] for me to eat, giving me the same welcome as the others had done, since they understood who I was. And I gave them the same crosses with the same ritual as the others. Then traveling farther upstream, I reached a land where I found greater orderliness. [This was] because the inhabitants completely obey only one [lord].

Now, speaking again with the interpreter about the dwellings of the [people] of Cíbola, he told me that the lord had a dog similar to the one I was bringing [with me]. Then, since I wanted to eat, I saw the interpreter carry some plates back and forth, about which he told me the lord of Cíbola also had some similar to them, but they were green. He had never seen that any other [people] there had them, except the lord. [The interpreter said] that there were four of them and that [the lord] obtained them with that dog and some other things from a black man who wore a beard.[74] However, he did not know from what direction [the black man] had gotten there. According to what [the interpreter] had heard them say, the lord had him killed.

I asked [the interpreter] whether he knew of some land there in the vicinity. He replied that going upriver, he was familiar with some. Among [those] others there was a lord of a place called Quicama and one of another land called Coama.[75] And [he said] that there were many people under them. After he had given me this information, he asked me for permission to return to his companions.

From here I launched myself by boat again, and after a day's journey I came across an abandoned place. When I went into it perhaps five hundred Indians came suddenly with their bows and arrows. Together with those Indians there was, as *principal,* the aforementioned interpreter whom I had left [farther back].[76] They brought some rabbits and cassava-like roots to give me.[77] When I had welcomed everyone, because I wanted to depart, I gave them permission to return to their houses.

When I had traversed the uninhabited area, I reached some rude shelters from which many people came out toward me with an old man before them. He called out in a language my interpreter understood well. He said to those men, "Brothers, you see here the lord; let us give him some of what we have, because he is doing [something] good for us. He has passed by so many ill-mannered people to come to see us." When he had said this, he made an offering to the sun and then to me, in the very same way the others had.

These [people] have some large, well-made bags made from the inner bark of reeds.[78] I understood that this land was that of the lord of Quicoma. They came there in the summer only to harvest the produce of their seeds. Among them I encountered one who understood my interpreter very well. As a result, I very easily made [known] to them the same [367v] obligation toward the cross that I had to those downstream.

These people had cotton, but they did not take much interest in working it, because there was no person among them who knew how to weave in order to make clothing. They asked me in what way they had to set up the cross once they had returned to their house[s], which were in the mountains. And [they asked] whether it was good to build a house around it, so that it would not get wet. Further, [they asked] whether they should put something on the arms [of the cross]. I told them no, and that it was enough for them to put it in a place where it could be seen by everyone, until I might return.

They offered to send more people with me in case some warriors were to come, saying the men I would find farther upstream were vicious. I tried not to accept them, but twenty of them came along anyway. They warned me when I was nearing those who were their enemies. I found lookouts were posted on guard on their borders.

On Saturday morning I encountered a great company of people assembled under a very large ramada, and another [group] outside. When I saw that they did not rise to their feet, I continued by them on my journey. [But] when this was observed by them, an old man rose to his feet and said, "Lord, why do you not take something to eat from us, since you took it from the others?" I replied to him that I was not in the habit of taking it if it was not given to me. [I said] further [that] I was traveling only to those who asked me [to come].

Then, without hesitating, they brought me many items of food. And they said to me that since we were not in the habit of entering their houses and stayed day and night on the river, and since I was the son of the sun, everyone ought to consider me their lord. I gestured to them that they were

to sit down. And I called the elder who understood my interpreter and asked him whose that land was, and whether there was a lord there. They replied to me, saying yes.

So I had him summoned. When he had come, I embraced him, showing him great affection. Seeing that everyone was pleased by the embraces I gave him, I dressed him in a shirt and gave him some other small items. I directed the interpreter to tell that lord the same thing I had told the others. Afterward I gave him a cross, which he accepted most willingly, as the others [had done]. This lord went with me a long distance, until I was summoned from the other side of the river. There stood the same elder [as before], with many people. I gave them another cross, telling [the elder] the same thing I had told the others, namely, what they had to do [to venerate the cross].

Then, continuing my journey, I encountered another throng of people, with whom came the same elder who understood my interpreter. When I had seen the lord whom [the elder] pointed out to me, I asked him if he would like to come with me in the *barca,* which he did willingly. Thus I traveled, always ascending the river. And the old man continued to show me who the lords were. I always spoke to them with great affection, and everyone showed great happiness and said many good [words] about my coming.

At night I retired into the breadth of the river, and I asked [the lord] many questions about that land. In this I found him completely willing to tell me about it, and [I found] in myself a similar desire to learn about it. I asked him about Cíbola, and he told me he had been there. [He said] that it was an excellent place and its lord [was] very much obeyed. And that there were some other lords in that vicinity with whom he has constant war. I asked him whether [the Cíbolans] had silver and gold.[79] And when he saw some bells, he said, "[What they have] is the color of those." I wanted to know whether they produced [the metal] there. He answered no, but that they brought it from a mountain where an old woman lived.

I asked him whether he had information about a river called Totonteac. He replied to me no, but that he knew well there was another great river where such large *lagartos* were found that they made round shields out of their skins. {*Lagartos* are crocodiles.}

And [he said] that [his people] worshipped the sun neither more nor less than the others before. When they offer it the fruits of the earth, they say to it, "Take [this], because you have brought it forth." And [he said] that they prayed [to the sun] greatly because it warmed [them] and when it did not come out they felt cold. Then, later in the discussion, he began to express pain somewhat, saying to me, "I do not know why the sun imposes these limits on us: it doesn't provide us bread or thread or cloth, and other things it gives to many others." And he lamented that those [people] of [that] land did not allow him to enter it and refused to give him some of their seeds. I told him that I would fix this for him. He was very happy with this.

{They receive a report from the Indians [concerning] why the lords of Cíbola killed the Moor who traveled with fray Marcos, and many other things. And regarding the old woman called Guatazaca, who lives at a lake without eating. Description of an animal, the skin of which is used to make heart-shaped shields. [Concerning] a suspicion about them, [which the Indians] conceive, that they might be from those Christians seen at Cíbola and how cleverly they save themselves.}

The next day, which was Sunday, it was not yet fully daylight when a shout began that [the sun] should get itself up.[80] [The shouting] was from three or four crowds of people who had slept near the river, waiting for me. [368r] They took corn and other seeds in their mouths and sprayed me with them, saying that was the kind of offering they made to the sun. Afterward they gave me some of those foodstuffs to eat. Among other things, [they gave me] many beans.

I presented them with [a] cross, as I had done with the others. Meanwhile, the elder was telling them grand things about my accomplishments. He pointed at me with his finger, saying, "This is the lord, a son of the sun." They had my beard combed and the clothing I was wearing straightened. Such was the belief they had in me that everyone told me [about] the things that had happened and were happening among them, and the good or ill will they bore one another. I asked them for what reason they were telling me everything about themselves, and the old man replied to me, "You are the lord, and not a thing must be kept hidden from the lord."

After these things, while continuing the journey, I again began to ask him about things concerning Cíbola and whether they knew if the people of that land had ever seen people like us. He responded to me, saying, "No, except for a Black who wore certain things on his feet and arms that made sound." (Your Lordship[81] must remember how there was this Black[82] who traveled with fray Marcos who wore bells and feathers on his arms and legs and that he carried dishes of various colors. It was a little more than a year ago when he arrived there.)

I asked [the lord] the reason [the Black] was killed. He answered me that the lord of Cíbola had asked him whether he had brothers. And he replied that he had an infinite number [of brothers], that they had many weapons with them, and that they were not very far from there. When this had been heard, many lords came together in council, and they agreed to kill him. [That was] so he could not provide information to these brothers of his about where [the lords of Cíbola] were. They killed him for that reason. And they cut him into many pieces, which were distributed among all those lords, so they could know for certain he was dead. Also, [he told me] that [the Black] had a dog like mine, which they also killed many days later.

I questioned him about whether those [people] of Cíbola had enemies. He told me yes, and told me [of] fourteen or fifteen lords who were customarily at war with them. And [he said] that they had *mantas* and the bows typical of the aforementioned [people]. He told me clearly that I would have found people who did not make war against their neighbors or anyone else as I ascended the river.

He said [the people upriver] had three or four kinds of trees with very excellent fruit for eating. Also, that at a certain lake an old woman lived who was closely looked after and served by them. She dwelled in a certain small house that was there, and she never ate [anything]. [He said] that the things that made sounds were made there. Many *mantas* and feathers, and much corn, were presented to her. I asked him [what] her name [was], and he told me she was called Guatuzaca.[83] [He told me] there were many lords in the surrounding area who, in life and death, follow the same customs as [the people] of Cíbola. They had summer residences [made of] painted *mantas,* and in winter they lived in houses made of timbers, two or three stories high. And [he said] that he had seen all these things, except the old woman. When I returned to questioning him about more things later, he did not wish to respond, saying that he was worn out by me. While many of those Indians were stationed in the area, they were saying among themselves, "Let us observe him closely so that we can recognize him when he returns."

The next [day,] Monday, the river [edge] was packed with the same sort of people. I started again to ask the old man to tell me [about] the people there were in that land. He replied that he thought I might have forgotten about it. Then he told me [about] an infinite number of lords and more than two hundred peoples.[84]

Discussing arms and armor with me, he told me that some of them had certain very large, round shields made of leather more than two fingers thick. I asked him what animal['s hide] they make [them] from. And he described to me a very large animal like a cow, but more than a large *palmo* taller, with wide feet and forelegs as thick as a man's thighs. The head [is] seven *palmos* in length, the brow three spans wide, and the eyes [are] larger than a fist. The horn[s are] of the length of a [man's] shin. Their sharp points point outward and are a *palmo* in length. The rear feet and forefeet [are] more than [two] *palmos* [in width]. [It has] a [short] tail, but [it is] very thick. Extending his arm above his head, he said that it was even taller [than himself].[85]

He then provided information to me about another old woman who lived on the seashore. I spent this day giving crosses to those people, as I had done to the others.

The elder with me got out [of the *barca*] onto the land and began a conversation with another [man], who had hailed him many times that day. Then the amicable pair made many gestures while speaking, waving their arms and pointing at me. I sent my interpreter out [of the *barca*] in order that he could position himself near them and listen to them. A little while later I summoned him and asked him what they were talking about. He said that the one who was making the gestures was saying to the other [one] that in Cíbola there were other [men] like us with beards who said they were Christians. Further, they both were saying that we all must be one identical [368v] [people]. And [the one said] that it would have been well to kill us, so that those others [in Cíbola] would not know anything about us, "so that they would come to cause us trouble."

The elder had replied, "This one is a son of the sun and our lord; he does good [things] for us. He does not want to come to our houses even when we beg him [to]. He does not take anything from us, [and] he does not want our women." In conclusion, he had said many other things in praise of and complimentary to me.

[Even] with all that, the other [man] stubbornly maintained that we all must be one identical [people]. And [the interpreter related] that the old man said, "Let us go to him and ask him whether he is a Christian like the others, or instead a son of the sun."

Then the elder came to me and said to me, "Other men who have your traits are residing in Cíbola, the land you asked me about." Then I made [it appear that I was] astonished and replied that it was not possible. They assured me that it was true and that they had seen two men who had come from there.[86] They related [that the men at Cíbola], like us, carried firearms and swords. I asked them whether they had seen them with their own eyes, and they replied no, but some of their acquaintances had seen them.

Then [the old man on shore] asked me whether I was a son of the sun. And I answered yes. They said those Christians from Cíbola said the same thing, and I replied that it could well be. Then they asked me, if those Christians from Cíbola had come to join me, what I would have done. I responded to them that they should not be afraid of anything, because if those [men] were sons of the sun, as they said, they would be my brothers and would have employed the same politeness and affection toward everyone that I had. With this [explanation], it seemed they remained well satisfied.

{He is told they are ten days' journey away from Cíbola. And that there are Christians there who are making war against those lords. Concerning the sodomy practiced by those Indians, with four youths, who wear women's clothing, dedicated to such service. Since [Alarcón and his party] are not able to send news of themselves to those at Cíbola, they make their return to the *navíos* by way of the river.}

Then I asked again that they tell me how many days' travel it was from that *reino* of Cíbola. They had said it was far from that river. That man replied that there was an region of ten days' [travel] without settlements. From there on he made no estimate, because there were people there.

With this information, I conceived the desire to send news of myself to the captain [general]. I talked this over with my men-at-arms, among whom I found no one who was willing to go there, even though I offered them many things on Your Lordship's behalf. Only one Moorish slave volunteered to go, although grudgingly. But I was expecting those Indians to come whom I had been told about. With this, we went on our way against the current of the river, with the same procedure as previously.

At that point the old man showed me as an extraordinary thing a son of his dressed in women's clothing, doing his work.[87] I asked [the old man] how many similar to [the son] there were among them. He told me there were four, and when any one of them died, a survey was made of all the pregnant women there were in the land. And [when] the first one gave birth to a male [child], he was designated as having the obligation to perform that feminine role. The women dressed him in their clothing, saying that later he had to do whatever they were supposed to do, if he wore that clothing.

Such men cannot have carnal intercourse with any woman. Rather, if it [is] all right with them,[88] [they can have intercourse with] all the young men of the land who are marriageable. They do not receive anything for this whorish act from those [young men] from there, because they are free to take whatever they find in each house as necessities of living. Also I saw some women who were shamelessly cohabiting among the men. I asked the old man if they were married. He said no, but that they were "experienced" women, who live separately from the married women.

During these conversations I had been requesting that those Indians come who said they had been to Cíbola. They

told me that [those Indians] were eight days' journey from there. But there was one among [the local Indians] who had been an associate of theirs. He had spoken with [the Indians who had gone to Cíbola] when he met them at the time they were going to see the *reino* of Cíbola. They told him he should not go farther because there he would have come across a warlike people similar to ourselves, with our same manner and features. They were wrangling considerably with the men of Cíbola, because [the Cíbolans] had killed a Moorish companion of theirs. [The Christians] were asking, "Why have you killed him? What has he done to you? Has he perhaps stolen [your] bread or done you some other harm?"[89] And [the Christians said] other words to that effect.

[The local Indians] said, moreover, that these people called themselves Christians and customarily lived in a single very large residence. [The locals said] that many of them had cattle like those of Cíbola and other small black animals with wool and horns.[90] And [they said] that there were some of them who rode horseback who raced a great deal.

[The Indians who had gone to Cíbola said,] "One day, before we departed, from sunrise to sunset these Christians did nothing but get themselves there.[91] And they all stayed [369r] there where the others were [already] lodging."

These two [Indians who reported this] had met two Christians who asked them where they were from and whether they had planted areas. They had told them that they were from a distant land and that they had planted lands. Then [the Christians] gave each of them a small cape.[92] Then they gave [the Indians another] one that they were to take to their other companions. This they promised to do, and shortly thereafter they departed.

Having understood this, I again spoke with my companions to see whether any of them were willing to go there. But I found them with the same mind as before. And they confronted me with [even] greater obstacles. Afterward I summoned the elder to find out whether he was willing to furnish men to lead me and foodstuffs for that unsettled region. But he laid before me many obstacles and discomforts I would necessarily be subject to in that journey. [He] laid out for me the danger there was in going on because of a lord of Cumana[93] who was threatening to come and make war on them. [That was] because [the elder's] men had entered his land [Cumana] to take a deer. [He said] that therefore I should not leave here without punishing him [the lord of Cumana].

When I replied to him that I was compelled to go to Cíbola in any case, he told me I should give up doing that. [That was] because he expected that, in any event, this lord would come [to do] them harm. Therefore these [people] could not abandon their land to come with me. It would be better, [he said,] if I had put an end to that war for them. Then I would have been able to go to Cíbola accompanied [by some of them]. We ended up arguing so much about this that we began to get angry.[94] Irately, he wanted to leave the *barca*, but I held him back and began placating him with kind words, having understood that it was very important to have him as a friend. I was unable, however, to move him from his desire, which he persistently held to despite the affection I showed him.

In the meantime, I had already sent a man to the *navíos* to give them word of the route I had chosen to pursue. After that, I asked the elder to have him return, since I had already determined that I did not see any way of being able to go to Cíbola. And [I had decided] not to linger more among those people, so that they might not find me out. Also I wanted to go back to visit the *navíos*[95] in person, with the intention of returning upriver another time, bringing with me some other companions and leaving others who were ill. Telling the old man and the others that I would return, and leaving them as contented as I could, I went back down the river [that led] to Cíbola.[96] Even so, they would always say I was leaving out of fear. [By] the route I had taken going upriver against the current, [it had taken] fifteen and a half days, and I made the return in two and a half days, because the current was strong and very rapid.

While I was traveling downstream in this way, many people came to the banks to ask me, "Lord, why are you leaving us? What displeasure has been caused to you. Did you not say you must stay with us forever and be our lord? Come back! If anyone from the shore up above has caused you some injury, we will go with you with our arms and armor to kill him." And [they said] other words of the sort, full of affection, willingness, and politeness.

{Having rejoined the *navíos*, the captain has that coast named the Campaña de la Cruz. And he has a small chapel [dedicated] to Our Lady built there. He calls the river Buena Guía. From that [place] he returns upstream. When he has reached Quicama and Coano, [his people are] treated with great politeness by those lords.}

When I rejoined the *navíos*, I found all my men in good condition, although much distressed concerning my long sojourn [upstream] and also because the powerful current had broken four lines. They had also lost two anchors, which were recovered. When the *navíos* had come together, I had them placed in a sheltered area. And [I had] the *navío San Pedro* careened and [had] everything that was necessary put in order.

When all the men had assembled there, I laid out for them the information I had received about Francisco Vázquez and how it could be, with luck, that in the period of sixteen days I had been traveling by boat on the river he had received word about me. Further, [I told them] that I felt like returning upstream one more time to see whether it was possible to find any means of getting together with him.

Although they argued against me, I had all the *barcas* put in order, because they were not necessary to care for the *navíos*.[97] One of them I had filled with clothing, trade goods, wheat and other seeds, along with hens and roosters from Castile. I departed up the swollen river, having left an order that in that land called [Campaña] de la Cruz they were to build an oratorio or chapel and call it the Church of Nuestra Señora de la Buena Guía. Further, [I had directed] that they call the river Buena Guía, because ["Buena Guía"] is the emblem of Your Lordship.[98]

I took the chief pilot, Nicolás Zamorano,[99] with me, so that he could take latitude[s]. I departed on Tuesday, which was the fourteenth of September,[100] and on Wednesday I reached the dwellings of the first Indians. They ran to prevent my passage, for they believed we were different people, because we were bringing a fife and drum with us [369v] and I was dressed in different clothes from those I had worn when they saw me the first time. When they recognized me they stopped [that]. But I could not lead them [to be] good friends of mine again. Hence, I went among them giving out some of the seeds I had brought, showing them how they should plant them.

When I had traveled by boat three leagues, the first interpreter came with great happiness all the way to the *barca* to find me. I asked him why he had left me. He said that some of his companions had led him astray. I welcomed him and gave him the best treatment, so that he might come with me again when he saw how important it was to me to have him near. He excused his having stayed there in order to bring me some parrot feathers, which he [now] gave me.[101]

I asked him what people those were and whether they had a lord.[102] He answered yes and named three or four [lords] for me, and after that [he provided] the names of twenty-four or twenty-five groups of people he knew. They [all] had houses [that were] painted inside. Those people had commercial dealings with the people of Cíbola. [He said] that they customarily reached that *reino* in two complete moon cycles. Beyond this, he told me the names of many other lords and of other groups of people that I have described in a book of mine which I am carrying to Your Lordship in person. But I have wanted to provide this summary report to Agustín Guerrero at the port of Colima, so that he may send it by land to Your Lordship, to whom I have many other things to tell besides.[103]

But returning to my travel, I reached Quicama,[104] where those Indians came out to receive me with much pleasure and a great celebration. They told me their lord was waiting for me. When I had reached him, I found that he had five or six thousand unarmed men with him. He moved away from them with perhaps only two hundred, all of whom carried items of food as they approached me. [The lord] came with great authority in advance of the others. Before and beside him were some [men] who managed to move the people aside to form an aisle through which he could pass. He wore a garment closed in the front and back and open on the sides, fastened with buttons, and decorated with black and white checks. [It was] made from the inner bark of reeds and [was] very lightweight and well made.

When he had reached the water, his servants picked him up in their arms and put him in the *barca*. There I embraced and welcomed him with great ceremony, showing him much affection. His people, who were there watching,

showed great happiness over this action. This lord turned to his [people] telling them they were to bear my politeness in mind. And [he said] that since he had gone freely among such foreign people and they were able to see how I was good and had treated him with so much affection, therefore they were to know that I was their lord. Therefore they all had to serve me and do whatever I commanded them.

Then I had him sit down to eat some sugary preserves I was carrying. I told the interpreter to thank [the lord] in my name for the courtesy he had done me by coming to see me. [I] exhorted him to venerate the cross and [to do] all the rest that I had entreated the others [to do]. Namely, that they should live in peace, give up war, and always be good friends among themselves.

He replied that war with their neighbors had persisted among them for a very long time, but that from then on he would command that everyone who passed through his *reino* would be given food to eat and that [his people] would do them no injury. Further, even if some people came to make war against them, he would tell them I had commanded them to live in peace. But if they refused peace, he would defend himself. He promised me that he would never go out looking for war, as long as others did not come to wage it against him. Then I gave him some small items from among both the seeds I was carrying and the Castilian chickens. From this he took great happiness.

When I departed, I took some of his [people] with me, in order to negotiate friendship between them and the other people who were farther upstream. At that point the interpreter came to me, [wanting] to return to his home. I gave him some gifts, with which he left very content.

The following day I arrived at Coano. Many [of the people there] did not recognize me, because they saw me dressed in different clothing. But as soon as the elder who was there recognized me, he threw himself into the water, saying "Lord, here is the man you left with me." Thereupon [the man I had left][105] appeared, happy and very pleased. He told me of the many endearments those people had declared to him, saying that they had fought with each other trying to take him to their homes. And [he told me] that it was incredible, the concern they had in placing their hands together and kneeling before the cross at sunrise. I gave them some of those [same] seeds, thanking them very much for the good treatment they had given this Spaniard from my [company]. They begged me to leave him with them, which I granted them until my return. And [the Spaniard] stayed there among them very content.

In this way I ascended the river, taking that elder with me. He reported to me that two Indians had come from Cumana[106] to ask about the Christians. He had replied to them [370r] that he was not familiar with them, but he knew the son of the sun well. [The Indians from Cumana] had [tried to] convince him to join them in killing me and my companions.[107] I told him that he was to give me two Indians and that [the two] were to go to tell [the people of Cumana] that I would be going to visit them. And [they were to say further] that I desired their friendship, but that if instead they wanted war, I would wage war against them in such a way they would regret it.[108]

Thus I traveled among all those people. Some [people] came to ask me why I had not given them [a] cross as I had [done with] the others. So I gave one to them.

{They land and see that the people are venerating the cross they had given them. They have [a representation of] that land painted by an Indian. They send a cross to the lord of Cumana. And they descend the river a second time and rendezvous with the *navíos*. Concerning the error Cortés's pilots made in determining the location of that coast.}

The next day I wanted to land to see some rude shelters, and I found many children and women with their hands together, kneeling before a cross I had given them. When I had arrived [among them], I did the same also. When I spoke with the elder, he began giving me information about more people and lands he knew about. When the hour had become late, I summoned the old man to come sleep on the *barca*. He replied to me that he did not want to come, because I would tire him out asking him about so many things. I answered him that I would not ask him another thing except that he mark on a map what he knew about that river and who the people were who lived on the banks of the river on both sides. This he did willingly.

Then he said I should paint [a representation of] my country for him in the same way he had painted [one of] his for me. So to make him happy, I had a painting of some things made for him.[109]

The following day I entered some very high mountains, between which the river ran very narrow.[110] The *barcas* passed through there with considerable toil, because there was no one to pull the towrope. There, some Indians came to tell me they were people from Cumana. Among the others there was a wizard who asked which way we would have to travel. When I told him, "Along the river," he went about placing some reeds from one bank to the other. We passed through them without suffering any injury, which they thought this would do.

Traveling this way, I reached the home of the old man who was traveling with me. There I had a very tall cross set up and on it I had lettering engraved to the effect that I had reached that point.[111] I had this done so that if it should happen that any of the general's men reached there, they would have information about me.

When at that point I finally understood that I would not be able to find out about what I wanted to know, I decided to return to the *navíos*.[112] When I was about to depart, two Indians arrived there. By means of the old man's translation, they told me they were coming on my orders [and] that they were from Cumana. [They said] further that the lord [of that land] could not come because it was so far away from that place. But I was to tell [them] what I wanted. I told [one of the Indians from Cumana] that [the lord] was always to remember to desire peace. [I] also [said] that I had been traveling to visit that land, but since I was forced to return downriver, I would not do so. I would, however, return. In the meantime, they were to give that cross to their lord, which they promised to do. Further, they were going straight [back] to carry the cross to him, along with some feathers that were on it.

I wanted to find out from these [men] what people inhabited the banks of the river upstream. They gave me information about many peoples and told me the river rose much farther than I had seen. But these [men] were not familiar with where its origin was because it came from very far away and many other rivers entered it.

When this was done, in the morning the next day I went downriver. And the following day I arrived at the place I had left the Spaniard.[113] I spoke to him and said that things had gone well with me and that this time and the other I had penetrated inland more than thirty leagues.[114] The Indians of that place asked me why I was leaving and when I would return. I replied to them that it would be soon.

As I was thus traveling downriver by boat, a woman jumped into the water, yelling that we should wait for her. She entered the *barca*, getting under a bench from where we could never make her come out. I found out that she was doing this because her husband had another [woman], with whom he had children, when she said that she did not intend to stay longer with him because he had another woman. Thus, she and another Indian came with me of their own free will.

In this way I reached the *navíos*. When I had put them in order, we continued coastwise on our journey. We landed many times and penetrated a long distance inland to see whether we could learn anything about Captain Francisco Vázquez and his company. We obtained no other hint of them than what I had heard [already] on that coast.

I am bringing with me many acts of possession [executed] all along that coast and the river. Concerning the latitude[s] I determined, I find that the one the masters and pilots of the *marqués* determined is incorrect. They were mistaken by two degrees,[115] and we have traveled farther [north] than they did by more than four degrees. I traveled eighty-five leagues up the river.[116] There I saw [370v] and heard everything I have stated, and many other things, about which I will give a lengthy and complete report, if I am granted the ability to go to kiss Your Lordship's hand.[117]

I consider that I have had good fortune in having run across don Luis de Castilla and Agustín Guerrero[118] in the port of Colima, because the small *galera*[119] belonging to the *adelantado* [Pedro de Alvarado] was coming up on me and wanted [my] sails struck.[120] It was there with his [the adelantado's] *armada*.[121] Because this seemed out of the ordinary to me, and because I did not know in what state the affair was in Nueva España, I prepared myself for defense and not to comply. At this moment, don Luis[122] de Castilla arrived in a *batel* [*barca*] and spoke to me. I went to anchor on the other side of the port from where the *armada* was.

I gave [Castilla and Guerrero] this report, because, as it was night, I wanted to make sail to avoid any disturbances. I was carrying that report written in summary, because I had always assumed I would deliver it upon making landfall in Nueva España, in order to inform Your Lordship [immediately].

TRANSCRIPTION

[fol. 363r]

363

RELATIONE DELLA NAVIGATIONE / & scoperta
che fece il Capitano Fernando Alarcone per ordine / dello
Illustrissimo Signore Don Antonio di Mendozza / Vice Re
dellanuova Spagna, data in Colima, porto / della nuova
Spagna.

{Fernando Alarchon doppo (h)avere patito fortuna, giunge
con l'armata nel porto di sant'Iago, & / di quivi al porto
Aguaiaval scorre molto pericolo nel volere scoprire un Golfo,
di quello Uscito sco- / pre Un fiume nella costa con gran
correntia in quello entrato scorrendo scuopre gran / numero
d'Indiani armati. con cenni ha con quelli commercio, &
temendo di / qualche pericolo fa ritorno alla Nave.}

LA Domenica che fu alli nove di Maggio del MDXL. diedi
vela con due na- / vi, l'una chiamata San Pietro che era la
Capitana, et l'altra Santa / Catherina, et cene andammo
ricercando il porto di sant'Iago di buona speranza, dove /
prima che giungessimo (h)avemmo una fortuna terribile, per
la quale coloro / che si trovavano nella nave di santa Catherina, essendo piu spaventati di quel / che era il dovere,
gittarono via nove pezzi d'artiglieria, due anchore & un ca- /
nape, & molte altre cose, cosi necessarie per la impresa in che
andavano, co- / me la nave istessa. Giunti che fummo al
porto di Sant'Iago mi rifeci del danno che (h)ave- / vo ricevuto, mi providi delle cose necessarie, & tolsi nelle navi la
gente che quivi m'aspet- / tava, & drizzai il cammino verso il
porto di Aguaiavale, & quivi arrivato intesi come il Ge-. /
nerale Francesco Vazquez di Coronado era partito con tutta
la sua gente, onde tolta la na- / ve chiamata San Gabriel che

andava con vettovaglia per lo essercito, & la condussi meco
in / essecutione dell'ordine della. Signoria Vostra. Doppo
segui'il cammino per la costa senza partirmi da quel- / la, per
vedere se potevo trovare segno alcuno, ò qualche Indiano che
mi potessi dare noti- / tia di esso, & per andare cosi vicino à
terra venni à scoprire altri porti assai buoni perche non vid-
/ dero ne trovarono le navi che conduceva il Capitano
Francesco di Ulloa per il Marchese / di valle, & arrivati alli
luoghi bassi donde erano ritornate le dette navi, parve cosi à
me / come à gli altri, h)avere terra ferma innanzi, & essere
cosi pericolose & spaventose quelle bas- / se, che

[fol. 363v]

se, che era forte cosa di pensare ancho con battelli potere
entrare per esse, & i Piloti & l'altra / gente volevan che faces-
simo il medesimo che (h)aveva fatto il Capitano di Ulloa.
Ma per / (h)avermi vostra Signoria comandato che io gli
(h)avessi à rapportare il se(c)greto di quel golfo, / determinai,
ancora che (h)avessi saputo di perdere le navi, per cosa alcuna
non restare di vede- / re il capo, & perciò comandai à Nicola
Camorano Piloto maggiore, & à Domenico del ca- / stello
che pigliassero un battello per uno, & lo scandaglio in mano
& entrassero per quelle / basse per vedere di trovarvi il canale
onde potessero entrare le navi, à quali pareva che le na- / vi
potessero, (anchora che con gran fatica & pericolo passar)
innanzi, & in questo modo, io in- / sieme con lui cominciai
à seguire il cammino che essi presero, & indi à poco ci
ritrovammo / con tutte tre le navi piantati ne l'arena, di
maniera che uno non poteva soccorrere l'altro, ne / i battelli
potevan anco darci soccorso, imperoche era il corrente cosi
grande ch'era impossi- / bile accostarsi l'uno all'altro, onde
corremmo tanto gran rischio che stette molte volte l'orlo /

della Capitania sotto l'acqua, & se non fosse miracolosamente venito un gran colpo di ma- / re che ci ridrizzò la nave, & la fece respirare, noi ci saremmo annegati, & similmente l'al- / tre due navi si trovarono in assai gran rischio, pur per essere minore & ricercare meno ac- / qua, non fu tanto quanto il nostro. (H)or volse Iddio che crescendo la marea ritornarono / le navi à nuoto, & con questo andammo innanzi, & anchora che la gente volesse ritornare / à dietro, tutta via determinai che si andasse oltre, & si seguisse il viaggio presso, & passammo / innanzi con gran fatica, girando la prora, (h)or di qua, (h)or di la, per vedere di ritrovare il cana- / le, & piacque à Dio che in questo modo venimmo à dare nel capo del seno, dove trovam- / mo un fiume molto potente che menava cosi gran furia di corrente che à pena potevamo / navigare per esso. In questo modo determinai di andare al meglio che si potesse per il detto / fiume, & con due barche, lasciando l'altra con le navi & con venti compagni, & io in una / d'esse con Rodrigo Maldonato Tesoriero di questa armata, & Gaspar di Castilleia Conta- / dore, & con alcuni pezzi d'artiglieria minuti cominciai à montare il fiume, & comandai à / tutta la gente che niuno si movesse ne facesse segno alcuno, se non colui à ch'io l'ordi- / nassi, / anchora che trovassimo Indiani. Quel medesimo giorno che fu il giovedi à ventisei d'Ago- / sto, seguendo il navigare nostro col tirare dell'alzana,[123] andammo tanto quanto saria sei leghe, / & l'altro giorno che fu il venere nell'apparire dell'alba cosi seguendo il cammino alinsu, io / viddi alcuni Indiani che andavano à certe capanne vicine all'acqua, i quali subito che vidde- / ro noi, si levaron qualche dieci ò dodici di loro alteratamente, & gridando à gran voce quivi / concorsero altri compagni fino al numero di cinquanta, che à gran fretta trassero fuori cio- / che (h)avevano nelle capanne, & lo portavano sotto certi boschetti, & molti di loro veniva- / no correndo verso quella parte donde noi venivamo facendoci gran cenni che ci tornassi- / mo à dietro, con farci fiere minaccie, correndo chi da una banda & chi dall'altra. Io veduto- / gli cosi alterati feci ridurre le barche nel mezzo del fiume, perche quegli Indiani si assicuras- / sero, & andai à surgere, & posi la gente in ordine al meglio ch'io puoi, comandando che / niuno parlasse ne facesse segno ò movimentò alcuno, ne si movesse

dal suo luogo, ne si alte- / rasse per cosa che gli Indiani facessero, ne mostrasse maniera di guerra: & con questo modo gli / Indiani si venivano ogni volta accostando piu al fiume à vederci, & io me ne andai à poco / à poco dove il fiume mostrava maggiore fondo verso di loro. Tra questo mezzo erano in / essere meglio di dugentocinquanta Indiani con suoi archi & frezze, & con certe bandiere in / atto di guerra nella maniera che usano quelli della nuova Spagna, & veduto che io andavo / verso terra vennero con gran gridi alla volta nostra con archi & frezze poste in essi & con / la lor bandiere alzate, & io mi posi alla prora della barca con lo interprete che menavo me- / co, al qual comandai che gli parlasse, & parlando, ne essi lo intendevano, ne egli loro, anchora / che per vederlo essere al modo suo, si ritenessero, & veduto questo mi accostai piu à terra & essi / con gran gridare mi vennero à pigliare la riva del fiume, facendo cenni che io non dovessi pas- / sare piu avanti, mettendomi pali fra l'acqua & la terra piantati, & quanto piu io tardavo, piu / gente di continouo si vedeva giungere di loro. Al che (h)avendo io posto mente cominciai à / farlor segni di pace, & presa la spada & la rotella, le gittai in terra nella barca ponendovi sopra / i piedi dando lor ad intendere con questo & altri segni che io non volevo guerra con esso loro, / & che

[fol. 364r]

364

& che essi dovessero fare il medesimo. Presi doppo una bandiera, & la abbassai, & feci che / la gente che (h)avevo meco si abbassasse similmente, & pigliando delle cose da contracambia- / re che io portavo meco gli chiamavo per dargliele, ma con tutto ciò, niuno di loro si mosse / per venire à pigliarne, anzi si missero insieme, & cominciarono à fare fra loro un gran mor- / morio: & subito usci uno fra di loro con un bastone, nel quale erano poste certe cappe, & en- / trò nell'acqua à darmele, & io le tolsi, & gli feci cenno che mi si appressasse, il che (h)avendo egli / fatto, io lo abbracciai, & gli diedi in contracambio alcuni paternostri & altro, & egli tornato / con essi à suoi, cominciò à guardarli, & à parlare fra loro, & indi à poco vennero alla volta / mia molti di essi, à quali feci cenno che dovessero abbassare le bandiere, & lasciare l'armi, il che / fecero incontanente, poi gli accennai che le mettessero tutte in un luogo, & appartessero da / loro, il che similmente fecero, & à que gli Indiani che quivi comparivano, di nuovo, gliele fa- / cean lasciare, & porle insieme con l'altre. Doppo questo, io gli chiamai che venissero da me, / & à tutti quei che veniano io davo qualche cosa da contracambiare, trattando gli amorevol- / mente, & di gia erano tanti quei che mi si appressavano, che mi parea di non stare quivi piu / (h)ormai sicuro, & feci lor cenno che si ritirassero, & che si mettessino tutti da una parte d'un / colle che era quivi fra una pianura & il fiume, & che non si appressassero à me piu di dieci alla / volta, & incontanente i piu vecchi di loro gli chiamarono in voce alta, dicendogli che dovesse- / ro farlo, & vennero dove ero io qualche dieci ò dodici di essi, onde vedutomi quasi sicuro, / determinai dismontare in terra per piu assicurare loro, & per piu assicurarme, gl'acennai che / si assentassero in terra, il che fecero essi, ma veduto che dietro me veniano in terra dieci ò do- / dici de i miei, si alterarono, & io acennai loro che fra noi sarebbe pace, & che non dovessero / temere, & con questo si quietarono che si rimisero loro sedere come dianzi, & io mi accostai lo- / ro, & gli abbracciai dandogli alcune cosette, commettendo al mio Interprete che gli parlas- / si, perche io desideravo molto intendere il modo del parlarloro, et il gridare che mi faceano. / Et per sapere che sorte di cibo (h)avevano, feci loro cenno che (h)avevamo voglia di mangiare, / & mi portarono certe mazoche di Maiz, & un pane di Mizquiqui, & mi acennarono che / voleano vedere tirare un archibuso, il quale io feci disserrare, & tutti si spaventarono con ma- / raviglia, eccetto dua ò tre vecchi di loro che non fecero movimento alcuno, anzi gridavano / gli altri, perche (h)avevano (h)avuto paura, & per il dire d'uno di quei vecchi cominciavano à le- / varsi, di terra, & à ripigliare le loro armi, il quale volendo io placare, gli vol(s)i dare un cordon di / seta di variati colori, & egli in gran colera si morsicò il labro da basso forte, & mi diede con / un gombito nel petto, & tornò à parlare alla gente con maggiore furia. Io doppo che viddi al- / zare le bandiere, determinai di ridurmi dolcemente alle mie barche, & con un poco di ven- / to feci dare vela, con che potemmo rompere il corrente che era molto grande, anchora che à / miei compagni dispiacesse dovere andare innanzi. In tanto gli Indiani se ne venivano

segui- / tandoci longo la riva del fiume, facendo cenni che dovessi saltare in terra che mi darebbono / robba da mangiare, succiandosi le dita alcuni, & altri entravano nell'acqua con alcune maz(o)- / zoche di Maiz à darmele nella barca.

{Delli (h)abiti, arme, & statura dell'Indiani scoperti. Relatione di molti altri con quali egli ha con / cenni commercio, Vettovaglia, & molte cortesie.}

In questo modo andammo due leghe, et arrivai presso à una rottura di monte, sopra la quale / era una frascata fatta di nuovo dove mi accennavano, gridando ch'io dovessi andare, mostrando- / mela con le mani, & dicendomi che quivi era da mangiare. Io veduto che il luogo era atto / per esservi qualche imboscata, non vi vol(s)i andare, ma segui innanzi il mio viaggio. Indi à po- / co uscirono di quivi piu di mille (h)uomini armati dei loro archi & frezze, & poi comparsero / molte donne & fanciulli, à quali io non vol(s)i approssimarmi, ma gia che era per tramontare / il Sole, io sursi in mezzo il fiume. Venivano questi Indiani adornati in differente foggie, alcu- / ni venivano con un segnal che gli pigliava in coperta la faccia à longo, altri coperta la meta di / essa, ma tutti tinti di carbone, & ciascuno come meglio gli pareva. Altri poi portavano grem- / biali innanzi del medesimo colore che (h)avevano l'insegna della faccia, portavano in testa un / pezzo di cuoio di Cervo, di larghezza di duoi palmi posto à guisa di cimiero, & sopra certe / bacchette con alcune penne. Le armi loro erano archi & frezze di legno duro, & due & tre / sorte di mazze di legno brustolato. Questa gente è grande, ben disposta & senza alcuna cor- / pulentia

[fol. 364v]

pulentia hanno il naso da basso forato, dove sono attaccati alcuni pendenti, & altri ci porta- / no cappe, & le orecchie forate con molti busi,[124] nelli quali attachano pater nostri & cappe, por- / tano tutti piccoli & grandi un cordon all'ombilico fatto di varij colorij, & in mezzo vi è le- / gato un mazo di penne ritondo, il quale gli cade di dietro come coda. similmente nella pol- / pa delle braccia hanno un cordon stretto, alquale danno tante volte che viene à essere di larghez- / za di una mano. portano certi stecchi di osso di cervo ligati al braccio, con liquali si nettano il / sudore, & nell'altro certe cannelle di canna. portano similmente certi sacchetti lunghi di lar- / ghezza di una mano legati al braccio sinistro, che gli servano anchora per braccialetto per / l'arco pieni di certa semenza, della quale fanno un lor beveraggio. hanno il corpo segnato / col fuoco, i capegli tagliati dinanzi, & quelli di dietro fin alla cintura: le donne vanno ignude, / & portano un gran rinvolto di piume di dietro, & davanti dipinto & incollato, & i capelli / come gli (h)uomini. Erano fra questi Indiani tre ò quattro (h)uomini con il medesimo (h)abito / delle donne. (H)or l'altro giorno che fu sabbato di buon' (h)ora io mi missi à seguire il mio cam- / mino montando il fiume, (h)avendo tolti fuori duoi (h)uomini per ciascuno battello, perche / tirassero l'Anzana, & nel spuntare del sole udimmo un grandissimo gridare d'Indiani da una / banda & l'altra del fiume con le lor armi, però senza bandiera alcuna. A me parve ben fatto / di aspettargli, cosi per vedere quel che voleano, come per vedersi il nostro interprete gli (h)a- / vessi potuti intendere. aCostoro giunti al dritto nostro si gittavano dall'una & l'altra riva nel / fiume con i lor archi & frezze, & parlando lo interprete non gli intendeva, onde io comin- / ciai à farlor cenno che dovessero lasciare l'arme come (h)avevano fatto glialtri. Alcuni lo faceva- / no & alcuni no, & quei che le lasciavano io gli facevo accostare à me & donavo loro alcune / cose di cambio, onde questo veduto da glialtri per (h)averne anche essi la parte loro le lascia- / vano similmente. Io giudicando essere sicuro saltai con esso loro in terra & mi posi in mezzo / di essi, iquali conoscendo che io non volevo guerra mi cominciaron à dare di quelle conchole / & pater nostri, & chi mi portava alcune pelle ben aconcie, & altri del Maiz & una torta del / medesimo mal macinato, in modo che niuno vi fu che non venisse con robba, & prima che / me la dessero,[125] alquanto da me appartati cominciavano à gridare forte, & faceano cenno col / corpo & con le braccia, & poi si appressavano a darmi quel che portavano. Et gia che era tra- / montato il sole io mi feci alla larga, & sursi in mezzo il fiume. Il giorno seguente che ancho- / ra non era di chiaro quando dall'una & l'altra parte del fiume si sentiano maggiore gridi et di / piu Indiani e quali si gittavano[126] nel fiume à nuoto & venivano à portarmi alcune mazoche / di Maiz & di

quelle torte che ho detto: io mostravo alloro grano & fava, & altre semenze per / vederse ne (h)avevan alcuna di esse, ma mostravono di non ne (h)avere notitia, et di tutto si maravi- / gliavano, & per cenni venni io à conoscere che quello che (h)avevano in maggiore stima & riveren- / za, era il sole, & io davo ad intendere loro che venivo dal sole, di che essi si maravigliavano, & / all(h)ora si mettevano à contemplarmi dal capo alle piante & mostravanmi maggiore amore / che prima, & domandandogli io da mangiare me ne portavano tanto che fui sforzato di al- / leggerire duoi volte le barche, & da qui avanti di tutto quel che mi portavano ne lanciavano / una parte al sole, & poi si voltavano à me à darmi l'altra: & cosi fui sempre meglio servito & / istimato da loro cosi in tirare dell'Alzana, come in darmi da mangiare, & mi mostra- / vano tan- / to amore che nel fermarmi ci voleano portare di peso su le braccia alle lor case, & in niuna co- / sa eccedevano quel che io comandavo loro, & per mia sicurezza gli imposi che non do- / vessero portare arme al mio cospetto, & (h)avevan tanta avvertenza di farlo, che se alcuno ve- / niva quivi di nuovo con esse, subito gli andavano incontro à farglile lasciare molto lontane / da me, & io mostravo che (h)aveo di cio grandissimo piacere, & ad alcuni di essi de principali / io davo alcuni mantelletti & altre cosette, perche se (h)avessi (h)avuto da dare in generale à / tutti non saria bastata tutta la robba della nuova Spagna. Avvenia tal'(h)ora (tanto era l'amore / & buona volontà che mi mostravano) che se per sorte venivano Indiani quivi di nuovo / con arme et alcuno avisato di lasciarle, per negligenza ò non intendere alla prima parola, non / le (h)avesse lasciate, correvano essi & gliele leva- / vano per forza & gliele spezzavano alla mia / presenza, poi pigliavano l'Anzana con tanta amorevolezza, & à ragatta l'un dell'altro, che / non era necessario di commandarglielo, onde se non fusse stato questo aiuto essendo il cor- / rente del fiume grandissimo & chi tirava l'Alzana mal pratichi, sarebbe stato impossibi- / le di montare il fiume cosi contra acqua. Io, veduto che mi intendevano (h)ormai in tutte le / cose,

[fol. 365r]

3(56)65

cose, & che similmente intendevo io loro, mi parve di vedere per qualche via dare buon prin- / cipio per fare sortire buon fine al desiderio che io (h)avevo, & di alcune bacchette & carta feci / fare alcune croci, & fra gli altri dove io gli le dava per cose piu stimate, & le basciavo io, acen- / nando loro che le dovessero (h)onorare & àprezzare molto, & che se le portassero al collo, dan- / do gli à intendere che quel segno era dal cielo, & essi le pigliavano & basciavano & l'alzava- / no in alto, & mostravano di sentirne grande allegrezza & contento quando faceano questo, / & à costoro io tal(h)ora mettevo nella mia barca mostrando loro amore grande, & tal(h)ora / davo lor delle cosette che io vi portavo, & venne poi la cosa à tanto che non bastavano ne / carta ne bastoni per fare croci. In questo modo fui quel di assai bene accompagnato finche / venuta la notte mi vol(s)i allargare nel fiume, & venni à surgere nel mezzo, & essi veniano à / domandarmi licenza per partirsi, dicendo che sarebbono tornati à vedermi il giorno seguen-/ te con vettovaglia, & cosi à poco à poco si partirono che non vi restarono se non da cin- / quanta, i quali fecero fuochi all'incontro di noi, & stettero quivi tutta notte chiamandoci, / ne era ben chiaro il giorno quando si veniano à gittare à nuoto nell'acqua à domandarci / l'Anzana, & noi gliela dessimo di buona voglia, ringratiando Iddio del buono apparecchio / che ci dava di potere montare il fiume, perche erano gli Indiani tanti, che se (h)avessero voluto / impedirci il passaggio, ancora che noi fussimo stati assai piu di quei che eravamo, lo (h)avreb- / bono[127] fatto.

{Uno delli Indiani (h)avendo inteso il linguaggio dell'Interprete, fa à quello diverse dimande de l'origine / degli Spagnuoli, gli dice che il loro Capitano è figliuolo[128] del Sole, & che da quello è à loro man- / dato, & lo Vogliono accettare per loro Signore. Togliono tale Indiano in Na- / ve, & da lui hanno molte relationi di quel paese.}

In questo modo navigammo fino al martedi al tardi, andando come solevamo, facendo par- / lare dal mio Interprete alla gente per vedere se à caso alcuno l'(h)avesse inteso, senti che uno / gli rispose, onde feci fermare i battelli, & chiamai colui che intendevo, imponendo al mio In- / terprete che non dovesse parlare ne rispondere piu se non quel tanto ch'io gli dicesse, & vid- / di cosi stando che quell'Indiano cominciò à

parlare à quella gente con gran furia, onde tut- / ti si cominciarono à unire insieme, & l'interprete mio intese, che colui che venia nella bar- / ca, diceva loro, che volea sapere che gente eravamo, & donde venivamo, & se erava- / mo usciti di sotto l'acqua, ò della terra, ò caduti dal cielo, & à questo dire si mise insieme in- / finita gente, che si maravigliava di vedermi parlare, & questo Indiano ritornava di volta in / volta à parlargli loro in altra lingua che il mio Interprete non intendeva. A quel che mi do- / mandò chi eravamo, risposi che noi eravamo Christiani, & che venivamo di longe à veder- / gli, & rispondendo alla interrogatione di chi mi mandava, dissi essere mandato dal Sole, mo- / strandolo à cenno come prima, perche non mi pigliassero in bugia. Mi ricominciò egli à dire come / mi (h)aveva mandato[129] il Sole, andando egli per l'alto ne mai fermandosi, & essendo molti anni / che ne egli, ne i vecchi (h)avevano veduti altri tali come noi, de quali mai (h)avevano (h)avuto no- / titia veruna, ne il Sole fino à quell'(h)ora (h)aveva mai mandato alcun'altro. Io gli risposi che / era vero che il Sole cominciava cosi da alto, & che giamai si fermava, però che essi poteano / ben vedere che al coricarsi, & al levarsi la mattina si veniva appressarsi alla terra, dove era / il suo domicilio, & che sempre lo vedeano uscire da un medesimo luogo, & che mi (h)aveva / creato in quella terra & paese donde egli usciva, in quel modo che (h)aveva ancora creati molti / altri che egli mandava in altre parti, & che all'(h)ora (h)aveva mandato me à visitare & vedere / quel fiume & la gente che vi (h)abitava vicina, perche io le dovessi parlare, & gli congiungessi / in amicitia meco, & gli dessi di quel che non (h)avevano, & che gli dicessi che non dovessero fare / guerra fra loro, al che rispose egli, che gli dovessi dire la cagione perche il Sole non mi (h)aveva / mandato prima per quietare le guerre che erano fra loro di molto tempo & si uccideano mol- / ti, io gli risposi essere proceduto, perchio ero stato fanciullo. Poi domandò all'Interprete se / noi lo conducevamo forzatamente che lo (h)avessimo pigliato nella guerra, ò pur egli vi ve- / niva di sua buona volonta, gli rispose che era con noi di sua propia volonta, & molto soddis- / fatto della compagnia nostra. Tornò à dimandare, perche non menavamo con noi se non lui / solo che gli intendessi, & perche noi non intendevamo tutti gli altri, poi che eravamo figliuo- / li del Sole, gli rispose, che'l Sole ancora (h)aveva generato lui, & gli (h)aveva dato linguaggio per / potere intenderlui, & me, & gli altri, che il Sole sapeva bene che essi dimoravano quivi, / ma

[fol. 365v]

ma che per (h)avere da fare molte altre cose, & essere io piccolo non mi (h)aveva mandato prima. Et / egli rivolto à me disse subito, vieni[130] dunque tu qua per essere Signore nostro: & che ti (h)abbia- / mo à servire: Io pensando che non gli dovessi piacere che gli dicessi di si, gli risposi che non / per Signore, ma ben per fratello, & per dargli di quel che (h)avessi. Mi domandò se mi (h)aveva ge- / nerato il Sole come gli altri, & se ero suo parente ò suo figliuolo, gli risposi che ero suo figliuo- / lo. Seguitò egli à domandare se gli altri che erano meco, erano figliuoli anch'essi del Sole, / risposegli che no, ma che si erano creati con me nella medesima terra, dove io mi ero alleva- / to. All'(h)ora egli gridò con voce alta & disse, poi che ci fai tanto bene, et non vuoi che faccia- / mo guerra, & sei figliuolo del Sole, & vogliamoti tutti tenere per Signore nostro, & servirti / sempre, però[131] ti preghiamo che tu non te ne vadi ne ti parti da noi, & subito si voltò alla gen- / te, & gli cominciò à dire come io ero figliuolo del Sole, & però che tutti mi elegessero per Si- / gnore. Quegli Indiani udito questo, rimasero stupefatti oltre modo, & si veniano accostan- / do tuttavia piu à guardarmi. Mi fece quell'Indiano anco[132] altre domande, che per evitare di es- / sere troppo longo, io non le narro, & con questo ce ne passammo il giorno, & gia che si ap- / prossimava la notte, incominciai ad affaticarmi col migliore modo che potetti di mettere quel / l'(h)uomo con esso noi nella barca, & egli recusando di farlo, gli disse lo Interprete che l'(h)avrem- / mo lasciato dallaltra parte del fiume, & con questa conditione egli vi entrò, & quivi io gli fe- / ci molte carezze, & il migliore trattamento che potetti, assicurandolo tuttavia, & quando / giudicai che si fosse tolto da ogni sospetto, mi parve'di domandargli qualche cosa di quel pae- / se. Et tra le prime che io gli domandassi fu, se mai per innanzi (h)avevo veduti altri come noi, / ò sentito nominargli rispose di no, eccetto che (h)aveva inteso dalli vecchi che molto lontano / di quel paese vi erano altri (h)uomini bianchi, & con barbe come noi, & che altro non

sapeva. / Gli domandai se (h)aveva notitia di un luogo che si chiamava Cevola, & di un fiume che si chia- / mava Totontoac, & rispose di no, onde io veduto che non mi potea dare nuova di Francesco / Vazquez ne della sua gente, determinai di interrogarlo delle cose di quel paese & del loro / modo di vivere, & cominciai à dirgli se teneano che vi fosse un Dio creator del cielo & della / terra, ò pur alcun Idolo, & risposemi che no, ma che tenevano il Sole in maggiore stima & ve- / neratione di tutte l'altre cose, perche gli scaldava, & gli facea nascere le loro semenze, & che / di tutto quel che mangiavano gliene lanciavano un poco all'aere. Dissigli poi se (h)avevano Si- / gnore, & rispose di no, ma che ben sapeano che vi era un grandissimo Signore, ma non (h)a- / veano notitia à qual parte fusse, & io gli dissi che stava nel cielo, & che si chiamava Giesu / Christo, & non mi curai di stendermi in piu theologie con esso lui. Gli domandai se (h)avevano / guerra, & per qual cagione, mi rispose di si, & molta grande & sopra cose leggierissime, perche / quando non (h)avevano causa da farle, si univano insieme, et qualunche di loro dicea[133] andiamo à / fare guerra in tal parte, all'(h)ora tutti si moveano con l'armi. Gli dissi chi di loro comandava alla / gente, rispose che li piu vecchi & i piu valenti, & che quando questi dicevano che non facessero / piu, subito si ritiravano dalla guerra. Gli domandai che mi dicessi che facevano di quegli (h)uo- / mini che uccidevano in battaglia, risposemi che ad alcuni cavavano il cuore, & se lo mangiava- / no, & altri bruciavano, & soggiunse che se non fosse stato per la mia giunta in quel luogo / che gia essi sarebbono in guerra, et perche io gli comandavo che non la dovessero fare, & la- / sciassero l'armi, però fin tanto che io non dicessi loro che le ripigliassero, non si sariano mossi / à guerriggiare con altri, & che fra loro diceano,[134] che poi ch'io ero venuto alloro, (h)avevano ri- / mossa la volonta di fare guerra, & (h)avevano animo buono di seguire la pace. Si lamentò d'alcu- / ni che restavano à dietro in una montagna che loro faceano gran guerra, & uccideano mol- / ti di loro, gli risposi che da li avanti non dovessero piu temere, perche io gli (h)avevo comandato / che stessero in pace, & che quando non l'(h)avessero fatto, li castigaria, & ammazzeria. Mi rispo- / se in qual modo, essendo noi si pochi, & essi in tanto numero, gli potria uccidere. Et percio- / che era (h)oggimai tardi, & gia vedevo che riceveva molestia di stare piu meco lo lasciai uscire / fuori, & ne lo mandai molto contento.

{Da Naguachato & altri principali di quelli Indiani ricevono molte Vettovaglie, oprano che piantino / nelle loro terre la Croce, & insegnagli ad adorarla. Hanno relatione di molti popoli, di loro di- / versi linguaggi, & de costumi circa il Matrimonio, come puniscono l'adulterio, delle / opinioni che hanno de morti, & delle infermità che patiscono.}

L'altro giorno di buon'(h)ora venne il principal loro detto Naguachato, & dissemi che io / uscissi

[fol. 366r]
3(57)66

uscissi in terra perche (h)ave*v*a gran vettovaglia da darmi. Et percio che mi vedevo in parte si- / cura lo feci senza indugio, & incontinente venne un vecchio con torte di quel Maiz & cer- / te piccole Zucche & chiamandomi à dalta voce, & facendo molti atti con la persona & con / le braccia si venne ad accostarmisi, & fattomi rivoltar*e* verso quella gente & similmente ri- / voltatosi anch'egli le disse, SAGUEYCA & tutta quella gente à gran voce rispose, HU, & of- / ferse al Sole di quelche (h)ave*v*a quivi di ogni cosa un poco, & cosi à me un'altro poco (benche / poi mi desse il restante) & il medesimo ordine tenne con tutti quei che erano meco, & venu- / to fuori l'interprete, io per suo mezzo gliene resi gratie, dicendo loro che per esser*e* le barche / cosi piccole non (h)ave*v*a condotte meco molte cose da poter*e* darloro in contracambio, ma / che ritornando un'altra volta lo (h)avrei fatto, et che se fussero voluti venire con meco in quel- / le barche alle navi che (h)avevo à basso del fiume, gli (h)avrei dato molte cose. Essi risposero / che lo (h)averiano fatto molto allegri in vista. Quivi per il mezzo dello interprete vol(s)*h*i[135] lor / dare ad intender*e* che cosa era il segno della croce, & imposi loro che mi portassero un legno, / del qual feci fare una gran Croce, & comandai à tutti quei che erano meco che nel farla l'ado- / rassero, & supplicasser*o* il nostro Signor*e* che gli desse la gratia che tanta ge*n*te venisse in cogni- / tione della sua santa fe de Catolica, & fatto questo dissi loro per l'interprete che io li lascia- / vo quel segno, in

segnal che io gli tenevo per fratelli, & che me lo guardassero con diligen- / tia fin che io fussi ritornato, & che ogni mattina si dovessero tutti inginocchiare nel levar*e* / del sole innanzi di esso. Et eglino la tolsero incontanente, & senza tochar*e* terra la portarono / à piantar*e* nel mezzo delle case loro, dove tutti la potessero veder, & lor dissi che sempre la / adorassero perche quella sarebbe che gli guardarebbe da male. Mi domandaro*n*o fino aquan- / to l'(h)avevano essi à metter*e* sotto terra & io gl*i*elo mostrai. Fu molta la gente che andò à ac- / compagnarla, & quei che quivi restarono mi interrogarono in qual modo (h)ave*v*ano da giun- / ger*e* le mani & à che guisa si (h)ave*v*ano da inginocchiare per adorarla, & mostravano di (h)aver*e* / un gran pe*n*siero di impararlo. Questo fatto, presi quel principal della terra & con esso entra- / to nelle barche mi misi al mio cammino nel fiume, & tutti di qua & di la della riva mi accom- / pagna- vano con grande amorevolezza & mi servivano in tirar*e* l'alzana, & tirarci dalla / ghiaia dove spesso entravamo, perchio[136] che in molti luoghi trovavamo il fiume cosi basso che / non vi era acqua per le barche. Cosi anda*n*do venivano de gli Indiani che io (h)avevo lasciati à / basso à dirmi che io gli insegnassi bene la maniera come che (h)avevano da giun- gere le mani / nella adoratione di q*u*ella Croce: altri mostra- vano se le stavan bene post(e)*o* in quel modo, in mo- /do che no*n* mi lasciavan riposare. Vicino all'altra riva del fiume era maggior*e* qua*n*tità di gente / che à gran fretta mi chiamavono che dovessi pigliar*e* delle vettovaglie che mi portavano. Et / p*er*che mi accorsi che l'uno (h)aveva invidia à l'altro, p*er* non lasciar*e* costoro discontenti, lo feci, & / quivi comparse un'altro vecchio come il passato che mi porto della vetto- vaglia con le mede- / sime cerimonie & offer(t)*se*, & vol(s)*h*i da lui intender*e* qualche cosa come dall'altro. Costui simil- / mente diceva all'altra gente, questo è il Signor*e* nostro, gia voi sapete quanto tempo ha che / noi sentimmo dire dalli antichi nostri, che al mondo era gente barbata & bianca, & noi ce ne / facevamo beff(e)*a*. Io che sono vecchio & altri che qui sono non (h)abbiamo gia mai vedut(a)*o* al- / tra simil gente come questa, & se no*n* lo volete credere, guardate q*u*elle che sono in q*u*esto fiume, / diamo gli a dunque da mangiare, poi che essi danno anco à noi de i cibi loro, serviamo di / buon animo questo Signore che ha buono volontà, & vieta che non dobbiamo far*e* guerra, / & tutti ci abbraccia & ha*n*no bocca mani & occhi come (h)abbiamo noi, & parla(o)*n*o come noi. / A costoro diedi similmente un'altra Croce come (h)avevo fatto à quei da basso, & dissi lor le / medesime parole, le quali ascoltaron*o* essi di miglior*e* voglia, & usavano maggior*e* diligenza di / imparare quel che io gli dicevo. Passando poi piu sopra, trovai altra gente, da i quali l'in- / terprete non intendeva cosa alcuna, onde io diedi loro à intender*e* per cenni le medesime ce- / rimonie dell'adoration della Croce, che à gli altri. Et quel principale (h)uomo che io (h)avevo / tolto meco mi disse che piu alto (h)avrei trovat(a)*o* ge*n*te che (h)avrebbe inteso lo interprete mio, / & essendo gia tardi, alcuni di questi (h)uomini mi chiamarono per darmi della vettovaglia & / fecero il medesimo che gli altri, facendo feste & gi(u)ochi per darmi piacere. Io vol(s)*i* intender*e* / che gente vivevono alla riva di questo fiume, & da quello (h)uomo intesi che era (h)abitata da / ventitre linguaggi, & questi erano i vicini al fiume senza altri poco lontani, & che vi erano / oltre questi ventitre linguaggi, sul fiume anco*ra* altri che egli non conosceva. Gli domandai / se ogni

[fol. 366v]

se ogni popolo era in un solo ridotto, & mi rispose che non, ma che erano piu case sparse per / la campagna, & che ogni popolo (h)aveva il suo paese separato & conosciuto, & che in ogni / (h)abitatione era gente assai. Mi mostrò una villa che era in una montagna, che diceva esservi / gran moltitudine di gente & di mala sorte che dava à coloro continoua guerra, che essendo / senza Signore & (h)abitando quel luogo deserto dove si raccoglieva poco Maiz descendea- / no alla pianura à pigliarlo à baratto di pelle di cervo, delle quali andavan vestiti, con ve- / ste lunge, le quali tagliavano con rasoi & le cuscivano con aghi fatti di osso di cervo. Et che / (h)ave*v*ano le case grande di pietra. Io gli domandai se quivi vi era persona alcuna di quel pae- / se, & trovai una donna che portava un vestimento come una mantellina che le pigliava dal- / la cintura fino in terra, di cuoio di Cervo ben concio. Gli domandai poi se la gente che (h)abi- / tava la riva di quel fiume stava sempre ferma quivi, ò pur à qualche tempo andava à viver*e* / altrove, mi rispose che di state facevano l'(h)abitation quivi & vi seminavano, & fatto il rac- /

colto se ne andavano ad (h)abitar*e* ad'altre case che (h)avevano alla falda della mo*n*tagna lontani / dal fiume, & mi acenno che le case erano di legno i*n*terrazzate dalle parti di fuori, et seppi che / facevano una stanza to*n*da dove dimoravan tutti insieme (h)uomini & donne. Lo doma*n*dai / se essi (h)avevano donne à commune, mi disse di no, che colui che si maritava (h)aveva da te- / ner*e* una sola moglie. Vol(s)*i* intender*e* l'ordine che teneano nel maritarsi, & dissemi che se alcu- / no (h)aveva qualche figliuola se ne andava dove era la gente, & diceva, io ho una figliuola da / maritare, ci è qui persona alcuna che la voglia: & se quivi era chi la volesse, rispondeva volerla / & si concertava il matrimonio, & che il padre di quel che la voleva portava qualche cosa à / donar*e* alla giovane, & da quell'(h)ora avanti si intendeva esser*e* fatto il matrimonio & che can- / tavano & ballavano, & venuta la sera i parenti gli pigliavano, & gli lasciavano soli in luogo / che niuno gli potesse vedere. Et seppi che non si maritavano fratelli con sorelle, ne con pa- / renti, & che le donne prima che fussero maritate non prati-cavano ne parlavano con gli (h)uo- / mini, ma se ne stavano in casa loro e nelle sue possessioni à lavorare, et che se per caso, alcuna / (h)aveva (h)avuto commercio con gli (h)uomini prima che si maritasse, il marito la lasciava, & se / ne andava in altri paesi, & che quelle che cadevano in questo errore erano tenute cattive fe- / mine. Et che se dopo che eran maritati, alcuno fussi stato trovato co*n* altra do*n*na in adulterio, / l'uccidevano, & che niuno poteva (h)aver*e* piu che una moglie se non nascos*t*a. Mi dissero che / abbru-sciav(o)*an*o[137] i morti, & quei che rimanevan*o* vedovi, stavano mezzo anno, ò uno, senza / rimaritarsi. Vol(s)*i* intendercio che credevan de i morti. Mi rispose che se ne andavano all'al- / tro mondo, ma che non (h)avev*a*n ne pena ne gloria. La principale infirmità di che qu*e*lle gen- / ti muoiono, è di g(i)ettar*e* sangue per la bocca: & hanno i medici che gli curano con parole & sof- / fiar*e* che gli fanno: l'(h)abito di costoro era come de glialtri di sopra: portano le sue can*n*elle da / farsi profumi come li popoli Tavagi della nuova Spagna. Vol(s)*i* intendere se costoro (h)ave- / vano Signore alcuno, & seppi che no, ma che ciascuna casa faceva il suo Signor*e* da per se. / Costoro ha*n*no di piu del Maiz certe zucche, et un'altra seme*n*za à guisa di miglio, hanno pietre / da macinare, et pignatte, nelle quali cuocono quelle zucche et pesce del fiume che lo hanno assai / buono. Da qui innanzi non pote venire lo interprete, perche diceva che quei che noi (h)ave- / vamo da trovare nel cammino piu oltre, erano suoi n(i)emici, & percio io lo rimandai à dietro / molto sodisfatto. Non tardò molto che vidi venire molti Indiani gridando à gran voce & / correndo d(r)ietro di me. Io mi fermai per sapere quelche volevano, & mi dissero che la Croce, / che io (h)avevo lor data, (h)avevan posta in mezzo le (h)abitationi loro si come io gli (h)avevo ordi- / nato, ma che io dovessi sapere che quando il fiume inondava, soleva arrivare fin li, però che / io gli dessi[138] licentia per poterla mutare & collocare in altra parte dove non potessi aggiungere / il fiume & portarla via, ilche io concessi.

{Da Un'Indiano di quella riviera hanno relatione del stato di Cevola & della qualita & costumi di / quelle genti, & del lor Signore. et parimente delle terre ivi non molto distanti, dette l'una / Quicama, & l'altra Coana, da quelli di Quicama, & da altri Indiani indi / non molto distanti ricevono cortesia.}

Cosi navigando giunsi dove erano molti Indiani, & un'altro Interprete, ilquale io feci en- / trare con meco nella barca, & percioche faceva freddo, & la gente veniva bagnata, saltai in / terra, & comandai che si facessi fuoco, & stando cosi à scaldarci, arrivò un Indiano che mi det- / te nel braccio, mostrandomi col dito un bosco, fuori del quale viddi uscire duoi squadroni di / gente

[fol. 367r]

367

gente con le loro armi, & mi mostrò come venivano à darci alla fronte, & io perche non vo- / levo rompermi con niuno, raccolsi la mia gente nei battelli, & gl'Indiani che erano con esso me- / co si g(i)ettarono à nuoto, & si salvarono all'altra riva. Io in tanto domandai à quello Indiano / che (h)avevo con meco che gente era quella che era venuta fuori del bosco, mi disse che erano / suoi n(i)emici, & però che questi altri nel giungerloro senza dire motto si erano messi nell'acqua, / & ciò (h)avevan fatto, perche volevano tornare à dietro, trovandosi senz'armi, per non l'(h)avere por- / tate nel venire con

esso loro, (h)avendo inteso il comandamento & volermio, che non vole- / vo che si portassero. Vol(s)i domandare à questo Interprete il medesimo che (h)avevo doman- / dato all'altro delle cose di quel paese, perche in alcuni popoli io (h)avevo inteso che uno (h)uo- / mo usava d'(h)avere molte moglie, & in altri non piu di una. (H)or seppi da lui che era stato in / Cevola, che (c)si era il cammino d'un mese dalla terra sua, & che da quel luogo ag(g)iatamente per / un sentiero che andava seguitando quel fiume si andava in quaranta giorni, & che la cagione / che lo mosse à andarvi, era stata solo per vedere Cevola, per essere cosa grande, che (h)aveva le / case altissime di pietra di tre & quattro solari, & con finestre da ciascuna banda, circondate / all'intorno d'un muro d'una statura & mezza d'(h)uomo d'altezza, & che di sopra et da basso / erano (h)abitate da gente, & che usavano le medesime armi che usavano quegli altri che (h)avevo / veduti, cioè, archi, & fre(zz)cce, mazze, bastoni & rotelle: & che (h)avevano un Signore, & che an- / davano vestiti di mantelli, & con cuoi di vacche, & che i loro mantelli (h)avevano una pittura à / torno, & il Signore portava una camiscia lunga molto sottile cinta, & di sopra piu mantelli: & / le donne vestivano vestimenti molto lunghi, & che erano bianche, & andavano tutte coper- / te: & che ogni giorno stavano alla porta del Signore molti Indiani per servirlo, & che porta- / vano molte pietre azzurre, le quali si cavano di una rocc(h)ia di sasso, & che costoro non (h)ave- / vano piu d'una moglie con chi si maritavano, & quando che morivano i Signori si sep(p)elli- / vano con esso loro tutte le robbe che (h)avevano. Et similmente nel tempo che mangiano, / vi stanno molti dei suoi alla loro tavola à cortegiarlo, & à vederlo mangiare, et che mangiano / con tovaglie, à che hanno bagni. (H)or giovedi nel far del giorno venivano gl'Indiani col / medesimo grido alla riva del fiume, & con maggiore volonta di servirci, portandomi da man- / giare, & facendomi la medesima buona cera che mi (h)avevano fatto gli altri, (h)avendo inteso / che io ero, & dando loro le medesime croci col medesimo ordine che à glialtri. Et caminando / poi piu in su, pervenni à una terra, dove trovai migliore ordine, percioche obediscono total- / mente gli (h)abitatori che vi sono à un solo. (H)or ritornando à parlare di nuovo con lo Inter- / prete delle (h)abitationi di quei di Cevola, mi disse che quel Signore (h)aveva un cane simile à / quel ch'io menavo. Volendo io poi ma*n*giare vid(d)i questo Interprete portar*e* innanzi & in- / dietro certi piatti, onde mi disse che il Signor*e* di Cevola ne (h)aveva di simili anch'egli, ma che / erano verdi, & che niun'altro vi era che ne (h)avesse se non il Signore, & che erano quattro, / i quali (h)aveva (h)avuti con quel cane, & altre cose da un (h)uomo nero che portava la barba, / ma che egli non sapeva da qual banda fosse quivi capitato, & che il Signore poi lo fece ucci- / dere per quanto egli (h)aveva inteso dire. Gli domandai se sapeva che alcuna terra fosse quivi / vicina, mi rispose che nel montare del fiume, ne sapeva alcune, & che fra glialtri vi era un Si- / gnore d'un luogo chiamato Chicama, & uno d'un'altra terra chiamata Coama, & che (h)ave- / va sotto di loro molta gente: & dipoi datomi q*ue*sto avviso, mi chiese licentia p*er* potere ritornare / dai suoi compagni. Di qua mi posi à navigare di nuovo, & ap*p*resso à una giornata trovai un / luogo dis(h)abitato, dove essendo io entrato, sopra*vv*ennero forse cinquece*n*to Indiani con suoi / archi & fre(zz)c*c*e, & insieme con loro era quel principale Indiano detto Naguachato ch'io (h)a- / vevo lasciato, & mi portarono à donare certi Conigli, & yucas, & (h)avendo fatti à tutti buo- / na cera, volendo partirmi, gli diedi licentia di ritornare alle lor case. Passando il d(i)*e*serto piu in- / nanzi, arrivai à certe capanne, donde mi usci incontro molta gente con un vecchio innanzi, / gridando in linguaggio che il mio Interprete ben intendeva, & diceva à quegli (h)uomini, / fratelli, vedete qui il Signore, diamo gli di quel che (h)avemo, poi che ci fa del bene, & è passa- / to per tante genti discortesi per venirci à vedere, & detto questo offerse al Sole, & poi à me / medesimamente come (h)avevano fatto glialtri. Costoro (h)avevano certi sacchi grandi, & ben / fatti di scorze di bessuchi, & intesi che era q*ue*sta terra del Signor*e* di Quicoma, i quali veniano / solamente à raccogliere il frutto delle loro semenze quivi la *e*state, & fra loro trovai uno che / intendeva molto bene il mio Interprete, onde io con molta a facilità feci à costoro il medesi- / mo

[fol. 367v]
mo (o)*u*fficio[139] delle Croci che (h)avevo fatto con glialtri da basso. (H)avevano queste genti del / bambaso, ma non pigli-

avano molta cura di farlo per non essere fra loro persona che sapessi / tessere per farne vestimenti. Mi domandarono come (h)avevano da piantare la Croce quan- / do fossero ritornati à casa loro che era alla montagna, & se era bene di farle una casa à torno, / accio non si bagnass(i)e, & se gli dovevano porre cosa alcuna alle braccia. Io gli dissi di no, & / che solo bastava che la ponessero in luogo che da tutti fusse veduta, fin che io ritornassi, & se / per caso venissi alcuna ge*n*te da guerra, mi offers(on)*e*ro di mandare meco piu gente, dicendo che / erano cattivi (h)uomini quei che io troverei disopra, ma io no*n* vol(s)*h* accettarla, tuttavia vi ven- / nero venti di loro, i quali nell'avvicina(r)*ndo*mi à quei che erano n(i)*e*mici loro, me ne avisarono, & / io trovai le fue sentinelle poste alla guardia ne i loro confini. Sabbato di mattina trovai un / gran squadrone di gente assisa sotto una frascata grandissima, una parte, & l'altra di fuori, & / veduto che no*n* si levavono in pie, io me ne passai di l(o)*u*ngo al mio viaggio, ciò veduto da lor, / si levò in pie de un vecchio che mi disse Signor, perche no*n* vuoi pigliare da noi da mangiare: / (h)avendone pigliato da glialtri: Io gli risposi che non pigliavo se non quel che mi era dato, & / non andavo se non da quei che mi doma*n*davano. Quivi senza indugiare mi potarono mol- / ta vettovaglia, dicendomi che poiche no*n* entravamo nelle case loro & ci stavamo di di, & di / notte nel fiume & essendo io figliuolo del Sole, tutti mi dovessino tenere p*er* Signore. Io feci / lor ce*n*no che si ponessero à sedere, & chiamai quel vecchio che inte*n*deva l'Interprete mio, & / gli domandai di chi era quella terra, & se quivi era il Signore, mi risposero di si, & lo feci chia- / mare, & venuto, lo (h)abbracciai monstra*n*dogli grande amore, et vede*n*do io che tutti (h)avevano / piacere delle carezze ch'io gli facevo, lo vestì di una camiscia, & gli donai altre cosette, & or- / dinai allo Interprete che dicesse à quel Signore il medesimo che (h)aveva detto à glialtri, dop- / (p)o gli diedi una Croce, la quale egli prese di molto buona voglia come glialtri, & questo Si- / gnore se ne ve*n*ne un gran pezzo con meco fintantoche fui chiamato dall'altra parte del fiu- / me dove stava il medesimo vecchio con molta gente, alla quale io detti un'altra Croce, dicen- / dogli il med*e*simo che (h)avevo detto à glialtri, cioè, quel che ne (h)aveva à fare. Seguendo poi il / mio cam*m*ino inco*n*trai un'altra moltitudine di ge*n*te, co quali ve*n*ne il medesimo vecchio che in- / tendeva l'Interprete mio, & veduto il signor*e* loro che mi mostrava, lo pregai che se ne voles- / si venire con meco nella barca, il che egli fece di buona voglia, & cosi me n'andavo per il fiu- / me sempre montando, & il vecchio mi veniva mostrando quali erano i Signori, & io parla- / vo loro sempre con grande affe(tt)*z*ione, & tutti mostravano d'(h)aver*e* grande allegrezza, & di- / cevano molto bene della mia venuta. La notte mi ritiravo nel largo del fiume, & domanda- / vogli di molte cose di quel paese, & trovai in lui cosi buona voglia & dispositione nel dirme- / le come in me desisterio[140] di voler*e* saperlo. Gli domandai di Cevola, & mi disse che egli vi era / stato, & che era una nobil*e* cosa, & il Signor*e* di esso era molto ubbidi*t*o, & che v'erano altri si- / gnori all'intorno co quali egli (h)aveva continoua guerra. Gli domandai se (h)avevano arge*n*to / & oro, & egli veduti certi sonagli, disse che l'(h)aveva del color*e* di quelli, vol(s)*l*i intendere se lo / facevano li, & mi rispose di no, ma che lo portavano da una montagna, dove stava una vec- / chia. Gli domandai se (h)aveva notitia d'un fiume che si chiamava Totonteac, mi rispose che / {Laga*r*tos so- / no cocodril- / li.} no, ma si ben di un'altro fiume grandissimo, dove si trovavano Lagartos si gra*n*di, che di loro / cuoi si facevano rot(o)*e*lle, & che adorano il Sole ne piu ne meno come gli altri passati, & quan- / do gli offeriscono dei frutti della terra, gli dicono, piglia poiche tu ce gli hai generati, & che / lo amavano molto, perche gli scaldava, & che qua*n*do no*n* usciva sentivano freddo. Quivi poi / nel ragionare cominciò à dolersi alquanto, dicendomi non so perche il Sole usi questi termi- / ni con noi, che non ci da panni *ne chi gli fili* ne chi gli tessa, & altre cose che da à molti altri, & si lamenta- / va che quei del paese non gli lasciavano entrare dentro & non gli volevano dare delle loro / semenze, io gli dissi che ci (h)averei dato rimedio, di che rimase egli molto sodd*i*sfatto.

{Dalli Indiani hanno rela(t)*z*ione, perche gli Signori di Cevola Uccisero il moro qual ando con fra Marco, / & altre molte cose; & della Vecchia detta Guatazaca, qual Vive in Una lacuna senza / prender*e* cibo. Descrittione di Un'animale, con la pelle del quale fanno targhe. So- / spitione[141] che di lor*o* prendono che siano di quelli christiani Veduti in Ce- / vola, & come accortamente si salvano.}

L'altro di che fu la Domenica, non era ancor*a* ben giorno quando incominciò il gridar*e* co- / me si sol*l*eva, & era di tre ò quattro popoli che (h)avevano dormito vicino al fiume, aspetta*n*do- / mi

[fol. 368r]
368

mi, & prendevano il Maiz, & altre semenze in bocca, & mi spargevan*o* con quelle, dicendo / che quella era la maniera del sacrificio che facevano al Sole, dop(p)o dieronmi[142] di questa vetto- / vaglia da mangiare, & fra l'altre cose di molti fasuoli. Io donai à costoro la Croce come (h)ave- / vo fatto à glialtri, & intanto quel vecchio diceva loro cose grande del fatto mio, et mi segna- / lava col dito, dice*n*do, questo è il signore, figliuolo del Sole, & mi facevano pettinar*e* la barba, / & ben ordinare la veste che io portavo addosso. Et tanto era la credenza che (h)avevano in / me, che tutti mi dicevano le cose che erano passate, & passavano fra loro, & l'animo buono ò / cattivo che (h)avevano l'uno à l'altro. Io gli doma*n*dai per qual cagione essi dicevano à me tut- / te le cose loro, & quel vecchio mi rispose, tu sei Signore, & al Signore non si debbe tener*e* ce- / lato cosa veruna. Doppo queste cose seguendo il cam*m*ino, ricominciai à doma*n*dargli delle co- / se di Cevola, & se sapeva che quei di quel paese (h)avessino veduto mai gente simili à noi, mi / rispose di no, eccetto un negro che portava à piedi, & alle braccia certe cose che sonavano: / vostra Signoria debbe (h)avere in memoria come stava questo negro che andò con fra Mar- / co che portava li sonagli, & le penne nelle brazza, & gambe, & chel portava piatti di diversi / colori, & che era poco piu d'un anno che era capitato quivi. Gli doma*n*dai la cagione, perche / fu morto, & egli mi rispose, che il Signore di Cevola gli (h)aveva domandato se (h)aveva altri / fratelli, gli rispose che ne (h)aveva infiniti, & che (h)avevano molte arme co*n* loro, ne erano mol- / to lontani di li. Il che udito, si misero in consiglio molti Signori, & concertaron[143] di ucciderlo, / acciocche non (h)avessi da dar*e* nuova à questi suoi fratelli, dove essi stavano, & che per questa / cagione l'uccisero, & ne fecero molti pezzi, i quali furono divisi fra tutti quei Signori, accio / sapessero del certo essere morto, & che similmente (h)aveva un cane come il mio, ilquale fece / ancor*a* uccidere di li à molti giorni. Lo interrogai se quei di Cevola (h)avevano n(i)emici, & mi dis- / se che si, & mi raccontò quattordici ò quindici Signori, che (h)avevano guerra con esso loro, / & che (h)avevano mantelli, & gli archi propri(i) delli sopradetti, ben mi disse che (h)av(e)rei trova- / to nel montar*e* su il fiume, gente che no*n* (h)aveva guerra alcuna ne con vicini, ne con altri. Dis- / semi che (h)avevano tre ò quattro sorte di alberi di bonissimi frutti da mangiare, & che in una / certa laguna (h)abitava una vecchia, la quale era molto osservata, & servita da loro, & sta*n*(c)ziava / in una certa casetta che quivi era, & che no*n* ma*n*giava giam*m*ai, & che quivi si facevano di quel- / le cose che sonavano, & che allei erano donati molti mantelli, piume, & Maiz. Gli doman- / dai del nome, & mi disse che si chiamava Guatuzaca, et che erano in quel contorno molti Si- / gnori che nel loro vivere, & morire, usavano gli medesimi costumi di quei di Cevola, iquali / (h)avevano loro (h)abitationi di *e*state con mante dipinte, & d'inverno (h)abitavano in case di le- / gname di duoi ò tre solari d'altezza, et che tutte queste cose (h)aveva egli vedute, eccetto che / la vecchia. Et ritornando à domandargli anc*ora* piu cose, non vol*e*se rispondermi, dicendo che / era stanco di me, et essendosi posti molti di questi Indiani all'intorno, dicevano fra loro, guar- / diamolo bene, perche lo riconosciamo quando ritornera. Il lunedi seguente era il fiume cir- / condato di gente della medesima maniera, & io ricominciai à domandare il vecchio che vo- / lesse dirmi la gente che era in quel paese, il quale mi rispose che pensava che gia me ne fussi di- / menticato, & quivi mi raccontò di una infinita di Signori, & di popoli che passavano dugen- / to: & ragiona*n*domi dell'armi, mi disse che alcuni di loro (h)avevano certe rotelle grandissime / di cuoio, grosse piu di due dita. Gli domandai di che animali le facessero, & mi descrisse una / (una) bestia molto grande, à guisa di vacca, ma piu di un gran palmo piu l(o)u*n*ga, & li piedi lar- / ghi, i bracci grossi come una coscia d'(h)uomo, & la testa di lunghezza di sette palmi, il fronte / di tre span*n*e, & gli occhi piu grossi che un pugno, & le corna della lo*n*ghezza d'uno schincho,[144] / delle quali uscivan punte acute, lunghe d'un palmo, i piedi & le mani grandi piu di sette pal- / mi, co*n* una coda torta,[145] ma molto grossa, & diste*n*dendo le braccia sopra'l capo, diceva che era an- / co*ra* piu alta. Mi diede poi notitia di un'altra vecchia che (h)abitava dalla ba*n*da del

mare. Questo / giorno co*n*sumai in dar*e* delle croci à q*ue*lle ge*n*ti come (h)avevo fatto à glialtri. Quel mio vecchio / smontò à terra, & si mise à parlame*n*to con un'altro, che quel giorno lo (h)aveva chiamato mol- / te volte, & quivi ame*ni* dui facevano nel parlare molti atti, maneggiando le braccia, & mo- / stra*n*domi. Io mandai perciò fuori il mio interprete, perche si ponesse allato di loro, & gli / ascoltasse, & indi à poco lo chiamai, & gli domandai di che parlavan coloro, & egli disse che / colui che faceva quelli atti, diceva all'altro che in Cevola erano altri simili à noi con le barbe, / & che dicevano che erano christiani, & che ame*ni*dui dicevano che tutti dovevamo esser*e* una / cosa

[fol. 368v]

cosa medesima, & che sarebbe stato bene di ammazzarci, acciochè quelli altri non sapessero / cosa alcuna di noi, onde venissero à farci noia, & che il vecchio gli (h)aveva risposto, costui è / figliuol del sole, & Signor*e* nostro, ci fa del bene, ne vuol*e* venire alle case nostre anc(h)ora che / ne lo preghiamo, non ci toglie cosa niuna del nostro, non vuole le donne nostre, & che final- / mente (h)aveva dette molte altre cose in mia lode & favore, & con tutto ciò l'altro si ostinava / che noi dovevamo esser*e* tutti una cosa medesima, & che il vecchio disse andiamo da lui & / domandiamogli se è christiano come gli altri, ò pur*e* figliuol del sole, & il vecchio se ne venne / à me & dissemi nel paese che voi mi domandasti di Cevola dimora*n*o altri (h)uomini della qua- / lità vostra: io feci all'(h)ora del m(a)eraviglioso & risposi che non era possibile, & essi mi affirma- / rono[146] che era vero, & che (h)aveva*n*o veduti duoi (h)uomini venuti di la, iquali r(e)*i*feriva*n*o che por- / tavano come noi tiri di fuocho, & spade. Io gli domandai se coloro gli (h)avevan*o* veduti co- / propri(i) occhi, & mi risposero di nò, ma che gli (h)aveva*n*o veduti certi suoi compagni. All(h)ora / mi domandò se io ero figliuolo del sole, & gli risposi di si. Essi dissero che il medesimo dice- / van quei christiani di Cevola, & io gli risposi che sarebbe ben potuto essere. Mi interroga- / ron*o* poi se quei christiani di Cevola, fossero venuti à congiungersi meco ciò che (h)avremmo / fatto, & io risposi loro che non doveva*n*o temere di cosa veruna perche se essi fossero figli- / uoli / del sole come dicevano, sarebb*ero*(n) miei fratelli & (h)avrebb*ero*(n) usato verso di tutti la medesima / cortesia &

amore che io facevo, onde con questo parve che rimanessero sodisfatti alquanto.

{Gli è detto che sono distanti da Cevola dieci giornate, & che Vi sono delli christiani che à quelli Signori / fanno guerra. Della Sodomia che essercitano quelli Indiani con quattro giovani à tal servigio / dedicati, quali portano (h)abito muliebre. Non potendo dare di se novella à quelli / di Cevola à seconda del fiume fanno ritorno alle Navi.}

Gli richiesi poi che mi dicessero quante giornate era quel regno di Cevola, che dicevano / lunge da quel fiume, & quel (h)uomo rispose che ci era uno spatio di dieci giornate senza (h)a- / bitatione, & che da li avanti egli non ne faceva stima, perche si trova(v)rono gente, Io con questo / aviso venni in desiderio di dare notitia di me al Capitano, & lo comunicai con i miei soldati, fra / quali non ritrovai niuno che volesse andarvi, anc(h)ora che io offerisse lor molte cose da parte / della Signoria vostra, solo un schiavo moro anc(h)ora di mala voglia mi si offerse d'andarvi, ma / io aspettavo che venissero quelli Indiani che mi era stato detto, & con questo ce n'an- / damo / al nostro cammino pel fiume contra acqua con il medesimo ordine di prima. Quivi mi mostro / il vecchio per cosa maravigliosa[147] un suo figliuolo vestito in (h)abito di donna essercitando il / suo officio, io gli domandai quanti ve ne era di quei tali fra loro, & dissemi che eran quattro, / & che quando qualch'un di essi moriva, si faceva disc(ri)uttione di tutte le donne gravide che / eran nella terra, & che la prima di esse che partoriva maschio era deputato à dovere fare quello / essercitio muliebre, & le donne lo vestivano dell'(h)abito loro, dicendo che poi che (h)aveva da / fare quelche dovevano faresse si pigliasse quel vestimento: questi tali non possono (h)avere com- / mercio carnale con donna alcuna, ma si bene con essi, tutti i giovani della terra che son(o) da ma- / ritarsi. costoro non ricevono cosa veruna per questo atto meretricale da quei del luogo, percio- / che hanno libertà di pigliarcio che trovano in ciascuna casa per bisogno del viverloro. Viddi / similmente alcune donne che conversavano dis(h)onestamente fra gli (h)uomini, & domandai / il vecchio se eran maritate, il quale mi rispose di no, ma che eran femine del mondo che vive- / vano separata-

mente dalle donne maritate. Io venivo pure con questi ragionamenti solleci- / tando che venissero quegli Indiani che dicevano di essere stati à Cevola, & mi diss(ono)ero che / erano lontani à otto giornate di li, però che vi era bene fra loro uno che era compagno di essi & / che gli (h)aveva parlato essendosi incontrato in loro quando andarono per vedere il regno di / Cevola, & gli dissero che non dovesse ir[148] piu oltre, (im)per(o)che quivi (h)avrebbe trovata una / gente brava come noi & delle'medesime qualita & fatezze nostre, la quale (h)aveva molto / conteso con gli (h)uomini di Cevola, per che gli (h)avevano ucciso un lor compagno moro, di- / cendo perche l'(h)avete voi morto: che vi ha fatto egli: vi ha forse tolto il pane, ò fatto vi altro / male: & simile parole. Et dicevano di piu che questi tali si chiamavano christiani che (h)abitava- / no in un gran casamento & che molti di essi (h)avevano delle vacche come quelle di Cevola, / & altri piccoli animali negri & con lana & con corna, & che ne (h)avevono alcuni che loro / cavalcavano che correvano molto, & che un giorno prima che si partissi(n)mo non (h)avevano / fatto altro dal nascere al tramontare del sole, che arrivare questi christiani, & tutti si fermavano / quivi

[fol. 369r]

369

quivi dove stan(t)ziavano glialtri, & che questi duoi si erano incontrati in duo Christiani che / gli (h)avevano domandato donde erano, & se (h)avevano luoghi seminati, & essi gli (h)avevano / detto che erano di paese lontano, & che (h)avevano le seminate, & che all'(h)ora gli donarono / una picciola cappa per uno, & gliene dierono[149] una che la dovessero portare à gli altri compagni / loro, ilche promissero essi di fare, & si partirono tosto. Questo inteso, di nuovo parlai con i / miei compagni per vedere se qualch'uno volessi andarvi, ma gli trovai del medesimo volere / di prima, & mi opposero maggiori inconvenienti. Dop(p)o c(i)hiamai il vecchio per vederse / mi (h)avesse voluto dare gente da menare (con) meco, & vettovaglio per quel deserto, ma mi mis(s)e / innanzi molti inconvenienti & disaggi in che io (h)arei potuto incorrere in quel viaggio, mo- / strandomi il pericolo che era in andare avanti per un Signore di Cumana, ilquale minacciava / di venire à farloro guerra, perche i suoi

erano entrati nel suo paese per pigliar*e* un Cervo, & / che io
non dovevo perciò partirmi di qui senza castigarlo. Et repli-
cando io che ero forza- / to di andare in ogni modo à Cevola,
& egli mi disse che io lasciassi di farlo, perche si aspetta- / va
che in ogni modo questo Signore veneria¹⁵⁰ à *fare* i danni loro,
& però no*n* potevano essi abban- / donare la sua terra per
venire meco, & che sarebbe meglio che io (h)avessi dato per
loro fine / à quella guerra, & poi (h)arei potuto andare acco*m*-
pagnato à Cevola. Et sopra di ciò venimmo / à contendere
tanto, che ci cominciammo à (s)corr(o)*u*cciare, & in col*l*era
vol(s)*l*e uscire della barca, / ma io lo ritenni, & con buone
parole lo incominciai à placare, veduto che importava molto /
(h)averlo amico, ma per carezze che io gli facessi non potei
levarlo dal suo volere nelquale ri- / mase sempre ostinato. Io
intanto (h)avevo gia mandato uno (h)uomo alle navi per
dargli noti- / tia del ca*m*mino che (h)avevo disegnato di fare.
Doppo richiesi il vecchio che lo facesse torna- / re, perche
determinai che gia che no*n* vedevo alcun ordine di poter*e*
andare à Cevola, & di no*n* / ritardare piu fra quella gente,
acciò non mi scoprissero, & similmente vol(s)*l*i tornare in
perso- / na à visitare le navi, con determinatione di ritornar*e*
un'altra volta per il fiume ad alto, me- / nando con esso meco
altri compagni, & lasciarve ne altri che mi si erano ammalati,
& dice*n*do / al vecchio, & à glialtri che io sarei tornato, &
lasciandogli al meglio sodisfatti che poteti [an- / c(h)ora che
sempre dicessero che io mi partivo per paura] me ne to(t)*r*nai
p*er* il fiume à Cevola, & / quel ca*m*mino che (h)avevo fatto in
montare il fiume contra acqua in quindici giorni & mez- / zo,
feci nel ritornare in duoi di & mezzo, per essere il corrente
grande & rapido molto. In / questo modo ca*m*minando per il
fiume à basso, veniva alle rive molta gente à dirmi, perche ti /
parti Signore da noi: che dispiacere ti è stato fatto: non dicevi
tu che (h)avevi da star(t)ene sem - / pre con esso noi: & esser*e*
Signor*e* nostro: ritorna a dietro che se alcuno dalla banda di
sopra ci / ha fatto ingiuria alcuna, noi veniremo¹⁵¹ con le
nostre arme teco per ucciderlo, & simile parole / piene di
amore volezza & cortesia.

{Giunti alle navi il Capitano fa nominare quella costa la
Campagna della Croce, & Vi fa edificare Un / Oratorio à
nostra Signora & il fiume chiama Buona guida & all'insu di
quello fa ritorno, per- / Venuto à Quicama & à Coano da
quelli Signori glie Usata molta cortesia.}

Giunto ch'io fui alle navi trovai tutta la mia gente in buon*o*
essere quantun(ch)*que* molto af- / flitta per rispetto del lungo
tardar*e* mio & anco per che il gran corrente gli (h)aveva spez-
zati / quattro sartie, & (h)aveva*no* perso due Ancore lequali
si ricuperarono. Ragunate le navi in- / sieme le feci mettere
sotto un riparo, & dar*e* Carena alla nave san Pietro, & ridriz-
zar*e* tutto qu*e*l / che era necessario. Quivi fatta aduna*n*za di
tutta la gente, gli esposi loro la notitia che (h)avevo / (h)avuto
da Francesco Vazquez, & come potrebbe esser*e* che in quel
tempo delli sed(e)*i*ci gior- / ni che io ero ito navigando per il
fiume egli per aventura (h)avrebbe (h)avuto notitia di me, &
/ che ero di animo di ritornar*e* su un'altra volta per vederse si
fosse potuto trovar*e* qualche mez- / zo di congiungermi con
esso lui, & anc(h)ora che mi fusse contradetto, feci metter*e*
in ordine / tutte le barche, *per*che p*er* il servi(t)*z*io delle navi
no*n* erano necessarie. L'una di esse io feci empier*e* / di
rob(b)a¹⁵² con cose da contraca*m*biare, di f(o)*r*umento & altre
semenze con galline & galli di Casti- / glia, & mi parti su per
la fiumana, lasciato ordine che in quella ca*m*pagna chiamata
della croce / facessero un oratorio ov*v*ero capella & lo chiamassero la chiesa della Madonna della buona / guida, & che
chiamassero quel fiume la buona guida per esser*e* la divisa di
vostra Signoria, / menai con esso me Nicola Camorano
maggior*e* Piloto perche prendesse l'altezze, & parti il /
Martedi che fu il quattordici di Settembre, & il Mercoledi
giunsi nelle (h)abitationi de i pri- / mi Indiani, iquali corsero
per vietarmi il passo credendosi che fussimo altre genti
percioche / conducevamo

[fol. 369v]

conducevamo con esso noi un Piffero, & un Tamburino, &
io ero vestito di diversi pa*n*ni da / quei che portavo, quando
mi vid(d)ero la prima volta, & qua*n*do mi conobbero si
fermarono / anc(h)ora che non potessi ridur*r*emeli buoni
amici, onde io andavo lor*o* dando di quelle semen- / ze che
io portavo insegnandogli in qual modo le dovevano semi-
nare, & navigato che (h)eb- / bi tre leghe mi venne à trovare
fino alla barca il primo interpete con grande allegrezza, al-

/ quale domandai perche mi (h)ave*va* lasciato, disse che certi suoi compagni lo (h)aveva*no* disviato.[153] / Io gli feci buona c(i)era, & miglior*e* trattamento, acciocche fosse venuto di nuovo con meco, ve- / duto quanto m'importava di (h)averlo appresso. Si scusò poi che era quivi rimas*to* p*er* portarmi / alcune pe*n*ne di Papagallo, le quali mi diede. Gli dima*n*dai che gente era quella, & se (h)aveva Si- / gnor*e* alcuno, & mi rispose di si, & me ne nominò tre ò quattro, appresso à q*u*egli ventiquattro / ò venticinque nomi di popoli che egli sapeva, & che (h)aveva*no* le case dipinte di dentro, & che / costoro (h)ave*v*ano contrattation con quei di Cevola, & che in due lune giungeva in quel Re- / gno. Dissemi oltre di questo molti altri nomi di Signori, & di altri popoli, i quali io ho de- / scritti in un mio libro che io portero in persona à Vostra Signoria, ma questa relatione sum- / maria ho voluto dar*e* in questo porto di Colima à Agostino Guerriero, accioche la mandi per / terra à Vostra Signoria, allaquale ho da dire molte altre cose di piu. Ma tornando al mio ca- / mino giunsi à Quicama, donde q*u*elli Indiani uscirono à ricevermi con molto piacere, & gran / festa, dicendomi che il Signor*e* loro mi stava aspettando, alqual giunto trovai che (h)ave*v*a seco / cinque ò seimila (h)uomini senza arme, da i quali si appartò con forse dugento solamente, che / tutti portavano vetto-vaglia, si mosse verso di me, & egli veniva innanzi glialtri con grande / aut(t)orità, & innanzi di esso, & allato erano alcuni che face*v*ano venire scostando la gente, fa- / cendogli strada per donde potessi passare. Portava una veste serrata dinanzi, & di dietro, & / aperta da i lati, allacciata con bottoni, lavo-rata à scacchi bianchi & neri, era di scorze di bessu- / gos molta sottile, & ben fatta. Giunto che fui all'acqua, i suoi servitori lo presero à braccia, & / lo misero nella barca, dove fu da me abbra(a)cciato, & ricevuto con gran festa, mostra*n*-doli mol- / to amore, del qual atto la sua gente che quivi stava à vedere, mostrava grande allegrezza. / Questo Signore si rivolse à suoi dicendoli, che ponessero mente alla mia cortesia, che egli es- / sendo entrato alla libera con tal gente straniera, potevano vedere quanto io foss(e)*i* da bene, & / con quanto amore io lo trattavo, & perciò sapessero che io ero suo Signore, onde tutti mi (h)a- / vevano da servire, & far*e* quanto io gli (h)avessi comandato. Quivi lo feci sedere à mangiare / di alcune conserve di zucchero che io portavo, & dissi allo interprete che lo ringra(t)ziasse in / mio nome del

favor*e* che mi (h)aveva fatto in venire à vedermi, raccoman-dandogli l'adoratione / della Croce, & tutto il rimane*n*te ch'io (h)avevo raccoma*n*dato à glialtri, cioè che vivessero in pa- / ce, & lasciassero le guerre, & che fossero fra loro buoni amici sempre, egli rispose che era gran / tempo che fra loro continuava la guerra con vicini, ma che da li avanti egli comanderia che / fosse dato da mangiare à tutti quei che passassero per il suo Regno, & che no*n* gli facessero ma- / le alcuno, & che se pur*e* qualche popolo venisse à farli guerra, egli gli diria come io (h)avevo co- / ma*n*dato che si vivesse in pace, & che se no*n* la volessero, el se diffenderia, & che mi prometteva / che giam*m*ai non andrebbe à cercar*e* guerra se altri non venissero à dargliela. Quivi io gli do- / nai alcune cosette, cosi delle semenze che io portavo, come delle galline di Castiglia, di che / ricevet*te* grandissimo contento. Et partendo menai con esso meco alcuni de i suoi per con- / tra(h)*tt*ere amici(t)*z*ia fra loro, & quegli altri popoli che erano di sopra, & quivi venne à me lo In- / terprete per ritornarsene à casa sua, & io gli donai alcuni doni con che si partì molto conten- / to. Il giorno seguente giunsi à Coano, & molti non mi conobbero vede*n*domi con altri pan- / ni vestito, ma il vecchio che quivi era incontanente che mi riconobbe si g(i)*e*ttò nell'acqua, di- / cendomi Signore ecco con esso meco l'(h)uomo che mi lasciasti, ilquale comparse quivi alle- / gro, & molto contento, dicendomi le gran carezze che gli (h)ave*v*an fatto quella gente, dicen- / do che combattevano insieme ciascuno in volerlo menar*e* à casa sua, & che era cosa incredi- / bile il pensiero che (h)avevano nello apparire del Sole, di giunger*e* le mani, & inginocchiarsi / innanzi la Croce. Io donai loro di quelle semenze, ringratian-dogli molto del buon tratta- / mento che (h)aveva fatto al mio spagnuolo, & essi mi pregarono che lo volessi lasciare con lo- / ro, ilche gli concessi io fin*o* alla mia tornata, & egli vi rimase molto contento fra loro. In que- / sto modo me ne montai il fiume conducendo con meco quel vecchio, il quale mi r(e)*i*ferì che / erano venuti duoi Indiani da Cumana à domandar*e* de i Christiani, & che egli gli (h)aveva ri- / sposto

[fol. 370r]

370

sposto che non gli conosceva, ma che ben*e* conosceva il figliuolo del Sole, & che lo (h)avevano / persuaso che si fosse unito con esso loro per uccidermi, et i miei compagni. Io gli dissi che mi / dessi duoi Indiani, & che gli andassero à dire come io andrei à trovarli, & voleva la sua ami- / stà, ma che se essi allo incontro vol(e)iano guerra che io gli̯e la faria di modo che saria loro dispia- / ciuto, & cosi andavo fra tutta quella gente, & alcuni mi venivano à dire perche non davo lo- / ro la Croce come (h)avevo fatto à glialtri, & cosi glie ne davo.

{Smontano in terra & Ve(gg)dono che i popoli adoravano la Croce che gli (h)avevano data. Da Un Indiano / fanno dipingere quel paese, mandano Una Croce al Signore di Cumana, & discende à seconda del / fiume, giungono alle navi. Dell'errore che presero i Piloti del Cortese in situare quella costa.}

L'altro giorno vol(s)i̯ saltare in terra à vedere certe capanne, & trovai molti fanciulli & don- / ne con le mani giunte, & inginocchiati innanzi à una Croce che io gli (h)avevo data. Quivi giun- / to che fui, feci il medesimo anch'io, & parlando col vecchio, mi cominciò à dare informatione / di piu gente, & piu terre che egli sapeva. Et venuta l'(h)ora tarda chiamai il vecchio che venis- / si à dormire alla barca, mi rispose di non volere venire, perch'io lo stancheria interrogandolo / di tante cose: io gli risposi che non gli (h)averei domandato altro, se non che in una carta mi no- / tasse cioche egli sapeva di quel fiume, & di che essere era la gente che (h)abitavano su le rive di / esso da tutti i lati, ilche egli fece volentieri, & doppo mi disse ch'io gli dipingessi il mio paese in / quel modo che egli mi (h)aveva dipinto il suo. Et per contentarlo gli feci fare una pittura di al- / cune cose, & il giorno che venne poi entrai in certe montagne molto alte, fra le quali camina- / va quel fiume molto stretto, et le barche vi passarono faticosa- / mente per non (h)avere chi tirasse / l'anzana.[154] Quivi mi vennero à dire alcuni Indiani che ci erano gente di Cumana, & fra glial- / tri vi era un Incantatore che domandava per qual luogo noi (h)averiamo da passare, & dicendogli / che per il fiume, andava ponendo dall'una, & l'altra riva del fiume certe canne, fra le quali noi / passammo senza ricevere danno alcuno che pensavano essi di farci. Cosi caminando giunsi al- / la casa del vecchio che veniva con meco, & quivi feci porre

una Croce molto alta, & in essa / feci mettere lettere come io vi ero arrivato, & ciò feci perche se per caso fosse quivi capi- / tata gen- / te alcuna del generale, potessi (h)avere notitia di me. Veduto finalmente poi che non potevo / venire à cognitione di quel che io desideravo di sapere, determinai di ritornarmene alle navi, / & essendo in punto di partire sopragiunsero quivi duoi Indiani che per interpretatori del vec- / chio mi dissero che essi venivano per ordine mio, che erano di Cumana, & che il Signore per / essere da quel luogo lontano molto non poteva venire, però ch'io gli dicessi quel che volevo. / Io gli dissi che si ricordassi di vol(v)ere sempre pace, & come io andavo per visitare quel paese, / ma essendo forzato di ritornarmene per il fiume à basso, non lo facevo, ma che ritorneria, & che / intanto essi dessero quella Croce al suo Signore, ilche mi promisero di fare, & che se n'anda- / vano dritto à portarli la Croce con certe penne che in quella vi erano. Da costoro io vol(s)i̯ inten- / dere che gente (h)abitava le rive del fiume di sopra, iquali mi dierono notitia di molti popoli, & / dissonmi che il fiume montava assai piu che io non (h)avevo visto, ma che essi non sapeano il / principio di esso per venire molto lontano, & che in esso entravano molti altri fiumi. Ciò fat- / to, l'altro giorno di mattina me ne venni per il fiume à basso, & il di seguente giunsi dove (h)ave- / vo lasciato lo spagnuolo, alquale parlai, & dissi che le cose mi eran passate bene, & che in que- / sta & l'altra volta era entrato dentro in terra piu di trenta leghe. Gli Indiani da quel luogo / mi domandarono della cagione perche io mi partivo, & quando saria la mia tornata, a quali / risposi che sarebbe presto, cosi navigando à basso, una donna si g(i)ettò nell'acqua gridando / che la dovessimo aspettare, & entrò nella nostra barca mettendosi sotto una banca donde mai / la potemmo fare uscire. Seppi che ciò faceva, perche il marito ne teneva un'altra, della quale (h)a- / veva figliuoli, dicendo che non intendeva di stare piu con esso lui, poi che ne (h)aveva un'altra. / Cosi ella, & uno altro Indiano se ne vennero con meco di lor buona voglia. In questo mo- / do giunsi alle navi, & fattele por in ordine ce ne venimmo al nostro viaggio costeggiando, & / molte volte saltando in terra entrando adentro per gran spatio per vedere se si poteva intende- / re qualche cosa del Capitano Francesco Vazquez, & sua compagnia, dellaquale non (h)avem- / mo altro indi(t)zio se non quel che intesi in quella riviera. Io porto con meco molti atti di / possessione di tutta quella costa: & per il fiume, & per l'altezza che presi, truovo che quella / che fecero i Patroni, & Piloti del Marchese è falsa, & si inga*n*narono di duoi gradi. Et son pas- / sato piu oltra di loro meglio di quattro gradi. Montai per il fiume ottantacinque leghe, do- / ve viddi

[fol. 370v]

ve viddi & intesi tutto quel che ho detto, & molte altre cose, dellequali, concedendomisi di po- / ter*e* venir*e* à basciar*e* le mani alla Signoria vostra, le darò lunga & intera relatione. Mi reputai (h)a- / ver*e* gran sorte in (h)aver*e* trovato Don Luigi di Castiglia & Agostino Ghenero nel porto di Co- / lima,

percioche la Galeotta dello Adelantado se ne veniva sopra di me, qual era ivi con la sua ar- / mata, & voleva che si calasse le vele, & parendomi cosa nuova, ne sapendo in che stato fussero / le cose della nuova Spagna, mi posi in ordine di difendermi & non farlo: in questo tempo arri- / vo Don Alvise di Castiglia in un battello & mi parlo, & io sorsi dall'altra parte del porto dove / stava detta armata, & li detti questa relatione, & essendo di notte vol(s)*i* far*e* vela per levar*e* via gli / scand(o)*a*li, la qual relatione io portavo scritta in sommario, perche sempre (h)ebbi presuppos(i)to[155] / di darla tochando terra di questa nuova Spagna, per avisar*e* vostra Signoria.

Document 16

The Viceroy's Instructions to Hernando Alarcón, May 31, 1541

Biblioteca del Escorial, Códice &-II-7, Doc. no. LXVII

INTRODUCTION

On May 31, 1541, Viceroy Antonio de Mendoza issued formal instructions to Hernando de Alarcón[1] to make a second voyage to the head of the Gulf of California as part of the expedition seeking populous and prosperous places in the region of Cíbola.[2] Specifically, Mendoza reminded Alarcón that "the main purpose for which you are going is to find out about Captain General Francisco Vázquez de Coronado and the people who are with him."[3] When contact with the expedition had been made, Alarcón was to deliver messages and goods being sent by the viceroy and the captain general's wife.[4] In addition, he was to facilitate the sale of merchandise to members of the expedition and perhaps to native people also.[5] The viceroy enjoined the former captain of his personal guard several times not to pursue any other reconnaissance until the expedition had been located and contacted.[6]

Mendoza's detailed sailing instructions were based on and incorporated information Alarcón had obtained the previous year. For instance, the viceroy refers to the Río de Buena Guia, a name bestowed on the modern Colorado River by Alarcón during his earlier voyage.[7] And he admonishes the captain to be sure that the leaders of Quicama and Coama are not "disturbed or mistreated in any way."[8] These are persons and names the viceroyalty had become aware of through Alarcón's 1540 voyage.

The viceroy also reveals the principal aim of the combined sea and land expedition—namely, to look for large native communities that were producing valuable commodities. He directs Alarcón to "find out who the people are who inhabit that entire area" and to "find out what one can obtain in that land . . . through the Indian merchants."[9]

The important role of don Luis de Castilla in Alarcón's voyage is evident in Mendoza's 1541 instructions. It is becoming increasingly clear that don Luis was a key party to planning and probably financing the Cíbola enterprise as a whole. In addition to his provision of a ship for Alarcón's planned second voyage, don Luis is reported, for instance, to have paid for *tamemes*, or Indian porters, at Michoacán, who were to carry supplies for the Coronado expedition. And his close personal connections with Vázquez de Coronado and Viceroy Mendoza increase the likelihood of his having played a major part in both the land and sea components of the project.[10]

A year earlier, before Alarcón's initial trip up the Gulf, Mendoza doubtless gave the captain of the fleet another set of instructions of a similar tenor, minus many of the specifics, which had been unknown at that time. Those instructions are no longer known to exist. But certainly their concentration on establishing contact with the land expedition and determining where productive native peoples were living must have been the same.

The voyage of 1541, though we publish its formal instructions here, never took place.[11] The Mixtón War intervened, diverting resources and personnel against one of the most serious threats ever to Spanish sovereignty in Nueva España. Alarcón himself was dispatched with a company of men to Autlán, an indigenous community about 20 leagues northeast and inland from the port of La Navidad in what is now Jalisco.[12] His enterprise therefore suffered a fate similar to that which befell the joint plans of Viceroy Mendoza and Pedro de Alvarado, which were also supposed to have gotten under way in 1541.[13] By the time the sailing season of 1542 arrived, the decision had already been made to abandon the expedition to Tierra Nueva, and so Alarcón's mission, as detailed in Mendoza's instructions, lost its most pressing raison d'être.

Two copies of Mendoza's 1541 instructions to Alarcón are known to exist. They are preserved together in the Biblioteca del Escorial, outside Madrid. They can be found there under the numbers Códice &-II-7, Doc. no. LXVI, and Códice &-II-7, Doc. no. LXVII. The first of these manuscripts is an unsigned draft of the second, which is signed by the viceroy. There are important differences between the two versions. For instance, the draft copy includes marginal notes in Mendoza's own hand specifying the ships Alarcón was to take on his second voyage. This stipulation does not appear in the signed copy.[14] We transcribe and translate the signed copy (LXVII) here, but we also note differences between it and the draft.

In 1857 Buckingham Smith published a Spanish transcription of Mendoza's instructions made by José Amador de los Rios. There are a number of omissions and mostly minor copying errors in this transcript, which Hammond and Rey subsequently used in 1940 in preparing their English translation.[15] We have consulted both these publications in editing the transcription and translation that follow. Neither Smith nor Hammond and Rey indicated that they were aware of the existence of the draft version of the signed copy.

TRANSLATION

[1r]

{Item} What you, Captain Hernando de Alarcón, must do during the voyage on which we are sending you into the gulf is the following:[16]

{Item} First, you must travel to the port of La Navidad in the *provincia* of Colima.[17] There you will take charge[18] of a *navío* named [not filled in],[19] which we have designated for your journey, and a large-sized *barca*, which we have built for [the voyage] [and] is ready to sail.[20] The food supplies, artillery, and munitions for [the voyage] will be provided to you. You shall have all of this recorded in his [account] book by the *escribano* (whom you are to take on the ship), very especially what the master[21] takes charge of (as well as other persons you may entrust with it). [This is] so that there may be proper reckoning and accounting regarding everything, both what is aboard the *navío* and [what is] aboard the *barca*. You shall sign this [record], along with the *escribano*. You shall provide another exact copy to don Luis de Castilla, so that the reckoning for [the voyage] may remain here [in Nueva España].[22]

{Item} Item. In the [log] book you shall set down a list[23] of the sailors who must go on the *navío* and *barca*, and of the artillery and munitions there are aboard them. You shall provide this [list] as an inventory to the artillerymen. You shall order them to keep it with them safely and with care[24] for when it may be necessary. You shall take special care of this, since you will [then] see how it is going for you.

{Item} Item. You shall prepare a list of the notable people who are going on the expedition.[25] You shall supply what seems to you will probably be necessary to go in the *barca*.[26]

You shall examine the arms and armor each individual is taking and have that all recorded in the *escribano*'s record book. [This record is to be] signed with your name.

{Item}[27] Furthermore, I enjoin you to honor and revere the fathers, fray Reymundo and fray Antonio de Meno, who are traveling in your company, and to solicit their opinion in matters where it will be appropriate, in accordance with what His Majesty orders by means of his directives.[28] In addition [you are to do this] because they are entitled to it since they are such persons (which is reason [enough] that it is to be done this way; [to do] otherwise would not[29] be of service to Our Lord).

{Item} Item. Later, Our Lord willing, when you are ready to sail and make the voyage in relief of Francisco Vázquez de Coronado and the people who are with him, you shall travel in search of the town of San Miguel. There, with the *barca*, you shall try to find out whether there is any news of Captain General Francisco Vázquez de Coronado. In accordance with what you find out about him, you shall proceed on your voyage. [That is] because this is the main reason for which we are sending you. You shall take half the iron goods there are in the town of San Miguel de Culiacán and deliver [them] to the person in the port of La Navidad who will be in charge for us, so that with [them] he may do what he is ordered [to do].[30] The other half [of the iron] you shall leave in the town for what might be necessary [there].[31]

{Item} If in the *villa* of San Miguel de Culiacán[32] you do not receive news of the captain, [1v] you shall go on to Puerto de los Puertos.[33] From there onward you shall try to make land in all the harbors and places where it is possible and to see whether you acquire any news of the general or Captain Melchior Díaz, who left the valley of Corazones to reconnoiter the coast along which you will be traveling.[34]

If you run across [Díaz] or his people, you shall inform him about how you are traveling in search of him and in relief of the general. You shall learn what [Díaz's party] may know about [the general] and whether there is a way for [the general] to have word of you. If you find a way to [have communication with the general], you shall establish yourself in what will seem to you the most convenient place for being able to do it. And you shall not travel farther on from there until you have accomplished it. For this [purpose] you must employ all means possible, because it is very important to us to obtain news of them by sea and that there be communication and commerce between you and them.

{Item} If you do not find the means for learning about them in all the ports and lands [where you anchor], you shall go on to the Río de Buena Guía,[35] leaving markers and letters in all the ports behind you, in which you are to tell them that you have gone on to that river [the Buena Guía] and that you will be at it for as much time as you can, until you obtain information about the general. [That is] because, by our order, you are going in search and in quest of him.

In the event you are unable to find out what [the natives] know about [the general] there,[36] you shall dispatch [a boat] back through the same places, examining the markers you are to have left, to learn whether [Díaz's party] has encountered them. If they come across [the markers], they will know where you are. If they are unable to travel there, they may leave something in writing [telling] where they are. And thus those whom you are sending will be able to find them, so as to be able to learn by what route they will be able to establish commerce with you and the sea.

{Item} When you have reached the Río de Buena Guía, if you have not previously found information about and a suitable[37] [means of] commerce with the general and the people who are with him, you shall ascend the river with the *barca* by way of the estuary which you say penetrates the interior of the land. You shall always inquire after and endeavor to

learn about the [people] from Cíbola,[38] because according to what [the general] writes me from there,[39] it is impossible that they have not reached the river or are very close to it. While you are without knowledge of Francisco Vázquez, you shall not devote yourself to anything except searching for him and connecting with him, because in this you will be performing a great service for His Majesty and a good deed for us, as well as [affording us] very great joy.

{Item} If, with the help of Our Lord, you have encountered the aforesaid Francisco Vázquez or his people, you shall deliver or send to him by very secure means the dispatches you are carrying for him, because I am writing to him that because you have been the discoverer of that river, the [native] people have good will toward you,[40] and you have served His Majesty in what I have entrusted to you, and further because of the information[41] you have about some things farther on, he is to provide you with more people, if it is necessary. [This is] so that with those whom you are [already] taking, you shall attempt to go on farther. You shall have the consideration to obey him and perform what[ever] you might be ordered [to do] by him and adhere to [whatever] direction he may give you.

[2r] {Item} In the instruction given to Diego López de Zúñiga[42] (who is traveling along the coast as a captain) there is a paragraph in which he is told to be very attentive to learning about the people who are traveling on land and about those you are taking by way of the gulf. [He is instructed that] if he has any news and it is necessary to link up with [the people traveling by land] or with you, that he is to do so. You must [do] the same, since it is all the same [undertaking] and he is also looking for you. The same thing [applies to] those who are going to the islands.[43] Thus it is reason[able] that it be done on your part and that everyone try to help you and assist you, whenever there is an opportunity.

{Item} You shall afford benevolent treatment to the Indians whom you are taking in your company, so that when they are in their [own] land they may encourage the others to have affection for you.[44]

{Item} You shall take great care that the names of Our Lord, His Glorious Mother, and the saints [are] not blasphemed, but rather [that] they are revered. Christian doctrine is to be discussed very regularly by you and [the other members of the expedition]. And you are to live like Catholics in such a way that the natives of the land where you are do not suffer[45] a bad example. Rather, with your virtues and good deeds, you are to lead them to desire your friendship and companionship.[46]

{Item} You shall make an effort to see that the lords of Quicama and Coama are not disturbed or mistreated in any way, since they welcomed you so willingly.[47]

{Item} You shall endeavor to be more circumspect in communication and conversation with the Indians, because it seems that it was necessary to be more cautious with them than you were the last time.[48]

{Item} You shall be very careful that the people who go in your company not inflict injury on or [exercise] force against the Indians. They are not to take anything they may possess from them against their will, nor are they to enter their houses without your permission.

{Item} Item. You shall endeavor to investigate thoroughly the information you received about the sea and those islands which you mention and to find out who the people are who inhabit that entire area. And you shall try, through kindness, to find out what one can obtain in that land. You shall make an effort to do this through the Indian merchants or by whatever other means may seem best to you, refusing to make war against them except [when] it is compelled by necessity. You shall endeavor to obtain samples of all the things there may be in [the land].

{Item} If you have not discovered information about [or] any trace of the general [or] his people [and] if it thus seems appropriate to you to send the *navío* or the *barca*, in order to examine the markers and letters you shall leave behind or in order to give us news about what is there (either for this

[reason] or for [obtaining] appropriate supplies or to deliver[49] some information to us), this you shall do as you see [is] most suitable, [either] to keep or dispatch it.

[2v] {Item} Item. If you establish a settlement somewhere, it is not to be among the Indians but separate from them. You shall order that no Spaniard or any other of your people is to go to [that] place or to the Indians' houses, except with your express permission. You shall very severely punish whoever does otherwise. You must give [permission] [only] at those times when it is necessary for something that is important and [only] to persons who you are confident will do nothing wrong. You must be very careful to adhere to this order because it is a thing that is more important than you can imagine.

{Item} You must be well aware that the main purpose for which you are going is to find out about Captain General Francisco Vázquez de Coronado and the people who are with him and how it would be possible to communicate with them by sea. Further, [you are going] in order to locate the port or ports which [are] most suitable for this [purpose]. You must endeavor [to do] this by all methods and means that are possible to you, by sea and by land. Until you have learned this and accomplished it, you are not to devote yourself to anything else, nor are you to return from there without informing us first of what you have accomplished and achieved, so that we may decide what seems to us advisable [to do next].

{Item} Regarding the trade goods we are sending, we order the person who is in charge of them not to use or release them unless it is in your presence. You must maintain a systematic record in the book such person will keep. And also the trade goods he is taking are to be recorded individually in the [book] of the *escribano* whom you are taking in the fleet that is in your charge. You and the person who will be in charge of the trade goods, as well as the aforesaid[50] *escribano*, are to sign [the entry] in both record books. The same system shall be maintained in [them] concerning what will be consumed in trade and commerce, setting down individually what is dispensed during the aforesaid trading and exchange. What [is set down] in both books according to this [method] is to be signed following the same rule for both obligation and release of the person who is going to be in charge of it. You shall take care that this is entered very clearly item by item, by which [means] it may be easily followed.

{Item} Item. We have engaged Francisco Pilo,[51] a merchant, [to] send a person of his own with merchandise, hardware, and other items of supply, both for the people who are going with you and for those who are with Captain General Francisco Vázquez de Coronado. You shall deliver to [that person] the iron goods you will take possession of at Culiacán, so that he may dispense and ship [them] as if [they were] his own. This is on account of other [business] we have with the aforementioned Pilo and because he gladdens us by risking his property. Also it is appropriate for him to gain a reputation, so that others may risk [their property].

You shall provide him an excellent place in the *navío* you are taking, where he may transport his merchandise. And you shall treat him well and allow him to dispose of [his merchandise] freely and sell it as he wishes. You shall not permit any abuse or force to be used against him, either in word or deed, by yourself or any of the people of your company. When he has to unload the merchandise onto the land, you shall give him full assistance and aid. You shall adopt a system so that [his goods] are not put at risk, since the risk [3r] and danger will quickly devolve on us. Because [this is] a matter which affects us, we entrust it fully to you.

As to the written instruments which are necessary to employ in regard to what he will sell on credit,[52] if there is one of His Majesty's *escribanos* in the fleet, you shall direct him to prepare them. And if [the fleet] does not include [one], you (as captain and *justicia* of the aforesaid fleet) shall set up whatever [procedure] is necessary in His Majesty's name. For this I grant you complete authority.

It has been seen from experience, in regard to the carrying of crossbows, arquebuses, and other arms and armor supplied to men-at-arms,[53] that they are [often] lost, ruined, and damaged. Because they are supplied [at no cost], no particular care is taken of [them]. [Therefore] you shall furnish to the men-at-arms and sailors whom you are taking the crossbows, arquebuses, and round shields that will be necessary for them at moderate prices as their own. [You shall furnish these things] on account against their salaries to those who will be receiving a salary. And to those who will not be receiving [one] [you shall furnish the goods] when they execute promissory notes for [the arms].[54]

What is being supplied to the men-at-arms and [what is] extra you shall turn over to the person whom Pilo will thus be sending, in compliance with a legal arrangement[55] between him and Agustín Guerrero[56] (whom we have placed in charge of what concerns our fleets). The promissory notes which they will execute against those to whom arms and armor are furnished, and whatever [instruments] are provided to the person whom Pilo is sending, you shall deliver to don Luis de Castilla so that he may send [them] to the aforesaid Agustín Guerrero.

{Item} You shall take [with you] certain items which doña Beatriz de Estrada[57] is sending to the captain general, her husband. With regard to these [items] and whatever else you will be carrying for the other men-at-arms, you shall direct that they recommend friends or relatives of theirs to you to keep them safe.[58]

{Item} Executed in the Ciudad de México, the last day of the month of May one thousand five hundred and forty-one.

{rubric} don Antonio de Mendoza {rubric}

By the order of their lordships,
[Antonio de] Almaguer[59]

Directive to Captain Hernando de Alarcón

[3v and 4r] [blank]

[4v] Directive to Alarcón[60]

[fol. 1r]

395

{y*tem*} lo q*ue* Vos el capitan her*n*ando de Alarcon *h*aveys de hazer *en* *e*l Viaje del ancon adonde os *en*Viamos es / lo siguiente

{y*tem*} primeramente *h*abeys de yr al puerto de la naVidad de la provinçia de Colima y alli recibi- / reys el navyo nombrado {lacuna} que para V*uest*ra Jornada tenemos señalado / {+} y Una barca grande q*ue* puede navegar q*ue* para ello tenemos hecha y los bastimientos ar- / tilleria y muniçion q*ue* para ello os sera dada todo lo qual hareys assentar al escr*iv*a*no* / q*ue* llevaredes del naVio en su libro muy particularmentte lo q*ue* lleva a cargo el maestre / y otras per*S*onas a quien lo encargaredes para q*ue* de todo *h*aya buena Razon y q*uen*ta asi / de lo q*ue* fuere *en* *e*l dicho naVio como en la dicha barca lo qual firmareys Vos Juntam*ent*e / con el dicho escrivano y a la letra dareis otro tanto A don luis de ca*S*tilla para q*ue* / quede aca Razon de *e*llo

{y*tem*} yten *en* *e*l dicho libro hareys copia de la gente de la mar q*ue* *h*a de yr *en* *e*l dicho naVio y barca / y del artilleria y muniçion q*ue* Va *en* *e*llos la qual entregareys por inventario a los ar- / tilleros y dareys orden como la lleven a buen reca*u*do[61] y a punto para quando fuere ne- / ce*S*saria y de *e*sto te(r)n*d*reis especial cuydado pues Veys Lo q*ue* *en* *e*llo os va

{y*tem*} Iten hareys copia de la gente sobre*S*aliente q*ue* va en la dicha Armada y po(r)n*d*reys la q*ue* os pareçiere / en la barca q*ue* sera nece*S*sario yr *en* *e*lla y Vereys las Armas q*ue* cada Uno lleva y hareys / lo a*S*sentar todo *en* *e*l libro del dicho es*C*rivano firmado de V*uest*ro nombre

{y*tem*} otrosi os encargo q*ue* honrreys y reverencieys a los padres fray remundo y fray antonyo / de meno q*ue* Van en V*uest*ra compañia y tomeys su pareçer *en* las co*S*as q*ue* convyniere conforme / a lo q*ue* su mag*estad* manda por Sus ynstruciones porq*ue* demas de mereçello por ser tales / per*S*onas es Razon q*ue* asi se haga y de lo contra*r*io *n*o seria n*uest*ro se*ñ*or de Servydo

{y*tem*} Iten despues q*ue* queriendo n*uest*ro se*ñ*or q*ue* esteys a punto p*a*ra naVegar y hazer el ViaJe del soco- / rro de Fran*cis*co Vazquez de coronado y de la gente q*ue* con el esta yreys en demanda / de la Villa de San miguel y alli con la barca procurareys de Saber sy *h*ay alg*un*a nue- / va del capitan general fran*cis*co Vazquez de coronado y conforme a lo q*ue* de *e*l supieredes / asy hareys en V*uest*ro ViaJe porq*ue* *e*l principal fin a que os emViamos es este y del he- / rraJe q*ue* esta en la dicha Villa de sa*n* myguel de Culuacan tomareys la mitad y en- / tregalloeys a la per*S*ona q*ue* llevare a cargo por noSotros lo q*ue* esta *en* *e*l puerto de la naVi- / dad para q*ue* haga de *e*llo lo q*ue* le fuere mandado y la otra mytad dexareys *en* la di*c*ha Vi*ll*a p*a*ra lo q*ue* fu*e*re neç*e*sario

{y*tem*} y si en la dicha Villa de san miguel de culuacan no tuvyeredes nueVa del d*i*cho capitan

[fol. 1v]

pasareys Al puerto de los puertos y de ally adelante procurareys en todos los puertos y par- / ttes q*ue* fuere po*S*ible de tomar t*i*erra y mirar si hallaredes alguna noticia del dicho genera*L* / o del capitan melchior diaz el qual partio del Valle de los coraçones a des*C*ubrir / la costa por donde Vos ys y si toparedes con el o con gente suya dalleseys notiçia / como ys

en Su busca y en socorro del general E ynformaroseys de lo
q*ue* Saben de *e*L / y si podra *h*aber manera para q*ue e*l tenga
noticia de Vos y si hallaredes medio para ello / poneroseys *en*
la partte mas comoda q*ue* os pareçiere para podello hazer y
no paSareys / de alli hasta *h*avello effe*c*tuado y para esto
*h*abeys de tener todos los modos q*ue* fueren po- / sibles
porq*ue* nos importta mucho saber de *e*llos por la mar y q*ue*
*h*aya converSaçio*n* y con- / tratacion entre Vos y ellos

{*ytem*} Y si en todos los puerttos y tierras de s(e)*u* paraJe no
hallaredes apareJo de saber de *e*llos / paSareys al rio de buena
guia dexando en todos los puertos de atras señales y car- / tas
en q*ue* les digais como soys paSsado aquel rio y q*ue* estareys
*en e*l todo el tiempo q*ue* / pudieredes hasta tener notiçia del
general porq*ue* ys en Su busca y demanda por n*uest*ro /
mandado y que quando por ally no pudieredes Saber de *e*l
sepan q*ue* emViareys atras / por los mesmos lugares
requiriendo las señales q*ue h*ovieredes dexado para Saber si /
*h*an topado con ellas y q*ue* por tanto si toparen con ellas
sepan donde ys y si no pudieren / {+} yr alla dexen esCrito
donde estan y podran hallarlos los q*ue* Vos emViaredes para
/ poder Saber por donde podran tener contrataçio*n* con la
mar y con Vos

{*ytem*} llegado q*ue* seays al rio de buena guia q*ue h*a de ser[62] no
hallando antes lengua y contrat*ac*ion / mas Convenible con el
dicho general y gentte q*ue* con el esta con la barca Subireys
por / el dicho rio y por el estero q*ue* dezis q*ue* Va la ti*e*rra
adentro y siempre preguntareys / y procurareys de Saber
nue*V*as de los de çivola porq*ue* segun lo q*ue* de alla me esCrive
/ es ymposible q*ue* ellos no *h*ayan Venydo al rio o esten muy
çerca de *e*l y en tanto q*ue* no / supieredes de Fran*c*isco Vazquez
no os ocupareys en otra coSa sino fuere en busCalle y /
Juntaros con el porq*ue* en esto hareys muy gran *servy*cio a Su
mag*estad* y a noSotros muy / gran plazer y buena obra

{*ytem*} y como con el ayuda de n*uest*ro señor *h*ayays topado
con el dicho francisco Vazquez o co*n* / gente Suya dalleeys o
emVialleeys a muy buen reca*u*do los despachos q*ue* para el
llevays / porq*ue* yo le esCrivo q*ue* por *h*aber sido Vos el
desCubridor de aquel rio y teneros la gen- / te de(l) buena
Voluntad y *h*aber *ser*vydo A su mag*esta*d en ello q*ue* os encar-

guelo de ally y por / la notiçia q*ue* teneys de algunas coSsas
adelante sy fuere neceSsario os de mas gente p*ar*a / q*ue* Con
la q*ue* vos llevays procurareys de paSar adelante y Vos
te(r)nd*r*eys respetto de obedeçell*e* / y hazer lo q*ue* por el oS
fuere mandado y guardar la orden q*ue* os diere

[fol. 2r]
396
{*ytem*} En la Ynstrucion q*ue* se dio a diego lopez de çuñiga
q*ue* Va por capitan por la costa lleva Un cap*itul*o en q*ue* / se
le dize q*ue* tenga mucho cuydado de saber de la gente q*ue h*a
ydo por tierra y de la que Vos / llevays por el Ancon y si
tuviere alguna noticia y fuere neç*esar*io Juntarse con ellos o /
con Vos q*ue* lo haga lo mismo *h*abeys Vos de tener porq*ue*
pues es tod(o)*a* Una mysma / coSsa y tanbien busCa el para
VoSotros y lo mysmo los q*ue* Van a las yslas / asi es razon q*ue*
Se haga por V*uest*ra partte y q*ue* todos procureys de ayudaros
y reme- / diaros syempre q*ue h*aya lugar para ello

{*ytem*} A los yndios q*ue* llevays en V*uest*ra compañia hazelles-
eys buen tratamy*ent*o para q*ue* qu*a*ndo es- / ten en Su ti*e*rra
atraygan a los demas A teneros amor

{*ytem*} Te(r)nd*r*eys mucho cuydado q*ue* no sea blasFemado el
nombre de n*uest*ro s*eñ*or ny de su madre / GlorioSa ny de los
san(c)tos Antes q*ue* sean muy reverençiados y la doctrina
*crist*iana en / Vos y en ellos se trate muy ordinaria y vivays
como catholicos de manera q*ue* los na- / turales de la ti*e*rra
donde estuvieredes no reciban mal exemplo antes los atray-
gais / con V*uest*ras Virtudes y buenas obras a deSear V*uest*ra
Amistad y converSacion

{*ytem*} procurareis q*ue* aquel s*eñ*or de quicama y de coama no
sean molestados ny maltratados en / nada pues de tan buena
Voluntad os recibieron

{*ytem*} procurareys de estar mas advertido *en* la comunica-
cion y conVerSacion de los yndios porq*ue* / pareçe q*ue* era
neceSsario estar mas recatado de *e*llos que lo estuvisteis la
Vez paSsada

{*ytem*} Estareys muy advertido q*ue* la gentte q*ue* va en

Vuestra compañia no haga ningun agravio ny fuer- / ça A los yndios ny les tomen nada de lo que tuvieren contra su Voluntad ny entren en / sus caSsas sin Vuestra licencia

{ytem} Yten procurareys de aVeriguar bien la noticia que tuvistes de la mar y de aquellas yslas / que dezis y saber que gente es la que habita en toda aquella comarca y por amor procurar de / saber la que puede haber en aquella tierra y esto tentareys con yndios mercaderes o por / otra qualquier Via que meJor os pareçiere esCusando de dalles guerra sino fuere cons- / trenydos de neçesidad y de todo lo que en ella huviere procurareys de haber muestras

{ytem} Si os pareciere que conviene asi para requerir las señales y cartas que dexaredes atras si no / huvieredes hallado lengua y raStro del general y de su gente o para darnos nueVas de / lo de alla que conViene emViar el naVio o la barca asy para esto como para algunas pro- / viSiones que convengan o darnos Algun aViSo esto hareys como Vieredes que mas con- / Viene detenello o emViallo

[fol. 2v]
{ytem} Iten si poblaredes en alguna partte no sea entre los yndios sino apartado de ellos y manda- / reys que ningun español ny otra perSona de las Vuestras Vaya al lugar ny a las caSsas de / los yndios sino fuere con expreSsa licencia Vuestra y al que lo contrario hiziere castigalleys / muy asperamente y la licençia habeys de dalla las Vezes que fuere neceSario para alguna coSsa que / conVenga y a perSonas de quien Vos esteys confiado que no haran coSsa malhecha y es- / tad muy advertido en guardar esta orden porque es coSsa que conViene mas de lo que Vos po- / deys penSar

{ytem} hAbeys de tener muy entendido que la principal coSsa a que Vays es a saber del capittan gene- / ral Francisco Vazquez de coronado y de la gentte que con el esta y a que se pueda contratar con / ellos por la mar y a desCubrir el puertto o puertos que para esto mas conVenga y que esto / habeys de procurar por todos los modos y Vias que os fuere poSsible por mar y por tierra / y que hasta saber esto y hazello no os habeys de ocupar en otra ninguna coSsa ni Venyr de / alla sin aViSarnos primero de lo que hovieredes hecho y

alcançado para que proveamos / lo que nos pareciere que conViene

{ytem} En lo de los resCattes que emViamos mandamos A la perSona que los lleva a cargo que no (h)uSe / de ellos ny resCatte sino fuere en Vuestra preSencia habeys de tener orden en el libro que la tal / perSona llevare y en el del escrivano que Vos llevaredes en el armada que Va a Vuestro cargo se pon- / gan espacificadamentte los resCattes que lleva y en el Un libro y en el otro lo firmeys Vos y / el que llevare a cargo los resCattes y el tal escrivano y la mysma orden se te(r)ndra en lo que / de ello se gastare en resCatar y contratar ponyendo espacificadamente lo que se gasta / en los dichos resCattes y contrataçiones y lo que por ello sea en el Un libro y en el otro / firmado por la mysma orden para cargo y desCargo de el que lo llevare a cargo y esto / te(r)ndreys orden que Se ponga muy claro y espacificado por que Se entienda bien

{ytem} Iten hemos procurado que francisco pilo mercader enVie perSona propia con mercaderias y he - / rraJe y otras coSsas de proviSiones asy para la gente que con Vos Va como para la que esta con / el capitan general francisco Vazquez de coronado al qual entregareys el herraJe que / en Culiacan tomaredes para que el lo gaste y despache como suyo porque es a cuenta de otras / {|} coSsas que Con el dicho pilo tenemos y porque el nos haze plazer en aVenturar su hazienda / Y conviene cobrar credito para que otros lo aVenturen dalleeys en el naVio que llevare- / des buen lugar donde lleve sus mercaderias y hazelleeys buen tratamyento y de- / Xalleeys libremente disponer de ellas y Vendellas a Su Voluntad y no consentireys / que le sea hecho ningun maltratamyento (^d) ny fuerça de palabra ny de obra por Vos ny por / nynguno de la gentte de Vuestra compañia y quando huvyere de sacar las mercaderias en tierra / dalleeys todo favor y ayuda y te(r)ndreys orden como no se aVenturen porque la aven-

[fol. 3r]
397
tura y peligro corren Sobre noSotros y como coSsa que nos toca os la encargamos mucho / y para las escrituras que fueren neceSario tomar de lo que Vendiere fiado si en el

armada / fuere escri*va*no de su mag*estad* mandalleeys q*ue* las haga y si no le huviere crialloeys / como capitan y Justicia de la d*i*cha armada q*ue* Si ne*çe*sario es en nombre de Su mag*estad* p*ar*a / ello os doy poder cumplido

Y porq*ue* por experiencia se *h*a Visto q*ue* de lleVar ballestas y arcabuzes y otras armas de / municion se pierden y diSminuyen y dañan porq*ue* por ser de municio*n* no se tiene de *e*llo / particular cuydado las ballestas *y* arcabuzes y rodelas q*ue* fueren ne*çe*s*ar*ias p*ar*a la gente de / guerra q*ue* llevays y marineros hazerselaseys entregar por suyas en precios moderados / a los q*ue* tuvieren Sueldo a cuenta de Su sueldo y a los q*ue* no lo tuvyeren obligalles por ello / y lo q*ue* fuere de mas y por muniçio*n* entregalloeys a la perSona q*ue* asi el d*i*cho pilo emViare / para Cuenta entre agustin guerrero y el a quien tenemos encargado lo de n*uest*ras Armadas / y las obligaciones q*ue* hizieren a quien se diere*n* las dichas armas y lo q*ue* asi se entre- / gare a la persona q*ue* *e*l d*i*cho pilo emVia dalloeys a don luys de castilla para q*ue* lo emVie / al dicho agustin guerrero

{*ytem*} llevareys ciertas coSsas q*ue* doña beatriz de *e*strada emVia para el capittan general su / marido y mandareys q*ue* en ello y en lo que mas llevaredes para algunos de los soL- / dados q*ue* Con el estan q*ue* os *h*ayan recomendado amigos o parientes suyos *h*aya *a* buen / recaudo

{*ytem*} F*e*cha En la Çiudad de mexico A postrero dia del mes / de mayo de myll y q*ui*nientos y quarenta E Una(s)

{rúbrica} don antonyo / de mendoça {rúbrica}

Por mandado de sus s*eñori*as / Almaguer

y*n*stru*cci*on para el Capitan H*ernan*do de alarCon

[fol. 3v-4r] [blank]

[fol. 4v]
yntruysyon de alarco*n*

Document 17

The Viceroy's Letter to the King, Jacona, April 17, 1540

AGI, Patronato, 184, R.31

INTRODUCTION

Before 1536 there had been occasional indications of the existence of a marvelous land far north of México-Tenochtitlan. But it was with the arrival of Álvar Núñez Cabeza de Vaca, Andrés Dorantes, Alonso del Castillo Maldonado, and Esteban de Dorantes at San Miguel de Culiacán on April 1, 1536, that the image of wealth and great population centers to the north became focused on towns beyond a native settlement called Corazones. According to the so-called Joint Report prepared during the fall of 1536 by the three Europeans of that company, there were "towns with many people and very large houses." Cabeza de Vaca later amplified these statements, writing that in those towns there were "cotton shirts" and a source of metal that the natives smelted.[1]

During the four years from April 1536 to July 1540, the allure of Tierra Nueva brightened, then dimmed, and finally was snuffed out. Following the Joint Report, the documentary record reveals three discrete steps in that change. Although the stories of the four Narváez expedition survivors caused a stir throughout the viceroyalty of Nueva España, the viceroy moved circumspectly. Before committing money and effort to attempting to take control of such a distant land, he wanted confirmation that it existed and lived up to the reports. Even so, it was not until slightly more than a year after the arrival of the four survivors that Viceroy Mendoza began negotiations with Andrés Dorantes to retrace his route from the north at the head of "forty or fifty horse[men] to learn the secret of those regions." For reasons the viceroy said he did not understand, Dorantes eventually withdrew from the projected enterprise.[2]

Mendoza then turned to fray Marcos de Niza to seek the desired verification. After a seven-month sojourn in 1539, the friar returned to make a lengthy, written report. Repeatedly he told of being assured by natives along his route that Tierra Nueva was "the best and greatest thing that was ever heard of."[3] But the proof rested on hearsay, because Marcos had not personally seen most of what he wrote about the Seven Ciudades. In addition, the friar brought disturbing news that establishing royal dominion over Tierra Nueva probably could not be the peaceful undertaking the viceroy had envisioned. Unarmed priests acting as the king's agents might well only suffer martyrdom. Yet the north remained a tantalizing place.

The ink was barely dry on Marcos's *relación* when Mendoza dispatched another attempt to corroborate reports about Tierra Nueva. This time the *entrada*, a party of 16 horsemen[4] under Melchior Díaz and Juan de Zaldívar, would be armed.[5]

Díaz and Zaldívar were both veterans of Nueva Galicia. Díaz had been a captain with Nuño de Guzmán in the early 1530s during the conquest of Nueva Galicia. He was now *alcalde mayor* of Culiacán and had welcomed Cabeza de Vaca and his companions back to the king's jurisdiction two and a half years previously. He was later appointed captain in command at the Coronado expedition's Río Sonora supply base, San Gerónimo. From there he led an unsuccessful

233

attempt to rendezvous with Alarcón's seaborne arm of the expedition in 1540 and died in the process, as the result of an accident.[6]

Zaldívar, also later a captain in the Coronado expedition, had arrived in Nueva Galicia in 1533[7] and was appointed a *regidor* of Guadalajara in 1538 by Francisco Vázquez de Coronado in his capacity as governor.[8] Zaldívar continued to serve as *regidor* until at least the middle 1560s.[9] He was a nephew of Vázquez de Coronado's lieutenant governor Cristóbal de Oñate and became a prominent figure in Nueva Galicia as one of the founders of Zacatecas.

As the viceroy records in the letter published here, Díaz, Zaldívar, and the rest of their company departed from Culiacán on November 17, 1539.[10] The lateness of the season, though, brought snowfall ahead of them along their route, which prevented their reaching Cíbola. Instead, they spent a good part of the winter in the vicinity of Chichilticale.[11] Both Zaldívar and Díaz reported that they made assiduous efforts to obtain information about Cíbola and Tierra Nueva, both by scouting and by interviewing local natives who had been there. In this way, they assembled a portrait of the people and towns of Cíbola that was much less enticing than the one given by fray Marcos. Their report culminated in the revelation that "[the Indians] are unable to give me information about any metal, nor do they say that [the people of Cíbola] possess it."[12] With this sobering news the Díaz party returned south bearing a formal, written report.

En route they met the northward bound Coronado expedition at Chiametla and disclosed their discouraging news. Captain Diego López later testified that "after the day they met Melchor Díaz, the witness [López] held no hope that they would come across anything [worthwhile]."[13] Vázquez de Coronado attempted to put a good face on the Díaz-Zaldívar report, but many expeditionaries besides López were disheartened.[14]

Zaldívar and three companions continued south in search of the viceroy.[15] They found him at Colima in March 1540 and delivered the written report to him, providing other details orally.[16] Although it is not apparent in the letter published here, Mendoza was chagrined. He immediately ordered Zaldívar to return north (going by ship to travel faster), intercept Vázquez de Coronado, and tell him "that the army was not to continue on. Instead, the general was first to send a captain to reconnoiter as far as Cíbola and to learn what it was." Although Zaldívar did not reach Culiacán before the captain general left, Vázquez de Coronado had already put into effect a plan similar to what the viceroy had ordered.[17] He had left most of the European contingent at Culiacán, proceeding northward with only 75 to 80 Europeans and most of the Indian allies.[18]

The final blow to the reputation of Cíbola came when that advance guard reached the first of the Seven Ciudades in July 1540. The full extent of the captain general's resulting disillusionment and anger are manifest in the letter he sent to the viceroy from Cíbola a month after his arrival there.[19]

Four months before that, however, when Viceroy Mendoza wrote to the king after Zaldívar had delivered his and Díaz's report, his tone was matter-of-fact. The letter seems untroubled, with no intimation of an unprofitable conclusion to the expedition. The better part of the letter comprises a lengthy, and purportedly verbatim, excerpt from the Díaz-Zaldívar report. It is copied into the letter without comment on its significance or trustworthiness. Nor is its relation to fray Marcos's earlier report even hinted at. The letter appears to serve only as a conduit, without recording the viceroy's reaction to what, for the expeditionaries, had been demoralizing news.

The letter is preserved in the Archivo General de Indias in Sevilla under the *signatura* (catalog number) AGI, Patronato, 184, R.31. It bears Mendoza's signature and a closing in his scrawling hand. The remainder of the letter was set down by an unidentified *escribano*. It was published in French translation in 1838.[20] About 25 years later, Joaquín Pacheco, Francisco de Cárdenas, and their associates published a Spanish transcription.[21] On the basis of that transcription, George Parker Winship published the first English translation in 1896.[22] Also deriving from the Pacheco and Cárdenas transcript was the 1940 translation published by George Hammond and Agapito Rey.[23]

The new transcription and translation that follow are based on the letter held in the Archivo General de Indias. In editing both, we have consulted all of the publications just mentioned, and we note major departures from them in the accompanying notes.

TRANSLATION

[1r]²⁴

Holy Catholic Imperial Majesty

I wrote to Your Majesty from Compostela²⁵ on the last day of February,²⁶ giving you a report of my arrival there and the departure of Francisco Vázquez with the people whom (in Your Majesty's name) I was sending for the pacification and settlement²⁷ of the newly discovered land. And [I wrote] that *alcaide* Lope de Samaniego went as *maestre de campo*,²⁸ both because he is a trustworthy person and a very good Christian and because he understands things [undertakings] of this sort, which Your Majesty had ordered [me] to pay attention to.

What must be said once more after this is that when the expedition had crossed the unsettled region [beyond] Culu-acán [Culiacán] [and] had arrived altogether at Chiametla, the *alcaide* went off with some horsemen to search for food supplies.²⁹ One of the soldiers who was going with [Samaniego], who had strayed off, yelled that [the Indians] were killing him. The *alcaide* rushed to help him, and [the Indians] wounded [Samaniego] with an arrow in the eye, from which he died.³⁰

Concerning the fortress [in the Ciudad de México], since it is dilapidated and of poor quality, it seems to me that its cost is becoming too great and that Your Majesty could avoid further [expense] by having one man who would be in charge of the munitions and artillery, one armorer who would keep them in repair, and a single artilleryman. This would [all] remain as it is now in the building of the *audi-encia*, until fortresses are built in accordance with what I have written Your Majesty. The other [expenses are] unnecessary, since that fortress was built for *bergantines* and for no other purpose.³¹ And since the lake [Lake Texcoco] is so dry, it cannot be used in any way at the present time.³² For this reason I am of the opinion that the expense [of the fortress]

is needless. Further, I believe that before Your Majesty's reply can arrive, [the fortress] will have collapsed.³³

{Item} Days ago I wrote Your Majesty that I had ordered Melchior Díaz, who was in the *villa* of San Miguel de Culu-acán, to go with some horsemen to learn whether the report Father fray Marcos brought was in agreement with what he would see.³⁴ [Díaz] left Culuacán with fifteen horsemen on the seventeenth [1v] of the month of November of last year [1539]. On the twentieth of March this year I received a letter of his which he sent with Juan de Zaldívar and three other horsemen.³⁵

What it says is that after he left Culuacán and crossed the Río de Petatlán,³⁶ he was always received well by the Indians. The system he employed was that he sent a cross [ahead] to the place where he was going to have to lodge, as a sign [of his coming]. The Indians received [the crosses] with extreme veneration. [The Indians] had the habit of erecting a building made of straw mats, where they put [the cross]. At some distance from [the building for the cross] they built a lodging for the Spaniards. They planted stakes [in the ground] where they tied the horses. There they set grass and a great quantity of corn for [the horses] (at those places where they had [corn]). [Zaldívar and the other horsemen] say that because the year had been bad, [Díaz] experienced the hardship of hunger at many places.

When he had traveled a hundred leagues from Culu-acán, he began to find the land cold and to experience hard frosts. As he went farther it became even colder, until it so happened that some of his Indians froze [to death], from among those they were taking in their company.³⁷ And two Spaniards survived great risk [of death]. When [Díaz] saw this he decided not to travel farther until winter was over and to send those whom I mention[ed] with the report of what he had learned about Cíbola and the land beyond. [What he reported] is this, which is extracted verbatim from his letter {scribal punctuation}:[38]

Since I have given a report[39] to Your Lordship about what has happened to me along the way, and having understood that it is impossible to cross the unsettled region there is between here and Cíbola because of the excessive snow and cold there is, I will give Your Lordship a report about what I have found out about Cíbola.[40] I have inquired into it through many people who have been there for fifteen [to] twenty years. I have attempted [to do] this in many different ways, making use of the Indians together and separately, and all [of them] eyewitnesses. They end up agreeing on what I will [now] tell.

Once they have left this large uninhabited region behind there are seven *lugares*. It is probably a short day's journey from one [*lugar*] to another. [The native informants] call all of them together Cíbola.

They have crudely worked buildings made of stone and mud. They are built in this way: [there is] one long wall, and from each end several sleeping rooms extend, partitioned into [spaces] of twenty square *pies*.[41] According to what [the informants] indicate, the [rooms] are roofed with wood over *vigas* [ceiling timbers]. In order to put up the other buildings they make use of the flat roofs with their ladders from the streets.[42] The buildings are three and four stories high. [The informants] declare there are a few [buildings] of [only] two stories.

The stories are more than one and a half *estados* high, except the first, which is the ground floor, which is probably not [that high], but something just over [2r] one *estado*.[43] Ten or twelve houses communicate together by means of one ladder. They make use of[44] the ground floors as is appropriate, and they live in the higher floors. In the lowest floor of all they have some loopholes at oblique angles, as in fortresses in Spain.

The Indians say that when [their enemies] come to make war on them, everyone goes into the buildings, and they fight from there. When they go [elsewhere] to make war, they carry round shields and wear some hide garments which come from bison of several colors. They fight with arrows, a few small stone maces, and other weapons made from poles which I have not been able to understand. They eat human flesh.[45] And those whom they capture in war they keep as slaves.

There are many domesticated native chickens [turkeys]. [The people of Cíbola] have large quantities of corn, beans, and melons. In their houses they have a few animals with tangled hair, similar to large Castilian bird dogs.[46] They clip them and make colored wigs/falls from the hair, which they put on; [they are] like this [one] I am sending to Your Lordship.[47] They also add the same [hair] to the clothing they make.[48]

FIGURE 17.1. We-Wha, a Zuni berdache, Zuni Pueblo, showing the traditional woman's hairstyle, dress, and boots. Photograph by John K. Hillers, 1886. Courtesy Museum of New Mexico, neg. no. 29921.

The men are of small stature. The women are fair-complected and good-tempered.[49] They go about dressed in chemises that reach to their feet.[50] Their hair is parted to the sides with twists which leave their ears exposed.[51] Many turquoises are hung from their ears and around their necks and wrists. The men's clothing consists of *mantas* and [bison] hides on top [of them]. [The hides are] like the one which Cabeza de Vaca and Dorantes brought and which Your Lordship probably saw.[52] They wrap scarves around their heads.[53] In summer they wear shoes made of painted or colored hide, and in winter {scribal punctuation} high buskins [decorated] in the same way.[54]

[The Indians] are unable to give me information about any metal, nor do they say that [the people of Cíbola] possess it. They do have turquoises in quantity, although not as many as the Father Provincial says. They have a few small crystals like this [one] I am sending to Your Lordship.[55] Your Lordship [has] seen plenty of these there in Nueva España.

They work the land in accordance with the practices of Nueva España. Loads are carried on their heads as in [the Ciudad de] México. The men weave the cloth[56] and spin the cotton. They eat salt from a lake that is two days' journey from the *provincia* of Cíbola.[57] The Indians perform their dances and songs accompanied by flutes they have. Their holes, where they place their fingers, yield many tunes.[58] They sing along with those who play [the flutes]; those who sing also clap their hands in the same way we do. I saw an Indian (from among those whom Esteban, the Black,[59] took), who was a captive there, [2v] play [the flute], which [is something] they taught him there. Others sing, as I [have said], although not very skillfully. [The former captive] says that five or six [flutists] join together to play and that some flutes are larger than others.

[The Indians who have been to Cíbola] say that the land is excellent for corn and beans and that [the people of Cíbola] do not have fruit trees, nor do they know what they are. There are very excellent woodlands. It is a *provincia* short of water. Cotton is not harvested [there]; they secure it from Totonteac.[60] They eat in

FIGURE 17.2. Zuni Salt Lake from the north, 2002. Photograph by the authors.

earthenware bowls, as in [the Ciudad de] México. They harvest a great quantity of corn, beans, and other seeds such as sage.[61] They know nothing about fish from the sea, nor have they heard of [them].

Regarding the [bison], there is no word except that they are beyond the *provincia* of Cíbola. There are a great many wild goats, and they are the same color as gray horses.[62] Everywhere here where I am there are large numbers of them. I have asked the Indians {scribal punctuation} whether [the bison] are like these [goats], and they tell me they are not.

{scribal highlighting}[63] Of the seven *lugares,* three are very large, four [are] not as big. [The informants] indicate, as it seems to me, [that] each *lugar* [is] three crossbow shots square.[64] According to what the Indians say and indicate about the buildings (namely that they are joined) and their size, and the [number of] people who reside in each building, [the population] must be a large multitude.

It has been determined that Totonteac is seven short days' travel from the *provincia* of Cíbola and that it is the same sort [of place], and the houses and people are also [the same]. And that there is cotton [there], [but] I doubt it since it is a cold land. [The informants] say that there are twelve *pueblos* [in Totonteac] [and] that each one is larger than the biggest one in Cíbola. Also they tell me that there is a *pueblo* which is a single day's journey from Cíbola and [that] they are at war with each other.[65] The houses, people, and trade are of the same sort. They assert that [it] is larger than any of the aforementioned [*pueblos*]. I hold it as true that [the population of this *pueblo*] is a great multitude of people. [The people of this region] are so famous because they have buildings, food, and turquoises in abundance.[66]

I have been unable to learn more than what I am telling [here], even though I have brought with me Indians who have been there [in Cíbola] for fifteen and [even] twenty years, as I have said.

{Item} The death of Esteban, the Black, took place in the way Father fray Marcos must have related it to Your Lordship. For that [reason] I do not refer to it here more than [to say] that the [people] of Cíbola sent [a messenger] to tell the [people] of this *pueblo* and its environs[67] that if Christians came, they were to consider them of no importance and were to kill them, since they were mortal. This [they said] they knew because they had the bones of the one who had gone there [Esteban]. [They said further] that if [the Indians where Díaz was writing] did not dare [to kill the Spaniards], they were to send [the messenger] to tell [the people of Cíbola], because they would come to do it right. {scribal punctuation} I believe that this has transpired in just that way and that [the people of Chichilticale]· have communicated {scribal punctuation} with [the people of Cíbola], considering the coolness with which they received us and the mean face they have shown us.[68]

[3r] {Item} Melchior Díaz says that the people he found along [his] route have no permanent townsite except in one valley which is a hundred and fifty leagues from Culuacán.[69] It is well settled, and [the people there] have buildings [with] flat roofs.[70] And [he says] that there are many people along the trail, but that they are not suited to any other use besides making them Christians (as if this were [of] small [importance]).[71]

May Your Majesty consider what to arrange in the service of God and may you be mindful of the deaths and destruction of peoples and *provincias* which have occurred in these Indies. [This is necessary] because up to the present none of what Your Majesty has ordered, which has been very holy and good, has been adhered to.[72] May you supply ecclesiastics, considering both that [fact] and what [must be done] from now on,[73] {scribal highlighting}[74] because I attest

to Your Majesty that in those places they have not reached, there is no trace of Christianity, neither slight nor considerable. The poor people are ready to receive the ecclesiastics. Where they flee from us [lay Spaniards] like deer [running] to the forests, they come back to them. I say this as an eyewitness who on this outbound trip has seen it clearly. I was importuning Your Majesty for friars [before], and now I cannot refrain from doing it much more, because I would not be doing what I am obligated [to do] if I did not do so.

{Item} [When I have] arrived in [the Ciudad de] México I will make a report to Your Majesty about everything concerning these *provincias,* because [right] now, even if I tried to, I would be unable to, because I am very weak from a persistent fever which I suffered in Colima.[75] Although it did not [last] more than six days, it afflicted me severely. It pleased Our Lord that I am now better and have traveled as far as Jacona, where I am.[76]

May Our Lord protect and glorify the Holy Catholic Imperial person of Your Majesty with an increase of grander kingdoms and dominions, as we, your servants, desire.

From Jacona, 17th of April in 1540[77]

Holy Catholic Imperial Majesty

Your Holy Majesty's humble servant, who kisses your royal feet and hands,
don Antonio de Mendoza [no rubric][78]

[3v–4r] [blank]

[4v]
Item: to the Holy Catholic Imperial Majesty of the most invincible Emperor [and] King of Spain,
Lords [of the Consejo de Indias]

{1540}
{to His Majesty from don Antonio de Mendoza}
{Report from the Consejo de las Indias with the letter from the viceroy and the [one] from Doctor Bernal}[79]

[fol. 1r]

Sacra Catolica Cesarea MagestaD

Desde conpostela a postrero de hebrero *e*Screvi a V*uestra* m*a*gesta*d* haziendole Rela- / çion de mi Venida alli y partida de franc*is*co Vazquez con la gentte q*ue* en nonbre / de V*uestra* m*a*gesta*d* EnViava a la paçificaçion y asientto de la t*ie*rra nueVamentte / desCubiertta y como yba por maese de Canpo El all*cai*de lope de samaniego asy / por ser persona de confiança y muy buen *cris*t*i*ano como Por *en*tendersele / las cosas de *e*Sta calidad como V*uestra* m*a*gesta*d h*abra⁸⁰ mandado Ver y lo que / de nueVo despues aca *h*ay que dezir es q*ue* pasando El canpo El despoblado / de culuaCan llegando juntto a chiametla El all*cai*de Se apartto con çiertta / gentte de Cavallo a buscar bastimentos y Un soldado de los q*ue* con el yban / que se *h*avia desmandado dio Vozes q*ue* le mataban y El all*cai*de acudio a socorre- / lle y dieronle Un flechazo por Un ojo de q*ue* murio en lo q*ue* toca a la forta- / leza segun(d) ella esta malparado y es Ruyn paresçeme q*ue* la coSta q*ue* se haze / es demasiada y q*ue* V*uestra* m*a*gesta*d* puede *e*SCusarla mas de *e*lla porq*ue* con ttener Un / honbre q*ue* tenga cargo de las muniçiones y artilleria y Un armero q*ue* las / Repare y Un artillero y q*ue e*Sto se este como se *e*Sta en la casa del au- / dien*ci*a / *h*aSta q*ue* se hagan las fortalezas conforme a lo q*ue* tengo *e*Scri(p)to a V*uestra* m*a*gesta*d* / es escusado lo demas porque aquella fortaleza se hizo para los bergan- / Tines y no para otro efe*c*tto y por estar tan seca la laguna no puede ser- / Vir de *e*llo al presentte por ningu*n*a Via y por *e*Sto digo⁸¹ q*ue* la costa es su- / perflua y creo q*ue* anttes q*ue* la Respuesta de V*uestra* m*a*gesta*d* venga estara / cayda

{y*tem*} los dias pasados *e*Screvi a V*uestra* m*a*gesta*d* como *h*abia mandado a melchior diaz / q*ue e*Stava en la Villa de san miguel de Culuacan fuese con algunos de Cavallo / a Ver Si conformava la R*elaci*on q*ue e*l padre fray marcos traya con lo q*ue e*l / Viese El qual se parttio de Culuacan con quinze de Cavallo a diez

[fol. 1v]

y siete del mes de novienbre del año pasado y en Veyntte del mes de março / de *e*Ste presentte Resçebi Una cartta Suya la qual enVio con Juan de çaldy- / Var y otros Tress de Cavallo lo que dize es q*ue* despues q*ue* de CuluaCan p*ar*tio / y paso El Rio de petatlan Sienpre fue muy bien Resçebido de los yndios / la (h)orden q*ue* tenia (h)era q*ue* enViava al lugar donde *h*avia de yr a posar Una / cruz por seña la qual Resçibian los yndios con hartta Veneraçion y / hazian Una casa de eSteras donde ponella y algo apartado de *e*lla hazian / El aposentto para los españoles E hincaban palos donde atasen los Cavallos / y alli les ponian yerva y mayz en abundançia en las partes q*ue* lo tenian / dizen q*ue* a causa de *h*aver sido El año malo paso nesçesidad de hanbre en / muchas partes y q*ue* pasados çien(t) leguas de CuluaCan q*ue* começo a hallar / la t*ie*rra Fria y a hazelle buenas *h*eladas y quantto mas adelant(r)e yba tan- / to mas frio les hazia *h*aSta que llego la cosa a *h*elarsele algunos yndios / de los q*ue* lleVaban en su conpañia y doS españoles pasaron harto Riesgo Visto / *e*Sto determino *h*aSta pasado El ynVierno de no pasar adelante y enViar / estos q*ue* digo con la Relaçion de lo que *h*abia Sabido de çivola y de la t*ie*rra / de adelant(r)e la qual es esta Sacada de su Cartta a la letra {scribal punctuation} ya que⁸² he dado / cuentta a V*uestra* s*eñori*a de lo q*ue* me ha su(b)çedido por el Camino y Visto q*ue* es / ynposible pasar el despoblado q*ue h*ay desde aqui a çivola a causa de las / grandes nieVes y frios q*ue* haze dare R*elaci*on a V*uestra* s*eñori*a de lo

que he sabido / de çivola lo qual Tengo aVeriguado por
muchas personas que han eStado / alla quinze y Veyntte años
y eSto he procurado por muchas y diversas Vias / Tomando a
los yndios Juntos y otros apartte y todos de ViSta Vienen a
Con- / çertar en lo que dire Salidos de eSte despoblado
grande estan siette lugares / y habra Una Jornada pequeña del
Uno al otro a los quales Todos Juntos / llaman çivola Tienen
las casas de piedra y barro toscamentte labradas / son de eSta
manera hechas Una pared larga y de eSta pared a Un cabo y
a otro sa- / len Unas Camaras ataJadas de Veyntte pies en
quadra segun(d) Señalan las / quales eStan maderadas[83] de
Vigas por labrar las mas casas se mandan / por las açoteas con
sus esCaleras a las calles Son las casas de treS y de quatro /
altos afirman haber pocas de doS altos los altos son de mas de
estado y / medio en alto eçebto El primero que eS baxo que
no te(r)ndra Sino algo mas que

[fol. 2r]

Un estado mandanse diez o doze casas juntas por Una
esCalera de los / bajos se sirven y en los mas altos habitan en
el mas bajo de todos tienen / Unas saeteras hechas al soslayo
como en fortalezas en eSpaña dizen los yn- / dios que quando
les Vienen a dar guerra que se meten en sus Casas Todos y /
de alli pelean y que quando ellos Van a hazer guerra que
lleVan Rodelas / y Unas Cueras VeStidas que Son de Vacas
de colores y que pelean Con flechas / y con Unas maçetas de
piedra y con otras armas de palo que no he podido / entender
comen Carne hUmana y los que prenden en la guerra
Tienen- / los por esclavos hay muchas gallinas de la tierra
mansas tienen mucho ma- / yz y frisoles y melones tienen en
sus casas Unos animales Vedijudos / como grandes podencos
de caStilla los quales tresquilan y del pelo hazen / Cabelleras
de Colores que se ponen como esa que enVio a Vuestra
señoria y tan- / bien en la Ropa que hazen (h)echan de lo
mismo los honbres son de pe- / queña eStatura las mugeres
Son blancas y de buenos gestos andan / Vestidas con Unas
Camisas que les llegan haSta los pies y los Cabellos /
partenselos a manera de lados con çiertas Vueltas que les
quedan las / orejas de fuera en las quales se Cuelgan muchas
TurqueSas y al cuello / y en las muñecas de los braços El
VeStido de los honbres Son mantas / y ençima Cueros de
Vaca como El que Vuestra señoria Veria que lleVo cabeça / de

Vaca y dorantes en las cabeças se ponen Unas tocas Traen /
en Verano çapatos de Cuero pintados o de color y en el
ynVierno / {scribal punctuation} borzeguies altos de la
misma manera no me saben dar Razon de / metal ninguno
ni dizen que lo tengan Turquesas tienen en Cantidad /
aUnque no tantas Como El padre provinçial dize Tienen
Unas pe- / drezuelas de cristal como esa que enVio a Vuestra
Señoria de las quales / Vuestra señoria habia Visto hartas en
esa nueVa españa labran las tierras / a USo de la nueVa
españa Carganse en la cabeça como en mexico los / honbres
Tejen la rropa E hilan El algodon comen sal de Una lagu- /
na que eSta a doS jornadas de la provinçia de çivola los
yndios hazen / Sus bayles y cantos Con Unas Flauttas que
tienen Sus puntos / do ponen los dedos hazen muchos Sones
Cantan Juntamentte / con los que tañen y los que Cantan
dan palmas a nuestro modo a Un / yndio de los que llevo
eSteban el negro que eStuvo alla Cautivo le Vi ta-

[fol. 2v]

ñer que Se lo mostraron alla y otros Cantaban como digo
aUnque no muy / desenVueltos dize que se Juntan çinco o
seys a tañer y que son las flauttas / Unas mayores que otras las
tierras dizen ser buenas para mayz y frisoles / y que no tienen
arboles de frutta ni saben que cosa es hay muy buenos
montes es / la provyncia Faltta de agua no se coge algodon
Traenlo de totonteac comen en / caxettes como en mexico
cogen mucho mayz y frisoles y otras Simillas / como chia no
saben que cosa es pescado de mar ni tienen notiçia de ello de
las / Vacas no hay notiçia mas de que las hay adelant(r)e de la
provinçia de çivola hay / mucha abundançia de cabras
Salvajes y son de color como Cavallos Ruzios / por aqui
donde yo estoy hay hartas[84] de ellas aUnque[85] he preguntado
a los yndios / {scribal highlighting} Si son como eStas y
dizenme que no de los siete lugares ^los tres hazen muy
grandes los / quatro no tanto Señalan a mi Ver Como tres
tiros de ballesta en quadra / cada lugar y segun(d) los yndios
dizen y señalan las Casas y el grandor y / como eStan Juntas
y la gentte que hay en cada casa deve ser Una gran mul- /
Titud aVeriguase que totonteac esta de la provyncia de çivola
siete JoR- / nadas pequeñas y que es de la misma manera y
casas y gentte y hay / algodon dudolo porque me dizen que
es Tierra Fria dizen que hay doze pueblos / que cada Uno es

mayor q*ue* El m*a*yor de çivola Tanbien me dizen q*ue* *h*ay /
Un pueblo que *e*sta Una Jornada de çivola y tienen guerra los
Unos con los / otros Son las casas y gentte y contrataçion de
Una manera afirman / Ser mayor q*ue* ning*u*no de los d*i*chos
yo los tengo q*ue* Son Una gran multitude de gent*e* / y como
tienen aquellas Casas y comida y turq*ue*Sas en abundançia
son / Tan nonbrados no he podido saber mas de lo q*ue* digo
aUnq*ue* he traydo / comigo yndios q*ue* han eStado alla
quinze y Veyntte añosS como he d*i*cho

{y*tem*} la muertte de esteban El negro paso de la manera q*ue*
*e*l padre fray marcos / lo contaria a V*uestra* Señori*a* y por eso
no lo Refiero aqui mas de q*ue* los / de çivola enViaron a dezir
a los de *e*ste pueblo y su Comarca q*ue* Si alg*u*nos / cris*t*ianos
VinieSen q*ue* no los Tuviesen en nada y q*ue* los mataSen
porq*ue* / (h)eran mortales y q*ue* *e*llos lo sabian pues tenian los
huesos del q*ue* *h*abia / ydo alla y que si ellos no Se atrevyesen
q*ue* Se lo enViaSen a dezir porq*ue* *e*llos / Ve(r)nd*r*ian a
hazello {scribal punctuation} bien creo q*ue* ha pasado eSto
asy y q*ue* se *h*an conVerSado⁸⁶ {scribal punctuation} / eStos
Con ellos segun(d) la tibieza con que nos rresçibieron y el
Ruyn / RoStro q*ue* nos han moStrado

[fol. 3r]
{y*tem*} Dize melchior diaz q*ue* la gentte q*ue* hallo por el
Camino no tiene Asientto ning*u*no / eçebto en Un Valle que
*e*sta çiento y çinquenta leguas de CuluaCan q*ue* eSta / bien
poblado y tienen casas de terrado y que es Mucha la gentte
q*ue* *h*ay por el Camin*o* / mas q*ue* no son para otro provecho
Sino para hazellos cris*t*ianos Como si este fuese / pequeño
V*uestra* m*a*gesta*d* por serviçio de dios mire lo q*ue* provee y
tenga memoria de las / muerttes y destruyçion de genttes y
provy*n*cias q*ue* ha *h*abido en eStas yndias y / como haSta el
dia de *h*oy nada de lo que V*uestra* m*a*gesta*d* *h*a mandado q*ue*
*h*a sido muy / santto y bueno se *h*a guardado y provea de
Religiosos asy para aquello como / {scribal highlighting}
para lo de aqui porque çertifico a V*uestra* m*a*gesta*d* que

donde ellos no han llegado ningun(d) / RaStro de cris*t*iandad
*h*ay *ni* poco ni mucho y la pobre gentte estan apareJado /
para Reçibir Religiosos y donde huyen de noStros Como
Çiervos a los / monttes Se Vienen a ellos y eSto hablo como
TeStigo de ViSta q*ue* *en* eSta / Salida lo he ViSto claro yo
ynportunava a V*uestra* m*a*gesta*d* por frayles / y agora no
puedo dexar de hazello mucho mas porque no haria lo q*ue* /
soy obilgado Si asy no lo hiziese

{y*tem*} llegado a mexico hare Relaçion a V*uestra* m*a*gesta*d* de
todo lo de eStas / provinçias porque agora aUnque quisiese
no podria a causa de *e*star / muy flaco de Una Calenttura
continua q*ue* tuve en Colima q*ue* aUn- / q*ue* no fue mas de
seys dias me apretto muy Rezio a n*uest*ro señor plazi- / do
q*ue* ya eStoy bueno y *h*e Caminado haSta aqui en Jacona
donde eStoy / n*uest*ro Señor la S*acra* C*atolica* C*esarea*
persona de V*uestra* m*a*gesta*d* guarde y ensalçe con / acresçen-
tamy*ento* de mayores Reynos y Señorios como Sus criados
de- / seamos de Jacona XVij de abril de MDXL

S*acra* C*atolica* C*esarea* M*a*gest*a*d

humil criado de V*uest*ra s*acra* m*a*gesta*d* qu*e*/ sus Reales pies y
ma*n*os besa / don antonyo / de mendoça

[fols. 3v–4r] [blank]

[fol. 4v]
y*tem* A la S*acra* C*atolica* C*esarea* Magestad / Del YnVic-
tisimo emp*era*d*o*r Rey de *e*spa*ñ*a / Señores

{1540}
{a Su m*a*gesta*d* / de don antonyo de mendoça / (^don
antonio del)}
{que*n*ta del *consej*o de las Indias co*n* / la Carta del Virrey y la
del / doctor bernal}

Document 18

Hernán Cortés's Brief to Carlos V concerning the Injuries Done to Him by the Viceroy of Nueva España, June 25, 1540

AGI, Patronato, 21, N.2, R.4\2

INTRODUCTION

During Holy Week of 1519, Hernán Cortés, leading a large force of Europeans, made landfall near the site of modern Veracruz, Mexico. He and his companions were about to set off toward the interior of the continent. At the time, Cortés, an *hidalgo* from Medellín in Extremadura, was 34 years old and a partner of Governor Diego Velázquez of Cuba in an enterprise of reconnaissance in the Gulf of Mexico. He was soon to dissolve that partnership unilaterally, because he received news of a vast, extremely populous, and fabulously wealthy polity centered on a huge metropolis called Tenochtitlan. Within two years, Cortés, his European followers, and his Native American allies had forcibly taken control of that indigenous state and destroyed much of its capital.[1]

The resulting booty, combined with Cortés's own eyewitness accounts of the sumptuousness and high civilization of the Valley of Mexico, brought him unprecedented renown. For years he was a celebrity throughout Europe and a major power in the New World. Young Carlos I of Spain, newly named Holy Roman Emperor Carlos V, showered him with rewards and honors. Nearly a decade after the celebrated conquest of Tenochtitlan, by a royal *cédula* dated July 6, 1529, Carlos granted Hernán Cortés the title of Marqués del Valle de Oaxaca, a princely territory comprising some 23,000 adult male vassals.[2] Just over three months later Queen Juana, the emperor's mother and joint sovereign with her son, conceded to the *marqués* the right to "reconnoiter, conquer, and settle whatever islands there are in the Mar del Sur that are within Nueva España and all those you may encounter toward the west, provided they are not within territories for which governors have already been provided."[3]

On the basis of this concession, between June 1532 and May 1539 the *marqués* dispatched four small fleets northward into the Gulf of California. He himself sailed in one of the fleets, establishing an abortive settlement at Bahía de Santa Cruz in what is now Baja California Sur.[4] The last of these fleets was commanded by Francisco de Ulloa and overlapped in time fray Marcos de Niza's overland trip in anticipation of the Coronado expedition. Indeed, Cortés had tried to enlist Marcos to lead a northward reconnaissance on his own behalf before Viceroy Mendoza did the same. And the *marqués* claimed that he had actually furnished much of the information contained in the friar's official report and that Marcos had not seen those things himself.[5]

With the return of fray Marcos in August 1539, Mendoza launched final preparations for a full-scale land expedition to locate and subjugate the settlements of Cíbola. Cortés protested that his prerogatives were thus being infringed. Without a channel of likely redress in Nueva España, he returned to Spain in 1540. There he and his representatives pursued challenges to the viceroy's authority before the Consejo de Indias and attempted to recover rights and privileges that had been retracted from Cortés over the years since his initial triumph. The issue of Mendoza's authority to mount an expedition was settled definitively in the viceroy's favor in 1541.[6] Many other contentions remained, however, and were still pending when Cortés died in Castilleja de la Cuesta, just outside Sevilla, in December 1547, without again returning to his *marquesado* del Valle de Oaxaca.[7]

Whereas in the early 1520s Cortés was viewed in Spain as a glorious instrument of imperial expansion, by the late 1530s and early 1540s he and other powerful New World conquistadores seemed instead to be agents of fragmentation of the empire. Their incredible wealth, influence over large and unruly followings, and geographical distance from the empire's seat in Spain threatened to dissolve the hold of the emperor and his government over the far-flung realm. The vivid example of civil war then ravaging Peru drove home the point that men of immense achieved status, such as Cortés, had to be reined in. This was certainly a major factor in what the *marqués* felt was an unjust abrogation of richly deserved rights and honors. Whether unjust or not, it had been, in fact, an important motivation behind the establishment of a viceroyalty in Nueva España in 1535.

Included in the lengthy case file of litigation before the Consejo de Indias concerning the respective rights of Cortés, Mendoza, Pedro de Alvarado, Nuño Beltrán de Guzmán, and Hernando de Soto is the statement of Cortés's argument published here. The original document, drafted by an unknown *escribano* and signed by the Marqués del Valle, is preserved in the Archivo General de Indias in Sevilla under the *signatura* (catalog number) AGI, Patronato, 21, N.2, R.4\2, fols. 4r–6r. It has not previously been published in English, although José Luis Martínez included a Spanish transcription of it in his four-volume *Documentos Cortesianos* (1992), and transcriptions have appeared in several other collections.[8] We consulted Martínez's edition in vetting our transcription, which follows, after our translation.

TRANSLATION

[4r]

{Filed in Madrid on the 25th of June in [the year 15]40 by the *procurador* Iñigo López de Mondragón in the name of the Marqués del Valle {rubric}}[9]

Very powerful Lords:

I, the Marqués del Valle, declare that I have come from Nueva España to these *reinos* principally to inform Your Majesty and [the officials] of [your] royal Consejo de las Indias of the harm and widely known injury that don Antonio de Mendoza, viceroy of Nueva España, has done and is doing to me by seeing that I am impeded and hindered in the conquest of a certain land which is included within the limits and confines of [the territory] that has been agreed to and contracted with me by order of Your Majesty since the year one thousand five hundred and twenty nine.[10] [That land] has been reconnoitered long before this by me and my captains, whom I have sent with fleets launched at my own expense. And I have taken possession of it in fulfillment of the aforementioned compact made with Your Majesty.

The viceroy has tried to justify the harm and trouble he has caused and is causing to me by claiming that a fray Marcos de Niza has reconnoitered that land anew, having been sent by the viceroy for that [purpose], about which a distorted report has been and is being made to Your Majesty.[11] But what is actually happening is that in observance and fulfillment of the aforementioned compact and at the time the concession was granted to me by Your Majesty and considerably before that, I have had the intention and have occupied myself with the reconnaissance and conquest of this land. For that [purpose] I have launched four armed expeditions, all at my own expense. I have spent more than two hundred thousand *ducados* on them. I went myself in

person on one of them and endured very great hardships and dangers.[12] My captains always pursued and conducted the journey in accordance with what [was] written down and agreed to with Your Majesty[13] and [took] the direct route, which is [toward] where the aforesaid land and islands seem to be.

The first expedition I launched, in which Diego Hurtado de Mendoza[14] went as my lieutenant [and] captain general, departed in [one thousand five hundred and] thirty-two and sailed along nearly the whole coast. It arrived very near the first and principal [place] which is populated in the explored part of this land. Because the *navío* in which the aforesaid captain was traveling ran aground, the conquest was not completed at that time.

When I went in person on the next expedition I followed the same channel and coast [of the Mar del] Sur.[15] And I reached the land of Santa Cruz and remained in it.[16] This is very near the land that is being talked about and borders on it. No one else had reached this place other than my captain Diego Hurtado de Mendoza. When I was in the land of Santa Cruz I gained a full understanding of this land, which is somewhat farther along in the same piece of land [or] coast [of the Mar del] Sur. Since at the time I did not have an interpreter through whom I could understand [the natives], I could not reach an understanding of all the details of that land. For this reason and because I lacked supplies, I headed back to Nueva España in order to refit and enlarge the *armada*.

I brought [with me] some native Indians from the land of Santa Cruz who, after they had learned the language of Nueva España, informed me in great detail about things concerning that land, about which they had complete knowledge because they were closer to it. [These are things] which, until then, no one else was aware of.

When I departed [from Santa Cruz], I left in the aforesaid land nearly all the people I had taken [there],[17] along with [the] twelve horses that were still alive, and with the plan to send them [4v] supplies and more people, so that from there they could continue the journey by land to the land that is being talked about.[18]

Don Antonio de Mendoza ordered that I remove all the people I had established in the aforesaid land from [there]. By his order [this] was done and carried out. At the time I returned from the aforementioned land, fray Marcos spoke with me (I was in Nueva España). I gave him information about this land and its reconnaissance, because I had determined to send him in my ships to proceed and subjugate the aforesaid coast and land. [That was] because it appeared that he understood something about navigation. The friar passed [that information] on to the viceroy. Then with [Mendoza's] license he says he traveled by land in search of the same coast and land I had reconnoitered, which was and is mine to reconnoiter.

After the friar returned, it was made public that he said he had arrived within sight of the aforesaid land. I deny that he has seen or reconnoitered that [place]. On the contrary, what the friar reports to have seen, he has asserted and [continues to] assert only on the basis of the report I made to him concerning the information I was receiving from the Indians of the land of Santa Cruz whom I brought [to Nueva España]. [This is true because] everything it is said the friar is reporting is identical to what the Indians told me.

By his behaving in this [matter] without respect [for my prior exploration], fray Marcos has done nothing new in putting himself forward as something he is not and relating what he neither knows nor has seen. [That is because] he has done it many other times and makes a habit of it, as is widely known in the *provincias* of Peru and Guatemala.[19] More than enough information about this will be given soon in this court, if it is necessary.

Within a very few days after I had arrived in Nueva España from the land of Santa Cruz I finished building certain ships, which I had left in the shipyard. And I bought others. I provisioned them with many supplies, people, arms and armor, and ammunition. [Then] I sent Francisco de Ulloa as their captain.[20] He carried my instruction that he

was always to follow the coast [of the Mar] del Sur in search of the land about which I was receiving information.

While [Ulloa] was pursuing his voyage and after he had navigated many days by sea, the viceroy, under pretext of the report which fray Marcos had made to him, dispatched and stationed men in Nueva España at the ports of the Mar del Sur, wherever he suspected the ships of the *armada* of Francisco de Ulloa could put in. [This was] so they could detain them and take [their] sails so that they could not continue the voyage. [They did this] also so that they might learn from them the knowledge and information that had been kept secret about the land, as actually happened.

When one of the ships which Francisco de Ulloa had taken returned to the port of Santiago de Buena Esperanza, which is in the *provincia* of Colima,[21] he disembarked a sailor so that he might come to me from there to give a report of what had happened during the expedition. Don Rodrigo Maldonado,[22] who (by order of the viceroy) was in that port as a guard for this purpose, apprehended him and tortured him so that he could find out what information he was bringing.[23] When he was unable to extract [anything] from him, he went with horsemen to the port to seize the ship in order to learn [the secrets] from its men. [The ship] was already leaving the port, and they followed it along the coast more than a hundred and twenty leagues.

Because of fear, the ship did not dare enter any port, so it was anchoring off those rugged coasts. Thus [it was that] a storm took it in its grip, during which it lost its anchors and its boat. Out of necessity it entered the port of Guatulco, and there [Mendoza's men] apprehended the pilot and sailors, and the ship was lost.[24]

Likewise, under stiff penalties, [the viceroy] issued an order prohibiting[25] any person from leaving Nueva España without his license. [He did this] so that I could not outfit other ships I have built to go to the aid of the *armada* I had sent with Francisco de Ulloa. And he sent Gómez de Villafañe, *corregidor* of Guamelula, [5r] to my *villa* of Tecoantepeque, where I maintain the shipyard for my ships.[26] By [the viceroy's] order, he seized from me all the ships I had there, plus the sails, rigging, rudders, and all their other tackle. He imposed heavy penalties on the officials and persons who were in charge of[27] the *armada* by my order, [under which] they were not to do any [further] work on it or launch any ship. Nor was the viceroy content with this. In order to do me greater injury and harm, he sent a Francisco Vázquez de Coronado with certain people, so it is said, to penetrate inland in search of the aforesaid land discovered by me, which is included within the limits of my jurisdiction.

In addition to the widely known harm and dispossession which would be done to me if what the viceroy has begun is continued, disservice to Your Majesty will ensue from it. [That is] because the people sent by the viceroy are few in number and nearly without experience and because the land to which they say they are going is large. And [further] its people [are] warlike and more intelligent and clever[28] than any other [people] who have yet been discovered in the Indies. If mistakes are made at the beginning of such an important undertaking, very great harm will likely result from it because of the knowledge and intelligence the natives of that land would be able to obtain. And more importantly, if don Antonio pursues this exploration, he will not be able to do so without leaving Nueva España unprotected and at great risk and danger, since he is the governor of Nueva España. And as a result [of the expedition], there would be the same problem in Nueva Galicia, where Francisco Vázquez is governor.[29]

In confirmation of this, since I arrived in these *reinos* letters have come from Nueva España in which is written news concerning these people sent by the viceroy. [This news] tells and affirms that those he sent first, which were twelve horsemen, are dead.[30] Further, some native *pueblos* in Nueva Galicia in which Francisco Vázquez has been have risen in arms. [The natives] have killed six horsemen and other Christians because of the abuse which has been inflicted on them. Because I consider [this information] very reliable and commonly known, as I did [before], I maintain that Your Majesty and the members of your royal Consejo de Indias needed to and [still] must rectify the harm and such obvious wrong which I have received and am receiving in this [matter].

Now, it has recently come to my notice that Your Majesty, it is said, has ordered or is ordering that a royal commission of yours be issued so that don Antonio de Mendoza can have the aforementioned conquest made and

can take with him the people, arms and armor, horses, and provisions he may need from the whole land of Nueva España. This, it is said, is ordered [to be] stipulated by Your Majesty.

I humbly ask and, with the respect I ought [to show], request[31] that for the time being the aforesaid decree or *cédula*, in which may be included what is stated above or part of it or anything whatsoever which may be or could be to my detriment, all be nullified and voided and that it ought to be annulled and revoked, since it is to my detriment and that of my rights and territory.[32]

Because of all I have stated above (which I consider as requested again[33] here), and because [the commission] has been issued without my having been notified or heard, and because neither the right nor the territory (which I have acquired by virtue of the aforesaid contract and compact executed by Your Highness and by your royal order) could and can now be taken away, [and] because [this] is a contract in which pledge money has been paid[34] which involves mutual obligation, according to the law Your Highness [5v] is obligated to fulfillment of what has been contracted and formally concluded with me in your royal name so many years ago.

[This is true because,] in particular, I, on my part, have executed and performed everything as completely as I was and am obligated to do, have spent on it more than two hundred thousand *ducados*, and have endured great and innumerable hardships and dangers to my person and life; because I have reconnoitered this land at such cost and hardship, and formal documents of possession [have been] prepared in the towns which lie within the boundaries of this [land] and within my territorial limits and [the extent of my] conquest (as is so well known); because I have the gear that I have to enable me to conquer it and bring it into submission to Your Majesty (with the aid of Our Lord God); also, because of the experience I have in similar matters in this part of the world (as is well known to Your Majesty); because I have much more knowledge of the matters of that land than anyone else; and because I have gotten [so close] and have been so near to it.

The temporary measure [now being applied] was not provided for by law in order to deprive and dispossess a rightful holder, but rather in order to preserve and protect what is in his possession. This measure must not have an effect on me opposite to that for which it was provided, nor must Your Majesty permit [such an effect].

I have come in person to humbly petition Your Majesty for relief from the harm and injury the viceroy has done and is doing to me and so that the contract and compact with me may be adhered to and my territory of jurisdiction may be preserved.[35] Not only does the [present] measure not achieve [that], but greater wrongs are being inflicted on me by approving and confirming what the viceroy has done so unjustly and by bestowing upon him a new title and commission without hearing me.

Neither is this a litigation or action in which there must be an informal hearing[36] or judicial examination[37] or some interim determination, nor do I consent to that, but rather immediately and without delay I offer to present my documents of right and jurisdiction. Then without causing [any] delay, Your Majesty can judge from the compact and contract documents which [are] presented on my behalf. I am presenting herewith these documents in proof of my having effected fulfillment of what has been and is my responsibility under the compact, as well as [others prepared] by a cosmographer and persons expert in the art of navigation and cosmography who are present in this court.

When it is apparent, as it will be apparent, that my right is so manifest, may Your Highness then order me to exercise[38] it. [This is] because as soon as the rights and jurisdiction of whichever of the parties [to a dispute] [are] certain and can be certain (as in the present case my right and juris-

diction are obvious), the aforesaid temporary measure is revoked and is not in effect and [because] I need to be protected as regards the aforesaid jurisdiction. Then, when an interim measure must be put into effect, it must be issued to me, since I hold the aforementioned title, contract, and document of jurisdiction.

I ask and humbly request that it be done and ordered in this way. Therefore, since [it is] best that the petition be granted according to law, I ask and humbly request that Your Highness order annulled or revoked any commission, *cédula*, or judgment to my detriment which may exist in [this case]. May you order that [any such document] not be dispatched and, if it has been dispatched, that it cannot be executed nor is it to be executed. May Your Majesty order that I [6r] can continue and complete the conquest of the aforesaid land, which is within the limits of my territory, jurisdiction, and [extent of] conquest, in accordance with the aforementioned compact. And [may Your Majesty direct that] the viceroy [be] given an order that he is not to hamper or impede me in it, either personally or through other individuals; that Francisco Vázquez is not to travel farther nor is the viceroy or any other person to meddle in [the conquest] any more; and that I may use and employ the people whom the viceroy sent with Francisco Vázquez in pacifying Nueva Galicia (which is nearly fully subjugated) and in another undertaking very important to Your Majesty's service, about which I will provide information soon.

Above all, I request justice and, in that regard, I commend [the matter] to Your Majesty's royal conscience.

Marqués del Valle {rubric}

TRANSCRIPTION

[fol. 4r]

iij

muy poderosos señores[39]

{*presenta*da en madrid a xxV de Junyo de xL del *procurador* yñygo lopez de mo*nd*ragon / en no*mb*re del marq*ue*s del Valle {rúbrica}}[40]

El marques del valle Digo que yo he Venido desde la nueVa españa a estos Rey- / nos prinçipalmente para dar notiçia A Vuestra mag*estad* y a los de su Real consejo de las / yndias de la fuerça y notorio agravio q*ue* don antonio de mendoça Vissorrey / de la nueVa *e*spaña me *h*a hecho y haze en *h*averme ympidido y enbaraçado la / conquista de çierta ti*e*rra que se compre(he)nde en los limites y demarcaçion / de lo que por mandado de V*uestra* mag*estad* esta comigo capitulado y contratado desde / el Año paSado de mil y quinientos y Veinte y nueVe a*ñ*os y que por mi y por mis / capitanes q*ue* yo he emViado con armadas hechas a mi costa se *h*a descubierto / munchos dias ha y de que yo tengo tomada la possesion en cumplimiento / de la d*i*cha capitulaçion hecha con V*uest*ra mag*estad* y el d*i*cho Vissorrey *h*a querido / dar color a la d*i*cha fuerça y oppression q*ue* me *h*a hecho y haze pretendiendo q*ue* / dizque Un fray marcos de niça *h*a descubierto de nueVo la d*i*cha ti*e*rra siendo / para ello emViado por el d*i*cho Vissorrey en lo qual se *h*a hecho y haze siniestra / Relaçion A V*uest*ra mag*estad* porque[41] lo que passa Verdaderamente es que en / guarda y cumplimiento de la d*i*cha capitulaçion y en el tiempo q*ue* por V*uest*ra / mag*estad* me fue limitado[42] y muncho antes yo he entendido y me he ocupado / en el descubrimiento y conquista de *e*sta ti*e*rra y para ello he hecho

quatro ar- / madas todas a mi costa en las quales he gastado mas de (^tre)^*do*zientos[43] mill duca- / dos y en la Una de *e*llas fui yo en perssona y padesçi muy grandes travajos y / peligros y siempre mis capitanes siguiero*n* y llevaron el Viaje y camino derecho / conforme A lo assentado y capitulado con V*uest*ra mag*estad* que es donde la d*i*cha tierra / E yslas paresçen estar y la primera armada que yo hize en que fue por mi / lugarteniente de capitan general diego hurtado de mendoça partio en el / año passado de treinta y dos y corrio casi toda la costa y llego muy çerca de lo / primero E prinçipal que esta poblado en esta ti*e*rra descubierta y porque el / navio en que *e*l d*i*cho capitan yva dio al traves no se acabo por entonçes la d*i*cha / conquista y quando yo en persona fui en otra armada porsegui el mismo / passaje y costa del sur y llegue a la ti*e*rra de santa cruz y estuve en ella q*ue* es / muy çercana a esta d*i*cha ti*e*rra y que confina con ella y que ninguno otro llego / alli[44] sino el d*i*cho mi capitan diego hurtado de mendoça y estando en la d*i*cha / tierra de santa cruz tuVe entera notiçia de *e*sta d*i*cha ti*e*rra q*ue* esta algo mas / adelante en el mismo paraje y costa del sur y por no tener a la sazon len- / gua con quien me pudiese entender no pude alcançar a saber todas las cosas / particulares de la d*i*cha ti*e*rra y por esto y porque me faltaro*n* los mantenimy*ento*s / di la Vuelta a la nueva españa para Rehazer e acresçentar la d*i*cha armada / y truxe algunos yndios de los naturales de la d*i*cha ti*e*rra de santa cruz los / quales despues que aprendieron la lengua de la nueVa españa me ynformaro*n* / muy particularmente de las cosas de la d*i*cha ti*e*rra de que ellos tenian en- / tera notiçia por estar mas çercanos a ella que a otros ningunos que hasta ento*n*çes / se supiesse y dexe en la d*i*cha ti*e*rra Quando de *e*lla parti cassi toda la gente q*ue* *h*abia / llevado con doze cavallos que Quedaro*n* Vivos y con presupuesto de les emViar

[fol. 4v]

bastimentos y mas gente para que desde alli prosiguiesen por tierra el dicho Viaje a esta / dicha tierra y el dicho don antonio de mendoça mando que yo sacase de la dicha tierra / toda la gente que en ella tenia y por su mandado se hizo y executo y al tiempo / que yo Vine de la dicha tierra el dicho fray marcos hablo comigo estando yo ya[45] en la / nueva españa E yo le di notiçia de esta dicha tierra y descubrimiento de ella porque / tenia determinaçion de emViarlo en mis navios en proseguimiento y conquista / de la dicha costa y tierra porque paresçia que se le entendia algo de cosas de naVega- / çion el qual dicho frayle lo comunico con el dicho Vissorrey y con su liçençia / dizque fue por tierra en demanda de la misma costa y tierra que yo habia descubierto / y que era y es de mi conquista y despues que Volvio el dicho frayle ha publicado / que dizque llego ^a vista[46] de la dicha tierra la qual yo niego haver el visto ni descubierto antes / lo que el dicho frayle Refiere haver visto lo ha dicho y dize por sola la Relaçion / que yo le habia hecho de la notiçia que tenia de los yndios de la dicha tierra de santa / cruz que yo truxe porque todo lo que el dicho frayle se dize que Refiere es lo mis- / mo que los dichos yndios a mi me dixeron y en haverse en esto adelantado el dicho fray / marcos fingiendo y Reseferiendo[47] lo que no sabe ni vio no hizo cosa nueVa por- / que otras muchas Vezes lo ha hecho y lo tiene por costumbre como es notorio en las / provinçias del peru y de guatimala y se dara de ello ynformaçion bastante luego en / esta corte siendo necessario y de(n)sde a muy pocos dias que yo llegue a la dicha nueVa / españa desde la dicha tierra de santa cruz hize acabar de hazer çiertos naVios que / tenia puestos en astillero y compre otros y los basteçi de munchos mantenimientos / y gente y armas E muniçion E ynVie por capitan de ellos a francisco de Ulloa / el qual llevo instruçion mia para que prosiguiese siempre la dicha costa del / sur en demanda de la dicha tierra de que yo tenia notiçia y continuando su / Viaje y haViendo navegado muchos dias por la mar el dicho Vissorrey so color / de la dicha Relaçion que el dicho fray marcos le havia hecho emVio y puso gente en los puer- / tos de la mar del sur de la nueVa españa dondequiera que sospechava que podian llegar / los navios de la armada del dicho francisco de ulloa para que los detuViessen y tomassen / las Velas para que no prosi-

guiessen el dicho Viaje y assimismo que supiessen de ellos / el secreto y aViso de la tierra como en efecto passo que Volviendo Uno de los na- / Vios que llevo el dicho francisco de ulloa al puerto de santiago de buena esperança / que es en la provinçia de colima echo desde alli en tierra Un marinero para que / me Viniesse a dar aVisso de lo que passava en la dicha armada y lo prendio don / Rodrigo maldonado que estava en el dicho puerto para guarda del para este / efecto por mandado del dicho Vissorrey y lo atormento para que descubriese la / nueva que traya y no lo pudiendo sacar del fue con gente de cavallo al dicho puerto / a tomar el dicho navio para se informar de la gente de el el qual era ya salido del dicho / puerto y le siguieron por la costa mas de çiento y Veinte leguas y no (h)osando el / dicho naVio entrar en puerto alguno de temor surgia en las costas bravas y assi le / tomo Un temporal en que perdio las anclas y batel y de necessidad entro en el / puerto de guatulco y alli prendieron al piloto y marineros y se perdio el naVio / y assimismo mando y defendio so grandes / penas que ninguna persona saliese / de la nueva españa sin su liçençia a fin de que yo no pudiese armar otros naVios / que tengo hechos para yr en socorro de la dicha armada que habia emViado con el / dicho francisco de ulloa y emVio a gomez de Villafañe corregidor de guamelula

[fol. 5r]

iiij

a mi Villa de tecoantepeque donde tengo el (h)astillero de mis naVios y me tomo / por su mandado todos los navios que alli yo tenia y las Velas y xarçias y / Governalles y todos los otros aparejos de ellos y puso grandes penas a los / offiçiales y personas que entendian por mi mandado en la dicha armada que no hiziesen / cosa alguna en ella ni echassen ningun(d) navio al agua y no contento con esto / el dicho Vissorrey y para me hazer mayor daño y fuerça emVio a Un francisco Vazquez / de coronado con çierta gente para que dizque entrase la tierra adentro en demanda / de la dicha tierra por mi descubierta y que se compre(he)nde en los limites de mi governa- / çion y de mas de que se me haria notoria fuerça y despojo si se continuase lo que el dicho / Visorrey ha començado se siguiria de ello desserviçio a

Vuestra magestad por ser poca y casi syn / esperiençia la dicha gente emViada por el dicho Vissorrey y porque la tierra adonde / dizen que Van es mucha y la gente de ella belicosa y de mas entendimiento y saber / que otra ninguna que hasta hoy se haya descubierto en las yndias E si en cosa de / tanta calidad se (h)errasse al prinçipio suçederian de ello muy grandes inconVini- / entes por el aviso E ynteligençia que los naturales de aquella tierra podrian tomar / mayormente que el dicho don antonio como es governador de la dicha nueva españa / si prosiguiese la demanda no la podria hazer sin dexar desmamparada y en mucho / Riesgo y peligro la dicha nueva españa y por consiguiente habria el mismo / ynconviniente en la nueva galizia de que es governador el dicho francisco Vazquez / y en confirmaçion de esto despues que yo llegue a estos Reynos han Venido cartas de la / nueva españa en que se escrive (^va de) la nueva⁴⁸ de esta gente enViada por el dicho / Visorrey y que dize y afirma ser muertos los que primero emVio que fueron doze de / cavallo y que assimysmo algunos pueblos de los naturales de la nueva galizia / donde el dicho francisco Vazquez estava se han alçado y que han muerto seis de cavallo / y otros cristianos por caUsa de los malostratamientos que se les han hecho

E teniendo yo por cosa muy çierta y notoria como la tuve y tengo que Vuestra magestad / y los de su Real consejo de las yndias habian y han de Remediar la dicha fuerça y / agravio tan manifiesto que yo he Recebido y Recibo en lo susodicho ha Venido / agora a mi notiçia nuevamente que Vuestra magestad dizque ha mandado o manda / dar su provission Real para que el dicho don antonio de mendoça pueda emViar / a hazer la dicha conquista y llevar consigo de toda la tierra de la nueva españa / la gente y armas y cavallos y provissiones que hoviere menester lo qual dizque / se manda proveer por Vuestra magestad por via del entretanto De la qual dicha / provision o çedula en que se contenga lo susodicho o parte de ello o otra qualquier / cossa que sea o pueda ser en mi perJuizio yo supplico y con el acatamiento que / devo (^?)⁴⁹ digo ser todo ello ninguno y de ningun(d) Valor y que se deve anular / y Revocar en quanto es en mi perjuizio y de mi derecho y possesion por todo lo / que de suso tengo dicho que he aqui por Repetido y porque ha

s(e)ido proveydo⁵⁰ / sin ser yo çitado ni oydo y porque no se pudo ni puede quitar ni suspender / el derecho ni la possesion que yo tengo adquirido por virtud de la dicha con- / trataçion y capitulaçion hecha por Vuestra alteza y por su Real mandado / porque es contrato oneroso que contiene Reçiproca obligaçion y Vuestra alteza

[fol. 5v]

segun(d) derecho es obligado al cumplimiento de lo que en su Real nombre ha sido / contratado y capitulado comigo tantos años ha mayormente haViendo yo / por mi parte complido y hecho tan enteramente todo aquello que fuy / y soy obligado de hazer y haViendo en ello gastado los dichos dozientos⁵¹ / mill ducados y mas y padesçido grandes E ynumerables travajos / y peligros de mi persona y Vida y teniendo yo descubierta esta tierra / con tanta costa y travajo y hechos aUtos⁵² de possesyon en pueblos tan / confines de ella y siendo Como es tan notoriamente de mi demarcaçion / y conquista y teniendo el aparejo que tengo para la poder conquistar y / suJetar a Vuestra magestad mediante el ayuda de nuestro señor dios assi por la esperien- / çia que yo tengo en cosas semeJantes en aquellas partes segun(d) que es no- / torio a Vuestra magestad como porque tengo mucha mas notiçia que otro ninguno / de las cosas de aquella tierra y porque he llegado y estado tan çerca de ella / y el Remedio del entretanto no se establecio en derecho para privar y des- / pojar al poseedor syno para conservarlo y ampararlo en su possesyon / y no ha de obrar Comigo este Remedio contrario efecto de aquel para que / fue estableçido ni ha de permitir Vuestra magestad que Viniendo yo en persona a su- / plicar a Vuestra magestad por el Remedio de las fuerças y agravios que el dicho Visso- / rrey me ha hecho y haze y para que se me guarde el dicho asiento y capitula- / çion y la dicha mi possesion Vel casi que no solamente no consiga el dicho Reme- / dio pero que se me hagan mayores agravios aprovandose y confirmandose / lo que tan inJustamente el dicho Vissorrey ha hecho y conçediendosele para ello / nuevo titulo y provision sin oyrme y este no es pleyto ni negoçio en que / ha de haver pleyto (h)ordinario ni tela de Juizio ni cosa del entretanto ni yo con- / siento en ello sino que luego incontinente (^y) sin dar⁵³ lugar a dilaçion me ofrez- / co A mostrar mi derecho y possesion y sin dar lugar a dilaçion Vuestra magestad / lo puede Ver y por la *escri*ptura de la dicha capitulaçion y contrataçion / que por mi parte esta presentada y estas escripturas que agora presento / para en prueva del cumplimiento que yo tengo hecho de la dicha capitu- / laçion de lo que ha sido y es a mi cargo y por Cosmografos y personas es- / pertas en el arte de la navegaçion y cosmographia que estan en esta / corte y paresçiendo como paresçera ser tan notoria mi Justiçia Vuestra / alteza me la mande luego administrar porque Quando luego inconti- / nente consta y puede constar del derecho y posesion de qualquier de las / partes como en el presente caso consta de mi derecho y posesion cessa / y no ha lugar el dicho Remedio del entretanto yo tengo de ser amparado / en la dicha possesion y quando hoViese de haver lugar cosa del entretanto / se ha de dar a mi que tengo el dicho titulo y asiento y possesion y assi lo pido / y suplico se haga y mande

Por ende como mejor ha lugar de derecho pido y supp*l*ico a Vuestra alteza / mande anular o rrevocar qualquier provision o çedula o consulta / que sobre ello haya en mi perJuizio y mande que no se despache y que si esta / despachada no se pueda Usar ni Use de ella y Vuestra magestad mande que yo

[fol. 6r]

v

pueda proseguir y acabar la dicha conquista de la dicha tierra que esta en mi / demarcaçion y governaçion y conquista y dentro de los limites de ella / conforme a la dicha capitulaçion y *estar* mandado[54] al dicho Visorrey que por sy / ni por otras personas no me ponga enbarço ni ympedimento en ello / y que el dicho francisco Vazquez no pase mas adelante ni se entremeta mas / en ello el dicho Vissorrey ni otra persona alguna y podriase emplear / y ocupar la gente que el dicho Vissorrey emVio con el dicho francisco Vazquez en / paçificar la dicha nueva galizia que casi toda esta por conquistar y en / otra cosa bien ymportante al serviçio de Vuestra magestad de que yo dare aViso / luego y pido sobre todo Justiçia y sobre ello encargo a Vuestra magestad su Real / conçiençia

{rúbrica} el marques / del Valle {rúbrica}

Document 19

Vázquez de Coronado's Letter to the Viceroy, August 3, 1540

History Library, Museum of New Mexico, Santa Fe

Ramusio, *Terzo volume delle navigationi et viaggi*, 1556, fols. 359v–363r

INTRODUCTION

Modern study of the Coronado expedition owes a great debt to the sixteenth-century Venetian collector and publisher Giovanni Battista Ramusio.[1] Four documents included in the present volume are known today only from Ramusio's Italian translations, the Spanish originals having disappeared centuries ago.[2] The last of the four such documents now being published is a lengthy excerpt from a letter (perhaps nearly the totality of it) written by Vázquez de Coronado to Viceroy Mendoza from Cíbola in early August 1540, less than a month after its capture by the expedition's advance guard.[3]

The letter, as we have it, is one of thinly veiled bitterness over Marcos de Niza's written report of August 1539 and oral statements he evidently made both before and after that date. Repeatedly, Vázquez de Coronado punctuates the letter with the refrain, "Everything the friar had said was found [to be] the opposite."[4] Finally, his anger overflows, and he writes bluntly that fray Marcos "has not spoken the truth in anything he said."[5] As a result, the captain general, though he has just reached the edge of Tierra Nueva, already foresees the fruitlessness of the remainder of the expedition and contemplates "abandoning this enterprise."[6]

There had already been intimations of loss of confidence in the friar earlier. Melchior Díaz and Juan de Zaldívar had been sent north late in 1539 to confirm fray Marcos's reports. Prevented from reaching Cíbola by heavy winter snow, they turned back south and met the northward-trekking expedition at Chiametla in the spring of 1540. Their ensuing report resulted in "poor expectations that were held about Cíbola."[7] As Pedro de Castañeda de Nájera later put it, "the bad news was soon rumored."[8] And thereafter, testified Diego López, "it was publicly known and widely held that fray Marcos had not seen things previously that he had pretended to."[9] Nevertheless, the captain general wrote that he "tried to lift [the expeditionaries'] spirits the best I could."[10] He evidently remained unconvinced himself.

Within weeks of dispatching the August letter from Cíbola, however, Vázquez de Coronado received news from Captain Hernando de Alvarado that moderated his pessimism. Stories told to Alvarado by a Plains Indian called El Turco reopened the possibility that large populations of wealthy and sophisticated people existed in Tierra Nueva. For nearly another year and a half, then, that possibility glimmered, though with decreasing likelihood.

In August 1540, as the captain general wrote to the viceroy, before receiving reports of people far to the east who ate off golden dishes, Vázquez de Coronado was profoundly disheartened. In his letter he ticks off, one by one, his disappointments. First, there was the *abra*, the wide valley off to one side of the main route north, where Marcos said he had been told there were "many very grand settlements in which there are people who wear cotton clothing" and use gold.[11] In evident disgust, the captain general reports to Mendoza that instead of "grand settlements," Melchior Díaz found "two or three impoverished little settlements with twenty or thirty rude shelters each."[12] Vázquez de Coronado follows that disillusioning item with similarly dismal news about the reportedly easy route north, the vaunted *ciudades* of Cíbola, and other reputedly marvelous polities named Totonteac, Marata, and Acus.

It is noteworthy that the captain general's focus is on population centers, and it is those that he appraises in his letter. Despite his mention of gold and silver as having been found at Cíbola, Vázquez de Coronado gives no indication that "those who understand mining" have gone out prospecting or that they may in the future. Instead, he laments that he has "been unable to extract from these people where they dug it up." And he expresses the hope that the people of Cíbola will relent and disclose the location of a source of precious metals.[13] The captain general devotes no space in his letter to appraisal of ore samples or sites deemed promising for mines. His interest is manifestly not in mining, but rather in locating people who already mine precious metals or produce other valuable commodities. In this, Vázquez de Coronado and the expedition as a whole fit the norm of Spanish-led expeditions of the first half of the sixteenth century.

Thus, what momentarily piques the captain general's interest is that "the population of these towns seems relatively large and intelligent to me."[14] This holds out the possibility that *encomiendas* might be established among them. Implicit in Vázquez de Coronado's assessment is that the people of Cíbola might be incorporated into the Spanish world with relative ease and begin paying tribute. But then he sets against the appearance of "intelligence" his observation that "for the most part they go about completely naked."[15] This seems to scuttle an expectation of their "civilization" and therefore of the "civilized" industries that would make *encomiendas* profitable. The captain general plunges back into discouragement.

Even in the face of anger with fray Marcos and rude disenchantment with Tierra Nueva, Vázquez de Coronado pledges to do his duty and pursue all leads. He writes that he will "not be lacking in diligence until Your Lordship orders what I am to do."[16] But he cannot disguise his lack of enthusiasm. One month after the capture of Cíbola, the captain general holds little hope of grand discoveries.

Despite the letter's tone of disillusionment, it provides numerous details of life among the ancestral Zunis and records behavior and reveals attitudes that prevailed among the Coronado expeditionaries and others of the period. Given Ramusio's dubious reputation for fidelity to sources, how far can those descriptions be trusted? As with all his published documents, readers need to be alert to Ramusio's occasional alteration and embellishment of original texts. Many of the statements included in his text of Vázquez de Coronado's letter, however, can be cross-checked and compared with parallel information from other documents—for example, the account of the attack on Cíbola contained in Document 22.[17] Such comparisons reveal substantial congruence between information provided in the August 1540 letter and other, contemporaneous documentary sources, although discrepancies exist.

Ramusio or his translator is the author of the document's title and the headings that organize the excerpt. To indicate that the headings and title were not part of the original manuscript, in the transcript and translation that follow they are enclosed in flourished brackets { }. Whoever the Italian translator was (and it may well not have been Ramusio himself), he seems to have been less than fully literate in that language. As we have discussed in relation to the other Ramusio documents included in this volume, frequent errors appear in the formation of verb forms throughout all four texts.[18] The Ramusio text of the August 1540 letter includes several instances of awkward and erroneous Italianization of Spanish words, strongly suggesting the translator's greater familiarity with Spanish than with Italian.

Three previous English translations of the August 1540 letter have been published, beginning with Richard Hakluyt's version from 1600.[19] That stood as the authoritative English text until George Parker Winship published a new translation in 1896. It was followed in 1940 by a version by George Hammond and Agapito Rey.[20] We consulted all three of these previous translations in editing the current English translation by Larry D. Miller and Richard Flint, which follows. In vetting our transcription of the original Italian publication, we consulted the 1988 Italian edition of Ramusio by Marica Milanesi.[21] In both translation and transcription, folio numeration conforms to the published 1556 Italian edition.

TRANSLATION

[359v]

{A report sent by Francisco Vázquez de Coronado, captain general of the company of people that was sent to the newly discovered land in His Majesty's name. Concerning what occurred during the expedition that departed from Culiacán, from the twenty-second of April of this year, 1540, onward.[22] Also concerning what he found in the land where he traveled.}

{Francisco Vázquez departs with the armed force from Culiacán. And after suffering various problems during the difficult journey, he reaches the valley of Los Corazones, where he finds there is no corn. In order to obtain [corn], he sends [someone] to the valley called "del Señor [Señora]." He obtains a report of the grandness of the valley of Los Corazones, about those peoples, and about some islands located off those coasts.}

On the twenty-second of the month of April just passed, I set out from the *provincia* of Culiacán with part of the armed force, holding to the plan I wrote about to Your Lordship. To judge by what happened, I am certain I have guessed right in not engaging all the combined armed force in this undertaking. [That is] because there have been such great difficulties and such a shortage of foodstuffs that I believe the enterprise could not have been carried out during this entire year. Further, if it had been completed [by the whole force], it would have been with a huge loss of people.

As I wrote Your Lordship, I made the trip from Culiacán [to Cíbola] in eighty days of travel.[23] During [this time] my companions, those gentlemen on horseback, and I carried [only] a small amount of foodstuffs on our backs and on our horses. Because of this I ordered that we not carry any other necessary items that weighed more than a *libra*.[24] In

spite of everything, and even though I had imposed as much regulation and control as possible on the few foodstuffs we were carrying, they proved insufficient. This is no wonder because the route is rough and long. What with the arquebuses that were carried when we climbed down from the mountains and slopes and that most of the corn was ruined when we crossed the rivers. Because I am sending Your Lordship a painting from this [portion of the] journey, I am not describing for you in this [letter] what is in the other [the painting].[25]

Thirty leagues before [the company] reached the place the father provincial describes so thoroughly in his report, I sent Melchior Díaz with fifteen horsemen on ahead.[26] I directed him to make [each] two-day journey in one, so that I would have everything [already] looked over when I arrived. He traveled four days through some very rugged mountains and found nothing to subsist on there. [Nor did he find] people or information about anything, except he did find two or three impoverished little settlements with twenty or thirty rude shelters each.[27] And he learned from their inhabitants that from there on, there was nothing but very rugged mountains, which continued on unsettled by any people. Since [this] was a waste of time, I chose not to send a messenger to Your Lordship [with information] about this. I gave the disappointing news to the entire company,[28] that a place so highly touted and about which the father had told so many things should be found [to be] so contrary. And [from this] the conclusion was drawn that all the rest [that fray Marcos had told about] would be things of that sort.

When I understood this, I tried to lift their spirits the best I could by telling them that Your Lordship had always held the opinion that this [side] trip[29] would be wasted travel and that we should focus our anticipation on those [360r] seven *ciudades* [of Cíbola] and the other *provincias* about which we had information, which [were] the goal of our undertaking.

With this resolve and intention, we all cheerfully traveled along a very difficult trail that could not be traversed without either [ourselves] preparing one or restraightening the track that was there. This distressed the men-at-arms not a little, [especially] when they saw that everything the friar had said was found [to be] the opposite. [This was so] because among other things the father said and attested was that the route was excellent and flat and that there was only one insignificant grade half a league long. The truth is that there are mountains. And even if the trail is well repaired, it cannot be traversed without great danger of the horses rolling there.

It was such that a great number of the livestock Your Lordship sent as provisions for the armed force remained behind at this [point of the] journey, because of the roughness of the rock. The lambs and wethers lost their hooves because of the [roughness of the] ground. And I left the greater part of those I had brought from Culiacán at the Yaquimí River because they could not travel.[30] Because they were proceeding slowly they stayed with four horsemen who have [just] now arrived. They have not brought more than twenty-four lambs and four wethers. The rest were left behind dead because of that cliff,[31] even though they had traveled no more than two leagues and had rested there several days.[32]

Then I reached the valley of Los Corazones on the twenty-sixth day of the month of May.[33] From Culiacán to there I obtained nothing more than a large supply of bread made from corn. Since the cornfields were not ripe, it was proper for me to leave all that. In this valley of Los Corazones we found more people than in any other part of the land we had left behind. And a large quantity of seed [corn], but there [was] no [fresh] corn for eating among them.

However, I understood rightly that there was [ripe corn] in another valley known as "del Señor" [Señora], which I did not want to disturb by exercising force. Instead, I sent Melchior Díaz there to obtain [corn] with trade goods, in order to give it to the Indian allies whom we were bringing with us. And also to [people] who, during the journey, had lost some of the beasts of burden they had brought and had been unable to carry provisions beyond what they had carried [themselves] from Culiacán as far as there. It pleased Our Lord that a small amount of corn was obtained with these trade goods. With it the Indians allies and some Spaniards were helped. As far as this valley of Los Corazones, some ten or twelve of our horses died from exhaustion. Because they had been carrying heavy loads and eating little, they could not endure the labor. Some of our Moors[34] and Indians ran away for the same reason, which resulted in no small deficiency among the servants for the enterprise.

They tell me this valley of Los Corazones is five days' travel from the Mar del Oeste.[35] I sent [someone] to summon Indians from the coast to tell me about their existence. While I was waiting for them, the horses rested. I remained there four days. During this time, the Indians from the sea[coast] came. They told me that two days' travel from the seacoast there were seven or eight islands directly across from them. [They were] heavily populated but deficient in foodstuffs, and they were brutish people. They told me they had seen a *navío* pass, not far from land. I do not know whether it was [one] of those that were sailing to reconnoiter the land or [whether] it belonged to the Portuguese.[36]

{They reach Chichilticale.[37] After having taken two days' rest, they enter a land very barren of foodstuffs and characterized by difficult travel for thirty leagues. Beyond that they again find a very pleasant land and the river called "del Lino."[38] They fight against the Indians when they are assaulted by them. As a result of victory, they take over [the Indians'] *ciudad* and are relieved from the discomfort of hunger.}

I departed from Corazones. According to my estimation, I was continually approaching the sea, but in fact I always found myself farther away. Thus, when I reached Chichilticale, I found myself fifteen days' travel from the sea. The father provincial had been saying that the distance [to the sea] was only five leagues and that he had seen it. We all experienced great distress and confusion on seeing that we found everything to be contrary to what he had told Your Lordship.

The Indians of Chichilticale say that whenever they travel to the sea for fish and other things they bring back, they travel cross-country, and they take ten days' travel [to get] there. It appears to me that the information I obtained from the Indians was true. The sea turns to the west directly opposite Los Corazones for ten or twelve leagues.[39]

I understood that Your Lordship's *navíos* had appeared at that place, the ones that were traveling in search of the port of Chichilticale, which the father said was located at thirty-five degrees.[40] God knows the concern I feel for them because I am anxious lest no misfortune befall them.[41] If they follow the coast, as they said [they would], so long as the foodstuffs they took with them hold out (for which reason I left them provisions at Culiacán), and if they are not subject to some mishap, I trust fully in God that they have already discovered something excellent. On this account, the delay they have caused will be forgiven.[42] At Chichilticale [360v] I rested for two days, and it was really necessary to have stayed longer, since we found the horses worn out at that point. But because the food supplies were short, it did not permit us to rest longer.

I crossed the boundary of the unsettled region on the eve of San Juan's [feast] day.[43] With [no] relief from the previous difficulties,[44] during the first days we found no grass, but rather a worse mountain route and more dangerous passes than any we had negotiated behind us. Because the horses were traveling exhausted, they felt it greatly there, and we lost more horses in this last unsettled region than we had farther back. Some of my Indian allies died, as well as a Spaniard named Espinosa[45] and two Moors, who died from eating a certain plant because they were lacking food supplies.

From this place I had the *maestre de campo,* don García López de Cárdenas,[46] go one day's journey ahead of me with fifteen horsemen to reconnoiter the land, and so that they might straighten the route. At this [task] he has toiled like the man he is and in keeping with the confidence Your Lordship has placed in his ability. I know that he did not stint in doing it, because, as I have told you, the route is very bleak for at least thirty leagues and more, since the mountains are unscalable. But when we had traversed these thirty leagues and more, we found running rivers and, at one

[river,] plant[s] like those of Castilla, and especially a kind we call *escaramujo,*[47] [and] many walnut and mulberry trees,[48] but the leaves of the walnut trees are different from those of Spain. I saw that there was flax in very large quantity on the bank of one river, and therefore it is called Río del Lino.

Not a single Indian was found until after one [more] day's travel. Then from a place there four Indians came out peacefully, saying that they were there because they had been sent to that unsettled place to tell us we were welcome, and that on the next day all their people would be coming out along the trail with food. The *maestre de campo* gave them a cross [and] told them they should tell the [people] of their *ciudad* that they should not be afraid. [And further,] that they should also let it be known that the people were to stay in their own houses, since I was coming in His Majesty's name only to protect and help them.

When this had been done, Fernando Alvarado[49] returned to tell me that some Indians had come peacefully and that two of them were waiting for me with the *maestre de campo.* Hence, I went to them. I gave them some rosary beads and cloaks, telling them they were to return to the *ciudad* and that they should all remain calm in their houses and should not be afraid.

Once this was done, I ordered the *maestre de campo* to go to find out whether there was a dangerous pass the Indians could defend. And [I directed] him to occupy and defend it until the following day, when I would join [him] there. So he went and found a very dangerous pass along the trail where we could have suffered great injury. Therefore he remained there with the force he was leading. That same night the Indians came to occupy that pass in order to defend it. When they discovered it was occupied, they attacked our people there.

According to what [the *maestre de campo*'s men] told me, they attacked like courageous men. Yet in the end they withdrew in flight because the *maestre de campo* was standing watch and was ready with his men. The Indians sounded a small trumpet[50] as a signal to assemble and did no harm to the Spaniards.

The *maestre de campo* sent me word about that the same night. Thus, the next day I got under way with the best order I could, [but] with such a shortage of food that I was worried that if we had to delay one more day, we would all be dead of hunger. [This was] especially [true of] the Indians because among us all we had no more than two *mine* of corn.[51] Therefore it behooved me to push on farther without delay.

From time to time the Indians sent up their smoke clouds, which were answered from a distance with as much coordination as we would have known how to do ourselves. Thus, they were notified that we were traveling and where we had reached.

As soon as I arrived within sight of the *ciudad*, I sent *maestre de campo* don García López, fray Daniel, fray Luis, and Fernando Bermejo some distance ahead with some horsemen, so that the Indians might see them. [I ordered them] to tell [the Indians] that [the purpose of] our coming was not to do them injury but to protect them in the name of the emperor, our lord. The *requerimiento* was made intelligible to the natives of that land through an interpreter, in accordance with instructions [and] in the way His Majesty commands.[52] However, [the Indians], being arrogant people, showed it little respect.[53] [They acted this way] because it seemed to them that we were few in number and they would have no difficulty killing us. They struck fray Luis in his robe with an arrow, which it pleased God did him no harm.

At that [moment] I arrived with all the rest of the horsemen and footmen. I found a large portion of the Indians in the country outside the *ciudad*. They began shooting arrows at us. In order to comply with Your Lordship's advice, and that of the *marqués*,[54] I did not want them to be attacked. So I prohibited the company from pursuing them, when they asked me if they could do so. And [I said] that what [our] enemies were doing was nothing and that it was not [right] to do battle with so few people.

On the other hand, the [361r] Indians, because they saw that we were not pursuing them, gained more courage and arrogance. So much so that they approached the horse's legs to shoot their arrows. When I saw there was no more time to stand in place, and it seemed the same to the ecclesiastics, [the company] attacked. [Then] there was little to do to them because some of them fled quickly to the *ciudad*, which was nearby and well fortified. And others [fled] into the countryside, to which chance led them.

Some Indians died, and more would have if I had

allowed them to be followed. But I saw that little benefit could come from that. [That was] because the Indians who were outside were few in number and those who had retreated within the *ciudad*, together with those who had remained there before, were numerous. Because that was where the foodstuffs were that we needed so sorely, I gathered all my men and divided them as seemed best to me to do battle against the *ciudad*. Then I surrounded it.

Because the hunger we were suffering did not permit delay, I dismounted with some of those gentlemen and men-at-arms. And I ordered that the crossbowmen and arquebusiers make an assault and remove [our] enemies from the defensive structures, so that they could not do us injury. I attacked the wall on one side at a place where they told me a movable ladder was leaning. And I saw that an entrance was there. However, in short order the strings of the crossbowmen's weapons broke, and the arquebusiers accomplished nothing because they were so weak and debilitated that they could hardly stay on their feet.

Because of this, the people who were on the roof defending themselves had no difficulty at all inflicting the injury on us that they had power [to do]. With an infinity of large stones they hurled from the roof, they knocked me to the ground twice. If I had not been protected by the excellent helmet I wore, I think the result would have been grim for me. Even so, [the men] removed me from the field with two small wounds to the face, an arrow in one foot, and many blows from stones to my arms and legs. In this way I left the battle extremely worn out. I think that if don García López de Cárdenas had not, like an excellent *caballero*, sheltered me the second time they knocked me to the ground by placing his body on top of mine, I would have run much greater risk than I did.[55] But it pleased God that the Indians surrendered. And Our Lord saw fit that this *ciudad* was captured. In it was found as great an abundance of corn as [we] were seeking [in] our necessity.

The *maestre de campo*, don Pedro de Tovar, Hernando de Alvarado, and Pablo de Melgosa, captains of the footmen, left [the battle] with some blows from stones, although none of them was wounded. [Gómez] Suárez was wounded by an arrow in one arm.[56] [Francisco] Torres, an *estante* of Pánuco,[57] [was wounded] in the face by another [arrow]. And two other footmen received two arrow wounds, although [only] slight [ones].

Because my armor was gilded and shiny, all [the Indians] assaulted me.[58] [It was] for this reason that I was wounded worse than the others, not because I had done more and set myself ahead of the others, since all these *caballeros* and men-at-arms acquitted themselves very well, as was expected of them. I am now well, God be praised, although still somewhat battered by the stones. Also, in the battle we had in the countryside, two or three other companions-in-arms were wounded. And three horses were killed, one belonging to don [García] López, another to [Juan de] Villegas, and the third to don Alonso Manrique.[59] There were seven or eight other horses wounded, but now these men, and the horses as well, have recovered and are quite healthy.

{Concerning the location and condition of the seven *ciudades* of the *reino* of Cíbola, the customs and capacity of their people, and the animals that were found there.}

It now remains for me to give an account of the seven *ciudades*, the *reinos*, and the *provincias* about which the father provincial reported to Your Lordship. So as not to beat around the bush, I can say truthfully that he has not spoken the truth in anything he said. Instead, everything has been quite contrary, except the name of the *ciudad* and the large, stone houses. Although they may be decorated with turquoise, [they are made] from neither mortar nor brick.[60] They are, nevertheless, very good houses, of three, four, and five stories. In them there are good lodgings, rooms with galleries, and some underground rooms [that are] very excellent and paved, which have been built for winter. They are almost like sweat baths.[61]

The ladders they have for their houses are almost all removable and portable. They are raised and set in place when it suits them. They are made of two timbers with rungs like ours.

The seven *ciudades* are seven small towns, all consisting of the [sort of] houses I describe [here].[62] They are all located within close proximity, within four leagues.[63] All [together] are called the *reino* of Cíbola. Each one has its own name, and no single one is called Cíbola. Instead, all as a whole are called Cíbola. [To] this one that I call a *ciudad* I have given the name Granada. [I have bestowed] such [a name] because [361v] there is some similarity about it [and] in commemoration of Your Lordship.[64]

FIGURE 19.1. Zuni Pueblo about 1890. Photograph by Ben Wittick. Courtesy Museum of New Mexico, neg. no. 16437.

In this one, where I am now lodged, there could be some two hundred houses, all encircled by a wall.[65] It seems to me that together with the other [houses] that are not [encircled] in this way, they could reach [a total of] five hundred hearths [households]. There is another neighboring town, one of the seven, [that] is somewhat larger than this one. [There is] another one the same size as this [one], and the remaining four are somewhat smaller. I am sending paintings of all this to Your Lordship, along with the route.[66] The finely prepared hide on which the painting is was found here, along with other such hides.

The population of these towns seems relatively large[67] and intelligent to me, but I am not certain [that is] so. [That is] because it would seem to me that they have attained [sufficient] judgment and intellect to know how to build these houses in the way they are [built],[68] [but] for the most part they go about completely naked,[69] with [only] their shameful parts covered. They also have *mantas* painted in the way [the one is that] I am sending to Your Lordship.

They do not harvest cotton, because the land is extremely cold. However, they wear *mantas*, like the one you will see as an example. And it is true that some spun cotton was found in their houses. They wear the hair on their heads in the same way [the people] from [the Ciudad de] México [do].[70] And they are all very well brought up and tractable.[71]

I think they have turquoise in quantity. By the time I arrived, this had disappeared, along with the rest of their possessions, except the corn. As a result, I did not find a single woman or any young men less than fifteen years old or [men] older than sixty, except for two or three elders who remained to command all the other youths and fighting men. Two bits of emerald were found in some paper,[72] also some very worthless, small, red stones that tend toward the color of garnets, along with other [bits] of rock crystal, [all of] which I gave to a *criado* of mine to put away in order to send to Your Lordship. [But] according to what they tell me, he has lost them.

[Turkeys] were found, but only a few, although we have some. In all seven of these towns the Indians tell me that they do not eat them, but keep them only to avail themselves of the feathers. I do not believe them about this, because [the turkeys] are very excellent and larger than those from [the Ciudad de] México.

FIGURE 19.2. Hawikku ruins near Zuni Pueblo, 1925. Photograph by Edward S. Curtis. Courtesy Museum of New Mexico, neg. no. 144697.

The weather in this land and the temperature of the air are almost like [those of Ciudad de] México, since now it is raining and hot.[73] Up until now, however, I have never seen it rain heavily; rather, a little shower has come with wind, like those that customarily fall in Spain. The snow and the cold are usually very severe. [I report this] because the natives of the land say this, and it seems likely that it is so. And also because of the nature of the country, the type of rooms they have, and the hides and other things these people have to protect themselves from the cold.[74]

There are no kinds of fruit or fruit trees here. It is all a land of plateaus, and in no direction are mountains visible, although there are some hills and a difficult pass. Birds are scarce here, which must be on account of the cold and because there are no mountains nearby. There are not many trees for making firewood here. They may obtain enough [wood] to burn for their own use [only by getting it] four leagues away, from a forest of very small juniper trees. Very good grass for our horses was located a quarter of a league from here, both for them to graze and for being cut for hay. Of this we were in great need, because our horses had arrived there exhausted and worn out.

The food which the people of this land have consists of corn (of which they have a great abundance here), beans, and small game, which they must eat (although they say they do not), because many pelts of deer, hares, and rabbits were found. They eat the best tortillas I have seen anywhere. And generally everyone eats them. They maintain the finest order and cleanliness in grinding [their corn] that may be seen anywhere. One woman from among the people of this land grinds as much as four [women] from among the Mexica. They have excellent granular salt that they bring from a lake one day's journey from here.[75]

No information has been supplied by them concerning the Mar del Norte or the one in the west. I cannot tell Your Lordship which we may be closer to, although logically they must be nearer to the one in the west. I imagine [I am] a hundred and fifty leagues away from it and that the one in the north must be much farther away. Your lordship may see how much the land widens here.[76]

There are many animals: bears, tigers, lions,[77] and porcupines, and some wethers the size of horses, with very large horns and a small tail.[78] I have seen the horns of these [animals], and their size is something to be marveled at. There are wild goats,[79] heads of which I have also seen, and the claws of the bears and hides of the wild boars.[80] There are game animals such as deer, leopards, [and] very large deer.[81] Everyone has concluded that some may be larger than the beast [horse] that had belonged to Juan Melaz, which Your Lordship made me a gift of.

They have made eight days' journey toward the lands in the direction of the Mar del Norte.[82] In that place there were some well-tanned hides. [The Indians] do the tanning and painting in the place where they kill the [bison]. Those [who went there] tell [it] this way.

[362r]
{Concerning the condition and nature of the *reinos* of Totonteac, Marata, and Acus, [which are] contrary in every way to fray Marcos's report.[83] [Concerning] the conversation [the Christians] have with the Indians of the city of Granada ([which] had been captured by them). [How] for fifty years [the Indians] had expected the Christians' arrival in their lands. A report which they obtain from [the Indians] concerning another seven *ciudades*, of which the principal one is Tucano.[84] And how they dispatch [a unit] to reconnoiter it. A gift of various samples obtained under these circumstances [is] sent from Vázquez [de Coronado] to Mendoza.}

[First,] the *reino* of Totonteac, extolled so highly by the father provincial, who said that there were such marvelous things and such grandness there. And [further,] that [the natives] there made *paño*.[85] The Indians say, [instead,] that it is a hot lake, around which there are five or six dwellings. [They] also [say] that there used to be some others, but they have been destroyed during the wars. There is no *reino* of Marata here, nor do the Indians have any information about it. The *reino* of Acus is only one small *ciudad* called Acucu, where cotton is harvested. I say that this is a town, because Acus, with aspiration or without, is not a word [known] in [this] land, and because it seems to me that [the Indians] believe that Acucu is derived from Acus. I say that it is this town that has been transformed into the *reino* of Acus.[86] Farther beyond this settlement, they say, there are other small ones that are near a river I have understood and heard about from the Indians.[87]

God knows I would have wished to have better news to write Your Lordship, but I have to tell the truth. And as I have written you from Culiacán both about success and the opposite, I must inform you about this. You may be certain that [even] if all the wealth and treasure of the world were here, I would not have been able to do more in His Majesty's service and [that of] Your Lordship than I have done in coming to where he has directed me [to come]. My companions and I carried our food supply on our backs and on our horses for three hundred leagues, traveling on foot many days.[88] [We] made routes across cliffs[89] and through rugged mountains, along with other hardships I will omit telling. Nor do I intend to leave here short of death, if it be of service to His Majesty or Your Lordship that it be so.

When three days had passed after this *ciudad* was captured, some Indians came from those settlements to offer me peace. They brought some turquoises and poor, little *mantas*. I welcomed them in His Majesty's name with the best speeches I could, making them understand that my purpose in coming to this land, in His Majesty's name and by Your Lordship's command, is so that they and all the others in this *provincia* may be Christians and know the true God as their lord and His Majesty as their king and earthly lord. With this they returned to their houses.

But suddenly, on the next day, they packed up their belongings and food[90] and fled to the hills [with] their women and children, leaving their towns almost deserted, so that none remained except a few of them. Having seen this, when I had finished recovering from my wounds, some eight or ten days later, I traveled from here to the town I have said is larger than this one,[91] and I found a few of them there. I told them that they should not be afraid and that they were to summon their lord [to come] to me, although from what I have concluded and understood, none of these towns has one [a lord]. [I say this] because I have not seen even one important house here, from which the superiority of any [person] over another might be distinguished.

Later, an elderly man came. He said he was the lord and [brought] part of a *manta* made of many pieces. I reasoned with him some, so that he stayed with me. He said that in three days he would return with the rest of the *principales* of the town, in order to see me and arrange the form [of relations] that would be necessary with them. They did so and brought me some small, old *mantas* and some turquoises.

They agreed that they would have to come down from their hills and return here with their wives and children to their houses. And [further], that they would be Christians and recognize His Majesty as their king and lord. But up to the present they are still keeping their wives and children and all the goods they have in their fortified places.

I directed them, if they were willing, to paint [images] on cloth of the animals they know about in that land. Thus, [although they are] poor painters, and they are, they quickly painted me two cloths, one [depicting] the animals and the other, the birds and fishes. They say they will bring their children, so that our ecclesiastics may teach them. And [further,] that they are anxious to know our laws. They assert that it was said among them more than fifty years ago that a people like us must come, from the direction we have come, and that they would subjugate this whole land.

According to what has been understood up to the present, what these Indians venerate is water. [I say this] because they say it generates their corn and sustains life. And they know of no other reason except [362v] that their forefathers did likewise.

I have made every possible effort to learn from the natives of these settlements whether they have information concerning other peoples, *provincias,* and *ciudades.* And they tell me about seven towns that are far from here and are like these. However, [those people] do not live in houses like these. Instead, they are small and made of earth. And much cotton is harvested among them.[92] The first of these four places they know about they say is called Tucano. They are not being clear to me about the other ones. I believe they are not telling me the truth, thinking that in any case I would have to leave them soon and turn back from here. But they will soon be disabused about that.

I am sending don Pedro de Tovar to see it with his company and some other horsemen. I would not have dispatched this bundle of documents to Your Lordship as long as I had not learned what [that place] is, if I had thought that within twelve or fifteen days it would have been possible to have word from him.[93] [But] because he will take at least thirty days, and when I considered that this information may be of little importance, and that already the cold and rains are approaching, it seemed to me that I should do what Your Lordship directed me [to do] in your instruction. Namely, that as soon as I was here, I should notify you. I am doing so by sending the single report about what I have seen, which is quite poor, as will be seen.

I have determined, next, to dispatch [parties] throughout the whole environs to obtain information about everything and first to suffer every disaster before abandoning this enterprise;[94] to be of service to His Majesty, if it happens it can be done here; and not to be lacking in diligence until Your Lordship orders what I am to do.

We have a great need of pasture. You are to know also that among all [of the people] who are here there is not a pound of raisins, nor [is there] sugar, oil, or wine, except for about half a *quarta,*[95] which is reserved for mass. [This is] because everything has been consumed and part of it lost along the way. Now, you can supply us whatever will seem [appropriate] to you. If you think you want to send us livestock, be aware that they will need to spend at least a year en route. [That is] because [if it is done] in some other way and more quickly, not a single one will be seen here.

With this dispatch I would have liked to send Your Lordship many samples of things there are in this land, but the journey is so long and rough that it is difficult for me to do so. However, I am sending you twelve small *mantas* of the type the people of [this] land customarily wear and a garment that seems to me to be well made. I kept it because it appears to me to be very nicely embroidered [and] because I do not believe that anything has been seen [before] in these Indies embroidered with a needle, except since the Spaniards have been living there. I am also sending you two cloths painted with [images of] the animals there are in this land, even though, as I say, the picture may be very poorly done. [That is] because the "master" took no more than a day to paint it. I have seen other paintings on the walls of the houses[96] of this *ciudad* with much better proportions and better done.

I am sending you a [bison] hide, some turquoises, two ear pendants made of the same [material], fifteen combs the Indians [use], some tablets decorated with turquoise, and two small, decorated, wicker baskets, of which the Indians have a great abundance. I am also sending you two small [bearer's rings] that the women here customarily wear on their heads when they carry water from the spring, in the same way as [the women do] in Spain. One of these Indian women, with one of these rings on her head, will carry a jar of water up a ladder without touching it with her hands. In addition, I am sending you an example of the arms and armor the natives of this land fight with: a round shield, a club, and a bow with some arrows. Among the latter there are two with certain bone points, which, according to what the conquistadores who are here report, are different from those that have been seen before.[97]

From what I am able to conclude, there does not appear to me to be any prospect of obtaining gold and silver, but I trust in God that if it exists here we will obtain it.[98] And it will not remain [unlocated] for lack of seeking it.[99]

I cannot tell Your Lordship about the women's clothing with any certainty. [That is] because the Indians keep [the women] so carefully guarded that until now I have seen no more than two elderly women, and these had two long shifts [that hang] to their feet. [They are] open in front and belted.[100] And they are fastened with some cotton cords. I asked the Indians to give me one of those [garments the women] customarily wore to send to you, since they did not want to show me the women. And they brought me two

mantas, which are these I am sending you. [They look] almost as if they were painted.[101] [The women] wear two earrings, like the women [do] in Spain. Some hang down their backs.

The death of the Moor is a certainty, because many of the things he was carrying have been found here. The Indians told me they [had] killed him here because the Indians from Chichilticale [had] told them he was a wicked man and not like the Christians. [That was] because the Christians did not kill anyone's women, but he did kill them. And [they killed him] also because [363r] he was touching their women, whom the Indians love more than themselves. Therefore they decided to kill him, but they did not do it in the way that was reported.

[I say this] because they did not kill any of those who had come with him. Nor did they wound the youth from the *provincia* of Petatlán who was with him. Instead, they took him prisoner and have held him closely guarded up until now. When I tried to get him back, they refused to give him up for two or three days, saying that he was dead. And other times [they said] that the Indians of Acucu had led him away. But finally, when I told them I would become extremely angry if they did not give him to me, they turned him over to me. He is [now] acting as interpreter. Although he may not be fluent at speaking, he nevertheless understands [the language] well.

In this place some gold and silver have been found.[102] Those who understand mining have thought it not bad.[103] To this point I have been unable to extract from these people where they dug it up. And I see that they refuse to tell me the truth about everything, imagining, as I have said, that soon I will have to depart from here. Nevertheless, I trust in God that they will not be able to avoid it any longer.

I beg Your Lordship to report to His Majesty about the outcome of this journey, because I have no more to say than I have [already] said. In the meantime, may it please God that we find that which we desire. May [the Indians] not do it [continue to obstruct us]. May God, Our Lord, protect and preserve Your Most Illustrious Lordship.

From the *provincia* of Cíbola and this *ciudad* of Granada, the third of August 1540. Francisco Vázquez de Coronado kisses Your Most Illustrious Lordship's hands.

TRANSCRIPTION

[fol. 359v]

{RELATIONE CHE MANDÒ FRANCESCO / Vazquez di Coronado, Capitano Generale della gente che fu mandata / in nome di Sua Maesta al paese nuovamente scoperto, quel che / successe nel viaggio dalli ventidua d'Aprile di questo anno / MDXL. che parti da Culiacan per innanzi, & di quel che / trovò nel paese dove andava.

Francesco Vazquez con essercito parte di Culiacan, et dop(p)o il patire diversi incommodi nel mal Viag- / gio, gi(o)*u*nge alla Valle de i Caraconi, la ritrova sterile di Maiz: per (h)averne, manda nella Valle / detta del Signore, ha relatione della grandezza della Valle di Caraconi, & di / quelli popoli, & di alcune Isole poste in quelle costiere.}

ALli ventiduoi del Mese d'Aprile passato, parti dalla provincia di Culiacan / con parte dell'essercito & con l'ordine che io scrissi à V*ostra* S*ignoria* & secondo il suc- / cesso tengo per certo che si indovino à non metter*e* tutto l'essercito unito in / questa impresa, perche sono stati cosi grandi i travagli & mancamento della / vettovaglia che credo che in tutto questo anno non si potesse effettuar*e* la / impresa, et gia che si effettuasse sarebbe con gran perdita di gente, perche co- / me scrissi à V*ostra* S*ignoria* io feci il viaggio di Culiacan in ottanta giorni di strada, la- / quale, io & quei gentil'(h)uomini à cavallo miei compagni portam*m*o su le spalle & ne nostri ca- / valli, un poco di vettovaglia, in modo che da questa impo*si* no*n* portammo niun di noi d'altre / rob(b)e necessarie tanto che passasse una libra, & con tutto cio, & con l'essersi messa in questa / poca vettovaglia che portammo tutta quella regola & ordine possibile, ci mancò, & non è / da farsene maraviglia, perche il ca*m*mino è aspro & lungo, & fra gli archibusi che si portavano / nel sal(l)ire

delle montagne & coste, & nel passar*e* de i fiumi ci si guastò la maggior parte del / Maiz: & perche io mando à V*ostra* S*ignoria* dipinto *di* questo viaggio no*n* le diro in cio altro per q*ue*sta mia.

Trenta leghe prima che si arrivasse al luogo che il padre Provinciale nella sua relatione / cosi ben diceva, mandai Melchior Diaz con quindici da cavallo innanzi, ordinandogli che / facesse di due giornate una, acciocche (h)avessi esami-nato[104] il tutto quando io gi(o)*u*ngessi: ilqua- / le, camminò quattro giorni per certe montagne asprissime, et non trovò quivi ne da vivere, / ne ge*n*te, ne information di alcuna cosa, eccetto che trovò due ò tre povere villette, di venti / ò trenta capanne l'una, & da gli (h)abitatori di essa seppe che da li avanti non si trovava se non / asprissime montagne che continovavano, disabitate da tutte le genti, & perche era cosa per- / duta, non vol*l*(s)i di qui mandar*e* di cio messo à V*ostra* S*ignoria* diedi dispiacere à tutti i compagni, che una / cosa tanto lodata, & di che il padre (h)aveva detto tante cose si fosse trovato tanto al contra- / rio, & si fece giudi(c)zio che il rimanente fosse tutto di quella sorte. Et veduto io questo, procu- / rai di rallegrargli al meglio che io potei, dicendogli che V*ostra* S*ignoria* sempre (h)ebbe oppinione che / questo viaggio fosse una cosa g(i)*e*ttata via, & che dovessimo metter*e* il nostro pe*n*siero in quelle / sette

[fol. 360r]

360

sette Citta, & l'altre provincie di che (h)avevamo noti(t)zia che quivi sarebbe il fine della nostra / impresa, & con questa resolu(t)zione, et disegno tutti cam*m*inam*m*o con allegrezza per molto mal / cam*m*ino che non si poteva passar*e* senza ò farne uno, ò rindrizzare[105] quel sentiero che vi era, di / che non eran poco afflitti i soldati, veduto che tutto quel che (h)aveva detto il frate si trovava / al rove(r)scio, perche fra l'altre cose che il padre diceva, et affermava, era che il camino fosse pia- / no, & buono, & che non ci era senon[106] una picciola costa di mezza lega. Et è vero, che vi sono / montagne, che con tutto che si racconciasse ben la strada, non vi si poteva passare senza gran / pericolo di traboccarvi i cavalli, & era tale che del bestiame che *Vostra Signoria* mandò per provisione / dell'essercito ve ne rimase gran parte in questo viaggio, per l'asprezza del sasso: gli agnelli, / & castrati, lasciavano l'ungie per terra, & di quei che condussi da Culiacano, la maggior parte / lasciai nel fiume di Lachimi, perche non potevan caminare, & perche venissero pian piano, / rimasero con essi quattro (h)uomini à cavallo che son arrivati (h)ora, ne (h)avevano condotti piu di / ventiquattro agnelli, & quattro castrati, che il rimanente rimase morto per quella balza, se ben / non si caminò se non due leghe, & riposato ci qualche di, arrivai poi alla valle de i Coraconi, / alli ventisei di, del mese di Maggio, & da Culiacano fino li, non mi prevalsi, se non di una gran / massa di pane di Maiz, perche non essendo i maizali stagionati mi convenne lasciarli tutti. / In questa valle de Coraconi trovammo piu gente che in niuna parte di tutto il paese che (h)ave- / vamo lasciato à dietro, & gran quantià di semenze, ma non ci è fra loro Maiz da mangiare, / ma si ben intesi esserne in un'altra valle chiamata del Signor, che non voll(s)i molestare con for- / za ma vi mandai con robba di baratto per (h)averne, Melchior Diaz, per darne à gli Indiani / amici che conducevamo con noi, & per alcuni che (h)avevano perdute delle bestie nel viaggio, / & non (h)avevano potuto portarsi vettovaglia dietro che condussero fuori di Culiacano fino li: / piacque à nostro Signor che si (h)ebbe con questi baratti qualche poco di Maiz, con che si r(e)i- / mediarono gli Indiani amici, & alcuni Spagnuoli, & fino à questa valle di Coraconi rimase- / ro morti di stracchezza qualche dieci ò dodici nostri cavalli, perche portando gran carichi, / & mangiando poco, non poterono sopportare la fatica. Similmente ci si partirono alcuni no- / stri mori, & alcuni Indiani che non ci fu di poco mancamento per il servigio della impresa. / Questa valle de i Coraconi mi dicono essere lunga cinque giornate dal mare di ponente, / mandai à chiamare gli Indiani della costa per

informarmi dell'essere loro, & in tanto che gli / aspettavo, si riposassero i cavalli: & vi dimorai quattro giorni, ne quali vennero gli Indiani / del mare, che mi dissero, che due giornate da quella costa di mare, erano sette, ò otto Isole al / dritto di loro, bene popolate di gente, ma povere di vettovaglia, & era gente brutta, & mi dis- / sero (h)avere veduto passare una nave non molto lunge da terra, che non so pensare se era di quei / che andavano à scoprire il paese, ò pur di Portugallesi.

{Giungono a Chichilticale dop(p)o l'(h)avere preso due giornate di riposo, entrano in paese molto sterile di / Vettovaglie, & difficile Viaggio per trenta leghe; oltra'l quale ritrovano paese assai ameno, & / il fiume detto del Lino, combattono contra gli Indiani essendo da lor assaltati, et con / Vittoria acquistata la lor città, si sollevano dal disagio della fame.}

Mi parti da i Coraconi, & sempre mi accostavo piu al mare al mio giudi(c)zio, & con effet- / to sempre me gli ritrovavo piu lontano, in modo che quando giunsi à Chichilticale, mi ritro- / vavo lunge dal mare quindici giornate, & il padre provinciale diceva che vi era distantia so- / lamente da cinque leghe, & che egli l'(h)avea veduto. Ricevemmo tutti grande affanno, & con- / fusione con vedere che ogni cosa trovavamo al rove(r)scio di quel che (h)aveva detto à *Vostra Signoria*. Gli / Indiani di Chichilticale, dicono che se vanno mai al mare per pesce, & altre cose, che portano, / vanno traversando, & vi fanno dieci giornate, & mi pare che fosse vera l'informatione ch'io (h)eb- / bi da gli Indiani. Il mare si rivolta à ponente à quel dritto de i Coraconi per dieci ò dodici le- / ghe, dove compresi che f(u)ossero comparse le navi di *Vostra Signoria* che andavano à cercare il porto di / Chichilticale che il padre disse che stava in trentacinque gradi, Iddio sa la pena che io ne ho, / perche temo che non gli avvenga qualche disgratia, et se essi seguiranno la costa, come dissero, fino / che loro durera il vivere che portano con esso loro, di che io gli lasciai provisione in Culiaca- / no, & se non saranno incorsi in qualche contrarietà sperero bene in Dio che (h)abbiano gia sco- / perto qualche cosa buona, & con questo se gli perdonera il tardare che hanno fatto. In Chichilti- / cale

[fol. 360v]

cale mi riposai duoi giorni, & sarebbe bisognato che ce ne fosse stato piu, secondo che ci tro- / vavamo stanchi i cavalli, ma perche ci mancava la vettovaglia non ci fu dato luogo à riposare / piu: entrai nel fine del paese disabitato la vigilia di San Giovanni, & per rifrigerio de i tra- / vagli passati, ne i primi giorni non trovammo (h)erba, ma peggior cammino di montagne & / cattivi passi, che non (h)avevamo fatto per l'ad*d*ietro, & venendo i cavalli stanchi, se ne sentirono / molto, in modo che in questo ultimo deserto perdemmo piu cavalli che non (h)avevamo fat- / to per l'ad*d*ietro, & mi morirono alcuni Indiani amici & uno Spagnuolo che si chia- / mava / Spinosa, & duoi mori che morirono mangiando certe (h)erbe per esserli mancata la vettova- / glia. Da questo luogo feci andare innanzi à me una giornata il mastro di campo Don Gar- / zia Lopez di Cardena con quindici cavalli perche discoprisero il paese, & perche ridrizzas- / sero il cammino, al quale si è affaticato da quel (h)uomo che egli è & conforme alla confidanza / che vostra Signoria (h)aveva nella sua persona. So che non gli mancò da fare, perche come / gl'ho detto, il ca*m*mino è tristissimo, almeno le trenta leghe & piu, per essere montagne inaccessi- / bili, ma passate q*u*este trenta leghe, trova*m*mo fiumi freschi, et del (h)erba come q*u*ella di Castiglia, et / specialme*n*te di una sorte che noi chiamiamo scaramoio, molti alberi di noce & di mori, ma le / noci sono differenti da quelle della Spagna nella foglia, & vi*di* era lino massimame*n*te alla riva / di una fiumana, & perciò si chiama il fiume del lino. Non si trovò quasi niuno Indiano fino à / una giornata, di quivi poi uscirono, 4. Indiani in atto di pace, dicendo che eran stati mandati / fino à quel luogo deserto à dirche noi fossimo i benvenuti, che l'atro giorno saria uscita al- / la strada tutta la gente con vettovaglia. Et il mastro di campo diede loro una croce, dicendo- / gli dovessero dire à quei della lor città che non dovessero temere, et che dovessero pure lasciare che / la gente se ne stess(i)e nelle proprie case, perche io venivo sola- mente in nome di sua Maesta / per difendergli & ai*u*targli: & cio fatto ritornò Ferrando Alvarado à dirmi che erano venuti / certi Indiani in atto di pace: & che duoi di essi mi aspettavano col mastro di campo, onde io / andai à loro, & gli donai de i paternostri & certi mantelli, dicendogli che

ritornassero alla / città & dicessero che dovessero stare tutti cheti nelle lor case & che non dovessero temere, & / cio fatto ordinai al mastro di campo che andasse à vedere se vi fosse qualche mal passo che gli / Indiani (h)avesser potuto difendere, & che lo pigliasse & difendesse fino all'altro di che io / vi sarei giunto, & cosi andò, & trovò nella strada un passo ben cattivo, dove (h)avremmo po- / tuto ricevere gran male, onde quivi si pose egli con la gente che conduceva, & quella mede- / sima notte vennero gli Indiani à pigliare quel passo per difenderlo, & trovatolo preso, assal- / taron i nostri quivi, & secondo che mi dicono, gli assaltaron da (h)uomini valorosi anc(h)ora / che alla fine ritornassero à dietro fuggendo, perche il mastro di campo veg(h)*i*ava et era all'or- / dine con i suoi, toccarono una trombettina gli Indiani in segno di raccolta, & non fecero al- / cuno danno ne gli Spagnuoli. La notte medesima mi diede di cio aviso il mastro di campo, / onde il di seguente col miglior ordine che potei parti con tanto mancamento di vettovaglia / che pensai che dovendo aspettare piu un giorno saremmo morti di fame tutti, massimamen- / te gli Indiani perche fra tutti noi non (h)avevamo due mine di Maiz, onde mi convenne / spingere oltra senza tardare. Gli Indiani à passo per passo facevano i lor fumi, & gliera da / lunge risposto con tanto concerto quanto (h)avessimo saputo fare noi, acciocche si fosse dato / aviso come noi andavamo & dove eravamo giunti. Subito che io arrivai à vista di questa / città mandai Don Garzia lopez mastro di campo, frate Daniello, & frate Luigi, et Ferrando / Vermizzo alquanto innanzi con alcuna gente da cavallo perche ritrovassero gli Indiani & / gli dicessero che la venuta nostra non era per farlor danno, ma per difendergli in nome del- / lo Imperatore Signor nostro, il ric*h*er(c)amento in forma come sua Maesta comanda per in- / struttione, il che si diede à intendere per interprete à i naturali di quel paese, ma essi lo stima- / ron poco come gente superba, perche pareva lor che noi fossimo pochi, & che non (h)avreb- / bono (h)avuto difficulta di ucciderci, & ferirono fra Luigi di una fre(zz)*c*cia nell'(h)abito, che piac- / que à Dio che non li fece male: in questo giunsi io con tutto il resto de i cavalli & pedoni, & / trovai in campagna gran parte de gli Indiani che si mossero à tirarci con le fre(zz)*c*ce, & io per / ob*b*edire il parere di vostra Signoria & del Marchese non vol*l*(s)i che si desse dentro, pro(h)iben- / do à compagni, che mi sollecitavano à farlo, che non dovessero muoverli, & che quel che / facevano i nimici non era niente, & che non era d'affrontar*e* si poca gente. Dall'altra ban- / da gli

[fol. 361r]

361

da gli Indiani per veder*e* che noi non ci movevamo piglia-vano maggior animo & alterez- / za tanto che si appressa-vano alle gambe de i nostri cavalli à tirarci delle fre(zz)*cc*e, onde vedu- / to che non era piu tempo da stare, & che cosi pareva à i religiosi, diede dentro & ci fu poco / che fare, perche subito fuggirono in parte alla Città che era vicina, & ben fortificata, & altri / per la campagna, dove gli guidava la ventura, & morirono alcuni Indiani, & piu sarebbono / morti se io l'(h)avessi consentito che si fossero seguitati, però veduto che di ciò ci poteva venir*e* / poco frutto, perche gli Indiani che erano fuori, eran*o* pochi, & quei che si erano riti-rati nella / Citta con quei che vi erano rimas*ti* prima erano molti, dove era la vettovaglia di che (h)aveva- / mo tanto di bisogno, raccolsi tutta la mia gente, & la divisi come meglio mi parve per com- / batter*e* la Città, & la circundai: & perche la fame che noi (h)avevamo non pativa dila(t)zione, io / smontai con alcuni di questi gentill'(h)uomini, & soldati, & comandai che i balestrieri, & ar- / chibusieri facessero empito, & levassero dalle dif(f)ese i nimici, accioche no*n* ci facessero danno, / & io assaltai le mura da una banda, dove mi dissero che era stata appoggiata una scala leva- / toia, & che vi*di* era una porta, ma à balestrieri si ro*m*perono tosto le corde delle balestre, & gli ar- / chibusieri no*n* fecero nulla, percio che venivano cosi deboli, & fiacchi, che quasi non si pote- / vano sostenere in piedi, & in questo modo le genti che erano all'alto per difendere non (h)eb- / bero disturbo alcuno di poter*e* far*e* sopra di noi il danno che potevano, onde à me, mi g(i)ettaron / due volte in terra con infinite pietre grande, che gittavano dall'alto, & se io non fosse stato / difeso da una bonissima armatura di testa che io portavo, penso che mi sarebbe successo ma- / le, tuttavia mi tolsero di terra con due picciole ferite in faccia, & una fre(zz)*cci*a nel piede, & con / molte sassate nelle braccia, & gambe, & in questa maniera usci della battaglia ben stanco, / pe*n*so che se Don Garzia lopez di Cardena*s* la seconda volta che mi

gittarono per terra no*n* mi / (h)avesse aiutato con por*re* la sua persona come ḅuon cavaliero sopra la mia, (h)av(e)rei corso assai / maggior pericolo di quel che corsi, ma piacque à Dio che gli Indiani ci si resero, & fu nostro / Signor servito che si prese questa città, & si trovò in essa tanta abbondanza di Maiz, quanto / la nostra necessità ricercava. Uscendo[107] il Mastro di Campo, & Don Pietro di Tovar, & Fe- / r*n*ando di Alvarado, & Paulo di Melgosa Capitani della fanteria con alcune sassate, anc(h)ora / che non fussino[108] feriti niun di essi, fu ferito Agoniez quarez in un braccio di una fre(zz)*cci*ata, & / à Torres (h)abitator*e* di Panuco in faccia di un'altra, & altri duoi pedoni furon*o* feriti di due fre(z)- / (z)*cci*ate ancora picciole: & perche eran le mie armi dorate, & rilucenti tutti car(r)icavono[109] addos- / so à me, & per questa cagione rimasi piu ferito de glialtri, no*n* per (h)aver*e* *f*atto piu, & messomi / piu innanzi de gli altri, perche tutti questi gentil'(h)uomini, & soldati si portarono cosi be- / ne, come si sperava di loro. Io (h)ora sto bene lodato sia Iddio, anchora che alquanto pesto dal- / le pietre. Nella battaglia che (h)avemmo in campagna similmente, rimasero feriti duoi ò tre / altri compagni, & vi rimasero morti tre cavalli, l'un di Don Lopez, & l'altro di Vigliega, & / il terzo di Don Alfonso Manrich, & vi furono altri sette ò otto cavalli feriti, ma (h)ora cosi / gli (h)uomini, come i cavalli sono guariti, & ben sani.

{Del sito, & stato delle sette Città dette il Regno di Cevola, & de costumi, & qualità de suoi popoli, & / delli animali che quivi si ritr(u)ovano.}

Restami (h)ora à dar*e* conto delle sette città, & Regni, & Provincie, di che il padre Provin- / ciale diede relatione à Vostra Signoria, & per non dilatarmi molto, posso dirle in verità che / in niuna cosa che disse, ha detto il vero, ma è stato tutto al rove(r)scio, eccetto nel nome delle cit- / tà, & delle case grandi di pietra, perche avve*n*ga che sian lavorate di turchino, ne di calcina, ne / di mattoni sono, nondimeno bonissime case, di tre, di quattro, & di cinque solari, dove sono / boni alloggiamenti, & belle stanze con cor*r*ido(r)i, & certe stanze sotto terra assai buone, & / mattonate, le quali son fatte per lo inverno, & sono quasi alla maniera delle stufe, & le scale / che hanno per le lor case son*o* quasi tutte levatoie, et portatili, che si levano & mettono quan- / do lor piace, & sono fatte di dua legni con i lor scaloni[110] come le nostre. Le sette città, sono sette / terre[111] picc(i)ole tutte di queste case che io dico, & stano tutte vicine à quattro leghe, & si chiama- / no tutti Regno di Cevola, & ciascuna ha il suo nome, & niuna si chiama Cevola, ma tutte in / insieme si chiamano Cevola, & questa che io chiamo città, gli ho posto nome Granata, cosi, / perche

[fol. 361v]

perche ne ha qualche simiglianza come per la memoria di vostra Signoria. In questo dove / io sto (h)ora alloggiato poss(i)ano esservi qualche dugento case tutte circondate di muro, & / parmi che con l'altre che non sono cosi, poss(i)ano arrivare à cinquecento fuochi. Vi è un'altra / terra vicina, che è una delle sette, & è alquanto maggior di questa, et un'altra della medesima gran- / dezza di questa, & le altre quattro sono alquanto minori, & tutte io le mando dipinte à / vostra Signoria con il viaggio: & pergamino dove va la pittura si trovo qui con altri per- / gamini. La gente di queste terre mi pare ragionevolmente grande, & accorta, però non / l'ho per tale che mi paia che arriv(i)a col giudicio & intelletto à sapere fare queste case nel modo / che sono, per la maggiore parte van tutti nudi, pero coperti delle vergogne loro, & hanno / mantelli dipinti della maniera che io mando à vostra Signoria, non raccolgono bombaso / per essere il paese frigidissimo, però ne portano mantelli come ella vedra per la mostra, & è / vero che si ritrovò nelle lor case certo bambaso filato: portano in testa cap(p)elli come quei di / Messico, & sono tutti ben creati & disposti, & hanno delle Turchine pensò in quantita, le- / quali col rimanente delle rob(b)e che (h)aveano eccetto il Maiz, (h)avevano fuggito quando io / giunsi, perche non vi trovai donna alcuna ne giovane di quindici anni à basso, ne da sessanta / in su, eccetto dui ò tre vecchi quivi rimas(i)ero per comandare à tutti gli altri giovanni & (h)uomi- / ni da guerra, si trovarono in una carta due punte di smeraldi & certe picciole pietre rotte che / tirano al color di granate assai cattive & altre pietre di cristallo che io diedi à riporre à un / mio creato per mandarle à Vostra Signoria & le ha perdut(u)e secondo che mi dicono: si trovarono galline però / poche, pur ce ne sono: in tutte queste sette terre mi dicono gli Indiani che non le mangiano,

ma / che solo le tengono per prevalersi della penna, io non gli(e)lo credo perche sono bonissime & / maggiori che quelle di Messico. Il tempo che è in questo paese & la temperie dell'aere è / quasi come quella di Messico, percioche (h)ora è caldo & (h)ora piove, però non ho veduto insino / à qui piovere mai, ma si ben è venuta una piovegina picciola con vento come quelle che so- / gliono cadere in Spagna. Le neve & i freddi sogliono essere molto grandi, perche cosi dicono i / nativi del paese, & pare ben che sia cosi & nella maniera della terra & nella sorte delle stanze / loro & le pelli & altre cose che queste genti tengono per difendersi dal freddo. Non vi è / niuna sorte di frutti ne di alberi di essi. E paese tutto piano & da niuna banda si scorge essere / montagne anc(h)ora che vi sia qualche poggi(o) & passo cattivo. Uccelli ve ne sono pochi, de(b)- / (b)velo causare il freddo, & per non vi essere montagne vicine. Quivi non sono molti alberi / per fare legna, postoche per abbruciarne[112] per loro uso ve ne (h)abbiano à bastanza[113] à quattro / leghe lunge da una selva di cedri molto picciole. Si trovò bonissima (h)erba à un quatro di / legha di qua per i nostri cavalli cosi per pascerli in passata in (h)erba, come segata per fieno, di / che (h)avevamo gran bisogno per essere giunti quivi i nostri cavalli cosi stanchi & lassi. La / vettovaglia che hanno quelli di questo paese è il Maiz, di che ne hanno essi grande abbondan- / (ti)za, & di fa(su)gioli & cacciagione che essi debbono mangiare (postoche dicono che no), per- / che si trovarono molte pelle di cervi, di lepri, & di conigli. Mangiono le migliori tortelle che / io (h)abbia veduto in alcuna parte, & le mangiano generalmente tutti. Hanno il piu bello or- / dine & pulitezza nel macinare che si sia veduto altrove, & macina tanto una Indiana di / quelle di questo paese quanto quattro di quelle di Messico. Hanno bonissimo sale in grano / che levano da un lag(ume)o che è lunge una giornata di qua. Niuna noti(t)zia è appres(s)to di loro / del mare del settentrione ne di quel di ponente, ne saprei dire à vostra Signoria a qual siamo / piu vicini, postoche ragionevolmente siano piu vicini à quel di ponente: & al piu vicino mi tr(u)o- / vo lontano da esso à centocinquanta leghe, et quel di settentrione deve essere assai piu lontano. / Veda vostra Signoria quanto si allarga qui la terra. Vi sono di molti animali, orsi, tigri, Leo- / ni, & porciSpin(os)i, & certi castrati della grandezza d'un cavallo, con corni molto grandi & / code picciole. Ho veduto i corni di essi che è cosa di maraviglia la sua grandezza. Vi sono / delle capre salvati che, delle quali ho similmente vedute le teste, & le branche de gli orsi, & le / pelli de i cing(g)hial(i)e. Vi sono cacciagioni di Cèrvi, Pardi, Cavrioli molto grandi: & tutti Hanno / giudicato che ve ne si(e)ano alcuni maggiori di quel animale di che Vostra Signoria mi fece gratia che era di / Giovan melaz fanno otto giornate verso le campagne[114] al mare di settentrione. Quivi sono certe / pelli ben conci(e)ati, & la concia & pittura gli danno dove uccidono le vacche, che cosi riferiscono essi / Del stato

[fol. 362r]
363
{Del stato & qualita delli Regni di Totonteac, Marata, & Acus, in tutto contraria alla relatione di / fra Marco, il parlamento che hanno con gli indiani della città di Granata da lor presa, iquali (h)a- / veano gia cinquanta anni preveduto la andata de Christiani ne loro paesi. Relatione che / da lor hanno di altre sette Città, delle quali è la principale Tucano, & come / mandano à discoprirle: presente di Varie mostre (h)avuto in quelli stati / dal Vazquez mandato al Mendozza.}

Il Regno di Totonteac tanto lodato dal padre provinciale, che diceva che vi erano cose si / maravigliose, & tante grandezze, & che vi si facevano panni: dicono gli Indiani essere un la- / go caldo, à torno alquale sono cinque ò sei case, & che ve ne soleavano essere certe altre, però che / sono state rovinate per le guerre. Il Regno di Marata non vi è, ne gli Indiani hanno di esso no- / titia alcuna. Il Regno di Acus è una città sola picciola, dove si raccoglie bombaso, che è chia- / mata Acucu, & dico che questa è una terra, perche Acus con aspiratione, ne senza non è vo- / cabolo del paese, & perche mi pare che Acucu vogliano tirarsi da Acus, dico che è questa ter- / ra, nellaquale si è convertito il Regno di Acus. Piu oltre di questo popolo, dicono che ve ne / sono altri piccioli che stanno vicino à un fiume che io l'ho veduto, & ho (h)avuto per relatione / da gl'Indiani. Iddio sa s'io (h)avessi voluto (h)avere miglior nuova da scrivere à Vostra Signoria: / però ho da dire il vero, & come l'ho scritto da Culiacano, cosi del prospero come dell'avver- / so io l'ho da avvisare: però sia certo che se quivi fossero tutte le ricchezze, & tesori del

mon- / do, io non (h)averei potuto fare piu in servi(t)zio di Sua Maesta, & di vostra Signoria, di quel che / ho fatto in venire dove mi ha comandato, portando i miei compagni & io, sopra le spalle tre- / cento leghe la vettovaglia, & ne i nostri cavalli: et molti giorni caminando à piedi, facendo ca- / mini per balze, & aspre montagne, con altri travagli che io lascio di dire, ne penso di partirmi / fino alla morte, se Sua Maesta, ò Vostra Signoria, sarà servita che cosi sia.

Passati tre giorni che si prese questa Città, vennero alcuni Indiani di quei popoli à offerir- / mi pace, & mi portarono alcune Turchine, & mantelletti cattivi, & io gli ricevetti in nome / di Sua Maesta con tutte le migliore parole ch'io potetti, dandogli à intendere il fine della mia / venuta in questo paese che è in nome di Sua Maesta, & per comandamento di Vostra Signo- / ria, perche essi, & tutti gliáltri di questa provincia debbono essere Christiani, & conoscono / il vero Iddio per lor Signore, & Sua Maesta per Re, & per lor Signore terreno, & con que- / sto se ne ritornarono alle lor case, & subito il giorno seguente posero in ordine le robbe, & so- / stanze loro, donne & figliuoli, et se ne fuggirono à i colli, lasciando quasi abbandonate le ter- / re loro, che non vi rimasero se non alcuni pochi di loro. Veduto questo di li à otto ò dieci / giorni che fui finito di guarire delle mie ferite, me n'andai alla terra che ho detto, che è mag- / gior di questa, & vi trovai pochi di loro, à quali dissi che non dovessero (h)avere paura, & che / chiamassero à me il Signore loro, ancora che per quel che ho inteso, & compreso, niuna di que- / ste terre lo (h)abbia, che non vi ho veduta niuna casa principale, dove si conosca niun vantag- / gio dall'altre. Venne poi un vecchio che disse che era il Signore con un pezzo di mantello fat- / to di molti pezzi, col quale io ragionai alquanto che restò con meco, & disse che di li à tre giorni / sarebbe venuto egli, & il resto de i principali della terra à vedermi, & à dare ordine del modo / che si ha da tenere con esso loro. Il che fecero, perche mi portarono certi mantelletti rotti, & alcu- / ne Turchine: rimasero di (h)avere à descendere da i loro poggi, & ritornarsene con le lor mo- / glie, & figliuoli alle lor case, & che sarebb(on)ero Christiani, & che (h)averiano[115] ricosciuto Sua / Maesta per lor Re, & Signore. Et fin qui ancora tengono in quei lor forti le donne, & fi- / gliuoli, & tutto il bene che hanno. Gli comandai che mi volessero dipingere un panno degli / animali di che hanno noti(t)zia in quel paese: & cosi cattivi pittori come sono, mi dipinsero pre- / sto due tele, una de gli animali, & l'altra di uccelli, & pesci. Dicono che condurranno i loro / figliuoli, accioche i nostri religiosi gli insegnino, & che desiderano di sapere la nostra legge, & / affermano che sono piu di cinquanta anni, che si disse fra loro che doveva venire una gen- / te de la sorte di noi altri, & dalla banda che siamo venuti, & che (h)avea à soggiogare tutto que- / sto paese. Quel che adorono questi Indiani secondo che si ha inteso fin qui, è l'acqua, perche / dicono che la gli genera il lor Maiz, & gli sostenta la vita, & che non sanno altra ragione se / non

[fol. 362v]

non che cosi facevano gli antichi loro. Ho procurato con ogni sforzo possibile di sapere / da i Naturali di questi popoli, se hanno noti(t)zia d'altre genti, provincie & citta, & mi dicono di / sette terre che stanno lontane di qua, che sono come queste, ancora che non (h)abitono case co- / me queste, ma sono di terracci(a)o,[116] & picciole, & che fra loro si raccoglie molto bombaso. Il pri- / mo di questi quattro luoghi di che hanno noti(t)zia, dicono che si chiama Tucano, & non mi / danno chiarezza d'altri, & credo che non mi dicano il vero, con pensiero che in ogni modo / io mi (h)abbia da partire presto da loro, & tornarmene à dietro. Ma di ciò rimarranno presto in- / gannati. Mando Don Pietro di Tovar à vederlo con la sua compagnia, & con alcuni altri / da cavallo, & non (h)av(e)rei spacciato questo plico alla Signoria vostra, finche non (h)avessi sa- / puto quel che n'è, se (h)avessi considerato che in dodici ò quindici giorni si fosse potuto (h)avere / nuova da lui, perche per il meno si tardera trenta *di*, & esaminato che questa noti(t)zia importi / poco, & che gia i freddi, & la'acque si av(v)icin(o)ano, mi parve di dovere fare quelche Vostra Si- / gnoria mi comandava per sua instru(tt)zione, che è, che subito, che io fosse quivi, la dovesse avisare, / & cosi faccio con mandare la sola relatione di quel che ho veduto, che è ben cattiva, come ella / vedrà. Io ho determinato di quivi mandare per tutto il contorno per (h)avere noti(t)zia d'ogni / cosa, & patire prima ogni esterminio,[117] prima che lasciare questa impresa, di fare il servi(t)zio di Sua / Maesta, se qua si trovera à farlo, & non mancarvi di diligenza: intanto che Vostra Signoria mi /

ordini quello ch'av(e)ro à fare. Noi (h)abbiamo gran carestia di pascoli, & sapere ancora che fra tut- / ti quei che sono quivi non vi'e una libra d'uva passa, ne zucchero, ne olio, ne vino, eccetto qual- / che mezza quarta che vi è riserbata per le messe che tutto si è consumato, & parte perduto / per la strada. (H)ora ella potra provederci di quelche le par(e)ra, & se pensera di volerci man- / dare bestiame, sappia che bisognera per il meno tardare un'anno nel camino, che in altro mo- / do & piu presto non vi ve(r)dra niuno. Io (h)av(e)rei voluto mandare à Vostra Signoria con questo / *di*spaccio molte mostre di cose che sono in questo paese: però il viaggio è si lungo, & aspro che / mi è difficile à farlo, però mandole dodici mantelli piccioli di quei che le genti del paese so- / gliono portare, et una veste, ancora che à me pare che sia ben fatta, guardaila, che à me pare che / la sia molto ben lavorata,[118] perche non credo che in queste Indie sia stata veduta cosa alcuna / lavorata à ago, se non doppo che gli Spagnuoli vi (h)abitano. Et le mando ancora duoi panni / dipinti de gl'animali che sono in questo paese, ancora che come dico la pittura sia molto mal / fatta, perche in dipingerla non vi consumò il mastro piu di un giorno. Io ho vedute altre pit- / ture nelle mura delle case di questa città con assai miglior proportione, & meglio fatte. / Le mando una pelle di vacca, certe Turchine, & duoi pendenti d'orec- / chie delle medesime, / & quindici pettin(i)e de gl'Indiani, & alcune tavolette guarnite di queste Turchine, & duoi / canestretti di vim(e)ine lavorati, di che gli Indiani hanno grande abbondanza. Le mando / similmente due coroglie di quelle che accostumano quivi le donne portare in testa, quando / portano l'acqua dalla fontana, alla maniera di quei di Spagna. Et una Indiana di queste con / una di queste coroglie[119] in testa, portera un Cantaro d'acqua senza tocarlo con mano superando / una scala. Le mando similmente la mostra dell'armi con che combattono i Naturali di que- / sto paese, una rotella, una mazza, & un'arco con alcune fre(zz)cce, fra le quali ve ne sono due di / certe punte di osso, che secondo che riferiscono questi conquistatori, non se ne sono vedute / simili. per quel che posso considerare non mi pare che vi sia speranza di (h)avere oro ne argen- / to, però spero in Dio che se ve ne sara noi ne (h)av(e)remo ne si rest(a)era per mancamento di cer- / carne. De i vestimenti delle donne non posso dire à Vostra Signoria certezza alcuna, perche / gli Indiani le tengono con tanta guardia che fin qui non ho veduto se non due vecchie, & / questa (h)ave*v*ano due camicie lunghe fino à piedi aperte davanti, & cinte, & sono affibbiate, / con cert(i)*e* cordon(i)*e* di bambaso. Domandai à gli Indiani che me ne dessero una di quelle che / portavano per mandargliela poiche non mi volevano mostrare le donne, & mi portarono / duoi manti che so*n*o questi, che gli mando, quasi come dipinti, hanno duoi pendenti come le / donne di Spagna, che pendono alquanto sopra le spalle. La morte del moro è cosa certa, / perche qua si sono trovate molte cose di quelle che portava, & mi dicono gli Indiani che l'uc- / cisero quivi, perche gli Indiani di Chichiticale gli dissero che era un tristo, & no*n* come i Chri- / stiani, perche i Christiani non uccidono le donne à niuno, & egli le uccideva, & perche anco[120] / toccava

[fol. 363r]
363
toccava le donne loro che gli Indiani le amano piu che s(e)*i* stessi, pero determinaron di ucci- / derlo, ma non lo fecero nel modo che fu ri(s)*f*erito, perche non uccisero niuno altro di quei che / veniva*n*o co*n* esso lui, ne ferirono quel giovanetto che era seco della provincia di Petatlan, ma / ben

lo presero & lo han*n*o tenuto con buona guardia fino adesso, & qua*n*do io ho procurato di / (h)averlo, si sono (e)scusati du*o*i ò tre di, di darlo, dice*n*domi che era morto, & altre volte che lo (h)a- / vevano menato via gli Indiani di Acucu. Ma al fine dicendogli io che mi adir(er)ei molto se / non me l'(h)avesse*r*o dato, me lo dierono.[121] E interprete che ancora che non sia atto à parlare / però intende molto bene. In questo luogo si è trovato alquanto oro & argento, che quei / che si intendo*n*o di miniera non lo ha*n*o reputato per cattivo: fin qui non ho potuto cavar*e* da / q*u*este genti donde se lo cavino, & vedo che negano di dirmi il vero in tutte le cose, con pensar*e* / che io in breve come ho detto mi debb(i)*a* partir*e* de qui, però spero in Dio che non potran*n*o piu / scusarsi: supplico vostra Signoria che faccia relatio*n*e à sua Maesta del successo di questo viag- / gio, perche per no*n* (h)aver*e* piu di quel che ho detto & fintantoche piacera à Dio che ci incon- / triamo in quel che desideriamo non lo facci*a*no. Nostro Signor Dio guardi & conservi vo- / stra Signoria Illustrissima. Dalla provincia di Cevola & da questa città di Granata il / terzo di Agosto. 1540. Francesco Vazquez di Coronado bacia le mani / di vostra Signoria Illustrissima.

Document 20

Formation of a Company between Mendoza and Pedro de Alvarado, Tiripitío, November 29, 1540

AGI, Patronato, 21, N.3, R.2

INTRODUCTION

Expansion of Spanish sovereignty in the New World was accomplished almost entirely by private initiative, often sanctioned by the royal court.[1] There was no royal master plan for occupation of the Western Hemisphere. Instead, backers and organizers of an expedition of reconnaissance and conquest typically petitioned the monarch for permission to undertake their proposed enterprise. Granting of such permission did not ordinarily result in royal financial support for the undertaking. But it did serve to discourage others from infringing on the target territory of the planned *entrada*, and the king handsomely rewarded the successful incorporation of large numbers of sophisticated and affluent people into the Spanish orbit. Sometimes, with hindsight, the king's rewards to conquistadores seemed too sweeping or too lavish, necessitating the tricky business of subsequently amending agreements and scaling back grants, as occurred most famously in the case of Hernán Cortés.[2]

The course of Spanish conquest was thus driven by personal and local ambition. The existence of two huge, populous, and previously unknown continents presented the prospect of incredibly rich prizes to be earned in pursuit of what seemed an obviously righteous cause: enlargement of the Spanish Empire and swelling of the congregation of the Catholic Church. One result was a nearly feverish pace of ferreting out prosperous native populations throughout the 1500s, but especially in the first half of the century. According to our tally, by the time of the Coronado expedition, at least 58 major Spanish-led expeditions had been conducted in the New World.

The combination of fervid ambition and plentiful opportunity repeatedly unleashed intense and bloody competition among the monarch's minions. Oversight and regulation of the activities of conquistadores and on-site resolution of disputes among them was almost completely on the honor system. Only haltingly and at an agonizingly slow pace was an effective apparatus of enforcement of royal mandates and broader norms of behavior established in the New World. The virtual absence of royal control left the empire's frontier regions in frequent chaos. Civil war was often threatened and sometimes became a gruesome reality.

The early history of Spanish America is punctuated again and again by incidents of mutiny and civil strife arising from contention over rights to subjugate and benefit from native peoples. Most spectacular was the civil war that overwhelmed Peru in 1537 and lasted more than a decade, in which all of the principal leaders were killed.[3] Perhaps less well known, though nearly as bloody, were the killing of Vasco Núñez de Balboa and a number of his associates in Panamá under orders from his father-in-law, Pedrarias Dávila, and the battle on the Gulf of Mexico coast between forces of Hernán Cortés and Pánfilo de Narváez.[4]

The latter conflict had its origins in Cortés's decision to defy the authority of Diego Velázquez, the royal governor of

Cuba, and establish his own separate government in what is now Mexico. One of Cortés's supporters during his violent confrontation with Velázquez's representative, Narváez, was Captain Pedro de Alvarado, already with 10 years of experience in the Indies.[5] The result of the confrontation was an overwhelming victory for Cortés and his followers and the subsequent royal recognition of Cortés as governor in his own right. That example did not go unheeded by Alvarado.

Late in 1522, just a year and a half after Cortés's conquest of the Mexica capital of Tenochtitlan, the still jubilant conqueror dispatched his fellow *extremeño* (someone from the *comunidad* of Extremadura) Alvarado with a sizable force to reconnoiter and subdue the region of Tehuantepec. In December 1523 Cortés sent Alvarado farther south to Guatemala.[6] By late 1524 the strategy of pitting native groups against each other had reduced Guatemala to a Spanish province.[7] And by September 1527 Alvarado had returned to Spain, both to fight accusations of malfeasance and to urge establishment of Guatemala as a separate jurisdiction, independent of Cortés. In both respects Alvarado was successful. He returned to Guatemala in 1530 with the title *adelantado*.

In 1536 Alvarado again sailed to Spain. This time one of his purposes was to lay before the king a proposal to construct a fleet and sail to the Molucca Islands in the Orient. When he returned to Guatemala three years later he had in hand a contract with Carlos V, dated the previous year, that conceded to him exclusive right to make seaborne reconnaissance from Guatemala on the Pacific Ocean toward the west and north over a distance of 1,500 leagues (about 4,000 miles).[8]

While Alvarado had been away in Spain, the survivors of Narváez's disastrous 1528 expedition to La Florida, Álvar Núñez Cabeza de Vaca and his companions, had made their way to Spanish-controlled territory with reports of wealthy population centers possibly accessible from the Mar del Sur, or Pacific Ocean. As a result, don Antonio de Mendoza, exercising his prerogative as viceroy of Nueva España, was preparing a coordinated sea and land *entrada* in an effort to locate those places. The independent plans of Mendoza and Alvarado both involved sea voyages on the Pacific, posing the possibility of conflicting claims and resultant confrontation.

In light of the civil war then raging in Peru, which had arisen over just such rival claims, the king and his counselors issued a series of *cédulas* in July 1540 to forestall such an outcome in Nueva España.[9] Among the provisions of those *cédulas* was recognition of the viceroy's precedence in mounting a reconnaissance of Tierra Nueva. But he was also admonished to come to an accommodation with Alvarado over the associated sea voyages.

In early November 1540, Alvarado and his fleet reached the port of Santiago de Buena Esperanza in Colima in preparation for launching into the Pacific. But the viceroy's friends and agents Agustín Guerrero and don Luis de Castilla prevented the loading of provisions and supplies. Instead, they showed the *adelantado* the royal *cédulas* and entered into negotiations with him aimed at resolving his differences with Mendoza. The upshot of those discussions was that Alvarado and Mendoza met in person in late November at Tiripitío in Michoacán.[10] There they concluded and signed a formal agreement creating a partnership, a copy of which is transcribed and translated here.

The partnership effectively put to rest the immediate and most serious challenge to Mendoza's expedition, which, however, was already in Cíbola by the time the document was signed. Not until six months later, though, did the Consejo de Indias finally and definitively end the cluster of disputes that had arisen between the viceroy and a swarm of rivals, including not only Alvarado but also Hernán Cortés, Hernando de Soto, and Nuño Beltrán de Guzmán.[11]

The text of the partnership agreement comprises 18 articles, most of which are devoted to formulaic language expressing the customary promises and guarantees required for such a contract. Articles 1–6, however, delineate what for the two parties was the meat of the agreement. They specify in what proportions and by whom the proceeds and expenses of activities undertaken by the partnership were to be split. Those arrangements were as follows: (1) Viceroy Mendoza was to pay Alvarado one-fourth of all the profits deriving from the Coronado and Alarcón expeditions, plus one-half of everything discovered along those routes, plus one-half of all profits deriving from grants resulting from those *entradas* or their joint reconnaissance; (2) Alvarado was to pay Mendoza one-half of everything deriving from their joint exploration of the islands of the Far East and the Pacific coast of the Americas; (3) Alvarado was to transfer ownership of one-half of his fleet to Mendoza; and (4) all expenses incurred in the course of activities under the partnership were to be shared equally by the two men.

Other articles specify materials and supplies that each partner was to furnish and where the building, repair, and loading of their fleet were to take place. As is typical of legal documents of the period, the language is convoluted. The sentences are extremely long and thoughts are interrupted by lengthy parenthetical insertions. For ease in reading the translation, we have rearranged the sequence of many elements of these seemingly endless, jumbled sentences. The English translation provided here is the first to appear in print.

Although the original partnership agreement is no longer known to exist, a sixteenth-century copy by an unidentified *escribano* is preserved in the Archivo General de Indias in Sevilla. Its *signatura* (catalog number) is AGI, Patronato, 21, N.3, R.2. Somewhat unusually, the copyist did not include in his transcript the customary attestation by the two *escribanos* listed in the body of the text, Juan de León and Diego de Robledo, as responsible for preparation of the original document. They were the *escribanos* associated with Mendoza and Alvarado, respectively. It is possible, though, that the AGI copy is one of those authorized to be made by the agreement itself.[12]

Two Spanish transcripts of the AGI document are included in Pacheco, Cárdenas, and Torres de Mendoza's *Colección de documentos inéditos,* 3:351–62 and 16:342–55. The first is, unfortunately, replete with errors, omissions, and gratuitous additions, the most significant of which we point out in the notes to the document. Nevertheless, we used that transcript in vetting our transcription.

TRANSLATION

[1r]

{Number 2}

In God's name, amen. Be it known to all those who may see[13] the present partnership agreement, contract, and compact: that on Monday the twenty-ninth day of November, in the one thousand five hundred and fortieth year since the birth of Our Savior, Jesus Christ, the very illustrious lord don Antonio de Mendoza,[14] viceroy and His Majesty's governor in this Nueva España and president of the royal *audiencia* which has its seat in the Ciudad de México, and the very magnificent lord *adelantado* don Pedro de Alvarado, His Majesty's governor in the *provincias* of Guatemala and Honduras, were present in the town of Tiripitío in Nueva España.[15]

In our presence, Juan de León and Diego de Robledo,[16] Their Majesties' *escribanos,* and [in the presence] of the undersigned witnesses who were present during [the formation of the partnership], the aforementioned lords declared that: whereas His Majesty commanded [Antonio de Mendoza] to enter into [it],[17] he has entered into a contract and agreement with the aforesaid lord *adelantado* Pedro de Alvarado concerning the reconnaissance which [Alvarado had] offered to make in the Mar del Sur toward the west and along the bend made by the land of Nueva España, in order to learn the secrets of its coast.[18] [This is] as it is laid out in the aforesaid contract and written compact[19] concerning it.

They declared that [the documents] referred to have been and were considered as inserted and written here[in] just as though they were [in fact] inserted and written here verbatim. In [the written compact], in one article concerning the aforesaid reconnaissance, conquest, and pacification, His Majesty orders that the viceroy is to have a one-third share in the partnership with the *adelantado* don Pedro de Alvarado, in accordance with the aforesaid compact.

In fulfillment of [the compact] the lord *adelantado* has made ready and initiated the journey with nine *naos* which he has at present anchored in the port of Santiago de Buena Esperanza in Colima.[20] With them [will be] one *galera* and one *fusta,* as well as one *fragata* which is beached in the port of Acapulco.[21] The aforementioned [nine] ships have the following names: the flagship [is] *Santiago,* another [is] named *San Francisco,* another [is] named *San Jorge,* another [is] named *San Antón,* another [is] named *Diosdado,* another [is] named *Juan Rodríguez,* another [is] named *Álvar Núñez,* another [is] named *Antón Hernández,* [and] another [is] named *Figueroa.*[22] [Yet] another [is] called the *galera,* [1v] another the *fusta,* and another the *fragata.* These make a total of twelve sailing ships.[23] With good luck, [they are] ready to continue their journey in carrying out the aforesaid reconnaissance and the contract His Majesty called for. [They are] manned with [both] footmen and horsemen.

Further, the viceroy has sent by land Francisco Vázquez de Coronado, governor and captain general of Nueva Galicia in His Majesty's name, with footmen and horsemen [and with] equipment and food supplies, to bring to the service of God and His Majesty the lands, *provincias,* and people which Father fray Marcos de Niza and others sent by His Lordship discovered. And also [they go] to reconnoiter anywhere else they can and to place [such land] under the dominion and rule of His Majesty.

[The viceroy has] also sent Captain Hernando de Alarcón by sea with three *navíos* and sufficient crew on them to make a reconnaissance.[24] [Alarcón] has already returned from the aforesaid reconnaissance, on which he has spent a large sum of gold pesos. Because of that and for what in [the reconnaissance] has been of service and may possibly be of service [in the future], His Majesty has written to [Alarcón, telling] him that he will reward him and make him a grant commensurate with his services.[25]

Being entrusted with carrying out the pacification and reconnaissance of [the land], the aforesaid lords viceroy and *adelantado* therefore declared that: because it was thus advantageous to the service of God and His Majesty, and in order to avoid any difficulties that might ensue if there were no pact and agreement between them and [if they were not to] enter into a partnership, they were executing and did execute this contract, agreement, and writ of partnership between themselves in the following manner with the articles and conditions that will be specified hereafter.

{Item} First, the lord viceroy concedes to the lord *adelantado* a fourth part of all the profits from what Francisco Vázquez de Coronado has gone to pacify and subjugate [with] his captains and men, both [any] offices and properties [the viceroy] may obtain through grants from His Majesty as well as the profits from whatever in any way [the viceroy] has [already] obtained and possesses from what Francisco Vázquez de Coronado has discovered during the subjugation of the Tierra Nueva up to the present time, [either] in person or through his captains and men.[26]

[2r] In like manner, the lord viceroy concedes to the lord *adelantado* a fourth part of all the profits and grants he may have obtained in any way from His Majesty or from the land which Captain Hernando de Alarcón reconnoitered by land and by sea with the three *navíos* and crew which the lord viceroy sent and which are presently in the port of Acapulco.

{Item} [Second] article: From this day forward, without dispute, the lord viceroy must concede and does concede to the lord *adelantado* one-half of all the profits he may obtain and [one-half] of all the grants His Majesty may make to him in any way as a result of [the reconnaissance], in accordance with what is stated above. This applies to what Francisco Vázquez de Coronado and the captains and men of his expedition, or any other captain or troop [going] by order of

and in [Vázquez de Coronado's] name, may reconnoiter, subjugate, settle, or pacify. [This is] exclusive of what they may have reconnoitered in the aforesaid land up until today (as is specified [above]). [This is to be done] without either one having more than the other, either in the form of offices, properties, or grants or as other profits he may come by in any way.

In like manner, the lord viceroy concedes to the lord *adelantado* one-half of everything any of his *navíos* may discover at the places and along the routes stipulated in the compact which the aforesaid lord *adelantado* entered into with His Majesty.

Concerning all that is stated above, the lord viceroy don Antonio de Mendoza declared that by his own free will he is making [this] concession to the aforesaid lord *adelantado* don Pedro de Alvarado and to his heirs and successors and any one of them who may have authority and right. The concession [is] indivisible, unrestricted, and irrevocable, now and forevermore. Because of the excellent work [the viceroy] has gotten from the lord *adelantado*, he makes all of the aforesaid concession to him. [This] applies both to the quarter part of what [derives] from the Tierra Nueva and to the half [share], which he thus concedes to [the *adelantado*] in accordance with what is specified in these two articles. And in like manner [it applies to] the expenditures the aforesaid lord viceroy has made in what has been stated above.

[2v] In recompense for the fleet and its expenses (as appears in the articles which will be specified hereafter) and [as] part of the compact the lord *adelantado* enters into with the lord viceroy, from this moment on, the viceroy conveys and transfers to the *adelantado* possession, control, and ownership of [the fleet] with all the obligations and guarantees that he can and by law must [include].

{Item} [Third article]: Heedful of what is stated above, and respecting that the lord viceroy is conceding to the lord *adelantado* one-fourth of what His Majesty may thus grant him and [one-fourth] of the profits and properties that he may possess in the Tierra Nueva and {Note} in what[ever land] Captain Alarcón has thus [far] reconnoitered and one-half of the profits and grants that he may derive in any way from what Francisco Vázquez, his captains, men, and *navíos* may discover from today (the date of this [document]) onward, [and] in accordance with what is stated in the articles preceding this one:

In return for what is outlined above, since [the *adelantado*] (just like the lord viceroy) owns one-third of [what has resulted from] his reconnaissance and conquest through a grant from His Majesty, the lord *adelantado* don Pedro Alvarado considers it good and it is pleasing to him that by means of this [document] he concedes to the lord viceroy don Antonio de Mendoza one-half of [what he may derive from] the aforementioned compact, signed document, and contract he has entered into with His Majesty concerning the aforementioned reconnaissance of the continent, islands, and coast.

[His Majesty has] granted him [the right] to concede [this]. That is evident according to [what] is contained at greater length in the aforesaid compact and in all the other provisions and powers which His Majesty conceded to him. [It is] to these, he declared, that reference was being and was made. And further that they were considered as being stated here as if they were written down verbatim. [He declared] that [the viceroy and himself] were to possess and enjoy equally the use of everything that may be reconnoitered, subjugated, and pacified on the continent, [on the] islands, and [on the] coast (as specified in the contract and written compact). [This is to be done] without either one obtaining more than the other, either in the form of offices, properties, or grants (as specified in the compact) or as other profits [either of them] may come by in whatever way from what may be discovered by the fleet the aforesaid lord *adelantado* has prepared or by its [individual] *navíos* or [by] others which the aforesaid lord *adelantado* and lord viceroy may dispatch to make reconnaissance for marking out territories in accordance with the aforesaid compact.

[3r] {Item} [Fourth] article: The lord *adelantado* don Pedro de Alvarado, in compensation for what is stated above, further concedes to the lord viceroy don Antonio de Mendoza one-half of all those *naos*, the *galera*, the *fusta*, and the *fragata* which are named above, with all the equipment, sails, rigging, arms and armor, and accouterments pertaining to them, [as well as] the food supplies. [These ships are] manned just as the lord *adelantado* has them in the port[s] of Coliman and Acapulco.[27] [They] are [Mendoza's] property in the same way they [are] the lord *adelantado* don Pedro de Alvarado's.

This [is done] by his own free and voluntary will, without his being compelled or pressured by [anyone],[28] but rather because he declares it was good and agreeable to him. [The *adelantado*] declared that he was making and did make [this] grant and concession of aid to the lord viceroy, his heirs, and successors and to any one of them who may have authority and right. [This applies] both to the one-half share of the fleet and to what is specified above in the preceding article. The concession [is] indivisible, unrestricted, and irrevocable, now and forevermore. Because of the debt he stated he was in to the lord viceroy and [because of] the many and excellent works he has gotten (which are worthy of greater compensation), and because of what has been stated above, [the lord *adelantado*] was conveying and did convey, was transferring and did transfer to the aforesaid lord viceroy from now on, possession, control, and ownership of the full one-half of his *naos* and fleet, as has been set forth. [The viceroy] possesses neither more nor less of the fleet than [the *adelantado*] possesses, [just] as if he were put in possession of the fleet by the order of a lawful judge.

Inasmuch as [the *adelantado*] conveys, transfers, and cedes [possession of the ships] to [the viceroy] from now on by means of what is stated above, accordingly it is [so] set down, with all the guarantees that he can and by law must [include]. [This is] so that by this means the entire fleet may be and is to be both [of theirs], without one having more [of an interest] than the other in it. [And so that] under this partnership [and] in fulfillment of the aforementioned compact, they may send [the fleet] wherever it may seem to them most appropriate, [either] in separate units or all together.

{Item} [Fifth] article: [This] constitutes an agreement between the lords viceroy and *adelantado* that the expenditures which up until today have been made on their fleets and in making them ready and provisioning them (both on the part of the lord viceroy in regard to the aforementioned

Tierra Nueva and in regard to the *navíos* he sent with Captain Hernando de Alarcón and expenditures he made in regard to the personnel he sent via land, as well as the expenditures which the lord *adelantado* has made in assembling and purchasing [3v] the aforementioned *navíos* and [providing] sailors and food supplies, and in regard to his entire fleet and crews) may sometimes exceed others in such a way that neither [the viceroy nor the *adelantado*] would be obligated to pay the other anything or any part of [the expenses], but rather some [expenses] would be offset by others and some [ships] might have departed [instead of] others without the lord viceroy's asking for anything from the lord *adelantado* or the lord *adelantado*'s asking for anything from the lord viceroy. [That is,] until today, as is stated [above].

{Item} [Sixth] article: From this day forward, the expenses which may be incurred both by sea and by land on the part of the lords viceroy and *adelantado* are to be halved and shared by both parties. Each one must pay and is to pay half of them. The arrangement which must be maintained in this is to conform to the agreement, arrangement, and contract which is to be established concerning it between them.

{Item} [Seventh] article: It is a condition [of this agreement] that this partnership, contract, and compact must last and is to last for the period and time of the immediately succeeding twenty full years.[29] [The years] are to run and be counted from today (the date of this partnership agreement). Within this time the lords viceroy and *adelantado*, their heirs, and whichever of them may have authority and right, must fulfill and abide by [the contract] and are to fulfill and abide by [it] in accordance with and in the manner specified and stated.

{Item} [Eighth] article: It is a condition [of this agreement] that if any one of the aforesaid lords viceroy and *adelantado*, or their heirs, or whichever of them may have authority and right, may desire, by whatever means, to transfer ownership of the aforesaid partnership agreement or what he possesses or may possess through it, or any part of it, he is to be obligated to notify his partner [in order to learn] whether he might

want [to purchase] it at the same price. If [any one of them] were to sell [the partnership agreement] without notifying his partner, such a sale would be null as far as he is concerned, and the other party could purchase [the partnership agreement] at the same price within the first two months immediately following [the sale's] coming to his notice.

{Item} [Ninth] article: Neither of the parties may introduce nor is to introduce any other partner into this partnership without the consent of both.

[4r] {Item} [Tenth] article: The port of Acapulco is to be designated and by the present [document] is designated for the loading and unloading of what may be necessary for the partnership until [such time as] another arrangement may seem [appropriate].

{Item} [Eleventh] article: Concerning the loading and unloading of what was mentioned above, it may not occur in any place other than the port of Acapulco. In accordance with this, the captains of the fleet who may be named {item} by the aforesaid lords are to be given [this] directive and [these] instructions.

{Item} [Twelfth] article: The shipyard where the ships must be made ready must be in the port of Xirabaltique, which is in the *provincia* of Guatemala.[30]

{Item} [Thirteenth] article: The lord *adelantado* will provide the necessary buildings for the shipyard in the aforesaid port and will take responsibility for [the shipyard] and will maintain in it the officials His Majesty orders in the contract which he entered into with the lord *adelantado*.

{Item} [Fourteenth] article: The lord *adelantado* will provide pitch, tar, rigging, carts, oakum, and sails and will take responsibility for doing this and will do [it].

{Item} [Fifteenth] article: The lord viceroy will provide and will order nails, anchors, cables, boarding pikes, and artillery to be provided for the aforestated purpose.

{Item} [Sixteenth] article: In the same manner, the lord viceroy must order and will order the necessary buildings to be built for loading and unloading at the port of Acapulco.

{Item} [Seventeenth] article: All the expenditures, both those the lord viceroy may make in doing and ordering done what was stated above and those that likewise the lord *adelantado* may make for that [purpose], are to be and must be shared equally.

{Item} [Eighteenth] article: Each year each of the lords may spend and is to spend as much as one thousand *castellanos de minas* in this [partnership] without consulting the other [partner] about it. If they must spend more, it is to be with the consultation and approval of the other. Concerning what the one and the other [partner] will spend, there is to be an account book and register with the day, month, and year. Each year in the month of December [each partner] is to be obligated to complete a report of what they [each] may have spent and to pay what each party may owe the other.

[4v] In this way and with the aforestated articles, contract, and conditions, the lords viceroy don Antonio de Mendoza and *adelantado* don Pedro de Alvarado pledged as gentlemen and by [that pledge] thus obligated themselves to fulfill, adhere to, and abide by the aforestated partnership agreement, contract, and covenant [and the] articles and conditions contained therein, in accordance with and in the manner which is stated and specified hereafter and is stipulated in this instrument.

[This is to be done] without [the parties] contravening [the partnership agreement] in any way, nor anyone else on their behalf, either now or at any time during the period of the aforesaid partnership, under penalty of fifty thousand *ducados* of genuine Castilian money. [Of this penalty] half [is] for His Majesty's treasury and the other half for the dutiful party who supported, abided by, and adhered to it. [Whether] the penalty is paid or not, [the parties] are still obligated to abide by and fulfill what is specified in this contract and partnership agreement in accordance with what is stated.

Thus, in order to adhere to, abide by, fulfill, and guar-

antee it, they declared that they were obligating and did obligate their persons and goods, [both] movable and fixed, [those] they possess and [those they are] yet to possess, as well as the rest of it. [In the same way, they obligated] the persons and goods of their heirs and successors.

Thus, in the event that they do not adhere to, abide by, and fulfill [the partnership agreement], as stated, [the partners] conceded a full power of attorney to any and all of Their Majesties' judges and *justicias*, both in their palace, court, and *chancillerías* and in all the *ciudades, villas,* and *lugares* in their *reinos* and dominions before whom this instrument may be presented. On the basis of that [instrument] and what is contained in it, the execution of justice may be petitioned for and requested, so that all the remedies and force of the law may constrain, compel, and oblige them thus to adhere to, abide by, and fulfill it and to pay [what is required] until [such time as] what is set forth above may have its complete and rightful conclusion, exactly as if it were thus settled by the definitive decision of a lawful judge. This was requested and agreed to by [the partners], and at their request it was granted and conceded as if [it were] something adjudicated.

For this reason they declared that they were waiving any laws, privileges, rights, and codes of laws, [whether] royal, canonical, civil, common, or municipal, [whether] special [or] general,[31] as well as any prerogatives, exemptions, and indemnities which they could take advantage of because of being *caballeros* of the [5r] Order of Santiago,[32] since they are not to avail themselves of [them] in any way whatever in these agreements, either in legal action or extralegally. Furthermore, they declared that they were waiving and did waive their personal resident privilege and jurisdiction. As is stated, they submitted to the royal laws and jurisdiction of Their Majesties. In particular, they declared that they were waiving and did waive the law and principle of rights in which they say the general waiving of laws is invalidated.

Beyond this, for [even] greater surety, obligation, and guarantee of what was stated above, the lords viceroy don Antonio de Mendoza and *adelantado* don Pedro de Alvarado pledged and swore by God, Santa María, and the words of the Holy Gospel[33] wherever they are written at greatest length, and by the habit of the lord Santiago, which they were wearing over their chests (where they placed their right hands). As *caballeros* and *hidalgos* they swore a solemn oath of fidelity to the king. [They swore] once, twice, and three times; once, twice, and three times; and once, twice, and three times in accordance with the usage, custom, and code of laws of Spain, while shaking hands in the grasp of don Luis de Castilla, a *caballero* and *hidalgo* of the Order of the lord Santiago.[34] From him [they] received [the charge] to adhere to, abide by, and fulfill this partnership agreement, contract, and compact, [and] the articles and conditions contained herein, in accordance with what is here specified and stated.

[The partners] declared that they were agreeing and did agree that one copy or two or more of this instrument and partnership agreement, which they executed before us, be prepared for the parties in the usual way, marked with our signs and authenticated by us, the aforementioned *escribanos*. As is stated, they executed it before us, and it is done and executed on the aforesaid day, month, and year, [all of us] being in the town of Tiripitío.

The witnesses who were present at what is related [are] the most reverend lord don Francisco Marroquín, first bishop of Guatemala, the lord *licenciado* Alonso Maldonado, the *veedor* Peralmindez Cherino, Gonzalo López, Hernán Pérez de Bocanegra, and Antonio de Zárate, *vecinos* of the Ciudad de México.[35] Present in the aforesaid town [Tiripitío were] don Antonio de Mendoza [and] *adelantado* Alvarado; as witness[es]: the bishop of Guatemala and *licenciado* Maldonado; don Luis de Castilla.

[5v and 6r] [blank]

[6v]
{Contract between the viceroy and the *adelantado* Alvarado / concerning the *provincia* of Guatemala and Honduras}
{40 Nueva España}

TRANSCRIPTION

[fol. 1r]

Numero segundo[36]

En el nonbre de dios Amen manifiesto sea A Todos los que la / presente carta de conpañia Asiento y conÇierto Vieren / como en el Pueblo de tiripitio de la nueVa españa lunes Veynte / e nueVe dias del mes de noVienbre Año del naÇimyento de nuestro saL- / Vador jesu cristo de myll e quinyentos e quarenta Años estando presentes / el muy ylustre señor don Antonyo de mendoça VisoRey e gover- / nador / por su magestad en esta nueVa españa e presydente en el / aUdienÇia[37] Real que Resyde en la ÇiUdad de mexico y el muy / magnifico señor Adelantado don pedro de alVarado Gobernador Por / su magestad de las ProVinÇias de guatimala y honduras / y en presenÇia de nos Juan de leon y diego de Robledo escribanos De / sus magestades y de los testigos ynfra(e)scritos que a ello fue- / ron presentes los dichos señores dixeron que por quanto su magestad / mando tomar y tomo Asyento y conÇierto con el dicho señor Ade- / lantado don pedro de alVarado sobre el desCubrimiento que se o- / Fresçio A hazer en la mar del sur hazia el Ponyente y en la Vuel- / Ta que faze la tierra de esta nueVa españa y para saber los se- / cretos de la costa de ella como se contiene en el dicho asyento / Y capitulaÇion[38] de ella A que dixeron que se Referian / e habian e hobieron Aquy por ynsertos y escritos como si de / Verbo Ad Verbum fuesen Aquy ynsertos y escritos en la quaL / por Un capitulo de ella su magestad manda que en el dicho descu- / brimyento conquysta y paçificaÇion el dicho señor VisoRey / Tenga la terÇia parte conforme A la dicha caPitulaÇion / en conpañya con el dicho señor Adelantado don pedro de alVarado / y en cumPlimyento de ella el dicho señor Adelan- / tado ha hecho y / començado A fazer el dicho Viaje con nueVe naos que Al presen- / te tiene surt(a)os en el Puerto

de sanTiago de buena esperança / de colima y Una galera y Una fusta con ellas y Una fragata / que esta Varada en el puerto de acaPulco las quales dichas / naos han nonbre la capitana santiago[39] otra nonbrada san francisco / otra nonbrada san jorGe otra nonbrada san(t) anton/ otra nonbrada diosdado otra nonbrada Juan Rodriguez[40] / otra nonbrada AlVar nunez otra nonbrada de anton her- / nandez otra nonbrada de Figueroa otra nonbrada la Galera

[fol. 1v]

otra la fusta otra la fra(t)ga(g)ta que son todas Doze Velas prestas / para seguir su Viaje con la buena Ventura marinadas con / Gente de pie y de caballo en prosecuÇion del dicho descubri- / myento[41] e asyento que su magestad[42] Asy dio y el dicho señor Viso- / Rey hA enViado a francisco Vazquez de coronado gobernador e capitan / General de la nueVa galizia en nonbre de su magestad por tieRa / con Gente de pie y de caballo y pertrechos y bastimentos / A traer Al serViÇio de dios y de su magestad las tierras e pro- / VinÇias y Gentes que el padre fray marcos de niça y otros / por su señoria enViados descubrieron y asymysmo A des- / cubrir todo lo que mas pudiesen y ponello debaxo del domy- / nyo y señorio de su magestad e ansymysmo enVyo por / mar Al capitan hernando de alarcon con tres naVios y Gen- / te bastante en ellos A descubrir el qual es ya Venydo del / dicho descubrimiento en que ha gastado[43] mucha suma de pesos de / oro por lo qual y para lo que en ello hA serVido y syrViere su / magestad le ha escrito que le (f)hara GratificaÇion y merced conforme / A sus serViÇios y enCargado la prose- / cuÇion de la PaÇifyca- / Çion y descubrimiento de ella por tanto los dichos señores Vi- / soRey y adelantado Dixeron que porque ConVenia Asy Al / serViÇio de dios y de su magestad y por eVitar Algunos yn- / conVinyentes que se podrian seguir sy no[44] *h*obiese Acuer- / do y con*Ç*ierto entre *e*llos y hiziesen conpañia fazian / e fizieron la di*ch*a conpañia Asyento y con*Ç*ierto entre *e*llos / *en* la forma syGuyente e con los capitulos y condi*Ç*iones q*ue* / de yuso se (f)*h*ara m(y)*en*Çion

{*ytem*} primeramente que *e*l di*ch*o señor VisoRey dA Al di*ch*o senor / Adelantado la quarta Parte de todos[45] los AproVechamyentos / que *en* lo q*ue* asy es ydo A pa*Ç*ificar y descubrir el di*ch*o fran*cis*co Vaz- / quez de coronado y capi-tanes y Gente *h*obiere Ansy por m*erce*des / de su mag*esta*d ofi*Ç*ios e tenen*ç*ias como de los AproVe- / chamyentos que en qualquyer manera *h*obiere e tuViere / de todo lo que *e*l di*ch*o fran*cis*co Vasquez de coronado *h*obiere / descubierto por su *per*sona o por sus caPitanes y Gente / en la conquysta de la di*ch*a tierra nueva hasta el dia de

[fol. 2r]

*h*oy e ansymysmo el di*ch*o señor VisoRey da Al di*ch*o señor / adelantado la quarta parte[46] de todos los a*pro*Vechami*ent*os / y mer*Ç*ed*e*s que de su m*agesta*d e de la tierra en qualquyer mane- / ra *h*obiere de lo q*ue por* mar e por tierra descubrio el di*ch*o Ca- / pitan hernando de alarcon con los tres naVyos y Gente / que *e*l di*ch*o señor VisoRey enVyo q*ue* Al *pre*sente estan en el / puerto de acaPulco

{*ytem*} yten que de lo que *h*oy dia en Adelante descubrieren o conquys- / t*ar*en o poblaren o pa*Ç*ificaren el di*ch*o fran*cis*co Vazquez / de coronado e capitanes e Gente de su Armada fuera / de lo que fasta el dia de *h*oy tuVieren descubierto o otro / qualquyer capitan[47] o Gente por mandado del di*ch*o señor Viso- / Rey o en su nonbre demas de lo q*ue* tienen descubierto o / poblado o pa*Ç*ificado hasta el dia de *h*oy como di*ch*o es en la di*ch*a / tierra el di*ch*o señor VisoRey ha por byen de dar e da Al di*ch*o / señor Adelantado la mytad de todos los AproVechamy*ent*os / que en ella *h*obiere y de las m*erce*des que su mag*esta*d en ello le hiziere / en qualquyer manera seGun(d) ARiba es di*ch*o syn que *e*l Uno ten- / ga mas que *e*l otro ny el otro mas que *e*l otro Asy en los ofi*Ç*ios / t(h)enen*ç*ias e mer*ç*edes como de los demas AproVechamyen- / tos que en qualquyer manera *h*obiere e ansymysmo el di*ch*o señor / VisoRey da Al di*ch*o señor

Adelantado la mytad de todo lo que / descubrieren de *h*oy dia de la fe*ch*a de *e*sta carta[48] *en* Adelante qua- / lesquyer naVios suyos en los paraJes y deRotas cont(h)enidas / en la capitula*Ç*ion que *e*l di*ch*o señor Adelantado tomo con su / mag*esta*d de todo lo susodi*ch*o el di*ch*o señor don Antonyo de mendo*ç*a / VisoRey dixo que de su *pro*pia Voluntad faze dona*Ç*ion Al / di*ch*o señor Adelantado don p*edro* de alVarado e a sus herederos e su(b)- / *Ç*esores e a quyen de lo de *e*llos *h*obiere caUsa y Razon dona*Ç*ion / pura e perfe*c*ta e no ReVocable para agora e para syenpre / Jamas por buenas obras q*ue* del di*ch*o señor Adelantado *h*A Re- / *Ç*ibido Ansy de la quarta parte q*ue* ansy le da de lo de la di*ch*a ti*err*a / nueVa como de la mytad seGun(d) que *en e*stos dos caPitu-los / se faze myn*Ç*ion e ansymismo en los Gastos que *en* lo su- / sodi*ch*o el di*ch*o señor VisoR*ey h*A hecho le faze la di*ch*a dona*Ç*ion

[fol. 2v]

de todo ello y en Reconpensa de la Armada y par- / te de capitula*Ç*ion que *e*l di*ch*o señor Adelantado da Al di*ch*o señor / VisoRey y Gastos de *e*lla como paresçe por los caPitu-los / q*ue* de yuso se hara myn*Ç*ion y le çede y traspasa desde aGora / la posesyon e señorio e *pro*piedad de *e*llo con todas las fuer- / *ç*as y firmezas que puede y de d*erech*o debe

{*ytem*} y atento lo susodi*ch*o e tenyendo Respe*c*to que *e*l di*ch*o señor Vi- / soRey da Al di*ch*o señor Adelantado la di*ch*a quarta Parte de lo / que ansy su magestad le hiziere m*erce*d y de los AproVechamien- / tos e yntereses que *h*obiere en la di*ch*a tierra nueVa y en lo / {*ojo*} q*ue* asy descubrio el di*ch*o capitan Alarcon y la mytad de los Apro- / Vechamyentos y mer*ç*edes que en qualquyer manera *h*obiere / de lo que descubrieren dende *h*oy dia de la fe*ch*a de *e*st*e en* Ad*e*lante / el di*ch*o fran*cis*co Vazquez e sus capitanes e Gente y naVios seGun(d) / se contiene en los capitulos Antes de *e*ste que en ReconPen- / sa de lo susodi*ch*o el di*ch*o señor Adelantado don p*edro* alVarado / ha por byen y le plaze q*ue* Ansy como el di*ch*o señor VisoRey tiene / por m*erce*d de su magestad la ter*Ç*ia parte de su conquysta e des- / cubrymyento por la presente le da Al di*ch*o señor don Ant*oni*o de / mendo*ç*a VisoRey la mytad de la di*ch*a capitula*Ç*ion e con- / trata*Ç*ion e asyento q*ue* con su mag*esta*d tomo e le fizo[49] m*erce*d de dar / sobre *e*l d*i*cho descubrimyento de las d*i*chas tierra firme yslas / e costa segun(d) mas largamente se contiene en la d*i*cha capi- / tula*Ç*ion y en todas las demas proVisyones y poderes q*ue* su m*a*g*es*t*ad* / le dio A que dixo que se Referia y Refirio y *h*abian Aquy / por e(s)xpresadas como sy de Verbo A Verbo fuesen escrit*a*s / e q*ue h*ayan e gozen yGualment*e* en todo lo que se descubriere / y conquystare y pa*Ç*ificare en las d*i*chas tierra fyrme yslas / e costa en el d*i*cho Asyento e capitula*Ç*ion contenydas syn / que *e*l Uno tenga mas q*ue e*l otro ny el otro mas que *e*l otro / Asy en los ofi*Ç*ios tenen*ç*ias y mer*ç*edes contenidas *en* la / d*i*cha capitula*Ç*ion como de los demas AproVechami*ento*s / que en qualquyer manera *h*obiere en lo q*ue* descubriere con la / Armada q*ue* tiene fecha el d*i*cho señor Adelantado o con los / naVios de ella o de fuera de *e*lla que *e*l d*i*cho señor Adel*a*nt*a*do⁵⁰ / y el d*i*cho señor Visorrei enViare A descubrir por las demarCa*Ç*io- / nes conForme A la d*i*cha capitula*Ç*ion

[fol. 3r]

{*ytem*} yten el d*i*cho señor Adelantado don p*edr*o de alvarado *en* Reconpensa / de lo susod*i*cho da mas Al d*i*cho señor don Antonyo de mendo*Ç*a / Visorrey la mytad de todas las d*i*chas naos Galera e fusta e fragata / q*ue* de suso Van nonbradas con todos los p(r)ertrechos Velas e aparejos / e armas e adere*Ç*os A ellas perteneçientes con los basti- mentos / marin*e*radas segun(d) e de la manera que *e*l d*i*cho señor Adelan- / tado las tiene en el d*i*cho puerto de coliman e acapulco q*ue* *e*s la p*r*opia / suya como lo es del d*i*cho señor Adelantado don p*edr*o de alVarado / el qual de su p*r*opia libre y espontanea Voluntad syn ser yndu- / zido ny apremiado para ello syno porque ansy dixo que le esta- / ba bien y le conVenia dixo q*ue* fazia e hizo Gra*ç*ia e dona*Ç*ion / Al d*i*cho señor VisoRey e a sus herederos e sus*Ç*esores e a quyen / de *e*l o de *e*llos *h*obiere caUsa e Razon Ansy de la mytad de la / d*i*cha Armada como de lo que d*i*cho es de suso en el capitulo An- / tes de *e*ste dona*Ç*ion pura e perf*e*cta e no ReVocable para / aGora e para syenpre jamas por cargos en que dixo ser Al d*i*cho / señor VisoRey e muchas y buenas obras que de *e*l *h*Abia Re*çib*i*do* / que son dignas de mayor Remunera*Ç*ion y por Razon de lo / susod*i*cho y le *Ç*edia e çedio e traspasaba e traspaso des- / de agora Al d*i*cho señor

VisoRey la posesyon e señorio e Propie- / dad de toda la d*i*cha mytad de sus naos e armada q*ue* como / d*i*cho es tiene ny mas ny menos que *e*l la tiene como sy por man- / damyento de Juez conpetente le fuese dada la posesyon / de *e*lla por quanto el desde agora se la *Ç*ede e trespasa e da / por lo susod*i*cho segun(d) que *e*s declarado con todas las fir- / mezas q*ue* puede y de d*erech*o debe para que de por medio este / toda la d*i*cha Armada e sea de *en*tranbos syn q*ue e*l Uno tenga / mas q*ue e*l otro en ello para en la d*i*cha conpañia en cum- / plimyento de la d*i*cha capitula*Ç*ion ynVialla donde les / pares*Ç*iere q*ue* mas conVenGa diVidida o junta

{*ytem*} yten es con*Ç*ierto⁵¹ *en*tre los d*i*chos señores VisoRey e adelan- / tado q*ue* los gastos que hasta el dia de *h*oy se *h*an hecho en las d*i*chas / sus Armadas y en Adere*ç*allas y *a*baste*ç*ellas ansy por / parte del d(e)*i*cho señor VisoRey en lo de la d*i*cha tierra nueVa / y en los naVios q*ue* enVyo con el d*i*cho capitan hernando de alar- / con y Gastos que hizo con la gente que *en*Vyo por tierra como⁵² / los gastos que *e*l d*i*cho señor Adelantado *h*A f*e*cho *en* fazer⁵³ e conprar

[fol. 3v]

los d*i*chos naVyos e marineallos y *a*baste*Ç*ellos y con toda la / d*i*cha su Armada y Gente de *e*lla hasta *h*oy d*i*cho dia se VayAn / Unos por otros de manera q*ue e*l Uno al otro ny el otro Al otro / sea obligado a pagar nynguna cosa ny parte de *e*llos syno / que los Unos se conpensen con los otros y se Vayan Unos por / otros syn que *e*l d*i*cho señor VisoRey pida nynguna cosa⁵⁴ Al / d*i*cho señor Adelantado ny el d*i*cho señor Adelantado Al d*i*cho señor / VisoRey hasta el dia de *h*oy como es d*i*cho

{*ytem*} yten que los Gastos que dende *h*oy d*i*cho d*i*a en adelante / se hizieren Ansy por mar como por tierra por parte de los / d*i*chos señores VisoRey e adelantado sean de Por medio / e comunes de *en*tranbas partes e q*ue* cada Uno *h*aya de Pagar / e pague la mytad de *e*llos y la (h)orden q*ue* en esto se *h*a de t(h)ener / sea conforme Al con*Ç*ierto (h)orden e asyento que sobre ello se / diere *en*tre *e*llos

{*ytem*} yten es condi*Ç*ion que *e*sta d*i*cha conpañia Asyento y Capi- / tula*Ç*iones de *e*lla *h*Aya de (du)durar y dure por espaÇio / e tienpo de Veynte Años cumPlidos primeros siguyen- / tes los quales coRan e se quentan desde *h*oy dia / de la *fe*cha de *e*sta conpañia y que en este tienpo los / di*c*hos señores VisoRey e adelantado e los di*c*hos sus he- / rederos e quyen de *e*llos *h*obiere caUsa y Razon lo *h*an / de cumplir e Guardar e cumplan e Guarden seGun(d) e / de la manera esta esp(a)*e*Çificado y declarado

{y*tem*} yten es condiÇion q*ue* si alguno de los di*c*hos señores Viso- / Rey e adelantado e sus herederos e quyen de *e*llos *h*o- / biere caUsa e Razon quysyere disponer por qualquyer / Via de la di*c*ha conpañia e de lo q*ue en e*lla tiene e tuViere toda / o de alguna parte de *e*lla sea obligado A Requerir Al / conpañero sy la quysyere por el tanto e sy la Vendiere syn lo / Requerir Al di*c*ho conpañero que la tal Venta sea en sy / nynguna e la otra parte lo pueda tomar Por el tanto / dentro de dos meses primeros syGuientes q*ue* Viniere / A su notiÇia

{y*tem*} yten q*ue* en esta di*c*ha conpañia nynGuna de las di*c*has partes / pueda meter ny meta otro nyngun(d) conpañero syn con- / sentimi*ent*o de ambos A doS

[fol. 4r]
{y*tem*} yten q*ue* se nonbre y por la presente se nonbra el puerto de aca- / pulco para el cargo y descargo de lo que fuere neÇesario para la / di*c*ha conpañia hasta q*ue* otra cosa parezca

{y*tem*} yten que *e*l cargo y descargo de lo susodi*c*ho no pueda ser en / otra parte syno en el di*c*ho puerto de acapulco y Conforme / A esto se den la yn(y)stru(y)*c*Çion e yn(y)strucÇiones Al los ca- / pitanes que por los di*c*hos señores fueren nonbrados / {y*tem*} *en* la di*c*ha Armada

{y*tem*} yten que *e*l Astillero donde se *h*an de hazer los naVyos *h*An de ser / en el puerto de xirabaltiq*ue* que *e*s en la p*rovi*n*c*ia de Guatimala

{y*tem*} yten que *e*l di*c*ho señor Adelantado (f)*h*ara las casas neÇesarias / para el di*c*ho Astillero en el di*c*ho puerto y te(r)nd*r*a cargo de *e*llo / y te(r)nd*r*a en el los ofiÇiales que su

magestad manda en el / Asyento q*ue* tomo con el di*c*ho senor Adelantado

{y*tem*} yten que *e*l di*c*ho señor Adelantado dara pez y al(cr)q*ui*tran y xar- / Çia y carretas y estopa e Velas y de *e*sto te(r)nd*r*a cargo De / (f)*h*azer (fazer) e (f)*h*ara

{y*tem*} yten que *e*l di*c*ho señor VisoRey p*ro*Veera y mandara p*ro*V(e)eer / de claVazon e anclas y cables y botaraen[55] y artilleria / para el di*c*ho efe*c*to

{y*tem*} yten q*ue* Asymysmo el di*c*ho señor VisoRey *h*A de mandar / e mandara (f)*h*azer las casas neÇesarias para el cargo y / descargo en el di*c*ho puerto de acapulco

{y*tem*} yten q*ue* todos los Gastos Ansy los que *e*l señor VisoRey / hiziere en fazer y mandar fazer lo susodi*c*ho como los / q*ue* asy hiziere en ello el di*c*ho señor Adelantado sean e *h*an / De ser de Por medio

{y*tem*} yten que los di*c*hos señores pueda Gastar e Gaste cada Uno / de *e*llos en cada Un año hasta myll castellaños de / mynas *en e*sto syn consultallo el Uno con el otro e sy / mas *h*obieren de gastar que sea con consulta y pare- / Çer del otro y de lo que *e*l Uno y el otro Gastare *h*aya / libro quenta e Razon con dia e mes e año e q*ue* cada Un año / por el mes de diz*iemb*re de *e*l sea obligado A feneÇer quenta de / los q*ue h*obieren Gastado e pagar lo q*ue* debiere la Una parte / A la otra

[fol. 4v]
E de *e*sta manera e con estos di*c*hos capitulos Asyento e / condiÇiones los di*c*hos señores don ant*o*nio de mendoça / VisoRey e adelantado don p*edr*o de alVarado prometieron como / caballeros e se obligaron de lo ansy cumPlir e t(h)ener / e Guardar esta di*c*ha conpañia Asyento e conÇierto ca- / pitulos e condiÇiones en ella cont(h)enidas seGun(d) e de / la manera que de suso Va declarado y espeÇificado y en es- / ta escritura se faze mynÇion e de no yr ny Venyr ellos ny / otr(e)o por ellos contra ella Agora ny en tienpo Alguno / ny por alguna manera durante el t*iem*po de la di*c*ha conpañia / so pena de çinquenta myll ducados de

buena moneda / de castilla la mytad para la camara e fysco
de su magestad / y la otra mytad para la parte obidiente que
por ello estu- / Viere e lo Guardare y mantuViere e la pena
pagada o non[56] / que todaVia sean obligados de Guardar e
cumplir lo con- / t(h)enydo en este dicho Asyento e
conpañia segun dicho es e / para lo Ansy t(h)ener e guardar
e cumplir e haber por firme / dixeron que obligaban e
obligaron sus personas e byenes e an- / symysmo las personas
e byenes de los dichos sus herederos e / susÇesores muebles
e Rayzes hAbidos e por haber e de- / mas de esto sy lo ansy
no tuVieren e Guardaren e cumplieren / como dicho es
dieron poder cumplido A todos e qualesquier jue- / zes e
justiÇias de sus magestades Ansy de la su casa[57] e corte / e
chanÇillerias como de todas las ÇiUdades Villas e lu- / gares
de los sus Reynos e señorios Ante quyen esta / escritura
paresÇiere e de ella e de lo en ella contenido fue- / re pedido
e demandado cumplimyento de justiÇia para / que por todos
los Remedios e Rigores del derecho les cons- / tringan
conpelan e apremyen A lo asy t(h)ener e guardar / e cumplir
e pagar hasta que lo susodicho haya su cumplido e / debido
efecto byen asy como si asy fuese jusgado por sentencia[58] /
difynytiVa de juez conpetente la qual fuese por ellos / pedida
e consentida e a su pedimiento dada e pasada en / cosa
juzgada en Razon de lo qual dixeron que Renunçia- / ban
qualesquier leyes fueros y derechos e (h)ordenamyentos
Reales / canonyCos e ÇiViles comunes e munyÇipales es- /
peçiales y Generales e qualesquyer libertades e pre- /
emynençias e (ç)cauÇiones que por ser caballeros de la

[fol. 5r]
(h)orden del señor santiago les pueden AproVechar / como
en otra qualquyer manera que les no Vala / en esta Razon en
Juicio ny fuera de el otrosy dixeron que / Renunçiaban e
Renunçiaron su propio fuero e jurisdi- / Çion dom(e)iÇilio[59]
e como dicho es se sometieron Al fuero e ju- / risdiÇion Real
de sus magestades y espeçialmente dixe- / ron que Renunçiaban e Renunçiaron la ley e Regla del derecho / en que dizque

general Renunçiaçion de leyes (f)hecha non Vala / e de mas
de esto para mayor abundamyento e ValidaÇion / e
f(e)irmeza de lo susodicho los dichos señores don Antonyo de
/ mendoça VisoRey e adelantado don pedro de alVarado pro- /
metieron e Juraron A dios e a santa maria e a las palabras /
de los santos eVanGelios doquyer que mas largamente / son
escritos y por el habito del señor santiago que en sus Pe- /
chos tenian donde pusyeron sus manos derechas e hizieron /
pleyto homenaje[60] como caballeros hijosdalgo una dos e tres /
Vezes Una dos e tres Vezes Una dos e tres Vezes seGun(d)
Uso / e costumbre e fuero de españa en manos de don luys de
cas- / tilla caballero hijodalgo de la (h)orden del señor san- /
tiago que de el ReÇibyo de lo ansy mantener Guardar e cum- /
plir esta dicha conpañia e asyento e conÇierto capitulos / e
condiÇiones en ella contenydos seGun(d) que aquy Va /
esp(a)eÇificado e declarado e dixeron que consentian e con- /
syntieron que de esta escritura y conpañia se saque Un
traslado / o dos o mas en publica forma para las dichas partes
/ e siGnados e aUtorizados de nos los dichos escribanos lo
quaL / otorgaron ante nos como dicho es que es (f)hecho e
paso en eL / dicho dia mes e año susodicho estando en el dicho
pueblo / de tiripitio testigos que fueron presentes A lo que
dicho es / el Reverendisimo señor don francisco marro(n)quin
primero obispo de Gua- / timala y el señor licenÇiado Alonso
maldonado[61] y el Veedor / perarmylldeZ cherino e Gonzalo
lopez[62] e hernan perez de boca- / neGra e antonio de çarate
Vesynos de la ÇiUdad de mexico / y estantes en este dicho
pueblo don antonio de mendoza el / adelantado AlVarado
por testigo episcopus Cua(s)hutimalensis[63] por / testigo el
licenÇiado maldonado[64] don luys de castilla

[fols. 5v–6r] [blank]

[fol. 6v][65]
{asYento entre el ViSorrey y el / adelantado alvarado}
{sobre la provyncia de guate- / mala y honduras}
{40 Nueva españa}

Document 21

Account of Pedro de Alvarado's Armada, 1541

Biblioteca Real, Madrid, II/3042

Gonzalo Fernández de Oviedo y Valdés, *Historia general y natural de las Indias*,
Tercera Parte, Libro XL, Capítulo II, 1547, fols. 23v–24r

INTRODUCTION

In Santo Domingo on the Caribbean island of Española, Gonzalo Fernández de Oviedo y Valdés, in his capacity as official chronicler of the Indies, was always alert for news of major events occurring in the New World. So when Bernardo de Molina, a *criado* of *adelantado* Pedro de Alvarado, reached Santo Domingo sometime early in 1541, the chronicler interviewed him and even, evidently, managed to get a look at and copy a portion of a report he was carrying from Alvarado to the king.[1]

The report, destined for Spain, told of the launching of a major sea voyage under Alvarado's command in August 1539. The voyage began from Guatemala and slowly progressed up the Pacific coast to Acapulco and the Port of Colima, soon to be known as La Navidad.[2] It was undertaken initially under authority granted to Alvarado by means of a contract between himself and the king, which had been formalized in 1538. The contract specified that for a period of eight years Alvarado was to have the exclusive right to make seaborne reconnaissance from Guatemala on the Pacific Ocean toward the west and north over a distance of 1,500 leagues (about 4,000 miles).[3]

That arrangement had been made more than a year before fray Marcos de Niza returned from his trek to the north with word of the Seven Ciudades of Cíbola. Such an enticing discovery lured the *adelantado* and put him into immediate conflict with Viceroy Mendoza, who was planning his own land expedition with the same destination. Contention between the two men was settled in November 1540 with the signing of an agreement of partnership that had been mandated by the king.[4]

It was after this resolution was reached that Alvarado finally put to sea in search of the seven *ciudades*. The date was probably in December 1540, not the best season for sailing up the Pacific Coast. And indeed, as Oviedo later reported, the ships "returned to port because of violent weather [*rribaron por tiempos forzosos*]."[5] Before repairs could be made and the fleet could reembark, the viceroy appealed by letter to Alvarado for reinforcements in Cristóbal de Oñate's effort to put down the native uprising in Jalisco known as the Mixtón War. The *adelantado* went to Oñate's aid, with a force from his fleet, and was killed when a horse fell on him during a retreat.[6] As a result, the voyage never continued.

Oviedo is ordinarily clear about which passages in his *Historia* represent his own opinions or conjectures and those that are verbatim reports from participants or observers of the events under consideration. In the case of the message carried by Bernardo de Molina, he is more ambiguous than usual. He fails to introduce the excerpt from the report with any phrase such as so-and-so "wrote exactly these words," as he does in Document 7 of this volume.[7] It seems most likely, however, that the direct quotation begins with the words, "After he had pacified the jurisdiction of Honduras."[8] The end of the quoted passage is much easier to discern; it is followed immediately by the statement, "This report was made known, exactly as it is stated."[9] The quoted material therefore consists of two paragraphs giving details of the plans for and start of Alvarado's reconnaissance.

The Molina message does not reveal the precise intended course of the fleet. But because it launched after the return of Hernando de Alarcón's three-ship squadron, it is not difficult to imagine that Alvarado and Mendoza's plan was to have part of the huge force retrace Alarcón's earlier route, then disembark a large party that would head overland to link with Vázquez de Coronado's land expedition.

Besides his inclusion of the transcribed excerpt from the Molina message, Oviedo provides valuable information as a witness himself. He reports that he talked with the messenger and saw at least some of the ancillary items with which he had been entrusted. These included "a painting . . . depicting the types and number of ships the *adelantado* was taking."[10] This is a tantalizing potential source of data about the Coronado expedition and the wider enterprise of which it was a part. Although it may still exist, its modern location is unknown. Nor is it evident who the artist was who made the painting—not even whether the artist was a European or a Native American.

Like Document 7 in this volume, the folios from Oviedo's *Historia* transcribed and translated here derive from the manuscript copy preserved in the Biblioteca Real in Madrid under the designation II/3042, folios 23v and 24r. Folio numbers from the Biblioteca Real document have been retained in the translation and transcription that follow, in order to facilitate location of the passages in the original document. It may be written in the chronicler's own hand.[11] The English translation provided here is the first available in print.

TRANSLATION

[23v]

[...]

Chapter 2

{How the *adelantado* don Pedro de Alvarado readied[12] an excellent fleet along the Mar del Sur (or, to express it better, along the Western [Sea]) and another part [of it] on Tierra Firme, in order to reconnoiter those areas in accordance with what he has contracted with the emperor, our lord, and is ordered [to do]; and other things that concern the present history.}[13]

After he had pacified the jurisdiction of Honduras {as was told in Book 31}, the *adelantado* don Pedro de Alvarado traveled from Spain and returned thereafter to the same jurisdiction [Honduras]. When he had gone from there to the [jurisdiction] of Guatemala, he made great haste to complete certain ships which by his order were being built on the coast of the other (southern) sea. [This was] in order to carry out and perform a certain reconnaissance which he [had] offered to make and [had] contracted that he would make with the emperor [and] king, our lord, and the lords of his very distinguished Consejo de las Indias.[14]

In the month of August, in the *provincia* and [from the] port of Istapa, where those ships were built, he departed for Acajutla, a port on the Mar del Sur, from where it was necessary to begin his voyage in search of the seven *ciudades*, which occurred in the next year, the year one thousand five hundred and forty.[15] [He sailed] with thirteen ships, including [both] large and small [ones].[16] Three of them [were] *galeones* of more than two hundred *toneladas* each. [There were] one very excellent *galera* [24r] and two *fustas*, and all the rest of the ships [were] of about a hundred *toneles* or more.[17] All those and the others [were] very well provided with large stores of food, arms and armor, artillery, and ammunition. Also with very excellent people for both sea and land, numbering more than a thousand men, including those who came with him from Spain and those who were already acclimated to [the] Indies.[18]

{This report was made known, exactly as it is stated, here in this *ciudad* of Santo Domingo by a *criado* of the *adelantado* himself, whom he sent to the emperor to give him information about what is stated [therein].[19] [The *criado*] was even carrying a painting, which he showed me, depicting the types and number of ships the *adelantado* was taking.[20] Regarding [the expedition], he told me and many others optimistically that a great result was certain to be forthcoming, if God were served that the enterprise and voyage continue. It was ordained by God, however, that the journey and conquest be suspended at that time, that the *adelantado* not make the voyage, and that his life be ended disastrously, as will be told at greater length in the following book, number 41, in chapter 3, as its most appropriate place in these histories.}

TRANSCRIPTION

[fol. 23v]

Tercera parte

[…]

Capitulo segundo {como El Adelantado don Pedro de / alvarado se puso en (h)orden con Una hermosa / Armada por la mar del sur o miJor diziendo / (por la oçidental) E de la otra parte de la tierra / Firme Para descubrir por aquellas partes con- / forme A lo que por el emperador nuestro Señor / Tiene capitulado E le esta mandado E otras / cosas que competen A la historia presente}

El Adelantado don pedro de Alvarado despues que / huvo paçifficado la Gobernaçion de honduras como / se dixo en el libro xxxi fue de (h)españa e Vuelto des- / Pues A la mism(o)a gobernaçion e desde alli pasado A la de / Guatimala dio mu(n)cha priesa a acabar çiertos naVios / que por Su mandado se hazian en la costa de la otra mar Austral / para Efectuar e cumplir²¹ çierto desCubrimyento que se / offrezçio de hazer E capitulo que haria con el Emperador / Rey nuestro señor e los Señores de su muy Alto / conseJo de las Yndias E en la proVinçia e puerto de ystapa / donde se hiZieron los dichos naVios²² salio de alli para aca- / yucla {ytem Acaxucla} puerto de la mar del sur desde donde habia de començar / su viaje en demanda de las siete çiUdades en el mes de agosto / que paso del año proximo de myll e quynientos e quarenta años / con treze naVios entre grandes e pequeños / los tres galeones de mas de cada dozientas toneladas / cada Uno de ellos: e una galera muy hermosa

[fol. 24r]

libro xL

24

Y Dos Fustas: y todos los demas naVios de çient / Toneles o mas muy bien proVeydos todos los Unos / y los otros de mu(n)chos bastimentos e armas e artilleria / E muniçiones e con muy buena gente para la mar e para / la tierra en numero de mas de myll hombres entre los / que con el Vinieron de (h)españa e los que ya estaban curssados / en yndias {esta RelaÇion a(n)si como esta dicho se supo / aqui en esta çiUdad de santo domingo de un criado del mismo Adelantado / Que le enVio²³ a çesar a le dar notiçia de lo que es dicho e aun lleVaba / Una pin(c)tura que el mesmo me enseño de la forma e cantidad / De los naVios que el dicho adelantado lleVaba de que / a mi e a otros muchos dexo²⁴ con esperança que habia de / salir gran fru(c)to si dios fuese serVido que aquella enpresa / E ViaJe se continuase: pero (j)ordenose por dios que / aquel camino E conquista se suspendiese por entonçes E que el / Adelantado no hiziese el Viaje e que su Vida se acabase desas- / Tradamente como mas largamente se dira en el siguiente libro / del numero xli en el capitulo terçero como en parte mas apropiada / a estas historias}

Fin del libro

Document 22

Traslado de las Nuevas (Anonymous Narrative), 1540

AGI, Patronato, 20, N.5, R.8

INTRODUCTION

Bundled together with Juan Jaramillo's narrative (Document 30) and the "Relación del Suceso" (Document 29) in the Archivo General de Indias under *signatura* (catalog number) AGI, Patronato, 20, N.5, R.8, is the "Traslado de las Nuevas," which, like its companion documents, was probably collected by Carlos V's royal chronicler, Juan Páez de Castro.[1] The handwriting of the text, however, does not match that of Jaramillo's report or the Relación del Suceso, nor does it match that of the notes it bears indicating origin in Páez's collection. Both the Jaramillo document and the Traslado do, though, bear incorrect dates at the heads of the first folio and the cover sheet (1531 in the case of the Traslado) that seem to be in the same hand. When the dates were added to the two documents and by whom are unknown and thus may have nothing to do with the royal chronicler's ferreting out of documents in preparation for his anticipated but never realized history of the emperor's reign. It has become common practice to call this document the "Traslado de las Nuevas." These are the first four words in the legend at the head of the first folio, probably added by a clerk or other functionary and meaning "copy of the news."

The name of neither the author of the original document nor the copyist who evidently prepared the Traslado in the Ciudad de México is indicated in the document itself. Frederick Webb Hodge suggested that the author of the original message on which the Traslado is based was García López de Cárdenas, the Coronado expedition's *maestre de campo*.[2] This seems unlikely because, for one thing, the author refers to the *maestre de campo* in the third person. That López de Cárdenas was not the author is further indicated by the author's reporting that the captain general came out of the fighting at the first *ciudad* of Cíbola "on his own [two] feet," whereas, according to Juan Troyano, Pedro de Ledesma, and Vázquez de Coronado's own later testimony concerning the fighting that day, "other Spaniards lifted him up and carried him to camp" unconscious.[3] López certainly would have been aware of this, because he had thrown himself on top of the general to protect him from further injury.[4]

Even though the author of the Traslado message was probably not López de Cárdenas, internal evidence from the document permits the certain conclusion that it was written by one of the 75 horsemen and 30 footmen whom Vázquez de Coronado took with him in the advance guard that traveled from Culiacán to Cíbola between April and July 1540. Whoever the author was, he was likely to have been someone from the captain general's personal retinue. The most likely candidate may be Ramos (probably Juan de Ramos), the captain general's surgeon, because the author seems to have as his purpose in writing the message to reassure the addressee that Vázquez de Coronado has been restored to health after his nearly fatal head injury during the advance guard's attack on Cíbola. He even states that *he* is sending the letter, rather than anyone else, "because it is fitting that I be the one who writes to Your Grace and my lady about everything which may occur concerning the health of the general."[5]

Not wholly certain either is to whom the message was sent. The author addresses that person as "Vuestra merced," or "Your Grace," indicating an exalted personage, perhaps the viceroy. The author also appears familiar with Beatriz de Estrada, the captain general's wife. He refers to the couple as *mi señor* and *mi señora*, my lord and my lady.[6] The original message was, then, a personal letter probably written in August 1540, certainly after July 19. It may have traveled to the Ciudad de México with the same courier who carried the captain general's own letter to the viceroy of August 3 (Document 19).

A careless transcription of the Traslado was published by Joaquín Pacheco and Francisco de Cárdenas in 1873.[7] It was republished in 1992 by Carmen de Mora.[8] George Winship used the flawed 1873 transcription in preparing his 1896 English translation, as did George Hammond and Agapito Rey in theirs of 1940.[9] The new translation and transcription that follow are therefore the first to be based directly on the original document from the Archivo General de Indias since Pacheco and Cárdenas's production-line work of 130 years ago.

TRANSLATION

[1r]

{1531}[10]

{scribal highlighting}

{Copy of the news that came from the *ciudad* of Cíbola, which is in Tierra Nueva}[11]

His Grace [Francisco Vázquez de Coronado] left most of the expeditonary force in the valley of Culiacán, and with only seventy-five companions on horseback and thirty footmen, he departed for this place [Cíbola] Thursday, April 22 [1540].[12] The [main body of the] expeditonary force, which remained [in Culiacán], was supposed to depart at the end of May. [That was] because [Vázquez de Coronado] had obtained information that until then they would find no food of any sort along the whole route as far as this *provincia* of Cíbola (which is more than[13] three hundred and fifty leagues).[14] For this reason he dared not start the whole expeditonary force on its way.

He ordered provisions prepared for eighty days for the troop he selected. These were carried on horseback, each man [carrying provisions] for himself and his followers.[15] Given the great danger of suffering from hunger and the equal [danger] from labor (since every day they were locating and breaking trails [through] dense undergrowth [and across] rivers and difficult passes), they [each] carried their share.[16] Along the entire route as far as this *provincia* there was only one *celemín* of corn.[17]

[Vázquez de Coronado] reached this *provincia* on Wednesday, the seventh of this past July, with the whole troop he took from the valley [of Culiacán] (highest praise to Our Lord), except one Spaniard who died of hunger four days' journey from here and some Blacks and Indians who also died of hunger and thirst. The Spaniard was one of the footmen and was called Espinosa.[18] In this way His Grace spent seventy-seven days en route until arriving here. During that [whole] time God knows how we lived on reduced rations and that we could have eaten much more [food] than we ate.

On the day His Grace arrived at this *ciudad* of Granada[19] (he has given it this name in honor of the viceroy and because they say that it looks like the Albaicín),[20] he was not

FIGURE 22.1. The Albaicín, Granada, Spain, 1998. Photograph by the authors.

welcomed in the way the people he brought needed, since they all arrived very worn out from their great toil on the lengthy route, from loading and unloading (like regular muleteers), and from not eating as much as they wanted. Because [of this] they had greater need of resting for a few days than of fighting, although in the entire camp there was not a single man who, for all that, was unwilling to try, if the horses (which had the same need as their owners) would assist them.

The *ciudad* had been cleared of men older than sixty years and younger than twenty [years] and of women and children.[21] All that remained were fighting men, who stayed in order to defend the *ciudad.* Many [of them] came forth from it about the [distance] of a crossbow shot, making fierce threats.

My Lord the general advanced with two churchmen and the *maestre de campo* to summon them to obedience, as is the custom in new lands.[22] The response they made to him was [1v] many arrows they let fly. They wounded Hernando Bermejo's[23] horse. And with an arrow they pinned together the skirts of the habit of Father fray Luis, who was an associate of the lord bishop of México.[24] When [the general] saw this, calling on Lord Santiago as intercessor, he attacked them with all his men. He kept [his men] in very good order. Even though the Indians retreated and intended to take refuge in the *ciudad,* since they were close to it, before they reached [it] many of them were overtaken and killed.[25] [The Indians] killed three horses and wounded seven or eight.

When my lord the general had reached the *ciudad,* he saw it was all surrounded by a stone wall like a city wall.[26] The houses [were] very tall, of four and five [stories] and [some] even of six stories, each one with its flat roof and covered passageways.

Since the Indians had fortified themselves in [the *ciudad*] and would not permit a man to reach the wall whom they did not shoot with arrows, and [since] we did not have [anything] to eat unless we took it from them (because on the day we arrived here I do not believe there was [anything]

FIGURE 22.2. Dowa Yalanne, the mesa overlooking Zuni Pueblo from the southeast. Photograph by W. T. Mullarky. Courtesy Museum of New Mexico, neg. no. 4998.

to eat for the next day), His Grace determined[27] to enter the *ciudad* on foot and encircle it with horsemen, so that none of the Indians who were inside could get away.

Because [the general] stood out from everyone [else], with his golden armor and a plume on his helmet,[28] all the Indians launched their missiles at him, as a man distinguished from all [the rest]. They knocked him to the ground twice with errant stone[s][29] [thrown] from the flat roofs. They dented his helmet, and if it had not been as excellent [as it was], I doubt he [would have] gotten out alive from where he went in. [Even] with all this, it pleased Our Lord that he got out on his own [two] feet.[30] They hit him many times with stones on the head, shoulders, and legs. He received two small wounds on the face and an arrow wound in the right foot. [Even] with all this, His Grace is as healthy and well as on the day he left that Ciudad [de México]. Your Grace can certify it thus to my lord.[31]

It must be on the 19th of this past July that [the general] traveled four leagues from this *ciudad* to see a steep, rugged hill of rock[32] where [people from Cíbola] told him that the Indians of this *provincia* were fortifying themselves. He returned the same day, during which he traveled eight leagues there and back.

It seemed [appropriate] to me to give Your Grace a report concerning everything, because it is fitting that I be the one who writes to Your Grace and my lady[33] about everything which may occur concerning the health of the general, my lord. My lady can be certain, without any doubt, that he is as well and healthy as the day he departed from that Ciudad [de México] for this place and [is now] quartered within the *ciudad* [Cíbola/Granada]. [This last is so] because when the Indians saw His Grace's determination in his desire to gain entry to their *ciudad,* they immediately abandoned it. So [the Spaniards] permitted [the Indians] to go with their lives. In [the *ciudad*] we found what we had more need of than gold or silver, that is, a great quantity of corn, beans, [turkeys] (larger than those of Nueva España), and the best and whitest salt I have seen in my whole life.[34]

[2r] [blank]

[2v]
{(^1531)}
{Notice!}
{Copy of the news about the Tierra Nueva that came from Cíbola}

TRANSCRIPTION

[fol. 1r]

{1531}

{scribal mark}

TRaslado de las nueVas q*ue* Vinieron de la / çiUdad de
Çibola q*ue* es en la ti*er*ra nueVa

En el Valle de Culiacan dexo su m*erced* la mayor p*ar*te d*el*
exerçito y Con sola- / m*en*te setenta y çinco companeros de
Cavallo y treynta peones / partio para aCa JueVes xxij de abril
y *h*abia de partir el exerçito / q*ue* alla q*ue*do *en* fin de mes de
mayo porq*ue* tuVo nueVa³⁵ q*ue* hasta e(s)*n*tonçes *en* todo / El
camino hasta esta provy*nc*ia de çibola q*ue h*ay trezi*en*tas y
Çinq*uen*ta leguas largas / no hallarian nynguna man*er*a de
ma*n*tenymy*en*to y a esta CaUsa no (^quedo) / oSSo meter
todo El exerÇito En el camino y para la gent*e* q*ue* saco
mando / hase*r* matalotaJe para ochenta dias lo qual se traxo
en Cavallos cada / Uno para sy y su gent*e* con muy gran peligro d*e* padesçer d*e* hambre / y no menos trabajo q*ue* Como
Venian abriendo y d*es*Cubriendo cada / dia Caminos los
arcabucos y rrios y malos paSos se lleVaban / su part*e* y en
todo el camino hasta esta provy*nc*ia no se *h*Uvo solo Un /
çelemin de mayz llego a esta p*ro*vy*nc*ia miercoles syet*e* d*e e*ste
mes de / Jullio paSado con toda la gent*e* q*ue* saco d*el* Valle
muy b*uen*os loores / A n*uest*ro señor Eçepto Un español q*ue*
murio d*e* hambre quatro jornadas / De aqui y algunos negros
e yndios q*ue* tanbien muriero*n* de hambre / y de Sed El
español (h)era d*e* los d*e* pie y llamabase espinosa / por manera q*ue* tardo su m*erced* en el camino hasta llegar aqui setenta
y siete / dias en los quales sabe dios quan por taSa ViVimos
y si comieramos mucho / mas de lo q*ue* Comiamos El dia q*ue*
llego su m*erced* a esta çiudad de granada / q*ue* asy le *h*a puesto
por nonbr*e* En mem*or*ia d*el* Visorrey y porq*ue* dizen q*ue*

pareçe / al albayzin no fue rreçibido como lo *h*Uviera menester la gent*e* q*ue* traya / porq*ue* todos Venian muy fatigados
d*el* gran trabaJo d*el* camino largo y de / cargar y d*es*Cargar
como b*uen*os (h)arry*er*os y de no comer ta*n*to como q*ui*sieran
/ q*ue* trayan mas neçesydad de desCansar algunos dias q*ue* no
de pelear / aUnq*ue* no *h*abia en todo El campo hombr*e* q*ue*
para todo no traxese buenas / ganas sy los cavallos les ayu-
daran q*ue* trayan la misma neçesydad / q*ue* los Amos estava la
çiudad d*es*poblada de hombres d*e* seSenta años / Arriba y de
Veynt*e* abaxo y de mugeres y niños todo lo q*ue h*abia (h)era*n*
/ hombres d*e* guerra q*ue* quedaron para defender la Çiudad y
muchos salie- / ron d*e e*lla obra de Un tiro de ballesta haziendo grandes fieros y el gen*er*al / mi señor se adelanto con doS
rreligiosos y el maestre d*e* Campo A / rrequerirlos como se
Usa en ti*er*ras nueVas y la rresp*ues*ta q*ue* le daban (h)era

[fol. 1v]

muchas Flechas q*ue* soltavan y hirieron a herna*n*do bermejo
su Cavallo / y al padre fray luys compañero q*ue* (h)era d*el*
señor ob*is*po d*e* mexico le Cosyeron³⁶ / las faldas de los
*h*Abitos con Una flecha y Como esto Vio tomando por /
Abogado al señor s*an*tiago arremetio a ellos con toda su
gente q*ue* la / traya³⁷ muy bien (h)ordenada y aUnq*ue* los
yndios Volvyeron las espaldas y se / penSavan acoger a la çiudad q*ue* estavan çerca d*e* ella a*n*tes q*ue* llegasen fuero*n* /
alcançados y muertos muchos d*e e*llos y ellos mataron treS
cavallos y hiri- / eron syete o ocho llegado El general mi
señor a la çiudad Vi(d)o q*ue* toda (h)era / çercada de piedra
a Casamuro y las Casas muy altas de quatro y Çinco y / aUn
de seys altos cada Una con sus açuteas y Corredores y Como
los yn- / dios se hizieron fuertes en ella y no dexasen llegar a
la çerca a hombre q*ue* / no flechasen y no tuViesemos q*ue*

Comer syno se lo tomabamos porq*ue e*l dia / q*ue* aqui llegamos no creo q*ue h*abia q*ue* comer para otro dia[38] aCordo su
m*erce*d d*e en*trar / la çiudad a pie y çercarla de gent*e d*e
Cavallo porq*ue* no se fuese yndio de los q*ue* / dentro estavan
y Como entre todos yva senalado con sus Armas doradas / y
un plumaJe en la armadura d*e* Cabeça todos los yndios tiravan a el como / A hombre señalado entre todos y de las
açuteas a piedra perdida le / Derribaron En el suelo doS
Vezes y le abollaron la Armadura d*e* cabeça / q*ue* a no ser tan
buena du(b)do q*ue* saliera Vivo de donde entro y Con todo
esto / plazo[39] a n*uest*ro señor q*ue* salio por sus pies dieronle
En la Cabeça y hombros / y piernas muchos golpes d*e* piedra
y en el rrostro saco doS heridas peq*ue*nas / y en el pie d*ere*-
c*h*o Un flechazo de todo esta su m*erce*d tan sano y b*ue*no
como El dia / q*ue* de *e*Sa çiudad salio y asy lo puede V*uestra*
m*erce*d certificar A mi señor *h*ay q*ue* a xjx / del mes de Julio
paSado fue quatro leguas d*e e*sta çiUdad a Ver Un piñol /
donde le dixeron q*ue* los yndios d*e e*sta provy*n*çia se hazian
fuertes y Volvyo / El mesmo dia q*ue* anduVo En yda y
Venida ocho leguas paresçiome / dar a v*uestra* m*erce*d (^A)

cuenta de todo porq*ue* es Justo q*ue* yo sea El au(c)tor con /
V*uestra* m*erce*d y mi señora[40] de todo lo q*ue* paSare En la
salud d*e*l general mi señor / y sin ning*un*a sospecha puede
creer mi señora[41] q*ue* esta tan b*ue*no y sano como El / dia q*ue*
de *e*Sa çiudad p*ar*tio para aCa y aposentado dentro d*e* la çiudad porq*ue* como / los yndios Vieron la determinaçion d*e* su
m*erce*d En quererles entrar la çiUdad / luego la desmam-
pararo*n* conq*ue* les dexaron yr con las Vidas hallamos / En
ella lo q*ue* mas q*ue* oro ni plata *h*abiamos menester q*ue* es
mucho (^Sa) ma- / yz y frisoles y gallinas mayores q*ue* las de
*e*sa nueVa esPaña y sal la / mejor y mas blanCa q*ue* he Visto
en toda mi Vida

[fol. 2r] [blank]

[fol. 2v]
{(^1531)}
{ojo}
traslado de las nue- / Vas q*ue* Vinieron de çi- / bola de la *ti*e-
rra nueva

Document 23

La Relación Postrera de Cíbola
(Fray Toribio de Benavente's Narrative), 1540s

University of Texas, Austin, Benson Collection, JGI 31 XVI C, fols. 123v–124v

INTRODUCTION

Fray Toribio de Benavente was one of "Los Doce," the cadre of 12 friars dispatched to Nueva España in 1524. They were all in the "observant" wing of the Order of Friars Minor, also known as Franciscans. Fray Toribio later adopted the Nahuatl nickname Motolinía, meaning "mendicant or poor," in reference to this strict observance of the founder of his order's rule of poverty.[1] Despite his humble image, on his arrival in Nueva España at age 34 Motolinía was an accomplished scholar well versed in languages, grammar, and law, both civil and canon.[2] In 1536 the Franciscan chapter directed him to prepare a history of the Indians of Nueva España. To do this he would draw on notes he had been keeping for more than a decade.[3] The process took until at least 1541, during which time he continued to acquire letters and reports from throughout the viceroyalty that bore on his subject.

The result of Motolinía's labors has come down to us in the form of three manuscripts, all closely contemporaneous copies of the friar's original works. One is known as the "Memoriales," and the other two bear the title "Historia de los indios de la Nueva España." The two copies of the Historia indicate that their original was a later production than the Memoriales.[4] Each of the three manuscripts is introduced by a dedicatory letter, all dated in February 1541.[5] The three dedicatory prefaces present slightly different versions, all of which state something like

letters have arrived recently [saying] that [Spaniards] have found the beginning of grand *pueblos* and many people. The first *ciudad* is called Cíbola, in which the Spaniards were residing. It is believed to be an excellent gateway to what lies beyond.[6]

Only the Memoriales develops that mention of Cíbola in the body of its text. Nearly at the end of the manuscript is Capítulo 96, titled "la Relación postrera de sivola y de más de quatrocientas leguas adelante."[7] The short chapter is a compendium or digest of information obtained from several sources, including the letters referred to in the prefaces. Like the rest of all three manuscripts, the "Relación Postrera," or "latest *relación* regarding Cíbola," was assembled from "sources having different aims and purposes," which Motolinía sought "to blend together with smooth transitions."[8]

Nancy Joe Dyer has suggested that many of fray Toribio's sources were fellow friars who communicated with him by letter.[9] That could be the case with the Relación Postrera, although Motolinía makes no explicit statement to that effect, as he frequently does in other, similar instances. It has even been suggested that his fellow Franciscan and head of the order's province of the Santo Evangelio, fray Marcos de Niza, was the principal informant for the Relación Postrera.[10] Although this may be true, information provided by the Relación differs from fray Marcos's formal report in several instances. For example, the Relación states that "little of the route [is] populated,"[11] whereas, according to Marcos, in the Sonora Valley "an inordinate number of people came out to receive me," and it was "heavily settled by splendid people."[12]

On this same point the Relación Postrera conflicts markedly with a number of other contemporary reports. Castañeda de Nájera writes, "Señora is a river and valley heavily populated by very intelligent people," and the "Relación del Suceso" has, "This whole route is settled up to fifty leagues from Cíbola."[13] Likewise, the Relación Postrera's characterization of the territory along the expedition's route as "an unproductive land"[14] ignores the fact, reported by a number of members of the Coronado expedition, that there was plenty of food, especially corn, but it was too early in the season for it to be ripe.[15] Such discrepancies may have their origin in Motolinía's method of extracting bits of information from their original, variant sources and combining them to create his own summary.

Because the Relación Postrera is a derivative patchwork, truly Motolinía's creation, it must be used cautiously as historical evidence. What the friar innocently added or omitted often cannot be ascertained, although occasionally his intrusion into the narrative is manifest, as on folio 124r and in the final three paragraphs of the report.[16] In those last entries fray Toribio adds, for comparison, information derived from his own extensive reading, summarizing two passages from Marco Polo's *Travels* and an untitled report by Nicolo di Conti. These three entries epitomize the notational character of the document as a whole. They are very choppy, with many short, disconnected thoughts, as though recording temporarily loosely connected bits of information intended to be expanded and incorporated into a more finished, but hybrid, report.[17] Despite these cautions, most details recorded in the Relación Postrera are consistent with those in other, contemporary accounts of the Coronado expedition.

Nominally, the Relación Postrera is addressed to Antonio Pimentel, the sixth Conde de Benavente, a younger relative of fray Toribio's and patron of his order. It is clear, nevertheless, that Motolinía envisioned a much wider readership.[18] The themes he selected for the Relación are ones that had proved popular in Europe: a miscellany of the "strange" customs of the Indians of the Valley of Mexico, with reference also to Guatemala and Michoacán; the work of the friars and consequent miracles; portraits of exotic landscapes and animals; and narration of episodes from Spanish conquests.

The sole surviving sixteenth-century manuscript of the Memoriales, and hence of the Relación Postrera, is held today in the Nettie Lee Benson Latin American Collection at the University of Texas in Austin. It makes up part of the "Libro de Oro" acquired by the University of Texas library in 1937 from Joaquín García Pimentel, grandson of the great Mexican scholar Joaquín García Icazbalceta. The manuscript of the Memoriales bears the call number JGI 31 XVI C, of which folios 123v–124v are transcribed and translated here.[19] Two different *escribanos* prepared the manuscript of the Memoriales, although the folios of the segment that is the Relación Postrera are all in a single hand.[20]

A folio in the Libro de Oro indicates that it had been sold in Madrid in 1702 by one Lucas Cortés. It was later purchased, also in Madrid, in 1862 by Joaquín María Andrade, who gave it to Joaquín García Icazbalceta 17 years later. If either of these men knew the earlier history of the manuscript, it disappeared with their deaths. Three editions of the Memoriales have been published in Spanish: one in 1903 by Luis García Pimentel, one in 1971 by Edmundo O'Gorman, and most recently a stricter paleographic transcription by Nancy Joe Dyer in 1996.[21] As a separate excerpt, the Relación Postrera de Cíbola has been previously published once in Spanish[22] and twice in English.[23] Differences between these transcripts and translations and ours, which follow, are pointed out in the annotations. Folio numbers from the Libro de Oro manuscript have been retained.

TRANSLATION

[123v]

[. . .]

{Item}[24] This is the latest *relación* regarding Cíbola and more than four hundred leagues farther on.

From Culiacán to Cíbola it is more than three hundred leagues.[25] Little of the route [is] populated; there are very few people.[26] It is an unproductive land.[27] There are very poor trails. The people along [that route] go about completely naked, except the women, who wear white, cured deerskins, from the waist down all the way to their feet, like little skirts. The houses they have are built of mats made from reeds. The houses are round and small, [so] that a standing man hardly fits inside.[28] The land is sandy where [the natives] are congregated and where they plant [their crops]. They harvest corn (although only a little), beans, and squash. They also sustain themselves by hunting cottontails, jackrabbits, and deer. They do not have sacrifices. This applies from Culiacán to Cíbola.

{Item} Cíbola is a town of up to two hundred houses.[29] They are two, three, four, and five stories [high]. [124r] They have walls one *palmo* thick. The poles used in the woodwork [of the roofs] are round and as big around as a wrist. In place of plank[s], very thin reeds with their leaves form the closure, and on top [is] compacted earth. The walls are made of earth and clay.[30] The doors of the houses are like the hatchways of ships.[31] The houses adjoin and abut each other.[32] In front of their houses they have some *estufas* made of clay-earth, where they take shelter from the cold in winter. [That is] because [the cold] is very severe since it snows six months of the year.

Some of these people wear *mantas* of cotton, maguey,[33] and cured deerhides. [Some] wear shoes made of the same hides, [which extend] over their knees. They also have *mantas* made of cottontail and jackrabbit pelts with which they cover themselves.[34] The women go about dressed in *mantas* made of maguey [which extend down to] to their feet. [The *mantas*] are bound about [them]. They wear their hair gathered above their ears like wheels.[35]

They harvest corn, beans, and squash.[36] This is plenty for them for their sustenance because the people are few. The land where they plant is all sand. The water sources are brackish. The land is very arid. [The natives] have some [turkeys], although only a few. They do not know what an edible fish is. There are seven *pueblos* in the *provincia* of Cíbola in a space of five leagues.[37] The principal one probably consists of two hundred houses. Another two consist of two hundred [houses each], and the others of sixty, fifty, and thirty houses.

{Item} From Cíbola to the river and *provincia* of Tiguex it is sixty leagues. The first *pueblo* is forty leagues from Cíbola. It is called Acuco.[38] This *pueblo* is situated on top of a steep, rugged hill of rock, [and is] very strong. It probably consists of two hundred houses built like [those] of Cíbola, which, [however, speaks] another language.[39]

From there to the Río de Tiguex it is twenty leagues. The river is nearly as wide as the one at Sevilla, although it is not as deep.[40] It flows through level land. It is a good water source. It has some fish. It originates in the north. The [person] who states this saw twelve *pueblos* within a certain distance along the river.[41] Others saw more.[42] They say [that] upstream and downstream along the river all the *pueblos* are small except two, which probably have two hundred houses [each]. These [are] houses with structural walls like free-standing walls made of sandy earth. They are very strong [and] as thick as one palm of a hand.[43] The houses are two and three stories [high]. They have roof woodwork like [that] in Cíbola. The land is very cold. It has its *estufas* as in Cíbola. The footing [of] the river being made firm,[44] loaded pack animals routinely crossed through it, and wagons would be able to cross.[45] [The natives] harvest [the] corn that they need, and beans and squash. They have a few [turkeys] which they keep in order to make *mantas* from [their] feathers. They harvest cotton, though only a little.[46] They wear *mantas* made of it and hide shoes as in Cíbola. They are a people who defend their property quite well from their houses, since they take care not to come outside [to do it]. The land is completely sandy.

{Item} After four days' journey from the *provincia* and river of Tiguex [the expedition] came across four *pueblos*.[47] The first probably has thirty houses; the second is a fine, large *pueblo*, destroyed during their wars. The third had as many as thirty-five inhabited houses. As far as those three, [the *pueblos*] are generally like those along the river. The fourth is a large *pueblo* which is situated among some woodlands. They call themselves Cicuic.[48] It had as many as fifty houses with an equal number of flat terrace-roofs like those in Cíbola.[49] The walls are made of earth and clay, like those of Cíbola. [The people of Cicuic] have plenty of corn, beans, and squash and a few [turkeys].

Four days' journey from this *pueblo* [the expedition] encountered a land level like the sea.[50] On those plains there is such a multitude of [bison] that they have no number. These cattle are like those of Spain. Some of the larger ones have a small hump on their withers. They are, however, more red, which tends to black. A very long fleece, one *palmo* [long], hangs from them between their horns and ears, [from the] chin, downward from the dewlap, and from the shoulders like manes. From the knees downward [and] all the rest is [covered] by very, very short wool, like [124v] merino.[51] They have very good, tender meat, and much fat.[52]

After traveling many days through these plains, [the expedition] came across a *ranchería* consisting of as many as two hundred houses, with people. The houses were made of cured [bison] hides. [They were] white like campaign or military tents. Food for the nourishment of these Indians comes entirely from the [bison], since they neither plant nor harvest corn. They make their houses from the hides; they clothe themselves and make shoes from the hides; they make cords from the hides and also from the wool; from the sinew they make thread with which they sew their clothing and also their houses; they make awls from the bones. The [bison] dung serves them in place of firewood, since there is none in that land. Their stomachs are useful to them as jars and jugs from which they drink.

With the meat they nourish themselves. They eat it partly roasted over the [bison] dung [and] still slightly hot; the rest [they eat] raw. Taking it in their teeth, they pull with one hand and in the other they have a large flint *navaja*[53] and cut off a mouthful. In this way they swallow it like birds, partly chewed. They eat the fat raw without [even] heating it. They drink the blood as soon as it comes from the [bison] and other times [they drink it] cold and uncooked [some time] after it has come out. They do not have any other food.[54]

These people have dogs like those in this land,[55] except that they are somewhat larger. They load up those dogs like beasts of burden and make them light packsaddles, [which are] like saddles for breaking horses.[56] They cinch them with hide strips. [The dogs] go about with galls on their withers like beasts of burden. When [these people] go hunting, they load the [dogs] with food. And when these Indians move (since they are not established in [any] one place, because they go where the [bison] go in order to sustain themselves), these dogs take their houses and transport the poles for the houses, dragging [them] tied to the saddles.[57] [These they carry] in addition to the load[s] they carry on top. Depending on the dog, the load can probably be an *arroba* and a half [or] two.

It is thirty leagues from Cíbola to where [the expedition] reached these plains. Moreover, the plains continue on, it is not known how far. Captain Francisco Vázquez went on across the plains with thirty horsemen, and fray Juan de Padilla [was] with him.[58] All the rest of the people [of the expedition] returned to the settlement on the river in order to await Francisco Vázquez because he ordered it [done] that way. It is not known whether he has returned, etc.[59]

{Item} The land is so level that men became lost when they were separated by [only] half a league. For instance, one horseman became lost who never turned up again, also two horses, saddled and bridled, which never appeared again. Where [people] travel no trace at all remains. For this reason they needed to mark the route by which they were going with piles of [bison] dung in order [to be able] to return. There are no stones or anything else [to mark with].

{Item}[60] In chapter 15 of his treatise, the Venetian Marco Polo mentions and states he has seen the same cattle, similar in regard to the hump.[61] In the same chapter he states that there are also rams the size of horses.

{Item} The Venetian Nicolao[62] gave a report to the Florentine *micer* Poggio.[63] In the second book, near the end, he states that in Ethiopia there are oxen with a hump such as camels [have] and they have horns the length of three *codos*.[64] They throw their horns [back] over their backbone. One of these horns holds a *cántaro* of wine.[65]

{Item} In chapter one hundred and thirty-four Marco Polo states that in the land of the Tartars, toward the north, doglike animals are found [which are] as large as donkeys.[66] [The Tartars] attach to [the animals] a [thing] like a cart, and they go into a very boggy land with them, all quagmires, which other animals would not be able to enter or get out of without drowning. For that [reason] they take dogs.

TRANSCRIPTION

[fol. 123v]

[. . .]

{Y*tem*} Esta es la Relacion postrera[67] de sivola / y de mas de quatrocientas leguas adelante

Desde culhuacan A sivola *h*ay mas de trecientas leguas poco del camino poblado / *h*ay muy poca gente es tierra esteril *h*ay muy malos caminos la gente anda del todo / desnuda salvo las mugeres que desde la cintura Abaxo traen cueros de Venados adobados / blancos A manera de faldillas hasta los pies las cassas que tienen son de petlatles / hechos de cañas son las casas redondas y pequeñas que Apenas cabe Un hombre en pie / dentro donde estan congregados y donde siembran es tierra Arenosa cogen mayz aUn- / que poco y frisoles y calabaças y tanbien se mantienen de caça conejos lie*b*res y ve- / nados no tienen sacrificios esto es desde culhuacan (^hasta) a sivola

{Y*tem*} Sivola es un pueblo de hasta ducientas casas son A dos y tres y quatro y cinco / sobrados

[fol. 124r]

sobrados tienen las paredes de Un palmo de ancho los palos de la maderacion / son tan gruesos como por la muñeca y redondos por tabla contienen cañas muy / menudas con sus hojas y encima tierra p(r)esada[68] las paredes son de tierra y barro / las puertas de las casas son de la manera de escotillones de navios estan las casas / juntas Asidas Unas con otras tienen delante de las casas Unas estufas de barro de / tierra donde se guarecen en el ynvierno del frio porque le haze muy grande que / ni(^a)eva seys meses del año De *e*sta gente algunos traen mantas de algodon y de / maguey y cueros de Venados Adobados y traen çapatos de los mesmos cueros hasta / encima de las Rodillas tanbien hazen mantas de pellejos de liebres y de conejos / con

que se cubren andan las mugeres Vestidas de mantas de maguey hasta los / pies andan çeñidas Traen los cabellos cojidos ençima de las orejas como rodajas / coxen mayz y frisoles y calabaças lo que les basta para su mantenimiento por- / que es poca gente La tierra donde siembran es toda arena son las aguas / salobres es tierra muy seca tienen algunas gallinas Aunque pocas no / saben que cosa es pescado son siete pueblos en esta provincia de sivola en espacio / de cinco leguas el mayor sera de duzientas casas y otros dos (dos) de a ducientas / y los otros A sesenta y A cincuenta y A treynta casas

{Y*tem*} Desde sivola al rio y provincia de tig*U*ex[69] *h*Ay sesenta leguas el primer pueblo / es quarenta leguas de sivola llamase acuco Est(a)*e* pueblo esta encima de / Un peñol muy fuerte sera de ducientas casas asentado A la manera de sivola que / es otra lengua Desde alli al rio de tiguex *h*ay veynte leguas El rio es quasi / tan ancho como el de sevilla Aunque no es tan hondo Va por tierra llana es / buen agua tiene algun(d) pescado nasçe al norte el que esto dize Vio ^*doze* (^çiertos) pueblos / en çierto compas del rio otros Vieron mas dizen el rio Ar*r*iba abaxo todos son / pueblos pequeños salvo dos que te(r)n*d*ran A duzientas casas estas casas con las pare- / des como A manera de tapias de tierra De Arena muy Rezias son tan anchas / como Un palmo De una mano son las casas de a dos y tres terrados tienen la / maderacion como en sivola es tierra muy fria tiene sus estufas como en sivola / y el asentando el rio[70] que pasavan bestias cargadas por el y pudieran pasar carre- / tas cogen mayz lo que *h*an menester y frisoles y calabaças tienen algunas / gallinas las quales guardan para hazer mantas de la pluma coxen algodon (^trae) / Aunque poco traen mantas de *e*llo y capatos del cuero como en sivola es gente / que defiende bien su capa y desde sus casas que no curan de[71] salir fuera es tierra / toda Arenosa

{Y*tem*} Desde la provincia y rio de tiguex A quatro jornadas toparon quatro pueblos / el primero te(r)n*d*ra treynta (^y cinco) casas el segundo es buen pueblo grande destruydo de / sus guerras t(h)enia hasta treynta y çinco casas pobladas el terçero hasta / estos tres son de la manera de los del rio en todo el quarto es Un pueblo grande / el qual esta entre Unos montes llamanse⁷² cicuic t(h)enia hasta cinquenta casas / con tantos terrados como los de sivola son las paredes de tierra y barro como / las de sivola tienen harto mayz y frisoles y cala- baças y algunas gallinas A / quatro Jornadas de *e*ste pueblo toparon Una tierra llana como la mar en los q*ua*les / llanos *h*Ay tanta multitud de Vacas que no tienen numero estas Vacas son como / las de castilla y algunas mayores que tienen en la cruz Una cor*co*Va pequeña y son / mas bermejas que tira*n* A negro cuelgales Una lana mas larga que Un palmo entre / los quernos y orejas y barba y por la papada Abaxo y por las espaldas como cri- / nes y desde las Rodillas Abaxo todo lo demas es de lana muy pequeñita A manera

[fol. 124v]

De merino tienen muy buena carne y tierna y mucho sebo Andando muchos / dias por estos llanos toparon con Una rancheria de hasta duzientas casas con gente / (h)eran las casas de los cueros de las Vacas adobados blancas A manera de pave- llones / o tiendas de campo el mant(h)enimiento A susten- tamiento de *e*stos yndios es todo / de las Vacas porque ni siem- bran ni coxen mayz de los cueros hazen sus casas de los / cueros Visten y calçan de los cueros hazen sogas y tanbien de la lana de los / n(i)er*v*ios hazen hilo con que cosen sus Vestiduras y tanbien las casas de los huesos / hazen alesnas⁷³ las boñigas los sirven de leña porque no *h*Ay otra en aquella tierra / los buches les sirven de jarros y Vasijas con que beben de la carne se mantienen / comen la medio Asada Aun poco caliente encima de las boñigas la otra cruda / y tomandola con los dientes tiran con la una mano y en la otra tienen Un (^Va) naVa- / jon de ped(r)e*r*nal y cortan el bocado a(n)si lo tragan como Aves medio mazcado comen el / sebo crudo sin calen- tallo beben la sangre A(n)si como sale de las Vacas y otras Vezes / despues de salida fria y cruda no tienen otro mantenimiento esta gente tiene perros / como los de esta tierra salvo que son algo mayores los quales perros cargan como A / bestias y les

hazen sus en(s)*j*almas como albardillas y las cinchan con sus correas / y andan matados como bestias en las cruzes quando Van A caça carganlos de man- / tenimientos y quando se mueven estos yndios porque no estan de Asiento en una parte / que se andan(^d) donde andan (^V)⁷⁴ las Vacas para se man- tener estos perros les llevan / las casas y llevan los palos de las casas arrastrando Atados A las albardillas allen- / de de la carga que llevan ençima podra ser la carga segun(d) el perro Ar*r*oba y media y / dos *h*Ay desde sibola A estos llanos Adonde lle- garon treynta leguas y aUn mas los / llanos proçeden adelante ni se sabe que tanto el capitan francisco Vazquez fue por los / llanos Adelant(r)e con treynta de A caballo y fray juan de pa- dilla con el toda la de- / mas gente se Volvieron A la poblacion del rio para esperar A francisco Vazquez por- / que a(n)si se lo mando no se sabe si es Vuelto et*cetera*

{Y*tem*} Es la tierra tan llana que se pierden los hombres Apartandose media legua como / se perdio Uno A cavallo que nunca mas parescio y dos cavallos en(^l)syllados y enfre- / nados que nunca mas parescieron no queda Rastro ninguno por donde Van y A / esta causa t(h)enian nesçesidad de Amojonar el camino por donde yvan para / Volver con boñi- gas de Vacas que no *h*Avia piedras ni otra cosa

{Y*tem*} Marco polo Veneciano en su tratado en el capitulo XV trata y dize que *h*A *visto*⁷⁵ las / mesmas Vacas y de la mesma manera en la corcoVa y en el mesmo capitulo dize / que tanbien *h*Ay carneros tamaños como caballos

{Y*tem*} Nicolao Veneciano dio Relacion A Miçer pogio florenti- no en el libro / segundo çerca del fin dize como en la etiopia *h*Ay bueyes con cor*co*va como / camellos y tiene*n* los quernos largos de tres codos y (h)echan los quernos ençima / sobre el (^pes- cueço) espinazo y haze Un querno de *e*stos Un cantaro de Vino

{Y*tem*} Marco polo en el capitulo çiento y treynta y quatro dize que en la tierra / de los tartaros hazia el norte se hallan canes⁷⁶ tan grandes o poco menos / que asnos A los quales (h)echan Uno como carro y entran con ellos en Una t*ie*rra / muy lodosa toda cenagales que otros Animales no podrian entrar ni salir / sin se Anegar y por eso llevan perros

Document 24

Hernando de Alvarado's Narrative, 1540

AGI, Patronato, 26, R.23

INTRODUCTION

Toward the end of August 1540, a trading or diplomatic party of seven or eight people from Cicuique Pueblo arrived at the newly renamed pueblo of Granada.[1] This may have been just after Vázquez de Coronado had dispatched García López de Cárdenas west, to follow up Pedro de Tovar's brief reconnaissance of Tusayán.[2] The party from Cicuique had made the 70-league trip, in Castañeda de Nájera's words, "because of the report they had been given," and "they were coming to be of service to [the captain general]."[3] The principal Cicuique spokesman, a man the Spaniards nicknamed Bigotes, said that "[the people of Cicuique] would consider [the Spaniards] allies" and offered to guide the expedition through the eastern pueblos.[4]

So, on August 29, within two or three days of the arrival of the emissaries, Captain Hernando de Alvarado departed from Granada with some 20 horsemen, led by Bigotes.[5] Among the Europeans included in the party were Melchior Pérez, Juan Jaramillo, Juan Troyano, and possibly Juan Cordero. Very likely this group was accompanied by a contingent of *indios amigos* from what is now central and western Mexico.

Their reconnaissance commission was for a period of 80 days. During that time the newcomers and their native guides toured much of the Río de Tiguex/Rio Grande Pueblo area. As Melchior Pérez recalled later, Bigotes "went ahead, making sure that the Indians of those pueblos came out in peace."[6] And as a result of Bigotes's diplomacy, it was said that "all [of the people] came forth in peace."[7] Along the Río de Tiguex, for instance, Alvarado's own report has it that "the principales and people came from twelve pueblos. [They came] in order, those from one [pueblo] behind the other."[8] Not all the Pueblo people, however, may have been as acquiescent as these statements indicate. For example, the expeditionary Rodrigo de Frías testified in 1544 that the people of all the pueblos "had come out to [Alvarado] in peace, with the exception of two pueblos where they came forth in war and which he had pacified."[9]

Despite such hostilities, Alvarado "made a report to Francisco Vázquez about this river" and "sent word to the general to come to that land to spend the winter."[10] As Castañeda de Nájera told it later, "the general relaxed more than a little with news that the land was improving," and he "sent don García López de Cárdenas to Tiguex with a troop to prepare quarters, in order to take the expedition there to spend the winter."[11]

It is a contemporaneous copy of a fragment of that report that is published here. The author of the original, though not named in the document, was almost certainly Hernando de Alvarado himself. In the report the author writes that "[the Indians] came into the tent and presented me with food, *mantas*, and hides they were carrying. I gave them a few small items."[12] Such a statement could have been made only by the leader of the reconnaissance party, Captain

Alvarado, who would have been the person with authority to carry out a formal gift exchange.

Alvarado had been born in 1517 in the small town of Las Montañas in the municipality of Torrelavega in the *provincia* of Santander in the modern Spanish *comunidad* of Cantabria. He had arrived in Nueva España in 1528, at the age of only 11, with the returning Hernán Cortés and went with him on a reconnaissance of the Mar del Sur. As a *caballero* of the Order of Santiago, Alvarado was an elite person, whom Vázquez de Coronado, in consultation with the viceroy, appointed captain of artillery for the expedition to Tierra Nueva. It was he who was first told the story of gold in Quivira by El Turco shortly after the events narrated in the letter that follows. He imprisoned the native leader Bigotes and transported him to Tiguex to be examined there. That examination involved physical intimidation and torture of the erstwhile ally. Charges stemming from the resulting dog attack against Bigotes were later recommended against Alvarado. However, none is known to have been filed. He was a *vecino* of the Ciudad de México by 1547, if not well before, and died on July 16, 1550.[13]

The report that Alvarado sent from Tiguex to Vázquez de Coronado in Cíbola in September 1540 survives only in this incomplete scribal copy, which is curated in the Archivo General de Indias under the *signatura* (catalog number) AGI, Patronato, 26, R.23. When and by whom the copy was made is unknown, although it was likely within a few months of Alvarado's preparation of the original report. The copyist was probably responsible for the document's title; certainly Alvarado was not. The copy breaks off rather abruptly, as though interrupted and never resumed. How much more there might have been to the original is impossible to gauge. We can say with assurance, though, that

Alvarado's recommendation that the expedition establish winter quarters along the Río de Tiguex is missing. And presumably he also indicated his choice for the particular pueblo that would best serve.

In the surviving fragment Alvarado seems uncommonly interested in construction details. He reports heights of walls on several occasions and frequently refers to building materials. Regarding the ruins of a very large *ciudad* in the Cíbola area, for example, he writes that "the outside wall [was] well built of excellent stone, [which was] shaped around its doorways and sewers, as [in] a *ciudad* in Castilla." Just a little farther along he writes about a particularly well-built wall in which "the first *estado* was made of very large granite stones and from there up of very good cut stone."[14] Alvarado's interest in stone masonry may have arisen in part from the common notion of the day that it, like the wearing of textiles and the use of metal, was a reliable indicator of a sophisticated and prosperous society.

In 1857 Thomas Buckingham Smith published a Spanish transcription of a copy of the Alvarado report that had been made in the 1770s by Juan Bautista Muñoz, founder of the Archivo General de Indias.[15] Eight years later, Joaquín Pacheco and Francisco de Cárdenas republished the same transcript.[16] The Muñoz transcript (Smith publication) was used by George Parker Winship to prepare his 1896 English translation.[17] In 1940 George Hammond and Agapito Rey used the Pacheco and Cárdenas version of the Muñoz transcript as the basis for their English translation.[18] Most recently, Carmen de Mora re-published the Pacheco and Cárdenas version in Spanish.[19] We consulted all of these earlier sources in editing the new transcription and translation that follow. Unlike the previous editions, however, this one is based directly on the sixteenth-century manuscript.

TRANSLATION

[1r]
{Reconnaissance}
{Mar del Sur, 1540}[20]

{Item} {Report of what Hernando de Alvarado and fray Juan de Padilla found during their search for the Mar del Sur}[21]

{Item} We departed from Granada [Cíbola] on Sunday, the twenty-ninth of August 1540, the day of the beheading of San Juan, [on] the route to Acoco.[22] When two leagues had passed, we encountered an ancient building like a fortress. A league farther on we found another one, and a little farther another one. Farther beyond these we found an ancient *ciudad.* [It was] exceedingly large [and] completely destroyed, although a great part of the perimeter wall was [still] standing, which was probably six *estados* tall.[23] The

FIGURE 24.1. Acoma Pueblo atop its mesa, about 1923. Courtesy Museum of New Mexico, neg. no. 57804.

outside wall [was] well built of excellent stone, [which was] shaped around its doorways and sewers, as [in] a *ciudad* in Castilla.

Half a league beyond this [*ciudad,* or] about one league, we found another ruined *ciudad.* The wall of this [one] must have been very good; the first *estado* was made of very large granite stones and from there up of very good cut stone.[24]

Here two routes divide; one [goes] to Chia [Zia] and the other to Coco [Acoma].[25] We took this [latter] one and arrived at the aforesaid place. It is one of the strongest things that have been seen, because the *ciudad* is located on a very high, steep, rugged hill of rock and its ascent is so difficult that we regretted having climbed up to that place. The houses are three and four stories high.[26] The people are the [same] kind [as those] from the *provincia* of Cíbola. They have an abundance of food: corn, beans, and [turkeys like] those of Nueva España.

From here we went to a very fine lake, at which there are trees like those of Castilla.[27] From there we went to a river which we named for Nuestra Señora, since we reached it on the eve of her [feast] day in the month of September.[28] We sent a cross with a guide to the *pueblos* farther on.

The next day the *principales* and people came from twelve *pueblos.* [They came] in order, those from one [*pueblo*] behind the other. They walked around our tent playing a flute, and an old man [was] speaking. In this [same] way they came into the tent and presented me with food, *mantas,* and hides they were carrying. I gave them a few small items, and with this they returned to their houses.

[1v] {Item} This Río de Nuestra Señora flows through a very wide, level, and fertile land, planted with cornfields. There are some groves of cottonwoods. There are twelve towns. The

houses are made of earth [and have] two terraced stories.[29] The people seem excellent, more like farmers than warriors. They have much food: corn, beans, melons, and [turkeys] in great abundance. They dress in cotton, [bison] hides, and long robes made of [turkey] feathers. They wear their hair trimmed short. It is the old men who have most authority among them. We consider them sorcerers because they say that they mount up to heaven and other things of this nature. In this *provincia* there are seven other deserted towns which were destroyed by those Indians whose eyes are dyed yellow.[30] The guides gave Your Grace an account of them. [The native Indians] say [the Indians with painted eyes] border on the [bison] and have corn and houses made of thatch.[31]

{Item} The [people] of the neighboring *provincias* came to this place to offer me their friendship.[32] These are [the *provincias*] Your Grace will understand from that account.[33] In them there are probably eighty towns of the sort I have [previously] told about. Among them [there is] one situated on some stream banks, [in which] there were twenty sections, which are something worth seeing.[34] The houses consist of three stories made of mud walls and another three built of small planks of wood. Around the outside of each of those three stories made of mud there is a covered walkway made of wood. These [walkways] encircle the whole section, on the perimeter. Now, it seemed to us that there were probably as many as fifteen thousand persons in this town. It is a very cold land. Neither [turkeys] nor cotton is raised [there]. They venerate the sun and rain. Outside that place we found earthen mounds where [their dead] are buried.

{Item} In those places where crosses were erected, we showed them [how] to venerate them. They offer their powders and feathers [to the crosses], and some leave the *mantas* they are wearing.[35] [They venerate the cross] with such great ardor that some climbed on top of others in order to reach the arms of the crosses so they could place feathers and roses [there]. Others brought ladders, holding them, [and still] others climbed up to tie on yarn in order attach the roses and feathers.[36]

[2r] [blank]

[2v][37]
{1540}
{Report for His Majesty regarding what Hernando de Alvarado and fray Juan de Padilla found}
{Copy}

[fol. 1r]

{descubrimy*entos*}

{Mar del sur 1540}

{*ytem*} R*e*La*ç*ion de Lo que Hernando de aLvarado y frai Joan de padilla descu- / brieron en demanda de la mar del sur

{*ytem*} Partimos de Granada domingo dia de san Joan / de(c)golla*ç*io*n* (treynt*a*) *veinte* y nueVe de agosto de *1*540 la Via / de acoco y andadas doss leguas dimos en Un (h)e- / defi*ç*io Antiguo como fortaleza y Una Legua / Adelante hallamos otro y poco mas Adelante / otro y adelante de *e*stos hallamos Una *ç*iudad / Antigua (f)*h*arto grande toda destruida AUnq*ue* / mucha parte de la muralla estaba en*h*yesta La / qual te(r)nd*r*ya seys estados en Alto el muro bien / labrado de buena piedra labrada de sus puer- / t*a*s y albanares[38] como Una *ç*iudad de castilla / media legua Adelante de *e*sta obra de Una le- / gua hallamos otra *ç*iudad destruyda la Çer- / ca de la qual debia ser muy buena hasta Un / estado de piedras berroquenas muy grandes / y de alli Arriba De muy buena piedra de Canteria / Aquy se apart*a*n doss Camyn*o*s Uno para chia y / otro para coco tomamos este y allegamos Al d*i*cho / lugar el qual es Una de las mas fuertes Cosas que / se *h*an Visto porq*ue* esta la *ç*iudad en Un peñol muy Alto / y tiene la subida tan mala que nos Arrepenti- / mos de *h*aber subido Al lugar las casas son de tress / y quatro sobr(e)ados la gente es de la manera de *e*sa / pro*v*in*ç*ia de *ç*ibola tienen Abundan*ç*ia de comyda / De mays e frisoles y gallinas de las de la nueVa / españa de aqui fuymos a Una laguna muy buena / en la qual *h*ay arboles como los de castilla de / Alli fuymos A Un Rio el qual

llamamos De / n*uest*ra senora porq*ue* llegamos A el la Vispera De / su dia en el mes de se*p*tienbre y enViamos la / Cruz con Una guia A los pu*ebl*os de Adelante y / otro dia Vinyeron de doze pu*ebl*os pren*ç*ipaLes y / gente en orde- / nan*ç*a los de Un pueblo tras / de otro y dieron Una Vuelt*a* A la tienda ta- / nendo con Una flaUta y Un Viejo hablando y / de *e*sta manera entraron en la tienda y me prese*n*- / taro*n* la comyda y mant*a*s y Cueros q*ue* traya*n* E yo / les di algu*n*as cosillas y con esto se VolViero*n* a sus caSas[39]

[fol. 1v]

{*ytem*} este Rio de n*uest*ra señora Corre por Una Vega muy ancha / senbrada de maizaLes *h*ay algunas Alamedas son / doze pu*ebl*os Las casas son de ti*er*ra de doss terrados La / gente pares*ç*e buena mas Como labradores q*ue* / gente de guerra tienen mucha comyda de mays E / Frisoles y melones y gallinas en gran(d) Abun- / dan*ç*ia Vistense de Algodon y de cueros de Vacas / y pellones de la pluma de las gallinas traen el / Cavello cort*a*do los que mas entre ellos manda*n* / son los VieJos tenemos(^y)los por hechizeros porq*ue* / dizen que suben Al *ç*ielo E otras cosas de *e*sta ca- / lidad en est*a* pro*v*in*ç*ia *h*Ay otros siete pu*ebl*os Des- / poblados y destruydos de Aquellos yndios en- / biJados Los oJos de quyen A V*uestra* m*erce*d hazian Rela- / *ç*ion las guyas dizen que confina*n* con las Vacas / y que tienen casas de paJa y mays

{*ytem*} Aquy Vinyeron A darme la paz los de las provyn- / *ç*ias comarcanas que son las que V*uestra* m*erce*d Vera / por esa memoria en q*ue* *h*Abra ochent*a* pu*ebl*os de la / Calidad que tengo dicho y entre ellos Uno que esta / Asent*a*do entre Unas rriVeras[40] *h*Ab(i)ia Veynte barrios / que son cosa de Ver las casas son de tress altos / De t*a*pia y otros tress de madera de Unas tablas / pequenas y en los tress Altos de t*a*pia por De- / fuera tienen tress Corredores de madera y estos / Dan Vuelt*a* A todo el barrio A la rredonda[41] pares- / çianos ya que *h*abria en este pu*ebl*o hasta quynze myll / personas es t*i*erra muy fria no se cria*n* gallinas / ny Algodon Adoran Al sol y al agua hallamos / montones de t*i*erra fuera del lugar donde se en- / Tierran

{y*tem*} en las partes q*ue* se leVant*a*ron Cruzes Les mostra- / bamos Adorallas y ellos ofresçen sus polVos / y plumas y algunos dexan las mant*a*s que / lleVan Vestidas y con t*a*nta agonya que subian / Unos ençima de otros por alcançar A los

braços / De las cruzes para poner plumas y rroSas / y otros trayendo esCaleras teniendolas ot*r*os / subian A atar *h*ylos para poner las Rosas / y las plumas

[fol. 2r] [blank]

[fol. 2v]
{1540}
{R*e*laci*o*n de lo q*ue* Hern*an*do d*e* alVarado y / fray Ju*an* de padilla desCubriero*n*
P*a*ra Su mag*es*ta*d*}
{Dup*lica*da}

Document 25

Letter from Viceroy Mendoza to Fernández de Oviedo, October 6, 1541

Segunda Parte, Libro XXXIII, Capítulo LII, *Historia general y natural de las Indias*, 1547

Academia Real de la Historia, Madrid

Colección Salazar y Castro, 9/555 (H-32)

INTRODUCTION

In response to a petulant letter from the royal chronicler, Gonzalo Fernández de Oviedo y Valdés, insisting on current information about events unfolding in Nueva España, Viceroy Mendoza drafted a reply in October 1541. Deeming the viceroy's response a "noteworthy report," Oviedo copied it into the manuscript of his *Historia general y natural de las Indias,* where it makes up Capítulo 52 of Libro 33 in the Segunda Parte.[1]

Oviedo had evidently gotten wind of the viceroy's having sent letters and reports to Venice and León, bypassing him at Santo Domingo in the Caribbean. That raised Oviedo's ire and launched his badgering letter to Mendoza. Word from Venice about Mendoza's communiqués quite likely came to Oviedo from his business partner, Giovanni Battista Ramusio, who was also a voracious collector and publisher of documents relating to contemporary voyages and expeditions. Ramusio, in turn, might well have gotten his information from the Spanish ambassador to Venice, Antonio de Mendoza's brother Diego Hurtado de Mendoza.[2]

Both the range of Oviedo's curiosity and the provisional state of knowledge of the New World are evident in the viceroy's responses to his queries. Those questions ranged from the origin of the Nahuas of the Valley of Mexico to the possible existence of giants. Oviedo's principal question,

however, as well as Mendoza's chief concern, focused on the coordinated land and sea expeditions led by Francisco Vázquez de Coronado and Pedro de Alvarado. Nearly half the viceroy's letter deals with those two enterprises.

Mendoza attempts to mask his annoyance over Oviedo's pestering with phrases such as "I will not break off this friendship."[3] Nevertheless, his irritation is apparent in his cursory replies directed only to Oviedo's specific questions. The viceroy seems loath to volunteer additional information, partly because to share intelligence with the chronicler was to broadcast it to all of Europe. Even about the northbound expeditions he insists that "there is little to say."[4]

Regarding "gold and silver and fair-complected and handsome women and food," Mendoza suspends his reticence just enough to write that they have been found "in abundance."[5] In this the viceroy is evidently relying on a now-lost letter that Vázquez de Coronado had dispatched to him from Tiguex in April 1541, before departing with the full expedition for Quivira.[6] Thus, Mendoza can still express optimism about the existence of "jars of gold and pearls, as well as grand *ciudades*" farther on.[7] Given that the Coronado expedition had not located large, prosperous communities at the time of the April letter and in fact had been repeatedly disappointed in following up rumors of their existence, the viceroy's optimism is an expression more of hope than of fact.

He indicates that he is awaiting the imminent arrival of a "detailed report" from the captain general.[8] This suggests a regular, prearranged schedule of spring and fall communiqués from the Coronado expedition to the viceroy, undoubtedly matched by equally regular courier packets from Mendoza to the north. Concluding this portion of his letter to Oviedo, the viceroy promises to forward to the chronicler a copy of the anticipated report. Whether he did or not is unknown, although if he did, Oviedo did not include a copy of it in his *Historia,* which seems out of character.

The viceroy then tells Oviedo about the accidental death of Pedro de Alvarado, which had scuttled their two joint sea ventures, including the one headed for Cíbola. The remainder of the letter is devoted to a potpourri of topics, including interesting information about efforts to determine the latitude and longitude of places in Nueva España.

Oviedo's transcript of Mendoza's letter is preserved as folios 457v–459v in a contemporary manuscript copy of Parts 1 and 2 of the *Historia* that is held by the Real Academia de la Historia in Madrid. There the manuscript is found in the Colección Salazar y Castro under the identifying *signatura* (catalog number) 9/555 (H-32). Folio numbers from the Real Academia document have been retained in the transcription and translation that follow, in order to facilitate location of the passage in the original document. María Victoria Alberola Fioravanti, director of the library of the Real Academia, graciously furnished photocopies of the manuscript to us for the preparation of its first published English translation.

The letter has been published previously in Spanish in the various editions of the *Historia.*[9] We consulted the 1992 edition by Juan Pérez de Tudela Bueso in editing our own transcription.

TRANSLATION

[457v]

[. . .]

Chapter 52

In which a particular, noteworthy report is dealt with, which Viceroy don Antonio de Mendoza[10] made in writing by means of a personal letter to the author of this history[11] about these subjects in response to another [letter] that the author had written to him for his information. Because it is necessary and fitting for exposition of these histories, it is placed here, verbatim.

"To the very noble lord Gonzalo Hernández de Oviedo, *alcaide* of the fortress of Santo Domingo on the island of Española[12] and His Majesty's chronicler, Very Noble Lord,

"I received your letter by way of the archdeacon of this church. It is true that I did not respond to what Father fray Antonio de León brought me. The reason was [my] being out of this *ciudad*. In accordance with how much needed to be said that would be left out, I made up my mind to return before beginning [a reply].

"As for the rest, it was sufficient that you are the lord you are and that you engage in the practice of the humanities for me to desire your friendship. [And] all the more so for being able to inherit [your friendship] from my father. And [for] remembering seeing you, [my] lord, in Madrid many times, conversing very familiarly with him. For my part, I will not break off this friendship; rather I will renew it. And if anything presents itself in this part of the world which may concern you, I will perform it with my complete willingness.

[458r] "Regarding what you, [my] lord, say ([namely,] that from Venice they sent you a report which I had sent to His Majesty concerning some matters in this land and that among them I said that the *mexicanos*[13] come from the region

of Peru), it is true that I have written some things that seemed worthwhile to me to make note of. But [this one] is not certain, because I hold a contrary opinion, since as far as I am concerned they came from the region to the north. They [themselves] say this, and where they came from is evident in the ancient buildings and the names of places. Inasmuch as they came as far as Guazacalco[14] with a leader called Quezalcoatl,[15] I do not put much stock [in the story about Peru].

"Other [reports of mine] went to León. What I remember myself having written in this case is that they brought me certain human bones and molars so large that proportionally [the man] would be eighteen or nineteen *pies* tall.[16] This is told by the natives: namely, that [the giants] numbered as many as five hundred men whom they killed and distributed to various places.[17] We have received no word that there are giants, except at the Strait of Magellan. I suspect that those [giants] come from there, because from the region to the north I have received no news of people so large, although there are [people] of very large proportions.

"[Regarding] the report about matters in this land, I have sought to learn about it in very great detail. I have encountered a variety of opinions. Because there were many leaders in each *provincia* and they relate things in their [own] way, I have been collecting and verifying [the various opinions]. When this is done I will send [the result] to you, for it seems to me that it would be very embarrassing were I to send you a report and you were to cite me, as its author, as not being very truthful. What [might come] from here [now] is so little that you might not be able to produce a book from it. [In the future, though,] it will not be [458v] inconsequential. [That is] because although Montezuma and México[18] [are] what has caused a stir among us, the

Cazonzi[19] of Michoacán was no less a lord, nor [are] others who did not recognize either the one [Montezuma] or the other [the Cazonzi] as their overlord.[20]

"Regarding what concerns the reconnaissance missions I have initiated, since they are all in the early stages, it seems that there is little to say. I only wish you to know, [my] lord (since you may touch upon the excesses in this part of the world), that my people do not gamble[21] or blaspheme or take anything from the Indians against their will. Nor do they indulge in transgressions of the sort that men-at-arms are accustomed to indulge in. It is true that some will say that [a situation] has not been presented to them in which they could prove [their good behavior]. [And] I acknowledge that.

"Regarding what concerns gold and silver and fair-complected and handsome women and food, up to the present [those engaged in reconnaissance] have found [them] in abundance.[22] And they have not taken anything against the will of their owners, if it has not been given or traded. Even with this, today they are farther than nine hundred leagues from this *ciudad*,[23] with news that farther on there are many jars of gold and pearls, as well as grand *ciudades* and houses and a land very productive of food (especially cattle, of which they say there are more than in España). This coming month of November I am expecting the detailed report about all of this. With the help of Our Lord it may [already] have arrived. I will take care to send it to you, because that will be [an] eyewitness report, and what [I have] now is hearsay.

"His Majesty was pleased by[24] a contract that was executed with the *adelantado* don Pedro de Alvarado for reconnaissance of this Mar del Sur,[25] which I would have had a part in even though there was some discord over it between him and me. In order to bring us together, His Majesty made me the grant[26] without my asking for it or being aware of it. In the end, having before my [459r] eyes what happened in Peru,[27] I came to an agreement with him.[28] We came to an understanding to send out two fleets, one to reconnoiter the coast of this Nueva España and another which was to travel to the west in search of the Lequios and Cathay.[29] The *adelantado* was going to be in charge of the latter.

"It happened in Nueva Galicia that through the carelessness of a captain, some Indians thwarted [the planned reconnaissance]. Because [Alvarado] was nearby with the people from the fleets, he determined to go to serve His Majesty in pacifying that [land].[30] As he was approaching a steep, rugged hill of rock where the Indians were fortified, he was skirting around [it] in order to see by what route he would attack it. [His] people strayed away from him, and [the Indians] killed five of his Spaniards before he could bring them together. So much rain and such severe weather occurred that he was forced to withdraw to Guadalajara. While he was in a difficult passage a *criado* of his was traveling along a slope above where [the *adelantado*] was traveling. [The *criado*] tumbled down and ended up colliding with the *adelantado*. [The *criado*] carried him for three or four revolutions down the slope without being able to separate himself. [The *adelantado*] was so broken that after three days he died.

"I have decided to go [myself] to pacify that [land],[31] not so much because of the straits in which the Indians have put us as because of the discord that existed among the captains who were there. [This] has been the cause of [my] not being able to dispatch the fleets as soon as I would have if this had not happened.

FIGURE 25.1. The death of Pedro de Alvarado, 1541, after *Codex Telleriano-Remensis*, fol. 46r. This representation, by a native artist, shows Alvarado with closed eyes, indicating death. It is associated with a depiction of fighting at Nochistlán in 1541, during the retreat from which the *adelantado* was fatally injured. The solar glyph near Alvarado's head signifies his nickname, Tonatiuh, meaning "the sun."

"Regarding the rest of this land, thanks to God each day it is improving[32] in what concerns both matters of the faith and those of civilized order.

"You suggest, [my] lord, that I send you the latitudes[33] and locations in which these lands lie which have now been newly discovered. [But] I do not have [that information]. [That is] because by means of two eclipses of the moon that there have been since I have been in this part of the world, I have verified the longitudinal distance there is to Toledo.[34] [It is] eight hours, two minutes, and thirty-four seconds.[35] Taking this into account, I find that all the data concerning this Mar del Sur are incorrect because the pilots' books were prepared in Spain.[36] [459v] I have sought to have [this] corrected. Because of this I have not certified [what you ask for] before now. I fully believe that you, [my] lord, and other persons in that *ciudad* will have made a calculation on the basis of the eclipse. I would be happy if you would pay me in the same coin by informing me in writing of the time when [the eclipse] began there, in order to determine the [longitudinal] distance this land is from that one.

"You wish, [my] lord, to know who my mother was. There is no reason to keep it from you because by enlightening you about my father along with the other lords of Spain, I cannot fail to do my duty, [on] my part. Since she is now among so much virtue and goodness, I would be doing ill to conceal her name, which was doña Francisca Pacheco, daughter of *maestre* don Juan Pacheco.[37]

"May Our Lord protect your very noble person and household. From [the Ciudad de] México, the sixth of October in the year 1541. [My] lord, you may send [this] to whomever [you wish].

don Antonio de Mendoza"

[. . .]

TRANSCRIPTION

[fol. 457v]
{libro xxxiij}
[. . .]

{¶} Cap*itul*o lij
En q*ue* se tra(c)ta Una çierta E nota- / ble Relaçion
q*ue* *e*l visorrey don Antonio de me*n*- / doça por su Carta
mesiva escrivio Al historiador / de *e*stas materias En
R*e*spuesta de otra q*ue* *e*l Au(c)tor / le *h*avia escri(p)to para
su informaçion: y por ser / nesçessaria y Al proposito del
discurso de *e*stas / historias se pone aqui A la letra

Al muy noble señor gonçalo Hernandez de oviedo / Alcayde
d*e* la fortaleza de san(c)to domingo En la ysla / española y
C(o)ronista de su mag*estad*:

Muy noble senor

Resçebi Una Carta V*uest*ra Con el arçediano de *e*sta yglesia /
y es Verdad q*ue* el no rresponder A la q*ue* me truxo[38] el pa- /
dre frey antonio de leon fue la Causa estar fuera de *e*s- / ta
çiUdad y segun lo mucho q*ue* *h*abia q*ue* dezia q*ue* se partia /
yo pensse de ser Vuelto antes q*ue* *e*l Embarcara q*ue* por / lo
demas bastava ser Vos señor quy*en* soys y El exer- / çiçio de
letras q*ue* t(h)eneys p*ar*a desear yo V*uest*ra amistad: / quanto
mas pudiendola *h*Eredar de mi padre y A- / cordandome de
Veros S*eñor* En madrid Conversar muy / familiarmente Con
el muchas vezes: y por my p*ar*te / no q*ue*brara esta amistad
antes la rrenovare y si Al- / guna Cosa se ofresçiere en estas
p*ar*tes q*ue* os toq*ue* la hare Con / muy Entera Voluntad.

[fol. 458r]
{Segunda p*ar*te}

{¶} Quanto A lo q*ue* Señor dezis q*ue* os EmViaro*n* de
Veneçia / Una rrelaçio*n* q*ue* yo EmVie A su mag*estad* de
Algunas Cosas / d*e* las de *e*sta ti*e*rra y q*ue* entre *e*llas dezia
Venir los Mexica- / nos d*e* la parte del peru Es Verdad q*ue*
yo he escri(p)to / algunas Cosas q*ue* me paresçian de notar
mas no esta / porq*ue* tengo la opinion Contraria: porq*ue* p*ar*a
mi Ellos / Vinieron de la parte del norte y Asi lo dizen y Se
/ muestra En (h)edefiçios antiguos y En nombres de /
lugares por donde Viniero*n*. y pues allegaro*n* hasta /
guaçaqualco Con Un señor q*ue* se llamava queçalcoatl / no
tengo A mucho q*ue* pasasen otros A leon lo q*ue* se me /
Acuerda *h*aber escri(p)to En este Caso es q*ue* A mi me
truxe- / ron çiertos huesos y muelas de *h*ombre tan grandes
/ q*ue* A la proporçion Seria de xViij o diez E nueve / pies de
Alto y estos dizen los naturales q*ue* fueron / hasta çinq*ue*nta
*h*ombres los quales rrepartieron por / diverSos lugares y los
mataron. No tenemos / notiçia que *h*aya gigantes sino es Al
estrecho de Ma- / gallanes: sospecho yo q*ue* Aq*ue*llos
Vendrian de Alli / porq*ue* d*e* la parte del norte yo no tengo
notiçia de / gente tan grande: aUnque la *h*Ay harto bien dis-
/ puesta:

{¶} La Relaçion de las Cosas de *e*sta ti*e*rra yo he p*r*ocurado /
de sabello muy Particularmente y hallo diversas / opiniones:
porq*ue* Como *h*abia muchos señores En Cada / provinçia
Cuentan las Cosas de su manera. yo las An- / do recogiendo
y Verificando y hecho os lo EmVia- / re porq*ue* me paresçe
q*ue* seria Cosa muy Vergonçosa / q*ue* os EmViase yo
Relaçion y q*ue* me Alegassedes por / au(c)tor de *e*llo no
siendo muy Verdadera. y lo de Aquy / no es tan poco q*ue* no
podays hazer libro de *e*llo y no sera

[fol. 458v]

{libro xxxiij}

pequeño: porque aUnque motecçuma y Mexico Es lo que / Entre nosotros ha Sonado no Era menor Senor El / Caçonçi de Mechuacan y otros que ni Reconoçian / al Uno ny Al otro:

{¶} En lo que toca A los descubrimientos que yo tengo Comen- / çados Como todos son prinçipios pareçe que hAy poco que / dezir. Solamente quiero Senor que sepays pues tocays / En las desordenes[39] de estas partes que mi gente ni juega / ni Reniega ni toman A los indios nada Contra Su / Voluntad ni hazen exçesos de los que gente de guerra / suelen hazer: Es Verdad que Algunos diran que no se les / ha ofresçido En que lo puedan mostrar: Confessarlo (h)e / En lo que toca Al oro y A la plata mas mugeres blan- / cas y hermosas y Comida hasta Agora han halla- / do En Abundançia: y no han tomado Cosa Contra Vo- / luntad de sus dueños si no ha sido dada o Rescata- / da. y con esto Estan El dia de hoy[40] passadas de nueve- / çientas leguas de esta çiUdad Con notiçia de haber A- / delante muchas Vasijas de oro: y perlas: y grandes / çiUdades y Casas y tierra muy Abundante de Comida / En espeçial Vacas. que dizen haber mas que En españa / la Relaçion particular de todo esto espero para / Este mes de noviembre Con Ayuda de nuestro Senor Como / sea Venida yo te(r)ndre Cuydado de EmViarosla porque / aquella sera de Vista y lo de Ahora es de oydas:

{¶} Su magestad fue servido En Un Asiento que se tomo Con el A- / delantado don pedro de Alvarado para los descubrimyentos / de esta mar del Sur en que yo toviesse parte:[41] y aUnque / entre el E mi huvo Alguna discordia Sobre El Con- / çertarnos A Causa que su magestad me hizo la merçed sin yo / pedillo ny sabello A la fin[42] t(h)eniendo delante los / ojos

[fol. 459r]

{Segunda parte}

ojos lo suçedido En el peru yo me Convine Con eL / y Acordamos de despachar dos armadas una para / descubrir la

Costa de esta nueva españa y otra que / fuese Al poniente En demanda de los lequios y Catayo / y yendo el adelantado A Entender en esto Suçedio / que En la nueva galizia Unos indios por descuydo de Un / Capitan le desbarataron: Como se hallo Çerca Con la gen- / te de las armadas quiso yr a servir A su magestad En paçifi- / car aquello y allegando a Un peñol donde los indios Es- / tavan fuertes En tanto que el dava Vuelta para Ver por / donde le Combatiria se le desmando la gente y mata- / ronle çinco españoles antes que pudiesse rrecogerlos Su- / çedio tanta agua y tan Rezio tiempo que Le fue forçado / Retirarse a guadalajara y haziendolo En Un mal paso / yva Un Criado suyo por Una ladera mas Alto que eL yva / El qual rrodo y Vino A topar Con el adelantado y llevole / tres o quatro Vueltas la ladera Abaxo sin que se pudiesse / Apartar: quedo tan quebrantado que desde A tres dias mu- / rio. yo he determinado de yr A paçificar aquello / no tanto por la nesçessidad En que nos ponen los indios / quanto por la discordia que quedo Entre los Capitanes / que tenia Alli ha sido Causa de no poder despachar las / Armadas En tan breve tiempo Como se hiziera si esto no / hovyera suçedido. De lo demas de esta tierra a dios graçias / Cada dia Va en Aumento Asi En lo que toca a las Cosas / de la fee Como En las de poliçia.

{¶} Dezis Senor que os EmVie las alturas y sitio En que estas / tierras que agora nuevamente se descubren estan no lo / hago porque por dos Eclypsis de luna que ha havido despues / que yo estoy En estas partes he verificado la longitud / que hay hasta toledo y son ocho horas y dos minutos y tre- / inta y quatro Segundos: y teniendo Rexpe(c)to A esto / hallo que todo lo de esta mar del Sur esta falsso por / Causa de los rregim(i)entos ser hechos En españa: y / LLLLj

[fol. 459v]

{libro xxxiij}

procuro de hazello Corregir: y por esto no hago CaudaL[43] / de lo de antes de Ahora. Bien Creo que En essa çiUdad Vos Senor / y otras perSonas te(r)ndriades Cuenta Con el Eclypsi holgaria / que me pagassedes En la misma moneda En escrevirme A la / hora que alla Començo para saber lo que esta tierra dista de essa.

{¶} qu*e*reis S*eñ*or saber quien fue mi madre y no es Razon de ne- / garoslo pues q*ue* esclaresçiendo Vos a mi padre entre esotros / Señores de españa no me puede dexar de Caber mi parte / y Siendo ella tal En Virtud y En bondad mal haria de / Callar su nombre El qual fue doña fran*cis*ca pacheco hija / d*el* maestre don joh*an* pacheco. Nuestro S*eñ*or V*uest*ra muy

/ noble p*er*Sona y Cassa guarde. de Mexico A Vj de o*c*tu- / bre de (^1542)⁴⁴ 1541. A lo q*ue* Señor mandared*e*s

Don Antonio de Mendoça:

[. . .]

Document 26

Vázquez de Coronado's Letter to the King, October 20, 1541

AGI, Patronato, 184, R.34

Introduction

As close to events of the Coronado expedition as any document that survives is the letter that follows. It was written to the king of Spain (or, perhaps more accurately, was "dictated" or "ordered composed") by Francisco Vázquez de Coronado himself at Tiguex along the modern Rio Grande within days of his return from Quivira. It is written not in Vázquez de Coronado's own hand but in that of an *escribano,* possibly his secretary, Hernando Martín Bermejo. The original letter, dated October 20, 1541 (Julian), and signed by the·captain general, resides in the Archivo General de Indias in Sevilla under the *signatura* (catalog number) AGI, Patronato, 184, R.34.

As in all scribal products, the words and phrasings of this letter cannot be assumed to be verbatim those of its signatory. *Escribanos* always played a role in the composition of the documents they prepared. Generally speaking, they did not act simply to render into script exactly, completely, and solely what their clients or employers had communicated orally. Yet even with that caveat, this document brings us as close to the captain general's own mode of expression, his own observations and reactions, as we are likely ever to get.[1] And certainly the gist of the letter is the captain general's.

Its tone is one of duty faithfully executed. It portrays Vázquez de Coronado as having performed the task of getting to Quivira, which required hundreds of leagues of difficult and dangerous travel, "because it seemed important to Your Majesty's service that it be examined."[2] He did this, the letter states, even though "I did not give them [El Turco and his other Plains Indian informants] credence" when their reports were first obtained; they seemed "very exaggerated to me."[3] Even with this initial skepticism, the letter reports that when the early descriptions were contradicted by Indians known as Teyas on the eastern margin of the Llano Estacado, "I received the utmost pain."[4] Despite discouragement, the captain general chose 30 men who—certainly also accompanied by servants, slaves, and a contingent of Indian allies—followed the stories to their bitter end. "It seemed best to me to find out whether I could be of service to Your Majesty by going on," reads the letter.[5]

What remains of the document (more than half its length) then details the dogged effort expended by Vázquez de Coronado and his companions to verify their anticipated disappointment and frustration "in order to make a truthful report to Your Majesty."[6] Principally, that report is one of how Quivira failed to live up to its early billing and was nothing of particular interest to the expedition. The houses there were of thatch, and on top of that, "the people of [the *provincia* of Quivira] are as uncivilized as all those I have seen and passed until now."[7] The captain general had harbored only the most modest expectations of Quivira to begin with, and they were never exceeded.

After having recited the captain general's great expenditure of effort "to find a land where God, Our Lord, might be served and Your Majesty's royal patrimony might be enlarged," the letter concludes with its central message: "I have done everything I possibly could."[8] And in passing, with evident exasperation, it takes a swipe at Marcos de Niza, saying that "there were none of the things fray Marcos [had] told about."[9] Nowhere, even among the most populous and "civilized" people encountered, the Tiguex and their Pueblo neighbors, could *encomiendas* support a Spanish settlement.[10] As if that were not enough, Tiguex was also too cold and much too far from any ocean port.

Apparently located, copied, and added to his research collection by the eighteenth-century royal chronicler Juan Bautista Muñoz, the original letter, together with his copy of it, was subsequently deposited in the Archivo General, for whose establishment Muñoz had lobbied King Carlos III. There it was transcribed for publication in 1865 by the team of Joaquín Pacheco and Francisco de Cárdenas.[11] The tran-scription of Muñoz's copy is one of the cleanest and most accurate in Pacheco and Cárdenas's monumental multi-volume edition. Meanwhile, their transcription of the orig-inal 1540 letter contains the usual numerous, mostly small copying errors.[12] Using both of these transcripts, George Winship prepared an English translation that was published in 1896.[13] Forty-four years later, George Hammond and Agapito Rey published another English translation, based on Pacheco and Cárdenas's transcription of the Muñoz copy.[14] The new transcription and translation that we have prepared disagree on a number of points with both of these published translations, disagreements that are noted in the appropriate annotations. In 1992 Carmen de Mora, professor of Spanish American literature at the Universidad de Sevilla, published her own modernized transcription of the letter, which suffers from numerous, mostly minor omis-sions and errors.[15]

TRANSLATION

[1r]

Holy Catholic Imperial Majesty

On the twentieth of April of this year [1541] I wrote to Your Majesty about this *provincia* of Tiguex in response to a letter from Your Majesty dated in Madrid on the eleventh of June last year [1540].[16] I gave you a detailed[17] report and account of this expedition (which the viceroy of Nueva España ordered me to make in Your Majesty's name) to this land which fray Marcos de Niza, the provincial of the Order of Lord San Francisco, discovered. [I also reported] everything about what [the *provincia*] is and the character of its people, which Your Majesty has probably ordered reviewed from my letters.[18]

While I was overseeing the subjugation and pacification of the natives of this *provincia*, some native Indians from other *provincias* beyond these gave me a report that in their land were much grander towns and buildings, better than those of the natives of this land. [They reported] that there were lords who ruled them, that they ate out of golden dishes, and other things of great magnificence.[19]

However, as I wrote to Your Majesty, since it was a report from Indians and mostly by signs, I did not give them credence until I could see it with my own eyes (their report seeming very exaggerated to me).[20] Because it seemed important to Your Majesty's service that it be examined, I decided to go with the company I have here to see [it].

I left this *provincia* [Tiguex] on the twenty-third of this past April, [going] by the route on which the Indians chose to lead me.[21] After I traveled nine days I reached some plains so extensive that wherever I traveled on them I did not find their end, even though I traveled across them [for] more

than three hundred leagues.[22] On [the plains] I found such a multitude of [bison] that to count them is impossible. [I say this] because never for a single day did I lose sight of them as I traveled through the plains, until I returned to where I [first] found them. [These are the cattle] which I told Your Majesty in writing there [are] in this land.

After seventeen days of travel I came upon a *ranchería* of Indians who travel with these [bison], whom [the guides] call Querechos.[23] These [people] do not plant [crops], and they eat the meat [of the bison] raw and drink the blood of the [bison] they kill. These [Indians] dress the hides of the [bison], with which all the people in this land clothe themselves. They have very well made pavilion-like tents made of dressed and greased [bison] hides, in which they have their privacy.[24] They travel behind the [bison], moving with them. They have dogs which they load [and] on which they transport their tents, poles, and lesser effects.[25] The people are the best disposed[26] I have seen in the Indies up until now.

These [Querechos] did not know how to give me a report about the land to which the guides were taking me or the route by which they wished to lead me.[27] I traveled another five days until I arrived at some plains so without landmarks[28] that it was as if we were in the middle of the sea. There [the guides] became confused,[29] because on all of [the plains] there is not a single stone or hill or tree or bush or [1v] anything that looks like that. There are numerous, very beautiful pasture lands of excellent grass.

Some horsemen who went out hunting [bison], while lost on these plains, encountered some Indians who were also hunting. Those [Indians] are enemies of the ones I [had] encountered at the last *ranchería* and [are] another tribe of people who are called Teyas.[30] All [their] bodies and faces [are] decorated.[31] [They are] also a numerous people

[and] very well disposed. These [Indians] also eat their meat raw, as the Querechos do. [And] they live and travel with the [bison] in the same way as [the Querechos] do.

From [the Teyas] I obtained an account of the land to which the guides were leading me, which was not the same as [the guides] had told me.[32] [That is] because these [Teyas] made me [understand that][33] in [the land I was going to] the houses [were made] of thatch and hides and not of stone, nor [were they] multistoried, as the guides I was taking had made me imagine them. And in them [there was] little corn for eating. With this news I received the utmost pain, seeing myself in those tiresome, endless plains, where I had an extreme need of water.[34] I drank [water] so bad it contained more mud than water.

At that place the guides stated to me under oath that only in the grandness of the houses had they not told me the truth, since they were made of thatch. [They said that] concerning the multitude of people and the other things about civilization, they were telling [the truth]. The Teyas disputed this. Because of the disagreement there was between the one [group of] Indians and the others, and also because there had already been some days on which many of the people I was taking with me had eaten nothing except exclusively meat (because we had run out of the corn we had taken from this *provincia* [Tiguex]), and because from where I came upon these Teyas to the land where the guides were taking me, they made me understand [that it was] more than forty days of travel, [and] although the difficulty and danger there would be on the journey from lack of water and corn were made clear to me,[35] it seemed best to me to find out whether I could be of service to Your Majesty by going on with only thirty horsemen until I managed to examine the land, in order to make a truthful report to Your Majesty about what I might see in it.

[So] I sent all the rest of the people I was taking with me [back] to this *provincia* [of Tiguex] with don Tristán de Arellano as leader.[36] Because there was a lack of water and, additionally, they needed to kill [bison] bulls and cows with which to feed themselves, since they had no other food, it [would have been] impossible to prevent many people from dying if everyone [had gone] on.

With only thirty horsemen whom I took as my company I traveled forty-two days after I left the troop.[37] We maintained ourselves for all that time with only the meat of the [bison] bulls and cows we killed. [This was] at the cost of some of our horses which [the bison] killed, since they are very dauntless, fierce animals (as I have written to Your Majesty). [We] traveled for many days without water, cooking our food with [bison] dung because there is no firewood of any sort in all these plains away from the streams and rivers, of which there are very few.[38] It pleased Our Lord that at the end of having traveled seventy-seven days through those empty lands, I reached the *provincia* they call Quivira, to which the guides were leading me.[39]

They had indicated to me [that there would be] multistoried houses made of stone. Not only are there none made of stone (rather [they are made] of thatch), but the people of [the *provincia* of Quivira] are as uncivilized as all those I have seen and passed until now. [I say this] because they have neither *mantas* nor cotton from which to make them, rather hides from the [bison] they kill, which they dress. [This is possible] because they are settled among [the bison] on quite a large river. They eat the meat raw as the Querechos and Teyas [do]. They are enemies [of] one another, but they are all a single kind of people.

These [people] of Quivira have an advantage over the others because of the houses they have and because they plant corn. [The people] in this *provincia*, of which the guides who led me [were] natives, received me in peace. Although when I left for there [the guides] told me that I would not finish seeing it all in two months, in [Quivira] and all the rest [of the *provincias*] I saw and learned about there are not more than twenty-five *pueblos*, consisting of houses made of [2r] thatch.[40] Those [people] rendered obedience to Your Majesty and were placed under your royal dominion.[41] The people of [the *pueblos*] are large. I had some Indian men measured and found that they were ten *palmos* tall. The women are well proportioned.[42] They have faces more like Moorish women than Indians.[43]

There the natives gave me a piece of copper which an Indian *principal* wore hanging from his neck.[44] I am sending it to the viceroy of Nueva España, because I have seen no other metal in these places except that [piece], some small copper bells[45] which I sent to him, and a very small [piece] of metal that appears [to be] gold. I have not found out where the latter comes from, although I think that the Indians who gave it to me obtained it from those whom I brought here as servants.[46] [I say this] because I am unable to discover the truth about its source from the previously mentioned individual,[47] nor do I know from where it may originate.

I have suffered because of the diversity of languages there are in this land and [because of] having lacked someone who understands them (since in each town they speak their own [language]).[48] Because [of this] I have been forced to send captains and men in many directions in order to find out whether there might be some place[49] in this land where Your Majesty would be served. Even though [such a place] has been sought with utmost diligence, it has not been found, nor has any report been obtained of an inhabited place except [the report] about these *provincias,* which are a very insignificant thing.

The *provincia* of Quivira is nine hundred fifty leagues from [the Ciudad de] México by the route I traveled.[50] It is at forty degrees [north latitude].[51] The soil itself is the most suited for growing all the [crops] of Spain that has been seen. [This is] because in addition to its being deep and black and having very excellent water from streams, springs, and rivers, I found plums like those in Spain, walnuts, excellent sweet grapes, and mulberries.[52]

I treated the natives of that *provincia* and the others I have encountered where I traveled with the greatest possible benevolence, in compliance with what Your Majesty has ordered. In no way have they received harm from me or from those who have traveled in my company.[53] In this *provincia* of Quivira I spent twenty-five days, both to see and ride about the land and to obtain a report as to whether there was[54] anything farther on which might be of service to Your Majesty. [This was] because the guides who were leading me had provided information about other *provincias* beyond this one. [The report] I was able to obtain is that there was no gold or other metal in that whole land. The rest they gave me reports about are nothing but small *pueblos.*[55] And in many of them [the people] do not plant crops, nor do they have houses, except [shelters] made of hides and grass straw.[56] And they travel about, moving with the [bison].

Thus[57] the report [the guides] gave me was false. [And] because it might have induced me to go there with the whole company, I believe[58] (because the route passed through so many empty and unsettled areas and [because of] the absence of water sources) that [the guides] may have directed us to a place where our horses and ourselves might die of hunger.[59] The guides confessed to just this and that they did it by the advice and order of the natives of these *provincias* [Tiguex, Cicuique, and perhaps others].[60]

With this, after having examined the land of Quivira and having obtained the report I mentioned earlier about what might be ahead, I returned to this *provincia* [Tiguex] to look after the safety[61] of the company I [had] sent [back] to it and to make a report to Your Majesty about what that land is, because I wrote to Your Majesty that [a report] would be made when I had seen it.

As your loyal servant and vassal, I have done everything I possibly could to serve Your Majesty and to find a land where God, Our Lord, might be served and Your Majesty's royal patrimony might be enlarged.[62] [I say this] because since I reached the *provincia* of Cíbola (to which the viceroy of Nueva España sent me in Your Majesty's name) and saw that there were none of the things fray Marcos [had] told about, I have endeavored to reconnoiter this land [for] two hundred leagues and more around Cíbola. And the best [place] I have found is this Río de Tiguex on which I am [now] located.[63] The [2v] settlements along it are not [such] as to allow [Spaniards] to settle [here] because they are more than four hundred leagues from the Mar del Norte and more than two hundred from the [Mar] del Sur.[64] It is impossible to have any sort of communication [from] there [either ocean]. As I have written to Your Majesty, the land is so cold that it seems impossible that we can pass the winter in it, because there is no firewood or clothing with which the men could protect themselves from the cold, except hides with which the natives clothe themselves and some cotton *mantas* [which are] in short supply.

I am sending the viceroy of Nueva España a report about everything I have seen in the lands [where] I have traveled. Because don García López de Cárdenas (who has worked diligently and served Your Majesty very well on this expedition) will soon kiss Your Majesty's hands, he, as a man who has seen it himself, will give Your Majesty an account of everything about this place.[65] I defer to him [in this].

May Our Lord preserve the Holy Catholic Imperial person of Your Majesty with an increase of grander kingdoms and dominions, as we, your loyal servants and vassals, desire. From this *provincia* of Tiguex, the 20th of October in the year 1541.[66]

Holy Catholic Imperial Majesty

Your Majesty's humble servant and vassal who kisses your royal feet and hands,
Francisco Vázquez de Coronado [no rubric][67]

{Nueva España, Tiguex}
{Francisco Vázquez de Coronado, 20th of October 1541}

[fol. 1r]

Sacra Catolica Cesarea Magestad

a Veynte de abryll de este año escrivi a Vuestra magestad de esta proVinçia de tiguex en rres- / puesta de Una letra de Vuestra magestad hecha en madrid a (h)onze de Junio del año pa- / sado y le di particular cuenta y rrazon de esta Jornada que el Visorrey de la nueVa / españa me mando hazer en nonbre de Vuestra magestad a esta tierra que descubrio fray / marcos de niça proVinçial de la (h)orden de señor san francisco y de lo que es toda ella / y de la calidad de la gente como Vuestra magestad lo habra mandado Ver por mis cartas y que / entendiendo en la conquista y paçificaçion de los naturales de esta provincia / çiertos yndios naturales de otras provincias adelante de estas me habian dado rrela- / çion que en su tierra habia muy mayores pueblos y casas meJores que las de los na- / Turales de esta tierra y que habia señores que los mandavan y que se sirVian en Va- / siJas de oro y otras cosas de mucha grandeza y aUnque como a Vuestra magestad esCrivi / por ser rrelaçion de yndios y mas por señas no les di credito hasta que por los / oJos[68] lo Viese pareçiendome la rrelaçion muy grande y que ynportava al servyçio / de Vuestra magestad que se Viese me determine con la gente que aqui tengo de ylla a Ver[69] / y parti de esta proVinçia a Veynte y tres del mes de abryll pasado por donde / los yndios me quisieron guiar[70] y a los nueVe dias que camine llegue a Unos lla- / nos tan grandes que por donde yo los anduVe[71] no les halle[72] cabo aUnque camine por / ellos mas de trezientas leguas y en ellos halle tanta cantidad de vacas / de las que a vuestra magestad esCrivi que habia en esta tierra que numerallas es ymposible / porque ningun dia camine por los llanos hasta que Volvi donde las halle que las

/ perdiese y a los diez y siete dias de camino tope Una rrancheria de yn- / dios que andan con estas vacas que los llaman querechos[73] los quales no sienbran / y comen la carne cruda y beben la sangre de las Vacas que matan esstos ado- / ban los cueros de las vacas de que en esta tierra se Viste[74] toda la gente de ella tie- / nen pabellones de cueros de vacas adobados y ensebados muy bien hechos / donde se meten y andan tras las Vacas mudandose con ellas[75] tienen pe- / rros que cargan en que lleVan sus tiendas y palos y menudençias es la gente / mas bien dispuesta que yo hasta hoy he Visto[76] en yndias esstos no me su- / pieron dar rrazon de la tierra a donde me lleVaban las guias[77] y por donde / me quisieron guiar camine otros çinco dias hasta llegar a Unos llanos / Tan sin seña como si estoVieramos engolfados en la mar donde desa- / Tinaron porque en todos ellos no hay Una piedra ni cuesta ni arbol ni mata ni

[fol. 1v]

Cosa que lo parezca hay muchas y muy hermosas dehesas de buena yerva[78] y estando / perdidos en estos llanos çiertos hombres de cavallo que salieron a caça de vacas to- / paron Unos yndios que tanbien andaban a caça los quales son enemigos de los que / Tope en la rrancheria pasada y otra naçion de gente que se llaman los teyas to- / dos labrados los cuerpos y rrostros gente asimismo creçida de muy buena dis- / pusiçion tanbien comen estos la carne cruda como los querechos ViVen y an- / dan por la misma manera que ellos con las Vacas de estos tuVe rrelaçion de la / Tierra donde me llevaban las guias que (h)era no como me habian dicho porque estos / me hizieron en ella las casas de paja[79] y de cueros y no de piedra y de altos como / me las hazian las guias que llevava y en ellas poca comida de mayz y con esta / nueVa rreçibi harta pena[80] por Verme en aquellos llanos sin cabo donde tuVe harta / nesçesidad de agua y hartos la bebi[81] tan mala que tenia mas parte de çieno que / de agua alli me confesaron las guias que en sola la grandeza de las casas no me / habian dicho Verdad porque (h)eran de paja que en la muchedunbre de gente y otras / cosas de poliçia la dezian y los teyas esstaban contra esto y por esta diVi- / sion que habia entre los Unos yndios y los otros y tanbien porque ya habia algunos / dias que mucha de la gente que comigo lleVaba no comian sino sola carne porque se nos / acabo[82] el mayz que de esta proVinçia sacamos y porque desde donde tope esstos te- / yas hasta la tierra donde me llevaban las guias me hazian mas de quarenta / dias de camino aUnque se me rrepresento el trabaJo y peligro que en la Jornada ha- /bria por la falta de aguas y de mayz me pareçio por Ver si habia en que serVyr a / Vuestra magestad pasar adelante con solos treynta de cavallo hasta llegar a Ver la tierra / para hazer Verdadera rrelaçion a Vuestra magestad de lo que en ella Viese y enVie toda la / demas gente que comigo llevava a esta proVinçia y por caudillo a don trystan / de arellano porque sigun la falta hubo de aguas[83] de mas que habian de matar toros / y Vacas con que se sustentar que no tenia otra comida (h)era ynposible dexar de / pereçer mucha gente si todos pasaran adelante y con solos los treynta de / cavallo que tome para mi conpañia camine quarenta y dos dias despues que dexe / la gente sustentandonos en todos ellos de sola la carne que matabamos de toros / y Vacas a costa de algunos cavallos que nos mataban porque son como he esCrito / a Vuestra magestad muy braVos y fieros animales y pasando muchos dias sin agua / y guisando la comida con freça de Vacas porque no hay ningun genero de leña / en todos esstos llanos fuera de los arroyos y rrios que hay bien pocos plugo / a nuestro señor que al cabo de haber caminado por aquellos desiertos setenta y siete / dias llegue a la proVinçia que llaman quiVira donde me lleVaban las guias y / me habian señalado casas de piedra y de muchos altos y no solo no las hay de / piedra sino de paJa pero la gente de ella(s) es tan barbara como toda la que he Visto / y pasado hasta aqui que no tienen mantas ni algodon de que las hazer sino Cueros / que adoban de las Vacas que matan porque esstan poblados entre ellas en Un rrio bien / grande comen la carne Cruda como los querechos y teyas son enemigos Unos / de otros pero toda es gente de Una manera y estos de quiVira hazen a los o- / Tros VentaJa[84] en las casas que tienen y en senbrar mayz en esta proVinçia de / donde son naturales las guias que me lleVaron me rreçibieron de paz y aUnque quando / parti para alla[85] me dixeron que en dos meses no la acabaria de Ver toda no hay en / ella y en todo lo demas que yo Vi y supe mas de Veynte y Çinco pueblos de casas de

[fol. 2r]

(de casas de) paJa los quales dieron la obidiençia a Vuestra magestad y se pusieron debaxo / de su rreal señorio la gente de ellos es creçida y algunos yndios hize medir y / halle que tenian diez palmos de estatura las mugeres son de buena dispusiçion / Tienen los rrostros mas a manera de moriscas que de yndias alli me dieron / los naturales Un pedaço de cobre que Un yndio prinçipal traya colgado del Cuello / enViolo al Visorrey de la nueVa españa porque no he Visto en estas partes otro me- / Tal sino aquel y çiertos caxcabeles de cobre que le enVie[86] y Un poquito de me- / Tal que pareçia oro que no he sabido de donde sale mas de que Creo que los yndios que / me le dieron le hubieron de los que yo aqui traygo de serViçio porque de otra parte / yo no le puedo hallar el nasçimiento ni se de donde[87] sea la diVersidad de / lenguas que hay en esta tierra y haber tenido falta de quien los entienda porque en cada / pueblo hablan la suya me ha hecho daño porque me ha sido forçado enViar capita- / nes y gentes por muchas partes para saber si en esta tierra habria donde vuestra magestad / pudiese ser serVido y aUnque con toda diligençia se ha buscado no se ha hallado / ni tenido rrelaçion de ningun (^pl) poblado sino es de estas pro- / Vinçias que es harta / poca cosa la proVinçia de quiVira essta de mexico noVeçientas y çinCuenta leguas / por donde yo Vine essta en quarenta grados la tierra en si es la mas apareJada / que se ha Visto para darse en ella todas las cosas de españa porque de mas de ser / en si gruesa y negra y tener muy buenas aguas[88] de arroyos y fuentes y rrios / halle çiruelas como las de españa[89] y nuezes y (h)uVas dulçes y muy buenas / y moras a los naturales de aquella proVinçia y a los demas que he topado por / do pase he hecho todo el buen tratamiento posible conforme a lo que Vuestra magestad / Tiene mandado y en ninguna cosa han rreçibido agraVio de mi ni de los que / han andado en mi conpañia en esta proVinçia de quiVira me detuVe Veynte y / çinco dias asi por Ver y pasear la *tie*rra como por *h*aber rrela*çi*on si adelante *h*a- / bia alguna cosa en q*ue* pudiese serVyr a V*ues*tra mag*est*ad porq*ue* las guias q*ue* lleVabame / *h*abian dado noti*çi*a de otras p*ro*Vin*çi*as adelante de *e*lla y la q*ue* pude *h*aber es / q*ue* no *h*abia oro ni otro metal en toda aq*ue*lla *tie*rra y las demas de q*ue* me dieron / rrela*çi*on no son syno pueblos peq*ue*ños y en muchos de *e*llos no sienbran ni / Tienen casas sino de Cueros y cañas y andan mudandose con las Vacas / por manera q*ue* la rrela*çi*on q*ue* me diero*n* fue falsa porq*ue* me mo*V*iese a yr alla / con toda la gente creyendo q*ue* por ser el Camino[90] de tantos desiertos y despo- / blados y falto de aguas nos metieran en parte donde n*uest*ros cavallos y nos- / otros murieramos de hambre y asi lo confesaron las guias y q*ue* por conseJo / y mandami*ent*o de los naturales de estas p*ro*Vin*çi*as lo *h*abian hecho[91] y con esto / despues de *h*aber Visto la *tie*rra de quiVira y *h*abida la rrela*çi*on q*ue* arriba digo / de lo de adelante VolVi a esta p*ro*Vin*çi*a a poner rrecaudo en la gente q*ue* en- / Vie a ella y a hazer rrela*çi*on a V*ues*tra mag*est*ad de lo q*ue* es aq*ue*lla *tie*rra porq*ue* en Viendola / es*C*ri*V*i a V*ues*tra mag*est*ad q*ue* se la haria yo *h*e hecho todo lo a mi posible por serVyr / a V*ues*tra mag*est*ad y descubryr *tie*rra donde dios n*uest*ro señor fuese serVido y ampliado / el rreal patrimonio de V*ues*tra mag*est*ad como su leal criado y Vasallo porq*ue* desde q*ue* / llegue a la p*ro*Vin*çi*a de çibola a donde el Visorrey de la nueVa españa me ynVio / en nonbre de V*ues*tra mag*est*ad Visto q*ue* no *h*abia ninguna cosa de las q*ue* fray marcos dixo *h*e / pro*C*urado descubryr essta *tie*rra dozientas leguas y mas a la rredonda / de çibola y lo meJor q*ue* *h*e hallado es esste rrio de tiguex en q*ue* esstoy y las

[fol. 2v]

pobla*çi*ones de *e*l q*ue* no son para poderlas poblar porq*ue* demas de estar quatroÇientas le- / guas de la mar del norte y de la del sur mas de duzientas donde no puede *h*aber / ninguna manera de trato la *tie*rra es tan fria como a V*ues*tra mag*est*ad tengo es*C*rito q*ue* pareçe / ynposible poderse pasar el ynVierno en ella porq*ue* no *h*ay leña ni rropa con que / se puedan abrigar los honbres sino cueros de q*ue* se Visten los naturales y al- / gunas mantas de algodon en poca cantidad yo enVio al Visorrey de la nueVa / españa rrela*çi*on de todo lo q*ue* *h*e Visto en las *tie*rras q*ue* *h*e andado y porq*ue* don / garçi lopez de cardenas[92] Va a besar las manos (a)*de* V*ues*tra mag*est*ad el qual en esta Jornada / *h*a trabajado mucho y serVido muy bien a V*ues*tra m*a*g*est*ad y dara rrazon a V*ues*tra mag*est*ad de / Todo lo de aca como honbre q*ue* lo *h*a Visto a el me rremito y guarde n*uest*ro señor / la *S*acra *C*atolica *C*esarea persona de v*ue*s*t*ra m*a*g*est*ad con a*C*reçentami*ent*o de mayores rreynos y se- / ñorios como sus leales criados y Vasallos deseamos de *e*sta p*ro*Vin*çi*a de / Tiguex xx de o*c*tubre de 1UDxli años

*S*acra *C*atolica *C*esarea M*a*g*est*ad

humyl criado y Vasallo de V*ues*tra m*a*g*est*ad / q*ue* sus Reales pyes y manos besa
Fran*cis*co Vazq*ue*z / de coronado

{nueva *e*spaña tiguez}
{Fran*cis*co Vazquez de Corunado de / 20 de o*c*tubre <u>1541</u>}

Document 27

Disposal of the Juan Jiménez Estate, 1542 (Copy, 1550)

AGI, Contratación, 5575, N.24

Introduction

The winter of 1541–42 was especially hard on the Coronado expedition. Food and clothing were scarce; people and animals were sick and dying.[1] Among the ill that February of 1542 at the pueblo called Coafor (or Coofor, as it was also spelled) was a man named Juan Jiménez, who was suffering from an unidentified malady. Jiménez, a native of Guadalcanal in the modern Spanish *comunidad* of Andalucía, had mustered into the expedition two years earlier as a horseman not yet assigned to a company.[2]

During the night watch of February 16–17 a crisis occurred, and Jiménez sensed that he would not recover. In fear that he would not survive the night, he sent for the sentinels making their rounds and asked them to witness the naming of *albaceas* (executors) of his last will and testament. Saying that he was in no condition to dictate a will, Jiménez asked that his long-time friends Antón Negrín and Jorge Báez prepare one on his behalf, in accordance with what he had told them on many occasions. They were to do as they knew he would wish for the unburdening of his soul and the disposal of his 200 pesos' worth of worldly goods. If he lived through the night, he would make a proper statement to that effect before Hernando Bermejo, the secretary of the expedition, come daylight. But before morning, Jiménez died.

Within a matter of days, on February 25, Negrín and Báez appeared before the *maestre de campo* and the secretary to present a report of what had occurred at Coafor on the night of Jiménez's death, together with the four witnesses to their appointment as executors: Alonso Álvarez, Gerónimo Ramos, Antonio Álvarez, and Antón Pérez Buscavida. Don Tristán de Luna y Arellano examined the witnesses, who certified that Jiménez had indeed designated Negrín and Báez to handle his affairs, in preference to all others.

A little over a month after Jiménez's death, with authorization from the *maestre de campo*, Negrín and Báez made an inventory of their deceased friend's stock and the goods in his room at Coafor. Three days later, on March 18, 1542, all of Jiménez's goods except horseshoeing tools, a hat, a hide, a packsaddle, spurs, a machete, and a lance point were sold at public auction. A black *pregonero* (crier) named Pedro was the auctioneer for this sale in Coafor. If the auction (*almoneda*) proceeded like others of the time, Pedro either stationed himself in a public place at Coafor or circulated through the pueblo, calling out the items for sale and keeping track of the bids offered by expedition members.[3] The goods that sold were purchased by five men, with the promise to pay within six months, indicating an understandable scarcity of cash money at this point late in the course of the expedition.

After his return to Nueva España, Antón Negrín, the only surviving executor,[4] dutifully prepared and executed a will for Juan Jiménez, arranging for payment of his debts and collection of his loans, giving bequests to the hospital and several *cofradías*, or religious confraternities, in the Ciudad de

México and Puebla de los Ángeles, and paying for masses to be said for his dead friend's soul and those of his parents.

The record of these events was eventually copied into a later document and preserved in the Archivo General de Indias in Sevilla as AGI, Contratación, 5575, N.24, "Bienes de difuntos, Juan Jiménez, Tenancingo, November 19, 1550." The document is a 1550 copy of an accounting made in 1545 at the direction of the *visitador* Francisco Tello de Sandoval, one of a series conducted in the process of investigating the discharge of duties by officials in overseeing the dispersal of estates, only a small part of his three-year *visita* of the royal officials of Nueva España. It was into that 1545 accounting that copies of documents from 1541 and 1542 were incorporated. The 1550 copy was made in accordance with a royal *cédula*, for what purpose is not said.[5] The copy is published here in its entirety for the first time.[6]

The bundle in the AGI consists of eight short documents prepared while the Coronado expedition to Tierra Nueva was under way. It more than doubles the number of known surviving documents that are strictly contemporaneous with the expedition (that is, prepared during its course)[7] and is the only known group of documents dealing with mundane activities of the expedition's rank and file. In contrast, most of the other extant documentary sources concerning the expedition were drafted years after the fact as formal reports and legal testimony focused on the momentous events of the expedition as a whole. Thus, the Jiménez documents offer an important vantage on the day-to-day workings of the expedition and contribute significantly to what has previously been known about it.

Thirty-eight members of the expedition (perhaps slightly over 10 percent of the total European contingent) figured in the events relating to Jiménez's affairs, including seven who have been previously unknown (they do not appear in the muster roll of the expedition prepared in February 1540 or in any of the other known surviving Coronado expedition documents). The previously unknown members now brought to light are the executor Antón Negrín himself, Diego Gallego, Pedro de Lasojo, Pedro de Huerve (Huelva), Juan Barragán[8] (from Llerena), Juan Pedro, and Pedro, the black *pregonero* (crier).

About Juan Jiménez himself, we learn from the docu-

FIGURE 27.1. The types of clothing worn by Juan Jiménez, including native head armor, a quilted cotton tunic, and *alpargates* (hemp sandals). He carries a sword and a *rodela*, or round shield. Although not mentioned in the inventory of Juan Jiménez's possessions, a *rodela* would have been standard protection for a swordsman. Drawing by Richard Flint.

ment that he possessed no metal armor at the time of his death, but only a native tunic (presumably of quilted cotton in the precolumbian style of central Mexico), a piece of native head armor, and a jerkin with hide sleeves. He had both shoes and sandals and an old hat. In all likelihood his shirt and breeches and whatever else he was wearing when he died were buried with him; at least they were not inventoried. Even the European members of the Coronado expedition relied heavily on gear from indigenous central Mexican traditions.[9] In this respect, Juan Jiménez was typical.[10]

The nails and horseshoes owned by Jiménez at the time of his death were readily purchased by another member of the expedition at the auction of his property. His tools for horseshoeing (hammer, tongs, and hoof parer), however, went unsold. What this indicates is that most horsemen of the expedition, if not all of them, had their own minimal kits of horseshoeing tools and individual stocks of shoes and nails. This does not rule out the existence of another central, reserve supply of horseshoes and nails or the presence of one or more farriers. But no one seemed in sore need of another hammer, tongs, and parer. Nor was there apparently any particular shortage of iron, even more than two years into the expedition. If there had been, surely a blacksmith or farrier would have snapped up the metal tools for refabrication into other items. But no one wanted the tools, even at bargain prices with deferred payment. The ready-made and exhaustible resources of horseshoeing (shoes and nails), on the other hand, were desirable and sold readily.

The will eventually prepared by Antón Negrín on Jiménez's behalf made no bequests to family members, indicating that the dead man had neither surviving spouse nor children and that any siblings, cousins, or grandchildren he might have had were unknown to his executor. Further, Jiménez's parents were evidently both already deceased, because the will provides that masses be said for their souls. This lack of close relations explains the concern expressed by licenciado Sandoval during the first judicial review of Negrín's performance that Jiménez's assets be "placed in the possession of the person who has the right to hold them . . . When such a person has come to light."[11] Negrín himself states that "he does not know of them and is not acquainted with them."[12]

The bulk of evidence from the Jiménez document demonstrates the importance and frequency of intraexpeditionary commercial activity and the existence and preservation of associated paperwork. The unfortunate man himself had engaged in a number of business deals while on the expedition; in this he was probably not unusual. In his possession at the time of his death were six financial documents completed during the course of the expedition, principally loans to other members. Or these may represent credit slips for goods Jiménez sold to others on the expedi-

tion. Which of these possibilities is correct cannot be said with certainty, because only the inventory entries are included in the document and not the instruments of credit themselves. Some of the transactions involved moderate sums of money.

Among the business papers copied into the Jiménez document is the record of a purchase he himself made in the provincia of Tiguex on April 6, 1541, shortly before the expedition left the Pueblo world in search of the fabled ciudad of Quivira far to the east. From expedition member Juan Barragán, Jiménez bought 50 pesos worth of hose, shirts, and other valuable goods (preseas). The transfer of such a quantity of clothing (more than a single individual would have been likely to need) raises the possibility that Jiménez was a mercader, or merchant.[13] Barragán, the other party to this transaction, almost certainly was. At any rate, Jiménez was probably buying the clothing for resale to other members of the expedition, even if retailing was not his normal trade. Jiménez, who was profoundly illiterate, not knowing even how to sign his name, nevertheless recognized the value of having this transaction recorded in writing and employed the escribano Hernando Gómez de la Peña to prepare a formal document.[14]

In addition to what the Jiménez document reveals about the parties directly involved in the disposal of the dead man's possessions, several facts about the expedition as a whole are evident. First, in the late winter of 1542 the expedition was housed in at least two camps at abandoned pueblos in Tiguex. It has been known previously that during the winter of 1540–41 the expedition had occupied several sites among the Tiguex pueblos, specifically while battles were in progress. It has not been known that a similar practice was followed the next winter. The 2,000 or so members of the expedition[15] may have been dispersed among several Tiguex pueblos for better resource acquisition, for defense in an area where a hostile standoff existed between the Tiwa people and the expeditionaries, or out of physical necessity because of the large size of the expedition relative to the smallness of the available abandoned pueblos. The average Rio Grande pueblo at the time normally accommodated something on the order of 300 residents, according to the Spaniards' own figures.[16]

Second, the presence of sentinels making their rounds on the night of Juan Jiménez's death confirms Pedro de Castañeda de Nájera's report that Tiguex was still a land at war and that there had been little if any improvement in relations between the expeditionaries and the Tiwas since the previous year, when open warfare flared. As Castañeda de Nájera wrote, while the expedition was on the Great Plains seeking Quivira during the summer of 1541, some of the Tiwas returned to their pueblos, but they fled and never returned when the expedition came back to spend a second winter along the Rio Grande.[17] It was at the end of that winter that Juan Jiménez died.

Jiménez was not alone in suffering the ravages of illness in Tierra Nueva. In an *interrogatorio* prepared by Vázquez de Coronado and his attorney in 1544, the captain general indicates that during the winter of 1541–42 "the horses were dying and the soldiers were falling sick."[18] During the expedition's return march south the following spring there was an unusual die-off of horses, and in the midst of that episode Jorge Báez, one of the executors of Jiménez's estate, died of an illness.[19] This suggests that poor health was seriously affecting the expedition after two and a half years on the trail. What sorts of illnesses were besetting people and animals are impossible to determine from the tiny amount of evidence available. Were they familiar maladies from the Old World or strange ones from the New? And how were the Pueblos of the Rio Grande region and other natives of Tierra Nueva affected by the sicknesses experienced by the expedition? For now those questions must go unanswered.

Within two months after the appointment of Antón Negrín and Jorge Báez as executors, the expedition began its long, irregular return trip to the Ciudad de México. Three dates in the Jiménez document bracket that journey: on March 18, 1542, the expedition was still in Tiguex; on April 9, 1542, it was on the Río Frío (five days out from Cíbola, between there and Chichilticale); and on September 13,

1542, at least some of the expeditionaries were in the Ciudad de México and probably had been for a number of days or even weeks. Castañeda de Nájera writes that the expedition began its return trip in the early days of April 1542.[20] Judging from the expedition's encampment on the Río Frío on April 9, however, the departure date from Tiguex must have been in March, because Juan Jaramillo provides a travel time of nine days from Tiguex to Cíbola and a five-day travel time from there to the Río Frío.[21]

Revealing widely held attitudes of expeditionaries and the larger society about the enterprise of conquest and reconnaissance is the request included in Jiménez's will that "a bull of indulgence as a participant in a holy crusade . . . be obtained."[22] This is an explicit statement that the Coronado expedition and the many other similar endeavors in the New World were equated with the Old World holy crusades against infidels that were then ongoing in Spain, North Africa, and Turkey.

The Jiménez document is unique among the known records of the Coronado expedition because it provides the only glimpse we have so far into the day-to-day appearance and activities of the expedition. In the document the epic events of the watershed first encounter between Europeans and Indian peoples in what became the American Southwest and northwest Mexico fade into the background. We are left with a picture of individuals far from their place of origin faithfully maintaining the rites and protocols of sixteenth-century Spanish life and death, even in the face of hardship, deprivation, and profound disappointment.[23] Above all, we see the inescapable obligation for Spaniards of the day to assure that every step in every transaction involving money be duly recorded and authenticated. This was as imperative for Juan Jiménez, Antón Negrín, Juan Barragán, and Francisco Vázquez de Coronado, off to seek a new and fabulous land, a *tierra nueva*, as it was for their erstwhile neighbors content at home in Guadalcanal, Llerena, and Salamanca.

TRANSLATION

{The file of the case concerning the property of Juan Jiménez, deceased, a native of Guadalcanal, in Coafor in the *provincia* of Tiguex, Nueva España, 32 folios}[24]

[1r]
{Juan Jiménez, deceased, a native of Guadalcanal}
{Number 15, 1550}
This is a copy correctly and faithfully extracted from a case file of accounts concerning the assets of Juan Jiménez, deceased. According to [and] by means of the case file it appears that its substance is what follows:

{Item} In the *ciudad* of [Puebla] de los Ángeles in this Nueva España on the thirteenth day of the month of August in the one thousand five hundred and forty-fifth year since the birth of Our Savior, Jesus Christ, Antón Negrín, a *vecino* of this *ciudad,* appeared in person before the magnificent lord *licenciado* Hernando Caballero, *residencia* judge and His Majesty's *justicia mayor* in this *ciudad* and judge of the estates of the deceased here, by special commission from the very magnificent and very reverend lord *licenciado* Tello de Sandoval, *visitador general* of this Nueva España and its judge of the estates of the deceased, and in my presence, Sebastián Vázquez, His Majesty's *escribano* and *escribano* of the aforementioned *residencia, audiencia,* and court of the lord judge.[25]

[Negrín] stated that, in fulfillment of and in compliance with what His Grace ordered and was proclaimed in this *ciudad* last Monday, the tenth day of the present month, namely, that all custodians of estates of the deceased were to come before him and give [an] accounting of those estates, he brought and presented two documents for the aforesaid purpose. One of them, a will, appears to be and is signed by

His Majesty's *escribano* Melchior Gómez, and the other by Andrés de Herrera, public *escribano* and, according to [the document], apparently former *escribano* of the *cabildo* of this *ciudad.*[26] [1v] [These documents] are the following:

{Item} In the great city of Tenuxtitan-México in Nueva España on the thirteenth day of the month of September in the one thousand five hundred and forty-second year since the birth of Our Savior, Jesus Christ,[27] Antón Negrín appeared in person before the very noble lord Gerónimo Ruiz de la Mota, His Majesty's *alcalde* in the Ciudad de México, and in my presence, Juan de Zaragosa, registered public *escribano* in [this *ciudad*].[28] [Negrín] presented a written petition along with a *probanza,* an inventory, and a record of auction, the sum and substance of which [are] as follows.
Juan de Zaragosa, public *escribano*

{Item} Very Noble Lord,
I, Antón Negrín, an *estante* in this *ciudad* and a *vecino* of the *ciudad* of [Puebla] de los Ángeles, appear before Your Grace and declare that while going to Tierra Nueva with Captain Francisco Vázquez [de Coronado], one Juan Jiménez (may God, Our Lord, forgive him) died in Tiguex.[29]

One night during the time when he was sick, fearing that he could not escape [death], and because he had need of an *escribano* in order that he could have his will prepared and there was none in that *pueblo,*[30] he declared in front of four witnesses that he was conferring his full power of attorney on me and Jorge Báez, so that we could prepare his will as seemed [right] to us.[31] [This he did because] he was a friend of mine and of Jorge Báez and [because] at the time he was prepared to die and earlier he had communicated to me and

Jorge Báez what would be proper for his soul and for the unburdening of his conscience.

This is a matter of record and can be seen [2r] in this *probanza* I am presenting. Because Jorge Báez, who is also executor, has died,[32] and because I am obliged by my conscience to do what I am obligated [to do], inasmuch as it is possible that I could die during the delay and leave with this responsibility, I ask and beg Your Grace to issue your judicial decree and to do in this case what is just and in [good] conscience, heedful that the dead man gave me [his] power of attorney in order that I could arrange his will as he discussed it with me, and that he gave me permission and authority to arrange and execute it as I am obliged [to do]. In what is necessary, I implore your noble office and request what in this case is most appropriate for me to ask.
Antón Negrín

{Item} The lord *alcalde* stated that he was accepting[33] [the petition] and will provide what would be just in the case.

{Item} In the town of Coafor in the *provincia* of Tiguex on the twenty-fifth day of the month of February in the year one thousand five hundred and forty-two, Antón Negrín and Jorge Báez, being *estantes* in the expeditionary force,[34] appeared in person before the very magnificent lord don Tristán de Arellano, *maestre de campo* of this expeditionary force (of which the captain general is the very magnificent lord Francisco Vázquez de Coronado, governor of the *provincia* of [Nueva] Galicia in Nueva España), and before me, Hernando Bermejo, His Majesty's *escribano*, and the witnesses listed below.[35] [Negrín and Báez] presented before His Grace a document, the substance of which is what follows:

[2v] {Item} Very Magnificent Lord don Tristán de Arellano, *maese de campo* of this expeditionary force,

We, Jorge Báez and Antón Negrín, *estantes* in [the expeditionary force], appear before Your Grace and state that Juan Jiménez, an *estante* in this expeditionary force, has passed from this present life. Because there was no *escribano* where he was, the aforesaid Juan Jiménez did not prepare and execute his will, nor did he ease his soul.

The night before he died, this Juan Jiménez, in the presence of witnesses, conferred his full power of attorney on us as friends and companions of his, which we have always been. This was so that we might prepare and execute his will for him and put his intention and conscience into effect in accordance with what the deceased discussed with us for this purpose on many occasions. Moreover, he left us as his executors and directed that his possessions not fall into the power of [other] custodians and instead that we hold them and look after them and administer them as seems best to us, in conformance with his wishes.

Because the aforesaid Juan Jiménez left a few possessions in this expeditionary force, as such administrators and persons whom the deceased named as suitable to administer them, we ask and request Your Grace to order them delivered to us. [This is] so that with them and with their administration we might discharge the wish of the deceased in the way that he discussed with us. For this we beseech Your Grace's very noble office and ask for justice.
Antón Negrín
Jorge Báez

{Item} When the document was presented in the way that is recorded, [3r] the aforesaid don Tristán de Arellano, *maestre de campo*, stated that they were to present and produce witnesses for examination of what they say. When that is delivered and reviewed he will do what is fair.
Witnesses: the aforesaid [names omitted].

{Item} {February 25}
After what has been stated, on the twenty-fifth day of February in the aforesaid year, Antón Negrín appeared in person before the lord don Tristán de Arellano, *maestre de campo* of this expeditionary force, and before me, Hernando Bermejo, His Majesty's *escribano*, and presented as witnesses for this purpose Alonso Álvarez, Gerónimo Ramos, and Antonio Álvarez, *estantes* in this expeditionary force. From them and each one of them the oath was received in the form required by law, by virtue of which they promised to tell the truth. When they were questioned in accordance with the aforementioned petition, they stated and declared the following:

{Item} Alonso Álvarez,[36] a witness presented for this purpose, having given his oath in the form required by law and being questioned in accordance with the petition, stated that one night in this month of February, which was the day before Juan Jiménez died, while he was walking about on watch,[37] the aforesaid Juan Jiménez, who was an *estante* in the expeditionary force, sent [someone] to call this witness and other individuals.

He said to [the witness], "Sir, you are to serve as witness because at present there is no royal *escribano* in the camp on this side of the river, [since it is] away from where the general is.[38] Because I feel very ill and think that I will not survive until morning, I declare that I grant my full and complete power of attorney, [3v] in the same way I possess it, to Jorge Báez and Antón Negrín, *estantes* in this expeditionary force. [This is] so that they may prepare my will for me and ease my soul in the way I have discussed with them several times, since I do not feel myself healthy enough to do it. And [so that] they may look after the possessions I have in this expeditionary force. [I declare that] they are to be my executors. I say this because I do not want my possessions to come under control of caretakers other than Antón Negrín and Jorge Báez, who are to take possession of them. They are to do with them as they wish. If God allows me to survive until morning, I will, before an *escribano*, grant to Jorge Báez and Antón Negrín my full power of attorney for the stated purpose, because that is my aim and desire."

[Alvarez] stated this, which is what he knows, in accordance with the oath he swore. And he signed it with his name. Also, he knows and saw that Juan Jiménez died in the morning [after] the night he sent to have the witness called in order to tell him what is stated.
Alonso Álvarez

{Item} The aforesaid Antonio Álvarez, a witness presented for this purpose by Antón Negrín, having given his oath in the form required by law and being questioned in accordance with the petition, stated that what he knows about this case is that this witness, while walking about on watch one night in this month of February (it was the day before Juan Jiménez, an *estante* in this expeditionary force, died), Juan

Jiménez sent [someone] to call this witness and other individuals.

He said to him, "Sir, you are to act as witness because at present there is no [4r] royal *escribano* in this camp where I am. I feel very ill and do not think I will survive until the morning. I declare that I grant my full power of attorney, in the same way I possess it, to Jorge Báez and Antón Negrín, *estantes* in this expeditionary force. This is so that they may prepare and execute my will for me and ease my soul in the way I have many times discussed it with them, because I do not feel well enough to do it. And [so that] they may look after the possessions I have on this expedition, and they are to be my executors. If God brings me to tomorrow, I will, before an *escribano*, grant my full power of attorney for the aforesaid purpose to Jorge Báez and Antón Negrín, because this is my intention and desire."

This witness believes that Juan Jiménez did this so that his possessions would not fall into the hands of [other] caretakers. Asked how he knows this, he declared that [it is] because in his sickness the aforesaid Juan Jiménez had said to this witness that if he were to die, he would not want his possessions to fall into the hands of [other] caretakers. Thus, this witness then saw Juan Jiménez die in the morning [after] the night he sent to have him called in order to tell him what is stated. And he signed it with his name.
Antonio Álvarez

{Item} The aforesaid Gerónimo Ramos, a witness presented for this purpose, having given his oath in the form required by law and being questioned in regard to what is stated, said that what he knows about this case is that one night in this month of February, while this witness [was] walking about on watch, the aforesaid Juan Jiménez sent [someone] to call this witness and other [4v] individuals.

He said to him, "Sir, you are to act as witness because at present in this camp where I am there is no *escribano* and because I feel very ill and do not think I will survive until the morning. I declare that I grant my total and complete power of attorney, in the same way I possess it, to Jorge Báez and Antón Negrín, *estantes* in this expedition. This is so that they may prepare and execute my will for me and ease my soul in the way I have many times discussed it with them. They are to look after the assets I have on this expedition and are to be my executors. If God brings me to tomorrow I will, before an *escribano,* grant the aforesaid full power of attorney to Jorge Báez and Antón Negrín for the stated purpose."

This witness then saw that in the morning Juan Jiménez died. This is what he knows about it. And he signed it with his name.

Gerónimo Ramos

{Item} After the aforementioned, [on] the aforesaid day, month, and year, Antón Negrín presented as a witness Antón Pérez Buscavida, an *estante* in this expeditionary force.[39] After having given his oath in the form required by law and being questioned in regard to what is stated, he said that what he knows about this case is that one night in this month of February, when this witness was walking about on watch, the aforesaid Juan Jiménez sent [someone] to call him and other individuals.

He said to this witness, "Sir, you are to act as witness, since [5r] I do not think I will survive until the morning because I feel ill. I grant my total and complete power of attorney, in the same way I possess it, to Antón Negrín and Jorge Báez, *estantes* on this expedition. [This is] so that, for me and in accordance with what I myself would [ordinarily] be able to do, they may prepare and execute my will and ease my soul in the way I have discussed it with them many times. [This is] because it is better that they prepare it than I [do], since I am of weak mind and nearly on the point of death. They are to prepare and dispose of my assets as they wish, because I name them my executors for that purpose. I desire that they take possession of them and look after them as they wish, in accordance with what is stated, because this is my intention and desire."

He knows this about it by the oath he swore. And he signed it with his name.

Antón Pérez

{Item} After the aforementioned, [on] this day, month, and year, lord don Tristán de Arellano, *maestre de campo* of this expeditionary force, having examined the petition and record

of inquiry recorded above, said that [he was] mindful that it was the wish of Juan Jiménez that his assets not fall into the hands of [other] caretakers [but] that Jorge Báez and Antón Negrín hold them and administer them, as it seems [best] to them.

[And he was mindful] that Jorge Báez and Antón Negrín have been very good friends and associates of the deceased and members of the lord don Tristán de Arellano's company. And that they hold the power of attorney to prepare his will. He is aware, as it is apparent from the record of inquiry, [that] the deceased communicated [5v] with them his wish and what was conducive to the discharge of his conscience. And [further] that Jorge Báez and Antón Negrín are men who will look after the deceased's assets like assets of their friend and [like] men who have the duty [to look after] his intention.

[Arellano] declared [that] he was ordering and did order that, in conformance with the inventory that is being made of those assets, they be delivered to the aforesaid Jorge Báez and Antón Negrín and that they are to look after them and administer them as they see is advantageous to the deceased. [He ordered further] that in everything they are to obtain[40] his advantage and profit and recoup his losses. They are to provide an accounting of [the losses] and the increase, along with true and faithful payment, each and every time they are requested [to do so] by the lord don Tristán de Arellano, *maestre de campo* of this expeditionary force, or by [any] other judge or individual who may make [such a request]. [This is] under penalty of making good [the shortfalls] or whatever part of them by means of their assets or their labor, [and under the] additional penalty of being subjected and liable to the punishments [customarily] incurred by persons who do not provide an accounting of the assets which are entrusted to them for safekeeping and administration.

Thus, he stated that he was ordering and did order me, the aforesaid *escribano,* to deliver the assets to Jorge Báez and Antón Negrín (in accordance with the inventory which is being made of them).

don Tristán de Arellano

{Item} After the aforesaid, on the fifteenth day of the month

of March of the aforesaid year, I, Hernando Bermejo, His Majesty's *escribano,* notified the aforementioned Antón Negrín [6r] and Jorge Báez in person [of] the order of the other party [Arellano] recorded [above]. They stated that they were ready and able to receive the assets listed on the inventory in accordance with and in the way lord don Tristán ordered it. Witnesses: Juan Pérez de Vergara, Jaque de Brujas, and Diego Gallego.[41]
Hernando Bermejo

{Item} I, Hernando Bermejo, His Majesty's *escribano* and public *notario,* was present at what is recorded [above].[42] In accordance with the petition from Antón Negrín, I set this down in writing in the way it transpired before me. There-

fore, in testimony of the truth [of what is recorded], I affixed here this sign of mine [made] in this way.[43]
Hernando Bermejo, His Majesty's *escribano*

{Item} In the town of Coafor in the *provincia* of Tiguex of this newly discovered land on the eighteenth day of the month of March in the year one thousand five hundred and forty-two, before the very magnificent lord don Tristán de Arellano, *maestre de campo* of this expeditionary force, and before me, Hernando Bermejo, His Majesty's *escribano,* Antón Negrín, executor of the deceased, Juan Jiménez, as it was said he was, conducted an auction of the possessions the deceased left in this expedition. It was done in the following way [in *pesos de minas*]:

---

minas

{Item} 40 *pesos*	First, one chestnut horse was sold at auction to Rodrigo de Trujillo,[44] son of Jorge Báez, for forty *pesos de minas* on credit for the period of six months from [today's] date.[45] Antón Negrín stood surety for [the debt].
[6v] {Item} 2 *pesos*	{Item} One sword with a leather belt was sold at auction to the Vizcayan Juanes de Guernica for two *pesos.*[46]
{Item} 2 *pesos*	{Item} Some shoes and sandals were sold at auction to Diego de Mata for two *pesos.*[47]
{Item} 5 *pesos*	{Item} One native tunic, one jerkin with leather sleeves, one breastband for a horse, two sacks (one leather and one wool), and one *caperuza* for war were sold at auction to Juan Pérez de Vergara for five *pesos.*[48]
{Item} 1 *peso*	{Item} Eleven new horseshoes and five worn ones, as well as three hundred nails [were sold at auction] to Cristóbal Pérez from Ávila for one *peso.*[49]
{Item} 4 *tomines*	{Item} One old [bison or] cowhide jacket was sold at auction to the Vizcayan Juanes de Guernica for four [*tomines de oro de minas*][50]
{Item} 30 *pesos*	{Item} One white-footed horse the color of blood sausage,[51] with saddle and bridle, was sold at auction to Juan Pérez de Vergara for thirty *pesos,* to be paid later.

{Item} All the possessions listed above[52] were sold and delivered during public auction when there was no one who offered to pay more within six full months from the date of this [document]. [7r] [It was conducted] before the lord *maestre de campo* by means of the booming voice of Pedro, the black public crier. Witnesses: Juan Pérez de Vergara, Melchior Pérez, and Miguel Sánchez de Plasencia.[53] The lord *maestre de campo* signed his name in the registry [entry] for this instrument, which is dated the aforesaid day, month, and year.
don Tristán de Arellano

I, Hernando Bermejo, His Majesty's *escribano* and public *notario,* was present for all that has been stated. At the request of Antón Negrín I recorded it in the way it transpired before me. Therefore, in testimony of the truth [of what is recorded], I affixed here this registered mark of mine, which is thus.[54]
Hernando Bermejo

{Item} {February 17} In the *provincia* of Tiguex of this newly discovered land, on the seventeenth day of the month of February in the year one thousand five hundred and forty-two, before me, Hernando Bermejo, His Majesty's *escribano,* and the witnesses listed below, the very magnificent lord don Tristán de Arellano, *maese de campo* of this expedition, made an inventory of the assets left in this expedition [by] Juan Jiménez, deceased, who died on this aforementioned day. It was done in the following manner:[55]

{Item}   First, a white-footed horse, bluish black with a stripe on its forehead, with its bit and an old saddle

{Item}   Another horse, chestnut with a stripe on its forehead, shod

{Item}   One native tunic

[7v]
{Item}   Two sacks, one made of leather and the other of wool

{Item}   One old [bison or] cowhide jacket

{Item}   One sword

{Item}   One jerkin with hide sleeves

{Item}   One [bison or] cowhide with hair

{Item}   One *caperuza* for war

{Item}   One worn hat

{Item}   Eleven new horseshoes and three hundred nails

{Item}   One lance point

{Item}   Some sandals

{Item}   One large packsaddle

{Item}   One breastband for a horse

{Item}   Some old shoes

{Item}   Some small spurs

{Item}   A promissory note against Alonso González in the amount of twenty-four *pesos de minas,* signed by Alonso González and [by] witnesses Miguel Torres and Antón Negrín[56]

{Item}   Another promissory note against Pedro de Benavides[57] in the amount of thirty-four *pesos de minas,* which he owes to the deceased, signed by Pedro de Benavides and by [witnesses] Pedro de Lasojo and Pedro de Huelva

{Item}   Another promissory note against Alonso González in the amount of forty-two *pesos de oro de minas,* which he owes [8r] the deceased, signed by the aforesaid Alonso González and [by] Alonso López[58] and Antón Negrín, witnesses

{Item}   Another promissory note against Juan Francés[59] in the amount of eight *pesos de minas,* which he owes the deceased, signed by Antón Negrín, witness for the promissory note

{Item}   Another promissory note against Alonso Jiménez[60] in the amount of eight *pesos de oro de minas,* which he owes the deceased, signed by Alonso Jiménez and [by] Antón Negrín and Jorge Báez, witnesses

{Item}   Another promissory note against Juan Galleas[61] in the amount of twenty-five *pesos de minas,* signed by the aforementioned Juan Galleas

{Item}   A broken machete

{Item}   A hammer, some tongs, and a hoof parer[62]

{Item} All of the assets recorded and declared above were found in the lodging of Juan Jiménez, and no other assets of his came to light.[63] Nor was there [any] person who was aware of other assets the aforesaid Juan Jiménez might have had on this expedition. [These items] were inventoried in the way that has been stated. The lord *maese de campo* signed [the entry] in the registry with his name. Witnesses who were present for it: Velasco de Barrionuevo,[64] [8v] Jorge Báez, and Antón Negrín.

{Item} {March 15} In the town of Coafor in the *provincia* of Tiguex on the fifteenth day of the month of March in the aforesaid year, I, Hernando Bermejo, His Majesty's *escribano,* by order of lord don Tristán de Arellano, *maese de campo* of this expedition, before the witnesses recorded below, delivered all the assets of this other party [Jiménez] listed and declared in this inventory to Jorge Báez and Antón Negrín, *estantes* in [the expedition].

They stated that they regarded themselves as recipients of them all for the purpose of selling them in the way that seems to them to be most advantageous and profitable for the deceased, Juan Jiménez.

{note} They will obtain everything that is to his benefit and profit and will avoid injury to him. Concerning [the assets] and what is added to them, they will give an accurate accounting, along with reliable and truthful payment, whenever it is requested from them by the lord *maese de campo* or another judge or person who has the right to request it. Whenever it is requested of them [it is to be] under penalty that they pay for the assets and the amount they have increased with their persons and property, movable and fixed, [both] [that] already in their possession and [what they] will come to possess.

For this purpose they declared they were expressly obligating [themselves] and granted full power of attorney to whichever of His Majesty's judges so they may have it carried out thus. They waived any [9r] laws which in this case they could make use of, as well as the general law. Antón Negrín signed his name in the register, and Jorge Báez signed it with his customary rubric.[65] Witnesses: Juan Pérez de Vergara, Diego Gallego, Jaque de Brujas, Diego Sánchez.[66]
Antón Negrín
Jorge Báez

I, Hernando Bermejo, Their Majesties' *escribano* and their *notario,* was present during everything which is related and recorded it in writing at the request of Antón Negrín. Therefore, in testimony of its truth [of what is recorded], I affixed here my registered mark, which is thus.[67]
Hernando Bermejo, Their Majesties' *escribano*

{Item} The aforementioned lord *alcalde* [Gerónimo Ruiz de la Mota], having considered what was requested and presented on behalf of Antón Negrín, stated and declared [that] the petition on behalf of the aforementioned was denied.[68] Neither the power of attorney nor the authorization from the deceased which he is presenting for the aforementioned [purpose] is sufficient for suspending within the power of attorney and appointment from the deceased the stipulations required by law.[69]

Therefore, [he declared] that he was considering and did consider everything which was presented by Antón Negrín concerning the aforesaid appointment without merit.[70] He was ordering and did order that Antón Negrín show[71] and make clear under oath which assets of the deceased he has in his possession and state whether he knows in whose possession they are, so that, with ample documentation, they may be placed in the possession of the person who has the right to hold them. [That is to be done] until a person to whom the assets belong may present himself. When such a person has come to light, the lord *alcalde* will order what he determines under the law and what is just for assistance [9v] of the soul of the deceased. Rendering his opinion in this way, he declared that he was ordering and did order it.

Gerónimo Ruiz de la Mota
licenciado [Tello de] Sandoval

{Item} This ruling concerning the [issue] referred to above was delivered and announced on the thirteenth day of the month of September in the year one thousand five hundred and forty-two in a public hearing. Witnesses: Sancho López and Alonso Sánchez.[72]

The aforementioned Antón Negrín stated that he was appealing and did appeal the judgment[73] to and before His Majesty, president, and *oidores*. He requested it by affidavit in this way:

Juan de Zaragosa, public *escribano*

{Item} Very powerful Lords,

I, Antón Negrín, appear before Your Majesty and state that the *alcalde ordinario* delivered an unjust ruling very injurious to me, in that I asked him to permit me and grant me authority so I could prepare a will in the name of Juan Jiménez, and he declared that [my] petition that [a will] be prepared was being denied. I request and entreat Your Highness to order that the *escribano* at long last make a report and that what in accordance with conscience and justice ought to be done be decided in the case. I implore your very royal office.

{Item} In the Ciudad de México on the fourteenth day of September in the aforesaid year, when this case file had been reviewed by the lords president and *oidores,* they declared, in regard [to it], that they were revoking and did revoke the ruling delivered and announced by the *alcalde.*

They decreed that Antón Negrín and Jorge Báez and each of them separately has authority [10r] to prepare a will in the name of the deceased, Juan Jiménez, as seems [best] to them, just as the testator discussed it with them. For this [the *oidores*] granted them, each one of them, jointly and severally, full authority, with the additional proviso and clarification that in regard to this will they may not name nor are they to name or establish an heir.[74] Thus they declared and decreed it.

Juan de Zaragosa, public *escribano*

{Item} This case file is taken over by me, the *escribano* Andrés de Herrera, a public *escribano* and [*escribano*] of the city council of [Puebla] de los Ángeles, so I can do everything that is most suitable and nothing else, insofar as it [was] entrusted to him in the first place.[75]

Juan de Zaragosa, public *escribano*

{Item} Following what has been related, in this *ciudad* of [Puebla] de los Ángeles in Nueva España on the twenty-seventh day of the month of February in the one thousand five hundred and forty-third year since the birth of Our Savior Jesus Christ, the aforementioned Antón Negrín, a *vecino* of this *ciudad,* appeared in the presence me, Andrés de Herrera, a public *escribano* and Their Majesties' *escribano* for the council of this *ciudad,* and [in the presence] of the witnesses recorded below.

By virtue of all that has been done and the authorization attached below, which he holds from the royal *audiencia* (which, on behalf of His Majesty, has its seat in the Ciudad de México), he stated that, in the name of the deceased, Juan Jiménez (may he be with God), and as his executor and agent, he was preparing and arranging and did prepare and arrange the last will and testament of that same Juan Jiménez, deceased. [This he did] exactly as he had discussed and talked it over with the deceased, [10v] which is in the following manner and form:

{Item} First, I commend the soul of the deceased to God, Our Lord, who nourished and redeemed it with his precious blood, in order that he may be pleased to find his soul worthy and carry it to his holy kingdom. Amen.

{Item} I direct that public masses of prayer for the soul of the deceased, Juan Jiménez, be said for thirty days. {note} They are to be said by the parish priest Father Alonso Maldonado, priest of the principal church of this *ciudad.* For saying [the masses], he is to be paid the customary amount from the deceased's assets.

{Item} I direct that the same priest, Alonso Maldonado, say another ten masses of prayer for the souls of the deceased's parents. The saying of them is to be paid for in the customary amount.

{Item} I direct that five *ducados* of bona fide Castilian gold be paid from the deceased's assets to the hospital of the Ciudad de México. [This is to be done] for the soul of the deceased, so that it may earn and obtain the indulgences which by this means may be earned.

{Item} I direct that four *pesos de oro que corre* be paid from the assets of the deceased to the hospital of this *ciudad,* as alms on behalf of the soul of the deceased.

[11r] {Item} I direct that one *peso de oro que corre* [be paid] from the assets of the deceased to each of the confraternities of this *ciudad.* These are the Confraternity of the Most Holy Sacrament, the Confraternity of the True Cross, and the Confraternity of the Angels.

{Item} I direct that the obligatory bequests (each one on behalf of the soul of the deceased) be paid from the assets of the deceased [at the rate of] one *tomín de oro que corre.*[76]

{Item} On behalf of the soul of the deceased, I direct that a bull of indulgence as a participant in a holy crusade[77] (which is ongoing at present) be obtained and be paid for from his assets.

{Item} {scribal mark} I direct that 50 *pesos de oro de minas* be given and paid from the assets of the deceased to Juan Barragán, which the deceased owed him by means of a promissory note.[78]

{Item} I direct that three *pesos de oro de minas* be paid from the assets of the deceased to Antón García, which the deceased owed and does owe him.[79]

{Item} I direct that two *pesos de oro de minas* be given and paid from the assets of the deceased to Juan Cordero, a tailor, which the deceased owed and does owe him.[80]

{Item} I direct that all debts owed by the deceased according to outstanding loan documents be paid. Because at present it is not known that he has any [other] debts, and in order to unburden the soul of the deceased, [Negrín] declared that, if any person will swear that the deceased is indebted to him and the amount due is up to one *peso de oro que corre,* he was directing and did direct that it be paid to him from the assets of the deceased on the basis of his oath alone.

[11v] The aforesaid Antón Negrín made it clear and directed, in the name [of the deceased], that all outstanding debts owed to the deceased, Juan Jiménez, are to be collected. Because all the debts thus owed to him are those which were entered into in Tierra Nueva and are exactly what [Negrín] talked with the deceased, Juan Jiménez, about, [Negrín] stated that all debts owed to the deceased, whether by means of loan documents or bills, or from auction of [the possessions of] the deceased, are to be collected at two-thirds [of their value], and the [remaining] one-third [the debtors] are not to pay; it is waived.[81]

He is pleased [to do this] in the name of the deceased because, as has been stated, he said that he had discussed it with [the deceased]. [He stated] that, as has been said, two-thirds of all the debts are to be collected except 40 *pesos de oro de minas* which Rodrigo de Trujillo owes to the deceased for a horse, through a loan document. All of the 40 *pesos de oro de minas* is to be collected from Rodrigo de Trujillo because he rightly owes them [and they are] owed to the deceased.

All that is mentioned above [Negrín] stated that he was doing and did do in order to unburden the soul of the deceased, and [it was done] just as he discussed and talked it over with [Jiménez], as was stated.

{Item} In order to fulfill, pay, collect, and execute the will and what is referred to in it, Antón Negrín stated that he was naming and did name himself as executor and agent of the deceased. [This is] so that what is referred to in this aforesaid will [may be done] and whosoever may possess his power of attorney [12r] can recover the possessions, debts, and property of the deceased.

Also the aforesaid Antón Negrín stated that he was naming and did name [himself] as caretaker and administrator of the money, debts, and property of the deceased in order to receive and collect it all and to give an accounting of it in the manner and to whomever he rightly should, to either the heir or heirs of the deceased, Juan Jiménez. He does not indicate or specify those individuals because he does not know of them and is not acquainted with them. Nor does he have authority to specify them.

Beyond what has been stated, Antón Negrín stated and conceded that, in case God were to take him from this present life, he was naming and did name Alonso Grande and Gregorio Genovés (*vecinos* of this *ciudad* who are not present), or either of them separately, as executors and agents of the deceased and as caretakers of his assets which remain and belong or did belong [to him].[82] [Negrín] granted them his full power of attorney, exactly as he [himself] has it according to law in this case, as well and completely as he can and ought to give it, in the form [required by law].

{Item} By means of this instrument the aforesaid Antón Negrín stated that he was revoking and did revoke all and any previous will or wills, codicil or codicils, [12v] in whatever form the deceased Juan Jiménez may have prepared and executed [them]. [And he stated] that none is valid except this one which now, in the name of [Juan Jiménez], he makes and executes exactly as he discussed with the deceased, as has been stated. [He stated] that it is valid as the

last will and testament of the deceased, Juan Jiménez. [Negrín] stated that he was making and did make and execute [it] in [Jiménez's] name, in accordance with what is referred to above. It is made and executed on the aforesaid day, month, and year. Antón Negrín signed his name in the register.

Witnesses who were present during all that has been related [are] Francisco de Orduña, Pedro de Villanueva, Juan de San Vicente, the priest Juan Valadés, and Juan Sánchez, [all] *vecinos* of this *ciudad*.[83] All those who knew how to write signed their names in the register, together with the one issuing the document.

Antón Negrín

Francisco de Orduña

Pedro de Villanueva

Juan de San Vicente

Juan de Valadés, priest

Juan de San Vicente, on behalf of Juan Sánchez

{Item} I, Andrés Herrera, public *escribano* and [*escribano*] for His Majesty of the council of this *ciudad* of [Puebla] de los Ángeles in this Nueva España, had what is recorded above written out and extracted from the original, which remains in my possession. I prepared it in accordance with what transpired before me.

Therefore, in testimony of the truth [of what is recorded], I here affixed my registered mark, which is thus. Andrés de Herrera, public *escribano* and [*escribano*] of the council

[13r] {Item} This is a copy well and faithfully extracted from a petition presented by Antón Negrín before the lords president and *oidores,* with [a] certain resolution [and] ruling executed by the lords, in which they decree that Antón Negrín and Jorge Báez (or either one of them) can prepare a will in the name of Juan Jiménez.

These (their verbatim substance), the one following the other, along with the will which Antón Negrín prepared in the name [of the deceased] (in accordance with what seemed proper for it), are what follows:

[. . .][84]

[16r]
[...]
{Item} When this copy had been prepared and extracted, [it] was corrected and reconciled with the authorized copy from which it was extracted in this Ciudad de México on the twenty-second day of October in the year of [Our] Lord one thousand five hundred and forty-three. Witnesses who were present to see it corrected and reconciled with the aforesaid copy: Diego Gómez and Juan Polido, *vecino* and *estante*[85] in this *ciudad*.

{Item} I, Melchior Gómez, Their Majesties' *escribano*, and their *escribano* and public *notario* in their court and in all their *reinos* and dominions, together with the aforementioned witnesses, was present at what has been related, and I extracted it from the authorized copy exactly as it is contained in it.

I wrote it out [16v] and, in testimony of the truth [of what is recorded], I affixed here my registered mark, [which is] thus.
Melchior Gómez, Their Majesties' *escribano*

{Item} When the documents (the will and judicial decrees included above in the aforementioned manner) had been presented, Antón Negrín stated that he was ready to give an accounting of the assets of the aforesaid Juan Jiménez, deceased, which are referred to in the aforementioned documents (which he is ordered [to do]). [He is ready to do this] immediately and exactly as he is ordered [to do].
Witnesses: Diego de Ordás;[86] Sebastián Vázquez, His Majesty's *escribano*.

{Item} After what is related above, in the aforesaid *ciudad* of [Puebla] de los Ángeles, on the ninth day of September in the year one thousand five hundred and forty-five, Antón Negrín appeared in person before the lord *residencia* judge and *justicia mayor* and judge of the assets of the deceased and in my presence, the aforementioned *escribano*. He stated that he is at last providing an accounting of the assets of Juan Jiménez.[87] Because he is obliged and has been ordered [to do] it by His Grace, he requested [that] it be received from him.

{Item} Then, in view of the aforesaid, the lord judge held Antón Negrín responsible for the assets of the deceased, [that is,] the following assets:

[17r]
minas   *tepuzque*[88]
{Item} First, he reviewed and checked the inventory with the auction [record] which was made of the assets. By this [comparison] it appears that the following failed to sell from the inventoried assets: one cow [or bison] pelt; item, one worn hat; one lance point; one large packsaddle; some small spurs; a broken machete; a hammer, some pliers, and a hoof parer. [Negrín] is held responsible for those assets that thus remain to be sold from those listed in the inventory, so that he must produce them and pay for them or their value.

{Item}
80 *pesos*
4 *tomines* Item. He is held responsible for eighty *pesos* and four *tomines de oro de minas*, which [is what] the payment and proceeds for the assets which were sold at the public auction added up to and amounted to. He was responsible for them since it is obvious and apparent from [the auction record].

{Item}
24 *pesos*

Item. He is held responsible for a promissory note which the deceased had [and is] listed in the inventory of the assets, in the amount of twenty-four *pesos de oro de minas,* for which Alonso González is liable. [It is] signed by the aforesaid Alonso González, Miguel de Torres, and Antón Negrín. He must produce the promissory note or pay the twenty-four gold *pesos.*

[17v]
minas   *tepuzque*
{Item}
30 *pesos*

Item. He is held responsible for another promissory note for which Pedro de Benavides is liable in the amount of thirty *pesos de oro de minas,* which the aforesaid owed the deceased. [It is] signed with his name and [those of] Pedro de Lasojo and Pedro de Huelva. He must produce the promissory note or pay the thirty gold *pesos* referred to in it.

{Item}
42 *pesos*

Item. He is held responsible for another promissory note for which Alonso González is liable in the amount of forty-two *pesos de oro de minas,* which the aforesaid owed the deceased. [It is] signed by the aforementioned and Antón Negrín and Alonso López. He must produce the promissory note or pay the forty-two *pesos* referred to in it.

{Item}
8 *pesos*

Item. He is held responsible for another promissory note {note} for which Juan Francés is liable. He was indebted to the deceased in the amount of eight *pesos de oro de minas.* [It] was signed by the aforesaid Antón Negrín. He must produce the promissory note or pay the eight *pesos de minas* referred to in it.

{Item}
8 *pesos*

Item. He is held responsible for another promissory note for which Alonso Jiménez is liable, in the amount of eight *pesos de oro de minas,* which he owed the deceased. [It] is signed by the aforesaid Alonso Jiménez, Antón Negrín, and Jorge Báez. He must produce the promissory note or pay the eight *pesos de minas* referred to in it.

[18r]
minas   *tepuzque*
{Item}
25 *pesos*

Item. He is held responsible for another promissory note for which Juan [Galeras] is liable, in the amount of twenty-five *pesos de oro de minas.* [It is] signed by Juan [Galeras]. He must produce the promissory note or the gold *pesos* referred to in it.

{Item}

All these promissory notes were inventoried as assets of the deceased, Juan Jiménez, in addition to the assets referred to in [the inventory document]. An oath was taken from

Antón Negrín by the lord judge in the form required by law. Under the obligation of [that oath], [Negrín] stated and declared that he is not aware of nor does he have information about, nor are there in his possession, any other assets of the deceased beyond those listed in the inventory. He signed it with his name. And the lord judge [did] likewise.

licenciado Caballero

Antón Negrín

Sebastián Vázquez, His Majesty's *escribano*

{Item}
217 *pesos*
4 *tomines*

As a result, as stated in the entries above, the aforesaid obligation totals and amounts to two hundred seventeen *pesos* and four *tomines de oro de minas*. [And] he is held responsible for them, in accordance with what has been stated. They signed it with their names. [This] does not include the other things referred to above.

licenciado Caballero

Antón Negrín

Sebastián Vázquez, His Majesty's *escribano*

[18v] {Item} After the aforementioned, {note} in the *ciudad* of [Puebla] de los Ángeles on the same day, month, and year (at the hour of vespers, since what was related above was done and transpired in the morning), the lord *residencia* judge and *justicia mayor* and Antón Negrín met again to scrutinize the calculation, deductions, and balance and to resolve them.

What transpired today, the aforesaid day, and was done in my presence, the aforementioned *escribano*, is the following:

Antón Negrín's ledger adjustments[89]

[*minas*]   [*tepuzque*]
{Item}
50 *pesos*

First, [Negrín] declared as a ledger adjustment that he had given and paid Juan Barragán fifty *pesos de oro de minas* which the deceased owed him under a public document, which he transferred in the presence of Hernando Gómez de la Peña, His Majesty's *escribano*.[90] [This was done] by virtue of an executory order, according to what is recorded by means of a receipt from Juan Barragán, which is on the reverse side of the order. [Negrín] presented the document, the order, and the receipt. In view of this, the fifty *pesos de oro de minas* are accepted for him in the reckoning.

{Item}

Item. [Negrín] stated that he was declaring and did declare as a ledger adjustment that he gave and paid to the priest Alonso Maldonado, [who is] parish priest of this holy church, twenty *pesos de oro que corre* for thirty days' worth of masses, plus ten masses, which [19r] [the priest] said for the deceased. He swore in the form required by law that it is so. {note} In accordance with what he has stated, he presented a letter from Alonso Maldonado. These twenty *pesos de oro común* are accepted for him in the reckoning.   20 *pesos minas*   *tepuzque*

{Item}   Item. [Negrín] declared as a ledger adjustment that he had given and paid Andrés de   2 *pesos*
Herrera, a public *escribano* who was from this *ciudad,* two *pesos de oro que corre* for registra-
tion and copying of the will, inventory, and auction record. [This is] just as it is recorded
by what is written in Andrés de Herrera's hand at the foot of the aforementioned documents. In view of that and the assessment that was made of it, the two *pesos de oro común*
are accepted for him in the reckoning.

{Item}   Item. [Negrín] stated that he was declaring and did declare as a ledger adjustment that he   2 *pesos*
gave and paid an *escribano,* Melchior Gómez, and an attorney, Álvaro Ruiz, for certain   5 *tomines*
documents dealing with the deceased, Juan Jiménez, which he executed before Melchior
Gómez. And [he paid] Álvaro Ruiz because through him the collection of certain gold
pesos pertaining to the deceased is being requested. With regard to all this (the aforementioned two *pesos* and five *tomines de oro común*), he presented and showed receipts for the
aforesaid. In view of this and that he gave his oath in the form required by law that [the
receipts] are reliable and genuine, the aforementioned gold *pesos* are accepted for him in the
reckoning.

[19v]

minas   *tepuzque*

{Item}   Item. [Negrín] declared as a ledger adjustment the promissory note for thirty *pesos de minas*
30 *pesos*   for which Pedro de Benavides is liable [and] for which [Negrín] was held responsible. He
presented this without a receipt because he said the [*pesos*] had not been collected from
[Benavides].[91] In view of this, the thirty *pesos de oro de minas* of the promissory note are
accepted for him in the reckoning.

{Item}   Item. [Negrín] declared as a ledger adjustment another promissory note, in the amount of
42 *pesos*   forty-two *pesos de oro de minas,* for which Alonso González is liable [and] for which
[Negrín] was held responsible. He presented and delivered the promissory note without a
receipt. In view of that, the forty-two *pesos de oro de minas* of the promissory note were
accepted from him in the reckoning.

{Item}   Item. [Negrín] declared as a ledger adjustment another promissory note in the amount of
24 *pesos*   twenty-four *pesos de oro de minas,* for which Alonso González is liable [and] which he was
held responsible for. He presented and delivered the promissory note without a receipt
because he said he had not collected the aforesaid gold *pesos.* In view of this, the twenty-
four gold *pesos* are accepted for him in the reckoning.

{Item}   Item. [Negrín] declared as a ledger adjustment another promissory note in the amount of
25 *pesos*   twenty-five *pesos de oro de minas,* for which Juan [Galeras] is liable. It is written on the back
of the promissory note about which mention was made in the immediately preceding entry.
[20r] He presented and delivered the promissory note on the same sheet of paper [and]

minas   *tepuzque*

without a receipt because he said he had not collected the [*pesos*]. In view of this, the aforementioned gold *pesos* are accepted for him in the reckoning.

{Item}

8 *pesos*

Item. [Negrín] declared as a ledger adjustment the promissory note for which Alonso
Jiménez is liable, in the amount of eight *pesos de oro de minas,* which he was held responsible for. He delivered the promissory note without a receipt. In view of this, the eight
pesos de oro de minas of the promissory note are accepted for him in the reckoning.

{Item}

8 *pesos*

Item. [Negrín] declared as a ledger adjustment another promissory note for which Juan
Francés is liable, in the amount of eight *pesos de oro de minas,* which he was held responsible
for. He delivered the promissory note without a receipt. In view of this, the eight *pesos de
oro de minas* are accepted for him in the reckoning.

{Item}

40 *pesos*

Item. [Negrín] declared as a ledger adjustment the forty *pesos de oro de minas* for the horse
which was sold on credit at auction to Rodrigo de Trujillo, a son of Jorge Báez, in the public
auction which was held of the assets of the deceased. He has seized [the horse] from the
aforementioned [Rodrigo Trujillo] and sold the property to pay the debt in the presence of
the lord *justicia mayor.*[92] [20v] Accordingly, he stated that it is recorded in and apparent
from the legal case file pertaining to the seizure and sale. Because it is recorded that it is so,
they are accepted for him in the reckoning and [as] a ledger adjustment.

{Item}

As a result, the ledger adjustment which Antón Negrín declares against what he is held
responsible for (as is specified in the entries recorded above) totals and amounts to two
hundred and twenty-seven *pesos de oro de minas* and an additional twenty-four *pesos de oro
común* and five *tomines.*

    As a result, Antón Negrín is owed[93] by the deceased the amount of nine *pesos de oro de
minas* and four *tomines* and twenty-four *pesos* and five *tomines de oro que corre.* [That amount
is due] when Antón Negrín has paid for the assets for which he was held responsible, namely,
those he had left to sell from the ones listed in the inventory and which remain as assets of
the deceased; all the debts recorded in the promissory notes which have been mentioned
above; and the forty *pesos de minas* from the seizure and sale which has been executed against
Rodrigo de Trujillo. The aforesaid lord *residencia* judge and Antón Negrín signed it.
licenciado [21r] Caballero
Antón Negrín
[This] took place before me,
Sebastián Vázquez, His Majesty's *escribano*

{Item} In the *ciudad* of [Puebla] de los Ángeles in this Nueva
España on the twenty-seventh day of the month of October
in the year one thousand five hundred and forty-five,

Sebastián Vázquez, His Majesty's *escribano,* appeared before
the lord Diego Ramírez, *juez visitador de agravios y bienes de
difuntos*[94] in the aforementioned *ciudad* for the very magnif-

icent lord *licenciado* Tello de Sandoval, *visitador general* in this whole Nueva España, etc., and in my presence, Cristóbal de Heredia, His Majesty's *escribano* and *escribano* of the court of the lord judge.[95]

[Vázquez] presented before His Grace and gave and delivered to me, the aforesaid *escribano,* this case file concerning the accounting which was executed by the *licenciado* Caballero, *residencia* judge of the aforementioned *ciudad.* [This] took place before [Vázquez] as the *escribano* of his court. He presented it in fulfillment of the order which was presented to him by the lord judge. Witnesses: Gaspar de Arana, an *alguacil* named by the lord judge, and Diego, his servant, who said he was a native of the *villa* of Almonte. Cristóbal de Heredia, Their Majesties' *escribano*

[21v] {Item} Afterward, on the aforesaid day, the lord judge having reviewed the case file concerning the accounting, stated that he was approving and did approve [it] and considered this accounting as properly prepared by the *residencia* judge. As the authorized judge of the *bienes de difuntos,* which he is, he was taking and did take charge of this file and case himself, in order to conclude and finish it in accordance with the commission he has for its [completion] from the lord *visitador general* and in order to do justice in the case. Witnesses: the aforementioned.[96]
Diego Ramírez

{Item} Know all those who may see this promissory note that I, Juan Jiménez, a native of Guadalcanal, which is in the *reinos* of Castilla, at present an *estante* in this expeditionary force, do grant and acknowledge by this document that I am obligated (myself personally and by means of my assets, [both] movable and fixed, [those I now] possess and [those I] will possess [in the future]) to give and pay [you], and I will give and pay you, Juan Barragán, a native of the *villa* of Llerena, who is now present, or whoever may have your power of attorney.

By this document I will make known a debt (acknowledged and truthful) to you, namely, in the net amount of fifty *pesos de oro de minas* (of maximum purity of four hundred and fifty *maravedís* each), each one [of the] *pesos* [to be] cast and stamped with Their Majesties' mark.

Those [*pesos*] are payment for some hose, two shirts, and other valuable items which I will purchase from you. Because of this I consider myself satisfied. I am delivering [the debt document] and [am] well and willingly compensated inasmuch as I received [the goods][97] and they truly and in reality are transferred from your possession to mine.

On the basis of the delivery (which at the present time has not occurred), [22r] I waive the two regulations governing rights which apply to this case, in their entirety and all [their parts], as is recorded in them. Further, [I waive] the law concerning the two years and the thirty days.[98]

I set the time limit for delivering and paying you these fifty gold *pesos* at fifteen months from today, [meaning] from the date of this document. [They will be] handed over and paid into your possession or into the possession of whoever is to hold them for you, without suit[s] and without dispute, under penalty of doubling [the amount] and [paying] the additional costs, interest, damages, and depreciation which on this account may be incurred by you.

Because of everything that has been stated it is thus best to adhere to, observe, and fulfill [the agreement] and pay [the debt]. I grant and confer my full power of attorney on all and whichever judges and *justicias* of Their Majesties (from whatever regions and places they may be). I submit to their jurisdiction and that of each one of them with my person and assets, waiving (as in this case I am waiving) my own privilege [the right to adjudication in my own] jurisdiction and home locale, as well as the law "*si convenerit juresdicione*" [if it will be agreed upon by the judicial authority . . .].[99] [This is] so that once this document is examined by the aforementioned judges, [or] by any one of them whatsoever, they may thus constrain, compel, and oblige me to adhere to, observe, and fulfill [the agreement] and pay [the debt] by means of seizure and selling of property as well. [They may do this] exactly as if everything that has been stated were reviewed, heard, considered, ordered, adjudged, and a verdict were rendered by means of a trial and definitive decision of an authorized judge.

Such a decision would be consented to and accepted by me as something settled, from which there could be no appeal, no petition for reversal, and no other remedy [22v] or any recourse whatsoever regarding what I am forswearing, relinquishing, and abjuring for myself and my aid, assistance, and remedy. All laws, privileges, rights, and ordinances whatsoever, [both] written [and] unwritten, both in general and individually, by which I might be benefited in this case are to be of no value to me. [This] includes the two laws, numbers five and six [of] Title 13,[100] and the statute and law in which it is stated that a man might make use of the general waiver of laws, [which] is to be of no value [to me].

In testimony of this, I executed this document in the presence of the current *escribano* and witnesses listed below. It was prepared and executed within this expeditionary force of which the very magnificent lord Francisco Vázquez de Coronado is captain general for Their Majesties, while it was quartered in the *provincia* of Tiguex, on the sixth day of April in the one thousand five hundred and forty-first year since the birth of Our Savior, Jesus Christ.

Witnesses who were present at what is recorded: Diego Hernández, Jorge Báez, and Lope de la Cadena, *estantes* in the expeditionary force.[101] Because the person executing the document (whom I, the *escribano*, swear to know) did not know how to write, he asked Diego Hernández to sign it for him. [Hernández] signed in the register as witness of this document: Diego Hernández.

I, Hernando Gómez, Their Majesties' *escribano*, was present [23r] during everything that is recorded, along with the aforementioned witnesses. By request of the individual executing the document, I wrote it out in accordance with what transpired before me. Therefore, in testimony of the truth [of what is recorded], I here affixed this, my registered mark, [which is] thus.[102]
Hernando Gómez de la Peña

{Item} After the aforementioned, in the *ciudad* of [Puebla] de los Ángeles on the fourth day of November in the year one thousand five hundred and forty-five, the aforesaid Sebastián Vázquez, His Majesty's *escribano*, appeared in person before the lord judge and in my presence, the aforementioned *escribano*, and presented this petition. He requested what is recorded in it. Witnesses: Gaspar de Arana and Diego de Padilla, *criados* of the lord judge.

{Item} My Magnificent Lord,

I, Sebastián Vázquez, His Majesty's *escribano*, state that I was employed in the accounting which was taken from Antón Negrín, executor of Juan Jiménez, deceased, concerning the assets which, in accordance with what is recorded above, [are] in his possession.

I spent two days and wrote out a document of four and a half folios, as is recorded and evident in the account record. I request that Your Grace order me paid my wages and for [preparing] the document from the assets of the aforementioned [Juan Jiménez]. I ask for justice.

Inasmuch as I am going to [the Ciudad de] México, I request that Your Grace order that it be delivered to Ana de Terrazas, my wife, because [thus] I [will] consider [it] properly paid.
Sebastián Vázquez

[23v] When the request had been presented in the form which is recorded and had been reviewed by the lord judge, he declared that he would review it and do justice. Witnesses: the aforementioned Cristóbal de Heredia, Their Majesties' *escribano*.

{Item} In the *ciudad* of [Puebla] de los Ángeles in this Nueva España on the thirty-first of July in the one thousand five hundred and forty-fifth year since the birth of Our Savior, Jesus Christ, Antón Negrín, a *vecino* of this *ciudad*, appeared in person before the magnificent lord *licenciado* Hernando Caballero, *residencia* judge and *justicia mayor* in this *ciudad* for His Majesty, and in my presence, Sebastián Vázquez, His Majesty's *escribano* of the *audiencia* and the court of the lord judge, and [in the presence] of the witnesses listed below.

[Being] (which he is said to be) both executor and the person assigned to fulfill the will of the deceased, Juan Jiménez, and the custodian of his assets, [Negrín] presented a promissory note, signed by Hernán Gómez de la Peña, His Majesty's *escribano*, which is as follows:

{Item} Know all those who may see this document that I, Rodrigo de Trujillo, a native of the *ciudad* of Veracruz in Nueva España, at present an *estante* in this expeditionary force, do grant [24r] and acknowledge by this document that I am obligated (myself personally and by means of my assets, [both] movable and fixed, [those I now] possess and [those I] will possess [in the future]) to give and pay [you], and I will give and pay you, Antón Negrín, a *vecino* of the *ciudad* of [Puebla] de los Ángeles (which you are at present), as heir, executor, and the person assigned to fulfill the will dealing with the assets which remained and were left by the deceased, Juan Jiménez, either {note} to the heirs of the aforesaid Juan Jiménez or to whoever may possess your power of attorney or their power of attorney, [the amount which] this document specifies, namely forty *pesos de oro de minas* of bona fide money. Each *peso* [is to be] valued at four hundred and fifty *maravedís*. Those [*pesos*] are payment for a horse, chestnut-colored, both feet having a different color from the body, with a stripe on the forehead. I bought and acquired it during the public auction of the aforesaid assets which was conducted in the presence of Hernando Bermejo, Their Majesties' *escribano*. That [amount] was fair value for the horse.

I consider myself and concede [that I am] satisfied. I am delivering [the debt document] and [am] well and willingly compensated, inasmuch as I received [the horse] and it truly and in reality was transferred into my possession. On the basis of the delivery, if it is necessary, I waive the exemption concerning money and the statute concerning two years and the thirty days in their entirety and all [their parts], [24v] as is recorded in them.

I set the time limit for delivering and paying you the aforementioned forty gold *pesos* at five months from today, [meaning] from the date of this document.

When [the *pesos*] have been placed and paid into your possession or into the possession of whoever is to hold them for you or the aforementioned heirs, they will possess [them] in peace and safety, without suit[s] and without any dispute, under penalty of doubling [the amount] and [paying] the costs, interest, damages, and depreciation which on this account may be incurred by you.

In order that everything which has been stated may be adhered to, observed, fulfilled, and paid, by this document I grant and confer my full power of attorney on all and whichever judges and *justicias* of Their Majesties (from whatever regions and places they may be). I submit to their jurisdiction and that of each one of them with my person and assets, waiving (as in this case I am waiving) my own privilege [the right to adjudication in my own] jurisdiction and home locale, as well as the law "*sid convenerit juresdicione anium judicium*" [if it will be agreed upon by the judicial authority in each jurisdiction]. [This is] so that once this document is examined by the judges, *justicias,* or by any one of them whatsoever, they may thus constrain, compel, and oblige me to adhere to, observe, and fulfill [the agreement] and pay [the debt] exactly [25r] as if by definitive decision of an authorized judge [and as if] it were reviewed, heard, considered, ordered, and adjudged. And [as if] it had come about as a settled matter, agreed to and approved by me, from which there could be no appeal, no petition for reversal, and no other remedy or any recourse whatsoever regarding everything that has been recorded.

I am forswearing, relinquishing, and abjuring for my aid, assistance, and remedy all laws, privileges, rights, and ordinances whatsoever, [both] written [and] unwritten, both in general and individually, by which I might be aided and benefited in this case. They are to be of no value to me. [This includes] the two laws, numbers five and six [of] Title 13, and in particular I forswear the statute and general law in which it is stated that a man might make use of the general waiver of laws, [which] is to be of no value [to me].

In testimony of this, I executed this document in the presence of the current *escribano* and witnesses listed below. The document was prepared within this expeditionary force of which Francisco Vázquez de Coronado is captain general for Their Majesties, while it was quartered on the banks of the river which is called Río Frío, which is between Chichiltiqueale and Çibola, on the ninth day of the month of April in the one thousand five hundred and forty-second year since the birth of Our Savior, Jesus Christ.[103] Witnesses who were present during what is recorded: Rodrigo de Ysla, Juan Pedro, and [25v] Francisco de Parada, *estantes* in this expeditionary force.[104] Because the person executing the document did not know how to write, he asked Rodrigo de Ysla to sign it for him. [Ysla] signed in the register as witness of this document at his request. As witness, Rodrigo de Ysla.

I, Hernando Gómez de la Peña, Their Majesties' *escribano,* was present during everything that is recorded, along with the witnesses. By request of the person executing the document, whom I swear I know, I wrote it out in accordance with what transpired before me. Therefore, in testimony of the truth [of what is recorded], I here affixed this my registered mark, which is thus.[105]

Hernando Gómez de la Peña

{Item} In the *ciudad* of [Puebla] de los Ángeles in this Nueva España on the thirty-first day of July in the one thousand five hundred and forty-fifth year since the birth of Our Savior, Jesus Christ, Antón Negrín, a *vecino* of this *ciudad,* appeared in person in the presence of me, the *escribano,* and the witnesses listed below.

He declared that he was granting and did grant his full and complete power of attorney, just as he [himself] holds and possesses it, which is required by law and, further, can and ought to be of worth in this case, to Diego González, a trial attorney in this *ciudad,* [26r] who was present.[106] [González] accepted it specifically so that for [Negrín] and in his name and just as he himself [would do it], [González] can receive, hold, and collect (either by legal judgment or without it) from the person and assets of Rodrigo de Trujillo, who legally owes the forty *pesos de oro de minas* which he owes [Negrín] by virtue of this promissory note.[107] And [so that] he may provide and execute receipts for [the *pesos*] or of whatever portion of them he may be able to collect, and [may provide and execute the documents] for closing the account. These [documents] which he will execute and will be necessary, are to be valid, have as much force, and be as sufficient as if [Negrín] himself were present and provided and executed them.

[González accepted this power of attorney] so that he can appear before whichever *justicias* of Their Majesties, in regard to [the debt], and file whatever claims, petitions, injunctions, judicial decrees, protestations, process papers, summons, oaths of no malice and stipulation,[108] sequestrations, restitution documents, seizures and sales of property to pay debts, imprisonments, sales of assets, and auctions of [assets are necessary]. [And so that he can] present whatever exemptions, evidence, and documents which by his right

may be appropriate. And finally [González accepted this power of attorney] to do all he would and could do, even being present (if his personal presence was required for it), until he has obtained and collected the gold *pesos.*

[Negrín] grants and conveys to the aforesaid Diego González as full and sufficient a power of attorney [as] he possesses for what is recorded above, [26v] [and] another like it, with its components and adjuncts. In accordance with the law, [Negrín] released [González]. And so that he would possess [the power of attorney] in force, [Negrín] obligated his person and assets, [those he now] possesses and [those he] will possess [in the future]). And he signed it with his name. Being present as witnesses: Bartolomé Hernández and Antón Pérez, *estantes* in this *ciudad.*

Antón Negrín

[This] took place before me,
Sebastián Vázquez, His Majesty's *escribano*

{Item} When the aforementioned public and legally binding agreement (included above in the way which has been stated) had been presented, the aforesaid Antón Negrín, executor and the person assigned to fulfill the will of Juan Jiménez, stated that since it is recorded in and apparent from [the agreement], the aforementioned Rodrigo de Trujillo owes him and is obligated to deliver and pay the forty *pesos de oro de minas* of highest purity. Nevertheless, the term referred to in [the agreement] has elapsed,[109] and many days more, when [Trujillo] was obligated to pay [the *pesos*] to [Negrín].

[Trujillo] had refused and was refusing to pay them to him. Therefore [Negrín] was asking and did ask the aforesaid lord *justicia mayor* to order that he be given his writ, so that by virtue of it, he could seize and sell property from the person and assets of Rodrigo de Trujillo for the aforementioned amount.

[27r] [Negrín] swore in the form required by law that [the *pesos*] were owed to him. For the purpose of paying the gold *pesos* and under obligation of the aforementioned oath, he promised not to give or pay me, the aforementioned *escribano,* any excess money in any amount whatsoever nor any other thing, except these [*pesos*] which are likely to come to me and pertain to me rightly in accordance with the legal

fee. [Neither] he nor any other person for him [may pay such additional amount] to me or to anyone else for me. If I receive, request, or demand them from him, he will deliver and show [them] to the lord *justicia mayor* in order that he may impose punishment for it in accordance with the law, under penalty of perjury.

Sebastián Vázquez, His Majesty's *escribano*

{Item} Because what is recorded above was reviewed by the lord *residencia* judge and *justicia mayor*, and in view of this and his having reviewed and examined the aforesaid legally binding agreement, he declared that he was decreeing and did decree that his implementing order be issued against the person and assets of Rodrigo de Trujillo for the amount of forty *pesos de oro de minas* referred to in [the agreement]. This order was issued in the form required by law and is the following:

Sebastián Vázquez, His Majesty's *escribano*
licenciado Caballero

{Item} [To the] *alguacil mayor* of this *ciudad* of [Puebla] de los Ángeles or to your lieutenant in the office,

I [27v] order you to make restitution [and] seize and sell assets of Rodrigo de Trujillo for the amount of forty *pesos de oro de minas* of bona fide money. [This is] because it appears that he owes [it] and is obligated to deliver and pay [it] to Antón Negrín, a *vecino* of this *ciudad*, as heir, executor, and the person assigned to fulfill the will concerning the assets which remained and were left [with him] by Juan Jiménez, deceased, by virtue of a public and legally binding agreement, the term of which has expired. Diego González presented [the agreement] before me, along with the power of attorney of the aforesaid. He, in the name of his party, swore that [the *pesos*] were owed to him and were to be paid.

The assets which you are to seize and sell are movable ones and such that may be worth the aforesaid amount, plus costs, at the time of the auction, with enough bond for total freeing of the debt, which you are to be provided from [the movable assets]. If [they are] not, [then they are to be provided] from his real property, including the bond. If he does not have either the one or the other [type of] assets or he will not surrender [them] to you, [you may] seize him bodily. When he has been arrested, you are to place him in the public jail of this *ciudad*, from which he may not be set free or released on bail without my license and order. You are to notify him [about] the [provision concerning] ten days from the Law[s] of Toledo[110] and designate a house and known attorney in this *ciudad* where and with whom the case files concerning this seizure and sale are to be held until its final litigation, serving notification on him in the form required by law.

Executed in the *ciudad* of [Puebla] de los Ángeles on the thirty-first of July in the year one thousand five hundred and forty five.

licenciado Caballero
By order of His Grace,
Sebastián Vázquez, His Majesty's *escribano*

[28r] {Item} In the *ciudad* of [Puebla] de los Ángeles in this Nueva España on the first day of August in the year one thousand five hundred and forty-five, Rodrigo de Coria,[111] *alguacil mayor* of this *ciudad*, by virtue of this order naming {note} Diego González on behalf and in the name of Antón Negrín, seized for sale one chestnut-colored horse which bears a recently made brand on the right hip in the form of a cross, without any other mark. [He seized the horse] because [it was] property of the selfsame Rodrigo de Trujillo referred to in [the order] in order [to recover] the amount of forty *pesos de oro de minas*, plus costs, with the stipulation that he would do likewise with additional assets, [either] movable or fixed, which he may find and appear to be his.

Concerning the aforementioned, he took the aforesaid horse from the house where it was and [from the] possession of Luisa, an Indian, who they say is Rodrigo de Trujillo's mother.[112] He placed it for safekeeping in the house and possession of Antón Martín Breva, a *vecino* of this *ciudad*.[113] [Martín Breva] took and received it into custody and was assigned as its caretaker. He pledged himself to turn over, deliver, and be present with [the horse] at the time when the auction must be conducted, so that [the auction] could be carried out, under the penalties to which caretakers are subjected and are liable who do not appear with what has been placed in their custody. For this, to thus adhere to, live up to, and fulfill [his charge], he pledged himself and his assets. And he granted [his] full power of attorney to any of

Their Majesties' judges [28v] and waived [recourse to] whatever laws might be of assistance to him, as well as the law and regulation concerning the right which they call the general waiver made according to the laws, [which] is to be of no value [to him].

He signed it with his name. Witnesses: Andrés Núñez, *alguacil*.[114]

Antón Martín stated that he stipulates that he will collect the costs of feeding the horse from [sale of the] horse.
Antón Martín
[This] transpired before me,
Sebastián Vázquez, His Majesty's *escribano*

Assessment of costs to this point

{Item}	For presentation of the promissory note	12 [*maravedís*]
{Item}	For the power of attorney which he granted to Diego González before me, in order to collect the debt referred to in [the promissory note]	18 [*maravedís*]
{Item}	For the petition for an order to be given to him and a certification that everything was done	6 [*maravedís*]
{Item}	For the judicial decree ordering him to be given the order	6 [*maravedís*]
{Item}	For the aforesaid order which was given to him	12 [*maravedís*] {note}
{Item}	For the judge's signature on the order	17 [*maravedís*]

{Item} [This] all totals seventy-one *maravedís* of bona fide money, which Diego González paid. He gave his oath in the form required by law that neither he nor anyone else on his behalf has delivered or paid to me, the *escribano*, or to any other person for [29r] me, or to the lord judge, more fees than those listed above, nor any other thing. Nor will he give [excess fees] for the judicial decrees which are specified above.

He signed it, as did the lord judge and I, the *escribano*.
Diego González
licenciado Caballero
Sebastián Vázquez, His Majesty's *escribano*

{Item} In the *ciudad* of [Puebla] de los Ángeles in this Nueva España on the fourth day of the month of November in that aforesaid year one thousand five hundred and forty-five, Sebastián Vázquez, *escribano* of His Majesty and of the court of *licenciado* Caballero (*residencia* judge in the aforementioned *ciudad*), appeared in person before the magnificent lord Diego Ramírez, *juez visitador de agravios y bienes de difuntos* in the aforesaid *ciudad*, and in my presence, Cristóbal de Heredia, *escribano* of Their Majesties and of the court of the lord judge.

[Vázquez] presented before the lord judge and gave and delivered to me, the *escribano*, a case record concerning a seizure and sale of property which was handled[115] before the *licenciado* and before him as his *escribano*. [It] consisted of an order for seizure and sale which the aforesaid *licenciado* directed [be] issued as a consequence of a promissory note against Rodrigo Trujillo in the amount of forty *pesos de oro de minas*, which the aforementioned appears to owe to Juan Jiménez, deceased, and to his [29v] heirs. The substance of which is what follows:

{Here [is inserted] this case record}
{Item} When the case record concerning seizure and sale of property had been presented in the manner recorded and had been reviewed by the lord judge, he declared that he was taking and did take charge of this action and case

himself in order to conclude, proceed with, and finish it.

Because he approved, confirmed, and considered proper everything which had been done and ordered by the aforesaid *licenciado* Caballero, as the authorized judge (which he is), for this reason he was ordering and did order that the aforementioned horse, which had been ordered seized and sold, be sold at public auction and [by] public announcement {note}, at the third [announcement] on the third day. It is to be auctioned to the person who will give the most for it. Payment of its value in gold *pesos* is to be made to the party of the deceased, Juan Jiménez, and to his heirs {note}.

Inasmuch as the principal legal action concerning the audit which was conducted of Antón Negrín, Juan Jiménez's executor, is pending before His Grace, he was ordering and did order that this case be combined and joined with it. He declared thus that he was ordering and did order it. And he signed it with his name.

Diego Ramírez

First public announcement

{Item} Then, on this same day, by order of the lord judge and before me, the aforementioned *escribano,* [30r] and by means of the booming voice[116] of Pedro, the Black,[117] the first public announcement about the horse was delivered, [Pedro] declaring in a loud voice [that] if there was anyone [who] might buy it and agree to a price, that the bid would be accepted from him. [He declared further] that it was being sold as assets of Rodrigo de Trujillo because of an order for seizure and sale which had been issued against him on the petition of the heirs and executor of Juan Jiménez, deceased. [He also declared] that it was being auctioned for nine days and a bid would be accepted from [anyone] as late as the third public announcement.

While the aforesaid public announcement was in progress, Juan Ruiz, a merchant and *estante* in the aforementioned *ciudad,* appeared and declared that he was offering and did offer eight *pesos de minas.* No one else appeared this day who might give more for it.

At the conclusion of the aforesaid public announcement the Black declared, "This is the first public announcement, and everything must be auctioned off by the third one [at the]

highest bid." There were present as witnesses Pedro de Meneses and Alberto de Cáceres, *vecinos* of the aforesaid *ciudad.*[118]
Diego Ramírez
Cristóbal de Heredia, Their Majesties' *escribano*

Second public announcement

{Item} After what is recorded above, in the *ciudad* of [Puebla] de los Ángeles on the seventh of the aforesaid month of November in the aforesaid year, before me, the [30v] aforementioned *escribano,* and by means of the booming voice of Juan, a black slave of Alberto de Cáceres, who was stationed in the public plaza of the aforementioned *villa,*[119] the second public announcement concerning the horse was delivered in the [same] form and manner as the first.

No person was found who offered a greater price for it. At the conclusion of the public announcement the black declared, "This is the second public announcement."

There were present as witnesses who heard it Hernando Ladrón and Hernando Veedor, *vecinos* of the aforesaid *ciudad.*
Cristóbal de Heredia, Their Majesties' *escribano*

Third public announcement

{Item} After what is recorded above, in the *ciudad* of [Puebla] de los Ángeles on the eleventh day of the aforesaid month and year and before me, the aforementioned *escribano,* and by means of the booming voice of Antón, the Black, who was stationed in the public plaza of the aforementioned *ciudad,* the third and final public announcement concerning the horse was delivered. Many people being present and involved in the auction, Juan de Sotomayor,[120] a *vecino* of the aforementioned *ciudad,* appeared and offered eleven and a half *pesos de oro de minas* for the horse. It was auctioned off at the highest and final bid, as [he was] the highest bidder, since there was no one who offered more.

[31r] Serving as witnesses for [the auction] were Alonso Valiente[121] and Rodrigo de Coria, *alguacil,* and others. I immediately gave and delivered the aforementioned gold *pesos* to the lord judge. From them, by order of the lord judge, were paid the following costs.
Cristóbal de Heredia, Their Majesties' *escribano*

{Item} After what is recorded above, in the *ciudad* of [Puebla] de los Ángeles on the twelfth day of November in the aforesaid year of one thousand five hundred and forty-five, the lord judge declared that he was ordering and did order [that], from the amount collected from seizure and sale of the horse, nine and a half gold *tomines común* be delivered and paid to Rodrigo de Coria, *alguacil mayor* of the aforementioned *ciudad*, for the food and [other] expense which the horse amassed during the period of the public announcements. Likewise, he ordered [that] one *peso de oro común* be delivered and paid to me, the *escribano*, as my fee for the public announcements and other legal documents prepared in this case. He ordered us to be paid.

Another *peso de oro común* was paid to Sebastián Vázquez, *escribano*, [31v] for [the time] he spent while preparing the accounting of Antón Negrín, which he recorded in writing in the account record. I, the aforementioned *escribano*, accepted this and gave it to the wife of Sebastián Vázquez, as the aforementioned ordered.

All this was delivered and paid in the manner recorded, and because Rodrigo de Coria received it, he signed it here with his name, along with me, the *escribano*.

Rodrigo de Coria

Cristóbal de Heredia, Their Majesties' *escribano*

tepuzque

3 *pesos*, 1 *tomín*, 6 *granos*

{Item} Because three *pesos*, one *tomín*, and six *granos* for the aforementioned fees [were] subtracted and deducted from the eleven and a half *pesos de [oro] de minas*, the amount for which the horse was sold, [that] yields and leaves fifteen *pesos*, seven *tomines*, and six *granos* of gold as the assets of the deceased.

{Item} Half a *peso* was subtracted for the public crier. [32r] [That] leaves a net [of] fifteen *pesos*, three *tomines*, and six *granos*.[122] [This] transpired before me, Cristóbal de Heredia, Their Majesties' *escribano*.

15 *pesos*, 3 *tomines*, 6 *granos*

TABLE 27.1

Tally Sheet for the Juan Jiménez Estate

Entry	Debit	Credit
Odds and ends not auctioned off	80 ps 4 tom	—
Uncollected IOU from Alonso González	42 ps	—
Uncollected IOU from Alonso González	24 ps	—
UncollectedIOU from Pedro Benavides	30 ps	—
Uncollected IOU from Juan Francés	8 ps	—
Uncollected IOU from Alonso Jiménez	8 ps	—
Uncollected IOU from Juan Galleas	25 ps	—
Paid debt to Juan Barragán	—	50 ps
Paid fray Maldonado for masses	—	20 ps
Paid scribe	—	2 ps
Paid scribe and attorney	—	2 ps 5 tom
Surrended uncollected González IOU	—	42 ps
Surrended uncollected González IOU	—	24 ps
Surrended uncollected Benavides IOU	—	30 ps
Surrended uncollected Francés IOU	—	8 ps
Surrended uncollected Jiménez IOU	—	8 ps
Surrended uncollected Galleas IOU	—	25 ps
Repossession of horse sold to Rodrigo Trujillo	—	40 ps
Total	**217 ps 4 tom**	**251 ps 5 tom**
Credit remaining	**—**	**34 ps 1 tom**

Note: The credit remaining consisted of 9 *pesos* 4 *tomines* in *pesos de minas* and 24 *pesos* 5 *tomines* in *pesos de tepuzque* (see Document 27, note 88).

This copy [was] prepared and extracted from the original case file by order of His Majesty and in fulfillment of one of his royal *cédulas*, in the *pueblo* of Tenancingo,[123] which is located in Nueva España, on the nineteenth day of the month of November in the one thousand five hundred and fiftieth year since the birth of Our Savior, Jesus Christ. Witnesses who were present to see it corrected and reconciled with the original: Pedro de Gamboa and Melchior de Legazpí, [who are] presently *estantes* in the aforementioned *pueblo*.

{It is corrected where it says "had discussed" [in 14r]. [It] is [written] between the lines and is valid where it says "my aim" [in 3v]; where it says "priest" [in 10v]; where it says "of gold" [in 11r]; where it says "thus" [in 13v]; where it says "what [Negrín] talked with the deceased Juan Jiménez about. He said that all" [in 15r]; where it says "Francés" [in 17v]; where it says "said" [in 19r]; where it says "on behalf and in the name" [in 28r]; where it says "at" [in 29v]; where it says "the principal legal action concerning the audit which was conducted of Antón Negrín" [in 29v].

It is valid [as] struck out where it said "ese" [location unknown]; where it said "l" [in 8v]; where it said "le" [in 10v]; where it said "de" [in 11r]; where it said "el" [in 14r]; where it said "Gutiérrez" [in 14v]; where it said "funto" [in 24r]; where it said "[word omitted]"; where it said "señal" [in 28r].[124]

I, Miguel López de Legazpí, His Majesty's *escribano* and His *escribano mayor* of the council and municipal court of the great Ciudad de México, had all that is recorded above extracted from the original by virtue of a *cédula* from His Majesty. Just as is stated above, it is corrected and reconciled with [it]. Therefore, in testimony of the truth [of what is recorded], I affixed here my registered mark, [which is] thus {the sign is made}.

{rubric} Miguel López {rubric}, *escribano* of the council

[fols. 32v–34r] [blank]

[34v] 1550
{Juan Jiménez, number 15}

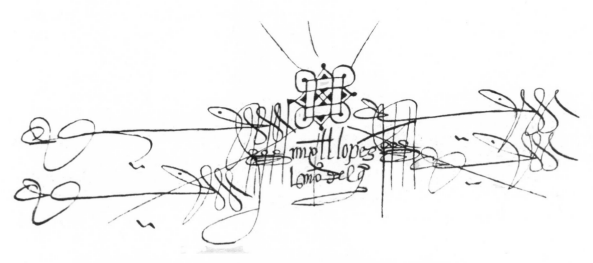

FIGURE 27.2. The signature and registered sign (*signo*) of Miguel López de Legazpí.
AGI, Contratación, 5575, N.24, fol. 31r. Reproduced courtesy of Spain's Ministerio de Educación, Cultura y Deporte.

TRANSCRIPTION

{Autos sobre los bienes de Juan Jiménez, natural de Guadal-canal, difunto en Coafor, en la provincia de Tiguex, en Nueva España}

[fol. 1r]
{32}
{Juan ximenez difunto natural de / GuadalCanal}
{Numero 15}
{1550}[125]
Este es Un treslado bien e fielmente sacado de Un / Proçeso de quentas de los bienes de Juan ximenez difunto / Segun por el dicho proçeso pareçe Su tenor del / qual es este que Se sigue

{ytem} En la ÇiUdad de los Angeles de esta nueVa españa A tre- / ze dias del mes de agosto Año del naçimyento de nuestro / salVador Jesu cristo de mill e quinientos e quarenta e çinco / Años Ante el magnifico Señor el licençiado hernando Caba- / llero Juez de Residençia e justiçia mayor en esta dicha / ÇiUdad por su magestad e juez de los bienes de los difuntos / en ella por espeçial comision del muy magnifico e muy Reverendo / señor el liçençiado tello de sandoVal Visitador general / de esta dicha nueVa españa e juez de los dichos bienes / de difuntos de ella y en presençia de mi s(a)ebastian Vaz- / quez escrivano de Su magestad e de la dicha Residençia / Audiençia e juzgado del dicho señor juez pareçio pre- / sente Anton negrin Vezino de esta dicha çiUdad e dixo que / en cumplimyento y conforme a lo que por Su merced fue man- / dado y se pregono en esta dicha çiUdad el lunes proxy- / mo pasado que se contaron diez dias de este presente / mes Açerca de que Vinyesen Ante el a dar quenta de los / dichos bienes de los difuntos todos los tenedores de ellos / y para el dicho efecto traxo y presento dos escritu- / ras

la una de testamento que pareçe y esta signada / de melchior gomez escribano de su magestad y la otra / de Andres de heRera escribano publico y del cabildo / que fue de esta dicha ÇiUdad Segun por ella se pareçia / {rúbrica}
{corregido}
1

[fol. 1v]
las quales Son las Siguientes
{ytem} En la gran ÇiUdad de tenuxtitan mexico de la nue- / Va españa A treze dias del mes de Septiembre Año / del naçimyento de nuestro salVador Jesu cristo de mill e quinientos / e quarenta e dos años Ante el muy noble Señor gero- / nymo Ruiz de la mota Alcalde en la dicha çiUdad de / mexico por Su magestad e en preSençia de my Juan de / Çaragoça escribano publico del numero de ella pareçio / Presente Anton negrin e presento un escrito de pe- / dimyento con Una probança y un ynVentaryo e al- / moneda Su tenor de lo qual es esto que se Sigue / Juan de Çaragoça escribano publico

{ytem} muy noble Señor Anton negrin estante en esta / ÇiUdad e Vezino de la ÇiUdad de los angeles parezco an- / te Vuestra merced e digo que yendo a la tierra nueva con el ca- / pitan francisco Vazquez falleçio en tiguex un Juan xime- / nez que dios nuestro Señor perdone (y)^el qual al tiem- / Po que estuVo enfermo una noche con temor de no / poder escapar Siendo como (h)era Amigo de mi y de / Un Jorge baez y por haber neçesidad y no se hallar / en el dicho pueblo escribano para que se pudiese ha- / zer el dicho Su testamento y al tiempo que quiso / e(s)xpirar y antes tenya començado[126] comigo y con el di- / cho Jorge baez lo que conViniese A su anyma y al / descargo de su conçiençia dixo delante de quatro *testigos* / q*ue* nos daba poder cumplido A mi y al dicho Jorge / baez para q*ue* pudiesemos hazer Su testamento / como a nosotros pareçiese como consta e pareçe / {rúbrica}

[fol. 2r]

de *e*sta probanÇa de q*ue* hago presentaÇion y porq*ue* / el dicho Jorge baez es albaçea A(n)simismo es falle- / Çido y porq*ue* en quanto A lo q*ue* me obliga conçien- / Çia y hazer lo q*ue* soi obligado porq*ue* podria ser / q*ue* en la dilaçion yo me muriese y fuese con este Car- / Go pido y suplico a V*uestra* m*erced* q*ue* atento q*ue* el dicho difun- / to me dio poder para q*ue* pudiese ordenar Su tes- / tamento como comigo lo conSulto q*ue* se me de[127] li- / Çençia e facultad para q*ue* lo haga y (h)ordene como Soi / obligado y en ello V*uestra* m*erced* ponga su decreto JudiçiaL / y V*uestra* m*erced* *en* *e*l caso haga lo q*ue* sea Justiçia y conçiençia y / en lo neçe- sario su muy noble ofiçio ymploro y / pido lo q*ue* en este caso lo q*ue* mas me conviniere pe- / dir Anton negrin

{y*tem*} El señor alcalde dixo q*ue* lo oya y en el caso pro- / Veera lo q*ue* fuere Justiçia

{y*tem*} En el pueblo de coafor de la proVinçia de tiguex *en* / Veinte e çinco dias del mes de hebrero de mill e qui*nient*os / e quarenta e dos años Ante *e*l muy mag*nifi*co Señor don / tristan de arellano maestre de campo de este exerçito / de q*ue* es capitan general el muy mag*nifi*co Señor Franci*s*co / Vazquez de coronado governador de la proVinçia de ga- / liçia de la nueVa españa por ante my hernando / bermejo escrivano de Su mag*estad* e de los testigos de / yuso escritos pareçieron presentes Anton negrin / e Jorge baez estantes en el dicho exerçito e preSen- / taron Ante su merÇed Un escrito Su tenor del / qual es este q*ue* se sigue / {rúbrica}
2

[fol. 2v]

{y*tem*} muy mag*nifi*Co Señor don tristan de arellano maese / de campo de este exerçito Jorge baez e anton negrin / estantes en el pareçemos Ante V*uestra* m*erced* e dezimos q*ue* / Ju*an* ximenez estante *en* este exerçito es falleçido de *e*s- / ta presente Vida el qual por falta de no *h*aber es- / cribano Adonde el dicho Ju*an* ximenez estaba no hizo / ni otorgo su

testamento ni (h)ordeno Su alma E / porq*ue* como amigos y compañeros q*ue* nosotros hemos / Sido Siempre del dicho Ju*an* ximenez Una noche an- / tes q*ue* muriese por ante testigos nos dio Su po- / der cumplido para q*ue* por el hiziesemos y otorga- / semos Su testamento y (h)orden- asemos su(^s) anyma / e conçiençia Segun el dicho difunto para este efe*c*- / to muchas Vezes lo comunico con nosotros de mas de / q*ue* nos dexo por sus albaçeas e mando q*ue* sus bie- / nes no *en*trasen *en* poder de ten(o)edores sino q*ue* no- / sotros los tuViesemos e mirasemos por ellos E / los bene- fiçiasemos como mejor nos pareçiese con- / Forme A su Voluntad e porq*ue* el dicho Ju*an* ximenez / dexo en este exerçito algunos bienes y A ellos co- / mo tales albaçeas e personas q*ue* el dicho difunto / para ello nonbro ConViene La administraçion de *e*llos / pedimos e Requerimos a V*uestra* m*erced* nos los mande *en*- / tregar para q*ue* nosotros con ellos e con la Admi- / nistraçion de *e*llos descarguemos el anyma del d*i*cho / difunto de la manera q*ue* el lo comunyco con noso- / tros e para ello el muy noble ofiçio de V*uestra* m*erced* ym- / Ploramos e pedimos justiçia anton negrin Jorge baez

{y*tem*} E asi preSentado el dicho escrito *en* la manera q*ue* / {rúbrica}

[fol. 3r]

d*i*cha es el dicho don tristan de Arellano maestre de canpo / dixo q*ue* presenten e den testigos de ynformaçion / de lo q*ue* dizen e q*ue* dada e visto hara lo q*ue* sea Jus- / tiçia *testig*os los d*i*chos

{y*tem*} E despues de lo Susodicho *en* este dicho dia Veinte {25. Febr*ero*} / e çinco de hebrero e año Susodicho Ante el dicho / Señor don tristan de arellano maestre de Campo / de *e*ste exerçito e por ante mi el dicho hernando *b*er- / mejo escribano de Su mag*estad* pareçio presente / el dicho anton negrin e presento por testigos / *en* la dicha Razon A alonso alvarez e a geronymo / Ramos e a Antonyo alvarez estantes en este exer- / Çito de los quales e de Cada Uno de *e*llos se / Reçibio Ju- / ramento *en* forma debida de d*e*rech*o* So Virtud deL / qual prometieron de dezir Verdad e lo q*ue* dixeron / E depusieron Siendo Preguntados por el di- / cho pedimiento es lo Siguiente

{ytem} El dicho Alonso alVarez testigo presentado *en* / la dicha rrazon *h*Abiendo Jurado *en* forma de d*e*rec*h*o / e siendo preguntado por el dicho pedimyento dixo q*ue* / Andando este testigo Velando Una noche de *e*ste mes de / hebrero q*ue* fue Un dia Antes q*ue* Ju*an* ximenez estante / en este exerçito muriese el d*i*cho Ju*an* ximenez *en*Vio A / llamar A este testigo e otras personas e le dixo / Señor sereis testigo como porq*ue* Al presente *en* / este Real q*ue* esta de *e*sta banda del Rio fuera de don- / de *e*sta el general no *h*ay escrivano de Su mag*e*stad e por- / q*ue* yo me Siento muy malo e pienso no llegar a la / mañana digo q*ue* yo doy todo mi poder cumplido se- / {rúbrica}
3

[fol. 3v]
Gun q*ue* lo yo tengo A Jorge baez e anton negrin / estantes *en* este exerçito para q*ue* hagan por my / mi testamento porq*ue* yo no me Siento *en* dis- / Pusiçion para hazello e (h)ordenen my Alma de / la manera q*ue* algunas vezes yo he comunica- / do con ellos e miren por los bienes q*ue* yo tengo *en* / este exerçito q*ue* sean mis albaçeas lo qual digo q*ue* / hago porq*ue* no quiero q*ue* mis bienes *en*tren *en* po- / der de tenedores Sino q*ue* los tengan los dichos An- / ton negrin e Jorge baez e hagan de *e*llos A Su volun- / tad e si dios me dexare llegar a la mañana por an- / te escribano yo dare A los dichos Jorge baez e an- / ton negrin my poder bastante para lo q*ue* dicho es por- /{ojo} q*ue* esta es ^*mi yntençion* (^m)y Voluntad y esto dyxo q*ue* es lo q*ue* sabe / Para el Juramento q*ue* hizo y firmolo de Su non- / bre e q*ue* a(n)simismo Sabe e Vio q*ue* el dicho Ju*an* xi- / menez murio por la mañana la noche q*ue* le emVio / a llamar para dezille lo q*ue* dicho es Alonso alVarez

{ytem} El d*i*cho antonyo AlVarez testigo presentado *en* / la dicha Razon por el dicho anton negrin *h*Abien- / do Jurado *en* forma de d*e*rec*h*o e siendo preguntado / por el dicho pedimyento dixo q*ue* lo q*ue* sabe de *e*ste Caso / es q*ue* andando este t*e*stigo(s) Velando Una noche de *e*ste mes / de hebrero q*ue* fue un dia Antes q*ue* Ju*an* ximenez estan- / te *en* este exerçito muriese el qual dicho Juan xi- / menez *en*Vio A llamar A este testi(^i)go e a otras perso- / nas e le dixo señor

sereis t*e*sti*g*os como porq*ue* al presen- / te *en* este Real donde yo estoi no *h*Ay escribano de / {rúbrica}

[fol. 4r]
Su mag*e*stad e yo me Siento muy malo e no pienso llegar / a la mañana digo q*ue* yo doi todo my poder cumpli- / do Segun lo yo tengo A Jorge baez e anton ne- / grin estantes *en* este exerçito para que hagan E / otorguen por my mi testamento porq*ue* yo no me / Siento *en* dispusiçion para hazello e (h)ordenen mi / Alma de la manera q*ue* yo algunas vezes lo he comu- / nicado con ellos e myren por los bienes q*ue* yo tengo / *en* este exerçito e sean mis albaçeas e si dios me lle- / gare a la mañana por ante escrivano yo dare A los / dichos Jorge baez e anton negrin mi poder bastan- / te para lo q*ue* dicho es porq*ue* esta es mi ynten- / Çion e Voluntad lo qual cree este testigo q*ue* el di- / cho Juan ximenez hizo porq*ue* sus bienes no *en*tra- / sen *en* poder de los tenedores preguntado como lo / Sabe dixo q*ue* porq*ue* en su *en*fer- medad el dicho / Ju*an* ximenez le *h*avia dicho A este testigo q*ue* si mu- / riese querria q*ue* sus bienes no *en*trasen *en* poder / de los tenedores e a(n)si Visto este testigo q*ue* el d*i*cho / Ju*an* ximenez murio luego por la mañana La noche / q*ue* le *en*Vio A llamar para dezille lo q*ue* dicho es / e firmolo de Su nonbre Antonyo alvarez

{ytem} El dicho geronymo Ramos testigo presentado *en* / la d*i*cha Razon *h*Abiendo Jurado *en* forma de d*e*rec*h*o E / siendo preguntado Açerca de lo q*ue* dicho es dixo q*ue* / lo q*ue* sabe de *e*ste Caso es q*ue* una noche de *e*ste mes de / hebrero Andando este testigo Velando el dicho Ju*an* /ximenez *en*Vio A llamar A este testigo e a otras per- / {rúbrica}
4

[fol. 4v]
sonas E le dixo Señor Sereis testigos q*ue* porq*ue* Al / Presente en este rreal Adonde yo estoy no *h*ay es- / cribano e porq*ue* yo me Siento muy malo e no pien- / So llegar a la mañana digo q*ue* doy todo my po- / der cumplido Segun q*ue* le yo tengo A Jorge baez / E anton negrin estantes *en* este exerçito para / q*ue* por mi (^oto) hagan e otorguen mi testa- mento / e (h)ordenen mi alma de la manera q*ue* yo algu- /

nas Vezes he comunicado Con ellos e miren por / los bienes *que* yo tengo en este exerçito e Sean / mis albaçeas e Si dios me llegare a la mañana yo / Por ante escribano dare el dicho poder bastan- / te A los d*i*chos Jorge baez e anton negrin para lo / *que* dicho es e *que* Vi(d)o este testigo *que* luego por la / mañana murio el dicho Juan ximenez e *que* esto / es lo *que* sabe e firmolo de Su nonbre gerony- / mo Ramos

{y*tem*} E despues de lo Susodicho este dicho dia mes E / año susodicho el dicho anton negrin preSento / Por testigo a Anton perez buscaVida estante / en este exerçito el qual despues de *h*Aber Jurado / en forma de d*e*rec*h*o e Siendo preguntado *en* Razon / de lo *que* dicho es dixo *que* lo *que* sabe de *e*ste Caso es / *que* una noche de *e*ste mes de hebrero Andando / este testigo Velando le *en*Vio a llamar el dicho Ju*an* / ximenez e A otras perSonas e le dixo A este / testigo Señor sereis testigo como yo por Razon / {rúbrica}

[fol. 5r]
que me Siento malo *que* no pienso llegar a la mañana / doi todo mi Poder cumplido Segun *que* yo lo ten- / Go A anton negrin e a Jorge baez estantes *en* este / exerçito para *que* por my Segu*n* *que* mi perSona / Propia lo podria hazer hagan e otorguen mi tes- / tamento e (h)ordenen mi Alma de la manera *que* yo / Algunas Vezes lo he Comunicado Con ellos por*que* me- / Jor lo haran ellos *que* yo por*que* me hallo flaco de / Juizio e muy a punto de muerte e hagan e dis- / pongan de mis bienes A su Voluntad por*que* para E- / llo les nonbro por mis albaçeas e quiero *que* ellos / los tengan e miren por ellos A su Voluntad Se- / gun dicho es por*que* esta es mi yntençion e Vo- / luntad E *que* esto Sabe para el Juramento *que* hi- / zo e firmolo de Su nonbre Anton Perez

{y*tem*} E depues de lo Susodicho este dicho dya mes / e año Susodicho Visto por el dicho Señor don / tristan de arellano maestre de campo de *e*ste exerçito / el dicho pedimy*ent*o e ynformaçion Arriba contenida / dixo *que* atento *que* la Voluntad del dicho Ju*an* xime- / nez fue *que* sus bienes no *en*trasen *en* poder de / tenedores *que* los tuViesen los dichos Jorge baez / e anton negrin e los benefiçiasen como A ellos les / Pareçiese e *que* los dichos Jorge baez e anton ne- / grin

*h*An sido siempre muy amigos e compañeros / del dicho difunto e compañeros de la compañya del / dicho Señor don tristan de arellano e *que* tienen / Poder para hazer Su testamento e pareçe por la / dicha ynformaçion *que* sabe y el d*i*cho difunto comu- / {rúbrica}
5

[fol. 5v]
nico Con Ellos Su Voluntad e lo *que* le conVenia / Para el descargo de Su conçiençia e *que* los d*i*chos / Jorge baez e anton negrin Son hombres *que* mi- / raran por los bienes del dicho difunto como bie- / nes de Su amigo e hombres *que* tienen Cargo de Su A- / nyma *que* mandaba e mando A los d*i*chos Jorge baez e an- / ton negrin *que* conforme al ynVentario *que* esta / hecho de los dichos bienes Se *en*treguen *en* ellos e los / miren e benefiçien como Vieren *que* conVenga Al d*i*cho / difunto e *que* en todo Su pro e provecho lleguen / E su daño Ri(e)*nd*i*e*ren[128] e *que* de *e*llos e de lo multiplicado / de *e*llos den quenta Con pago leal e Verdadera cada E / quando *que* les fuere pedida por el dicho Señor don / tristan de arellano maestre de Campo de *e*ste exerçito / o por otro Juez o persona *que* se la pueda pedir So / pena *que* los pagaran todos o qualquier parte de *e*llos / Por sus personas e bienes de mas de caer e yncurrir *en* las / penas *que* caen e yncurren las personas *que* no dan quen- / ta de los bienes *que* les Son dados *en* guarda e adminis- / traçion A(n)si dixo *que* lo mandaba e mando (e man- / do) a mi el d*i*cho escribano *en*tregue los dichos bie- / nes conforme Al ynVentario *que* de *e*llos esta hecho / A los d*i*chos Jorge baez e anton negrin don tristan / de arellano

{y*tem*} E despues de lo Susodicho *en* qu*i*nze dias del mes / de março del dicho año yo el d*i*cho hernando berme- / Jo escribano de su mag*estad* notifique el mando de *e*sta / otra parte contenydo A los dichos anton negrin / {rúbrica}

[fol. 6r]
E Jorge baez *en* sus personas los quales dixeron *que* / estaban prestos e aparejados de Reçebir los dichos / bienes por el d*i*cho ynVentaryo Segun e de la ma- / nera *que* el dicho señor don tristan lo manda tes- / tigos Juan perez de Vergara e Jaque de b(u)r*u*jas / e diego gallego hernando bermejo

{*ytem*} Yo hernando bermejo escribano de Su mag*es*T*ad* e su no- / tario pu*bli*co presente fui a lo q*ue* dicho es e de pedi- / miento del d*i*cho anton negrin lo escrebi Segun / q*ue* ante my paso e por ende fize aqui este mi Sig- / no q*ue* es (a)tal *en* testimonio de Verdad hernan- / do bermejo escribano de Su mag*es*tad

{*ytem*} En el pueblo de coafar de la proVinçia de tiguex / de *e*sta tierra nueVamente descubierta *en* diez / E ocho dias del mes de março de mill e quinientos E / quarenta e dos años Ante el muy mag*nifi*co Señor / don tristan de arellano maese de campo de *e*ste exer- / Çito por ante mi hernando bermeJo escriba- / no de Su magestad Anton negrin Albaçea q*ue* / Se dixo Ser de juan ximenez difunto hizo almo- / neda de los bienes q*ue* el d*i*cho difunto dexo *en* este / exerçito la qual Se hizo *en* la manera Siguiente

mynas
{*ytem*}   Primeramente Se Remato un cavallo / castaño
xl p*eso*s   *en* Rodrigo de truxillo hijo de Jor- / ge baez *en*
                quarenta pesos de mynas fia- / do A plazo de
                seis meses de la d(^ich)^*eud*a de la / hecha de
                *e*sta fiolo el dicho Anton negrin / {rúbrica}

6

[fol. 6v]
{*ytem*}   yten se Remato Una espada con Un talabar- /
ij p*eso*s   te de cuero *en* Juanes de garnica Viz- / caino
                en dos pesos

{*ytem*}   yten se Remato *en* diego de mata Unos /
ij p*eso*s   Çapatos y Unos Alpargates *en* dos / p*eso*s

{*ytem*}   yten un sayo de armas de la tierra e / Un jubon
V p*eso*s   con Unas mangas de cuero / e Un pecho de
                cavallo e dos costales Uno / de quero e otro de
                lana y Una caperu- / Ça de armas *en* Ju*an* perez
                de Vergara / *en* Çinco pesos

{*ytem*}   yten onze herraduras nueVas e çin- / co Viejas
j p*eso*s   e trezientos claVos *en* crist*o*bal / perez de aVila
                en un p*eso*s

{*ytem*}   yten se rremato Una quera de Vaca
p*e*sos iiij to*mines*   Vie- / Ja *en* Juanes de garnyca Vizcaino
                        en iiii *tomines* / 0 peso

{*ytem*}   yten se Remato Un caballo morzillo /
xxx p*eso*s   quatralVo *en*sillado y *en*frenado *en* Juan
                / Perez de Vergara *en* treinta pesos A
                lue- / go pagar

{*ytem*} Todos los quales dichos bienes Suso declarados se / Vendieron e Remataron *en* almoneda publica por no / *h*Aver persona q*ue* mas por ellos diese a pagar del dia / de la fecha de *e*sta *en* seis meses cumplidos primeros / {rúbrica}

[fol. 7r]
Siguientes por Voz de pedro color negro pregonero pu*bli*co / por ante el dicho señor maestre de Campo testigos / Ju*an* perez de Vergara e melchior perez e miguel / sanchez de plazençia y el dicho señor maestre de Canpo / lo firmo de su nonbre *en* el Registro de *e*sta Carta / q*ue* es fecha *en* el d*i*cho dia mes e año Susodicho / don tristan de arellano e yo hernando berme- / Jo escribano de Su mag*es*tad e su notario pu*bli*Co presen- / te fui A todo lo q*ue* d*i*cho es e de pedimy*ent*o del dicho / Anton negrin lo escrebi Segun q*ue* ante mi paso / e por *en*de fize aqui este mi Signo q*ue* es (a)tal / *en* testimonyo de Verdad hernando bermejo

{*ytem*} En la proVinçia de tiguex de *e*sta tierra nueVame*n*- / te descubierta *en* diez y siete dias del mes de hebrero {17 Febr*ero*}[129] / de mill e qui*nient*os e quarenta e dos años el muy mag*nifi*co Se- / ñor don tristan de arellano maeSe de campo de *e*ste / exerçito por ante mi hernando bermejo escribano de / su mag*es*tad e de los t*e*s*ti*gos de yuso escritos hizo ynVen- / tario / de los bienes q*ue* en este exerçito dexo Juan ximenez di- / Funto q*ue* murio *en* este dicho dia el qual se hizo *en* la / manera Siguiente

{*ytem*}   Primeramente Un cavallo quartalVo *en*drino con
                Una / lista *en* la frente con su freno e silla Vieja

{*ytem*}   otro Caballo castaño calçado de los pies con
                Una lis- / ta *en* la frente

{y*tem*}
7

Un sayo de armas de la tierra / {rúbrica}

[fol. 7v]

{y*tem*} Dos Costales Uno de quero e otro de lana

{y*tem*} Una quera de Vaca Vieja

{y*tem*} Una espada

{y*tem*} Un Jubon Con Unas mangas de quero

{y*tem*} Un quero de Vaca de pelo

{y*tem*} Una caperuça de armas de la tierra

{y*tem*} Un Sombrero Viejo

{y*tem*} (h)onze herraduras de cavallo nueVas y trezientos / claVos

{y*tem*} Un hierro de lança

{y*tem*} Unos alpargates

{y*tem*} Un albardon

{y*tem*} Un pecho de cavallo

{y*tem*} Unos Çapatos Viejos

{y*tem*} Unas espuelas chicas

{y*tem*} Un conoçimy*ento* contra Alonso Gonçalez de can- / tia de veinte y quatro p*es*os de mynas firmado del / d*ic*ho alonso gonçalez e de miguel torres e anton / negrin t*estig*os de *e*llo

{y*tem*} otro conoçimy*ento* contra pedro de benavides de qua*n*- / tia de treinta p*es*os de minas q*ue* debe Al dicho dif*unt*o / firmado del d*ic*ho pedro de

benaVides e de pedro de / lasoJo e de pedro de huerVe[130]

{y*tem*} otro conoçimy*ento* contra alonso gonçalez de quantia / de quarenta e dos p*es*os de oro de mynas q*ue* debe Al / {rúbrica}

[fol. 8r]
(Al) d*ic*ho difunto firmado del d*ic*ho alonso gonçalez / e de alonso lopez e anton negrin t*estig*os de *e*l

{y*tem*} otro conoÇimy*ento* contra Ju*an* frančes de quantia / de (de) ocho p*es*os de mynas q*ue* debe al d*ic*ho difunto q*ue* / estaba firmado del d*ic*ho anton negrin testigo del / dicho conoçimy*ento*

{y*tem*} otro conoçimy*ento* contra Alonso ximenez de quantia / de ocho p*es*os de oro de mynas q*ue* debe al d*ic*ho difunto q*ue* / esta firmado del d*ic*ho alonso ximenez e de anton ne-◆ grin e Jorge baez testigos de *e*l

{y*tem*} otro conoÇimy*ento* contra Ju*an* galleas de quantia de Ve- / {ojo} inte e Çinco p*es*os de minas firmado del d*ic*ho Ju*an* galleas

Un machete quebrado

{y*tem*} Un martillo e unas tenazas e Un puJaVante

{y*tem*} Todos los quales dichos bienes Suso Conteny- / dos e declarados Se hallaron *en* la posada del d*ic*ho / Ju*an* ximenez e no pareçieron otros bienes Suyos / ningunos ni *h*obo persona q*ue* supiese de otros bie- / nes q*ue* el dicho Ju*an* ximenez tuViese *en* este exer- / Çito los quales fueron ynVentaryados *en* la ma- / nera q*ue* dicha es y el dicho Señor maese de campo / lo firmo de su nombre *en* el rregistro testigos q*ue* / A ello fueron presentes Velasco de barrionueVo E / {rúbrica}
8

[fol. 8v]
Jorge baez e anton negrin

{ytem} En el pueblo de Coafor *en* La proVinçia de / {15. Marzo} tiguex *en* quynze dias del mes de março e del d*i*cho / año yo hernando bermejo ecribano de Su mag*estad* / por ante los testigos de yuso escritos *en*tregue / todos los bienes contenidos E declarados *en* este yn- / Ventario de *e*sta otra parte por mandado del se- / ñor don tristan de arellano maese de Campo de *e*s- / te exerçito A Jorge baez e anton negrin estan- / tes *en* el los quales dixeron q*ue* se daban e dieron / por *en*tregados *en* todos ellos para los benefiçiar / de la manera q*ue* les pareçiere q*ue* sea mas Util / e proVechoso para el dicho Ju*an* ximenez difunto E / q*ue* todo su bien e provech(an)*o* Allegaran e Su daño / {ojo} arredraran e q*ue* de *e*llos e de l(^l)o multiplicado de *e*llos / daran buena quenta Con pago leal e Verdadera ca- / da e quando les fuere pedida por el dicho Señor mae- / se de canpo o por otro Juez o persona q*ue* se lo pue- / da pedir cada e quando les fuere pedida So pe- / na q*ue* pagaran los d*i*chos bienes e multiplico de *e*llos / por Sus personas e bienes muebles e Raizes *h*A- / bidos e por *h*aber q*ue* para ello dixeron q*ue* obliga- / ban espresamente e dieron poder Cumplido A qua- / lesquier Justiçias de su(^s) mag*estad* para q*ue* a(n)si Se / lo hagan cumplir e Renunçiaron qualesquier / {rúbrica}

[fol. 9r]

leyes de q*ue* en este caso se puedan Aprovechar e la ley / General y el d*i*cho Anton negrin lo firmo de Su no*m*- / bre *en* el rregistro y el d*i*cho Jorge baez lo firmo de / su rrubrica Acostumbrada testigos Ju*an* perez de Ver- / gara e diego gallego e Jaque de brujas e diego sanchez / Anton negrin Jorge baez e yo hernando berme- / Jo escribano de Sus mag*estade*s e su notario pu*bli*Co presen- / te fui A todo lo q*ue* d*i*cho es e de pedimy*ent*o del d*i*cho An- / ton negrin lo escribi e por *en*de fize aqui este / myo signo q*ue* es (a)tal *en* testimonyo de Verdad her- / nando bermejo escribano de Su mag*estad*

{ytem} El d*i*cho señor alcalde *h*Abiendo Visto lo pedido e / presentado por parte del d*i*cho Anton negrin dixo y de- / claro no *h*aber lugar lo pedido por parte del Su- / sodicho ni el poder ny facultad q*ue* presenta para lo / Susod*i*cho del d*i*cho difunto Ser bastante por no ynter- / Venyr *en* el d*i*cho poder e comysion del dicho difunto / la sole*m*nidad q*ue* de

d*erech*o Se Requiere por tanto q*ue* da- / ba e dio por nynguno todo lo presentado Çerca de la / d*i*cha Comision por parte del d*i*cho Anton negrin / y mandaba y mando Al d*i*cho anton negrin esiba y / aclare con juramento los bienes q*ue* tiene *en* su po- / der del d*i*cho difunto o diga si sabe *en* cuyo poder / estan para q*ue* se pongan *en* poder de la persona / q*ue* tuViere derecho de tenellos con Recaudos bas- / tantes hasta tanto q*ue* parezca persona q*ue* le / pertenezcan los dichos bienes y pareçida la tal per- / sona el Señor alcalde mandara para *en* cumplimy*ent*o / {rúbrica}

9

[fol. 9v]

del Anyma del d*i*cho difunto lo q*ue* de d*erech*o hallare / e fuere justiçia y juzgando Asi dixo q*ue* lo manda- / ba e mando geronymo Ruiz de la mota el liçençia- / do sandoVal

{ytem} Diose E proñunçiose este auto de Suso Contenydo / *en* treze dias del mes de Se*p*tiembre de mill e qui*nient*os E / quarenta e dos años estando *en* audiençia publi- / ca testigos sancho lopez e alonso Sanchez el d*i*cho / anton negrin dixo q*ue* apelaba e apelo de la d*i*cha Sen- / tençia para y Ante su magestad presidente E / oydores e a(n)si lo pidio por testi- / monyo Ju*an* de ça- / ragoça escribano publico

{ytem} muy poderosos Señores Anton negrin parezco ante / V*uestra* mag*estad* e digo q*ue* el alcalde (h)ordinario / pronunçio Un / auto ynJusto y muy agraviado contra mi *en* / Razon / q*ue* le pedi me diese liçençia e facultad para poder / hazer un testamento *en* nonbre de Ju*an* ximenez E / declaro no *h*aber lugar de se hazer pido e suplico A / V*uest*ra alteza(s) mande q*ue* el escribano Venga A ha- / zer Relaçion y en el caso Se determyne lo q*ue* de con- / Çiençia e Justiçia deba ser hecho e ymploro Su muy / Real ofiçio

{ytem} En la ÇiUdad de mexiCo A catorze dias del mes de / Se*p*- / tiembre del d*i*cho año visto este proçeso por los Seño- / res presidente e oydores *en* rrelaçion dixeron / que rreVo- / caban y rreVocaron El auto dado y pronu*n*- / Çiado por el Alcalde e mandaron q*ue* los d*i*chos Anton / negrin e Jorge baez e cada Uno de *e*llos Puedan / {rúbrica}

[fol. 10r]

hazer testamento *en* nonbre del dicho Ju*an* ximenez /
difunto como les pareçiere y segun y como el d*i*cho /
testador con ellos lo comunyco para lo qual Les / dieron
a cada Uno de *e*llos yn solidun poder Cumpli- / do Con
aditamento y declaraçion q*ue* en el tal testa- / mento no
puedan nonbrar ni nonbren ni co*n*s- / tituyan heredero e
a(n)si lo dixeron e mandaron / Ju*an* de Çaragoça
escribano pu*bli*Co

{y*tem*} Este proçeso se comete por mi el dicho escri- / bano
Andres de herrera escribano pu*bli*Co y del / conçejo de la
çiUdad de los angeles para q*ue* pueda / hazer todo lo mas q*ue*
conVenga y no otro Algu- / no por quanto se le comete
oreginalmente / Ju*an* de Çaragoça escribano pu*bli*Co

{y*tem*} E despues de lo susod*i*cho *en* esta çiUdad de los ange-
/ les de esta nueVa españa *en* Veinte e siete dias deL / mes de
hebrero Año del naçimy*ento* de n*uest*ro SalVador / Jesu *cristo*
de mill e qui*nientos* e quarenta e tres años *en* / Presençia de
mi Andres de herrera escribano pu*blic*o / Y del conçejo por
su mag*estad* de *e*sta d*i*cha ÇiUdad e de los / testigos de yuso
escritos pareçio el d*i*cho anton ne- / grin V*e*zino de *e*sta d*i*cha
çiUdad e por Virtud de todo lo / a(u)ctuado e de la facultad
q*ue* tiene de la Real audien- / Çia q*ue* en la çiUdad de
mex*i*Co Reside por Su mag*estad* de / suso encorporada dixo
q*ue* en nonbre del dicho Ju*an* xi- / menez difunto q*ue* dios
*h*aya segun q*ue* con el d*i*cho / difunto lo tenia platicado e
comunycado hazia / E (h)ordenaba e hizo e (h)ordeno el
testamento e pos- / {rúbrica}
10

[fol. 10v]

trimera Voluntad del d*i*cho Ju*an* ximenez difunto / como Su
albaçea e testamentario q*ue* es *en* la for- / ma E manera Siguiente

{y*tem*} Primeramente mando el anyma del d*i*cho difun- / to
A dios n*uest*ro señor q*ue* la crio e Redimyo por / su preçiosa
Sangre para q*ue* el sea servido de / *h*aber merito de ssu anyma
e la lleVe a su santo Rei- / no Amen

{y*tem*} yten mando q*ue* por el anyma del d*i*cho Ju*an* xi- /
{ojo} menez difunto se (^le) diga un tre*i*ntenario de my- / sas
Rezadas abierto el qual diga el padre Cu- / {ojo} ra Alonso
maldonado ^*clerigo en* la yglesia mayor de *e*s- / ta d*i*cha
ÇiUdad e se le pague por lo dezir de los bie- / nes del d*i*cho
difunto lo q*ue* es Costunbre

{y*tem*} yten mando por Las anymas de sus Padres del d*i*cho
/ difunto q*ue* el d*i*cho alonso maldonado clerigo diga / otras
diez misas rrezadas e se paguen por las de- / zir lo q*ue* es
Costumbre

{y*tem*} Yten mando al hospital de la ÇiUdad de mex*i*Co por
el / anyma del d*i*cho difunto porq*ue* consiga e gane las /
yndulgençias q*ue* en el se ganan los Çynco ducados / de buen
oro de castilla e se pague*n* de los bienes del d*i*cho / difunto

{y*tem*} yten mando Al hospital de *e*sta d*i*cha ÇiUdad *en* li(s)- /
mo*s*na por el anyma del d*i*cho difunto quatro p*es*os / del oro q*ue*
corre q*ue* se paguen de los bienes del dicho / difunto / {rúbrica}

[fol. 11r]

{y*tem*} Yten mando a cada Una de las cofradias de *e*sta d*i*cha
/ ÇiUdad q*ue* son del santisimo sacramento e Ve- / ra cruz e
de los angeles A cada Una de los bienes / del dicho difunto
Un peso del d*i*cho oro q*ue* corre

{y*tem*} Yten mando a las mandas Forçosas E a cada Una / de
*e*llas por el anyma del d*i*cho difunto Un tomyn deL / oro q*ue*
corre e se paguen de los bienes del d*i*cho difunto

{y*tem*} yten mando q*ue* por el anyma del dicho difunto se /
tome Una bula de la santa cruzada q*ue* al presen- / te *h*ay e
se pague lo q*ue* es de sus bienes

{y*tem*} {scribal mark} yten mando de los bienes del d*i*cho
difunto se den / {ojo} e paguen A Ju*an* (^de) barragan
Çinquenta p*es*os ^*de oro* de my- / nas q*ue* el d*i*cho difunto le
debia por Una obligaçion

{y*tem*} Yten mando q*ue* de los bienes del d*i*cho difunto se pa-

/ guen a Anton garçia tres p*es*os de oro de mynas / q*ue* el d*ic*ho difunto le debia e debe

{y*tem*} yten mando q*ue* de los bienes del d*ic*ho difunto se den / e paguen a Ju*an* cordero sastre dos p*es*os de oro de my- / nas q*ue* el dicho difunto Se los debia e debe

{y*tem*} Yten mando q*ue* todas las deudas q*ue* el d*ic*ho dif*unto* / debe por escrituras liquidas se paguen e porq*ue* / de presente no se sabe q*ue* deba ninguna deuda e por / descargo del anyma del d*ic*ho difunto dixo q*ue* man- / (^v)daba e mando q*ue* si alguna persona Jurare q*ue* / el d*ic*ho difunto le debe y es a cargo hasta *en* cantia / de Un peso del oro q*ue* corre se le pague de los bienes / del d*ic*ho difunto con solo Su Juramento / {rúbrica}
11

[fol. 11v]
Yten El d*ic*ho Anton negrin *en* el d*ic*ho nonbre A- / claro e mando q*ue* se cobren todas las deudas / q*ue* al d*ic*ho Ju*an* ximenez difunto le deben liquydamen- / te E porq*ue* las deudas q*ue* a(n)si le deben son q*ue* se hi- / Zieron *en* la tierra nueVa e segun q*ue* el lo platico / con el d*ic*ho Ju*an* ximenez difunto dixo q*ue* de todas / las deudas q*ue* le deben al d*ic*ho difunto A(n)si por / escrituras conoçimy*ent*os o de almoneda del d*ic*ho dif*unto* / se Cobren las dos terçias partes e la Una ter- / Çia parte no paguen e se lo Suelta e haze gra- / Çia de *e*lla *en* nonbre del d*ic*ho difunto porq*ue* como / d*ic*ho es A(n)si dixo q*ue* lo comunyco con el e q*ue* las / dos partes de todas las deudas Se cobren Como / d*ic*ho es eç*ep*to q*ue* quarenta p*es*os de oro de mynas / q*ue* debe al d*ic*ho difunto Rodrigo de truxillo por / escritura de Un Caballo q*ue* todos los d*ic*hos qua- / renta p*es*os de mynas se cobren del d*ic*ho Rodrigo / de truxillo porq*ue* los debe bien debidos Al d*ic*ho di- / Funto lo qual de suso Contenido dixo q*ue* hazia / e hizo por descargo del anyma del d*ic*ho dif*unto* / e segun con el lo platico e comunico como di- / cho es

{y*tem*} E para Cumplir e pagar e cobra*r* y execu- / tar el d*ic*ho testamento e lo *en* el contenydo el / d*ic*ho anton negrin dixo q*ue* se nonbraba e no*m*- / bro A si propio por albaçea y testa-

mentario deL / d*ic*ho difunto para lo Contenido en este dicho / testamento e para quien Su poder *h*obiere / {rúbrica}

[fol. 12r]
Pueda Cobrar Los bienes e deudas e hazienda deL / d*ic*ho difunto y a(n)simysmo dixo q*ue* el d*ic*ho an- / ton negrin se nonbraba e nonbro por tene- / dor e admynistrador de los dineros deudas E / hazienda del d*ic*ho difunto para todo lo Reçebir / E cobrar *en* si e para dar quenta de *e*llo Segun / e a quien e con derecho deba o al heredero o he- / rederos del d*ic*ho Ju*an* ximenez difunto los quales / no señala ni estableçe porq*ue* no los Sabe ni co- / noÇe e porq*ue* no tiene facultad de los Señalar / E demas de lo Susod*ic*ho dixo e otorgo q*ue* si dios / le lleVare Al d*ic*ho anton negrin de *e*sta presente / Vida q*ue* nonbraba(n) e nonbro por albaçeas e tes- / tamentarios del d*ic*ho difunto e por tenedores / de los bienes q*ue* suyos quedaron e perteneçieron / e perteneçen A alonso grande e a gregorio / ginoVes V*ezin*os de *e*sta d*ic*ha ÇiUdad q*ue* estan Ausen- / tes o a qualquier de *e*llos yn solidum a los / quales dio poder Cumplido Segun q*ue* lo tiene / e de derecho *en* el d*ic*ho caso meJor e mas Cum- / Plidamente lo puede e debe dar e otorgar *en* / Forma

{y*tem*} E por esta carta el d*ic*ho anton negrin dixo / q*ue* ReVocaba e ReVoco todos e qualesquier / testamento o testamentos codeçilio(^s) o code- / {rúbrica}
12

[fol. 12v]
Çilios q*ue* antes de *e*ste *en* qualquier manera eL / d*ic*ho Ju*an* ximenez difunto *h*aya hecho e otor- / Gado q*ue* no Vala salvo este q*ue* agora *en* su / nonbre el d*ic*ho anton negrin haze e otor- / Ga segun q*ue* como d*ic*ho tiene lo comunico con / el d*ic*ho difunto e q*ue* Valga por tal testame*n*- / to e postrimera Voluntad del d*ic*ho Ju*an* xime- / ne(x)z difunto *en* cuyo nonbre dixo q*ue* lo hazia / e hizo e otorgo segun de suso Se contiene q*ue* / es Fecho e otorgado *en* el d*ic*ho dia mes e año / Susod*ic*ho y el d*ic*ho anton negrin lo firmo de / su nonbre *en* el Registro testigos q*ue* fuero*n* / Presentes a todo lo q*ue* d*ic*ho es franc*is*co de (h)orduña / e pedro de VillanueVa e Ju*an* de san Viçente E / Ju*an* Valades clerigo e Ju*an* sanchez

vezinos de *e*sta / d*i*cha ÇiUdad los quales los q*ue* supieron escrebir / lo firmaron de Sus nonbres *en* el Registro Jun- / tamente con el d*i*cho otorgante Anton negrin / Fran*ci*sco de (h)orduña pedro de VillanueVa Juan / de san Viçente Ju*an* de Valades clerigo por Ju*an* / sanchez Ju*an* de san Viçente

{*ytem*} E yo el d*i*cho andres de herrera escribano pu*bli*Co / e del Conçejo por Su mag*estad* de *e*sta d*i*cha ÇiUdad / de los angeles de *e*sta dicha nueVa españa lo su- / sodicho fize escribir e sacar del oreginal q*ue en* / mi poder queda e lo di segun q*ue* ante mi paso e por *en*de / fize aqui este myo Signo q*ue* es (a)tal *en* testimonyo de Verdad / Andres de herrera escrivano pu*bli*co y de Conçejo / {rúbrica}

[fol. 13r]
{*ytem*} Este Es Un treslado bien e fielmente Sacado de Una / petiçion presentada por anton negrin Ante los Se- / ñores presidente e oydores Con Çierto ProVeimy*ento* man- / do por los d*i*chos Señores fecho *en* que mandan A / Anton negrin e a Jorge baez o a qualquier de *e*llos / puedan hazer Su testamento *en* nonbre de Ju*an* xime- / nez lo qual Uno *en* pos de otro con el testamen- / to q*ue* (h)ordeno el d*i*cho Anton negrin *en* el d*i*cho nonbre / Segun q*ue* por ello pareçia Su tenor de lo qual de Ver- / bo ad Verbo es esto q*ue* se Sigue

{*ytem*} muy poderosos Señores anton negrin parezco an- / te V*uestra* mag*estad* e digo q*ue* el alcalde (h)ordinario pronun- / Çio Un auto ynJusto e muy agraviado Contra my *en* / rrazon q*ue* le pedi me diese liçençia e facultad para / poder hazer Un testamento *en* nonbre de Ju*an* xime- / nez e declaro no *h*aber lugar de se hazer pido e su- / plico a V*uestra* alteza mande q*ue* el escribano Venga A / hazer Relaçion y en el Caso Se determine lo q*ue* de / conçiençia e justiçia deba Ser hecho e ynploro su / muy Real ofiçio

{*ytem*} En la ÇiUdad de mexico A catorze dias del mes de Se*p*tien- / bre del d*i*cho año Visto este proçeso por los Se- / ñores presidente e oydores *en* rrelaçion dixeron / que ReVo-caban e ReVocaron el auto dado e pronunçia- / do por el alcalde y mandaron q*ue* los d*i*chos anton / negrin e Jorge baez y cada Uno de *e*llos puedan / hazer testamento *en* nonbre del

d*i*cho Ju*an* ximenez / difunto como les pareçiere y segun y como el d*i*cho / {rúbrica}
13

[fol. 13v]
testador con Ellos Lo Comunyco para lo qual les / dieron A cada Uno de *e*llos yn solidum poder Cum- / {ojo} plido con aditamento y declaraçion q*ue en* el ^*tal* testamen- / to no puedan nonbrar ni nonbren ni Constitu- / yan heredero e asi lo dixeron e mandaron Ju*an* de ça- / ragoça escribano pu*bli*co

{*ytem*} Este proçeso se comete por mi el dicho escribano / (A) andres de herrera escribano pu*bli*co y del conçejo de / la ÇiUdad de los angeles para q*ue* pueda hazer to- / do lo q*ue* mas ConVenga y no otro alguno por qua*n*- / to se le comete oreginalmente Ju*an* de Çaragoça es- / cribano pu*bli*co

{*ytem*} E despues de lo Susod*i*cho *en* esta ÇiUdad de los an- / geles de *e*sta nueVa españa en Veinte y siete dias del / mes de hebrero año del naçimy*ento* de n*uest*ro salvador Je- / su *cri*s*t*o de mill e qui*nient*os e quarenta (e quarenta) e tres A- / ños *en* presençia de mi andres de herrera escriba- / no pu*bli*co y del conçejo por Su mag*estad* de *e*sta d*i*cha çiUdad / E de los *testi*gos de yuso escritos pareçio el d*i*cho anton ne- / grin V*e*zi*n*o de *e*sta d*i*cha ÇiUdad e por Virtud de todo lo a(u)c- / tuado e de la facultad q*ue* tiene de la Real audiençia / q*ue en* la ÇiUdad de mexico Reside por Su mag*estad* de su- / so yncorporada dixo q*ue* en nonbre del dicho Ju*an* / ximenez difunto q*ue* dios *h*aya Segun q*ue* con el d*i*cho / difunto lo tenia (^f) platiCado e comunicado fazia / e (h)ordenaba e hizo e (h)ordeno el testamento E / Postrimera Voluntad del d*i*cho Ju*an* ximenez difunto / {rúbrica}

[fol. 14r]
Como Su albaçea e testamentario q*ue* es *en* la for- / ma e manera Siguiente

{*ytem*} Primeramente mando el anyma del d*i*cho difunto / A dios n*uest*ro Señor q*ue* la crio e Redimyo por su pre- / Çiosa Sangre para q*ue* el sea SerVido de *h*aber merito de / su anima e la lleVe A su santo Reino amen {*ytem*} yten mando q*ue* por el anyma del d*i*cho Ju*an* ximenez difu*n*to / Se diga Un trentenario de misas Rezado abierto / el qual diga el padre Cura Alonso maldonado cle- / rigo *en* la yglesia mayor de *e*sta d*i*cha ÇiUdad e se le pague / por lo dezir de los bienes del d*i*cho difu*n*to lo q*ue* es costu*m*bre

{*ytem*} Yten mando Por las anymas de Sus padres deL / d*i*cho difunto (^el) *el* qual d*i*cho alonso maldonado clerigo / diga otras diez misas Rezadas e se pague*n* por / las dezir lo q*ue* es Costumbre

{*ytem*} yten mando Al hospital de la ÇiUdad de meXico por / el anyma del d*i*cho difu*n*to porq*ue* consiga e gane las / yndulgenç*i*as q*ue* en el se ganan los çinco ducados / de buen oro de Castilla e se pague*n* de los bienes deL / d*i*cho difunto

{*ytem*} yten mando al hospital de *e*sta d*i*cha ÇiUdad *en* li(^s)mos- / na por el anyma del d*i*cho difunto quatro p*e*sos del oro / q*ue* corre e se paguen de los bienes del dicho difunto

{*ytem*} yten mando A cada Una de las cofradias de *e*sta / d*i*cha ÇiUdad q*ue* son del santisimo Sacramento / (o)*e* Vera cruz e de los angeles A cada Una de los bie- / {rúbrica}
14

[fol. 14v]
nes del d*i*cho difunto Un p*e*so del d*i*cho oro q*ue* corre

{*ytem*} Yten mando a las mandas forçosas e a cada Una / de *e*llas por el anyma del d*i*cho difu*n*to un tomin del oro q*ue* / corre e se pague de los bienes del d*i*cho difunto

{*ytem*} Yten mando q*ue* por el anyma del dicho difunto Se to- / me Una bula de la santa cruzada q*ue* al presente *h*ay / e se pague lo q*ue* *dic*ho es de Sus bienes

{*ytem*} yten mando de los bienes del d*i*cho difunto se den / e paguen A Ju*an* barragan Çinquenta p*e*sos de oro / de mynas q*ue* el d*i*cho difu*n*to le debia por Una obligaç*i*on

{*ytem*} yten mando q*ue* de los bienes del d*i*cho difunto / {ojo}

Se paguen A anton (^gutierrez) garçia tres p*e*sos de / oro (de oro) de mynas q*ue* el d*i*cho difu*n*to se los debia y debe

{*ytem*} yten mando q*ue* de los bienes del d*i*cho difunto se den / e paguen A Ju*an* cordero sastre dos p*e*sos de oro de my- / nas q*ue* el dicho difunto se los debia e debe

{*ytem*} yten mando q*ue* todas las deudas q*ue* el d*i*cho difu*n*to / debe por escrituras liquidas Se paguen E / porq*ue* de presente no se sabe q*ue* deba ninguna deu- / da e por descargo del anyma del d*i*cho difunto / dixo q*ue* mandaba e mando q*ue* si aLguna perso- / na Jurare q*ue* el d*i*cho difunto le debe y es a / cargo hasta *en* quantia de Un p*e*so del oro q*ue* corre / le paguen de los bienes del d*i*cho difunto con solo su Jurame*n*to

{*ytem*} Yten el d*i*cho anton negrin en el d*i*cho nonbre A- / claro e mando q*ue* se cobren todas las deudas q*ue* / {rúbrica}

[fol. 15r]
Al d*i*cho Ju*an* ximenez difunto le deben liquidamente / e porq*ue* las deudas q*ue* asi le deben Son q*ue* se hizieron / {*ojo*} *en* la tierra nueVa e Segun q*ue* ^*el lo platico con el dicho Juan Ximenes difunto diXo que de todas* las deudas q*ue* le deben / al d*i*cho difunto Asi por escrituras o conoçimy*en*tos e deL / Almoneda (del Almoneda) del d*i*cho difunto Se cobren / las dos terçias partes e la Una terçia parte no pa- / Guen e se la Suelta e haze graçia de *e*lla *en* nonbre / del d*i*cho difunto porq*ue* como dicho es Asi dixo q*ue* lo / comunico con el e q*ue* las dos partes de todas las / deudas Se Cobren como d*i*cho es eçep*t*o q*ue* quare*n*- / ta p*e*sos de oro de minas q*ue* debe al d*i*cho difunto Rodrigo / de truxillo por escritura de Un caballo q*ue* todos los / d*i*chos quarenta p*e*sos de minas Se Cobren del d*i*cho R*o*drig*o* / de truxillo porq*ue* los debe bien debidos Al d*i*cho difu*n*to / lo qual de suso contenido dixo q*ue* hazia e hizo por / descargo del anyma del d*i*cho difunto e Segun q*ue* con eL / lo platico y comunico como d*i*cho es

{*ytem*} E para cumplir e pagar y cobrar y *e*xecutar eL / d*i*cho testamento e lo en el Contenido el d*i*cho anton / negrin dixo q*ue* se nonbraba e nonbro A si propio / Por albaçea e testa- / mentario del d*i*cho difunto pa- / ra lo contenido *en* este

dicho testamento e para quien / Su poder *h*obiere pueda
cobrar los bienes e deu- / das e hazienda del di*c*ho difunto y
asimismo dixo / q*ue* el di*c*ho anton negrin Se nonbraba e
nonbro por te- / nedor e administrador de los dineros deudas
e ha- / Zienda del di*c*ho difunto para todo lo Reçebir E /
{rúbrica}
15

[fol. 15v]
Cobrar en si e para dar quenta de *e*llo Segun E / a quien e
con d*erec*ho deba o al heredero o herederos / del di*c*ho Ju*an*
ximenez difunto los quales no señala / ni estableçe porq*ue* no
los sabe ni conoçe e porq*ue* / no tyene facultad de los Señalar
e demas de lo Su- / sodi*c*ho dixo e otorgo q*ue* si dios le
lleVare al di*c*ho an- / ton negrin de *e*sta presente Vida q*ue*
nonbraba E / nonbro por albaçeas e testamentarios del di*c*ho
/ difunto e por tenedores de los bienes q*ue* suyos q*ue*- / daron
e perteneçieron e perteneçen A alonso gran- / de e a
Gr*egorio* ginoVes V*ezino*s de *e*sta di*c*ha ÇiUdad q*ue* estan /
Ausentes o *a* qualquier de *e*llos yn solidum a los / quales dio
poder cumPlido Segun q*ue* lo tiene e de / d*erec*ho en el di*c*ho
caso mejor e mas Cumplidamen- / te lo puede e debe dar e
otorgar *en* forma

{y*tem*} E por esta carta el di*c*ho anton negrin dixo q*ue* ReVo-
/ caba e ReVoco todos e qualesquier testamento(^s) / o testamentos Codeçilio(^s) o Codeçilios q*ue* antes de *es*- / te *en*
qualquier manera el di*c*ho Ju*an* ximenez / difunto *h*aya
hecho e otorgado q*ue* no Vala / salVo este q*ue* agora *en* su
nonbre el di*c*ho anton ne- / grin haze e otorga Segun q*ue*
como di*c*ho tiene lo / comunico con el di*c*ho difunto e q*ue*
Valga por taL / testamento e postrimera Voluntad del di*c*ho
Ju*an* / ximenez difunto *en* cuyo nonbre dixo q*ue* lo hazia / E
hizo e otorgo Segun de suso Se contiene q*ue* / es hecho e
otorgado *en* el di*c*ho dia mes e año Suso- / di*c*ho y el di*c*ho
anton negrin lo firmo de Su nonbre / *en* el Registro testigos
q*ue* fueron presentes A todo / {rúbrica}

[fol. 16r]
lo q*ue* di*c*ho es Franci*s*Co de (h)orduña e pedro de
VillanueVa / e Juan de san Viçente e Ju*an* Valades clerigo e

Ju*an* / sanchez V*ezino*s de *e*sta di*c*ha ÇiUdad los quales los
q*ue* su- / pieron escrebir lo firmaron de sus nonbres *en* / el
Registro Juntamente con el otorgante / Anton negrin fran-
*cis*co de (h)orduña p*edr*o de VillanueVa / Ju*an* de san Viçente
Ju*an* valades clerigo por Ju*an* san- / chez Ju*an* de San(t)
Viçente e yo el di*c*ho andres / de herrera escribano del
Conçejo por su mag*estad* / de *e*sta di*c*ha çiUdad de los
angeles de *e*sta di*c*ha nueVa espa- / ña lo susodi*c*ho fize
escribir e sacar del oreginal / q*ue* *en* mi poder queda e lo di
Segun q*ue* ante mi paso / E por *en*de fize aqui este mi Signo
q*ue* es (a)tal *en* / testimonio de Verdad Andres de herrera
escribano / publico y del Conçejo

{y*tem*} Fecho y sacado corregido y conçertado fue este / treslado con el treslado autorizado de donde fue sa- / cado *en*
esta ÇiUdad de mexi*C*o *en* Veinte y dos dias deL / mes de
octubre Año del señor de mill e qui*nient*os e qua- / renta e
tres años *testigo*s q*ue* fueron presentes A lo *ver* / corregir y
conçertar con el di*c*ho treslado diego go- / mez e Ju*an* polido
V*ezino* y estantes *en* esta di*c*ha ÇiUdad

{y*tem*} E yo melchior gomez escribano de sus mag*estade*s E
/ su escribano e notario pu*bli*Co *en* la su corte y en to- / dos
los Sus Reinos e señorios en Uno con los di*c*hos / *testigo*s
presente fui a lo q*ue* di*c*ho es e lo saque del di*c*ho tresla- / do
aUtorizado Segun e como *en* el se contiene e lo / {rúbrica}
16

[fol. 16v]
Escrebi E fiz*e* aqui mi Signo (A)tal *en* testimo- / nio de
Verdad melchior gomez escribano de Su*s* / mag*estade*s

{y*tem*} Y presentadas Las di*c*has Escrituras de testamento / e
autos Suso *en*coporadas *en* la manera q*ue* di*c*ha / Es luego el
di*c*ho anton negrin dixo q*ue* estaba / presto de dar la quenta
q*ue* le es mandada de los / bienes del di*c*ho Ju*an* ximenez
difunto q*ue* le es man- / dada contenidos *en* las di*c*has escrituras luego Se- / gun y como le es mandado *testigo*s diego de
ordas Se- / bastian Vazquez escribano de Su mag*estad*

{y*tem*} E despues de lo susodi*c*ho *en* la di*c*ha ÇiUdad de los an- / g̃eles A nueVe dias del mes de septiembre del dicho año / de mill e quinientos e quarenta e çinco años Ante el dicho / señor Juez de Residençia e Justiçia mayor e Juez / de los dichos bienes de difuntos y en presençia de mi / El dicho escribano pareçio presente el dicho anton negrin / Y dixo que el Venia a dar la dicha quenta de los dichos / bienes del dicho

Juan ximenez Segun esta ofreçi- / do y por su merced le ha sido mandado y pidio Se le / tomase

{ytem} E luego el dicho señor Juez Atento a lo Susodicho / hizo Al dicho Anton negrin Çerca de[131] los bienes / del dicho difunto El Cargo y de los bienes Sigui- / entes / {rúbrica}

[fol. 17r]

mynas   tepuzque

{ytem}   Primeramente Vio E cotejo El dicho / ynVentario con el almoneda que de los / dichos bienes se hizo y pareçe por Ellos / que faltaron por vender de los bienes / YnVentariados lo Siguiente Un cue- / ro de Vaca de pelo yten Un sonbrero / Viejo e Un hierro de Lança e Un albar- / don e Unas espuelas chicas e Un mache- / te quebrado e Un martillo e Unas tena- / zas e Un pujaVante de todos los qua- / les dichos bienes que asi quedaron por Ven- / der de los Contenidos en el dicho ynVenta- / rio se le haze Cargo para que los ha de / dar y pagar o su Valor

{ytem}   Yten se le haze Cargo de ochenta pesos / y quatro tomines de oro de minas que sumo / y
Lxxx pesos   monto el preçio y proçedido de los dichos / bienes que se Vendieron en la dicha almo- / neda
iiij tomines   publica que de ellos Se hizo como por Ella / consta y pareçe

{ytem}   Yten se le haze cargo de Un conoçimyento / contra alonso gonçalez que el dicho difunto
xxiiij pesos   tenya / de cantia de Veinte y quatro pesos de oro de / mynas firmado del dicho alonso gonçalez e de / miguel de torres y anton negrin Conte- / nido en el ynVentario de los dichos bienes / hA de dar el dicho Conoçimyento o pagar los / dichos Veinte y quatro pesos del dicho oro / {rúbrica}

17

[fol. 17v]

minas   tepuzque

{ytem}   yten se le haze Cargo de otro conoçi- / myento contra pedro de benaVid(o)es de Cantia
xxx pesos   de / treinta pesos del dicho oro de mynas que / El susodicho debia al dicho difunto firma- / do de Su nonbre y de pedro de lasojo E de / Pedro de huelVe hA de dar el dicho Cono- / Çimiento o pagar los dichos treinta pesos del / dicho oro en el contenidos

{*ytem*} xlij pesos	yten se le haze cargo de otro conoçimyento / contra Alonso gonçalez de quantia de / quarenta y dos pesos del dicho oro de minas que el / susodicho debia al dicho difunto firmado / del Susodicho y del dicho anton negrin y a- / lonso lopez hA de dar el dicho Conoçimyento o / Pagar los dichos quarenta y dos pesos en el con- / tenidos

{*ytem*} Viij pesos	yten se le haze cargo de otro conoÇi- / {ojo} myento Contra Juan ^françes que debia Al dicho difunto / de Cantia de ocho pesos del dicho oro de mi- / nas que estaba firmado del dicho Anton ne- / Grin hA de dar el dicho conoçimyento o pagar / los dichos ocho pesos de mynas en el conte- / nidos

{*ytem*} Viij pesos	yten se le haze cargo de otro conoçimyento con- / tra alonso ximenez de cantia de ocho / Pesos de oro de mynas que debia al dicho difunto / que esta firmado del dicho alonso ximenez / y del dicho anton negrin y del dicho Jorge / baez ha de dar el dicho conoçimyento o pagar los / dichos ocho pesos de mynas en el contenidos / {rúbrica}

[fol. 18r]

mynas   tepuzque

{*ytem*} xxV pesos	Yten se le haze Cargo de otro cono- / Çimyento contra Juan galleas de cantia de / Veinte e çinco pesos del dicho oro de my- / nas firmado del dicho Juan galleas hA de / dar el dicho Conoçimiento o los dichos pesos de / oro en el contenidos

{*ytem*}	Todos los quales dichos Conoçimyentos se ha- / llaron estar ynVentariados por bienes / del dicho Juan ximenez difunto de mas de / los dichos bienes en el contenidos e fue to- / mado por el dicho señor Juez Juramen- / to en forma de derecho del dicho anton ne- / Grin y so cargo de el dixo y declaro que no / Sabe ni tiene notiçia ni en su poder es- / tan otros ningunos bienes del dicho dy- / Funto de mas de los Contenidos en el dicho / ynVentario y lo firmo de su nonbre y / el dicho señor Juez asimysmo el liçen- / Çiado Caballero anton negrin s(a)ebas- / tian Vazquez escribano de Su magestad

{*ytem*} ccxVij pesos iiij tomines	Por manera que suma y monta el dicho / cargo como se contiene en las dichas par- / tidas dozientos y diez y siete pesos y qua- / tro tomines del dicho oro de mynas de los qua- / les se le(^s) haze Cargo segun dicho es y / lo firmaron de sus nonbres Sin las o- / tras cosas suso contenidas el liçen- / Çiado caballero Anton negrin S(a)e- / bastian Vazquez escribano de su magestad / {rúbrica}

18

[fol. 18v]

{*ytem*} E despues de lo Susdicho en la dicha çiUdad de los / {ojo} angeles (^d)el dicho dia mes e año Susodicho A hora de Vis- / Peras porque lo susodicho se hizo e paSo por la maña- / na Se tornaron a juntar A hazer y aVeriguar la / dicha quenta descargo Alcançe y Resuluçion de ellas / el dicho señor Juez de Residençia e Justiçia mayor / y El dicho anton negrin e lo que hoy dicho dia paSo e se hizo / en presençia de my el dicho escribano Es lo Siguiente descargo de anton negrin

{*ytem*} L p*esos*	Primeramente dio Por descargo q*ue* dio / e pago a Ju*an* barragan Çinquenta p*esos* / de oro de mynas los quales le debia el / d*ic*ho difunto por Una escritura pu- / blica q*ue* paso ante hernando gomez / de la peña ecribano de su mag*estad* e por / Virtud de Un mandamy*ento* executorio se- / gun q*ue* consta por Una carta de pago / del d*ic*ho Ju*an* barragan q*ue* esta A las espal- / das del d*ic*ho mandamy*ento* hizo presenta- / Çion de la d*ic*ha escritura y del d*ic*ho man- / damy*ento* y carta de pago atento a lo qual / se le rreçiben *en* quenta los d*ic*hos çinque*n*- / ta p*esos* del d*ic*ho oro de mynas
{*ytem*}	Yten dixo q*ue* daba e dio por descar- / Go q*ue* dio y pago A alonso maldona- / do clerigo cura de *e*sta santa ygle- / sia Veinte pesos del oro q*ue* corre / Por un trentenario y diez misas q*ue* / {rúbrica}

[fol. 19r]

mynas

		tepuzq*ue*
	dixo por El d*ic*ho difunto Juro *en* / Forma de d*erec*ho q*ue* es asi Segun tie- / {ojo} ne ^*dicho* dio Carta del d*ic*ho Alonso mal- / donado Reçibensele *en* quenta los / d*ic*hos Veinte p*esos* del d*ic*ho oro Comu*n*	xx p*esos*
{*ytem*}	Yten dio por descargo q*ue* dio y pago / A andres de herrera Esribano pu*bl*ico q*ue* / fue de esta d*ic*ha ÇiUdad dos p*esos* de oro q*ue* co- / rre por Razon del testamento ynVen- / tario e almoneda de Registro y saca / Segun consta por lo q*ue* esta Asentado / al pie de las d*ic*has Escrituras de mano / del d*ic*ho andres de herrera Atento A / lo qual y a la tasaçion q*ue* de *e*llo se hizo / se le Reçiben *en* quenta los d*ic*hos dos p*esos* / del d*ic*ho oro Comun	ij p*esos*
{*ytem*}	yten dixo q*ue* daba e dio por descar- / go q*ue* pago a melchior gomez ecribano / e a Alvaro Ruiz procurador por rra- / zon de Çiertas escrituras q*ue* otorgo / ante el d*ic*ho melchior gomez tocantes / al d*ic*ho Ju*an* ximenez difunto e al di- / cho alVaro Ruiz porq*ue* por el Soli- / Çitase la cobrança de çiertos p*esos* de oro / tocantes al d*ic*ho difunto de todo ello / a los Susod*ic*hos dos p*esos* y çinco to*mine*s del di- / cho oro comun de q*ue* dio y mostro car- / tas de pago de los susod*ic*hos atento a lo / qual e a que Juro *en* forma de d*erec*ho ser / Çiertas y verdaderas se le Reçiben *en* / quenta los d*ic*hos p*esos* de oro / {rúbrica}	ij p*esos* V to*mines*

19

[fol. 19v]

mynas

		tepuzq*ue*
{*ytem*} xxx p*esos*	Yten dio por descargo El d*ic*ho cono- / Çimy*ento* contra pedro de benaVides de trein- / ta p*esos* de mynas de q*ue* se le hizo cargo / el qual dio sin carta de pago porq*ue* / dixo no *h*aber los cobrado de *e*l aten- / to a lo qual se le Reçiben *en* quenta los / d*ic*hos treinta p*esos* del d*ic*ho oro de mynaS / del d*ic*ho Conoçimy*ento*	

{y*tem*}
xLij p*esos*

Yten dio por descargo otro conoçimy*ento* / contra alonso gonçalez de cantia de / quarenta y dos p*esos* de oro de mynas / de q*ue* se le hizo cargo dio y entrego el / d*icho* conoçimy*ento* sin carta de pago A- / tento a lo qual se le Reçiben *en* quen- / ta los d*ichos* quarenta y dos p*esos* del / d*icho* oro de mynas del d*icho* conoçimy*ento*

{y*tem*}
xxiiij p*esos*

yten dio por descargo otro conoçimy*ento* / Contra otro alonso gonçalez de cantia / de Veinte y quatro p*esos* de oro de mynaS / q*ue* se le hizo cargo dio y entrego el di- / cho conoçimy*ento* sin carta de pago por- / q*ue* dixo no *h*aber cobrado los d*ichos* p*esos* / de oro Atento a lo qual se le Reçibe*n* / *en* quenta los d*ichos* Veinte y quatro / p*esos* del dicho oro

{y*tem*}

yten dio por descargo Asimismo o- / tro conoçimy*ento* contra Ju*an* gall*e*as de can- / tia de Veinte y çinco p*esos* del d*icho* oro / de mynas el qual esta escrito a las es- / paldas del conoçimy*ento* de q*ue* de suso se ha- / Ze mynçion en la partida antes de *e*sta / {rúbrica}

[fol. 20r]
mynas   tepuzque
xxv pesos

En el mesmo papel dio y entrego el / d*icho* conoçimy*ento* Sin carta de pago por- / q*ue* dixo no *h*abellos cobrado Atento A / lo qual se le rreçiben *en* quenta los / dichos p*esos* de oro

{y*tem*}
Viij p*esos*

yten dio por descargo el conoçimy*ento* de q*ue* / se le hizo cargo contra alonso xime- / nez de cantia de ocho p*esos* de oro de / minas *en*trego el d*icho* conoçimy*ento* Sin / carta de pago Atento a lo qual se le / Reçiben *en* quenta los d*ichos* ocho / p*esos* del d*icho* oro de mynas del d*icho* Conoçi- / myento

{y*tem*}
Viij p*esos*

yten dio por descargo otro conoçimy*ento* / contra Ju*an* franç*e*s de cantia de ocho / P*esos* del d*icho* oro de mynas de q*ue* se / le hizo cargo *en*trego el d*icho* Conoçimy*ento* / Sin carta de pago Atento a lo qual / se le rreçiben *en* quenta los d*ichos* ocho / P*esos* del d*icho* oro de mynas

{y*tem*}

yten dio por descargo q*ue* los quaren- / ta p*esos* de oro de mynas del cavallo q*ue* / se Remato fiado a Rodrigo de truxi- / llo hijo de Jorge baez por el almone- / da q*ue* se hizo de los bienes del d*icho* di- / Funto tiene hecha execuçion por E- / llos Ante el d*icho* señor Justiçia mayor / {rúbrica}

20

[fol. 20v]
mynas   tepuzque
xl p*esos*

Al susod*icho* Segun dixo q*ue* consta y pa- / reÇe por los autos de la d*icha* execuçio*n* / q*ue* porque consto ser asi Se le Reçi- / ben *en* quenta y descargo {*ytem*}   Por manera q*ue* suma y monta El / dicho descargo q*ue* el d*i*cho anton ne- / grin da al d*i*cho cargo q*ue* le esta he- / cho como Se contiene *en* las parti- / das Susodichas dozientos y Vein- / te e siete p*es*os de oro de mynas E mas / Veinte y quatro p*es*os y çinco to*mine*s de oro / Comun por manera q*ue* el d*i*cho anto*n* / negrin Alcança al d*i*cho difunto / Por cantia de nueVe p*es*os y quatro / tomynes de oro de mynas e Veinte / e quatro p*es*os e çinco to*mine*s del oro q*ue* co- / rre pagando el d*i*cho anton negrin / los bienes de q*ue* se le hizo cargo q*ue* / dexo de Vender de los contenydos / En el ynVentario y quedan por bie- / nes del d*i*cho difunto todas las deu- / das contenidas En los d*i*chos conoçi- / my*ento*s de q*ue* de Suso se haze mynçion / y los d*i*chos quarenta p*es*os de mynas de / La d*i*cha execuçion q*ue* esta hecha al / d*i*cho Rodrigo de truxillo y firmolo / el dicho Señor Juez de Residençia / y El d*i*cho anton negrin El liçençia - / {rúbrica}

[fol. 21r]

do Caballero Anton negrin pa- / so ante my Sebastian Vazquez / Ecribano de Su mag*estad*

{*ytem*} En la ÇiUdad de los Angeles de *e*sta nueVa es- / paña A veinte y siete dias del mes de o*c*tubre / de mill e qui*niento*s e quarenta e çinco años ante *e*l se- / ñor diego rramirez Juez Visitador de AgraVios / e bienes de difuntos En la d*i*cha ÇiUdad por EL / muy magni*fi*Co señor liçençiado tello de SandoVaL / Visitador general en toda esta nueVa españa / *etcetera* y en presençia de mi *crist*obal de heredia escri- / bano de su mag*estad* E del Juzgado del d*i*cho Señor Juez / pareçio Sebastian Vazquez Escribano de Su mag*estad* / e presento Ante Su m*erce*d e dio y entrego A mi EL / d*i*cho escribano este proçeso de quenta q*ue* fue to- / mada por el licençiado Caballero Juez de rre- / sidençia de la d*i*cha ÇiUdad e paso Ante el como / escribano de su Juzgado lo qual presento *en* cum- / Plimy*ento* del mandamyento q*ue* para ello le fue da- / do por el d*i*cho señor Juez *testigo*s gaspar de arana / Alguazil nonbrado por el d*i*cho señor Juez E / diego su criado natural q*ue* dixo Ser de la Villa / de almonte *crist*obal de heredia ecribano de / sus mag*estade*s / {rúbrica}
21

[fol. 21v]
{*ytem*} E luego El d*i*cho dia El d*i*cho señor Juez *h*Abiendo Vis- / to el dicho proçeso de quenta dixo q*ue* aprobaba E / aprobo e *h*abia por buena esta d*i*cha quenta toma- / da por el

d*i*cho Juez de Residençia e q*ue* como Juez / competente q*ue* es de los bienes de los dichos difuntos / tomaba e tomo *en* si este dicho proçeso e causa pa- / ra lo feneçer e acabar conforme A la comision / q*ue* para ello tiene del d*i*cho señor Visitador generaL / e hazer en el caso Justiçia *testigo*s los dichos diego / rramirez

{*ytem*} Sepan quantos esta carta de obligaçion Viere*n* / Como yo Ju*an* ximenez natural de guadalcanal / q*ue* es en los rreynos de castilla estante al presente / En este exerçito otorgo e conozco por esta presen- / te carta q*ue* me obligo por mi persona e bienes mue- / bles e Raizes *h*Abidos E por *h*aber por dar e pagar / E que dare e pagare A vos Ju*an* barragan natural / de la Villa de llerena q*ue* estais presente o a quien / V*uest*ro poder *h*obiere y esta carta por Vos mostrare / deuda bien liquida conoçida e Verdadera ConViene / A saber Çinquenta p*es*os de oro de mynas de lei perfe*c*- / ta de A quatroÇientos e çinquenta maraVedis cada / Un p*es*os fundidos e marcados con la marca de Sus / mag*estade*s los quales son por Razon de[132] Unas calças E / dos camisas e otras preseas q*ue* de Vos Compre de / q*ue* me doi por contento entrego e bien pagado A / toda mi Voluntad por quanto lo Reçebi e pasa- / ron de V*uest*ro poder Al mio rreal- / mente e con efe*c*- / to y en rrazon de la entrega q*ue* de presente no pa- / {rúbrica}

[fol. 22r]

reçe Renunçio Las dos Leyes del derecho que en este caso / hablan en todo e por todo como en ellas Se contie- / ne e la lei de los dos años e los treinta dias e pongo / plazo para Vos dar e pagar estos dichos Çinquenta / pesos del dicho oro para desde hoy dia de la fecha de es- / ta carta En quinze meSes cumplidos primeros / Siguientes puestos e pagados en Vuestro poder o en / poder de quien por Vos los hobiere de haber Sin / pleito e sin contienda alguna so pena del doblo e de / las costas e daños yntereses e menoscabos que so- / bre la dicha rrazon se Vos ReCreçieren para lo quaL / todo que dicho es mejor a(n)si tener e guardar e cum- / plir e pagar doy e otorgo todo mi poder cumpli- / do A todos e qualesquier Juezes e Justiçias de / Sus magestades de qualesquier partes e lugar que sean / A la Juresdiçion de las quales e de cada Una de ellas me / someto con la dicha my persona e bienes Renunçian- / do como en este caso Renunçio mi propio fuero / Juresdiçion e domeçilio E la Ley Si ConVenerit Ju- / resdicione para que luego que esta carta sea Vista / Por los dichos Juezes e por qualquiera de ellos me Cons- / tringan[133] Conpelan e apremien A lo a(n)si tener E guardar / Cumplir e pagar por Via de execuçion bien a(n)si[134] / o A tan Cumpli- damente como si todo lo que dicho / es fuese a(n)si Visto e oydo dado e mandado Juz- / gado e sentençiado por Juizio e sentençia difiniti- / Va de Juez conpetente e la tal sentençia fuese por / mi consentida e pasada en cosa Juzgada de la quaL / no hobiese apelaçion ni suplicaçion ni otro Reme- / {rúbrica}

22

[fol. 22v]

dio ni Recurso alguno Çerca de lo qual Renunçio E / aparto e quito de mi e de mi faVor e ayuda e Re- / medio todas e qualesquier leyes Fueros E / derechos E (h)ordenamyentos escritos o non escri- / Tos A(n)si En general como en espeçial de que / en este caso me pudiesen aproVechar que me / non Valan e las dos leyes quinta e sesta titulo / treze e la ley e derecho en que dizque generaL / Renunçiaçion de leyes que home[135] Faga non vala en / testimonio de lo qual otorgue esta carta / Por ante El presente escribano e testigos de yu- / so escritos que fue fecha e otorgada en este / exerçito de que es capitan general por sus ma- / gestades el muy

magnifico señor Françis- / co Vazquez de coronado estando AloJado en la / proVinçia de tiguex A seis dias del mes de abril A- / ño del naçimiento de nuestro salvador Jesu cristo de / mill e quinientos e quarenta e Un años tes- / tigos que fueron presentes A lo que dicho es die- / go hernandez e Jorge baez e lope de la cadena / estantes en el dicho exerçito e porque el dicho o- / torgante Al qual yo el dicho escribano doy fee / conoçer no sabia escrebir Rogo al dicho diego her- / nandez lo firmase por el qual lo firmo / En el Registro de esta carta por testigo die- / go hernandez e yo hernando gomez de la pe- / ña escribano de sus magestades presente fui / {rúbrica}

[fol. 23r]

A todo lo que dicho es en Uno con los dichos testigos / e de pedimyento del dicho otorgante La escri- / bi Segun que ante mi paso e por ende fize aqui / este mio Signo (A)tal en testimonyo de Verdad / hernando gomez de la peña

{ytem} E despues de lo Susodicho En la dicha çiUdad de los an- / geles A quatro dias del mes de noViembre de mill / E quinyentos e quarenta e çinco Años Ante el dicho / señor Juez y en presençia de mi el dicho escri- / bano pareçio presente el dicho sebastian Vazquez / ecribano de su magestad e presento esta petiçion / e pidio lo en ella contenido testigos gaspar de arana E / diego de padilla criados del dicho señor Juez

{ytem} magnifiCo mi señor sebastian Vazquez escribano de su / magestad digo que yo me ocupe en la quenta que / se tomo a Anton negrin albaçea de Juan ximenez / difunto de los bienes que del susodicho En su / poder tenya dos dias y escrebi quatro hojas y / media de escritura como por las dichas quentas / consta y pareçe A Vuestra merced suplico de los bienes / del susodicho me mande pagar el dicho sala- / rio y escritura y pido Justiçia y por quanto yo / Voy a mexico Suplico a Vuestra merced lo mande dar a Ana / de terrazas mi muger que yo los doy por bien / Pagados Sebastian Vazquez / {rúbrica}

23

[fol. 23v]

E presentada La dicha petiçion En la manera / que dicha es

e Vista por el dicho señor Juez dixo / que el lo Vera e hara
Justiçia testigos los di- / chos cristobal de heredia escribano
de Sus / magestades

{ytem} En la ÇiUdad de los angeles de esta nueVa es- / paña
A treinta e Un dias del mes de Julio A- / ño del naçimyento
de nuestro salvador Jesu cristo de mill / E quinientos e
quarenta e çinco Años Ante el mag- / nyfico señor el
liçençiado hernando cavallero / Juez de Residençia e Justiçia
mayor en esta dicha / ÇiUdad por su magestad y en presençia
de mi / s(a)ebastian Vazquez escribano de su magestad / E
del audiençia e Juzgado del dicho señor Juez y de / los testigos
de yuso escritos pareçio presente anton / negrin Vezino de
esta dicha ÇiUdad Asi como albaçea y / testamentario que se
dixo ser de Juan ximenez / difunto y tenedor de sus bienes e
presento / Una escritura de obligaçion Signada de her- / nan
gomez de la peña escribano de su magestad / la qual es la
Siguiente

{ytem} Sepan quantos esta carta Vieren Como / yo Rodrigo
de truxillo natural de la ÇiU- / dad de la Vera cruz de la
nueVa españa es- / tante Al presente En este exerçito otorgo
/ {rúbrica}

[fol. 24r]
E conozco por esta presente Carta que / me obligo por mi
persona e bienes muebles / e Raizes hAbidos e por haber por
dar e pagar / e que dare E pagare A vos anton negrin Ve- /
zino de la ÇiUdad de los angeles que estais presen- / te como
heredero albaçea e testamentario de / los bienes que
quedaron e fincaron[136] de Juan / ximenez difunto o a los
herederos del dicho Juan / {ojo} (^Funto) ximenez o a quien
Vuestro poder o EL / Poder de ellos hobiere y esta carta
mostrare / conViene a saber quarenta pesos de oro de mi- /
nas de buena moneda de Valor cada Un / Peso de A
quatroÇientos e çinquenta mara- / Vedis los quales Son por
Razon de Un ca- / ballo color castaño calçado de entranbos
/ Pies Con Una lista en la Frente que compre e / saque del
almoneda que de los dichos bienes Se / hizieron En presençia
de hernando bermejo / ecribano de sus magestades que los
muy bien / Valio del qual dicho caballo yo me doy e otor- /

Go por bien contento entrego e bien pagado / E entregado
A toda mi Voluntad por quanto lo Re- / Çebi e paso A mi
poder Realmente E con E- / Fecto y en Razon de la entrega
Si neçesario es / Renunçio la exebçion de la pecunya e la ley
de los / dos Años e los treinta dias en todo e por todo /
{rúbrica}
24

[fol. 24v]
Como en ellas Se contiene e pongo plazo / para Vos dar e
pagar los dichos quarenta pe- / sos del dicho oro para desde
hoy dia de Fecha / de esta carta en çinco meses cumplidos
prime- / ros Siguientes puestos e pagados en Vuestro / Poder
o en poder de quien por Vos o por / los dichos herederos los
hobiere de hAber en / paz y en salvo Sin pleyto e Sin
contien- / da Alguna So pena del doblo e de las costas / e
daños yntereses e menoscabos que sobre / la dicha rrazon se
Vos Recreçieren para / lo qual todo que dicho es A(n)si tener
e guar- / dar e cumplir e pagar por esta carta doy / e otorgo
todo mi poder Cumplido A to- / dos e qualesquier Juezes e
Justiçias de sus / magestades de qualesquier partes e lugar que
/ sean A la Juresdiçion de las quales e de cada Una / de ellas
me someto con la dicha mi persona E / bienes Renunçiando
como en este caso Renun- / Çio mi propio fuero Juresdiçion
e domeçi- / lio e Ve(n)zindad e la lei Sid convenerit Jures- /
diçione anium Judiçium para que luego que es- / ta carta sea
vista por los dichos Juezes o / Justiçias o por qualquiera de
ellos me constrin- / gan compelan E apremyen A lo A(n)si
tener / E guardar e cumplir e pagar bien Como / {rúbrica}

[fol. 25r]
Si por sentençia difinitiva de Juez compe- / tente fuese Visto
e mandado Juzgado e sen- / tençiado e la tal sentençia fuese
pasada en cosa / Juzgada e por mi consentida e aprobada de
la quaL / no hobiese apelaçion ni Suplicaçion ni otro /
Remedio ni rrecurso Alguno Çerca de lo qual / todo que
dicho es Renunçio e aparto e quito de / mi FaVor e ayuda e
Remedio todas e quales- / quier leyes fueros e derechos e
(h)ordenamien- / tos Escritos o non escritos a(n)si en
generaL / Como en espeçial de que en este Caso me puedan
/ ayudar e aproVechar que me non Valan e las dos / leyes

quinta e sesta titulo treze y en espe- / Çial Renunçio la lei e
Regla general en q*ue* / dizque general Renunçiaçion de leyes
q*ue* home haga / non Vala en testimonio de lo qual otorgue
esta / Carta por ante el presente escribano e testi- / Gos *de*
yuso Escritos fecha la carta En este / (h)exerçito de q*ue* es
capitan general por Sus / magestades Franc*is*Co Vazquez de
coronado estando / Alojado en la Ribera del Rio q*ue* se dize
de Rio frio / q*ue* es Entre chichiltiqueale e çibola A nueVe /
dias del mes de abril Año del naçimiento de / n*uest*ro
Salvador Jesu *cristo* de mill e quinient*os* e quaren- / ta e dos
años testigos q*ue* fueron presentes / A lo q*ue* dicho es
Rodrigo de ysla e Ju*an* pedro E / {rúbrica}
25

[fol. 25v]
Franc*is*Co de parada Estantes en este d*ich*o exerçito E /
porq*ue* el dicho otorgante no sabia escrebir Ro- / Go al d*ich*o
Rodrigo de ysla lo firmase por / el el qual lo firmo en el
Registro de *e*sta car- / ta A su Ruego e por testigo Rodrigo
de ys- / La E yo hernando gomez de la peña es- / cribano de
Sus magestades presente fui A / todo lo q*ue* dicho es en Uno
con los dichos tes- / tigos e de pedimyento del dicho
otorgan- / te Al qual yo doy fee conoçer la escrebi Se- / gun
q*ue* ante mi paso E por ende fiz*e* Aqui / este mio Signo q*ue*
es (a)tal en testimonio / de Verdad hernando Gomez de la
peña

{y*tem*} En la ÇiUdad de los angeles de *e*sta nueVa espa- / ña
A treinta e Un dias del mes de Julio Año / del naçimiento de
nuestro SalVador Jesu *cristo* / de mill e quiny*ent*os e quarenta
e Çinco años en / presençia de mi el escribano y testigos de
/ yuso escritos pareçio presente Anton / negrin V*ezino* de
*e*sta d*ich*a çiUdad y dixo q*ue* daba / Y dio todo Su poder
Cumplido Segun q*ue* / el lo ha y tiene y de derecho en tal
Caso / se Requiere y mas puede y debe Valer A diego /
Gonçalez procurador de Causas de *e*sta d*ich*a çiU- / {rúbrica}

[fol. 26r]
dad q*ue* estaba presente y lo aÇepto espeçialmente / para que
por el y en su nonbre y como Su per- / sona misma pueda
Recaudar Reçebir *h*Aber / E cobrar en Juizio e fuera de *e*l de

la persona E / bienes de Rodrigo de truxillo y de quien Con
de- / recho deba los quarenta p*e*sos de oro de mynas q*ue* / le
debe por Virtud de *e*sta obligaçion y de *e*llos / o de qualquier
parte que de *e*llos Cobrare dar y / otorgar sus cartas de pago
y de finequito las / que cumplieren y menester fueren las
qua- / les Valan y sean tan firmes y bastantes como / Si el
propio las diese e otorgase Siendo pre- / sente y para q*ue*
pueda pareçer Sobre Ello Ante / qualesquier Justiçias de sus
magestades e hazer / qualesquier demandas pedimi*ent*os
Requirimientos / Autos y protestaçiones Çitaçiones
enplazamy- / entos Juramentos de calu*m*nia y deÇisorio
enbargos en- / tregas execuçiones prisiones Ventas de bienes
y Rema- / tes de *e*llos y presentar qualesquier derechos /
ProbanÇas y escrituras q*ue* a su derecho ConVengan / y
finalmente hazer todo aquello q*ue* el haria / y hazer podria
presente Siendo Aunque pa- / ra ello se Requiera su
presençia personal has- / ta *h*Aber y cobrar los dichos pesos
de oro e quan / Cumplido y bastante poder el tiene para lo
Su- / {rúbrica}
26

[fol. 26v]
sodicho otro tal lo dio e otorgo Al d*ich*o di*e*go gon- / çalez
con sus ynçidençias y conexidades y lo / ReleVo Segun
derecho e para lo *h*Aber por fir- / me obligo Su persona y
bienes *h*Abidos y por / *h*Aber y lo Firmo de su nonbre
Siendo pre- / sentes por testigos bartolome hernandez y
anton / perez estantes en esta d*ich*a ÇiUdad Anton negrin /
Paso ante mi sebastian Vazquez escribano de su / magestad

{y*tem*} E presentado el d*ich*o Contrato publico Su- / so
encorporado en la manera q*ue* dicha es el di- / cho anton
negrin albaçea y testamentario deL / dicho Ju*an* ximenez
dixo q*ue* como por ella Cons- / ta y pareçe el dicho Rodrigo
de truxillo le / debe y es obligado A dar y pagar quaren- / ta
p*e*sos de oro de mynas de ley perfe*c*ta y no en- / bargante q*ue*
es pasado el plazo en ella Conte- / nido y muchos dias mas
q*ue* estaba obliga- / do a se los pagar no se los *h*abia querido
ni que- / rya pagar por tanto q*ue* pedia y pidio AL / d*ich*o
señor Justiçia mayor le mandase / dar y diese Su
mandamyento para por Vir- / tud de *e*l hazer execuçion por

la dicha Cantia / en la persona y bienes del dicho Rodrigo de truxillo / {rúbrica}

[fol. 27r]
E juro en forma de derecho ser le debidos y por / pagar los dichos pesos de oro y so cargo del di- / cho Juramento prometio de no dar ni pagar A / mi el dicho escryvano el ny otra ninguna persona por / el A mi ny a otro por my ningunos dineros dema- / siados en ninguna cantidad que sea ni otra cosa / Alguna Salvo aquellos que Justamente me vi- / nieren y perteneçieren Conforme al aranzel E / que si yo se los llevare pidiere o demandare lo di- / ra y manyfestara Al dicho señor Justiçia mayor pa- / ra que lo Castigue conforme A derecho so pena de / perjuro S(a)ebastian Vazquez escribano de su magestad

{ytem} E por el dicho señor Juez de Residençia e Jus- / tiçia mayor Visto lo susodicho e atento A ello / E habiendo Visto y esaminado el dicho Contrato / dixo que mandava y mando dar su mandamien- / to executorio Contra la persona y bienes del dicho / Rodrigo de truxillo por la dicha Cantia de los / dichos quarenta pesos de oro de mynas en el Con- / tenidos el qual dicho mandamiento Se dio en / Forma y es el Siguiente Sebastian Vazquez / escribano de Su magestad el liçençiado ca- / vallero

{ytem} Alguazil mayor de esta ÇiUdad de los angeles o / A Vuestro lugartenyente en el dicho ofiçio yo / {rúbrica}
27

[fol. 27v]
os mando que hagais entrega execuçion en / bienes de Rodrigo de truxillo por cantia de qua- / renta pesos de oro de mynas de buena moneda / que pareçe que debe y es obligado A dar y pagar / A anton negrin Vezino de esta dicha ÇiUdad Como / A heredero albaçea y testamentario de los bienes / que quedaron e fincaron de Juan ximenez di- / funto por Virtud de Un Contrato publico de / plazo pasado que ante mi presento diego / gonçalez con poder del susodicho el qual en / nonbre del dicho su parte Juro Ser le debidos y / por pagar y los bienes en que hizieredes la dicha / Execuçion sean muebles

y tales que Valgan la di- / cha Cantia y costas Al tiempo del Remate con / Fiança bastante de todo saneamyento que a ellos Vos de / y si no en Raizes con la dicha fiança y si Unos / ni otros bienes no tuViere o no Vos diere / Prende(l)r de el cuerpo y preso le poned en la car- / Çel publica de esta dicha ÇiUdad de la qual no / sea suelto ni enfiado Sin mi liçençia y man- / do y notificadle los diez dias de la ley de toledo / e que señale casa y procurador Conoçido de esta / dicha ÇiUdad donde E con quien se hagan los au- / tos de esta dicha execuçion hasta la final con- / t(^d)ension de ella Çitandole para ello en forma fe- / cho en la ÇiUdad de los angeles A treinta y Uno / de Julio de mill e quinyentos e quarenta e çinco años / el liçençiado cavallero por mandado de su merced Sebas- / tian Vazquez escribano de su magestad / {rúbrica}

[fol. 28r]
{ytem} En la ÇiUdad de los angeles de esta nueVa es- / paña A primero dia del mes de agosto de mill / e quinientos e quarenta e çinco años Rodrigo de / coria Alguazil mayor de esta ÇiUdad por Vir- / tud de este mandamiento de nonbramiento de die- / {ojo} go gonçales ^por y en nonbre de anton negrin hizo execuçion en Un ca- / ballo castaño que tiene Un hierro Rezien (h)e- / chado en (^e)la cadera derecha A manera de cruz sin / señal ninguna (^señal) por bienes propios de / Rodrigo de truxillo en el Contenido por can- / tia de los quarenta pesos de oro de mynas en / el contenidos y mas las costas con protes- / taçion de hazerla en mas bienes muebles / o Raizes que hallare y pareçieren ser suyos / del susodicho el qual dicho caballo saco de casa / y poder de luisa yndia madre que dizque es del di- / cho Rodrigo de truxillo donde estaba y lo deposi- / to en casa y poder de Anton martyn breVa vezi- / no de esta dicha ÇiUdad el qual lo tomo y Reçi- / bio en el dicho deposito y se constituyo por / depositario de el y se obligo de lo dar y entregar / e acudir Con el Al tiempo que se hobiere de hazer / El Remate para que se pueda hazer en el So / las penas en que caen y encurren los deposita- / rios que no acuden con los depositos que en ellos / Son hechos para lo qual Asi tener e guardar / y cumplir obligo su persona y bienes y dio / poder Cumplido A qualesquier Justiçias de / {rúbrica}
28

[fol. 28v]

Sus magestades y Renunçio qualesquier / leyes q*ue* en su faVor sean y la ley y Regla / del derecho en q*ue* dizque general Renunçiaçion / Fecha de leyes non Vala y lo firmo de su nom- / bre testigos andres nuñez alguazil y dixo EL / d*ic*ho anton m*art*yn q*ue* las costas q*ue* el dicho Caba- / llo hiziere de Comer protesta de las Cobrar deL / dicho Caballo Anton martin paso Ante my / S(a)*e*bastian Vazquez escribano de su mag*estad*

tasaçion de Costas Hasta Aqui

{y*tem*}	De presentaçion de la ecritura de obligaçion	Xij
{y*tem*}	Del poder q*ue* dio Ante my A diego gonçalez para / cobrar la deuda en ella contenida	XViij
{y*tem*}	Del pedimyento para q*ue* se le diese mandamyen- / To e Jura- mento q*ue* hizo de todo	Vj
{y*tem*}	Del auto de mandarle dar el dicho mandamy*ento* (^que) / {ojo} D*e*l(^e) d*ic*ho mandamy*ento* q*ue* se le dyo	Vj Xij
{y*tem*}	de la fyrma del Juez del dicho mandamy*ento*	Xvij

{y*tem*} Todo lo qual monta Setenta y Un maraVedis / de buena moneda los quales pago el dicho diego / Gonçalez e Juro en forma de derecho q*ue* no *h*A / dado ni pagado el ni otro por el A mi el dicho / escribano ni A otra persona Alguna por / {rúbrica}

[fol. 29r]

mi ni Al d*ic*ho señor Juez mas derechos de los / susodichos ni otra Cosa Alguna ni los da- / ra por los dichos autos q*ue* de suso se declaran / y firmolo y el dicho señor Juez

Asimismo / y yo el dicho escribano diego gonçalez EL / liçençiado cavallero Sebastian Vazquez es- / cribano de Su mag*estad*

{y*tem*} En la ÇiUdad de los angeles de *e*sta nueVa españa / A quatro dias del mes de noViembre e del dicho / año de mill e qui*niento*s e quarenta e çinco años An- / te el magnifico señor diego Ramirez Juez / (^Juez) Visitador de agraVios e bienes de difuntos en / la dicha ÇiUdad y en presençia de mi *crist*obal de he- / redia escribano de sus magestades e del Juzga- / do del dicho señor Juez pareçio presente s(a)*e*bas- / tian Vazquez ecribano de su magestad e del Juz- / gado del liçençiado caballero Juez de Residen- / Çia de la dicha ÇiUdad presento Ante el dicho se- / ñor Juez e dio y entrego A mi el dicho escrybano / Un proçeso de execuçion q*ue* paso Ante el dicho li- / Çençiado e ante el como Su escribano de Un man- / damiento de execuçion q*ue* el dicho liçençiado man- / do dar por Virtud de Una obliga- / çion Contra / Rodrigo de truxillo por cantia de quaren- / ta pesos de oro de minas q*ue* el susodicho pa- / reçe deber A Juan ximenez difunto e a sus / {rúbrica}
29

[fol. 29v]

herederos el tenor del qual Este q*ue* se sigue

Aqui este proçeso

{y*tem*} E presentado el dicho proçeso de execu- / Çion en la manera q*ue* dicha es e Visto por / el dicho señor Juez dixo q*ue* tomava e tomo / en si este dicho proçeso e causa para lo fene- / Çer proseguir e acabar e aprobando e Retifican- / do e *h*abiendo por bueno todo lo hecho e mando / por el dicho liçençiado cavallero Como Juez con- / petente q*ue* es de *e*sta causa mandaba e mando q*ue* / el dicho cavallo en q*ue* fue hecha la dicha execu- / Çion se Venda en publica Almoneda y publi- / {ojo} co pregon ^dentro de terçero en terçero dia e / a la per- / sona q*ue* mas por el diere se Remate e de los pe- / sos de oro de su Valor sea hecho pago a la parte / del dicho Juan ximenez difunto e a sus / {ojo} herederos e q*ue* por quanto el ^(el) *proçeso prinçipal de la quenta que Se tomo al* /

dicho anton / *negryn* albaçea del di- / cho Ju*a*n ximenez esta pendiente ante su m*erce*d / mandaba y mando q*ue* este dicho proçeso Sea / co*n*mu(l)*t*e E Junte Con ello e asi dixo q*ue* lo man- / daba e mando e lo Firmo de su nonbre die- / go rramirez

primero pregon

{*ytem*} E luego en este dicho dia e por mandado deL / dicho señor Juez e por ante mi el dicho es- / {rúbrica}

[fol. 30r]
Cribano e por Voz de pedro negro Se dio el pri- / mero pregon Al dicho Caballo diziendo en / altas Vozes si *h*abia quien lo comprase e pu- / siese en preçio q*ue* se le Reçebiria la postura / q*ue* se Vendia por bienes de Rodrigo truxillo por / execuçion q*ue* en el *h*avia sido hecha A pedimi- / ento de los herederos e albaçea de Juan xime- / nez difunto q*ue* se *h*abia de Rematar dentro de / nueVe dias e al terçero pregon q*ue* se le Reçe- / beria la postura e andando en el dicho pre- / gon pareçio Juan Ruiz mercader estante / en la dicha ÇiUdad e dixo q*ue* el le ponia e puso / en ocho pesos de mynas e no pareçio este dia / quien mas por el diese y en fin del dicho pre- / gon dixo el dicho negro este es el primero / pregon e al terçero se *h*a de Rematar de todo / Remate E fueron presentes por tes- / tigos pedro de meneses e Alberto de ca- / Çeres Vezinos de la dicha ÇiUdad diego / Ramirez *crist*obal de heredia escriba- / no de sus mag*estade*s

Segundo pregon

{*ytem*} E despues de lo susodicho en la dicha / ÇiUdad de los angeles en siete dias del dicho mes / de noViembre e del dicho Año por Ante my EL / {rúbrica} 30

[fol. 30v]
dicho escribano e Por Voz de Juan negro / EsclaVo de Alberto de caçeres estando en / la plaça publica de la dicha Villa se dio EL / segundo pregon Al dicho caballo en la for- / ma E manera q*ue* el primero e no se hallo per- / sona q*ue* lo pusiese en mas preçio y en fin / del dicho pregon dixo el

dicho negro este es / el segundo pregon testigos los q*ue* lo oyen / e fueron presentes por testigos hernan- / do ladron E hernando Veedor Vezinos de la / dicha ÇiUdad *cist*obal de heredia escriba- / no de sus magestades

Terçero PreGon

{*ytem*} E despues de lo susodicho En la dicha ÇiU- / dad de los angeles onze dias del dicho mes E / Año susodicho e por Ante mi el dicho escri- / bano e por Voz de anton negro estando en la plaça / publica de la dicha ÇiUdad se dio el terçero e UL- / timo pregon al dicho Cavallo estando presen- / te mucha gente e andando en la dicha almoneda / pareçio Juan de sotomayor Vezino de la dicha / ÇiUdad e puso el dicho cavallo en (h)onze pesos / y medio de oro de minas en el qual se Remato / de Ultimo e postrimero Remate Como En ma- / yor ponedor porq*ue* no *h*obo quien mas diese / {rúbrica}

[fol. 31r]
Por El Siendo testigos Alonso Valiente e Ro- / drigo de Coria Alguazil e otros los quales di- / chos pesos de oro yo di y entregue luego al di- / cho señor Juez de los quales Se pagaron en las / Costas Siguientes por mandado del dicho se- / ñor Juez *crist*obal de heredia escribano de Sus / magestades

{*ytem*} E despues de lo susodicho en la dicha ÇiUdad / de los Angeles A doze dias del mes / de noViembre e del dicho año de mill / E qui*n*ient*o*s e quarenta e Çinco Años / el dicho señor Juez dixo q*ue* man- / daba e mando se de y pague A / Rodrigo de coria alguazil mayor / de la dicha ÇiUdad de los derechos de / la execuçion del dicho Cavallo e del / gasto e comida q*ue* el dicho cavallo / hizo en el termino de los pregoneS / nueVe tomines e medio de oro comu*n* / Y asimismo mando se de y pague / A mi el dicho escribano de mis de- / rechos de los pregones e otros au- / tos hechos en esta causa Un peso / de oro comu*n* e nos mando pagar / E se pago a sebas- / tian Vazquez es-/ {rúbrica}

31

[fol. 31v]

cribano de lo que se ocupo en to- / mar la quenta Al dicho anton ne- / grin e de lo q*ue* escribio en la dicha / quenta otro peso de oro Comun lo / qual yo el dicho escribano Recebi / y di a la muger del dicho sebasti- / an Vazquez como el susodicho ma*n*- / do todo lo qual se dio e pago en la / manera susodicha y el dicho Ro- / drigo de coria de Como lo Reçibio / lo firmo aqui de su nonbre Jun- / ta(^n)mente Comigo el dicho escriba- / no Rodrigo de Coria *crist*obal / de heredia escribano de sus ma- / Gestades

*tepuzqu*e iij p*es*os j to*min* vj *granos*

{y*tem*} Por manera que sacados e desco*n*- / tados de los dichos (h)onze p*es*os e me- / dio de minas en q*ue* fue Vendido / el dicho Caballo los dichos tres / Pesos y un tomyn e seis granos de / los dichos derechos Resta e que- / da por bienes del dicho diFunto / quinze pesos e siete tomynes E / seis granos del dicho oro

{y*tem*} Sacose para el pregonero medio / {rúbrica}

[fol. 32r]

Peso y queda liquido quinze Pe(^s)- / sos e tres tomines e seis granos / Paso ante mi *crist*obal de heredia / Escribano de sus magestades

xv p*es*os iij to*mines* Vj *granos*

---

fecho e sacado fue este dicho traslado del proçeso ori- / Ginal por mandado de su mag*estad* y en cumplimy*ent*o de Una su / Real Çedula en el pueblo de tenanÇingo q*ue* es en la nue- / Va españa a diez e nueVe dias del mes de noViembre A- / ño del nasÇimy*ent*o de n*uest*ro salvador *jesu crist*o de mill e quy*niento*s / e Çinquenta años testigos q*ue* fueron presentes a lo *ver* corre- / Gir e conçertar con el dicho original pedro de Gamboa / e melchior de legazpi estantes al presente en el dicho pueblo / Va enmendado *donde* diz platicado Vala Va entre Renglones *donde* diz my / yntençion e *donde* diz clerigo e *donde* diz de oro e *donde* diz tal e *donde* diz / el lo platico con el d*i*cho ju*an* ximenez dif*unt*o dixo q*ue* de todas e *donde* diz / françes e *donde* diz d*i*cho e *donde* diz por y en nombre e *donde* diz dentro e *donde* diz / el proÇeso prinÇipal de la quenta q*ue* se tomo al dicho anton negrin / Vala Va testado *donde* dezia ese e *donde* dezia 1 e *donde* dezia le e *donde* dezia de / e *donde* dezia el e *donde* dezia Gutierrez e *donde*

dezia funto e *donde* dezia [missing] e *donde* de- / zia señal[137]

yo miG*ue*ll lopez de leGazPi es*crib*ano de su m*agestad* e su es*crib*ano / mayor del conçeJo e ayuntamy*ent*o de la Gran Çiudad de meXico FiZ*e* saCar / del oreGinal todo lo susodicho por Virtud de Una Çedula / de su m*agestad* seGun de suso es dicho e Va CorreGido E Çierto Con[138] / Por ende FiZ*e* aquy my sYGno (a)tal {signo} en testim*on*Yo de *ver*dad[139]

{rúbrica} miG*ue*ll lopes {rúbrica} / es*crib*ano del *consej*o
32

[fols. 32v–34r] [blank]

[fol. 34v]
Año de 1550
Juan ximenez Num*ero* 15[140]

Document 28

The Relación de la Jornada de Cíbola, Pedro de Castañeda de Nájera's Narrative, 1560s (copy, 1596)

New York Public Library, Rich Collection, no. 63

INTRODUCTION

Born about 1515,[1] Pedro de Castañeda de Nájera (or simply Pedro de Nájera, as he usually identified himself) was among the scores of residents of Baeza in Andalucía who left their homes for the New World during the late 1520s and 1530s.[2] He thus represented part of a tide of migration from Andalucía and the rest of southern and western Spain that rose during that period.

Precisely when and how he made his way to the northwestern frontier of Nueva España is unknown. In the early days of 1540, though, when the expedition to Tierra Nueva led by Francisco Vázquez de Coronado passed through the new *ciudad* of Guadalajara, Pedro de Nájera was in residence on its outskirts.[3]

From Guadalajara he accompanied the expedition to Compostela, where he passed muster before the viceroy and other dignitaries on February 22, 1540. He was listed in don Diego de Guevara's company of horsemen, taking with him two horses and a chain mail jacket, in addition to native arms and armor. As a member of that company, he traveled with the main body of the expedition under the leadership of Tristán de Luna y Arellano and evidently never with the advance guard or any of the reconnaissance parties dispatched to scout such places as the coast of the Mar del Sur, Tusayán, or Tiguex.[4]

Thus, much of what he reports in his *relación* he did not witness firsthand. For instance, he knew of the death of Melchior Díaz, the storming of Cíbola, the descent into the Grand Canyon, the climb to Acoma, the occupation of Tiguex, the garroting of El Turco, and the uprising at San Gerónimo only through the accounts of others. This makes the detail with which he narrates these events and many others all the more remarkable. On the other hand, he personally experienced the northward trek of the van of the expedition from Culiacán under Luna y Arellano, the fruitless march across the southern Great Plains in 1541, and at least some of the fighting in Tiguex the preceding winter.[5]

Even though the expedition located no source of tapable wealth in Cíbola, Quivira, or anywhere else it reconnoitered, Pedro de Nájera found the land to be "the beginning of a good land to settle."[6] Perhaps in the early 1540s, and certainly 20 years later, the chronicler maintained that the reasons Vázquez de Coronado and his advisers gave for leaving those northern lands and returning to Nueva España were "not legitimate."[7] It is even possible that he might have been among the "seventy chosen men" who would have stayed in the north, had the captain general not forbidden it.[8]

But return south the expedition did. The future chronicler stopped and settled at Culiacán as the disintegrating expedition passed through, one of the "people who refused to follow [the captain general]" farther.[9] The seventeenth-century historian fray Antonio Tello identified Pedro de Nájera as a *poblador antiguo,* or old-time settler, of San Miguel de Culiacán.[10] Castañeda de Nájera lived to regret the decision to remain in Culiacán, complaining, as he wrote his *relación*, that "both they [certain other expeditionaries] and I, as well as the rest who halted in this *provincia*, have had no lack of hardships pacifying and maintaining this land, catching rebels and living in poverty and want."[11] During his long years in Culiacán, Cíbola and Quivira came to represent for him a prosperous life of ease that might have been. Speaking for himself and other former members of the expedition, the chronicler writes: "Their hearts weep because they have lost such an opportunity of a lifetime."[12] And he reveals that "some of those who came back from there would today be happy to go back, in order to continue farther so as to recover what was lost."[13] Perhaps Pedro de Nájera was among those anxious for another opportunity in the north, even though he was now in his middle to late forties.[14]

It was in Culiacán, the chronicler himself tells us, that he drafted his *relación*.[15] By the time he wrote, it was "about twenty years and more ago that the expedition was made"— that is, it was now the early 1560s.[16] The highly literate former expeditionary was then a *vecino* of San Miguel de Culiacán. Later, in 1566, at age 51, he declared that he had lived there for the full 24 years since the return of the expedition.[17] This is the last glimpse we have of Pedro de Nájera. To what age he lived, what his subsequent activities were, and whether he remained in San Miguel are all unknown.

Pedro de Nájera opens his *relación* by addressing it to a "muy magnifico señor [very magnificent lord],"[18] whom he later calls "Vuestra merced [Your Grace]."[19] Who that exalted person was is not evident from the *relación* itself. We are nearly certain, though, that it was doctor Alonso de Zorita, one of the *oidores* of the Real Audiencia de Nueva España.

We say this because, first and foremost, it is certain that during the late 1550s and early 1560s a return expedition northward was in the wind, and Zorita, as its potential leader, was extremely interested in the *entrada* the Coronado expedition had made to Cíbola approximately 20 years before. Indeed, beginning in 1558 and continuing through 1562, Zorita, together with the Franciscan fray Cyndos (Jacinto) de San Francisco, made a series of proposals to the king and Consejo de Indias to mount a new expedition of 100 Spaniards and at least 20 Franciscan friars, in order to return to the land of the Chichimecas—from which access could be gained, as Zorita put it in 1561, to "the Tierra

Nueva to which Francisco Vázquez Coronado went, and to Nuevo México . . . *provincias* . . . heavily populated by people, very productive, and showing strong indications of sources of gold and silver."[20]

As he looked forward to the proposed *entrada*, Zorita, as *oidor*, had access to considerable information about the Coronado expedition. This came to him in the form of at least six *probanzas de méritos y servicios* (proofs of worthiness and service) that were submitted to the *audiencia* in the late 1550s and early 1560s, during Zorita's tenure, by former participants in the *entrada*. Zorita himself signed documents dealing with the *probanzas* of three of the former expeditionaries: Juan Gallego, Juan Troyano, and Tristán de Luna y Arellano.[21] In addition, Zorita's intended partner, fray Cyndos, made a trip to the region of Zacatecas in 1559 in company with an Indian *donado*, or lay brother, named Lucas, who had been a companion of fray Juan de Padilla's during the Coronado *entrada*.[22] Undoubtedly it was from Lucas that Cyndos learned much of the news of the far north about which he subsequently was enthusiastic.[23]

In preparing for their intended expedition, Zorita and fray Cyndos surely must have solicited information about Cíbola and how to get there from other former members of the Coronado expedition.[24] Their call for reports likely explains the writing at that time of Pedro de Nájera's *relación*, as well as the one prepared nearly simultaneously by Juan Jaramillo, also addressed to an unidentified illustrious personage who most likely was Zorita.[25]

Pedro de Nájera's inclusion of the *apellido*, or surname, Castañeda on the title page of his manuscript adds further credence to our suggestion that the manuscript was prepared for and perhaps even at the request of Alonso de Zorita. Undoubtedly Castañeda was a name associated with Pedro de Nájera and his family, although he did not customarily use it. He might well have done so on this occasion in order to distinguish himself from Pedro Gómez de Nájera, a young interpreter who had worked for, even lived with, and was well known to doctor Zorita in Guatemala and the Ciudad de México.[26]

Although the chronicler does not explicitly reveal that he is writing to provide planning information in support of Zorita's proposed *entrada*, he does give several hints to that effect. The ninth chapter of Part 3 states the veteran's principal reason for writing his account: to provide information "should people leave again from Nueva España in search of that land."[27] And at the opening of the manuscript the chronicler offers the hope that he may do "this little service" for the "magnificent lord" whom he is addressing.[28]

Pedro de Nájera composed his lengthy and sophisticated *relación* to perform this service for Zorita or whomever. Earlier historians have taken Pedro de Nájera's self-deprecation much too seriously, saying, for instance, "As a rhetorician and geographer Castañeda was not a paragon."[29] More recent scholars have rightly recognized the chronicler's skill.[30] His is far and away the most literary of the known documents deriving from the Coronado expedition. It is a crafted piece of writing by a sophisticated author, one who seems comfortable with the language. His use of an intricate and lengthy prologue to the manuscript is perhaps only the most conspicuous instance of his familiarity and ease with the formal writing and publishing conventions of his day.

Division of the narrative into chapters for dramatic effect is a potent literary device that the chronicler employs with masterful results. Meanwhile, the macro-organization of the *relación* into three parts is a skilled manipulation of the author's subject matter, taking the work far beyond the level of simple narrative. Part 1 details "The Exploration" to its farthest limit. As Castañeda de Nájera himself writes, "The first [part] will give an account of the reconnaissance and the armed force or expedition which made [it], including the entire journey and the captains who went there."[31] Part 2 outlines "What Was Found," the disappointingly small size and poverty (by European standards) of the native populations. In the author's own words, "I want to give individual report[s] about the entire inhabited region which was seen and reconnoitered during this expedition."[32]

Maureen Ahern has recently pointed out the cartographic aspect of Part 2 of the *relación* "in establishing a spatial and cultural order for resolving the articulation of alterity and territoriality from Culiacán to Quivira."[33] That aspect is certainly present and not insignificant, especially in light of the *relación*'s potential use in planning a new expedition, as previously outlined. Part 2, however, is more fundamentally the candid and critical appraisal of the populations of Señora, Cíbola, Tusayán, Tiguex, the buffalo plains, and Quivira from the vantage of an aspiring *encomendero*. Over and over he reveals those lands as too sparsely populated and too much consumed by bare subsistence to support the kind of tributary settlement envisioned by most sixteenth-century conquistadores.

Finally, Part 3 follows "The Results of that Disappointment," the fitful disintegration of the expedition, offset somewhat by the promise of *más allá, plus ultra* (more, farther on). Pedro de Nájera expresses it thus: "This was the conclusion that those reconnaissances had, and the expedition which was made to Tierra Nueva."[34]

In order to ensure the reader's awareness of simultaneous events, the chronicler several times interrupts himself and breaks the thread of his narrative to insert reports of separate units of the expedition.[35] This is a technique of an experienced writer, far removed from the more common, strictly linear accounts given by other expedition members, again suggesting Pedro de Nájera's comfort with and experience at formal written expression. On occasion he uses the editorial "we,"[36] and several times he has recourse to nautical figures of speech.[37] All these examples point to the chronicler's being a practiced writer fully able and willing to select and arrange story elements for discursive effect.

That effect was, first, to dispel any misconceptions his readers might harbor that the Coronado expedition had encountered exceedingly populous and wealthy towns. Second, it was to make clear that both Cíbola and Quivira were, nonetheless, likely jumping off points for the discovery of such places. And third, it was to delineate two routes for a possible new *entrada*: a western one up the coast of the Mar del Sur, which was likely to lead to Greater India, and an eastern route northward from Pánuco, which would lead eventually to Arahe and other places in the interior of the continent, which the Coronado expedition had heard about but not reached.

Through his use of imagery and metaphor, Pedro de Nájera conveys a sense of the proximity of the realms of India and China. He does this by repeatedly associating Native American groups of Tierra Nueva with traits and behaviors of Islamic peoples of northern Africa and the Middle East. People in the towns of Suya and the pueblos of the Rio Grande, but more especially the Querechos and Teyas of the Great Plains as groups, are likened to Bedouins, Arabs, Moors, and Turks.[38] This accomplishes two things. First, it identifies natives of Tierra Nueva as "heathens" hostile to Christianity and "civilization" and rightfully subject to conquest. Such a view of Native Americans was far from peculiar to Pedro de Nájera; rather, it was the majority view of Europeans in the New World at the time.

Beyond that, and more importantly for the argument the chronicler is making, encounters with people looking like Arabs and Turks imply that the Coronado expedition had progressively approached the Orient. Readers of the *relación* would have been familiar with Marco Polo's *Travels*, still immensely popular in the sixteenth century, more than 300 years after it was written. In that "best seller," published anew in Spanish in 1518, Polo delineated a social geography of the route to the kingdom of the great kahn, characterized by a succession of Islamic polities.[39] For Pedro de Nájera, the appearance of Arab-like peoples among the bison is convincing evidence that Cathay (China) and Cipango (Japan) were close at hand. Even stronger confirmation of Polo's geography was the fact that the Teyas of the southern Great Plains ate "only meat," just as did the Turkomans who lived on the very threshhold of the realms of the khan, and seemed like "Tartars with their herds, dwelling in tents on the plain."[40] Thus, a new *entrada* to the north could expect brilliant success.

In accomplishing his persuasive purpose, Pedro de Nájera coincidently reveals to unanticipated readers four and a half centuries later the most powerful motives behind sixteenth-century expeditions such as the one led by Francisco Vázquez de Coronado. The chronicler's most succinct indication of the principal motivation of lay expeditionaries comes during his explanation of the reasons for abandonment of the *entrada* in 1542. The majority of the leadership and rank-and-file members, he writes, concluded that "they should return to Nueva España, because nothing of wealth had been found and there was no settlement in what had been reconnoitered where *repartimientos* [*encomiendas*] could be made to the whole expedition."[41] Earning the right to collect tribute from prosperous peoples newly brought under the Spanish king's dominion was the primary goal of nearly

every lay expeditionary. If all went well for them, that would mean a sumptuous life of ease and status.

But, as Castañeda de Nájera demonstrates in Part 2 of his *relación*, the realities of Tierra Nueva were not such as to support a manorial existence for even a handful of people, let alone the hundreds who hoped for such an outcome from the expedition. In speaking of the pueblos of the Rio Grande as a whole—the most populous and prosperous area the expedition encountered—the chronicler writes, "There are *repartimientos* in Nueva España with a greater number of people, and not just one but many."[42] Clearly, even at its best (from the expeditionaries' perspective), Tierra Nueva was a bust.

We cannot stress enough that the Coronado expedition and scores of others like it that took place during the 1500s were not primarily exploring parties bent on simply charting the unknown. Empty land was of little interest to them, regardless of its mineral or agricultural potential. Instead, they sought out people—specifically, people who possessed or produced high-value goods that might be appropriated by means of a kind of taxation. Thus, Part 2 of Pedro de Nájera's *relación* is a description not of the land through which the expedition moved but rather of the peoples it met.[43] It had, after all, been news of wealthy people far to the north that had launched the expedition.

The reasons for such sanguine expectations about the northern lands were many, including, at the end of a long chain of events, fray Marcos de Niza's 1539 report.[44] But Pedro de Nájera's *relación* exposes another contributing factor, a fanciful geography that sought to reconcile the landmass of the Americas with medieval notions of the physical layout of the world. Even as late as the 1560s, when the *relación* was written, and more strongly 20 years before, at the time of the Coronado expedition itself, many people believed, as Pedro de Nájera did, that the wealthy lands of the Far East, known then as Greater India, were contiguous with and within easy reach of America's northern continent. The chronicler insists, "Just as this land of Nueva España is a [continuous] landmass with El Perú, so is it also with Greater India or China."[45] According to him, "if those mountain ranges where that river [the Rio Grande] has its headwaters were crossed and [if] the lands from which those people originate were entered, magnificent news would probably be obtained. [That is] because, according to the direction, [that land] is the beginning of Greater India."[46] And Greater India was, according to the chronicler, "what was being sought when the expedition set out to go there."[47]

No wonder, then, that Pedro de Nájera is highly critical of the expedition's leader for choosing to give up the search so near the source of fabulous wealth. He levels the accusation that Vázquez de Coronado "made it appear he was ill, traveling with a guard,"[48] in order not to have to confront those who disagreed with his decision in the spring of 1542 to turn back south. In recounting events following the determination to abandon Tierra Nueva, the chronicler repeatedly portrays the captain general as deceitful and underhanded. Fray Marcos de Niza fares no better in the relación: "His report had turned out to be incorrect about everything."[49] In both cases the chronicler's central displeasure arises from what he sees as the thwarting of the "reasonable" expectations of most members of the expedition that lives as encomenderos awaited them in the north.

The strength of Castañeda de Nájera's complaints, as well as the logic of his geography, arises from the torrent of detail he is able to marshal about every phase of the expedition. Although he occasionally protests that "with time I have lost the memory,"[50] he much more often displays a phenomenal remembrance of events two decades in the past, perhaps aided by notes made during the course of the expedition and augmented by the recollections of some of his companions in arms with whom he maintained contact. Evidently these powers of observation and retrospection were not limited to events of the 1539–42 entrada. Pedro de Nájera exhibited the same extraordinarily detailed memory in 1566 when he made a long statement about the whereabouts of former residents of Nueva Galicia in a petition from the ayuntamiento (municipal council) of Culiacán to the audiencia in the Ciudad de México. On that occasion his statement was far more extensive and detailed than those of others who were deposed at the same time.[51] To the same degree, his relación concerning the journey to Cíbola far exceeds all others in wealth of detail.[52] He provides information about countless episodes that cannot now be corroborated from other sources.[53] The relación is, however, broadly compatible with other accounts on those points where they overlap.

Early in his manuscript Castañeda de Nájera insists that "it is not my aim to earn favors as a fine author or rhetorician."[54] Nevertheless, he employs the forms and style of a polished writer throughout. And he openly expresses the assumption that his work will have a much wider audience than just the illustrious person to whom it is formally addressed. Indeed, he writes that one of his aims is "to give a brief overall account for all those who are driven by this inquisitive trait."[55] And his is undoubtedly the most often cited and quoted document deriving from the Coronado expedition. It is also, by a considerable margin, the longest contemporary narrative of the entrada.

The relación has come down to us, however, not as a popular book of its day but in the form of a handwritten copy made in 1596 in Sevilla by licenciado Bartolomé Niño Velázquez, either for or from the library of Hernando González, Conde de Castilla.[56] Pedro de Nájera's original document is not known to exist. Once drafted and delivered to its intended recipient (probably Alonso de Zorita), the relación seems to have suffered neglect for centuries, except for the preparation of Niño Velázquez's copy in the 1590s. That may well have been because Zorita lost interest in and abandoned his project before returning to Spain in 1566, where he spent some time in Sevilla, perhaps even depositing some of his papers there, including the "Relación de la Jornada de Cíbola." His partner, fray Cyndos, joined forces with Francisco de Ibarra in his 1564 entrada to Copala and certainly would have shared information about Cíbola and the rest of the north with that governor and captain.[57]

Although seemingly written with an eye to publication, the relación did not find itself in print until 1838, and then only in a French translation. Henri Ternaux-Compans, a French collector and bibliographer who was preparing a multivolume series of original narratives of European colonial activity in the Americas,[58] came across Niño Velázquez's transcription of the relación in the collection of Antonio de Uguina, which he had purchased perhaps during the first decade of the nineteenth century.[59] Ternaux-Compans translated and published the lengthy manuscript and, in doing so, according to George Winship 60 years later, "rendered the language of the original accounts with great freedom . . . and in several cases . . . entirely failed to understand what the original writer endeavored to relate."[60] So Pedro de Nájera's report for Alonso de Zorita finally rolled off the presses, altered but still recognizable, as "Relation du voyage de Cibola" in volume 9 of *Voyages, relations et memoires originaux pour servir a l'histoire de la decouverte de l'Amerique.*[61]

Around 1844 the Massachusetts-born bookseller and bibliographer Obadiah Rich purchased all of Ternaux-Compans's Spanish manuscripts, including the Niño Velázquez copy of the *relación.* The 142 volumes of the Rich collection then passed, only four years later, to James Lenox, who donated them to the New York Public Library. There, the 1596 copy of the *relación* is conserved today in the Manuscripts and Archives Section as Rich Collection no. 63.[62]

In the late 1880s or early 1890s George Parker Winship, an undergraduate at Harvard University, seeking to improve on Ternaux-Compans's effort, transcribed and translated into English Rich no. 63 (all except, unaccountably, the first three folios, which appear in print for the first time here). His work was published in 1896 in *The Coronado Expedition, 1540–1542,* which appeared in Part 1 of the *Annual Report of the Bureau of American Ethnology of the Smithsonian Institution for 1892–1893.* Winship's transcription was the first publication of the *relación* in the author's native tongue, approximately 330 years after he wrote it. Winship's English translation has been reprinted several times, most recently in 1990 by Dover Publications under the title *The Journey of Coronado,* a facsimile re-publication of a 1933 edition issued by Grabhorn Press of San Francisco. In the same year Fulcrum Publishing of Golden, Colorado, reprinted Winship's translation, along with his historical introduction and a modern introduction by Donald C. Cutter, under the title *The Journey of Coronado, 1540-1542.*

As part of the national Coronado Cuarto Centennial commemoration in 1940, the historian George P. Hammond, then of the University of New Mexico, and the linguist Agapito Rey, of Indiana University, published their own English translation of the *relación* among the documents included in *Narratives of the Coronado Expedition,*

1540–1542. Although that volume was reprinted by AMS Press of New York in 1977, it has now long been out of print.

Most recently, in 1992, Carmen de Mora, a professor of Hispanoamerican literature at the Universidad de Sevilla, published another transcription of the *relación* in her *Las Siete Ciudades de Cíbola: Textos y testimonios sobre la expedición de Vázquez Coronado.* Using Mora's transcription as a base, in 1998 Jerry L. Craddock, a philologist and romance linguist at the University of California, Berkeley, prepared detailed philological annotations for the *relación* for use in an undergraduate course in Spanish literature that he was teaching. Those notes have not been published, but Craddock generously shared them with us.[63]

All of these editions, as well as Craddock's notes, proved useful to us in reviewing the annotated transcription and translation we publish here. As is clear from our notes and is inevitable when a fresh look is taken at a whole corpus of documents, we have often disagreed with the readings and interpretations of these deservedly renowned scholars. In other cases their work has served to confirm and occasionally cause us to revise our own choices.

The hundreds of ways in which the present text and translation differ from those of our predecessors do not alter the fact that the astonishingly detailed narrative by Pedro de Castañeda de Nájera is an impressive piece of historical writing. It exhibits a number of the characteristics that we have come to expect of such work. Like the best of modern histories, it has a strong, easy-to-follow story line and is rich in relevant detail, but it also provides context for and attempts to explain the events it recounts. The extent to which that contextualization is adequate and those explanations are convincing can now be judged by comparison with other, less polished contemporary documents that are included in this volume, as well as scores of other "minor" documents that remain unpublished. With each "discovery" of a "new" document, assessment of the chronicler's work shifts at least slightly, like barely perceptible slippage along a geologic fault.

TRANSLATION

[ir]

{note}[64]

Report on the expedition to Cíbola, authored by Pedro de Castañeda Nájera, wherein are discussed those settlements and [their] habits and customs. Which [expedition] took placed in the year 1540. A history belonging to *conde* Hernando González, set to paper.[65]

[iv] [blank]

[iir]

licenciado Bartolomé Niño Velásquez {rubric}

[iiv] [blank]

[iiir]

Report on the expedition to Cíbola, authored by Pedro de Castañeda de Nájera, wherein are discussed all those settlements and [their] habits and customs. Which [expedition] took placed in the year 1540.

[iiiv] [blank]

[1r]

Prologue

Very Magnificent Lord, it seems certain to me that it is a legitimate [undertaking] and occupation of virtuous men to want to know and to try to acquire for their memory factual news of things and events that have occurred in distant places of which little is heard. For this I do not blame some inquisitive persons who have often taken the opportunity to importune me very earnestly, begging me not infrequently to elucidate and clarify for them some uncertainty they had concerning specific things they had heard from the common people about things and events that occurred during the expedition to Cíbola, or Tierra Nueva. [Which was an expedition] ordered and put into execution by the good viceroy Antonio de Mendoza, may God have him in his heaven.[66] [1v] (He sent Francisco Vázquez de Coronado as captain general.)

Truly they have good reason in wanting to learn the truth, because very often the things the common people have heard by chance from someone who does not have even rudimentary knowledge of them are turned into things that are greater or lesser than they [really] are. Things that are important they make insignificant, and those that are not so they turn into things so astonishing as to seem incredible. What may also have caused this is that because [the expedition] did not stay [in] that land, there was no one who was willing to spend the time to write down its details.[67] For this reason, knowledge may have been lost [2r] of that which it did not suit God (he knows why) to have them enjoy.

In truth, whoever would be willing to employ himself in writing down both the things which happened in the course of the expedition and the things which were seen in those lands (the habits and manner of life of the natives) would have plenty of material with which to express his mind. I am convinced that he who would discuss them truthfully would not lack things to report which would be so surprising that they would seem incredible. I also think that some falsehoods that are told are because it is about twenty years and more ago that the expedition was made. I mention this because some people turn it into an uninhabitable land, others [2v] [make it] contiguous with La Florida, and [still] others with Greater India, which seems no small nonsense. They are able to seize some rationale and reason on which to establish their reliability. There is someone who reports very unlikely animals which others, having been on the expedition, declare to be untrue and assert there are none such nor have they seen them. Other [persons] differ as to the direction to the *provincias* and even as to the behavior and dress [there], attributing that of one [people] to others.

All of this, or much [of it], Very Magnificent Lord, has motivated me, though tardily, to try to give a brief overall account for all those who are driven by this inquisitive trait. And also in order to spare [myself] [3r] the time when I am plagued with requests. Therein will certainly be found things exceedingly difficult to believe, all or most of which [I have] seen with my own eyes and other things (about which the natives themselves were asked) understood through true reports.

Believing and having come to understand, as I have, that by itself this little work of mine would be worthless or unconvincing unless it were supported and protected by a person whose authority is such as to check the impudence of those who, without respect, give free rein to their gossiping tongues, and being aware of how much I am and have always been indebted to Your Grace, I humbly beg, as a true [3v] servant and *criado,* that this little work be admitted to your protection.

It is divided into three parts so that it may be better understood. The first will give an account of the reconnaissance and the armed force or expedition which made [it], including the entire journey and the captains who went there. The second [will tell of] the *pueblos* and *provincias* and in which directions they were found; the habits and customs; the animals, fruits, and pastures; and in what parts of the land [they were found]. The third [will tell of] the return made by the expedition and the reasons there were for leaving [the land] unsettled (although [they are] not legitimate, since it is the best location there is for reconnaissance in those western regions, the most central part of [4r] the land, as has been understood since then and as will be seen).

In the final [part] some astonishing things that were seen will be dealt with, as will the route by which it would be possible to return more easily to reconnoiter the [land] we did not see (which was the best [land]). [This route] would be more than a little suitable for entering the land which the Marqués del Valle, don Hernando Cortés, went in search of toward the western star.[68] This cost him not a few maritime expeditions.

[I] pray[69] to Our Lord to grant me such favor that, with my rudimentary understanding and slight ability and by putting down the truth, I may be pleasing with this [4v] small work of mine to the wise and prudent reader. If it is accepted by Your Grace, it is not my aim to earn favors as a fine author or rhetorician, but to try to give a truthful report and to do Your Grace this little service. May you receive it as from a true servant and a man-at-arms who was there. Even though I do not write what happened in a polished style, I have heard, felt, seen, and dealt with it.

I always see (and it is so) that for the most part when we have some precious thing within our grasp and use it without difficulty, we do not value it or hold it in as much value as [we do] when we understand the deficiency we would suffer if we were to lose it. [5r] Therefore, we invariably start holding it in contempt. When, however, we have lost it and are in need of its benefits, we have great pain in our hearts, and we always go around imagining [and] searching for ways and means that we might again recover it. It seems to me that it happened thus to all or most of those who went on the expedition that Francisco Vázquez Coronado made in search of the seven *ciudades* in the year of Our Savior Jesus Christ one thousand five hundred and forty. {1540}

Although they did not find the wealth of which they had been told, they found the beginning of a good land to settle and the wherewithal [5v] to search for [wealth] and to go onward and, afterward, to come here through the land they had conquered and left unsettled. Time has made clear to them where the route and supplies were, and also the beginning of a fine land they had in their grasp. Their hearts weep because they have lost such an opportunity of a lifetime. As it would be certain that men see more when they go up to the highest seats[70] than when they are in the bullring [itself], [just so] now that they are away, [those who went on the expedition] know and understand where the routes and supplies were. Now that they see they cannot enjoy or recover it, nor [6r] the time that has passed, they take pleasure in recounting what they saw and even what they understand they lost. This is especially so for those who find themselves as poor today as when they went there, [even though] they have not stopped laboring and have spent their time without profit.

I say this because I have understood [that] some of those who came back from there would today be happy to go back, in order to continue farther so as to recover what was lost. Others would enjoy hearing and learning the reason for which it was reconnoitered. So I have volunteered to undertake the telling of it from the beginning, which goes like this:

[6v] [blank]

[7r]

First Part

First Chapter

in which is related how the first settlement of the seven *ciudades* became known and how Nuño de Guzmán mounted an armed force in order to reconnoiter them[71]

In the year [one thousand] five hundred and thirty, when he was president of Nueva España, Nuño de Guzmán had in his possession an Indian [who was] a native of the valley or valleys of Oxitipar, whom the Spaniards named Tejo.[72] This Indian said that he was the son of a merchant and that his father was dead. When he was young, however, his father used to go into the interior of the land [7v] as a merchant, with sumptuous feathers to use as ornaments.[73] In exchange, he brought back a great amount of gold and silver, of which there is much in that land. [Tejo also said] that once or twice he went with [his father] and saw *pueblos* so grand[74] that he liked to compare them with [the Ciudad de] México and its environs. [He said] he had seen seven very grand *pueblos* where there were streets of silver workshops.[75] [And he said] that in order to journey to them, it took them forty days [of travel] from their land, all [across] unsettled land. The land through which they went did not have pasture grass, except some [that was] very short (one *jeme*).[76] The course which

FIGURE 28.1. Street sign definition of a *jeme*, the distance between the outstretched thumb and forefinger, in Almagro, Ciudad Real, Spain, 2002. Photograph by the authors.

they pursued was lengthwise through the land between the [two] seas, following [8r] the route to the north.

On the basis of this news, Nuño de Guzmán mustered nearly four hundred Spaniards and twenty thousand [native] allies from Nueva España. Because he was then in [the Ciudad de] México, he crossed the Tarascan [land], which is {/} the land of Michoacán, in order to locate the provisions the Indian told about. Returning across the land toward the Mar del Norte, they came across the land where they traveled in search of what they already called the Seven Ciudades. For the forty days (in accordance with what El Tejo said), [Guzmán] found that, having traveled two hundred leagues, they were usually able to traverse the land easily.[77]

Leaving aside some events which transpired [8v] during this journey, as soon as they had arrived in the *provincia* of {/} Culiacán (which was the most remote [place] of [Guzmán's] jurisdiction and now is [in] the Nuevo Reino de Galicia) they tried to cross the land.[78] But there was a very severe difficulty because the mountain chain that comes down toward the sea is so rugged that as much as [Guzmán] toiled, it was impossible to find a way in that area.[79] For this reason the whole expedition was detained in that land of Culiacán for so long that powerful men who were traveling with him and had *repartimientos* in the land of México changed their minds, and with each day they sought to return from there.

[9r] Nuño de Guzmán received news that the Marqués del Valle, don Hernando Cortés, had come from Spain with [that] new title and substantial concessions and commissions. Because, during the time Nuño de Guzmán was president, he had been a very strong rival of [Cortés's] and had done much damage to his properties and those of his friends, he was afraid {+} that he would be despoiled by don Hernando Cortés repaying him with similar deeds, or worse. [So] he decided to settle that *villa* of Culiacán and return [to the Ciudad de México] with the rest of the men, without there being any other result of his expedition. During the return journey he settled Jalisco, which [today] is the Ciudad de Compostela, and Tonalá, which [now] they call [9v] Guadalajara.[80] Today [these places] are [in] the Nuevo Reino de Galicia. The guide whom they took along, called Tejo, died during the time between these two events.

Thus the name of the Seven Ciudades and the search for them have endured. [Still] today they have not been reconnoitered.

Second Chapter
how Francisco Vázquez [de] Coronado came to be governor and the second report that Cabeza de Vaca made[81]

When eight years had passed since this expedition had been made by Nuño de Guzmán, he was arrested by a *residencia* judge who had come from Spain with [10r] ample commission specifically for that purpose [conducting the *residencia*]. Afterward the judge, named *licenciado* Diego de la Torre, died [although] he had already assumed control of the government of that land.[82] The good don Antonio de Mendoza, viceroy of Nueva España, appointed a *caballero* from Salamanca, Francisco Vázquez de Coronado, as governor in that jurisdiction. At that time [Vázquez de Coronado] was married in the Ciudad de México to a lady who was the daughter of Alonso de Estrada, who had been treasurer and governor of México.[83] (The common people say about him that he was the son of the Catholic king don Fernando, and many persons assert that as a certainty.)

I say that at the time [10v] Francisco Vázquez was appointed governor he was serving as *visitador general* of Nueva España. Through that office he had dealings and friendship with many noble persons who later followed him on the expedition he made.

At that time, it happened that three Spaniards, named Cabeza de Vaca, Dorantes, and Castillo Maldonado, and a Black arrived in [the Ciudad de] México. They had been shipwrecked during the expedition that Pánfilo de Narváez took to La Florida.[84] These [four] emerged from there by way of Culiacán, having traversed the land from sea to sea, as those who desire to learn about it will see in a treatise [11r] that Cabeza de Vaca himself wrote, addressed to Prince don Felipe, who is now our lord and king of Spain. They informed the good don Antonio de Mendoza how, in traversing those lands, they used an interpreter and obtained marvelous news of some wealthy, four- and five-storied[85] *pueblos* and other things very different from what was found to be true.

[All of] this the good viceroy made known to the new governor. For this reason he hurried and left [unfinished] the *visita* he had under way. Then he departed for the seat of his government, taking with him the Black (whom [the viceroy] had bought),[86] as well as the three [11v] friars of the Franciscan order, one of whom was named fray Marcos de Niza (a theologian and priest). Another [was named] fray Daniel (a lay brother), and the other, fray Antonio de Santa María.[87] [Vázquez de Coronado] reached the *provincia* of Culiacán, [where] he then bid farewell to the three friars already named and the Black, who was named {note} Esteban, so that they could go in search of that land. [That was] because fray Marcos de Niza was given preference to go to see it, since this friar had been in Peru when don Pedro de Alvarado passed through the land.[88]

When the aforesaid friars and the Black, Esteban, had gone, it seems that the Black was not going with the support of the friars because [12r] he [was in the habit of] taking the women [the Indians] gave him, collecting turquoises, and amassing a quantity of both. Still, the Indians of those settlements through which they were going understood the Black better, because they had already seen him before. For this reason [the friars] had sent him ahead, to reconnoiter and pacify [the land], so that when they arrived they would have nothing to think about other than collecting reports about what they were searching for.

Third Chapter
how the [Indians] of Cíbola killed the Black, Esteban, and fray Marcos returned in flight

When Esteban parted [12v] from the aforesaid friars, he anticipated that in all of this he would win renown and honor and that the daring and boldness of having alone discovered those multistoried settlements, so famous throughout that land, would be ascribed to him. {discovered} Taking with him [some] of the people who were following him, he tried to cross the unsettled areas there are between Cíbola and the settled land, which he had walked through [before]. He got so far ahead of the friars that when they reached Chichilticale, which is [at] the beginning of the unsettled land, he was already in Cíbola. The unsettled area is eighty leagues across.[89] From Culiacán to the [13r] beginning of the unsettled land [there are] two hundred and twenty leagues, plus the eighty that are in the unsettled land, making three hundred, plus or minus ten.

As I say, when the Black, Esteban, reached Cíbola, he came loaded with numerous turquoises and some beautiful women, [all of which the Indians] had given him. And the Indians who had accompanied him and followed him from all of the settled land he had passed through brought [these things]. The [Indians], traveling under his protection, believed they could traverse the whole land without any risk. However, because the people of that land [Cíbola] may have been more [13v] intelligent than those who were following Esteban, they lodged him in a certain small shelter they had outside the *pueblo*.

The oldest men and those who governed heard his explanations and sought to learn the reason for his coming to that land.[90] When they were fully informed, they went into deliberation for a period of three days. Because of the report the Black gave them, that behind [him] were coming two white men,[91] sent by a great lord, [men] who were well versed in the things of heaven, and that they were coming to instruct them about things divine, [the Indians of Cíbola]

concluded that he must be a spy or guide for some people who were trying to come to conquer them. [This was] because [14r] it seemed nonsense to them to say that the land he was coming from was one of white people who had sent him, when he was black. And they went [back] to him. After [he had offered] other explanations, they resolved to kill him because he asked them for turquoises and women, [which] to them seemed offensive. So they did it, without killing any of those who came with him.[92] And they seized some boys, but they let the rest, who were about sixty persons, return to their lands free.

When these [people], who were returning in terrified flight, managed to find and come across the friars in the unsettled land [14v] sixty leagues from Cíbola,[93] and they delivered the sad news, they made the [friars] so fearful that, not trusting these people, even though they had gone in the Black's company, [the friars] opened the hampers they were carrying and distributed to [the Indians] everything they were bringing. Thus, nothing was left to them except the vestments for saying mass. And they returned from there without examining the land more than [hearing] what the Indians told them.[94] Rather, they traveled by doubling their daily rate, [with] the skirts [of their habits tucked] in their sashes.

Fourth Chapter
how the good Antonio de Mendoza arranged an expedition for the reconnaissance of Cíbola

[15r] After Francisco Vázquez [de] Coronado had dispatched fray Marcos de Niza and his company on the search already reported, he remained in Culiacán occupied in business pertaining to his governorship. He received a particular report of a *provincia* which was to the north on the road traversing the land of Culiacán, which was called Topira.[95] He left immediately, in order to go reconnoiter it with some conquistadores and [native] allies.[96] His going had little result, because they had to cross the mountain range, [which] was very difficult for them. And they found that [Topira] did not match the report, nor [did they find] signs of a good [15v] land. So he returned.

When he reached [Culiacán] he found the friars, who

had just arrived.[97] So great was the magnificence of what they told [him], concerning what the Black, Esteban, had found and what they had heard from the Indians and other reports about the Mar del Sur and islands they had been told of and concerning other wealth, that without further delay the governor departed for the Ciudad de México.[98] He took with him fray Marcos de Niza, so that he could provide information about it to the viceroy. By refusing to inform anyone, except certain persons stealthily and under great [16r] secrecy, he enhanced those things.

When they had arrived in [the Ciudad de] México and met with don Antonio de Mendoza, it immediately began to be spread abroad that the Seven Ciudades Nuño de Guzmán had searched for had been discovered. And the raising of an armed force and the assembly of people began, in order to go to conquer them. The good viceroy had such influence with the friars of the Order of San Francisco that they made fray Marcos provincial. As a result, the pulpits of that order were full of so many marvels, and such magnificent ones, that in a few days more than three hundred Spaniards were assembled and about eight hundred Indians native to Nueva [16v] España.[99] Among the Spaniards [there were] so many men of such great status that I doubt such a noble group of persons has [ever] been assembled in the Indies among such a small number of men, which was three hundred.

Captain general of them all [was] Francisco Vázquez [de] Coronado, the governor of Nueva Galicia, who had been the instigator of everything. The good viceroy don Antonio [de Mendoza] arranged all this because Francisco Vázquez was then the person closest to him by [his own] preference, since he considered [Vázquez de Coronado] an astute and capable man of good judgment. And furthermore, a *caballero*, which he was held to be. [Thus], he would likely give [17r] more attention[100] and concern to the position in which [the viceroy] placed him and the duty he bore (or at least to the honor he had earned and was yet to earn) in leading such [a group of] *caballeros* under his command than to the income he was leaving behind in Nueva España.[101] But it did not turn out that way, as will be seen hereafter at the end of this treatise. He did not know how to maintain that position or the governorship he held.

Fifth Chapter
which deals with who went as captains to Cíbola

Because the viceroy don Antonio de Mendoza saw the very [17v] noble group of people he had assembled and the spirit and willingness with which they all had offered themselves to him, and knowing their individual worth, he would have wanted to make each of them captain of an armed force. Because, however, the total number of [people] was small, he could not do what he wished. Thus he arranged the contingents and captaincies as it seemed [best] to him. Because it was arranged by his hand [and] he was so much loved and obeyed, no one would stray from his order.

Once everyone understood who the general was, he appointed as *alférez general* don Pedro de Tovar, a *caballero* and the young son of don [18r] Fernando de Tovar, a guard and the *mayordomo mayor* of doña Juana, the queen, our natural mistress (may she be in glory).[102] As *maestre de campo*, Lope de Samaniego, the *alcaide* of the dockyards of [the Ciudad de] México [and] a *caballero* very suitable for [that] post.[103] [The] captains were don Tristán de Arellano, don [Diego] de Guevara (the son of don Juan de Guevara and nephew of the Conde de Oñate), don García López de Cárdenas, don Rodrigo Maldonado (brother-in-law of the Duque del Infantado), Diego López (one of the twenty-four councilmen of Sevilla), [and] Diego Gutiérrez de la Caballería.[104] [18v] All the rest of the *caballeros* went under the standard of the general, because they were distinguished persons. Some of them later were captains and continued in that [rank] by order of the viceroy, and others [by order of] the general Francisco Vázquez. I will name some of those whom I remember; they were {+} Francisco de Barrionuevo (a *caballero* from Granada), {+} Juan de Zaldívar, Francisco de Ovando, Juan Gallego, Melchior Díaz (who had been captain and *alcalde mayor* of Culiacán, who, although he was not a *caballero*, personally merited the post [19r] he held.)[105] {/} The other notable *caballeros* were don Alonso Manrique de Lara, don Lope de Urrea (a *caballero* from Aragón), Gómez Suárez de Figueroa, Luis Ramírez de Vargas, Juan de Sotomayor, Francisco Gorbalán, the *factor* Riberos, and other *caballeros*, men of high status, whom today I do not remember.[106] The captain of footmen was Pablo de Melgosa (a native of Burgos), and [the captain] of artillery [was] Hernando de Alvarado (a *caballero* from Santander).[107]

I say [again] that with time I have lost the memory of many fine *hidalgos* whom it would have been [19v] good to name, because [then] the reason could be seen and understood why I must say that on this expedition there was the most splendid group of people that has [ever] been assembled in the Indies to go in search of new lands. Except they may have been unfortunate in having a captain who was leaving income and an excellent young and noble wife behind in Nueva España. [These things] were no small spurs for what he ended up doing.

Sixth Chapter
how all of the captaincies came together at Compostela and departed in formation for the journey

As soon as don Antonio de Mendoza had arranged and set in order [20r] what we have told about, and established the captaincies or the captains, he provided assistance to the men-at-arms ([those] individuals most in need) from His Majesty's treasury.[108] Because it seemed to him that if the expedition departed from [the Ciudad de] México en masse, it would do some injury [as it passed] through the lands of the [native] allies,[109] he decreed that they were to go [separately] to meet in the *ciudad* of Compostela, the seat of government of the Nuevo Reino de Galicia, a hundred and ten leagues from [the Ciudad de] México, in order to start the expedition in an orderly manner from there. There is nothing to report that occurred during this trip [to Compostela].[110] [20v] Finally, on the Tuesday of Carnival in the year [one thousand five hundred and forty {1540}],[111] everyone came together.

When [the viceroy] had dispatched the whole company from [the Ciudad de] México, he arranged how [Hernando] de Alarcón was to depart with two *navíos* which were in the port of Navidad on the Costa del Sur and travel to the port of Jalisco, in order to carry the clothing the men-at arms could not take [with them].[112] [And] so he would travel coastwise behind the expedition, because it was understood, according to the report [of fray Marcos], that they had to

travel through the land near the seacoast and that, by means of the rivers, [21r] we would get to the ports and the *navíos* would always have news of the expedition. It later became apparent that this was untrue, so that all of the clothing went astray or, rather, it was lost to its owners, as will be told farther on.

As soon as the viceroy had sent [Alarcón] off and put the finishing touches on everything, he [himself] departed for Compostela, accompanied by many *caballeros* and noblemen. He spent New Year's Day of [one thousand five hundred and forty] at Pátzcuaro, which is the episcopal seat of Michoacán.[113] From there he crossed the entire land of Nueva España, met by great pleasure and happiness and splendid receptions, [21v] all the way to Compostela (which is, as I have said, [a distance of] a hundred and ten leagues). There he found the whole company assembled, well cared for and given lodging by Cristóbal de Oñate, who at the time was the person who had sole charge of that jurisdiction.[114] He had supported and was captain of all that land, even though Francisco Vázquez was governor.

When [Mendoza] had arrived to the great joy of everyone, he conducted a muster of the people he was sending and found all those whom we have pointed out.[115] And he distributed the captaincies. The next day after that was done, following mass, [22r] the viceroy made a brief and eloquent speech to everyone assembled, both captains and fighting men, imposing on them the loyalty owed to their general. He made them understand fully the benefits that could result from making that expedition, both from the conversion of the peoples there and in profit to those who conquered that land.[116] [He also made clear] the service it would be to His Majesty and the obligation they were placing [the king] under to always aid and support them.

That finished, he took everyone's oath at large (although according to rank), [sworn] on the Gospels contained in a missal, both [22v] {/} by captains and fighting men. [They swore] that they would follow their general and would do [so] throughout the expedition. [Further], that they would fulfill everything that they were ordered [to do] by him. Thereafter they complied faithfully with what [they swore], as will be seen.

The following day after this was done, the expedition

departed with its banners unfurled. The viceroy don Antonio accompanied it for two days' travel, at which point he bade it farewell, returning to Nueva España attended by his friends.

{*/*}   *Seventh Chapter*
how the expedition reached Chiametla[117] and how [the natives of Chiametla] killed the *maestre de campo* and what else happened until [23r] they arrived at Culiacán

When the viceroy don Antonio had left, the expedition traveled according to its daily marches. Because each person was compelled to carry his belongings on horseback[118] and not everyone knew how to harness [a horse], and [because, further,] the horses were wide and fat when they set off,[119] there was great difficulty and annoyance during the first days' travel. Many [persons] left behind many costly objects and gave them, at no charge, to who[ever] wanted them, in order not [to have] to load them. [But] in the end and with time, necessity (which is a teacher) made masters of [the inexperienced]. From that point on, many *caballeros* could be seen [who had] turned into muleteers, and anyone who [23v] rejected that work was not held to be a man.

With other difficulties, which, at the time, they took to be great, the expedition arrived at Chiametla. There, because of a lack of foodstuffs, it was compelled to halt for several days. During that time the *maestre de campo*, Lope de Samaniego, with a certain company, went in search of food. At one *pueblo*, because he imprudently entered a thicket in pursuit of enemies, they shot him in the eye with an arrow and pierced his brain,[120] from which he died immediately, right there.[121] They also shot another five or six of his companions with arrows.

As soon as he was dead, Diego López, one of the twenty-four councilmen [24r] of Sevilla, gathered the troop together and dispatched [a man] to make the general aware [of what had happened]. And he set a guard around the *pueblo* and the supply of food. When this was known in the camp it caused a great disturbance. [Samaniego] was buried. They made several *entradas*, as a result of which they brought back supplies of food and several native prisoners. At least those who seemed to be from the area where the *maestre de campo* died were hung.[122]

It seems that when the general Francisco Vázquez had left Culiacán with fray Marcos to give the previously mentioned report to the viceroy don Antonio de Mendoza, he left [24v] it arranged that the captain Melchior Díaz and Juan de Zaldívar would go forth from Culiacán with a dozen good men, in search of what fray Marcos had seen and heard. They departed and traveled as far as Chichilticale, which is at the beginning of the unsettled region two hundred and twenty leagues from Culiacán, and they found nothing of worth.[123] They returned just as the expedition was planning to leave from Chiametla. They arrived and talked with the general. Despite the privacy in which it was discussed, the bad news was soon rumored.[124] There were some statements [made] which, although embellished, did not [25r] disguise what the news was.

Fray Marcos de Niza, being aware that some [people] were upset, dispelled that danger by vowing that what they had seen [so far] was excellent and that he had gone there and would place the expedition in a land where they would fill their hands.[125] With this [the disturbance] was quelled, and [those who were discontented] put on good faces.

The expedition traveled on from there until arriving at Culiacán, making several *entradas* in the *tierra de guerra*[126] in order to seize supplies of food. They arrived two leagues from the *villa* of Culiacán on the evening before Easter. The *vecinos* [of Culiacán] came out to that place to welcome their governor. [25v] They requested that he not enter the *villa* until the second day, [the day] after Easter.[127]

Eighth Chapter
how the expedition entered the *villa* of Culiacán and the welcome that was given and what else happened until its departure

It being the second day, [the day] after Easter, the expedition set out in the morning to enter the *villa*. In a cleared space at the entrance [of the *villa*] the [men] of the *villa* sallied forth, making a show of trying to defend the *villa*. [They were] arranged according to the practices of war in squadrons, on foot and on horseback, with their artillery leveled (which was [26r] seven bronze pieces). With them was a portion of our fighting men. Our side, in the same order, opened a skirmish with them. Thus they advanced, attacking after the artillery had been discharged on both sides, so that the *villa* was taken from them by force of arms. This was a lighthearted show and reception, though not for the artilleryman who lost a hand because the order to light [the charge] had been given before he finished removing the ramrod from [26v] an artillery piece.[128]

When the *villa* had been taken, [the people of the expedition] were soon well lodged and quartered by the *vecinos*. Even though quarters for everyone had been set up outside the *villa*, [the *vecinos*] placed all the *caballeros* and persons of rank who went on the expedition in their own houses because they were all highly respected men. Some *vecinos* were not badly recompensed for this hospitality, because everyone came decked out in rich dress and from that point they had to take food supplies on their pack animals and necessarily had to leave their [27r] valuables behind.[129] Many [people] preferred to give them to their hosts, instead of putting them at risk at sea (or having them carried by the *navíos* which had come along the coast, following the expedition, in order to take the baggage, as has already been said).

Thus, when they had all arrived and been lodged in the *villa*, the general, under instructions from the viceroy don Antonio, installed Fernandarias de Saavedra as captain and lieutenant [governor] there. [He was] an uncle of Hernandarias de Saavedra, the Conde de Castellar, who was *alguacil mayor* of Sevilla.[130]

The expedition rested there for several days [27v], [because] the *vecinos* had collected a great supply of food-stuffs that year. They split them with the people of our expedition, each one with his guests, with great and special affection, so that not only was there a great quantity for consumption there but even to take away. Because of this, at the time of departure, more than six hundred loaded pack animals left, as well as the [native] allies and servants, who amounted to more than a thousand persons.

When fifteen days had passed the general announced that he would go on ahead with as many as fifty horsemen and a few footmen, as well as most of the [native] allies.[131] He would leave the [rest of the] expedition, which would follow him [28r] after fifteen days. And he left don Tristán de Arellano as his lieutenant [general].

During the time before the general departed, a "charming"[132] event occurred. Because it was such, I give an account of it. [What happened] was that a young man-at-arms called Trujillo pretended to have had a prophetic vision while bathing in the river and defecating. With his appearance altered, he was brought before the general, at which point he explained that the devil had told him that he [Trujillo] would kill the general and marry his wife, doña Beatriz, and that she would give him great treasures. And [he said] other crude things. [28v] From [this event] fray Marcos de Niza drew several sermons, ascribing it to the devil, who, envious of the benefit that was sure to result from that expedition, was trying to ruin it by that means. And it did not end with that only. The friars who went on the expedition wrote about [the event] to their monasteries, because of which complete falsehoods were told about it from the pulpits of [the Ciudad de] México. The general ordered Trujillo to remain in that *villa* and not to make the journey, which is what he was after when he concocted that [29r] hoax, according to what afterward appeared to be true.[133]

The general departed with the people already mentioned, continuing his journey, and afterward the [rest of the] troop [departed], as will be told.

Ninth Chapter
how the [main body of the] expedition left
Culiacán and [arrived at] Señora and the general
reached Cíbola and what else occurred

As has been told, the general departed from the valley of Culiacán, continuing his travel at a fairly rapid pace [and] taking with him the friars, none of whom wanted to stay behind with the [main body of the] expedition. After three days' travel a [29v] friar named fray Antonio Vitoria, who was a preaching friar, broke a leg.[134] In order that he might recover, he was sent back along the route, and later he traveled with the [main] expedition, which was no small comfort to everyone.

The general and his troop crossed the land without opposition, because they found everyone to be at peace because the Indians were familiar with fray Marcos and some of those who had traveled with Captain Melchior Díaz when he and Juan de Zaldívar went to make a reconnaissance.

Because the general had traversed the populated land and arrived at Chichilticale, [which is at the] beginning [30r] of the unsettled land, and saw nothing worthwhile, he did not fail to feel some distress. [This was] because although the news of what lay ahead was marvelous, there was no one who had seen it,[135] except the Indians who had gone with the Black, [Esteban], who already had been caught in several lies. [And] it grieved everyone to see that the renown of Chichilticale was reduced to a ruined roofless house, although in former times, when it was inhabited, it appeared to have been a strongly fortified building.[136] It was well understood that it had been built by civilized [and] warlike foreigners who had come from far away.[137] This building was [30v] made of bright red earth.

From there they proceeded [through] the unsettled land and in fifteen days arrived eight leagues from Cíbola at a river which they named Río Bermejo because its water flowed muddy and bright red.[138] In this river there were whiskered carp like [those] in Spain.[139] It was here that the first Indians of that land were seen. They were two, who fled and went to spread the news [of the Spaniards' arrival]. The next day at night, two leagues from the *pueblo*, a number of Indians taunted [them] from a safe place.[140] Although the troop had been warned, some [of them] became so flustered [31r] that there were some who put their saddles on backward. {/} These were persons [who were] untried. The skilled [men] immediately mounted and the company charged off. The Indians fled in the way that one who knows the land [does], so that none [of them] could be caught.

The following day they entered the settled land in good order. When they saw the first *pueblo*, which was Cíbola, such were the curses that some of them hurled at fray Marcos that may God not allow them to reach [his ears]. It is a small *pueblo* crowded together and spilling down a cliff.[141] In Nueva España there are *estancias* which from a distance have [31v] a better appearance. It is a *pueblo* with three and four upper stories and with up to two hundred fighting men. The houses are small and not very roomy. They do not have [individual] patios; a single patio serves a neighborhood.[142]

The people of the area had come together there, because it is a *provincia* of seven *pueblos* in which there are other *pueblos* very much larger and stronger than Cíbola.[143] These people waited in the countryside in view of the *pueblo*, arranged in their units. Because in response to the *requerimientos* which [the Spaniards] made to them through interpreters they refused to come to peace, but instead showed themselves to be angry, [the general] gave the order to attack [32r] them.[144] They were very quickly routed, and then [the troop] moved to take possession of the *pueblo*. This was more than a little difficult because [the Indians] have a narrow entryway [with] twists and turns.[145]

When the general entered, they knocked him down flat with a large rock. And they would have killed him if it were not for don García López de Cárdenas and Hernando de Alvarado, who threw themselves over him and took him away, [meanwhile] receiving blows from stones, which were not insignificant. But because there is no way to resist the utmost fury of the Spaniards, in less than an hour the *pueblo* was entered and taken.[146] [32v] Food supplies were found [there], which is what there was most need for.

From that time on the whole *provincia* came to peace.

The [main body of the] expedition, which had stayed [at Culiacán] under don Tristán de Arellano, departed [from there] loaded with food, following the general [Arellano],[147] all of them on foot with their lances over their shoulders. This was so that they could take the horses loaded down. Following day after day of travel and with no little difficulty, they arrived at a *provincia* which Cabeza de Vaca had named Corazones [hearts] because there [the Indians] offered [Cabeza de Vaca and his companions] many animal hearts.[148] Then [Arellano] [33r] began settling a *pueblo*, calling it San Gerónimo de los Corazones. And immediately he began settling it. When he saw that [the *pueblo*] could not be supported, he afterward transferred it to a valley which [the Indians] call Persona, I mean Senora. The Spaniards called it Señora, and I will call it that from here on.[149]

From there [Maldonado] left to look downriver for {to look for} the port along the seacoast, in order to learn about the *navíos*. They did not find [them]. When he returned, don Rodrigo Maldonado, who had gone as leader of the search for the *navíos,* brought with him an Indian so large and tall that the tallest man [33v] in the camp did not reach his chest.[150] It was said that on that coast there were other Indians even taller.

At that place [Señora] [the main expedition] rested [during] the rains, and afterward the expedition and the *villa* of Señora moved, in order to be able to await the general's order, because there were food supplies in the area [to which they moved].

Halfway through the month of October, Captains Melchior Díaz and Juan Gallego came from Cíbola. Juan Gallego [was going] to Nueva España, and Melchior Díaz [was coming] to stay in the new *villa* of Los [34r] Corazones as captain of the people who were staying there, and [also] to go to find the *navíos* along that coast.

Tenth Chapter

how the [main expedition] departed from the *villa* of Señora, leaving the *villa* settled, and how it reached Cíbola; what happened to Captain Melchior Díaz along the way while going in search of the *navíos,* and how he reconnoitered the Río del Tizón[151]

As soon as Melchior Díaz and Juan Gallego arrived at the *villa* of Señora,[152] [34v] the departure of the expedition for Cíbola was announced. {Cíbola} And [it was also announced] that Melchior Díaz was to remain as captain in that *villa* with eighty men and that Juan Gallego was going to Nueva España with a message for the viceroy.[153] [Gallego] was taking in his company fray Marcos, who, seeing that his report had turned out to be incorrect about everything, did not consider himself safe staying in Cíbola. [That is] because the *reinos* he had told about had not been found, nor [had the] populous *ciudades* or wealth of gold or rich jewels that had been publicized, nor [the] brocades or other things that had been told about from the pulpits.[154]

[35r] So as soon as this was announced, the people who were to remain [at Señora] were picked out. The rest loaded up food supplies and, in the middle of September, they departed in order, [taking] the route to Cíbola, following their general, don Tristán de Arellano. [Díaz][155] stayed in the new *villa* with the lower-class people. As a result, from that time on there never failed to be quarrels and mutinies. {/} [That happened] because when the main expedition had left, Captain Melchior Díaz took twenty-five of the choicest

men, leaving in his stead one Diego de Alcaraz, a man not well prepared [35v] to have people under his command.[156]

[Díaz] went forth in search of the seacoast with guides, [traveling] between north and west.[157] Having traveled about a hundred and fifty leagues, they came upon a *provincia* of exceedingly tall and muscular people, like giants.[158] However, [they are] naked people and make their residence in long thatched *chozas* excavated into the ground in the same way pig pens [are], so that nothing rises above the ground except the thatch.[159] [The natives] entered [them] at one end and exited at the other. [36r] More than a hundred persons, both young and old,[160] slept in a single *choza.* When they bore loads, they carried the weight of more than three or four *quintales* on top of their heads.[161] It was observed, [once when] our people wanted to bring a log to the fire and six men could not bring it, that one of [the natives] came and lifted it in his arms and by himself placed it on his head and carried it very easily.

[These people] eat cornbread that is baked under embers in the ashes. [They make it] bigger than the large Castilian *hogazas.*[162] [36v] In order to walk from place to place, because of the great cold, they take along a smoldering stick in one hand, with which they travel, warming the other [hand] and their body.[163] They travel in this way, exchanging it [for a fresh stick] from time to time. Because of this [the expedition members] named a great river that runs through that land the Río del Tizón [firebrand].

It is a powerful river which was half a league across more than two leagues from its mouth.[164] There the captain understood [from] an interpreter that the *navíos* had been three days' journey downstream toward the sea. When they reached a place where the *navíos* had been (which was more than fifteen leagues upriver [37r] from the port at its mouth) they found written on a tree, "Alarcón reached this point. At the foot of this tree there are letters."[165] The letters were extracted, and by means of them they understood that [Alarcón's party] had been there for some time waiting for news of the expedition. Alarcón had returned from there to Nueva España with the *navíos,* since he could not sail farther, because the sea was [instead] a gulf. He was returning along the Isla del Marqués, which they [now] call

California. And they reported that California [37v] was not an island but a cape of the continent, [arising] from the bend of that gulf.[166]

When the captain understood this he returned upriver (without seeing the sea), in order to search for a ford by which to cross to the opposite bank so as to follow that other shore. Because they [then] walked for five or six days [without finding a ford], it seemed [best] to them to cross on rafts. In order to do this, they summoned many people of that land. [The natives] had been trying to arrange to make an assault on our people and had been looking for the suitable occasion. Seeing that [Díaz's company] was trying to cross over, [the natives] came quickly and at full speed to build the rafts. [38r] [This was] because they [could] thus catch them in the water and drown them. Or else, being divided in such a way, they would not be able to aid or help each other.

During the time when the rafts were being built, a man-at-arms[167] who had gone to scout the countryside, while crossing through a forest, saw many armed people [natives] waiting for [Díaz's] people to cross [the river]. He reported this, and secretly an Indian was confined in order to learn the truth from him. Because they inflicted pain on him, he told about the whole plan they had arranged for when [Díaz's company] was crossing.[168] {/} The plan was that when [38v] part of our people had crossed and part was crossing the river and [another] part was waiting to cross, the [natives] on the rafts would try to drown those they were carrying across. And the remainder of the [native] people would come forth to attack both the groups on land. If they had [had] good judgment and spirit, they would have succeeded in their enterprise, because they had the manpower.[169]

When he understood their intention, the captain secretly had the Indian killed who confessed what was afoot. And he was thrown into the river that night with a weight, so that the Indians would not realize they had been discovered. Because they sensed the suspicion of our people the next day, [39r] they revealed themselves as hostile, firing showers of arrows. Because the horses began to catch up with them and the lances hurt them pitilessly and also the arquebusiers were making good shots, they had to leave the field and take to the forest, until it seemed not a man of them remained around there.

Thus the troop crossed [the river] safely. The [native] allies were ferrymen, and on their return the Spaniards crossed the horses[170] at the same time[171] as the rafts. Which is where we will leave them, walking [around], in order to relate how the company that was traveling to Cíbola fared.[172]

Because the [expedition] traveled in an orderly way and the general [39v] had left everything peaceful, {/} everywhere they found the native people happy [and] without fear, and they willingly allowed themselves to be directed. In one *provincia*, called Vacapan,[173] there were vast numbers of cactus fruits, from which the natives make a great amount of preserves. And they presented much of this conserve [to the expedition]. When the people of the expedition ate it, they all collapsed as though sleepy, with headaches and fever, so that if the natives had tried, they could have done much harm to the people. This lasted twenty-four hours,[174] after [40r] which they departed from there.

Traveling on, they reached Chichilticale. After they had left there, one day the guards saw a herd of rams pass by. I saw them and followed them.[175] They were large bodied; their coats [were] exceedingly long; their horns [were] very large and heavy. In order to run, they lift their faces and throw their horns over their backs. They run much [of the time] over rough land, so that we were unable to lance them and had to let them go. After three days' travel into the unsettled area, a horn was found on the bank of a river which is in a very deep canyon.[176] [40v] After the general had seen it, he left it there, so that those of his expedition would see it. It was one *braza* in length and, at its base, as thick as a man's thigh.[177] In features[178] it seemed more likely to be from a goat than from [any] other animal. It was something to see.

Passing onward, the company traveled as far as one day's journey from Cíbola. A great whirlwind of very cold air came up late that afternoon. Then it was followed by a heavy snowstorm, which meant great confusion for the servants. The [41r] expedition traveled on with great risk to the [native] allies, until it reached some hollows among very large boulders, at which [the company] arrived when it was fully dark. [The allies were in such peril] because since they were from Nueva España and most of them from hot climates, they suffered the cold badly that day. So much so that the next day there was much done looking after them and carrying them on horseback, while the men-at-arms went on foot. With this difficulty, the expedition reached Cíbola, where its general awaited it. Once lodgings were prepared, [the expedition] was again united there, although some captains and [other] persons who had gone to reconnoiter [41v] other *provincias* were missing.

Eleventh Chapter

how don Pedro de Tovar found Tusayán, or Tutahaco, and don García López de Cárdenas saw the Río del Tizón and what else occurred

While the things already narrated were happening, because Cíbola was at peace,[179] General Francisco Vázquez sought to learn from the [natives] of that land what *provincias* there were in the vicinity and to have them inform their neighbors and allies that Christians had come to their land. Also, that they wanted nothing other than to be their friends and to have news of fine lands [42r] to settle. Further, [they were to be asked] to come and see [the Christians] and talk [with them]. And thus [the Cíbolans] made it known in those places that traded and had contact with them.

{/} They provided information about a *provincia* of seven *pueblos* of the same sort as theirs, although there was some disagreement [between them], so that they did not have dealings with them. This *provincia* is called Tusayán. It is twenty-five leagues from Cíbola.[180] The *pueblos* are multistoried, and the people are quarrelsome among themselves. The general had sent don Pedro de Tovar to them with seventeen horsemen and three or four footmen. One Franciscan friar, fray Juan de Padilla, went with them. [42v] In his youth he had been a combative fellow.[181]

When [Tovar's company] had arrived in that land, they entered it so stealthily that they were not noticed by anyone. That was because between *provincias* there are no settlements or isolated houses, nor do the people leave their *pueblos* more than [to go] to their properties.[182] This was especially true at that time because they had received word that Cíbola had been overrun by the most ferocious people who rode animals that ate people. Among those who had not seen horses this information was so extraordinary that it threw them into amazement. This was so much the case that our people

FIGURE 28.2. Walpi Pueblo, Hopi (Castañeda de Nájera's Tusayán), Arizona. Courtesy Museum of New Mexico, neg. no. 74864.

arrived late at night and [43r] were able to conceal themselves at the base of the cliff below the *pueblo* and to be there listening to the natives talking in their houses.[183] However, they were discovered early in the morning.

The [people] of that land set themselves in formation and came forth against them on the flank, in good order with bows and shields and wooden clubs, without losing their order. There was an opportunity for the interpreters to talk with them and recite the *requerimiento* to them, because they are people of good understanding.[184] After all this, though, they marked out lines, demanding that our people not cross them toward their *pueblos*, which were some distance away. [43v] [But Tovar's people] walked on, crossing some of the lines and talking to [the natives]. [It] went so far that one of them became upset and struck a horse on the fittings of the bit with a club.

Fray Juan, angered by the time that was being wasted with them, said to the captain, "Truly, I don't know why we have come here."[185] {/} In view of this, [Tovar's company] attacked. This was so sudden that they knocked down many Indians. They were immediately thrown into confusion and fled to the *pueblo*. But [Tovar's company] did not attack others at that time. Such was the speed with which the [people in the] *pueblo* came out in peace with gifts that immediately [44r] the troop was ordered to disengage and not to do them any more harm.

The captain and those who were with him looked for a place to establish their *real* near the *pueblo*.[186] There they were,

I mean there where they dismounted, the people [of the *pueblo*] came in peace, saying that they were coming to render obedience on behalf of the whole *provincia*,[187] that they wanted [Tovar's company] to consider them friends, and that they should accept the gift they were giving them. That was some cotton clothing, although not much because in that land there is not any [cotton].[188] They [also] gave some dressed hides, much flour, *pinole*,[189] corn, and [44v] native fowl. Afterward they gave[190] some turquoises, although only a few.

That day the people of that land were gathered together, and they came to render obedience. They freely relinquished their *pueblos* and allowed [Tovar's company] to enter them in order to trade, buy, sell, and exchange. [The land] is governed in the same way as Cíbola, by a council of the oldest persons.[191] They have their designated governors and captains. At that place word of a large river was received. Several days' journey downstream along the river there were marvelous peoples with large bodies. Because don Pedro de Tovar [45r] did not have a commission for a longer period, he returned from there and gave this report to the general.

Promptly, [Vázquez de Coronado] dispatched don García López de Cárdenas there, with about twelve companions, to reconnoiter this river. When he reached Tusayán [López de Cárdenas] was well received and lodged by the natives. They gave him guides in order to continue his travels. [López de Cárdenas and his company] left there loaded with food supplies because they had to travel through unsettled land until [they reached] a settlement which the

Indians said was more than twenty days' travel [farther on]. When they had walked for twenty days they arrived at the canyons of the river.[192] When [the company] was camped at its edge it appeared [45v] that it was more than three or four leagues through the air to the opposite edge. It is an elevated land covered by forests of short, gnarled pines. [It is] very cold to the north.[193] Even though it was [then] the hot season, it was not possible to live at this canyon because of the cold. For three days they searched for the way down to the river.

From that height the stream appeared to be one *braza* across, but from the reports of the Indians it stretched half a league wide.[194] Descent [to the river] was impossible, because at the end of three days the most agile [men] set themselves to climbing down at a place that seemed to them the least difficult. [They were] Captain Melgosa, [46r] a Juan Galeras,[195] and another companion. They descended a long time in view of those [who remained] above, until their forms were lost from sight. Because of the height,[196] [one] was unable to see them. They returned at the hour of four in the afternoon.[197] They did not complete the descent, because of great obstacles they found. What from above seemed easy was not, but rather very rugged and rough. They said that they had descended a third of the way. From where they had reached, the river appeared to be very large. In accordance with what they saw, what the Indians said about its width was true. From the [46v] top they had distinguished several smallish blocks broken off from the cliff, apparently the

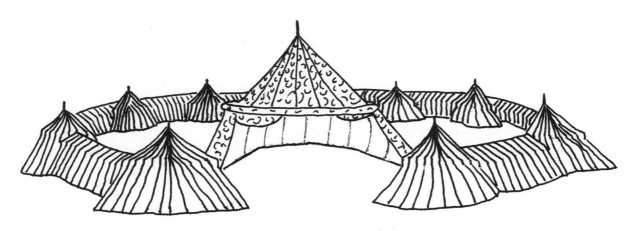

FIGURE 28.3. A *real,* or tent encampment, after *Field of the Cloth of Gold,* painting by unknown artist, about 1545, in the Royal Collection at Hampton Court Palace, England.

height of a man. The [men] who climbed down swore that when they got to them, they were larger than the principal [church] tower in Sevilla.[198]

[López de Cárdenas's company] did not travel any farther, near to and along the canyon of the river, because there was no water. Until that point, every day in the late afternoon they had made a side trip of one or two leagues into the interior in search of streams. When they had traveled another four days the guides said it was impossible to go on because there was no water in [the next] three or four days of travel. Because of that, when [47r] [the Indians themselves] traveled that way, they brought women along loaded with water in gourd jars. They buried the gourd jars of water for their return. [They also said] that the distance our people traveled in two days they traveled in one.[199]

This river was the [Río] del Tizón, much closer to its source than at the place beyond which Melchior Díaz and his company did not pass. According to what was later apparent, these Indians were at the same level [of society]. [López de Cárdenas's company] turned around at that point, so that trip had no further result. En route they saw a string of beads [made by] water that fell from a [47v] great rock. They learned from the guides that some of the clusters that hung like crystal breasts[200] were salt. They went [up] to it and gathered a quantity, which they brought back and distributed when they reached Cíbola. There they gave a written report of what they had seen to their general, because one Pedro de Sotomayor had gone with don García López. And [Sotomayor] was going along as chronicler of the expedition.[201]

The *pueblos* of that *provincia* remained at peace even though they were never visited again. Nor did [the members of the expedition] learn about or try to find other settlements along that route.

Twelfth Chapter
how [48r] people from Cicuyc came to see the Christians and how Hernando de Alvarado went to see the [bison]

During the time they were involved in these reconnaissances some Indians came to Cíbola from a *pueblo* that is seventy leagues from that *provincia*, eastward toward the interior. They call it by the name Cicuyc.[202] Among them came a

captain to whom our people gave the name {+} Bigotes, because he had long mustaches.[203] He was a tall young man, well disposed and with a vigorous expression. {/} This [man] told the general that because of the report they had been given they were coming to be of service to him [48v] [and] in order to present themselves to [the Christians] as allies. [He said] that if [the Christians] had to travel through their land, they would consider them allies.[204] They made a gift of cured hides, shields, and head armor,[205] [which] was received with much affection. The general gave them drinking vessels of glass, glass beads, and hawksbells, which they esteemed greatly as something never before seen by them.[206]

They gave a report of [bison]. It was deduced from [the image of] one which [an Indian] bore tattooed on his body[207] that it was a cow [they were referring to]. By means of the hides this could not be determined, because the hair was curly and so gray[208] that it was impossible to learn what [animal] those hides came from.

The general ordered [49r] that Hernando de Alvarado go with [Bigotes's company] with twenty companions and a commission for eighty days. He was to return to make a report of what they found. This Captain Alvarado [then] pursued his journey. After five days' travel they arrived at a *pueblo* called Acuco which was situated on top of a great rock.[209] It was [a *pueblo*] of about two hundred warriors, marauders feared throughout the land and region. The *pueblo* was extremely strong because it was [immediately] above the entrance to the rock, which everywhere was sheer stone of such great height that it would take a well-handled arquebus to shoot [49v] a ball onto the top. There was only one way up, a stairway cut out by hand. It began at the top of a short, steep incline which that part formed. Near the ground this stairway was wide for about two hundred steps, until it reached the rock [itself]. Then there is another [stairway from that point], narrow and next to the rock, of about one hundred steps. At the top of this they have to climb up on the rock [itself for a distance of] about three times the height of a man by means of cavities[210] into which they insert their toes. And [the same] is done with their hands. At the top is a large, dry-laid stone wall. From there, without exposing themselves, they can [50r] knock down so many [people] that no armed force would be strong [enough] to win entrance from them.[211]

Figure 28.4. Women at water hole, Acoma Pueblo, 1904. Photograph by Edward S. Curtis. Courtesy Museum of New Mexico, neg. no. 76958.

On top there is space for planting and harvesting a very large amount of corn. And [there are] cisterns for collecting snow and water.[212]

These people came out on the plain below [prepared] for war.[213] [Even] the best reasoning was of no avail with them. They marked lines, intending to stop our people from crossing them.[214] When, however, they saw themselves attacked [with] a sudden rush, they immediately surrendered the plaza, I mean came to peace.[215] Before they could be hurt, they performed their peace rituals, which [were] to come up to the horses, take their sweat and smear themselves with [50v] it, and form crosses with the fingers of their hands. The surest [guarantee] of peace, though, is to join hands, one with the other. This [promise] these [people] hold inviolate. [The people of Acuco] presented a great many very large roosters with wattles [turkeys], much bread, many cured deer hides, *pinole,* flour, and corn.

{note} From there, after three days' journey, they reached a *provincia* called Triguex.[216] All [of the people] came forth in peace, seeing that men feared throughout all those *provincias* were traveling with Bigotes. From that place Alvarado sent word to the general to come to that land to spend the winter. [51r] The general relaxed more than a little with news that the land was improving. After five days' travel from there [Alvarado] reached Cicuyc, a very strong *pueblo* with four-storied [buildings]. The [people] of the *pueblo* came out to welcome Hernando de Alvarado and their [own] captain with demonstrations of happiness. They took [Alvarado] into the *pueblo* with drums and flutes, of which there are many there similar to fifes. And they offered him a large gift of clothing and turquoises, of which there are a great many in that land.

{note} [Alvarado's company] rested there for several days, and they acquired as interpreter an Indian slave,[217] a native of that [51v] part of the land which extends toward La Florida, the interior land (which is the area don Fernando de Soto reconnoitered at the end [of his travels]).[218] This [man][219] gave a report of grand settlements, which he should not have. Hernando de Alvarado took him [with him] to the [bison] as a guide. Such and so many were the things that he said about riches of gold and silver[220] that there were in his land that [Alvarado's company] did not diligently pursue the search for [bison] beyond seeing a few. Then they returned in order to give the general the magnificent news. They called the Indian Turco because by his appearance he seemed like one.[221]

At that time the general had sent don García[222] López de [52r] Cárdenas to Tiguex with a troop to prepare quarters, in order to take the expedition there to spend the winter. [The main body of the expedition] had arrived by then from Señora. When Hernando de Alvarado reached Tiguex on returning from Cicuyc, he found don García López de Cárdenas. And [therefore] it was unnecessary for him to go farther. Because it was important that the natives see, I mean give up a place where the Spaniards would be lodged, they were forced to abandon one *pueblo* and were given shelter in the other *pueblos* of their friends.[223] They did not take [with them] more than their persons and clothing.

Information came to their knowledge there about many *pueblos* [52v] toward the north,[224] because of which I believe it would have been much better to follow that route rather than El Turco (which was the cause of all the poor results which [the expedition] had).[225]

Thirteenth Chapter
how the general arrived by way of Tutahaco
with a few people and how he left the expedition with
don Tristán, who led it to Tiguex

All of the things already mentioned had occurred when don Tristán de Arellano reached Cíbola from Señora.[226] Because of a report the general had received of a *provincia* of eight *pueblos*, as soon as [Arellano] arrived [Vázquez de Coronado] took thirty of the best rested men [53r] and went, with good guides whom he took along, to see it and from there to take the route to Tiguex. He left orders that when

the people had rested for twenty days, don Tristán de Arellano was to set out with the expedition on the direct trail to Tiguex.

Thus he pursued his route, on which it happened that from the day they set out from [their] lodging until noon of the third day they did not drink water. [Then] they saw a snow-covered mountain range to which they went in search of water. Neither their horses nor the servants could stand it because of the severe cold. Nevertheless, after eight days' travel they reached Tutahaco with great difficulty.[227] There it was learned that downstream on that river there were [53v] other *pueblos*. [The people of] these [*pueblos* of Tutahaco] came forth in peace. They are multistoried *pueblos* like those of Tiguex, with the same clothing.

The general departed from there, visiting the whole *provincia* upstream along the river until he arrived at Tiguex. There he found Hernando de Alvarado and El Turco. The celebrations he made were not few as a result of such good news. [This was] because [El Turco] said that in his land there was a river in a plain which was two leagues wide. There were fish as large as horses there. And [there were] a great many exceedingly large canoes with more than twenty rowers on each side, which also carried sails.[228] The lords traveled on the poop, seated [54r] beneath awnings. On the prow [there was] a large eagle of gold. He said further that the lord of that land slept during siesta under a great tree on which a great number of small golden bells hung. In the breeze they gave him pleasure. Further, he said that generally everyone's common serving dishes were worked silver. And the pitchers, plates, and small bowls were [made] of gold. [El Turco] called gold "acochis."

He was given credence, [and is even] now, because of the ease with which he spoke and because they showed him tin jewelry and he smelled it and said that it was not gold. He was very familiar with gold and silver, and [54v] he took no notice of the other metals.

The general sent Hernando de Alvarado to Cicuyc again to ask for some golden arm bands which this Turco said they had taken from him when they captured him. Alvarado went, and the [people] of the *pueblo* welcomed him as an ally. When he asked for the arm bands they denied [their existence] by every means, saying that El Turco was deceiving them and was lying. Captain Alvarado, seeing that there was no resolution, sought to [have] the captain Bigotes and the governor [of the *pueblo*] come to his tent.[229] When they came he took them captive [and put them] in chains. The [people] of the *pueblo* came out prepared for war, shooting arrows [55r] and insulting Hernando de Alvarado, saying that he was a man who was breaking their trust and friendship.

Hernando de Alvarado left with them, [going] to the general in Tiguex. There they were subsequently held prisoner more than six months. This was the beginning of bringing discredit on [the Spaniards'] word when they offered peace from then on, as will be seen by what happened afterward.

Fourteenth Chapter
how the expedition left Cíbola for Tiguex and what happened to them en route regarding snow

We[230] have already related that when the general departed from Cíbola [55v] he left orders for don Tristán de Arellano to leave [there] after twenty days, which he did. When he saw that the people were rested, supplied with food, and eager to depart in search of their general, he left with his troop on the route to Tigues.[231] On the first day they traveled to where they established quarters, which was at the largest, best, and most beautiful *pueblo* of that *provincia* [of Cíbola].[232] Only this *pueblo* has seven-story buildings. They are special buildings which serve as strongholds in the *pueblo*. They are taller than the others and rise over [them] like [56r] towers. In them there are loopholes and embrasures for defense of the roofs. [This is necessary] because the *pueblos* do not have streets; the roofs are level, and they come and go among themselves by first climbing up to the roofs.[233] These taller buildings [then] protect them.

At that place it began to snow on us.[234] The people [of the *pueblo*] gave [us] shelter under the *aves,* I mean *alaves* [edges of the roofs] of the *pueblo*, some of which extend out like balconies with wooden pillars beneath.[235] [This is] because usually they communicate with each other by means of ladders which ascend to those balconies, because they do not have doors at ground level. When it stopped snowing the expedition left there on its route.

[56v] Because this took time, it was the first days of December. During the ten days the expedition expended [in going to Tiguex] it did not stop snowing in the late afternoons and almost every night, so that in order to establish quarters wherever they reached, they had to pry up a *codo* of snow and more.[236] The trail was not discernible, but the guides, being familiar with the land, led [us] gropingly. Throughout all the land there are junipers and pine trees. Great bonfires were made from them, and the smoke and heat melted the snow that was falling so that it was kept away for the distance of a *braza* or two around the fire. It was dry snow, so that although half an *estado* fell on top of the baggage, [57r] it did not get wet. When it was shaken it fell [off], and the herd stayed clear [of snow]. When it fell all night, it covered the baggage and the men-at-arms in their bed[roll]s[237] in such a way that if someone had come upon the camp unexpectedly, he would not have seen anything other than mounds of snow and the horses. Even though it was half an *estado* [deep] it was endured; in fact, it provided warmth to those who were beneath [it].

The expedition passed by Acuco, the great steep, rugged hill of rock. Because [the people of Acuco] were at peace, they hosted [the expedition] well, providing food supplies and fowl, {/} even though the people are few. As I have said, many companions [of mine] went up to the top to see [the *pueblo*] and the stairs in the rock. [57v] [They did it] with great difficulty, because they were not accustomed to [the

FIGURE 28.5. Acoma women carrying water jars, Acoma Pueblo, 1904. Photograph by Edward S. Curtis. Courtesy Museum of New Mexico, neg. no. 144502.

stairway], by which the natives, who bore loads of food supplies, and the women water, went up and down so easily. It appeared that they did not [even] touch [their loads] with their hands.[238] In order to climb up, our people had to pass their weapons from one to another on the ascent.

From there they went on to Tiguex, where they were well received and lodged. Such excellent news from El Turco gave [them] no little happiness, as it smoothed the troubles, even though when the main expedition arrived [in Tiguex] we found that land or *provincia* had risen up.[239] The reason [58r] for this had to be something not insignificant, as will be told. Already our people had burned one *pueblo* the day before the main expedition arrived and were returning to their quarters.[240]

Fifteenth Chapter
how Tiguex rose up in arms and the punishment that was [inflicted] on them without [any] being [inflicted] on the instigator[241]

It may be told [again] how the general reached Tiguex, where he found don García López de Cárdenas and Hernando de Alvarado, how [Vázquez de Coronado] sent [Alvarado] to Cicuye[242] again, and [further, how] [Alvarado] made prisoners [of] the captain Bigotes and the [58v] governor of the *pueblo* (who was a very old man).

The [people of] Tiguex did not have a positive opinion about this imprisonment. In addition to this, the general tried to collect some clothing to distribute to the men-at-arms. For this purpose he had an Indian summoned [who was] a *principal* of Tiguex and who was already well acquainted and had had much conversation with him. Our people called him Juan Alemán, after a Juan Alemán who was in [the Ciudad de] México, whom they said he resembled.[243] The general talked with this [man], saying that [Alemán] was to furnish him three hundred pieces of clothing or more. This he had need of to [59r] give to his people. [Alemán] said that was not for him to do, but rather for the governors, and that above all it was necessary to engage in consultation and to distribute [the burden] among the *pueblos*. Further, [he said] that it was necessary to make the request individually to each *pueblo*.

The general himself ordered [that it be done] that way and that certain men chosen from among those who were with him were to go to make the request. Because the *pueblos* numbered twelve,[244] some [men] were to go on one side of the river and the others on the other. Because [each man] went unexpectedly, [the *pueblos*] were not given an opportunity to consult or discuss [the request]. Further, because [an expeditionary] arrived at [a] *pueblo* and immediately made the request to [the leaders], [59v] they had to deliver [the clothes right away], because [the expeditionary] had to have time to go on. In this situation, they had no more time than to take off their outer fur robes and hand them over until the number they were asked for was reached. The collectors gave *mantas* and robes to some of the men-at-arms who went there [to Tiguex], who, if [the clothes] were not just so and they saw an Indian with another, better one, they exchanged with him without having greater respect and without ascertaining the rank of the [man] they were despoiling. So that [the Indians] were not a little angry over this.[245]

In addition to what [has already been] told, a notable person (who in consideration of his honor I will not name) left the *pueblo* [where his] quarters [were] [60r] and went to another *pueblo* a league from there. Seeing a beautiful woman, he called to her spouse to hold his horse by the reins for him. [Then] he climbed up to the roof. Because communication in the *pueblo* is by way of the roof, the Indian believed that [the Spaniard] was going to another part [of it]. As he [the husband] waited there, there was a certain vague noise. [Then the Spaniard] came down, took his horse, and went away. The Indian climbed up and found out that [the Spaniard] had raped or tried to rape his wife.[246]

In the company of the high-ranking people of the *pueblo*, he came [to the *pueblo* of Tiguex] to make a complaint, stating that a man had raped his wife. And he related how it had happened. When the general [60v] had all the men-at-arms and [other] persons who were with him come before him, the Indian did not recognize [the rapist], either because he had changed clothes or for some other reason.[247] But he said that he would recognize the horse, because he had held it by the reins. He was [then] taken through the stable areas. [There] he found a blanketed, peach-colored horse, and he said that the owner of that horse was [the rapist]. The owner denied [it]. Seeing that [the husband] had not recognized [the Spaniard] and it could have been that he was in error about the horse, in the end he went away without the redress he asked for.[248]

The next day an Indian from the expedition who had been guarding the horses came [to the *pueblo* of Tiguex] [61r] wounded and in flight, saying that the Indians of that land had killed a companion [of his] and had taken the horses and driven them toward their *pueblos*. [The Spaniards] went to gather up the horses, but many were missing, as well as seven mules belonging to the general.

The following day don García López de Cárdenas went to inspect the *pueblos* and to get an interpreter from them. He found the *pueblos* closed by palisades. [There was] a great shout inside, [where they were] fighting the horses[249] (as in a bullring) and shooting them with arrows. [They were] all up in arms. [López de Cárdenas] could do nothing because [the Indians] did not come out into the countryside. Because the *pueblos* are fortified, [61v] [the men-at-arms] could not [even] hurt them.

Without delay, the general ordered that don García López de Cárdenas go to lay siege to one *pueblo* with all the rest of the troop. This *pueblo* was [the one] where the most harm had been done and where the [episode] concerning the Indian woman had occurred.[250] Many were the captains who went ahead with the general [López de Cárdenas],[251] such as Juan de Zaldívar, Barrionuevo, Diego López, and Melgosa. They took the Indians so much by surprise that they immediately reached the roofs, [but] with great risk because they wounded many of our people from inside the houses through the loopholes. Our people were [62r] on top [of the roofs] for that day and night and part of the next day at great risk, making accurate shots with crossbows and arquebuses. The horsemen and many allies from Nueva España in the space outside the *pueblo* started large, smoky fires[252] [in] the ground-floor rooms[253] [into] which they had broken, so that [the Indians] sued for peace.

Pablo de Melgosa and Diego López (one of the twenty-four councilmen of Sevilla) were at that place and replied to them with the same signs they were making [to indicate] peace, which is to form a cross. Then [the Indians] dropped

their weapons and gave themselves up without submitting to [the Spaniards'] will.[254] [Melgosa and López] took them to don García's tent. According to what was said, he [62v] was unaware of the [promise of] peace and believed that [the Indians] were surrendering involuntarily as vanquished men.[255] Because the general[256] had ordered that the [Indians] not be taken alive, so as to be a punishment and to make the rest [of the Indians] afraid, [López de Cárdenas] ordered that two hundred posts be planted in the ground right away in order to burn the [Indians] alive. There was no one who told him about the [promise of] peace which [Melgosa and López] had given to them. Nor did the men-at-arms know about it. And those who made it kept their mouths shut, in order not to make an issue of it.[257]

When the enemy [Indians] saw that the [others] were being tied [to the posts] and [the men-at-arms] were beginning to burn them, about a hundred men who were [63r] in the tent began to fortify and defend themselves with what was [there] inside [the tent] and with sticks that they came out to get.[258] Our footmen attacked the tent from all sides. Sword thrusts forced them [the Indians] to abandon the tent. Then the horsemen attacked them. Because the land was flat no man remained alive, except some who had remained hidden in the *pueblo* and fled that night.[259] They spread the word throughout the land that [the Spaniards] did not keep the promise of peace that had been given to them. Thereafter it was very unfortunate that this was done.[260]

Then it snowed on [the attackers]. [63v] They left the *pueblo* and returned to their quarters [just] at the time when the main expedition arrived from Cíbola.[261]

Sixteenth Chapter
how Tiguex was besieged and captured and
what else occurred as a result of the siege

As I have already related, just as they subdued that *pueblo* it began to snow in that land. And it snowed so much that for two months nothing could be done except to travel along the trails to notify [the Indians] that they should come to peace, giving them the fullest assurance that they would be pardoned.[262] [64r] They replied to this [by saying] that they could not trust [people] who did not know how to keep the promise they had given. [And they said] they remembered that [the Spaniards] were holding Bigotes prisoner and that at the *pueblo* that had been burned they had not kept their promise of peace.

Don García López de Cárdenas was one of those who went to make these summonses to them. One day he left with about thirty companions and went to the *pueblo* of Tiguex to talk with Juan Alemán.[263] Even though they were at war, they ended up talking to him. They told [López de Cárdenas] that if he wanted to talk with them, he should dismount, and they [would] come to him to talk peace. [They also said] that [64v] the horsemen should go off to one side, and they would have their people move away. [Then] Juan Alemán and another captain from the *pueblo* came to him.

It was done just as they requested. [López de Cárdenas] was close to them, and they said that because they were not carrying weapons, he should remove his. With the desire he had to bring them to peace, don García López did so, in order to give them more assurance. When he reached them, Juan Alemán came forward to embrace him. As he did that, the two [others][264] who came with him withdrew two small clubs they were secretly carrying behind their backs and struck him on the helmet, two such [powerful] blows that they nearly stunned him. [65r] Two men-at-arms on horseback were nearby (because they had refused to withdraw even though they were ordered to) and attacked with such speed that they snatched him from [the Indians'] grasp. [The horsemen] were unable to harm their enemies, though, because [the Indians] had a refuge nearby and also because of the thick showers of arrows which immediately fell upon them. And [the arrows] pierced the horse of one [of the men-at-arms] through the nose. The horsemen arrived all in a mad rush and extricated their captain from the fighting, [but] without being able to harm their enemies. Many of our people, though, came out [of the fighting] badly wounded. Thus they withdrew, several staying [65v] to oppose [the Indians].

Don García López de Cárdenas, with a part of the force, went to another *pueblo* which was half a league farther on,[265] because in those two places most of the people of those *pueblos* had gathered. Because they did not heed the summonses made to them, nor did they surrender in peace, but rather, with great shouts, fired arrows from the roof, [López de Cárdenas] returned to the company that had stayed to oppose the *pueblo* of Tiguex.[266] Then the [people] of that *pueblo* came forth in large numbers. Our people made a show of fleeing, [but] with checked reins, so that they drew their enemies [66r] out onto the flats. [Then the horsemen] turned on them in such a way that some of the most notable [Indians] were thrown to the ground. The rest retired to the *pueblo*, to the roofs. Thus, this captain [López de Cárdenas] returned to [the expedition's] quarters.

As soon as this happened, the general ordered them to go besiege [the *pueblo*]. One day [López de Cárdenas] departed with his troop well ordered and with several ladders. When he had arrived, he established his *real* next to the *pueblo* and promptly gave battle. Because, however, the enemies had had many days to prepare themselves, they threw so many stones onto our people that they knocked many [of them] to the ground, and they wounded [66v] about a hundred men with arrows. Afterward several died from [their wounds], because of poor treatment by an unskilled surgeon who was traveling with the expedition.[267]

The siege lasted fifty days, during which [the Indians] were occasionally given several scares.[268] What most troubled them was that they had no water. They dug an exceedingly deep well within the *pueblo*, but they could not obtain water.[269] Instead, it collapsed on them while they were digging it and killed thirty persons. Of the besieged, two hundred men died within [the *pueblo*] during the battles. One day when they were engaged in fierce battle [67r] they killed, from among our people, Francisco de Ovando, a captain [who had served as] *maestre de campo* the entire time that don García López de Cárdenas was occupied in the reconnaissances already related. And [they killed] Francisco de Pobares, an excellent *hidalgo*.[270] Because our people were unable to protect him, they pulled Francisco de Ovando into the *pueblo*. This was not a little regretted, as he was, indeed, a distinguished person and so respected, pleasant, and well liked in his own right that it was a marvel.

One day, before capture of [the *pueblo*] was complete,

[the Indians] summoned [the Spaniards] to talk. It was learned that their request was [made] in order to say that they had [67v] noticed that we did not harm the women and children. For this reason, they wanted to give up their women and children because they were using up the water. It was not possible to conclude [an agreement] with them whereby they would come to peace; they said that we would not keep our word with them. Thus, they turned over [only] about a hundred persons, children and women, because more did not want to leave. While they delivered them, our horsemen were in line in front of the *pueblo*.

Don Lope de Urrea, on horseback and without a helmet, had been receiving the boys and girls in his arms. When [the Indians] did not want to turn over any more, don Lope pleaded that they [68r] give themselves up peacefully, making them numerous promises of security. They told him to move away, because it was not their wish to trust people who did not preserve the friendship or keep the word they had given. Because [Urrea] refused to move away, a man came forth with a bow and arrow to shoot. He threatened [Urrea] with it, [indicating] that he would shoot it unless he went away from there. [Urrea's companions] shouted that he should put on his helmet, [but] he refused, saying that while he was there, [the Indians] would do him no harm. Because the Indian saw that he refused to go, he shot, and the arrow stuck [in the ground] between his horse's front feet. [68v] [The Indian] immediately nocked another [arrow] and again told [Urrea] that he should go, otherwise they would truly shoot him. Don Lope put on his helmet and returned, step by step, to his place among the horsemen without receiving [any] harm from them. When [the Indians] saw that he was now out of danger, with a great yell and war cry they let loose a rain of arrows.

The general refused to do battle with them that day, in order to see whether [the Spaniards] could bring them to peace by some means. [But] they never chose to [come to peace].

One night, fifteen days later, [the Indians] decided to leave [the *pueblo*], and so they did. Taking [69r] the women in the middle [of the group], they came forth during the quarter just before daybreak.[271] Forty horsemen were keeping watch during that quarter, and they gave the call to arms. The [men-at-arms] in don Rodrigo Maldonado's camp[272] attacked [the Indians]. The enemies knocked one Spaniard and one horse down dead and wounded others. But [the men-at-arms] happened to break through and work slaughter among them until, [when] [the Indians] were withdrawing, [the men-at-arms] attacked them in the river, which was flowing rapidly and was extremely cold. Because the troop from the *real* arrived very soon, those [Indians] who escaped death or injury were few.

The next day the people from the *real* crossed over the river [69v] and in the countryside found many wounded [Indians] whom the severe cold had felled. They brought them back in order to heal [them] and to be served by them. Thus that siege came to an end, and the *pueblo* was taken. Some [Indians], however, who had remained in the *pueblo*, made a stand[273] in one section [but] were captured in a few days.

Two captains had overcome the other large *pueblo* by means of a siege. They were don Diego de Guevara and Juan de Zaldívar, who had planned to lay a trap at dawn one [day], in order to catch in it some [Indian] men-at-arms who [70r] were accustomed to sallying forth each morning to make a show [of combat], so as to throw fear into our *real*.[274] The spies whom [the Spaniards] had stationed (so that they would return when they saw [the Indians]) saw that people were coming forth and walking into the [surrounding] land. [The Spaniards] came out of their ambush and went to the *pueblo*. They saw the people [of the *pueblo*] fleeing and followed them, working slaughter among them. When news of this was delivered, the troop left the *real* and went through the *pueblo*, looting it and taking prisoner all the people who were in it. There were about one hundred women and children.[275]

This siege was concluded at the end of [70v] March {1542 rubric}[276] of the year [one thousand five hundred and] forty-two, by which time other things had occurred of which I could have given a report, [but] in order not to cut the thread [of the narrative] I have left them out. Now, though, they must be told, because it is advisable that they be known in order to understand what [comes] later.

Seventeenth Chapter

how messengers came to the expedition from the
Valley of Señora and how Captain Melchior Díaz died
during the journey from the [Río] del Tizón

We have already related how Captain Melchior Díaz had crossed the Río del Tizón on rafts [71r] in order to continue reconnaissance farther along that coast. Now, at the time when the siege was concluded, messengers reached the expedition from the *villa* of San Gerónimo with letters from Diego de [Alcaraz],[277] who remained there in Melchior Díaz's place. They brought reports that Melchior Díaz had died during the search he was leading. The people [he had taken with him] had returned without seeing anything of what they sought. The affair [of Díaz's death] happened in this way.

When they had crossed the river they traveled in search of the coast, which in that area now turned to the south or between [71v] south and east.[278] That gulf of the sea penetrates [the land] in a due northerly direction, and this river enters the gulf at its head. It brings its current out of the north and flows to the south.

Traveling as they were on foot, they encountered some dunes of steaming cinders, which no one could enter, because to enter [them] would be [like] being swamped in the sea. The land they were walking on vibrated like a drumhead, so that it seemed as though caverns[279] were beneath it. It seemed an extraordinary thing that in some places the ash was steaming that way, which appeared to be a hellish thing. He detoured around this place because of the [72r] the danger they were running and because of the lack of water.[280]

One day a whippet which a man-at-arms had ran ravenously after several rams [the Spaniards] were bringing along for food. When the captain saw it, he hurled his fighting lance[281] at it as he was galloping. [The lance] stuck in the ground. Unable to stop the horse, he ran onto the lance, and [Díaz's] thigh was pierced by it, so that the iron tip exited at his groin and his bladder was ruptured.

When the men-at-arms saw this, they returned [to San Gerónimo] with their wounded captain, every day fighting skirmishes with the Indians, who were still [72v] up in arms. [Díaz] lived about twenty days, during which [his companions] endured great hardship because they were carrying him. In this way they returned, in good order without losing a [single] man, until [Díaz] died.[282] At that point they were freed of their greatest hardship.

When they had arrived at Señora, Alcaraz dispatched the messengers previously mentioned, who made [the general] aware of [the return of Díaz's party] and that some men-at-arms were restless and [had] attempted insurrection several times. Further, that he had condemned two [men] to hanging, who thereafter had fled from confinement. When the general understood this, he sent don Pedro de Tovar to that *villa* to cull out some persons and to [73r] take with him messengers whom [Vázquez de Coronado] was sending to the viceroy don Antonio de Mendoza with messages about what had happened and about the promising report of El Turco.[283]

Don Pedro de Tovar left and, when he had arrived, found that the natives of that *provincia* had killed a man-at-arms with a poisoned arrow. [He had suffered only] a very small wound in one hand. In addition to this, several men-at-arms had gone there [to an unidentified place] and had not been well received. Don Pedro de Tovar dispatched Diego de Alcaraz with a troop to take the leaders and lords of one *pueblo* captive. [The Spaniards] called it the Valle de Bellacos [scoundrels]. [The *pueblo*] is on a height. When [the Spaniards] reached there, they took [the Indians] captive. When they had been confined, [73v] it seemed to Diego de Alcaraz that they should be released in exchange for some yarn, clothing, and other things which the men-at-arms had need of.

When [the leaders] were seen to be free, [the Indians] rose up in arms. [The Spaniards] ascended to them. Because they were strongly fortified and had poison, they killed several Spaniards [outright] and wounded others, who died en route while retreating to their *villa*. If they had not taken allies from Los Corazones with them, it would have gone worse.[284] They returned to the *villa*, leaving [behind] seventeen men-at-arms dead from the poison. [Even] with only a small wound, they died screaming with pain, [and] their bodies burst open with a unbearable pestilential stench.[285]

[74r] When the harm was seen by don Pedro de Tovar [and] it seemed to them that they [could] not remain secure

in that *villa*, [Tovar] moved it forty leagues closer to Cíbola to the Valley of Suya.[286] There we will leave them in order to relate what transpired with the general and the expedition following the siege of Tiguex.

Eighteenth Chapter
how the general tried to leave the land calm in order to go in search of Quisvira,[287] which El Turco said was where wealthy [lands] began

Midway through the siege of Tiguex the general decided to go to Cicuyc, taking with him the governor. [This he did] in order to set him free [74v] with promises that when he set out for Quivira he would [also] release Bigotes and leave him in his *pueblo*. When he reached Cicuye he was welcomed peacefully, and he entered the *pueblo* with several men-at-arms. [The people of Cicuyc] received their governor with great affection and celebration. When he had seen how the *pueblo* acted and had talked with the natives, he returned to his camp, leaving Cicuyc at peace and with the expectation of getting its captain Bigotes back.

The siege being concluded, as we have already told, [Vázquez de Coronado] sent a captain to Chia, an excellent *pueblo* of many people.[288] It had [previously] sent [a representative] to render [75r] obedience [to the king]. It was situated away from the river four leagues toward the west. [The captain and his company] found it at peace. Four bronze artillery pieces which were in poor condition were delivered to this place for safekeeping.[289]

Six comrades in arms also went to Quirix, a *provincia* of seven *pueblos*.[290] In the first *pueblo*, which probably had one hundred *vecinos*, [the people] fled because they did not dare wait for our people. [The Spaniards] went at full speed to intercept them, and they returned [the Indians] to their houses in the *pueblo* with complete assurance [of peace]. From there they informed the rest of the *pueblos* and reassured them. Thus, little by little, the whole region began to be reassured. In the meantime, the river was thawing, [which] permitted it [75v] to be forded, making travel possible. None of the twelve *pueblos* of Tiguex, however, was [re]settled during the entire time the expedition was there, despite the assurance [the Indians] were given.[291] The river

had been [frozen] for nearly four months, so that it was regularly crossed on horseback on top of the ice.[292] [But] because it had [now] thawed, the departure for Quivira was ordered. [That was] where El Turco said there was some gold and silver, although not as much as in Arehe and Los Guaes.[293]

Already there were some among the members of the expedition [who were] suspicious of El Turco. [That was] because during the siege a Spaniard who was named Cervantes[294] had [El Turco] in custody, [and] this [76r] Spaniard swore under oath that he had seen El Turco speaking into a jar of water with the devil. [He] also [said] that he was holding [El Turco] under [lock and] key, so that no one could talk to him. El Turco had asked [Cervantes] who among the Christians had been killed by the [people] of Tiguex. He told him, "No one." El Turco replied to him, "You are lying, because five Christians and one captain have died." Cervantes, seeing that he spoke the truth, admitted it to him, in order to learn from him who had told it to him. El Turco said to him that he had learned it by himself and that he had not needed anyone [76v] to tell it to him. Because of this, [Cervantes] spied on him and saw him talk to the devil in the jar, as I have said.

Nevertheless, a muster was conducted in order to leave Tiguex.[295] {+} At this time people from Cíbola came to see the general and [he] entrusted them with the good treatment of the Spaniards[296] who would be coming from Señora with don Pedro de Tovar. And he gave them letters they were to deliver to don Pedro. In [those letters] he gave [Tovar] instructions about what he should do and that he was to go in pursuit of the expedition. [Vázquez de Coronado wrote] that [Tovar] would find letters beneath the crosses at the daily encampments the expedition would have to make.[297]

The expedition departed from Tiguex on the fifth [77r] of May,[298] returning to Cicuyc, which is twenty-five days' travel, I mean leagues, from there, as I have said. [Vázquez de Coronado] took Bigotes from there [Tiguex]. When he had reached there [Cicuyc], he delivered their captain to them. [Bigotes] was already going about unfettered with a guard. The *pueblo* celebrated with him. They were at peace and supplied foodstuffs. Bigotes and the governor furnished the general [with] a youth called Xabe, a native of Quivira, so that [the members of the expedition] would be informed by him about the land [Quivira].[299] [Xabe] said that there were gold and silver, but not as much as El Turco was saying. El Turco [himself] still held fast [to his statements] and went [along] as guide. Thus, the expedition departed from there.

[77v]

Nineteenth Chapter
how [the expedition] departed in search of
Quivira and what happened en route

The expedition departed from Cicuyc, leaving the *pueblo* at peace, because their governor and captain had been returned to them. Accordingly, the people seemed satisfied and obligated to remain friendly.

They traveled so as to go to the plain that is beyond all the mountains. After four days walking on the trail [the expedition] encountered a swift, deep river that came down from the direction of Cicuye.[300] For that reason it was called the Río de Cicuyc. [The expedition] halted [78r] here in order to build a bridge to cross it. With the utmost diligence and speed [the bridge] was finished in four days.[301] When it was finished, the entire expedition and all the livestock crossed over on it.

After ten more days of travel they came upon some *rancherías* of Arab-like people who are known there as Querechos.[302] [Bison] had been seen two days earlier. These people live in tents made of cured [bison] hides, [and] they travel along behind the [bison], preparing meat. Although these [people] saw the expedition, they did not move nor did they make any commotion. Instead, they came out of their tents to look [at us] openly. Afterward, they came to talk with the advance guard, asking what [78v] the expedition was.

The general spoke with them, but because they had already talked with El Turco (who traveled in the advance guard), they confirmed everything he said. They were a people very skillful with [hand] signs,[303] such that it seemed as if they were talking. And they made a thing understood so that there was no longer need for an interpreter. These [people] said that proceeding downstream[304] toward where the sun rose there was a very large river. One could travel along its bank through settled land for ninety days, from settlement to settlement without a break. [They said] that the first settlement was called Haxa[305] and that the river was more [79r] than a league wide.[306] [On it] there were many canoes. The next day these [people] departed from there with droves of dogs on which they transported their belongings.

For two days,[307] during which the expedition continued to travel on the course it had taken on leaving the settled land[308] (which was between north and east, more toward the north), other Querechos were seen encamped.[309] And a huge number of [bison] that seemed like something unbelievable. These [Querechos] gave the grandest report of settlements, all to the east of where we were. Here don García [López de Cárdenas] broke an arm. Also, a Spaniard was lost when he went out hunting and did not find his way back to the *real* because the land was very [79v] flat.[310]

El Turco said that it was one or two days' travel to Haya [from there].[311] [So] the general sent Captain Diego López and ten members of his company [to go] quickly ahead, setting his course toward where the sun rose with a sea compass and traveling at full speed for two days to locate Haxa. [Then] he was to find the expedition again. The next day [the expedition itself] set off on the same course. There were so many grazing animals [bison] that, with some difficulty, those who traveled in the advance guard overtook a large number of bulls ahead of them. Because [the bulls] fled and were pushing one another, [when] they came upon a ravine, so many of the animals fell in that they filled it level and the rest crossed over on top [of them]. The horsemen [80r] who went in pursuit of them, without knowing what [the bulls] had done, fell on top of them. Three saddled and bridled horses, among those that fell, went in among the [bison] and could not be retrieved.[312]

Because it seemed to the general that Diego López should have been back already, he ordered six members of the company to follow the bank of a small river upstream and an equal number [to follow] the bank downstream to look for tracks of the horses at the ingresses to and egresses from the river.[313] [That is] because on the [solid] ground it is not possible to locate tracks, because when the grass is trampled it straightens back up. Traces were found of the way by which [López's company] had traveled. [But] it was by luck that, on returning [to camp] [80v] after having gone a full league from there looking for fruit, Indians from the expedition found the tracks and stumbled on [the missing men].[314] They descended the river to the camp and gave their report to the general. [This was] that in the twenty leagues they had traveled they had seen nothing except [bison] and sky.[315]

Another tattooed[316] Indian was traveling with the expedition, a native of Quivira called Sopete. This Indian always said that El Turco was lying. Therefore, no credit had been given to him. Even though at this time he said that the Querechos had reported the same thing to him, Ysopete was not believed.[317]

From here the general sent don Rodrigo Maldonado in advance with his company. He traveled for four days and reached a [81r] great *barranca* like those of Colima.[318] He found in the bottom of it a large *ranchería* of people. Cabeza de Vaca and Dorantes had passed this way.[319] [The Indians] here presented a heap[320] of cured hides and other things to don Rodrigo, along with a tent as large as a house in height. [Maldonado] ordered that it be guarded until the expedition arrived and sent members of his company to guide the expedition toward that place, so that [it] would not become lost, even though [Maldonado and his company] had set up markers of bone and [bison] dung as they traveled, so that the expedition could follow. By this means the expedition had already been guided in the wake of the advance guard.

The general arrived with his expedition, and seeing such a huge quantity [81v] of hides, he intended to distribute them among the people [of the expedition]. He had guards posted to watch over [the hides]. However, the people arrived and members of the company saw that the general was sending certain men with passwords, so that the guards would give them hides, and they went about selecting them. Angered that [the mound of hides] was not being distributed in an orderly way, they stole[321] them. In less than a quarter of an hour nothing was left but bare ground. The natives who saw that also took part in the work. The women and some others cried because they had believed that [the members of the expedition] would not take anything from them but would bless [their things], as Cabeza [82r] de Vaca and Dorantes had done when they passed through this place.[322]

There was an Indian woman there as white as a woman of Castilla except that she had tattooed her chin like a Moorish woman from Barbary.[323] In general, all the women's chins are decorated in that way there. [And] they accent their eyes with kohl.[324]

Twentieth Chapter
how large hailstones fell on the camp and
how another gorge was found where the expedition
was divided into two parts

One afternoon while the expedition was resting in the *barranca* we have told about, a whirling storm arose with the strongest of winds and hail.[325] In a brief while [82v] such a huge number of hailstones came down, as large as small bowls and larger and as dense as rain, that in one place they covered the ground [to a depth of] two and three *palmos* and more.

One was missing his horse. I mean there was not a single horse that did not get loose unless it was two or three which Blacks went to hold, protected by helmets and round shields.[326] All the rest were carried before [the storm] until it drove them against the scarp [of the gorge]. And some of them climbed to where they were brought down [only] with great effort. If [the storm] had caught them on the plains above, as it did within [the *barranca*], the expedition would have been placed at great risk, without horses, because many could not have been recovered.

The hail tore through [83r] many tents, dented many helmets, and hurt many horses. It also broke all the expedition's pottery and gourd [containers], which put [them] in no small predicament, because there is no pottery, and neither pottery nor gourd [containers] are made there.[327] Corn is not planted, nor do [the natives] eat bread. Rather, [they eat] only meat that is raw or partly roasted, as well as fruits.[328]

From there the general dispatched [individuals] to make a reconnaissance. After four days' travel they came upon other *rancherías* resembling those of Bedouins.[329] It was a densely settled land where there were abundant beans and plums like those of Castilla, and grapevines.[330] These *pueblos* of *rancherías* extended over a territory covered by three days' travel. [The land] was called Cona.[331]

From this place[332] [83v] some Teyas (which is what those people were called) departed with the expedition and traveled with their droves of dogs and their women and children until the encampment at the end of the last day's journey, [at a settlement] of other [Teyas]. There they provided guides for traveling on. From there the expedition went to a[nother] great *barranca*. [Members of the expedition] did not allow these guides to talk with El Turco, and they did not receive the [same] reports as before. [Instead], [the Teyas] said that Quivira was toward the north.[333] And because we were not finding [any other] good route, Ysopete began to be believed.

In this way, the expedition reached the last *barranca*, which was a league from rim to rim. [There was] a small river in the bottom and level ground covered with [84r] a grove of trees, and with plentiful grapes, mulberries, and rosebushes [or gooseberries] which is a fruit there is in France [that] they serve unripe.[334] It was ripe in this *barranca*. There were walnuts and [turkeys] equal in quality to those of Nueva España.[335] And plums like those in Castilla [were] in abundance.

En route [to the last *barranca*] a Teya was seen to make a shot [with an arrow] that passed through both shoulders of a [bison] bull, which is something that an arquebus would do well to accomplish. These are very intelligent people. The women are treated well and fully cover their bodies out of shame. They wear shoes and ankle boots made of cured hide. The women wear *mantas* over their tunics with the ends [of the *mantas*] wrapped around [84v] their shoulders. All of this is made of hide. Some [of the hides] resemble small hair shirts of penitents with fringe on them that reaches to mid-thigh. [They are worn] over the tunics.[336]

In this *barranca* the expedition rested for many days in order to explore the region. Up to this point [the members of the expedition] had completed thirty-seven days of travel of six to seven leagues each.[337] [This is known] because one person was given the responsibility of making an estimate, and one was counting the paces. They said that it was two hundred and fifty leagues to the settled land.[338]

When General Francisco Vázquez saw this and understood that until that point they had been deceived by El Turco and that the expedition was short of provisions [85r]

and {+} that there was no place around there where they could be supplied, he called the captains and the *alférez* [*general*] to a meeting.[339] [This was] so that they could decide on what seemed to them ought to be done. That was, by unanimous agreement, that the general would go [on] in search of Quivira with thirty horsemen and half a dozen footmen and that don Tristán de Arellano would return to Tiguex with all [the rest of] the expedition.

When this was known to the people of the expedition and that it had already been agreed upon, they appealed the decision (that they would not be allowed to be taken along) to their general. And [they said] they all preferred to die with him and not to turn back. This was to no avail, although the general granted them that, within eight days, he would send messengers to [tell] them whether it was advisable [85v] to follow him or not. With this, he departed with the guides he took and with Ysopete. El Turco went [along], safely in chains.

Twenty-first Chapter
how the main body of the expedition returned to
Tiguex and the general reached Quivira

The general departed from the *barranca* with the guides the Teyas had provided to him. He appointed Diego López, one of the twenty-four councilmen of Sevilla, as his *maestre de campo*. From [among] the personnel he took those who seemed to him most distinguished, and [he took] the best horses. The [main body of the] expedition remained [behind] with some [slight] hope that they would be summoned by the general. They again sent [a message] of appeal to the general with two horsemen traveling [86r] quickly and posthaste.

The general arrived, I mean the guides fled from him during the first days of travel. So Diego López had to return to the [main] camp for [new] guides. [He came] with the order that the [main body of the] expedition return to Tiguex to seek food supplies and await the general. The Teyas willingly gave him other guides. The [main body of the] expedition waited for their messengers and [remained] there fifteen days, preparing dried [bison] meat to take [with them].[340] By all accounts, there must have been five hundred bulls killed during those fifteen days. The number of [bulls] there were without cows was an unbelievable thing.

Many of the people who went out to hunt during this time got lost. They did not [86v] return to the camp for two or three days, foolishly traveling from one place to another without knowing how to return to the place from which they had departed. [This happened] even with that *barranca* being such that either upstream or down they had to hit upon [it]. Because every night a report was made of [those] who were missing, they fired the artillery, sounded trumpets, and beat drums. And they built huge, bright bonfires. Some [of the lost men] were so far away and so imprudent that none of this benefited them, although it was worthwhile for others. The solution was to return to where they had killed the beasts and to set a course to one place and [then] another until they encountered the *barranca* or came across someone [else] who guided them.

It is something worth noting that because the land is so flat, if at midday [87r] they have wandered foolishly following their prey from one place to another, they must stay calmly near their prey until the sun lowers, in order to see by what course they must return to where they departed from. Even so, these had to be knowledgeable men. Those who were not had to entrust [themselves] to others [who were].

The general followed his guides until he reached Quivira. In this he expended forty-eight days of travel because of the great deviation from the meridian toward La Florida which they had made. He was welcomed peacefully because of the guides he took.

He asked El Turco why he had lied[341] and had guided the [people of the expedition] so tortuously. He replied that his land was toward that area, and besides, the [people] of Cicuyc had [87v] begged him to get the [Spaniards] lost on the plains.[342] [That was] so that, lacking food supplies, the horses would die. And [the people of Cicuyc] could kill [the Spaniards] without difficulty when they returned, [because they would be] weak. And [they would be able] to avenge what [the Spaniards] had done. Because of this he had led the [Spaniards] off course, thinking that they would not know how to hunt or how to sustain themselves without corn. Regarding what [he had said previously] about gold, he

[now] said that he did not know where there was any. He said this now as [one who was] hopeless. He was ashamed that [the Spaniards] had believed Ysopete and that [Ysopete] had guided them better than he had.

Because the [Spaniards] who had gone there [to Quivira] were concerned that [El Turco] not give any warning from which some harm might come to them, they garrotted him.[343] Ysopete was pleased about that, because [El Turco] had always said that Ysopete was a scoundrel and that he did not know [88r] what he was talking about. And [the Spaniards] had always blocked him from talking with anyone.

Neither gold nor silver was seen among those people, nor [was there] news of it. The lord[344] wore a copper medallion [suspended] from his neck, [which] he esteemed more than a little.[345]

The messengers whom the [main body of the] expedition had dispatched after the general [now] returned, as I said [previously]. Then, because they did not bring any message different from the one [Diego López,] one of the twenty-four councilmen of Sevilla, had related, the [expedition] left the *barranca* and returned to the Teyas.[346] There they acquired guides, who took them back by a more direct route.[347] [The Teyas] provided the [guides] voluntarily. [They knew of a more direct route] because, since they are people who do not stop [permanently] [88v] in those lands, [but travel] in pursuit of the [bison] herd, they know everything.

They showed the way by this means. First thing in the morning they observed where the sun was rising and chose the course they had to take. [Then] they shot an arrow. Before they reached it, they shot another one over [it].[348] They traveled the whole day this way until [reaching] the water sources where the daily encampment had to be made. By this method, what had been traveled in thirty-seven days' journey on the way out was [covered] in twenty-five on the return, hunting [bison] en route.

Along this route were many salt lakes which had [salt] in great quantity.[349] [89r] On top of the water there were slabs of it, four and five fingers thick and larger than tabletops. Two and three *palmos* beneath the water [there was] granular salt [which was] more flavorful than the [salt] in the slabs, because this [slab salt] tasted a little bitter. [The granular salt] was clear. On those plains there were some animals, like squirrels, [which were] very numerous.[350] And [there were] a great number of their burrows.

On this return trip the expedition ended up reaching the Río de Cicuyc more than thirty leagues below it, I mean below the bridge which had been built on the outbound trip.[351] [The expedition] went upstream along it. In general, [89v] nearly all its banks had rosebushes. [The fruits] taste like muscatel grapes [and] grow on thin canes an *estado* [in length]. [The plant] has a leaf like parsley.[352] There were immature and very juicy grapes and oregano.[353] The guides said that river joined the [Río] de Tiguex more than twenty days' journey from that point and that its flow turned to the east.[354] It is believed that it flows to the powerful Río del Espíritu Santo, which the [members of the expedition] of don Hernando de Soto discovered in La Florida.[355]

During the outbound leg of this journey a tattooed Indian woman hid from Captain Juan de Zaldívar and fled downstream through the canyons. [90r] [This was] because she had been a slave in Tiguex, where she had been captured [by the Spaniards], and [now] she recognized the land. Certain Spaniards among those who had penetrated that region making a reconnaissance from La Florida [later] had this Indian woman in their possession.[356] I heard them, when they returned to Nueva España, say that the Indian woman had told them that nine days earlier she had fled from other [Spaniards].[357] And she gave the names of captains. Because of this it ought to be believed that we [the expedition of Vázquez de Coronado] had reached [an area] not far from where they made [their] reconnaissance, although [the Soto expedition] said that then [at the time of the woman's story] they were more than two hundred leagues inland. It is [therefore] believed that the land [90v] is more than six hundred leagues across in that region, from sea to sea.

Now, as I said, the expedition traveled upstream along the river until it reached the *pueblo* of Cicuye. It was prepared for war, so that [the people of Cicuye] refused [even] to make a show of peace or to provide food assistance. From there [the expedition] went to Tiguex. There, some *pueblos* had now been resettled, [but] they were immediately again abandoned out of fear.[358]

Twenty-second Chapter
how the general returned from Quivira and [how] other *entradas* were made toward the north

[91r] As soon as don Tristán de Arellano reached Tiguex in the middle of the month of July in the year [one thousand five hundred and forty-one {1541}],[359] he had food supplies gathered for the coming winter. And he dispatched Captain Francisco de Barrionuevo with several people upstream along the river toward the north. There he saw two *provincias,* one of which, of seven *pueblos,* was called Hemes and the other Yuque Yunque.[360] The [people of the] *pueblos* of Hemes came out in peace and provided food supplies. While the [Spanish] camp was being set up, those of Yuque Yunque abandoned two very beautiful *pueblos,* between which was the river, [91v] and went to the mountain chain, where they had four very strong *pueblos* in rugged land.[361] It was impossible to go to them on horseback.

In these two *pueblos* there were many provisions and very beautiful pottery, glazed, intricately worked, and in many shapes. Also, many jars were found full of choice shiny metal, with which [the Indians] glaze their pottery. This was an indication that in that land there were sources of silver, if they had been looked for.[362]

Twenty leagues farther upstream along the river there was a strong and wonderful river, I mean *pueblo,* which was called Uraba, to which our people gave the name Valladolid.[363] [92r] It had the river in the middle.[364] It is crossed by wooden bridges made from very tall, heavy pines, [which had been] squared. In this *pueblo* were seen the largest and most magnificent *estufas* in all that land, because they [each] had twelve pillars, every one of which was two *brazas* in circumference and two *estados* in height. Hernando de Alvarado had visited this *pueblo* when he reconnoitered toward Cicuye. It is a very elevated land and extremely cold. The river runs deep [in the earth] and with a heavy flow, without any ford.[365]

Captain Barrionuevo returned, leaving those *provincias* at peace.

Another captain went downriver [92v] in search of the settlements which the [people] of Tutahaco said were several days' journey from there. This captain descended [the river]

FIGURE 28.6. Taos Pueblo, north building, about 1949. Castañeda de Nájera referred to this pueblo as Uraba. Courtesy Museum of New Mexico, neg. no. 90747.

for eighty leagues and found four large *pueblos*, which he left in peace.[366] He traveled [on] until he found that the river sank underground {a river that vanishes} like [the] Guadiana in Extremadura.[367] He did not go on to where the Indians said it emerged [again] very powerful, because he was not carrying a commission [for] more than eighty leagues of travel.

Because this captain returned and the time was approaching when the captain [general] had to return from Quivira but had not [yet] returned, don Tristán selected forty companions and, leaving the camp in charge of Francisco [93r] de Barrionuevo, departed with them in search of the general. When he reached Cicuye, the [people of the] *pueblo* came forth prepared for war. That caused [Arellano's] company] to halt there four days in order to inflict some injury on [the people of Cicuique]. With shots fired at the *pueblo* they killed several people, so that [the Indians] did not come forth against the [Spanish] camp. [That was because,]

on the first day, [Arellano's company] killed two distinguished men.

While this was happening, news arrived that the general was coming.[368] For this reason also don Tristán had to wait there, so as to secure that pass.[369] When the general arrived, he was welcomed heartily by everyone with great [93v] happiness.

With don Tristán de Arellano was the Indian Xabe, who was the youth the [people of] Cicuye had provided to the general when he was going in search of Quivira.[370] When he was aware that the general was coming he showed that he was pleased. He said, "Now that the general is coming, you will see that in Quivira there are gold and silver, although not as much as El Turco said." When the general arrived and [Xabe] understood that [the general's company] had found nothing, he became sad and dumbfounded, insisting, in such a way that he convinced many [people], that [the result of the general's trip] was such because the general had not penetrated the land farther into the interior, which he did not dare [to do], because [that land] was heavily populated and [his company] was not [94r] powerful.[371] [The general] had returned in order to take his [full] troop [back] once the rainy season was over. [That was] because in that region it was already raining, because it was the first days of August when [the general] set out. They returned by traveling rapidly with excellent guides. The return consumed forty days.

When the expedition had departed from Tiguex, El Turco had said that, because they had loaded the horses with such a great supply of food, they were becoming exhausted and later would not be able to bring back the gold and silver. From this it seems clear that [El Turco] had trickery in mind.

Once the general reached Cicuyc with his company, he promptly left for Tiguex, leaving the *pueblo* calmer (seeing that [the people of Cicuyc] promptly came out to him peacefully [94v] and talked with him). Having arrived at Tiguex, he intended to spend the winter there in order to return [to Quivira] with the whole expedition, because he said he was bringing news of great settlements and extremely powerful rivers. And [he said] that the land was very similar to that of Spain in its fruits, grasses, and weather. Further, [he said] that they were not content with thinking there was no gold. Rather, they suspected that it was in the land farther into the interior, because [the Indians] did not deny it and understood what [gold] was, and [because, further,] it had a name among them, which was pronounced "acochis."

With that we will conclude this first part and will try to give an account of the *provincias*.

[95r]

Second Part

in which are discussed the multistoried *pueblos*
and *provincias* and their habits and customs; compiled
by Pedro de Castañeda, a *vecino* of the *ciudad* of Naxara[372]
laus deo [glory to God]

[95v] It seems to me that the reader is probably not satisfied to have comprehended and understood [only] what I have related about the expedition. It is, however, well to point out the disparity between the [various] reports. [That is] because there was such a wonderful report of great treasures, even though in the place itself [we] found no [reliable] account or [even any] probability that they exist.[373] It is something worth noting that instead of inhabited areas, [we] found great unsettled regions, and instead of populous *ciudades*, we found *pueblos* of two hundred *vecinos*, the largest [being] of eight hundred or a thousand.

I do not know whether this [what I am about to write] will give [readers] a basis to consider and reflect on the variety in this life, but in order to humor them, I want to give individual report[s] [96r] about the entire inhabited region which was seen and reconnoitered during this expedition. As well as some [of the] customs [the natives] have and [their] habits, in accordance with what we were able to learn about them. Also, in what direction each *provincia* lies, so that afterward it may be understood in what region La Florida is and in what region Greater India lies.

Just as this land of Nueva España is a [continuous] landmass with El Perú, so is it also with Greater India or China, unless there is a strait in that direction which divides it. Rather, the width of the land is so great that it leaves room for there to be such large unsettled areas [96v] as there are between the two seas. [That is] because the coast of the [Mar] del Norte beyond La Florida turns toward Los Bacallaos[374] and then turns toward Norway. And that of the [Mar] del Sur [turns] to the west, forming another peninsula toward the south,[375] in its curve nearly like the bend of India.

The result of this is that the lands which conform to the mountain chains on both coasts diverge, the ones from the others, to such an extent that they leave great plains between them. [The plains are] such that, because they are uninhabitable [by humans], they are populated by grazing animals and many other animals of various sorts. [They are,] however, not [inhabited] by snakes, because they are as open and without forests as they are.[376] [97r] Instead, [they are] populated] by every sort of game animal and birds, as will be told later.

Leaving narration of the return to Nueva España which the expedition made until the scanty reason there was for it is understood, we begin by describing the *villa* of Culiacán.

And from the difference between the one land and the other, it will be seen that one [land] is worth being settled by Spaniards and the other [is] not. As regards Christians, it needs to be the reverse. [That is] because in the one land there is human civilization and in the other the barbarity of animals (as opposed to [the barbarity] of brutish men).[377]

[97v]

First Chapter
concerning the *provincia* of Culiacán and
its habits and customs

Culiacán is the most remote [place] in the Nuevo Reino de Galicia. And it was the first [place] that Nuño de Guzmán settled when he conquered this *reino*.[378] It is two hundred and ten leagues to the west of [the Ciudad de] México. In this *provincia* there are three principal languages, not counting several others to which [the natives] of [the *provincia*] respond.[379]

The first is [the language] of [the] Tahus, who were the most excellent people, the most intelligent, and the [ones] who at this time are the most settled and are the most enlightened by the Faith.[380] These [people] practiced idolatry and made offerings to the devil from their possessions and wealth.[381] [This] was clothing and turquoises. They did not eat human flesh, nor did they sacrifice it.[382] They were in the habit of raising very large snakes, and they held [98r] them in veneration. Among them there were men in women's clothing, who were married to other men and functioned for them as wives.[383]

With a grand celebration, they legitimated the women who chose to live unmarried. [This was done] with a grand *areito*, or dance,[384] at which all of the lords of the region came together. They brought [the woman to be legitimated] out to dance naked. When all of them had danced with her, they put her in a *rancho* which is lavishly decorated for that purpose.[385] Then the women adorned her with clothing and arm bands of fine turquoise. Then, one by one, the lords came in to enjoy her, and after them, all the rest [of the men] who wanted to. From then on [the legitimated women] were not allowed to deny anyone. [The men] paid them a certain amount which was [98v] established for this. Even if later they took husbands, they were not for this reason exempt from satisfying whoever paid it.

Their greatest diversions are markets. There was a custom that the husbands who were marrying women bought them from their parents and relatives for a large price. Then [the relatives] took her to an important man whom they hold as a priest to deflower her and find out whether she was a virgin. If she was not, [the relatives] had to return the full price to [the husband]. And it was his choice whether he [still] wanted her as a wife or not. Or [whether] to abandon her, so that she would be legitimated [as a single woman]. Sometimes[386] they went on long drunken binges.

The second language is [that] of [the] Pacaxes, who are a people who inhabit the land that is between [99r] the plain and the mountains.[387] These are a more uncivilized people. Some [of them] eat human flesh. These are the ones who border on the mountains. They are flagrant homosexuals. They take many wives, even if they are sisters. They worship stones decorated with carvings. And they are well-known diviners and wizards.

The third language is [that] of [the] Acaxes. These [people] control much of the rugged land and all of the mountain range.[388] They go about hunting men in the same way they hunt deer. They all eat human flesh.[389] Whoever has the most human bones and skulls hanging around his house is the most feared and the most esteemed. They live in clusters of houses and in very rugged terrain. They avoid the plain. Midway traveling from one [99v] cluster of houses to another there must be a gorge. Although they talk [across it] to each other, it is not possible to cross it as easily. At a single call, five hundred men come together. For the slightest reason they kill and eat each other. They have been difficult to subdue because of the ruggedness of the land, which is very severe.[390]

In this land are many rich sources of silver. They are not deep [and] play out quickly. From [this point] on the coast of the *provincia* begins the gulf which the sea extends toward the north. It penetrates the land to the interior two hundred and fifty leagues and terminates at the mouth of the Río del Tizón. {California} This land [of Culiacán] is the eastern extremity [of the gulf], and the western extremity is La California. From [one] extremity [100r] to [the other] [across the gulf] it is thirty leagues,[391] according to what I have heard from men who have sailed it, because just as they lose sight of this land they spot the other. They say the size [length] of the gulf reaching from the land [at the head] to the land [at the end] is a hundred and fifty leagues and more.[392] At the Río del Tizón the coast turns to the south, forming an arc to La California, which [subsequently] turns to the west, forming that peninsula which was previously taken to be an island. [That was] because it is a low, sandy land. [It is] settled by a brutish and bestial people [who go about] naked.[393] They eat their own feces. A man and woman have sexual intercourse publicly like animals, the female positioning herself on all fours.

Second Chapter
concerning the [100v] *provincia* of Petlatlán[394] and the whole populated region as far as Chichilticale

Petlatlán is a settlement of houses covered with a sort of matting made from reeds. {-} [The houses are] congregated into *pueblos*.[395] [They] extend all along a river from the mountains to the sea.[396] They are a people of the same social level and habits[397] as the Tahues of Culiacán.[398] There are many homosexuals among them. They have a large population and a neighboring area of other *pueblos* toward the mountainous region. They differ [only] somewhat in language from the Tahues, because the ones and the others understand each other.[399] [The *provincia*] was called Petlatlán because the houses were made of mats [*petates*]. [101r] [Use of] this type of house is continuous throughout that region for two hundred and forty leagues and more, as far as the beginning of the unsettled area [before] Cíbola. At Petlatlán that land clearly forms a boundary; that is because from there onward there are no trees without spines, and there are no fruits except prickly pears, mesquite [beans], and *pitahayas*.

From Culiacán to there [Petlatlán] it is twenty leagues, and from Petlatlán to the valley of Señora it is a hundred and thirty. In between there are many rivers settled by the same sort of people. [These rivers] are [ones] such as Sinaloa, Boyomo, Teocomo, Yaquimí, and other, much smaller

ones.[400] Also [there] is Los Corazones, which is [101v] our base[401] downstream from the valley of Señora.

Señora is a river and valley heavily populated by very intelligent people.[402] {*Naguas*} The women wear petticoat-like skirts made of cured deerskin and little *sambenitos* ([which reach] to the middle of the body).[403] In the mornings those who are lords of the *pueblos* station themselves on small elevations which they have built for this purpose.[404] In the manner of public proclamations, [that is to say] town criers, they make announcements for the space of an hour, as though directing [the people of the *pueblo*] as to what they must do [that day]. They have several small buildings which serve as shrines, into which they thrust many arrows, which they put [102r] on the outside like [the bristles of] a hedgehog.[405] They do this when they expect to have war.

Around this *provincia*, toward the mountains, there are large settlements in separate small *provincias*. They are composed of ten or twelve and seven or eight clustered *pueblos*. Of these that I know, the names are Comu, Patrico, Mochilagua, Arispa, and Vallecillo.[406] There are other *pueblos* toward the mountainous region which were not seen.

From Señora to the valley of [S]uya there are forty leagues.[407] The *villa* of San Gerónimo was settled in this valley. Afterward [the natives] rose up and killed part of the people who were settled [there], as will be seen farther on in the [102v] third part. In this valley there are many *pueblos* which they control in their neighborhood. The people are of the [same social] level as those of Señora. And [they are the same] as all the rest [of the people] who are found as far as the unsettled region beginning at Chichilticale, with regard to clothing, language, habits, and customs. The women are tattooed on the chin and around their eyes, like Moorish women of Barbary. They are flagrant homosexuals.

They drink a wine made from *pitahayas* (which are the fruits of giant cacti).[408] [The fruits] are opened like pomegranates. They become stupid from the wine. They make great quantities of a preserve from prickly pears. [The prickly pears] are preserved in large quantity in their juice, without other sweetener. From mesquite beans they make a bread [that looks] like cheese. It keeps the entire year. There are melons in this land [103r] so large that it requires a person to carry just one.[409] They make strips from them and cure them in the sun. When eaten they have the flavor of dried figs. When cooked they are very good and sweet. They are saved all year dried that way.

In this land {Eagles} golden eagles were seen. The lords keep them for their magnificence.[410] In all of these *pueblos* no gallinaceous birds of any sort were seen, except in this valley of [S]uya. There, chickens like those of Spain were found.[411] It is not known how [the chickens] [could have] penetrated so much *tierra de guerra*, being at war as all [the *pueblos*] are with each other. Between [S]uya and [103v] Chichilticale there are many rams and mountain goats with exceedingly large bodies and horns.[412] There were Spaniards who claim to have seen a herd of more than a hundred together. They run so fast that they quickly disappear.

At Chichilticale the land again forms a boundary, and the spiny forest disappears.[413] That is because the gulf reaches about as far as that place [and then] the coast turns and the mountain chain turns likewise.[414] There one finally crosses the mountainous land, [which] is broken to permit passage to the land's region of plains.

Third Chapter
concerning what Chichilticale is and the
unpopulated region; concerning Cíbola, its [104r]
customs and habits, and other things

Chichilticale was so called because the friars found in this vicinity a building that in former times was inhabited by people who split off from Cíbola.[415] It was made of reddish or bright red earth. The building was large and clearly seemed to have been strong. It must have been abandoned because of the [Indians] of that land, who are the most uncivilized people of those that had been seen until then. They live in *rancherías*, without permanent habitations.[416] They live by hunting.

All the rest [of the region] is uninhabited,[417] covered by great pine forests. There are huge quantities of piñon nuts. The pines there are [104v] spreading [and] from two to three *estados* tall.[418] There are oak forests with sweet acorns and juniper trees that yield a fruit [that looks] like dry coriander candy. It is very sweet, like sugar.[419] At several springs there are watercress, rosebushes, pennyroyal, and

oregano.[420] In the rivers of this unsettled region there are whiskered and freshwater carp like [those] in Spain. There are leopards [jaguars],[421] which were seen from the beginning of the unsettled region.

The land rises continually until Cíbola is reached, which is eighty leagues toward the north.[422] From Culiacán, until reaching there [Cíbola], [the expedition] had traveled keeping the North Star over the left eye.[423]

[105r] Cíbola comprises seven *pueblos*.[424] The largest is called Mazaque. Usually the buildings are three- and four-storied. At Mazaque there are buildings of four and [even] seven stories. These people are very intelligent. They go about with their genitals and all their indecent parts covered with cloths similar to table napkins with fringes and a tassel at each corner. They fasten them above their hips. They wear long robes made of feathers and rabbit fur and [they wear] cotton *mantas*. The women are dressed in *mantas* which they tie or tie together over the left shoulder, and they expose the right arm.[425] On top [the *mantas*] are cinched around the body. They wear cloaks made of hide and finished in an excellent [105v] way. They gather their hair above both ears. [The hair] is formed into two wheels, which look like the buns of a [Spanish] hairdo.[426] [See fig. 17.1.]

This land is a valley between short ranges of mountains [which are] like bluffs.[427] They plant in holes.[428] The corn plant[s] do not grow tall from the base. Concerning the ears, [there are] three or four on each stalk, fat and long and with about eight hundred kernels.[429] [That is] something not seen [elsewhere] in this region. In this *provincia* there is a great number of bears, lions, and short-tailed cats.[430] And there are very fine beavers.

They trade turquoises, though not in the quantity [the reports] said.[431] They collect and store piñon nuts for the year.

A man does not have more than one wife. In the *pueblos* {patios} there are *estufas*, which are in the patios [106r], or plazas. [This is] where they come together for deliberation. There are no lords like [those] throughout Nueva España. [Instead], they are governed by a council of the oldest [persons].[432] They have their priests, whom they call *papas* and who preach to them. These [persons] are elderly. They climb to the highest roof of the *pueblo*, and from there, in the mornings when the sun rises, they make proclamations to the *pueblo*, like town criers. Everyone in the *pueblo* remains silent, sitting in the covered passageways, listening. [The priests] tell them how they must live. And I think they enunciate some rules they have to adhere to. [That is] because among them there is no drunkenness or homosexuality or sacrifices, nor do they eat human flesh or steal.[433] They work communally [106v] in the *pueblo*. The *estufas* are shared. It is a sacrilege for the women to go into the *estufas* to sleep. They form a cross as a sign of peace. They burn their dead and cast into the fire with them the implements they possess for use in their trades.

Tusayán is twenty leagues [in a direction] between north and west.[434] It is a *provincia* of seven *pueblos* of the same sort (dress, habits, and customs) as those of Cíbola.[435] In these two *provincias* there are probably fourteen *pueblos* and as many as three or four thousand men. To Tiguex it is forty or more leagues by the northern route.[436] In between [Cíbola and Tiguex] there is the steep, rugged hill of rock of Acuco, which we told about in the first part.

[107r]

Fourth Chapter
how the [people] of Tiguex live, about the
provincia of Tiguex and its environs

Tiguex is a *provincia* of twelve *pueblos* [on the] banks of a great and copiously flowing river, some *pueblos* on one side and others on the other.[437] It is a broad valley two leagues in width. To the east is a snow-covered mountain range, very high and rugged. At the foot of it on the backside there are seven *pueblos*, four [of them] in the flats and three situated in the foothills of the mountain range.[438]

Seven leagues to the north is Quirix, [which] has seven *pueblos*.[439] To the [northwest] forty leagues is Hemes, [which] has seven *pueblos*.[440] [107v] To the north or east four leagues is Acha.[441] To the southeast is Tutahaco, a *provincia* of eight *pueblos*.[442] In general, all these towns have the same habits and customs, although they do have some distinctive things which the others do not have. They are [all] governed by a council of the oldest [persons].

They erect their buildings communally. The women are in charge of making the mortar and putting up the walls. The men bring the wood and set it in place. There is no lime, but they make a mortar of charcoal ash and soil. This [mortar] is [only] slightly inferior to [that made] from lime, because when the building must have four stories, they build the [108r] the wall no wider than half a *vara*. They assemble a great quantity of sage twigs and reeds and set fire to them. When it is between charcoal and ash, they throw in much soil and water and mix it. From it they form round lumps which they use in place of stone, after they have dried. They cement them with the same mixture, so that afterward it is like mortar.

The young men of marriageable age serve the *pueblo* as a whole. They bring the firewood that must be consumed, and they set it in a pile in the patios of the *pueblo*, from which the women take it to carry to their houses. The place of residence of the young men is in the [108v] *estufas*, which are underground in the patios of the *pueblo*. [They are] square or circular, with pine pillars. Some were seen with twelve pillars, some with four [forming a] central space, each [pillar] of two *brazas* in girth. The usual [*estufas*] were of three or four pillars. The floors [were made] of large, smooth stone slabs, as [in] the baths which are the fashion in Europe. Inside, they have a fireplace [that looks] like a compass cabinet on a ship. There they light a handful of sage, with which they maintain the heat. They can be inside like [being] in a bath. The roof [is] level with the ground. One [*estufa*] was seen [which was] so spacious that it probably would accommodate a *juego de bolas*.[443]

When anyone needs to marry [109r] it must be [done] in accordance with the rules of those who govern. The young man must spin yarn and weave a *manta* and lay it before the woman. If she covers [herself] with it, she is regarded as his wife. The houses belong to the women, the *estufas* to the men. If the young man spurns his wife, he must for that reason go to the *estufa*. It is an irreverent act for [a woman] to sleep in the *estufa* or [even] to enter on any business other than to take food to her husband or her sons. The men spin and weave. The women raise the children and cook the food.

The land is so productive that they do not pull up the stubble during the whole year other than in order to plant.[444] [That is] because then the snow falls and covers what has been planted, [and] the ears of corn sprout beneath the snow.

[109v] In one year they harvest [enough] for seven.[445] There is a huge number of cranes, geese, ravens, and robins which live off the planted land.[446] [Even] with all this, when they plant again for the next year the fields are covered with corn which they have not been able to finish storing away. There are in these *provincias* a great many native chickens and roosters with wattles [turkeys]. When they are dead, they were customarily kept for sixty days without a foul odor, [if] they are not plucked or opened up. Dead men [last] the same [length of time], and longer when it is winter.

The *pueblos* are free of waste because [110r] [the residents] go out [of the *pueblo*] to defecate, and they urinate in clay vessels and take them outside [the *pueblo*] to empty. They have houses that are excellently divided up [and] very clean, where they cook food and where they grind flour. The [latter place] is a separate room or small secluded room[447] where they have a large grinding bin with three stones set in mortar,[448] where three women go, each one to her stone. One of them breaks the grain,[449] the next grinds [it], and the next grinds [it] again. Before [the women] go through the door,

they remove their shoes and gather up their hair. They shake their clothes and cover their heads. While they grind, a man is seated at the door playing [music] with a flute. [110v] To the melody they draw their stones and sing in three parts. On a single occasion they grind a large quantity [of flour], because they make all their bread, like wafers, from flour mixed with hot water. All year they gather and dry a great quantity of small plants for cooking. In the land there are no fruits to eat except piñon nuts.[450]

They have their preachers. There is no homosexuality among them, nor do they eat human flesh or sacrifice it. They are not a bloodthirsty people. [This is known] because Francisco de Ovando was left dead in Tiguex for about forty days, and when the town had been completely overcome, [members of the expedition] found him intact, among [the Indians' own] dead, without any injury other than the wound from which he died.[451] [He was] white like snow [111r] and without a foul odor.

One of our Indians [allies], who had been a captive among [the Pueblos] for one year, succeeded in learning

FIGURE 28.7. Woman grinding corn, Cochití Pueblo. Courtesy Museum of New Mexico, neg. no. 40791.

something about their customs.⁴⁵² When I asked him in particular why the young women in that *provincia* went about naked, even when it was so very cold, he told me the virgins must go about that way until they take husbands. Once they had carnal relations with a young man, they covered themselves. The men in that area wear short shirts made of cured deer hide. Over those [they wear] their robes. Throughout all of these *provincias* there is pottery glazed with lead⁴⁵³ and jars of consummate workmanship and very many shapes. That was something to see.

[111v]

Fifth Chapter
concerning Cicuyc and the towns of its environs and about how some peoples came to conquer that land

We have already told about Tiguex and all of the *provincias* which are on the bank of that river. Because the people are all of one social level and state, with the same customs, it will not be necessary to distinguish anything among them. I want to tell only about the site of Cicuye and about several depopulated *pueblos* which are situated near the direct route which the expedition followed to [go] there. Also [about] others which are behind the snow-covered mountain range of Tiguex. These [latter] [112r] are also in that region, away from the river.

Cicuye is a *pueblo* of as many as five hundred fighting men. It is feared throughout that whole land. With regard to its site, it forms a square situated on a rocky headland.⁴⁵⁴ In the middle [there is] a great patio, or plaza, with its *estufas*.

The buildings are all of the same height, [which is] four stories. At that height one walks through the whole town without there being a street which might hinder that. At each of the first two stories [the *pueblo*] is completely surrounded by covered passageways.⁴⁵⁵ [It is] by means of them that one walks through the whole town. They are like balconies that extend outward. Beneath them [the people] can take shelter. The buildings do not have doors at ground level. Ladders that can be raised up are used, [by which] they mount to the passageways [112v] that are within the town. Things are arranged there so that the doors of the buildings open onto the passageway on that level. The passageway

functions as a street. The buildings that face the countryside are back to back with those within, on the patio.

In time of war [the people] communicate with each other by means of the interior doors. [The *pueblo*] is surrounded by a low stone wall.⁴⁵⁶ Within [the *pueblo*] there is a spring of water which [the people] can impound. The people of this *pueblo* boast that no one has been able to subjugate them and that they subjugate [whichever] *pueblos* they want to.

They are of the same state and [have the] same customs as the other *pueblos*. [For instance], the virgins [there] also go about naked until they take husbands. They say [this is] because if they perform any improper act, it will immediately be [113r] seen. Thus, [the young women] will not do it. Nor are they to be ashamed that they go about as they were born.

Between Cicuye and the *provincia* of Quirix there is a small, strong *pueblo* to which the Spaniards gave the name Ximena⁴⁵⁷ and another *pueblo* almost entirely depopulated, of which only one section is inhabited. This [latter] *pueblo* was important, judging by its location. It seemed as if it had recently been destroyed. This [*pueblo*] was called Los Silos [underground storerooms]⁴⁵⁸ because great underground storerooms of corn were found in it.

Farther on there was another great *pueblo*, totally destroyed and devastated.⁴⁵⁹ In its patios [there were] many stone balls as large as one-*arroba* jugs,⁴⁶⁰ which [113v] appeared to have been hurled by [some] war machine⁴⁶¹ or catapult. With them [the attackers] had destroyed the *pueblo*. Concerning this, [the Spaniards were] able to learn that it was probably sixteen years earlier,⁴⁶² when some people called Teyas had come into that land in large numbers and had destroyed those *pueblos*. They had also besieged Cicuye but had been unable to take [it] because it was strong. When [the Teyas] left that land, they had made pacts of friendship with the whole land.

It seems as though they must have been a mighty people and they must have had war machines in order to demolish the *pueblo*. [The Pueblos] did not know how to say from what area [the Teyas] came, except to gesture toward the north. Generally these peoples [the Pueblos] characterize these [114r] Teyas as brave people, in the same way the Mexicanos [Nahuas] portray Chichimecas or Teules.⁴⁶³

Because [of those pacts] the Teyas that the expedition encountered, although they were fierce, were on good terms with the people from the settlements and [were] their allies, because they go to spend the winters there [at the *pueblo*], beneath the edges of the roofs of the settlement. [They stay there] because [the residents] do not dare welcome [the Teyas] inside, since they do not trust them. Although [the Pueblos] receive them in friendship and trade with them, [the Teyas] do not remain in the *pueblos* at night, but rather outside beneath the edges of the roofs. And [the people of] the *pueblos* keep watch, [sounding] a conch shell and calling out, as [in] the fortresses of Spain.[464]

There are seven other *pueblos* off to the side [114v] of this trail toward the snow-capped mountain range.[465] One was half destroyed by these people previously mentioned [the Teyas], who are under allegiance to Cicuyc.

Cicuye is in a small valley between mountain ranges and lands forested with great stands of pine. It includes a small stream which has many fine trout and beavers.[466] Many large bears and excellent falcons flourish around there.

Sixth Chapter
in which is made known how many *pueblos* were seen in the terraced settlements, and their population

It seems to me that before setting out [115r] to tell about the [bison] plains and their population and *ranchería* settlement, it would be good that it be known how large the population was that was seen in multistoried buildings in aggregated *pueblos*. And also what extent of land [was occupied].

I say that Cíbola is the first [*provincia*].

Cíbola [comprises] seven *pueblos*.
Tusayán, seven *pueblos*.
The steep, rugged hill of rock of Acuco, one.
Tiguex, twelve *pueblos*.
Tutahaco, eight *pueblos*. These *pueblos* [Tutahaco] are downstream along the river.

Quirix [comprises] seven *pueblos*.
By the snow-covered mountain range, seven *pueblos*.
Jimena, three *pueblos*.

Cicuye, one *pueblo*.

Jemez, seven *pueblos*.

[115v] Aguas Calientes, three *pueblos*.[467]

Yuque Yunque, [including the pueblos] in the mountain range, six *pueblos*.[468]

Valladolid, called Uraba, one *pueblo*.

Chia, one *pueblo*.

In all they total sixty-six *pueblos*.[469] It appears that Tiguex is at the heart of the *pueblos*. Valladolid is the [settlement] farthest upriver to the northeast. The four *pueblos* [which are farthest] downriver [are] to the southeast, because the river turns toward the east. From the point from which the lower river was seen to the other from which the upper river was seen, in which [stretch] the entire population [lives], there are a hundred and thirty leagues, ten [leagues] more or less.[470]

All the *pueblos*, including [116r] those [located] in the areas transverse [to the river], total sixty-six, as I have said. In them all there may be about twenty thousand men, which can be considered and understood as the population of the *pueblos*.[471] Between the various *pueblos* there are no isolated houses or other dwellings. Instead, [it is] all uninhabited.

Because they are a people of small numbers and are so different in behavior, government, and civilization from all the peoples which have been seen and discovered in these western regions, it is understood that they are foreigners from that part of Greater India, the coast of which lies toward the west of this land.[472] They may have [116v] descended through that region, crossing those mountain ranges, coming downstream along that river [Río de Tiguex],[473] and settling in the place that seemed best to them. Because they had been increasing in numbers, they were establishing [more] settlements until they found no more river, because it disappears underground, flowing toward La Florida and descending from the northeast.[474]

From that region [the northeast], news of *pueblos* continued to be received [even] when El Turco (who was reporting it) ceased to be followed. I think that if those mountain ranges where that river has its headwaters were crossed and [if] the lands from which those people originate were entered, magnificent news would probably be obtained. [That is] because, according to the direction, [that land] is the beginning of Greater India, although [in] remote regions, [117r] unfamiliar and unknown. [And also] because, as is proven by the coast, the land is very far to the interior between Norway and China, in the middle of the land[mass]. The width from sea to sea is great, according to what the directions of both coasts make clear (both what Captain Villalobos discovered traveling across this Mar de Poniente in search of China and what may be discovered in the Mar del Norte on the route to Los Bacallaos, which is located upward along the coast of La Florida toward Norway).[475]

In order that [we may] return to the subject of what [had already been] begun, I state that in a space of seventy leagues [117v] across[476] that settled land and of a hundred and thirty leagues lengthwise along the Río de Tiguex, no more peoples or settlements were seen or found than those already related. There are *repartimientos* in Nueva España with a greater number of people, and not just one but many.[477] In many of those *pueblos* [along the Río de Tiguex] there was silvery metal,[478] which they had in order to glaze pottery and paint their faces.

Seventh Chapter
which deals with the plains which were crossed [and] with the [bison] and peoples who inhabit them

We have already spoken about the settled area [118r] with multistoried [*pueblos*]. As it appears, that is in the center of the mountain chain, in the most level and spacious [part] of it. [We know that] because there is a crossing of a hundred and fifty leagues before one enters the plain which is between the two mountain chains, I mean the one that is toward the Mar del Norte and the one that is toward the Mar del Sur (which along this coast could better be called the Mar de Poniente).[479] This mountain chain [where Tiguex is] is the one that is toward the Mar del Sur. In order to understand how, as I say, the settled area is in the middle

of the mountain chain, I state that it is eighty leagues to Cíbola from Chichilticale (which is [at] the beginning of the crossing to Cíbola). [118v] From [Cíbola] (which is the first *pueblo*) to Cicuye (which is the last in the transverse crossing) it is seventy leagues.[480] From Cicuyc to the plains it is thirty leagues, to the beginning of them.[481]

It may be that [the plains] were crossed somewhat transversely or obliquely, from which cause it appears that there is a greater extent of land than if [they] were crossed through the middle. [That] might possibly be more difficult and rugged [land]. This may not be well understood because of the turn which the mountain chain makes away from the coast of the gulf of the Río del Tizón.[482]

Now we will speak about the plains, which are a level and wide land. It is [119r] more than four hundred leagues in width across that region between the two mountain chains: the one that Francisco Vázquez [de] Coronado crossed toward the Mar del Sur, and the other that don Fernando de Soto's people crossed toward the Mar del Norte, entering by way of La Florida.

All of the plain which was seen was unsettled.[483] On traveling through [the plains] for two hundred and fifty leagues, the other mountain chain could not be seen, nor could a range of mountains or [even] a hill with a height of three *estados*. At intervals there were some lakes, round like plates [and] a stone's throw [119v] and more across.[484] Some [were] freshwater and some [were] salty. At these lakes there is some grass growing. Away from them all [the grass] is very short, [only] one *jeme* and less.[485]

The land is in the form of a ball, so that wherever a man stands, the sky encloses him at the distance of a crossbow shot. There are no groves of trees except along the rivers, which are in several *barrancas*. [The *barrancas*] are so hidden that they are not seen until [the people] are on their edge. They are of barren earth.[486] There are entrances [into the *barrancas*] which the [bison] make in order reach the water, which is deep [in the bottoms].

As I have said in the first part, across these plains[487] travel [120r] people in pursuit of the [bison], hunting and curing hides. [This latter they do] in order to take them [the hides] to the settled areas to sell during the winters, because they go there to spend the winter. Each band [goes] to wherever it finds itself closest, some to the settlements of Cicuye, others toward Quivira, [and] others toward La Florida, to the settlements that are toward that region and port.[488] They are people whom [the guides] call Querechos and Teyas.

They provided information about marvelous settlements. According to what was understood from these people[489] and from others who were in other places who gave information, [120v] the population there is exceedingly more numerous than that of the [Río de Tiguex] settlements.[490] Also [they are] more intelligent, better men-of-war, and more feared.

[The Querechos and Teyas] travel around like Arabs[491] with their tents and droves of dogs equipped with pads, packsaddles, and cinch[es]. When their load[s] twist on them [the dogs] howl, summoning someone to fix them. These people eat raw meat and drink the blood [of the bison]. They do not eat human flesh. They are a kind people and not violent. They hold faithfully to friendship. They are very skillful with signs.

They dry their meat in the sun, cutting it thin [121r] like a sheet of paper. When it is dry, they grind it like flour in order to store it and to make porridge. To eat [it] they throw a handful into a pot. [The pot] is filled because [the meat meal] swells up considerably. They cook it with lard, which they always try to render when they kill [a bison]. They emptied a large intestine and filled it with blood. They slung it around their neck[s] in order to drink when they [were] thirsty. When they have opened the stomach of a [bison], they press the chewed grass to the bottom and drink the juice that remains on top. They say that is the whole essence of the stomach.

They [cut] open the [bison] [121v] along the back and cut them apart at the joints with a flint as large as a finger, tied to a small stick. [They do this] as easily as if it were [done] with a very good [metal] implement, giving a cutting edge to [the flints] on [the bison's] own teeth.[492] The speed with which they do [the process] is something to see and observe.

Throughout these plains there is a great number of wolves that travel along behind the [bison].[493] They have white fur. The deer are streaked with white [and] the fur [is]

thick. When [the deer] has died, while [it is still] hot, [the skin] is peeled off with the hand. [The skinned deer] are left like peeled pig[s]. The rabbits, which exist [122r] in great multitudes, run about so stupidly that [the Spaniards] kill them with lances while riding horseback. That is to say [these things] were done among the [bison]. They run away from the footmen.

Chapter Eight
concerning Quivira and the direction in which it lies
and the news [the residents of Quivira] give

Quivira lies to the [northeast][494] of those canyons, in the middle of the land[mass], somewhat close to the mountain chain of the Mar [del Norte]. [This is known] because as far as Quivira the land is level, but at that place there begin to be some mountain ranges. The land is heavily populated. As [it was] from the beginning, [122v] this land was seen to be very much like the [land] of Spain, in regard to its types of plants and fruits. There are plums like the ones in Spain, grapes, walnuts, blackberries, rye grass, oats, pennyroyal, oregano, and flax in great quantity. They do not make use of [the flax] because they do not know how to use it.[495]

The people are of nearly the [same] sort and [have nearly the same] dress as the Teyas. They have towns of the same type as those in Nueva España:[496] the houses are round, without fence[s]; they have upper stories like buildings on stilts; [up there] underneath the roof [is] where they sleep and have their belongings; the roofs are made of thatch. In its environs there are other very populous *provincias* [123r] with large numbers of people.

A friar called fray Juan de Padilla stayed here in this *provincia* [Quivira], along with a Portuguese Spaniard,[497] a Black, a mestizo, and certain Indians from the *provincia* of Zapotlán in Nueva España. [The people of Quivira] killed the friar because he wanted to go to the *provincia* of the Guas, who were their enemies. The Spaniard escaped, fleeing on a mare, and afterward arrived in Nueva España. He made his exit by way of Pánuco.[498] The Indians from Nueva España who had gone with the friar buried him with [123v] the consent of his murderers. Then they traveled in

FIGURE 28.8. A Wichita grass lodge under construction at the Trans-Mississippi International Exposition, Omaha, Nebraska, 1898. The houses Castañeda de Nájera reported for Quivira must have been similar to this. Courtesy Museum of New Mexico, neg. no. 4852.

Hercules knew about the location where Julius Caesar was to found Sevilla, or Hispalis.[501] {This says nothing.}

It is granted to the all-powerful Lord to be served by everything. It is certain that if it had been His will, Francisco Vázquez would not have returned to Nueva España without cause or reason, nor would the [people] of don Fernando de Soto [125r] have failed to settle such excellent land as they have, [land which is] also so heavily populated and abundant.[502] Especially having received, as they had, news of our expedition.

Third Part

in which is related what befell
Francisco Vázquez [de] Coronado while he
was passing the winter; how he abandoned the
expedition and returned to Nueva España
laus deo [glory to God]

[125v] [blank]

[126r]

First Chapter
how don Pedro de Tovar came from Señora
with a troop and [how] don García López de Cárdenas
left for Nueva España

At the end of the first part of this book we told how, when Francisco Vázquez [de] Coronado had returned from Quivira, he arranged that [the expedition] would spend the winter in Tiguex and [that], when the winter had passed, he would return with his entire expedition to reconnoiter all those settlements.[503] In the meantime, don Pedro de Tovar (who, as we said, had gone to get a troop from the *villa* of San Gerónimo) arrived [126v] with the troop which he was bringing. Because, in truth, he thought he would be going to the land of the Indian called Turco [by the Spaniards], in search of his general, it suited him to bring good people. He did not choose the seditious or rebellious ones but rather the most experienced and best men-at-arms, [the most] trustworthy men he could.

Because, however, when they reached Tiguex they

pursuit of the Spaniard until they overtook him. This Spaniard was Portuguese. He had the name Campo.

The great river Espíritu Santo, which don Fernando de Soto reconnoitered in the land of La Florida, flows from this land and, according to what was taken as truthful information there, passes through a *provincia* called Arache.[499] Its sources were not seen, because, according to what [the people there] say, it comes from a faraway land of the southern mountain chain (from that region which drains to the plains). It crosses the entire plain, [124r] breaks through the mountain chain of the [Mar del] Norte, and goes to where the [men] of Fernando de Soto navigated it.[500] It is more than three hundred leagues to the sea from where [Soto] embarked. Because of this and because of the great tributaries it has, it flows so strongly out into the sea that [even when Soto's men] had lost sight of land, the water was fresh.

This land of Quivira was the most distant [place] that was seen and about which I can now provide information or make a report. Now it is appropriate for me to return to speak about the expedition, which I left in Tiguex, resting for the winter, in order to be able to go farther or seek again these [124v] settlements of Quivira. Afterward, this did not happen, because God was pleased to have these discoveries left to other people and to have us, who went there, be content with saying that we were the first who reconnoitered [Quivira] and received news of [the settlements beyond]. In the same way found the expedition there, it did not please them very much. [That is] because they arrived cocksure, believing they would find the general in the wealthy land of the Indian called Turco. They consoled themselves with the expectation of the return [to Quivira] which surely would be made, and they lived in great pleasure and happiness with the expectation [127r] of the return which surely would be made and that the expedition would very soon go to Quivira.

With don Pedro de Tovar came letters from Nueva España, both from the viceroy don Antonio de Mendoza and from private individuals.[504] Among the latter, they gave one to don García López de Cárdenas in which [an unnamed correspondent] informed him of the death of a brother of his, possessor of the family estate. [They] summoned him to Spain to take up the inheritance. He had a license for this purpose and departed from Tiguex with a few other people who held license[s] to leave in order to rest at their homes. Many others would have wanted to go, [but] they abandoned [the idea] in order not to show [127v] weakness.

During this time an effort was made to bring to peace several *pueblos* of the region that had not fully come to terms and to summon the [people] of Tiguex [itself] to peace.[505] [An effort was also made] to locate some native clothing, because the men-at-arms at this point were going about very poorly dressed,[506] in a poor state, and full of lice. Obviously,[507] they were not able to eliminate or get rid of [the lice].

Among his captains and men-at-arms, General Francisco Vázquez [de] Coronado had been the best liked and obeyed captain who could ever have gone forth in the Indies. But because necessity is in need of regulation and the captains who distributed the clothing did it unfairly (taking the best [128r] for themselves and their friends and *criados* and distributing the leftovers to the men-at-arms), there began to be grumblings and sourness. Some of it [was] because of what has been related and some because it was seen that several notable persons were exempted from work and from standing watch, but were given a better share of what was distributed (both from the clothing and from the food supplies). Because of this, it is thought, [the discontented men-at-arms] were now saying to each other that there was nothing in Quivira for which to return. As will be seen, this was no small reason for what came later.

Second Chapter
how the general fell and the return to Nueva [128v] España was ordered

When winter was over, the return to Quivira was announced, and the people started collecting the necessary items. Because, [however], nothing in this life is under the control of humans, but rather [everything is] under the direction of all-mighty God, it was His will that our [plans] did not come to fruition. What happened was that on one day of celebration the general went out to enjoy himself on horseback, as he was in the habit of doing. He was on a strong horse, and his *criados* had put on a new cinch which, with the passage of time, must have been rotten. While [the general was] racing side by side with Captain don Rodrigo Maldonado [129r] it burst in the midst of the race. [The general] ended up falling to the side don Rodrigo was on and he ran over [Vázquez de Coronado]. The horse ended up striking him in the head with its hoof.[508] He came to the brink of death from [the blow]. His convalescence was long and fearful.[509]

While [the general] was bedridden, don García López de Cárdenas, who had left to go to Nueva España, returned from [S]uya. [He was] in flight because he had found the *villa* abandoned and the people, horses, and livestock dead. He reached Tiguex. When he had learned the sad news that the general was in the condition already described, [129v] [he and those with him] did not dare tell [Vázquez de Coronado about Suya] until he was well. At last, when he recovered, he learned of [the news] and was so affected by it that he fell ill again.

According to what was later believed, because of [this] piece of bad luck he came to do what he did.[510] [This] was because when he found himself in that situation, the memory came to him that in Salamanca an astrologer[511] friend of his had told him that he was certain to find himself a lord in foreign lands, and influential. And that he was certain to suffer a fall from which he could not recover. This mental image of his death gave him the desire to go back to where he had a wife and children, to die.

His own physician and surgeon,[512] who was treating him (and was also a gossip), [130r] learned about the grumblings

that were going on among the men-at-arms. He spoke
secretly and surreptitiously with several *caballeros* who shared
his opinion. They were to bring about the return to Nueva
España by holding meetings and small gatherings among
the men-at-arms, so that they could be asked for advice.
[The men-at-arms] were to petition the general through
their *alféreces* with open letters signed by all the men-at-
arms. This [the *caballeros*] discussed very thoroughly. It was
not necessary to spend much time [to bring this about],
because many [persons] already held [that opinion] willingly.

As soon as they petitioned him about it, the general
made a pretense of not wanting to do it [return to Nueva
España] unless all the *caballeros* and captains concurred by
giving their [130v] signed formal opinion[s].[513] Because
several [men] were involved in [the original plan], they
immediately gave it and even persuaded the others to do the
same. Thus, they gave their formal opinion, [which was] that
they should return to Nueva España, because nothing of
wealth had been found and there was no settlement in what
had been reconnoitered where *repartimientos* could be made
to the whole expedition.[514]

As soon as [the general had] gathered the signatures, the
return to Nueva España was announced. Because nothing
can be concealed, the [general's] duplicity began to be
exposed, and many *caballeros* found themselves insulted and
embarrassed. They tried in every way to retrieve their signatures [131r] from the general. [But] he guarded them so
[carefully] that he did not leave one room, pretending that
his ailment was much worse and posting guards over himself
and the room, and at night [posting guards] on the roofs
where he was sleeping. [Even] with all this, [the disgruntled
caballeros] stole his trunk[515] from him. But it is said that they
did not find their signatures in it because he was keeping
them in his mattress.[516] On the other hand, it is [also] said
that they did retrieve them.

[The disgruntled *caballeros*] requested that the general
leave seventy chosen men.[517] They would stay there and hold
the land until the viceroy sent them aid or summoned them
[to return]. Alternatively, [they requested] that the general
leave the main body of the expedition and choose seventy
men, with whom he would depart. The men-at-arms,
however, [131v] refused to stay under either the one [plan]

or the other. [That was] because, for one thing, they had
already "set their prow" toward Nueva España and, for
another, they saw clearly the conflict which was sure to arise
over who must be in command.

The *caballeros*, it is not known whether because they had
sworn loyalty or because they believed the men-at-arms
would not support them, had to endure it and abide by what
had been decided, despite being humiliated. From then on,
however, they did not obey the general as had been their
habit. And he was disliked by them, while he held the men-
at-arms in high regard and rewarded them. This was going
to make ready [132r] the result he wanted: that the return of
the entire expedition would be carried out.

Third Chapter
how [S]uya rose up in arms and the provocations
for it [that] the [Spanish] settlers gave

In the preceding chapter we already told how don García
López de Cárdenas returned in flight from [S]uya, because
he found the land up in arms. It remains to tell how and why
that *villa* was abandoned. It happened as I will narrate. The
situation was that already no one remained in that *villa*
[132v] except the inferior, venal people, rebellious and seditious men. Although a few upright individuals remained in
the public offices in order to govern the rest, the wickedness
of the inferior [people] was stronger. Every day they were
conspiring and conniving illegally, saying that they were
betrayed, because communication with that land [Tierra
Nueva] was being conducted through another area more
convenient to Nueva España than that one was.[518] [They
did] not [conspire] in order to take unscrupulous advantage.
And they were nearly correct.

Driven by this, [133r] a certain company, having chosen
one Pedro de Ávila as leader, mutinied and returned to Culiacán. This left Diego de Alcaraz as their captain with a few
sick people in that *villa* of San Gerónimo,[519] so that there
was no one who could go after [the mutineers] and compel
them to come back. In a few *pueblos* along their route [the
mutineers] killed some people. {Saavedra} Finally they
appeared at Culiacán, where Hernando Arias de Saavedra
stopped them.[520] They were delayed with words [133v]

because [Saavedra] was waiting for Juan Gallego, who was certain to come with a troop from Nueva España and would take [the mutineers] back [to San Gerónimo]. A few, being afraid of what was sure to happen, fled toward Nueva España in the night.

Diego de Alcaraz, who had stayed [in San Gerónimo] with a few sick people, could not maintain himself there, even though he wanted to.[521] [That was] because of danger from the deadly poison[522] the natives are accustomed to prepare in that area. [The natives], sensing the Spaniards' weakness, no longer allowed themselves to be treated as they used to be.[523] Prior to this, sources of gold had been discovered, [134r] but because they were in the *tierra de guerra* and there was no possibility [of working them], they were no longer being worked. Being in this uncertain situation, [the Spaniards at San Gerónimo] did not cease standing watch and were more diligent than they used to be.

The *villa* was established near a small river.[524] One night [the Spaniards] unexpectedly saw fires, which were not usual or customary. This caused them to double the guard. But because during the whole night they noticed nothing [else], they became careless at dawn. Their enemies entered the *pueblo* so silently that they were not seen until they were going about killing and robbing. [134v] A few people got out to the plain when they had the opportunity. During the exodus [the natives] fatally wounded the captain. When a few Spaniards rallied on some horses, they attacked their enemies again and went to the aid of some [other] people. Although [the Spaniards] were few, their enemies withdrew with their booty without receiving injury, leaving three Spaniards, many servants,[525] and more than twenty horses dead.

The Spaniards who remained set out that day, on foot [and] without horses, to return to Culiacán, [keeping] away from the trails.[526] [They were] without food supplies until [135r] they reached Los Corazones, where those Indians aided them with food, like [the] friends they always were.[527] [Going] from there, after having endured great difficulties, they reached Culiacán. There, *alcalde mayor* Hernandarias de Saavedra received and accommodated them as best he could until Juan Gallego arrived with the relief supplies he was bringing in order to go on in search of the expedition.

It weighed not a little on [Gallego] that the pass had been

abandoned, because he thought the expedition was in the wealthy land that had been told about by the Indian called Turco (because he seemed like one from his appearance).[528]

[135v]

Fourth Chapter
how fray Juan de Padilla and fray Luis stayed in the [northern] land and the expedition prepared for the return to [the Ciudad de] México

Because General Francisco Vázquez saw that everything was calm and his plans had been set under way according to his wishes, {1542} he ordered that once the beginning[529] of the month of April of the year [one thousand] five hundred and [forty-two][530] had arrived, everyone was to be prepared to set out on the return to Nueva España.

Seeing this, fray Juan de Padilla, a preaching friar of the Order of [Friars] Minor,[531] and another [136r] friar, Luis,[532] a lay brother, told the general that they wanted to stay in that land. Fray Juan de Padilla [wanted to stay] in Quivira because it seemed to him that there his teaching would bear fruit. And fray Luis [wanted to stay] in Cicuye. Because at the time it was Lent, one Sunday [fray Juan] preached the sermon about the priest of the company of soldiers. He based his argument on the authority of Holy Scripture. Because his great passion was to convert those people [of Quivira] and bring them to the Faith, and because he held a license, although for this it was not necessary, the general dispatched a company [of men-at-arms] with them to take them as far as Cicuyc.

There fray Luis remained. And fray Juan [136v] went on along the route to Quivira, taking the Portuguese we mentioned,[533] and the Black,[534] the mestizo, and the Indians from Nueva España,[535] along with the guides the general had brought from there [Quivira]. When [fray Juan] had arrived there, within a very short time [the natives] martyred him, as we related in the Second Part, Eighth Chapter. And it can be believed that he truly died a martyr, because his devotion was holy and complete.

Fray Luis remained at Cicuyc. Nothing has been learned about him to this day. Before the expedition left Tiguex, however, those who were taking a certain number of ewes to him (so they would be left with him) ran into him, accompanied by people [from Cicuyc], going to visit [137r] other towns that were fifteen and twenty leagues from Cicuye. [This] gave not a little positive expectation that he was in the good graces of the *pueblo* and that his preaching would bear fruit. He was complaining, however, that the elders were abandoning him, and he believed that in the end they would kill him. For my part, I maintain that because he was a man of good and holy life, Our Lord would protect him and grant him the favor of converting some of those people and, at the end of his days, of leaving someone to direct them in the Faith. It is not to be believed otherwise, because the people of that area are merciful and not the least bit violent.[536] Rather, they are friends [of the Spaniards] (or enemies of violence), and they keep their pledge and maintain loyalty to their friends.

[137v] When the friars had been sent off, the general, fearing lest his taking [native] people from that land to Nueva España harm him,[537] ordered that the native servants whom the men-at-arms had were to be allowed to go freely to their *pueblos* [or] to wherever they wanted. In my view, that was not correct, because it would have been better that they be taught among the Christians.[538]

The general now was cheerful and happy. When the [departure] date arrived and everyone had been supplied with what was necessary for their journey, the expedition departed from Tiguex [on] the return route to Cíbola.[539] On this trail one thing occurred which is not a little worth noting. It was that upon setting out, [although] the horses were accustomed to the work and were fat and beautiful, [138r] during the ten days it took to reach Cíbola more than thirty [of them] died. [That is] because there was not a day when two or three or more did not die.[540] And after that, until [the expedition] reached Culiacán, a great many of them died, which was something that had not happened during the entire [rest of] the journey.

When the expedition had arrived at Cíbola, it regrouped in order to set out across the unsettled land, because that place is the last of the settlements of that land. [It was] leaving the entire land pacified and calm. And some of our [Indian] allies stayed behind among [the settlements].[541]

Fifth Chapter
how the expedition left the settled land and traveled to Culiacán and what happened on the way

[138v] Now "leaving astern"[542] (we can say) the settlements which had been found in Tierra Nueva (which I have said were the seven *pueblos* of Cíbola, the first to be seen and the last to be left), the expedition set out, traveling across the unsettled region. For two or three days' journey the natives never stopped following the expedition, behind the rear guard, in order to pick up a little of the baggage or a few servants. [They did this] because, even though they had come to peace and had been excellent and loyal friends, still when they saw that the land was being left to them without restraints, they enjoyed seeing some of our people in their hands. [139r] It is believed, however, that [it was] not [done] to vent their anger on them.[543] This was learned from some [of the servants] who refused to go with [the people of Cíbola] but were constantly urged and begged by them [to go with them]. Even so, they persuaded a few people, and [there were] others who had remained of their own free will. Among those [who stayed] there are probably excellent interpreters today.

The unsettled region was traversed without opposition. They left Chichilticale, [and] Juan Gallego reached the expedition during the second day's travel.[544] He was coming from Nueva España with reinforcements of people and things necessary for the expedition, supposing that he would find it in the land of the Indian called Turco. When Juan Gallego saw that the expedition was returning, the first [139v] word out of his mouth was not to say, "What good luck that you are coming [back],"[545] and he did not feel any less [disappointed] after having talked with the general.

When [Gallego and his company] had reached the expedition, I mean its quarters, there probably was sedition among the *caballeros,* what with the new reinforcements, which had reached there with no small difficulty. Every day they had skirmishes with the Indians of those areas (who were up in arms, as has been said).[546] There were some negotiations and discussions about establishing a settlement somewhere around there until a report of what was happening was delivered to the viceroy. The troop of men-at-arms who were coming from Tierra Nueva, [however], consented to nothing except [140r] returning to Nueva España.

Because of this, nothing of what was proposed during [the *caballeros'*] deliberations came about, although there were some disturbances. In the end a few of the mutineers who had abandoned the *villa* of Los Corazones [and] who came with Juan Gallego were pacified. [They were] given guarantees by him, on his word. Even though the general might have wanted to impose some punishment, his authority was slight, because now he was disobeyed and little respected. From that point on [Vázquez de Coronado] again began to be afraid and made it appear he was ill, traveling with a guard.

At a few places there were some shrieks, [some] from Indians, [some] from [those who were] wounded, and [some from] the deaths of horses, until [the expedition] reached Batuco.[547] There, [140v] Indian allies from the valley of Los Corazones came to the camp in order to see the general, like [the] friends they always were. They had always treated all the Spaniards who had passed through their lands that way, supplying them with what they needed, with regard to food supplies, and people if that were necessary. Thus, they were always well treated and rewarded by our [people] during this expedition.

Concerning the juice of the quince, it was shown to be effective against the [poisonous] herb of these regions. [That was] because at a pass a few days' journey before [the expedition] reached the valley of Señora the enemy Indians wounded a Spaniard named Mesa.[548] Because the wound was life threatening because of [141r] fresh poison, they spent more than two hours treating it with the juice. [And] he did not die, although the [area] which the poison had infected was rotten, and the flesh fell away, until the bones and sinews were left bare, with a pestilential stench. Although the wound was in the wrist, the poison had reached all the way to the shoulder when he finally recovered. The flesh fell away from all of this [part of his body].

The expedition was traveling without taking rest because already at this time there was a lack of food.[549] Because [the people of] those areas were up in arms, there

was nowhere to get provisions until [the expedition] reached Petlatlán.[550] [They did, however] make several forays to the [141v] side [of their route] looking for food supplies.

Petlatlán is in the *provincia* of Culiacán. For that reason it was at peace, although afterward there have been some surprises here.[551] The expedition rested there for a few days in order to [re]supply. Having left there with greater speed than previously, they sought to cross those thirty leagues which there are to the valley of Culiacán. There [the settlers] once again gave them shelter, as people who were coming with their injured governor.

Sixth Chapter
how the general departed from Culiacán in
order to give the viceroy a report of the expedition
of which he had put him in command

[142r] Having reached the valley of Culiacán, it now seem[ed] that the difficulties of this expedition were at an end because, on the one hand, the general was governor [there] and, on the other, they were in a land of Christians. Thus, some [men] began to chafe under the authority and control their captains exercised over them. And some captains [likewise began to chafe] under their obedience to the general. And each one put his plans first, so that when the general went to the *villa*, which was ten leagues from there, many people, or [even] most of them, stayed in the valley resting, some with the aim of not following him.

[142v] The governor sensed full well that he was no longer strong by simple force. The authority of being governor, however, conferred on him another, different authority. And he made up his mind to accomplish what [he desired] by another [and] better means, which was to order that all the captains be given food supplies and meat from what there was in a few *pueblos* which were under his jurisdiction as governor. And he made a show of being incapacitated, taking to bed. Because of this, those who needed to confer with him could speak with him or he with them more freely and without reticence or interference. He did not stop sending [people] to summon a few special friends to ask and assign them to talk with the men-at-arms and encourage them to

leave there [the valley] in his company on the return to Nueva [143r] España. [His friends] were to tell them that he was taking it on himself to see that those who chose to remain in his jurisdiction were given preferment, both by the viceroy don Antonio de Mendoza and within his jurisdiction itself.

When [Vázquez de Coronado] had negotiated this, he set out with his expedition in severe weather at the beginning of the rainy season. This was around the day of San Juan, at which time it rains heavily.[552] The rivers of that unsettled region, which are crossed as far as Compostela, are numerous, very dangerous, and full of large, ferocious crocodiles.[553] When the expedition was encamped at one of those rivers, a man-at-arms was crossing from one side to the other. In view of everyone he was seized by a caiman and carried off without any possibility of being helped.

The general traveled along, everywhere leaving people [143v] who refused to follow him. He reached [the Ciudad de] México with fewer than a hundred men to give Viceroy don Antonio de Mendoza a report.[554] He was not well received by [Mendoza], although he offered his justifications. From then on, he lost his reputation, and he held office only a short while [longer] in the jurisdiction of Nueva Galicia, which had been entrusted to him.[555] [This was] because the viceroy took charge of it himself until an *audiencia* came to [Nueva Galicia], as it [continues] to be there up to the present.[556] This was the conclusion that those reconnaissances had, and the expedition which was made to Tierra Nueva.

Now it is left to us to tell by what route it would be possible to enter [Tierra Nueva] by a more direct route. I say, however, that there is no shortcut without difficulty and [that] what is best is always what [144r] is known. [That is] because people prepare [themselves] well for what they know must come and the exigencies in which they find themselves once again.

And [it is left to us] to tell in what region Quivira lies and what the route is that the expedition took. Also in what region Greater India lies, which was what was being sought when the expedition set out to go there.[557] Because Villalobos has reconnoitered this coast of the Mar del Sur (which is west of this route), it is recognized and clearly

understood that it was necessary to turn, keeping as we were [at first], to the west of north, and not to the east, as we went. With this, we will leave this subject and conclude this treatise when I have given a report of a few notable things [144v] which I neglected to recount in order to discuss them separately in the following two chapters.

Seventh Chapter
concerning the things that happened to
Captain Juan Gallego as he was carrying relief supplies
through the land [which was] up in arms

One is probably distressed that in the last chapter I passed over in silence the feats Captain Juan Gallego accomplished with twenty companions he took with him. [That] is to be told in the present chapter so that in times to come those who read about it and give account of it may have an informed author they can consider trustworthy. [An author] who does not write fables like some of the things we read in our [145r] day in the books of chivalrous deeds.[558] Were it not for [the fact that] they contain fables of sorcery, there are things which have occurred in the present in these regions, to our own Spaniards, in conquests and skirmishes they have had with the natives, that surpass in wondrous deeds not only the books already mentioned but [also] those which are written about the twelve peers of France.[559] [That is] because when the deadly powers the authors of those times attribute to [the peers of France] are scrutinized and considered, as well as the shining and glittering arms and armor[560] that adorn them, and the small stature of the men of our day and the few and inferior arms and armor [145v] [there are] in these places, the singular things our people undertake and accomplish with such arms and armor in the present day [are] more to be admired than what they write about the ancients. [That is] because [the ancients] fought against barbarous and naked people, as [do] our people [against people] such as Indians. [In those places] there is no lack of men among [the Indians] [who] are brave and courageous, as well as very accurate archers. [That is known] because we have seen them shoot down birds that are flying, and [we have seen them] shoot jackrabbits[561] while running after them.

I have said this at the end because some things we hold to be fictitious can be true. And because in our times every day we see more marvelous things, such as those [performed] by don Fernando Cortés, [146r] who, with three hundred men,[562] ventured to penetrate the very heart of Nueva España, where [there was] such a great multitude of people as there is [in] México [Tenochtitlan].[563] Then, with five hundred Spaniards, in two years he ended up conquering and taking control of it, an extremely amazing thing. [So also were] the deeds of don Pedro de Alvarado in the conquest of Guatemala and those of Montejo in Tabasco. [And] the conquests of Tierra Firme and Peru.[564]

[Such] were all these things that I ought to omit and pass over in silence what I now want to relate. Because, however, I am obliged[565] to give a report of the things which transpired during this expedition [to Tierra Nueva] and [it is] desired that they be [146v] known, I will also now narrate those things, along with the rest I [already] related.

Thus it is that Captain Juan Gallego reached the *villa* of Culiacán with very few people and gathered there those he could from among those who had escaped from the *villa* of Los Corazones or, to say it more accurately, from [S]uya.[566] From all these places there were twenty-two men. With these he traveled through that entire settled land, in which he went two hundred leagues,[567] and a *tierra de guerra* [among] people who were up in arms, [people] who had previously been on good terms with the Spaniards.[568]

Every day, or a little less frequently, they had skirmishes with their enemies. [147r] Always he traveled so as to leave the baggage behind with two-thirds of the people. [He was] continually leading the advance guard with six or seven Spaniards without [any] allies from among those they took [with them], entering the towns by force, killing, laying waste, and setting fire.[569] They set upon their enemies so suddenly and with such speed and boldness that they did not give [the Indians] an opportunity to come together or [even] understand what had befallen them. Because [of this] they were so feared that there was not a *pueblo* that dared to await their [arrival].

Thus, they fled from [the Spaniards] as though from a powerful armed force. So much so that it happened that [the Spaniards] traveled for a full ten days through a settled land without having an hour's [147v] rest. [Gallego] did all this with seven companions, so that when the baggage arrived with all the rest of the troop, they had nothing to do except despoil those whom [Gallego and his party] had already killed and taken prisoner, [and] the people whom they were able to catch. The rest had fled. Because [Gallego and his party] did not stop to rest, even when the *pueblos* ahead had some warning, they were upon them so quickly that they did not give them an opportunity to assemble. This was especially [true] in that area where the *villa* of Los Corazones had been, so that there [Gallego] killed and hung a considerable number of people in punishment for their rebellion.

In all of this he did not lose a single companion, though [148r] [the Indians] wounded one. [That is,] except the one who, while he was despoiling an Indian who was nearly dead, [that same Indian] wounded him in the eyelid as he tore a hide from him.[570] Because [the wound] was [made] with the [poisonous] herb, he would necessarily have died, except that he was treated with quince juice.[571] And he did lose the eye.

Such were these *hijos*, I mean *hechos* [deeds], that those people will retain everything in [their] memory for as long as [their] lives last, especially four or five Indian allies who departed with [Gallego and his company] from Los Corazones. They were so amazed by this that they considered [the Spaniards' deeds] more as a divine thing than a human [one].[572] If our expedition had not run into them, as it did, [Gallego and his company] would certainly have reached the land of the Indian whom [the Spaniards] called [148v] Turco. [Which is] where they were on their way to. And they would have crossed [the land] without danger, judging by the excellent control and command [Gallego] was exercising and [by how] well trained and practiced [his troop was] in warfare.

Some of those [men] remained in this *villa* of Culiacán, where at present I am writing this narrative and report.[573] There we, both they and I, as well as the rest who halted in this *provincia*, have had no lack of hardships pacifying and maintaining this land, catching rebels and living in poverty and want. [Which] is worse right now because the land is poorer and shorter of money than it ever was.

Eighth Chapter
in which [149r] are recounted several amazing
things that were seen on the plains, together with the
distinguishing features of the [bison] bulls

It is no secret [that] in the Second Part of this book, in the Seventh Chapter (which speaks of the plains), I kept quiet and concealed the things about which I will make mention in this special chapter where [they] might be found all together, because they were notable things and not seen in other places. I venture to write them because I am writing at a time when many men are alive today who saw [them] and will verify my manuscript.

Who will be able to believe that when [149v] a thousand horses and five hundred of our cattle, more than five thousand rams and ewes and more than one thousand five hundred persons among the allies and servants [of the expedition] were traveling across those plains [and had] finished crossing [an area] they left no more trace than if no one had ever crossed there.[574] So much [was this so] that it was necessary to put up large heaps of bones and [bison] dung at intervals in order that the rearguard could be guided behind the [main body of the] expedition and not get lost.[575] When the grass is walked on, although [it is] very short, it returns upright, as unmarked and straight as it was before.

Another thing, which was found on the shore of a salt lake, on the [150r] south side, in an area where there are no people who could have created it, [was] a great accumulation of [bison] bones which had the length of a crossbow shot or a little less and a [height] of nearly two *estados* in places and [was] three *brazas* and more wide in one place.[576] What was thought about it was that, with the retreat of the waves [which] the lake or pond must have formed during a time of north winds, it has amassed the [bones] of the grazing animals that died within the pond. On entering [the water] they [could] not get out, because of [being] either old or weak. What must be noted is what a number of animals would be necessary for so many skeletons.

Now, I also want to recount the distinguishing features of the [bison] bulls. It is [150v] amazing that at first there was not a horse that looked them in the face that did not flee from their gaze. [That is] because they have a wide and short face. From eye to eye [it is] two *palmos* across the forehead. The eyes [are] protuberant from the side [of the head], so that when they are running in flight they [can] see whoever is chasing them. They have very large beards, as billy goats [have]. When they run away they carry the head low, the beard dragging across the ground. From the middle of the body to the rear, they are narrow-waisted [with] very fine, dense, and short hair, like ewes. From the waist forward the hair [is] very long in the manner of a raging lion. [It has] a great hump, larger than [that] of a camel. The horns [are] short and stout; [151r] they are exposed [only] a little above the hair. About May they shed their hair from the middle of the body to the rear in a fleece, which turns them into veritable lions. In order to get rid of their hair, they rub against the few small trees there are in some small ravines. There they scrape themselves until they cast off the fleece, as a snake [does] its skin. They have [a] short tail and a small brush at the end. They carry it high when they run, in the way a scorpion [does]. It is something to see that when they are young calves, they are bright red and like our cattle. With time and age they change in color and [other] features.

There is one more thing, which [is] that all the bulls that were killed had their [151v] left ear split, although they have them undamaged when [they are] young.[577] This was a mystery of which it was not possible to understand the cause. Concerning the wool, judging by its fineness, excellent fabrics would be made [from it], although not in colors because it is of a dark red color.

Another thing of note is that the bulls go about without cows in such great numbers that there is no one who could count them. They are separated so far from the cows that from where we began to see bulls to where we began to see cows it was more than forty leagues. The land where they were was so level and clear that wherever [the members of the expedition] looked at them, the sky was seen [152r] between their legs, so that if they were a little way off, they looked like trimmed pine trees which joined their crowns at the top.[578] Furthermore, if a single bull was [a little way off], it looked like four pine trees. When one was close [to them] it was impossible to see the land beyond, [even] looking over [them]. All this was caused by the land being so round that wherever a man positioned himself, he seemed to be on the highest point, and he saw the sky all around himself at the distance of a crossbow shot. The view of the land was blocked from him by [any] small object which was set in front of him.

Other things were seen that, because they were not of as great importance, I am not writing down, nor do I make mention of them. It seems, however, that it is not [good] to omit [152v] [the Indians'] holding the sign of the cross in veneration, because they do so hold [it] in some places among the multistoried settlements. [That is known] because at Acuco, at a spring which was in the plain, they have a cross made from a stick, two *palmos* tall and of the thickness of a finger, with its stone [base] a *vara* square. And [there are] many small sticks decorated with feathers surrounding it, and many crumbled dry flowers.[579]

{A cross among the Indians} At Tutahaco, at a grave outside the *pueblo*, in which it appeared that someone had recently been buried, was another cross at the head end, made from two small sticks tied together with cotton thread. And [there were] crumbled dry flowers. I say that, in my opinion, in [153r] some way they possess some knowledge of the cross of Christ, Our Redeemer.[580] It could be by way of India, from where [the Indians] originate.

Ninth Chapter
which deals with the route the expedition took and how it would be possible to find another way that would be more direct, if it were necessary to return to that land

In order to make what I want to say understood, I very much wish that I now had available within myself some modicum of cosmography or geometry. That way I could calculate or measure the advantage there is and could be (should people leave again from Nueva España in search of that [153v] land) in going there through the middle of the land or following the route which the expedition took. Instead, with the Lord's grace helping me, I will state what I understand, making it comprehensible in the best way possible for me.

It seems to me that it is already understood that the Portuguese [named] Campo was the man-at-arms who escaped when the [people] of Quivira killed fray Juan de Padilla. He ended up coming away [from there] to Nueva España by way of Pánuco, after traveling through the land of the plains until finally he crossed the mountain chain toward the Mar del Norte, always keeping the land which don Fernando de Soto reconnoitered on his left hand. [This is known] because this man never saw [154r] the Río del Espíritu Santo. When he finally finished crossing the mountain chain toward the Mar del Norte, he came out at Pánuco in such a way that if he had not set out to look for the Mar del Norte, he would have had to come out in the vicinity of the frontier region or land of the Zacatecas, about which information now has been received.[581]

For the purpose of having to return in search of Quivira, that route would be very much better and more direct. Then there are guides in Nueva España among those who came with the Portuguese. I say, however, that it would be [even] better and more direct [to go] by way of the land of the Guachichiles, always staying close to the mountain chain toward [154v] the Mar del Sur.[582] [That is] because it is more settled and there would be a food supply, because getting far out on the flat land would get one lost, owing to its breadth and its being devoid of foods. It may be true, however, that when one encountered the [bison], one would not suffer much want.

This [route] is [useful] only to go in search of Quivira and those towns that the Indian whom [the Spaniards] called Turco told about. [That is] because to travel by way of where the expedition of Francisco Vázquez [de] Coronado went results in a very wide loop, because they depart[ed] from [the Ciudad de] México toward the west, [traveling] a hundred and ten leagues.[583] And then to the north[west][584] a hundred leagues, and to the north two hundred and fifty. All of this is as far as [155r] the *barrancas* among the [bison]. After having traveled eight hundred and fifty leagues,[585] they had not gotten [even] four hundred leagues away from [the Ciudad de] México by a direct route.

If going to the land of Tiguex is desired, in order to turn from there toward the west in search of the land of India, it is necessary to take the route the expedition took, because although one might want to take another route, there is none. [That is] because the gulf of the sea (which penetrates inland toward the north along this coast) does not allow that possibility. That is, unless one has to send a sea *armada* which could cross this gulf of [the] sea to disembark at the anchorage on the Isla de Negros.[586] From there [155v] [one must] enter the land by crossing the mountain chain in search of the land where the [people] of Tiguex or other peoples who could be civilized have their origin.[587]

[This route is best] because if one had to enter through the land of La Florida, by way of the Mar del Norte, it has already been seen and understood how many expeditions have been made through there [and] have been unfortunate and not very lucky. Beyond that, the land in that region is full of swamps and under water. [It is] barren and the worst [land] warmed by the sun. [This route is best] unless [the members of an expedition] are going to disembark beyond the Río del Espiritu Santo, as don Hernando de Soto did. All in all, I declare that, although much difficulty would be entailed, it is best [to go] through the land which has already been traveled [156r] and [where] the water sources are known. [That is] because the necessary items could be taken along more easily and more plentifully.

In new lands horses are the most necessary thing and what most puts fear in one's adversaries and those who are masters of the countryside.[588] Also, artillery is feared where its use is unknown. With regard to settlements such as those Francisco Vázquez found, some piece of heavy artillery would have been useful to demolish [them], because he took [nothing] except the smallest *versillos*[589] and no skilled man

for building a catapult or other machine which would have frightened the [Indians]. This is very necessary.

I say, then, that with the knowledge [156v] that is possessed today regarding the routes that the ships have sailed along this coast of the Mar del Sur [and] have traveled, reconnoitering throughout this western region, and what is known about the Mar del Norte toward Norway (which is the [same as] the coast of La Florida northward), those who today would enter to reconnoiter by way of the area that Francisco Vázquez penetrated would find themselves in the land of Cíbola or of Tiguex. They would know well in which direction they had to go in search of the land the Marqués del Valle, don Hernando Cortés, was searching for. [And they would know] the bend of the gulf of the [Río] del Tizón, so that they could take the true route.

This will suffice to bring our [157r] report to an end. In everything else, the powerful Lord of all things, omnipotent God, will provide. He knows how and when these lands will be reconnoitered and for whom this good fortune is reserved.

laus deo [glory to God]

Transcription was completed in Sevilla on Saturday, the twenty-sixth of October, in the year one thousand five hundred and ninety-six.

[157v] [blank]

[fol. ir]

{ojo} {Relaçion de la Jornada de Cibola / compuesta por P*edr*o de Castañeda / Nacera Donde se trata de (de) aq*ue*- / llos poblados y ritos y costumbres / la qual Fue el año de 1540 / Historia del Conde Fernando Gon- / zales impressa}

[fol. iv] [blank]

[fol. iir]

llic*encia*do b*artolo*me /niño velasques {rúbrica}[590]

[fol. iiv] [blank]

[fol. iiir]

{Relacion de la jor- / nada de Cibola con- / puesta por Pedro de / Castañeda de Naçe- / ra donde se trata de / todos aquellos pobla- / dos y ritos y costumbres la qual fue / el Año De 1540}

[fol. iiiv] [blank]

[fol. 1r]

1

proemio {rúbrica} / cosa por sierto me parece muy / magnifico señor liçeta y que es / exerçiçio de hombres virtuo- sos / el desear saber y querer adqui- / rir para su memoria la notiçia / Verdadera de las cosas i casos a- / conteçidos en partes rremotas / de que se tiene poca notiçia lo / qual ya no culpo algunas per- / sonas especulativas que por ven- / tura con bien çelo por muchas / veces me han sido inportunos / no poco rroga*n*dome les dixese / y aclarase algunas dudas que / tenian de cosas particulares q*ue* / al Vulgo *h*avian oydo en cosas y / casos aconteçidos en la jorna- / da de cibola *o* tierra

nueVa / que el buen Visorrey que dios / *h*aya en su gloria don Antonio

[fol. 1v]

de mendoça ordeno y hiço ha- / çer emVio por gene- / ral capitan a francisco vasques / de coronado y a la Verdad e- / llos tienen rraçon de querer / saber la verdad porque como / el Vulgo muy muchas veçes / y cosas que *h*an oydo y por ven- / tura a quien de ellas no tuVo / noticia ansi las haçen mayo- / res o menores que ellas son y / las que son algo las hacen na- / da y las no tales las hacen ta*n* / admirables que parecen cosas / no creederas podria tanbien / causarlo que como aquella / tierra no permanecio no *h*Ubo / quien quisiese gastar tienpo / en escrebir sus particularida- / des por que se perdiese la no- / tiçia

[fol. 2r]

2

tiçia de aquello que no fue dios / servido que gosasen el sabe por- / que que en Verdad quien qui- / siera exercitarse en escrebir / asi las cosas acaeçidas en la jor- / nada como las cosas se Vieron / en aquellas tierras los rritos y / tratos de los naturales tuViera / harta materia por donde pa- / reçiera su juiçio y creo que no / le faltara de que dar relaçion / que tratar de Verdad fuera tam / admirable que pareciera in- / creyble

y tambien creo que algunas no- / Velas que se quentan el *h*aber / como *h*a veinte años y mas que / aquella jornada se hiço lo cau- / sa digo esto porque algunos la / haçen tierra in*h*abitable otros

[fol. 2v]

confinante a la florida otros / a la india mayor que no parece

/ pequeño desVario pueden to- / mar alguna ocaçion y causa / sobre que poner su fundamen- / to tambien *h*ay quien da noti- / çia de algunos animales bi- / en rremotos que otros con *h*aber- / se hallado en aquella jorna- / da lo niegan y afirman no *h*aber / tal ni *h*aber los Visto otros varia*n* / en el rrumbo de las provincias / y aun en los tra(c)tos y trajes atri- / buyendo lo que es de los Unos a / los otros todo lo qual *h*a sido / gran parte muy magnifico / señor a me moVer aunque / tarde a querer dar Una bre- /Ve noticia general para todos / los que se arrean de esta virtud / especulativa y por ahorrar / el

[fol. 3r]
3
el tiempo que con importuni- / dades soy aquexado donde se / hallaran cosas por sierto harto / graves de cre*e*r todas o las mas /Vistas por mis ojos y otras por noti- / çia Verdadera inquiridas de /los propios naturales creyendo / que Veniendo entendido como lo / tengo que esta mi pequeña obra / seria en si ninguna o sin autori- / dad sino fuese faVoreçida y an- / parada de tal persona que su / autoridad quitase el atre- Vimien- / to a los que sin acatamiento / dar libertad a sus murmurado- / res lenguas y conoçiendo yo en / quanta obligaçion siempre / *h*e sido y soy a Vu*estr*a m*erce*d humil- / mente suplico debaxo de su / anparo Como de Verdadero

[fol. 3v]
servidor y criado sea rrece- / bida esta pequeña obra la qu- / al Va en tres partes rrepartida / para que mejor se de a enten- / der la primera sera dar noticia / del descubrimiento y el arma- / da o campo que hiço con toda / la jornada con los capitanes / que alla fueron la segunda / los pueblos y provinçias que / se hallaron y en que rrum- / bos y que rritos y costumbres / los animales fru(c)tas y yer- / bas y en que partes de la tie- / rra la terçera la Vuelta que / el campo hiço y las ocaciones / que *h*Ubo para se despoblar / aunque no liçitas por ser el / mejor paraje que *h*ay para / se descubrir el meollo de / la

[fol. 4r]
4
la tierra que *h*ay en estas partes / de poniente como se vera y

/ despues aca se tiene entendi- / do y en lo ultimo se tratara / de algunas cosas admirables / que se Vieron y por donde con / mas façilidad se podra tornar / a descubrir lo que no Vimos / que fue lo mejor y que no poco / haria al caso para por tierra / entrar en la tierra de que / yba en demanda el marques / del valle don fer*nan*do cortes de- / baxo de la estrella del ponien- / te que no pocas armadas le / costo de mar plega a n*uest*ro se- / ñor me de tal graçia que con / mi rrudo entendimiento y poca / *h*abilidad pueda tratando Verdad / agradar con esta mi pequeña

[fol. 4v]
obra al sabio y prudente le- / ctor siendo por Vu*estr*a m*erce*d acepta- / do pues mi intinçion no es ga- / nar gracias de buen compone- / {/} dor ni rretorico salVo querer / dar Verdadera notiçia y haçer / a Vu*estr*a m*erce*d este pequeño serviçio / al qual rreciba como de Verda- / dero servidor y soldado que se / hallo presente y aunque no por / estilo pulido escrebo lo que pa- / so lo que *h*a oydo palpo y Vi(d)o / y tratato {rúbrica}

siempre Veo y es ansi que por / la mayor parte quando tene- / mos entre las manos alguna / cosa preçiosa y la tratamos sin / inpedimento no la tenemos / ni la preçiamos en quanto / vale si entendemos la falta / que nos haria si la perdiesemos / y por

[fol. 5r]
5
y por tanto de continuo la Vamos / teniendo en menos pero des- / pues que la *h*abemos perdido y carecemos del bene- / fficio de / ella *h*abemos gran dolor en el / coraçon y siempre andamos y- / maginatiVos buscando modos / y maneras como la tornemos / a cobrar y asi m*e* pareçe aca- / eçio a todos aquellos o a los / mas que fueron a la jornada / que *e*l año de n*uest*ro salVador je- / su c(h)risto de mill y quinien- / tos y quarenta hico françisco {1540} / Vasques coronado en deman- / da de las siete çiudades que / puesto que no hallaron aque- / llas rriqueças de que les *h*avian / dado notiçia hallaron apare-

[fol. 5v]
jo para las buscar y principio de / buena tierra que poblar

para / de alli pasar adelante y como / despues aca por la tierra que / conquistaron y despoblaron / el tiempo les *h*a dado a entender / el rrumbo y aparejo donde es- / taban y el prinçipio de buena / tierra que tenian entre ma- / nos lloran sus coraçones por / *h*aber perdido tal oportuni- / dad de tiempo y como sea / sierto que Ven mas lo*s* honbres / quando se suben a la talanque- / ra que quando andan en el co- / so agora que estan fuera co(g)no- / çen y entienden los rrumbos / y el aparejo donde se halla- / van y ya que Ven que no lo / pueden goçar ni cobrar y / el

[fol. 6r]
6
el tiempo perdido deleytanse / en contar lo que Vieron y aun / lo que entienden que perdie- / ron especial aquellos que se / hallan pobres *h*oy tanto como qu- / ando alla fueron y no *h*an dexa- / do de trabajar y gastado el tien- / po sin proVecho digo esto porque / tengo entendido algunos de / los que de alla Vinieron holga- / rian *h*oy como fuese*n* para pasar / adelante Volver a cobrar lo / perdido y otros holgarian oyr / y saber la causa por que se des- / cubrio y pues yo me *h*e ofrecido / a contarlo tomarlo e del / prinçipio que pasa asi {rúbrica}

[fol. 6v] [blank]

[fol. 7r]
7

primera parte / {rúbrica}
Capitulo primero donde se / trata como se supo la prime- / ra poblaçion de las siete çiu- / dades y como Nuño de guz- / man hiço armada para des- / cubrir (l)las

en el año y quinientos y trein- / ta siendo presidente de la nue- / Va españa Nuño de guzman / *h*Ubo en su poder Un indio natu- / ral del valle o valles de oxi- / tipar a quien los españoles / nombran tejo este indio dixo / que el era hijo de Un merca- / der y su padre era muerto pe- / ro que siendo el chiquito su / padre entrava la tierra aden-

[fol. 7v]
primera / {rúbrica}

tro a mercadear con plumas / rricas de *h*aver para pluma- / ges y que en returno trayan / mucha cantidad de oro y plata / que en aquella tierra lo *h*ay / mucho y que el fue con el Una / o dos veçes y que Vi(d)o muy / grandes pueblos t(r)anto que / los quiso comparar con mexi- / co y su comarca y que *h*avia / visto siete pueblos muy gran- / des donde *h*avia calles de / plateria y que para ir a ellos / tardavan desde su tierra qua- / renta dias y todo despobla- / do y que la tierra por do*nde* yban / no tenia yerba sino muy / chiquita de Un xeme y que / el rrumbo que llevaban e- / ra al largo de la tierra entre / las dos mares siguiendo la / via

[fol. 8r]
8
parte

(la) via del norte debaxo de esta / notiçia Nuño de guzman jun- / to casi quatrosientos hombres / españoles y veinte mill amigos / de la nueva españa y como se ha- / llo a el presente en mexico a- / traVesando la tarasca que es / {/} tierra de mechuacan para / hallandose el aparejo que *e*l in- / dio deçia Volver atraVesan- / do la tierra haçia la mar del / norte y davan en la tierra que / yban a buscar a la qual ya / nombravan las siete ciudades / pues conforme a los quarenta / dias que *e*l texo decia hallava[591] / que *h*abiendo andado doçien- / tas leguas podian bien atraVe- / sar la tierra quitado aparte / algunas fortunas que pasaron

[fol. 8v]
primera / {rúbrica}

en esta jornada des*de* que fue- / ron llegados en la provinçia / {/} de culiaCan que fue lo Ulti- / mo de su governaçion que es / agora el nuevo reyno de ga- / liçia quisieron atraVesar la / tierra y *h*ubo muy gran dificu- / ltad porque la cordillera de / la sierra que cae sobre aque- / lla mar es tan agra que por / mucho que trabajo fue inpo- / sible hallar camino en aque- / lla parte y a esta causa se de- / tuVo todo su campo en aque- / lla tierra de culiacan hasta / tanto que como yban con el /

hombres poderosos que teni- / an rrepartimientos en tie- / rra de mexico mudaron las / Voluntades y de cada dia se / querian Volver fuera de esto / nu

[fol. 9r]
9
parte / {rúbrica}

Nuño de guzman tuVo nueva / como *h*avia Venido de españa / el marques del valle don fer- / nando cortes con el nuevo titu- / lo y grandes faVores y proviçio- / nes y como Nuño de guzman / en el tiempo que fue presiden- /te le *h*Ubiese sido emulo muy / grande y hecho muchos daños / en sus haçiendas y en las de sus / amigos temiose que don fer*nan*do {+} / cortes se quitiese pagar en otras / semejantes obras o peores y de- / termino de poblar aquella / villa de culiacan y dar la Vu- / elta con la demas gente sin / que *h*Ubiese mas efecto su jorna- / da y de Vuelta poblo a xalis- / co que es la çiudad de conpos- / tela y a tonala que llaman

[fol. 9v]
primera

guadalaxara y esto es agora / el nueVo reyno de galiçia la / guia que llevaban que se de- / çia texo murio en estos come- dios / y ansi se quedo el nombre de / estas siete ciudades y la deman- / da de ellas hasta *h*oy dia que no / se *h*an descu- bierto {rúbrica}

Capitulo segundo como Vi- / no a ser governador francisco / vasques coronado y la segun- / da relaçion que dio cabeça / de vaca {rúbrica}

pasados que fueron ocho años / que esta jornada se *h*avia he- / cho por Nuño de guzman / *h*abiendo sido preso por Un juez / de rresidençia que vino de / españa para el efecto con pro- / vicio

[fol. 10r]
10
parte

viçiones bastantes llamado el / lic*encia*do diego de la torre que des- / pues muriendo este juez que ya / tenia en si la governaçion de / aquella tierra el buen don Antonio de mendoça Visorrey / de la nueva españa puso por / gover- nador de aquel*l*a gover- / naçion a francisco vasques de / coronado Un cavallero de sa- / lamanca que a la saçon era ca- / sado en la çiudad de mexico co*n* / Una señora hija de Alonso de / estrada T(h)esorero y governador / que *h*avia sido de mexico Uno / por quien el Vulgo diçe ser hi- / jo del rrey cat(h)olico don fernan- / do y muchos lo afirman por / cosa sierta digo que a la saçon

[fol. 10v]
primera / {rúbrica}

que francisco vasques fue proVe- / ydo por governador andaba por / visitador general de la nue- / va españa por donde tuVo a- / mistad y conversaçiones de / muchas *p*ersonas nobles que / despues le siguieron en la jor- / nada que hiço aconteçio a / la saçon que llegaron a mexi- / co tres españoles y un negro que / *h*avian por nombre cabeça de / vaca y dorantes y castillo / maldonado los quales se *h*avian / perdido en la armada que me- / tio pamfilo de narVaes en la / florida y estos salieron por la / via de culiacan *h*abiendo a- / traVesado la tierra de mar a / mar como lo Veran los que lo / quisieren saber por Un tratado / que

[fol. 11r]
11
primera / {rúbrica}

que el mismo cabeça de va- / ca hiço dirigido a el principe / don phelipe que agora es rey / de españa y señor n*uest*ro y estos die- / ron notiçia a el buen don Anto- / nio de mendoça en como por las / tierras que atraVesaron toma- / ron lengua y noticia grande de / Unos poderosos pueblos de altos / de quatro y çinco doblados y o- / tras cosas bien difer- entes de lo / que pareçio por Verdad esto co- / munico el buen Visorrey con el / nueVo governador que fue cau- / sa que se apresurase dexando / la Visita que tenia entre manos / y se partiese para su governa- / çion llevando consigo el negro / que *h*avia Vendido con los tres

[fol. 11v]
primera

frayles de la orden de san fran*cis*co / el Uno *h*avia por nombre fray / marcos de niça t(h)eologo y sa- / serdote y el otro fray daniel / lego y otro fray Antonio de san- / ta maria y como llego a la pro- / vinçia de culiacan luego / despidio a los frayles ya non- / brados y a el negro que *h*avia / {-} por nombre estevan para que / fuesen en demanda de aquella / tierra porque el fray marcos de / niça se prefirio de llegar a Ver- / la porque este frayle se *h*avia / hallado en el peru a el tienpo / que don pedro de alVarado pa- / sso por tierra ydos los dichos / frayles y el negro estevan pa- / reçe que el negro no yba a / faVor de los frayles porque / lle

[fol. 12r]
12
parte / {rúbrica}

llevaba las mugeres que le da- / ban y adquiria turquesas y ha- / cia Volumen de todo y aun los / indios de aquellos poblados por / do*nde* yban entendiasen mejor / con el negro como ya otra vez / lo *h*avian visto que fue causa / que lo *h*Ubieron (h)echar delante / que fuese descubriendo y paçifi- / cando para que quando ellos / llegasen no tuViesen mas que / entender de en tomar la rrela- / çion de lo que buscavan {rúbrica}

Capitulo terçero como ma- / taron los de cibola a el negro / estevan y fray marcos VolVio / huyendo {rúbrica}

{/} apartado que se *h*Ubo el este-

[fol. 12v]
primera / {rúbrica}

van de los dichos frayles presu- / mio ganar en todo rreputaci- / on y honrra y que se le atribu- / yese la osadia y atre-Vimiento / {descubierto} de *h*aver el solo des(V)*c*ubierto / aquellos poblados de altos tan / nombrados por aquella tie- / rra y llevando consigo de a- / quellas gentes que le seguian / procuro de atraVesar los des- / poblados que *h*ay entre

çibola / y lo poblado que *h*avia andado y *h*aviaseles adelan-tado tanto / a los frayles que quando ellos lle- / garon a chichi(e)/ticale que *e*s / prinçipio del despoblado ya / el estava e*n* cibola que son o- / chenta leguas de despobla- / do que *h*ay desde culiacan / a el

[fol. 13r]
13
parte

a el principio del despoblado / docientas y veinte leguas y en / el despoblado ochenta que son trecientas diez mas o menos / digo ansi que llegado que fue / el negro estevan a çibola llego / cargado de grande numero de / turquesas que le *h*avian dado / y algunas mugeres hermosas / que le *h*avian dado y llevavan / los indios que le acompañavan / y le seguian de todo lo poblado / que *h*avia pasado los quales en / yr debajo de su amparo cre- / yan poder atraVesar toda la / tierra sin rriesgo ninguno pero / como aquellas gentes de aque- / lla tierra fuesen de mas rra-

[fol. 13v]
primera

çon que no los que seguian a el / estevan aposentaronlo en una / sierta (h)ermita que tenian fue- / ra del pueblo y los mas viejos / y los que governavan oyeron / sus rraçones y procuraron saber / la causa de su Venida en aque- / lla tierra y bien informados por / espaçio de tres dias entraron / en su consulta y por la notiçia / que *e*l negro les dio como atras ve- / nian dos hombres blancos em- / Viados por Un gran señor que / eran entendidos en las cosas / del çielo y que aquellos los / venian a industriar en las co- / sas divinas consideraron / que debia ser espia o guia de / algunas naçiones que los que- / rian yr a conquistar porque / les

[fol. 14r]
14
parte / {rúbrica}

les pareçio desVario decir que / la tierra de donde venia era *de* la / gente blanca siendo el negro / y enViado por ellos y

fueron a / el y como despues de otras rra- / çones le*s* pidiese
turquesas y /mugeres pareçioles cosa dura / y determinaronse
a le ma- / tar y ansi lo hicieron sin que / matasen a nadie de
los que / con el yban y tomaron algu- / nos muchachos y a
los demas / que serian obra de sesenta per- / sonas dexaron
VolVer libres / a sus tierras pues como estos que / Volvian ya
huyendo atemori- / sados llegasen a se topar y Ver / con los
frayles en el despoblado

[fol. 14v]
primera / {rúbrica}

sesenta leguas de çibola y les / diesen la triste nueVa
pusieron- / los en tanto temor que aun no / se fiando de esta
gente con *h*a- / ber ydo en compañia del ne- / gro abrieron
las petacas que / llevaban y les rrepartieron / quanto trayan
que no les que- / do salVo los (h)ornamentos de / deçir misa
y de alli dieron / la Vuelta sin Ver la tierra mas / de lo que los
indios les deçian / antes caminaban dobladas / jornadas
(h)*f*aldas en sinta {rúbrica}

Capitulo quarto como el / buen don Antonio de men- / doça
hiço jornada para / el descubrimiento de cibo- / la {rúbrica}
/ des

[fol. 15r]
15
parte / {rúbrica}

despues que francisco vas- / ques coronado *h*Ubo emViado
/ a fray marcos de niça y su con- / paña en la demanda ya di-
/ cha quedando el en culia- / can entendio en negocios que /
conVenian a su governaçio*n* / tuVo sierta rrelaçion de Una /
provincia que corria en la tra- / Vesia de la tierra de culiacan
/ a el norte que se decia topira / y luego salio para la ir a des-
/ cubrir con algunos conquista- / dores y gente de amigos y
su / yda hiço poco efecto porque / *h*avian de atraVesar las
cordi- / lleras y fue les muy dificul- / toso y la notiçia no la
halla- / ron tal ni muestra de buena

[fol. 15v]
primera

tierra y ansi dio la Vuelta y llega- / do que fue hallo a los
frayles que / *h*avian acabado de llegar y fue- / ron tantas las
grandeças que / les dixeron de lo que el este- / van el negro
*h*avia descubi- / erto y lo que ellos oyeron a / los indios y
otras noticias de / la mar del sur y de y*s*las que / oyeron deçir
y de otras rrique- / sas que e*l* governador sin mas / se detener
se partio luego pa- / ra la ciudad de mexico lle- / vando a el
fray marcos consi- / go para dar notiçia de ello / a el Visorrey
engrandesien- / do las cosas con no las querer / comunicar
con nadie sino de- / baxo de puridad y grande se- / cre

[fol. 16r]
16
parte / {rúbrica}

{/} creto a personas particulares y / llegados a mexico y Visto
con don / Antonio de mendoça luego se / començo a
publicar como ya se / *h*abian descubierto las siete ciu- / dades
que Nuño de guzman / buscaba y haçer armada y jun- / tar[592]
gente para las yr a conquis- / tar el buen Virrey tuVo tal or-
/ den con los frayles de la orden / de san françisco que
hiçieron a / fray marcos provincial que fue / causa que andu-
Viesen los pul- / pitos de aquella orden llenos / de tantas
maraVillas y tan gra*n*- / des que en pocos dias se junta- / ron
mas de tresientos hombres / españoles y obra de ochoçien- /
tos indios naturales de la nue*va*

[fol. 16v]
primera / {rúbrica}

españa y entre los españoles hon- / bres de gran calidad tantos
y / tales que dudo[593] en indias *h*aber- / se juntado tan noble
gente y / tanta en tam pequeño nu- / mero como fueron
treçientos / hombres y de todos ellos ca- / pitan general francisco vas- / ques coronado governador de / la nueVa galiçia
por *h*aber si- / do el autor de todo hico todo / esto el buen
virrey don Antonio / porque a la saçon era fran*cis*co / vasques

la persona mas alle- / gada a el por priVança porque / tenia entendido era hom- / bre sagaz *h*abil y de buen con- / sejo allende de ser cavalle- / ro como lo era tenido tuViera / mas

[fol. 17r]
17
parte / {rúbrica}

mas atençion y rrespe(c)to a el / estado en que lo ponia y cargo / que lleVava que no a la rrenta / que dexaba en la nueVa espa- / ña o a lo menos a la honrra / que ganaba y *h*avia de ganar / llevando tales cavalleros de- / baxo de su bando pero no le sa- / lio ansi como adelante se Vera / en el fin de este tratado ni el su- / po conserVar aquel estado ni / la governaçion que tenia {rúbrica}

Capitulo quinto que trata / quienes fueron por capita- / nes a çibola {rúbrica}

ya que *el*⁵⁹⁴ Visorrey don Antonio / de mendoça Vi(d)o la muy

[fol. 17v]
primera / {rúbrica}

noble gente que tenia junta / y con los animos y voluntad q*ue* / todos se le *h*avian ofreçido co- / (g)noçiendo el valor de sus per- / sonas a cada Uno de ellos / quisiera haçer capitan de / Un exerçito pero como el nu- / mero de todos era poco no pu- / do lo que q*u*isiera y ansi orde- / no las condu*c*tas y capi- tanias / que le pareçio porque yendo / por su mano ordenado era / tam obedeçido y amado que / nadie saliera de su manda- / do despues que todos ente*n*- / dieron quien era su gene- / ral hiço alferez general / a don pedro de tovar cava- / llero mançebo hijo de don / fer

[fol. 18r]
18
parte / {rúbrica}

fernando de toVar guarda y / mayordomo mayor de la rey- /

na doña juana n*uest*ra natural / señora que sea en gloria y ma- / estre de campo a lope de sama- / niego alcayde de las ataraça- / nas de mexico cavallero pa- / ra el cargo bien sufiçiente ca- / pitanes fueron don tristan de / arellano don (pedro) *diego* de gue- / vara hijo de don juan de gue- /vara y sobrino del conde de o- / ñate don garçi lopes de car- / denas don rodrigo maldona- / do cuñado del duque del / infantado diego lopes veinte / y quatro de sevilla diego gu- / tierres de la cavalleria to-

[fol. 18v]
primera / {rúbrica}

dos los demas cavalleros y- / ban debajo del guion del ge- / neral por ser personas seña- / ladas y algunos de ellos / fueron despues capitanes / y permanecieron en ello por / ordenaçion del Virrey y otros / por el general françisco vas- / ques nombrare algunos de / aquellos de que tengo me- / moria que fueron françisco / de barrionueVo Un cavalle- / {+} ro de granada {+} juan de sal- / diVar françisco de ovando / juan gallego y melchior di- / as capitan y alcalde mayor / que *h*avia sido de culiacan q*ue* / aunque no era cavallero me- / reçia por su persona el cargo / que

[fol. 19r]
19
parte / {rúbrica}

{/} que tuVo los demas cavalle- / ros que fueron sobre- salientes / fueron don Alonso manrrique / de lara don lope de Urrea / cavallero aragones gomes / suares de figueroa luis rra- / mires de vargas juan de / sotomayor francisco gorba- / lan el factor rriberos y otros / cavalleros de que agora no me / acuerdo y hombres de mu- / cha calidad capitan de in- / fanteria fue pablo de mel- / gosa burgales y de la arti- / lleria hernando de alVara- / do cavallero montañes di- / go que con el tiempo *h*e perdi- / do la memoria de muchos / buenos hijosdalgo que fuera

[fol. 19v]
primera / {rúbrica}

bueno que los nombrara por- / que se Viera y co(g)noçiera la / rracon que tengo de deçir que / havia para esta jornada la / mas lucida gente que se ha / juntado en indias para yr / en demandas de tierras nue- / Vas sino fueran desdichados / en llevar capitan que de- / xaba rrentas en la nueVa es- / paña y muger moça noble / y generosa que no fueron po- / cas espuelas para lo que Vi- / no a haçer {rúbrica}

Capitulo sexto como se jun- / taron en conpostela todas / las capitanias y salieron en / orden para la jornada {rúbrica}

hecho y ordenado por el Virrey / don

[fol. 20r]
20
parte

don Antonio de mendoça lo que / habemos dicho y hechas las capi- / tanias o capitanes dio luego / a la gente de guerra socorros / de la caxa de su magestad a las / personas mas menesterosas y por / pareçerle que si salia el cam- / po formado desde mexico / haria algunos agravios por / las tierras de los amigos orde- / no que se fuesen a juntar a la / çiudad de conpostela cabeça / del nueVo reyno de galiçia / çiento y diez leguas de mexi- / co para que desde alli orde- / nadamente comencasen su / jornada lo que paso en este / viaje no hay para que dar de

[fol. 20v]
primera

ello rrelaçion pues al fin to- / dos se juntaron en conposte- / la el dia de carnestollen- / das del año de quarenta (y / {1541} Uno) y como hUbo (h)echado to- / da la gente de mexico dio / orden en como (pedro) Hernando de alar- / con saliese con dos navios que / estaban en el puerto de la / naVidad en la costa del sur / y fuese a el puerto de xalis- / co a tomar la rropa de los / soldados que no la pudiesen / llevar para que costa a costa / fuese tras del campo porque / se tuVo entendido que segun / la notiçia havian de ir por / la tierra çerca de la costa de / el mar y que por los rrios sa- / ca

[fol. 21r]
21
parte / {rúbrica}

cariamos los puertos y los navi- / os siempre tendrian notiçia / del campo lo qual despues / pareçio ser falso y ansi se perdio / toda la rropa o por mejor de- / çir la perdio cuya era como a- / delante se dira asi que des- / pachado y concluido todo el / visorrey se partio para con- / postela acompañado de mu- / chos cavalleros y rricoshonbres / y tuVo el año nueVo de qua- / renta (y uno) en pasquaro / que es cabeça del obispado / de mechuacan y de alli con / mucha alegria y plaçer y / grandes rreçebimientos a- / traVeso toda la tierra de la

[fol. 21v]
primera / {rúbrica}

nueVa españa hasta conposte- / la que son como tengo dicho / çiento y diez leguas adonde / hallo toda la gente junta y bi- / en tratada y hospedada por / c(h)ristobal de oñate que era / a la saçon la persona que te- / nia en peso aquella gover- / naçion y la havia sostenido y / era capitan de toda aquella / tierra puesto que[595] francisco / vasques era governador y / llegado con mucha alegria / de todos hiço alarde de la gen- / te que emViaba y hallo toda / la que habemos señalado y / rrepartio las capitanias y es- / to hecho otro dia despues de / misa a todos juntos ansi ca- / pi

[fol. 22r]
22
parte

pitanes como a soldados el / visorrey les hico Una muy elo- / quente y breve oraçion en- / cargandoles la fidelidad que / debian a su general dando- / les bien a entender el proVe- / cho que de haçer aquella / jornada podia rredundar a- / si a la converçion de aque- / llas gentes como en pro de / los que conquistasen aque- / lla tierra y el servicio de su / magestad y la obligaçion / en que le havian puesto pa- / ra en todo tiempo los faVore- / çer y socorrer y acabada to- / mo juramento sobre los evan- / gelios en un libro misal a / todos generalmente asi

[fol. 22v]
primera / {rúbrica}

{/} a capitanes como a soldados / aunque por orden que
sigui- / rian a su general y harian / en aquella jornada y obe-
/ decerian todo aquello que / por el les fuese mandado lo /
qual despues cumplieron fi- / elmente como se Vera y esto /
hecho otro dia salio el campo / con sus banderas tendidas /
y el virrey don Antonio le a- / compaño dos jornadas y de /
alli se despidio dando la Vuel- / ta para la nueva españa a- /
conpañado de sus amigos {rúbrica}

{/} Capitulo septimo como el / campo llego a chiametla y /
mataron a el maestre de canpo / y lo que mas acaeçio hasta / lle

[fol. 23r]
23
parte / {rúbrica}

llegar a culiacan {rúbrica}

partido que fue el virrey / don Antonio el campo cami- / no
por sus jornadas y como era / forçado llevar cada Uno sus *ha*-
/ beres en cavallos y no todos / los sabian aparejar y los cava-
/ llos salian gordos y holgados / en las primeras jornadas
*h*Ubo / grande dificultad y trabajo y / muchos dexaron
muchas pre- / seas y las daban de gracia a / quien las queria
por no las car- / gar y a el fin la necesidad que / es maestra
con el tiempo los hi- / ço maestros donde se pudiera*n* / Ver
muchos cavalleros torna- / dos (h)arrieros y que el que se

[fol. 23v]
primera / {rúbrica}

despreçiaba del officio no era / tenido por hombre y con
otros / trabajos que entonçes tuVie- / ron por grandes llego
el can- / po en chiametla donde por / faltar bastimentos fue
forçado / detenerse alli algunos dias / en los quales el maestre
de / campo lope de samaniego / con sierta compañia fue a /
buscar bastimentos y en un / pueblo por entrar indiscre- /
tamente por Un arcabuco / en pos de los enemigos lo /
flecharon por Un ojo y le pa- / saron el celebro de que lue- /

go murio alli y flecharon / otros çinco o seis compañeros / y
luego como fue muerto / diego lopes veinte y quatro / de

[fol. 24r]
24
parte / {rúbrica}

de sevilla rrecogio la gente / y lo emVio a haçer saber a el /
general y puso guarda en el / pueblo y en los bastimentos sa-
/ bido dio gran turbacion en el / campo y fue enterrado y
hiçie- / ron algunas entradas de do*n*- / de truxeron bastimentos y al- / gunos presos de los naturales / y se ahorcaron
a lo menos los / que pareçieron ser de aque- / lla parte ado*nde*
murio el maes- / tre de campo {rúbrica}

pareçe que a el tiempo que / el general françisco vasques /
partio de culiacan con fray / marcos a dar la notiçia ya di- /
cha a el Visorey don Antonio / de mendoça *h*avia dexado

[fol. 24v]
primera / {rúbrica}

ordenado que saliese el capi- / tan melchior dias y juan de
sal- / diVar con Una doçena de bue- / nos hombres de culiacan en / dema*n*da de lo que fray mar- / cos *h*avia Visto y
oydo los qua- / les salieron y fueron hasta / chichilticale que
es prinçipio / del despoblado doçientas y / veinte leguas de
Culiacan / y no hallaron cosa de tomo / VolVieron y a el
tiempo que / el campo queria salir de / chiametla llegaron y
ha- / blaron a el general y por / secreto que se trato la mala /
nueva luego suena *h*Ubo / algunos dichos que aunque / se
doraban no dexaban / de

[fol. 25r]
25
parte / {rúbrica}

de dar lustre de lo que eran / fray marcos de niça co(g)noci-
/ endo la turbaçion de algu- / nos deshaçia aquellos nubla- /
dos prometiendo ser lo que Vie- / ron lo bueno y que el yba
alli / y po(r)ndria el campo en tierra / donde hinchesen las
manos / y con esto se aplaco y mostra- / ron buen semblante

y de alli / camino el campo hasta llegar / a Culiacan haçiendo algunas / entradas en tierra de guerra / por tomar basti- / mentos llega- / ron a dos leguas de la villa / de culiacan vispera de pas- / qua de rresurreçion adon- / de salieron los vecinos a rre- / cebir a su governador y le

[fol. 25v]
primera / {rúbrica}

rrogaron no entrase en la vi- / lla hasta el segundo dia de / pasqua {rúbrica}

Capitulo octavo como el / campo entro en la villa / de culia- can y el rrecebimi- / ento que se hiço y lo que mas / acaeçio hasta la partida {rúbrica}

como fuese segundo dia de / pasqua de rresurreçion el / campo salio de manaña pa- / ra entrar en la villa y en / la entrada en Un campo / esconbrado los de la villa or- / denados a uso de guerra⁵⁹⁶ / a pie y a cavallo por sus ex- / quadrones teniendo ase- / tada su artilleria que eran / sie

[fol. 26r]
26
parte / {rúbrica}

siete pieças de bronce salieron / en muestra de querer defen- / der la villa estaban con ellos / alguna parte de nuestros solda- / dos nuestro campo por la misma / orden comencaron con ellos / Una escaramuça y ansi fue- / ron e rompiendo despues de / haber jugado el artilleria de / ambas partes de suerte que / les fue tomada la villa por fu- / erça de armas que fue Una / alegre demostraçion y rreçe- / bimiento aunque no para / el artillero que se lleVo Una / mano por haber mandado po- / ner fuego antes que acabase / de sacar el atacador de

[fol. 26v]
primera / {rúbrica}

Un tiro tomada la villa / fueron luego bien aposen- / tados y hospedados por los / veçinos que como eran to- / dos hombres muy honrrados / en sus propias posadas me- /

tieron a todos los cavalleros / y personas de calidad que / yban en el campo aunque / havia aposento hecho para / todos fuera de la villa y no / les fue algunos veçinos mal / gratificado este hospedaje / porque como todos Venian / aderesados de rricos ataVios / y de alli havian de sacar bas- / timentos en sus bestias y de / fuerça havian de dejar sus / pre

[fol. 27r]
27
parte / {rúbrica}

preseas muchos quisieron an- / tes darlas a sus huespedes que / no ponerlas a la Ventura de / la mar ni que se las lleVasen / los naVios que havian Veni- / do por la costa siguiendo el / campo para tomar el fardaje / como ya se dixo ansi que lle- / gados y bien aposentados en / la villa el general por orden / del Visorrey don Antonio pu- / so alli por capitan y tinien- / te a fernandarias de saaVe- / dra tio de hernandarias de / saaVedra conde del castellar / que fue alguaçil mayor de / sevilla y alli rreposo el can- / po algunos dias porque

[fol. 27v]
primera / {rúbrica}

los veçinos havian cogido aqu- / el año muchos bastimentos y / partieron con la gente de nuestro / campo con mucho amor espe- / çial cada Uno con sus huespe- / des de manera que no sola- / mente hubo abundançia para / gastar alli mas aun hubo pa- / ra sacar que a el tiempo de / la partida salieron mas de / seiçientas bestias cargadas y / los amigos y serviçio que fue- / ron mas de mill personas pa- / sados quinse dias el general ordeno de se partir delante / con hasta sinquenta de a ca- / vallo y pocos peones y la ma- / yor parte de los amigos y de- / xar el campo que le siguiese / des

[fol. 28r]
28
parte / {rúbrica}

desde a quinse dias y dexo / por su teniente a don tristan / de arellano {rúbrica} en este comedio antes que se / partiese el general aconte- / çio Un caso donoso y yo por / tal lo quento y fue que Un / soldado mançebo que se de- / cia trugillo fingio *h*aber Visto / Una Viçion estando bañando- / se en el rrio y façiendo de / *e*l dis- / figurado fue traydo ante el ge- / neral adonde dio a entender / que le *h*avia dicho el demo- / nio que matase a el general / y lo casaria con doña beatris / su muger y le daria grandes / t(h)esoros y otras cosas bien do-

[fol. 28v]

nosas por donde fray marcos / de niça hiço algunos sermo- / nes atribuyendolo a que el / demonio con emVidia del bi- / en que de aquella jornada / *h*avia de rresultar lo queria / desbaratar por aquella via / y no solamente paro en esto / sino que tambien los frayles / que yban en la jornada lo es- / cribieron a sus conVentos y fue / causa que por los pulpitos / de mexico se dixesen hartas / fabulas sobre ello {rúbrica}

el general mando quedar / a el truxillo en aquella vi- / lla y que no hiciese la jorna- / da que fue lo que el preten- / dio quando hiço aquel / em

[fol. 29r]
29
parte / {rúbrica}

embuste segun despues pare- / çio por Verdad el general sa- / lio con la gente ya dicha sigui- / endo su jornada y despues el / campo como se dira {rúbrica}

Capitulo nueve como el can- / po salio de culiacan y llego / el general a çibola y el cam- / po a señora y lo que mas a- / caeçio {rúbrica}

el general como esta dicho / salio del valle de culiacan / en seguimiento de su viaje / algo a la ligera llevando / consigo los frayles que nin- / guno quiso quedar con el / campo y a tres jornadas Un

[fol. 29v]
primera / {rúbrica}

frayle llamado fray Antonio / vitoria se quebro Una pier- / na y este frayle era de misa / y para que se curase lo VolVi- / eron del camino y despues / fue con el campo que no fue / poca consolaçion para todos / el general y su gente atra- / Vesaron la tierra sin contras- / te que todo lo hallaron de / pax porque los indios co(g)no- / çian a fray marcos y algunos / de los que *h*avian ydo con el / capitan melchior dias quan- / do *h*avia ydo el y juan de sal- / diVar a descubrir como / el general *h*Ubo atraVesa- / do lo poblado y llegado a / chichilticale prinçipio / del

[fol. 30r]
30
parte / {rúbrica}

del despoblado y no Vio cosa / buena no dexo de sentir al- / guna tristesa porque aunque / la notiçia de lo de adelante / era grande no *h*avia quien / lo *h*ubiese visto sino los indi- / os que fueron con el negro que / ya los *h*avian tomado en algu- / nas mentiras por todos se sin- / tio mucho Ver que la fama de / chichilticale se rresumia / en Una casa sin cubierta a- / rruynada puesto que pare- / çia en otro tiempo *h*aber sido / casa fuerte en tiempo que fue / poblada y bien se co(g)noçia / ser hecha por gentes estran- / geras pulíticas y guerr*e*ras Ve- / nidas de lejos era esta casa

[fol. 30v]
primera / {rúbrica}

de tierra bermeja desde alli / prosiguieron el despoblado / y llegaron en quinse dias / a ocho leguas de çibola a un / rrio que por yr el agua tur- / bia y bermeja le llamaron / el rrio bermejo en este rrio se / hallaron barbos como en es- / paña aqui fue adonde se Vi- / eron los primeros indios de a- / quella tierra que fueron dos / que huyeron y fueron a dar / mandado y otro dia a dos le- / guas del pueblo siendo de / noche algunos indios en / parte segura dieron Una / grita que aunque la gen- / te estaba aperçebida se al- / teraron algunos en tanta / ma

[fol. 31r]
31
parte / {rúbrica}

manera que *h*Ubo quien hecho / la silla a el reVes y estos fueron / {/} gente nueVa que los diestros lu- / ego cavalgaron y corrieron / el campo los indios huyeron / como quien sabia la tierra que / ninguno pudo ser *h*abido {rúbrica}

otro dia bien en orden entraron / por la tierra poblada y como / Vieron el primer pueblo que / fue çibola fueron tantas las / maldiciones que algunos / (h)echaron a fray marcos qua- / les dios no permita le compre- / (he)ndan {rúbrica}

el es Un pueblo pequeño a- / rriscado y apeñuscado que / de lejos *h*ay estancias en la nue- / va españa que tienen me-

[fol. 31v]
primera / {rúbrica}

jor apar*i*ençia es pueblo de / hasta doçientos hombres de / guerra de tres y de quatro al- / tos y las casas chicas y poco es- / paciosas no tienen patios Un / patio sirve a Un barrio *h*avia- / se juntado alli la gente de la / comarca porque es Una pro- / vinçia de siete pueblos don- / de *h*ay otros harto mayores / y mas fuertes pueblos q*ue no* / çibola estas gentes esp*eraron*[597] /en el campo (h)ordenados con / sus exquadrones a vista del / pueblo y como a los rreque- / rimientos que le hicieron / con las lenguas no quisie- / ron dar la paz antes se mos- / traban bravos diese santia- / go

[fol. 32r]
32
parte / {rúbrica}

go en ellos y fueron desba- / ratados luego y despues fue- / ron a tomar el pueblo que / no fue poco dificultoso que / como tenian la entrada an- / gosta y torneada a el entrar / derribaron a el general con / Una gran piedra tendido y / ansi le mataran si no fuera / por don garçi lopes de carde- / nas y

hernando de alVara- / do que se derribaron sobre / el y le sacaron rrecibiendo e- / llos los golpes de piedras que / no fueron pocos pero como a la / primera furia de los españo- / les no *h*ay rresistençia en me- / nos de Una *h*ora se entro y ga-

[fol. 32v]
primera / {rúbrica}

no el pueblo y se descubrieron / los bastimentos que era*n* de lo que / mas neçesidad *h*avia y de a*h*y a- / delante toda la provinçia Vi- / no de pax {rúbrica}

el campo que *h*avia quedado / a don tristan de arellano par- / tio en seguimiento del ge- / neral cargados todos de bas- / timentos las lanças en los *h*on- / bros todos a pie por sacar car- / gados los cavallos y no con pe- / queño trabajo de jornadas en / jornadas llegaron a Una pro- / vinçia que cabeça de va- / ca puso por nombre cora- / çones a causa que alli les o- / frecieron muchos coraçones / de animales y luego la co- / men

[fol. 33r]
33
parte / {rúbrica}

menço a poblar Una villa y / ponerle nombre sant hiero- /nimo de los coraçones y luego / la començo a poblar y Visto que / no se podia sustentarla paso / despues a Un valle que llama*n* / persona digo[598] senora y los espa- / ñoles le llamaron señora y an- / si le llamare de aqui adelan- / te desde alli se fue a *buscar* {buscar / {rúbrica}}[599] / el puerto el rrio abajo a la cos- / ta de la mar por saber de los / naVios y no los hallaron don / rodrigo maldonado que yba / por caudillo en busca de los / naVios de Vuelta truxo con- / sigo Un indio tam grande y / tam alto que el mayor hon-

[fol. 33v]
primera / {rúbrica}

bre y tan alto que *e*l hom-[600] / bre del campo no le llegava / a el pecho deçiase que en a- / quella costa *h*avia otros indios /

mas altos alli rreposaron las / aguas y despues paso el cam- / po y la villa señora[601] porque / *h*avia en aquella comarca / bastimentos para poder a- / guardar mandado del gene- / ral {rúbrica}

mediado el mes de octubre mel- / chior dias y juan gallego / capitanes Vinieron de çibo- / la el juan gallego para / nueVa españa y melchior / dias para quedar por capi- / tan en la nueVa villa de / los

[fol. 34r]
34
parte / {rúbrica}

los coraçones con la gente que / alli quedase y para que fue- / se a descubrir los naVios por / aquella costa {rúbrica}

Capitulo deçimo como / el campo salio de la villa / de señora quedando la vi- / lla poblada y como llego a / çibola y lo que le avino en / el camino a el capitan mel- / chior dias yendo en deman- / da de los naVios y como des- / cubrio el rrio del tison {rúbrica}

luego como fue llegado en / la villa de señora melchior / dias y juan gallego se publico

[fol. 34v]
primera / {rúbrica}

la partida del campo para cibo- / {cibola / {rúbrica}} la y como *h*avia de quedar en / aquella villa melchior dias / por capitan con ochenta hon- / bres y como juan gallego y- / ba con mensaje para la nue- / Va españa a el Visorrey y / lleVaba en su compania / a fray marcos que no se tuVo / por seguro quedar en cibola / Viendo que *h*avia salido su re- / laçion falsa en todo porque / ni se hallaron los reynos q*ue* / deçia ni ciudades populosas / ni rriquesas de oro ni pedre- / ria rrica que se publico ni / brocados ni otras cosas que / se dixeron por los pulpitos / pues

[fol. 35r]
35
parte / {rúbrica}

pues luego que esto se publico / se rrepartio la gente que *h*a- / via de quedar y los demas / cargaron de bastimentos y por / su orden mediado se*p*tiembre / se partieron la via de çibola / siguiendo su general don / tristan de arellano *Dí*az quedo / en esta nueVa villa con la gen- / te de menos estofa y asi nun- / ca dexo de *h*aber de alli ade- / lante motines y contrastes por- / {/} que como fue partido el canpo / el capitan melchior dias to- / mo veinte y çinco hombres de / los mas escogidos dexando en / su lugar a Un diego de alca- / raz hombre no bien acondi-

[fol. 35v]
primera / {rúbrica}

cionado para tener gente / debaxo de su mando y el / salio en demanda de la cos- / ta de la mar entre norte y / poniente con guias y *h*abien- / do caminado obra de çien- / to y sinquenta leguas die- / ron en Una provinçia de ge*n*- / tes demasiadamente de / altos y membrudos ansi / como gigantes aunque gen- / te desnuda y que hacia su / *h*abitaçion en choças de pa- / ja largas a manera de sa- / hurdas metidas debaxo / de tierra que no salia sobre / la tierra mas de la paja entra- / ban por la Una parte de largo / y salian por la otra dormian / en

[fol. 36r]
36
parte / {rúbrica}

en Una chosa mas de çien per- / sonas chicos y grandes lleva- / ban de peso sobre las cabeças / quando se cargavan mas / de tres y de quatro quinta- / les Viose querer los *nuest*ros tra- / er Un madero para el fue- / go y no lo poder traer seis / hombres y llegar Uno de a- / quellos y levantarlo en / los braços y ponerselo el solo / en la cabeça y llevallo m- / uy livianamente {rúbrica}

comen pan de mais cosido / so el rrescoldo de la senisa / tam
grandes como hogasas / de castilla grandes {rúbrica}

[fol. 36v]
primera / {rúbrica}

para caminar de Unas par- / tes a otras por el gran frio /
sacan Un tison en Una / mano con que se Van calentan- / do
la otra y el cuerpo y ansi / lo Van trocando a trechos y / por
esto a Un gran rrio que / Va por aquella tierra lo nom- / bran
el rrio del tison es pode- / roso rrio y tiene de boca mas / de
dos leguas por alli tenia / media legua de traVesia / alli tomo
lengua el capitan / como los naVios havian esta- / do tres
jornadas de alli por / bajo hacia la mar y llega- / dos adonde
los naVios es- / tuVieron que era mas de / quinçe leguas el
rrio arriba / de la

[fol. 37r]
37
parte / {rúbrica}

de la boca del puerto y ha- / llaron en un arbol escri(p)to /
aqui llego alarcon a el pie / de este arbol hay cartas saca- /
ronse las cartas y por ellas / Vieron el tiempo que estuVie- /
ron aguardando nueVas de / el campo y como alarcon ha- /
via dado la Vuelta desde / alli para la nueVa españa / con los
naVios porque no / podia correr adelante por- / que aquella
mar era ancon y / que tornaba a VolVer sobre / la isla del
marques que di- / cen California y dieron rre- / laçion como
la california

[fol. 37v]
primera / {rúbrica}

no era isla sino punta de tie- / rra firme de la Vuelta de /
aquel ancon {rúbrica}

visto esto por el capitan torno / a VolVer el rrio arriba sin Ver
/ la mar por buscar Vado pa- / ra pasar a la otra banda pa- /
ra seguir la otra costa y co- / mo anduVieron cinco o seis /
jornadas parecioles podri- / an pasar con balsas y pa- / ra esto

llamaron mucha / gente de los de la tierra los / quales querian
ordenar / de hacer salto en los nuestros y / andaban buscando
ocaçion / oportuna y como Vieron que / querian pasar acudieron a / haçer las balsas con toda pres- / tesa

[fol. 38r]
38
parte / {rúbrica}

tesa y diligençia por tomar- / los ansi en el agua y aho- /
garlos o diVididos de suerte / que no se pudiesen faVore- /
çer ni ayudar y en este co- / medio que las balsas se haci- /
an Un soldado que havia y- / do a campear Vi(d)o en Un
mon- / te atraVesar gran numero / de gente armada que
aguar- / daban a que pasase la gente / dio de ello notiçia y
secreta- / mente se ençerro Un indio pa- / ra saber de el la
Verdad y co- / mo se apretasen dixo toda / la orden que
tenian ordena- / da para quando pasasen que / era que como
hUbiesen pa-

[fol. 38v]
primera / {rúbrica}

{/} sado parte de los nuestros y parte / fuesen por el rrio y
parte que- / dasen por pasar que los de / las balsas procurasen
aho- / gar los que llevaban y la / demas gente saliese a dar /
en ambas partes de la tie- / rra y si como tenian cuerpos / y
fuerças tuVieron discriçi- / on y esfuerço ellos salieran /con
su empresa {rúbrica}

Visto su intento el capitan / hiço matar secretamente el /
indio que confeso el hecho / y aquella noche se (h)echo / en
el rrio con Una pesga⁶⁰² por- / que los indios no sintiesen que
/ eran sentidos y como otro dia / sintieron el rreçelo de los
nuestros / mos

[fol. 39r]
39
parte / {rúbrica}

mostraronse de guerra (h)echan- / do rroçiadas de flechas

pero / como los cavallos los comen- / çaron a alcançar y las lanças / los lastimaban sin piadad[603] y los / arcabuçeros tambien hacian / buenos tiros *h*Ubieron de dexar / el campo y tomar el monte / hasta que no pareçio honbre / de ellos Vino por alli y an- / si paso la gente a buen rre- / caudo siendo los amigos bal- / seadores y españoles a las Vu- / eltas pasando los cavallos a / la par de las balsas donde los / dexaremos caminando {rúbrica}

por contar como fue el campo / que caminaba para çibola / que como yba caminando / por su orden y el general

[fol. 39v]
primera / {rúbrica}

lo *h*avia dexado todo de pax / por doquiera hallaban la / gente de la tierra alegre sin / {/} temer y que se dexaban bien / mandar y en Una provinçia / que se diçe vacapan *h*avia gr- / an cantidad de tunas que / los naturales haçen conser- / va de ellas en cantidad y / de esta conserva presenta- / ron mucha y como la gente / del campo comio de ella / todos cayeron como amo- / dorridos con dolor de ca- / beça y fiebre de suerte que / si los naturales quisieran / hicieran gran daño en la / gente duro esto veinti y qu- / atro *h*oras naturales despues / que

[fol. 40r]
40
parte / {rúbrica}

que salieron de alli cami- / nando llegaron a chichil- / ticale despues que saliero*n* / de alli Un dia los de la gu- / ardia Vieron pasar Una ma- / nada de carneros y yo los / Vi y los segui eran de gran- / de cuerpo en demasia el / pelo largo los cuernos muy / gruesos y grandes para correr / enhiest(r)an el rrostro y (h)echa*n* / los cuernos sobre el lomo co- / rren mucho por tierra agra / que no los pudimos alan- / çar y los *h*Ubimos de dexar {rúbrica}

entrando tres jornadas por / el despoblado en la rrive- / ra de Un rrio que esta en un- / as grandes honduras de

[fol. 40v]
primera / {rúbrica}

barrancas se hallo Un cuer- / no que *e*l general despues / de *h*aberlo visto lo dexo a- / lli para que los de su canpo / le Viesen que tenia de lar- / go Una braça y tam gordo / por el naçimiento como el / muslo de Un hombre en la / faicion parecia mas ser de / cabron que de otro anim- / al fue cosa de Ver pasando / adelante y aquel canpo / yba Una jornada de çibo- / la començo sobretarde Un / gran torbellino de ayre / frigidissimo y luego se si- / guio gran *ll*uVia de nieVe / que fue harta confuçion[604] pa- / ra la gente de serviçio el / can

[fol. 41r]
41
parte / {rúbrica}

campo camino hasta llegar / a Unos peñascos de socarre- / nas donde se llego bien noche / y con harto rriesgo de los / ami- / gos que como eran de la nu- / eVa españa y la mayor parte / de tierras calientes sintieron / mucho la frialdad de aqu- / el dia tanto que *h*Ubo harto / que haçer otro dia en los / rre- / parar y lleVar a cavallo y- / endo los soldados a pie y / con es- / te trabajo llego el campo a / çibola donde los aguarda- / ba su general hecho el a- / posento y alli se torno a ju*n*- / tar aunque algunos ca- / pitanes y gente faltava / que *h*avian salido a descu-

[fol. 41v]
primera / {rúbrica}

brir otras provinçias {rúbrica}

Capitulo onçe como don / pedro de tovar decubrio a / tusayan o tutahaco y don / garci lopes de cardenas Vi*o* / el rrio del tison y lo que mas / acaecio(n) {rúbrica}

en el entretanto que las cosas / ya dichas pasaron el gene- / ral *fran*çisco vasques como estaba / en cibola de pax procuro sa- / ber de los de la tierra que pro- / vincias le cayan en comarca / y que ellos diesen noticia a / sus amigos y vecinos como / era*n*

Venidos a su tierra cris- / tianos y que no querian otra cosa salVo ser sus amigos y ha- / ber notiçia de buenas tierras / que

[fol. 42r]
42
parte / {rúbrica}

que poblar y que los Viniesen / a Ver y comunicar y ansi lo / hiçieron luego saber en aque- / llas partes que se comunica- / ban y trataban con ellos y die- / ron notiçia de Una pro- / vinçi- / {/} a de siete pueblos de su mis- / ma calidad aunque estaban / algo discordes que no se trata- / ban con ellos esta provincia se / diçe tusayan esta de cibola ve- / inte y çinco leguas son pueblos / de altos y gente belicosa en- / tre ellos {rúbrica}

el general havia emViado / a ellos a don pedro de tovar / con desisiete hombres de a / cavallo y tres o quatro peones / fue con ellos Un fray juan / de padilla frayle françisco

[fol. 42v]
primera / {rúbrica}

que en su mosedad havia sido / hombre belicoso llegados que / fueron entraron por la tierra / tam secretamente que no fue- / ron sentidos de ningun hon- / bre la causa fue que entre / provincia y provinçia no hay / poblados ni caserias ni las / gentes salen de sus pueblos / mas de hasta sus heredades / en espeçial en aquel tienpo / que tenian noticia de que çi- / bola era ganada por gentes / ferosissimas que andaban / en Unos animales que co- / mian gentes y entre los que / no havian Visto cavallos e- / ra esta notiçia tam grande / que les ponia admiraçion / y tanto que la gente de los / nuestros llego sobrenoche y / pu

[fol. 43r]
43
parte / {rúbrica}

pudieron llegar a encubrirse / (se) debajo de la barranca del / pueblo y estar alli oyendo ha- / blar los naturales en sus casas / pero como fue de manana fue- / ron descubiertos y se

pusie- / ron en orden los de la tierra / salieron a ellos bien ordena- / dos de arcos y rrodelas y porras / de madera en ala sin se des- / consertar y hubo lugar que / las lenguas hablasen con e- / llos y se les hiçiese rrequerri - / mientos por ser gente bien / entendida pero con todo es- / to hacian rrayas rrequirien- / do que no pasasen los nues- / tros aquellas rrayas hacia / sus pueblos que fuesen por-

[fol. 43v]
primera / {rúbrica}

te^{605} pasaronse algunas rrayas / andando hablando con ellos / Vino a tanto que Uno de ellos / se desmesuro y con Una porra / dio Un golpe a Un cavallo en / las armas del freno^{606} {rúbrica}

el fray juan enojado del ti- / empo que se malgastaba / con ellos dixo a el capitan / en Verdad yo no se a que Ve- / nimos aca Visto esto dieron san- / {/} tiago y fue tam supito que / derribaron muchos indios y / luego fueron desbaratados / y huyeron a el pueblo y a / otros no les dieron ese lugar / fue tanta la prestesa con que / del pueblo salieron de pax / con presentes que luego se / ma

[fol. 44r]
44
parte / {rúbrica}

mando rrecoger la gente y / que no se hiçiese mas daño / el capitan y los que con el / se hallaron buscaron sitio / para asentar su rreal çer- / ca del pueblo y alli se ha- / llaron^{607} digo se apearon don- / de llego la gente de pax / diciendo que ellos Venian / a dar la obidiençia por toda / la provinçia y que los queria / tener por amigos que rreci- / biesen aquel presente que / les daban que era alguna / rropa de algodon aunque / poca por no lo haber por aque- / lla tierra dieron algunos cue- / ros adobados y mucha hari- / na y pinol y mais y aVes de

[fol. 44v]
primera / {rúbrica}

de la tierra despues dieron / algunas turquesas aunque /

pocas aquel dia se rrecogio / la gente de la tierra y Vinie-
/ ron a dar la obidiençia y die- / ron abiertamente sus pue-
/ blos y que entrasen en ellos / a tratar comprar y Vender / y
cambiar {rúbrica}

rrigese como çibola por a- / yuntamiento de los mas an- /
çianos tienen sus governa- / dores y capitanes señalados
/ aqui se tuVo notiçia de Un / gran rrio y que rrio abajo a /
algunas jornadas havia gen- / tes muy grandes de cuerpo /
grande {rúbrica}

como don pedro de tovar / no

[fol. 45r]
45
parte / {rúbrica}

no lleVo mas comiçion VolVio / de alli y dio esta notiçia al
ge- / neral que luego despacho / alla a don garçi lopes de car-
/ denas con hasta doçe conpa- / ñeros para Ver este rrio que
/ como llego a tusayan siendo / bien rreçebido y hospedado
de / los naturales le dieron guias / para proseguir sus jornadas
/ y salieron de alli cargados de / bastimentos porque havian de
/ yr por tierra despoblada has- / ta el poblado que los indios
de- / çian que eran mas de veinte / jornadas pues como
hUbieron an- / dado veinte jornadas llegaron / a las barrancas
del rrio que pu- / estos a el b(a)ordo⁶⁰⁸ de ellas pare-

[fol. 45v]
primera / {rúbrica}

çia al otro bordo que havia mas / de tres o quatro leguas por
el / ayre esta tierra era alta y lle- / na de pinales bajos y encor-
/ Vados frigidissima debajo / del norte que con ser en ti- /
empo caliente no se podia Vi- / vir de frio en esta barranca /
estuVieron tres dias buscando la / bajada para el rrio que pa-
/ reçia de lo alto tendria Una / braçada⁶⁰⁹ de traVesia el agua
/ y por la notiçia de los indios ten- / dria media legua de
ancho / fue la baxada cosa inposi- / ble porque a cabo de
estos / tres dias pareciendoles Una / parte la menos dificul-
tosa / se pusieron a bajar por mas / ligeros el capitan melgosa
/ y un

[fol. 46r]
46
parte / {rúbrica}

y un juan galeras y otro con- / pañero y tardaron baxando /
a Vista de ellos de los de arri- / ba hasta que los perdieron de
/ vista los bultos que el Viso no los / alcansaba a Ver y
VolVieron / a hora de las quatro de la tarde / que no pudieron
acabar de / bajar por grandes dificulta- / des que hallaron
porque lo / que arriba parecia façil no / lo era antes muy
aspero y a- / gro dixeron que havian ba- / xado la terçia parte
y que / desde donde llegaron pare- / cia el rrio muy grande y
que /conforme a lo que Vieron era / Verdad tener la anchura
/ que los indios deçian de lo

[fol. 46v]
parte / {rúbrica}

alto determinaban Unos pe- / ñolsillos desgarrados de / la
barranca a el pareçer de / Un estado de hombre juran / los
que baxaron que llega- / ron a ellos que eran mayo- / res que
la torre mayor de / sevilla no caminaron mas / arrimados a la
barranca de / el rrio porque no havia agua / y hasta alli cada
dia se des- / Viaban sobretarde Una le- / gua or dos la tierra
adentro / en busca de las aguas y co- / mo anduViesen otras
qua- / tro jornadas las guias dixe- / ron que no era posible
pa- / sar adelante porque no ha- / via agua en tres ni quatro
/ jornadas porque ellos quan- / do

[fol. 47r]
47
primera / {rúbrica}

do caminavan por alli saca- / ban mugeres cargadas de a- /
gua en calabaços y que en / aquellas jornadas enterra- / ban
los calabaços del agua / para la Vuelta y que lo que /
caminaban los nuestros en dos / dias lo caminaban ellos en
U- / no {rúbrica}

este rrio era el del tison mucho / mas hacia los nacimientos
de el / que no por donde lo havian pa- / sado melchior dias
y su gente / estos indios eran de la misma / calidad segun

despues pare- / çio desde alli dieron la Vuel- / ta que no tuVo
mas efecto a- / quella jornada y de camino / Vieron Un
descolgadero de a- / guas que baxaban de Una

[fol. 47v]
primera / {rúbrica}

peña y supieron de las guias / que Unos rrasimos que colga-
/ van como s(i)*e*nos de c(h)ristal / era sal y fueron alla y
cogie- / ron cantidad de ella que tru- / geron y rrepartieron
quando / llegaron en çibola donde / por escri(p)to dieron
quenta a / su general de lo que Vieron / porque *h*avia ydo con
don gar- / çi lopes Un pedro de sotoma- / yor que yba por
c(o)ronista de / el campo aquellos pueblos / de aquella provinçia que- / daron de paz que nunca mas / se Viçitaron ni
se supo ni procu- / ro buscar otros poblados por / aquella via
{rúbrica}

Capitulo doçe como Vinie- / ron

[fol. 48r]
48
parte / {rúbrica}

ron a çibola gentes de cicuyc / a Ver los c(h)ristianos y como
fue / her*nan*do de alvarado a Ver las / vacas {rúbrica}

en el comedio que andaban / en estos descubrimientos Vini-
/ eron a çibola siertos indios de / Un pueblo que esta de alli
se- / tenta leguas la tierra aden- / tro al oriente de aquella
pro- / vinçia a quien nombran ci- / cuyc Venia entre ellos Un
ca- / pitan a quien los *nuestr*os pusie- / {+} ron por nombre
{+} bigotes por- / que traya los mostachos largos / era
mançebo alto y bien dis- / puesto y rrobusto de rrostro / {/}
este dixo al general como e- / llos Venian a le servir por

[fol. 48v]
primera / {rúbrica}

la noticia que les *h*avian dado / para que se les ofreçiese por a-
/ migos y que si *h*avian de yr por / su tierra los tuViesen por

tales / amigos hicieron sierto presen- / te de cueros adobados
y rro- / delas y capaçetes fue rreçebi- / do con mucho amor y
dioles el / general Vasos de Vidrio y que*n*- / tas margaritas y
caxcabeles / que los tuVieron en mucho co- / mo cosa nunca
por ellos Vista / dieron notiçia de vacas que / por Una que
Uno de ellos tra- / ya pintada en las carnes se sa- / co ser vaca
que por los cueros / no se podia entender a causa / que *e*l pelo
era merino y bur*ie*- / lado tanto que no se podia / saber de
que eran aquellos / cueros ordeno el general / que

[fol. 49r]
49
parte / {rúbrica}

que fuese con ellos hernando / de alvarado con veinte com-
/ pañeros y ochenta dias de co- / miçion y quien VolViese a
dar / rrelaçion de lo que halla- / van este capitan alvarado
pro- / siguio su jornada y a çinco jor- / nadas llegaron a Un
pue- / blo que estaba sobre Un peñol / deciase acuco era de
obra de / doçientos hombres de guerra / salteadores temidos
por toda / la tierra y comarca el pueblo / era fortissimo
porque estaba / sobre la entrada del peñol / que por todas
partes era de / peña tajada en tan grande / altura que tuViera
Un arca- / buz bien que haçer en (h)echar

[fol. 49v]
primera / {rúbrica}

una pelota en lo alto de *e*l te- / nia una sola subida de esca-
/ lera hecha a mano que co- / mençaba sobre Un rrepecho
/que haçia aquella parte / haçia la tierra esta escalera / era
ancha de obra de doçien- / tos escalones hasta llegar a la /
peña *h*avia otra luego angos- / ta arrimada a la peña de o-
/ bra de cien escalones y en el / rremate de ella *h*avian de /
subir por la peña obra de / tres estados por agugeros do*n*-
/ de hincaban las puntas de / los pies y se *h*asian con las ma-
/ nos en lo alto *h*aVia Una al- / barrada de piedra seca y gra*n*-
/ de que sin se descubrir po- / dian

[fol. 50r]
50
parte / {rúbrica}

dian derribar tanta que no / fuese poderoso ningun exerçito / a les entrar en lo alto *h*avia / espacio p*ara* sembrar y coger / gran cantidad de maix y cister- / nas para rrecoger nieve y a- / gua esta gente salio de gue- / rra abajo en lo llano y no / aproVechaba con ellos ningu- / na buena rraçon haçiendo / rrayas queriendo defender / que no las pasasen los nuestros / y como Vieron que se les dio / Un apreton luego dieron la / plaça digo la pax antes / que se les hiçiese daño hicie- / ron sus serimonias de pax / que llegar a los cavallos y to- / mar del sudor y untarse con

[fol. 50v]
primera / {rúbrica}

el y hacer cruçes con los dedos / de las manos y aunque la pax / mas figa es trabarse las ma- / nos Una con otra y esta guar- / dan estos inViolablemente di- / eron gran cantidad de / gallos de papada muy grandes mu- / cho pan y cueros de Venado / adobados y pinoles y harina / y mais {rúbrica}

{ojo} de alli en tres jornadas lle- / garon a una provinçia que / se dice triguex salio toda de / pax Viendo que yban con / bigotes hombres temido*s* por / todas aquellas provinçias / de alli emVio alvarado / a dar aviso a el general / para que se Viniese a inVer- / nar

[fol. 51r]
51
parte / {rúbrica}

nar aquella tierra que no po- / co se holgo el general con la / nueVa que la tierra yba me- / jorando de alli a çinco jorna- / das llego a cicuyc Un pueblo / muy fuerte de quatro altos / los del pueblo salieron a rre- / cebir a her*nan*do de alvarado y a / su capitan con muestras de a- / legria y lo metieron en el pue- / blo con atambores y gaitas / que alli *h*ay muchos a mane- / ra de pifanos y le hiçieron gra*n*- / de presente de rropa y tur- / quesas que las *h*ay en aque- / lla tierra en cantidad alli (^lle) / {ojo} holgaron algunos dias y to- / maron lengua de un indio es- / claVo natural de la tierra

[fol. 51v]
primera / {rúbrica}

de aquella parte que Va hacia / la florida que *e*s la parte que / don fer*nan*do de soto descubrio en / lo Ultimo la tierra adentro / este dio notiçia que no debiera / de grandes poblados lleVolo / hernando de alvarado por / guia para las vacas y fueron / tantas y tales cosas las que di- / xo de las rriqueças de oro y / plata que *h*avia en su tie- / rra que no curaron[610] de buscar / las vacas mas de quanto Vi- / eron algunas pocas luego / VolVieron por dar el gene- / ral la rrica notiçia a el indio / llamaron turco porque lo pa- / reçia en el aspecto y a esta sa- / con el general *h*avia emVi- / ado a don garcia lopes de / car

[fol. 52r]
52
parte / {rúbrica}

(lopes de) cardenas a tiguex / con gente a haçer el aposen- / to para llevar alli a inVer- / nar el campo que a la sason / *h*avia llegado de señora y qu- / ando hernando de alVara- / do llego a tiguex de Vuel- / ta de cicuyc hallo a don gar- / cia lopes de cardenas y fue / neçesario que no pasase / adelante y como los natura- / les les inportase que Viesen / digo diesen a donde se apo- / sentasen los españoles fueles / forçado desamparar Un pu- / eblo y rrecogerse ellos a los / otros de sus amigos y no lle- / Varon mas que sus personas / y rropas y alli se descubrio / notiçia de muchos pueblos

[fol. 52v]
primera / {rúbrica}

debajo del norte que creo fue- / ra harto mejor seguir aque- / lla via que no a el turco que / fue causa de todo el mal su- / seso que *h*Ubo {rúbrica}

Capitulo trece como el / general llego con poca gen- / te la via de tutahaco y / dexo el campo a don tristan / que lo lleVo a tiguex {rúbrica} todas estas cosas ya dichas ha- / vian pasado quando don / tristan de arellano llego / de señora en cibola y como lle- / go luego el general por no- / ticia que tenia de Una pro- / vincia de ocho pueblos tomo / treinta hombres de los mas / des

[fol. 53r]
53
parte / {rúbrica}

descansados y fue por la ver y de / alli tomar la Vuelta de tiguex / con buenas guias que llevaba / y dexo ordenado que como des- / cansase la gente veinte dias don / tristan de are- / llano saliese con el / campo la via derecha de tiguex / y asi siguio su camino donde le / acontecio que desde Un dia q*ue* / salieron de Un aposento hasta / terçero dia a mediodia que Vie- / ron Una sierra neVada donde / fueron a buscar agua no la be- / bieron ellos ni sus cavallos ni el / servicio pudo soportarla por / el gran frio aunque con gran / trabajo en ocho jornadas lle- / garon a tutahaco y alli se supo / que aquel rrio abaxo havia

[fol. 53v]
primera / {rúbrica}

otros pueblos estos salieron de / pax son pueblos de terrados co- / mo los de tiguex y del mismo / traje salio el general de alli / Visitando toda la proVinçia el / rrio arriba hasta llegar a ti- / guex donde hallo a hernan- / do de alvarado y a el turco / que no pocas fueron las ale- / grias que hiço con tam buena / nueVa porque deçia que ha- / via en su tierra Un rrio en ti- / erra llana que tenia dos le- / guas de ancho adonde havi- / a peçes tan grandes como cava- / llos y gran numero de cano- / as grandissimas de mas de a / veinte rremeros por banda y / que llevaban velas y que los / señores yban a popa senta- / dos

[fol. 54r]
54
parte / {rúbrica}

dos debajo de toldos y en la / proa Una grande aguila de / oro deçia mas que *e*l señor de / aquella tierra dormia la

sies- / ta debajo de Un grande ar- / bol donde estaban colgados / gran cantidad de caxcabeles / de oro que con el ayre le daba*n* / solas deçia mas que *e*l comun ser- / vicio de todos en general era / plata labrada y los jarros pla- / tos y escudillas eran de oro lla- / maba a el oro Acochis diose- / le a el presente credito por la / eficaçia con que lo deçia y por- / que le enseñaron joyas de (a-) / laton y oliolo y deçia que / no era oro y el oro y la pla- / ta co(g)noçia muy bien y de los

[fol. 54v]
primera / {rúbrica}

otros metales no hacia caso de / ellos {rúbrica}

emVio el general a hernan- / do de alVarado otra Vez a ci- / cuyc a pedir Unos brasaletes / de oro que deçia este turco que / le tomaron a el tiempo que / lo prendieron alVarado fue / y los del pueblo lo rrecibieron / como amigo y como pidio los / bracaletes negaronlos por to- / das vias diciendo que *e*l turco / los engañaba y que mentia / el capitan alvarado Viendo / que no havia rremedio procu- / ro que Viniese a su tienda el / capitan bigotes y el governa- / dor y Venidos prendioles en / cadena los del pueblo salie- / ron de guerra (h)echando fle- / chas

[fol. 55r]
55
parte / {rúbrica}

chas y denostando a hernando / de alVarado diçiendole de hon- / bre que quebrantaba la fee y / amistad her*nan*do de alVarado par- / tio con ellos a tiguex al gene- / ral donde los tuVieron presos / mas de seis mese(i)s despues que / fue el principio de desacredi- / tar la palabra que de alli / adelante se les daba de paz / como se vera por lo que des- / pues suçedio {rúbrica}

Capitulo catorce como el / campo salio de sibola para / tiguex y lo que les acaeçio en / el camino con nieVe {rúbrica}

ya habemos dicho como quan- / do el general salio de çibola

[fol. 55v]
primera / {rúbrica}

dexo mandado a don tristan / de arellano saliese desde / a
veinte dias lo qual se hiço / que como Vi(d)o que la gente /
estaba ya descansada y pro- / Veydos de bastimentos y ga- /
nosos de salir en busca de / su general salio con su gen- / te
la Vuelta de tigues y el / primero dia fueron a haçer /
aposento a Un pueblo de / aquella proVinçia el mejor /
mayor y mas hermoso solo / este pueblo tiene casas de / siete
altos que son casas par- / ticulares que sirven en el / pueblo
como de fortaleças / que son superiores a las otras / y salen
por encima como / to

[fol. 56r]
56
parte / {rúbrica}

torres y en ellas *h*ay troneras / y saeteras para defender los /
altos porque como los pue- / blos no tienen calles y los te- /
rrados son parejos y comuni(s)c- / anse⁶¹¹ de ganar primero
los al- / tos y estas casas mayores es la / defença de ellos alli
nos co- / menço a neVar y faVoreçio- / se la gente so las las
aves di- / go alaves del pueblo que / salen afuera Unos como
bal- / cones con pilares de madera / por baxo porque
comunme*n*- / te se mandan por escaleras / que suben a aquellos balco- / nes que por baxo no tienen / puertas {rúbrica}

como dexo de neVar salio / de alli el campo su camino

[fol. 56v]
primera / {rúbrica}

y como ya el tiempo lo llevaba / que era entrada de
diçiembre / en diez dias que tardo el can- / po no dexo de
neVar sobre- / tarde y casi todas las noches / de suerte que
para haçer los / aposentos donde llegaban / *h*avian de
apalancar Un co(l)- / do de nieVe y mas no se Vio / camino
empero las guias / a tino guiaban co(g)nociendo / la tierra
*h*ay por toda la tie- / rra savinas y pinos hacia- / se de ello
grandes hogue- / ras que *e*l humo y calor haçia / a la nieVe
que caya que se / desViase Una braça y dos / a la rredonda

del fuego e- / ra nieve seca que aunque / cay*o* medio estado
sobre el far- / da

[fol. 57r]
57
parte / {rúbrica}

daje no mojaba y con sacudi- / lla caya y quedaba el hato lin-
/ pio como caya toda la noche / cubria de tal manera el far-
/ daje y los soldados en sus le- / chos que si de supito algui-
/ en diera en el campo no Viera / otra cosa que montones de
ni- / eVe y los cavallos aunque fue- / se medio estado se
soportaba / y antes daba calor a los que es- / taban debajo
{rúbrica}

paso el campo por Acuco el / gran peñol y como estaban de
/ paz hiçieron buen hospedaje / dando bastimentos y aV*es*
au*n*- {/} / que ella es poca gente como / tengo dicho a lo alto
subie- / ron muchos companeros por / lo Ver y los pasos de
la peña

[fol. 57v]
primera / {rúbrica}

con gran dificultad por no lo / *h*aber usado por que los
natu- / rales lo suben y bajan tam li- / beralmente que Van
carga- / dos de bastimentos y las mu- / geres con agua y
parece que / no tocan las manos y los n*uest*ros / para subir
*h*avian de dar las / armas los Unos a los otros por / el paso
arriba {rúbrica}

desde alli pasaron a tiguex / donde fueron bien rrecebidos /
y aposentados y la tam buena / nueVa del turco que no dio /
poca alegria segun aliVia- / ba los trabajos aunque qu- / ando
el campo llego halla- / mos alçada aquella tierra / o
proVincia por ocaçion que / pa

[fol. 58r]
58
parte / {rúbrica}

para ello *h*Ubo que no fue peque- / ña como se dira y *h*avian ya / los n*uest*ros quemado Un pueblo / Un dia antes que el campo / llegase y VolVian a el aposen- / to {rúbrica}

Capitulo quinçe como se / alço tiguex y el castigo que / en ellos *h*Ubo sin que lo *h*Ubie- /se en el causador {rúbrica}

dicho sea[612] como el general / llego a tiguex donde hallo / a don garci lopes de carde- / nas y a hernando de alVa- / rado y como lo torno a em- / Viar a cicuye y truxo preso / a el capitan bigotes y a el go-

[fol. 58v]
primera / {rúbrica}

vernador del pueblo que / era Un hombre ançiano de / esta pricion los tiguex no sin- / tieron bien juntose con esto q*ue* / el general quiso rrecoger / alguna rropa para rrepar- / tir a la gente de guerra y / para esto hiço llamar a Un / indio prin- / cipal de tiguex / que ya se tenia con el mu- / cho conosimiento y conVer- / saçion a quien los nuestros / llamavan juan aleman / por Un juan aleman que / estaba en mexico a quien / {çer} deçian pare*çe*r aqueste / hablo el general diciendo / que le proVeyese de tresi- / entas pieças de rropa o mas / que *h*avia menester para / dar

[fol. 59r]
59
parte / {rúbrica}

dar a su gente el dixo que a- / quello no era a el haçerlo / sino a los governadores y que / sobre ello era menester entrar / en consulta y rrepartirse por / los pueblos y que era menes- / ter pedirlo particularmen- / te a cada pueblo por si orde- / nolo ansi el general y que / lo fuesen a pedir siertos hom- / bres señalados de los que con / el estaban y como eran doçe / pueblos que fuesen Unos por / la Una parte del rrio y otros / por la otra y como fuese de / manos a boca no les dieron / lugar de se consultar ni tra- / tar sobre ello y como llegava / a el pueblo luego se les pedia

[fol. 59v]
primera / {rúbrica}

y lo *h*abian de dar porque *h*Ubi- / ese lugar de pasar adelante / y con esto no tenian mas lu- / gar de quitarse los pellones / de ençima y darlos hasta que / llegase el numero que se les pe- / dia y algunos soldados de los / que alli yban que los cogedo- / res les daban algunas man- / tas o pellones si no eran tales y V*e*ian algun indio con otra / mejor trocabansela sin tener / mas rrespecto ni saber la ca- / lidad de *e*l que despojaban / que no poco sintieron esto / allende de lo dicho del pue- / blo del aposento salio un / sobresaliente que por su / honrra no le nombrare / y fue

[fol. 60r]
60
parte / {rúbrica}

y fue a otro pueblo Una legua / de alli y Viendo Una muger / hermosa llamo a su marido / que le tuViese el cavallo de / rrienda en lo bajo y el subio / a lo alto y como el pueblo se / mandaba por lo alto creyo / el indio que yba a otra parte / y detenido alli *h*Ubo sierto rru- / mor y el bajo y tomo su cava- / llo y fuese el indio subio y su- / po que *h*avia forçado o queri- / do forçar a su muger y junta- / mente con las personas de ca- / lidad del pueblo se vino a / quexar diçiendo que Un / hombre le *h*avia forçado a su / muger y conto como / *h*avia pasado y como el general

[fol. 60v]
primera / {rúbrica}

hiço pareçer todos los soldados / y personas que con el estaban / y el indio no lo conoçio o por *h*a- / berse mudado la rropa o por / alguna otra ocaçion que pa- / ra ello *h*Ubo pero dixo que / conoçeria el cavallo porq*ue* / lo tuVo de rrienda fue lleva- / do por las cavallerisas y ha- / llo Un cavallo enmanta- / do hoVero y dixo que su due- / ño de aquel cavallo era el / dueño nego Viendo que *e*l no / *h*abia conoçido y pudo ser que / se (h)erro en el cavallo final- / mente el se fue sin *h*aber en- / mienda de lo que pedia otro / dia vino Un indio del canpo / que guardaba los cavallos / he

[fol. 61r]
61
parte / {rúbrica}

herido y huyendo diciendo que / le *h*avain muerto Un compañe- / ro y que los indios de la tierra / se lleVavan los cavallos an- / tecogidos hacia sus pueblos / fueron a rrecoger los cavallos / y faltaron muchos y siete mu- / las del general {rúbrica}

otro dia fue don garci lopes de / cardenas a Ver los pueblos y / tomar de ellos lengua y ha- / llo los pueblos serrados con / palenques y gran grita de*n*- / tro corriendo los cavallos co- / mo en coso de toros y flechan- / dolos y todos de guerra no / pudo haçer cosa porque / no salieron a el campo que co- / mo son pueblos fuertes no

[fol. 61v]
primera / {rúbrica}

les pudieron enojar luego or- / deno el general que don gar- / çi lopes de cardenas fuese a / çercar Un pueblo con toda / la demas gente y este pue- / blo era donde se hiço el ma- / yor daño y es donde acaeçio / lo de la india fueron muchos / capitanes que *h*avian ydo / delante con el general co- / mo fue juan de saldivar y / barrionueVo y diego lopes / y melgosa tomaron a los in- / dios tam de sobresalto que / luego les ganaron los altos / con mucho rriesgo porque / les hirieon muchos de los / nuestros por saeteras que / haçian por de dentro de las / casas estuVieron los nuestros / en

[fol. 62r]
62
parte / {rúbrica}

en lo alto a mucho rriesgo el / dia y la noche y parte de otro / dia haçiendo buenos tiros de / b(e)*a*llestas y arcabuçes la gente / de a cavallo en el campo con / muchos amigos de la nueVa / españa y daban por los sotanos / que *h*avian aportillado gran- / des humasos de suerte que p*i*- / dieron la paz hallaronse aque- / lla parte pablos de melgosa / y diego lopes veintiquatro de / sevilla y rrespondieronles co*n* / las mismas

señales que ellos / haçian de paz que es haçer / la cruz y ellos luego soltaron / las armas y se dieron a m*erce*d / lleVabanlos a la tienda de / don garçia el qual segun se

[fol. 62v]
primera / {rúbrica}

dixo no supo de la paz y cre- / yo que de su Voluntad se da- / ban como hombres Vençidos / y como tenia mandado del / general que no los tomase / a vida porque se hiçiese cas- / tigo y los demas temiesen / mando que luego hincasen / doçientos palos para los que- / mar Vivos no *h*Ubo quien le / dixese de la paz que les havi- / an dado que los soldados tan- / poco lo sabian y los que la di- / eronselo callaron que no / hiçieron caso de ello pues co- / mo los enemigos Vieron que / los yban atando y los comen- / çaban a quemar obra de / çien hombres que estaban / en

[fol. 63r]
63
parte / {rúbrica}

en la tienda se començaron a / haçer fuertes y defenderse con / lo que estaba dentro y con palos / que salian a tomar la gente / nuestra de a pie dan en la tie*n*- / da por todas partes estocadas / que los hacian desmanparar / la tienda y dio luego la gente / de a cavallo en ellos y como / la tierra era llana no les quedo / hombre a vida sino fueron al- / gunos que se *h*avian quedado / escondidos en el pueblo que / huyeron aquella noche y die- / ron mandado[613] por toda la tie- / rra como no les guardaron la / paz que les dieron que fue / despues harto mal y como esto / fue hecho y luego les neVase

[fol. 63v]
primera / {rúbrica}

des*m*ampararon el pueblo y Vol- / Vieronse a el aposento a / el tie*m*- / po que llegaba el campo de / cibola {rúbrica}

Capitulo desiseis como se / puso cerco a tiguex y se gano / y lo que mas aconte(n)cio / mediante el cerco {rúbrica} como ya *he* contado quando / acabaron de ganar aquel / pueblo començo a neVar / en aquella tierra y neVo / de suerte que en aquellos / dos meses no se pudo haçer / nada salVo yr por los cami- / nos a les aVisar que Vinie- / sen de pax y que serian per- / donados dandoles todo segu- / ro

[fol. 64r]
64
parte / {rúbrica}

ro a lo qual ellos respondieron / que no se fiarian de quien no / sabia guardar la fe que da- / ban que se acordasen que / tenian preso a bigotes y que / en el pueblo quemado no / les guardaron la paz fue Uno / de los que fueron a les haçer es- / tos rrequerimientos don gar- / cia lopes de cardenas que sa- / lio con obra de treinta compa- / ñeros Un dia y fue a el pue- / blo de tiguex y a hablar con / juan aleman y aunque / estaban de guerra Vinieron / a hablalle y le dixeron que / si queria hablar con ellos q*ue* / se apease y se llegavan a el / a hablar de paz y que se des-

[fol. 64v]
primera / {rúbrica}

Viase la gente de a cavallo y / harian apartar su gente y / llegaron a el el juan ale- / man y otro capitan del pue- / blo y fue hecho ansi como lo / pedian ya que estaba çerca / de ellos dixeron que ellos / no trayan armas que se las / quitase don garcia lopes lo / hiço por mas los asegurar co*n* / gana que tenia de los traer / de paz y como llego a ellos el / juan aleman lo Vino a abra- / çar en tanto los dos que con / el Venian sacaron dos maçe- /tas que secretamente tray- / an a las espaldas y dieron- / le sobre la çelada dos tales / golpes que casi lo aturdie- / ron

[fol. 65r]
65
parte / {rúbrica}

ron hallaronse dos soldados / de a cavallo çerca que no / se

*h*avian querido apartar a- / unque les fue mandado y arre- / metieron con tanta preste- / ça que lo sacaron de entre / sus manos aunque no pudie- / ron enojar a los enemigos / por tener la acogida çerca / y grandes rrosiadas de flechas / que luego Vinieron sobre e- / llos y a el Uno le atraVesaron / el cavallo por las narises / la gente de a cavallo llego / toda de tropel y sacaron a / su capitan de la priesa[614] sin po- / der dañar a los enemigos / antes salieron muchos de / los n*uest*ros mal heridos y asi se / rretiraron quedando algunos

[fol. 65v]
primera / {rúbrica}

haçiendo rrostro don garçia / lopes de cardenas con parte / de la gente paso a otro pue- / blo que estaba media legua / adelante porque en estos / dos lugares se *h*avia rrecogi- / do toda la mas gente de a- / quellos pueblos y como de los / rrequerimientos que les hi- / çieron no hiçieron caso ni de / dar la paz antes con grandes / gritos tiraban flechas de lo / alto y se VolVio a la compa- / ñia que *h*avia quedado ha- / çiendo rrostro a el pueblo de / tiguex entonçes salieron los / del pueblo en gran canti- / dad los n*uest*ros a media rrienda / dieron muestra que huyan / de suerte que sacaron los e- / ne

[fol. 66r]
66
parte / {rúbrica}

nemigos a lo llano y rreVolVi- / eron sobre ellos de manera / que se tendieron algunos de / los mas señalados los demas / se rrecogieron al pueblo y a / lo alto y ansi se VolVio este / capitan a el aposento {rúbrica}

el general luego como esto / paso ordeno de los yr a çer- / car y salio Un dia con su gen- / te bien ordenada y con algu- / nas escalas llegado asento / su rreal junto a el pueblo / y luego dieron el combate / pero como los enemigos ha- / via muchos dias que se pertre- / chaban (h)echaron tanta pie- / dra sobre los n*uest*ros que a mu- / chos tendieron en tierra y hi-

[fol. 66v]
primera / {rúbrica}

rieron de flechas cerca de çien / hombres de que despues mu- / rieron algunos por mala cu- / {jano} ra de Un mal s(u)irugano que / yba en el campo el çerco duro / sinquenta dias en los quales / algunas veces se les dieron / sobresaltos y lo que mas les a- / quexo fue que no tenian a- / gua y hiçieron dentro del / pueblo Un poso de grandi- / ssima hondura y no pudie- / ron sacar agua antes se les / derrumbo a el tiempo que lo / hacian y les mato treinta per- / sonas murieron de los çer- / cados doçientos hombres de / dentro en los combates y Un / dia que se les dio Un conbate / rre

[fol. 67r]
67
parte / {rúbrica}

rrecio mataron de los nuestros a / francisco de oVando capitan / y maestre de campo que havi- / a sido todo el tiempo que don / garcia lopes de cardenas an- / duVo en los descubrimien- / tos ya dichos y a un francisco / de pobares buen hidalgo / a francisco de oVando metie- / ron en el pueblo que los nuestros / no lo pudieron defender que / no poco se sintio por ser co- / mo era persona señalada / y por si tam honrrado afable / y bien quisto que era mara- / villa antes que se acaba- / se de ganar Un dia llama- / ron a habla y sabida su de- / manda fue deçir que tenian

[fol. 67v]
primera / {rúbrica}

co(g)noçido que las mugeres / ni a los niños no haciamos / mal que querian dar sus mu- / geres y hijos porque les gasta- / ban el agua no se pudo acabar / con ellos que se diesen de paz / diçiendo que no les guarda- / riamos la palabra y asi dieron / obra de çien personas de ni- / ños y mugeres que no quisie- / ron salir mas y mientras las / dieron estuVieron los nuestros a / cavallo en ala delante / del pueblo don lope de U- / rrea a cavallo y sin çelada / andaba rreçibiendo en los /

braços los niños y niñas y co- / mo ya no quisieron dar mas / el don lope les inportunaba / que

[fol. 68r]
68
parte / {rúbrica}

que se diesen de pax haçien- / doles grandes promeças de se- / guridad ellos le dixeron que / se desViase que no era su vo- / luntad de se fiar de gente / que no guardaba la amistad / ni palabra que daban y co- / mo no se quisiese desViar / salio Uno con Un arco a fle- / char y con Una flecha y a- / mena- solo con ella que / se la tiraria sino se yba de / alli y por Voçes que le die- / ron que se pusiese la çela- / da no quiso diçiendo que / mientras alli estuViese no / le harian mal y como el in- / dio Vi(d)o que no se queria / yr tiro y hincole la flecha / par de las manos de el ca-

[fol 68v]
primera / {rúbrica}

vallo y enarco luego otra y / tornole a deçir que se fuese / sino que le tirarian de Veras / el don lope se puso su çelada / y paso ante paso se vino a / meter entre los de a cavallo / sin que rreçibiese enojo de / ellos y como le Vieron que ya / estaba en salVo con gran gri- / ta y alarido comencaron / a rroçiar flecheria el ge- / neral no quiso que por a- / quel dia se les diese bate- / ria[615] por Ver si los podian tra- / er por alguna via de paz / lo qual ellos jamas quisie- / ron {rúbrica}

desde a quinçe dias deter- / minaron de salir Una noche / y ansi lo hicieron y tomando / en

[fol. 69r]
69
parte / {rúbrica}

en medio las mugeres salie- / ron a el quarto de la modo- / rra velavan aquel quarto / quarenta de a cavallo y / dando a el arma los del qu- / artel de don rrodrigo maldo- / nado dieron en ellos los ene- / migos derribaron Un espa- / ñol muerto y Un cavallo y hi- / rieron a otros pero *h*Ubieron los / de rromper y haçer matan- / ça en ellos hasta que rreti- / randose dieron consigo en / el rrio que yba corr*i*ente y / frigidissimo y como la gente / del rreal acudio presto fueron / pocos los que escaparon de / muertos o heridos otro dia pa- / saron el rrio la gente del rreal

[fol. 69v]
primera / {rúbrica}

y hallaron muchos heridos / que la gran frialdad los *h*a- / via derribado en el campo / y trayanlos para curar y / servirse de ellos y ansi se a- / cabo aquel çerco y se gano / el pueblo aunque algunos / que quedaron en el pueblo / se rreci(h)*b*ieron en Un barrio / y fueron tomados en pocos / dias {rúbrica}

el otro pueblo grande media*n*- / te de çerco le *h*avian gana- / do dos capitanes que fueron / don diego de guevara y ju*an* / de saldiVar que yendoles / Una madrugada a echar / Una çelada para coger en / ella sierta gente de guerra / que

[fol. 70r]
70
parte / {rúbrica}

que acostumbraba a salir ca- / da mañana a haçer muestra / por poner algun temor en / n*uest*ro rreal las espias que tenia*n* / puestas para quando los Vie- / sen Venir Vieron como salia*n* / gentes y caminaban haçia / la tierra salieron de la çe- / lada y fueron para el pue- / blo y Vieron huir la gente / y siguieronla haciendo en / ellos matança como de esto / se dio mandado salio gente / del rreal que fueron sobre el / pueblo y lo saquearon pre*n*- / diendo toda la gente que en / el hallaron en que *h*Ubo obra / de çien mugeres y niños a- / cabose este çerco en fin de

[fol. 70v]
primera / {rúbrica}

marco del año de quarenta / {1542 / {rúbrica}} y dos en el

qual tiempo a- / caecieron otras cosas de que / podria dar notiçia que por / no cortar el hilo las he dexa- / do pero *de* deçir se *h*an agora / porque conViene se sepan / para entender lo de ade- / lante {rúbrica}

Capitulo desisiete como / Vinieron a el campo mensa- / jeros del valle de señora / y como murio el capitan / melchior dias en la jornada / del tizon {rúbrica} {rúbrica}

ya diximos como melchior / dias el capitan *h*avia pasa- / do en balsas el rrio del tiçon / para

[fol. 71r]
71
parte / {rúbrica}

para prosequir adelante el / descubrimiento de aquella / costa pues a el tiempo que se / acabo el cerco llegaron men- / sajeros a el canpo de la villa / de san hieronimo con cartas / de diego de (alarcon) *alcaraz* que *h*a- / via quedado alli en lugar / del melchior dias trayan nue- / Vas como melchior dias *h*avia / muerto en la demanda que / llevaba y la gente se *h*avia / Vuelto sin Ver cosa de lo que / deseaban y paso el caso de *e*s- / ta manera {rúbrica}

como *h*Ubieron pasado el rrio / caminaron en demanda / de la costa que por alli ya da- / ba la Vuelta sobre el sur o en-

[fol. 71v]
primera / {rúbrica}

tre sur y oriente porque aqu- / el ancon de mar entra dere- / cho al norte y este rrio entr(^e)^a / en el rremate del ancon tra- / yendo sus corrientes debaxo / del norte y corre a el sur yen- / do como yban caminando / dieron en Unos medanos de / çenisa ferViente que no po- / dia nadie entrar a ellos por- / que fuera entrarse ahogar / en la mar la tierra que ho- / llaban temblaba como ten- / pano que pareçia que esta- / ban debaxo algunos lagos / pareçio cosa admirable / que asi herVia la çenisa / en algunas partes que pa- / reçia cosa infernal y des- / Viandose de aqui por el / pe

[fol. 72r]
72
parte / {rúbrica}

peligro que pareçia que lle- / Vavan y por la falta del a- / gua
Un dia Un lebrel que / llevaba Un soldado anto- / josele dar
tras de Unos car- / neros que lleVavan para / bastimentos y
como el capi- / tan lo Vi(d)o arro(n)jole la lan- / ça de
enquentro yendo co- / rriendo y hincola en tierra / y no
pudiendo detener el ca- / vallo fue sobre la lança y en- /
claVosela por el muslo que / le salio el hierro a la ingle y / le
rrompio la Vejiga Visto / esto los soldados dieron la / Vuelta
con su capitan heri- / do teniendo cada dia rrefri- / egas con
los indios que havian

[fol. 72v]
primera / {rúbrica}

quedado rebelados ViVio obra / de veinte dias que por le
traer / pasaron gran trabajo y asi Vol- / Vieron hasta que
murio con / buena orden sin perder Un hon- / bre ya yban
saliendo de lo / mas trabajoso llegados a seño- / ra hiço
alcaraz los mensaje- / ros ya dichos haciendolo sa- / ber y
como algunos solda- / dos estaban mal asentados / y procuraban algunos moti- / nes y como havia sentenciado / a la
horca a dos que despues / se le havian huydo de la pri- / çion
{rúbrica}

el general Visto esto enVio a / aquella villa a don pedro de /
tovar para que entresaca- / se alguna gente y para / que

[fol. 73r]
73
parte / {rúbrica}

que lleVase consigo mensajeros / que emViaba a el visorey
don / Antonio de mendoça con rreca- / (u)dos de lo acon-
teçido y la bue- / na nueVa del turco {rúbrica}

don pedro de tovar fue y lle- / gado alla hallo que havian los
/ naturales de aquella pro- / Vinçia muerto con Una flecha /

de yerba a Un soldado de Un- / a muy pequeña herida en /
Una mano sobre esto havian / ydo alla algunos soldados / y
no fueron bien rrecebidos / don pedro de toVar emVio a /
diego de alcaraz con gente a / prender a los prinçipales y /
señores de Un pueblo que lla- / man el valle de los vella- /
cos que esta en alto llegado / alla los prendieron y presos

[fol. 73v]
primera / {rúbrica}

pareciole a diego de alcaraz / de los soltar a trueque de que /
diesen algun hilo y rropa y / otras cosas de que los soldados
/ tenian necesidad Viendose / sueltos alsaronse de guerra / y
subieron a ellos y como esta- / ban fuertes y tenian yerba /
mataron algunos españoles / y hirieron otros que despues /
murieron en el camino Vol- / Viendose rretirandose para /
su villa y si no llevaran con- / sigo amigos de los coraçones / lo
pasaran peor VolVieron / a la villa dexando muertos /
desisiete soldados de la yer- / ba que con pequeña herida /
morian rrabiando rrompi- / endose las carnes con Un pes- /
telencial hedor inconporta- / ble

[fol. 74r]
74
parte / {rúbrica}

ble Visto por don pedro de tovar / el daño pareçiendoles que
no / quedaban seguros en aque- / lla villa la paso quarenta /
leguas mas haçia çibola al / valle del suya donde los de- /
xaremos por contar lo que / aVino a el general con el / campo
despues del cerco de / tiguex {rúbrica}

Capitulo desiocho como el / general procuro dexar asen- /
tada la tierra para ir en de- / manda de quisvira donde / deçia
el turco havia el prin- / çipio de la rriqueça {rúbrica}

mediante el çerco de tiguex / el general quiso yr a cicuyc /
lleVando consigo a el gover- / nador para lo poner en li-

[fol. 74v]
primera / {rúbrica}

bertad con promesas que qu- / ando saliese para quivira / daria libertad a bigotes y / lo dexaria en su pueblo y / como llego a cicuye fue rre- / çebido de paz y entro en el / pueblo con algunos solda- / dos ellos rreçibieron a su go- / vernador con mucho amor / y fiesta Visto que hUbo el pue- / blo y hablado a los natura- / les dio la Vuelta para su can- / po quedando cicuyc de paz / con esperança de cobrar su / capitan bigotes {rúbrica}

acabado que fue el çerco co- / mo ya habemos dicho emVio / Un capitan a chia Un buen / pueblo y de mucha gente / que havia emViado a dar la / obi

[fol. 75r]
75
parte / {rúbrica}

obidiençia que estaba desVia- / do del rrio al poniente qua- / tro leguas y hallaronle de / paz aqui se dieron a guardar / quatro tiros de bronçe que es- / taban mal acondiçionados / tambien fueron a quirix / proVincia de siete pueblos / seis compañeros y en el prim- / er pueblo que seria de çien / veçinos huyeron que no osa- / ron a esperar a los nuestros y / los fue- / ron atajar a rrienda suelta / y los VolVieron a el pueblo a / sus casas con toda seguridad / y de alli aVisaron a los de- / mas pueblos y los asegura- / ron y asi poco a poco se fue / asegurando toda la comar- / ca en tanto que el rrio se des- / helaba y se dexaba Vade-

[fol. 75v]
primera

ar para dar lugar a la jor- / nada aunque los doçe pue- / blos de tiguex nunca en to- / do el tiempo que por alli es- / tuVo el campo se poblo nin- / guno por seguridad ningu- / na que se les diese {rúbrica}

y como el rrio fue deshelado / que lo havia estado casi qua- / tro meses que se pasaba por / ençima del hyelo a cavallo / ordenose la partida para qui- / Vira donde decia el turco que / havia algun oro y plata a- / unque no tanto como en / Arehe y los guaes ya havia / algunos del campo sospe- / chosos del

turco porque me- / diante el cerco tenia cargo / de el Un español que se lla- / mava servantes y este es- / pa

[fol. 76r]
76
parte / {rúbrica}

pañol juro con solemnidad que / havia Visto a el turco hablar en / Una olla de agua con el de- / monio y que teniendolo el de- / baxo de llave que nadie po- / dia hablar con el le havia pre- / guntado el turco a el que a / quien havian muerto de los / cristianos los de tiguex y / el le dixo que a no nadie y / el turco le respondio mientes / que çinco c(h)ristianos han mu- / erto y a un capitan y que el / çervantes Viendo que deçia / Verdad se lo conçedio por saber / de el quien se lo havia dicho y / el turco le dixo que el lo sabia / por si y que para aquello no / havia neçesidad que nadie

[fol. 76v]
primera / {rúbrica}

se lo dixese y por esto lo espio / y Vio hablar con el demonio / en la olla como he dicho {rúbrica}

con todo esto se hiço alarde / para salir de tiguex a este / tiempo {+} llegaron gentes / de cibola a Ver a el general / y el general les encargo el / buen tratamiento de los es- / pañoles que Viniesen de se- / ñora con don pedro de tovar / y les dio cartas que le diesen / a don pedro en que le daba / aViso de lo que debia de ha- / çer y como habia de yr en / busca del campo y que ha- / llaria cartas debajo de las / cruçes en las jornadas que / el campo habia de haçer sa- / lio el campo de tiguex a çin- / co

[fol. 77r]
77
primera[616] / {rúbrica}

co de mayo la Vuelta de cicuyc / que como tengo dicho son ve- / inte y cinco jornadas digo / leguas de alli llevando de / alli a bigotes llegado alla / les dio a su capitan que ya / andaba suelto con guardia / el pueblo se holgo mucho con / el y estu-

Vieron de paz y die- / ron bastimentos y bigotes y / el governador dieron a el / general Un mancebete que / se deçia xabe
natural de / quivira para que de *el* se in- / formasen de la
tierra este de- / çia que *h*abia oro y plata pe- / ro no tanto
como deçia el tu*r*- / co todavia el turco se afir- / mava y fue
por guia y a- / si salio el campo de alli {rúbrica}

[fol. 77v]
primera / {rúbrica}

Capitulo desinueve como / salieron en demanda de / quivira
y lo que aconteçio / en el camino {rúbrica}

salio el campo de cicuyc de- / xando el pueblo de paz ya / lo
que pareçio contento / y obligado a mantener / la amistad por
les *h*aber res- / tituydo su governador y / capitan y caminando
para / salir a lo llano que esta pa- / sada toda la cordillera a /
quatro dias andados de ca- / mino dieron en Un rrio de / gran
corriente hondo que / baxaba de hacia cicuye / y a que *e*ste se
puso nombre / el rrio de cicuyc detuVieron- / se

[fol. 78r]
78
parte / {rúbrica}

se aqui por haçer puente pa- / ra le pasar acabose en qua- /
tro dias con toda diligençia / y prestesa hecha paso todo el /
campo y ganados por ella y a / otras diez jornadas dieron en
/ Unas rra*n*cherias de gente a- / larabe que por alli son lla- /
mados querechos y *h*avia dos / dias que se *h*avian visto vacas
/ esta gente Viven en tiendas de / cueros de vacas adobados
/ andan tras las vacas haçien- / do carne estos aunque Vieron
/ n*uest*ro campo no hiçieron muda- / miento ni se alteraron
an- / tes salieron de sus tiendas a / Ver esentamente⁶¹⁷ y luego
Vi- / nieron a hablar con la avan- / guardia y dixeron que sea

[fol. 78v]
primera / {rúbrica}

el campo y el general hablo / con ellos y como ya ellos *h*av-
/ ian hablado con el turco que / yba en la avanguardia co*n*- /
formaron con el en quanto / deçia era gente muy enten- /

dida por señas que pareçia / que lo deçian y lo daban tan- /
bien a entender que no *h*avi- / a mas necesidad de interpre-
/ te estos dixeron que baxan- / do haçia do*nde* sale el sol *h*avia
/ Un rrio muy grande y que / yria por la rrivera de *e*l por /
poblados noventa dias sin / quebrar de poblado en po- /
blado deçian que se decia / lo primero del poblado ha- / xa y
que el rrio era de mas / de

[fol. 79r]
79
parte / {rúbrica}

de Una legua de ancho y que / *h*avia muchas canoas estos sa- /
lieron de alli otro dia con (h)a- / rrias de perros en que lleVaba*n*
/ sus *h*aberes desde a dos dias que / todavia caminaba el campo
/ a el rrumbo que *h*avian sali- / do de lo poblado que era entre
/ norte y oriente mas haçia el / norte se Vieron otros querechos
/ rrancheados y grande nume- / ro de vacas que ya pareçia /
cosa increib(^l)le estos dieron / gra*n*dissima notiçia de pobla- /
dos todo a el oriente de don- / de nos hallamos aqui se que- /
bro don garçia Un braço y se / perdio Un español que salio / a
casa y no aserto a Volver / al rreal por ser la tierra muy

[fol. 79v]
parte / {rúbrica}

llana decia el turco que *h*avia / a haya Una o dos jornadas el
/ general emVio adelante a / el capitan diego lopez a la li- /
gera con diez compañeros dan- / dole rrumbo por Una
guia de / mar haçia adonde salia el sol / que caminase dos
dias a toda / priesa y descubriese a haxa / y VolViese a se
topar con el can- / po otro dia salio por el mesmo / rrumbo
y fue tanto el ganado / que se topo que los que yban / en la
avanguardia cogiero*n* / por delante Un gran nume- / ro de
toros y como huyan y u- / {xa} nos a otros se rrenpugaban⁶¹⁸
die- / ron en Una barranca y cayo / tanto ganado dentro que
la / emparejaron y el demas ga- / nado paso por ençima la
ge*n*- / te

[fol. 80r]
80
parte / {rúbrica}

de a cavallo que yba en pos de ellos / cayeron sobre el ganado sin sa- / ber lo que haçian tres cavallos / de los que cayeron ensillados y / enfrenados se fueron entre las / Vacas que no pudieron mas ser / habidos {rúbrica}

como a el general le parecio que / seria ya de Vuelta diego lopes hi- / ço que seis compañeros siguiesen / Una rriVera arriba de Un peque- / ño rrio y otros tantos la rrivera / abajo y que se mirase por el rras- / tro de los cavallos en las entra- / das o las salidas del rrio porque / por la tierra no es posible hallar- / se rrastro porque la yerva en / pisandola se torna a levantar / hallose por donde havian ydo / y fue Ventura que a las Vueltas

[fol. 80v]
primera / {rúbrica}

havian ydo indios del campo en / busca de fruta Una gran legua / de donde se hallo rrastro y toparon / con (c)ellos y ansi bajaron el rrio / abajo a el rreal y dieron por nu- / eva a el general que en ve- / inte leguas que havian anda- / do no havian visto otra cosa sino / vacas y çielo yba en el campo o- / tro indio pintado natural de qui- / vira que se deçia sopete este in- / dio siempre dixo que el turco men- / tia y por esto ^no haçian caso de el y a- / unque en esta saçon tambien lo / deçia como los querechos havian / informado con el y el ysopete no / era creydo {rúbrica}

desde aqui emVio el general / delante a don rrodrigo maldo- / nado con su compañia el qual ca- / mino quatro dias y llego a Una / ba

[fol. 81r]
81
parte / {rúbrica}

barranca grande como las de coli- / ma y hallo en lo bajo de ella / gran rrancheria de gente por / aqui havia atraVesado cabeça / de vaca y dorantes aqui presen- / taron a don rrodrigo Un monton / de cueros adobados y otras cosas / y Una tienda tan grande como / Una casa en alto la qual man-

/ do que asi la guardasen hasta / que el campo llegase y emVio con- / pañeros que guiasen el campo / haçia aquella parte porque / no se perdiesen aunque havian / ydo haçiendo mojones de guesos / y boñigas para que el campo se / siguiese y de esta manera se gui- / aba ya el campo tras la aVangu- / ardia {rúbrica}

llego el general con su campo / y como Vio tan gran multitud

[fol. 81v]
primera / {rúbrica}

de cueros penso los rrepartir con / la gente y hiço poner guardas / para que mirasen por ellos pe- / ro como la gente llego y Vieron / los compañeros que el general / emViaba algunos hombres par- / ticulares con señas para que les / diesen las guardas algunos cue- / ros y los andaban a escoger eno- / jados de que no se rrepartia con / orden dan sacomano y en me- / nos de quarto de hora no dexa- / ron sino el suelo limpio {rúbrica}

los naturales que Vieron aque- / llo tambien pusieron las ma- / nos en la obra las mugeres y / algunos otros quedaron lloran- / do porque creyeron que no les / havian de tomar nada sino ben- / deçirselo como havian hecho ca- / beça

[fol. 82r]
82
parte / {rúbrica}

beça de vaca y dorantes quan- / do por alli pasaron aqui se ha- / llo Una india tam blanca como / muger de castilla salvo que te- / nia labrada la barva como mo- / risca de berberia que todas se / labran en general de aquella / manera por alli se alcogolan / los ojos {rúbrica}

Capitulo veinte como cayeron / grandes piedras en el campo y / como se descubrio otra barran- / ca donde se diVidio el campo / en dos partes {rúbrica}

estando descansando el campo / en esta barranca que

*h*abemos / dicho Una tarde començo Un / torbellino con grandissimo a- / yre y graniço y en pequeño es-

[fol. 82v]
primera / {rúbrica}

paçio Vino tam grande multi- / tud de piedra tam grandes como / escudillas y mayores y tam espe- / sas como l*lu*Via que en parte / cubrieron dos y tres palmos y / mas de tierra y Uno dexo el ca- / vallo digo que ningun cava- / llo *h*ubo que no se solto sino fue- / ron dos o tres que acudieron a los / tener negros enpaVesados y / con seladas y rrodelas que to- / dos los demas lleVo por delan- / te hasta pegallos con la barran- / ca y algunos subio donde con gra*n* / trabajo se tornaron a bajar y / si como los tomo alli dentro fue- / ra en lo llano de arriba queda- / ra el campo a gran rriesgo sin / cavallos que muchos no se pu- / dieran cobrar rrompio la piedra / mu-

[fol. 83r]
83
parte / {rúbrica}

muchas tiendas y abollo muchas / çeladas y lastimo muchos cava- / llos y quebro toda la losa del can- / po y calabaços que no puso po- / ca neçesidad porque por alli / no *h*ay losa ni se haçe ni calabaços / ni se siembra maiz ni comen pan / salVo carne cruda o mal asada / y fru(c)tas {rúbrica}

desde alli emVio el general / a descubrir y dieron en otras / rrancherias a quatro jornadas / a manera de alixares era tie- {Alixeres} / rra muy poblada adonde *h*avia / muchos frisoles y siruelas como / las de castilla y parrales dura- / ban estos pueblos de rrancherias / tres jornadas desiase cona / desde aqui salieron con el

[fol. 83v]
primera / {rúbrica}

campo algunos teyas porque / asi se deçian aquellas gentes / y caminaron con sus (h)arrias de / perros y mugeres y hijos

hasta / la p(r)ostrera jornada de las otras / donde dieron guias para pasar / adelante adonde fue el can- / po a Una barranca grande es- / tas guias no las dexaban hablar / con el turco y no hallavan[619] las / notiçias que de antes deçian / que quivira era hacia el nor- / te y que no hallavamos buena / derrota con esto se començo a / dar credito a ysopete y ansi lle- / go el campo a la p(r)ostrera barra*n*- / ca que era Una legua de bor- / (b)*d*(o)*e* a bord(o)*e* y un pequeño rrio / en lo bajo y un llano lleno de / ar

[fol. 84r]
84
parte / {rúbrica}

arboleda con mucha uVa mo- / rales y rrosales que es fruta que / la *h*ay en françia y sirven de / agraz en esta barranca la *h*a- / via madura *h*abia nueses y ga*l*- / linas de la calidad de las de / la nueVa españa y siruelas co- / mo las de castilla y en cantidad / en este camino se Vio a Un te- / ya de Un tiro pasar Un toro por / ambas espaldas que Un arca- / buz tiene bien que haçer es ge*n*- / te bien entendida y las muge- / res bien tratadas y de Verguença / cubren todas sus carnes traen {traen} / çapatos y borseguiez de cue- / ro adobado traen mantas / las mugeres sobre sus faldelli- / nes y mangas cogidas por

[fol. 84v]
primera / {rúbrica}

las espaldas todo de cuero y / Unos como sanbenitillos con rra- / pasejos que llegan a medio mus- / lo sobre los faldellines {rúbrica}

en esta barranca holgo el cam- / po muchos dias por buscar co- / marca hicieronse hasta aqui / treinta y siete jornadas de ca- / mino de a seis y de a siete le- / guas porque se daba cargo a / quien fuese tasando y un con- / tando por pasos deçian que / *h*avia a el poblado doçien- / tas y sinquenta leguas Visto / ya y co(g)noçido por el general / fran*c*isco vasques como hasta a- / lli *h*avian andado engañados / por el turco y que faltavan / los basti- / mentos a el campo / y que

[fol. 85r]
85
parte / {rúbrica}

{+} y que por alli no havia tierra {+} don- / de se pudiesen
proVeer llamo a / los capitanes y alferes a junta / para acordar
lo que les paresi- / ese se debiese haçer y de acuer- / do de
todos fue que el general / con treinta de a cavallo y medi- / a
doçena de peones y fuese en / demanda de quivira y que don
/ tristan de arellano VolViese con / todo el campo la Vuelta
de tiguex / sabido esto por la gente del can- / po y como ya
se sabia lo acorda- / do suplicaron de ello a su gene- / ral y
que no los dexase de lle- / var adelante que todos que- / rian
morir con el y no VolVer / atras esto no aprovecho aun- / que
el general les conçedio que / les emViaria mensajeros den- /
tro de ocho dias si conViniese se-

[fol. 85v]
primera / {rúbrica}

guirle o no y con esto se partio / con las guias que llevaba y
/ con ysopete el turco yba a rre- / caudo en cadena[620] {rúbrica}

Capitulo veinte y uno como / el campo VolVio a tiguex y /
el general llego a quivi- / ra {rúbrica}

partio el general de la barran- / ca con las guias que los teyas
/ le havian dado hiço su maes- / tre de campo a el veinte y
qua- / tro diego lopes y lleVo de la gen- / te que le pareçio
mas escogida / y de mejores cavallos el canpo / quedo con
alguna esperança / que emViaria por el el gene- / ral y
tornaronselo a emViar / a suplicar a el general con / dos
hombres de a cavallo a / la

[fol. 86r]
86
parte / {rúbrica}

la ligera y por la posta {rúbrica}

el general llego digo que se / le huyeron las guias en las pri-

/ meras jornadas y hUbo de Vol- / Ver diego lopes por guias
a el / campo y con mandado que el can- / po VolViese a
tiguex a buscar / bastimentos y a aguardar a / el general
dieronle otras gui- / as que les dieron los teyas de / Voluntad
aguardo el campo / sus mensajeros y estuVo alli / quinçe dias
haçiendo carna- / je de Vacas para llevar tuVo- / se por
quenta que se mataron / en estos quinse dias quinien- / tos
toros era cosa increyble el / numero de los que havia sin /
Vacas perdiose en este comedio / mucha gente de los que
salian / a caça y en dos ni tres dias no tor-

[fol. 86v]
primera/ {rúbrica}

naban a VolVer a el campo an- / dando desatinados a Una
parte / y a otra sin saber VolVer por don- / de havian ydo y
con haber aquella / barranca que arriba o abaxo / havian de
atinar y como cada / noche se tenia quenta con qui- / en
faltava tiravan artilleria / y tocavan trompetas y (a)tambo- /
res y haçian grandes hogare- / das[621] y algunos se hallaron /
tam desViados y habian desati- / nado tanto que todo esto
no les / aproVechava nada aunque a / otros les Valio el
rremedio era tor- / nar adonde mataban el ganado / y haçer
Una via a Una parte / y a otra hasta que daban con / la
barranca o topaban con qui- / en los encaminava es cosa / de
notar que como la tierra es / tam llano en siendo mediodia /
como

[fol. 87r]
87
parte / {rúbrica}

como han andado desatinados en / pos de la caça a Una parte
y a o- / tra se han de estar cabe la caça que- / dos hasta que
decline el sol pa- / ra Ver a que rrumbo han de Vol- / Ver
adonde salieron y aun estos / havian de ser hombres entendi-
/ dos y los que no lo eran se havian / de encomendar a otros
{rúbrica}

el general siguio sus guias has- / ta llegar a quivira en que /
gasto quarenta y ocho dias de ca- / mino por la grande

cayda[622] que / havian hecho sobre la florida y / fue reçebido
de paz por las gui- / as que llevaba preguntaron / a el turco
que por que havia men- / tido y los havia guiado tam aVie-
/ so dixo que su tierra era haçia / aquella parte y que allende
de / aquello los de cicuyc le havian

[fol. 87v]
primera / {rúbrica}

rrogado que los truxese perdidos / por los llanos porque
faltando- / les el bastimento se muriesen los / cavallos y ellos
flacos quando / VolViesen los podrian matar sin / trabajo y
Vengarse de lo que ha- / vian hecho y que por esto los habia
/ desrrumbado[623] creyendo que no / supieran caçar ni
mantenerse / sin maiz y que lo del oro que no sa- / bia
adonde lo havia esto dixo ya co- / mo desesperado y que se
hallaba / corrido[624] que havian dado credito a / el ysopete y
los havia guiado me- / jor que no el y temiendose los que /
alli yban que no diese algun a- / Viso por donde les Viniese
algun / daño le dieron garrote de que / el ysopete se holgo
porque siem- / pre solia deçir que el ysopete / era Un bellaco
y que no sabia / lo

[fol. 88r]
88
parte / {rúbrica}

lo que se deçia y siempre le es- / torba(n)ban que no hablase
/ con nadie no se Vio entre aque- / lla gente oro ni plata ni
noti- / çia de ello el señor traya a el / cuello Una patena de
cobre / y no la tenia en poco {rúbrica}

los mensajeros que el campo / emVio en pos del general Vol-
/ Vieron como dixe y luego co- / mo no truxeron otro
rreca(u)do / que el que el veintiquatro / havia dicho el campo
salio de / la barranca la Vuelta de los te- / yas adonde
tomaron guias / que los VolViesen por mas de- / recho
camino ellas las die- / ron de Voluntad porque co- / mo es
gente que no para

[fol. 88v]
primera / {rúbrica}

por aquellas tierras en pos / del ganado todo lo saben gui- /
aban de esta manera luego / por la mañana miraban / adonde
salia el sol y toma- / ban el rrumbo que havian de / tomar y
tiraban Una flecha / y antes de llegar a ella tira- / van otra
por ençima y de es- / ta manera yban todo el dia / hasta las
aguas adonde se / havia de haçer jornada / y por este orden
lo que se ha- / via andado a la yda en tre- / inta y siete
jornadas se Vol- / Vio en veinte y çinco caçan- / do en el
camino vacas ha- / llaronse en este camino / muchas lagunas
de sal que / la havia en gran cantidad / havia

[fol. 89r]
89
parte / {rúbrica}

havia sobre el agua tablones / de ella mayores que mesas /
de quatro y de çinco dedos de / grueso debajo del agua a /
dos y tres palmos sal en gra- / no mas sabrosa que la de / los
tablones porque esta a- / margaba Un poco era cris- / talina
havia por aque- / llos llanos Unos animales / como (h)ardillas
en gran nu- / mero y mucha suma de / cuevas de ellas vino
en es- / ta Vuelta a tomar el campo / el rrio de cicuyc mas de
tre- / inta leguas por baxo de ella / digo de la puente que se
/ havia hecho a la yda y subio- / se por el arriba que en ge- /

[fol. 89v]
primera / {rúbrica}

neral casi todas sus rriveras / tenian rrosales que son co- / mo
UVas moscateles en el / comer naçen en Unas varas /
delgadas de Un estado tie- / ne la hoja como peregil ha- / via
UVas en agraz y mucho / vino y oregano deçian las / guias
que se juntaba este rrio / con el de tiguex mas de ve- / inte
jornadas de alli y que / Volvian sus corrientes a el / oriente
creese que Van a el / poderoso rrio del espiritu san- / to que
los de don hernando / de soto descubieron en la flo- / rida
en esta jornada a la y- / da se hundio Una india la- / brada a
el capitan juan de sal- / diVar y fue las barrancas / aba

[fol. 90r]
90
parte / {rúbrica}

abajo huyendo que recono- / çio la tierra porque en tigu- / ex donde se hUbo era esclava / esta india hUbieron a las ma- / nos siertos españoles de los de / la florida que havian entra- / do descubriendo hacia aque- / lla parte yo les oy deçir quan- / do VolVieron a la nueVa espa- / ña que les havia dicho la in- / dia que havia nueVe dias que / se havia huydo de otros y que / nombro capitanes por don- / de se debe creer que no lle- / gamos lejos de lo que ellos des- / cubrieron aunque diçen que / estaban entonçes mas de do- / sientas leguas la tierra adentro / creese que tiene la tierra de

[fol. 90v]

primera / {rúbrica}

traVesia por aquella parte / mas de seicientas leguas de mar / a mar {rúbrica}

pues como digo el rrio arriba / fue el campo hasta llegar a el / pueblo de cicuye el qual se / hallo de guerra que no qui- / sieron mostrarse de paz ni / dar ningun socorro de basti- / mento de alli fueron a tigu- / ex que ya algunos pueblos / se havian tornado a poblar / que luego se tornban a des- / poblar de temor {rúbrica}

Capitulo veinti y dos como / el general VolVio de qui- / vira y se hiçieron otras entra- / das debajo del norte {rúbrica} / lue

[fol. 91r]

91

parte / {rúbrica}

luego que don tristan de are- / llano llego en tiguex me- / diado el mes de jullio del año de quarenta y dos hiço {1542} / rrecoger bastimentos para / el inVierno Venidero y en- / Vio a el capitan francisco de / barrionueVo con alguna gen- / te el rrio arriba debajo del / norte en que Vio dos provin- / çias que la Una se decia he- / mes de siete pueblos y la o- / tra yuque yunque los pue- / blos de hemes salieron de paz / y dieron bastimentos los de / yuque yunque en tanto que / el rreal se asentaba despobla- / ron dos muy hermosos pueblos / que tenian el rrio en medio

[fol. 91v]

primera / {rúbrica}

y se fueron a la sierra adonde / tenian quatro pueblos muy / fuertes en tierra aspera que / no se podia yr a ellos a cava- / llo en estos dos pueblos se (U) / hUbo mucho bastimento y lo- / ça muy hermoça y Vedriada / y de muchas labores y hechu- / ras tambien se hallaron / muchas ollas llenas de me- / tal escogido rreluciente / con que Vedriaban la losa / era señal que por aquella / tierra havia minas de plata / si se buscaran {rúbrica}

veinte leguas adelante el / rrio arriba havia Un pode- / roso y grande rrio digo pue- / blo que se decia Uraba a qu- / ien los nuestros pusieron va- / lla

[fol. 92r]

92

parte / {rúbrica}

lladolid tomaba el rrio por / medio pasabase por puentes / de madera de muy largos / y grandes pinos quadrados / y en este pueblo se Vieron las / mas grandes y braVas estufas / que en toda aquella tierra / porque eran de doçe pilares / que cada Una tenia dos braças / de rruedo de altura de dos / estados este pueblo havia visi- / tado hernando de alvarado / quando descubrio a çicuye es / tierra muy alta y frig(r)idissi- / ma el rrio yba hondo y de / gran corriente sin ningun va- / do dio la Vuelta el capitan ba- / rrionueVo dexando de pax / aque- / llas provinçias {rúbrica}

otro capitan fue el rrio abajo

[fol. 92v]

primera / {rúbrica}

en busca de los poblados que / deçian los de tutahaco havia / algunas jornadas de alli este / capitan bajo ochenta leguas / y hallo quatro pueblos gran- / des que dexo de paz y an- / duVo hasta que hallo que el / rrio se sumia debajo de tie- / {Rio que se hunde} rra como guadiana en ex- / tremadura no paso adelan- / te donde los indios decian que / salia muy poderoso por no / lleVar mas comiçion de ochen- / ta leguas de camino y como / VolVio este capitan y se llega- / ba el plaço en que el capitan / habia de VolVer de quivira / y no VolVia don tristan seña- / lo quarenta conpañeros / y dexando el campo a francisco / de

[fol. 93r]
93
parte / {rúbrica}

de barrionueVo salio con ellos / a buscar el general y como / llego a cicuye los del pueblo / salieron de guerra que fue ca- / usa que se detuViesen alli qu- / atro dias por les haçer algun / daño como se les hiço que con ti- / ros que se asentaron a el pue- / blo les mataron alguna gen- / te porque no salian a el can- / po a causa que el primer dia les / mataron dos hombres señala- / dos {rúbrica}

en este comedio llegaron nue- / Vas como el general Venia y / por esto tambien hUbo de agu- / ardar alli don tristan para / asegurar aquel paso llega- / do el general fue bien rre- / çebido de todos con grande

[fol. 93v]
primera / {rúbrica}

alegria el indio xabe que era / el mançebo que havian dado los / de cicuye a el general quan- / do yba en demanda de qui- / vira estaba con don tristan / de arellano y como supo que / el general Venia dando mu- / estras que se holgaba dixo a- / gora que Viene el general / Vereis como hay oro y plata en / quivira aunque no tanta / como deçia el turco y como / el general llego y Vio como / no havian hallado nada que- / do triste y pasmado y afirman- / do que la havia hiço creer a / muchos que era asi porque / el general no entro la tierra / adentro que no oso por ser / muy poblada y no se hallar / po

[fol. 94r]
94
parte / {rúbrica}

poderoso y dio la Vuelta por lle- / var sus gentes pasadas las a- / guas porque ya por alla llo- / Via que era entrada de agos- / to quando salio tardo en la / Vuelta quarenta dias con bue- / nas guias con Venir a la ligera / como VolVieron deçia el turco / quando salio de tiguex el can- / po que para que cargavan / los cavallos tanto de bastimen- / tos que se cansavan y no po- / drian despues traer el oro y la / plata donde parese bien anda- / ba con engaño {rúbrica}

llegado el general con su gen- / te a cicuyc luego se partio / para tiguex dexando mas / asentado el pueblo porque / a el luego salieron de paz

[fol. 94v]
primera / {rúbrica}

y le hablaron llegado a tiguex / procuro de inVernar alli pa- / ra dar la Vuelta con todo el / campo porque deçia traya no- / ticia de grandes poblaciones / y rrios poderossissimos y que / la tierra era muy pareciente / a la de españa en las frutas y / yerbas y temporales y que no / Venian satisfechos de creer que / no havia oro antes trayan sos- / pecha que lo havia la tierra a- / dentro porque puesto que lo / negavan entendian que co- / sa era y tenia nombre entre / ellos que se deçia acochis / con lo qual daremos fin a es- / ta primera parte y tratare- / mos en dar rrelaçion de las / provinçias {rúbrica}

[fol. 95r]
95
Segunda parte en / que se trata de los pueblos / y provincias de altos y de / sus rritos y costumbres rre- / copilada por pedro de cas- / tañeda Veçino de la ciu- / dad de Naxara {rúbrica}

laus deo / {rúbrica}

[fol. 95v]
segunda / {rúbrica}

no me parece que quedara sa- / tisfecho el lector em haber Vis- / to y entendido lo que he conta- / do de la jornada aunque en / ello *h*ay bien que notar en la / discordança de las noticias / porque *h*aber fama tan gran- / de de grandes t(h)esoros y en el / mismo lugar no hallar memo- / ria ni aparençia de *h*aberlo*s* / cosa es muy de notar en lu- / gar de poblados hallar gran- / des despoplados y en lugar / de ciudades populosas hallar / pueblos de doçientos vecinos / y el mayor de ochocientos o / mill no se si esto les dara ma- / teria para considerar y pe*n*- / sar en la Variedad de esta / vida y para poderlos agra- / dar les quiero dar rrela-

[fol. 96r]
96
parte / {rúbrica}

çion particular de todo lo pobla- / do que se Vio y descubrio en es- / ta jornada y algunas costun- / bres que tienen y rritos confor- / me a lo que de ellos alcança- / mos a saber y en que rrumbo / cae cada provinça para que / despues se pueda entender a / que parte esta la florida y a / que parte cae la india mayor / y como esta tierra de la nueVa / españa es tierra firme con el / peru ansi lo es con la india ma- / yor o de la china sin que por / esta parte *h*aya extrecho que / la diVida ante(e)s es tan gran- / de la anchura de la tierra / que da lugar a que *h*aya tan / grandes despoplados co-

[fol. 96v]
segunda / {rúbrica}

mo *h*ay entre las dos mares por- / que la costa del norte sobre la / florida VuelVe sobre los baca- / llaos y despues torna sobre / la nuruega y la del sur a el / poniente haciendo la otra / punta debaxo del sur casi / como enarco^625 la Vuelta de la / india dando lugar a que las / tierras que siguen las cordi- / lleras de anbas costas se des- / Vien en tanta manera Unas / de otras que dexen en medio / de si grandes llanuras y ta- / les que por ser in*h*abitables so*n* / pobladas de ganados y o- / tros muchos animales de / diVersas maneras aunque / no de serpientes por ser co- / mo son esentos y sin montes / an

[fol. 97r]
97
parte / {rúbrica}

antes de todo genero de caça / y aves como adelante se dira / dexando de contar la Vuelta / que *e*l campo dio para la nue- / Va espana hasta que se Vea / la poca ocaçion que para e- / llo *h*Ubo començaremos a tra- / tar de la villa de culiacan / y Verse a la diferença que *h*ay / de la Una tierra a la otra pa- / ra que meresca lo Uno estar / poblado de españoles y lo o- / tro no *h*abiendo de ser a el con- / trario quanto a cristianos por- / que en los Unos *h*ay rraçon de / hombres y en los otros barba- / ridad de animales y mas / que de bestias {rúbrica}

[fol. 97v]
segunda / {rúbrica}

Capitulo primero de la pro- / vincia de culiacan y de sus / rritos y costumbres {rúbrica}

Culiacan es lo Ultimo del nue- / Vo reyno de galiçia y fue lo / pri- / mero que poblo Nuño de guz- / man quando conquisto este rey- / no esta a el poniente de mexi- / co doçientas y diez leguas en es- / ta provinça *h*ay tres le*n*guas prin- / çipales sin otras Variables que de / ella rresponden la primera es de / tahus que era la mejor gente / y mas entendida y los que en esta / saçon estan mas domesticos y tie- / nen mas lumbre de la fe estos y- / dolatraban y haçian presentes / a el demonio de sus *h*aberes y rrique- / ças que era rropa y turquesas no / comian carne humana ni la sa- / crifiçavan aco(n)stumbraban a / criar muy grandes culebras y / te- / nia

[fol. 98r]
98
parte / {rúbrica}

nianlas en Veneraçion *h*avia entre / ellos hombres en *h*abito de muge- / res que se casaban con otros hon- / bres y les servian de mugeres / canonicaban con gran fiesta / a las mugeres que querian ViVir / solteras con Un gran*de* arey- / to o bayle en que se juntaban / todos los señores de la comarca y sacabanla a baylar en cue- / ros y des*de* que todos *h*abian bayla- / do con ella metianla en Un / rrancho que para aquel efecto / esta bien adornado y las seño- / ras la adereçaban de rropa y / braçaletes de finas turquesas / y luego entraban a usar con e- / lla los señores Uno a Uno y tras / de ellos todos los demas que que- / rian y desde alli adelante no ha- / bian de negar a nadie pagan- / doles sierta paga que estaba

[fol. 98v]
segunda / {rúbrica}

constituyda para ello y aunque / despues tomaban maridos no / por eso eran rreservadas de cum- / plir con quien se lo pagaba sus / mayores fiestas son mercados / havia Una costumbre que las mu- / geres que se casaban los maridos / las compraban a los padres y pa- / rientes por gran preçio y luego / la lleVaban a Un señor que lo / tenian como por saserdote pa- / ra que la(s) desVirgase y Viese si es- / taba donçella y si no lo estaba le / habian de VolVer todo el preçio y / estaba en su escoger si la queria / por muger o no o dexalla pa- / ra que fuese canoniçada ha- / çian grandes borracheras a sus / tiempos {rúbrica}

la segunda lengua es de paca- / xes que es la gente que habi- / tan en la tierra que esta entre / lo

[fol. 99r]
99
parte / {rúbrica}

lo llano y las serranias estos son mas / barbara gente algunos comen / carne humana que son los que / confinan con las serranias son / grandes someticos toman muchas / mugeres aunque sean herma- / nas adoran en piedras pintadas / de entalladura son grandes a- / buçioneros y hechiçeros {rúbrica}

la tercera lengua son acaxes a- / questos poseen gran parte de la / tierra por la serrania y toda la / cordillera y asi andan a caça de / hombres como a caça de Venados / comen todos carne humana y / el que tiene mas guesos de hom- / bre y calaVeras colgadas a el rre- / dedor de su casa es mas temido / y en mas tenido ViVen a barrios y / en tierra muy aspera huyen de / lo llano para pasar Un ba-

[fol. 99v]
segunda / {rúbrica}

rrio a otro ha de haber quebrada / en medio que aunque se hablen / no puedan pasar tam ligeramen- / te a Una grita se juntan qui- / nientos hombres y por peque- / ña ocaçion se matan y se comen / estos han sido malos de sojuzgar / por la aspereça de la tierra que / es muy grande {rúbrica}

han se hallado en esta tierra mu- / chas minas de plata rricas no / Van a lo hondo acabanse en bre- / ve desde la costa de esta provin- / çia comiença el ancon que me- / te la mar debajo del norte que / entra la tierra adentro doçien- / tas y sinquenta(s) leguas y fene- / se en la boca del rrio del tiçon / esta tierra es la Una punta a / el oriente la punta del poni- / {california / {rúbrica}} ente es la California hay de punta / a pu

[fol. 100r]
100
parte / {rúbrica}

a punta segun he oydo a hombres / que lo han naVegado treinta le- / guas porque perdiendo de Vis- / ta a esta tierra Ven la otra el an- / con diçen es ancho dentro a te- / ner de tierra a tierra çiento y sin- / quenta leguas y mas desde el rrio / del tiçon da la Vuelta la costa / a el sur haçiendo arco hasta la ca- / lifornia que Vuelve a el poni- / ente haçiendo aquella punta / que otro tiempo se tuVo por isla / por ser tierra baxa y arenosa / poblada de gente bruta y bes- / tial desnuda y que comen su mis- / mo estiercol y se juntaban hom- / bre y muger como animales po- / niendose la hembra en quatro / pies publicamente {rúbrica}

Capitulo segundo de la

[fol. 100v]
segunda / {rúbrica}

provinçia de petlatlan y to- / do lo poblado hasta chichil- / ticale {rúbrica} petlatlan es Una poblaçion de / casas cubiertas con Una mane- / ra de esteras hechas de cariso {-} / congregadas en pueblos que / Van a el lue*n*go[626] de Un rrio des- / de las sierras hasta la mar son / gente de la calidad y rritos de / los tahues culhacaneses *h*ay en- / tre ellos muchos someticos tie- / nen grande poblaçion y co- / marca de otros pueblos a la se- / rrania difieren en la lengua / de los tahues algun tanto pu- / esto que se entienden los Unos / a los otros dixose petlatlan por / ser las casas de petates dura / esta

[fol. 101r]
101
parte / {rúbrica}

esta manera de casas por aque- / lla parte docientas y quarenta / leguas y mas que *h*ay hasta el / principio del despoblado de çi- / bola desde petlatlan[627] hace rraya / aquella tierra co(g)noçidamen- / te la causa por que desde a- / lli para adelante no *h*ay arbol / sin espina ni *h*ay frutas sino son / tunas y mesquites y pitahayas / *h*ay desde culiacan alla vein- / te leguas y desde petlatlan a / el valle de señora ciento y / treinta *h*ay entremedias muchos / rrios poblados de gente de la / misma suerte como son sino- / loa boyomo teocomo yaqui- / mi y otros mas pequeños estan tambien los caraçones que *e*s

[fol. 101v]
segunda / {rúbrica}

nuestro caudal abajo del va- / lle de señora {rúbrica}

señora es Un rrio y valle / muy poblado de gente muy / dispuesta las mugeres Visten / {Nagues} naguas de cuero adobado / de Venados y sanbenitillos has- / ta medio cuerpo los que son se- / ñores de los pueblos se ponen / a las mañanas en Unos alti- / llos que para aquello tienen / hechos y a manera de prego- / nes o pregoneros estan pre- / gonando por espaçio de Una / *h*ora como administrandoles / en lo que *h*an de haçer tiene*n* / Unas casillas pequeñas de a- / doratorios en que hincan / muchas flechas que las ponen / por

[fol. 102r]
102
parte / {rúbrica}

por de fuera como Un eriso y / esto haçen quando esperan / tener guerra a el rrededor / de esta provincia hacia las / sierras *h*ay grandes poblaçio- / nes en proVincillas aparta- / das y congregadas de diez / y doçe pueblos y ocho o siete / de ellos que se los nombres so*n* / comu patrico mochilagua / y arispa y el vallecillo *h*ay o- / tros pueblos haçia la serrania / que no se Vieron {rúbrica}

desde señora a el valle de ffu- / ya *h*ay quarenta leguas en este / valle se vino a poblar la villa / de san hieronimo que despues / se alcaron y mataron parte de / la gente que estaba poblada / como se Vera adelante en la

[fol. 102v]
segunda / {rúbrica}

terçera parte en este valle *h*ay / muchos pueblos que tienen en / su torno[628] son las gentes de la / calidad de los de señora y de / Un traje y lengua rritos y cos- / tumbres con todo los demas / que *h*ay hasta el despoblado de / chichilticale las mugeres se la- / bran en la barba y los ojos como / moriscas de berberia ellos son / grandes someticos beben Vino / de pitahayas que es fruta de / cardones que se abre como / granadas hacense con el Vi- / no tontos haçen conserva / de tunas en gran cantidad / conservanse en su sumo en / gran cantidad sin otra miel / haçen pan de mesquites co- / mo quesos conservase todo / el año *h*ay en esta tierra me- / lo

[fol. 103r]
103
parte / {rúbrica}

lones de ella tam grandes que / tiene Una persona que llevar / en Uno haçen de ellos tasajos y / curanlos a el sol son de comer / del sabor de higos pasado*s* gui- / sados son muy buenos y dulces / guardanse todo el año asi pa- / sados {rúbrica} y por esta tierra se Vieron a- / guilas caudales tienen las / los señores por grandeça en to- {Aguilas} / dos estos pueblos no se Vieron / gallinas de ninguna suerte / salVo en este valle de fuya / que se hallaron gallinas co- / mo las de castilla que no se su- / po por donde entraron tanta / tierra de guerra teniendo co- / mo todos tienen guerra Unos / con otros entre ffuya y chi-

[fol. 103v]
segunda / {rúbrica}

chilticale *h*ay muchos carneros / y cabras montesas grandissimas / de cuerpos y de cuernos espa- / ñoles *h*Ubo que afirman *h*aber / Visto manada de mas de çiento / juntos corren tanto que en / breVe se desparesen {rúbrica}

en chichilticale torna la tie- / rra a haçer rraya y pierde / la arboleda espinosa y la cau- / sa es como el Ancon llega / hasta aquel paraje y da Vu- / elta la costa asi da Vuelta la / cordillera de las sierras y alli / se Viene atraVesar la serrania / y se rrompe para pasar a lo / llano de la tierra {rúbrica}

Capitulo tercero de lo / que *e*s chichilticale y el des- / pobldo de çibola sus cos- / tun

[fol. 104r]
104
parte / {rúbrica}

tumbres y rritos y de otras co- / sas {rúbrica}

chichilticale dixose asi por- / que hallaron los frayles en es- / ta comarca Una casa que fue / otros tiempos poblada de gen- / tes que rresquebraban de çi- / bola era de tierra colorada o / bermeja la casa era grande / y bien pareçia en ella *h*aber / sido fortaleça y debio ser des- / poblada por los de la tierra / que es la gente mas barbara / de las que se Vieron hasta a- / lli Viven en rrancherias sin / poblados ViVen de casar y to- / do lo mas es despoblado y de / grandes pinales *h*ay piñones en / gran cantidad son los pinos

[fol. 104v]
segunda / {rúbrica}

don(^o)de se dan parrados de has- / ta de dos a tres estados de alto *h*ay / ençinales de bellota dulce y / sav(o)*i*nas que dan Una fru- / ta como confites de culantro / seco es muy dulce como asu- / car *h*ay berros en algunas fue*n*- / tes y rosales y poleo y orega- / no {rúbrica}

en los rrios de *e*ste despoblado / *h*ay barbos y picones como en / españa *h*ay leones pardos que / se Vieron desde el prin- / cipio / del despoblado siempre se / Va subiendo la tierra hasta / llegar a çibola que son ochen- / ta leguas la via del norte / y hasta llegar alli desde cu- / liacan se *h*avia caminado lle- / vando el norte sobre el ojo is- / quierdo / çibo

[fol. 105r]
105
parte / {rúbrica}

çibola son siete pueblos el mayor / se dice maçaque comunmen- / te son de tres y quatro altos las / casas en maçaque *h*ay casas de / quatro altos y de siete estas gen- / tes son bien entendidas andan / cubiertas sus Verguenças y todas / las partes deshonestas con paños / a manera de serVilletas de me- / sa con rrapasejos y Una borla / en cada esquina atanlos sobre / el quadril Visten pellones de / plumas y de pelo de liebres ma*n*- / tas de algodon las mugeres se / Visten de mantas que las a- / tan o añudan sobre el honbro / isquierdo y sacan el braço de- / recho por ençima siñense- / las a el cuerpo traen capotes / de cuero pUlidos de buena

[fol. 105v]
segunda / {rúbrica}

fayçion[629] cogen el cabello sobre / las dos orejas hechos dos rrue- / das que paresen papos de / cofia {rúbrica}

esta tierra es Un valle entre sie- / rras a manera de peñones / siembran a hoyos no crese el / maiz alto de las maçorcas des- / de *e*l pie tres y quatro cada caña / gruesas y grandes de a ochoçie*n*- / tos granos cosa no Vista en es- / tas partes *h*ay en esta provin- / cia osos en gran cantidad leo- / nes gatos çervales y nutrias *h*ay / muy finas tratan turquesas / aunque no en la cantidad / que deçian rrecogen y entro- / {xan} gan piñones para su año no / tiene Un hombre mas de u- / na muger *h*ay en los pueblos / {patios / {rúbrica}} estufas que estan en los patios / o pla

[fol. 106r]
106
parte / {rúbrica}

o placas donde se juntan a / consulta no *h*ay señores como / por la nueVa españa rrigense / por consejo de los mas Viejos / tienen sus saserdotes a quien lla- / man papas que les pre- / dican es- / tos son viejos subense en el terra- / do mas alto del pueblo y desde / alli a manera de pregoneros / predican a el pueblo por las ma- / ñanas quando sale el sol estan- / do todo el pueblo en silençio a- / sentados por los corredores escu- / chando dicenles como *h*an de Vi- / Vir y creo que les diçen algunos / mandamientos que *h*an de guardar / porque entre ellos no *h*ay borra- / chera ni sodomia ni sacrificios / ni comen carne humana ni / hurtan de comun trabajan

[fol. 106v]
segunda / {rúbrica}

en el pueblo la*s* estufas son co- / munes es sacrilegio que las / mugeres entren a dormir en / las estufas por señal de paz dan / cruz queman los muertos (h)e- / chan con ellos en el fuego los ins- / trumentos que tienen para / usar sus officios {rúbrica}

tienen a tusayan entre norte / y poniente a veinte leguas es / provinçia de siete pueblos de / la misma suerte trajes rritos / y costumbres que los de çibola / *h*abra en estas dos provinçias / que son catorçe pueblos hasta / tres or quatro mill hombres y *h*ay / hasta tiguex quarenta leguas / o mas la Vuelta del norte *h*a- / y entremedias el peñon de a- / cuco que contamos en la pri- / mera parte {rúbrica} / cap

[fol. 107r]
107
parte / {rúbrica}

Capitulo quarto como se tra- / tan los de tiguex y de la pro- / vincia de tiguex y sus coma- / rcas {rúbrica}

tiguex es provinçia de doçe pue- / blos rriberas de Un rrio grande / y caudaloso Unos pueblos de / Una parte y otros de otra es va- / lle espaçioso de dos leguas en / ancho tiene a el oriente Una / sierra neVada muy alta y as- / pera a el pie de ella por las espal- / das *h*ay siete pueblos quatro en / llano y los tres metidos en la (h)*f*al- / da de la sierra {rúbrica}

tiene a el norte a quirix siete / pueblos a siete leguas tiene / a el nordeste la provincia de he- / mes siete pueblos a quarenta

[fol. 107v]
segunda / {rúbrica}

leguas tiene a el norte o (l)este / a Acha a quatro leguas a el su- / este a tutahaco provinçia / de ocho pueblos todos estos pue- / blos en general tienen Unos / rritos y costumbres aunque / tienen algunas cosas en par- / ticulares que no las tienen los / otros gobiernanse por acuer- / do de los mas viejos labran / los edificios del pueblo de co- / mun las mugeres entienden / en haçer la mescla y las pare- / des los hombres traen la made- / ra y la asientan no *h*ay cal pe- / ro haçen Una mescla de çe- / nisa de carbon y tierra que *e*s / poco menos que de cal por- / que con *h*aber de tener quatro / altos la casa no hacen la pa- / red

[fol. 108r]
108
parte / {rúbrica}

red de mas gordor[630] que de media / Vara juntan gran cantidad de / rrama de tomillos y carriso / y ponenle fuego y como esta en- / tre carbon y çenisa (h)echan mu- / cha tierra y agua y haçenlo / mescla y de ella hacen pellas / rredondas que ponen en lugar / de piedra despues de seco y / traban con la misma mescla / de suerte que despues es como / argamasa los mançebos por / casar sirven a el pueblo en / general y traen la leña que se / ha de gastar y la ponen en rrima / en los patios de los pueblos de / donde la toman las mugeres / para llevar a sus casas su habi- / taçion de los mançebos es en las

[fol. 108v]
segunda / {rúbrica}

estufas que son en los patios de / el pueblo debajo de tierra / quadrados o rredondos con pi- / lares de pino algunas se Vie- / ron de doçe pilares de qua- / tro por naVe de gordor de dos / braças los comunes eran de / tres o quatro pilares los suelos / de losas grandes y lisas como / los baños que se usan en euro- / pa tienen dentro Un fogon / a manera de Una bita- / cora / de naVio donde ensienden / Un puño de tomillo con que / sustentan la calor y pueden / estar dentro como en baño lo / alto en pareja con la tierra / alguna se Vio tan espaçiosa / que tendra juego de bola qu- / ando alguno se ha de casar / ha de

[fol. 109r]
109
parte / {rúbrica}

ha de ser por orden de los que go- / biernan ha de hilar y texer / Una manta el Varon y poner- / le la muger delante y ella / cubre con ella y queda por su / muger las casas son de las mu- / geres las estufas de los hombres / si el varon rrepudia la muger / ha de ir a ello a la estufa es Viola- / ble cosa dormir las mugeres en / la estufa ni entrar a ningun / negoçio mas de meter de co- / mer a el marido o a los hijos los / hombres hilan y texen las mu- / geres crian los hijos y guisan / de comer la tierra es tan fertil / que no desyerban en todo / el año mas de para sembrar / porque luego cae la nieVe y cu- / bre lo senbrado y debajo de la

[fol. 109v]
segunda / {rúbrica}

nieVe cria la maçorca cogen / en Un año para siete hay gran-

/ dissimo numero de grullas / y de ansares y cuerVos y tor- / dos que se mantienen por los / sembrados y con todo esto qu- / ando Vuelven a sembrar pa- / ra otro año estan los campos / cubiertos de maiz que no lo / han podido acabar de ence- / rrar {rúbrica}

havia en estas provincias gran / cantidad de gallinas de la / tierra y gallos de papada sus- / tentabanse muertos sin pelar / ni abrir sesenta dias sin mal / olor y los hombres muertos / lo mismo y mas tiempo sien- / do inVierno los pueblos son / limpios de inmundiçias por- / que

[fol. 110r]
110
parte / {rúbrica}

que salen fuera a estercolar y / desaguan en Vasijas de barro / y las sacan a Vasiar fuera del / pueblo tienen buen rreparti- / das las casas en grande linpie- / ça donde guisan de comer y / donde muelen la harina que / es Un apartado o rretrete don- / de tienen Un (f)harnal con tres / piedras asentado con arga- / masa donde entran tres muge- / res cada Una en su piedra que / la Una frangolla y la otra mue- / le y la otra rremuele antes que / entren dentro a la puerta se des- / calçan los sapatos y cogen el ca- / bello y sacuden la rropa y cubren / la cabeça mientras que muelen / esta Un hombre sentado a la / puerta tañendo con Una gayta

[fol. 110v]
segunda / {rúbrica}

al tono traen las piedras y cantan / a tres Voçes muelen de Una Vez / mucha cantidad porque todo / el pan haçen de harina des- / leyda con agua caliente a ma- / nera de obleas cogen gran can- / tidad de yervas y secanlas / para guisar todo el año para / comer no hay en la tierra fru- / tas salvo piñones tienen sus / predicadores no se hallo en e- / llos sodomia ni comer carne / humana ni sacrificarla no / es gente cruel porque en ti- / guex estuVieron obra de qua- / renta dias muerto a françisco / de ovando y quando se acabo / de ganar el pueblo lo halla- / ron entero entre sus muertos

/ sin otra liçion mas de la herida / de que murio blanco como nie- / Ve

[fol. 111r]
111
parte / {rúbrica}

Ve sin mal olor de Un indio de / los nuestros que havia estado Un / año cautiVo entre ellos alcanse / a saber algunas cosas de sus cos- / tumbres en especial preguntan- / dole yo que por que causa en / aquella provincia andaban / las mugeres moças en cueros / haçiendo tam gran frio dixo- / me que las donçellas havian / de andar ansi hasta que to- / masen maridos y que en co(g)no- / çiendo varon se cubrian tray- / an los hombres por alli camise- / tas de cuero de Venado adoba- / do y ençima sus pellones hay por / todas estas provinçias loça Vedri- / ada de alcohol y jarros de ex- / tremadas labores y de hechuras / que era cosa de Ver {rúbrica}

[fol. 111v]
segunda / {rúbrica}

Capitulo quinto de cicuyc / y los pueblos de su contorno / y de como Unas gentes Vinie- / ron a conquistar aque- / lla tierra {rúbrica}

ya habemos dicho de tiguex / y de todas las provinçias que / estan en la costa de aquel rrio / por ser como son todas de Una / calidad de gente y una condi- / çion y costumbres no sera me- / nester en ellos particulariçar / ninguna cosa solo quiero de- / çir del açiento de cicuye y / Unos pueblos despoblados que / le caen en comarca en el cami- / no derecho que el campo lleVo / para alla y otros que estan tras / la sierra neVada de tiguex / que

[fol. 112r]
112
parte / {rúbrica}

que tambien caen en aquella / comarca fuera del rrio {rúbrica}

cicuye es Un pueblo de hasta / quinientos hombres de guerra / es temido por toda aquella tie- / rra en su sitio es quadrado a- / sentado sobre peña en medio / Un gran patio o plaça con sus / estufas las casas son todas pare- / jas de quatro altos por lo alto / se anda todo el pueblo sin que / haya calle que lo estorbe a los / dos primeros doblados es todo / çercado de corredores que se / anda por ellos todo el pueblo / son como balcones que salen afuera y debajo de ellos se / pueden amparar no tienen / las casas puertas por lo bajo / con escaleras levadisas se / sirven y su(^s)ben a los corredo-

[fol. 112v]
se(n)gunda / {rúbrica}

res que son por de dentro del / pueblo y por alli se mandan / que las puertas de las casas / salen a aquel alto al corredor / sirve el corredor por calle las / casas que salen a el campo ha- / çen espaldas con las de dentro / del patio y en tiempo de gue- / rra se mandan por las de den- / tro es çercado de Una çerca ba- / ja de piedra tiene dentro Una / fuente de agua que se la pue- / den quitar la gente de este pu- / eblo se preçia[631] de que nadie los / ha podido sojuzgar y los sojuz- / gan los pueblos que quieren / son de la misma condiçion / y costumbres que los otros pue- / blos tambien andan las donce- / llas desnudas hasta que toman / maridos porque diçen que si / haçen maldad que luego se / Ve

[fol. 113r]
113
parte / {rúbrica}

Vera y ansi no lo haran ni tienen / de que tener Verquença pues / andan qual naçieron {rúbrica}

hay entre cicuye y la provinçia / de quirix Un pueblo chico y / fuerte a quien los españoles / pusieron nonbre ximena y o- / tro pueblo casi despoblado que / no tiene poblado sino Un barrio / este pueblo era grande se- / gun su sitio y fresco pareçia ha- / ber sido destruydo aqueste se / llamo el pueblo de los çilos por- / que se hallaron en el grandes / silos de maiz {rúbrica} adelante *h*avia otro pueblo / grande todo destruido y asola- / do en los patios de *e*l muchas / pelotas de piedras tan grandes / como botijas de arroba que

[fol. 113v]
segunda / {rúbrica}

pareçia *h*aber sido (h)echadas / con ingenios o trabucos con que / destruyeron aquel pueblo / lo que de ello se alcanso a sa- / ber fue que *h*abria desiseis a- / ños que Unas gentes llama- / dos teyas en gran numero / *h*avian Venido en aquella / tierra y *h*avian destruydo a- / quellos pueblos y *h*avian teni- / do çercado a cicuye y no lo *h*avi- / an podido tomar por ser fuer- / te y que quando salieron de a- / quella tierra *h*avian hecho / amistades con toda la tierra / pareçio debio de ser gente / poderosa y que debia de te- / ner ingenios para derribar / los pueblos no saben decir de / que parte Vinieron mas de / señalar debajo del norte ge- / neralmente llaman estas / gen

[fol. 114r]
114
parte / {rúbrica}

gentes teyas por gentes valie*n*- / tes como diçen los mexi- / canos / chichimecas o teules porque / los teyas que el campo topo pu- / esto que eran valientes eran / co(g)noçidos de la gente de los / poblados y sus amigos y que se / Van a inVernar por alla los / ynViernos debaxo de las ala- / ves de lo poblado porque de*n*- / tro no se atreVen a los rreçe- / bir porque no se deben fiar / de ellos y puesto que los rreçi- / ben de amistad y tratan con e- / llos de noche no quedan en los / pueblos sino fuera so las ala- / ves y los pueblos se Velan a bo- / cina y grito como las fortaleças / de españa {rúbrica}

otro siete pueblos *h*ay a la orilla

[fol. 114v]
segunda / {rúbrica}

de *e*ste camino haçia la sierra / neVada que el Uno quedo

me- / dio destruydo de estas gen- / tes ya dichas que estan deba- / jo de la obidiençia de cicuyc / esta cicuye en Un pequeño / valle entre sierras y monta- / ñas de grandes pinales tiene / Una pequeña rrivera que / lleVa muy buenas truchas / y nutrias crianse por aqui / muy gra*n*des osos y buenos / halcones {rúbrica}

Capitulo sexto en que / se declara quantos fueron / los pueblos que se vieron / en los poblados de terra- / dos y lo poblado de ellos {rúbrica}

pareçiome antes que salga / deçir

[fol. 115r]
115
parte / {rúbrica}

deçir de los llanos de las Vacas / y lo poblado y rrancheado de / ellos que sera bien que se se- / pa que tanto fue lo poblado / que se Vio de casas de altos en / pueblos congre- gados y en que / tanto espaçio de tierra digo / çibola es lo primero {rúbrica}

çibola siete pueblos
tucayan siete pueblos
el peñon de acuco Uno
tiguex doçe pueblos
tutahaco ocho pueblos
por abajo del rrio estavan / estos pueblos {rúbrica}

quirix siete pueblos
a la sierra neV(e)*a*da siete pueblos
ximena tres pueblos {rúbrica}

cicuye Un pueblo {rúbrica}

hemes siete pueblos

[fol. 115v]
segunda / {rúbrica}

aguas calientes tres pueblos {rúbrica}

yuque yunque de la sierra / seis pueblos {rúbrica}

valladolid dicho Uraba Un / pueblo {rúbrica}

chia Un pueblo {rúbrica}

por todos son sesenta y seis pu- / eblos como parece tiguex
es / el rriñon de los pueblos valla- / dolid lo mas alto el rrio
arriba / a el nordeste los quatro pue- / blos a el rrio abaxo al
sueste / porque el rrio Voltea hacia / levante que desde la Una
/ punta de lo que se Vio el rrio / abajo a la otra que se Vio el
/ rrio arriba en que esta todo / lo poblado *h*ay çiento y trein-
/ ta leguas diez mas o menos / que por todos los pueblos con
/ los

[fol. 116r]
116
parte / {rúbrica}

los de las traVesias son sesenta / y seis como tengo dicho y
en to- / dos ellos puede *h*aver como ve- / inte mill hombres
lo qual se / puede bien considerar y en- / tender por la
poblaçion de / los pueblos y entremedias de / Unos y otros
no *h*ay caserias ni / otra *h*abitaçion sino todo des- / poblado
por donde se Ve que / segun son poca gente y tan di- /
ferençiados en trato govier- / no y poliçia de todas las naçio-
/ nes que se *h*an Visto y descu- / bierto en estas partes de po-
/ niente son Venediços[632] de aque- / lla parte de la india
mayor que / cae su costa debaxo del poni- / ente de esta tierra
que por / aquella parte pueden *h*aber

[fol. 116v]
segunda / {rúbrica}

baxado atraVesando aquellas / cordilleras baxando por aqu(e)-
/ el rrio abajo poblando en lo / mejor que les pareçia y como /
*h*an ydo multiplicando *h*an y- / do poblando hasta que no ha-
/ llaron rrio porque se sume de- / baxo de tierra haciendo sus
/ corrientes hacia la florida ba- / xando del nordeste donde se
/ hallava notiçia todavia / de pueblos que se dexo de / seguir al

turco que lo deçia / si(n) aquellas cordilleras do*nde* / nace aquel
rrio se atraVesa- / ran yo creo se tomaran rricas / notiçias y se
entrara en las / tierras de donde aquellas gen- / tes proçeden
que segun el rru*m*- / bo es principio de la india ma- / yor
aunque partes rr(in)*em*otas / y no

[fol. 117r]
117
parte / {rúbrica}

y no sabidas ni co(g)nosidas por- / que segun la
demostraçion de / la costa es muy la tierra aden- / tro entre
la nuruega y la chi- / na en el comedio de la tierra / de mar
a mar es grande an- / chura segun demuestran los / rrumbos
de ambas costas asi / lo q*ue* descubrio el capitan villa- / lobos
yendo por esta mar de / poniente en demanda de / la china
como lo que sea des- / cubierto por la mar del nor- / te la
Vuelta de los bacalla- / os que es por la costa de la flo- / rida
arriba hacia la nurue- / ga {rúbrica}

ansi que tornado a el propo- / sito de lo començado digo q*ue*
/ en espaçio de setenta leguas

[fol. 117v]
segunda / {rúbrica}

en el ancho de aquella tie- / rra poblada y de ciento y tre- /
inta leguas al lue*n*go del rrio / de tiguex no se Vieron ni ha-
/ llaron mas poblados ni gen- / tes de las ya dichas que *h*ay /
rrepartimientos en la nue- / Va españa no Uno sino mu- /
chos de mayor numero de / gentes en muchos pueblos de /
ellos se hallaron metales de / plata que los tenian para /
Vedriar y pintar los rrostros {rúbrica}

Capitulo septimo que / trata de los llanos que se / atraVesaron de Vacas y de / las gentes que los habitan {rúbrica}

dicho *h*abemos de lo poblado / de

[fol. 118r]
118
parte / {rúbrica}

de altos que segun parese es- / ta en el comedio de la cordi- / llera en lo mas llano y espa- / çioso de ella porque tiene de / atraVesia çiento y sinquenta / leguas hasta entrar en la tie- / rra llana que esta entre las / dos cordilleras digo la que / esta a la mar del norte y la que / esta a la mar del sur que por / esta costa se podria mejor de- / çir a la mar de poniente esta / cordillera es la que esta a el / mar del sur pues para enten- / der como lo poblado que digo / esta en el comedio de la / cordi- / llera digo que desde chichil- / ticale que es el prin- / cipio de / la traVesia a çibola *h*ay ochen-

[fol. 118v]
segunda / {rúbrica}

ta leguas de çibola que es el pri- / mer pueblo a cicuye que es / el p(r)ost*r*ero en la traVesia *h*ay se- / tenta leguas de cicuyc a los / llanos *h*ay treinta leguas has- / ta el prinçipio de ellos pue- / de ser *h*aberse atraVesado al- / go por traVesia o a el sesgo por / do*nde* parece *h*aber mas tierra que / si se atra- / Vesara por medio y / pudiera ser mas dificultoso / y aspero y esto no se puede bie*n* / entender por la Vuelta que / la cordillera *h*açe tras[633] de su / costa del Ancon del rrio del / tizon {rúbrica}

agora diremos de los lla- / nos que es Una tierra llana / y espaçiosa que tiene en / an

[fol 119r]
119
parte / {rúbrica}

anchura mas de quatro cien- / tas leguas por aquella parte / entre la dos cordilleras la / Una la que atraVeso françis- / co vasques coronado a la mar / del sur y la otra la que atra- / Veso la gente de don fernando / de soto a la mar del norte en- / trando por la florida lo que / de estos llanos se Vio todo e- / ra despoblado y no se pudo / Ver la otra cordillera ni çe- / rro ni çierra que tuViese de / altura tres estados con andar / doçientas y sinquenta le- / guas por ellos a trechos se / hallavan algunas lagu- / nas rredondas como platos / de Un tiro de piedra de an-

[fol. 119v]
segunda / {rúbrica}

cho y mayores algunas dul- / çes y algunas de sal en estas / lagunas *h*ay alguna yerba / cresida fuera de ellas to- / da es muy chica de Un ge- / me y menos es la tierra de / hechura de bola que don- / dequiera que Un hombre / se pone lo çerca el çielo a ti- / ro de ballesta no tiene arbo- / leda sino en los rrios que / *h*ay en algunas barrancas / que son tam encubiertas que / hasta que estan a el bord(o)*e* de / ellas no son Vistas son de tie- / rra muerta tienen entra- / das que *h*açen las Vacas pa- / ra entrar a el agua que esta / honda por estos llanos andan / gen

[fol. 120r]
120
parte / {rúbrica}

gentes como tengo dicho en la / primera parte en pos de las / Vacas haçiendo caça y adoba*n*- / do cueros para llevar a Ven- / der a los poblados los inVier- / nos porque Van a inVernar / a ellos cada compañia adon- / de mas çerca se halla Unos a / los poblados de cicuye otros ha- / çia quivira otros haçia la flo- / rida a los poblados que estan / haçia aquella parte y puer- / to estan gentes que los llama*n* / quere- / chos y teyas dan rre- / laçion de grandes poblados / y segun lo que de estas gen- / tes se Vio y de otros que ellos / daban notiçia que *h*avia

[fol. 120v]
segunda / {rúbrica}

por otras partes ella es harto / mas gente[634] que no la de los / poblados mas dispuesta y / mayores hombres de gue- / rra y mas temidos andan / como alarabes con sus tien- / das y (h)arrias de perros apa- / rejados con lomillos y en- / xalmas y sincha quando / se les tuerçe la carga aullan / llamando quien los adere- / se comen esta gente la / carne cruda y beben la sa*n*- / gre no comen carne huma- / na es gente amoros(o)*a* y no / cruel tienen fiel amistad / son muy entendidos por / señas secan la carne a el / sol cortandola delgada / como

[fol. 121r]
121
parte / {rúbrica}

como Una hoja y seca la mue- / len como harina para guar- / dar y haçer maçamorras pa- / ra comer que con Un puño / que (h)echan en Una olla se / hinche porque creçe mucho / guisanlo con manteca que / siempre proc(a)uran traer qu- / ando matan la Vaca vaçian / Una gran tripa y hinchenla / de sangre y (h)echanla a el / cuello para beber quando t(^e)ie- / nen sed quando han abierto la / pança de la Vaca aprietan / para abajo la yerva mas- / cada y el sumo que queda / arriba lo beben que diçen / que es toda la sustançia de / el Vientre abren las Vacas

[fol. 121v]
segunda / {rúbrica}

por el lomo y deshaçenlas por / sus coyunturas con Un pe- / dernal grande como Un / dedo atado en Un palito con / tanta façilidad como si fue- / se con Una muy buena he- / rramienta dandoles los fi- / los en sus propios dientes es / cosa de Ver y de notar la pres- / teça con que lo haçen {rúbrica}

hay por estos llanos muy gran / cantidad de lobos que andan / tras de las Vacas tienen el pe- / lo blanco los siervos son rre- / mendados de blanco el pelo / ancho y que muriendo an- / si con la mano se pelan en / caliente y quedan como puer- / co pelado las liebres que son / en

[fol. 122r]
122
parte / {rúbrica}

en gran numero andan tan / abobadas que yendo a ca- / vallo las matan con las lan- / ças esto es de andar (h)echas / entre las Vacas de la gente de / pie huyen {rúbrica}

Capitulo ocho de quivi- / ra y en que rrumbo esta / y la notiçia que dan {rúbrica}

quivira es a el poniente / de aquellas barrancas por / el medio de la tierra algo a- / rrimada a la cordillera de / la mar porque hasta qui- / vira es tierra llana y alli / se comiençan haber algu- / nas sierras la tierra es muy / poblada segun el princi-

[fol. 122v]
segunda / {rúbrica}

pio de ella se Vio ser esta tie- / rra muy aparente a la de / españa en su manera de / yervas y frutas hay siruelas / como las de castilla UVas / nueçes moras vallico y aVe- / na poleo oregano lino en / gran cantidad no lo beneffi- / cian porque no saben el uso de / ello la gente es casi de la / manera y traje de los te- / yas tienen los pueblos a la / manera como los de la nue- / Va españa las casas son rre- / dondas sin çerca tienen U- / nos altos a manera de bal- / {barbacoas} bacoas por baxo la techum- / bre adonde duermen y tie- / nen sus haberes las techum- / bres son de paja hay en su / contorno otras provinçias / muy

[fol. 123r]
123
parte / {rúbrica}

muy pobladas en grande / numero de gente y aqui / en esta provinçia quedo Un / frayle que se deçia fray juan / de padilla y Un español por- / tugues y Un negro y Un mes- / tiso y siertos indios de la pro- / vinçia de çapotlan de la / nueVa españa a el frayle / mataron porque se queria / yr a la pro- / vinçia de los gu- / as que eran sus enemigos / el español escapo huyendo / en Una yegua y despues a- / porto en la nueVa espa- / ña saliendo por la via de / panuco los indios de la nue- / Va españa que yban con / el frayle lo enterraron con

[fol. 123v]
segunda / {rúbrica}

consentimiento de los matado- / res y se Vinieron en pos del / español hasta que lo alcan- / çaron este español era por- / tugues havia por nombre / campo {rúbrica} el gran rrio del espiritu san- / to que descubrio don fer*nan*do / de soto en la tierra de la flo- / rida lleva sus corrientes de / aquesta tierra pasa por U- / na provinçia que se diçe a- / rache segun alli se tuVo por / notiçia Verdadera que no / se Vieron sus naçimientos por- / que segun deçian Vienen de / muy lejos tierra de la cordi- / llera del sur de la parte / que desagua a los llanos / y atraVesa toda la tierra / lla

[fol. 124r]
124
parte / {rúbrica}

llana y rompe la cordillera / del norte y sale adonde lo / nave- / garon los de don fer- / nando de soto esto es mas / de treçientas leguas de don- / de el Va a salir a la mar y por / esto y por las grandes acogi- / das que tiene sale tam po- / deroso a el mar que *h*an perdi- / do la vista de la tierra y no / el agua de ser dulçe {rúbrica}

hasta esta tierra de quivi- / ra fue lo Ultimo que se Vio / y de / lo que ya puedo dar no- / tiçia o rrelaçion y agora me / conViene dar la Vuelta a ha- /blar del campo que dexe / en tiguex rreposando el / inVierno para poder pasar / o VolVer a buscar estos po-

[fol. 124v]
segunda / {rúbrica}

blados de quivira lo qual / despues no suçedio ansi por- / que fue dios servido que estos / descubrimientos quedasen / para otras gentes y que nos / contentasemos los que a- / lla fuimos con deçir que fui- / mos los primeros que lo des- / cubrimos y tuVimos notiçia / de ellos {rúbrica}

{no dice nada} como hercules conoçer el / sitio adonde jullio çesar / *h*avia de fundar a sevilla / o hispalis plega a el se- / ñor todo poderoso se sir- / va con todo que sierto es / que si su voluntad fuera / ni fran*cis*co vasques se VolVie- / ra a la nueVa españa tan / sin causa ni rraçon ni los / de don fernando de soto / de

[fol. 125r]
125
parte / {rúbrica}

dexaran de poblar tan bue- / na tierra como tenian y / tambien poblada y larga / mayormente *h*abiendo te- / nido como tuVieron notiçia / de nuestro campo {rúbrica}

terçera parte como y en / que se trata[635] aquello que / aconteçio a françisco vas- / ques coronado estando in- / Vernando y como dexo / la jornada y se VolVio a / la nueVa españa {rúbrica}

laus deo / {rúbrica}

[fol. 125v]
tercera / {rúbrica}
[blank]

[fol. 126r]
126
parte / {rúbrica}

Capitulo primero como Vi- / no de señora don pedro / de tovar con gente y se par- / tio para la nueVa espa- / ña don garci lopes de car- / denas {rúbrica}

en el fin de la primera par- / te de este libro diximos como / françisco vasques coronado / Vuelto de quivira *h*avia or- / denado de inVernar en ti- / guex y Venido el inVierno / dar la Vuelta con todo su can- / po para descubrir todos a- / quellos poblados en estos co- / medios don pedro de tovar / que como diximos *h*avia y- / do a sacar gente de la vi- / lla de san hieronimo llego

[fol. 126v]
tercera / {rúbrica}

con la gente que traya y a / la Verdad considerando / que p*ar*a ir en demanda de / su general a la tierra del / indio que

llamavan turco le / conVenia llevar buena gen- / te no saco
de alla los cediçiosos / ni rreVoltosos sino los mas ex- / peri-
mentados y mejores solda- / dos hombres de confiança que
/ pudo y llegados a tiguex aun- / que hallaron alli el campo /
no les plugo mucho porque / Venian y a el pico a el Viento /
creyendo hallar a el gene- / ral en la tierra rrica del in- / dio
que deçian turco consola- / ronse con la esperança de la /
Vuelta que se havia de ha- / çer y Vivian en gran plaçer / y
alegria con la esperanca / de

[fol. 127r]
127
parte / {rúbrica}

de la Vuelta que se havia de / hacer[636] y de que presto yria / el
campo a quivira con don / pedro de tovar Vinieron cartas /
de la nueVa españa ansi del / virrey don Antonio de mendo-
/ ça como de particulares entre / los quales dieron una a don
gar- / çia lopes de cardenas en que / le hiçieron saber la
muerte de / Un su hermano mayorazgo / llamandole fuese a
heredar / a españa por donde hUbo li- / çençia y salio de
tiguex con / algunas otras personas que / hUbieron liçençia
para se yr a / rreposar a sus casas otros mu- / chos se
quisieran yr que lo / dexaron por no mostrar fla-

[fol. 127v]
tercera / {rúbrica}

queça procurabase en estos co- / medios apasiguar algunos
pu- / eblos de la comarca que esta- / ban no bien asentados
y lla- / mar a los de tiguex a paz y / buscar alguna rropa de la
/ tierra porque andaban ya / los soldados desnudos y maltra-
/ tados llenos de piojos y no los / podian agotar ni
des(h)echar / de si {rúbrica}

el general francisco vasques / coronado havia sido entre / sus
capitanes y soldados el / mas bien quisto y obedeçido /
{capitan / {rúbrica}} capitan que podia haver sa- / lido en
indias y como la neçe- / sidad careçe de ley y los capi- / tanes
que rrecogian la rropa / la rrepartiesen mal tomando / para

[fol. 128r]
128
parte / {rúbrica}

para si y sus amigos y criados / lo mejor y a los soldados se
les / rrepartiese el des(h)echo comen- / ço a haber algunas
murmura- / çiones y desabrimientos Unos / por lo dicho y
otros por Ver que / algunos sobresalientes eran / rreservados
del trabajo y de / las velas y mejor rrepartidos / en lo que se
rrepartia asi de / rropa como de bastimentos / por donde se
cree p(r)laticaban ya / no haber en la tierra para que / VolVer
a quivira que no fue / pequeña ocaçion para lo de / adelante
como se vera {rúbrica}

Capitulo segundo como ca- / yo el general y se (h)orde- / no
la Vuelta para la nueVa / españa / {rúbrica}

[fol. 128v]
parte / {rúbrica}

pasado que fue el invierno / se publico la Vuelta para / quivira
y la gente se comen- / çava a perçebir de las co- / sas neçesarias y como ningu- / na cosa esta en esta vida a / la
dispusiçion de los hombres / sino a la ordenaçion de dios /
todo poderoso fue su volun- / tad que las nuestras no se
efectua- / sen y fue el caso que el gene- / ral Un dia de fiesta
se salio / a holgar a cavallo como so- / lia y corriendo parejas
con / el capitan don rrodrigo mal- / donado el yba en Un
pode- / roso cavallo y sus criados havi- / an le puesto Una
çincha nu- / eVa que del tiempo debia / de

[fol. 129r]
129
tercera / {rúbrica}

de estar podrida en la carre- / ra rreVento y Vino a caer de
/ lado a la parte que yba don / rrodigo y a el pasar (a)(^e)
^alcanso- / le el cavallo con el pie en la / cabeça de que
llego a punto / de muerte y su cura fue larga / y temida
{rúbrica}

en este comedio que *e*l estaba en / la cama don garçi lopes de / cardenas que *h*avia salido pa- / ra salir a la nueVa españa Vol- / Vio de ffuya huyendo que ha- / llo despoblada la villa y / muerta la gente y cavallos / y ganados y llego a tiguex / y sabida la triste nueVa co- / mo el general estaba en los / terminos ya dichos no se lo (o)

[fol. 129v]
tercera / {rúbrica}

osaron deçir hasta que estuVi- / ese sano y al cabo ya que se / leVantava lo supo y sintio lo / tanto que *h*Ubo de tornar a / rrecaer y por ventura para Ve- / nir a haçer lo que hiço segun des- / pues se creyo y fue que como se / Vio de aquella suerte Vino- / le a la memoria que en sala- / manca Un mat(h)ematico su / amigo le *h*avia dicho que se *h*a- / via de Ver en tierras estrañas / señor y poderoso y *h*abia de dar / Una cayda de que no se *h*avia / de poder levantar y con esta / inmaginacion de su muer- / te le dio deseo de Volver a / morir adonde tenia muger / y hijos y como del mismo fiçi- / co y su s(u)irujano que lo cura- / va y servia tambien de chis- / mo

[fol. 130r]
130
parte / {rúbrica}

moso supiese las murmuraçio- / nes que andaban entre los sol- / dados trato secreta y oculta- / mente con algunos cavalleros / de su opinion pusiesen en prac- / tica la Vuelta de la nueva espa- / ña entre los soldados haçien- / do juntas y corrillos que se hi- / çiesen consultas y lo pidiesen / con sus alferes*es* a el general co*n* / carteles firmados de todos sus / soldados lo qual ellos trata- / ron muy por entero y no fue / menester gastar mucho tien- / po segun ya muchos lo teni- / an en voluntad el general / mostro desque se lo pidieron / que no lo queria haçer sino lo / confirmavan todos los cava- / lleros y capitanes dando su

[fol. 130v]
tercera / {rúbrica}

pareçer firmado y como algu- / nos eran en ello dieronlo lue- / go y aun persuadieron a los / otros a haçer lo mismo y ansi / dieron pareçer que se devi- / an de Volver a la nueVa espa- / ña pues no se *h*avia hallado / cosa rrica ni *h*avia poblado / en lo descubierto donde se / pudiesen haçer rrepartimi- / entos a todo el campo y como / les cogio las firmas luego se / publico la Vuelta para la nue- / va españa y como no puede / *h*aber cosa encubierta come*n*- / çose a descubrir el trato do- / ble y hallaronse muchos de / los cavalleros faltos y corri- / dos y procuraron por todas / vias tornar a cobrar sus fir- / mas

[fol. 131r]
131
parte / {rúbrica}

mas del general el qual las guar- / do tanto que no salia de Una / camara haçiendo su dolençia / muy mayor poniendo guardas / en su persona y camara y de / noche en los altos adonde dor- / mia con todo esto le hurtaron / el cofre y se dixo no hallaron / en el sus firmas que las tenia / en el colchon por otro cabo se / dixo que las cobraron ellos pi- / dieron que *e*l general les die- / se sesenta hombres escogidos / y que ellos quedarian y sus- / tentarian la tierra hasta que / el virrey les emViase socorro / o a llamar o que el general / dexase el campo y escogiese / sesenta hombres con que se / fuese pero los soldados ni de

[fol. 131v]
tercera / {rúbrica}

Una ni de otra manera no quisi- / eron quedar lo Uno por *h*aber / ya puesto la proa a la nueVa / españa y lo otro porque Vieron / clara la discordia que se *h*a- / via de levantar sobre quien / *h*avia de mandar los cava- / lleros no se sabe si porque / *h*avian jurado fidelidad / o por tener creydo que los / soldados no los faVoreçeri- / an aunque agraViados lo / *h*Ubieron de sufrir[637] y pasar p*or* / lo determinado aunque / desde alli no obedeçian / al general como solian y / el era de *e*llos mal quisto / y haçia caudal de los solda- / dos y honrra- / balos que fue / a Ve

[fol. 132r]
132
parte / {rúbrica}

a Venir a el efecto de lo que *el* / queria y que se efe*c*tuase la / Vuelta de todo el campo {rúbrica}

Capitulo terçero como se / alço fuya y las causas que / para ello dieron los po- / bladores {rúbrica}

ya diximos en el capitulo / pasado como don garçia / lopes de cardenas VolVio / huyendo de ffuya desque / hallo alçada la tierra y que*da* / de deçir como y por que se / despoblo a la aquella villa / lo qual paso como contare / y fue el caso que como ya / en aquella villa no (a)

[fol. 132v]
tercera / {rúbrica}

*h*avia quedado sino la gente / rruyn entereçada honbres / rreVoltosos y sediciosos pu- / esto que quedaron algunos / honrrados en los cargos de / rrepublica y para gover- / nar a los demas podia mas / la maliçia de los rruynes / y cada dia hacian munipu- / dios y tratos diçiendo que es- / taban Vendidos y no para / ser aproVechados pues en / aquella tierra se manda- / ba por otra parte mas a / proposito de la nueVa es- / paña que no aquella es- / tava y ellos quedaban / casi por derecho y con esto / mo

[fol. 133r]
133
parte / {rúbrica}

movidos sierta compañia / haciendo caudillo a Un pe- / dro de avila se amotina- / ron y fueron la Vuelta de / culiacan dexando a diego / de alcaraz su capitan con / poca gente doliente en a- / quella villa de sant hie- / ronimo que no *h*Ubo quie*n* /los pudiese seguir para los / apremiar a que VolViese*n* / en el camino en algunos / pueblos les mataron al- / guna gente y al cabo sa- / lieron a culiacan adonde / hernando arias de saya- / Ve(n)dra los detuVo entrete- / ni(^e)dos con palabras por {saaVedr*a* / {rúbrica}}

[fol. 133v]
terçera / {rúbrica}

porque aguardaba a juan / gallego que *h*avia de Venir / alli con gente de la nueva / españa y que los VolVeria[638] / algunos temiendo lo que / *h*avia de ser se huyan de no- / che para la nueVa españa / diego de alcaraz que *h*avi- / a quedado con poca gente / y doliente aunque quisie- / ra no podia alli sustentar- / se por el peligro de la yerva / mortal que por alli Usan / traer los naturales los qua- / les sintiendo la flaqueça / de los españoles ya no se de- / xaban tratar como solian / *h*abianse ya descubierto an- / tes de *e*sto mineros de oro / y co

[fol. 134r]
134
parte / {rúbrica}

y como estaban en tierra de / guerra y no tenian posibili- / dad no se labravan estando / en esta confuçion no se dexa- / ban de Velar y rrecatar mas / que solian {rúbrica}

la villa estaba poblada çer- / ca de Un rrio pequeño y Una / noche a des*h*ora Vieron fuegos / no Usados ni acostum- brados / que fue causa que doblaron / las velas pero como en toda / la noche no sintieron nada a / la madrugada se descuidaro*n* / y los enemigos entraron tan / callados por el pueblo que no / fueron vistos hasta que anda- / ban matando y rrobando algu-

[fol. 134v]
terçera / {rúbrica}

nas gentes salieron a lo lla- / no que tuVieron lugar y a el / salir hirieron de muerte a / el capitan y como algunos / españoles se rrehiçieron en / algunos cavallos VolVieron / sobre los enemigos y socorrie- / ron alguna gente aunque / fue poca y los enemigos se fue- / ron con la presa sin rreçebir / daño dexando muertos tres / españoles y mucha gente de / serviçio y mas de veinte ca- / vallos {rúbrica} los españoles que quedaron / salieron aquel dia a pie sin / cavallos la Vuelta de culia- / can por fuera de caminos y sin /ningun bastimento hasta lle- / gar

[fol. 135r]
135
parte / {rúbrica}

gar a los coraçones adonde a- / quellos indios los socorrieron / de bastimentos como amigos / que siempre fueron y de alli con / grandes trabajos que pasaron / llegaron a Culiacan adonde / hernandarias de saaVedra al- / calde mayor los rrecibio y hos- / pedo lo mejor que pudo hasta / que juan gallego llego con el / socorro que traya para pasar / adelante en busca del cam- / po que no poco le peso se hUbiese / despoblado aquel paso cre- / yendo que el campo estaba / en la tierra rrica que havia / dicho el indio que llamaron / turco porque lo parecia en / su aspecto {rúbrica}

[fol. 135v]
tercera / {rúbrica}

Capitulo quarto como se / quedo fray juan de padilla / y fray luis en la tierra y el / campo se aperçibio la Vuel- / ta de mexico {rúbrica}

ya que el general francisco / vasques vi(d)o que todo esta- / ba pacifico y que sus negoçios[639] / se havian encaminado a su / voluntad mando que para / entrado el mes de abril del / año de quinientos y quaren- / {1543} ta y tres estuViesen todos aper- / çebidos para salir la Vuelta / de la nueVa españa {rúbrica}

Viendo esto Un fray juan de / padilla frayle de misa de la / orden de los menores y otro / fray

[fol. 136r]
136
parte / {rúbrica}

fray luis lego dixeron a el ge- / neral que ellos querian que- / darse en aquella tierra el / fray juan de padilla en quivi- / ra

porque le parecia haria a- / lli fru(c)to su doctrina y el fray / luis en cicuye y para esto como / era quaresma a la saçon pre- / dico un domingo aquel sermon / del padre de las compañas[640] y / fundo su proposito con autori- / dad de la sagrada escritura / y como su çelo era comVertir / aquellas gentes y traerlos a / la fe y como tuVieron liçençia / que para esto no era menester / emVio el general con ellos U- / na compañia que los sacasen / hasta cicuyc donde se quedo / el fray luis y el fray juan

[fol. 136v]
tercera / {rúbrica}

paso la Vuelta de quivira / llevando el portugues que / diximos y el negro y el mes- / tiso y indios de la nueVa es- / paña con las guias que havia / traydo el general donde / en llegando alla dentro de / muy poco tiempo lo martiri- / çaron como contamos en la / segunda parte capitulo octavo / y ansi se puede creer murio / martir pues su çelo era santo / y bueno {rúbrica}

el fray luis se quedo en cicuyc / no se ha sabido de el mas / hasta hoy / aunque antes que el campo sa- / liese de tiguex llevandole sier- / ta cantidad de oVejas para que / se le quedasen los que las lleVa- / van lo toparon acompañado / de gente que andaba viçitando / otros

[fol. 137r]
137
parte / {rúbrica}

otros pueblos que estaban a quin- / çe y a veinte leguas de cicuye / y no dio poca buena esperanca / que estaba en graçia del pue- / blo y haria fruto su doctrina aun- / que se quexaba que los viejos lo / desamparaban y creyo al fin / lo matarian yo para mi tengo / que como era hombre de buena / y santa vida nuestro señor lo guar- / daria y daria gracia que conVir- / tiese algunas gentes de aque- /llas y dexase despues de sus dias / quien los administrase en la fee / y no es de creer otra cosa porque / la gente de por alli es piadosa y / ninguna cosa cruel antes son / amigos o enemigos de la cruel- / dad y guardan la fee y lealtad / a los amigos {rúbrica}

[fol. 137v]
tercera / {rúbrica}

el general despachados los / frayles temiendo no le daña- / se
el traer gente de aquella / tierra a la nueVa españa ma*n*- /
do que *el* serviçio que los sol- / dados tenian de los natura- / les
lo dexasen yr libres a sus / pueblos adonde quisiesen que / a
mi Ver no lo aserto que mas / valiera se do*c*trinaran entre /
c(h)ristianos {rúbrica}

andaba ya el general alegre / y contento llegado el plaço y to-
/ dos proVeydos de lo necesario pa- / ra su jornada el campo
salio / de tiguex la Vuelta de cibola a- / conteçio en este
camino Una co- / sa no poco de notar y fue que con / salir
los cavallos exerçitados / a el trabajo gordos y hermosos / en

[fol. 138r]
138
parte / {rúbrica}

en diez dias que se tardo en lle- / gar a cibola murieron mas de
/ treinta que no *h*Ubo dia que no / muriesen dos y tres y mas
y des- / pues hasta llegar a culiacan mu- / rieron gran numero
de ellos co- / sa no aconteçida en toda la / jornada {rúbrica}

llegado que fue el campo a çibo- / la se rrehiço para salir por
el / despoblado por ser alli lo Ulti- / mo de los poblados de
aquella / tierra quedando toda aquella / tierra paçifica y llana
y que se / quedaron algunos amigos en- / tre ellos de los
nuestros {rúbrica}

Capitulo quinto como el canpo / salio del poblado y camino
/ a culiacan y lo que acon*t*eçio / en el camino / {rúbrica}

[fol. 138v]
tercera / {rúbrica}

dexando ya por popa pode- / mos deçir los poblados que
se / *h*avian descubierto en la tie- / rra nueVa que como
tengo / dicho eran los siete pueblos / de çibola lo primero

que se / Vio y lo p(r)ost*r*ero que se dexo sa- / lio el campo
caminando por el / despoblado y en dos o tres jorna- / das
nunca dexaron los natu- / rales de seguir el campo tras /
la rretaguardia por coger al- / gun fardaje o gente de
servi- / çio porque aunque daba*n* / de paz y *h*avian sido
buenos y le- / ales amigos todavia como Vie- / ron que se
les dexaba la tierra / libre se holgavan de Ver en su / poder
gente de la nuestra a- / un

[fol. 139r]
139
parte / {rúbrica}

aunque se cre*e* no para los enojar / como se supo de algunos
que no / quisieron yr con ellos que fue- / ron de ellos inpor-
tunados y / rrogados todavia llevaron al- / guna gente y otros
que se *h*avi- / an quedado voluntariame*n*- / te de los quales
el dia de *h*oy / *h*abra buenas lenguas el despo- / blado se
camino sin contraste / y como salieron en chichilti- / cale en
la segunda jornada lle- / go a el campo juan gallego que / yba
de la nueVa españa con / socorro de gente y cosas neçe- /
sarias para el campo pensan- / do de lo hallar en la tierra /
del indio que llamavan turco / y como juan gallego Vi(d)o
que / el canpo se VolVia la prime*ra*

[fol. 139v]
tercera / {rúbrica}

palabra que dixo no fue deçir / norabuena Vengais y no lo /
sintio tan poco que despues de / *h*aber hablado al general y
lle- / gados a el campo digo a el apo- / sento no *h*Ubiese
algunos moVi- / mientos en los cavalleros con / aquel nueVo
socorro que no con / poco trabajo *h*avian llegado *h*as- / ta alli
teniendo cada dia rre- / cuentros con los indios de aque- /
llas partes como se *h*a dicho que / estaban alcados *h*Ubo
algunos / tratos y platicas de poblar por / alli en alguna parte
hasta / dar rrelaçion a el Visorrey de / lo que pasaba la gente
de los / soldados que venian de la / tierra nueVa a ninguna
cosa / daban consentimiento sino / en

[fol. 140r]

140

parte / {rúbrica}

en VolVer a la nueVa españa / por donde no *h*Ubo efecto
nada / de lo que se proponia en sus con- / sultas y aunque
*h*Ubo algunos al- / borotos al cabo se apasi(a)guaro*n* / *los que*
yban con juan gallego algu- / nos de los amotinados que des-
/ poblaron la villa de los cora- / çones asegurados por el y
deba- / jo de su palabra y puesto que / el general quisiera
*h*açer al- / gun castigo era poco su poder / porque ya era
desobe- (d*e*sobe) / decido y poco acatado y de / alli delante
de nueVo comen- / ço a temer y haciase doliente / andando
con guarda en algu- / nas partes *h*Ubo algunas gri- / tas y de
indios y de heridos y / muertes de cavallos hasta lle- / gar a
batuco donde salieron

[fol. 140v]

tercera / {rúbrica}

a el campo indios amigos del va- / lle de *los* coraço*nes* por Ver
a el ge- / neral como amigos que sien- / pre fueron y ansi
*h*avia tra- / tado a todos los españoles que / por sus tierras
*h*avian pasado / proVeyendolos en sus neçesida- / des de
bastimentos y gente / si necesario era y ansi fueron / de los
n*uest*ros siempre muy bien / tratados y gratificados en esta /
jornada se aprobo del agua / del menbrillo ser buena con- /
tra la yerba de estas pa*r*tes / porque en Un paso algu- / nas
jornadas antes de lle- / gar a el valle de señora los / indios
enemigos hirieron a / Un español llamado mesa / y con ser
la herida mortal de / yer

[fol. 141r]

141

parte / {rúbrica}

yerba fresca y tardarse mas de / dos *h*oras en curar con el agua
/ no murio puesto que quedo lo / que la yerba *h*avia
infiçiona- / do podrido y se cayo la carne / hasta dexar los
guesos y n(i)er- / V*i*os desnudos con pestilençial / hedor que
fue la herida en la / muñeca y *h*avia llegado la pon- / soña

hasta la espalda qua*ndo* / se vino a curar y todo esto des- /
amparo la carne {rúbrica}

caminaba el campo sin tomar / rreposo porque ya en esta sa-
/ çon *h*avia falta de bastimentos / que como aquellas
comarcas / estaban alçadas las Vituallas / no *h*avia adonde las
tomar has- / ta que llego a petlatlan *h*açien- / do algunas
entradas en las

[fol. 141v]

terçera / {rúbrica}

traVesias por buscar bastimen- / tos patlatlan[641] es de la pro-
/ vinçia / de culiacan y a esta causa es- / taba de paz aunque
despues / aca *h*a *h*abido algunas noVeda- / des alli descanso
el campo / algunos dias por se *a*basteçer / y salidos de alli con
mayor / presteça que de antes procu- / raron pasar aquellas
trein- / ta leguas que *h*ay al valle de / culiacan donde de
nueVo / los acogieron como gente / que Venia con su
governa- / dor maltratado {rúbrica}

Capitulo sexto como el ge- / neral salio de culiacan pa- / ra
dar quenta a el visorrey / del campo que le encar- / go
{rúbrica} / ya

[fol. 142r]

142

parte / {rúbrica}

ya parece que en *h*aber llega- / do a el valle de culiacan / se
da fin a los trabajos de esta / jornada lo Uno por ser el ge- /
neral governador y lo otro por / estar en tierra de
c(h)ristianos / y ansi se començaron luego / (^e)asentar[642]
algunos de la supe- / rioridad y dominio que sobre / ellos
tenian sus capitanes y a- / un algunos capitanes de la / obe-
di*e*ncia del general y ca- / da Uno *h*açia ya cabeça de / su
juego de manera que pa- / sando el general a la villa / que
estava de alli diez legu- / as mucha de la gente o la / mas de
ella se le quedo en / el valle rreposando y algu- / nos con
proposito de no le se-

[fol. 142v]
tercera / {rúbrica}

guir bien sintio el general que / por via de fuerça ya no era pode- / roso aunque la autoridad de ser / governador le daba otra nueVa / autoridad determino lleVarlo / por otra mejor via que fue man- / dar proVe*e*r a todos los capitanes / de bastimentos y carne de lo que / *h*avia en algunos pueblos que / como governador estaban en / su cabeça y mostrose estar dolien- / te haçiendo cama por que los que / con el *h*Ubiesen de negoçiar pudie- / sen hablarle o el con ellos mas li- / bremente sin enpacho ni o(b)cu- / pacion⁶⁴³ y no dexaba de emViar / a llamar algunos particulares / amigos para les rrogar y encar- / gar hablasen a los soldados y los / animasen a salir de alli en su / compañia la Vuelta de la nue- / Va

[fol. 143r]
143
parte

Va españa y les dixesen llevaba / muy a cargo de los faVoreçer an- / si con el visorrey don Antonio de / mendoça como en su governa- / çion a los que con el quisiesen / quedar en ella y desque *h*Ubo / negoçiado salio con su campo en / tiempo rreçio y principio de las / aguas que era por san juan en / el qual tiempo llueVe braVamen- / te y los rrios de aquel despoblado / que se pasan hasta conpostela so*n* / muchos y muy peligrosos y cauda- / losos de grandes y bravos lagar- / tos en Un rrio de los quales estan- / do asentado el campo pasando Un / soldado de la Una parte a la o- / tra a Vista de todos fue arrebata- / do de Un lagarto y lleVado sin / poder ser socorrido el general / camino dexando por todas par-

[fol. 143v]
tercera / {rúbrica}

tes gentes que no le querian seguir / y llego a mexico con menos de / çien hombres a dar quenta a el / visorrey don Antonio de mendoça / no fue de *e*l bien rrecebido aun- / que dio sus descargos y desde a- / lli perdio rreputaçion y gover- / no poco tiempo la governaçion / que se le *h*avia encargado

de / la nueVa galiçia porque el vi- / sorrey la tomo en si hasta que / vino a ella audiençia como a el / presente la *h*ay y este fue el fin que / *h*Ubieron aquellos descubrimi- / entos y jornada que se hiço de / la tierra nueVa {rúbrica}

quedanos agora deçir por que / via se podria entrar por mas de- / recho camino en ella aunque / digo que no *h*ay atajo sin trabajo / y siempre es lo mejor lo que / se sa

[fol. 144r]
144
parte / {rúbrica}

se sabe porque preVienen bien / los hombres lo que saben que *h*a / de Venir y necesidades en que / ya otra vez se Vieron y decir sea / a que parte cae quivira que *e*s / el rrumbo que lleVo el campo / y a qual parte cae la india / mayor que era lo que se preten- / dia buscar quando el campo sa- / lio para alla que agora por / *h*aber villalobos descubierto / esta costa de la mar del sur que / es por esta via de poniente se co- / (g)noçe y Ve claramente que se *h*a- / via de VolVer estando como esta- / bamos debajo del norte a el po- / niente y no haçia oriente co- / mo fuimos y con esto dexaremos / esta materia y daremos fin a es- / te tratado como *h*aya hecho rre- / laçion de algunas cosas notables

[fol. 144v]
tercera / {rúbrica}

que dexe de contar por las tra- / tar particularmente en los dos / capitulos siguientes {rúbrica}

Capitulo septimo de las co- / sas que le aconteçieron al ca- / pitan juan gallego por la tie- / rra alçada llevando el so- / corro {rúbrica}

bien se sufrira pues en el ca- / pitulo pasado pase en silen- / çio las haçañas que *e*l capitan / juan gallego hiço con veinte / compañeros que llevaba se / diga en el presente capitulo / para que en los tiempos Veni- / deros los que lo leyeren y de / ello dieren notiçia tengan a- / utor sierto⁶⁴⁴ quien aprobar /

y que no escribe fabulas co- / mo algunas cosas que en / nuestros⁶⁴⁵

[fol. 145r]
145
parte / {rúbrica}

tiempos leemos en los libros de ca- / vallerias que si no fuese por lle- / var aquellas fabulas de encan- / tamientos hay cosas el dia de hoy / acontesidas en estas partes por / nuestros españoles en conquistas y / rrecuentros habidos con los na- / turales que sobrepujan en he- / chos de admiraçion no solo a los / libros ya dichos sino a los que / se escriben de los doçe pares / de françia porque tanteado y / mirado las fatales fuerças que / los autores de aquellos tienpos / les atribuyen y las lucidas y / rresplandesientes armas de / que los adornan y las peque- / ñas estaturas de que agora son / los hombres de nuestros tiempos y / las pocas y rruynes armas de

[fol. 145v]
tercera / {rúbrica}

en estas partes mas es de admirar / las cosas estrañas que con tales ar- / mas los nuestros acometen y hacen / el dia de hoy que las que escriben / de los antiguos pues tambien / peleaban ellos con gentes bar- / baras y desnudas como los nuestros / como indios donde no dexa de / haber hombres que entre ellos son / esforcados y valientes y muy / çerteros flecheros pues l(e)os habe- / mos visto derribar las aves / que Van Volando y corriendo / tras las liebres flecharlas todo / esto he dicho a el fin que algu- / nas cosas que tenemos por fa- / bulosas pueden ser Verdade- / ras y pues cada dia Vemos / en nuestros tiempos cosas mayores / como han sido las de don fernando / cortes en los Venideros tienpos / que

[fol. 146r]
146
parte / {rúbrica}

que con tresientos hombres osase / entrar en el rriñon de la

nue- / Va españa donde tan grande / numero de gentes como es me- / xico y con quinientos españo- / les la acabase de ganar y se- / ñorear en dos anos cosa de gran- / de admiraçion {rúbrica}

los hechos de don pedro de al- / varado en la conquista de / guatimala y los de montejo / en tabasc(^a)o las conquistas de / tierra firme y del peru cosas / eran todas estas para que / yo hUbiera de callar y pasar / en silençio lo que agora quie- / ro contar pero porque estoy / obligado a dar rrelacion de / las cosas en esta jornada a- / contecidas e querido se se-

[fol. 146v]
tercera / {rúbrica}

pan tambien las que agora / dire con las demas que ten- / go dicho {rúbrica}

y es ansi que el capitan juan / gallego llego a la villa de / culia- can con bien poca gen- / te y alli rrecogio la que pu- / do de la que se havia escapa- / do de la villa de los coraço- / nes o por mejor decir de ffu- / ya que por todos fueron ve- / inte y dos hombres y con estos / camino por toda aquella / tierra poblada en que an- / duVo doçientas leguas y de tie- / rra de guerra y gente alça- / da que havian estado ya en / el amistad de los españoles te- / niendo cada dia o poco menos / rrecuentros con los enemigos / y sie

[fol. 147r]
147
parte / {rúbrica}

y siempre caminava dexan- / do atras el fardaje con las dos / partes de las gentes llevando / continuamente la avanguar- / dia con seis o siete españoles sin / otros amigos que los lle- / vaban / entrando en los pueblos por / fuerça matando y destruyen- / do y poniendo fuego dando en / los enemigos tam de supito y / con tanta presteça y denuedo / que no les daban lugar a que / se juntasen ni entendiesen / de suerte que eran tan temi- / dos que no havia pueblo que / esperarlos osase que ansi hu- / yan de ellos como de Un pode- / roso exercito tanto que les a- / conteçio yr diez dias todo por / poblado que no tenian *h*ora

[fol. 147v]
tercera / {rúbrica}

de descanso y todo lo haçia con / siete compañeros que quando / llegava el fardaje con toda / la demas gente no tenian en / que entender salvo en rrobar / que ya ellos *h*avian muerto / y preso la gente que *h*avian po- / dido *h*aver a las manos y la / demas *h*avia huydo y como no / paraban aunque los pueblos / de adelante tenian algun / aViso eran con ellos tam presto / que no les daban lugar a se / rrecoger en espeçial en aque- / lla parte donde *h*avia sido / la villa de los coraçones que / alli mato y ahorco buena / cantidad de gente en castigo / de su rrebelion y en todo esto / no perdio companero sin se / lo

[fol. 148r]
148
parte / {rúbrica}

lo hirieron salvo Uno que por / despojar a Un indio que casi es- / taba muerto le hirio en el pa- / rpalo⁶⁴⁶ del ojo quando le rron- / pio el pel*l*ejo y por ser con yer- / ba *h*obiera de morir sino fue- / ra socorrido con el agua del / membrillo y perdio el ojo fue- / ron tales estos hijos digo hechos / que aquella gente tendra en / memoria todo quanto la vida / les durare en espeçial quatro / o çinco indios amigos que salie- / ron con ellos de los coraçones / que quedaron de *e*sto tam admi- / rados que los tenian mas por cosa / diviña que humana y si co- / mo n*uest*ro campo los topo no los / topara *h*Ubieran de llegar a la / tierra del indio que llamavan

[fol. 148v]
tercera / {rúbrica}

turco do*nde* yban encaminados / y lo pasaran sin rriesgo segu*n* / la buena orden y govierno / llevaba y bien do*c*trinada y / exerçitada en la guerra de / los quales algunos quedaron / en esta villa de culiacan don- / de yo a el presente escribo esta

/ rrelaçion y notiçia adonde / ansi ellos como yo y los demas / que en esta provincia para- / mos no nos *h*a faltado trabajos / apasiguando y sustentando / esta tierra tomando rrebeldes / y Viviendo en p(r)ob*r*eça⁶⁴⁷ y neçe- / sidad y en esta *h*ora mas por estar / la tierra mas p(r)ob*r*e y alcança- / da que nunca lo fue {rúbrica}

Capitulo o*c*tavo en que se / que

[fol. 149r]
149
parte

quentan algunas cosas admi- / rables que se Vieron en los / llanos con la façion⁶⁴⁸ de los / toros {rúbrica}

no ser⁶⁴⁹ misterio calle y dicimu- / le en la segunda parte de *e*s- / te libro en el capitulo septimo / que habla de los llanos las co- / sas de que hare mençion en / este capitulo particular adon- / de se hallase todo junto pues / eran cosas señaladas y no vis- / tas en otras partes y atreVome / a las escrebir porque escribo / en tiempo que son *h*oy Vivos mu- / chos hombres que lo Vieron y / haran Verdadera mi escri- / (p)tura quien podra cre*e*r que / caminando por aquellos

[fol. 149v]
tercera / {rúbrica}

llanos mill cavallos y quinien- / tas vacas de las nuestras y mas / de çinco mill carneros y oVe- / jas y mas de mill y quinien- / tas personas de los amigos y / serviçio que acabando de pa- / sar no dexaban mas rrastro / que si nunca por alli *h*Ubieran / pasado nadie tanto que era / menester haçer montones / de guesos y boñigas de vacas / a trechos para que la rreta- / guardia guiase tras del can- / po y no se perdiesen la yerba / aunque menuda en pisan- / dola se en- / hiestava tam lim- / pia y derecha como de antes / lo estaba {rúbrica}

otra cosa que se hallo a la ori- / lla de Una laguna de sal a la / par

[fol. 150r]

150

parte / {rúbrica}

parte del sur Un grande ayun- / tamiento de guesos de vacas / que tenia de largo Un tiro de / ballesta o muy poquito menos / y de esto⁶⁵⁰ casi dos estados en par- / tes y en ancho tres braças y mas / en parte donde no *h*ay gente / que lo pudiese haçer lo que de / ello se entendio fue que con / la rresaca que debe de ha- / çer el lago o laguna en tiem- / po de nortes los *h*a juntado de / el ganado que muere dentro / en la laguna que de viejo y / flaco entrando no puede salir / lo que se *h*a de notar es que nume- / ro de ganado seria menester pa- / ra tanta osamenta {rúbrica}

pues querer contar la façion / de los toros tambien es de ad-

[fol. 150v]

terçera / {rúbrica}

mirar que ningun cavallo *h*Ubo / a los principios que los Viese de / cara que no huyese de su Vis- / ta porque ellos tienen el rros- / tro ancho y corto de ojo a ojo / dos palmos de frente los ojos sa- / lidos por el lado que yendo / huyendo Ven a quien los si- / gue tienen barbas como cabro- / nes muy grandes quando hu- / yen llevan la cabeça baxa / la barba arrastrando por el / suelo del medio cuerpo para / atras son señidos el pelo muy / merino como de ovejas muy / finas y de la sinta⁶⁵¹ para adelan- / te el pelo muy largo de faicion / de leon rraspante⁶⁵² y Una gra*n* / corcoVa mayor que de came- / llo los cuernos cortos y gordos / que

[fol. 151r]

151

parte / {rúbrica}

que se descubren poco por cima / del pelo mudan el pelo de / medio cuerpo atras por mayo en / Un Vellon y que dan perfectos / leones para mudarse arrima*n* / a algunos arboles pequeños / que *h*ay en algunas barranqui- / llas y alli se rre- friegan hasta / que dexar el Vellon como la / culebra el pel*l*ejo

tienen la cola / corta y un pequeño *h*ysopo a / el cabo llevanla quando co- / rren alta a manera de alacra*n* / es cosa de Ver que quando son / beçerricos son bermejos y de / la manera de los nuestros y / con el tiempo y la edad se mu- / dan en color y faiçion {rúbrica}

*h*ay otra cosa que todos los toros / que se mataron tenian a la o-

[fol. 151v]

tercera / {rúbrica}

reja isquierda hendida tenien- / dolas sanas quando chiquitos / este fue Un secreto que no se / pudo alcançar la causa de / ello de la lana segun la fi- / nesa se harian buenos pa- / ños aunque no de colores por / ser ella de color de buriel {rúbrica}

otra cosa es de notar que an- / dan los toros sin Vacas en tan- / to numero que no *h*ay quien / los pueda numerar y tam a- / partados de las vacas que des- / de donde començamos a Ver / toros Jasta adonde comença- / mos a Ver vacas *h*avia mas / de quarenta le*g*uas y la tie- / rra adonde andaban era tan / llana y esconbrada que por do- / quiera que los mirasen se V*e*ia / el

[fol. 152r]

152

parte / {rúbrica}

el çielo por entre las piernas de / suerte que si estaban algo lejos / pareçian escombrados pinos que / Juntaban las copas por lo alto / y si Un solo toro estaba pareçia / quatro pinos y por serca que estu- / Viese no se podia mirando por / encima Ver tierra de la otra par- / te causaba todo esto ser la tierra / tam rredonda que doquiera que / Un hombre se ponia pareçia que / estaba en la cumbre y v*e*ia el / çielo a el rrededor de si a tiro de ba- / llesta y por poca cosa que se le po- / nia delante le quitaba la vis- / ta de la tierra {rúbrica}

otras cosas se Vieron que por no / ser de tanta calidad no las es- / cribo ni hago de ellas minçion / aunque no parece es de callar

[fol. 152v]
tercera / {rúbrica}

el tener como tienen en Vene- / raçion en algunas partes de / los poblados de altos la señal / de la cruz porque en acuco / en Una fuente que estaba en / lo llano tenian Una cruz de / dos palmos de alto de gordor de Un dedo hecha de palo con / su peña de Una vara de qua- / dro y muchos palitos adorna- / dos de plumas a el rrededor / y muchas flores secas desme- / nuçadas {rúbrica}

{Cruz entre los Indios} en tutahaco en Un sepulcro / fuera del pueblo parecia haber- / se enterrado en el frescamen- / te alguien estava otra cruz / a la cabeçera de dos palitos a- / tados con hilo de algodon y / flores desmenusadas secas yo / digo que a mi pareçer por / al

[fol. 153r]
153
parte / {rúbrica}

alguna via tienen alguna lun- / bre de cruz de c(h)risto nuestro / rredentor y podria ser por la / via de la india de donde ellos pro- / çeden {rúbrica}

Capitulo nono que trata el / rrumbo que lleVo el campo y / como se podria yr a buscar o- / tra via que mas derecha fuese / habiendo de Volver aquella tie- / rra {rúbrica}

mucho quisiera yo agora que / para dar a entender lo que quie- / ro deçir hUbiera en mi alguna / parte de cosmografia o Jume- / tria⁶⁵³ para que pudiera tante- / ar o compasar la Ventaja que / puede haber y hay si otra vez sa- / liesen de la nueVa españa gen- / tes en demanda de aquella

[fol. 153v]
tercera / {rúbrica}

tierra en yr alla por el rriñon / de la tierra o seguir el camino / que el campo lleVo pero ayu- / dandome la graçia del señor / dire lo que alcanso dandolo a / entender lo mejor que a mi se- / a posible {rúbrica}

ya me pareçe que se tiene enten- / dido que el portugues campo / fue el soldado que se escapo qu- / ando los de quivira mataron / a fray juan de padilla el qual / vino a salir a la nueVa espa- / ña por panuco habiendo anda- / do por la tierra de los llanos has- / ta que vino atraVesar la cor- / dillera de la mar del norte / dexando siempre la tierra que / descubrio don fernando de / soto sobre mano isquierda por- / que este hombre nunca Vio / el

[fol. 154r]
154
parte / {rúbrica}

el rrio del espiritu santo y quan- / do Vino acabar de atra- / Vesar la cordillera de la mar del / norte cayo sobre panuco de / manera que si no se pusiera / a demandar por la mar del / norte hUbiera de salir por la co- / marca de la marca o tierra / de los sacatecas de que ya a- / gora se tiene lumbre⁶⁵⁴ {rúbrica}

y para haber de Volver en de- / manda de quivira seria a- / quella via harto mejor y mas / derecha pues hay guias en la / nueVa españa de las que Vini- / eron con el portugues aun- / que digo que seria mejor y / mas derecho por la tierra de / los guachichiles arrimandose / siempre a la cordillera de

[fol. 154v]
tercera / {rúbrica}

la mar del sur porque es mas / poblada y habria bastimento / porque engolfarse en la tie- / rra llana seria perderse por / la gran anchura que tiene / y ser esteril de comidas aun- / que sea Verdad que dando en / las vacas no se pasaria mu- / cha necesidad y esto es sola- / mente para yr en deman- / da de quivira y de aque- / llos pueblos que decia el in- / dio que llamavan turco por- / que yr por donde fue el cam- / po de francisco vasques coronado / es grandissimo rrodeo porque / salen de mexico a el ponien- / te siento y diez leguas y des- / pues a el nordeste çien le- / guas y a el norte docientas y / sin- / quenta y todo esto es hasta / los

[fol. 155r]
155
parte / {rúbrica}

los barrancos de las vacas y con / *h*aber andado ocho*ç*ientas
y sin- / quenta leguas por rrumbo de- / recho no se *h*an
desViado de / mexico quatrosientas leguas / si es querer yr a
la tierra de ti- / guex para desde alli VolVer / a el poniente en
demanda de / la tierra de la india *h*ase[655] de lle- / var el
camino que *el* campo lle- / Vo porque aunque se quiera /
tomar otro camino no lo *h*ay que / no da lugar el ancon de
mar / que entra por esta costa aden- / tro hacia el norte sino
es que / se *h*Ubiese de hacer armada / de mar que fuese
atraVesan- / do este ancon de mar a des- / embarcar en el
paraje de / la isla de negros y por alli

[fol. 155v]
tercera / {rúbrica}

entrar la tierra adentro atra- / Vesando la cordillera en busca
/ de la tierra do*nde* pro*ç*eden los de / tiguex o de otras gentes
que / tengan aquella poli*ç*ia por- / que *h*aber de entrar por
tierra / de la florida por la mar del / norte ya se *h*a visto y
conosi- / do que quantas jornadas por / alli se *h*an hecho *h*an
sido infeli*ç*es / y no bien afortunadas allen- / de de que *es* la
tierra de aque- / lla parte llena de cienegas y / ahogadi*ç*a
esteril y la mas ma- / la que calienta el sol sino Van / a
desembarcar pasado el rrio / del espiritu santo como hi*ç*o /
don hernando de soto y con to- / do me afirmo que aunque
/ se pase mucho trabajo es lo me- / jor por la tierra que *h*a ya
anda- / do

[fol. 156r]
156
parte / {rúbrica}

do y se sepan los aguajes porque / se llevarian las cosas nece-
sari- / as con mas fa*ç*ilidad y mas a- / bundosamente y en las
tierras / nuevas los cavallos es lo mas ne- / *ç*esario y lo que
mas ha*ç*e temer / a los enemigos y los que son se- / ñores del

campo tambien es te- / mida el artilleria donde no sa- / ben
el uso de ella y para pobla- /dos como los que fran*c*isco
vasques des- / cubrio fuera buena alguna / pie*ç*a de artilleria
gruesa pa- / ra derribar porque el no lle- / Vo sino versillos
menores y no / hombre ingenioso para que / hi*ç*iese Un
trabuco ni otra maqui- / na que los atemorisas*e lo* qu- / al es
muy necesario {rúbrica}

digo pues que con la lunbre

[fol. 156v]
tercera / {rúbrica}

que el dia de *h*oy se tiene de los / rrumbos que *h*an corrido
los na- / vios por esta costa de la mar / del sur *h*an andado
descubrie*n*- / do por esta parte de ponie*n*- / te y lo que se
sabe de la mar / del norte hacia la nuruega / que *es* la costa
de la florida a- / rriba los que agora entrasen / a descubrir por
donde fran*c*isco / vasques entro y se hallasen en / tierra de
*ç*ibola o de tiguex bi- / en sabrian a que parte *havian* / de yr
en demanda de la tie- / rra que *el* marques del valle / don
hernando cortes busca- / ba y la Vuelta que da el ancon / del
ti*ç*on para tomar el rru- / mbo Verdadero y esto bas- / tara
para dar fin a nues- / tra

[fol. 157r]
157
parte / {rúbrica}

tra rrela*ç*ion en todo lo demas / proVea aquel poderoso señor
/ de todas las cosas dios omni- / potente que *el* sabe el como
/ y quando estas tierras seran / descubiertas y para quien /
esta guardada esta buena / ventura {rúbrica}

laus deo / {rúbrica}

acabose de tresladar sabado / a veinte y seis de o*c*tubre / de
mill y quinientos y nove*n*- / ta y seis anos en sevilla / {rúbrica}

[fol. 157v] [blank]

Document 29

The Relación del Suceso (Anonymous Narrative), 1540s

AGI, Patronato, 20, N.5, R.8

Introduction

The "Relación del Suceso" ("report of the outcome") is second in the bundle of documents in the Archivo General de Indias that also includes Juan Jaramillo's narrative (Document 30) and the "Traslado de las Nuevas" (Document 22). Like the Traslado, the author of the Relación is not known with any certainty, although he was among the advance guard that made first contact with Cíbola, and he also participated in Hernando de Alvarado's reconnaissance to the bison plains in the late summer of 1540 and the captain general's march to Quivira in 1541.[1] The author displays knowledge of when and to whom Vázquez de Coronado sent messages and when and from whom he received reports. This suggests someone involved directly in the processing of such communications. Certainly the captain general's secretary, Hernando Bermejo, or a scribal assistant of his cannot be ruled out as author of the Relación del Suceso. He certainly would have had the necessary literary skill and would have been privy to the information about travel distances and latitude measurements now discussed in detail.

More than any other known Coronado expedition document, the Relación del Suceso devotes significant and consistent attention to distances and latitude measurements. It is the most geographically oriented of the surviving documents of the expedition. On 19 occasions the author provides information on the travel distances along segments of the expedition's route (in the process covering its entirety). He relates data such as that the valley of Los Corazones lies halfway between Cíbola and the valley of Culiacán, 150 leagues each way.[2] Four times the author reports latitude readings: for Cíbola, Quivira, a river (either at Tiguex or in Quivira), and the point where the northward route to Cíbola made a decided long dogleg to the northeast.[3] He also records the general bearing of the two major segments of the route from Culiacán to Cíbola and the direction of flow of the Río de Tiguex and of an unnamed river at the beginning of the bison plains.[4]

Assuming that the author of the Relación was reporting distances in the *legua legal,* or old league of Burgos, 2.63 miles in length (as he seems to be), then those distances seem quite accurate, within a margin of error of 10 to 15 percent.[5] For example, the Relación states that it is 300 leagues from Culiacán to Cíbola. In *leguas legales* this would be about 790 miles, in comparison with the straight-line modern map distance of about 730 miles. The distance between Tiguex and the *barrancas* reached by the expedition during the early summer of 1541 is given as 100 leagues to the east and 50 to the southeast.[6] On the modern map that would place the *barrancas* in the vicinity of Lubbock, Texas, uncannily close to the archaeologically located campsite of the expedition situated in southern Floyd County, only about 35 miles northeast of Lubbock.[7] A third example is even more remarkable. The Relación lists the distance from Acuco (Acoma Pueblo, New Mexico) to the Río de Tiguex (the Rio Grande in the immediate vicinity of Albuquerque, New Mexico) as 20 leagues, the equivalent of about 53 miles, which happens to match the modern straight-line map distance.[8]

It is worth noting in this regard that the distance of 150 leagues reported in the Relación from Culiacán to Los Corazones, when converted to miles (395) and applied as a straight line to the modern map, falls nearly exactly at Ures, Sonora, the location most frequently suggested for Corazones.

Such attention to and accuracy of distances traversed by the expedition raises the possibility that the author of the Relación was one of the two men who were assigned to keep track of the daily distances covered, one by making an estimate, the other by actually counting his steps.[9] Unfortunately, the identity of neither of those persons is known, but one of them certainly could have been the secretary.

The document called the "Relación de Suceso" is assuredly a sixteenth-century copy of the original report, a copy perhaps made for Juan Páez de Castro, royal chronicler to Carlos V.[10] Its status as a copy is shown by two circumstances, both highly unusual in an original document as short as this one, unless it was written for publication. First, the document is titled. Most titles of such manuscript documents are products of the copying process, to allow rapid location of the document within a collection or archive. Second, the title is in the same sixteenth-century hand as the text, which indicates that the title was not added to an original document but was an element of the composition of this version. Moreover, the text seems to begin after the events it recounts are already under way, in the midst of the action, as though it is an excerpt from a larger document, perhaps a letter. All of these facts point to the document's being a copy more or less contemporaneous with the original.

That the surviving document is a copy, not the original, may be relevant in accounting for what appears to be a rare error in a distance number cited by the author. The Relación states, "The [first is] two hundred and forty leagues [from Culiacán] to the north. This is as far as thirty-four and a half degrees [north latitude]. And from there to Cíbola, [it is] to the northeast."[11] Shortly before this we have been told that the total distance from Culiacán to Cíbola is 300 leagues,

meaning that from the dogleg to Cíbola was 60 leagues. Pedro de Nájera and Marcos de Niza agree, however, that it was 80 leagues from Chichilticale to Cíbola, requiring 15 long days of travel, and Juan Jaramillo records that Chichilticale was two days of travel (that is, 10 to 12 leagues) toward Cíbola from the dogleg point.[12] All this indicates that the dogleg, according to these three expeditionaries, was situated 90 leagues or so from Cíbola, rather than the 60 implied by the Relación del Suceso. If the original Relación text gave the distance from Culiacán to the dogleg as 210 leagues in arabic numerals and the copyist read the "1" as a "4" (an easy and common error in reading sixteenth-century numerals, even for sixteenth-century *escribanos*), then all sources would be in essential agreement.[13]

There is a circuitous way to verify the copyist's error in this case. The Relación gives the latitude of the point where the dogleg occurred as 34.5 degrees north.[14] Like virtually all other latitude readings of the day, this one is probably badly in error. But the direction of the error can be determined and its size estimated. Two known locations for which the Relación also provides latitude readings are Cíbola (37 degrees) and Quivira (40 degrees).[15] Today these places are widely and with good reason thought to be Hawikku (just short of 35 degrees) and Rice County, Kansas (about 38.5 degrees), respectively. Thus, it appears that the latitude figures given in the Relación are consistently 1.5 to 2.0 degrees too high. If that holds true for the location of the route's dogleg, then it must actually have lain at about 32.0 to 32.5 degrees north. That would place the expedition's right-hand, or eastward, turn along the San Pedro River between about Benson and Redington, Arizona. Benson lies some 214 straight-line miles, 82 *leguas legales,* from Hawikku, which would be much more consonant with the figures from the remaining expedition documents. We therefore suppose that the figure of 240 leagues quoted earlier must be a copyist's error for 210 leagues.

Despite paying particular attention to certain geographical details, the author of the Relación ignores many others. He makes almost no mention of topography and, with the exception of bison, describes none of the native flora and fauna of Tierra Nueva. Description of rocks, minerals, and soils is left out, too. His geographical information would permit the creation of only a rudimentary map. The Relación cannot be regarded as a full-fledged *derrotero*, or detailed pilot's book. Such books include much more detailed descriptions of the land and are often accompanied by sketches.[16] To return to Cíbola, Quivira, the Río de Tiguex, and other places in the north, the reader of the Relación would still have required human guides.

Beyond the author's evident concern for reporting quantitative data regarding locations and distances, his other goal seems to be to portray briefly the various peoples encountered by the expedition and their principal products. This is in keeping with the then still-popular model for travel reports that had been provided by Marco Polo and Rustichello's thirteenth-century composition of *The Travels*.[17] Further, such a focus is consistent with the leading motivation behind the expedition, to secure comfortable *encomiendas* of native peoples.

Thus, the author makes observations about the cultural practices of some of the peoples encountered by the expedition that can be correlated with more modern ethnographic information. As one example, he refers to "little painted sticks, feathers" that the people of Cíbola placed at springs and other water sources.[18] These were prayer plumes, which have been described by many ethnologists who have worked among the Zunis, including Frank Hamilton Cushing and Matilda Coxe Stevenson in the late 1800s. Stevenson reported the Zuni name for these offerings as *te'likinawe*.[19] In addition, the author of the Relación tells of the production of sun-dried jerky by Querechos and Teyas, dog nomads of the southern Great Plains, where the practice was still in evidence until the late nineteenth century.[20]

In 1870 Joaquín Pacheco and Francisco de Cárdenas published a very poor transcription of the Relación del Suceso that is riddled with errors and omissions, even more than is usual for this unfortunate series.[21] Sadly, Carmen de Mora, not suspecting this transcription's poor quality, republished it in 1992.[22] In preparing his 1896 translation into English, George Winship, perhaps aware of the dismal state of the Pacheco and Cárdenas transcription, used instead the nineteenth-century printed version of one made in the eighteenth century by the royal chronicler Juan Bautista Muñoz that is now curated in the Archivo Histórico Nacional in Madrid. It is a much better rendition.[23] Besides Winship's translation, there exists another from 1940 done by George Hammond and Agapito Rey.[24] Although they claimed to have made their translation from a photographic copy of the AGI document, it is difficult to see how, in that case, they could have made the error of substituting "sur" for "sueste" on folio 4r, just as Pacheco and Cárdenas did but which Muñoz did not. We have consulted all of these earlier editions in vetting the new translation and transcription that follow.

[1r]

Report of the outcome of the expedition which Francisco Vázquez made in reconnaissance of Cíbola.

{+} When the expedition had reached the valley of Culiacán, because of the poor expectations that were held about Cíbola[25] and [because] (according to the statement of Melchior Díaz, who had just returned from examining it) food supplies were scarce along the route, Francisco Vázquez divided and split the expedition.[26] He took eighty horsemen, twenty-five footmen,[27] and part of the artillery and departed from Culiacán, leaving the rest of the troop with don Tristán de Arellano and an order that it leave twenty days after he [did].[28]

{+} When [Arellano] had arrived, as he did, in the valley of Los Corazones,[29] he was to wait there for [Vázquez de Coronado's] letter, which would [come] after he had reached Cíbola and had seen what it was.[30] And he did so. This valley of Los Corazones is situated a hundred and fifty leagues from the valley of Culiacán and the same distance from Cíbola.[31]

{+} This whole route is settled up to fifty leagues from Cíbola, although [the people] are away from the trail in some places.[32] The population is all [of] one type of people. [This can be said] because their houses are all made of cane mats and some among them [have] low, flat roofs. They all have corn, even though not much, and in some places very little. They have melons and beans. The best of all the settled places is a valley they call Señora, which is ten leagues farther on from Los Corazones.[33] A [Spanish] *villa* was later settled there. Among these [people] there is some cotton. What they dress in most is deerskins.

{+} Francisco Vázquez traveled through this entire [region].[34] Because the planted crops were [still] young, there was no corn on the entire route,[35] except that [the members of the expedition] got[36] a little from this valley of Señora. With what [the expedition] took along from Culiacán, it had enough for eighty days. On the seventy-third [day] we reached Cíbola,[37] although with extreme difficulty, the loss of many horses, and the deaths of some Indians.[38] When we saw [Cíbola] [the difficulties] doubled for us, even though we found more than enough corn. [Along] this whole route we found the natives at peace.

{+} The day we arrived at the first *pueblo* [of Cíbola], some of them came out against us in war, and the rest stayed fortified in the *pueblo*. [1v] It was not possible to conclude peace with them, although [peace] was eagerly sought. For this reason attacking them was unavoidable. When some of them had died, the rest immediately withdrew to the *pueblo*, which was then besieged and attacked to gain entry. Because of the great injury they were doing to us from the flat roofs, we were compelled to draw back.[39] From a distance the artillery and arquebuses began to do them harm.[40] That afternoon they surrendered. Francisco Vázquez ended up badly injured by stones and I am even sure he would have died there[41] if it were not for the *maestre de campo*, don García López de Cárdenas, who went to his aid.[42] As soon as the Indians surrendered, they abandoned the *pueblo* and went to the other *pueblos*. Because they left their houses to us, we took up quarters in them.

{+} Father fray Marcos[43] had understood or made [it] understood that the [entire] area and environs in which the seven *pueblos* are situated was a single *pueblo*, which he was calling El Cíbola. This entire settlement and [its] environs

[are] called Cíbola. The *pueblos* comprise three hundred, two hundred, and a hundred and fifty households.[44] [In] some [of them] the buildings of the *pueblos* are joined, although in some *pueblos* they are separated into two or three sections. For the most part, however, [the buildings] are joined. Their patios [are] interior [to those sections], and in them [are] their *estufas* for winter. Outside the *pueblos* they have the [*estufas*] for summer. The buildings are of two and three stories; their walls are made of stone and mud, and some [are] walls of mud alone.[45] In many places the *pueblos* present defensive walls formed by the buildings. For Indians, [the *pueblos*] consist of exceedingly good buildings, particularly for these [Indians], who are brutish and uncivilized, except in regard to their buildings.[46]

{+} The food they have is a great amount of corn, beans, melons, and some [turkeys] like the ones in [the Ciudad de] México. They keep these [turkeys] more for their plumage than to eat, because they make long robes out of it. [That is] because they have no cotton. They dress in *mantas* made of henequen,[47] deer hides, and some [made] of [bison hides].

{+} The ceremonies and sacrifices they have involve some idols, but mostly what they employ in that role is water, to which they offer some [2r] little painted sticks, feathers, and yellow powder from flowers.[48] This occurs most commonly at the springs. They also offer some turquoises they have, although inferior [ones].

{+} From this valley of Culiacán as far as Cíbola [the route] runs on two bearings. The [first is] two hundred and forty leagues to the north. This is as far as thirty-four and a half degrees [north latitude]. And from there to Cíbola, [it is] to the northeast.[49] This is at just short of thirty-seven degrees.[50]

{+} When an interpreter had been obtained from the natives of Cíbola, they told about what [is] farther on. [They said] there was a settled area to the west. Francisco Vázquez immediately sent don Pedro de Tovar to examine it. He found it to consist of seven more *pueblos* which [are] called the *provincia* of Tuzan.[51] It is thirty-five leagues to the west.[52] The *pueblos* are a little better[53] than those of Cíbola. Regarding the rest, the food and everything, they are of one type, except that these [Indians of Tuzan] harvest cotton.[54]

While don Pedro de Tovar went to see this [place],

Francisco Vázquez dispatched messengers to the viceroy with a report about what had happened up to that point.[55] He sent an order with these same [messengers] [to deliver] on the way to don Tristán (who, as I have said, was at Los Corazones). [Namely, that he was] to travel on to Cíbola. And he was to leave a town established in the valley of Señora, which he did.[56] In it he left eighty horsemen. All of them, to a horse and man, [were] very weak. And with them [he left] Melchior Díaz as captain and *alcalde mayor*, because Francisco Vázquez had arranged it thus. He ordered [Díaz] to travel from there with half the troop to reconnoiter toward the west.

This he did and traveled a hundred and fifty leagues, as far as the river which Hernando de Alarcón had entered by sea and called Buena Guía.[57] The settlement[s] and people who exist along this route are nearly the same as those of Los Corazones, except [along] the river and its environs.[58] They are a most capable people and have more corn, although the houses they live in are huts like pigsties, nearly [entirely] underground. The roof[s] [are] made of thatch, without any order.

They say this river is large. [The Díaz party] reached it thirty leagues from the coast. Alarcón had ascended this far and as many [leagues] more upstream with his boats two months before they arrived.[59] In this area the river flows from north to south.

Melchior Díaz went five or six days' journey farther to the west. [2v] From there he returned because he found neither water nor grass. Instead, [he found] many sand dunes. On the way back, he returned along the river and in its vicinity. He engaged in some fighting, because when he crossed the river [the Indians] tried to take advantage of them. On the return trip Melchior Díaz died because of a mishap, since he was killed while throwing a lance at a dog.[60]

{+} Don Pedro de Tovar returned [to Cíbola]. As soon as he had been given a report about those *pueblos*, [Vázquez de Coronado] dispatched the *maestre de campo*, don García López de Cárdenas, along the same route don Pedro had come [on].[61] [He ordered López de Cárdenas] to go on beyond that *provincia* of Tuzan toward the west.[62] He designated a period of eighty days for the outbound and return journeys and the reconnaissance. [López de Cárdenas] went and passed beyond Tuzan with native guides, who were saying there was a settled area farther on, although distant.

[Having] traveled fifty leagues from Tuzan toward the west and eighty from Cíbola, he found a gorge of a river.[63] There, at one place and another, it was impossible to find a way down by horse, or even on foot. [That is], except at one very difficult place, by which there was a descent of nearly two leagues. The gorge was so vertical [and] rocky that they could hardly see the river. Although, according to what [the natives] say, it is as large and larger than the one in Sevilla,[64] from above it looked like a stream. [It was so vertical and rocky] that although a way [down] was sought with the utmost diligence and in many places, none was found. [The people in López de Cárdenas's party] were at [this gorge] an inordinate number of days.[65] [This was] with an extreme shortage of water, which they did not find. They could not avail themselves of [water] from the river even though they saw it. For this reason don García López was forced to return to [a place] where they found [water]. This river was coming from the northeast and turned to the south-southwest, so that without doubt it is the one which Melchior Díaz reached.[66]

{+} As soon as Francisco Vázquez had dispatched don García López on this reconnaissance, he sent Hernando de Alvarado from there four days later to reconnoiter the way east.[67] [Alvarado] departed and found a steep, rugged hill of rock and a *pueblo* on top thirty leagues from Cíbola.[68] [It is] the strongest place ever seen in the world. In their language [the natives] call it Acuco. Father fray [3r] Marcos called it the *reino* of Hacus. They came out to us in peace, although they well could have refused to do it[69] and could have stayed on their rugged rock without our being able to harm them. They gave us cotton *mantas*, [bison] and deer hides, turquoises, [turkeys], and the rest of the food[s] they have. [These are] the same as in Cíbola.

{+} Twenty leagues to the east of this rugged rock we found a well-settled river which flows north and south.[70] It probably has seventy *pueblos* in all, more or less, [counting both] small and large [ones].[71] Their design [is] like those of Cíbola, except that they are nearly all made of well-built mud walls. The food [includes] neither more nor fewer [items than at Cíbola]. These [people] harvest cotton, I

mean those who live near the river.[72] The rest do not. Here there was much corn. They are not people who have *tiánguez* [markets].[73] This settled area is situated along fifty leagues of this river, north [to] south, and off to the sides fifteen or twenty leagues.[74] Some *pueblos* [are] on one side [of the river] and [others are on] the other.

This river arises at the end of the settled area toward the north, from the foothills of those jagged mountains.[75] A *pueblo* is located there, large and different from the others. It is called Yuraba. It is arranged as a settlement in this way: it has eighteen sections. Each one occupies as much space as two *solares* [Spanish house sites]. The buildings abut each other [and] are of five and six stories, three made of mud walls and two or three made of thin wooden walls. [The buildings] get narrower as they rise. On the exterior, on the levels made of mud walls, *portales* [covered passages] made of wood extend out all the way around on each [level], one above the other. Because they are in the mountains, the people in this *pueblo* do not harvest cotton or raise [turkeys]. They dress only in [bison] and deer hides. It is the *pueblo* [with] the most people in all that land. We concluded there would be fifteen thousand souls in it.[76]

Of the other sort of *pueblos*, there is one, better and stronger than all [the rest], which is called Cicuique.[77] It is four and five stories high and has eight large patios, each one with its *portal*. There are excellent buildings in it. [The natives of Cicuique] neither harvest cotton nor keep [turkeys], because [the pueblo] is fifteen or twenty leagues to the east away from the river.

[3v] After having made a report to Francisco Vázquez about this river, [Alvarado] reached the plains where the [bison] are.[78] He continued onto those plains. At the beginning of them he found a small river which flows to the southeast.[79] After four days' journey he found the [bison], which are the most extraordinary kind of animal that has been seen or read [about]. He followed this river a hundred leagues, each day finding more [bison].[80] We availed ourselves of them [for meat], although at first [it was] at the horses' peril, until we had experience.[81] There is such a quantity [of bison] that I do not know what I might compare [them] to, except the fish in the sea. [I say this] because both on this trip and on the one the entire expedition subse-

quently made, going to Quivira, there were so many [bison] that many times we were traveling right through the middle of them.[82] Even though we may have wanted to go another way, we could not, because the countryside was covered with them.

The meat of [the bison] is as good as that of the [cattle] of Castilla and some were even saying [it was] better. The bulls are large and ferocious, although they do not chase [one] much. They have wicked horns, however, and [with] a sudden charge they deliver a strong assault. Making an effective rush, they killed some of our horses and wounded many. We found that the best weapon[s] for exploiting them [are] pole weapon[s] for hurling at them and the arquebus for when [they are] standing still.

{+} When Hernando de Alvarado had returned from these plains to the river that is called Tiguex, he found the *maestre de campo*, don García López de Cárdenas, preparing quarters for the whole expedition, which was coming there. And it arrived soon afterward.[83] Even though this entire population [of Tiguex] had come out to Hernando de Alvarado in peace, [when] the whole troop came, part of [the native people] rose up in arms. The [places which took up arms] were twelve *pueblos* which were located together. One night they killed forty of our horses and mules which were roaming free in the countryside.[84] [And] they fortified themselves in their *pueblos*.

{+} Immediately, war was waged against them. The first [to engage them] was don García López. [4r] He took [one *pueblo*] and inflicted punishment on many of them.[85] When the rest [of the Tiguex people] had seen this they abandoned their *pueblos*, except for two. One [was] the strongest of them all, at which the expedition spent two months.[86] As soon as we besieged them,[87] in a single day we gained entry and occupied part of the flat roof. But because there were many wounded and it was so hazardous to maintain ourselves [there], [López de Cárdenas] was forced to abandon it. Even though once more during this same time we again gained entry, in the end it could not be completely overrun. Because of this [the *pueblo*] was besieged for that much time [two months]. We overcame them because of thirst. They lasted as long as they did because it snowed twice for them just as they were about to surrender. Finally

we overcame them, and many died because they went away [fled] at night.

{+} From some Indians who were found at this *pueblo* of Cicuique[88] Francisco Vázquez obtained a report which, if it were true, was [about] the richest thing that has been found in the Indies. The Indian who provided the information and report was from three hundred leagues east of this river, from a *pueblo* he called Haraee.[89] He was in the habit of providing very detailed information about what he was saying, as if it were true and he had seen it. Afterward it appeared certain, however, to have been the devil who was speaking through him. Francisco Vázquez and all the rest of us gave him a great deal of credence.

Although he was counseled by some *caballeros* not to move the whole expedition farther,[90] but to dispatch a captain to find out what [Haraee] was, he refused. Instead, [he chose] to take it all and even to send don Pedro de Tovar to Los Corazones for half the people who were in that *villa*.

Thus, he departed with the whole expedition. When they had traveled a hundred and fifty leagues, one hundred to the east and fifty to the southeast,[91] and with the Indian now failing to produce what he had told about (namely, that there was a settlement there and corn so that they could travel farther), [Vázquez de Coronado] cross-examined the other two guides[92] about how that was. One of them declared that what the Indian was saying was a lie, except that there was a *provincia* called [4v] Quivira and that there were corn and buildings made of thatch. It was very far, though, because they had taken us away from the [right] route.

When this was understood by Francisco Vázquez and he saw the scant food supplies he had, he decided, with the consent of the captains,[93] to go onward with thirty of the best and most well-equipped [men] and that the [remainder of the] expedition was to return to the Río [de Tiguex]. Thus it was done. At that time, two days before this, it had happened that don García López's horse fell with him and his arm was dislocated.[94] Because of this he was greatly incapacitated. On this account don Tristán de Arellano returned to the river with the [main body of the] expedition.

En route they endured extreme hardship because nearly everyone [had] nothing more than meat to eat, and [that] was causing many [people] harm. A multitude of [bison] cows and bulls was being killed. There were days when they brought sixty and seventy head into camp. It was necessary to go hunting every day. Because of that and not eating corn in all this time the horses were suffering badly.

{+} When Francisco Vázquez had set out across those plains in search of Quivira, [it was] more on account of the information which we had been given along the Río [de Tiguex] than because of [any] credence we then gave the guide. After many days following the compass ourselves,[95] God was pleased that after thirty days' journey we found the Río de Quivira. Its crossing is thirty leagues before the settlement.[96] There [at the crossing] we found people[97] who were hunting, [some] of the natives of Quivira themselves. {Quivira}

{+} What there is in Quivira is a very brutish people without the least [indication of] civilization, in their houses or anything else.[98] [Their houses] are made of thatch like Tarascan shelters.[99] In some *pueblos* [composed of] houses close together [there are] about two hundred households. They have corn, beans, and squash. They do not have cotton or [turkeys], nor do they make the bread that is baked on a *comal* [stone griddle];[100] rather, [it is baked] under the ashes.

Francisco Vázquez went twenty-five leagues into this settled area, to where he obtained information about what [was] farther on.[101] They said that the plains ended, that downriver there were people who did not plant [but] who sustained themselves by hunting.

[5r] {+} They also provided information about two other large *pueblos*, one of which was called Tareque and the other Arae. Tareque[102] had houses made of thatch, and [in] Arae some of it was thatch and the rest of the houses [were] made of hide. There was copper in this place.[103] They said it was farther on, close to this *pueblo* of Arae. The Indian had told us that there was more, according to the excellent signs he made about it. Here, [though], we found neither indications of it nor information about it.

Francisco Vázquez returned from here to the Río de Tiguex, where he found the [main body of the] expedition. We[104] returned by a more direct route, because on the route we took going out we traveled three hundred and thirty leagues,[105] and by the [way] we returned there were no more

than two hundred.[106] Quivira is at forty degrees [north latitude], and the river [is] at thirty-six.[107]

On these plains it is as though one is traveling by sea, because there are no roads except [those made] by [bison]. Because it is so flat and without either mountain range or hillock, it was so dangerous a route that if one got separated from the expedition, on losing sight of it one became lost. {scribal highlighting} In this way one man was lost by us[108] and others, going out to hunt, traveled three and four days lost on these plains.

Two types of people travel with these [bison]; one is called Querechos and the other, Teyas.[109] They are very capable and [are] painted [or tattooed and are] enemies of one another. They do not have other husbandry or fixed location other than traveling with the [bison], of which they kill all they want. And they dress the hides, with which they clothe themselves and [from which] they make [their] tents. They eat the meat, even sometimes raw, and they even also drink the blood when they are thirsty. The tents they carry are like a type of *pabellón*.[110] They set them up on some poles which they carry [already] made for that purpose. When they are planted [in the ground], they are probably all tied together at the top.

When they travel from one place to another they carry what they have on a few dogs.[111] They have many of those [dogs] and load them with the tents, poles, and other things. This is made possible because the land is so flat. [The dogs] are used in this by [the Indians] because, as I say, they transport the poles, dragging [them]. What they most revere is the sun.[112] The hide of the tents is dressed on both sides, without hair. They trade their surplus [bison] and deer hides and sun-dried jerky for corn and *mantas* with the natives of the Río [de Tiguex].[113]

[5v] When Francisco Vázquez had arrived at the river where he found the camp, very shortly afterward don Pedro de Tovar came with half the troop from Los Corazones. And don García López de Cárdenas left for [the Ciudad de] México. Besides being very crippled in his arm, he had a permit to go from the viceroy because of the death of his brother.[114] With him went ten or twelve persons there were who were ill. Among them [there was] not a man who was able to fight. [López de Cárdenas] reached the Spanish *villa*[115] and found it burned. Two Spaniards and many

Indians and horses [were] dead.[116] For this reason he returned to the Río [de Tiguex]. He [had] escaped from [the natives of the San Gerónimo area only] with plenty of luck and great effort.

The reason for this destruction was that when don Pedro had departed and left forty men there, half of them mutinied and fled. The Indians, remembering the abuse they had received, attacked them one night. Because of their negligence and carelessness, [the Indians] routed them, and they returned in flight to Culiacán.

One day during this period, Francisco Vázquez fell while racing a horse, and was incapacitated for many days. When winter had passed, he decided to return [to the Ciudad de México].[117] Even though [others] might say something else, he returned because he was more motivated than anyone [else].[118] Thus we returned all together to Culiacán, from where each one went wherever he wished.[119]

Francisco Vázquez came here to [the Ciudad de] México to give a report to the viceroy. [The viceroy] was not at all happy with his return, although at first he feigned [happiness].[120] He was pleased that Father fray Juan de Padilla (who went to Quivira) had remained there, along with a Spaniard and a Black. And fray Luis, a lay brother [and] very holy person, remained in Cicuique.[121]

Along this river we spent two winters of severe cold, much snow, and such hard frosts that the river froze one night and remained so more than a month. Loaded horses crossed over on top of the ice.[122] The reason for these *pueblos* being this type of settlement is, I believe, the great cold. It is also, however, due in part to the wars they fight against each other.

In that entire land this is what was seen and [about which] information was obtained. That [land] is very barren of fruits and stands of trees. Quivira is the best land,[123] with many savannas, and [it is] not as cold [as Tiguex], even though it is farther north.

[fol. 1r]

{1}

{+} Relaçion del suçeso de la Jornada que Francisco Vazquez hizo En el descubrimiento de çibola

{+} llegado El canpo al Valle de culuacan A causa de la rruyn Esperança / que de çibola se tenia y de los bastimentos ser pocos En el camino / por dicho de melchior diaz que A la sazon VolVio de Verlo Francisco Vazquez / deVidio e partio El canpo El qual tomo ochenta de A caballo / e Veynte e çinco peones e çierta parte de la Artilleria e / partio de culuacan dexando con la demas gente A don tris- / tan de Arellano e mandado partiese Veynte dias despues / de el e llegado que Fuese Al Valle de los coraçones Esperase Ally / su carta que serya despues de llegado A çibola e Visto lo que / Era e A(n)si lo hizo Este Valle de los coraçones Esta / çien(t) e çinquenta leguas del Valle de culuacan e otras / tantas de çibola

{+} todo este camino hAsta çinquenta leguas Antes de çibo- la Es / Poblado AUnque (^en) (h)en algunas partes Esta Apartado / del camino la poblaçion Es toda Una suerte de gente por- / que las casas son todas de petates e alguna Entre ellas / de Açuteas baxas tienen mayz todos AUnque no mucho / Y En Algunas partes muy poco tienen melones e Frisoles / lo mejor de todo lo poblado Es Un Valle que lla- man de señora / que Es diez leguas mas Adelante de los coraçones Adonde / despues se poblo Una Villa tienen Entre Estos AL- / gun Algodon de lo que mas se Visten Es de cueros de Venados

{+} Francisco Vazquez paso por todo esto E A causa de estar las sementeras[124] / pequeñas no hubo mayz En todo El

camino sino Fue de este / Valle de señora que sacaron Un poco e con lo que saco de / culuacan que se cargo para ochenta dias A los setenta / e tres llegamos A çibola AUnque con hArto trabaJo e perdida / de muchos cavallos e muerte de algunos yndios e doblaron- / senos[125] quando la Vimos AUnque hAllamos mayz hArto todo este / camino hAllamos los naturales de paz

{+} El dia que llegamos Al primer pueblo nos salieron de guerra parte / de ellos e los demas quedaban En el pueblo(s) fortalesçido(s) con los

[fol. 1v]

quales no se pudo Acabar AUnque se procuro hArto la paz por lo / qual Fue forçoso rronpellos e muertos Algunos de ellos los / demas luego se rretraxieron Al pueblo El qual se çerco / luego e se Acometio A Entrar e A causa del mucho / daño que nos hazian de las (h)açuteas nos fue forçado rre- tirar- / nos y de Fuera se les començo hazer daño con la Artilleria / e Arcabuzes y Aquella tarde se dieron Francisco Vazquez salio / maltratado de Algunas piedras y AUn tengo por çierto que- / daria Alli si no Fuera por El maestre de canpo don garçi lopez de car- / denas que le socorrio luego que los yndios se dieron des- / mampararon El pueblo e se Fueron A los otros pueblos / e como nos dexaron las casas Aposentamosnos En ellas

{+} El padre Frai marcos hAbia Entendido o dio A Entender / que el çercuito e comarca En que Estan siete pueblos (h)era / Un solo pueblo que llamaba El çibola e toda esta poblazon / e comarca se llama çibola los pueblos son de A trezientas / e dozientas e de A çien(t) e çinquenta casas en Algunos Estan / las casas de los pueblos todas Juntas AUnque En Al-

/ gunos pueblos estan partidos En dos e tres barrios pero / por la mayor parte son juntos y dentro sus patios y En / Ellos sus EstuFas de ynVierno e Fuera de los pueblos / las tienen de Verano las casas son de dos e tres Altos / las paredes de piedra e lodo y Algunas de tapias los / pueblos por muchas partes son casamuro para yndios / son demasiados de buenas casas mayormente para estos / que son bestiales e no tienen otra poliçia sino En las / casas

{+} la comida que tienen Es mucho mayz e Frisoles e me- lones / e Algunas gallinas de las de mexico y estas las tienen / mas para la pluma que para comer porque hazen de ella / pellones A causa que no tienen ningun Algodon e se / V(e)ist(i)en de mantas de henequen e de cueros de Venado / e Algunos de Vaca

{+} los rrytos e sacrefiçios que tienen son Algunos ydolos pero a lo / que mas (h)usan Es A la (h)agua A la qual ofresçen Unos

[fol. 2r]
Palillos pintados e plumas e po(V)lvos Amarillos de Flores y esto / Es lo mas ordinario En las fuentes tanbien ofresçen / Algunas turquesas que las tienen AUnque rruynes

{+} de este El Valle de culuacan hAsta çibola se corre A dos derrotas / las dozientas e quarenta leguas que Es hAsta treynta e qua- / tro grados e medio Al norte y desde Alli A çibola Al nordeste / la qual esta En treynta e siete grados Escasos

{+} tomado lengua de los naturales de çibola de lo de Adelante dix(i)eron / que Al poniente hAbia poblado fran- cisco Vazquez EnVio luego A don / pedro de toVar A Verlo El qual hAllo ser otros siete pueblos / que se llama la proVinçia de tuçan Esta treynta e çinco leguas / Al poniente los pueblos son Algun tanto mayores que los / de çibola y En lo demas En comyda y En todo son de Una / manera salVo que estos coxen Algodon Entretanto que don / pedro de toVar fue A Ver Esto Francisco Vazquez despacho / mensaJeros Al Visorrey con rrelaçion de lo de hAsta Ally / suçedido y EnVio A mandar con Ellos mismos de camino /

A don tristan que como dicho tengo Estaba En los coraçones / que fuese A çibola e dexase poblada Una Villa En el Valle / de señora El qual lo hizo y En ella dexo ochenta de A caballo / todos los de A Un caballo e gente mas Flaca y con Ellos / A melchior diaz por capitan e Alcalde mayor porque A(n)si / le hAbia proVeydo Francisco Vazquez y le mando que desde Alli con / la m(e)ytad de la gente Fuesen A des- cubrir Al poniente / e A(n)si lo hizo y AnduVo çien(t) e çin- quenta leguas hAsta El / rryo En que Entro hernando de Alarcon por la mar El / qual llamo de buena guia y (^El) la poblazon e gente que hay En / este camino (h)es casi como la de los coraçones salVo El rryo / e su comarca que Es gente mas bien dispuesta e tienen / mas mayz AUnque las casas En que ViVen son choças o como / çahurdas casi debaxo la tie- rra la cobyja Es de paja sin / poliçia ninguna Este rryo dizque (h)es grande llegaron A El / treynta leguas de la costa las quales y otras tantas / mas Arryba hAbia s(o)ubido Alarcon con las barcas / dos meses Antes que Ellos llegasen este rrio corre Alli de / norte sur melchior diaz paso çinco o seys jor- nadas Al poniente

[fol. 2v]
De donde se VolVio A causa de no hAllar agua ni yerba sino / muchos medaños de Arena e A la Vuelta que VolVia En el / rryo e su comarca tuVo çierta guerra porque Al pasar / del rryo se quisieron AproVechar de ellos De esta Vuelta / morio melchior Diaz por Un desastre que se mato El mismo / tirando Una lança A Un perro

{+} Vuelto Don pedro de toVar e dada rrelaçion de Aquellos pueblos / luego despacho A don garçi lopez de cardenas maestre de canpo / por El mesmo camyno que hAbia Venido don pedro e que pasa- / se de Aquella proVinça de tuçan Al poniente e para yda / e Vuelta de la Jornada e descubrimien- to le señalo ochenta / Dias de termino de yda e Vuelta El qual Fue e paso / Adelante de tuçan con guias de los natu- rales que / Dezian que hAbia Adelante poblado AUnque lexos / Andadas çinquenta leguas de tuçan Al poniente e ochenta / de çibola hAllo Una barranca de Un rryo que Fue ynposible / por Una parte ni otra hAllarle baxada para ca- ballo / ni AUn para pie sino por Una parte muy trabaxosa / por donde tenia casi dos leguas de baxada Esta- / ba la

barranca tan Acanty(^l)lada de peñas que Apenas / podian
Ver El rio El qual AUnque Es segun dizen / tanto e m*a*s
mayor[126] que *e*l de seVilla de Arriba aparesçia / Un (h)arr(a)*o*yo
por manera que[127] AUnque con *h*Arta deligençia / se busco
pasada e por muchas partes no se *h*allo En la(s) / qual
EstuVieron *h*Artos dias e con mucha nesçesidad / de agua que
no la *h*Allaban e la del rrio no se podian / AproVechar de *e*lla
AUnque la V*e*ian e A Esta causa / le Fue forçado A don garçi
lopez Volverse A donde *h*Allaron / Este rryo Venia del
nordeste e VolVia Al sur sudues- / te por manera que sin Falta
ninguna Es Aquel donde / llego melchior Diaz

{+} luego como Franc*is*co Vazquez despacho A don garçi
lopez A este descubrimi- / ento desde Alli A quatro dias
despacho A *h*Ernando de / AlVarado A descubrir la Via de
l(V)ev(l)ante El qual partio y / A treynta leguas de çibola
*h*Allo Un peñol e Un pueblo En- / çima la cosa mas fuerte
que ser (^de) A Visto En el mundo El / qual Ellos llaman
En su lengua Acuco y El padre frai

[fol. 3r]

marcos le llamaba El rreyno de hacus salieron nos de paz
AUnque / bien pudieran Escusarlo e quedarse En su peñol
sin que / les pudieramos (h)enoJar dieronnos mantas de
Algodon / cueros de Venado e de Vaca e turquesas e gallinas
e la / demas comida que tienen que Es lo que (h)en çibola

{+} Veynte leguas Al leVante de *e*ste peñol *h*Allamos Un rryo
/ que corre norte i sur bien poblado *h*Abra En todo El chicos
/ e grandes setenta pueblos poco(s) mas o menos la manera /
de *e*llos como de los de çibola salVo que son casi todos de
tapias / bien *h*Echas la comida ni mas ni menos Estos coxen
Algodon / Digo los que ViVen çerca del rryo que los demas
(^d) no Aqui / *h*Abia mucho mayz no son gente que tienen
tianguez Esta / Este poblado En çinquenta leguas de norte
sur En / Este rrio e quinze o Veynte leguas Apartado
Algunos / pueblos de *e*l A Una parte y A otra Este rrio nasçe
/ En el cabo de la poblazon Al norte de las *f*Aldas de /
Aquellas sierras Adonde esta Un pueblo e diferente / de los
otros y grande llamase yuraba Esta poblado / de *e*sta manera
tiene Diez e ocho barri*o*s cada Uno / tiene tanto sitio como
dos solares las casas muy jun- / tas (^E) son de çinco e seys

Altos los tres de tapias / e dos e tres de tabique de madera e
Van (Ens)an- / gostando[128] Arriba e por Fuera En los Altos
de tapia / salen En cada Uno su corredorçillo Uno sobre otro
to- / Dos A la rredonda de madera Estos En este pueblo / por
estar En las sierras no coxen Algodon ni crian gally- / nas solo
Visten de cueros de Venado e de Vacas / Es El pueblo de mas
gente de toda Aquella t*i*erra Juz- / gabamos *h*Abrya En el
quinze mill Animas de la / otra manera de pueblos *h*Ay Uno
mayor que todos / muy fuerte que se llama çicuyque Es de
quatro e çinco / Altos tiene ocho patios grandes cada Uno
con su corre- / Dor e *h*Ay En el buenas casas tanpoco coxen
al- / godon ni tienen gallinas porque esta Apartado del rryo

[fol. 3v]

quinze leguas Al leVante llegado a los llanos donde Andan /
las Vacas despues de *h*Aber alVarado *h*Echo rrelaçion / de *e*ste
rrio a Franc*is*co Vazquez paso Adelante A estos llanos / e al
prençipyo de *e*llos *h*Allo Un rrio pequeño que corre / A el
sueste e A quatro Jornadas *h*Allo las Vacas que son / la cosa
mas mo*n*struosa de Animales que se *h*A Visto ni / leydo siguio este rrio çien(t) leguas *h*Allando cada dia mas / Vacas de
las quales nos AproVechabamos AUnque / A los prençipios
*h*Asta que toVimos Esperençia con rryes- / go de caballos *h*Ay
tanta cantida*d* que no se A que lo / conpare sino A pescados
En la mar porque Ansy / de *e*sta Jornada como En la que
despues todo El canpo / hizo yendo A quiVira hubo tantas
que muchas Vezes / (h)ibamos A pasar por medio de *e*llas e
AUnque quisiera- / mos yr por otro cabo no podiamos porque
estaban / los canpos cubiertos de *e*llas Es la carne de *e*llas / tan
buena como de la de castilla y AUn Algunos / dezian que
mejor los toros son grandes e braVos AUn- / que no siguen
mucho pero tienen (^d) malos cuernos y / Un Apreton danle
bueno Arremetiendo bien / mataronnos Algunos caballos e
*h*yrieron muchos / la mejor Arma para AproVecharse de *e*llos
*h*Allamos / que Es Arma EnAstada para (h)arroJarsela e /
Arcabuz para quando esta parado (^la fig)

{+} Vuelto hernando de AlVarado de *e*stos llanos Al rryo que
/ se llama de tiguex *h*Allo Al m*aestr*e de canpo don garçi
lopez de / cardenas *h*Aziendo El Apos(i)ento para todo / El
canpo que Venia Alli e luego Vino y aUnque toda / esta
poblazon *h*Abia salido de paz A *h*Ernando de Al- / Varado

Venida toda la gente parte de ellos se Alçaron / que Fueron
doze pueblos que Estaban Junto e Una noche / nos mataron
quarenta caballos e mulas que Andaban / sueltos Al canpo
hizieronse Fuertes En sus pueblos / Dioseles luego guerra y
El primero fue don garçi lopez

[fol. 4r]
e le tomo e hizo Justiçia de muchos de ellos los demas Visto
Esto / desmanpararon los pueblos salVo dos El Uno El mas
fuerte / de todos sobre El qual EstuVo El canpo dos meses y
AUn- / que luego que les pusimos çerco les Entramos Un dia
e les / tomamos Un pedaço de Açutea A causa de los muchos
/ heridos que hubo e de ser tan peligroso de sustentar- / nos
fue forçado desmanparalle e AUnque otra / Vez En este
mismo tienpo tornamos A Entralle Al / fin no se pudo ganar
todo y A Esta causa EstuVo çer- / cado todo Este tienpo e los
tomamos por sed e / duraron tanto A causa que les neVo dos
Vezes / ya que¹²⁹ Estaban para rrendirse Al fin los tomamos /
e murieron muchos porque se salian de noche

{+} de Unos yndios que se hAllaron En este pueblo de
çicuyque / tuVo francisco Vazquez Una rrelaçion que si fuera
verdad / Era la mas rrica cosa que se hA hAllado En yndias /
El yndio que daba las nueVas e rrelaçion (h)era de tre- / zien-
tas leguas de este rrio Al leVante de Un pueblo / que llamaba
haraee daba tanta rrazon de lo que dezia / como si Fuera verdad e lo hobiera Visto que bien paresçio / despues ser El diablo El que hAblaba En el / Francisco Vazquez e todos le
dabamos mucho credito AUn- / que Fue AconseJado de
algunos caball(a)er(^e)^os no mo- / Viese todo El canpo mas
Antes EnViase Un capitan / A saber lo que (h)era e no quiso
sino lleVarlo todo e AUn / ynViar A don pedro de toVar A
los coraçones por la / m(e)ytad de la gente que estaba En
Aquella Villa e / A(n)si partio Con todo El canpo e Andadas
çien(t) / e çinquenta leguas las çien(t) A leVante y las çin- /
quenta Al sueste¹³⁰ e Faltando ya El yndio En lo / que hAbia
dicho que Alli hAbia poblazon e mayz para pasar / Adelante
rrepreguntado A las otras dos guias como / (h)era Aquello El
Uno confeso que (h)era mentira lo que el / yndio dezia salVo
que hAbia la proVinçia que se llamaba

[fol. 4v]
QuiVira e que hAbia mayz e casas de paJa pero que Era muy
lexos / porque nos hAbian traydo por fuera de camino Visto
/ Esto y El poco bastimento que hAbia A Francisco Vaz- /
quez con Acuerdo de los capitanes se determino pasar /
Adelante con treynta de los meJores e mas bien / proVeydos
e que El canpo Volviese Al rrio y A(n)si se hizo / A la sazon
Dos dias Antes de esto hAbia suçedido A don / garçi lopez
que cayo Un caballo con El e se le (^quebro) des- / conçerto Un braço de lo qual estuVo muy malo y A esta causa /
VolVio don tristan de Arellano con El canpo Al rryo / En el
qual camino pasaron hArto trabajo A causa de / no comer
mas de carne casi todos e A muchos hazia / daño matabase
El mundo¹³¹ de Vacas e toros que / hubo Dias que Entraban
En el rreal sesenta y seten- / ta rreses e cada dia Era menester de yr A caça de lo / qual e de no comer mayz En todo
este tienpo los / caballos lo pasaban mal

{+} partido Francisco Vazquez por Aquellos llanos En busca
/ de quiVira mas por la rrelaçion que En el rryo nos hAbia /
dado que por El credito que alli le dabamos A la guia /
muchos Dias seguiendonos por AguJa fue dios serVido / que
(^tr)^A treynta jornadas hAllamos El rrio de quiVira que
esta / treynta leguas Antes de la poblazon El paso de el e Alli
/ hAllamos gente que Andaba A caça de los mesmos / naturales de quiVira / {quiVira}

{+} lo que En quiVira hAy Es Una gente muy bestial sin
poliçia / ninguna En las casas ni En otra cosa las quales son
/ de paja A manera de rranchos tarascos ^En Algunos pueblos / juntas las casas de A doçientas casas tienen mayz / e
frisoles e calabaças no tienen Algodon ni gallinas / ni hazen
pan que se cueza En comal sino debaxo de la / çeniza Entro
francisco Vazquez por este poblado Veynte / e çinco leguas
Adonde tomo rrelaçion de lo de Adelante / e dix(i)eron que
se Acababan los llanos que por El rryo Abaxo / hAbia gente
que no senbraba que se mantenia de caça

[fol. 5r]
{+} tanbien dieron rrelaçion de otros dos pueblos grandes que
se llama- / ba El Uno tareque y El otro Arae de casas de paJa
/ los tareques y Arae parte de el de paja e lo demas de ca- / sas

de cuero Aqui se *h*Allo cobre e dezian que lo *h*Abia / Adelante cabe[132] este pueblo de Arae nos *h*Abia di*ch*o / El yndio que *h*Abia mas segun las buenas señas que daba / de *e*lla Aqui no *h*Allamos señal ni nue*V*a de *e*lla Fran*cis*co / Vazquez se Vol*V*io desde Aqui Al rrio de tiguex Adonde / *h*Allo El canpo Vol*V*imos por mas d*erech*o cAmino porque A la / yda por El que Fuimos Ando*V*imos tre*ç*ientas e treynta / leguas e por El que Vol*V*imos no *h*Ay mas de dozientas / queVira Esta En quarenta grados Y El rrio En treyn- / ta e seys En estos llanos que son como quien Anda por la / mar por no *h*Aber camino sino de Vacas como por ser tan / llano e sin Una sierra ni mogote Era tan peligroso camino / ni Apartarse[133] del canpo q*ue* En perdiendole de Vista / {//} se que daba perdido e A(n)si se nos perdio Un *h*onbre e otro*s* / saliendo A ca*ç*a Andaban tres e quatro Dias / perdidos En estos llanos e con estas Vacas Andan / dos maneras de gente los Unos se llaman querechos / e otros teyas son muy bien Dispuestos e pintado*s* / Enemigos los Unos de los otros no tienen otra / granjeria ny Asiento mas de Andarse con las / Vacas de las quales matan todas las que quieren e / Adoban los cueros de que se Visten e *h*Azen tien-das / e comen la carne y AUn Algunas Vezes cruda y aUn / tanbyen beben la sangrre quando *h*an sed las tiendas q*ue* / traen son como a manera de pabellones y armanlas sobre / Unas Varas q*ue* p*a*ra Ello trAen hechas y despues de *h*yncadas[134] / Van a atarse todas Junt*a*s arryba y quando Van de Una / p*ar*te a otra las lleVan En Unos perros q*ue* tienen de los / q*ue* les tienen muchos y los c*ar*gan con las tiendas / y palos y otras cosas por ser la tierra tan llana Çu- / fre y se aproVechan en esto de *e*llos como digo porq*ue* / lleVan los palos Arrastrando a lo q*ue e*stos mas adoran / es al Sol El Cuero(^s) de las tiendas esta adobado por *en*tranbas / p*ar*tes syn pelo y estos de los Cueros q*ue* les sobran de Vac*a* y Venado y t(r)asajo*s* / secos al soL[135] rresc*a*tan[136] algun mayz y mant*a*s con los naturales del ryo[137]

[fol. 5v]

llegado Fran*cis*co Vazquez al rryo donde *h*allo EL canpo luego Vyno Don / p*edr*o de toVar Con la myt*a*d de la gente de los cora*Ç*ones y don Gar- / Çi lopez de cardenas se p*ar*tio p*ar*a mexico q*ue* demas de *e*star muy ma- / lo de su bra*Ç*o tenya lyc*encia* del Vysorrey a c*a*Usa de la muerte / de su her-m*an*o con El q*ua*l Venyan dieZ o doze Dolyentes q*ue h*abya / y entre Ellos no honbre q*ue* pudiese pelear y llego a la Vylla de / los españoles y la *h*allo quemada y muertos dos españoles / e muchos yndios y Caballos y a esta c*a*Usa VolVyo al rryo El / q*ua*l se esc*a*po de *e*llos con hart*a* Ventura[138] y buena delygen*Ç*ia / la c*a*Usa de *e*ste desbarato Fue q*ue* partido don p*edr*o y dexado / ally quarent*a* honbres la mytad de *e*llos hi*Ç*ieron motin y se / huyeron y acordandose los yndios de los malostratamy*ent*o*s* / q*ue h*abyan rre*Ç*ebydo dieron Una noche sobre Ellos y por su des- / Cuydo y FloGedad los desbarataron y se Venyeron *h*Uyendo a cu- / ly*aca*n Fran*cis*co Vazquez en este *ti*e*m*po corryendo Un dia Un caballo / c*a*yo y estuVo malo muchos dias y pasado El ynVyerno se deter- / myno de Venyrse y aUnq*ue* digan otra cosa El se Vyno q*ue* tenya / mas Gana q*ue* nadie y a(n)si Venymos todos Juntos *h*asta Culyac*a*n / De donde c*a*da Uno Fue por donde quyso y Fran*cis*co VaZquez / se Vyno aquy a mexico a dar q*uen*ta al Vyrrey El qual nada se *h*olgo / con su Venida aUnq*ue* al pren*Ç*ipio (^de) desimulaba[139] *h*olgose / de q*ue* se *h*Ubiesen quedado alla El padre Fray Ju*an* de padilla / El qual fue a queVyra y Un espanol y Un negrro *con* El / y Fray luys Un lego muy sant*a* persona quedo en Çiquyque / en este rryo tuVymos Dos ynVyernos de muchos fryos y nyeVes / e *h*yelos Grandes tanto q*ue* aquel rryo se *h*Elo Una noche y lo / estuVo y mas de Un mes y pasaban por en*Ç*ima del *h*yelo / los caballos c*ar*gados la c*a*Usa de *e*stos pueblos estan de *e*sta ma- / nera de poblazon se cree es los muchos fryos aUnq*ue* tanbyen / es p*ar*te las g*ue*rras q*ue* Unos con otros tienen y este es lo q*ue* se Vyo / y tuVo noti*Ç*ia en toda aquella tierra la q*ua*l es muy este- / ryl de frutas y arboledas quyVyra(s) es m(y)*e*Jor tierra de / muchas Ç*a*Vanas y no tan Frrya aUnq*ue e*sta mas al norte

Document 30

Juan Jaramillo's Narrative, 1560s

AGI, Patronato, 20, N.5, R.8

INTRODUCTION

Often confused with the Captain Juan Jaramillo who participated in the conquest of Tenochtitlan under Cortés,[1] the man of the same name who was a member of and wrote the following *relación* about the Coronado expedition was only about 10 years old at the time of the famous conquest of the Mexica/Aztec capital.[2] He was known as "el Mozo," or "the younger," to distinguish him from the better-known captain and from several other contemporaries of the same name. His parents were Gómez Méndez and Ana de Toro. A native of Villanueva de Barcarrota in southern Extremadura, Spain, Jaramillo, during a period of 10 years, served King Carlos in Italy, Tunis, and France before coming to the New World, perhaps at about the time of Viceroy Mendoza's arrival in 1535.[3] Also from Barcarrota were expedition members Alonso Álvarez del Valle and Rodrigo Álvarez (likely Alonso's father), but there is no evidence that Jaramillo was otherwise linked with them.[4]

In order to outfit and support himself on the Coronado expedition, Jaramillo spent more than 3,000 *pesos*.[5] Judging from the size of this expenditure and the three horses and at least two slaves or servants he took with him, he was certainly moderately well off at the time of the expedition.[6] During the *entrada* he served as a horseman. He does not stand out in any of the surviving contemporary documents, not even particularly in his own chronicle. He did, however, often travel with the captain general in the advance guard and thus was present at the capture of Cíbola and was among the few people who reached Quivira.[7] According to his own narrative, Jaramillo was one of a small group of people who opposed returning from Tierra Nueva in 1542.[8] It appears that he lived with his wife, Ana de Andrada, in the Cuidad de México following the end of the expedition and was a *vecino* and still living there as late as 1578.[9] By the time he wrote his chronicle, Jaramillo was himself a captain.[10]

Like Castañeda de Nájera, Jaramillo addresses his narrative to an unnamed illustrious person whom he calls "vuestra señoría" (your lordship), whom "His Majesty directed . . . to find out about or locate a route by which to connect that land with this."[11] And like Castañeda de Nájera, Jaramillo probably wrote in the 1560s (although the existing unsigned copy of the document is incorrectly dated at 1537), quite likely also to doctor Alonso de Zorita.[12]

The narrative itself, though, is very unlike Castañeda de Nájera's *relación*. Jaramillo displays no particular literary flair or experience, and the information he provides is most often unembellished and usually unelaborated. The first half of the narrative is, indeed, little more than the spare recital of daily direction, distance, and destination of travel. Once the events of the narration reach the plains inhabited by bison, however, that changes radically. From that point, Jaramillo dedicates nearly half the *relación* to Quivira and the plains. Nearly two and a half folio sides of text are devoted to Quivira, in comparison with less than a single folio side to Cíbola, about a paragraph to Tiguex, and only a passing mention to Cicuique.[13]

This glaring contrast between the two halves of the chronicle is reminiscent of the style of a famous book of the day, *El Viaje de don Fadrique Henríquez a Jerusalén*. Recording the Marqués de Tarifa's 1518–20 pilgrimage to the Holy Land,[14] it opens with many pages of entries such as "On Monday we reached Abreol, which is five leagues," providing only the barest of information defining his travel.[15] But once the pilgrim reaches the goal of his voyage, each day's entry swells to pages in length as he visits shrine after shrine of the life and death of Christ.

Like don Fadrique, Juan Jaramillo wrote sparingly until it came time to report on the region he considered most significant in his travels, Quivira and the buffalo plains. Bison and bison hides run through Jaramillo's narrative, at first as a seemingly accidental motif, but finally as the dominant theme. Rather than gold, it was clearly hides that represented potential wealth to this chronicler. Over and over again it is bison, their hides, and the nomads who harvested, processed, and traded them that occupy the narrative. About the plains and Quivira, Jaramillo writes, "[We were] always among the [bison]," referring to "the multitude [of bison] that is there, which is as large a quantity as you care to imagine."[16] In addition, there are plums, flax, sumac, and grapes—but it is bison hides that take center stage.

The chronicler takes time to observe and mention the fact that the leather seen at Cíbola was produced by painstaking tanning.[17] Evidently the tanning of those hides was done elsewhere, almost certainly on the Great Plains where the animals were killed, since Jaramillo reports that the tanned bison hides were "obtained" (*alcanzados*) by the Cíbolans, rather than being tanned by them.[18] Nearly 60 years later, a party led by Vicente de Zaldívar to the plains also remarked on the tanning done by Querechos/Vaqueros so skillfully that the resulting leather, soaked in water and then dried again, was "as soft and pliable as before."[19] Jaramillo, too, was impressed by the chamois-soft, water-repellant hides, for which Europe and many areas in the Western Hemisphere would have been lucrative markets. By the 1560s, when Jaramillo was writing, silver was being energetically mined at a number of places on the northern frontier of Nueva España such as Zacatecas, San Martín, and Sombrerete. Durable hides, used as bags for carrying ore,

were indispensible to mining operations of the day. What Jaramillo points out in his narrative is that there exist peoples on the Great Plains who have many years of experience as suppliers of hides. They were, as Judith Habicht-Mauche has put it, "highly specialized commodity producers."[20]

Thus, Jaramillo's narrative flies through the population centers of Sonora, the western pueblos of Zuni and Hopi, and the Rio Grande pueblos without the least stir of excitement. His enthusiasm blossoms and his descriptions become much more generous when the expedition begins "to enter the plains where the [bison] are."[21] It is this resource, both *vacas* (bison) and *vaqueros* (the Indians who harvest the bison and process its products), that constitutes the land's principal value as a royal dominion. And it is this that Jaramillo is at pains to impress upon his narrative's addressee.

Clearly, Jaramillo, as one of the expedition members who wanted to stay in Tierra Nueva, had thought it worth taking permanent possession of in 1541. Twenty years later, in the veteran's view, it still was. Like his fellow expeditionary Pedro de Castañeda de Nájera, Jaramillo seems steadfastly of the opinion that Tierra Nueva is a region worthy of Spanish occupation, and without doubt a new expedition there is warranted. Both for the anticipated return expedition and to facilitate exploitation of the hide-producing buffalo plains once authority over their resident hunters and tanners has been achieved, Jaramillo underscores the existence of "a different route and course more direct than the one I have told about."[22] That is the route traced by Andrés de Campo when he fled from Tierra Nueva to Pánuco following the killing of fray Juan de Padilla, who had stayed behind when the expedition returned south. The chronicler states that he has informed two men—presumably officials or associates of his addressee—about the shorter route because "it seems an important thing to me" for delineating "a route by which to connect that land with this."[23] A substantially shorter route to Quivira might make feasible *encomiendas* based on tribute in hides that could subsequently be shipped to Spain or anywhere else in the empire for sale.

In contrast to the author's certainty about the value of Tierra Nueva, he is often tentative and unsure about the distances and directions the Coronado expedition traveled in getting to and traversing it. He blames his hesitation about such crucial information on a memory overtaxed by the long years that have intervened since the expedition. He expresses his uncertainty through frequent use of the imperfect subjunctive forms of verbs and the future tense to express probability.[24] Furthermore, he often has recourse to phrases such as "creo" (I think), "a mi paresçer" (in my opinion), "si bien me acuerdo" (if I remember rightly), and "no se" (I do not know).[25]

This raises a question for modern historians about how far and on what subjects Jaramillo's information can be trusted. His memory is clearly fixated, for instance, on northeast as the direction of the expedition's travel. And he is at pains to demonstrate that the expedition traveled in a wide arc, starting west from the Ciudad de México, then north and northwest to Culiacán and Señora, and from there northeast to Cíbola and Quivira. Thus, he shows that the distance traveled by the expedition greatly exaggerates the straight-line distance from the Ciudad de México and other towns in Nueva España to hide-rich Quivira. But is Jaramillo's drumbeat repetition of northeast as the course of the expedition's travel always accurate?

Seven times he specifies portions of the route of the *entrada* as being to the northeast.[26] Indeed, northeast appears to be his orienting direction; on one occasion Jaramillo even directs the reader to visualize the location of Tusayán by first facing northeast.[27] In several cases, however, his references to northeast are clearly erroneous. For instance, expressing some uncertainty, Jaramillo writes, "it seems to me that, in order to get [from Cicuique/Pecos] to this river [Río de Cicuique/Pecos River] by the route we followed, we went somewhat beyond northeast."[28] As reported in other contemporary documents such as the "Relación del Suceso" (Document 29) and supported by recent archaeological finds associated with the expedition far to the southeast of Pecos Pueblo, it is apparent that the direction of travel here was generally southeast, not northeast.[29] The Jaramillo narrative continues to route the expedition erroneously in a northeasterly direction beyond the Río de Cicuique, a route that is again contradicted by contemporaneous documents and modern archaeology.[30]

Does this call into question Jaramillo's other references to northeast or his directional information in general? At the least it must counsel caution about blindly accepting his directions as accurate. And indeed, there is at least one other case in which his report of a northeasterly direction is suspect. That is in the portion of the expedition's route from the Río Nexpa/San Pedro River to the Río Bermejo/Little Colorado River. Although Herbert Bolton and others have routed the expedition steadily northeastward from a proposed Eagle Pass, Arizona, location of Chichilticale across the White Mountains to the Little Colorado and on to Cíbola/Zuni, a route that kept to generally lower elevations seems more likely, judging in part from Castañeda de Nájera's detailed description of vegetation along the way.[31] Such a lower-elevation route would mean that the expedition probably circled eastward around the higher terrain, finally approaching the Little Colorado while traveling briefly in a northwesterly direction, even though the overall direction of travel was northeasterly. If this was indeed the case, it would mark an instance in Jaramillo's narrative when the unidentified copyist likely misread "nordeste" for "noroeste," as seems to have been the case several times in the Castañeda de Nájera *relación*.[32]

In addition to the direction of the expedition's travel, Jaramillo admits uncertainty on a number of occasions about distances traveled, which he most frequently expresses in numbers of *jornadas*, or days of travel. Because much of the first half of the narrative consists of statements about direction and distance of travel with few other details, the chronicler's lack of confidence in the information he is providing regarding both these elements ought to serve as a caveat: "historians beware." Even more than is usually the case, corroboration of Jaramillo's testimony about the expedition's travel needs to be developed. Firm establishment of some point along the route from Señora to Cíbola would make an important difference. Identification of the location of Suya or Chichilticale or both, for instance, would permit at least partial testing of Jaramillo's statements about that particular segment.

In light of the overall purpose of the narrative—promoting the buffalo plains and demonstrating that they are much closer to Nueva España than was generally thought—some modern readers will be disappointed to find in it so little else about the Coronado expedition. Descriptions of topographic features are largely absent from what Jaramillo wrote, as they are from other contemporary accounts of the expedition. So, too, is information about the makeup, motives, and operations of the expedition. Almost wholly ignored are contacts between the expeditionaries and the indigenous peoples of Tierra Nueva, except those on the Great Plains. In particular, there is little indication of hostility between native groups and the expeditionaries, which would likely have affected any future attempt to establish Spanish occupation and dominion there.

Nevertheless, Jaramillo's narrative is replete with information recorded unselfconsciously as the author develops his major theme. For example, he provides the only information known to exist about slaves he had taken with him on the expedition, young men named Cristóbal and Sebastián. Furthermore, we are told of another black slave, who stayed in Tierra Nueva with his wife and children.[33] Such information, peppered throughout the narrative, is otherwise extremely difficult to come by. Even if the purposeful data the chronicler provides about the expedition's route were all in error (and they are not), the document would be of major importance as a source of details that probably survive in no other way.

Jaramillo's narrative was first published in Spanish tran-

scription in 1870 in the long series *Collección de documentos inéditos relativos al descubrimiento, conquista y organización de las antiguas posesiones españolas de América y Oceania.*[34] This transcription is riddled with errors, as are Pacheco and Cárdenas's transcriptions in general. Unfortunately, in 1992 Carmen de Mora re-published their flawed transcript.[35] On the other hand, Winship and Hammond and Rey attempted to correct many of those errors.[36] Our notes to the following transcription and translation of the manuscript document point out many of Pacheco and Cárdenas's errors and misreadings, as well as points at which our work differs significantly from that of Winship and Hammond and Rey.

The manuscript preserved in the Archivo General de Indias (AGI, Patronato, 20, N.5, R.8) is an unsigned copy made in the sixteenth century by an unidentified *escribano*. According to marginal notes on both the head and title sheet, the copy was transmitted by Juan Páez de Castro, the king's official chronicler, who may have employed the *escribano*.[37] This is another example of the debt we owe to sixteenth- and seventeenth-century historians for preserving documents that otherwise would probably not have survived, despite the contemporary Spanish bureaucracy's policy of archiving official documents.

TRANSLATION

[1r]

{1537}

{from Juan Páez}[38]

{Quivira and Cíbola}[39]

{Item} {*Relación* concerning the expedition made to Tierra Nueva, of which Francisco Vázquez de Coronado was general, presented by Captain Juan Jaramillo.}[40]

{Item} We departed from [the Ciudad de] México [going] directly to Compostela [by a] route fully populated and at peace. The direct route is approximately toward the west, and the distance is one hundred and twelve leagues.[41] From there we went to Culiacán, which is about eighty leagues.[42] It is a well-known and much-traveled route because in that valley of Culiacán is a *villa* settled by Spaniards with *repartimiento* from Compostela.[43] At this *villa* [the route] turns and goes approximately to the northwest.[44]

From here [only] we sixty horsemen went with the general, because we had received word that the route was almost completely unpopulated and without food.[45] He left his armed force and traveled with those aforesaid on reconnaissance of that route and in order to leave [food] for those who were coming behind. He must have taken that course, although with some meandering, until we crossed a mountain chain I knew about [even] from here in Nueva España more than three hundred leagues away. At this pass we gave [the mountains] the name Chichilticale, because we were informed that they were so called by some Indians we had passed.

{Item} Having left the valley of Culiacán, he [went] to a river called Petlatlán, which is probably about four days' travel. We found these Indians at peace, and they gave us a small amount of food. From here we went to another river called Sinaloa. From the one [river] to the other it is probably about three days' travel. From here the general ordered ten of us horsemen to double the daily journeys, by [traveling] light, until we arrived at the Arroyo de los Cedros. From there we were to go through an opening which the mountains formed to the right of [our] route and see what was in those [mountains] and behind them.[46] If more days were necessary [for this] than we had been allotted, he would wait for us at the Arroyo de los Cedros. It happened just that way. All that we saw there were a few Indians in some valleys settled in something like *rancherías*. [It is] a lean land. From the river [Petlatlán] to this Arroyo [de los Cedros] there is probably about another five days' travel.

From here we went to the river called Yaquimí, which is probably approximately three days' travel from this [stream].[47] [The route was] by way of a dry arroyo, traveling on the route about another three days. The dry arroyo, however, probably lasts only about one league. [There] we reached another stream[48] where some Indians were settled who had shelters of thatch and planted fields of corn, beans, and squash. {Dorantes} Having departed from here, we went to the stream and place called Los Corazones. Dorantes, Cabeza de Vaca, Castillo, and the Black, Estebanillo, named it that because the [people there] gave them hearts of animals and birds to eat and as a gift.[49] [1v] This is probably about two days' journey.[50]

At this *pueblo* of Los Corazones is a stream used for irrigation, [and it is] a *tierra caliente* [hot lowlands]. They have their dwellings, which are several huts. After setting up poles very much in the manner of ovens, though much larger, they cover them with mats. For their food, which I think never fails them, they have corn, beans, and squash. They clothe themselves in deer hides. Because this place appeared to be well disposed, it was ordered [that] a *villa* be settled here by Spaniards who were coming behind. They lived there almost until the expedition ended.

There is the [poisonous] herb here.[51] {Poisonous herb} According to what was seen of it and the action by which it works, it is the most harmful [herb] that can be found. From what we understood, it came from the sap of a small tree similar to the mastic tree. It sprouts up among slate and on barren ground.

We went from here going through a sort of small pass[52] and, very near this stream, to another valley[53] {+} formed by the same stream, which is called [Arroyo] de Señora. It is also irrigated and [is inhabited] by more Indians than the others.[54] There are the same sorts of settlements and food [here]. This valley probably extends about six or seven leagues, a little more or less.[55] At first these Indians were peaceful, but afterward [they were] not. Rather, they and those they were able to call together from around there [were] very hostile. They have [the poisonous] herb, with which they killed some Christians. There are mountain ranges that are little vegetated on both sides [of the valley].

From here we travel[ed] beside this same stream, crossing it at the bends it makes, to another Indian settlement called Ispa.[56] There is probably one day's journey from the last [valley] to this one. [The people there] have the same mode of life as those before.

{Item} From here one travels in about four days [through] unsettled land to another stream which we understood to be called Nexpa.[57] {-} Just a few Indians came out to see the general with gift[s] of little value, some roasted maguey stalks and *pitahayas*.[58] We went downstream along this rivulet for two days. Once we left the stream, we went to the right to the foot of the mountain range in two days of travel, where we were told it was called Chichiltiecally.[59] Once the mountain range had been crossed, we went to a deep arroyo and canyon, where we found water and pasture for the horses.[60]

To my mind, from this stream [or] from the Nexpa farther back, about which I have told, we turn[ed] nearly to the northeast. From here we went in the same direction in three days, I think, to a river we named San Juan, because we

arrived at it on this day.[61] Having left here, we went more toward the north through land [that is] somewhat broken to another river we called [Río] de las Balsas,[62] for we crossed it on [rafts, or *balsas*] because it was swollen. It seems to me we took two full days [going] from the one river to the other. I say this because it has been so long since we crossed that [river] that I could be mistaken about some days' travel, which I did not discuss among the rest.

From [2r] here we went to another stream we called [Arroyo] de la Barranca. There are two short days' travel from the one [stream] to the other, and the direction [is] nearly northeast.[63] From here we traveled in one day to another river to which we gave the name Río Frío because the water proved to be so [cold].[64] Then from here we traveled through a pine forest, almost at the end of which we found a stream and small flow of fresh water, where [we arrived] after probably another day's travel.[65]

{They died from eating poisonous herbs.} At this stream and place a Spaniard called Espinosa[66] and two other persons died from poisonous herbs which they ate owing to the great shortage [of food] they were suffering.

From here we went in two days of travel on the same [general] course, but rather to the north[west],[67] to another stream we named Bermejo. Here we saw one Indian and [another] pair who afterward appeared to be from the first settlement of Cíbola.[68]

{Here they killed Estebanico.}[69] {Item} From here we traveled in two days to that *pueblo*, the first one of Cíbola. The houses have flat roofs, and the walls are made of stone and mud.[70] {The *provincia* of Cíbola and what is there} Here they killed the Black, Estebanillo, who had come with Dorantes from La Florida and was returning with fray Marcos de Niza.[71] In this *provincia* of Cíbola there are five small *pueblos* including this one.[72] As I say, they all have flat roofs and are built of stone and mud. It is a cold land. So it is clear that they have plenty of food for themselves (corn, beans, and squash) in the houses and *estufas* they have. These *pueblos* are separated from each other by about a league or more, which probably turns out to form a circuitous route of about six leagues.[73]

{What the land of Cíbola is like, and their dress.} It is a somewhat sandy land and not well covered by pasture.[74] The forests around there are of juniper trees for the most part. The clothing of the Indians is made from deerskins. The tanning [is] very painstaking. They obtain some tanned [bison] hides with which they protect themselves. They are like *bernias*[75] and provide much protection from the cold. They have square cotton *mantas,* the largest of which [are] a *vara* and a half long. The Indian women wear them over one shoulder, as Gypsy women do, and encircled[76] at the waist with a sash also made of cotton, wrapped around twice.

Being in this first *pueblo* of Cíbola, facing the northeast or not quite,[77] a *provincia* called Tusayán, which has seven flat-roofed *pueblos,* is on the left five days' journey from it.[78] It has food that is as good as and better than that of these others and an even greater population. They, too, have the [bison] hides, deerskins, and cotton *mantas* that I have told about.

{Item} Whatever running water we found, the rivers and streams, as far as this one at Cíbola (I do not know whether even one or two days' journey farther) flow to the Mar del Sur. From here on they [flow] to the Mar del Norte.[79]

{Item} From this first *pueblo* of Cíbola we went, as I have said, to another one of them, which is probably about one short day's journey.[80] By the road to Tihuex [2v] it is nine days' journey, of the sort we were used to making, from this settlement of Cíbola to the Tihuex River.[81] A *pueblo* made of earth and cut stone and called Tutahaco is in a very strong position.[82] I do not know whether [it is] one day's journey more or less from the midpoint [of this route]. All these Indians thoroughly welcomed us, except the first ones of the first *pueblo* of Cíbola.

{note} When we had successfully arrived at the Tihuex River [we found] there are 15 *pueblos* within a distance of 20 leagues along it.[83] They are all of flat-roofed houses built of earth and not of stone, in the same way *tapias* [free- standing mud walls] are.[84] Away from the river, on other streams that join this one, there are other *pueblos.* For being Indian [*pueblos*], three of them in particular are very much worth seeing. {Uraba} {Uraba, two-story houses} One is called Chia, another Brava, and another Cicuique.[85] This Brava and Cicuique have houses fully two stories tall. These [three] and all the rest have corn, beans, squash, hides, and some feather robes. [These latter] they make by twisting together feathers and strands of yarn, from which then they make an excellent cloth in the same way they make the *mantas* with which they protect themselves from the cold. All [of the *pueblos*] have underground *estufas.* Although [they are] not beautiful, they [are] very good shelter from the cold. They gather and have some small amount of cotton,[86] from which they make the blankets I have told about earlier.

This river comes approximately from the northwest, flowing approximately to the southeast, which indicates, as is certain, that it empties into the Mar del Norte.

Having left this area of settlement and the aforesaid river, we travel[ed] by way of two other *pueblos,* the names of which I do not know, in four days to Cicuique, which I have already mentioned.[87] The direction of travel is to the northeast. From here we [went], if I remember correctly, in three days' travel to another river which we Spaniards called [Río] de Cicuique.[88] It seems to me that, in order to get to this river by the route we followed, we went somewhat beyond northeast. Thus, when [the river] had been crossed, we turned more to the left, which was more [directly] toward the northeast, and we began to enter the plains where the [bison] are. {The [bison]} However, we did not find them until more than four or five days' travel.[89] After that we began to encounter bulls, which there are in great quantity. Having traveled in the same direction two or three days, meeting bulls, we probably found ourselves after that among a huge multitude of [bison] cows, calves, and bulls, all intermingled.

Where the [bison] cows began we found Indians who were called Querechos by the [Indians] from the flat-roofed houses.[90] They lived without houses other than some like humble shelters that serve as houses.[91] In order to erect them at their transient camps, they take with them some poles leaned together. They tie the poles together overhead, [3r] and they spread them apart at the bottom, enclosing them with [bison] hides that they carry. As I have said, they serve them as houses. According to what was understood about these Indians, they obtain all of their human necessities from the [bison]: because of the [bison], they eat and dress and cover their feet. They are men who move here and there, to wherever it seems best to them, at the water sources that there are among the [bison].

We traveled in the aforesaid direction as many as eight or ten days. From this point the Indian who was guiding us,[92] since it seems he desired to go to his own land, exceeded himself in saying things which we found not to be true. I do not know whether it was for this reason or because he was put up to it that he took us by way of other places, going by a roundabout road (although throughout that [region] there were no [roads] except those of the [bison]).[93] He had informed us that the land of Quivira and Arahey was very wealthy and [possessed] much gold and other things.[94] He and the other Indian were from this land that I am telling about and to which we were going. These two Indians were found at the flat-roofed *pueblos*. {The Indian's deception} We understood [later] that he [had] led us away from the course which we needed to take and got us onto those plains as he did so that we would consume our food.[95] Then, because of a lack of [food], we and the horses would become weak. As a result, whether we turned back with him or went forward, eventually we would not have strength to resist whatever they might want to do with us.

From the time we entered onto the plains, as I mentioned, [that is], from this Querecho *ranchería*, he led us away farther to the east until we came to the brink of disaster from lack of food. When the other Indian, a companion of his from his land, whose opinion we never had heeded (only that of Turco, which was what we were calling him), saw that he was not leading us by the way we needed to go, he dropped [to the ground] in the path, indicating to them to cut off his head so that he would not have to go that way and [indicating] that it was not our route either.[96]

I think that we were traveling in that direction for 20 days or more,[97] at the end of which we found another *ranchería* of Indians who had the same dwellings and mode of living as those before. {The blind Indian; with whom days before} Among them was an old, bearded, blind Indian who made us understand through signs he made to us that many days before he had seen four of us.[98] And he indicated he had seen them near there and closer to Nueva España. Thus we understood and assumed they were Dorantes and Cabeza de Vaca, and those I have told about.

At this *ranchería*, when the general saw our hardship, he ordered us to assemble, [3v] meaning the captains and persons whose opinion he customarily consulted, so that we would express [our opinions] to him together with his own.[99] The [opinion] of everyone was that it seemed to us that, in order to free itself from danger, the whole force should return in search of food to the area we had departed from. And further, that 30 horsemen, certain persons, should go in search of the place the Indian had told about. We resolved on this way of thinking.

We all traveled onward one day's journey to a stream that was hemmed in by cliffs and had good meadows between [them].[100] [This was] in order to decide who had to go on from there and how the rest had to return. Here the Indian Ysopete, whom we were calling a companion of the aforesaid Turco, was asked whether he would tell us the truth and lead us to the land we were going in search of. {-} He said yes, he would do that, and that it was not as El Turco had told us. Because what he had told us and made us understand in Tihuex were certainly excellent things (both about gold and how it was mined and about buildings and the [people's] mode of living and their commerce, and many other things which I omit because they take too much space), we had been induced to search for [that land] with the consent of all those who offered their opinions, and the religious. [Ysopete answered] in such a way that he asked that as a reward for guiding us he wanted us to leave him in that land afterward, since it was his homeland. And also that El Turco not travel with him because he was quarreling with him and interfered with him in everything he tried on our behalf. The general promised him that. And [Ysopete] answered that he wanted to be the first one of the 30, and he was.

When we were ready to leave and the others were ready to stay, we pursued our journey, from here turning always toward the north for 30 days or nearly 30 days of travel.[101] {The horsemen, 30 days among the [bison]} However, [they were] not long days of travel, [and] we never lacked water during any of them. [We were] always among the [bison], some days more numerous than others, depending on the streams we encountered. In this way we ended up striking a river there on the day of San Pedro and San Pablo, which we named accordingly.[102] {Quivira} We traveled along this river and, having arrived below Quivira,[103] the Indian recognized it and said it was that one and that the settlements were downstream. We crossed it there and traveled downstream along the opposite (northern) bank, turning our course to the northeast. After traveling three days we found some Indians who were out hunting, killing [bison] to supply meat [4r] to their *pueblo,* which was about three or four days of our travel farther downstream.[104]

Here where we found the Indians and they saw us, they became agitated, yelling and indicating they would flee. Some [of them] also had their wives with them there. The Indian Ysopete began to call them in their language. Thus they came to us without indication of fear. When we and they had halted, the general revealed the Indian Turco, whom all along we had brought clandestinely in the rear-guard. When we arrived where the lodgings were prepared, it was done in such a way that the other Indian called Ysopete did not see him. [This was done] to give him the satisfaction he asked for.

{The *provincia* of Quivira} Seeing the fine appearance of the land, both that place and from there onward (which certainly is fine and which is among the [bison]), the general got some satisfaction. Here he wrote a letter to the governor of Harahey and Quivira, having understood that he was a Christian from the shipwrecked fleets bound for La Florida.[105] [This was] because the mode of government and the orderliness which the Indian had told about led us to believe that. So then the Indians left to [go to] their houses, which were at the distance [already] reported. And we did likewise, by our [own] daily rate of travel, until we reached the settlement. {The *pueblos* which they found} We found [the houses] on pleasant streams, although not with much water, with good riverside gardens. [These streams] flow into the other, larger one I have mentioned. If I remember correctly, the settlements numbered six or [seven], separated from each other.

We traveled through them for four or five days, by which it is to be understood[106] that between one stream and the next was unsettled territory. We arrived at what they said was the end of Quivira, to which they led us with reports that it was a great thing. In order to tell us about it, they called it Teucarea.[107] It was a river with more water and a larger population than the rest. When [they] were asked whether there was anything else farther on, they said, not

beyond Quivira, except for Arahey, which would be of the same mode of living, the same sorts of settlements, and the same size as [Quivira].

The general sent [a message] summoning the lord of those Indians and the others, who, they said, lived in Arahey. And he came with about two hundred men. They were all naked and [had] bows. I do not know what things [they wore] on their heads, and their genitals [were] barely covered. [The lord] was a big, well-proportioned Indian with a huge trunk and limbs.

Having heard the arguments of one and another [of the men], [4v] {item} the general asked them what we should do.[108] It seemed to all of us, who were in agreement, that because he had left the armed force and we were there [in Quivira], his grace should return in search of them. [This was especially so] since it was nearly the beginning of winter (because, if I remember correctly, it was {+} past the middle of August), and we were few to [attempt] overwintering there and had little equipment for doing so.[109] And further, [we agreed to do this] because of our uncertainty about the successful outcome for the expedition that had been left behind and in order that winter [weather] not close the route to us with snow and the rivers not permit us to cross, and also so that we could see what had happened to the other people who had been left [behind]. Once they were found and it was known how they were, he should spend the winter there and at the beginning of summer return to that land [Quivira] to get to know it and to plow it.[110]

{Conflict in Quivira} Here, which as I say was the farthest point we reached, having realized that [we knew] he had lied to us, El Turco summoned and called together the entire populace in order to attack and kill us one night. We became aware of it and it put us on guard. That night he was put to the garrote, so that he did not wake the next day.[111]

With the aforementioned accord we turned back, I do not know whether for two days' travel or three, to where we packed our supply of shelled green corn and dry corn, so that we could return.[112] At this campsite the general raised a cross, at the foot of which some letters were carved with a chisel.[113] They said that Francisco Vázquez de Coronado, general of that armed force, had reached there.

{Quivira, a fine land} This land has a very beautiful

appearance, such that I have not seen better in the entirety of Spain, nor in Italy or part of France, nor even in other lands where I have traveled in His Majesty's service.[114] That is because it is not a very broken land, rather [one] of hills, plains, and beautiful-looking rivers and streams, which certainly pleased me. I expect that [the land] probably is very productive of every kind of fruit. As far as livestock goes, my knowledge is certain, because of the multitude [of bison] that is there, which is as large a quantity as you care to imagine. {plums} We found a type of Castilian plum which is not totally red, but between red and somewhat black and green.[115] It is certain that both the tree and the fruit are Castilian, [and the fruit] has a very pleasant flavor. {flax} Among the [bison] we found a flax which the land yields; the stalks [are] separated from each other.[116] Because the grazing animals do not eat it, it is left throughout the area, with its little head and blue flower. {Sumac} Also, [we found] a genuine sumac, although [it is] small, [5r] [with] the form of our [sumac] in Spain. [And] along some streams [we found] grapes with decent flavor, considering they are not tended.

The houses which those Indians had were made of thatch.[117] Many of them were round. The thatch reaches the ground [and serves] as a wall. [The houses] are not of the same type and size as the ones here.[118] Outside of and in addition to which, [the house] has a sort [of place] like a chapel or little porter's room with an entrance, where the Indians keep a lookout, either sitting or lying down.

The Indian Ysopete was left here, where the cross was raised. Five or six Indians were taken from these *pueblos* who led and guided us to the flat-roofed houses. Thus it was that we returned by the same route until [the place] where I said earlier we had struck the river we named San Pedro and San Pablo. From this point we diverged from the one by which we had come, bearing to the right. They led us along streams and among the [bison]. [It was] a good path, although there is none through one area or another except the path of the [bison].

As I have said, we ended up leaving, and finally we recognized the land where at the beginning I said we had found the *ranchería* where El Turco led us away from the route we needed to take.[119] Thus, leaving out everything else,

we arrived in Tihuex, where we found the rest of the expedition. There, while racing a horse, the general fell and received a head wound, from which he showed signs of poor health.[120] And he concocted our return, which 10 or 12 of us were not party to, arguing with him about it in order to keep him from doing it.[121]

When the return [of the expedition] was ordered, the Franciscan friars who were with us (one preaching friar and a lay brother, who were called fray Juan de Padilla—the preaching friar—and fray Luis de Escalona—the lay brother) were prepared to stay [there] and already had a permit from their provincial [to do so].[122] Fray Luis wanted to remain among the flat-roofed houses, saying that with a chisel and adze that was being left to him, he would put up crosses throughout those *pueblos* and would baptize infants he would find on the point of death, in order to send them to heaven. For this he wanted no other company for his consolation than a young slave of mine called Cristóbal.[123] And [fray Luis] said [5v] that he would quickly learn the language of that land, with which [the people] would help him. There were so many things that he did to bring this about that I could not deny him [what he asked]. I do not know [if] anything more has been learned about him. I think that this friar's staying there was the reason some Indians from here and two Blacks remained [behind]. One [of the slaves was] mine called Sebastián, and the other belonged to Melchior Pérez, the son of *licenciado* de la Torre.[124] This [latter] Black was married, with his wife and children.[125] (Regarding Quivira, I remember that some Indians, including one from my company, a Tarascan called Andrés, also stayed.)[126]

Fray Juan de Padilla insisted on returning to Quivira, and he sought to have the Indians whom I mentioned we had brought as guides given to him. They were given to him and he took them. [He also took] a Portuguese and a free *ladino* Black, who was [then] a tertiary and became a Franciscan friar.[127] And [he took] a mestizo and two Indians who, I think, were from Zapotlán or thereabouts.[128] He had raised both of them together, and he took them in friars' habits. He took sheep, mules, one horse, vestments, and other small items. I do not know whether it was because of them or what the reason was that they killed him. It was [either] messengers or the very same Indians he took back from Tihuex who did it, in exchange for the good deeds he had done them.

As soon as [fray Juan had] died, the Portuguese fled, along with one of the Indians whom I said [fray Juan] was taking dressed in a friar's habit. Or I think [it was] both [of them]. I mention this because they came to this land of Nueva España by a different route and course more direct than the one I have told about. Eventually they got to the valleys of Pánuco. I have informed Gonzalo Solís de Meras and Isidro de Solís of this, because it seems an important thing to me, considering what you tell me and what I have understood. [Namely,] that His Majesty directed your lordship to find out about or locate a route by which to connect that land with this.[129] And also because it may be that this Indian Sebastián,[130] during the time he was in Quivira, may have had a clear idea of the environs and surrounding lands and also have information about the sea and the road by which he came and what there is on it and how many days' journey [it takes] to get here.

So certainly, if your lordship were to reach Quivira and Arahe from that place, you could bring many people from Spain, I understand, to settle the land without misgivings, owing to the [6r] appearance and indications the land shows.

[6v] {*Relación* by Captain Juan Jaramillo of the *entrada* to Cíbola and Quivira made by Francisco Vázquez Coronado}
{the, the very, the very illustrious}
{1537}
{*Relación* concerning the *entrada* to Cíbola and Quivira made by Francisco Vázquez Coronado}
{Juan Páez, 46}
{from Juan Páez}

TRANSCRIPTION

[fol. 1r]

{1537}

{de Ju*an* paez}

{QuiVira y Çibola}

{Y*tem*} Relaçion que dio El capitan Jhoan Jaramyllo de la hornada que / Hizo a la tierra nueVa de la qual fue general franci*s*co Vazquez / de coronado

{y*tem*} Salimos de mexico derechos a conpostela camino todo poblado y de paz / Y su dereçera[131] Es como al ponyente y es distançia de çiento y doze / leguas dende alli fu(^e)imos a culiacan seran como ochenta leguas / es camino muy sabido y Usado porque *e*sta En el di*c*ho Valle de / culiacan Una Villa poblada de *e*spanoles con rrepartimy*en*to / de conpostela A esta Villa se Vuelve y Va como al norrueste / de aquy los Sesenta de a cavallo que fuimos con el general por / tener notiçia ser El camino despoblado y sin comidas[132] casi todo / El dexo su exerçito y fue El con los di*c*hos En descubrimy*en*to del / di*c*ho camyno y para dexarlas[133] a los que atras Venyan lleVase / Esta derrota AUnque con algunas torçeduras hasta que / atravesamos Una cordillera de sierras que la conosci dende / aca de la nueVa españa de mas de trezçientas leguas A la qual / pusimos nonbre[134] En este paso chichiltecally porque ansi / tuVimos notiçia que se llamava de algunos yndios que atras / dexamos

{y*tem*} Salido del di*c*ho Valle de culiacan Vase[135] a Un rrio que se dize pe- / tlatlan que *h*abra como quatro hornadas Estos yndios halla- / mos de paz y nos dieron algunas cosillas de comyda dende aqui / fuimos a otro rrio que se dize çinaloa que *h*abra del Uno Al / otro como tres hornadas dende aqui nos mando El generaL / a diez honbres de caballo que

doblasemos las hornadas A la ligera /hasta llegar al arroyo de los çedros y de alli Entrasemos por Una / Abra[136] que las sierras hazian A mano derecha del camino y Viesemos[137] / lo que por ellas y detras[138] de *e*llas *h*Abia y que si fuese menester / mas dias de los que nosotros *h*Ubiesemos cobrado nos Esperaria En el / di*c*ho arroyo de los çedros fue ansi y todo lo que por ally Vimos fue / Unos yndiezuelos En algunos Valles poblados como En rrancheria / tierra esteril *h*Abra dende El rrio a este arroyo como otras çinco / hornadas de aquy fuimos al rrio que se dize yaquemy que *h*abra / como tres hornadas de *e*ste y se Va por[139] Un arroyo seco y salimos / En otros tres dias de camino aUnque El arro*y*o seco no durara / sino como Una legua y llegamos a otro arroyo adonde estavan / Unos yndios poblados que tenyan rranchos de paja y sementeras / de ma(h)iz y frisoles y calabaças salidos de aqui fuimos al arroyo / {*d*orantes} y pueblo que se dyze los coraçones El qual nonbre le pusieron dorantes y / cabeça de Vaca y castillo y estevanillo El negro y pusieronle Este / nonbre por les dar A comer y como *u*n presente coraçones de anymales y de / aVes

[fol. 1v]

*h*Abra como dos hornadas En este pueblo de los coraçones Es Un arroyo de / rriego y de tierra caliente y tienen sus ViViendas de Unos rranchos que / despues de armados los palos casi a manera de hornos aUnque muy / mayores los cubren con Unos petates tienen ma(h)iz y frisoles y ca- / labaças para su comer que creo que no le*s* falta Vistense cueros / de Venados y aquy por ser este puesto al paresçer cosa dicente se mando / poblar aquy Una Villa de los españoles que yban traseros donde / ViVieron hasta casi que la hornada peresçio Aquy *h*Ay yerva / {Yerba} y segun(d)[140] lo que de *e*lla se Vio y la operaçion que hazia es la mas / mala que se puede hallar y de lo que tuVimos Entendido (ser) / (h)era de la leche de Un arbol pequeno a manera de l(a)entisco / E nasç(i)e[141] En piçarilla y tierra esteril fuimos de aquy pasando / Una manera de portezuelo y casi çerca de este arroyo A otro Valle / {+} que El mysmo arroyo haze[142] que se dize de señora que es tanbien / de rriego y de mas yndios que los otros y de la mysma manera de / poblacion y comida turara[143] Este Valle como seis U siete leguas / poco mas U menos estos yndios estuVieron a los principios de paz / Y despues no sino antes muy Enemygos Ellos y los que mas pu- / dieron[144] por alli apellidar tienen yerba con la qual mataron / algunos cristianos tienen sierras de Una banda y de otra / y poco fructiferas de aquy Vamos por junto a este dicho arroyo / atraVesandole por Vueltas que haze a otra poblacion / de yndios que se dize (^la p) ^ispa que[145] habra de lo p(r)ostrero de esto- / tro a este Una hornada tienen la mesma manera de los pasados /

{ytem} dende aquy se Va como En quatro jornadas de despoblado / A otro arroyo donde Entendimos llamarse nexpa y salieron / {-} Unos yndizuelos a Ver al general y con presente de poca estima / con Unas pencas de mahuey asadas y pitahayas por este arroyo / abaxo fuimos dos hornadas y dexado El arroyo fuimos a la / mano derecha al pie de la cordillera En dos dias de camino / donde tuVimos notiçia que se llamaba chichiltiecally pasada / la cordillera fuimos a Un arroyo hondo y canada donde ha- / llamos agua y yerva para los cavallos dende Este arroyo / atras de nexpa que tengo dicho Volvemos a mi paresçer / casi al nordeste de aqui por la mysma derrota fuimos creo / que En tres dias a Un rrio que pusimos nonbre de san Juan / Por llegar Este dia A el salidos de aqui fuimos a otro rrio / por tierra Algo doblada y mas hazia El norte Al rrio que lla- / mamos de las balsas por lo pasar En ellas a causa de yr creçido / paresçeme que tardamos dos dias de el Un rrio al otro y esto digo por / haver tanto tienpo que aquello pasamos que podria ser En- / ganarme En alguna hornada que En lo demas no ver de[146]

[fol. 2r]

Aqui Fuimos a otro arroyo que llamamos de la barranca / hay dos pequenas hornadas de Uno a otro y la derrota casi / al

nordeste de aqui fuimos a otro rrio que pusimos El rrio / frio por el agua Venirlo ansi En Un dia de camino y despues / de aqui fuimos por Un monte de pinar donde hallamos casi al / cabo de el Un agua E arroyuelo fresco donde habra otro dia / {mueren de yer- / bas que Comieron} de camino y en este arroyo y puesto murio Un españoL / que se dezia espinosa y otras dos personas de yervas que / comieron por la grande nesçesidad que llevavan de aqui / fuimos a otro arroyo que pusimos bermejo En dos dias de camino / Y la mysma derrota menos que al nordeste Aqui Vimos Un yndio / {aqui mataron / a estebanico} e dos que paresçieron ser despues de la primera poblaçion de çibola

{ytem} de aqui fuimos En dos dias de camyno Al dicho pueblo y primero de / çibola son casas de açoteas y las paredes de piedra y barro y aqui / {la provyncia de /Çivola y / lo que en ella / hay} mataron A estebanillo El negro que habia Venydo con dorantes / de la florida y VolVia con fray marcos de niça hAy en esta proVin- / çia de çibola çinco pueblezuelos con este todos de acotea y piedra / y barro como digo es tierra fria y ansi En las casas y estufas / que tienen se demuestra tienen comyda harta para Ellos de / ma(h)iz y frisoles Y calabaças estan estos pueblos aparta- / dos El Uno del otro como a legua y a mas que Vendran A ser / como En çercuyto de seis leguas es la tierra algo arenysca / {como es la / tierra de / Cibola / su Vestido} y no muy solada de yerva y los montes que por alli hAy es la / mayor parte de sabinas el Vestido de los yndios es de cueros / de Venados estremadisimo El adobo alcançan ya Algunos / cueros de Vaca Adobados con que se cubixan que son A ma- / nera de bernyas y de mucho abrigo tienen mantas de algodon / quadradas Unas mayores que otras como de Vara y media En largo / las yndias las traen puestas por el honbro a manera de xitanas / y çenydas Una Vuelta sobre otra por su çintura con Una / çinta del mysmo algodon Estando En este pueblo primero de çibola / El rrostro al nordeste o Un poquyto me^nos esta A la mano y(r)zqui- / erda de el çinco hornadas Una proVinçia que se dize tuçayan / que tiene siete pueblos de acoteas y con comydas tan / buenas y mejores que estotros y aUn de mejor poblaçion / y tanbien tienen los cueros de Vaca y de Venados y las man- / tas de algodon que digo {y*tem*} todas quantas aguas hallamos y rrios E arroyos hasta / esto de çibola y aUn no se si Una hornada U dos mas corren / a la mar del sur y los dende aqui adelante a la mar del norte

{y*tem*} dende este primer pueblo de çibola como tengo di*c*ho fuimos a otro de *e*llos / mysmos (^y)^*que h*abra como Una hornada pequena y camino de tihues[147]

[fol. 2v]

*h*Ay[148] nueve hornadas de las que nosotros haziamos dende esta pobla- / çion de çibola hasta El rrio de tihuex esta En el medio / no se si Una hornada mas U menos Un pueblo En Un puesto[149] muy / fuerte de tierra y peña taxada que se dize tutahaco todos / estos yndios si no fueron los primeros ^*del primer pueblo* de çibola nos Resçibieron / bien llegado al rrio de tihuex *h*ay por el En distançia como Veynte / {//} leguas quinze pueblos todos de casas de acotea de tierra y no piedra / A manera de tapias *h*ay fuera de *e*l[150] En otros arroyos que se / juntan con este otros pueblos y los tres de *e*llos para Entre / yndios muy de Ver En espeçial Uno que se dize chia y otro / {uraba / Casas de a / dos altos} BraVa {Uraba} y otro çicuyque Este b(^z)^*r*aVa y çicuyque[151] que tienen / casas hartas de a dos altos todos los demas y estos tienen / ma(*h*)iz y frisoles y calabaças cueros Unos pellones de pluma / que la tuerçen acompanando la pluma con Unos hilos / Y despues las hazen a manera de texido Ralo[152] con que hazen / las mantas con que se abrigan tienen todos estufas deba- / Xo de tierra AUnque no muy pulidas muy abrigass / tienen y coxen algun poquillo de algodon del qual[153] hazen / las mantas que atras tengo di*c*ho este rrio Viene como del / norueste corriendo como al sueste dando muestra como / es çierto que Entra En la mar del norte dexada Esta / poblaçion y rrio di*c*ho Vamos por otros dos pueblos que no se / como se llaman En quatro hornadas a çicuyque[154] que / Ya he nonbrado Es la derrota de *e*sto al nordeste dende Aquy / Vamos a otro rrio que llamamos los Espanoles de çicuyque / En tres Hornadas si bien me acuerdo paresçeme que para / Venyr hasta este rrio por donde lo pasamos fuimos algo mas / q*ue* al nordeste y ansi pasado VolVimos mas a la mano yzquier- / da que (h)era[155] mas hazia El nordeste y començamos A Entrar / {las Vacas}

por los llanos donde *h*ay las Vacas aUnque no las hallamos / a mas de a quatro U çinco hornadas despues de las quales / començamos a topar con toros que *h*ay mucha quantidad / de *e*llos y con la mysma derrota y *h*abiendo andado dos U tres dias / topando toros fuimos despues de *e*llos a hallarnos Entre gran- / disima quantidad de Vacas bezerros y toros todo ReVuel- / to En estos prinçipios de las Vacas hallamos yndios que ^*les* lla- / mavan a estos los de las casas de açoteas quere- chos ViVian / sin casas Sino con Un(a)*o*s palos arrimados que traen consigo / para hazer ^*En* los puestos que se mudan Unas como cabañas / que les sirven de casas los quales palos atan por arriba

[fol. 3r]

Juntos y de abaxo los arriedran çercandolo*s* con Unos cueros de Vaca / que Ellos traen de que les Sirve*n* de casas como tengo di*c*ho / segun(d) Se Entendio de *e*stos yndios todo su menester humano / lo tienen de las Vacas[156] porque de *e*llas comen y Visten y cal- / çan son honbres que se mudan Aqui y alli donde mejor / les paresçe En aquellas aguas que Entre las Vacas *h*Ay / anduVimos como hasta ocho U diez dias por la derrota di*c*ha / Y dende aqui El yndio q*ue* nos guiava que (h)era El que nos *h*A- / bia dado las nuevas de queVira y arahey ser tierra[157] muy rrica / y de mucho oro y otras cosas y este y otro (h)eran de aquesta / tierra que digo y a que ybamos los quales dos yndios se ha- / llaron En los pueblos de açotea paresçe que como El di*c*ho / yndio deseava yr a su tierra Alargose a dezir En lo que ha- / llamos no ser verdad y no se si por esto si por ser aconsejado / que nos llevase por otras p*ar*tes torçiendo El camino AUnque / por todo Esto no los *h*ay sino son los de las Vacas Entendimos / Tanbien que nos de(s)truxo de la derrota que *h*abiamos de lle- / var y nos metiese por aquellos llanos como nos metio para / {El engano / del Yndio} que gastasemos la comyda y por faltos / de *e*lla Vinyesemos En / flaqueza nosotros y los cavallos por que si VolViesemos con este / atras U adelante no tuVier- amos rresistençia A lo que quisie- / ran hazer de nosotros finalmente que dende los dias que / Tengo di*c*ho Entrados por los llanos y dende Esta rrancheria / de querechos nos de(s)trae a mas que al este hasta que Venymos / En estrema nesçesidad de falta de comyda y Visto El otro / yndio

conpanero suyo y de su tierra que no nos llevava / por donde
*h*abiamos de yr que *h*abiamos sienpre seguido / no(^s) Su
paresçer sino El del turco que le llamavamos ansi / dexose
caer En el camino señalando que le cortasen la cabe- / ça que
El no *h*avia de yr por ally ny Era Aquel n*uest*ro Camyno /
creo que fuimos caminando Esta derrota Veynte dias U mas
/ En cabo de los quales hallamos otra rrancheria de yndios
de / la Vi*vi*enda¹⁵⁸ y manera de los de atras Entre los quales
Estava / Uno çiego y VieJo y barbado y nos dio A Entender
por senas que / {El Yndio Ciego / Con q*ue h*a dias}¹⁵⁹ nos
hazia que *h*abia Visto muchos dias *h*Abia otros quatro / de
nosotros que çerca de ally y mas hazia la nueva españa /
señalo *h*aver Visto y ansi lo Entendimos y presumymos ser /
dorantes y cabeca de Vaca y aquellos que tengo d*ich*o En esta
/ rrancheria y Visto n*uest*ro trabajo nos mando Juntar El
general

[fol. 3v]

a los capitanes y personas de quien solia t(h)omar paresçer /
para que se lo dixesemos Juntam*en*te con el suyo El qual / fue
de todos que nos paresçia que todo aquel Exerçito / se
VolViese Atras a las p*art*es donde *h*abiamos salido En /
busca de comida para que guaresçiesen y que treynta / de a
cavallo personas tales fuesemos En demanda de lo / que El
yndio *h*abia d*ich*o En el qual paresçer nos Re- / sumimos
fuimos Una hornada Adelante todos a Un / arroyo que *e*stava
metido Entre Unas barrancas y de / buenas Ve(^x)^gas¹⁶⁰
dentro para de alli acordar los que *h*a- / bian de yr y Como
se *h*abian de Volver los demas Aquy se le pregunto al yndio
ysopete que llamavamos conpa- / nero del d*ich*o turco que
nos dixese la *ver*dad y nos lleva- / se A aquella tierra En cuya
demanda ybamos y le dixo / que si haria y que no (h)era
como El turco nos *h*abia d*ich*o / {-} porque çiertamente Eran
braVas Cosas las que nos *h*abia / d*ich*o y dado a Entender En
tihuex¹⁶¹ ansi de oro y como Se sa- / cava y de Edificios y la
manera de *e*llos y las contrata- / çiones y otras muchas Cosas
q*ue* por¹⁶² prolixidad dexo /Por cuya causa nos *h*abiamos
moVido En busca de *e*llo / con paresçer de todos los que lo
daban y rreligiosos / de manera que pidio q*ue* En premyo de
nos guiar queria que / lo dexasemos despues En aquella
tierra por ser su patria / Y tanbien que no fuese con el El
turco porque le rreñya / Y le yba A la mano En todo lo que

En n*uest*ro p*ro* queria p*ro*me- / tioselo El general y dixo que
queria ser de los treynta / El Uno y ansi fue y aderesçados
para nos apartar y los / otros quedar seguimos n*uest*ro Viaje
VolViendo sienpre den- / de aqui al norte mas de treynta
dias U casi treynta dias de / camino aUnque no de
(^h)^jornadas grandes sin que nos fal- / {30 dias / por entre
/ Vacas los / de a cavallo} tase agua En nynguna de *e*llas y
sienpre por Entre Vacas / Unos dias mas cantidad q*ue* otros
conforme a las aguas En que / topavamos de manera que
Venymos a dar dia de san p*edr*o y san / pablo En Un rrio que
alli lla*ma*mos¹⁶³ ansi y abaxo de qui- / {QuiVira} Vira llegado
que fuimos al d*ich*o rrio lo conosçio El yndio / y dixo ser
aquel y estar abaxo las poblaçiones pasa- / moslo ally y por la
otra banda del norte fuimos por el / abaxo VolViendo la
derrota al nordeste y despues de / tres hornadas andadas
hallamos Unos yndios que anda- / van a caça matando de las
Vacas para llevar carne

[fol. 4r]

A su pueblo que Estava como tres U quatro hornadas de / las
n*uest*ras mas abaxo aqui donde hallamos los yndios / y nos
Vieron se començaron de alborotar con Voçes y muestras /
de huir y aUn tenyan alli algunos sus mugeres Consigo /
comencoles A llamar El yndio ysopete En su lengua y an- /
si se Vinyeron a nosotros sin muestra de t(h)emor y
parados¹⁶⁴ / que *e*stuVimos nosotros y ellos hizo muestra Alli
El general / del yndio turco El qual *h*Abiamos llevado
sienpre Escon- / didamente En rret(r)aguardia¹⁶⁵ y llegados
adonde Estava El / aposento hecho se hazia de manera por
que no lo Viese El otro / yndio que se dezia ysopete por dalle
El contento que pidio / Vista la buena Aparençia de tierra
como çierto lo es esta / de entre las Vacas y aquella y de alli
Adelante Rescibio- / {la p*rovy*nci*a* d*e* / quyVira} se algun
contento y escribio aqui Una carta El general / para El
governador de harahey y quiVira teniendo Entendido / que
(h)era c*rist*iano de las armadas de la florida perdidas / porque
la manera del govierno y pol(l)içia que El yndio *h*A- / bia
d*ich*o que tenya nos lo *h*avya hecho creer ansi que los yn- /
dios se fueron a sus cassas que Estavan A la distançia / d*ich*a
y nosotros por n*uest*ras hornadas ansimysmo hasta lle- / gar
a la poblaçion las quales hallamos En arroyos aUn- / que {los
pue- / blos q*ue* / hallaron} no de mucha Agua buenos y de

buenas rriberas que / Van a Entrar En estotro mayor que
tengo dicho fueron / si bien me acuerdo seis U (seis)[166]
poblaçiones arredradas Unas / de otras por las quales Andu-
Vimos quatro U çinco dias que / se Entiende ^ser
despoblado Entre El Un arroyo y el otro / llegamos a lo
p(r)ostrero de quiVira que dixeron ser a lo qual / nos llevaron
con nuevas de ser mucho que dezian Ellos para / signyficarnoslo teucarea[167] Este (h)era Un rrio de mas agua (^que)
/ y poblaçion que los demas preguntado que si habia
Adelante / otra cosa dixeron que de quiVira no sino arahey
y seria de la / misma manera y poblaçiones y tamaño que
aquello En- / Vio a llamar El general al señor de estos y los
otros yndios que / dixeron (^se) rresidir[168] En lo de arahey y
Vino con ^como dozientos honbres / y todos desnudos y
arcos y no se que cosas En las cabeças y poco co- / bixadas
sus Verguenças Era Un yndiazo de gran cuerpo y mien- /
bros y buena proporçion tomada la rrazon de lo que Uno y
lo otro

[fol. 4v]
{ytem} los pregunto El ge(^r)^neral que debiamos hazer
Acordandonos de como / habia quedado El Exerçito y (^q)
estavamos nosotros ally / ansi que nos paresçio a todos que
pues que (h)era ya casi la / boca del ynVierno porque si me
acuerdo bien (h)era media / {+} y mas de agosto y por ser
pocos para ynVernar alli y el poco / aparexo que para Ello
tenyamos y la duda del buen çucesso / del canpo que habia
quedado y porque El ynVierno no nos / çerrase los caminos
de nyeves y rrios que no nos dexasen / pasar y ansimysmo por
haver Visto El su(b)çeso de la otra jente / dexada debia su
merced Volver En busca de ellos y hallados y sa- / bidos como
Estavan ynVernar Alla y Volver a la boca / del Ver(e)ano a
Aquella tierra y sabella[169] y aralla Aqui / {guerra / En
QuiVira} que como digo fue lo p(r)ostrero a lo que llegamos
Visto El turco / que nos habia mentido apellido y muño toda
esta poblaçion / para que diesen En nosotros Una noche y
nos matasen su- / pimoslo y pusimonos En rrecaudo y a el
se le dio Aquella / noche Un garrote con que no amanesçio
con el acuerdo / dicho VolVimos atras no se si dos U tres
hornadas donde hizimos / nuestro matalotaxe de Elotes
desgranados y enxuto El ma(h)iz[170] / para Volvernos En este
puesto alço (^f)[171] El general Una cruz / En el pie de la qual

con Un escoplo se le hizieron Unas le- / tras que dezian
haber llegado ally francisco Vazquez de coronado / {quyVira
/ buena / tierra} general de aquel Exerçito esta tierra tiene
muy linda A- / parençia tal que no la he Visto yo mejor En
toda nuestra españa / ni En ytallya y parte de françia ni aUn
En otras tierras que / he andado En servyçio de su magestad
porque no es tierra muy doblada / sino de lomas y llanos y
rrios de muy linda Aparençia y aguas / que çierto me
contento y tengo presunçion que sera muy / fructifera y de
todos frutos En los ganados ya esta la (yn)espiri- / ençia En
la mano por la muchedunbre que hay que Es tanta / {ziru-
elas} quantia[172] quieran pensar hallamos çirhuelas de castilla
/ Un xenero de ellas que ny son del todo coloradas Sino
Entre / coloradas y algo ne(d)gras y Verdes El arbol y el fruto
es çierto / {lino} de castill(o)a de muy jentil sabor hallamos
Entre las Vacas lino / que produze la tierra hebrezitas[173]
arredradas Unas de otras / que como El ganado no lo come
se queda por alli con sus ca- / {Zuma- / que} bezuelas y flor
azul y aUnque pequeno muy perfecto çumaque[174]

[fol. 5r]
natural de el de nuestra españa En algunos arroyos UVas de
rra- / Zonable sabor para no benefiçiadas las casas que estos
yn- / dios tenian (h)eran de paxa y muchas de ellas Redondas
y la / paxa llegava hasta El suelo como pared que no tenyan
/ la proporcion y manera de las de aca por de fuera y encima
/ de esto tenya Una manera como capilla o garita con Una /
Entrada donde se asomavan los yndios sentados u Echados
/ Aqui donde se alço la cruz se dexo El yndio ysopete y se
toma- /ron de estos pueblos çinco U seis yndios que nos
truxesen / y nos guiasen a las casas de açotea y ansi fue que
nos / Volvieron por el mismo camino hasta donde dixe /
antes que habiamos topado con el Rio que llamamos / de san
pedro y san pablo y dende aqui dexaron El por donde / habiamos ydo y tomando a manderecha nos truxeron / por aguas
y entre Vacas y buen camino aUnque por Una / parte ny por
otra no hay nynguno sino El de las Vacas / como tengo dicho
Vinymos a salir y a rreconoscer la tierra / adonde al prinçipio
dixe que habiamos hallado la / rrancheria donde El turco nos
aparto El camyno que / habiamos de llevar ansi que dexado
lo demas aparte / llegamos a tihuex donde hallamos El
demas Exerçito / donde cayo El general corriendo Un

cavallo de que rresçibio / Una herida En la cabeça con la qual
dio muestras (^de no te- / ner El) de rruyn dispusiçion y
fabrico la Vuelta que / diez U doze de nosotros con
rrequerirselo no fuimos parte / para estorbarselo ansi que
(h)ordenada Esta Vuelta / los frayles françiscos que Estavan
con nosotros El Uno / de misSa y el otro lego que se
llamavan El de misa fray Juan / de padilla y el lego fray luis
de escalona Estavan Aperçe- / bidos y tenyan ya licençia de
su proVinçial para se poder / quedar quiso El fray luis[175]
quedarse En estas casas de / açotea diZiendo que con Un
escoplo y acuela que le quedava / alçar cruzes por aquellos
pueblos y bau(p)tizar algunas / criaturas que En articulo de
la muerte hallase para En- / Viallas Al çielo para lo qual no
quiso otra conpanya sino Un / esclavito myo que se dezia
cristobal para su consuelo y diziendo

[fol. 5v]
Aprenderia presto la lengua de ally con que le ayudasen / y
fueron tantas las Cosas que para esto hizo que no pude /
negarselo y ansi no se ha sabido mas de el Entiendo que la /
quedada de este frayle por ally fue causa de que
quedasen(mos) / algunos yndios de los de por aca y dos
negros Uno myo que / se dezia sebastian y otro de melchior
perez hijo del / (l)licençiado la torre y este negro Era casado
con su muger / Y hijos Y en lo de quiVira me acuerdo se
quedaron tan- / bien algunos yndios y Uno de my conpanya
tarasco que / se dezia Andres El fray Juan de padilla porfio
de Vol- / ver a quiVira y procuro que se le diesen aquellos
yndios / que dixe habiamos traydo por guias dieronsele y lle-
/ volos y mas Un portugues y Un negro ladino y horro / que
fue de terçero que se metio frayle françisco y Un mestizo / y
dos yndios creo que de çapotlan e de ally Junto los quales /
habia criado y los traya En habito de frayles llevo oVejas / Y
mulas y Un cavallo y (h)ornamentos y otras Cosillas que / ny

se si por ellas o por que causa paresçe que lo mataron /
Fueron munydores o los que lo hizieron los mysmos yndios
que / de tihuex VolVio En pago de las buenas obras que les
hA- / bia hecho ansi que muerto se huyo El portugues dicho
/ y Un yndio de los que dixe traya Vestidos En habito de
frayle / U creo que Entranbos digo Esto para que Ellos
Vinyeron / a esta tierra de la nueva españa por otro camyno
y de- / rrota mas çercana que la que yo tengo dicho y
Vinyeron / a salir a los Valles de panyco hE dado AViso de
esto A gonçalo / solis de meras y a ysidro de solis por me
paresçer cosa ynportan- / te para lo que me dize y tengo
Entendido que (^lo q) su magestad / mando a Vuestra
senoria supiese U descubriese camyno para / Juntar aquesa
tierra con esta para que tanbien podria / ser que este yndio
sebastian Entendiese En el tiempo que En / QuyVira
EstuVo la comarca y tierras de a la rredonda / de ella y
tanbien notiçia de la mar y el camino por donde Vino / y que
hay En el y quantas Jornadas hasta llegar Aca Ansi / que
ciertamente si Vuestra señoria Alcança dende Ese puesto / lo
de quyVira y arahe[176] tengo Entendido que puede traer /
mucha jente de españa A poblalla sin rresçelo segun la Apa-

[fol. 6r]
rençia y muestras la tierra tiene

[fol. 6v]
{Relaçion del capitan / Juan Jaramyllo de la en- / trada que
hizo francisco Vazquez / coronado A Çibola y a / quyVira}
{lo / los muy / los muy Yllustres}[177]
{1537}[178]
{Relaçion de la entrada / que hizo francisco Vazquez / Coronado A çibola y / a queVira}
{Juan paez 46}[179]
{De Juan PaeZ}

Document 31

Juan Troyano's Proof of Service, 1560

AGI, México, 206, N.12

INTRODUCTION

Had the Coronado expedition been successful in locating populous societies that produced valuable commodities marketable in Tierra Nueva or exportable to other parts of the world, most European members of the expedition likely would have become *encomenderos* or *criados*, employees, or other sorts of economic dependents of *encomenderos*. As such, they could have looked forward to comfortable, if not opulent, lives based ultimately on tribute and labor rendered by the native peoples of the region.

But that was not to be. As Castañeda de Nájera wrote, "there was no settlement in what had been reconnoitered where *repartimientos* could be made to the whole expedition."[1] Thus, the expedition returned to Nueva España, where many, probably most, of its members faced immediate debt and dim prospects for the future. There was a recourse available to the former expeditionaries, though, one that had a venerable tradition in Spain and the New World. That was to petition the king for recompense on the basis of one's *servicios* (deeds and exploits that had benefited the king) and *méritos* (the good reputation and earlier services of one's forebears).[2] If merit were recognized, recompense could be made in a variety of ways, from granting the right to use a coat of arms to conferring a title of nobility, or from assignment of a grant of land or jurisdiction to employment in a royal post. Most often, but by no means always, the petitioner sought direct improvement in economic circum-

stances. So it was with Juan Troyano in 1560. He asked for unspecified "grants with which he could maintain himself."[3]

Troyano had been a man of modest means when he enlisted in the Coronado expedition at his patron Antonio de Mendoza's request.[4] He was the only person on the expedition who can with any certainty be called a career military man, having served in many campaigns on behalf of the king, beginning in 1511, at age 15, in Italy.[5] During the Coronado expedition Troyano, as an experienced artilleryman,[6] was placed in charge of the force's ordnance, six small-bore *versillos*.

The long-time royal man-at-arms and native of Medina de Rioseco in the modern *provincia* of Valladolid had arrived in Nueva España in 1535 in the new viceroy's entourage, as a *criado* of his.[7] As a dependent of Mendoza's he was given a stipend for his support during the expedition to Tierra Nueva.[8] Throughout the expedition he served directly under Captain Hernando de Alvarado and was thus among the first Europeans to see Cíbola, the pueblos of the Rio Grande, and the tremendous bison herds of the Great Plains. According to fellow expeditionary Juan Cordero, "nothing was done without [hearing] Juan Troyano's opinion. [His opinion] was sought and solicited because he had (as he [still] has) very extensive experience in matters of war."[9]

While he was in Tierra Nueva, Troyano made a liaison with a native woman, who returned south with him in 1542. Whether their partnership was sanctioned in marriage by the Church is unknown, but they maintained a household for many years. As Troyano wrote in 1568 of his unnamed *compañera* (companion), "God was pleased to give me . . . a woman from that land." The former expeditionary may have felt he had a special rapport with American natives. For instance, in 1568 he asked to be named protector of the Indians in Nueva España,[10] and he had previously served as legal agent for several native communities in the region of Chalco and Tlalmanalco, southeast of the Ciudad de México.[11]

After the return of the fruitless expedition in 1542, Viceroy Mendoza directed Troyano "to build *bergantines* to bring supplies to the city by way of the canals and the lake." In conjunction with this responsibility, Troyano exercised three prerogatives: the sole right to build *bergantines* on the lake, the right to obtain stone and wood within 10 leagues of the Ciudad de México, and the right to hire whatever Indians he needed from the vicinity at the rate of 3 *tomines* per week. Despite that lucrative concession, he and his household remained dissatisfied with their economic state.[12] Whether this means that they lived in penury is not at all clear, although *de oficio* witness Juan Cordero asserted that Troyano was "poor and suffer[ed] deprivation."[13] This despite the fact that since the return of the Coronado expedition he had become a *vecino* of the Ciudad de México, a status that usually implied at least moderate social rank.[14]

Like any other petitioner for royal preferment, Troyano formulated an *interrogatorio* and requested that the authorities examine a specified list of witnesses using that set of questions. These *de parte* witnesses presumably would have supported Troyano's claim. The authority doing the first screening of the petition, in this case the Audiencia de Nueva España, was also responsible for calling its own, or *de oficio*, witnesses as an independent check on the petitioner's claims.

From the case record that was assembled as a result of Troyano's petition, only a contemporaneous copy of the testimony of two *de oficio* witnesses is known to survive—the statements offered by Captain Rodrigo Maldonado and Juan Cordero. The copy was signed and certified by Antonio de Turcios, chief *escribano* of the Real Audiencia de Nueva España, not quite three weeks after the final of the two testimonies was taken. The *escribano* who prepared the copy (not Turcios), although literate, often employed unusual word order and made a number of obvious omissions. Missing from the surviving copy of the case record (though their absence is not attributable to the *escribano*) are the original request to the *audiencia* that witnesses be examined; the *interrogatorio* submitted by Troyano; the record of testimony taken from *de parte* witnesses; additional *de oficio* testimony, if any; and the king's or Consejo de Indias's disposition of Troyano's request for grants.

It seems likely, though it is not documented, that the former artilleryman was made some concession or grant as compensation for his years of service, during which he had "shed his blood many times."[15] At any rate, he claimed later to have been granted by Viceroy Luis de Velasco the right to use Indian labor on a wheat farm that he owned.[16]

In 1544 he provided key testimony that helped clear Vázquez de Coronado of charges of abuse of Native Americans during the expedition to Tierra Nueva.[17] In later years he was imprisoned twice for lengthy periods, accused of fomenting rebellion among indigenous communities.[18] Every year for at least six in the 1560s Troyano sent letters to the king protesting what he claimed was his arbitrary incarceration. The letters are generally rambling and vague. He did, however, offer to return to Tierra Nueva, a place he called "otro nuevo mundo Tan bueno como Esta nueva españa" (another New World as excellent as this Nueva España).[19]

The two *de oficio* witnesses from 1560 whose testimony is published here provide very different assessments of Juan Troyano's contributions to the Coronado expedition. Don Rodrigo Maldonado portrays Troyano as a reliable but otherwise undistinguished man-at-arms. Juan Cordero, on the other hand, a companion of Troyano's and a fellow rank-and-file horseman on the expedition, gives a glowing testimonial to Troyano's abilities and accomplishments. In Cordero's view, as pointed out earlier, Troyano's knowledge and experience were indispensable to the expedition, and he was frequently consulted on military matters. From the fact that Troyano does not stand out in any of the other documentary accounts of the expedition, it may be that Maldonado's opinion was the more generally held.

The copy of the *de oficio* testimony presented here is preserved in the Archivo General de Indias in Sevilla under the *signatura* (catalog number) AGI, México, 206, N.12. It is published here for the first time in either English or Spanish.

TRANSLATION

[1r]
{1560}
{México}

In the Ciudad de México on the twentieth day of the month of February in the year one thousand five hundred and sixty,[20] because His Majesty has prescribed and ordered that when any persons desire to make proof[21] of their services, *de oficio* [testimony][22] is likewise to be received in opposition [to those claims], the very magnificent lord doctor Villalobos, *oidor* for His Majesty in the Real Audiencia de Nueva España, compelled don Rodrigo Maldonado, a *vecino* of this *ciudad,* to appear before him.[23] And his oath was taken and received: he swore by God, Santa María, the sign of the cross (which he made with the fingers of his hands), and the words of the Holy Gospels. Under that obligation, he promised to tell the truth.

Being questioned *de oficio* by the aforementioned [lord], this witness stated that he has known the aforesaid Juan Troyano[24] in this Ciudad de México for what may be twenty years, more or less.[25] [Troyano] was a *criado* of don Antonio de Mendoza, viceroy of Nueva España.[26] This witness knows and saw that Juan Troyano went on the expedition to Cíbola as a man-at-arms.[27] During that expedition he served with the help of a subsistence allowance which was given to him, as [it was] to the rest [of the viceroy's *criados*].[28] He served in Tierra Nueva with his arms and armor and horse in whatever was presented and ordered of him by the general.[29]

This witness considers the aforesaid Juan Troyano [to be] a responsible man.[30] And it seems to this witness that [Troyano] knows something about building bridges.[31] [Maldonado] considers him a man of excellent skill and judgment. As such, Hernando de Alvarado, the captain of artillery, took him as his artilleryman on the expedition to Cíbola.[32] In this [capacity] he served and was in charge of half a dozen *versillos* supplied by the viceroy.[33]

In the [course of] appointment[s] which General Francisco Vázquez made at Culiacán, from some captains he took with himself [some] of the men-at-arms they had [in their companies].[34] This witness maintains that Juan Troyano was among those. The general did not take with him [all] those he selected,[35] because in choosing, he left other persons among the *caballeros,* captains, and men-at-arms who remained, both captains and men-at-arms, with as much competence and courage for whatever [situation] might be presented as those he took with him. Thus it is not to be believed that those whom he took he selected because [they were] more outstanding than those who remained.

This is the truth because it happened this way, and the contrary falls short of [the truth].

As to telling how Juan Troyano was occupied during the reconnaissance of Cíbola [and] under whose command [he was], he would have been a subordinate of the *maestre de campo,* don Garci López,[36] or of another *caballero* who went on the reconnaissance. Thus, the aforesaid Troyano would have gone as a man-at-arms of [his company], as an excellent man-at-arms. But [this was] not because he showed himself to be outstanding on the expedition. During the *entrada* to Cíbola, [which] the general undertook with all the *caballeros* and the rest of the people who went with him, they wounded the general within the *pueblo* of Cíbola. Many *caballeros* and captains who went with him carried him out and ministered to him. Because of them [and] with the help of other men-at-arms, they brought him out wounded. And they subdued and took the *pueblo* and brought the *provincia* to peace.

As to what is relevant to the aforesaid Juan Troyano, this witness considers him competent and capable of many things. He demonstrated and confirmed this [1v] in what he was ordered [to do]. In the course of the entire expedition he did not make a single *entrada* or pacify [any single place], nor did he make any reconnaissance that was assigned to him; he did not demonstrate the truth [of his competence] except by being a responsible man-at-arms and proving his talents in [situations] which were presented during battle. Because of this the witness considers that if His Majesty were to concede him some office in keeping with [the services] he has elucidated, he would be capable of it.

This is the truth and what he knows concerning this case under the oath he swore. And he confirmed and certified it before the lord *oidor*. He signed it with his name.

He declared that he was more than forty-five years of age and that the questions regarding personal data do not apply to him.[37]

don Rodrigo Maldonado

Before me, Agustín Pinto, His Majesty's *escribano*[38]

{witness} In the Ciudad de México on the twenty-sixth day of the month of February in the year one thousand five hundred and sixty the very magnificent lord doctor Villalobos, *oidor* for His Majesty in the Real Audiencia de Nueva España, to whom this affair was entrusted, compelled Juan Cordero, a *vecino* of this *ciudad,* to appear before him as a *de oficio* [witness].[39] His Grace took and received the oath from him. He swore by God, Santa María, and the sign of the cross (which he made with the fingers of his hands). Under that obligation, he promised to tell the truth.

When he was questioned according to the aforementioned [*interrogatorio*] this witness declared that he has known the aforesaid Juan Troyano for what could be fifteen or sixteen years, both in this Ciudad de México and on the expedition to Cíbola.[40] He knows him in this *ciudad* and has known that he maintained his *casa poblada,* along with his arms and armor and horses, but he does not know whether he is married.[41] But this witness did see that [Troyano] went on the expedition to Cíbola at his own cost and expense.[42] He took his arms and armor, horses, and slaves on the expedition.[43] In addition to this, [Cordero knows that] during the whole expedition [Troyano] served as an artilleryman, being in charge (as he was) of the artillery on the expedition. Additionally, [he knows] that the aforesaid Juan Troyano was personally extremely valuable on the expedition, both [to] the general and [to] the rest of the captains who went on it.

Nothing was done without [hearing] Juan Troyano's opinion. [His opinion] was sought and solicited because he had (as he [still] has) very extensive experience in matters of war. [He has] very good judgment and understanding and provided very excellent solution[s] in all situations. He habitually served and did serve on the expedition with total fidelity as a very excellent man-at-arms, [was] personally brave, and endured much hardship.

This witness considers it certain that if His Majesty had been pleased to assign the expedition and conquest to the aforesaid Juan Troyano, it would have turned out very well and at less cost than [with] someone else. And even now this witness would resolve to make the journey because [Troyano] is the person he is.

This witness knows and saw that the general selected the aforesaid Juan Troyano [to be] among [a group of] sixty men [who were] to go in advance to reconnoiter the land.[44] This witness knows that he served His Majesty during this [*entrada*]. [Those who went in advance] endured many and great hardships, hunger, and deprivations. This witness knows and saw that the general ordered this witness and Juan Troyano to return to Cíbola from Tiguex for the artillery. [On this trip] [Troyano] suffered many and very great hardships [from] cold and snow and traveled lost through the forests.

This witness also knows and saw that the general ordered Juan Troyano [2r] to go search for a barber [named] Campo, who had become lost on the plains.[45] Always and continually they entrusted Juan Troyano with similar matters because he possessed (as he did possess in his person) the fullest judgment. He is a very notable[46] man in a variety of matters. He is the sort of person most needed and appropriate for this land because he has (as he does) the talents which [the witness] has stated and declared.

In addition to that, any grant His Majesty might be pleased to order made to him would be well held by him. [His Majesty knows this] because of the service he has [already] given. This witness knows that the aforesaid Juan Troyano is poor and suffers deprivation.

This is the truth and what he knows concerning this case, by the oath he swore. When his statement was read to him, he confirmed and certified it before His Grace. And he signed it with his name. He stated that he is more than fifty years old and that the questions regarding personal data do not apply to him. Asked how he knows what is contained in this statement, he replied that [it is] because he went on the expedition to Cíbola as a man-at-arms and was present during all this, as he has stated.

Juan Cordero

Before me, Agustín Pinto, His Majesty's *escribano*[47]

In the Ciudad de México on the eighteenth day of the month of March in the year one thousand five hundred and sixty, I, Antonio de Turcios, chief *escribano* of the Real Audiencia de Nueva España and its government for His Majesty, by the order of the lords president and *oidores* of the royal *audiencia*, had extracted and did extract this copy from the original, with [and against] which it was corrected and reconciled. Sancho López de Agurto de Murcia and Pedro García, *estantes* in this *ciudad*, were present to see it extracted, corrected, and reconciled.[48]

In confirmation of which I here affixed this, my registered mark, which is thus [sign made]. In testimony of the truth.

Antonio de Turcios {rubric}

[2v]

Holy Catholic Royal Majesty

On the request of Juan Troyano, a *vecino* of this Ciudad de México, a report of testimony was received in this royal *audiencia* in order to provide information to Your Majesty concerning the services [Troyano] has performed in this part of the world and his skill and competence, and to request that he be made grants with which he could maintain himself. [This is] because he is needy.

In addition to the testimony which was taken at his request, this [*de oficio* testimony] was received for the [same] purpose. [This was done] in conformance with what Your Majesty has recently prescribed and ordered. By this it appears that [Troyano] has been in this land for more than twenty-five years and that he went on the expedition to Cíbola with General Francisco Vázquez de Coronado, during which he performed services in what was ordered of him as a talented man. They say that currently he is in need. He is a foreigner[49] and a seaman. As such he has built a *bergantín*[50] in order to bring stone and other materials and supplies for provisioning the Ciudad [de México].

{rubric} Viceroy Luis de Velasco {rubric}

doctor Zorita {rubric}

{rubric} doctor Villalobos {rubric}

{rubric} doctor Orozco {rubric}

doctor Vasco de Puga {rubric}[51]

[3r–4r] blank

[4v]

{Report of *de oficio* testimony received in the Real Audiencia de Nueva España concerning the excellence of Juan Troyano. It is going before His Majesty and His Consejo de Indias.} {wax seal}

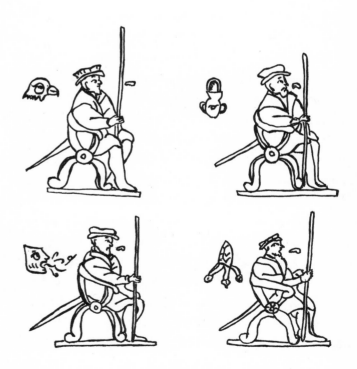

FIGURE 31.1. Four *oidores* of the Audiencia de México, 1565, after the *Codex Osuna*, fols. 22v–24r. Left to right: *doctores* Alonso de Zorita, Jerónimo de Orozco, Vasco de Puga, and Pedro de Villalobos.

TRANSCRIPTION

[fol. 1r]
{36}
{1560}
{mexico}

En la çiudad DE mexico Veinte dias del mes de / hebrero de
mill E quinientos E sesenta años por quanto / su magestad
tiene proVeydo E mandado que quando al- / Gunas personas quisieren hazer ynformaçion de / sus Serviçios se rreçi-
ba ansimismo de offiçio / Al contrario y el muy magnifico
señor doctor Villalobos oydor por su magestad / en el audiençia rreal de esta nueVa españa hizo paresçer Ante si de
ofiçio / A don Rodrigo maldonado Vezino de esta çiudad del
qual fue tomado E / Resçebido Juramento y el lo hizo por
dios E por Santa maria E por la señal / de la cruz que hizo
con los dedos de sus manos E por las palabras de los / Santos
EVangelios so cargo del qual prometio de dezir Verdad E
siendo / preguntado de offiçio por lo susodicho dixo que este
testigo conosçe al dicho Juan troyano / puede haber Veinte
años poco mas o menos en esta çiudad de mexico el qual /
(h)era criado de don Antonio de mendoça Visorrey de esta
nueVa españa y que / este testigo sabe E Vio que el dicho
Juan troyano fue a la Jornada de çibola / por soldado E sirVio
en la dicha Jornada con el ayuda de costa que se le dio como
/ a los demas E sirvio en la tierra nueVa con sus armas y cavallo en lo que / se ofresçia E por el general le (h)era mandado e este testigo tiene al dicho Joan / troyano por honbre
de bien E le paresçe a este testigo que al dicho Juan troyano
/ se le entiende alguna cosa de hazer puentes E le tiene por
honbre de buena / habilidad E Juyzio E que como (a)tal en
la dicha Jornada de çibola el capitan / del artilleria hernando
de alVarado le lleVo por su artillero en la dicha Jor- / nada en
la qual servia E tenia A cargo media dozena de Versillos de

muni- / çion E que en el nombramiento que el general
Francisco Vazquez hizo en culhuacan / entre algunos capitanes que lleVo consigo de los soldados que los suso- / dichos
tenian tiene este testigo que el dicho Juan troyano fue con
ellos y no es- / cogio el general los que lleVo consigo porque
para escoger dexo otras / personas ansi capitanes como soldados de tanta sufiçiençia y Valor / para toda qualquier cosa
que se ofresçiese entre los cavalleros capitanes / E soldados
que quedaron como los que lleVo consigo E ansi no es de
creer / que los que lleVo los escogio por mas aVentaJados que
los que quedaron / y esta es la Verdad porque ansi paso E lo
contrario caresçe de ella y en lo que / toca a dezir que en el
descubrimiento de çibola fuese el dicho Juan troyano / A
quien se encargase seria su(b)jeto E por soldado del maese de
canpo don / Garci lopez o de otro cavallero que fuese al dicho
descubrimiento E ansi el dicho / troyano yria por Soldado de
el como buen Soldado pero no porque en la Jor- / nada se
aVentaJase y en la entrada de çibola el general con todos los
cavalleros / E demas gente que con el yban Acometieron la
dicha entrada de la qual y en / ella hirieron al general dentro
en el dicho pueblo de çibola E le sacaron E so- / coRieron
muchos cavalleros E captianes que con el yban A causa de
los / quales con ayuda de otros Soldados le sacaron herido e
Vençieron E tomaron / el dicho pueblo E paçificaron la dicha
proVinçia y en lo que toca al dicho Juan troyano / este testigo le tiene por habil e sufiçiente para muchas cosas E ansi lo
mostro / {rúbrica}

[fol. 1v]
E aprobo en lo que le fue mandado ny entrada particular ni
paçificaçion / no la hizo ny descubrimiento a el encomendado no lo hizo en toda la Jornada / ny tal se probara por
Verdad mas de ser buen soldado E haber aprobado su per-

sona / en las cosas que se ofresçieron en la dicha guerra por lo qual tiene este testigo / que si su magestad le hiziese alguna merced de algun ofiçio conforme a lo que / tiene alegado cabra bien en su persona y esta es la Verdad E lo que sabe de / este caso para el Juramento que hizo en lo qual se afirmo E rrectifico ante su merced / del dicho senor oydor E firmolo de su nonbre E dixo ser de (h)edad de mas / de quarenta e Çinco años E no le tocan las Generales don Rodrigo maldonado / ante mi agustin Pinto escrivano de su magestad

{testigo} En la çiudad de mexico Veinte y seys dias del mes de hebrero de myll E quinientos / E sesenta años El muy magnifico senor doctor Villalobos oydor por su magestad / en el audiençia rreal de esta nueva españa de maner(o)a de ofiçio A quien fue / cometido este negoçio hizo paresçer ante si A Juan cordero Vezino de esta / ÇiUdad del qual Su merced tomo E rresçibio Juramento y el lo hizo por dios E por / Santa maria E por la señal de la cruz que hizo con los dedos de sus manos / so cargo del qual prometio de dezir Verdad E siendo Preguntado por lo suso- / dicho dixo que este testigo conosçe al dicho Juan troyano puede haber quinze / o diez y seis años en esta çiUdad de mexico y en la Jornada de çibola y en / esta çiudad le conosçe E ha conoçido tener su casa poblada con sus armas / y cavallos pero no sabe sy es casado mas de que Vio este testigo que fue en la / Jornada de çibola a su costa E mision el qual lleVo en la dicha Jornada sus / armas y cavallos y esclavos E de mas de esto en toda la Jornada sirvio de / artillero teniendo como tenia E tuVo A cargo la artilleria en la dicha / Jornada demas que el dicho Juan troyano se tuVo Gran quenta con su persona / en la dicha Jornada ansi el general como los demas capitanes que en ella yban / E no se hazia cosa ninguna sin paresçer del dicho Juan troyano del qual se / tomaba E tomo por tener como tiene muy gran yspiriençia en las cosas / de la guerra E de muy buen Juizio y entendimiento E a todo daba E dio / muy buena salida E servia E serVio en la dicha Jornada con toda fidelidad / E como muy buen soldado e Valiente de su persona E (para) paso mucho trabaJo / e tiene por çierto este testigo que si su magestad fuese servido de le encargar / la Jornada E conquista al dicho Juan troyano lo haria muy bien E a menos / costa que otro y aUn este testigo se determinaria a hazer la dicha Jornada / Por ser la persona que es E que

sabe este testigo E Vio que el dicho general esco- / Gio entre sesenta honbres al dicho Juan troyano para yr Adelante a descu- / brir la tierra E sabe este testigo que en ello sirvio a su magestad E pasaron muchos / e Grandes trabaJos hanbres E nesçesidades E sabe este testigo e Vio que / el dicho General mando a este testigo E al dicho Joan troyano que VolViesen / por la artilleria desde tiguex A çibola donde se padesçio muchos E muy / Grandes trabaJos e frios e nyeVes E anduVieron perdidos por los montes / E ansimismo sabe e Vio este testigo que el dicho General mando al dicho Juan troyano / {rúbrica}

[fol. 2r]

Fuese A buscar A Un canpo barbero que se hAbia perdido en los llanos / E siempre E a la continua le encargavan al dicho Juan troyano SemeJantes ne- / Goçios por tener como se tenia de su persona todo conçepto y es honbre / muy Gentil en diferentes cosas y muy nesçezaria E conViniente su persona / para esta tierra por tener como tiene las partes que tiene dichas E de- / claradas demas de que qualquier merced que su magestad fuere Servido de le / mandar hazer en el sera bien enpleada por lo haber Servido y este testigo / sabe que el dicho Juan troyano esta pobre E padesçe nesçesidad y esta es la / Verdad E lo que sabe de este caso para el Juramento que hizo e siendole leido su / dicho se afirmo en ello E rretifico ante su merced e firmolo de su nonbre / e dixo ser de (h)edad de mas de çinquenta años E que no le tocan las Generales / preguntado como sabe lo contenido en este dicho dixo que porque fue en la dicha Jor- / nada de çibola por soldado y se hallo presente a todo ello como dicho tiene / Joan cordero ante mi agustin pinto escrivano de su magestad

En la çiUdad de meXico En diez e ocho dias del mes de marÇo[52] / de myll e quinientos e sesenta años yo antonyo de turÇioS escrivano / mayor de la audiencia Real de nueVa españa e gobierno / de ella por su magestad de mandamyento de los señores presidente / e oydores de la dicha Real audiencia hize sacar e saque / este treslado de la original con la qual se corregio e / conÇerto e fueron presentes a lo ver sacar corregir e con- / çertar sancho lopez de agurto de murÇia e pedro Garcia estantes / en la dicha ÇiUdad

en Fee de lo qual Fiz Aquy este myo siGno q*ue* es (a)taL[53] /
[signo] *en* testim*on*io de *ver*dad / ant*on*io de turÇios / {rúbrica}

[fol. 2v]

Sacra Catolica Real Magestad[54]

A pedimiento de Juan troyano Vezino de *e*sta çiudad de me-
/ Xico se rresçibio En esta rreal audiençia ynformaçion para
/ dar notiçia a V*uestra* m*a*g*estad* de los Serviçios que en estas
partes *h*a / hecho y de su aVilidad y sufiçiençia y Suplicar se
le hagan al- / Gunas m*erced*es con que se pueda Sustentar
por estar pobre y / demas de la ymformaçion que se tomo de
su pedimy*ento* Se rres- / çibio esta de eff*ecto* Comforme a lo
q*ue* V*uestra* m*a*g*estad* nueVamente / tiene proVeydo E mandado por la qual paresçe que A mas / de Veinte E çinco añoS
que esta en esta tierra y fue a la / Jornada de çibola con el
general ffran*cis*co Vazquez de coronado / En donde Sirvyo
en lo que le fue mandado como hombre / yngenioso Al pre-

sente dizen estar nesçesitado es estran- / Gero y hombre de
la mar E asi *h*a hecho Un bergantin pa- / ra traer por Agua
piedra y otros materiales y baStimen- / Tos para el
proVeymy*en*to de la çiudad

{rúbrica} V*irrey* luys / de Ve*las*co {rúbrica}
doctor / çorita {rúbrica}
{rúbrica} el doctor / villalobos {rúbrica}
{rúbrica} el doctor / (h)orozco {rúbrica}
doctor vasco de puga {rúbrica}

[fols. 3r–4r] [blank]

[fol. 4v]

Ynformaçion R*ecibi*da *en* La / audiençia rreal de La nueva
esp*aña* / De oFiçio sobre la calidad de / Johan TroYano Va
Ante su / mag*estad* E su conseJo de yn- / Dias / {sello}[55]

Document 32

Melchior Pérez's Petition for Preferment, 1551

University of California, Berkeley, Bancroft Library, M-M 1714

INTRODUCTION

Even generations after the end of the Coronado *entrada*, descendants of the expeditionaries were still soliciting rewards from the king on the basis of their relatives' service in Tierra Nueva from 1539 to 1542.[1] One such instance resulted in the document presented here. Nearly 130 years after the expedition, Diego Flores de la Torre, a distant relative of expeditionary Melchior Pérez, submitted a petition for royal preferment.[2] As evidence of his family's *méritos* (worthiness), to support that petition he ordered copied into the file Pérez's own 1551 proof of service.[3] The 1551 document, in turn, had been prepared in the hope of securing an *encomienda* or *corregimiento* for Pérez in recognition of his suffering and financial loss as a result of the Coronado expedition.

Melchior Pérez was the son of Vázquez de Coronado's predecessor in the governorship of Nueva Galicia, *licenciado* Diego Pérez de la Torre.[4] He had gone to Nueva Galicia with don Luis de Castilla in 1536, ahead of his father, in a failed attempt to rescind *encomiendas* that had been distributed by Nuño de Guzmán.[5] Pérez was still in Nueva Galicia when Vázquez de Coronado arrived in December 1538 to take the *residencia* of Diego Pérez de la Torre and found that he had died.[6] Because Melchior Pérez could have been held financially responsible for his father's misdeeds in office, he must have been relieved when Vázquez de Coronado decided not to lodge any charges.[7]

Within a short time after the arrival of the new governor's entourage, Melchior befriended a member of Vázquez de Coronado's household, a man named Pedro de Ledesma. The two were to remain friends and close associates for the rest of their lives and even became relatives when, sometime around 1547, Ledesma married Pérez's daughter Catalina Mejía.[8] When the expedition to Tierra Nueva mustered at Compostela in February 1540, the two were listed among the unassigned horsemen. Already their friendship was such that only seven names intervene between theirs on the roster.[9] Later they both served in the company of Captain Juan de Zaldívar.[10] After the expedition the two frequently testified in legal cases, one immediately following the other.[11] Furthermore, Ledesma was one of those called by Pérez to testify in support of his 1551 petition.

Pérez was probably one of the wealthier members of the Coronado expedition. In preparation for its departure, he spent some 4,000 *pesos,* according to his son-in-law.[12] As he himself put it, "I took on the expedition more than a thousand head of livestock (pigs, sheep, and rams)."[13] Assuredly, this was done with the intention of turning a profit by selling meat animals to other expeditionaries either during the course of the *entrada* or once a permanent settlement had been established. But as he laments, they were all "lost and expended ... without any return."[14] Pérez also took two black slaves on the expedition; they were evidently also available for sale. As he phrases it in the 1551 *interrogatorio,* he took "two *ladino* Blacks (for one of whom four hundred gold *pesos* were offered to me)." But in the course of the *entrada* the two fled, making Pérez's purchase price unrecoverable and future profit unattainable.[15]

This loss of potential profit forms the centerpiece of Pérez's 1551 claim, the chief reason the king should award him an *encomienda* or *corregimiento*.[16] A further reason adduced by Pérez is that the *corregimiento* he already has pays very poorly. That is especially true, as his *de parte* witnesses testify, because prices have risen dramatically in the seven years since the salaries of *corregidores* were last adjusted.[17] In the royal office of *corregidor* Pérez received a annual salary as administrator and tribute collector for the king within an indigenous community that has not been identified. Pérez fails to mention in the 1551 petition that from the 1530s until recently he has been *encomendero* of Cuyupuztlan, 10 miles west of Guadalajara. About 1547 he transferred the *encomienda* as dowry to his daughter Catalina at the time of her marriage to Pedro de Ledesma.[18]

Modern historians agree that Nueva Galicia and all of Nueva España suffered increasing inflation during the sixteenth century.[19] This may have been due to the presence of a large volume of silver in the viceroyalty after the discovery of the Zacatecas mines in 1546 or to a decrease in production of native goods following the great epidemic of 1545–48, arguably the greatest disaster ever to befall the indigenous peoples of Nueva España.[20] Perhaps more likely, both factors played a role. In addition, inflation in Nueva Galicia was probably not unrelated to the parallel phenomenon in peninsular Spain. The parent country was then also feeling the effects of soaring inflation that would result in 1557 in the first of a series of royal bankruptcies.[21] The testimony about prices elicited from the 1551 *de parte* witnesses is evidence of the severity of inflation in Nueva Galicia at the time.

The result of Pérez's 1551 petition is not apparent from the surviving documentary record. But it seems that it was unsuccessful, or at least less successful than he wished. That is because in 1563 Pérez renewed his appeal for royal support. Again, the outcome is unknown.[22] Pérez was married at least twice, first about 1532 to an Indian woman, evidently given the name Francisca Xérez, and in 1555 to a Spanish woman, Juana de Cáceres.[23] His second wife's father, Bartolomé Gómez Catalán, was *encomendero* of Tepetitlan, north of the Ciudad de México. Around the time of his second marriage, Pérez left Guadalajara and took up residence as a *vecino* in the Ciudad de México.[24] Born in 1512 or 1513, he was still alive in 1566, after which time nothing is known of him.[25]

Even if it was included in the document held by his cousin Jacinto de Pineda y Ledesma, Diego Flores de la Torre did not have the testimony of *de oficio* witnesses concerning Melchior Pérez's services copied into his 1671 petition. Thus, what survives is only the testimony most favorable to Pérez.[26] If it were not for this seventeenth-century petition, however, Pérez's 1551 request for compensation probably would remain completely unknown. No other copy has been located. The single extant copy was acquired by the University of California's Bancroft Library in the 1950s from a private collector and resides there under the catalog number M-M 1714. Our Spanish transcription and English translation are the first to be published in either language.

TRANSLATION

[1r] {Copy:[27] certified copy[28] of the proof of status[29] which [Diego Flores de la Torre][30] provided to the royal *audiencia* concerning the merits and reputation of his forebears[31] and progenitors}

{Diego Flores de la Torre, archdeacon of the Church of Guadalajara}[32]

[1v] {coat of arms}

[2r]
In the *ciudad* of Guadalajara, in the Nuevo Reino de Galicia,[33] on the thirteenth day of the month of August in the year one thousand six hundred and seventy-one,[34] this petition was read before the lord *licenciado* don Juan de Bolívar y Cruz, [a member] of His Majesty's council, his *oidor* of the royal *audiencia* of this *reino,* and provincial judge in this court.[35] I present [here] its substance.

{Petition}
I, Diego Flores de la Torre, archdeacon of the Holy Cathedral Church of the *ciudad* of Guadalajara in this Nuevo Reino de Galicia, appear before Your Grace and declare that I need to extract a transcript, copy, and certified copy (in the way that is legally acceptable) of a proof of status which Melchior Pérez de la Torre executed.[36] [He was] a legitimate son of the lord *licenciado* Diego Pérez de la Torre, second governor and former captain general of this Reino de la Nueva Galicia, about whom I am making proof [of status].[37] This [proof of status] lies and rests among the papers and [proofs of] merit in the possession of Jacinto de Pineda y Ledesma, a *vecino* of this *ciudad* of Guadalajara.[38]

Therefore, I ask and humbly request that Your Grace be pleased to order that copies of the proof of status be provided to me. These should and will need to be authenticated[39] in a public and adequate form and way. [I also ask] that the originals be returned to me in order to return and deliver them to Jacinto de Pineda y Ledesma, to whom they belong. [Further, I ask] that I receive mercy with justice in this [matter]. And I give my oath *in verbo sacerdotis* [by my word as a priest] that I am making the request without malice and for it, etc.[40]
Diego Flores de la Torre

{Judgment}
When [the petition] had been reviewed by the lord *oidor,* he ordered that the certified copies to which the petition refers be supplied to [the individual] referred to. [Namely,] [the copies] of the responses[41] [Flores de la Torre] indicates by reference to Jacinto de Pineda y Ledesma, to whom they belong. Concerning this, by law, time must be made available [for doing it]. [2v] When the copy has been made, the originals are to be returned to him as he requests.
licenciado Juan de Bolívar y Cruz
before me, don Tomás de Orendaín, chief royal *escribano* of the *provincia*[42]

{Summons}
In Guadalajara on the thirteenth day of the month of August in the year one thousand six hundred and seventy-one, by virtue of the above ruling, I, the incumbent *escribano,* summoned Jacinto de Pineda y Ledesma in person in order to extract the responses referred to in the petition. When he had heard and understood [the ruling] he stated that he is

not providing what is requested voluntarily. He gave this as his response, and he signed it.

To this I attested.
Jacinto de Pineda y Ledesma
don Tomás de Orendaín, chief royal *escribano* of the *provincia*

In fulfillment of the ruling, I, don Tomás de Orendaín, His Majesty's chief *escribano* of the General Tribunal of Assets of the Deceased in this Reino de la Nueva Galicia and [chief *escribano*] of the court in this *provincia* for the king, our lord, caused to be extracted and did extract a certified copy of the responses to which the petition refers. Their verbatim substance is the following:

{Petition}
Very magnificent lord,

I, Melchior Pérez, a *vecino* of this *ciudad* of Guadalajara, appear before Your Grace and declare that I have need of executing a certain proof [of worthiness] *ad perpetuam Rey memoriam* [for the perpetual remembrance of the matter] in order to send [it] to the *reinos* of Castilla [and have it presented] before His Majesty or before His Royal Consejo [de las Indias].

I ask and humbly request Your Grace to order Baltasar de Montoya, His Majesty's *escribano,* together with Your Grace, to examine the witnesses by means of this *interrogatorio* which I am presenting. And [I ask that] you order that their statements and declarations be given to me, secured and sealed, in the way that is valid. [I ask further] that Your Grace exercise[43] your authority and judicial ruling on my behalf as much as the law allows and no more, neither at this time [nor] any other.
Melchior Pérez

In the *ciudad* of Guadalajara on the twenty-seventh day of the month of January[44] in the year of [Our] Lord one thousand five hundred and fifty-one, Melchior Pérez, a *vecino* of the *ciudad* of Guadalajara, appeared and [was] present before the magnificent lord Francisco Cornejo,[45] *alcalde* of the aforesaid *ciudad,* and in my presence, Baltasar de Montoya,[46] His Majesty's *escribano,* and [that]

of the witnesses recorded below, and presented this petition [3r] and *interrogatorio.*

He requested [that] the witnesses be examined by means of [the interrogatorio] and that he might present as witnesses on his behalf Juan Galeasso and Alonso de la Vera, *vecinos* of this *ciudad.*[47] Immediately the lord *alcalde* declared that he considers it presented. And he orders that the witnesses who are to be presented on [Pérez's] behalf be examined by means of the aforementioned *interrogatorio.*
Francisco Cornejo
[This] transpired before me, Baltasar de Montoya

In the *ciudad* of Guadalajara on the thirtieth day of the month of January in the year of [Our] Lord one thousand five hundred and fifty-one, the aforesaid Melchior Pérez presented as witnesses Francisco de Olivares, Andrés de Villanueva, Diego de Colio, [Juan] Galeasso, Hernán Flores, and Pedro de Ledesma.[48] From them the lord *alcalde* took and received [their] oath[s] in the form required by law, by the sign of the cross, that they would well and faithfully tell the truth about what might be asked of them concerning this case. When they had been asked [this] as witnesses in order to be cleared of guilt under the aforesaid oath, they each answered, "Yes, I swear, Amen."

What each of the witnesses stated and declared, each one for himself privately and separately, is the following:

{*Interrogatorio*}
By means of the following questions the witnesses who are or were presented on behalf of me, Melchior Pérez, are to be examined concerning the proof [of worthiness] I am making *ad perpetuam Rey memoriam* [for the perpetual remembrance of the matter]. [This is done] in order to send [it] to the *reinos* of Castilla so that [it may be presented] before His Majesty or before His Royal Consejo de Indias.

{1} First, they are to be questioned as to whether they know me, Melchior Pérez, a *vecino* (which I am) of this *ciudad* of Guadalajara in this Reino de Galicia in Nueva España.

{2} Item. Whether they know, have seen, [or] were acquainted with *licenciado* de la Torre, my father, *residencia* judge and former governor in this *reino* for His Majesty. And [that] he, my father, died in office in the service of His Majesty.

{3} Item. Whether they know that it was probably twenty-two years ago, more or less, that I, Melchior Pérez, traveled to Nueva España. [Whether] always, during all [3v] the time I have been here in it, I have served His Majesty in the situations which have presented themselves with my arms and armor, horses, and slaves, at my own cost, without taking wages from His Majesty. The witnesses are to state what they know.

{4} Item. Whether they know that I, Melchior Pérez, was present in this Nueva Galicia among those designated to come to settle it and diligently establish peace. [And that] together with the rest of the *vecinos* who are in [the *provincia*], I always have gone (with my arms and armor and horses, at my own expense) on the expeditions of pacification and *entradas* which have been made in [the *provincia*].

{5} Item. Whether they know that, as His Majesty's loyal servant, I went with Governor Francisco Vázquez de Coronado on the reconnaissance of Cíbola and the entire Tierra Nueva.[49] [That] because of the journey I spent more than three thousand *pesos de minas,* since I took on the expedition more than a thousand head of livestock (pigs, sheep, and rams)[50] and seven horses (four of which cost eight hundred *pesos de minas,* and the rest, ninety *pesos*). [That I took] two *ladino* Blacks (for one of whom four hundred gold *pesos* were offered to me). [And that I took] many other attendants (both men-at-arms and servants)[51] and other things necessary for war.

{6} Item. Whether they know that all of the aforementioned was lost and expended in His Majesty's service in the war, without any return from it. [That this is] because *maestre de campo* don García López[52] took the livestock from me in order to feed the expeditionary force at Culiacán[53] (because it lacked [food]). And [that] the Blacks fled from me in the *tierra de guerra,*[54] where they

were never seen again. These things the witnesses know because of having seen them.

{7} Item. Whether they know that as a result of having spent all [this] I ended up in debt for more than five hundred *pesos,* which I repaid after having returned from the expedition.
{8} Item. Whether they know that I, Melchior Pérez, am married and have a wife and legitimate children and grandchildren. [That] I do not hold Indians in *encomienda,* nor [do I possess] other assets or income, except [that there] is a *corregimiento* in this *ciudad* which the lords *oidores* [4r] are conceding to me in His Majesty's name in this Nuevo Reino, [which pays] a salary of about a hundred and thirty *pesos de oro que corre.*

{9} Item. Whether they know that it was probably seven years ago, more or less, that *licenciado* Tejada,[55] *oidor* of the Real Audiencia de México, came to this Nueva Galicia to take the *residencia* of Francisco Vázquez de Coronado and to place [the *provincia*] under the jurisdiction of México. [That] at the time and on the occasion when *licenciado* Tejada came he adjusted the low salaries of *corregimientos.* As a result, at that time they were more than a hundred *pesos,* which [should] now [be] four hundred, since they were paying one *tomín* for eight chickens, and now one [chicken] is worth one *tomín.* Likewise, a *fanega* of corn was worth half a *tomín* [seven years ago], and now it is worth half a *peso* and more.[56] A *manta* was valued at two *tomines* and now is worth four and a half *pesos.* One *fanega* of wheat was worth two *tomines* [then], and now it is worth two to two and a half *pesos.* A ram was valued at two *tomines* and now is worth five to six *tomines.* Likewise, all the other goods have risen in the same way to excessive prices, in [such] a way that one is able to maintain himself for [only] three months out of the year with the aforementioned salary. The witnesses are to state and declare what they know.

{10 Personal data} Item. Whether they know that I, Melchior Pérez, have always lived honorably. [That] I have maintained a household and have supported my mother and sisters until my mother died (which is probably seven years ago, more or less). [That] two sisters and three brothers reside with me. [That] those brothers became friars within the last few years; because *licenciado* de la Torre, my father, died they were left poor and in need. [That] with regard to my two sisters, I, Melchior Pérez, helped them to marry with the little that was left to me, giving them what I had [so that] they might marry honorably.[57] The witnesses are to state and declare what they know concerning this.

{11} Item. Whether they know that everything stated above is widely and commonly known.

Melchior Pérez

{Witness, Francisco de Olivares}
When the aforesaid witness Francisco de Olivares had given his oath and was asked [4v] the first question, he declared that he is familiar with the aforesaid Melchior Pérez, a *vecino* of the aforesaid *ciudad,* by appearance, voice, and conversation he has had with him for the last eighteen years and continues to have with him.

{1} Asked the questions concerning personal data,[58] he stated that he is more than forty years of age and that none of the other questions impede him [from testifying].

{2} In response to the second question, he stated that he did not know *licenciado* de la Torre, [Melchior's] father, but that he knows that he was the *residencia* judge and governor of this *reino,* and he knows that he died in office because it is widely and commonly known [to be] so.

{3} To the third question he answered that he is aware of it, as stated in [the question]. Asked how he knows it, he stated that [it is] because this witness came to Nueva Galicia in His Majesty's service with don Luis de Castilla,[59] and Melchior Pérez likewise came with his weapons in that company to serve His Majesty, at his own cost, without [receiving] any wages.

{4} To the fourth question [Olivares] said that the [individual] who is testifying knows that for the last fifteen years

he has seen Melchior Pérez always living in the aforesaid jurisdiction at his own cost, with his arms and armor and horses, [and] without [receiving] any wages.

{5} In answer to the fifth question, he stated that he is aware of it, as stated in [the question], because this witness went with Governor Francisco Vázquez de Coronado to the land of Cíbola. [Pérez] was well accoutered and took a quantity of livestock, and the horses and Blacks referred to in the question. He knows that none of it returned [and] that he expended it all during the journey without anything being left over.

{6} To the sixth question he said that he replies what he has stated in the previous question.

{7} To the seventh question he answered that he has heard it said, except that this [individual] who is testifying does not know the amount or how many, except that he knows that everyone ended up ruined and indebted.

[5r] {8} To the eighth question he replied that he is aware of it, as stated in [the question], because this witness lives in the *ciudad* of Guadalajara, and he knows that [Pérez] has a wife, and children and grandchildren from a legitimate marriage, and that he does not hold Indians [in *encomienda*], with the exception of one *corregimiento* worth the amount referred to in the question.

{9} In response to the ninth question, he declared that he is aware of it, as stated in [the question]. Asked how he knows it, he said that [it is] because he is a *vecino* of the aforementioned *ciudad* and has seen it and continues to see it, and it has happened as it is recorded in the question. And he knows that a hundred *pesos* were [worth] more than three hundred [are] now. With such a small salary a married man cannot maintain himself except with great privation.

{10} To the tenth question [Olivares] replied that he knows that Melchior Pérez has always lived and continues to live honorably. [That] he has supported his household as a responsible man. And that when his mother died this [individual] who is testifying was not in the land. As to the rest, concerning his siblings, the [witness] who is testifying was not aware of it.

{11} In reply to the eleventh question, he said that he states what he has said [previously] and that it is publicly and widely known. And he signed his name.

Francisco Cornejo
Francisco [de] Olivares

{Witness, Diego de Colio}
{1} When the aforesaid witness Diego de Colio had sworn his oath and was asked the first question, he stated that he has known Melchior Pérez for the last nineteen years, more or less.

{Personal data} When he was asked the questions concerning personal data required by law, he said that he is forty years of age, more or less, and that none of the other questions concerning personal matters impede him [from testifying].

{2} To the second question he replied that he was familiar with *licenciado* de la Torre and knows that he was the *residencia* judge in Nueva Galicia and [that] he died in office.

{3} In response to the third question, he stated that he knows that during that period of time [5v] [Pérez] has served His Majesty well in matters that have presented themselves, and he has seen that for this [service] he has not drawn or [been] paid any wages.

{4} To the fourth question he answered that he knows that Melchior Pérez has been in the land since[60] his father came to it, I mean in Nueva Galicia, since he was in México for a long while before [that].

{5} In reply to the fifth question, [Colio] declared that he knows that Melchior Pérez went on the aforesaid expedi-

tion. And that he who testifies did not see what he took, but he knows about it because he has heard from many people that he spent a great amount on the expedition and that he lost the aforementioned Blacks, along with the rest referred to in the question.

{6} To the sixth question he replied that he has heard the people who came from there say what is referred to in the question. He does not know the remainder.

{7} To the seventh question he said in response that he knows that Pérez returned from Tierra Nueva in debt, but he who testifies does not know in what amount.

{8} To the eighth question he answered that he knows that the aforesaid Melchior Pérez is married and has legitimate children and grandchildren and that he does not hold Indians in *encomienda*. [He said further] that he knows that he holds a *corregimiento* which yields very little remuneration.

{9} In response to the ninth question he stated that he is aware of it, as stated in [the question]. Asked how he knows it, he said that [it is] because at the time *licenciado* Tejada came, the items [referred to] were valued at the rate recorded in the question, and now [they] are available at the prices the question states. Further, that a hundred *pesos* then were worth more than three hundred now.

{10} To the tenth question [Colio] replied that he knows that Pérez has lived as a responsible man and has supported his household honorably. The rest he does not know because he was not in the land at the time [Pérez's] mother died. Nor does he know the rest. [6r] [But] he does know that the two brothers became friars.

{11} To the eleventh question he declares that he states what he has said [previously]. And he was confirming and did confirm it. He signed it with his name.

Francisco Cornejo
Diego de Colio

{Witness, Juan Galeasso}

{1} When the aforesaid witness Juan Galeasso had given his oath and was asked the first question, he stated that he has known Melchior Pérez for the last ten years by sight, speech, and conversation he has had and continues to have with him.

{Personal data} When he was asked the questions concerning personal data required by law, he stated that he is forty years of age, a little more or less, and that none of the other questions concerning personal matters impede him [from testifying], so that it would keep him from telling the truth.

{2} To the second question he said that he had heard [*licenciado* de la Torre] talked about, but he was not acquainted with him.

{3} In reply to the third question he declared that for the whole amount of time about which this individual testifies, he has seen [Pérez] serving His Majesty with his arms and armor and horses, at his own cost.

{4} To the fourth question he replied that he heard what is stated in the question said, and that he does not know the rest.

{5} To the fifth question he said in answer that he is aware of it, as stated in [the question]. Asked how he knows it, he said that [it is] because this [individual] who is testifying went on the journey and saw that [Pérez] took the horses, Blacks, and livestock referred to in the question. [He also said] that [Pérez] could not have avoided spending a large quantity of gold *pesos* on everything mentioned above. However, this [individual] who is testifying does not know the accurate value, because [Pérez] took many [things] with him.

{6} To the sixth question [Galeasso] stated that he knows it [is true] because this [individual] who is testifying ([who was] *alguacil mayor* and billeting officer for the expedition) seized the aforesaid livestock by order of don García López,

maestre de campo. [He was ordered to do this] because the people had need of the livestock. He knows that the Blacks fled, and [as to] the rest, [Pérez] expended everything [6v] and returned with nothing from it all.

{7} In answer to the seventh question, this [individual] who is testifying stated that Melchior Pérez probably could not have avoided coming back indebted, owing to his many expenses for [the] things which he was taking. [He also stated] that he does not know the amount [of his expenditures].

{8} To the eighth question this [individual] who is testifying replied that he knows that Melchior Pérez is lawfully married and has legitimate children and grandchildren. Further, [he stated] that [Pérez] does not hold Indians in *encomienda* nor [does he have] any other income, besides a meager *corregimiento*.

{9} To the ninth question he answered that he is aware of it, as stated in [the question], because he sees it occurring every day. And he knows that at that time a hundred *pesos* were worth more than four hundred [are] now. [He stated further] that everything has risen and increased in price.

{10} In response to the tenth question, [Galeasso] declared that he is aware of it, as stated in [the question], because he considers Melchior Pérez an honorable, married man and has heard said what is referred to in the question. The rest he does not know.

{11} To the eleventh question he said that he states what he has said previously and that everything stated above is publicly and commonly known. And he signed it with his name.

Francisco Cornejo
Juan Galeasso

{Witness, Hernán Flores}
{1} When the aforesaid witness Hernán Flores had given his oath and was asked the first question, he stated that he has

known Melchior Pérez for the last twelve years, a little more or less, and that he knew his father, *licenciado* de la Torre.

{Personal data} When he was asked the questions concerning personal data required by law, he stated that he is forty years of age, a little more or less, and is Melchior Pérez's brother-in-law and the son-in-law of *licenciado* de la Torre.

{2} In reply to the second question, he said that he knew *licenciado* de la Torre as the *residencia* judge and governor of this Nuevo Reino, and he knows that he died in office.

{3} To the third question [the witness] answered that during the time stated he has been aware that Melchior Pérez served His Majesty in everything which has presented itself, with his armor and arms and horses, without taking any wages.

[7r] {4} To the fourth question this [individual] who is testifying stated that he saw the aforesaid Melchior Pérez come to settle and live in this jurisdiction with his wife and children. Since then he has resided in this *ciudad*, in which he is currently a *vecino*. Concerning the rest, [he said] that he states what he has said previously.

{5} To the fifth question [Flores] said in response that he knows that Melchior Pérez went with Governor Francisco Vázquez de Coronado on the conquest of Cíbola and Tierra Nueva very well accoutered, as the question declares. And that what [Pérez] took [with him] was [certainly] worth the amount referred to in the question, or a little less.

{6} In answer to the sixth question he declared that he knows that when Melchior Pérez returned [from the expedition] he brought back nothing he had taken. Because of this the [individual] who is testifying believes that everything was used up during fighting and the *entrada*, as he has said previously.

{7} To the seventh question he declared that he knows that [Pérez] returned from the conquest in debt, but that he does not know in what amount.

{8} To the eighth question [Flores] responded by saying that he is aware of it, as stated in [the question], because he has seen and did see it.

{9} To the ninth question he answered that he is aware of it, as stated in [the question]. Asked how he knows it, he said that [it is] because he saw it and it happens and did happen just as it is recorded in the question.

{10} To the tenth question he stated that he knows [Pérez] lives honorably with his wife and legitimate children and grandchildren from a lawful marriage. [And he knows] the remainder of what is referred to in the question because, being married to his sister, he is [Pérez's] brother-in-law.

{11} To the eleventh question he states what he has said previously and that everything mentioned above is commonly and widely known. And he signed it with his name.

Francisco Cornejo
Hernán Flores
Baltasar de Montoya, His Majesty's *escribano*

{Witness, Andrés de Villanueva}
{1} The aforesaid Andrés de Villanueva, a *vecino* of the *ciudad* of Guadalajara, responding to the first question, said that he has known Melchior Pérez, a *vecino* of the aforementioned *ciudad*, for the last twelve years, a little more or less, and that he knew his father, *licenciado* de la Torre.

[7v] {Personal data} When he was asked the questions concerning personal data required by law, he stated that he is forty years of age, a little more or less, and that none of the other questions impede him [from testifying].

{2} To the second question he replied that he knew *licenciado* de la Torre [as] *residencia* judge and governor and knows that he died in office. He is aware that he had a son, Melchior Pérez, and saw him treated as such.

{3} To the third question this [individual] who is testifying answered that he knows that [Pérez] has been in this land a long time, but he does not know how long. And [he says] that during the time this witness has known him he has seen [Pérez] serving His Majesty in what[ever] has presented itself.

{4} To the fourth question [Villanueva] replied that he declares what he has stated in the previous question.

{5} In response to the fifth question, he said that he knows that Melchior Pérez went with Governor Francisco Vázquez de Coronado to Tierra Nueva. And he knows that [Pérez] went well accoutered with horses, arms and armor, Blacks, livestock, and everything else necessary. And he knows further that much money would have been spent, but this witness does not know how much.

{6} To the sixth question this [individual] who is testifying said that he knows that when [Pérez] returned, he brought back little or nothing because everything was used up during the fighting.

{7} To the seventh question [Villanueva] stated that he knows Pérez returned in debt, but he does not know in what amount.

{8} In answer to the eighth question, he declared that he knows that [Pérez] is married and has a wife and legitimate children and grandchildren. He also knows that [Pérez] does not hold an *encomienda* of Indians nor [does he have] assets, unless it would be the *corregimiento* referred to in the question, with the aforementioned salary.

{9} To the ninth question [the witness] answered that he is aware of it, as stated in [the question], because this witness knows it and saw it as recorded in the question.

{10} To the tenth question [Villanueva] declared that he knows the aforesaid Melchior Pérez has lived and continues to live honorably and that he is the son of a respected father and mother.

{11} To the eleventh question he replied that he says what he has stated previously. And he signed it with his name.

Francisco Cornejo
Andrés de Villanueva

[8r] {Witness, Pedro de Ledesma}
{1} When the aforesaid witness Pedro de Ledesma had sworn his oath and was asked the first question, he stated that he has known Melchior Pérez for the last twelve years, a little more or less, and that he knows he is a *vecino* of the aforementioned *ciudad*.

{Personal data} When he was asked the questions concerning personal data required by law, he stated that he is thirty-five years of age, a little more or less, and is [Pérez's] son-in-law, but he will not fail to tell the truth because of this.

{2} In reply to the second question, he said that he knew *licenciado* de la Torre, Melchior Pérez's father. And he knows that [de la Torre] was *residencia* judge and governor in the Nuevo Reino for His Majesty and died in office in His Majesty's service.

{3} To the third question this witness stated that he knows that for all the time he has known [Pérez] he has seen him serving His Majesty with his arms and armor, horses, and slaves, at his own cost and expense, without any wages.

{4} To the fourth question he answered that he had heard what is referred to in the question said by many persons, conquistadores of the land who saw it.

{5} To the fifth question [Ledesma] declared that he knows that Melchior Pérez went with the aforesaid governor to serve His Majesty, leaving his household, wife, and children. He knows that he expended and lost more than four thousand *castellanos* on the expedition, because he took many horses, Blacks, slaves, and livestock, all or most of which he lost. He ended up in debt and received no subsistence help or any salary.

{6} In reply to the sixth question he answered that he says what he has stated in the previous question.

{7} To the seventh question [Ledesma] stated that he knows [Pérez] ended up in debt because of the expedition, as did the others who went on the expedition.

{8} To the eighth question [the witness] declared that he knows [Pérez] is married and has a wife and legitimate children and grandchildren. [He knows] also that he does not hold Indians [8v] in *encomienda,* nor [does he have] other assets or income, unless it would be a *corregimiento* on the edge of this *ciudad* which the lords *oidores* granted to him in His Majesty's name. [The Indians] from there render him about one hundred and thirty *pesos de oro que corre.*

{9} To the ninth question he replied that he knows *licenciado* Tejada came to the Nuevo Reino to take the *residencia* of Francisco Vázquez de Coronado, as the question states. He knows that he assessed the *corregimientos,* to which assessment he refers. [He states] further that everything is now offered for sale at exorbitant prices. A *fanega* of corn is valued at two *pesos,* and the remuneration from the *corregimiento* is not enough to supply one's needs for corn. Consequently, all the other goods [are sold] for large sums, as the question maintains.

{10} To the tenth question he declared that he is aware of it, as stated in [the question], and that [Pérez's brothers] became friars out of necessity.

{11} To the eleventh question he answered that he says what he has stated previously and that everything related above is publicly and commonly known. And he signed it with his name.

Francisco Cornejo
Pedro de Ledesma

In fulfillment of the petition [made] by Melchior Pérez, I, the aforementioned *escribano,* provided and delivered the

written proof of worthiness, as it is called, for the stated purpose. Witnesses: Pedro de Ledesma [and] Bartolomé de Coca,[61] *vecinos* and *estantes* in this *ciudad.*

[This] transpired in my presence,
Baltasar de Montoya, His Majesty's *escribano*

Reconciled with the original proof of status for the purpose of extracting this certified written copy for the lord *licenciado* Diego Flores de la Torre, archdeacon of the Holy Cathedral Church of this *ciudad* of Guadalajara [in the] Nuevo Reino de Galicia. I returned it to him, [that is, the original] to which I am referring.

So that [this] may be a matter of record in accordance with [the archdeacon's] petition and the directive of the lord *licenciado* don Juan de Bolívar y Cruz, [a member] of His Majesty's council, his *oidor* in the royal *audiencia* of this *reino,* and provincial judge in this court, I delivered the present [copy], which is true and faithful [and] is incorporated above. Witnesses who saw it extracted, corrected, and reconciled were Jacinto de Pineda [y] Ledesma, don Luis [9r] de Níjar, and don Lorenzo Viscaíno, *vecinos* and *estantes* in this *ciudad* of Guadalajara, where it is being executed the twenty-third day of the month of August in the year one thousand six hundred and seventy-one.

[List of corrections][62]

I affix my registered mark in testimony of the truth.
don Tomás de Orendaín, chief royal *escribano* and [*escribano*] of the *provincia*

I certify [that] fees of sixty-four *maravedís* per sheet [were charged], and no more.

We certify that don Tomás de Orendaín, who, it is apparent, affixed his mark [to] and signed the testimony comprising seven folios preceding this [one], [who is] an *escribano* of His Majesty, chief [*escribano*] of the general court for the goods of the deceased in this *reino* of Nueva Galicia, and [*escribano*] of the *provincia* in this court and, as such, [*escribano* for] all the case files, testimonies, and other certified documents which have passed and are now passing before him, has certified and authenticated and is certifying and authenticating them fully, [sufficiently for the purposes] of court and [transactions] outside it.

Because it is a matter of record, we provide the present [certification]. In Guadalajara the twenty-third day of the month of August in the year one thousand six hundred and seventy-one.

Melchor de Medrano, royal *escribano*

Diego de la Parra Ardevol, royal *escribano* and public [*escribano*]

Diego de Galarreta, royal *escribano*

TRANSCRIPTION

[fol. 1r]

TANTO / TTESTIMONIO DE LAS INFOR- / MASIONES Q*UE* DIO EN LA R*EA*L AU*DIENCIA* / DE LOS MERITOS Y NO*MBRE* DE SUS / MAYORES Y PROGENITORES

El Arçediano de la Ig- / *le*çia de Guadalax*ar*a Diego / Flores de la Torre

[fol. 1v] {escudo de armas}

[fol. 2r]

En la Çiu*da*d de Guadalaxara NueVo Reyno de Galizia a treze / Diaz del mes de Agosto de mill seisçientos y Setenta / Y Un años ante El S*eñor* liz*encia*do Don Juan de / BoliVar y Cruz del Consejo de Su mag*esta*d Su oydor / de la R*ea*l aud*iencia* de este R*e*ino Y juez de Provy*nci*a En / esta Corte se ley*o* esta petiçion que present*o* El Contenido en ella

{P*e*tti*cion*} Diego Flores de la Torre Arçediano de esta santa / Iglesia Cat(h)edral de esta Çiu*da*d de Guadalaxara de este / NueVo R*e*ino de Galizia paresc*o* ante V*uestra* merc*e*d y digo q*ue* Yo / tengo neçesidad de sacar Un traslado tanto y testi- / monio En / manera q*ue* haga Fee de Una informacion que hizo Me*l*chor / Perez de la Torre hijo legitimo del S*eñor* liz*encia*do Diego Perez / de la Torre segundo governador y Capitan general que / fue de este d*i*cho R*e*ino de la nueVa galiçia de que hago demos- / traçion la qual esta y para en los papeles y meritos de Ja- / çinto de Pineda y ledesma Vezino de esta d*i*cha Çiu*da*d de Gua- / dalaxara por tanto A V*uestra* m*e*rc*e*d pido y suplico se sir- / va de mandar que de la d*i*cha informaçion se me den los testi- / monios q*ue* pudiere y

huviere menester aut(h)orizados En / Publica forma En manera que haga fee y que se me VuelVan / los originales para Volverlos y entregarlos al d*i*cho Jacinto / de Pineda y ledesma a q*uie*n pertenezen que en ello Rezcivi*er*e mer- / çed Con Justiçia y Juro in Verbo Saçerdotis q*ue* pido sin / maliçia y para ello *etcetera* Diego flores de la Torre

{Decreto} E Vista por el d*i*cho Señor oydor mando se le den al Contenido / los testimonios q*ue* El pedim*ien*to Refiere de los Recados de q*ue* / haze demostraçion Con Zitaçion de Jaçinto de Pineda / Y ledesma a quien pertenesen sobre lo q*ue* huviere lugar / {rúbrica}

[fol. 2v]

de derecho y f*e*cho se le VuelVan los originales como lo pide / Y lo firmo El lizençiado Juan de BoliVar y Cruz ante mi Don / Thomas de (H)orendayn *escri*b*a*no mayor R*ea*l y de Provy*nci*a

{Çitt*acion*} En Guadalaxara a trese diaz del mes de Agosto de mill Seisçien- / tos y Setenta y Un años Yo el presente *e*Scrivano Çite para la / saca de los Recados q*ue* este pedim*ien*to contiene En Virtud del / Auto de arriba a Jaçinto de Pineda y Ledesma en su persona / Y haviendolo oydo y entendido dixo que no se le ofreze / que pedir y esto dio por su Respuesta y lo firmo de q*ue* d*e* es*e* fee / Jaçinto de Pineda y ledesma Don Thomas de (H)o- / rendayn *e*Scrivano mayor R*ea*l de Provinzia

Y en cumplim*ien*to del d*i*cho auto Yo Don Thomas de (H)orendayn es- / crivano de su mag*esta*d mayor del Juzgado gen*era*l de bienes de di- / funtos de este R*e*ino de la nueVa galizia y de provinzia / En esta Corte por el Rey n*uest*ro Señor hize Sacar y Saq*ue* / Un tanto de los Recados que la petiçion contiene Cuyo the- / nor a la letra es El Siguiente

{Peti*cion*} Muy MagniFico señor Melchor Perez Vezino de esta Çiu*da*d / de Guadalaxara paresco ante V*uestra* m*erce*d y digo que Yo tengo ne- / çessidad de hazer Çierta probanza ad perpetuam Rey me- / moriam para emviar a los Reynos de Castilla ante Su / Mag*esta*d o ante su R*ea*l Consejo pido y suplico a V*uestra* m*erce*d q*ue* mande / a Balthazar de Montoya escrivano de su mag*esta*d Juntam*en*te / con V*uestra* m*erce*d que Examinen los testigos por este interrogatorio / de que hago presentaçion e sus d*i*chos y depossiçiones me / lo mande dar serrado y sellado En manera q*ue* haga / fee q*ue* para ello V*uestra* m*erce*d interponga su authoridad y decreto / Judiçial en tanto q*uan*to d*e*rech*o* haya lugar no mas ni aqui en- / de Melchor Perez

En la Çiu*da*d de Guadalax*ar*a a Veinte y siete diaz del mes / de Henero año del señor de mill quinientos Y / (^Z)^*C*inquenta y Un años ante el magniFico señor / Fran*cis*co Cornejo alcalde en la d*i*cha Çiu*da*d y en presenzia / de mi Balthazar de Montoya escrivano de su mag*esta*d / Y de los testigos de yusso escri(p)tos parezio y presente Melchor / Perez Vezino de la Çiu*da*d de Guadalax*ar*a y presento esta petiçion /{rúbrica}

[fol. 3r]
2
E interrogatorio y pidio por el sean examinadoS los testigos / que de su parte preSentare testigos J*u*an Gal(l)e*a*sso y Al*on*so de / la Vera Vezinos de la d*i*cha Ciu*da*d E luego el dicho señor / Alcalde dijo que lo *h*a por preSentado y manda que por el d*i*cho / Ynterrogatorio se examine los d*i*chos *testi*goS que de Su par- / te Se preSentaren testigos los d*i*chos Franc*i*Co Cornejo passo ante / mi Baltassar de Montoya

En la Ciu*da*d de Guadalax*ar*a a treinta diaz del mes *de* henero año / del señor de mil quinientos y sinquenta y Un años El / d*i*cho Melchor peres pressento por testig*o*s a Fran*ci*Co de Olivares / Y Andres de Villa Nueva y a D*i*ego de Colio y a (Franc*i*Co) *Juan* Gal(l)e*a*sso[63] / a Hernan Flores y

a Pedro de ledesma de los quales d*i*cho / señor Alcalde Tomo y ReSivio Juram*en*to En forma devido / de derecho Sobre la Señal de la cruz que bien y fielmente / diran la Verdad de lo que les fuere preguntado que Serca / de *e*ste Casso (an) preguntadoS por testigos a la a*b*Soluss*io*n de / d*i*cho Jura*me*nto dijeron Si juro y Amen E lo que los d*i*chos / testigos e Cada Uno de ellos dijeron y deClararon Cada / Uno por Si Secreta y apartadam*en*te es la Siguiente

{Ynterroga- / torio} Por las preguntas Siguientez Sean Examinados los testigos / que Son o fueren pressentadoS por parte de mi Melchor per*e*s / Sobre provanza q*ue* Hago ad perpetuan rei memorian p*a*ra EmViar / a los Reynos de Castilla para ante Su mag*esta*d o *an*te Su R*ea*l Consejo / de Yndiaz

{1} Prim*eramen*te Sean ExaminadoS Si conoSen a mi el d*i*cho Melchor / perez Vezin*o* que Soy de *e*sta ciu*da*d de Guadalax*ar*a de *e*ste reyno / de galiçia de *e*sta Nueva (h)eSpaña

{2} Yten Si saven Vieren Y ConoSieron al liz*encia*do de la torre juez / de reSidençia y Governador que fue en este dicho reyno por Su / Mag*esta*d y murio En el dicho Cargo En Serviçio de Su mag*esta*d / mi padre

{3} Yten Si saven q*ue h*abra Veinte Y dos años poco mas o menos que yo / el dicho Melchor perez passo a esta nueva eSpaña y todo el / {rúbrica}

[fol. 3v]
Tiempo que aqui *e*stoy en ella Siempre *h*e Servido a Su mag*esta*d En / laz cozaz q*ue* Se *h*an oFreçido Con mis armaz y Cavallos y eScla- / vos a mi Costa Sin llevar Salario de Su mag*esta*d digan los / testigos lo que Saven

{4} Yten Si saven q*ue* yo el d*i*cho Melchor perez me halle en / esta nueva galiçia En los aSignados que a ella Vinieron a poblarla / y Cuidarla a paSiFicar Con los demas Vezinos que en ella esta- / mos y siempre en la pasiFicass*io*n y entradas que en ella Se / Haçian Fue Con mis armaz y Cavallos a mi Costa

{5} Yten Si saven que Como leal Servidor de Su magestad Fui Con el gover- / nador FrancisCo Vasques de Coronado En el deScubrimiento de Sivola / y toda la tierra Nueva En que gaste en el dicho Viaje mas / de tres mil pessoS de minas (^por que lleve) porque lleve a la dicha / Jornada mas de mil cavessaz de Ganado puercos y oVejas / y CarneroS y Siete Cavallos de los Cuatro de ellos ^que Costaron ochoSientos / pessos de minaz y los demas a Noventa pesos y dos negros / ladinos que por el Uno me davan CuatroSientos pesoz / de dicho oro y otros muchos adherenteS de Armaz y Serviçio / y otraz Cozaz NeSes(es)arias para la guerra

{6} Yten Si saven que todo lo Susodicho Se perdio y Gasto en Serviçio / de su magestad en la dicha guerra Sin Volver de ello Coza al- / guna porque el ganado me tomo Don Garsi lopez maeSe / de Campo para Comer El exerssito en Culia-can porque / tuVo NeSesidad de ello y los negroS Se me huyeron a tierra / de Guerra donde nunca maS pareSieron lo qual los testigos / Sav(o)en por Haverlo Visto

{7} Yten Si Saven que al fin de haver gastado todo lo Susodicho Vine / adeudado en mas de quinientos pesos los quales pague deSpues / de haver Venido de la dicha jornada

{8} Yten Si Saven que Yo el dicho Melchor perez Soy Cassado y / tengo muger y hijos y nietos lejitimos y no tengo Yndios / de repartimiento ni otras haçiendas ni grangeriaz Sino / es Un Correjimiento en esta ciudad que los Señorez oydores / {rúbrica}

[fol. 4r]

3

Me haçen merced de este nuevo Reyno en nombre de Su magestad de / hasta Siento y treinta pessos del oro que Corre de Salario

{9} Yten Si Saven que habra Siete años poco mas o menoS que el lizenciado / tejada oydor de la audiencia Real de Mexico Vino a esta nue- / va Galiçia a tomar reSidençia a FrancisCo Vazques de Coronado / y meterla a la jurisdiçion de mexico y al tiempo y Sason que / el dicho lizenciado tejada

Vino modero los Correjimientos en / bajos SalarioS por que entonSes eran mas de Sien(t) pesos que ahora / CuatroSientoS por que davan por Un tomin ocho gallinas / y ahora Vale Una Un tomin y aSimismo Valia Una Fanega / de maiz medio tomin Y Vale ahora medio pesso y maz Valia / Una manta dos tomineS y ahora Vale Cuatro pesos y medio / y Valia / Una fanega de trigo dos tomines y Vale ahora dos pesos y dos / y medio y Un Carnero Valia dos tomines y ahora Vale sinco / y Seis tomineS y assimesmo todas las demaz Cozas han Subido / en por la mesma Manera en exesivos presios por Manera / que no Se puede Sustentar tres meses del año Con el dicho Sa- / lario y digan y declaren los testigos lo que Saven

{10 / generales} Yten Si saven que (^el)^Yo dicho Melchor Perez Siempre he Vivi- / do honrradamente y he tenido Cassa y he Sustentado a / mi madre y hermanaz Hasta que la dicha mi madre / murio que habra Siete años pocos maz o menoS y queda- / ron doS hermanaz y otros tres hermanos Conmigo los qualeS / dichos hermanos Se metieron frailez de(n)sde ha pocos años / que al dicho lizenciado de la torre mi padre murio por quedar / pobreS e neSesitadoS para las dichaz doS mis hermanas / yo el dicho Melchor perez las ayude a Cassar Con la / pobressa que me quedo dandolez A lo que tenia las quales / Casse honrradamente digan y declaren los testigos / lo que Saven aSerca de ello

{11} Yten Si Saven que eS publico y notorio todo lo Susodicho / Melchor perez

{testigo francisco de / olivares} El dicho Francisco de olivares testigo jurado y preguntado a la / {rúbrica}

[fol. 4v]

Primera pregunta dijo que Conoze al dicho Melchor peres / Vezino de la dicha ciudad por ViSta e habla e Conversasion / que Con el ha tenido e tiene de dies y ocho años a esta parte

{1} Preguntado por las preguntaz generalez de la ley dijo que / es de (H)edad de mas de quarenta años y que no le empesse / ninguna de las generalez

{2} A la Segunda pregunta dijo q*ue* no conoSio al d*i*cho liz*enci*ado / de la torre Su padre mas de que Save que fue jues de RE- / Sidençia y governador de *e*ste Reyno y save q*ue* murio en / el d*i*cho Cargo porque aSi es publico y notorio

{3} a la terSera pregunta dijo q*ue* la Save Como en ella Se Con- / tiene preguntado q*ue* Como la Save(r) dijo q*ue* porq*ue* / este testigo Vino a esta nueva galiçia en Serviçio de / su mag*esta*d Con Don luiz de Castilla y el d*i*cho Mel- / chor peres Venia aSimismo en la d*i*cha Compañia / Con sus armas a Servir a Su mag*esta*d a Su costa Sin Salario / alguno

{4} A la Quartta pregunta Dijo que Save este q*ue* depo- / ne q*ue* de quinçe años a esta parte Siempre *h*a visto / al d*i*cho Melchor perez reSidir Siempre en la / d*i*cha GovernaSion a Su Costa Con Sus armaz Y Cavallos / sin salario alguno

{5} A la quinta pregunta dijo que la Save Como en ella / se Contiene porque este testigo fue Con el d*i*cho gover- / nador Franc*is*Co Vazquez de Coronado a la tierra de / Sivola y fue bien adereSado y llevo Cantt*ida*d de ganado / y los Cavallos y Negros en la pregunta Contenidos / e Save que no Volvio Nada q*ue* todo Se gasto en el / dicho Viaje Sin que quedasse nada

{6} A la Sesta preguntta dijo q*ue* diçe lo q*ue* d*i*cho tiene / en la pregunta antes de *e*sta

{7} A la Septima pregunta dijo q*ue* lo oyo deçir pero este q*ue* de- / pone no Save la Cantt*ida*d de quantoz mas de q*ue* Save / que todoS Vinieron perdidos y adeudados / {rúbrica}

[fol. 5r]
4
{8} A la octava pregunta dijo q*ue* la Save Como en ella Se / Contiene porque *e*ste testigo Vive en la d*i*cha Ciu*da*d de guadala*ja*ra / y Save que tiene muger e hijos Y nietoS de lejitimo ma- / trimonio y que no tiene Yndios Salvo Un correjimiento / de la cantt*ida*d en la pregunta Contenido

{9} A la novena pregunta dijo que la Save Como en ella / Se

Contiene preguntado Como la Save dijo que por- / que es Vezi*n*o de la d*i*cha ciu*da*d y lo *h*a Visto y Ve y paza / Como en la pregunta Se Contiene y Save que era / mas entonses Sien(t) p*eso*s que a*h*ora treSientos y q*ue* Con / tan poco Salario no Se puede Sustentar Un hombre / Cassado Sino Con mui gran neSesidad

{10} A la dies pregunta dijo que Save que el d*i*cho Mel- / chor perez Siempre *h*a vivido y Vive honrradamentte / e *h*A Sustentado Su caza Como hombre de bien y q*ue* al / tiempo que murio su madre este que depone no / estava en la tierra y lo demas de Sus hermanos este / que depone no los ConoSio

{11} A la onsena pregunta dijo que diçe lo q*ue* d*i*cho / tiene y que es publico y notorio y firmolo de Su nom- / bre Franc*is*Co Cornejo, Franc*is*Co olivarez

{testigo D*i*ego de / Colio} {1} El d*i*cho D*i*ego de Colio testigo jurado e preguntado a la / primera pregunta dijo que Conoze al d*i*cho Mel- / chor peres de dies y nueve años a esta parte pocos mas / o menoS

{G*enerale*s} Preguntado por las preguntaz generaleS dijo que *e*s de (h)edad / de quarenta años pocos maz o menoS y que no le / empesse ninguna de laz generaleS

{2} A la Segunda pregunta dijo q*ue* le conoSio al d*i*cho lizen- / ciado / de la torre y save que fue jues de ReSidencia en esta nueva / galicia e murio en el d*i*cho Cargo

{3} A la terçera pregunta dijo q*ue* Save q*ue* del d*i*cho t*iem*po / {rúbricas}

[fol. 5v]
A esta parte en cozaz q*ue* se *h*an oFreçido *h*a Servido bien a Su mag*esta*d / y que no *h*a visto que por ello Se traiga dado Salario alguno

{4} A la quartta pregunta Dijo que Save que el d*i*cho Mel- / chor peres esta en la tierra deSpues q*ue* Su padre Vino a ella

/ digo en la Nueva galiçia porque en mexico estuVo antes / mucho *tiem*po

{5} A la quinta pregunta dijo que Save q*ue* el di*c*ho Mel- / chor perez Fue a la di*c*ha jornada y que este que depone / no Vio lo q*ue* llevo mas de que Save por Haverlo oydo a muchas / perSonaz q*ue* gasto mucho en la di*c*ha jornada y q*ue* / perdio los di*c*hos negros Con lo demaz Contenido / en la di*c*ha pregunta

{6} A la Sexta pregun*t*ta dijo q*ue h*a oydo deçir lo Contenido / en la di*c*ha pregunta a laz perSonaz q*ue* de alla Vinie- / ron y lo demaz no lo Save

{7} A la Setena pregunta dijo que Save q*ue* Vino adeudado de / la tierra Nueva pero que este que depone no Save en / q*ue* Can*tt*i*da*d

{8} A la octava pregun*t*ta dijo q*ue* Save q*ue* el di*c*ho Melchor / perez eS cazado e tiene hijaz e nietoS lexitimos e q*ue* / no tiene Yndios de repartim*ien*to e q*ue* Save q*ue* tiene Un / Correjim*ien*to de muy poco Salario

{9} A la novena pregunta dijo q*ue* la Save Como en ella Se / Contiene preguntado Como lo Save dijo que porq*ue* al / tiempo que el di*c*ho liz*encia*do texada Vino Valian laz Cozaz Como / en la pregunta Se Contienen y a*h*ora corre a los presios Como / la pregunta (Como la pregunta) lo declara e q*ue* Valia mas / en aquel tiempo Sien(t) p*es*os q*ue* a*h*ora treçientos

{10} A la dies pregunta dijo q*ue* lo Save q*ue h*a Vivido Como / hombre de bien e *h*a Sustentado Su cassa honrradamen- / tte e lo demaz q*ue* no lo Save porq*ue* no Se hallo / En la tierra al tiempo q*ue* Su madre murio y lo demaS no / {rúbrica}

[fol. 6r]

5

Lo Save y que save q*ue* los dos hermanos Se metieron Frayles

{11} A la onse preguntaz que diçe lo q*ue* di*c*ho tiene Y en ello Se aFir- / mava e aFirmo e Firmolo de Su nombre Fran*cis*Co Cor- / nejo Diego de Colio

{testigo Ju*an* / Galeasso} {1} El di*c*ho Juan Galeasso testigo Jurado e pregunta- / do a la primera pregunta dijo q*ue* Conose al di*c*ho Melchor perez / de diez años a esta partte por Vista e habla e Comunicasion / q*ue* Con el Susodicho *h*a tenido y tiene

{*G*enerale*s*} Preguntado por las preguntaz Generale*S* de la ley dijo que *e*s de (h)e- / dad de quarenta años pocos mas o menos y que no le em- / pesse ninguna de las generalez por q*ue* deje de deçir Verdad

{2} A la Segunda pregunta dijo q*ue* le oyo deçir mas q*ue* no le co- / noSio

{3} A la terSera pregunta dijo q*ue* Save q*ue* del *tiem*po que *e*ste depone / a esta partte Siempre le *h*a visto Servir a Su mag*esta*d Con sus armas / e Cavallos a Su costa

{4} A la quartta pregunta dijo q*ue* oyo deçir lo Contenido en / la dicha pregunta Y lo demaz no lo Save

{5} A la quinta pregunta dijo q*ue* la Save Como en ella Se Con- / tiene preguntado Como lo Save dijo que porque *e*ste / que depone fue al di*c*ho Viaje y Vio que llevo los di*c*hos Cava- / llos negros y ganadoS Contenidos en la di*c*ha pregun*t*ta / y q*ue* no pudo dexar de se gastar mucha Can*tt*i*da*d de pesos / de oro en todo lo Susodi*c*ho pero q*ue* este que depone no / Save el Verdadero Valor porque llevo muchos Consigo

{6} A la Sexta pregun*t*ta dijo que la Save porque este / (^porq*ue* este) q*ue* depone lo tomo el di*c*ho ganado por man- / dado de Don Garcia lopez maesse de Campo Siendo / este q*ue* depone Algua*ç*il mayor y apoSentador del Campo / porq*ue* tuVo neSesidad la gente del di*c*ho ganado y q*ue* Save / q*ue* los di*c*hos negroS Se huyeron Y lo demas Se gasto todo / {rúbricas}

[fol. 6v]
Y que no Volvio Con alguno de todo ello

{7} A la Septima pregunta dijo que Save este que depone que no po- / dra dexar de Venir adeudado Segun los muchoz gastoz / de Cos(t)az que el dicho Melchor pereZ llevava que la Cantidad / no la Save

{8} A la octava pregunta dijo que Save este que depone que el dicho / Melchor peres es cassado lejitimamente e tiene hijaz e nie- / tos lejitimos e que no tiene Yndios de repartimiento / y otraz Grangeriaz ningunaz maz de Un pobre Correjimiento

{9} A la novena pregunta dijo que Save lo Contenido / en la dicha pregunta Como en ella Se Contiene porque lo / Ve Cada dia pazar e Save que Valian maz Sien(t) pesoz en- / tonSes que ahora quatroSientos y mas y todaz las Cozas / han Subido en Creçido preçio

{10} A la deSima pregunta dijo que la Save Como en ella Se / Contiene porque tiene el dicho Melchor perez por hom- / bre honrrado y Cassado y que ha oydo deçir lo Contenido / en la dicha pregunta y lo demas no lo Save

{11} A la onSe pregunta dijo que diçe lo que dicho tiene e que / todo lo Susodicho es publico e notorio e Firmalo de su nom- / bre FrancisCo Cornejo Juan Galeasso

{testigo her- / nan florez} {1} El dicho Hernan flores testigo jurado e preguntado a la / primera pregunta dijo que Coneze al dicho Melchor peres / e ConoSio al lizenciado de la torre su padre de doSe años de / esta partte poco mas o menoS

{Generales} Preguntado por laz preguntaz generalez de la ley dijo / que es de (h)edad de quarenta años poco mas o menos / y que eS cuñado del dicho melchor peres e (h)ierno del dicho / lizenciado de la torre

{2} A la Segunda pregunta dijo que ConoSio al dicho lizenciado

de / la torre por jues de reSidençia e governador en este / nuevo Reyno e que Save que murio en el dicho Cargo

{3} A la terSera pregunta dijo que del tiempo que tiene dicho / Save que el dicho Melchor perez Servio a Su magestad en todo / le que Se ha oFreçido Con sus armaz e Cavallos Sin llevar Salario / {rúbricas}

[fol. 7r]
6
Alguno

{4} A la Cuartta pregunta dijo que Vio este que depone / Venir al dicho Melchor peres Con Su muger e hijas a poblar / E Vivir en la dicha Governaçion que dezpues aca ha reSedido / en esta ciudad a donde al pressente es Vezino e en lo demaz que diçe / lo que dicho tiene

{5} A la quinta pregunta dijo que Save que el dicho Melchor perez / fue Con el governador francisco Vasques de Coronado a la Conquista / de Sivola e tierra nueva muy bien adereSado Como la pre- / gunta lo deClara Y que Valia bien la canttidad en la preguntta / Contenida o poco menoS

{6} A la Sexta preguntta dijo que Save que quando el dicho Mel- / chor peres Volvio no traia coza alguna de lo que llevo por do / Cree este que depone que todo Se gasto en la dicha guerra / y entrada Como dicho tiene

{7} A la Septima pregunta dijo que Save que Vino adeudado de la dicha / Conquista pero que no Save en quanta Canttidad

{8} A la octava preguntta dijo que la Save Como en ella Se Con- / tiene porque lo ha Visto e lo Vei[64]

{9} A la novena preguntta dijo que la Save Como en ella Se Contiene / preguntado Como la Save dijo que porque la Vio y paza y paso / aSi Como en la pregunta Se Contiene

{10} A la deçima preguntta dijo que Save que Vive honrrada- / mentte Con Su muger e hijos e nietoS lejitimoS de lejitimo

/ matrimonio y todo lo demaS en la pregunta Contenido por- / que eS cuñado Cassado Con Su hermana

{11} A la onSe preguntta que diçe lo que dicho tiene e que todo lo Su- / sodicho es publico e notorio e Firmolo de su nombre / FrancisCo Cornejo Hernan floreS Balthassar de / Montoya eScrivano de Su magestad

{testigo Andrez / de Villanueva} {1} El dicho Andrez de Villanueva Vezino de la ciudad de guadalaxara / a la primera pregunta dixo Que ConoSe al dicho Melchor / Peres Vezino de la dicha ciudad e Que ConoSio al dicho lizenciado de la / torre su padre de doSe años a esta partte poco mas o menos / {rúbrica}

[fol. 7v]
{Generales} Preguntado por laz preguntaS generales de la ley dijo que es de / (h)edad de quarenta años poco mas o menos y que no le em- / pessen ninguna de las generalez

{2} A la Segunda preguntta dijo que ConoSio al dicho lizen- / ciado de la / torre jues de reSidençia e Governador e save que murio en / el dicho Cargo e Save que le tenia por su hijo al dicho Mel- / chor perez y por tal lo Vio tratar

{3} A la terSera preguntta dijo que Save este que depone que ha mucho / tiempo que esta en esta tierra pero que no Save quanto y que del tiempo / que este testigo le Conosse le ha Visto Servir a Su magestad en lo / que Se ha oFreçido

{4} A la Cuartta preguntta dijo que diçe lo que dicho tiene en la / pregunta antes de esta

{5} A la quintta pregunta dijo que Save que el dicho Melchor / perez Fue Con el governador FrancisCo Vazques de Coro- nado a la / tierra nueva y Save que fue bien adereSado de Cavallos y armaz / y negroS ganado Y todo lo demaz neSesario y que Save que / Se gastarian Muchos dineroS pero que este testigo no Save / quantos

{6} A la Sexta pregunta dijo que Save este que depone que al / tiempo que Volvio traia poco o nada porque Se gasto todo en / la dicha guerra

{7} A la Septena pregunta dijo que Save que Vino adeudado pero que no / save en quantta Canttidad

{8} A la octava preguntta dijo que Save que eS cazado e tiene / muger e hijaz e nietos lejitimos e Save que no tiene repar- / timiento de Yndios y haçiendaz Sino es el correjimiento / en la pregunta Contenido Con el dicho Salario

{9} A la novena pregunta dijo que la Save Como en ella Se Contiene / porque este testigo lo Save e lo Vey passa Como en la preguntta / Se Contiene

{10} A la deSima pregunta dijo que Save que dicho Melchor peres / ha Vivido e Vive honrradamente y que es hijo de honrrades / padre e madre

{11} A la onSe preguntta dijo que diçe lo que dicho tiene y (lo) firmolo de su / nombre FrancisCo Cornejo Andrez de Villanueva / {rúbrica}

[fol. 8r]
(^6)^7
{testigo Pedro / de ledezma} {1} El dicho Pedro de ledesma testigo Jurado e preguntado a la pri- / mera pregunta dijo que Conoze al dicho Melchor perez de dose añoz / a esta parte poco maz o menoS e que Save que es Vezino de la dicha Ciudad

{Generales} Preguntado por las preguntas generales de la ley dijo que es / de (h)edad de treinta y Sinco años poco mas o menoS e que es Su / (H)ierno pero que por esto no dejara de deçir Verdad

{2} A la Segunda pregunta dijo que Conoçio al dicho lizen- / ciado de la torre / padre de dicho Melchor perez e que Save que Fue jues de reSiden- / çia e Governador eN este nuevo reyno por Su magestad e que murio / en el dicho Cargo En Serviçio de Su magestad

{3} A la terSera pregunta dijo que Save que deSpues que del tiempo que este / testigo le Conosse Siempre le ha visto Servir a Su magestad Con suz / Armaz e Cavalloz e eSclavos a Su Costa Y m(en)içion Sin / salario alguno

{4} A la quartta pregunta dijo que havia oydo decir lo Contenido / en la dicha preguntta a muchaz perSonaz Conquistadorez / de la dicha tierra Que lo Vieron

{5} A la quinta pregunta dijo que Save que Fue El dicho Mel- / chor perez Con el dicho Governador a Servir a Su magestad / dexando Su cassa Y muger e hijos y que Save que gasto / En la dicha jornada y perdio mas de quatro mill Cas- / tellanos En la dicha jornada porque llevo Muchos Cava- / llos y negroS y eSclavoS Y ganadoS de lo qual todo Se le / perdio o la mayor parte de ello y Vino adeudado lo qual / no hUbo ayuda de Costa ni Salario alguno

{6} A la Sexta pregunta dijo que diçe lo que dicho tiene en / la pregunta antes de esta

{7} A la Septima preguntta dijo Que Save que Vino adeu- dado / de la dicha jornada Como los demaz que fueron a la dicha / Jornada

{8} A la octava preguntta dijo que Save que es Cassado e tiene / (^Hijos e) Muger ^e hijos e niettoS lejitimoS e que no tiene Yndios de / {rúbrica}

[fol. 8v]
(De) Repartimiento ni otraS haçiendaS ni Renta Sino eS Un / Correjimiento de en termino de esta ciudad que los Señores oydores le / Haçen merzed en nombre de Su magestad de que le dan Hasta Si- / ento y treinta pesos del oro que Corre

{9} A la Novena pregunta dijo que Save que el dicho lizen- ciado tejada / Vino a este nuevo reyno a tomar reSidençia a francisco Vazques / de Coronado Como la pregunta lo diçe e

Save que tazo los Co- / rrejimientoS y que a la taSaçion Se remitte y que todas / laz Cozaz Valen a exessivo preçio y que Vale Una fanega / de maiz doS pesos y que no basta el Salario de dicho Correjimiento / (^y) ^a Sustentarsse de maiz e por el Consiguiente todas las de- / mas Cozas en mucha Can- ttidad Como la pregunta lo deClara

{10} A la deçima pregunta dijo que la Save Como en ella Se / Contiene e Save que Se metieron fraylez por tener neSesidad

{11} A la onSena preguntta dijo que diçe lo que dicho / tiene e que todo lo Suso eS publico e notorio e firmolo / de su nombre Francisco Cornejo Pedro de ledesma

{//} E Yo el dicho eScrivano en Cumplimiento de lo pedido por / el dicho Melcjor pereS di y entregue al Susodicho la dicha / provança eScrita Segun dicho eS e para el dicho efecto / testigos Pedro de ledesma Barttolome de Coca Vezinos y estantes / en esta dicha çiudad Passo ante mi Baltazar de montoya / eScrivano de Su magestad

{/} Concuerda Con la Ynformaçion original que para efecto de / sacar este tanto esxri(p)to[65] el señor lizenciado Diego flores de la torre / Arçediano de la santa Ygleçia Catedral de esta Çiudad de guadalaxara / Nuevo Reyno de la galiçia a que la Volvi a que me remitto / y para que Conste en Virtud de Su pedimiento y mandato del / señor lizenciado Don Juan de Volivar y Cruz del Consejo de Su magestad / y Su oydor de la Real Audiencia de este dicho Reyno e Jues de provinçia En esta Corte que de SuSo Va Ynsertto di / El pressente que Va Sierto y Verdadero y a lo Ver Sacar Correjir Y / Consertar fueron testigos Jaçinto de pineda ledesma Don luiz / {rúbrica}

[fol. 9r]
de Nijar y Don Lorenço ViScaino Vezinos y estanttez / En esta ciudad de guadalaxara donde es fecho En Veinte y trez / diaz del mes de agosto de mil Seisienttos y Setenta Y Un / años testado Un {obliterated} - de - este = n Vuestra = han mandado - leasso / leaso - mercedes - g Sien - Vuestro - a - o

- pues V*uestr*a - hago mi Sig- / no En testim*oni*o de Verdad Don Thomaz de (h)orendayn / eScriv*a*no mayor R*ea*l y de provinçia derechos a SeSSenta y quatro / m*aravedie*s foxa y no mas doy fee = Damos fee q*ue* Don Tho- / mas de (h)orenday*n* de q*uie*n pareçe Signado y firmado el / {a*p*robaz*i*on} testim*oni*o de las Siete foxaz antes de *e*sta esScrivano de Su mag*esta*d / mayor del juzgado General de bienes de difuntos de / este reyno de la nueva galiçia y de provinçia en esta /

Cortte y Como tal a todos los autoS testimonioS y de- / maz reCaudoS q*ue* ante el *h*an passado y passan Se lez / *h*a dado y da Entera fee y Credito Judiçial y EXtrajudi- / çialmente y porQue Conste damos la press*en*te En guadalax*a*ra / a VEinte y tres diaz del mes de agosto de mil Seisientos / y Setenta y Un años = Melchor de Medra*n*o *e*Scriv*a*no R*ea*l / Di*e*go de la parra Ardevol *e*Scriv*a*no publico y R*ea*l = Diego / de Galarreta *e*Scriv*a*no R*ea*l

Document 33

Cristóbal de Escobar's Proof of Service, 1543

AGI, México, 204, N.14

INTRODUCTION

A third-generation *hidalgo*, 19-year-old Cristóbal de Escobar took a Spanish servant with him in 1540 on the expedition to Tierra Nueva.[1] In keeping with his *hidalgo* status, he was better accoutered than the average member of the expedition, possessing a chain mail vest and an unspecified type of European head armor, in addition to native arms and armor.[2] As a horseman in Vázquez de Coronado's personal guard, Escobar had two or three horses.[3] The typical horseman on the expedition had only one.[4] Befitting his at least moderate rank, he was given command of small units of men on several occasions during the expedition.[5] His social and economic status is also apparent in the fact that he, like Melchior Pérez, took a number of livestock with him on the expedition at his own cost.[6]

During the expedition to Tierra Nueva Escobar was among the advance guard when it reached Cíbola in July 1540, participated in the search for Hernando de Alarcón's ships with Melchior Díaz later that year, and was responsible for "a system and method for building a bridge across a very large river, by which the river was crossed." He also is reported to have carried relief supplies to the advance guard from San Gerónimo de los Corazones.[7] Later he testified as a *de oficio* witness regarding the expedition's treatment of indigenous peoples.[8]

Only a little over a year after the disintegrating expedition returned to the Ciudad de México, Escobar petitioned

the king for perquisites commonly awarded to an *hidalgo*, such as himself, who had served his sovereign at great expense and had been wounded in the process.[9] That request was recorded in the document transcribed and translated here, AGI, México, 204, N. 14. In the petition, Escobar's expressed desire is only for the right to display a coat of arms.[10] Much of the examination of witnesses, however, concerns Escobar's unremunerated expenses as a result of the expedition, suggesting that his appeal was implicitly for financial recompense.

Escobar's claims before the king and the Consejo de Indias are supported by the testimony of seven *de parte* witnesses, all but one of whom are fellow former expeditionaries. They all agree that their companion in arms is "suffering deprivation and hardship" and has been "in hardship and privation [ever] since he returned from the war."[11] His life-long acquaintance Hernando Gutiérrez states that Escobar "is worthy of whatever grants His Majesty may make him."[12]

Both financial recompense and a heraldic emblem were forthcoming, though it took several years for approval of the coat of arms. A royal *cédula* of July 20, 1551, granted Escobar the right to display a coat of arms described as follows:

> una torre de plata en campo colorado, y por orla ocho estrellas de oro en campo azul; por timb(l)re un yelmo cerrado, por devisa un brazo armado con una espada desnuda en las manos, con sus trascoles y dependencias

a follages de azul y oro [a silver tower on a field of red; as a border, eight stars on a field of blue; as an insignia at the top, a closed helmet; as device (crest), an armored arm with an unsheathed sword in hand; with its mantling and foliage of blue and gold].[13]

In the same year Escobar received his coat of arms, he was also made, by means of a personal grant from the king, *corregidor* of a native community called either Xicotepeque or Xilotepeque.[14] But he evidently had begun receiving appointments to royal offices as early as 1544. For instance, he served as *justicia mayor* of Guachinango and Pagautla.[15] By 1561 Antonio de Turcios could call Escobar one of the principal *vecinos* of the Ciudad de México. Nevertheless, he continued to be pressed for money and was granted a supplemental salary of 200 *pesos* because his *corregimiento* paid so little.[16] After 1561 Escobar drops from sight in the surviving documentary record.

The text of the former expeditionary's 1551 petition for a coat of arms survives as one of the copies Escobar requested immediately following the taking of supporting testimony. Missing from the record is any *de oficio* testimony that might have been taken in the case.[17] There are two signatures on the document, that of the *escribano* who prepared the copy, Antonio de la Cadena, and that of Sancho López de Agurto, the *escribano* who certified the copy.[18] The Spanish transcription and English translation that follow are the first to be published in either language.

FIGURE 33.1. Cristóbal de Escobar's coat of arms, reproduced from Sociedad de Bibliófilos Españoles, *Nobiliario de Conquistadores de Indias,* plate 41.

TRANSLATION

[1r]

Holy Catholic Cesarean Majesty

I, Cristóbal de Escobar, a *vecino* of the Ciudad de México, declare that I [am] one of the first settlers of this *ciudad* and have maintained and continue to maintain my *casa poblada* [here],[19] with my wife and children, always keeping my arms and armor, horses, and *criados* at the ready. I have served Your Majesty in everything that has presented itself and especially in the fighting and reconnaissance in Tierra Nueva, taking [with me] my arms and armor, horses, and servants.[20] And [I have served Your Majesty] on other *entradas* and missions of reconnaissance, all at my own expense and provisioning, taking people under my command. I have performed conspicuous services to Your Majesty in everything which has presented itself, [for instance,] traveling [with very few] people through large settlements [. . . traveling] quickly in order to relieve the expedition with supplies which it sorely needed on account of the large unsettled areas which were coming farther on. In addition to this, [I did outstanding service] by establishing a system and method for building a bridge across a very large river, by which the river was crossed.[21] During the aforementioned fighting and reconnaissance I suffered the loss of much of my assets because I have always traveled at my own cost and provisioning, as is all a matter of record and is apparent in this proof of worthiness I am presenting.

I humbly ask Your Majesty that I be granted a coat of arms and heraldic banners[22] which I could carry and place on my house. [This would be] in remuneration for my services and so that [some] memory of me and my descendants might remain. [The coat of arms would be] like and in the same design as this [drawing] which I am submitting [herewith].[23] [I ask that it be granted] so that I can enjoy the benefit of the concession Your Majesty may make to me in all Your Majesty's kingdoms and dominions.

[1v] {Cristóbal de Escobar, a *vecino* of the Ciudad de México, requests a coat of arms, [a drawing of which] he submits herewith.}

{to the lord doctor}[24]

[drawing is missing]

[2r] {México 1543}

A proof of worthiness *ad perpetuam rey memoriam* [for the perpetual remembrance of the matter],[25] executed before the *justicia ordinaria* of the great Ciudad de Tenuxtitan-México in Nueva España of the Indies of the Ocean Sea, at the request of Cristóbal de Escobar, a *vecino* of this *ciudad*, to inform His Majesty of the services he has performed.[26] {rubric}

It is secured and sealed, etc.

[2v] [blank]

[3r] In the great Ciudad de Tenuxtitan-México in Nueva España, on the fourteenth day of the month of November in the year of Our Lord one thousand five hundred and forty-three, Cristóbal de Escobar, a *vecino* of this *ciudad*, appeared in person before the very noble lord Antonio de la Cadena, *alcalde ordinario* in this *ciudad*, and in the presence of me, Sancho López de Agurto, registered public *escribano* of this *ciudad*.[27] He presented a petition accompanied by questions [in] an *interrogatorio*, the substance of which is the following:

Very noble lord,

Cristóbal de Escobar, a *vecino* of the Ciudad de México, appeared before Your Grace and stated, "I have need of executing a certain proof of worthiness *ad perpetuam rey memoriam* [for the perpetual remembrance of the matter] (or as [might] better [be said], in accordance with the law that time be set aside [for execution of such a proof]). [Namely,] concerning when [it was that] I came to Nueva España with my wife and household to lodge and reside in this part of the world. And the services I have performed for His Majesty since[28] I came [here]. And the expenditures I have made from my assets, and hardships I have personally [endured] in the aforementioned service of His Majesty, without [3v] taking wages, salary, or any recompense whatsoever, but at my own cost and provisioning. And about other things I need to prove, in order to make a report about [them] to His Majesty and his illustrious viceroy of Nueva España, or before whatever other judges it might be appropriate for me [to do so].

"Therefore I request of Your Grace that you order that the witnesses whom I will present for this purpose be queried and examined by means of the questions in the *interrogatorio* which I am presenting [herewith]. That you order that I be provided [a copy] of what they state and declare, signed, secured, and certified. And [that] for [the purpose of certification] you include [a copy of] the basis of your authority and the judicial ruling [establishing it], to the extent provided by law, not more or in excess, so that it is valid and fully certified both for a judicial hearing and outside it.

"I request [this] of Your Grace's very noble office, and ask [that] justice [be done]."

The witnesses who are or may be presented on behalf of Cristóbal de Escobar, a *vecino* of this *ciudad*, are to be queried and examined by means of the following questions:

[4r]
{1} {Item} First, whether they are acquainted with me and whether they have knowledge of how long ago I came to this part of the world with my wife and household. They are to state [what they know].

{2} {Item} Item. Whether they know that it could be six years, more or less, since I, Cristóbal de Escobar, came to Nueva España with my wife and household. And [that] I have maintained and continue to maintain a *casa poblada* in the Ciudad de México, where I presently reside. They are to state what they know.

{3} {Item} Item. Whether they know, etc., that I, Cristóbal de Escobar, went to Tierra Nueva in His Majesty's service in the company of Captain Francisco Vázquez de Coronado, His Majesty's captain general. [And that] I went there with my arms, double-thick armor, three horses, and a manservant to whom I was paying and did pay day wages.[29] They are to state what they know.

{4} {Item} Item. Whether they know, etc., that I, Cristóbal de Escobar, took part in[30] the aforementioned fighting for three years, more or less, serving His Majesty with my arms and armor and horses, at my own cost and provisioning. [That] I served for the whole time[31] during all the fighting and *entradas* which presented themselves in that land and [the leadership] assigned and entrusted to me, giving very excellent account of [myself]. [4v] And [that] since I came to this *ciudad*, I have always maintained my *casa poblada*, as well as arms and armor and horses. They are to state what they know.

{5} {Item} Item. Whether they know, etc., that I, Cristóbal de Escobar, had people under my command.[32] [That] with them I went in person to the aid of the expedition from the *provincia* of Los Corazones to the *provincia* of Cíbola, [a distance of] one hundred and fifty leagues.[33] [And that] by this means the expedition was relieved from danger with supplies of which it was in very great need because of the large unsettled areas there were along the way. They are to state, etc.

{6} {Item} Item. Whether they know that if I, Cristóbal de Escobar, had not gone and expended so much effort in seeing that the expedition was provided with supplies, many of our Indian allies, Spaniards, and Blacks would have died of hunger. That because of the few [supplies] they had come across, more than sixty of our Indian allies had [already] died along the way from hunger, as well as some Spaniards and Blacks.[34] [And that] because the expedition was resupplied, no one [further] died. They are to state what they know, etc.

{7} {Item} Item. Whether they know, etc., that in order to travel rapidly and arrive in time [5r] to aid the expedition, I left behind some fatigued horses, as well as some companions who were to protect them. [That] [those men] were expected to travel with the [main body of the] expedition. And [that] I, Cristóbal de Escobar, with four companions, traveled through very large settlements and very warlike people and arrived in time, [so] that the expedition, which was in very dire straits, was relieved. They are to state what they know.

{8} {Item} Item. Whether they know, etc., that I, Cristóbal de Escobar, went with the captain general and other captains to reconnoiter many areas, among which we reconnoitered the Mar del Sur[35] and many other settlements. [That] during that reconnaissance, I, Cristóbal de Escobar, often suffered severe hunger, going for more than sixty days without eating any sort of bread. And [that] I often endured severe thirst, spending four days without drinking or [even] coming across any water, traveling night and day, eating frozen sand in order to bear the thirst.[36] They are to state what they know.

{9} {Item} Item. Whether they know, etc., that for the entire time of three years I served in the war for His Majesty I traveled at my own cost and provisioning. And that for [the expedition] I took from Nueva España a certain number [5v] of livestock without being provided any salary or recompense by His Majesty or any other person.[37] They are to state what they know.

{10} {Item} Item. Whether they know, etc., that I, Cristóbal de Escobar, was present during all the fighting, skirmishes, [and] battles that we had during the aforesaid war, exposing my person to many and several dangers, as [did] the rest of

the *hidalgos* who participated in that fighting. They are to state what they know.

{11} {Item} Item. Whether they know that during that fighting [the Indians] killed a horse of mine which was worth four hundred *pesos de minas*. And [that] I lost many other things which I bought for the war and [my] service in it and which cost me much money. [This I did] without returning [with anything] to this *ciudad*, except my person alone, clothed in hides, and not another thing. They are to state what they know.

{12} {Item} Item. Whether they know, etc., that I, Cristóbal de Escobar, did not leave the war or return to this *ciudad* until the captain himself returned and brought me in his personal guard. They are to state what they know.

{13} {Item} Item. Whether they know that because of going to the war, I, Cristóbal de Escobar, [6r] am [now] impoverished, debilitated, and in debt because I expended (as I did) a large part of my assets without anything having been provided or given to me in recompense. They are to state what they know.

{14} {Item} Item. Whether they know, etc., that I, Cristóbal de Escobar, am an *hidalgo*, son of parents who are likewise, and grandson of grandparents who are also. [That my forbears] were considered and held to be such. [That] I, Cristóbal de Escobar, am [an *hidalgo*] and myself am well thought of, God-fearing, and desirous of increasing His Majesty's royal patrimony. And [that I am] not disobedient, but [am] of excellent conduct and reputation. They are to state what they know.

{15} {Item} Item. Whether they know, etc., that everything stated above is publicly and widely known and [is commonly held to be true].[38]

When the aforestated statement and *interrogatorio* had thus been presented, the lord *alcalde* declared that he was ordering and did order that Cristóbal de Escobar bring forward and present the witnesses whom he intends to make use of. [He also stated] that he is prepared to order [their testimony] to be taken. Because he is engaged in matters concerning the administration of justice [6v], he was delegating[39] and did delegate the authorizing and swearing in of the witnesses to me, the aforementioned public *escribano*. For this purpose he gave me a power of attorney and commission in the form [required by law].

After the aforementioned, on the aforesaid day, month, and year, Cristóbal de Escobar appeared in person before me, the aforesaid public *escribano*, and presented as a witness Lope de la Cadena, *estante* in this *ciudad*, from whom I, the aforesaid public *escribano*, took and received [his] oath, by the sign of the cross, in the form required by law, by virtue of which he promised to tell the truth. Witnesses: Lope de Madrid and Cristóbal Rodríguez Bilbao[40]

After the aforementioned, on the twentieth day of the month of November in the aforesaid year, Cristóbal de Escobar appeared in person before me, the aforesaid public *escribano*, and presented as a witness Juan de Zagala, *estante* in this *ciudad*, from whom I, the aforesaid public *escribano*, took and received [his] oath in the form required by law, by virtue of which he promised to tell the truth.

After the aforementioned, [7r] on the twenty-first day of the month of November in the aforesaid year, Cristóbal de Escobar appeared in person before me, the aforesaid public *escribano*, and presented as witness[es] in this case Miguel de Entrambasaguas and Domingo Martín,[41] from whom, each one of them, I, the aforesaid public *escribano*, took and received [their] oaths, by the sign of the cross, in the form required by law, by virtue of which [each one] promised to tell the truth.

After the aforementioned, on the fourth day of the month of December in the aforesaid year one thousand five hundred and forty-three, Cristóbal de Escobar appeared in person before me, the aforesaid public *escribano*, and presented as a witness in the case Juan López, *estante* in this *ciudad*, from whom I took and received [his] oath just as stated above.[42]

After the aforementioned, on the twelfth day of the month of December in the aforesaid year, Cristóbal de Escobar appeared before me, the aforesaid public *escribano*, and presented as witness[es] Alonso Álvares and Hernando Gutiérrez,[43] from whom I took and received [their] oath[s], by the sign of the cross, in the form required by law. [Each of them] promised to tell the truth, etc.

[7v] What the aforesaid witnesses stated and testified, each one for himself, is the following:

{Witness}
When Lope de la Cadena, *estante* in this *ciudad* and a witness presented in the case, had sworn his oath in accordance with the form required by law and was examined by means of the questions in the aforesaid *interrogatorio*, he declared the following:

{1} {Item} To the first question he replied that he has been acquainted with Cristóbal de Escobar for four years, more or less, during the fighting in Cíbola and in the *provincia* of Tierra Nueva to which Francisco Vázquez de Coronado went.

{2} {Item} To the second question he answered that he does not know.

{3} {Item} In response to the third question, he stated that what he knows is that he saw that, in His Majesty's service, Cristóbal de Escobar went on the conquest and pacification of the *provincia* of Cíbola and the other *provincias* of Tierra Nueva to which Francisco Vázquez de Coronado went as general. He also saw that he took along his arms and armor, two or three horses, and a Spaniard [8r] who was in service to him. During this [expedition] he saw that [Escobar] served very well, enduring many privations.

{4} {Item} To the fourth question [la Cadena] replied that he is aware of it, as stated in [the question]. Asked how he knows it, he stated that [it is] because he saw it happen, and it happen[ed] as the question states.

{5} {Item} To the fifth question he declared that he is aware of it, as stated in [the question]. Asked how he knows it, he stated that [it is] because he saw that it was and happened just as the question states.

{6} {Item} In answer to the sixth question, he said that he replies what he has stated in the previous questions. [And] that he knows that Cristóbal de Escobar employed great diligence and labored very concertedly to supply the expedition, so that it might not be in such dire straits. And that [the expedition] was in need of food supplies and some persons had died (but he does not know how many).

{7} {Item} To the seventh question he said that he is aware of it, as stated in [the question]. Asked how he knows it, he declared that [it is] because he saw it and was present during [Escobar's trip north]. It happen[ed] just as the question relates it.

[8v]
{8} {Item} To the eighth question he answered that he says what he has declared in the previous questions. And that he has heard the remainder of what is referred to in the question said on many occasions by many persons who were present, as something publicly and widely known.

{9} {Item} To the ninth question [la Cadena] declared that what he knows about it is that the aforesaid Cristóbal de Escobar served His Majesty in the war and conquest at his own cost and provisioning. For three years, more or less, he experienced many hardships. He and the rest who went to the war suffer[ed] hunger, [the] perils of risk, and mortal dangers.

{10} {Item} In reply to the tenth question, he said that he is aware of it, as stated in [the question], because at the points and places where this witness saw Cristóbal de Escobar, he saw him serving His Majesty very competently and courageously, like an *hidalgo*.

{11} {Item} To the eleventh question he answered that he is aware of it, as stated in [the question]. Asked how he knows

it, he stated that [it is] because he saw it happen as the question says. And he saw the aforesaid Cristóbal de Escobar return to this Ciudad de México [9r] very impoverished and needy. And he [had] lost and spent everything he [had] taken [with him] for his maintenance and support.

{12} {Item} To the twelfth question he replied that he is aware of it, as stated in [the question]. Asked how he knows it, he said that [it is] because he saw it happen, and it happen[ed] just as the question states.

{13} {Item} To the thirteenth question he answered that he says what he has stated in the previous questions. And this witness saw him return in a sad state. He considers it certain that [Escobar's] service has not been rewarded. For this reason he believes with certainty that he is suffering deprivation and hardship.

{14} {Item} To the fourteenth question this witness stated that he considers Cristóbal de Escobar to be such a person, an *hidalgo*, esteemed, and well thought of, as the question declares. Because he is as the question relates, he deserves that His Majesty reward his service, since he is a very capable person. By the oath he swore, [he stated that] this is the truth and what he knows concerning this case and for this purpose. And he signed it with his name, Lope de la Cadena.

[9v]
{Witness}
When Miguel de Entrambasaguas, a witness presented in the case, had given his oath in accordance with the form required by law and was examined by means of the questions in the aforesaid *interrogatorio*, he declared the following:

{1} {Item} To the first question he answered that he has been acquainted with the aforesaid Cristóbal de Escobar for the last five years, a little more or less.

{2} {Item} In reply to the second question, this witness stated that for the aforesaid period of five years during which he has known Cristóbal de Escobar, he has considered and continues to consider him [to be] a married individual in this *ciudad.* He knows this concerning the question.

{3} {Item} To the third question this witness responded that what he knows about it is that he saw the aforesaid Escobar go to the fighting in Tierra Nueva in the company of the captain referred to in the question. This witness saw him and was familiar with two horses and the double-thick armor he took [with him] to the war. And he saw that [Escobar] took a Spaniard as his servant, [at] his own cost. This is what he knows concerning the question.

[10r]
{4} {Item} To the fourth question [Entrambasaguas] stated that he is aware of it, as stated in [the question]. Asked how he knows it, he stated that [it is] because he saw it and was present at it and saw it happen, and it happen[ed] as the question relates.

{5} {Item} To the fifth question he said that he is aware of it, as stated in [the question]. Asked how he knows it, he declared that [it is] because he saw it happen as the question relates it. With regard to the long journeys, since Escobar was leading, he left a fatigued horse with this witness, and he lost it. At the time he lost it, this witness knows that they valued a horse [at] three hundred gold *pesos de minas*. He knows this.

{6} {Item} In answer to the sixth question, he declared that he is aware of it, as stated in [the question]. Asked how he knows it, he stated that [it is] because he saw it and was present at everything and saw it happen as the question states. If it had not been for the concerted diligence and persistence Cristóbal de Escobar exercised during the relief [expedition] which the question relates, this witness considers it certain and believes that the people of the armed force [10v] would have perished from the cold and hunger. [This was] due to the heavy snows there were and not knowing where they were. The aforesaid Cristóbal de Escobar was the great[est]

agent of relief (after Our Lord), so that they would not perish.

{7} {Item} To the seventh question he said that he is aware of it, as stated in [the question]. Asked how he knows it, this witness said that [it is] because he was present during it all. This witness is one of those who was traveling with the aforesaid Escobar. Regarding the three horses [Escobar] was taking, the one was worn out, and the expedition took care of the others because they were fatigued.

{8} {Item} To the eighth question [Entrambasaguas] declared that what he knows concerning the question is that Cristóbal de Escobar went with his captain to reconnoiter the Mar del Sur.[44] This witness heard it said as something publicly and commonly known [that] they endured much thirst and hunger during the aforementioned reconnaissance of the Mar del Sur. The rest that is referred to in the question this witness heard said as something publicly and widely known. This witness was present during many events in the course [of the expedition].

{9} {Item} In answer to the ninth question, he stated that he had heard what is referred to in the question said by many persons, as something publicly and commonly known, and it was [considered to be] so among many persons.

[11r]
{10} {Item} To the tenth question he said that he is aware of it, as stated in [the question]. Asked how he knows it, he stated that [it is] because he saw it and was present during everything referred to in the question, [and] it happen[ed] as related in it.

{11} {Item} To the eleventh question he stated that he says what he has declared in the previous questions. He knows [what is stated in] the question, just as it is referred to in it. Asked how he knows it, he said that [it is] because he saw that it was and happened as the question states it.

{12} {Item} To the twelfth question [Entrambasaguas]

replied that he is aware of it, as stated in [the question]. Asked how he knows it, he stated that [it is] because he saw it happen as the question says.

{13} {Item} To the thirteenth question he said that he knows [what is stated in] the question, just as it is referred to in it, because this witness has seen that Escobar has suffered and is suffering privation since he returned from the war without being rewarded for his service. This witness marvels at how the aforesaid Cristóbal de Escobar is able to maintain himself, given that he has seen him [11v] in hardship and privation [ever] since he returned from the war.

{14} {Item} To the fourteenth question this witness replied that during the time he has been acquainted with [Escobar] ([that is,] prior to today), he has considered and does consider him a person with the status of *hidalgo*, a person such as the question states. Out of respect [for this status], [Escobar's] captain commonly assigned *entradas* to him, since he was diligent (as [Entrambasaguas] considered that he certainly was) and [was] willing [to do] everything that dealt with His Majesty's service. By the oath he swore, [he stated] that this is the truth and what he knows about this matter. And he signed it with his name, Miguel de Entrambasaguas.

{Witness}
When Juan de Zagala, *estante* in this *ciudad* and a witness presented in the case, had given his oath in accordance with the law and was examined by means of the questions in the aforesaid *interrogatorio*, he declared the following:

{1} {Item} To the first question he stated that he has been acquainted with the aforesaid Cristóbal de Escobar for the last five years, a little more or less.

{2} {Item} In reply to the second question, he declared that for the period of five years [12r] this witness has known Cristóbal de Escobar, he has seen him living in this Ciudad de México, maintaining his wife and household [here], where up to the present he has seen him living and maintaining [it].

{3} {Item} To the third question he responded by saying that he knows it as stated in [the question]. Asked how he knows it, he said that [it is] because he saw it happen, and it happen[ed] just as the question relates it.

{4} {Item} To the fourth question he declared that he knows it as referred to in [the question]. Asked how he knows it, he stated that [it is] because he saw it happen, and it happen[ed] as the question says [it did].

{5} {Item} To the fifth question [Zagala] stated that he knows it as related in [the question]. Asked how he knows it, he stated that [it is] because he saw it and was present during it, and he saw it happen just as the question states.

{6} {Item} In answer to the sixth question, he said that what he knows about it is that this witness saw that when the general of the expeditionary force traveled ahead [to] the *provincia* of Cíbola, this witness and the rest who went with him suffered great privation and hardship from hunger and thirst that occurred along the way. Because of this [12v] many Indian allies and horses were left behind and died. The supplies which [Escobar and his party] took to them en route were a great benefit to those who were traveling in this way. He knows this concerning the question.

{7} {Item} To the seventh question he replied that he is aware of it, as stated in [the question]. Asked how he knows it, he stated that [it is] because he saw it happen, and it happen[ed] just as the question states.

{8} {Item} To the eighth question this witness declared that what he knows about it is that he saw that Cristóbal de Escobar was present during an *entrada* on which [Zagala] saw that he was without a drink of water for four days and suffer[ed] other hardships and hunger. [He knows this] because this witness saw it. He was present during [the *entrada*] and saw this. He also went sixty days without eating bread, during which they all suffered great hardship. Therefore, Escobar suffered it as the others [did].

{9} {Item} To the ninth question this witness stated that what he knows about it is that he saw that the aforesaid Escobar served His Majesty very well during the fighting, in all [13r] situations which presented themselves, at his own cost and provisioning. Regarding the livestock, he heard it said as something publicly and widely known that [Escobar] had taken livestock to the war.

{10} {Item} In reply to the tenth question, he declared that he knows it, as it is referred to in [the question]. Asked how he knows it, he stated that [it is] because he saw it and was present, and he saw it happen just as the question relates it.

{11} {Item} To the eleventh question [Zagala] answered that he is aware of it, as stated in [the question]. Asked how he knows it, he said that [it is] because he saw [it] happen in the way the question says. [And] that at the time some horses were commonly valued at a greater amount than is referred to in the question and others at less. Further, at that time [horses] were being sold at that price. The horse Escobar lost was worth that much. And everyone lost [what they had] during the fighting, as [did] Escobar, and returned very much in debt.

{12} {Item} To the twelfth question he responded by saying that he is aware of it, as stated in [the question]. Asked how he knows it, he said that [it is] because he saw it happen as the question states. And [that] [he and Escobar] returned together to this *ciudad.*

[13v]
{13} {Item} To the thirteenth question this witness declared that he believes and considers it certain that the aforesaid Escobar would have been impoverished and suffering deprivation because of having gone to the war and expended his assets on it. He knows that until the present Escobar has not been rewarded [for] the services he thus performed in His Majesty's service during the fighting.

{14} {Item} To the fourteenth question this witness said that he considers the aforesaid Cristóbal de Escobar to be a

person such as the question states. He has seen that he has been a peaceful, well thought of, and esteemed person and is considered and held to be such by many persons. He has seen that it is in this way something publicly and commonly known. By the oath he swore, [he declared] that this is the truth and what he knows about this matter. And he signed it with his name, Juan de Zagala.

{Witness}
When Domingo Martín, a *vecino* of this *ciudad* and a witness presented in the case, had given his oath in accordance with the law and was examined by means of the questions in the aforesaid *interrogatorio,* he declared the following:

{1} {Item} To the first question he answered that [14r] he has been acquainted with the aforesaid Cristóbal de Escobar for the last five years, a little more or less. And that this witness has been an *estante* for twenty-five years.

{2} {Item} To the second question he declared that (as he has said) for the aforementioned length of time of five years ([that is] before the present) that he has been acquainted with him, he has seen that he has maintained a *casa poblada* in this *ciudad* and [has] a wife, as the question says. [And that is true] at present [as well].

{3} {Item} In answer to the third question, [Martín] stated that he knows it as it is referred to in [the question]. Asked how he knows it, he stated that [it is] because he saw that it happen[ed] just as the question relates it, because this witness went on the aforesaid expedition. When they left this *ciudad,* this witness and Escobar left together. He saw that it happen[ed] just as the question states.

{4} {Item} To the fourth question he replied that he knows and saw that Cristóbal de Escobar was present in the fighting for a period of more than two and a half years, serving His Majesty in everything he was directed [to do]. And [that] he did everything that was presented and he was directed [to do], just as the question states. This witness saw and was present during [this].

[14v]
{5} {Item} To the fifth question this witness stated that what he knows about it is that he knows and saw that Cristóbal de Escobar traveled from the *provincia* of Los Corazones to Cíbola with some companions. When he arrived he brought some supplies that don Tristán de Arellano had been carrying, in order to relieve the [advance guard of the] expedition.[45]

{6} {Item} In response to the sixth question, he declared that he knows and saw that because Escobar came, food supplies were obtained. And this witness believes that if they had not been obtained, some Indians would not have failed to die from hunger. This is what he knows concerning the question.

{7} {Item} To the seventh question he answered that he says what he has stated in the previous question. Regarding what is referred to in the question about the horses that [Escobar] left behind, this witness heard it said (because he was at Cíbola) as something publicly and widely known among the persons [who were present] during the fighting.

{8} {Item} To the eighth question [Martín] said that he states what he has answered to the previous question. And he heard what is referred to in the question said [15r] as something publicly and commonly known. Further, he knows and saw that the aforesaid Cristóbal de Escobar went with the captain to the *provincia* of Tiguex, where he suffered hunger, hardships, and other privations.[46]

{9} {Item} In reply to the ninth question, [this witness] said that what he knows about it is that he knows and saw that Escobar took in his company some livestock that the witness had. [Martín] believes that [Escobar] went at his own cost and provisioning and without any salary or wages, because this witness did not see [such pay] given to any person who went to the war. If it had been given, this witness would not have failed to know about and see it.

{10} {Item} To the tenth question he responded by saying that he knows and saw that the aforesaid Escobar was present during all the fighting in the *provincia* of Tiguex.

And [that] he suffered great hardship there during the night watches in the fighting and other hardships incident to war. During [the fighting] he performed very well.

{11} {Item} To the eleventh question he stated that what he knows about it is that this witness knows that Cristóbal de Escobar [15v] lost a horse during the *entrada* referred to in the question. It seems to this witness that it was worth the three hundred *pesos* mentioned in the question. And that [Escobar] could not avoid losing many other things, as [did] the rest, who returned very much worn out and in debt.

{12} {Item} To the twelfth question he replied that he is aware of it, as stated in [the question]. Asked how he knows it, he stated that [it is] because he saw that when the captain returned to this *ciudad*, Escobar returned. And he did not leave [the expedition] nor was he sent away until the captain himself returned.

{13} {Item} In answer to the thirteenth question, he stated that he knows and has seen that Cristóbal de Escobar is impoverished and [suffers] deprivation and hardship. If [Escobar] had not gone to the war, he would have set his life in order, because of which he would not be in the straits [he is in]. In addition, up to the present he has not been given any reward for his service.

{14} {Item} To the fourteenth question this witness replied that he says what he has [previously] stated. What he knows concerning it is that he considers Cristóbal de Escobar [to be] a good Christian, esteemed and highly thought of. [16r] By the oath he swore, [he declared] that this is the truth. And he signed it with his name, Domingo Martín.

{Witness}
When Juan López, *estante* in this *ciudad* and a witness presented in the case, had given his oath in accordance with the law and was examined by means of the questions in the aforesaid *interrogatorio*, he declared the following:

{1} {Item} To the first question he answered that he has been acquainted with the aforesaid Cristóbal de Escobar for the last four years, a little more or less.

{2} {Item} To the second question he declared that for the aforementioned period of four years during which he has been acquainted with [Escobar] in this land, he has known and seen that he is married and maintains a house and keeps his wife in this *ciudad*.

{3} {Item} To the third question he stated that he knows and saw that Cristóbal de Escobar went to Tierra Nueva with his arms and armor and horses with the aforementioned captain in His Majesty's service. And he knew that [Escobar] was taking a young man with him. He knows this concerning the question.

{4} {Item} In reply to the fourth question, this witness said that he knows it as referred to in [the question]. Asked how he knows it, he stated that [it is] because he saw it happen, just as the question relates it.

[16v]
{5} {Item} To the fifth question [López] answered that he heard what is referred to in the question said as something publicly and commonly known among persons who went with [Escobar]. The witness does not remember their names.

{6} {Item} To the sixth question he stated that he knows it as referred to in [the question]. Asked how he knows it, he said that [it is] because he saw that it was and happened just as the question declares. [Escobar] performed a great service, in that the expedition was relieved.

{7} {Item} In response to the seventh question he said that he heard what is referred to in the question said as something publicly and widely known among persons present during the fighting. The aforesaid Escobar could not avoid suffering much hardship during the aforementioned *entradas*.

{8} {Item} To the eighth question [López] stated that he says what he has declared in the previous questions.

{9} {Item} To the ninth question he declared that what he knows about it is that he heard it said as something publicly and widely known that Escobar took livestock to the war. He believes and considers it certain that he went at his own cost and provisioning without being provided any salary on behalf of His Majesty or any another person. [17r] [López knows this] because if he had taken one or one had been given to him, this witness would have known it, and it could not be otherwise.

{10} {Item} To the tenth question he replied that he knows it, as it is referred to in [the question]. Asked how he knows it, he stated that [it is] because he saw that it was and happened just as the question says.

{11} {Item} In answer to the eleventh question, he declared that he knows and saw that [the Indians] killed one of Escobar's horses. It could have cost the three hundred *pesos de minas*, in accordance with [the way] its price was rising then, as [were the prices of] other things.[47] The rest [of the people] who went to the war [had to pay such prices].

{12} {Item} To the twelfth question he stated that he heard what is referred to in the question said as something publicly and commonly known. This witness [knows this] because he [went] ahead from Culiacán to Compostela and left Escobar [behind] in the fighting with the captain general.[48]

{13} {Item} To the thirteenth question [López] replied that he knows and has seen that Escobar is impoverished and suffering deprivation. And [further,] that his service has not been rewarded. He knows this concerning the question.

{14} {Item} To the fourteenth question this witness declared that he considers the aforesaid Cristóbal de Escobar [17v] a person [who is] a good Christian, esteemed, [and] well thought of, is of excellent conduct, and [is held in] high repute. And he sees that he is considered and held to be such. By the oath he swore, [he stated] that this is the truth and what he knows about this matter. And he signed it with his name, Juan López.

{Witness}

When Alonso Álvarez, *estante* in this *ciudad* and a witness presented in the case, had given his oath in accordance with the law and was examined by means of the questions in the aforesaid *interrogatorio*, he declared the following:

{1} {Item} To the first question he stated that he has known the aforesaid Cristóbal de Escobar for the last six years, a little more or less.

{2} {Item} To the second question he replied by saying that for the period of six years this witness has been acquainted with Cristóbal de Escobar, he has seen him being and living with his wife and household in this *ciudad*. He came from the *reinos* of Castilla in the same *nao* in which this witness came. He saw that it was and happened just as the question states.

[18r]

{3} {Item} In response to the third question, he said that he knows it as it is referred to in [the question]. Asked how he knows it, he stated that [it is] because he saw it, and it happen[ed] exactly as the question relates it.

{4} {Item} To the fourth question he answered that he knows it as it is referred to in [the question]. Asked how he knows it, he stated that [it is] because he saw it, and it happen[ed] this way, just as the question says.

{5} {Item} To the fifth question he stated that he heard what is referred to in the question said as something widely known among persons who went to the aforementioned war.

{6} {Item} To the sixth question [Álvarez] stated that he answers what he has declared in the previous questions. And that he knows that a Spaniard and [some] Blacks and Indians died. If the expedition had not been relieved, he does not know whether [more] would have died or not.

{7} {Item} In reply to the seventh question, he declared that what he knows concerning this case is that he knows that the aforesaid Cristóbal de Escobar traveled through the land of Indians, [through] both unsettled areas [18v] and dense settlements. He does not know about the remainder of what is referred to in the question.

{8} {Item} To the eighth question he answers that he knows and saw that the aforesaid Cristóbal de Escobar went to reconnoiter the Mar del Sur and [on] other *entradas* during which he suffered[49] great hunger and thirst, just as everyone suffered and endured them. He believes and considers it certain that Escobar would have endured [such lack], as one of those who went on [the *entradas*]. He knows this about this question.

{9} {Item} To the ninth question [Álvarez] stated that he heard it said as something publicly and commonly known that Cristóbal de Escobar took livestock to the war. And he knows that he served His Majesty during the war at his own cost and provisioning, without being paid a salary or anything for his expenses, either on His Majesty's behalf or [that] of any other person. He knows this.

{10} {Item} In answer to the tenth question, this witness said that he knows and saw that during the fighting and *entradas* in which he saw the aforesaid Escobar, [Álvarez] saw that he performed everything that was presented [19r] very well. And [that] [Escobar] went and was present during many [such *entradas*], which occurred over and again. And [he] suffer[ed] many hardships.

{11} {Item} To the eleventh question this witness stated that what he knows about it is that he knows and saw that [the Indians] killed one of Escobar's horses. [And that] at the time it was worth the three hundred *pesos* referred to in the question. This witness saw that [Escobar] had accoutered[50] his person well. But afterward he saw him return clothed in hides. He knows this concerning the question.

{12} {Item} To the twelfth question [Álvarez] replied that he is aware of it, as stated in [the question]. Asked how he knows it, he stated that [it is] because he saw it happen as the question states.

{13} {Item} To the thirteenth question he answered that he is aware of it, as stated in [the question]. Asked how he knows it, he stated that [it is] because he saw it, and it happen[ed] just as the question says.

{14} {Item} To the fourteenth question this witness stated that he considers the aforesaid Cristóbal de Escobar an *hidalgo* and holds him to be [such] a person. He considers him a good Christian, God-fearing and of excellent conduct, and [he is held in] high repute. [19v] He is considered and is such [a person]. This witness is certain of it. By the oath he swore, [he declared] that this is the truth and what he knows concerning this matter. And he signed it with his name, Alonso Álvarez.

{Witness}
When Hernando Gutiérrez, *estante* in this *ciudad* and a witness presented in the case on behalf of Cristóbal de Escobar, had sworn his oath in accordance with the law and was examined by means of the first and fourteenth questions in the aforesaid *interrogatorio*, he declared the following:[51]

{1} {Item} In reply to the first question, he declared that he has been acquainted with the aforesaid Cristóbal de Escobar for the last twenty-four years, a little more or less. And he knows that it could have been seven years, more or less, since Cristóbal de Escobar came to this part of the world with his wife and household.[52]

{14} {Item} To the fourteenth question (for which [reason] he was presented as witness), [Gutiérrez] replied that for the period of time he has stated in the previous question, he has been acquainted and still is acquainted with both Cristóbal de Escobar's parents and the aforementioned [individual himself]. [20r] Likewise, he knows and has known a great share of [the members of] his lineage.

And he knows that they were and are *hidalgos* and were considered and held as such in the *reinos* of Spain where they were living.

This witness considers the aforesaid Cristóbal de Escobar an *hidalgo* and has seen him considered and held in regard as such. [The witness] considers him a good Christian and a peace-loving and steady person, a stranger to lawsuits and controversies. He considers him a person who has always desired to increase His Majesty's royal patrimony during the time he has been present and this witness has known him in this part of world. And he has heard it said as something publicly and commonly known in this *ciudad* that [Escobar] has served His Majesty in this part of the world, performing what he was ordered to do by his captains and governors, like a person of *hidalgo* status.

[Gutiérrez] has known him to have his household and wife in this *ciudad*. [And that] he has suffered and continues to suffer privation [and] hardship here because his services have not been rewarded. [The witness] considers him [to be] a person so distinguished and of such repute who is worthy of whatever grants His Majesty may make him. [20v] By the oath that he swore, [he declared] that this is the truth and what he knows. And he certified it and signed it with his name, Hernando Gutiérrez.

When the evidence of worthiness had been received and recorded in the way that it is stated, the lord *alcalde* declared that he was ordering and did order me, the aforesaid public *escribano*, to extract and have extracted from it one, two, or more copies and furnish and deliver them to the aforesaid Cristóbal de Escobar, so that he might present them wherever and however is suitable within his rights. With those [copies] he stated he was including and did include the basis of his authority and the judicial ruling [establishing it], so that it may be valid and fully certified both in a judicial hearing and outside it. And he signed it with his name, Antonio de la Cadena.

Antonio de la Cadena

I, Sancho López de Agurto, their Cesarean Catholic Majesties' *escribano* and a registered *escribano* in this *ciudad,* was present and had [it] copied, corrected, and reconciled with the original. Therefore I affixed here this my sign, [which is] thus {sign}, in testimony of the truth.

{rubric} Sancho López de Agurto {rubric}

{Fees: no charge}

[21r and 21v] [blank]

FIGURE 33.2. The signature and registered sign (*signo*) of Sáncho López de Agurto. AGI, Patronato, 78A, N.1, R6\48. Reproduced courtesy of Spain's Ministerio de Educación, Cultura y Deporte.

TRANSCRIPTION

[fol. 1r]⁵³

Sacra Catolica Cesarea Magestad

*cristo*bal de *e*scobar Vezino de la Çiudad de mexico digo q*ue* yo he / sido Uno de los mas Antiguos pobladores d*e* la d*i*cha ÇiUda*d* / y he tenydo y tenGo my casa poblada co*n* my muger e hijos tenye*n*- / do A la continua mys Armas y Caballos y criados y he ser- / Vido A V*uest*ra mag*e*st*ad* en todo lo que se ha ofreçido y en espeÇial *en* la / Guerra y descubrimyento de la tierra nueVa lleVando mys / Armas y Caballos y *h*onbres de serViçio y en otras entradas / y desCubrimy*en*tos todo A my costa e mysio*n* e lleVando Gente A my / carGo y en todo lo q*ue* se ha ofreçido he hecho Senalados servyçios / A V*uest*ra mag*e*st*ad* and*a*ndo *con muy* poca gente por Grandes poblaÇio- / nes [. . .] *p*asando a⁵⁴ la ligera para hazer socorrer El Campo / *con* bast*im*entos q*ue* yba *en* muy Gran(d) nesçesydad A caUSa de / los Grandes despoblados q*ue* adelante se syGuya y de mas de *e*s- / to en dar (h)orden y manera para hazer una puente *en* / Un Rio muy Grande por donde se paso el d*i*cho Rio y en las / d*i*chas Guerras y descubrimy*en*tos he perdido muy Gran parte de / my hasyenda por *h*aber syenpre Andado A my costa e mysio*n* como / todo ello consta e pareÇer por esta ynform*ç*io*n* q*ue* prese*n*to / suplico A V*uest*ra mag*e*st*ad* q*ue* en Remuneraçio*n* de mys *ser*vyçios e para q*ue* / de my A de mys desÇendientes q*ue*de memoria se me haga m*erce*d / q*ue* pueda traer e poner *en* my Casa e Reposteros Un escudo de Ar- / mas segun(d) y de la manera q*ue* este q*ue* presento p*ar*a q*ue* pueda Gozar / d*e*sta m*erce*d *en* todos los Reynos y senorios de V*uest*ra mag*e*st*ad* en lo / qual V*uest*ra mag*e*st*ad* me hara m*erce*d

[fol. 1v]

{*cristo*bal de *e*scobar V*e*cin*o* de la Çiudad de mex*i*Co / pide Unas Armas / *p*or aqui *p*r*e*Senta}

{al S*eño*r doctor}

[fol. 2r]

{Mej*ic*o 15(5)43}

probança A perpetuan rrey memoria / fecha Ante la Justiçia (h)ordina- / ria de la gran(d) ÇiUdad (ÇiUdad) de / t(h)enuxtitan mexico de *e*sta / nueVa españa de las yndias / del mar oçeano A pedimy*ent*o / de *cristo*bal de escobar / Vezino de *e*sta ÇiUdad p*ar*a / ynformar A su mag*e*st*ad* / de los serViçios q*ue* / el *h*a (E) *h*echo {rúbrica}

Va çerrada y sellada *etcetera*

[fol. 2v] [blank]

[fol. 3r]

En la gran(d) ÇiUdad de t(h)enuxtitan / mexico de *e*sta nueVa es- / paña en Catorze dias del / mes de noVienbre año / del señor de myll E quy*nient*os E / quarenta E tres años Ante El muy / noble señor Antonyo de la cadena / alc*ald*e (h)ordinario En esta d*i*cha ÇiUdad / y en presençia de my sancho lopez / de agurto escri*ban*o publico E del numero / de *e*sta d*i*cha ÇiUdad paresçio p*re*sente / *cristo*bal de *e*scobar Vezino de *e*sta / ÇiUdad E presento Un pedimyen- / to con Un ynt(h)eRogatorio de pregun- / tas El t(h)enor de lo qual es esto / que se sigue

muy noble señor *cristo*bal de *e*scobar / Vezino de *e*sta ÇiUdad de mexico / paresco ante V*uest*ra m*erce*d E digo que yo / tengo nesçeÇidad de hazer Çierta / probança a perpetua(d)*n* Rey memo- / ria o como meJor de derecho *h*Aya / lugar del tienpo que a que pase / A esta nueVa españa con my muger / E casa Apo^*s*entar E Residir *en* *e*stas / p*ar*tes E de los serViçios que des- / pues que ahi pase *h*E hecho A su / mag*estad* / E de gastos de my hazienda E de / trabaJos de my persona que en el / d*i*cho serViçio de su mag*estad h*e hecho Sin por ello / {rúbrica}

[fol. 3v]
lleVar salario sueldo ny acostamy*ento* / Alguno sino A my costa E mysion E / de otras cosas que tengo nesçeçidad / probar para de *e*llo dar quenta a / su mag*estad* E a su yll*us*trisi*m*o VisoRey de es- / ta nueVa españa u ante otras / qualesquyer Justiçias que me / conVengan por tanto a V*uest*ra m*erce*d / pido que los *testig*os que presentare / en la d*i*cha Razon los mande p*re*Guntar / y esamynar por las preguntas / de *e*ste ynt(h)eRogatorio de que / hago presentaÇion E lo que dixe- / ren E depusieren me lo mande / dar signado E çeRado y en ma- / nera que haga fee E para Ello / Ynterponga V*uest*ra m*erce*d su aUtori- / dad E decreto JudiÇial en tan- / to quanto de derecho *h*A lugar / ny mas ny al(i)/*e*nde para que Val- / Ga E haga mas entera feé *en* Juyzio / E Fuera de *e*l y el muy noble ofiçio / de V*uest*ra m*erce*d ynploro E pido Jus- / tiÇia

E los testigos que son o fueren pre- / sentados por p*art*e de *crist*obal de es- / cobar Vezino de *e*sta ÇiUdad se pre- / gunten y esamynen po*r* las pre- / guntas siguyentes / {rúbrica} / 1

[fol. 4r]
{1} {y*tem*} primeramente si conosçen A my / E si tienen notiçia que tanto tienpo E a / que pase a estas p*art*es con my muger / E casa digan Et*ceter*a

{2} {y*tem*} yten si saben que puede *h*aber / Seys años poco mas o menos / tienpo que yo El d*i*cho *crist*obal de esco- / bar pase a esta nueVa españa / con my muger E casa E *h*E tenydo E / tengo *casa* poblada En esta ÇiUdad de / mexico donde al presente Re- / sido digan lo que saben

{3} {y*tem*} yten si saben Et*ceter*a que yo El d*i*cho / *crist*obal de *e*scobar fue en ser- / Viçio de su mag*estad* A la tieRa nueVa / *en* Conpañya del Capitan Franc*isc*o / Vazquez de coronado

capitan / general de su mag*estad* donde Fu(e)*i* con mys / Armas dobladas E tres caballos / E Un honbre de serViÇio A quyen / pagaba E pague s(ue)*o*ldada digan / lo que saben

{4} {y*tem*} Yten si saben Et*ceter*a que yo El d*i*cho / *crist*obal de *e*scobar AnduVe *en* la d*i*cha / gueRa tres años poco mas o m*en*os / tienpo sirV(^*d*)iendo A su mag*estad* con mys / Armas E caballos E A my costa E / mysion E serVi muy cumplidam*en*te / *en* toda la gueRa y entradas q*ue* / en la d*i*cha tieRa se ofresçieron / dando muy buena quenta de lo / {rúbrica}

[fol. 4v]
que me *en*Comendaban y encarga- / ban E Venydo A esta ÇiUdad sienpre / tengo my casa poblada con armas / E caballos digan lo que saben

{5} {y*tem*} yten si saben *etcetera* que yo El d*i*cho *crist*obal / de escobar tuVe A my cargo / gente con la qual E con my persona / Fue a socoRer El canpo desde la / proVinçia de los coraçones çiento / E çinquenta leguas E *h*asta la pro- / Vinçia de sibola de adonde se so- / coRio el d*i*cho canpo con bastimen- / tos que yba en muy gran(d) nesçe- / çidad A caUsa de los grandes des- / poblados que En el(l) d*i*cho camyno / *h*Abia*n* digan *etcetera*

{6} {y*tem*} yten si saben que si yo el d*i*cho / *crist*obal de *e*scobar no Fuera E pu- / siera tanta diligençia En hazer / proVe(h)er El d*i*cho canpo de bastimen- / tos que murieran muchos yndios / de n*uest*ros amygos y españoles / y negros de hanbre como en el d*i*cho / camyno de los pocos que *h*abian pa- / sado se *h*abian muerto mas de / Sesenta yndios de n*uest*ros amygos / y Çiertos españoles y negros / de hanbre y que por ser socoRido / El d*i*cho canpo no murio nynguno / digan lo que saben Et*ceter*a

{7} {y*tem*} yten si saben Et*ceter*a que por yr / Aprieça y llegar A tienpo / {rúbrica} / 2

[fol. 5r]
de socoRer Al d*i*cho canpo dexe / Çiertos caballos Cançados

E a Çiertos / conpañeros que los rreCoJesen / y se esperasen
A yr con el canpo / que Venya E yo El dicho cristobal de /
escobar con quatro conpañeros / pase por muy grandes
poblazones / y gente muy belicosa y llegue A / Tienpo que el
dicho Canpo fue socoRido / que yba en muy gran(d)
nesçeÇidad / Digan lo que saben

{8} {ytem} yten si saben etcetera que yo El dicho cristo- / bal
de escobar fue A descubrir con el / dicho capitan general E
con otros / capitanes A muchas partes donde / Descubrimos
la mar del sur E / otras muchas poblazones En el / qual
descubrimyento yo El dicho cristobal / De escobar padeçi
muy grandes / hanbres pasando mas de sesenta / Dias sin
comer nyngun(d) genero / de pan E sufri muy grandes /
çedes pasando quatro dias sin / beber ny topar nynguna agua
ca- / mynando noches E dias comyendo / El arena hElada
para suFrir la dicha / çed digan lo que saben

{9} {ytem} yten si saben Etcetera que todo El tiempo / de los
dichos tres años que en la dicha / gueRa A su magestad serVi
fu(e)i A my costa / E mysion E que para Ell(l)o lleVe / de
esta nueVa españa Çierta Can- / {rúbrica}

[fol. 5v]
tidad de ganados sin que de parte de / Su magestad ny de
otra persona me fuese / dado nyngun(d) sueldo ny
acostamyento / Digan lo que saben

{10} {ytem} yten si saben Etcetera que yo El dicho /
cristobal de escobar me halle en to- / da la gueRa Recuentros
batallas / que en la dicha gueRa tuVimos ofres- / çiendo
my persona a muchos E diVer- / sos peligros como los
demas hijos- / dalgo que en la dicha gueRa andaban /
digan lo que saben

{11} {ytem} yten si saben que en la dicha gueRa / me mataron
Un caballo que Va- / lia quatro çientos pesos de mynas / E
perdi otras muchas cosas que me / costaron muchos dineros
que para / la dicha gueRa y serViçio de ella / yo conpre sin
Volver A esta ÇiUdad / si sola la my persona Vestida / de
cueros y no otra cosa Alguna / Digan lo que saben

{12} {ytem} yten si saben Etcetera que yo el dicho / cristobal
de escobar no deXe la dicha / GueRa ny Vine A esta ÇiUdad
E has- / Ta que el dicho capitan se Vino E me / truXo en
Guarda de su persona digan / lo que saben

{13} {ytem} yten si saben que por yr yo El / dicho cristobal de
escobar a la dicha / {rúbrica} / 3

[fol. 6r]
gueRa E por gastar como gaste / gran(d) parte de my
hazienda es- / toy pobre gastado y enpeñado sin / que por
ello se me haya dado ny gra- / tiFycado nynguna cosa / digan
lo que saben

{14} {ytem} yten si saben etcetera que yo El dicho cristobal /
de escobar soy hiJodalgo E hiJo de / (^p)tales padres E nyeto
de tales A(h)bue- / los E los tales Fueron habidos E tenydos
/ por tales E yo El dicho cristobal de es- / cobar lo soy y si soy
bien quysto teme- / roso de dios y codiçioso de aUmen- /
Tar El patrimonyo Real de su / magestad y no ReVoltoso y
de buena Vida / E Fama digan lo que saben

{15} {ytem} yten si saben Etcetera que todo lo suso- / dicho es
publico E notorio E pu- / bliCa Voz E fama

E ansi presentado El dicho conos- / çimyento E
ynt(h)eRogatorio El dicho / señor alcalde dixo que mandaba
/ E mando que El dicho cristobal de es- / cobar trayga E
presente los testigos de / que se entiende aproVechar E que
eL / esta presto de los mandar tomar / E porque esta
ocupado en Cosas / Tocantes A la (h)exercicio de la Justiçia
/ {rúbrica}

[fol. 6v]
cometia E cometio la Resol(^z)- / Uçion E Juramentos de
los testigos / A my El dicho escribano publico para lo / qual
me dio poder E comysion / en forma

E despues de lo susodicho / En este dicho dia mes E año
suso- / dicho Ante my El dicho escribano publico / paresçio
presente El dicho cristo- / bal de escobar E presento por

testigo / A lope de la cadena estante *en* *e*sta / ÇiUdad del qual yo El *di*cho es*cri*ba*no* pu*bli*co / tome E Resçibi Juramento sobre / la señal de la cruz *en* fo*r*ma de de*r*echo / so Virtud del qual prometio / de *decir ver*dad *testigo*s lope de madrid / E *crist*obal Ro*drigue*s bilbao

E despues de lo susod*i*cho en / Veynte dias del mes de / noVienbre del d*i*cho año Ante my / El d*i*cho escri*ban*o publico paresÇio presente / El d*i*cho *crist*obal de escobar E pre- / sento por testigo a Juan de / zagala estante En esta d*i*cha ÇiUdad / Del qual yo El d*i*cho escri*ban*o pu*bli*co tome E / Resçibi Juramento *en* fo*r*ma de / derecho so Virtud del qual pro- / metio de *decir ver*dad

E despues de lo susod*i*cho en / {rúbrica} / 4

[fol. 7r]

Veynte E Un dias del mes de noVien*br*- / E del d*i*cho año Ante my El d*i*cho escri*ban*o pu*bli*co / paresçio presente El d*i*cho *crist*o- / bal de *e*scobar E *p*resento por tes- / tigo *en* la d*i*cha Razon (^a) A myguel / de *en*tranbasAguas E a domyngo / martin de los quales E de Cada / Uno de *e*llos yo El d*i*cho escri*ban*o pu*bli*co tome / E Resçibi Juramento sobre la señal / De la cruz *en* fo*r*ma de derecho so Vir- / Tud de *e*l prometio de *ver*dad *decir*

E despues de lo susod*i*cho *en* q*u*atro / dias del mes de dizienbre del / D*i*cho año de myll E quy*niento*s E quarenta / E treS años Ante my El d*i*cho escri*ban*o publico / paresçio presente El d*i*cho *crist*obal / De escobar E presento por *testig*o *en* la / D*i*cha Razon A Juan lopez es*tant*e *en e*sta ÇiUdad / Del qual tome E Resçibi Jura- / mento segun(d) de suso

E despues de lo susod*i*cho *en* doze / dias del mes de dizienbre del / D*i*cho año Ante my El d*i*cho escri*ban*o publico / Paresçio El d*i*cho *crist*obal de *e*scobar / E presento por testigo A Alonso / AlVares E a her*n*ando gutieRes de los / q*u*ales tome E Resçibi Juramento / sobre la señal de la cruz *en* fo*r*ma de / derecho E prometio de *decir ver*dad E*t*cetera / {rúbrica}

[fol. 7v]

E lo que los d*i*chos *testigo*s dixeron E de- / pusieron cada Uno por si es / lo siguyente

{*testigo*} El d*i*cho lope de la Cadena estante / En esta d*i*cha ÇiUdad testigo pre- / sentado En la d*i*cha Razon *h*abiendo / Jurado segun(d) fo*r*ma de derecho / E siendo preguntado por las pre- / Guntas del d*i*cho ynt(h)eRogatorio / Dixo lo siguiente

{1} {*ytem*} A la primera pregunta dixo que co- / nosçe Al d*i*cho *crist*obal de *e*scobar de la / guerra de sibola E de la proVinçia / de la tierra nueVa donde fue fran*ci*sco / Vazquez de coronado de quatro / años poco mas o menos

{2} {*ytem*} A la segunda pregunta dixo q*ue* la / non sabe

{3} {*ytem*} A la terçera pregunta dixo que / lo que de *e*lla sabe es E Vi(d)o q*ue e*L / Dicho *crist*obal de *e*scobar Fue en / serViçio de su mag*estad* A la conquysta / E paÇiFycaçion de la proVinçia / de Çibola E de las otras proVinçias / de la tierra nueVa donde Fue El d*i*cho / Fran*ci*sco Vazquez de coronado por / general E Vi(d)o q*ue* lleVo sus Armas / E dos o tres caballos E Un español / {rúbrica} / 5

[fol. 8r]

que le serVia donde Vi(d)o que sirVio / muy bien padessiendo muchas nes- / çeÇidades

{4} {*ytem*} A la quarta pregunta dixo que la / Sabe como *en e*lla se contiene pre- / Guntado como la sabe dixo que / porq*ue* lo Vi(d)o asi pasar E pasa / como (^p) la pregunta lo dize

{5} {*ytem*} A la quynta pregunta dixo que / la sabe como *en e*lla se contiene pre- / Gunt*a*do como la sabe dixo que porq*ue* / lo Vi(d)o ser E pasar como la pre- / Gunta lo dize

{6} {*ytem*} A la sesta pregunta dixo que / Dize lo que d*i*cho tiene *en* las pre- / Guntas Antes de *e*sta E que sabe / que El d*i*cho *crist*obal de *e*scobar / puso mucha diligençia E traba- / Jo muy bien porque no tuViese / nesçeÇidad El Canpo para ha- / zerlos prove(h)er E que hubo nes- / çeÇidad de basti- mentos E murie- / ron Çiertas personas que no sabe / que Cantidad

{7} {*ytem*} A la se*p*tima pregunta dixo / que la sabe como En ella se *contiene* / pregunt*a*do como la sabe dixo que / porque lo Vi(d)o E se hallo *p*resente / A ello E pasa Como la preg*u*n*t*a lo dize / {rúbrica}

[fol. 8v]
{8} {*ytem*} A la *oc*taVa pregunta dixo q*ue* dize lo / que d*i*cho tiene En las preguntas / Antes de *e*sta E que lo demas *en* la / pregunta *conteni*do lo oyo dezir por / publico E notorio A muchas per- / sonas que se hallaron *p*resent*e*s

{9} {*ytem*} A la noVena pregunta dixo / que lo que de *e*lla Sabe es q*ue e*l dicho / *crist*obal de *e*sCobar sirVio en la d*i*cha / guerra E conquysta A su mag*estad* A su / costa E mysion tienpo de tres años / poco mas o menos paso muchos / trabaJos El E los demas que a la / D*i*cha gueRa fueron padessiendo / hanbres y nesçesidades de Riez- / Gos E peli- gros de muertes

{10} {*ytem*} A la deçima pregunta dixo q*ue* la / sabe como En ella se contiene / porque *en* las p*a*rtes E lugares q*ue e*ste / Testigo Vi(d)o al d*i*cho (fray) *crist*obal de *e*scobar / le Vi(d)o serVir muy bien E anymo- / samente como hijodalgo A su mag*estad*

{11} {*ytem*} A la (h)onze pregunta dixo q*ue* la / sabe como En ella se contiene / preguntado como la sabe dixo / que porque lo Vi(d)o pasar co- / mo la pregunta lo dize E Vi(d)o / que El d*i*cho *crist*obal de *e*scobar / VolVio A esta ÇiUdad de mexico / {rúbrica} / 6

[fol. 9r]
E muy pobre(s) E nesçeÇitado(s) E perdio / E gasto todo lo que lleVo para man- / tenymy*en*to E suste(s)*n*tam*i*ento d*e* su p*e*rsona

{12} {*ytem*} A las doze preguntas dixo q*ue* la sa- / be como

En ella se *contiene* preguntado / como la sabe dixo que porq*ue* lo / Vi(d)o asi pasar E pasa como la / pregunta lo dize

{13} {*ytem*} A las treze preguntas dixo q*ue* / Dize lo que d*i*cho tiene *en* las pre- / guntas Antes de *e*sta E que *e*ste *testi*go / le Vi(d)o Venyr con mucha nesçe- / çidad E que tiene por çierto que / no se le *h*a gratiFycado su serViçio / E que por esta Razon cre(h)e por çierto/ que padesçera nesçeçidad E / TrabaJo

{14} {*ytem*} A las Catorze preguntas dixo / que *e*ste testigo tiene al d*i*cho / *crist*obal de *e*scobar por tal per- / sona hiJo- dalgo E honRado / E bien quysto tal como la preg*u*n*t*a / lo dize E que por ser tal como la / D*i*cha pregunta dize mere- *c*ese que / su mag*estad* le gratiFyque su ser- / ViÇio por ser persona en quye(r)*n* / cabe E que *e*sta es la *ver*dad E lo / que sabe de *e*ste *e*ffecto E caso para El / Juramento q*ue* hizo E firmolo de su n*o*mb*r*e / (pedro) *lope* de la Cadena / {rúbrica}

[fol. 9v]
{T*esti*go} Al d*i*cho myguel de EntranbasAguas / testigo presentado *en* la d*i*cha Ra- / zon *h*abiendo Jurado Segun(d) forma / de derecho E siendole pregun*t*ado / por las preguntas del d*i*cho ynt(h)e- / Rogatorio dixo lo siguyente (^a la)⁵⁵

{1} {*ytem*} A la primera pregunta dixo / que conosçe Al d*i*cho *crist*obal de *e*sco- / bar de çinco años a esta p*a*rte poco / mas o menos

{2} {*ytem*} A la segunda pregunta dixo q*ue* / Del d*i*cho Tienpo de Çinco años / que *e*ste testigo A que conosçe Al / D*i*cho *crist*obal de *e*scobar lo *h*a tenydo / E tiene por persona que esta *en* po- / sesion de casado En esta ÇiUdad / E que *e*sto sabe de *e*sta pregunta

{3} {*ytem*} A la terçera pregunta dixo q*ue* / lo que de *e*lla sabe es que *e*ste *testi*go / Vi(d)o yr A la gueRa de la d*i*cha t*i*erra / nueVa Al d*i*cho escobar *en* Conpañya / del d*i*cho capitan *en* la pregunta *conteni*do / E que *e*ste *testi*go le Vi(d)o E conosçio / DoS caballos que a la d*i*cha gueRa / lleVo E sus armas dobladas

E que / Vi(d)o q*ue* lleVo Un español p*ara* su / serViçio E su costa E q*ue* *e*sto sabe / de *e*sta pregunta / {rúbrica} / 7

[fol. 10r]
{4} {*ytem*} A la quarta pregunta dixo que la / sabe como *en* *e*lla se *contiene* pregunt*a*do / como la sabe dixo que porque lo / Vi(d)o E se hallo p*re*sente a Ello / E Vi(d)o pasar E paso como la pre- / gunta lo dize

{5} {*ytem*} A la quynta pregunta dixo que / la sabe como En ella se *contiene* pre- / Guntado como la sabe dixo que / porque lo Vi(d)o pasar como la / pregunta lo dize E que por Res- / pe*c*to de las largas Jornadas E / pu*e*sto que lleVaba El d*i*cho escobar / se le quedo Cançado Un caballo / A este testigo E lo perdio E que / A la sazon que lo perdio sabe / este testigo que val*i*an Un caballo / trezientos pesos de oro de mynas / E que *e*sto sabe

{6} {*ytem*} A la sesta pregunta dixo q*ue* la / sabe como En ella se *contiene* pre- / Guntado como la sabe dixo que / porque lo Vi(d)o E se hallo p*re*sente / A todo E Vi(d)o pasar como la / pregunta lo dize E si no Fuera / por la buena diligençia E soleÇitud / q*ue* el d*i*cho *cristo*bal de escobar puso / En el socoRo q*ue* la pregunta dize / este testigo tiene por Çierto E cre(h)e / q*ue* la gente de la d*i*cha armada peres- / {rúbrica}

[fol. 10v]
çiera de Frio E hanbre por caUsa de las / grandes nyeVes que *h*abia E no / saber donde (dond) estaban E / El d*i*cho *cristo*bal de escobar Fue gran / Remedio despues de n*uest*ro señor / para que no peresçiesen

{7} {*ytem*} A la Se*p*tima pregunta dixo q*ue* la / sabe como *en* *e*lla se *contiene* pregunt*a*do / como la sabe dixo que porque este t*e*stigo / se hallo A todo Ello E este t*e*stigo Es Uno / De los que yban con el d*i*cho escobar / E de treS caballos que lleVaba El / Uno se le CanÇo E los otros porq*ue* / se le Cançaban Aguardo El Canpo

{8} {*ytem*} A la o*c*taVa pregunta dixo ^*que lo* que sa- / be de la pregunta es que El d*i*cho / *cristo*bal de escobar Fue con su Ca- / pitan A descubrir la mar del sur / E que *e*ste testigo

oyo *decir* por pu*b*lico / E notorio *h*Aber pasado mucha / çed E hanbre En el d*i*cho descubrimy*ento* / *en* la mar del sur E que lo demas / *en* la pregunta *conteni*do oyo *decir* por pu*b*lico / E notorio este testigo que a muchas / cosas de *e*llo se hallo presente / este testigo

{9} {*ytem*} A la noVena pregunta dixo q*ue* / oyo *decir* lo *en* la pregunta *conteni*do A / muchas personas por pu*b*lico E / notorio E asi lo (h)era *en*tre muchas personas / {rúbrica} / 8

[fol. 11r]
{10} {*ytem*} A la deçima pregunta dixo q*ue* / sabe la pregunta como *en* *e*lla / se contiene preguntado co- / mo la sabe dixo que porq*ue* lo / Vi(d)o E se hallo presente a todo / lo *conteni*do *en* la pregunta SE pasa como / *en* *e*lla se *contiene*

{11} {*ytem*} A la (h)onzena pregunta dixo q*ue* / Dize lo que d*i*cho tiene *en* las pre- / Gunttas antes de *e*sta E que sabe / la pregunta como En ella se *contiene* / pregunt*a*do como la sabe dixo que / porq*ue* lo Vi(d)o ser E pasar como la / pregunta lo dize

{12} {*ytem*} A las dozena pregunta dixo que / la sabe como *en* *e*lla se contiene pre- / Gunt*a*do como la sabe dixo que por- / que lo Vi(d)o pasar como la pre- / Gunta lo dize

{13} {*ytem*} A las treze preguntas dixo que / sabe la pregunta como *en* *e*lla se *contiene* / porque *e*ste testigo *h*a Visto que / El d*i*cho escobar *h*a padeçido E pa- / Desçe nesçeÇidad despues / que de la d*i*cha gueRa Vyno sin que / se le *h*aya gratiFycado su serViÇio / E que *e*ste testigo se maraVylla / como el d*i*cho *cristo*bal de *e*scobar se pue- / de Sustentar Segun(d) le *h*a Visto / {rúbrica}

[fol. 11v]
en trabaJo E nesçeÇidad despues / que de la gueRa Vino

{14} {*ytem*} A las *catorze preguntas* dixo que *e*ste testigo del / Tienpo que a que le conosçe a es- / Ta p*ar*te le *h*a tenydo E tiene en / posesion de persona HiJodalgo / tal persona como la pregunta / lo dize E por este Respeto Su / capitan le *en*Cargaba *en*tradas / por tener como tenya por Çierto / que tenya zelo E deseo *en* todo de / serVir a su mag*esta*d E que *esta* es la / *ver*dad E lo que sabe de *este* *effect*o p*ar*a El / Jura-mento que hizo E fir*m*olo / de su nonbre myguel de *en*tran- / basAguas

{T*estigo*} {y*tem*} A El d*i*cho Juan de zagala estante / En esta ÇiUdad testigo p*re*sentado / en la d*i*cha Razon *h*abiendo Jurado / segun(d) derecho E siendo pregunt*a*do / por las preguntas del d*i*cho ynt(h)e- / Rogatorio dixo lo siguyente

{1} {y*tem*} A la primera pregunta dixo / que conosçe Al d*i*cho *crist*obal de *e*s- / cobar de Çinco años A esta p*ar*te / poco mas o menos

{2} {y*tem*} A la Segunda pregunta dixo / que del d*i*cho tienpo de Çinco años / {rúbrica} / 9

[fol. 12r]⁵⁶
que *e*ste testigo conosçe Al d*i*cho / *crist*obal de *e*scobar le *h*a Visto ViVir / E tener su muger E casa En esta / ÇiUdad de mexico donde al p*re*sente / se la *h*a Visto tener E ViVir

{3} {y*tem*} A la terçera pregunta dixo / q*ue* la sabe como *en* *e*lla se *contiene* / pregunt*a*do como la sabe dixo que / porq*ue* lo Vi(d)o pasar E pasa como / la pregunta lo dize

{4} {y*tem*} A la quarta pregunta dixo que / la sabe como En ella se contiene / preguntado como la sabe dixo / que porque lo Vi(d)o pasar E / pasa como la pregunta lo dize

{5} {y*tem*} A la quynta pregunta dixo q*ue* / la sabe como En ella se contiene / preguntado como la sabe dixo / que porq*ue* lo Vi(d)o E se hallo / presente a Ello E lo Vi(d)o pasar / como la pregunta lo dize

{6} {y*tem*} A la Sesta pregunta dixo q*ue* lo / que sabe de *e*lla es que *e*ste t*e*stigo / Vi(d)o como quando paso El general / de la d*i*cha armada primero de / la proVinçia de Çibola pasaron / *e*ste t*e*stigo e los demas que con el fue- / ron mucha nesçeÇidad E trabaJo / de hanbres E çed que En el Camyno / pasaron por caUsa de lo qual / {rúbrica}

[fol. 12v]
muchos yndios Amygos E caballos / se les quedaban atras E se les / murieron E q*ue* *e*l bastimento q*ue* les / sacaron al Camyno les hizo / mucho proVecho A los que asi / Venyan E q*ue* esto sabe de *e*sta pregu*n*ta

{7} {y*tem*} A la Se*p*tima pregunta dixo q*ue* / la sabe como En ella se contiene / preguntado como la sabe dixo q*ue* / porq*ue* lo Vi(d)o pasar E pasa como / la pregunta lo dize

{8} {y*tem*} A la octaVa pregunta dixo *que* lo / que de *e*lla sabe es q*ue* este testigo / Vi(d)o como El d*i*cho *crist*obal de *e*s- / cobar se hallo en Una *en*trada / donde Vi(d)o que *e*stuVo quatro / Dias sin beber Agua E pasando / otros trabaJos E hanbre porq*ue* lo / Vi(d)o este testigo E se hallo / En ello E que *e*sto Vi(d)o E que asi- / mysmo estuVo seSenta dias / sin comer pan donde pades- / Çieron todos mucho trabaJo E asi / lo padesÇio El d*i*cho escobar como / los demas

{9} {y*tem*} A la noVena pregunta dixo / que lo que de *e*lla sabe es q*ue* este / testigo Vi(d)o como El d*i*cho escobar / sirVio muy bien A su mag*es*tad *en* todas / {rúbrica}

[fol. 13r]
las cosas que se oFresçian *en* la / D*i*cha gueRa a su costa E mysion / E que *en* lo del ganado lo oyo *decir* / por publico E notorio que *h*abia / lleVado ganado A la d*i*cha gueRa

{10} {y*tem*} A la deçima pregunta dixo q*ue* la / sabe como En ella se *contiene* pregun- / Tado como la sabe dixo que porq*ue* / lo / Vi(d)o E se hallo presente E lo / Vi(d)o pasar como la pregu*n*ta lo dize

{11} {y*tem*} A las (h)onze preguntas dixo q*ue* la / sabe como En ella se *contiene* pre- / guntado como la sabe dixo que / porque Vi(d)o pasar Como la / pregunta lo dize E que Valian / los caballos a la d*i*cha sazon Unos / mas cantidad de la contenyda / *en* la pregunta E otros menos / E que a la sazon se Vendian / Al presçio E los valia El d*i*cho caballo / q*ue* *e*l d*i*cho escobar perdio E que todos / perdieron *en* la d*i*cha gueRa como / El d*i*cho escobar E Vinyeron muchos / AdeUdados

{12} {*ytem*} A las doze preguntas dixo que / la sabe como En ella se *contiene* pre- / Guntado como la sabe dixo q*ue* / porque lo Vi(d)o pasar como / la pregunta lo dize E Vinyeron / Juntos a esta ÇiUdad / {rúbrica}

[fol. 13v]
{13} {*ytem*} A las treze preguntas dixo q*ue* / por *h*aber ydo A la d*i*cha gueRa / E gastado En ella de su hazienda / cre(h)e E tiene por Çierto este tes- / tigo que *el* d*i*cho escobar estara pobre / E con nesçeÇidad E que sabe q*ue* / hasta agora no se le *h*a gratificado / Al d*i*cho escobar lo que asi sirVio / *en* la d*i*cha gueRa en serViÇio de su mag*estad*

{14} {*ytem*} A las Catorze preguntas dixo / que por tal persona como la / pregunta lo dize este testigo / Tiene al d*i*cho *cristo*bal de *e*scobar / E *h*a Visto que *h*a sido bien quysto E / paÇiFyco E persona honRada / E tenyda E *h*abida por tal *en*tre / muchas personas E asi *h*a Vis- / to q*ue* *e*S publico E notorio E que *es*- / ta es la *ver*dad E lo que sabe de *es*- / te *effecto* p*ar*a El Juramento q*ue* hizo E / Fir*m*olo Juan de Zagala

{*T*estigo} El d*i*cho domyngo martin Vezi*n*o de *es*ta / ÇiUdad testigo p*re*sent*ado en* la / D*i*cha Razon *h*abiendo Jurado / segun(d) derecho E siendo pregu*n*t*a*do / por las preguntas del d*i*cho yn- / teRogatorio dixo lo siguyente

{1} {*ytem*} A la primera pregunta dixo que / {rúbrica}

[fol. 14r]
conosçe Al d*i*cho *cristo*bal de *e*scobar / de Çinco años a esta p*ar*te poco mas / o menos E que *este* t*estigo* es est*ante* de / Veynte E Çinco años

{2} {*ytem*} A la segunda pregunta dixo que / como d*i*cho tiene del d*i*cho tienpo / a esta parte le conosçe de los / d*i*chos çinco años E que le *h*a Visto / al presente que tiene casa poblada / En esta ÇiUdad E muger como la / pregunta lo dize

{3} {*ytem*} A la terçera pregunta dixo q*ue* la / sabe como En ella se contiene pre- / Guntado como la sabe dixo que por-

/ que Vi(d)o que pasa como la / pregunta lo dize porq*ue* este t*estigo* / Fue a la d*i*cha armada E este t*estigo* E / El d*i*cho escobar en saliendo / de *e*sta ÇiUdad salieron Junto / E Vi(d)o que pasa Como lo dize la / pregunta

{4} {*ytem*} A la quarta pregunta dixo que sa- / be E Vi(d)o q*ue* *el* d*i*cho *cristo*bal de *e*scobar / AnduVo *en* la d*i*cha gueRa mas / Tienpo de doS años y medio sir- / Viendo a su mag*estad* en todo lo que le / (h)era mandado E hazia todo lo q*ue* / se ofresÇia E le (h)era mandado / como la pregunta lo dize E q*ue* est(o)*e* t*estigo* Vi(d)o / se hallo p*re*sente a Ello / {rúbrica}

[fol. 14v]
{5} {*ytem*} A la quynta pregunta dixo q*ue* lo / que de *e*lla sabe es que *e*ste t*estigo* sa- / be E Vi(d)o q*ue* *el* d*i*cho *cristo*bal de *e*scobar / Fue desde la proVinÇia de los / coraçones hasta Çibola con Çiertos / conpañeros E por su llegada se / saco Çierto bastimento para so- / coRer aL canpo q*ue* lleVaba don / Tristan de arell(l)año

{6} {*ytem*} A la sesta pregunta dixo que / sabe E Vi(d)o que por Razon de (^s)*ve*(^r)- / (^Ve)nir El d*i*cho esCobar se sacaron los / bastimentos E que si no se sacara / cre(h)e *e*ste testigo que no pudie- / ran deXar de peresçer Algunos / yndios de hanbre E que *e*sto sabe / de *e*sta pregunta

{7} {*ytem*} A la se*p*tima pregunta dixo que / dize lo que d*i*cho tiene *en* la pre- / gunta antes de *e*sta E que *en* lo / de los caballos que dexo *en* la / pregunta contenydo(s) este t*estigo* lo / oyo dezir por pu*b*lico E notorio / Entre las personas de la d*i*cha / gueRa porq*ue* *e*ste t*estigo* estaba en Çibola

{8} {*ytem*} A la octaVa pregunta dixo que dize / lo que d*i*cho tiene *en* las pregun- / Tas Antes de *e*sta E que oyo *decir* / {rúbrica}

[fol. 15r]
lo en la pregunta contenydo por / publico E notorio E que sabe / E Vi(d)o que Fue El d*i*cho *cristo*bal de / escobar con el d*i*cho capitan A la / proVinçia de tiguex donde paso / hanbres E trabaJos E otras nesçe- / (çi)sidades

{9} {ytem} A la noVena pregunta dixo que lo / que de ella sabe es que este testigo / sabe E Vi(d)o que El dicho escobar lle- / Vo Çierto ganado en Conpañya de el / que este testigo lleVaba E que cre- / (h)e que fue a su costa E mysion / E sin sueldo ny salario Alguno / porque este testigo no le Vi(d)o / Dar a nynguna persona que a la / dicha (^R)gueRa fue porque si se / Diera este testigo no pudiera de- / Xar de saberlo E Verlo

{10} {ytem} A la deçima pregunta dixo que / sabe E Vi(d)o que el dicho escobar se ha- / llo en toda la guerra de la proVin- / Çia de tiguex E donde paso mu- / cho trabaJo en Velas en la gueRa / E otros trabaJos tocantes a la guerra / donde lo hizo muy bien

{11} {ytem} A las (h)onze preguntas dixo / que lo que de ella sabe es que este / testigo sabe que el dicho cristobal de escobar / {rúbrica}

[fol. 15v]
perdio en la dicha entrada en la pregunta / contenyda Un caballo que le paresçe / A este testigo que Valia los treziento[s] / pesos en la pregunta contenido(s) E que no pu- / do deXar de perder otras / muchas cosas como los demas que / Vinyeron muy gastados E a- / deUdados

{12} {ytem} A las doze preguntas dixo que / la sabe como En ella se contiene preguntado / como la sabe dixo que porque / Vi(d)o que a la sazon que Vino El dicho / capitan Vino El dicho escobar a esta / ÇiUdad E no le deXo ny le enVio has- / Ta que el dicho capitan se Vino

{13} {ytem} A las treze preguntas dixo que / sabe E ha Visto que el dicho cristobal de es- / cobar esta pobre E con nesçeÇidad / E trabaJo E que si no hubiera ydo / A la dicha gueRa hubiera dado / (h)orden de su ViVir por donde no / TuViera la nesçeÇidad E que / no se ella GratiFycado cosa de su ser- / ViÇio hasta hoy

{14} {ytem} A las catorze preguntas dixo / que dize lo que dicho tiene E que / lo que de ella sabe es que este testigo tiene / Al dicho cristobal de escobar por buen cristiano / persona honRada E bien quysto / {rúbrica}

[fol. 16r]
E que esta es la verdad para El Ju- / ramento que hizo E Firmolo de su / nonbre domyngo martin

{Testigo} El dicho Juan lopez estante En es- / ta dicha ÇiUdad testigo presenta- / Do en la dicha Razon habiendo Jura- / do segun(d) derecho E siendo pre- / Guntado por las preguntas del / dicho ynt(h)eRogatorio dixo lo siguiente

{1} {ytem} A la primera pregunta dixo / que conosçe Al dicho cristobal de es- / cobar de quatro años a esta parte / poco mas o menos

{2} {ytem} A la segunda pregunta dixo / que del dicho tienpo de quatro años / A que le conosçe En esta tieRa / E que sabe E ha Visto que eS Casado E tiene / Su Casa E muger En esta ÇiUdad

{3} {ytem} A la terçera pregunta dixo / que sabe E Vi(d)o que el dicho cristobal / de escobar Fue con el dicho capi- / Tan en serViçio de su magestad A la / TieRa nueVa con sus Armas E / caballos E que le conosçio ll(l)eVar / Un moço e que esto sabe de esta pregunta

{4} {ytem} A la quarta pregunta dixo que / la sabe como En ella se contiene / preguntado como la sabe dixo / que porque este testigo lo Vi(d)o / pasar como la pregunta lo dize / {rúbrica}

[fol. 16v]
{5} {ytem} A la quynta pregunta dixo que / oyo dezir lo en la pregunta Contenydo / por publico E notorio entre las personas / que con el Fueron de cuyos nonbres / no se acuerda este testigo

{6} {ytem} A la sesta pregunta dixo que la sabe / como En ella se contiene pre- / guntado como la sabe dixo que / porque lo Vi(d)o ser E pasar como / la pregunta lo dize E que hizo mu- / cho proVecho porque se socoRio / El Canpo

{7} {ytem} A la septima pregunta dixo que / oyo dezir lo contenido en la pregunta / por publico E notorio entre las /

PerSonas de la dicho gueRa E que / no podia deXar de pasar / mucho trabaJo El dicho escobar *en* las / dichas *en*tradas

{8} {y*tem*} A la o*c*taVa pregunta dixo que / Dize lo que dicho tiene en las / preguntas Antes de *e*sta

{9} {y*tem*} A la noVena pregunta dixo q*ue* lo / que de *e*lla sabe es que *h*a oydo *decir* / por publico E notorio q*ue* *e*l dicho es- / cobar lleVo ganados A la dicha / gueRa E que cre(h)e E tiene por / çierto q*ue* fue a su Costa E mysion / sin que de p*ar*te de su mag*estad* ny otra / persona le fuese dado sueldo / {rúbrica}

[fol. 17r]
Alguno porque si lo lleVara o se / lo diera este t*estig*o lo supiera E no / pudiera ser menos

{10} {y*tem*} A la deçima pregunta dixo q*ue* / la sabe como *en* *e*lla se contiene / preguntado como la sabe dyxo / que porq*ue* lo Vi(d)o ser E pasar / Asi segun(d) la pregunta lo dize

{11} {y*tem*} A las (h)onze preguntas dixo que / sabe E Vi(d)o que le mataron / Al dicho escobar Un caballo que / podia Valer los trezientos p*e*sos de / mynas segun(d) A la sazon se apres- / çiaba E otras cosas como los de- / mas que a la dicha gueRa Fueron

{12} {y*tem*} A las doze preguntas dixo que o- / Yo *decir* lo *en* la pregunta contenydo / por pu*blic*o E notorio porque *e*ste / Testigo se Vino delante desde / Culuacan hasta Conpostela / E deXo al dicho escobar *en* la dicha gue- / Ra con el Capitan general

{13} {y*tem*} A las treze preguntas dixo q*ue* / sabe E *h*a Visto q*ue* *e*l dicho escobar / esta pobre E con nesçeÇidad E que / no se le *h*a gratiFycado su serViÇio / E q*ue* esto sabe de *e*sta pregunta

{14} {y*tem*} A las catorze preguntas dixo q*ue* este / testigo tiene Al dicho *crist*obal de *e*scobar / {rúbrica}

[fol. 17v]
por persona buen *crist*iano E hon- / Rada E bien quysto de

buena / Vida E fama E por tal Ve(h)e q*ue* es *h*a- / bido E tenydo E q*ue* esta Es la *ver*dad / E lo que sabe de *e*ste *effec*to para el Ju- / ramento que hizo E fi*rr*molo de su / nonbre Ju*an* lopez

{T*estig*o} El dicho Alonso alVares estante / En esta ÇiUdad testigo p*re*sent*ado* / *en* la dicha Razon *h*abiendo Jurado / segun(d) derecho E siendo pre- / Guntado por las preguntas / Del dicho ynteRogatorio dixo lo / siguyente

{1} {y*tem*} A la primera pregunta dixo / que conoSçe Al dicho *crist*obal de *e*s- / cobar de seys años a esta p*ar*te po- / co mas o menos

{2} {y*tem*} A la segunda pregunta dixo q*ue* del / dicho tienpo de los dichos seys años / que *e*ste testigo A q*ue* le conosçe / Al dicho (alonso) *crist*obal de *e*scobar le *h*a Vis- / To estar E ViVir con su muger E / Casa En *e*sta ÇiUdad E Vino de los / Reynos de Castilla *en* la nao / Donde este t*estig*o Vino E lo / Vi(d)o ser E / pasar como la pregunta lo / Dize / {rúbrica}

[fol. 18r]
{3} {y*tem*} A la terçera pregunta dixo q*ue* / la sabe como En ella se contiene / preguntado como la sabe dixo / que porque lo Vi(d)o E pasa A- / si segun(d) E como la pregunta / lo dize

{4} {y*tem*} A la quarta pregunta dixo / que la sabe como En ella se / contiene pregunt*ado* como la sa- / be dixo que porque lo Vi(d)o E / pasa Asi segu*n*(d) q*ue* la pregunta / lo dize

{5} {y*tem*} A la quynta pregunta dixo que / oyo dezir lo en la pregunta / contenydo por notorio *en*tre / las personas que a la dicha / GueRa Fueron

{6} {y*tem*} A la sesta pregunta dixo que / Dize lo que dicho tiene *en* las pre- / Guntas Antes de *e*sta E que sabe / que se murio Un español E ne- / Gros E yndios E que si no Fuera so- / coRido El Canpo no sabe si mu- / rieran o no

{7} {y*tem*} A la se*p*tima pregunta dixo que / lo que sabe de *e*ste Caso es que / sabe q*ue* *e*l d*ic*ho *crist*obal de *e*scobar / paso por tie*R*a de yndios E des- / {rúbrica}

[fol. 18v]
poblados de gran poblaçion⁵⁷ E q*ue* / lo demas *en* la pregunta contenydo / no lo sabe

{8} {y*tem*} A la oc*ta*Va pregunta dixo que / sabe E Vi(d)o q*ue* *e*l d*ic*ho *crist*obal de *e*s- / cobar Fue a descubrir la mar del / sur E otras *en*tradas donde Res- / Çibio grandes hanbres E çed E q*ue* / como todos los sufrian E pasa- / ban cre(h)e E tiene por çierto la pa- / saria El d*ic*ho escobar como Uno de / los que a *e*lla Fueron E q*ue* esto sabe / de *e*sta pregunta

{9} {y*tem*} A la noVena pregunta dixo q*ue* / oyo dezir por publico E notorio / q*ue* *e*l d*ic*ho *crist*obal de *e*scobar lleVo / Ganado A la gue*R*a E que sabe / que sirVio A su costa E mysion / *en* la d*ic*ha gue*R*a A su mag*estad* sin q*ue* le / Fuese dado sueldo ny costa al- / Guna de p*ar*te de su mag*estad* ny de otra / persona alguna E que *e*sto sabe

{10} {y*tem*} A la deçima pregunta dixo q*ue* / sabe E Vi(d)o que en la gue*R*a / y *en*tradas que *e*ste testigo Vi(d)o / Al d*ic*ho escobar q*ue* fue E se hallo / en muchas de las que *en* la d*ic*ha gue*R*a / se RecresÇieron Vi(d)o q*ue* lo hazia / {rúbrica}

[fol. 19r]
muy bien E todo lo que se ofresÇia / pasando muchos trabaJos

{11} {y*tem*} A las (h)onze preguntas dixo q*ue* / lo que de *e*lla sabe es que *e*ste *t*estigo / sabe E Vi(d)o como le mataron al / d*ic*ho escobar Un caballo que Valia / En el d*ic*ho tienpo los trezientos / pesos en la pregunta contenydos / E q*ue* este *t*estigo Vi(d)o que lleVo bien / Adereçada su persona E des- / pues le Vi(d)o Venyr Vestido de / cueros E q*ue* esto sabe de *e*sta pregunta

{12} {y*tem*} A las doze preguntas dixo / que la sabe como *en* *e*lla se *contiene* / preguntado como la sabe dixo / que porq*ue* lo Vi(d)o pasar como / la pregunta lo dize

{13} {y*tem*} A las treze preguntas dixo q*ue* la / sabe como En

*e*lla se contiene pre- / Guntado como la sabe dixo que / porq*ue* lo Vi(d)o E pasa como / la pregunta lo dize

{14} {y*tem*} A las catorze preguntas dixo / que *e*ste testigo tiene Al d*ic*ho *crist*obal / de escobar por hijodalgo E su / persona tuvies(a)*e* serlo E q*ue* lo tiene / por buen *crist*iano temeroso de dios / n*uest*ro se*ñ*or E de buena Vida E fama E / {rúbrica}

[fol. 19v]
por tal es *h*abido E tenydo E este tes- / tigo le tiene E que *e*sta es la *ver*- / dad E lo que sabe de *e*ste *effect*o p*ar*a El / Juramento que hizo E fi*r*molo / de su nonbre (lorenço) *alonso a*lVares

{T*estigo*} El d*ic*ho her*n*ando gutierres estante / En esta ÇiUdad testigo p*r*esentado / *en* la d*ic*ha Razon por p*ar*te del d*ic*ho / *crist*obal de *e*scobar *h*abiendo Jurado / segun(d) derecho E siendo pregunt*a*do / por la Primera E Catorzena pre- / Guntas del d*ic*ho ynt(h)eRogatorio / dixo lo siguyente

{1} {y*tem*} A la primera pregunta dixo q*ue* / conosçe Al d*ic*ho *crist*obal de *e*scobar / de Veynte E quatro años a esta / p*ar*te poco mas o menos E que sabe / que puede *h*aber siete años po- / co mas o menos q*ue* *e*l d*ic*ho *crist*obal / De *e*scobar paso a estas p*ar*tes / con su muger E casa

{14} {y*tem*} A las Catorze preguntas p*ar*a / en que fue presentado por t*e*stigo / dixo que *e*ste testigo conosçio E / conosçe Asi a sus padres del / d*ic*ho *crist*obal de *e*scobar como / Al / susod*ic*ho del d*ic*ho tienpo q*ue* tiene / {rúbrica}

[fol. 20r]
d*ic*ho *en* la pregunta Antes de *e*sta E asi- / mysmo Conosçe E conosçio A mucha / P*ar*te de su generaÇion E sabe que / (h)eran E son hiJosdalgo E por tales (h)eran / *h*Abidos E tenydos *en* los Reynos / De *e*spaña donde ViVian E que este / t*e*stigo tiene al d*ic*ho *crist*obal de *e*scobar por / hiJodalgo E *en* tal ReputaÇion / *h*A Visto que *h*a sido y es *h*abido E / tenydo E q*ue* lo tiene por buen *crist*iano E / persona paÇi- / Fyca quyeta E apar- / Tada de pleytos E debates E q*ue* lo / tiene por persona q*ue* sienpre / que se *h*a hallado En estas

partes / En el tienpo que *este* testigo le / *h*A Conosçido En
ella le *h*a conosçido / por persona que desea Aumen- / Tar
El patrimonyo Real *de* su mag*estad* / E que *h*a oydo *decir* por
publico E /notorio En esta ÇiUdad que *h*a / serVido A su
mag*estad* En estas p*ar*tes / haziendo lo que por sus capita- /
nes E gobernadores les (h)era / mandado como tal persona /
hiJodalgo E que le *h*a conosÇido te- / ner su Casa E muger
En esta ÇiUdad / donde *h*a padesçido E padesçe nesçe- /
Çidad de trabaJo A CaUsa de no le *h*aber / GratiFycado sus
serViÇios E q*ue* lo / tiene *en* tal ReputaÇion E p*er*sona / que
meresçe su mag*estad* le haga m*erced*es / {rúbrica}

[fol. 20v]
E que *esta* es la *ver*dad E lo que sabe / p*ara* El Juramento q*ue*
ff*ech*o tiene E / En ello se afi*r*mo E fi*r*molo d*e* su n*o*nb*r*e /
her*n*a*n*do GutieRes

E ansi tomada E ResÇibida la / d*ich*a probança *en* la manera
q*ue* / d*ich*a es El d*ich*o s*eñ*or al*cald*e dixo que manda- / ba E

m*a*ndo A my El d*ich*o es*cr*ibano pu*b*lico sacase / E hiziese
sacar de *e*lla Un treslado / o doS o mas E los diese y *en*tregase
/ Al d*ich*o *cristoba*l de *e*scobar para q*ue* los pre- / sente donde
E a su d*er*ec*h*o conVenga / en los quales dixo que ynterponya
/ E ynterpuso su aUtoridad E decreto / JudiÇial para que
Valga E haga / fee *en* Juyzio E fuera de *e*l E lo fi*r*mo / de su
nonbre Antonyo de la / Cadena / *an*tonyo d*e* la Cadena

E yo sancho lop*ez* de agurto[58] / escry*b*ano d*e* sus *e*Sarias
catolycas magestad*e*S / E pu*b*lico es*cr*ibano d*e* los d*e*l nu*m*ero
d*e* *e*sta d*ich*a ÇiUdad / Fuy p*r*eSente e fyze trasladar
coReGyr E /*con*sertar del d*ich*o (h)oriGynal E por ende fyze
Aquy / este myo syG- [signo] no (A)tal *en* testymo*n*yo / de
*ver*dad / {rúbrica} Sancho lop*e*Z / de agurto {rúbrica}

d*er*ec*h*os Gratyz

[fol. 21r-21v] [blank]

Document 34

Vázquez de Coronado's Petition for Recovery of Encomiendas, 1553

AGI, Justicia, 336, N.1, fols. i right–2 left

INTRODUCTION

For those who invested in the Coronado expedition or expended large sums to outfit themselves and their *criados*, servants, and slaves to participate in it, the return of the expedition without establishment of *encomiendas* in Tierra Nueva meant straitened economic circumstances. Documentary evidence is abundant that a sense of financial misfortune was common, perhaps typical, among the former expeditionaries.[1] There can be little doubt that as an economic enterprise the expedition was universally regarded as a failure.

Its captain general, though, could claim, with some legitimacy, that the expedition had succeeded in accomplishing many of its original objectives. It had in fact searched diligently over a huge territory for native populations of sufficient size and economic potential to warrant establishment of profitable *encomiendas*. Certainly neither Vázquez de Coronado nor any other member of the expedition could be blamed for the absence of such peoples in Tierra Nueva.

It was, then, doubly galling to the former captain general that he had not only lost his enormous investment of 50,000 *castellanos* but also was subsequently divested of *encomiendas* he had held as governor of Nueva Galicia at the time of the expedition. This combination deprived him of both former assets and future income. In 1552, by means of the petition published here, Vázquez de Coronado, acting through his long-time attorney Pedro Ruiz de Haro, sought reversal of both losses through restitution for his failed investment and return of the *encomiendas*.[2] This was in continuance of an appeal begun eight years before.

The divestiture of *encomiendas* comprising nine native communities in eastern Nueva Galicia had come about as a result of a routine *residencia* of the officials of that *provincia* conducted by *licenciado* Lorenzo de Tejada, an *oidor* of the royal *audiencia* during August and September 1544. Among the ensuing 34 charges lodged against the former governor were two relating to his awarding of *encomiendas* to himself and Álvaro de Bracamonte. Of greatest relevance to the 1552 petition is charge number 24:

> He is accused of holding, in partnership with Álvaro de Bracamonte, all the pueblos of the said Bracamonte and also those reverting on the death of Francisco de Villegas, and of having divided the said pueblos with Álvaro de Bracamonte and, knowing about the New Laws and Ordinances, after their publication, of giving the said Álvaro de Bracamonte thrice the number of Indians and thrice doubled the supply of [profit from] those that remained for His Majesty.[3]

On this charge and seven others, *oidor* Tejada rendered no decision, referring them instead to the king and Consejo de Indias for their verdict. There is no evidence that the Consejo ever acted on the case, either on initial appeal or in response to the 1552 petition. Nevertheless, the petition did occasion the taking of testimony from witnesses to support the former captain general's claims of having expended 50,000 *castellanos* on the expedition to Tierra Nueva and of having been wrongly deprived of *encomiendas.*[4]

The appeal was still pending at the time of Vázquez de Coronado's death 10 years after his *residencia.*[5] Thus, the *encomiendas* in question reverted to the Crown in 1544 and remained under royal jurisdiction thereafter. A similar fate befell the former governor's request for reimbursement for his costs in mounting the expedition to Tierra Nueva. His death closed the issue.

What survives of Vázquez de Coronado's 1552 petition is a contemporaneous copy made by *licenciado* Hernando Balbuena, secretary of the royal *audiencia* in Nueva Galicia. It was prepared to be forwarded to the Consejo de Indias in Spain, where it was received in March 1554. It is now preserved in the Archivo General de Indias in Sevilla under the *signatura* (catalog number) AGI, Justicia, 336, N.1, fols. i right through 2 left. We prepared the transcription and translation that follow on the basis of the copy in the AGI. This portion of AGI, Justicia, 336, N.1, uses an uncommon folio numbering system in which facing sheets bear the same number, rather than the more usual "recto-verso" designation of the two sides of a single sheet. In the transcription and translation that follow, the original folio numbers are retained.

This document has not been published previously in either Spanish or English.

TRANSLATION

[i right]⁶
{Guadalajara, the year 1553
   Francisco Vázquez Coronado, *vecino* and *regidor*
     of the Ciudad de México
        vs.
     His Majesty's *fiscal*
   Concerning certain Indians}

[ii left] [blank]

[ii right]
{Guadalajara, the year 1553
Francisco Vázquez Coronado vs. the fiscal concerning
certain Indians}⁷

[1 left] [blank]

[1 right]⁸
{Received in Valladolid the 22nd of March in the year 1554.
This case file, which the officials of his council sent to His
Highness, arrived in a sealed envelope.}⁹

In the *ciudad* of Compostela in the Nuevo Reino de Galicia¹⁰
on the fourth day of the month of February in the year one
thousand five hundred and fifty-two, when the lords *oidores*
(*alcaldes mayores* for His Majesty) of the royal *audiencia* were
sitting in open session and in my presence, *licenciado*
Balbuena (His Majesty's *escribano* and secretary of the royal
audiencia), Pedro Ruiz de Haro appeared in person in the
name of Governor Francisco Vázquez de Coronado and
presented the following petition, power of attorney, and
commissions:¹¹

Very powerful lords,

In the person of my attorney, I, Francisco Vázquez de
Coronado, formerly your governor in this *provincia* of Nueva
Galicia, appear before Your Highness and place a petition
before Your Majesty and before *licenciado* Juan Rodríguez,
your *fiscal* in your royal name. What I state is this: that when
I was governor in this *provincia* in your royal name, considering how to best serve Your Highness (since, in keeping
with the status of my person and with what was required as
such a governor of yours and [in keeping with] the custom
which like governors for Your Majesty in this region have
maintained, it was impossible to support myself, [my] wife,
[my] household, and the *criados* whom I was supporting
from the property I held in Nueva España and the salary
provided to me in the aforesaid office),¹² I assigned in
encomienda to myself in your royal name one-half of the
pueblo[s] of Aguacatlán and Xala, with their *estancias* and
sujetos, and one-half of the [*pueblos*] of Mezquitlán and
Guaxacatlán, which are in the valley of Guaxacatlán, with
their *estancias* and *sujetos*.¹³ [This was] in the same way Francisco de Villegas, deceased, held [them], the one and the
other, in their entirety.¹⁴ [I also assigned myself] one-half the
pueblos and *estancias* of Tepujuacán, Mezquitlán, Amaxaque,
and Amatlán, with their *sujetos*, in the same way Álvaro de
Bracamonte held [them].¹⁵ And further, [I assigned myself]
the *pueblo* of Quinsique, along with the Chichimeca Otomí
Indians who are in its vicinity.¹⁶

In Your Highness's name I issued myself titles and
cédulas of *encomienda* to these [places], signed with my name
and countersigned by Hernando Bermejo, who was my
secretary at the time.¹⁷ I am [herewith] submitting those
titles, by virtue of which I held and possessed the aforesaid

pueblos and *estancias*, with their *sujetos*, quietly and peacefully without opposition from any person, taking the tributes and services from those *pueblos* in accordance with the assessment which was levied against them.

While possession of the aforementioned *pueblos* was quiet and peaceful and while, as has been stated, I was your governor in the aforesaid *provincia* and exercising that office by your royal decree, sealed with your royal seal, I was chosen and appointed as your captain general of the people who by Your Highness's order were sent to reconnoiter and subjugate the *provincias* and Tierra Nueva about which fray Marcos de Niza said he had had news.[18] As such a captain general, I was ordered to conduct the aforementioned expedition in your royal name, as is recorded in the aforementioned royal commission.[19]

This [commission] I am [herewith] submitting. By it I was promised that because I was going, as I was, in your service, the *pueblos* of Indians that, in your royal name, I held in *encomienda* and in trust (in Nueva España and outside it) would not be taken or wrested from me at any time.[20]

Even though I was aware of the great expenses, hardships, dangers, and deprivations which were expected to present themselves to me during the aforesaid expedition, I accepted the appointment. Thus, since I was obedient to Your Highness's commands (both in order to secure the reward and grants which were promised to me by the aforesaid royal commission[21] and to obtain the excellent grants which the monarchs of glorious memory and Your Majesty are in the habit [of making] [and are] accustomed to make to those who serve them faithfully, loyally, and diligently), because [of this] I resolved to serve and did serve Your Highness, by whose command I conducted the expedition.

On [the expedition] I spent more than fifty thousand *castellanos* of my own wealth, for much of which I was left in debt and am [so now].[22] During the expedition I performed many and very outstanding services to Your Highness, placing my person at very great risk [and] danger and [enduring] hardships. I suffer[ed] many deprivations and was, and indeed arrived, at the very point of death because of [the] many wounds I received from the natives of Tierra Nueva during the aforementioned just conquest.[23]

I expect[ed] to be rewarded and remunerated because of

what has been stated, [and] expect[ed] the grants promised in the royal commission to be fulfilled, because I had served so loyally in the aforementioned conquest and pacification. During it I performed and fulfilled, in the service of God, Our Lord, and Your Highness, what I was directed [to do] by your instructions, executing and fulfilling them exactly as I was obligated [to do], on behalf and to the benefit of and as a good example to the natives of that land.

Not only have no grants been made to me, but failing to complete and fulfill what was promised to me by Your Majesty through your royal commission, [and] without cause or any reason that might be just, without [my] being heard or summoned, [and] not according to law or [even] superseded statute, precipitately and without order of law, but rather contrary to it, *licenciado* Lorenzo Tejada, *oidor* of your royal *audiencia* which has its seat in the [2 left] Ciudad de México and *residencia* judge in this *provincia*, seized from me the aforementioned *pueblos* and [took away my] possession of them.[24] [He did this] under the pretext of the New Laws issued for the good governance of these regions, in which it is ordered that Indians whom the governors held be seized [for the crown], without evidently considering the New Laws [specifically] in regard to this [matter] with me.[25] [Namely, what was guaranteed to me] by the promise Your Highness made to me by means of the aforesaid royal commission.

[This is] especially [irksome] because he has taken [the *pueblos*] from me, [and] I have committed no crime whatsoever, since [in consequence of] those [crimes] I was accused of by *licenciado* Benavente, your *fiscal*,[26] I was released, set free, and exonerated by Your Highness, as is recorded in this royal writ of final decision which I am submitting [herewith].[27]

Not only should the aforementioned injury not have been done to me, but I ought to be further rewarded because of the way I served Your Highness during the aforementioned expedition (as has been stated), because of what I spent from my own wealth in your royal service, because of the rest of the services I have performed for Your Highness, because I am (as indeed I am) a well-known *caballero hidalgo*, and [further] because my ancestors have truly served Your Highness.

{Item} Because of this I ask and beseech Your Highness to order [that] it be declared and to declare [that] the afore-mentioned *pueblos* and *sujetos* are under my control and [that] there is no cause or reason because of which they should be taken from me or because of which your royal commission to me should fail to be fulfilled (recording in writing what is stated above or as much of it as might effectively suffice for my purpose).

As a consequence of this I ask and beseech Your Highness to order that the aforementioned *pueblos* of Indians and [the Indians] in all their *sujetos* be returned and restored to me. [This is] so that I may hold and possess them in Your Highness's name, just as I held them at the time they were taken from me. Further, [that they be restored to me] along with the produce, income, services, and tribute they have yielded, could have yielded, and will yield until royal restitution [is made].[28]

In the event Your Highness does not order that what I have requested be done, [I ask that] you order that the fifty thousand *castellanos* I spent in your royal service be restored and paid to me, making Your Majesty and the *fiscal* in your royal name responsible for delivering and paying to me the fifty thousand *castellanos* and what I am to be rewarded and remunerated with because of my services and the blood I myself spilled in your royal service.

Because of this I implore and beseech your royal office for justice and costs in the required [form].

{Item} News of this litigation concerns His Highness, and by virtue of the royal commission which I am submitting [herewith], it must be dealt with in this royal *audiencia*. *licenciado* Caballero.[29] Pedro Ruiz de Haro

TRANSCRIPTION

[fol. i right]

{2 / Guadalaxara Año de 1553 / FrancisCo Vazquez Coronado Vecino y Regidor / de la Ciudad de Mexico / Con / El
Fiscal de su magestad / Sobre / Ciertos Yndios}

[fol. ii left] [blank]

[fol. ii right]

{Guadalaxara Año de 1553 / Francisco vazquez coronado
con eL fiscal sobre çiertos yndios}

[fol. 1 left] [blank]

[fol. 1 right]

{recibido en Valladolid A xxij de março de jUdLiiij años Vino
este proÇeSo en Un pliego que los officiales de / su consejo
enViaron A su alteza {rúbrica} 4}

En la çiUdad de conpostela del nueVo rreyno de galicia
quatro dias del mes de hebrero año de myll E quynientos / E
çinquenta E dos años Estando En aUdiencia publica los
señores oydores Alcaldes mayores por su magestad de la
dicha / Real aUdiençia E por presençia de my licenciado
balbuena escrivano de su magestad e Secretario de la dicha
rreal aUdiencia pareçio / presente pedro rruiZ de haro en
nonbre del gobernador Francisco Vazquez de coronado e
presento la petiçion e poder E proVisiones / {ytem}
Siguyentes

muy poderosos señores francisco Vazquez de coronado Vuestro
gobernador que fue de esta provyncia de la nueVa ga- / Lizia
por persona de my procurador parezco ante Vuestra alteza y

pongo demanda a Vuestra magestad y al lycenciado Juan
rrodriguez / Vuestro fiscal en Vuestro rreal nonbre y digo que
ansy es que siendo yo gobernador en esta provyncia en Vuestro
rreal nonbre con- / siderando que para meJor serVir a Vuestra
alteza por no me poder Sustentar con la hazienda que en la /
nueVa españa tenya y con el salario que en el dicho cargo se
me daba conforme a la calidad de my persona / muger y Casa
y criados que sustentaba E a lo que se Requeria como (a)tal
Vuestro gobernador y a la / Costumbre que los semeJantes
gobernadores de estas partes por Vuestra magestad hAn
tenido me enComende / En Vuestro rreal nonbre la mytad
de los pueblos de aguaCatlan y xala con sus Estançias y
Su(b)- / Jetos y la mytad de las Estançias de myzquytlan y
guaxaCatlan que Son en el Valle de guaxaCatlan / Con sus
Estançias y Su(b)jetos como lo Uno y lo otro todo entero lo
tenya Francisco de Villegas / difunto y la mytad de los
pueblos y estançias de tepuJuacan y myzquytlan y amaxaque
/ Y amatlan con sus su(b)jetos como lo tenya AlVaro de
braCamonte y el pueblo de quyn- / Sique con los yndios
chichimecas otomyes que estan en su comarca de los quales /
En nonbre de Vuestra alteza me di titulos y çedulas de
encomyenda fyrmadas de my nonbre e / Refrendadas de
hernando bermejo my secretario que a la sazon era de los
quales titulos / hago presentaçion por virtud de los quales
(Es)tuVe[30] y posey quyeta y paÇificamente / los dichos
pueblos y estançias Con sus su(b)Jetos syn contradiçion de
persona alguna / lleVando los tributos y servycios de los
dichos pueblos conforme a la tasaçion que de ellos estaba /
hecha y estando esta quyeta y paçifica posesion de los dichos
pueblos y siendo como dicho es en la / dicha provyncia
Vuestro gobernador y Resydiendo en el dicho cargo por
Vuestra Real proVision sellada con Vuestro / Real sello Fuy

Elexido y nonbrado por Vuestro Captian general de la
Jente que por mandado / de Vuestra alteza se enVio Al
desCubrimyento y Conquysta de las proVinÇias y tierra
nueVa / de que Fray marcos de nyça dixo haber tenydo
notiçia y me Fue mandado en Vuestro Real / nonbre hiziese
la dicha Jornada como tal Capitan general segun(d) que
Consta de la dicha rreal / Provysion e la qual hago presentaçion por la qual se me prometio que por yr como yba / en
Vuestro Real servycio no me serian quytados ny RemoVidos
en tienpo alguno los pueblos de / yndios que en Vuestro Real
nonbre tenya enComendados y depositados en la nueVa
españa Y / Fuera de ella y aUnque se me rrepresentaron[31] los
Grandes Gastos trabaxos peligros / y neçesidades que se me
habian de ofreçer en la dicha Jornada Açepte el dicho cargo
asy por ser / obidiente A los mandamyentos de Vuestra alteza
como por conseguyr el premyo y mercedes que / por la dicha
provysion Real se me prometieron y para conseguyr las
grandes mercedes / que los Reyes de gloriosa memoria y
Vuestra magestad suelen aCostumbrar a hazer a los que / Fiel
leal y diligentemente les syrVen como yo determyne de servir
e sirVi / a Vuestra alteza por Cuyo mandado hize la dicha
Jornada y en ella gaste de mys pro- / pias haziendas mas de
çinquenta myll Castellanos en mucha parte de loS / quales
quede adeUdado y lo estoy y en la dicha Jornada hize
muchos y muy / señalados servycios a Vuestra alteza
p(u)onyendo my persona a muy gran Riesgo peligro / y
trabaxos pasando muchas neçesidades y estando como
estuVe y llegue / A punto de muerte de muchas heridas que
en la dicha conquysta Justificada Reçebi / de los naturales de
la dicha tierra nueVa y habiendo de ser premyado y Re- /
(n)mu(m)nerado por rrazon de lo dicho habiendoseme de
guardar[32] las mercedes prome- / tidas en la dicha Real proVision por haber serVido tan lealmente en la / dicha Conquysta
y paÇificaçion donde en servycio de dios nuestro señor y de
Vuestra alteza / hize y guarde lo que por Vuestras
ynstruçiones Reales se me mando y guar- / dandolas y
Cumpliendolas segun(d) y Como era obligado En pro y
Utilydad / buen En exenplo de los naturales de la dicha tierra
no solamente no se me han / hecho Algunas mercedes mas no
guardando ny Cumpliendo lo que por Vuestra magestad / me
fue prometido por la dicha Vuestra Real proVision syn caUsa

ny rrazon / Alguna que justa fuese o syn ser oydo ny llamado
ny por fuero y derecho VenÇido[33] / ex abrruptamente[34] e sin
(h)orden de derecho antes contra ella El licenciado Lo- /
renÇo tejada oydor de Vuestra Real aUdiençia que Reside en
la / {rúbrica}

[fol. 2 left]
çiUdad de mexico E JueZ de ResydenÇia en esta proVinÇia
me quyto / los dichos pueblos y posesyon de ellos so color de
las nueVas leyes / Fechas para la buena Gobernaçion de estas
partes en que se manda / quytar los yndios que los gobernadores tuVieron no debiendo de entender- / se las dichas
nueVas leyes En quanto a esto conmygo por la promesa / que
por la dicha provysion Real Vuestra alteza me hizo mayormente que / para haberseme de quytar no Cometi delito
alguno porque los que / se me opusyeron por el licenciado
benaVente Vuestro fiscal yo fuy A / Suelto y dado por libre
E quyto por Vuestra alteza como consta / de esta exeCutoria[35]
Real de que hago presentaçion y no solamente / no se me
debiera hazer el dicho agraVio pero aUn debia ser / mas
premyado por lo que Como dicho es a Vuestra alteza servy en
la dicha / Jornada e por lo que de mys Haziendas gaste en
Vuestro Real servycio / e por los demas SerViÇios que a
Vuestra alteza hE hecho y por ser / Como soy Caballero hijodalgo notorio y por mis pasados haber SerVido Realmente A
Vuestra alteza

{ytem}   por que pido e suplico / a Vuestra alteza que
Constando de lo dicho o de tanta parte que baste profun-
damente / my yntençion mande declarar y declare los
dichos pueblos y estançias / y su(b)jetos perteneçerme y no
haber caUsa ny Razon por donde me / debiesen ser
quytados ny por donde se me debiese dexar de guardar /
Vuestra proVision Real En consequençia de lo qual pido /
y suplico a Vuestra alteza mande que los dichos pueblos / de
yndios y en todos sus su(b)Jetos me sean Vueltos y
Restituy- / dos para que yo los tenga y posea en nonbre de
Vuestra alteza / segun(d) que los tenya al tienpo que me
Fueron quytados con / mas los frutos Rentas e serViÇios e
tributos que han Rentado / y podido Rentar y Rentaren
hasta la Real Restituçion / y en defecto que Vuestra alteza

no mande hazer lo q*ue* tengo pedido / Se me mande Resti-
tuyr y pagar los d*ic*hos çinq*uen*ta myll Cas- / tellanos q*ue*
en V*uest*ro *servy*cio Real gaste condenando a V*uest*ra /
mag*estad* y al d*ic*ho fiscal En V*uest*ro Real nonbre a q*ue* me
den y paguen / los d*ic*hos Çinquenta myll Castellanos y a
que / yo sea premyado e Re(n)*m*u(m)*n*erado de mys *servy*-
*cio*s y my sangre / q*ue* en V*uest*ro Real SerViÇio dierame

por lo qual Y en lo / neÇesario V*uest*ro Real ofiçio ynploro
y pido JustiÇia e costas

{y*tem*}   El ConoÇimyento de *e*sta caUsa perteneçe A /
V*uest*ra alteza y se *h*a de tratar *en e*sta Real aUdienÇia / por
*vir*tud de la p*r*ovysion Real de que hago p*r*esentaÇion / El
lic*encia*do caballero p*edr*o Ruyz d*e* haro

Acknowledgments

It has taken the support and assistance of many persons and institutions to make this volume possible. The preparation of a documentary edition is extremely labor intensive. Our work on *Documents of the Coronado Expedition* was supported full-time for three years by a group of generous people, foundations, and governmental organizations.

First and foremost was the National Historical Publications and Records Commission of the National Archives and Records Administration, which has courageously stretched the scope of its original mandate by funding this and other projects not directly related to the "founding fathers" but nevertheless essential to understanding the history of the United States and the larger context within which it has evolved. Probably to no one at NHPRC do we owe greater thanks than to Roger Bruns, former deputy executive director. And we are extremely grateful for the encouragement and assistance of program officer Michael Meier.

Even with significant funding from NHPRC, it was continually necessary to raise sizable and crucial matching funds. During the first year of the project, matching monies came almost entirely from private donors, without whom the project would have been stillborn. They were E. Suzanne Flint, Joe H. Staley, Don Cushing and Associates, William K. Hartmann, Wid and Katherine Slick, Robert J. Flint, Harry C. Myers, Robert Krane, Nancy Jane Cushing, Forrest Fenn, Waldo M. Wedel, Richard Graham and Sandra Lauderdale Graham, Don Henkle, J. A. Whittenburg, Lester Strong, Sam Ballen, Glen W. Davidson, Harold Cushing, Caroline Everts, Gayle Harrison Hartmann, Mr. and Mrs. John Brittingham, Frances Webb, Dee Brechiesen, David and Irene Schneider, Walter and Isabel Davis, and Diana Stein.

For the second and third years of the project, in the midst of a deteriorating national economy, we were extremely fortunate in receiving enthusiastic and liberal support from the following foundations: Summerlee Foundation, The L. J. Skaggs and Mary C. Skaggs Foundation, Southwestern Foundation for Education and Historical Preservation, Clements Foundation, Southwestern Mission Research Center, Program for Cultural Cooperation between Spain's Ministry of Education, Culture and Sports and United States Universities, Santa Fe Art Foundation and the Gerald and Kathleen Peters Family Fund, and New Mexico Highlands University Foundation. Without the philanthropy of such institutions, scholarly work in the humanities would be all but impossible in the United States today.

New Mexico Highlands University, and especially its former vice president for academic affairs and provost, Glen W. Davidson, saw to it that the project had office space and other support facilities that made our work easier.

Although fund-raising was of necessity a major preoccupation of ours throughout the preparation of this volume, that was only one ingredient in a project involving, first, tracking down and securing facsimile copies of the documents to be included. Although the originals of the documents transcribed and translated here reside in 11 repositories in Europe and America, the bulk of them are preserved in the magnificent Archivo General de Indias (AGI) in Sevilla, Spain. Its spectacular collection and solicitous staff make the AGI a treasure for historians of the Americas. As in the past, our sincerest appreciation goes to the people of Spain who support such an important institution.

The remaining 10 institutions from which documents in this volume derive are the following: History Library,

Museum of New Mexico; John Carter Brown Library, Brown University; Biblioteca Real, Madrid; Mark Winters Collection, Santa Fe; Library of the British Museum; Biblioteca del Escorial, El Escorial; Nettie Lee Benson Collection, University of Texas, Austin; Academia Real de la Historia, Madrid; New York Public Library; and Bancroft Library, University of California, Berkeley. We thank all of them for their diligent work of conservation and for making the documents they hold available to scholars such as us.

We extend a special thanks to Dr. W. Michael Mathes for facilitating access to microfilm of the manuscript of the *Libro segundo de la Crónica miscelánea* by fray Antonio Tello, held by the John Carter Brown Library.

We were aided with translation of the four documents in Italian and the single one in Nahuatl by Larry D. Miller of the Spanish Colonial Research Center at the University of New Mexico and John Frederick Schwaller, vice chancellor for academic affairs and dean at the University of Minnesota, Morris, respectively. We are greatly in their debt for their excellent work. The final revisions and editing of their translations, though, are our responsibility.

A number of scholars reviewed individual translations, including Adrian Bustamante, Nancy Joe Dyer, William K. Hartmann and Gayle Harrison Hartmann, Rick Hendricks, John L. Kessell, Carroll L. Riley and Brent Locke Riley, Joseph P. Sánchez, Thomas E. Sheridan, and the members of the Santa Fe Seminar. They all made valuable suggestions that served to improve the final result.

In addition, David Weber and Donald Chipman both reviewed the manuscript as a whole. We are most grateful for the insightfulness of their comments. They both underlined the need for important clarifications.

Harry Myers, longtime friend and colleague as well as a staff member of the National Park Service's Long-Distance Trails Group, shared many a field trip in our effort to "ground-truth" the documents of the Coronado expedition. Keith Kintigh generously spent an extra day in El Morro Valley showing us the remains of ancestral Zuni pueblos. The late Benjamin Keen kindly introduced us to the underutilized work of Antonello Gerbi on Giovanni Battista Ramusio. Detailed recent correspondence with Dan Judkins and Richard S. Felger has sharpened our understanding of head injuries and the flora and fauna of the lower Colorado River.

Once again, we are in awe of the superb copyediting Jane Kepp does. With such a huge manuscript there is nearly infinite potential for inadvertent errors and inconsistencies. She patiently worked to keep those that remain to the minimum possible. The staff of SMU Press, Keith Gregory, Kathie Lang, and George Ann Ratchford, as well as their talented book designer, Tom Dawson, did a superb job with a handsome result.

All these friends and colleagues have been essential to getting *Documents of the Coronado Expedition* into print. May the material it contains prove of value to those seeking to understand and elucidate the full course by which we have gotten to where we are. May we in the future emulate what we find inspiring and shun what we are ashamed of from that past. And may we increasingly appreciate the inevitable complexity and tangledness of human affairs in any age.

Abbreviations Used in the Appendixes, Notes, and References

AGI   Archivo General de Indias, Sevilla, Spain

AGN   Archivo General de Nación, Ciudad de México

AGnot   Archivo General de Notarías, Ciudad de México

AGS   Archivo General de Simancas, Spain

AHN   Archivo Histórico Nacional, Madrid

Bolton   Herbert E. Bolton, *Coronado on the Turquoise Trail: Knight of Pueblos and Plains* (Albuquerque: University of New Mexico Press, 1949)

Boyd-Bowman   Peter Boyd-Bowman, *Índice geobiográfico de cuarenta mil pobladores españoles de América en el siglo XVI*, 2 vols. (Bogotá, Columbia: Instituto Caro y Cuervo, 1964, and México: Editorial Jus, 1968)

CDI   *Colección de documentos inéditos relativos al descubrimiento, conquista y organización de las antiguas posesiones españolas de América y Oceania*, Series 1, edited by Joaquín F. Pacheco, Francisco de Cárdenas, and Luis Torres de Mendoza, 42 vols. (Madrid: José María Pérez, 1864–84)

Covarrubias   Sebastián de Covarrubias Orozco, *Tesoro de la lengua castellana o española*, edited by Felipe C. R. Maldonado, 2nd ed. (Madrid: Editorial Castalia, 1995; originally published Madrid: Luis Sánchez, 1611)

DRAE   Real Academia Española, *Diccionario de la lengua española*, 21st. ed., 2 vols. (Madrid: Editorial Espasa Calpe, 1992)

H&R   George P. Hammond and Agapito Rey, eds. and trans., *Narratives of the Coronado Expedition, 1540–1542* (Albuquerque: University of New Mexico Press, 1940)

Icaza   Francisco A. de Icaza, *Conquistadores y pobladores de Nueva España: Diccionario autobiográfico sacado de los textos originales*, 2 vols. (Madrid: El Adelantado de Segovia, 1923)

Mora   Carmen de Mora, *Las Siete Ciudades de Cíbola: Textos y testimonios sobre la expedición de Vázquez Coronado* (Sevilla: Ediciones Alfar, 1992)

OED   *The Compact Edition of the Oxford English Dictionary*, 2 vols. (New York: Oxford University Press, 1971)

Pasajeros   Cristóbal Bermúdez Plata, *Catálogo de pasajeros a Indias durante los siglos XVI, XVII, y XVIII*, 3 vols. (Sevilla: Editorial de la Gavidia, 1940, 1942)

Pasajeros   Luis Romera Iruela and María del Carmen Galbis Díez, *Catálogo de pasajeros a Indias durante los siglos XVI, XVII y XVIII*, vols. 4 and 5 (Sevilla: Ministerio de Cultura, 1980)

Siete Partidas   Samuel Parsons Scott, trans., and Robert I. Burns, ed., *Las Siete Partidas*, 5 vols. (Philadelphia: University of Pennsylvania Press, 2001)

PTBOviedo   Gonzalo Fernández de Oviedo y Valdés, *Historia general y natural de las Indias*, edited by Juan Pérez de Tudela Bueso, 5 vols. (Madrid: Ediciones Atlas, 1992)

Tello   Antonio Tello, *Libro segundo de la crónica miscelánea, en que se trata de la conquista espiritual y temporal de la santa provincia de Xalisco en el nuevo reino de la Galicia y Nueva Vizcaya y descubrimiento del Nuevo México* (Guadalajara, México: Republica Literaria, 1891; reprint, México, DF: Editorial Porrúa, 1997)

Winship   George Parker Winship, ed. and trans., *The Coronado Expedition, 1540–1542*, in *Fourteenth Annual Report of the Bureau of American Ethnology of the Smithsonian Institution, 1892–1893*, Part 1, 329–613 (Washington, DC: Government Printing Office, 1896; reprint, Chicago: Rio Grande Press, 1964)

Appendix 1

Biographical Data

Almaguer, Antonio de. An *hidalgo* and a secretary to Viceroy Mendoza, Almaguer was a native of the *villa* of Corral de Almaguer in the *provincia* of Toledo in the modern Spanish *comunidad* of Castilla–La Mancha. He was married to doña Juana Briseño, the widow of Hernando de Torres. Sources: Icaza, 1: no. 405; Boyd-Bowman, 2: no. 10848.

Arellano, Tristán de (Luna y). Luna y Arellano was born at Borovia in the *provincia* of Soria in the modern Spanish *comunidad* of Castilla y León about 1515. He arrived in Nueva España in 1530 in the company of don Luis de Castilla. By 1546 he was married to the wealthy two-time widow doña Isabel de Rojas and was a *vecino* of Antequera in Oaxaca. Through his wife he acquired several *encomiendas*. He also had at least one sugar mill and an *estancia*. In 1559–61 Luna y Arellano served as captain general of an expedition to La Florida that ended in fiasco. He died in Madrid in 1573 as the sixth *mariscal* (originally the title given to the judge of the army and later an inherited title) of Castilla, despite published statements to the contrary.

During the expedition to Tierra Nueva, he was about 25 years old and was in charge of the main body of the expedition. In this role he led the bulk of the Spaniards, their livestock, and many of the Mexican Indians from Culiacán to Cíbola, from Cíbola to Tiguex, and from the buffalo plains back to Tiguex. He established the Spanish outpost of San Gerónimo at Corazones and later moved it to the Valley of Señora. Arellano became *maestre de campo* of the entire expedition following an injury to García López de Cárdenas in a fall in the summer of 1541.

Sources: Document 28, fols. 28r, 32v, 53r and 85r; Boyd-Bowman, 2: no. 10523; don Tristán de Luna y Arellano, *The Luna Papers: Documents Relating to the Expedition of don Tristán de Luna y Arellano for the Conquest of La Florida in 1559–1561*, 2 vols., trans. and ed. Herbert Ingram Priestley (Freeport, NY: Books for Libraries Press, 1971), 1:xxv, xxvii–lxvii; AGI, México, 1064, L.1\1, "Informes de los conquistadores," fol. 165v; Victor M. Álvarez, *Diccionario de conquistadores* (México, DF: Instituto Nacional de Antropología y Historia, 1975), 1:38–40; Doris M. Ladd, *The Mexican Nobility at Independence, 1780–1826* (Austin: Institute of Latin American Studies, University of Texas at Austin, 1976), 193–95.

Bermejo, Hernando, or **Hernando Martín Bermejo.** Bermejo was a native of Fuente del Arco in the *provincia* of Badajoz in the modern Spanish *comunidad* of Extremadura. He came to Nueva España in 1535 with his cousin Juan Martín (Bermejo) and Pero Martín Cano (a possible relative), both of whom who were also on the Coronado expedition. Given the date of their licenses to depart, they possibly traveled in the same fleet that carried Antonio de Mendoza to Nueva España. Prior to and during the expedition to Tierra Nueva, Bermejo served as principal *escribano* and secretary to Vázquez de Coronado. By sometime in late 1544 or early 1545 he was no longer serving in that capacity and had become a *vecino* in Santiago, Guatemala. Sources: *Pasajeros*, 2: no. 2201; H&R, 101 n. 76; Document 12, fol. 7v; Document 27, passim; AGI, Justicia 336, N.1, "Probança"; AGI, Patronato, 64, R.1, "Juan de Aguilar."

Cabeza de Vaca, Álvar Núñez. Cabeza de Vaca was the son of Francisco de Vera and grandson of Pedro de Vera, conqueror of Gran Canaria. His mother was doña Teresa Cabeza de Vaca. A native of Jerez de la Frontera in the *provincia* of Cádiz in the modern Spanish *comunidad* of Andalucía, he was one of four survivors of the Narváez expedition (see Narváez, Pánfilo de) who returned to Nueva España after seven years of traveling through coastal Texas and Mexico. His report spurred further exploration of northern New Spain. In 1540 he was appointed *adelantado* of the *provincia* of Río de la Plata (Argentina and Paraguay). He was arrested in 1544 and sent back to Spain to stand trial on charges of abuse of the natives. Convicted on a number of those charges, he was, however, soon released from confinement, and the conviction was eventually reversed. He died in 1559, evidently in his native Jerez de la Frontera.

For a full treatment of his life and extraordinary trek across North America, see Rolena Adorno and Patrick Charles Pautz, *Álvar Núñez Cabeza de Vaca: His Account, His Life, and the Expedition of Pánfilo de Narváez*, 3 vols. (Lincoln: University of Nebraska Press, 1999); Alex D. Krieger, *We Came Naked and Barefoot: The Journey of Cabeza de Vaca across North America* (Austin: University of Texas Press, 2002); and David A. Howard, *Conquistador in Chains: Cabeza de Vaca and the Indians of the Americas* (Tuscaloosa: University of Alabama Press, 1997).

Castilla, don Luis de. Luis de Castilla was a native of Valladolid in the modern Spanish *comunidad* of Castilla y León and a direct descendant of King Pedro I and doña Juana de Castro. "De Castilla" was not a true surname but rather an indication of his royal heritage—"House of Castilla"—and he was usually known by the honorific "don Luis." The 28-year-old arrived in Nueva España in 1530 as escort for his relative doña Juana de Zúñiga, the second wife of Hernán Cortés. He married doña Juana de Sosa, sister of the royal treasurer, Juan Alonso de Sosa, who in turn was the husband of Vázquez de Coronado's sister-in-law, Ana de Estrada. Don Luis served in the pacification of Jalisco, where he was briefly made prisoner by Guzmán in the ongoing dispute between Cortés and Guzmán over the right of conquest. He was *justicia mayor* of Nueva España, an *encomendero* by 1531, and a *regidor* of the Ciudad de México in 1534. He was also a personal friend of Viceroy Mendoza's and seems to have been instrumental in planning and executing the early stages of the expedition to Tierra Nueva.

Sources: Peter Gerhard, *The North Frontier of New Spain,* rev. ed. (Norman: University of Oklahoma Press, 1993), 39–55; Arthur Scott Aiton, *Antonio de Mendoza: First Viceroy of New Spain* (Durham, NC: Duke University Press, 1927), 166; Harry Kelsey, *Juan Rodríguez Cabrillo* (San Marino, CA: Huntington Library, 1998), 86; Boyd-Bowman, 2: no. 12093a; *Primera y segunda relaciónes anónimas de la jornada que hizo Nuño de Guzmán a la Nueva Galicia* (Mexico: Chimalistac, 1952), 17. See also the introduction to Document 16.

Cherino or **Chirinos, Pero Almíldez** or **Peralmíndez** or **Perarlmíndez.** A royal *cédula* issued in Valladolid and dated October 15, 1522, named Alonso de Estrada, Peralmíndez Cherinos, and Rodrigo Albornoz royal officials for Nueva España. Cherino was a native of Úbeda in the *provincia* of Jaén in the modern Spanish *comunidad* of Andalucía. He served in the Ciudad de México as *veedor* and also as lieutenant governor of Nueva España during Cortés's absences. He often sided with the royal *factor,* Gonzalo de Salazar, against the other two royal officials, Estrada and Albornoz, resulting in a contentious governmental atmosphere. He returned to Spain in 1544.

There is (and was in the sixteenth century) much disagreement about the spelling of his name. Document 14 spells it Almidrez Cherino (fol. 1r) and Almidez Cherino (fol. 1v). Robert Himmerich y Valencia spells it Pero Almíndez Chirinos; Herbert Bolton, Peralmíndez Cherinos; and Hammond and Rey, Peralmyndes Cherino. Sources: Francisco Fernández del Castillo, "Alonso de Estrada: Su familia," in *Memorias de la Academia Mexicana de la Historia* 1 (1942):398; John H. Parry and Robert G. Keith, eds., *New Iberian World,* vol. 1, *The Conquerors and the Conquered* (New York: Times Books, 1984), 3:316; Francisco López de Gómara, *Cortés: The Life of the Conqueror by His Secretary,* trans. and ed. Lesley Byrd Simpson (Berkeley: University of California Press, 1964), 339, 342–45; Boyd-Bowman, 2:no. 5761; Robert Himmerich y Valencia, *The Encomenderos of New Spain, 1521–1555* (Austin: University of Texas Press, 1991), 13; Bolton, 68; H&R, 87.

Consejo Real de las Indias, Consejo de las Indias. The Consejo de Indias was the highest institution of Spanish administration in the Americas and the Philippines and also the supreme tribunal of justice for those possessions. Originally these matters were the concern of the Consejo de Castilla, but eventually two institutions were formed to deal with the Indies: the Casa de la Contratación in Sevilla in 1503 and the Junta de Indias in 1511. The latter acted within the Consejo de Castilla and was guided by Carlos V's existing advisors (Cobos, Fonseca, García de Padilla, and Gattinara).

The actual date of establishment of a separate Consejo de las Indias is under debate, but it certainly existed by 1522. The date of its official establishment is the date of appointment of its first president, fray García de Loaysa, August 1, 1524. Its first counselors were Luis Cabeza de Vaca (bishop of Canarias), and doctors Gonzalo Maldonado, Diego Beltrán, and Pedro Mártir de Anglería. Its *fiscal* was Francisco de Prado; Francisco de los Cobos was its secretary; and its grand counselor was Mercurino de Gattinara (holder of the royal seal). During the period of the expedition to Tierra Nueva, the Consejo de Indias was peripatetic, functioning in whichever location the royal court happened to be.

The Consejo handled matters of administration for the Indies: naming governors and royal officials, supervising the fleets, and promulgating legislation concerning the treatment of the Indians. During the reign of Felipe IV it was reorganized into the Junta de Guerra de Indias, the Junta de Hacienda de Indias, and the Junta de la Cámara de Indias.

Source: Purificación Medina Encina, "El Consejo de Indias," in *Archivo General de Indias,* general editor Pedro González García (Madrid: Lunwerg Editores y Ministerio de Educación y Cultura, 1995), 169–247.

Díaz, Melchior. Prior to the expedition, Díaz had served as a captain under Nuño de Guzmán during the conquest of the *provincia* of Nueva Galicia. He was captain and *alcalde mayor* of Culiacán and lieutenant governor of Compostela. As such, he was the official, along with Diego de Alcaraz, who first received the survivors of the Narváez expedition to La Florida when they reached Culiacán in 1536. He held a *repartimiento* in Culiacán, which after his untimely death was transferred to Pedro de Tovar. While *alcalde* at Culiacán, Díaz allegedly sent three Indian women as servants to Vázquez de Coronado's wife, Beatriz, in Ciudad de México. Vázquez de Coronado was later found to have acted improperly in accepting the servants.

Vázquez de Coronado appointed Díaz *alcalde mayor* and administrator of the Spanish outpost of San Gerónimo and then sent him, with 25 men, to the coast of the Mar del Sur/Pacific Ocean to look for the supply ships under Hernando de Alarcón. In his absence, Díaz left Diego de Alcaraz in charge at San Gerónimo. While in modern northwestern Sonora, Díaz died of an accidental wound from his own lance in late 1540 or early 1541. Sources: Document 28, fols. 24v, 35v–39r, and 71r–72v; Bolton, 12; H&R, 106 n. 97; AGI, Justicia, 339, N.1, R.1, "Residencia"; Tello, 306, 327, 407–11.

Dorantes, Andrés. A survivor of the Narváez expedition along with Cabeza de Vaca, Alonso del Castillo Maldonado, and Esteban, Dorantes was a native of Béjar in the *provincia* of Salamanca in the modern Spanish *comunidad* of Castilla y León. He was the son of Pablo Dorantes. Source: Adorno and Pautz, *Núñez Cabeza de Vaca,* 1:279.

Esteban de Dorantes (Esteban, Estebanillo, Estebanico). A black, Arabic-speaking Christian slave from Azamor in Morocco, Esteban was a survivor of the Narváez expedition along with Cabeza de Vaca, Andrés Dorantes, and Alonso del Castillo Maldonado. Viceroy Mendoza bought him from Dorantes in 1537 and sent him with fray Marcos de Niza to reconnoiter Cíbola. He was killed at Zuni. Sources: Frank Hamilton Cushing, "A Lesson in History," in *Zuñi: Selected Writings of Frank Hamilton Cushing,* edited by Jesse Green (Lincoln: University of Nebraska Press, 1979), 174; Edmund J. Ladd, "Zuni on the Day the Men in Metal

Arrived," in *The Coronado Expedition to Tierra Nueva: The 1540–1542 Route across the Southwest,* edited by Richard Flint and Shirley Cushing Flint (Niwot, CO: University Press of Colorado, 1997), 225; Adorno and Pautz, *Núñez Cabeza de Vaca,* 1:xxii, 279; AGI, Patronato, 184, R.27, "Mendoza, Letter to the King, December 1537," fol. 14v.

Guzmán, Nuño Beltrán de. A native of Guadalajara in the modern Spanish *comunidad* of Castilla–La Mancha, Guzmán spent his early years in the Spanish royal court. He was appointed governor of Pánuco in 1525 and arrived to assume office in May 1527. He was president of the first *audiencia* for Nueva España. He launched *entradas* into Michoacán, Jalisco, Nayarit, and Sinaloa, pushing the frontier of Spanish jurisdiction west and north. Accused of extreme cruelty to Indians, he was recalled to Spain in 1538, where he remained under house arrest at the Spanish court. Sources: Himmerich y Valencia, *Encomenderos,* 170–71; Donald E. Chipman, *Nuño de Guzmán and the Province of Pánuco in New Spain, 1518–1533* (Glendale, CA: Arthur H. Clark, 1967).

López de Cárdenas, García or García Ramírez de Cárdenas. Don García was a native of Madrid and son of Nunfro Ramírez and Mencia de Cárdenas. His license to travel to the New World was dated May 15, 1535, which may place him in the same fleet as Mendoza (a kinsman of his) and Vázquez de Coronado. He was named *alguacil mayor* of the Audiencia and Chancillería de México on April 8, 1538, because of his ability and as recompense for past services.

After the death of Lope de Samaniego he served as *maestre de campo* on the Coronado expedition and was eventually held accountable for the cruelties to the Indians at Tiguex. He served some of his sentence in the Torre de Homenaje in Pinto, south of Madrid, and the rest in Vélez Málaga in the modern Spanish *comunidad* of Andalucía.

Sources: *Pasajeros,* 2: no. 1064; AGI, Patronato, 277, N.4, R.36, "Appointment of López de Cárdenas, Mexico City, April 8, 1538"; AGI, Justicia, 1021, N.2, Pieza 1, "Acusación e información"; Richard Flint, *Great Cruelties Have Been Reported: The 1544 Investigation of the Coronado Expedition* (Dallas: Southern Methodist University Press, 2002), 336–39.

Luis, fray, de Úbeda, or de Escalona. As his name might suggest, fray Luis may have been a native of Úbeda in the *provincia* of Jaén in the modern Spanish *comunidad* of Andalucia, or he might have taken his vows there. After arriving in Nueva España in 1535, he served in the household of the first bishop of México, fray Juan de Zumárraga. Upon joining the expedition to Tierra Nueva, fray Luis was responsible for erecting crosses in the indigenous communities through which it passed. When it was determined that the expedition would return to Nueva España, he remained in the north, going to Cicuique with the hope of converting its population. It is likely that within a short time he was killed. The historian fray Angélico Chávez determined that the fray Luis de Escalona referred to by expedition member Juan Jaramillo was the same person and that the name Escalona was erroneously attributed to fray Luis. Sources: fray Angélico Chávez, *Coronado's Friars* (Washington, DC: Academy of American Franciscan History, 1968), 28–29; Document 28, fols. 135v–147r; Document 30, fol. 5r; AGI, Contratación, 4675, L.5, "Account book," fols. 373v–374r.

Maldonado, licenciado Alonso. A native of Salamanca in the modern Spanish *comunidad* of Castilla y León and a member of the Colegial de Cuenca in Salamanca, Maldonado married doña Catalina de Montejo, daughter of Francisco de Montejo, conquistador of Yucatán. He received in dowry various *encomiendas, estancias,* and barrios. He was named an *oidor* in the Audiencia de México and served from 1530 to 1543. In June 1543 he was named first president of the Audiencia de los Confines (Audiencia de Guatemala). In March 1552 he was named president of the Audiencia de Santo Domingo and served there until 1557. Sources: Himmerich y Valencia, *Encomenderos,* 198; Boyd-Bowman, 2: no. 7481; Ernesto Schäfer, *El Consejo Real y Supremo de las Indias: Su historia, organización y labor administrativa hasta la terminación de la Casa de Austria,* 2 vols. (Sevilla: Universidad de Sevilla, 1935), 2:451.

Maldonado, Rodrigo. This native of Guadalajara in the modern Spanish *comunidad* of Castilla–La Mancha came to Nueva España in 1535. He married doña Isabel de Aux and through her became an *encomendero.* Through his sister he was the brother-in-law of the Duque del Infantado and thus also a relative of Viceroy Mendoza's. He was about 25 years old when the expedition departed from Compostela. Sources: AGI, Justicia, 1021, N.2, Pieza 6, "Probanza del fiscal Villalobos"; AGI, Justicia, 260, Pieza 1, "Cargos y descargos, visita contra Tejada, 1546"; AGI, Patronato, 291, R.37, "Emplazamiento a don Rodrigo Maldonado, vecino de México, y doña Isabel de Aux, su mujer, en un pleito con doña Isabel de Barrios, February 21, 1566"; Helen Nader, *The Mendoza Family in the Spanish Renaissance, 1350 to 1550* (New Brunswick, NJ: Rutgers University Press, 1979), xv.

Mendoza, Antonio de. Don Antonio de Mendoza was the first viceroy of Nueva España, from 1535 to 1550, although he had first been offered the post in 1529. The new viceroy brought a sizable entourage with him to Nueva España, including Francisco Vázquez de Coronado. At least 13 people who received licenses to travel to Nueva España between April 17 and September 26, 1535, stated that they were accompanying the viceroy. More than 170 others were granted such licenses during that period, many of whom were also in Mendoza's entourage. In 1536 he received the survivors of the Narváez expedition to La Florida and heard their reports of populous and wealthy *pueblos* far to the north. A little over two years later, he dispatched Esteban de Dorantes (one of the Narváez survivors) and fray Marcos de Niza to confirm those reports. Then he assigned Francisco Vázquez de Coronado, governor of Nueva Galicia, to lead a full-scale expedition to the Tierra Nueva reported by fray Marcos. Mendoza was reported to have spent the equivalent of 85,000 silver *pesos* as one of the expedition's three principal financial backers. According to the seventeenth-century historian fray Antonio Tello, Mendoza provided 30 *pesos* of aid to each horseman and 20 *pesos* to each footman. In 1545, he claimed still to be in debt because of his expenses for the expedition. In Vázquez de Coronado's absence while in Tierra Nueva, Mendoza led a large force of Indians and Spaniards to suppress a serious native uprising in Nueva Galicia known as the Mixtón War.

Mendoza also served as president of the Audiencia de Nueva España. At the instigation of Hernán Cortés, from 1544 to 1546 a sweeping *visita* was conducted of the performance in office of the viceroy and all the royal officials of Nueva España. The *visitador,* Francisco Tello de Sandoval, very much in accord with Cortés's complaints and perhaps in the hope of replacing the viceroy himself, determinedly sought indications of malfeasance by Mendoza. He eventually lodged 44 mostly petty charges against the viceroy. Mendoza responded with a massive documentary defense. In 1545, the viceroy's half-brother Luis Hurtado de Mendoza became president of the Consejo de Indias. Under his pressure, the king recalled Tello de Sandoval to Spain. In 1548 the Consejo absolved the viceroy and chastised the former *visitador*. In 1550 Mendoza, though suffering ill health, was ordered transferred to the viceroyalty of Peru in an effort to put a definitive end to the civil unrest there. Mendoza served briefly in Peru until his death in 1552.

Like his sometime business partner Lorenzo de Tejada, Antonio de Mendoza used his official position in Nueva España to further private business as part of a general effort toward economic development. He owned at least one *obraje*, or weaving shop, a sugar mill, and several *estancias*. Through third parties, especially his son Francisco, he controlled the supply of livestock and equipment used in the several enterprises of exploration he sponsored, and he also shipped horses to Peru for sale. Nevertheless, historical judgment has been almost uniformly that Mendoza was the most capable and effective viceroy that Nueva España ever had.

Mendoza was considered a native of Granada in the modern Spanish *comunidad* of Andalucía, having been born near there in 1490 or 1491. His father was Iñigo López de Mendoza, the Conde de Tendilla, Marqués de Mondéjar, and *alcaide* of the Alhambra. His mother was Francisca Pacheco, second wife of López de Mendoza and daughter of the Marqués de Villena. Antonio's half-brother Luis Hurtado de Mendoza, in addition to serving as president of the Consejo de Indias, succeeded to his father's titles, including that of captain general of Granada.

Antonio de Mendoza was married to Catalina de Vargas. Before becoming viceroy, he led royal forces at Huéscar during the Comunero Revolt. He had also served as ambassador to Hungary and as the queen's chamberlain. He was a knight of the Order of Santiago.

Sources: Aiton, *Mendoza*; AGI, Mexico, 1088, L.1, "Royal *cédula*, Madrid, November 9, 1529"; *Pasajeros*, 2:nos. 913 and 2213; AGI, Patronato, 57, N.2, R.1, "Antonio de Mendoza"; Tello, 2:324–26; Arthur S. Aiton, "The Secret Visita against Viceroy Mendoza," in *New Spain and the Anglo-American West: Historical Contributions Presented to Herbert Eugene Bolton*, vol. 1 (Los Angeles: privately printed, 1932), 1–7; Ethelia Ruiz Medrano, "La Política del Virrey Mendoza," in *Gobierno y sociedad en Nueva España: Segunda audiencia y Antonio de Mendoza* (Michoacán: Colegio de Michoacán, 1991), 162–205; Lewis Hanke, *Los Virreyes españoles en América durante el gobierno de la Casa de Austria, México*, 5 vols., in *Biblioteca de autores españoles desde la formación del lenguaje hasta nuestros días*, vols. 273–77 (Madrid: Ediciones Atlas, 1976), 1:18.

Narváez, Pánfilo de. Narváez was born about 1475 in Navalmanzano in the *provincia* of Segovia in the modern Spanish *comunidad* of Castilla y León. He came to the Indies around 1498, taking up residence first in Santo Domingo. He then served as second-in-command to Juan de Esquivel in Jamaica and afterward to Diego Velázquez in Cuba. He sailed from Cuba to Veracruz in March 1520 to apprehend Cortés but was defeated near Cempoallan on May 29, 1520, losing an eye in the process.

He was then placed in charge of an expedition organized in Spain that left in August 1527, arriving at Hispañola in September. Having been appointed in December 1527 as governor and captain general for life, *alguacil mayor*, and *adelantado* of Río de las Palmas and Florida, he set sail from Cuba for Florida in mid-March 1528. In early April his expedition landed in Florida.

After exploring inland and fighting the natives, he ordered rafts built

for his remaining men (those not killed by disease, starvation, or Indians). There were 49 men with Narváez when he embarked for the Spanish settlement of Pánuco. A second raft with Alonso Enríquez, the comptroller, and fray Juan Suárez held about 49 more. Alonso del Castillo and Andrés Dorantes were on a third raft with 48 men. Captains Téllez and Peñalosa manned a fourth with 47 others, and a fifth raft with 49 men was under the command of Alonso Solís and Álvar Núñez Cabeza de Vaca.

Narváez's raft disappeared one night in November 1528 off the Texas Gulf Coast near the island of Malhado (Galviston Island, Texas), and he was never seen again. Of the remaining men of his aborted expedition, only four are known to have survived more than a few months: Cabeza de Vaca, Castillo Maldonado, Dorantes, and Esteban de Dorantes. Sources: Hugh Thomas, *Conquest: Montezuma, Cortés, and the Fall of Old Mexico* (New York: Simon and Schuster, 1995), 354–56, 377; Adorno and Pautz, *Núñez Cabeza de Vaca*, 1:map 1, 21–22, 75, 2:21–22.

Oñate, Cristóbal de. A native of Vitoria in the *provincia* of Álava in modern País Vasco in Spain, Oñate arrived in Nueva España in 1520. He married doña Catalina de Salazar, daughter of the royal *factor*, Gonzalo de Salazar. He became a *vecino* of the Ciudad de México and held *encomiendas* in Michoacán, Culiacán, and in the vicinity of the Ciudad de México. He served as lieutenant governor of Nueva Galicia under Vázquez de Coronado and helped suppress the Mixtón War in the governor's absence in Tierra Nueva. His brother Juan de Oñate went to Perú, and Cristóbal's son of the same name, Juan de Oñate, led the permanent settlement of New Mexico in 1598.

In addition to participating in the conquest and pacification of Nueva Galicia, he was also its governor and captain general after Vázquez de Coronado's term. In 1547 he, Diego de Ibarra, and Juan de Tolosa founded Zacatecas. Oñate became a powerful silver mining magnate in that area. Sources: Icaza, 2:no. 1383; Himmerich y Valencia, *Encomenderos*, 207; Marc Simmons, *The Last Conquistador: Juan de Oñate and the Settling of the Far Southwest* (Norman: University of Oklahoma Press, 1991), 1–47.

Padilla, fray Juan de. Fray Juan may not have been in Nueva España until late 1533, although other evidence indicates he was there by 1529. Whenever he came, he arrived there from the *provincia* of Andalucía, possibly his home region in the modern Spanish *comunidad* of Andalucía. He served as guardian of the Franciscan convents at Tulancingo and Zapotlán before the expedition to Tierra Nueva was mounted. Fray Juan was deeply interested in, if not obsessed by, stories of the Seven Cities of Antillia. When the organization of the expedition was announced, he sought out Vázquez de Coronado and asked to join.

Fray Juan was the senior ecclesiastic with the expedition after fray Marcos de Niza returned to the Ciudad de México. As head of the religious component of the expedition, fray Juan was frequently consulted by the captain general when questions of the proper course of action arose. He supported attacks on the pueblos of Cíbola and Tiguex, recommended the interrogation of Bigotes, and confirmed the decision to execute El Turco.

When it was decided that the expedition would leave Tierra Nueva, fray Juan insisted on remaining to preach to the people of Quivira. He traveled there with the Portuguese, Andrés de Campo, a Black, a mestizo, and two Indian *donados* (lay brothers) but was killed within a short time. Sources: Boyd-Bowman, 2: no. 12928a; Document 28, fols. 123r–123v,

135r–136v, and 153v; AGI, Contratación, 4675, L.5, "Account book," fols. 335r–336r; Chávez, *Coronado's Friars*, 14–27.

Pérez de la Torre, licenciado Diego. *Residencia* judge Diego Pérez de la Torre was a native of Almendralejo in the *provincia* of Badajoz in the modern Spanish *comunidad* of Extremadura. Sent from Spain by the king, he arrived at Pánuco in 1536 to take the *residencia* of Nuño de Guzmán. After arresting Guzmán he became the governor of Nueva Galicia in 1537 and held the office briefly, until his death the following year. Vázquez de Coronado went to Nueva Galicia to take the *residencia* of the deceased Pérez de la Torre and then to assume the governorship. It was a common practice to take the *residencia* of one's predecessor. The *licenciado's* son, Melchior Pérez de la Torre, was a member of the expedition to Tierra Nueva. Sources: Boyd-Bowman, 2: no. 697; Document 1, fol. 1r. See also the introduction to Document 32.

Querechos. The Querechos were a nomadic Apachean people of the northern and western Llano Estacado of modern eastern New Mexico and the Texas Panhandle. Members of the Coronado expedition met them in the summer of 1541. Like their neighbors to the south and east, the Teyas, they subsisted primarily by hunting bison. They lived in hide tents, used the dog travois, and traded regularly with the Pueblo Indians of the Rio Grande region. They are thought to have been the people responsible for the remains identified archaeologically as the Tierra Blanca Complex. They had little interaction with the expedition to Tierra Nueva, packing up and moving off soon after their encounters. Sources: Judith A. Habicht-Mauche, "Coronado's Querechos and Teyas in the Archaeological Record of the Texas Panhandle," *Plains Anthropologist* 140 (1992), 247–59; Document 28, fols. 78r–79r and 120r–121v; Donald J. Blakeslee, Douglas K. Boyd, Richard Flint, et al., "Bison Hunters of the Llano in 1541: A Panel Discussion," in *The Coronado Expedition from the Distance of 460 Years,* edited by Richard Flint and Shirley Cushing Flint (Albuquerque: University of New Mexico Press, 2003), 164–86.

Samaniego, Lope de. Viceroy Mendoza appointed the long-time veteran of Nueva España, *regidor* of the Ciudad de México, and its *alcaide,* Lope de Samaniego, as *maestre de campo* of the expedition to Tierra Nueva. Indicative of his status within the expedition and Nueva España more generally were the 16 or 17 horses Samaniego took with him.

A native of Segovia in the modern Spanish *comunidad* of Castilla y León, Samaniego served on the *cabildo* of the Ciudad de México from about 1529 until his death in the *provincia* of Chiametla in 1540, shot with an arrow while trying to commandeer supplies from the Indians there. He had been a captain under Nuño de Guzmán in the conquest of Nueva Galicia and had been sent by Guzmán to pacify Chiametla. It is quite likely that his killing in 1540 was an act of revenge for his earlier violence against the natives there.

He was married to Isabel Flaces and had at least one son. For a short time he was *encomendero* of Calimaya, Metepec, and Tepemaxalco, southwest of the Ciudad de México. Sources: Boyd-Bowman, 2: no. 8024; Document 12, fol. 1r; AGI, Mexico, 203, N.13, "Report concerning Lope de Samaniego, México, 1531"; *Actas de Cabildo,* compiled by Ignacio Bejarano, 64 vols. (México, DF: Aguilar e Hijos, 1889–), 4:131–33; *Pasajeros,* 4: no. 2406; Anonymous, "Cuarta relación anónima de la

jornada de Nuño de Guzmán," in *Colección de documentos para la historia de México,* 2nd facsimile ed., ed. Joaquín García Icazbalceta (Mexico City: Editorial Porrúa, 1980), 2:472; Himmerich y Valencia, *Encomenderos,* 123.

Tejada, licenciado Lorenzo de. Tejada was a native of Santo Domingo de la Calzada in the modern Spanish *comunidad* of La Rioja. At age 35 he was appointed one of four *oidores* of the Audiencia de Nueva España during Mendoza's administration as viceroy, replacing Vasco de Quiroga. He served from 1537 to 1552. During his tenure in office he was a large employer of Indian labor for his building projects and was accused of mistreating the Indians he employed. After repeated conflicts with the second viceroy, Luis de Velasco, he left Nueva España in 1552 for Granada, Spain, where he had become a *vecino* by at least 1559. Source: Flint, *Great Cruelties,* 31–33.

Teyas, Teyvas. Like their fellow nomads of the Great Plains and sometime enemies the Querechos, with whom they shared the Llano Estacado, the Teyas lived by hunting bison, gathering wild plants, and trading bison products with the Pueblos of what is now New Mexico. They may also, however, have done some farming. Archaeologically identified village sites on the southeastern margin of the Llano Estacado, labeled the Garza Complex, are attributed to the Teyas. It has been suggested that the Teyas spoke either a Caddoan dialect or a language related to that of the Piro Pueblos.

According to members of the expedition to Tierra Nueva, Teyas routinely spent the winters at or in the vicinity of the easternmost pueblos, especially Cicuique. This did not prevent occasional hostility between Teyas and Pueblos. For instance, members of the expedition were told that Teyas had destroyed a pueblo in New Mexico's Galisteo Basin only a few years earlier. Although the expedition stole a large number of bison hides from Teyas met in a *barranca* at the edge of the buffalo plains, relations between the two groups during their brief encounter seem not to have been openly hostile.

Sources: Habicht-Mauche, "Coronado's Querechos and Teyas," 247–59; Carroll L. Riley, "The Teya Indians of the Southwestern Plains," in Flint and Flint, *Tierra Nueva,* 320–43; Document 28, fols. 83v, 85v–86r, and 113v–114v; Blakeslee, Boyd, Flint, et al., "Bison Hunters of the Llano."

Turcios, Antonio de. A native of Salinas de Añava in Spain, Turcios was the son of Pedro de Turcios and Maria Martínez de Aramayona. He arrived in Nueva España about 1527 and from the late 1530s until at least 1551 served as chief *escribano* of the Audiencia de Nueva España. Source: AGI, México, 1064, L.1\1, "Informes de los conquistadores," fol. 169r.

Turco. Documentary sources are ambiguous about El Turco's place of origin. The author of the "Relación del Suceso," however, explicitly states that he was "from a *pueblo* he called Haraee." According to modern reconstructions of the social geography of the Great Plains, he was thus a member of a proto-Pawnee people. His fellow guide, Ysopete, is usually considered to have been a native of Quivira and therefore a member of a proto-Wichita band. Testimony by a member of the Coronado expedition, however, states that the two were from the same land. Members of the expedition understood El Turco to say that precious metals were abundant in Quivira, which was governed by a wealthy elite.

Communication between the Spaniards and El Turco was imperfect at best, relying as it did primarily on hand signs. It is likely that the Spaniards never understood exactly what El Turco said about Quivira or why he led them as he did. It is even remotely possible that, as Mildred Mott Wedel suggested almost 20 years ago, El Turco's goal was the great tributary chiefdoms of the lower Mississippi Valley. More recently, Jane Walsh has raised the possibility that the name El Turco was applied to the guide ex post facto in reference to his lying. Under this suggestion, he was seen as "evil" like the Turks, enemies of the Christians of the time.

Sources: Document 29, fol. 4r; Document 30, fol. 3r; Carroll L. Riley, *Rio del Norte: People of the Upper Rio Grande from Earliest Times to the Pueblo Revolt* (Salt Lake City: University of Utah Press, 1995), 169; Mildred Mott Wedel, "The Indian They Called Turco," in *Pathways to Plains Prehistory: Anthropological Perspectives of Plains Natives and Their Pasts,* edited by Don G. Wyckoff and Jack L. Hofman (Duncan, OK: Cross Timbers Press, 1982), 153–62; Jane MacLaren Walsh, "Myth and Imagination in the American Story: The Coronado Expedition, 1540–1542" (Ph.D. diss., Catholic University of America, 1993), 207–8.

Appendix 2

Geographical Data

Acuco, Coco, Acoco. These are all renderings of the Keresan word *ák'u*, the native name of the New Mexico pueblo now usually referred to as Acoma. It lies in modern Cíbola County, approximately 60 miles west of the Rio Grande and 50 miles east of Zuni. Notable now as in the sixteenth century, Acoma occupies the top of an isolated, 350-foot-high, sheer-walled mesa in Acoma Valley. The pueblo has been occupied since at least the 1100s. Its population in 1540 included an estimated 200 adult males. Today it is only lightly populated on a full-time basis. Contact between Acoma and the expedition to Tierra Nueva was minimal.

Sources: Velma García-Mason, "Acoma Pueblo," in *Handbook of North American Indians*, vol. 9, *Southwest*, ed. Alfonso Ortiz (Washington, DC: Smithsonian Institution Press, 1979), 450, 456; Robert Julyan, *The Place Names of New Mexico* (Albuquerque: University of New Mexico Press, 1996), 3; Mrs. William T. Sedgwick, *Acoma, the Sky City: A Study in Pueblo Indian History and Civilization* (Cambridge, MA: Harvard University Press, 1927), 15. See map 3.

Acus. The polity to which this name applies has not been identified. See the entry for Marata.

Arahe, Arahey, Harahey, Arache, Arehe, Haraee, Arae. Members of the expedition to Tierra Nueva were told of a land to the east, and possibly north, of Quivira called Arahe or Harahey. It was supposed to be wealthier in precious metals than Quivira. Most students of the subject think Arahe was a region of ancestral Pawnee settlements in modern eastern Nebraska. Had the Coronado expedition continued another year, Arahe would have been among its destinations. El Turco was said to have been a native of Arahe. Sources: Document 28, fol. 75v; Carroll L. Riley, *Rio del Norte: People of the Upper Rio Grande from Earliest Times to the Pueblo Revolt* (Salt Lake City: University of Utah Press, 1995), 196; Bolton, 233.

Brava, Uraba, Yuraba, Valladolid. The place to which these names applied has been identified as modern Taos Pueblo, a northern Tiwa community, situated now, as in 1540–42, along Taos Creek, a small tributary flowing into the Rio Grande from the east in Taos County, New Mexico. It was in the sixteenth century and still is the northernmost Pueblo community. It was apparently visited only twice by the expedition,

evidently without incident. It was given the name Valladolid by the Spaniards. The name Brava was also occasionally written as Uraba. Sources: Albert H. Schroeder, "Pueblos Abandoned in Historic Times," in Ortiz, *Southwest*, vol. 9, 251; Document 28, fols. 91v–92r.

Chiametla. The *provincia* of Chiametla or Chametla comprised the coastal plain along the Río Baluarte in what is now southern Sinaloa. Like so many names used to refer to social entities in the Americas during the era of conquest, "Chiametla" was applied to both a region and a specific settlement within that region. The principal settlement may have been at a site known more recently as Cocoyolitos, on the north side of the Río Baluarte less than five miles from its mouth. For many years the river was known as the Río Chametla (spelled without an *i*). Tello, 212, says that Guzmán founded a *villa* there called Espíritu Santo in 1534. See, however, the entry for Compostela.

Characterized as a *provincia* by Nuño de Guzmán when he reached it late in 1530, Chiametla or Chametlán was a region densely populated by speakers of a Nahuatl-like language, Totorame. Farmers and fishermen, they suffered heavy depredations from slave raiders in the early 1530s and were devastated by an outbreak of measles in 1536. People of Chiametla killed former Guzmán captain Lope de Samaniego and wounded several other members of the expedition to Tierra Nueva when they attempted to commandeer food there early in 1540. In retaliation for the killing, Vázquez de Coronado had at least eight Chiametlans hung and drawn and quartered.

Sources: Peter Gerhard, *The North Frontier of New Spain*, rev. ed. (Norman: University of Oklahoma Press, 1993), 270–71; Document 28, fol. 23v; Isabel Kelly, *Excavations at Chametla, Sinaloa*, Ibero-Americana 14 (Berkeley: University of California Press, 1938), 4; Richard Flint, *Great Cruelties Have Been Reported: The 1544 Investigation of the Coronado Expedition* (Dallas: Southern Methodist University Press, 2002), 326, 330.

Chichilticale, Chichiltiecally. A landmark and stopover point for travelers between Sonora and the Pueblo region of New Mexico, both prehistorically and at the time of the Coronado expedition, Chichilticale was a ruined *casa*, or house, constructed of red earth. The name also applied to the region of the *casa*. Melchior Díaz and Juan de Zaldívar, with a small reconnaissance party, spent the winter of 1539–40 there or nearby. They had been sent north to verify the reports of fray Marcos de Niza. Later in 1540, the full expedition camped at Chichilticale, and it saw occasional traffic between the expeditionaries among the Pueblos and their shifting supply base in Sonora over the next two years. The *casa* of Chichilticale itself had been abandoned for more than 100 years, and the surrounding region was unsettled.

Researchers have differed widely in locating the site of Chichilticale, placing it at several points in modern southeastern Arizona, southwestern New Mexico, and northern Sonora. In 1940, Herbert Bolton and the archaeologist Emil Haury concluded that several Salado pueblo ruins in the Sulphur Springs Valley of Graham County, Arizona, were prime candidates for Chichilticale. That idea has gained new credence since recent reexamination of one of those ruins by William Duffen, William Hartmann, and Gayle Harrison Hartmann. However, we have posited that its location is either in or near Apache Pass, southeast of Willcox, Arizona.

Sources: Document 28, fols. 103v–104v; William A. Duffen and William K. Hartmann, "The 76 Ranch Ruin and the Location of Chichilticale," in *The Coronado Expedition to Tierra Nueva: The 1540–1542 Route across the Southwest*, edited by Richard Flint and Shirley Cushing Flint (Niwot, CO: University Press of Colorado, 1997), 190–211. See also Document 30, note 59.

Cíbola. The original goal of the expedition to Tierra Nueva, Cíbola had been heard of and possibly seen by fray Marcos de Niza in 1539. Marcos's guide Esteban de Dorantes was killed there. It was stories of the reputed size and wealth of Cíbola that launched the Coronado expedition. And in fact, Cíbola was at the time an important center of trade in turquoise, bison hides, and tropical feathers and shells between the Pueblo world and the northern fringes of Mesoamerica. The name referred to a group of related pueblos and, apparently, also to the principal pueblo of the group.

When Vázquez de Coronado and the advance unit of the expedition arrived there in July 1540, violence quickly flared when the people of Cíbola refused to allow the armed force to enter the principal pueblo, upon the reading of the *requerimiento*. In a short time the expedition overran the pueblo, and its residents abandoned it. The pueblo was renamed Granada by the Spaniards. For the next two years a tense peace existed between the Cíbolans and the expeditionaries. Probably as a result of news the Pueblos received of Spanish slaving habits in the Chiametla and Culiacán areas, women and children were kept largely out of sight while the expedition was in Cíbola. Nor did many men return to the pueblo.

Cíbola has for more than a century been identified as the Zunian-speaking culture area located in modern west-central New Mexico. In 1540–42 it comprised six or seven towns along the Zuni River in modern western McKinley and Cibola Counties. At that time the name was also applied to the most southwesterly town in the area, now usually identified as the ruined pueblo of Hawikku, about 12 miles southwest of modern Zuni Pueblo.

Historical references to Cíbola/Zuni appear again for 1581, when the Rodríguez-Chamuscado expedition took note of only five pueblos in the "valley called Suni," and just two years later the Espejo expedition counted six Zuni pueblos: Mazaque, Quaquema, Aguico, Alona, Quaquina, and Cana. Juan de Oñate in 1598 specifically confirmed the

identity of Cíbola as Zuni. Writing in the 1930s, the archaeologist Frederick W. Hodge agreed that there were only six Cíbolan pueblos. As identified by modern archaeology, though, the Cíbolan pueblos of 1540 may have numbered as many as nine: Hawikku, Kechiba:wa, Kwa'ki'na, Kyaki:ma, Mats'a:kya, Halona:wa north, and possibly Chalo:wa, Binna:wa, and Ah:kya:ya.

Information presented during testimony concerning the conduct of the expedition—that Vázquez de Coronado approached the first pueblo of Cíbola from the west—all but rules out the possibility that the ruined pueblo of Kyaki:ma was the pueblo attacked and overrun by the expedition, as Madeleine Rodack has suggested as a possibility.

Sources: Document 6; Document 28, fols. 30v–32v and 104r–106v; Riley, *Rio del Norte*, 113–14; James H. Simpson, "Coronado's March in Search of the 'Seven Cities of Cibola' and Discussion of their Probable Location," *Annual Report of the Board of Regents of the Smithsonian Institution for 1869* (Washington, D.C.: n.p., 1872), 309–40; Roger Anyon, "The Late Prehistoric and Early Historic Periods in the Zuni-Cíbola Area, 1400–1680," in *Current Research on the Late Prehistory and Early History of New Mexico*, ed. Bradley J. Vierra (Albuquerque: New Mexico Archaeological Council, 1992), 77; Madeleine Turrell Rodack, "Cíbola, from Fray Marcos to Coronado," in Flint and Flint, *Tierra Nueva*, 112–14; AGI, Patronato, 22, R.13\9, "Traslado de los ensayos que se hobieron de las minas de mohoque," fols. 12v–13v; Hernán Gallegos, "Gallegos' Relation of the Chamuscado-Rodríguez Expedition," in *The Rediscovery of New Mexico, 1580–1594: The Explorations of Chamuscado, Espejo, Castaño de Sosa, Morlete, and Leyva de Bonilla and Humaña*, eds. George P. Hammond and Agapito Rey (Albuquerque: University of New Mexico Press, 1966), 108; Diego Pérez de Luxán, "Diego Pérez de Luxán's Account of the Antonio de Espejo Expedition into New Mexico, 1582," in Hammond and Rey, *Rediscovery of New Mexico*, 183; Frederick Webb Hodge, *History of Hawikuh, New Mexico, One of the So-Called Cities of Cíbola* (Los Angeles: Southwest Museum, 1937), 57; Keith W. Kintigh, "Introduction," in *Hemenway Southwestern Archaeological Expedition*, vol. 6, *Selected Correspondence, June 1, 1888, through 1889*, ed. David Wilcox (in preparation). See maps 1, 2, and 3.

Cicuique, Cicuyc, Cicuye, Cicuic, Cicuyque. Accepting the offer of friendship from a trading or diplomatic party from Cicuique in summer 1540, Vázquez de Coronado dispatched Hernando de Alvarado to conduct a reconnaissance of the pueblos east of Cíbola and of the buffalo plains beyond. Alvarado imprisoned and tortured a *principal* of Cicuique in an effort to verify reports of a wealthy population center much farther east, called Quivira. Initially willing to link themselves with the expedition to Tierra Nueva, the people of Cicuique became increasingly hostile, finally openly attacking a group under Tristán de Arellano in the early fall of 1541. When the expedition departed from the Pueblo world, two Franciscan friars remained behind in the hope of converting the native people. One of them was fray Luis de Úbeda, who went to Cicuique and probably was later killed nearby.

Cicuique was a Towa-speaking pueblo situated in the upper Pecos River Valley in what is now extreme western San Miguel County, New Mexico. It had been inhabited since the 1300s. In 1540–42 it was the most populous of the pueblos and one with extensive trade contacts with buffalo-hunting Indians of the Great Plains. Now known as Pecos Pueblo, it has been abandoned since the 1830s.

"Cicúye," the spelling of this name favored by Winship, Hammond and Rey, Bolton, and Mora, is rare in the Coronado expedition documents. When it does appear, it seems to be a scribal miscopying of "Cicuyc," a variant of the much more common "Cicuique." Sources: Document 28, fols. 48r, 54v–55r, 92r–94v, 111v–114v, and 136r–137r; John L. Kessell, *Kiva, Cross, and Crown,* 2nd ed. (Albuquerque: University of New Mexico Press, 1987), 10–12, 459. See also Document 28, note 202. See maps 1 and 3.

Colima. Colima had been a Spanish settlement since the middle 1520s. The *villa* of this name was first established at the native community of Tecoman but was moved farther inland to its present site in 1525. It is located in what is now the Mexican state of Colima on the Pacific coast. In colonial times the *provincia* of Colima was nearly twice as extensive as the modern state is today and included southernmost Jalisco. Source: Peter Gerhard, *A Guide to the Historical Geography of New Spain,* rev. ed. (Norman: University of Oklahoma Press, 1993), 78–82. See map 1.

Compostela. Originally called Espíritu Santo, the settlement that soon came to called Compostela by royal decree was founded in 1531 at the site of modern Tepic in what is now the Mexican state of Nayarit. At that time it had 60 Spanish *vecinos,* most of whom subsequently abandoned it for Peru. In January 1532 Nuño de Guzmán renamed Espíritu Santo, his capital of Nueva Galicia at what is now Tepic, Santiago de Compostela. Shortly after the Coronado expedition's departure from there in February 1540, the *ciudad* of Compostela was moved to its final site, about 24 miles south of Tepic. By 1549 a separate *audiencia* for Nueva Galicia was established at Compostela, and in 1560 it was moved to Guadalajara.

Source: Gerhard, *North Frontier,* 39–55, 138–43. See also Donald D. Brand, "Erroneous Location of Two Sixteenth-Century Spanish Settlements in Western Nueva España," in *Across the Chichimec Sea: Papers in Honor of J. Charles Kelley,* eds. Carroll L. Riley and Basil C. Hedrick (Carbondale: Southern Illinois University Press, 1978), 200–01. See map 1.

Coofor, Coafor. Also known as the pueblo of Tiguex, Coofor was, in 1540, one of the largest, if not the largest, of the dozen or so Tiguex pueblos. The various names used by the Spaniards for this pueblo probably derived from the Tiwa name, *ghufoor,* meaning "parched corn." It was in the pueblo of Coofor that the expedition to Tierra Nueva took up quarters after its *maestre de campo* "asked" that its native residents vacate it.

There has been considerable disagreement among historians and archaeologists about which of the several ruins of Southern Tiwa pueblos represents Coofor. What can be said with assurance is that it was on the west side of the Río de Tiguex, or modern Rio Grande, in what is now northern Bernalillo County or southern Sandoval County, New Mexico.

The discovery and archaeological investigation in 1987 of part of a campsite likely associated with the expedition to Tierra Nueva focused attention on nearby Santiago Pueblo as the most likely candidate. The information on distances between the various Tiguex pueblos provided during Lorenzo Tejada's 1544 investigation supports that possibility. Melchior Pérez stated then that Coofor was next to the river, and Vázquez de Coronado indicated that other pueblos were one-half, one, two, and three leagues from Coofor. Juan Troyano said that Coofor was one or two leagues from the pueblo besieged by López de Cárdenas, Pueblo del Arenal. Castañeda stated, more precisely, that Arenal and Coofor were one league apart. Furthermore, Pedro de Ledesma declared that Pueblo de

la Alameda was "between" Coofor and Pueblo del Arenal, meaning intermediate in distance between the two. Together these statements imply that a cluster of at least three pueblos, including Coofor, lay in close proximity, two of them only half a league apart and the third no more than a league from one of the others, which was on the west bank of the Rio Grande. In addition, that cluster must comprise the pueblos called Coofor, Alameda, and Arenal by the expedition members, with Coofor somewhat closer to Alameda than to Arenal (since Vázquez de Coronado and López de Cárdenas were to meet at Alameda, which was "between" the other two).

Among the known pueblo ruins with mid-sixteenth-century occupations in the Southern Tiwa area, there is only one such tight cluster, the ruins known as Santiago, Kuaua, and Watche, near and within Bernalillo, New Mexico. On this reasoning, Santiago would be Coofor, Watche would be Alameda, and Kuaua would be Arenal.

Albert Schroeder's 1992 identification of Santiago as the site of Pueblo del Cerco, or Moho, must be incorrect, given the 1545 statement of Lorenzo Álvarez that Pueblo del Cerco was on a height, which Santiago decidedly is not; being in the floodplain, much of it has been lost to the Rio Grande. Further, although Schroeder referred to the clustering of Coofor, Alameda, and Arenal, the archaeological sites he identified them with are not clustered in that way at all.

In 1999 a collector and metal detector from Valencia County came forward with a group of 21 copper crossbow boltheads and a dozen pieces of fired lead shot he had recovered from the immediate vicinity of the ruins of Santiago Pueblo. Both the shot and several of the boltheads give evidence of having made impact, probably with the adobe of the pueblo. This suggests that fighting occurred between the Coronado expedition and residents of Santiago. In turn, this raises the possibility that Santiago may be the Pueblo del Arenal of the Coronado expedition documents. If so, then Kuaua would be Coofor. On the other hand, fighting at Santiago, if it is Coofor, would be consistent with evidence from Castañeda de Nájera's *relación* that the residents of Coofor were compelled to abandon it to the expedition, rather than surrendering it peacefully, as is often maintained.

Sources: Document 28, fols. 52r–54v, 58r–71r, 107r–111v, and 115r; Bradley J. Vierra, *A Sixteenth-Century Spanish Campsite in the Tiguex Province,* Laboratory of Anthropology Notes 475 (Santa Fe: Museum of New Mexico, Research Section, 1989); Bradley J. Vierra and Stanley M. Hordes, "Let the Dust Settle: A Review of the Coronado Campsite in the Tiguex Province," in Flint and Flint, *Tierra Nueva,* 249–61; Archeological Records Management System (ARMS), "Site files for LA 187, Kuaua Pueblo; LA 288, Corrales Pueblo; LA 289, Calabacillas Pueblo; LA 290, Piedras Marcadas Pueblo; LA 294, Sandia Pueblo; LA 326, Santiago Pueblo; LA 421, Alameda Pueblo; LA 677, Watche Pueblo; LA 716; LA 717, Maigua Pueblo; and LA 22765, Chamisal Pueblo," unpublished files, Laboratory of Anthropology, Museum of New Mexico, Santa Fe; Albert H. Schroeder, "Vásquez de Coronado and the Southern Tiwa Pueblos," in *Archaeology, Art, and Anthropology: Collected Papers in Honor of J. J. Brody,* eds. Meliha S. Duran and David T. Kirkpatrick, Papers of the Archaeological Society of New Mexico, no. 18 (Albuquerque: Archaeological Society of New Mexico, 1992), 185–91. See map 5.

Corazones, Los Corazones, de los Corazones. Like a number of other places referred to by members of the Coronado expedition, both a *pueblo* and a region were called by the name Corazones. In 1536, the four survivors of the expedition of Pánfilo de Narváez were feasted on dear hearts at this *pueblo* and thus applied the name Corazones to it. Under the leadership of Tristán de Arellano, the main body of the expedition to Tierra Nueva established a Spanish *villa* there early in 1540, adopting the name Corazones from their predecessors. The *villa* was later moved to another stretch of the same valley, called Señora by the Spaniards. The key documentary evidence on this point is Juan Jaramillo's statement, "We went from here [Corazones] going through a sort of small pass and, very near this stream, to another valley formed by the same stream, which is called [Arroyo] de Señora." Afterward, the *villa* was moved yet again to the Suya Valley, some 40 leagues closer to Cíbola.

The results of archaeological survey of the Río Sonora Valley support the proposition that Corazones was downstream from the Ures Gorge along the Río Sonora in what is now central Sonora. This would place Corazones in what has come to be known as the Pimería Bajo, or Lower Pima culture area. At the time of the expedition to Tierra Nueva the ancestral Lower Pimas maintained a sophisticated culture much influenced by their proximity to the northern reaches of Mesoamerica. Their population, though heavily agricultural, was clustered in substantial towns that also participated in long-distance trade. Exposure to European diseases decimated the Lower Pimas and radically altered their lifeway after the 1540s.

Sources: Document 28, fols. 32v–33r and 101r–101v; Document 30, fol. 1v; Álvar Núñez Cabeza de Vaca, *Naufragios y comentarios con dos cartas,* 9th ed. (México, DF: Espasa-Calpe Mexicana, 1985), 94; Richard A. Pailes, "An Archaeological Perspective on the Sonoran Entrada," in Flint and Flint, *Tierra Nueva,* 186; Carroll L. Riley, *The Frontier People: The Greater Southwest in the Protohistoric Period,* rev. ed. (Albuquerque: University of New Mexico Press, 1987), 68–76; Timothy Dunnigan, "Lower Pima," in Ortiz, *Southwest,* vol. 10, 218; Daniel T. Reff, *Disease, Depopulation, and Culture Change in Northwestern New Spain, 1518–1764* (Salt Lake City: University of Utah Press, 1991), 57, 59–60, 245. See map 2.

Culiacán, San Miguel de Culiacán.

In 1540, San Miguel de Culiacán was the northernmost Spanish settlement in Nueva Galicia. The site visited by the Coronado expedition was the town's second location, on the Río San Lorenzo, roughly 10 miles upstream from its mouth, in the west-central part of what is now the Mexican state of Sinaloa. Founded in 1532 by Nuño de Guzmán, San Miguel's population in 1540 was composed overwhelmingly of Indians transplanted from central Mexico, a number of whom joined the expedition to Tierra Nueva. The indigenous Taracahitan-speaking population of the region (called the *provincia* of Culiacán by the Spaniards) had been ravaged by slave hunters and disease. The Spanish citizenry of Culiacán was well represented in the expedition, including such captains as Diego de Alcaraz, Melchior Díaz, Diego López, and Pedro de Tovar. Following the conclusion of the expedition, a number of former expeditionaries settled at Culiacán, including Pedro de Castañeda de Nájera. Sources: Document 28, fols. 97v–100r and 148v; Gerhand, *North Frontier,* 39–55, 256–62. See map 1.

Guadalajara.

Guadalajara was established as a *villa* in 1535 in the colonial jurisdiction of Cuquío, now in north-central Jalisco. A royal *cédula* dated November 8, 1539, granted it the status of *ciudad.* In 1542 the site was moved about five leagues southwest to its present location. Guadalajara quickly became a rival of Compostela for the status of political and demographic hub of Nueva Galicia. The *audiencia* for the *provincia,* established at Compostela in 1549, was moved to Guadalajara only 11 years later. Source: Gerhand, *North Frontier,* 78–80, 90–92. See map 1.

Mar del Norte, Mar del Sur, Costa del Sur.

The names Mar del Norte and Mar del Sur applied to what are now known as the Atlantic and Pacific Oceans, respectively. The terminology originated on the east-west-oriented Isthmus of Panama, where indeed the Atlantic is to the north and the Pacific is to the south. The Gulf of California was included in the Mar del Sur designation. The Costa del Sur referred simply to the Pacific coast of the Americas.

Mar Océano, or Ocean Sea.

In medieval European cosmography and cartography, the Mar Océano was envisaged as the great sea that made up one-half of Earth's globe and encircled the inhabited land masses of Europe, Africa, and Asia.

Marata, Marate, Maratta, Matata.

It is our contention that the three polities that fray Marcos understood were called Marata, Totonteac, and Acus lay at a latitude considerably south of Cíbola. Marcos had obtained the locational directions he originally reported from an informant he found many leagues to the south of Cíbola, probably in what is now southern Arizona. We are convinced that the directions given by that informant orient those locations in relation to the place where he and Marcos were talking, and not to Cíbola. Thus, it is not surprising that neither the places themselves nor the names by which they were called (in Pima or some other language, not Zunian) were not readily identifiable by the people of Cíbola.

Given the apparent size, importance, and prosperity of these three southern polities, we are convinced that Marcos was hearing stories that related not to then-flourishing communities but to ones whose grandness lived only in memory. The reports were, on this assumption, of great florescences that had faded in the region 150 to 300 years before Marcos had the 1539 conversation with his informant—that is, Paquimé, the Hohokam area, and an unknown polity associated with the name Acus. In this hypothesis, Marata, to the southeast of Marcos, was Paquimé, and Totonteac, to the west, was the Hohokam communities of the Salt River valley.

The general notion that Marcos was receiving long out-of-date information meshes well with the Coronado expedition's subsequent experience concerning Chichilticale and Quivira. When it reached Chichilticale, much to its chagrin, the expedition found the famous place a ruin, quite possibly empty for 150 years. Likewise, some of the stories the expeditionaries heard about Quivira would fit well with Cahokia and the northern Mississippian mound-building cultures, which had also faded out about 150 years earlier.

Carroll Riley, too, has suggested that Totonteac, Acus, and Marata, located in the area of the modern U.S.-Mexico border near where the present states of New Mexico and Arizona abut, may have been largely or even completely deserted by Marcos's time and that he was being told stories about an earlier time. Riley also discusses the many other conjectural placements of these *reinos.*

Efforts to unravel the mystery of Marata are further complicated by the possibility that Marcos's wishful thinking led him to conflate or misinterpret the name he was told by native informants. "Marata" appears in the second-century geography of Claudius Ptolemy as the name of a town or village in Arabia Felix (the modern Arabian Peninsula) near the Persian Gulf.

Sources: Carroll L. Riley, "Marata and Its Neighbors," in *The Gran Chichimeca: Essays on the Archaeology and Ethnohistory of Northern Mesoamerica*, ed. Jonathan E. Reyman (Aldershot, UK: Avebury, 1995), 220; Claudius Ptolemy, *The Geography*, trans. and ed. Edward Luther Stevenson (New York: Dover, 1991), 139. See map 1.

Nueva Galicia, Nuevo Reino de Galicia. Nueva Galicia comprised what is now the Mexican states of Aguascalientes, Zacatecas, and Nayarit, much of Jalisco, and the northwest corner of San Luis Potosí. This vaguely defined *provincia* of Nueva España was subdued by Nuño de Guzmán in 1529–30. Guzmán's tenure as governor was followed by those of Diego Pérez de la Torre and Francisco Vázquez de Coronado. When Vázquez de Coronado was removed as governor in 1544, Viceroy Mendoza took direct control and governed the *provincia* as an *alcaldía mayor* (jurisdiction under a royal administrator) for four years. In January 1549 a separate *audiencia* was established at Compostela; it was moved to Guadalajara in 1560. The population in 1550 was slightly fewer than 224,000 persons. At European contact, at least 25 languages were spoken in Nueva Galicia, but by the late sixteenth century Nahuatl had become the lingua franca. Source: Gerhard, *North Frontier*, 39–55.

Petatlán, Petlatlán; Río de Petatlán. These place names derive from the Nahuatl word *petlatl*, meaning *estera*, or mat. *Petates* walled most of the indigenous houses of the region.

On his way north in March 1539, fray Marcos de Niza stopped for three days at the Indian community of Petatlán. He was received there cordially and from there on was joined by a large group of Petatleños. Similarly, the expedition to Tierra Nueva experienced no conflict at Petatlán, where it, too, stopped for a rest of several days on its return south in 1542. Petatlán was the home of Bartolomé, the young companion of Esteban de Dorantes, who later served as interpreter for the expedition because he knew Nahuatl and perhaps Ópata.

Castañeda's description of the *provincia* of Petatlán indicates a series of *ranchería* settlements on the coastal plain along a river either 20 or 30 leagues from Culiacán. Herbert Bolton put Petatlán in today's state of Sinaloa along the Río Sinaloa, of which the modern Río Petatlán is a tributary. This would conform with Castañeda de Nájera's longer estimate of 30 leagues from Culiacán to Petatlán. Charles Di Peso, on the other hand, placed Petatlán on the Río Evora de Mocorito, some 30 miles (about 12 leagues) south of the Río Sinaloa, which seems to be a better fit with Castañeda de Nájera's lower figure of 20 leagues from Culiacán.

Sources: Document 6, fols. 2r–2v; Document 28, fols. 100v–103r and 144v; Bolton, 26; Charles C. DiPeso, John B. Rinaldo, and Gloria J. Fenner, *Casas Grandes: A Fallen Trading Center of the Gran Chichimeca*, vol. 4, *Architecture and Dating Methods* (Dragoon, AZ: Amerind Foundation, 1974), 93; Alonso de Molina, *Vocabulario en lengua mexicana y castellana* (México, DF: Antonio de Spinosa, 1571; reprint, Madrid: Ediciones de Cultura Hispánica, 2001), fol. 81r. See also "map VII" in Baltasar de Obregón, *Historia de los descubrimientos antiguos y modernos de la Nueva España, escrita por el conquistador en el año de 1584*, ed. Mariano Cuevas (México, DF: Editorial Porrúa, 1988), facing page 164. See map 1.

Puebla de los Ángeles. Often called simply Puebla, this second *ciudad* in Nueva España still exists in its original location east of the Ciudad de México. As Peter Gerhard writes, it was "organized to accommodate Spaniards who had arrived in Mexico after the Conquest, too late to participate in the distribution of encomiendas." By 1534 it had 81 *vecinos*. Intertribal warfare had decimated the area before Spanish conquest. By 1570, though, there were some 1,000 Indian tribute payers in the *ciudad* and its environs. Source: Gerhard, *Historical Geography*, 220–23.

Quivira, Quisvira; Río de Quivira. The place known as Quivira was in 1540–42 a *provincia*, or culture area, along the middle Arkansas River (Río de Quivira) in what is now central Kansas, especially in Rice and McPherson Counties. It was described in 1541 as a well-settled area of six or seven towns, each of up to 200 circular straw houses. It was the "most remote land seen" by the expeditionaries to Tierra Nueva. The people there, Caddoan-speaking ancestors of the Wichita, dry-farmed a number of crops, most significantly corn, and lived in permanent, grass-thatched houses (a characteristic of protohistoric Caddoes of the central Great Plains). Archaeological remains of these people are known as the Little River focus of the Great Bend phase. The Coronado expedition's guide Ysopete was probably a native of Quivira. El Turco may have been also, despite the "Relación del Suceso's" explicit statement that he was from Arahe.

Some of the people of Quivira were said to have conspired with El Turco to kill Vázquez de Coronado and his select party, who arrived there in the summer of 1541. Nevertheless, the various Spanish accounts give little indication and no specifics about hostility between the Quivirans and members of the expedition. When the expedition returned to Nueva España, fray Juan de Padilla, together with a Portuguese, a Black, a mestizo, and two Indian lay assistants, journeyed back to Quivira to preach the Catholic faith. Fray Juan was soon killed, but the others escaped and returned eventually to central Mexico.

Sources: Waldo R. Wedel, "Coronado, Quivira, and Kansas: An Archeologist's View," lecture delivered Nov. 3, 1990, Coronado-Quivira Museum, Lyons, Kansas; Waldo R. Wedel, *Archeological Remains in Central Kansas and Their Possible Bearing on the Location of Quivira*, Smithsonian Miscellaneous Collections 101, no. 7 (Washington, DC: Smithsonian Institution, 1942); Document 28, fols. 122r–125r, 135v–136r, and 153v; Document 29, fol. 4v; William W. Newcomb, Jr., "Wichita," in *Handbook of North American Indians*, vol. 13, part 1, *Plains*, ed. Raymond J. DeMallie (Washington, DC: Smithsonian Institution Press, 2001), 548–66. See maps 1 and 4.

San Gerónimo, San Gerónimo de los Corazones. In the late spring of 1540, Vázquez de Coronado founded a Spanish community called San Gerónimo adjacent to or within the native settlement known as Corazones. With a detachment from the expedition left there, San Gerónimo was to serve as an intermediate supply base and communication link for the expedition. Within a matter of weeks, Tristán de Arellano, who was left temporarily in charge at San Gerónimo, found it necessary to move the *villa* because of lack of food supplies. He moved it upstream, or north, to the native community known to the Spaniards as Señora. Pedro de Tovar assumed charge of this second San Gerónimo when Arellano left to lead the main body of the expedition to Cíbola. Díaz, assigned to make a reconnaissance to the Mar del Sur, appointed Diego de Alcaraz to take command at San Gerónimo in his stead. Because of friction with the local people, Alcaraz subsequently moved the *villa* a second time, again northward, to the native *pueblo* of Suya. The people of Suya, promptly angered by activities of some of the Spaniards, rose up and destroyed the Spanish *villa*, severing the expedition's link with Nueva España. Sources: Document 28, fols. 33r and 102r. See Map 2.

Señora, Sonora, Senora, Arroyo de Señora. In the 1540s, a settlement, an area, a river, and a valley all went by an indigenous name recorded as Senora by members of the expedition to Tierra Nueva. The name was transmuted by the Spaniards into Señora and has become Sonora in more recent times. In the mid-sixteenth century the area of Señora was densely populated by Ópata peoples along the middle portion of today's Río Sonora. Andrés Pérez de Ribas, writing a hundred years after the Coronado expedition, positively identified this region as Señora. It was very prosperous agriculturally. The ruins of the town of Señora, likely the largest of the region, may now lie beneath Baviácora or Aconchi along the Río Sonora in modern central Sonora. As at Suya, the indigenous people of Señora and most of the other Ópatas rose up in early 1542 and expelled the members of the expedition who had been left there. Retaliation was soon to come when Juan Gallego made lightning strikes the whole length of Ópata country on his way north to join the expedition.

Sources: Andrés Pérez de Ribas, *History of the Triumphs of Our Holy Faith amongst the Most Barbarous and Fierce Peoples of the New World*, eds. and trans. Daniel T. Reff, Maureen Ahern, and Richard K. Danford (Tucson: University of Arizona Press, 1999), 419; Pailes, "Archaeological Perspective," 187. See maps 1 and 2.

Tierra Nueva. This was the name given to the undefined territory in the interior of North America comprising the communities of Cíbola, Tusayán, Marata, Totonteac, Tiguex, and others.

Tiguex, Triguex, Tigues, Tihuex, Coofor; Río de Tiguex, Río de Nuestra Señora. Tiguex was a *provincia*, or culture area, in 1540 comprising 12 or 13 Tiwa-speaking pueblos in the middle Rio Grande Valley in what is now central New Mexico. Tiguex pueblos of the sixteenth century were located on both sides of the Rio Grande (Río de Tiguex, Río de Nuestra Señora) from south of modern Isleta Pueblo (northern Valencia County) north to the confluence of the Rio Grande and the Jemez River and perhaps slightly farther north (in southeastern Sandoval County).

The Tiguex/Tiwas, the first of the Puebloan peoples to live along the Río Grande, had been in the middle Rio Grande Valley for more than 500 years when the expedition to Tierra Nueva arrived. It is no accident that their middle Rio Grande homeland has proved enduringly attractive to humans. A relative abundance of water and a mild climate—the area is largely sheltered from the frigid cold that can grip New Mexico's eastern plains and lies just on the northern margin of the land of blistering summers—made it probably the prime sedentary homeland of sixteenth-century New Mexico. There is abundant archaeological evidence that other agricultural peoples had been nibbling at the edges of Tiguex territory and actually intruding for hundreds of years.

In 1540 the Tiguex area was the most populous of those settled by town-dwelling agricultural peoples along and adjacent to the Rio Grande. Immediately to the west and north were the Keres Pueblos, to the east the Tano Pueblos, and to the south the Piro Pueblos. Farther north were the Tewas and more Tiwas; beyond the Keres to the west, the Jemez; to the east beyond the Tanos, the people of Cicique/Pecos Pueblo; and to the east and southeast, the Tompiros and the enigmatic and perhaps illusory Ubates. Though often unified under the name "Puebloans," these peoples spoke distinct languages, essentially mutually unintelligible. Yet despite their language differences, the Puebloan groups of the sixteenth century shared broad cultural similarities, including government by councils of elders and complex religious practices involving solicitation of activity on the part of deified ancestors in bringing beneficial weather and otherwise supporting the living. These similarities were noticed and commented on by members of the expedition to Tierra Nueva such as Pedro de Castañeda de Nájera. There was clearly much contact and interchange between the various Puebloan groups. See also the entry dealing with Coofor.

Albert Schroeder identified the remains of these pueblos as stretching from LA 50232 (south of the Jemez River) on the north to LA 290 (Piedras Marcadas, just north of modern Interstate 40) on the south. More recently, Elinore Barrett proposed that Tiguex did not extend that far north. The 12 pueblos she recognized as comprising Tiguex stretch along the Rio Grande from LA 187 (Kuaua at Coronado State Monument) on the north to LA 290 (Piedras Marcadas) on the south. The Schroeder and Barrett lists share 10 sites.

Sources: Schroeder, "Pueblos Abandoned," 238, 240; Elinore M. Barrett, *The Geography of the Rio Grande Pueblos Revealed by Spanish Explorers*, Research Paper Series no. 30 (Albuquerque: Latin American Institute, University of New Mexico, 1997), 7–11; Riley, *Rio del Norte*, 99–102, 170; Marc Simmons, "History of Pueblo-Spanish Relations to 1821," in Ortiz, *Southwest*, vol. 9, 178–79; Edward P. Dozier, *The Pueblo Indians of North America* (New York: Holt, Rinehart, and Winston, 1970; reprint, Prospect Heights, IL: Waveland Press, 1983), 43–44, 200; Document 28, fols. 52r–54v, 58r–71r, 107r–111v, and 115r; Albert H. Schroeder, "Vásquez de Coronado," in Duran and Kirkpatrick, *Archaeology, Art, and Anthropology*, 186; Elinore M. Barrett, *Conquest and Catastrophe: Changing Rio Grande Pueblo Settlement Patterns in the Sixteenth and Seventeenth Centuries* (Albuquerque: University of New Mexico Press, 2002), 25. See maps 1, 3, and 5.

Topira. Stories of the seven *ciudades* of Cíbola were not the only stimulus for expeditions in search of precious metals northwest of the Ciudad de México in the late 1530s. Much nearer to the seat of Vázquez de Coronado's administration in Nueva Galicia was Topira, or Topia, where the natives were rumored to wear ornaments of gold and precious jewels. An attempt by Vázquez de Coronado to lead an expedition there in 1539 was abandoned. By the 1590s silver veins had been discovered in the region, and as a result Topira came fully under Spanish control. Topira comprised an area in the extreme west of the modern state of Durango along tributary valleys of the Río Culiacán. Source: Gerhard, *North Frontier*, 238–39. See map 1.

Totonteac, Totinteac. The name Totonteac was, we suggest, applied to the Hohokam communities of the Salt River Valley, which at the time of the expedition would have been in ruins, though their reputation remained a matter of vivid lore. In recent years, some researchers have concluded that Totonteac was a name applied to the Hopi pueblos of modern Arizona, but that does not agree with the statements of members of the expedition. It is quite likely that two similar names were conflated in what fray Marcos heard and reported. Sources: Document 6, fols. 4r, 4v, and 5r; Document 17, fol. 2v; Document 19, fol. 362r; Bolton, 36; John C. Connelly, "Hopi Social Organization," in Ortiz, *Southwest*, vol. 9, 551; Hodge, *History of Hawikuh*, 64. See also the entry for Marata. See map 2.

Tusayán, Tuzan. Tusayán and its variants are names used by members of the expedition to Tierra Nueva for the Hopi pueblos of modern north-central Arizona. The names either dropped out of use after the 1540s or had been misunderstood in the first place. At any rate, the names were not used again until the late 1800s when Tusayán, in particular, was resurrected by anthropologists who had become familiar with some of the sixteenth-century Spanish documents.

Albert Schroeder lists the following pueblos in the *provincia* of Tusayán in 1540: Awatovi, Walpi, Mishongnovi, Shongopavi, Oraibi, and "two [unidentified] Jeddito Valley pueblos that might have been abandoned prior to the 1580s." Henry Dobyns, however, has argued that at least 30 Hopi/Tusayán pueblos might have been occupied in the 1540s, including 6 or more in the Little Colorado River drainage. He claims that evidence from the Coronado expedition documents indicates that it was these riverine Tusayán pueblos, closer to (but southwest of) Zuni, that Pedro de Tovar and García López de Cárdenas visited.

Sources: Connelly, "Hopi Social Organization," 551; John O. Brew, "Hopi Prehistory and History to 1850," in Ortiz, *Southwest*, vol. 9, 519; Schroeder, "Pueblos Abandoned," 253–54; Henry F. Dobyns, "Sixteenth-Century Tusayán," *American Indian Quarterly* 15, no. 2 (1991):187–200. See map 1.

Appendix 3

Known Members of the Coronado Expedition

In the following table, places of origin are given in terms of town and province (town: province). Italics indicate a possibility. Duplicate entries indicate more than one person (usually unrelated) of the same name.

Under the heading "Source or Sources," numbered documents are those published in this volume. Abbreviations used for additional sources are listed at the end of the appendix.

Name	Place of Origin	Age in 1540	Occupation	Residence Afterward	Source or Sources
Europeans					
Alarcón, Hernando de	Granada: Granada or Trujillo: Cáceres	—	—	—	Doc. 28; *Pasajeros,* 2: no. 1261
Alba, Hernando de	Salamanca: Salamanca	—	—	Puebla	Doc.12; MX 1064
Alcántara, Francisco de	—	—	—	—	Doc. 12
Alcántara, Pedro de	—	—	—	—	Doc. 12
Alcaraz, Diego de	—	—	—	Died 1541/42	Doc. 28
Alonso, Domingo	—	25	—	Purificación	Doc. 12; Just 339, N1, R1
Alonso de Astorga, Martín	*Astorga:* León	—	—		Doc. 12
Alvarado, Hernando de	Las Montañas: Torrelavega: Santander	23	—	Ciudad de México	Doc. 12; Just 1021, N2, Pieza 6
Álvarez, Antonio	—	—	—	—	Doc. 12
Álvarez, Gaspar	Portugal	—	—	—	Doc. 12
Álvarez, Lorenzo	—	25	—	Mines of Nuestra Señora de Buena Esperanza	Doc. 12; Patro 216, N2
Álvarez, Pedro	*Castilla La Vieja*	—	—	*Culiacán*	Doc. 12; Guad 46, N8
Álvarez, Rodrigo	Zafra or *Barcarrota:* Badajoz	—	—	Guadalajara	Doc. 12; Just 339, N1, R1
Álvarez, Roque	—	—	—	—	Doc. 12
Álvarez [del Valle], Alonso*	*Villanueva de Barcarrota:* Badajoz	15	—	Guadalajara and Chiametla	Doc. 12; Patro 74, N2, R2; *Pasajeros,* 2: no. 3193
Aranda, Alonso de	—	—	—	—	Doc. 12
Arjona, Gonzalo de	*Jerez de los Caballeros:* Badajoz	—	—	—	Doc. 12; *Pasajeros,* 2: no. 3477
Ávila, Pedro de	—	—	—	—	Doc. 28
Azebedo, Baltasar	—	—	—	—	Doc. 12
Báez, Jorge	—	—	Escribano	Died 1542	Doc. 12; Doc. 27
Barahona, Hernando de	*Fuente del Maestre:* Badajoz	—	—	—	Doc. 12; *Pasajeros,* 3: no. 235
Barbero, Juan	—	—	—	—	Doc. 12

Name	Place of Origin	Age in 1540	Occupation	Residence Afterward	Source or Sources
Barragán, Juan	Llerena: Badajoz	—	—	*Colima*	Doc. 27; Mathes
Barrionuevo, Rodrigo de	Granada: Granada	19	—	*Izatlán*	Doc. 12; Just 263, Pieza 1; MX 204, N33\2; Mathes
Barrionuevo, Velasco de	Granada: Granada	—	—	—	Doc. 12; Doc. 28
Benavente, Pedro de	—	—	—	—	Doc. 12
Benavides, Juan de	*Torrijos:* Toledo	—	—	Oaxaca	Doc. 12; *Pasajeros,* 2: no. 804; *Pasajeros,* 3: no. 3440; Contra 490, N1, R2
Benavides, Pedro de	Benavente: Zamora	—	—	Oaxaca	Doc. 12; MX 204, N33\2; Contra 490, N1, R2
Benítez, *Martín de Alfarache*	*San Juan de Aznalfarache:* Sevilla	—	—	Died 1540	Tello 2:424; Calvo, 107 n. 28
Bermejo, Juan	Torrelaguna: Madrid	20	—	Compostela	Doc. 12; Just 339, N1, R1
Bermúdez, Florián	—	23	—	Compostela	Doc. 12; Just 336, N1
Bernal de Molina, Pascual	—	—	—	—	Doc. 12
Berrugo, Andrés	—	—	—	—	Doc. 12
Bertao, Cristóbal	La Debornuel: Rouen: France	—	—	Ciudad de México	MX 1064
Beteta, Juan de	Torralba/Beteta: Cuenca	25	—	Tasco mines	Doc. 12; Just 1021, N2, Pieza 5; Just 262, N1
Blaque, Tomás	Scotland	<23	Hosier	Ciudad de México	MX 1064; Just 268, N2, Pieza 2
Bonilla, Juan Carlos de	*Guadalupe:* Cáceres	25+	—	Ciudad de México, *Zipotecas*	Patro 78A, N1, R6; MX 1064
Boo, Pero	—	—	—	—	Doc. 12
Botello, Hernando	Alcántara: Cáceres	23	Alcalde mayor of Ameca	Colima	Doc. 12; MX 1064; Patro 60, N5, R4; Patro 56, N3, R2
Brujas, Jaco*	*Bruges:* Flanders	—	—	—	Doc. 12
Bustamante, Juan de	—	—	—	—	Doc. 12
Caballero, Cristóbal	—	—	—	—	Doc. 12
Caballero, Lope	Lugo: Lugo	—	—	Puebla	MX 1064
Cadena, Hernando de la	Medillín: Badajoz	26	—	Ciudad de México	MX 1064; Just 1021, N2, Pieza 6
Cadena, Lope de la	—	—	—	—	Doc. 12
Cadena, Lope de la	—	—	—	Ciudad de México	Doc. 12
Calderón, Francisco	—	—	—	—	Doc. 12
Campo, Andrés de	Portugal	—	—	—	Doc. 12; Doc. 28
Campo, Bartolomé del	—	—	*Barber*	*Died 1541*	Doc. 12; Doc. 28; Doc. 31
Candía, Diego de	*Candia:* Crete	—	—	—	Doc. 12
Canseco, Alonso de	—	23	—	Ciudad de México	Doc. 12; MX 204, N33\2
Caravajal, Francisco de	*Cáceres:* Cáceres	—	—	*Died 1540–41*	Doc. 12; MX 1064; Tello 2:424
Castañeda, Machín de	—	—	—	*Died 1540–41*	Doc. 12; Tello 2:253
Castilblanco, fray Antonio	*Castilblanco:* Badajoz	—	Priest	—	Doc. 28
Castilla, Gonzalo de	—	—	—	—	Doc. 12
Castillo, Diego del	*Medillín:* Badajoz	—	—	—	Doc. 12; *Pasajeros,* 2: no. 2297
Castillo, García del	Sevilla: Sevilla	19	—	Guadalajara	Doc. 12; Just 1021, N2, pieza 5
Castro, Francisco de	—	—	—	—	Doc. 12
Castro, Miguel de	—	—	—	—	Doc. 12
Castro, Pedro de	—	16	—	Compostela	Just 336, N1
Castroverde, Hernando de*	*Medina de Ríoseco:* Valladolid	—	—	—	Doc. 12; *Pasajeros,* 2: no. 2566
Celada, Juan de	—	—	—	—	Doc. 12
Cepeda, Juan de*	Toledo: Toledo	—	—	Ciudad de México	Doc. 12; MX 1064

Name	Place of Origin	Age in 1540	Occupation	Residence Afterward	Source or Sources
Cerbatos, Diego de	—	—	—	—	Doc. 12
[Cés]pedes, Bartolomé de*	—	—	—	—	Doc. 12
Céspedes, Juan de	—	—	—	San Juan de Ulloa	Doc. 12; Patro 68, N2, R4
Chica, Luis de la	—	—	—	—	Doc. 12
Contreras, Juan de	*Lepe:* Huelva	20	Interpreter	Ciudad de México	Doc. 12; Just 267, N3; *Pasajeros,* 2: no. 5617
Cordero, Juan	—	25–30	Tailor	Ciudad de México	Doc. 12; MX 206, N12; Doc. 27
Cornejo, Francisco de	Salamanca: Salamanca	26	Alcalde	Guadalajara	MX 1064; Just 339, N1, R1; Doc. 32
Cortés, Pedro	Tendilla: Guadalajara	24	—	Michoacán	Just 263, Pieza 3
Covarrubias, Andrés de	—	—	—	—	Doc. 12
Cuevas, Juan de*	Aranda de Duero: Valladolid	—	—	—	Doc. 12; MX 1064
Daniel, fray	Italy	—	Priest	Guadalajara	Tello 3:30–31
Dávalos, Diego	—	—	—	—	Just 263, Pieza 1
Delgado, Antón	—	—	—	—	Doc. 12
Díaz, Diego	Isla de Santo Domingo	—	—	—	Doc. 12
Díaz, Francisco	—	14	—	Ciudad de México	MX 206, N35
Díaz, Melchior	—	—	—	Died 1541	Doc. 28
Écija, Pedro de	—	—	—	Ciudad de México	Doc. 12; MX 206, N12
Entrambasaguas, Miguel de	Burgos: Burgos	23	—	Quito	Doc. 12; Patro 121, R8; Patro 127, N1, R10
Escobar, Cristóbal de	Aracena: Huelva	19+	Corregidor	Ciudad de México	Doc. 12; Just 1021, N2, Pieza 6; MX 206, N35
Escobar, Rodrigo	—	—	—	—	Doc. 12
Escobedo, Luis	*Medinaceli:* Soria	—	—	—	Doc. 12; *Pasajeros,* 2: no. 3797
Espinosa, Francisco de	—	—	—	Died 1540	Doc. 12; Doc. 30
Esteban de Mérida, Alonso	*Mérida:* Badajoz	—	—	—	Doc. 12
Estepa, Martín de	—	—	—	*Colima*	Doc. 12; Mathes
Estrada, Gerónimo de	—	—	—	—	Doc. 12
Fernández, Domingo	—	—	—	Died 1541/42	Tello 2:438
Figueredo, Luis de	—	25	—	Culiacán	Patro 216, N2
Fioz, Juan	Worms: Germany	20–22	Trumpeter, escribano	Ciudad de México	Doc. 12; Just 1021, N2, Pieza 5; Patro 78A, N1, R6
Francés, Juan	*Béjar del Castañar: Salamanca*	—	—	*Tasco*	Doc. 12; MX 1064
Franco de Mentre, Juan	—	—	—	—	Doc. 12
Frías, Rodrigo de	Talavera: Toledo	23	—	Ciudad de México	Doc. 12; Just 1021, N2, Pieza 6
Fuenterrabia, Miguel de	—	—	—	*Ciudad de México*	Doc. 12; Patro 61, N2, R7
Galeras, Juan*	Almendralejo: Badajoz	23	—	Compostela and Ciudad de México	Doc. 12; Just 336, N1
Galiveer, ?*	*England*	—	—	—	Doc. 12
Gallego, Cristóbal	—	—	—	—	Doc. 12
Gallego, Diego	—	—	—	—	Doc. 27
Gallego, Juan	—	—	—	—	Doc. 12
Gallego, Lope	*Madrid*	—	—	—	Doc. 12; *Pasajeros,* 4: no. 2266
Gámez, Rodrigo de	—	—	—	Culiacán	Doc. 12; Mathes
García, Antón	*Sevilla:* Sevilla	—	—	—	Doc. 12; *Pasajeros,* 2: no. 4235
García, Cristóbal	*Sevilla:* Sevilla	—	—	—	Doc. 12; *Pasajeros,* 2: no. 4235
García, Hernán	*Llerena:* Badajoz	—	—	—	Doc. 12; *Pasajeros,* 3: no. 24
García, Simón	—	—	—	—	Doc. 12
Garrido, Bartolomé	Moguer: Huelva	33+	—	Colima	MX 1064; Just 263, Pieza 2

Name	Place of Origin	Age in 1540	Occupation	Residence Afterward	Source or Sources
Gastaca, Juan de	*Loyando:* Ávala	—	—	—	Doc. 12; *Pasajeros,* 2: no. 3585
Genovés, Lorenzo	*Genoa*	—	—	*Ciudad Real de Chiapas*	Doc. 12; MX 1064
Godoy, Francisco de	*Plasencia:* Cáceres	—	—	—	Doc. 12; *Pasajeros,* 2: no. 5128
Gómez, Francisco	—	—	—	—	Doc. 12
Gómez, Francisco	—	—	—	—	Doc. 12
Gómez, Francisco	—	—	—	—	Doc. 12
Gómez de la Peña, Hernán	Ledesma: Salamanca	—	Escribano	Culiacán	Doc. 12; MX 1064; Doc. 27
Gómez de Paradinas, Juan	Paradinas: *Salamanca* or *Segovia*	18+	Tailor	Ciudad de México	Doc. 12; Patro 63, R5; Just 1021, N2, Pieza 6
Gómez de Salazar, Juan	—	20	—	Ciudad de México	Patro 63, R5
González, Alonso (uncle or father to below)	*Villanueva de Fresno:* Badajoz	—	—	—	Doc. 12; Patro 61, N2, R7; MX 1064
González, Alonso (nephew or son to above)	*Villanueva de Fresno:* Badajoz	—	—	—	Doc. 12; Patro 61, N2, R7; MX 1064
González, Fernán	Isla de Santo Domingo	—	—	Colima	Doc. 12; MX 1064
González, Fernand	—	—	—	—	Doc. 12
González, Francisco	—	—	—	—	Doc. 12
González, Pedro	*Fuente del Arco:* Badajoz	—	—	—	Doc. 12; *Pasajeros,* 2: no. 2213
Gorbalán, Francisco	—	29	—	Guadalajara	Doc. 12; Just 1021, N2, Pieza 5
Górez, Francisco	—	—	—	—	Doc. 12
Guadalupe, Gaspar de	*Toledo*	—	—	—	Doc. 12; *Pasajeros,* 2: no. 2582
Guernica, Juan de*	Guernica: Vizcaya	—	—	*Culiacán*	Doc. 12; Doc. 27; Tello 2:136
Guevara, Diego de	*Vitoria:* Álava	19	Encomendero		Doc. 12; Doc. 28; Chipman, 299
Gurrea, don Lope de	Zaragosa	—	—	—	Doc. 12; *Pasajeros,* 2: no. 3804
Gutiérrez, Cristóbal	—	—	—	—	Doc. 12
Gutiérrez, Francisco	—	19+	—	Puebla	Doc. 12; MX 204, N33\2
Gutiérrez de la Caballería, Diego	Almagro: Ciudad Real	—	—	Died 1542	Doc. 12; MX 228, N23\1; Flint, 48
Hernández, Alonso	*Oropesa:* Toledo	—	—	—	Doc. 12; *Pasajeros,* 2: no. 1488
Hernández, Andrés	*Encinasola:* Salamanca or Sevilla	—	—	—	Doc. 12
Hernández, Diego	*Frenegal:* Badajoz	—	—	—	Doc. 12; *Pasajeros,* 3: no. 101; Patro 61, N2, R7
Hernández, Gonzalo	—	—	—	—	Doc. 12
Hernández, Graviel	—	—	—	—	Doc. 12
Hernández, Juan	Valle de Selorio de las Esturias: Oviedo	*32*	—	*Colima*	MX 1064; Just 198, N3
Hernández, Luis	—	—	—	Died 1541/42	Doc. 12; Tello 2:438
Hernández, Manuel	—	—	—	—	Doc. 12
Hernández, Martín	—	—	—	—	Doc. 12
Hernández, Martín	—	—	—	—	Doc. 12
Hernández, Miguel	—	—	—	—	Doc. 12
Hernández, Onofre	—	—	—	—	Doc. 12
Hernández, Pero	—	—	—	—	Doc. 12
Hernández, Pero	—	—	—	—	Doc. 12
Hernández Calvo, Pero	—	—	—	—	Doc. 12
Hernández Chillón, Martín	Guadalcanal: Sevilla	—	—	—	Doc. 12; *Pasajeros,* 1: no. 4383
Hernández Moreno, Cristóbal	—	—	—	—	Doc. 12
Hernández de Arriba, Francisco	—	37	—	Quito	Patro 127, N1, R10
Hernández de Guadalajara, Pero	*Guadalajara*	—	—	—	Doc. 12

Name	Place of Origin	Age in 1540	Occupation	Residence Afterward	Source or Sources
Homem, [H]orta*	Portugal	—	—	—	Doc. 12
Hoz, Cristóbal de la	—	—	—	—	Doc. 12
Hozes, Francisca de	Ciudad Real: Ciudad Real	—	—	Ciudad de México	Just 267, N3
Huerta, García de	*Sevilla*	—	—	—	MX 1064; *Pasajeros,* 1: no. 4005
Huelva/Huerve, Pedro de	—	—	—	—	Doc. 27
Jaramillo, Juan	Villanueva de Barcarrota: Badajoz	30	Captain	Ciudad de México	Doc. 12; MX 1064; Patro 87, N1, R5; Doc. 30
Jerónimo, Pedro*	—	—	—	Ciudad de México	Doc. 12; Patro 56, N3, R2
Jiménez, Alonso	*Guadalcanal:* Sevilla	—	—	Compostela	Doc. 12; *Pasajeros,* 1: no. 3071
Jiménez, Juan	Guadalcanal: Sevilla	—	—	Died 1542	Doc. 12; Doc. 27
Laredo, Antonio de	—	—	—	—	Doc. 12
Lasojo, Pedro de	—	—	—	—	Doc. 27
Lázaro	—	—	Drummer	—	Doc. 12
Ledesma, Pedro de	Zamora	24	Encomendero, regidor, lt. treasurer	Compostela, Colima, Guadalajara	Doc. 12; Just 339, N1, R1; Just 336, N1
Linares, Pedro	—	—	—	—	Doc. 12
López, Alonso	*Guadalcanal:* Sevilla	—	—	—	Doc. 12; *Pasajeros,* 2: no. 1058
López, Diego	Sevilla	25	Encomendero	Colima, mines of Nuestra Señora de los Remedios, Culiacán	Doc. 12; Patro 216, N2; Escorial
López, Francisco	—	—	—	—	Doc. 12
López, Gabriel*	—	25	Encomendero	Culiacán	Doc. 12; MX 1064; Patro 78A, N1, R6
López, Gonzalo	*Medillín:* Badajoz	—	—	—	H&R, 106 n. 105
López, Juan	—	—		Ciudad de México	Doc. 12; Doc. 33
López, Pedro	*Ciudad Real*	—	—	—	Doc. 12; *Pasajeros,* 2: no. 2578
López de Cárdenas, García	Madrid	—	Noble	Madrid	Doc. 12; Patro 281, N1, R34
López de la Rosa, Juan*	Sayago: Zamora	—	Small farmer	Puebla	Doc. 12; MX 1064; Dicc. de Conquist., 308
López de Urrea, Pedro*	—	16/28	—	Cuzco	Doc. 12; Patro 110, R7\1; Patro 56, N3, R2
Luna y Arellano, Tristán de	Borovia: Soria	<25	Encomendero	Oaxaca	Doc. 12; Just 144, N1; Boyd-Bowman 2: no. 10523
Madrid Avendaño, Diego de*	Toledo	25	Corregidor	Ciudad de México	Doc. 12; Just 1021, N2, Pieza 5; MX 1064
Maldonado, Alonso	—	—	—	—	Doc. 12
Maldonado, Cristóbal	Burguillos: *Toledo* or *Sevilla*		Encomendero	Pánuco	Doc. 12; MX 1064
Maldonado, María	—	—	—	Ciudad de México	Patro 63, R5
Maldonado, don Rodrigo	Guadalajara: Guadalajara	25	Encomendero	Ciudad de México	Doc. 12; Just 1021, N2, Pieza 6; Velasco, 34–35
Maldonado, ?	—	—	—	—	Díaz del Castillo, 830–31
Manrique de Lara, Alonso*	Valladolid	—	—	Phillipines	Doc. 12; MX 1064; Doc. 28; Boyd-Bowman 2: no. 12150
Marcos, fray	Nice: France	—	Priest	Ciudad de México	Doc. 28; Boyd-Bowman 2: no. 13383
Márquez, Pedro	*Orehuela:* Murcia	—	—	—	Doc. 12; *Pasajeros,* 2: no. 2132
Martín, Andrés	—	—	—	—	Doc. 12
Martín, Andrés	Portugal	—	—	—	Doc. 12
Martín, Antón	—	—	—	—	Doc. 12
Martín, Domingo	Las Broças: Cáceres	38	—	Ciudad de México	Doc. 12; Just 1021, N2, Pieza 6

Name	Place of Origin	Age in 1540	Occupation	Residence Afterward	Source or Sources
Martín, Esteban	Sevilla	17	Alcalde mayor	San Sebastian	Doc. 12; Patro 74, N2, R2; Tello 2:135
Martín, Francisco	*Fuente de Cantos:* Badajoz	—	Butcher	Culiacán	Doc. 12; Just 267, N3; *Pasajeros,* 1: no. 4190
Martín, Francisco	—	—	—	—	Doc. 12
Martín, Juan	*Fuente del Maestre:* Badajoz	—	—	—	Doc. 12; *Pasajeros,* 3: no. 236
Martín Bermejo, Hernando*	Fuente del Arco: Badajoz	—	Escribano	Guadalajara	Doc. 12; *Pasajeros,* 2: no. 2201; Doc. 27; Tello 2:515–16
Martín Bermejo, Juan*	Fuente del Arco: Badajoz	—	—	—	Doc. 12; *Pasajeros,* 2: no. 2211
Martín Cano, Pero	Fuente del Arco: Badajoz	*38*	—	*Purificación*	Doc. 12; *Pasajeros,* 2: no. 2208; Just 339, N1, R1
Martín Parra, Alonso	—	—	—	—	Doc. 12
Martín de la Bermeja, Pedro	Calzadilla: Cáceres	—	—	—	Doc. 12; *Pasajeros,* 1: no. 4191
Mata, Diego de	—	—	—	—	Doc. 12
Mayoral, Pedro	*Orehuela:* Murcia	—	—	—	Doc. 12; *Pasajeros,* 2: no. 2132
Mayorga, Cristóbal de	Benavente: Zamora	18	Encomendero	Ciudad de México	Doc. 12; Just 1021, N2, Pieza 6; Patro 205, R1\2; MX 1064
Mazuela, Florián de	—	—	—	—	Doc. 12
Medina, Alonso de	—	—	—	—	Doc. 12
Medina, Diego de	—	—	—	—	Doc. 12
Melgosa, Pablo de	Burgos	24	—	Burgos	Doc. 12; Just 1021, N2, Pieza 5
Méndez de Sotomayor, Pero	—	—	*Encomendero*	*Michoacán*	Doc. 12; MX 1064
Mercado de Sotomayor, Gerónimo	Carmona: Sevilla	20	Encomendero	Ciudad de México	Just 1021, N2, Pieza 5; MX 1064
Mesa, Antonio	*Almadén de los Azogues:* Ciudad Real	—	—	Ciudad de México	Doc. 28; Patro 56, N3, R2; *Pasajeros,* 2: no. 5095
Miguel, maestre	*Valladolid*	—	*Tanner*	—	Doc. 12; *Pasajeros,* 2: no. 2116
son of Miguel, *Miguel/Luis/Juan*	*Valladolid*	—	—	—	Doc. 12; *Pasajeros,* 2: no. 2116
Miguel, Antón	—	—	—	—	Doc. 12
Millero, Alonso	Galicia	—	—	—	Doc. 12
Miranda, Andrés de	—	—	—	—	Doc. 12
Mondragón, Francisco	—	—	—	—	Just 1021, N2, Pieza 2
Moral, Alonso del	—	—	—	—	Doc. 12
Morilla, Diego de	—	—	—	—	Doc. 12
Morillo, Juan	*Fuente del Arco:* Badajoz	—	—	—	Doc. 12; *Pasajeros,* 2: no. 2183
Muñoz, Francisco	Granja: Cáceres	21	—	Tlalmanalco	Doc. 12; MX 1064; MX 98, N33
Muñoz, Juan	*Utrera:* Sevilla	—	—	*Died 1542*	MX 1064; Tello 2:136, 443
Nájera, Pedro de Castañeda de*	Baeza: Jaén	25	—	Culiacán	Doc. 12; Guad 46, N8; Tello 2:135
Napolitano, Bartolomé	*Naples*	—	—	—	Doc. 12
Navarro, Juan	*Logroño:* La Rioja	—	—	—	Doc. 12; *Pasajeros,* 2: no. 3448
Navarro, Pedro	Estella: Navarra	30	—	Guadalajara	Doc. 12; Just 1021, N2, Pieza 5
Negrín, Antón			—	Puebla	Doc. 27
Nieto, Pedro	*Plasencia:* Cáceres	20	—	Ciudad de México	Doc. 12; Patro 63, R5; *Pasajeros,* 2: no. 3445
Núñez de Garbeña, Diego	—	—	—	—	Doc. 12
Núñez de Mirandilla, Diego	*Mirandilla:* Badajoz	—	—	—	Doc. 12
Olivares, Francisco de	Béjar del Castañar: Salamanca	26	Encomendero	Guadalajara	Doc. 12; MX 1064; Doc. 32; Just 339, N1, R1

Name	Place of Origin	Age in 1540	Occupation	Residence Afterward	Source or Sources
Ordóñez, Sancho	Alange: Badajoz	40	—	Puebla	Doc. 12; MX 1064; Just 265, Pieza 2
Orduña, Hernando de	Burgos	24	—	Ciudad de México	Just 1021, N2, Pieza 6
Orduña, Juan de	Toledo		—	Culiacán	MX 1064
Orejón, Andrés	Ávila	33	—	Pátzcuaro	MX 1064; Just 263, Pieza 3
Orozco, Gerónimo de	—	—	—	—	H&R, 106, n. 102
Ortega, Pedro de	*Segovia*	—	—	—	Doc. 12; Pasajeros, 2: no. 2454
Ovando, Francisco de	*Cáceres*	—	—	Died 1541	Doc. 12; *Pasajeros*, 2: no. 495
Padilla, Francisco de	—	—	—	—	Doc. 12
Padilla, fray Juan de	Andalucía	—	Priest	Died in Quivira	Doc. 28; Tello 2, 487–91
Páez, Fernán	Villafranca: Portugal	26	—	Ciudad de México	Doc. 12; Just 1021, N2, Pieza 5
Paniagua, Juan	Écija: Sevilla	27	Alcalde mayor	Culiacán	Doc. 12; MX 1064; MX 204, N33\2; Patro 60, N5, R4
Parada, Francisco de	—	—	—	—	Doc. 12
Paradinas, Alonso de	—	—	—	—	Doc. 12
Pascual, Pedro	—	28	—	Ciudad de México	Doc. 12; Patro 56, N3, R2
Pastor, Juan	—	16	—	Culiacán	Doc. 12; Just 336, N1
Paz Maldonado, Rodrigo de*	Salamanca	24	Encomendero	Quito	Doc. 12; Patro 112, R2\2
Pedro, a Black	—	—	Crier	*Colima*	Doc. 27; Mathes
Pedro, Juan	—	—	—	—	Doc. 27
Peñas, Juan de*	Sevilla	—	—	Ciudad de México	Doc. 12; MX 1064
Perea, García de	—	—	—	—	Doc. 12
Pérez, Andrés	—	22	Money dealer	Ciudad de México	Doc. 12; Patro 78A, N1, R6
Pérez, Cristóbal	Ávila	21+	—	Ciudad de México	Doc. 12; Just 339, N1, R1
Pérez, Hernán	*Azuaga:* Badajoz	20	—	Ciudad de México	Patro 79, N1, R2; *Pasajeros*, 2: no. 1142
Pérez, Juan	Aragon	—	—	—	Doc. 12
Pérez, Melchior	Villa de la Torre: Badajoz	26	Encomendero	Compostela, Colima, Guadalajara	Doc. 12; Just 336, N1; Patro 60, N5, R4; Doc. 32; MX 1064
Pérez Buscavida, Antón	Conil de la Frontera: Cádiz	—	Villager	Compostela	MX 1064; Doc. 27
Pérez de Bocanegra, Alonso*	*Trigueras:* Huelva	20	Regidor	Ciudad de México	Doc. 12; Patro 87, N1, R5; Indif 127, N51\1
Pérez de Vergara, Juan	*Mondragón: Guipúzcoa*	—	—	—	Doc. 12; *Pasajeros*, 4: no. 407
Pigredo, Luis de	—	—	—	—	Doc. 12
Plasencia, Juan de	—	—	—	—	Doc. 12
Pobares, Francisco de	*Sabiote:* Jaén	—	—	—	Doc. 12; *Pasajeros*, 2: no. 2673; Tello 2, 423
Puelles, Diego de	Miranda de Ebro: Álava	—	*Lt. alguacil mayor*	Ciudad de México	Doc. 12; MX 1064; Just 268, N2, Pieza 3
Quesada, Cristóbal de	Carmona: Sevilla	—	Painter	*Ciudad de México*	Doc. 12; MX 1064
Quexada, Luis de	—	—	—	—	Patro 216, N2
Ramírez de Vargas, Luis*	*Madrid*	21	*Residencia judge*	Ciudad de México, *Queretaro*	Doc. 12; Patro 68, N2, R4\1; MX 205, N12; MX 1064
Ramos, Gerónimo	—	—	—	—	Doc. 12
Ramos, Juan de	—	—	*Surgeon*	—	Doc. 12
Ramos, Pedro	—	—	—	—	Doc. 12
Ribadeneyra, Juan de	—	—	—	—	Doc. 12
Ribero, Antonio de*	Medina del Campo: Valladolid	18+	—	Ciudad de México	Doc. 12; *Pasajeros*, 2: no. 1262; MX 204, N33\2
Robles, Melchor de	*Almazan:* Soria	25	Encomendero	Antequera	Doc. 12; MX 97, R1; MX 1064

Name	Place of Origin	Age in 1540	Occupation	Residence Afterward	Source or Sources
Rodríguez, Francisco	*Alange:* Badajoz	—	—	—	Doc. 12; *Pasajeros,* 3: no. 212
Rodríguez, García	Alcaraz: Albacete	20	Priest (later)	Mines of Tasco	Doc. 12; Just 1021, N2, Pieza 6; Patro 87, N1, R5
Rodríguez, Gaspar	—	—	—	—	Doc. 12
Rodríguez, Juan	Alange: Badajoz	—	—	*Ciudad de México*	Doc. 12; MX 1064
Rodríguez, Sancho	—	—	—	—	Doc. 12
Rodríquez de Ávalos, Juan	—	—	—	—	Doc. 12
Rodríguez Parra, Alonso	—	—	—	Chiametla	Patro 74, N2, R2
Román, Gómez	—	—	—	—	Doc. 12
Romano, Marco	*Italy*	—	—	—	Doc. 12
Romero, Domingo	—	23	—	Ciudad de México	Doc. 12; Patro 56, N3, R2
Roxo, Sebastián	Sicily	—	—	—	Patro 60, N5, R4; MX 1064
Roxo Loro, Francisco	Sicily	14/17	Encomendero	Compostela	Doc. 12; MX 1064; Patro 60, N5, R4
Ruiz, Antón	Guadalacanal: Sevilla	—	—	—	Doc. 12; *Pasajeros,* 2: no. 2513
Ruiz, Domingo	—	—	—	—	Doc. 12
Ruiz, Juan	Hispañola	15+	Encomendero	Guadalajara	MX 1064; Just 336, N1
Ruiz de Rojas, Marcos	Madrid	—	—	—	Díaz del Castillo, 830–31
Salamanca, Diego de	—	—	—	—	Doc. 12
Salamanca, Gaspar de	*Melgar:* Burgos	*20*	*Lt. alcalde mayor*	*Tlalmanalco,* Ciudad de México	Patro 79, N1, R2; MX 98, N33; *Pasajeros,* 2: no. 4811
Salamanca, Juan de	—	—	—	—	Doc. 12
Saldaña, Gaspar de	Guadalajara	18+	Corregidor	Charcos	Doc. 12; Just 1021, N2, Pieza 5; Patro 110, R7\1
Salinas, Andrés de	Salinas: ?	—	—	*Ciudad de México*	MX 1064
Salinas, son of Andrés	Salinas: ?	—	—	—	Doc. 12
Samaniego, Lope de	*Segovia*	—	Former alcaide of the shipyard	Died 1540	Doc. 12; Doc. 28; Boyd-Bowman 2: no. 8024
Sámano, Julián de	Santa Gadea: Burgos	—	—	—	Doc. 12; Icaza 1: no. 403
Sánchez, Alonso	Ciudad Real: Ciudad Real	—	Merchant	Ciudad de México	Doc. 12; Doc. 14; MX 1064
Sánchez, son of Alonso: *Alonso de la Camara/Francisco de la Serna/Juan de Hozes*	*Ciudad de México*	—	—	Ciudad de México	Doc. 12; AGnot, 1
Sánchez, Bartolomé	*Azuaga:* Badajoz	—	*Painter*	—	Doc. 12; Contra, 199, N23
Sánchez, Damián	—	23	—	Ciudad de México	Patro 56, N3, R2
Sánchez, Diego	Fromista: Palencia	—	—	—	Doc. 12
Sánchez, Leonardo	—	—	—	—	Doc. 12
Sánchez, Martín	*Villanueva de Fresno:* Badajoz	—	—	—	Doc. 12; *Pasajeros,* 2: no. 4390
Sánchez, Miguel	—	—	—	—	Doc. 12
Sánchez, Miguel	—	—	—	—	Doc. 12
Sánchez, Pedro	El Barco de Ávila: Ávila	*26*	*Blacksmith*	*Guadalajara*	Doc. 12; Just 339, N1, R1
Sánchez, Rodrigo	Azuaga: Badajoz	—	—	Ciudad de México	MX 1064
Sánchez de Plasencia, Miguel	*Plasencia:* Cáceres	—	—	—	Doc. 12
Sandoval, Juan de	—	—	—	—	Calvo, 80
Santillana, Francisco de*	*Sevilla*	—	Gatekeeper	Ciudad de México	Doc. 12; *Pasajeros,* 2: no. 3447; Patro 79, N3, R2
Santovaya, Juan de	—	—	—	—	Doc. 12
San Vitores, Juan Bautista de	—	—	*Merchant*	—	Doc. 12; Contra 707, N1
Sayavedra, Alonso de	—	22	—	Quito	Doc. 12; Patro 117, R5
Serrano, Bartolomé	*Plasencia:* Cáceres	—	—	—	Doc. 12; *Pasajeros,* 2: no. 3443

Name	Place of Origin	Age in 1540	Occupation	Residence Afterward	Source or Sources
Simancas, Francisco de	—	—	—	—	Doc. 12
Simón, Rodrigo	Moguer: Huelva	33	Encomendero	Ciudad de México	MX 1064; Just 1021, N2, Pieza 6
Solís Farfán, Juan de	—	—	—	—	Doc. 12
Soto, Sebastián de	*Guadalajara*	—	—	—	Doc. 12; *Pasajeros,* 2: no. 1258
Sotomayor, Juan de	—	—	—	—	Doc. 28
Talavera, Pedro de	*Fuente del Maestre:* Badajoz	*25+*	—	*Ciudad de México*	Doc. 12; MX 1064
Tamarán, Rodrigo de	Espinosa de los Monteros: Santander	25	—	*Ciudad de México*	Doc. 12; Just 339, N1, R1
Temiño, Francisco de	—	*19+*	—	Ciudad de México	Doc. 12; MX 1064; Patro 79, N1, R2
Toro, Alonso de	Alcalá de Henares: Madrid	24–30	Small farmer	Purificación	MX 1064; Just 339, N1, R1; Just 339, N1, R3
Torquemada, Juan de	—	—	—	—	Doc. 12
Torres, Francisco de	Trujillo: Cáceres	—	Corregidor	Pánuco	MX 1064
Torres, Miguel de	—	—	—	—	Doc. 12
Torrez, Miguel de	—	—	—	—	Doc. 12
Tovar, Pedro de	*Villamartín:* León	22	Encomendero	Culiacán	Doc. 12; Patro 216, N2; Guada 46, N8; Boyd-Bowman 2: no. 6017
Troyano, Juan	Medina de Rioseco: Valladolid	44	Freighter	Ciudad de México	MX 206, N12; MX 168; MX 98, N33
Trujillo, Pedro de (ordered to stay in Culiacán)	—	—	—	—	Doc. 12; Doc. 28
Trujillo, Rodrigo de	Veracruz: Mexico	—	—	Puebla	Doc. 12; Doc. 27
Úbeda, fray Luis de	*Escalona:* Toledo or *Úbeda:* Jaén	—	Priest	*Died at Cicuique*	Doc. 28; Tello 2: 328
Ureña, *Diego*	*Sevilla*	—	—	—	Obregón, 153; *Pasajeros,* 1: no. 4315
Vaca, Juan de	—	—	—	—	Doc. 12
Valderreina, Alonso de	Astorga: León	38	—	—	Just 1021, N2, Pieza 6
Valdivieso, Francisco de	—	—	—	—	Doc. 12
Valencia, Alonso de	—	—	—	—	Doc. 12
Vallarra, Juan de	—	—	—	—	Doc. 12
Valle, Cristóbal del	Aranda de Duero: Valladolid	16+	—	Guadalajara	MX 1064; Just 339, N1, R1
Valle, Hernando de	Olmedo: Valladolid	23+	Small farmer	Purificación	Doc. 12; Just 339, N1, R1; MX 1064
Vargas, Francisco de	—	*33+*	—	*Ciudad de México*	Doc. 12; Just 268, N1
Vargas, Pedro de	—	—	—	—	Doc. 12
Vázquez, Gonzalo	—	—	—	—	Doc. 12
Vázquez de Coronado, Francisco	Salamanca	29	Regidor	Ciudad de México	Doc. 12; MX 1064; Just 260, Pieza 4
Vázquez de Garabel, Rosele	—	—	—	—	Doc. 12
Velasco, Alonso de	—	—	—	—	Doc. 12
Velasco, Cristóbal	—	—	—	—	Doc. 12
Velasco, ?	—	—	—	—	Doc. 12
Vera, Rodrigo de	—	—	—	—	Doc. 12
Villafranca, Francisco de	*Medina de Rioseco:* Valladolid	—	—	—	Doc. 12; *Pasajeros,* 2: no. 4813
Villareal, Juan de	Agudo: Ciudad Real	*31*	—	*Guadalajara*	Doc. 12; Just 339, N1, R1; MX 1064

Name	Place of Origin	Age in 1540	Occupation	Residence Afterward	Source or Sources
Villaroya, Martín de	—	—	—	—	Doc. 12
Villegas, Juan de	Zafra: Badajoz	*34*	—	—	Doc. 12; Just 258, Pieza 1
Vitoria, Juan de	Burgos	26	—	Madrid	Just 1021, N2, Pieza 5
Vos, Alonso	Ribadeo: Lugo	—	—	—	Doc. 12
Xuárez de Ávila, Juan	—	13+	—	Ciudad de México	Patro 78A, N1, R6
Xuárez de Figueroa, Gómez	—	—	—	—	Doc. 12
Yáñez, Gonzalo	*Guadalacanal:* Sevilla	—	Escribano	Quito	Doc. 12; *Pasajeros,* 2: no. 2513; *Pasajeros,* 3: no. 3332
Ysla, Rodrigo de	—	22+	—	Ciudad de México	Doc. 12; Patro 63, R5
Zagala, Juan de	—	—	—	Ciudad de México	Doc. 33
Zaldívar, Juan de	*Vitoria:* Álava	26	Encomendero	Guadalajara	Doc. 28; Patro 339, N1, R1; Boyd-Bowman 2: no. 13623; Chipman, 304–5
Zamora, Baltasar de	—	—	—	—	Doc. 12

Indios

Name	Place of Origin	Age in 1540	Occupation	Residence Afterward	Source or Sources
don Alonso	Michoacán	—	—	—	Just 263, Pieza 1
Andrés	Coyoacán	—	—	—	Espejo
Antón	Guadalajara	—	—	—	Espejo
Caballero, wife of Lope	Nueva España	—	—	—	MX 1064
Gaspar	México	—	—	—	Espejo
Jiménez, Francisco	Tlatelolco	—	—	—	Oroz Codex, 314
León, Luis de	Santiago *de Tlatelolco*	—	—	—	Just 21; Hanke 1:70, no. 75
Lucas	*Zapotlán*	—	—	—	Doc. 30
Luisa	Culiacán	—	—	—	Obregon, 71
Sebastián	*Zapotlán*	—	—	—	Doc. 30
Troyano, wife of Juan	Tierra Nueva	—	—	—	MX 168

Incorrect Additions by Hammond and Rey, 1940

Arce, Juan de	Witness: says he has known Vázquez de Coronado since only about 1542; also says he has been in Nueva Galicia only a year and a half; AGI, Justicia, 339, N.1, R.1, "Residencia." Makes no mention of going to Cíbola; AGI, México, 1064, L.1\1, "Informes de los conquistadores," fol. 255v, and Icaza, 2: no. 1191
Arias de Saabedra, Hernando	States that the viceroy sent him to Culiacán to provide for the expedition to Tierra Nueva; AGI, México, 1064, L.1\1, "Informes de los conquistadores," fol. 266r
Barrionuevo, Francisco de	There were two Barrionuevo brothers, Rodrigo and Velasco, on the expedition; however, a Francisco de Barrionuevo went to Peru, and Castañeda de Nájera may have confused him with Velasco; *Pasajeros,* 2: no. 3809
Castañeda, Alonso de	Died from his wounds at Tiguex and yet on August 2, 1541, was an *alcalde* in the *cabildo* in Guadalajara; Tello 2:253, 355. Does not state in 1547 that he went on the expedition; Icaza, 1: no. 473. States that he knows Vázquez de Coronado went to Tierra Nueva and left Oñate in charge; AGI, Justicia, 339, N.1, R.1, "Residencia." It seems clear that Alonso de Castañeda has been confused with Machín de Castañeda, a member of the expedition.
Cuevas, Juan de	See Document 12, note 115, for explanation.
González, Ruy	States specifically that he sent his brother and four others on the expedition; AGI, Patronato, 61, N.2, R.7\1, "Rui González." Does not state that he went, but only that he helped people to go; Icaza, 1: no. 52.
Méndez, Cristóbal	States that he was pursuing Vázquez de Coronado in order to go to Cíbola but was caught up in the Mixtón War in Jalisco; AGI, Patronato, 63, R.23\1, "Méritos y servicios, Cristóbal Méndez, November 7, 1559."
Ruiz, Juan	The Juan Ruiz from Agudo does not state that he went on the expedition, whereas the Juan Ruiz from Española did; Icaza, 2: nos. 1139 and 1304
Simón (Ximón), Diego	Not found as a witness; AGI, Justicia, 1021, N.2, Pieza 6, "Probanza del fiscal Villalobos." Possibly confused with Rodrigo Simón.

Abbreviations

AGnot 1	Archivo General de Notarías, Ciudad de México, 1, Diego de Isla, IV, "Distribution of inheritance from Alonso Sánchez, Ciudad de México, 1553"
Contra	AGI, Contratación
Guad	AGI, Guadalajara
Indf	AGI, Indiferente
Just	AGI, Justicia
MX	AGI, Mexico
MX 1064	AGI, México, 1064, L.1 \1, "Informes de los conquistadores"
Patro	AGI, Patronato
Escorial	Biblioteca del Escorial, Codíce &-2-7, Doc. no. LXXX
Chipman	Donald E. Chipman, "The Oñate-Moctezuma-Zaldívar Families of Northern New Spain," *New Mexico Historical Review* 52, no. 4 (1977):297–310
Dicc. de Conquist.	Victor M. Álvarez, *Diccionario de conquistadores* (México, DF: Instituto Nacional de Antropología y Historia, 1975)
Flint	Shirley Cushing Flint, "*La Sangre Limpiada* of Marina Flores Gutiérrez de la Caballería," *Colonial Latin American Historical Review* 11, no. 1 (2002):35–54
Hanke	Lewis Hanke, *Los Virreyes españoles en América durante el gobierno de la Casa de Austria, México* (Madrid: Ediciones Atlas, 1976)
Mathes	W. Michael Mathes, "New Research in Mexico regarding Francisco Vázquez de Coronado" (conference paper presented in Las Vegas, NM, 2000)
Oroz Codex	Fray Angélico Chávez, trans. and ed., *The Oroz Codex* (Washington, DC: Academy of American Franciscan History, 1972)
Velasco	Luis de Velasco, *Relación de las encomiendas de indios hechas en Nueva España a los conquistadores y pobladores de ella, año de 1564* (México, DF: Jose Porrúa e hijos, 1955)

* Name as it appears in Document 12, "Muster Roll": Álvarez, Alonso; Bermejo, Hernando; Bruges, Jaco de (aka, Brujas); Caso Verde, Hernando de; Cepeda (remained in Culiácan sick, did not go to Cíbola); Duero, Juan de; Galeras, Juan (aka, Galeas, Gallas, Galeasso, Galeaso); Galiveer, ? (possibly Gulliver); Gerónimo, Pero; Homem, Orta; López, Graviel; López, Juan; Madrid, Diego de; Manrique, Alonso; Martín, Juan; Nájera, Pedro de; Paz, Rodrigo de; Pedes, Bartolomé de; Peña, Juan de; Pérez, Alonso; Riber, Antonio de; Santillan, Francisco de; Urrea, Pedro de; Vargas, Luis de; Vizcaíno, Juan.

Appendix 4

Requerimiento

Strong ecclesiastical complaints about abuse of natives of the New World by conquistadores and *encomenderos* began as early as the second decade of the sixteenth century. As part of the Spanish royal court's response to those complaints, a legal code known as the Laws of Burgos was promulgated late in 1512. Concern for the rights of Indians was expressed in regulations governing their labor and provision to them of adequate shelter and instruction in the principles of the Christian faith.

The Laws of Burgos and their expansion less than a year later opened the door to further official consideration of the treatment of American natives, specifically the question of the conditions under which war could legitimately be waged against them. One result of these discussions was the drafting, probably in 1513, by the Spanish jurist Juan López de Palacios Rubios of the *requerimiento,* or formal summons to submit. For the next 60 years conquistadores were required to read this document, through interpreters and in the presence of notaries, to native leaders before hostilities could be opened against them. The *requerimiento* laid out the Spanish claim to sovereignty over all the peoples of the New World and demanded their peaceful submission to the authority of the king. It also promised dire consequences if submission was not made without delay.

Although the reading of the *requerimiento* was often grotesquely absurd, conscientious conquistadores such as Vázquez de Coronado went to extreme lengths to ensure that natives were given the opportunity to hear it three times before any attack against them was launched. The text of the *requerimiento* was set by law, although it varied slightly over time and from place to place. The precise text used by the Coronado expedition has not been located. We publish here, as representative of the *requerimiento* read on many occasions by members of the Coronado expedition, the text used by Alonso de Ojeda in 1514 or 1515. It was transcribed from a documentary record by the early-seventeenth-century historian Antonio de Herrera y Tordesillas. Other examples of the *requerimiento* have been published previously, including one by Ángel de Altoaguirre y Duvale in *Governación espiritual y temporal de las Indias: Códice publicado en virtud de acuerdo de la Real Academia de la Historia* (1927), demonstrating some of the variation between versions of the summons.

TRANSLATION

Description of the Western Indies, by Antonio de Herrera, chief chronicler for the Indies for His Majesty, and his chronicler of Castilla. Madrid: Nicolas Rodriguez Franco, 1725.
Decada I, Libro VII, Cap. 14, pp. 197–98

[197]
How Alonso de Ojeda[1] left the island of Española with his *armada* and went to Tierra Firme: the *Requerimiento* that the monarchs ordered to be read to the Indians

I, Alonso de Ojeda, *criado,* messenger, and captain of the very exalted and powerful monarchs of Castilla and León, subjugators of the barbarous peoples, inform and make known to you (as best I can) that God, Our Lord, the One and Everlasting, created Heaven and Earth and one man and one woman from whom you, we, and all the people of the Earth were and are begotten descendants, as well as all those who may come after us.

However, because of the multitude of descendants that has issued from them in the five thousand and more years since the world was created, it was necessary that some people go to one region and others to another and be divided into many *reinos* and *provincias,* because in one single place they could not be sustained and preserved.

From among all these peoples, God, Our Lord, appointed one called San Pedro to be lord and superior of all humankind, whom all were to obey. He was to be head of the whole human lineage, wherever people might exist and live and under whatever law, sect, or belief. [God] gave him to the whole world for its service and governance. [God] ordered him to establish his seat in Rome (as the most suitable place) in order to rule the world. Also He promised him that he could live and establish his seat in any other part of the world and that [he could] judge and govern all the people (Christians, Moors, Jews, Gentiles) and [those] who might adhere to any other sect or belief. They called this [individual] "Pope," that is to say, "Most Esteemed Father and Protector," because he is father and governor of all people.

Those who were living in those times obeyed this Holy Father and took [him] as lord, king, and superior of the universe. In the same way they have held all the others who were elected to the papacy after him. Thus it has continued until now and will continue until the world may end.

One of the pontiffs of the past, [of] those I have mentioned, made, as lord of the world, a grant of these islands and continent of the Mar Océano, along with everything that there is in [these lands], to the Catholic Sovereigns of Castilla, who were then don Fernando and doña Isabel (of glorious memory) and their successors, our lords. [This is] in accordance with what is recorded in certain documents that were issued concerning this (according to what is said). These you may view, if you wish.

Thus, His Majesty is king and lord of these islands and continent by virtue of the aforesaid grant. [The people of] some islands, nearly all [of those] who have been notified of this, have accepted His Majesty as such king and lord and have obeyed and served him and do serve [him], as subjects must do, willingly and without any resistance whatsoever. Thereafter, without any hesitation, once they were informed of what was referred to above, they obeyed the men of God whom [the king] sent to them so that they might preach and teach them our Holy Faith.

All of them, by their free and willing choice, without inducement or any reservation, became Christians and are now [Christian]. His Majesty has received them joyfully and benevolently. Therefore, he [has] ordered them to [be] treated just as are his other subjects and vassals. And you must and are obliged to do the same.

Therefore, as the best I can, I beg and summon you to consider fully what I have told you. In order to consider and deliberate on it, you may take the time that is reasonable. And if you acknowledge the Church as lord and superior of the universe [and] world, and the sovereign pontiff (called the pope) in its name, and His Majesty in his stead as superior, lord, and king of the islands and continent, by virtue of the aforesaid grant, and if you allow these religious fathers to preach and make known to you what was stated above, you will do well that which you must and [are] obliged [to do].

His Majesty and I, in his name, will receive you with complete affection and charity. [The people who are with me] will leave your wives to you and your children at liberty, without imposing servitude, so that they and you may do freely whatever you may wish and may think wise. [This will be] as nearly all the *vecinos* of the other islands have done. Besides this, His Majesty will extend many privileges and prerogatives to you and will make you many grants.

If, [however], you do not do [what I ask] or you maliciously delay [doing] it, I assure you that, with the help of God, I will attack you mightily. I will make war [against] you everywhere and in every way I can. And I will subject you to the yoke and obedience of the Church and His Majesty. I will take your wives and children, and I will make them slaves. As such, I will sell and dispose of them as His Majesty will order. I will take your property. I will do all the harm and damage to you that I can, [treating you] as vassals who do not obey and refuse to accept their lord and resist and oppose him.

I declare that the deaths and injuries that occur as a result of this would be your fault and not His Majesty's, nor ours, nor that of these *caballeros* who have come with me.

I request the *escribano* [who is] present to provide me a signed affidavit that I am informing you of this and summoning you [to comply].

TRANSCRIPTION

Descripcion de las Indias Ocidentales de Antonio de Herrera Coronista Mayor de su Magestad de las Indias, y su coronista de Castilla Madrid: Nicolas Rodriguez Franco, 1725.
Decada I, Libro VII, Cap. 14, p 197–98

Que Alonso de Ojeda saliò con su Armada de la Isla Española, i fue a Tierra-firme: i el Requerimiento, que los Reies mandaron hacer a los Indios

Yo Alonso de Ojeda, Criado de los/ mui Altos, i mui Poderosos Reies de Cas-/tilla, i de Leon, Domadores de las Gen-/tes Barbaras, su Mensagero, i Capitan,/ vos notifico, i hago saber, como mejor pue-/do, que Dios Nuestro Señor, Uno, i Eter-/no,

198
no, criò el Cielo, i la Tierra, i un Hom-/bre, i una Muger, de quien vosotros, i/ nosotros, i todos los Hombres del Mundo,/ fueron, i son descendientes procreados, i/ todos los que despues de nosotros vinieren:/ mas por la muchedumbre de generacion, que/ de estos ha procedido, desde cinco mil, i/ mas Años, que ha que el Mundo fue cria-/do, fue necesario, que los unos Hombres/ fuesen por una parte, i los otros por otra,/ i se dividiesen por muchos Reinos, i Pro-/vincias, porque en una sola no se podian/ sustentar, i conservar. De todas estas Gen-/tes Dios Nuestro Señor diò cargo à uno,

que/ fue llamado San Pedro, para que de todos/ los Hombres del Mundo fuese Señor, i Su-/perior, à quien todos obede-/ciesen, i fuese/ Cabeça de todo el Linage Humano, doquier/ que los Hombres estuviesen, i viviesen, i en/ qualquier Lei, Secta, ò Creencia: i diòle/ à todo el Mundo por su servicio, i jurisdic-/cion; i como quiera que le mandò, que pu-/siese su Silla en Roma, como en lugar mas/ aparejado, para regir el Mundo; tambien le/ prometiò, que podia estàr, i poner su Silla/ en qualquier otra parte del Mundo, i juz-/gar, i governar todas las Gentes, Christia-/nos, Moros, Judios, Gentiles, i de qual-/quiera otra Secta, ò Creencia, que fuesen./ A este llamaron Papa, que quiere decir,/ Admirable Maior, Padre, i Guardador,/ porque es Padre, i Governador de todos los/ Hombres. A este Santo Padre obedecieron,/ i tomaron por Señor, Rei, i Superior del/ Universo, los que en aquel tiempo vivian:/ i ansimismo han tenido à todos los otros, que/ despues de èl fueron al Pontificado elegidos,/ i ansi se ha continuado hasta aora, i se con-/tinuarà hasta que el Mundo se acabe./

Uno de los Pontifices pasados, que he/ dicho, como Señor del Mundo, hiço Dona-/cion de estas Islas, i Tierra-firme del Mar/ Occeano, à los Catolicos Reies de Castilla,/ que eran entonces D. Fernando, i Doña Isabel,/ de Gloriosa Memoria, i à sus Sucesores, nues-/tros Señores, con todo lo que en ellos hai,/ segun se contiene en ciertas Escrituras, que/ sobre ello pasaron, segun dicho es, que po-/deis vèr (si quisieredes.) Asi que su Ma-/gestad es Rei, i Señor de estas Islas, i/ Tierra-firme, por virtud de la dicha Do-/nacion, i como à tal Rei, i Señor, algu-/nas Islas, i casi todas, à quien esto ha/ sido notificado, han recibido à su Mages-/tad, i le han obedecido, i servido, i sir-/ven, como Subditos lo deben hacer, i con/ buena voluntad, i sin ninguna resistencia,/ luego, sin ninguna dilacion, como fueron/ informados de los susodicho, obedecieron à/ los Varones Religiosos, que les embiaba,/ para que les predicasen, i enseñasen nues-/tra Santa Fè: i todos ellos, de su libre, i/ agradable voluntad, sin premio, ni condi-/cion alguna, se tornaron Christianos, i lo/ son: i su Magestad los recibiò alegre, i be-/nignamente, i ansi los mandò tratar como/ à los otros sus Subditos, i Vasallos: i vo-/sotros sois tenidos, i obligados à hacer lo/ mismo. Por ende, como mejor puedo, vos/ ruego, i requiero, que entendais bien en es-/to que os he dicho, i tomeis para entende-/llo, i deliberar sobre ello, el tiempo que/ fuere justo, i reconozcais à la Iglesia por/ Señora, i Superiora del Universo Mundo,/ i al Sumo Pontifice, llamado Papa, en su/ nombre, i à su Magestad en su lugar, co-/mo Superior, i Señor Rei de las Islas, i/ Tierra-firme, por virtud de la dicha Do-/nacion: i consintais, que estos Padres Re-/ligiosos os declaren, i prediquen lo susodi-/cho: i si ansi lo hicieredes, hareis bien, i/ aquello que sois tenidos, i obligados, i su/ Magestad, i Yo en su nombre, vos recibi-/ràn con todo amor, i caridad, i vos dexa-/ràn vuestras Mugeres, i Hijos libres, sin/ servidumbre, para que de ellas, i de voso-/tros hagais libremente todo lo que quisiere-/des, i por bien tuvieredes, como lo han[2]/ hecho casi todos los Vecinos de las otras Is-/las: Y aliende de esto, su Magestad vos da-/rà muchos Privilegios, i Exempciones, i/ vos harà muchas mercedes; si no lo

hicie-/redes, ò en ello dilacion maliciosamente pu-/sieredes, certificoos, que con el aiuda de/ Dios, Yo entrarè poderosa-mente contra vo-/sotros, i vos harè guerra por todas las par-/tes, i manera que Yo pudiere, i vos suje-/tarè al iugo, i obediencia de la Iglesia, i/ de su Magestad, i tomarè vuestras Muge-/res, i Hijos, i los harè Esclavos, i como/ tales los venderè, i dispondrè de ello, co-/mo su Magestad mandare: i vos tomarè/ vuestros bienes, i vos harè todos los males,/ i daños que pudiere, como à Vasallos, que/ no obedecen, ni quieren recibir à su Señor,/ i le resisten, i contradicen. Y protesto, que/ las muertes, i daños, que de ello se recre-/cieren, sean à vuestra culpa, i no de su/ Magestad, ni nuestra, ni de estos Caba-/lleros, que conmigo vinieron. Y de como/ os lo digo, i requiero, pido al pre-/sente Escrivano, que me lo/ dè por testimonio/ signado.

Notes

General Introduction

1. Rolena Adorno and Patrick Charles Pautz, *Álvar Núñez Cabeza de Vaca: His Account, His Life, and the Expedition of Pánfilo de Narváez,* 3 vols. (Lincoln: University of Nebraska Press, 1999), 1:207, 231; PTBOviedo, 4:311.

2. Document 22, fol. 1r.

3. Document 19, fol. 360v.

4. For the full text of one of several extant versions of the *requerimiento,* see Appendix 4.

5. Document 28, fol. 31v.

6. Document 22, fol. 1v.

7. Richard Flint, *Great Cruelties Have Been Reported: The 1544 Investigation of the Coronado Expedition* (Dallas: Southern Methodist University Press, 2002), 353.

8. Document 28, fol. 130v.

9. Document 28, fols. 95r–125r.

10. Clinton P. Anderson, "Foreword," in *The Entrada of Coronado: A Spectacular Historic Drama,* by Thomas Wood Stevens (Albuquerque: Coronado Cuarto Centennial Commission, 1940), n.p.

11. Ibid.

12. Anonymous, "The Coronado Entrada Will Be Presented," in *The Coronado Magazine, The Official Program of the Coronado Cuarto Centennial in New Mexico* (Albuquerque: Coronado Cuarto Centennial Commission, 1940).

13. Stevens, *Entrada,* 122.

14. Ibid., 132.

15. A. Grove Day, *Coronado's Quest: The Discovery of the Southwestern States* (Berkeley: University of California Press, 1940), xvi.

16. Anonymous, "Publications of the Coronado Cuarto Centennial Commission," in Stevens, *Entrada,* 134–35.

17. Two other particularly influential publications from the 1930s and 1940s dealing with the Coronado expedition are A. Grove Day's *Coronado's Quest* and Paul A. Jones's *Coronado and Quivira* (Lyons, KS: Lyons Publishing Company, 1937).

18. For the sixteenth-century *entradas* into the American Southwest that followed the Coronado expedition, see George P. Hammond and Agapito Rey, *The Rediscovery of New Mexico* (Albuquerque: University of New Mexico Press, 1963). For the establishment of a "permanent" Spanish colony in New Mexico, see Hammond and Rey, *Don Juan de Oñate: Colonizer of New Mexico, 1595–1628,* 2 vols. (Albuquerque: University of New Mexico Press, 1953). For the first half of the seventeenth century in New Mexico, see Frederick W. Hodge, George Hammond, and Agapito Rey, *The Revised Memorial of Fray Alonso de Benavides, 1634* (Albuquerque: University of New Mexico Press, 1945). For the Pueblo Revolt of 1680, see Charles W. Hackett and Charmion C. Shelby, *Revolt of the Pueblo Indians of New Mexico and Otermín's Attempted Reconquest, 1680–1682,* 2 vols. (Albuquerque: University of New Mexico Press, 1942). For the reconquest of New Mexico, see J. Manuel Espinosa, *The First Expedition of Vargas into New Mexico, 1692* (Albuquerque: University of New Mexico Press, 1940).

19. A partial reprint of the Winship translations has been published by Dover Publications under the title *The Journey of Coronado,* and recently the Lakeside Classics Series has republished Winship's transcript of the *relación* by Pedro de Castañeda de Nájera in a single volume along with Hammond and Rey's translation of the same document. Pedro de Castañeda et al., *The Journey of Coronado,* trans. and ed. George Parker Winship (San Francisco: Grabhorn Press, 1933; reprint, New York: Dover, 1990); Pedro de Castañeda de Nájera, *Narrative of the Coronado Expedition,* ed. John Miller Morris (Chicago: R. R. Donnelley and Sons, 2002).

20. *CDI.*

21. Winship, 236.

22. Compare Document 28, fol. 82v: "protected by helmets and round shields."

23. Document 28, fol. 80r.

24. H&R, 236–37.

25. Bolton, 252.

26. Harry C. Myers, "The Mystery of Coronado's Route from the Pecos River to the Llano Estacado," in *The Coronado Expedition from the Distance of 460 Years,* eds. Richard Flint and Shirley Cushing Flint (Albuquerque: University of New Mexico Press, 2003), 140–50; Richard Flint, "Reconciling the Calendars of the Coronado Expedition: Tiguex to the Second Barranca," in Flint and Flint, *From the Distance of 460 Years,* 151–63.

27. Winship, 373.

28. Document 30, fol. 1v.

29. Bolton, 108–9. For an alternative reconstruction that better fits Jaramillo's description, see Document 30, note 60.

30. H&R, 91.

31. See the introduction to Document 12, and also Document 12, note 30. Nor did Arthur Aiton point out this relationship in his 1939 transcription of the muster roll. Arthur Scott Aiton, "Muster Roll," *American Historical Review* 64, no. 3 (1939):556–70.

32. Flint, *Great Cruelties.*

33. The 14 documents are numbers 7, 8, 10, 11, 13, 18, 20, 21, 25, 27, 31, 32, 33, and 34.

34. The *probanzas de méritos y servicios* (proofs of worthiness and service) published in this volume are Documents 31–33.

35. AGI, Justicia, 339, N.1, R.1, "Residencia que el licenciado Lorenzo de Tejada, oidor de la Audiencia Real de Nueva España, tomo a Francisco Vázquez de Coronado, Guadalajara, December 1544 and January 1545"; AGI, Justicia, 336, N.1, R.3, "Testimony concerning certain pueblos, Compostela, spring 1552."

36. AGI, Justicia, 1021, N.2, Pieza 1, "Acusación e información contra García Ramírez de Cárdenas, Madrid, 1546–1547."

37. W. Michael Mathes, "New Research in Mexico regarding Francisco Vázquez de Coronado," paper presented at the conference "Contemporary Vantage on the Coronado Expedition through Documents and Artifacts," Las Vegas, NM, April 15, 2000.

38. See, for example, the sections on "Archival Material" in the bibliographies of this volume and Flint, *Great Cruelties,* 607–11.

39. Herbert Bolton published a list of such documents in 1949. The fate and present location of most of them remain unknown. Bolton, 472–75. Document 10 is one of the few from Bolton's list that has subsequently been located.

40. H&R, 117–55.

41. See the section "Dates and Distances" later in this introduction for the suggestion that, without mentioning it, the copyist of Castañeda de Nájera's *relación* modernized dates throughout that manuscript. See also Flint, "Reconciling the Calendars."

42. For a detailed discussion of the various "standard" leagues in use in the Spanish world, see Roland Chardon, "The Linear League in North America," *Annals of the Association of American Geographers* 70, no. 2 (1980):129–53.

43. Document 28, fol. 23r; Document 5, fol. 406v.

44. "In the case of the bilabial fricative /b/, there was a further weakening of pronunciation so that by the fourteenth century, the bilabial had become in essence a semivowel. . . . *cibdad* [was] usually . . . *ciudad*" [emphasis added]. Paul M. Lloyd, *From Latin to Spanish*, vol. 1, *Historical Phonology and Morphology of the Spanish Language*, Memoirs of the American Philosophical Society, vol. 173 (Philadelphia: American Philosophical Society, 1987), 347.

45. This example, the first of numerous instances in the documents of this volume, comes from Document 1, fol. 1v.

46. This example is from Document 16, fol. 1r.

47. Rafael Lapesa, *Historia de la lengua española*, 9th ed. (Madrid: Editorial Gredos, 1981), 392: "También las formas *porné, verné, terné* sucumbieron, tras un período de alternancia que duró hasta fines del siglo XVI, ante *pondré, vendré, tendré* [emphasis added]." The example is from Document 6, fol. 1r.

48. Descending directly from its Latin root, the third-person singular preterit form of the verb *ver* in medieval Castilian was *vido*, which, with the disappearance of the intervocalic *d*, was gradually replaced by *vio*. That shift was still in progress in the sixteenth century. Lloyd, *Latin to Spanish*, 306–7.

Document 1. Letter of Vázquez de Coronado to the King, December 15, 1538

1. AGS, Camara de Castilla, 121–46, "Petition of Juan Vázquez de Coronado, Granada, December 5, 1516"; Arthur Scott Aiton, *Antonio de Mendoza: First Viceroy of New Spain* (Durham, NC: Duke University Press, 1927), 9.

2. *CDI*, 2:198–99.

3. AGI, Justicia, 127, N.2, "Investigation of treatment of Indians at Sultepec, February and March 1537."

4. Vázquez de Coronado is referred to as married (*ser casado*) in late 1536. This is quite likely, because in 1538 he and Beatriz already had two children. Silvio A. Zavala, *La encomienda indiana*, 2nd ed. (México, DF: Editorial Porrúa, 1973), 397; *Actas de Cabildo*, compiled by Ignacio Bejarano, 64 vols. (México, DF: Aguilar e Hijos, 1889–), 4:130.

5. A *comendador* was the administrator of an area under the control of one of Spain's religious-military orders. In this case, Juan Vázquez de Coronado was a *caballero* of the Order of San Juan. AHN, Órdenes Militares, 304, Expillo. 13408, "Order of San Juan to Juan Vázquez de Coronado," n.p., n.d.

6. AGI, Justicia, 259, Pieza 4, "Certification of suit concerning Tlapa, Mexico City."

7. *Actas de Cabildo*, 4:130–33; Bolton, 405; *Actas de Cabildo*, 5:152.

8. Fol. 1r; Bolton, 21.

9. Document 6, fol. 2r.

10. Arthur S. Aiton, "Coronado's First Report on the Government of New Galicia," *Hispanic American Historical Review* 19, no. 3 (1939):307.

11. Fol. 1r; Tello, 299–302.

12. Fol. 1r.

13. Ibid.

14. Fols. 1v–2v.

15. Fols. 2v–3r.

16. Two other documents in this edition also bear Vázquez de Coronado's signature, Documents 3 and 26. Document 3 was written in March 1539, and its text is in a hand that is decidedly different from the one used here. Document 26, written in October 1541, is in a hand closely related to, but not identical with, the one of this letter. The overall impression is that the three letters were drafted by three different *escribanos*, two of whom (those of Documents 1 and 26) might have been related to each other as teacher and pupil or employer and employee. There are many similarities between these two (especially in weight of line and size and uprightness of letters), even though the shaping of individual letters is often different. Presumably, though not positively, one of the preparers of these three letters was Hernando Martín Bermejo.

17. *Pasajeros*, 2: no. 2201.

18. See Document 12.

19. AGI, Patronato, 64, R.1, "Méritos y servicios, Juan de Aguilar, Santiago de Guatemala, December 7, 1564."

20. Fol. 1v. See also note 69, this document.

21. Fols. 1r–4r.

22. See notes 41, 44, 45, 51, 55, 57, and 60, this document.

23. Aiton, "Coronado's First Report," 306–13; H&R, 35–41.

24. For geographical information, see the entry for Nueva Galicia in Appendix 2.

25. For biographical information, see the entry for Diego Pérez de la Torre in Appendix 1.

26. For geographical information, see the entry for Ciudad de México in Appendix 2.

27. For geographical information, see the entry for Guadalajara in Appendix 2.

28. For geographical information, see the entries for San Miguel and Culiacán in Appendix 2.

29. For geographical information, see the entry for Compostela in Appendix 2.

30. For information about Ayapín, see the introduction to Document 3. In July 1539 Vázquez de Coronado reported that he had apprehended and executed Ayapín. Document 3, fol. 2r.

31. H&R, 36, interpret this sentence differently: "the residents of the town of San Miguel and the Indians living there peacefully are suffering great hardships."

32. Neither petition nor report is preserved with the letter in the Archivo General de Indias. However, the text of a similar petition made by *vecinos* of Guadalajara in December 1539 is transcribed in Tello, 322–24.

33. In March 1539 Vázquez de Coronado referred to this report as having already been dispatched to the king. The report itself has not been located. See Document 3, fol. 1r.

34. H&R, 36, incorrectly put this in the past tense: "I found it."

35. For biographical information, see the entry for Nuño Beltrán de Guzmán in Appendix 1.

36. This statement does not accord with Peter Bakewell's assertion that "some relief came in 1543 with the first mining strikes in the region. Gold was found at Xaltepec and silver at Espíritu Santo, both near Compostela on the western margin of New Galicia." Peter J. Bakewell, *Silver Mining and Society in Colonial Mexico: Zacatecas, 1546–1700* (Cambridge: Cambridge University Press, 1971), 6. Writing in the seventeenth century, fray Antonio Tello reported the early Spanish settlers and *encomenderos* of Nueva Galicia as being engaged only in agricultural pursuits, but because the land was poor, many left to go to Peru. Tello, 228. On the other hand, a mutilated sixteenth-century document written in Nahuatl refers to placer gold sources at Culiacán and Huichichila, seemingly at a time before 1540. These were evidently worked by gangs of Indians sent out by their *encomenderos*. Frequent mention is made of Domingo de Arteaga, who was an *encomendero* in the Tepíc area by 1548. Thomas Calvo et al., *Xalisco, la voz de un pueblo en el siglo XVI* (México, DF: Centro de Investigaciones y Estudios Superiores en Antropología Social and Centro de Estudios Mexicanos y Centroamericanos, 1993), 83–84; Peter Gerhard, *The North Frontier of New Spain*, rev. ed. (Norman: University of Oklahoma Press, 1993), 141, 144. In addition, Vázquez de Coronado himself indicates that the first sources of gold had been located in Nueva Galicia in 1536 or thereabouts (fol. 1v).

37. As provided in the *Siete Partidas*, the great medieval compilation of Castilian law: "There are three kinds of slaves. The first is those taken in war who are enemies of the faith." This notion was not formally rescinded with respect to Indians until issuance of the New Laws of the Indies in 1543, which proclaimed that no Indian could be enslaved by means of war. *Siete Partidas*, 4:977; *Leyes y ordenanças nuevamente hechas por Su Magestad para la governación de las Indias*, in *The New Laws of the Indies for the Good Treatment and Preservation of the Indians*, trans. and eds. Henry Stevens and Fred W. Lucas (London: Chiswick Press, 1893; reprint, Amsterdam: N. Isreal, 1968), fol. 6r. Nueva Galicia had been the scene of massive enslavement of thousands of native people during Nuño de Guzmán's tenure as governor. Perhaps the most lurid (but in the main accurate) account of his slaving activities is provided in Bartolomé de las Casas, *The Devastation of the Indies: A Brief Account*, trans. Herma Briffault (Baltimore, MD: Johns Hopkins University Press, 1992), 77.

38. The location of these mines in the general vicinity of Compostela is unknown, but naming mines after advocations of the Virgin Mary was common. For instance, by 1545 there were at least two in the Culiacán area, Nuestra Señora de la Esperanza and Nuestra Señora de los Remedios. Flint, *Great Cruelties*, 348, 360.

39. In 1537 Vázquez de Coronado had been sent to inspect conditions at another mine, at Sultepec. In that case he had lodged formal complaints against the mine owners. AGI, Justicia, 127, N.2, "Treatment of Indians at Sultepec."

40. Four years later a similar provision was included in the New Laws of the Indies. *Leyes y ordenanças*, fol. 6r.

41. This complimentary comment was probably written by an official in the Consejo de Indias. Such marginal comments are common and often served to formulate actions to be taken or replies to be made by the Consejo.

42. H&R, 38, unnecessarily restrict the meaning of *usar* and render it "heed."

43. At the time he received this charge, *licenciado* Pedraza was cantor in the Ciudad de México. In 1539 he was named bishop of Honduras and *protector* of the Indians. Ernesto Schäfer, *El Consejo Real y Supremo de las Indias: Su historia, organización y labor administrativa hasta la terminación de la Casa de Austria*, 2 vols. (Sevilla: Universidad de Sevilla, 1935), 2:578; Ralph H. Vigil, *Alonso de Zorita: Royal Judge and Christian Humanist, 1512–1585* (Norman: University of Oklahoma Press, 1987), 121. A *protector* was an official with responsibility for protecting the rights and interests of a community. It was often an abbreviation for the title *protector de indios*, the purview of which was indigenous rights and welfare. *DRAE*, 1681.

44. This is another note written by the Consejo official, presumably to be incorporated into a letter to the viceroy. H&R, 38, expand the sense of the word *jncha* and have "so he may assign the tribute with the governor." "Send it to him blank" was said of a document that was already signed but in which blanks were supposed to be filled in (*DRAE*, 297). Evidently the document referred to is the decree ordering the assessment of tribute.

45. The official of the Consejo again approves Vázquez de Coronado's work.

46. This represents a decision of the Consejo, but exactly what is meant is unclear.

47. This is the modern location of Compostela. The move took place in 1540. Gerhard, *North Frontier*, 142.

48. H&R, 40, interpret this as "on their *encomiendas*." At this time *encomenderos* were required to live among the Indians with whom they had been entrusted. Lesley Byrd Simpson, *The Encomienda in New Spain: The Beginning of Spanish Mexico*, rev. ed. (Berkeley: University of California Press, 1982), 115.

49. Aiton, "Coronado's First Report," 312, erroneously transcribed this as "bien." H&R, 39, accepted his reading without consulting the original document and translated this as "good."

50. Those councilmen were Diego Proaño, Santiago de Aguirre, Juan de Zaldívar, and Toribio de Bolaños. Tello, 303.

51. This is again a statement of approval from the Consejo official.

52. The treasurer in Compostela was Luis Salido, followed by Pedro Gómez de Contreras. Tello, 505. Pedro Gómez de Contreras, from Pedroche, Córdoba, was in the Ciudad de México by 1530. He was one of the founders of Compostela in 1531. He had become treasurer in the Ciudad de México by 1549. Boyd-Bowman, 2: no. 4153. Francisco de Godoy was treasurer in Compostela in 1544. AGI, Justicia, 339, N.1, R.2, "Residencia of Francisco Vázquez de Coronado, August 1544," fol. 29r.

53. Aiton, "Coronado's First Report," 313, has "senia," without expanding this common abbreviation. Juan Carlos Galende, *Diccionario General de Abreviaturas Españolas* (Madrid: Editorial Verbum, 1997), 226. H&R, 40, have "sentence" and imply that this is an imposition of penalty against Nuño de Guzmán. Instead, it is more likely de la Torre's conclusions after auditing the treasury accounts.

54. It is clear from subsequent passages that Vázquez de Coronado is removing documents from the treasurer's possession, since the treasurer asked that copies be made and given to him. H&R, 40, mistakenly translated this very differently: "by instructions and decrees of your Majesty, and he audited his accounts."

55. The official of the Consejo again approves Vázquez de Coronado's work. H&R, 40, interpolate two additional words, which result in "Let him examine them."

56. The port is Veracruz, which at the time was the only authorized port of entry in Nueva España for goods from Europe.

57. The Consejo official agrees that a salary needs to be provided.

58. The second copy of the document uses Roman numerals for the date, despite the fact that both copies were written by the same scribe. At the time it was not unusual to shift back and forth between Roman and Arabic numerals, with Arabic numerals becoming increasingly common.

59. This copy of the document is signed by Vázquez de Coronado, as is the second copy.

60. These are the final notes of the Consejo officials. "Respondida" is written by a hand not otherwise seen in the document.

61. Copy 2 has "que ha sido."

62. The *ll* is supplied from copy 2, which has "aquella Villa."

63. Necesidad. *DRAE*, 1431: "especial riesgo o peligro que se padece, y que se necesita pronto auxilio."

64. Andar = *haber*. *DRAE*, 138.

65. Traer. *DRAE*, 2004: "tener a uno en el estado o situación que expresa el adjetivo que se junta con el verbo."

66. Poder. *DRAE*, 1629: "tener expeditas la facultad o potencia de hacer una cosa."

67. Desocuparse. *DRAE*, 722: "desembarazarse de un negocio."

68. Copy 2 omits "aqui."

69. Copy 2 has "de paçificos." This may indicate an effort to euphemize the enterprise of subjugation that eventually culminated in exclusion of the word *conquistar* and its derivatives from official documents altogether, as ordered by the 1573 Ordenanzas sobre Descubrimientos. John H. Parry and Robert G. Keith, eds., *New Iberian World*, vol. 1, *The Conquerors and the Conquered* (New York: Times Books, 1984), 1:368.

70. *Vecinos* is clearly the correct word in this situation and is supplied from copy 2.

71. Copy 2 omits "toda."

72. "De ello" is omitted in copy 2.

73. Copy 2 has "cargados con mercaderias."

74. Copy 2 has "nadie."

75. Jncha = *hincha*.

76. "En esta" is supplied from copy 2.

77. "Su" is probably in error. The *escribano* employs both the second- and third-person plural to refer to the king.

78. Digan. The present subjunctive is evidently a scribal error for "dicen," since there is no need of the subjunctive here.

79. The scribe made many errors of tense and mood at the end of fol. 1v and the beginning of fol. 2v. In this case, what was intended was probably "mas . . . que deben dar y pueden dar," or "more than they should pay and are able to pay."

80. "Trabajare" is omitted from copy 2.

81. Copy 2 has "E dicho a."

82. En mas comarca, in greater proximity. *En comarca, DRAE*, 514: "cerca."

83. Rreçiben = *reciban*, because the subjunctive is necessary here.

84. Copy 2 omits "en ella."

85. Copy 2 has instead "cuenta a los oficiales que tienen cargo de la rreal hazienda de VM en esta provincia." This represents principally a rearrangement of word order.

86. Alcance. *DRAE*, 87: "en materia de cuentas, saldo que, según ellas, está debiendose."

87. "Muy" is supplied from copy 2.

88. "Y prospere" is omitted in copy 2.

Document 2. Letter of Vázquez de Coronado to Viceroy Mendoza, March 8, 1539

1. See *Actas de Cabildo*, 4:130–33; Document 5; Tello, 303.

2. See Document 6, fol. 1r; AGI, Patronato, 184, R.27, "Antonio de Mendoza, Letter to the King, Mexico City, Dec. 10, 1537," fol. 14v.

3. Fol. 354v.

4. Fol. 355r.

5. Documents 4, 15, and 19.

6. Bernardo Blanco-González, "Introducción, biográfica y crítica," in Diego Hurtado de Mendoza, *Guerra de Granada* (Madrid: Editorial Castalia, 1970), 27.

7. For biographical information about Oviedo, see the introduction to Document 7. The peak period of Oviedo's collecting of documents for preparation of his massive *Historia general y natural de las Indias* was the late 1530s and early 1540s. He finished writing the *Historia* in 1549. Juan Pérez de Tudela Bueso, "Vida y escritos de Gonzalo Fernández de Oviedo," in PTBOviedo, 1:cxviii, cxl.

8. Antonello Gerbi, *Nature in the New World: From Christopher Columbus to Gonzalo Fernández de Oviedo*, trans. Jeremy Moyle (Pittsburgh: University of Pittsburgh Press, 1985), 169, 172.

9. See the introduction to Document 15.

10. See also the introduction to Document 6.

11. Richard Hakluyt, ed. and trans., *The Principal Navigations, Traffiques, and Discoveries of the English Nation Made by Sea or Over-land to the Remote and Farthest Distant Quarters of the Earth at any Time within the Compasse of these 1600 Yeeres*, 12 vols. (Glasgow: James MacLehose and Sons, 1903–4), 9:116–18.

12. Fol. 354v.

13. See Document 6.

14. Hakluyt, *Principal Navigations*, 9:118–20.

15. Henri Ternaux-Compans, trans. and ed., "Vázquez de Coronado to Mendoza," in *Voyages, relations et memoires originaux pour servir a l'histoire de la decouverte de l'Amerique* (Paris: A. Bertrand, 1838), 9:352–54.

16. H&R, 42–44.

17. Ramusio's use of the term *naviga(t)zione* (sea voyage), with its clear implication of sailing, rather than *viaggio*, or trip, suggests confusion on his part about how Vázquez de Coronado and fray Marcos were traveling and where places such as Topira were located relative to the coast.

18. For biographical information on Viceroy Mendoza and fray Marcos de Niza, see Appendix 1. For geographical information on Topira, Compostela, Nueva Galicia, San Miguel de Culiacán, Petatlán, see Appendix 2.

19. Reference here is to the fuses, or "matches," necessary for discharging matchlock arquebuses, which were the gunpowder firearms of the day. Later, the Coronado expedition carried at least 26 such weapons. See Document 12.

20. Vázquez de Coronado's uncertainty here suggests that he has written at least one previous letter to the viceroy during his months in Nueva Galicia. No such letter has been located. H&R, 42, gratuitously add "or whether I have made any report."

21. This is a marginal note inserted by Ramusio or his translator.

22. What is being described here may be Paquimé, the great late prehistoric urban area in what is now northern Chihuahua (see map 1). It lies not far beyond the hundred-league distance from Topira/Topia, to which Vázquez de Coronado later refers. Archaeological excavation has revealed the presence of significant quantities of bison/cattle remains at Paquimé throughout its existence, and bison meat may have contributed a major share of the animal protein consumed there. Although it had collapsed as a polity and settlement nearly 150 years before the Coronado expedition, Paquimé might well have survived in memory as "another, larger provincia." Charles C. Di Peso, John B. Rinaldo, and Gloria J. Fenner, *Casas Grandes: A Fallen Trading Center of the Gran Chichimeca*, 8 vols. (Dragoon, AZ: Amerind Foundation, 1974), 8:245.

23. If, as appears to be the case, all of the footmen in this force were armed with crossbows and arquebuses, they would have been much better armed than the members of the subsequent expedition to Cíbola, who carried only 26 known arquebuses and 19 crossbows. Document 12.

24. This confirms that hogs such as those Juan Bermejo certified that he had purchased for Vázquez de Coronado were successfully herded at least as far as Culiacán. See Document 11, fol. 43r.

25. Marcos's own written report gives his starting date as March 7, rather than February 7. Document 6, fol. 2r.

26. For biographical information, see the entry for Esteban in Appendix 1.

27. H&R, 43, grossly mishandle this idiomatic expression, giving "they carried the padre on the palms of their hands." R. C. Melzi, *Langenscheidt's Standard Italian Dictionary* (Berlin: Langenscheidt, 1990), 240.

28. Neither of these letters is known to have survived.

29. This letter has disappeared.

30. H&R, 44, misinterpret this clause, giving "he must have traveled two thousand leagues."

31. This word derives from the Nahuatl *axin*, which fray Alonso de Molina defined in the sixteenth century as "a particular native unguent [pungent paste]." It is now usually spelled *aji* in Spanish and still applies to the chile, the spicy pepper native to the Americas. Alonso de Molina, *Vocabulario en lengua mexicana y castellana* (México, DF: Antonio de Spinosa, 1571; reprint, Madrid: Ediciones de Cultura Hispánica, 2001), fol. 10r (folio citation is to the reprint edition).

32. "A dosso" may be the translator's attempt to render *encima*, "in addition."

33. "Fare frutto" is the Italian rendition of the Spanish *hacer fruto*, "to derive profit." Covarrubias, 561–62.

Document 3. Letter of Vázquez de Coronado to the King, July 15, 1539

1. Fol. 2v.

2. For more detail, see note 10, this document.

3. Gerhard, *North Frontier*, 257.

4. In 1544 Vázquez de Coronado referred to these events during his formal

defense against charges of abuse committed against Indians at Chiametla. See Flint, *Great Cruelties*, 466–67.

5. For a discussion of the identities of the preparers of this group of documents, see Document 1, note 16.

6. H&R, 45–49.

7. "Nueva Galicia" is written in a more modern hand and may represent an archival label. It is in the same hand as the similar label on Document 1. At least ten different hands are represented by brief notes entered on the letter, primarily on the cover, indicative of the routing and filing of the message, as well as comments of Consejo de Indias staff. "Francisco Vázquez Coronado" is written in a sixteenth-century hand, but not that of Hernando Bermejo. "Audiencia" is in yet a third hand that is not Bermejo's.

8. For additional information about Ayapín, see the introduction to this document.

9. H&R, 45, misinterpret this passage with "the trip would redound to the service of your Majesty."

10. As early as 1536 the Indians of the *provincia* of Culiacán had risen up in arms against Spanish slaving activities attributed primarily to Diego Hernández de Proaño and Pedro de Bobadilla. Despite the efforts of the successor to these two at Culiacán, Cristóbal de Tapia, to restore peace between Spaniards and Indians, few Indians consented to work in Spanish enterprises. In addition, the Indians of the *provincia* suffered catastrophic mortality during this period caused by newly introduced Old World diseases. The native peoples of the region may have suffered a death rate of greater than 80 percent during this period. As a result, two-thirds of the *provincia*'s European settlers abandoned it. A renewal of conflict in the *provincia* had begun at about the time of Vázquez de Coronado's arrival in Nueva Galicia as governor. Tello, 249–51; Flint, *Great Cruelties*, 466.

11. H&R, 46, reverse the roles of actor and object with "through interpreters whom they understood well."

12. H&R, 46, give this a very different twist: "this execution completed the task of stabilizing and pacifying all that land."

13. For biographical information about fray Marcos, see the introduction to Document 6.

14. "Directed me," *me encomendo*. H&R, 46, have "recommended that I." *Encomendar, DRAE*, 825: "encargar a uno que haga alguna cosa." Certainly "recommend" is too timid a translation.

15. For geographical information, see the entry for Petatlán in Appendix 2.

16. Viceroy Mendoza, in reporting this success, wrote that more than 400 Indians came from the Petatlán region. Document 4, fol. 355v.

17. Mendoza's purchase of Esteban from Andrés Dorantes is confirmed in AGI, Patronato, 184, R.27, "Letter to the King," fol. 14v. Herbert Bolton wrote ambiguously that Mendoza "acquired the Negro Stephen." Bolton, 19.

18. "I pray to God." *Plegar* is related to *plegaría*, prayer or supplication. *Simon and Schuster's International Dictionary, English/Spanish, Spanish/English*, edited by Tana de Gámez (New York: MacMillan, 1973), 1430. Boyd-Bowman provides this similar example: "plega a Nuestro Señor." Peter Boyd-Bowman, *Lexico hispanoamericano del siglo XVI* (London: Tamesis Books, 1971), 708. *Pregar = suplicar*, Martín Alonso, *Enciclopedia del idioma*, 3 vols. (Madrid: Aguilar, 1958), 3:3379. H&R, 47, misconstrue this as "the Lord willed."

19. Although it has been traditional to read this sentence as implying that Marcos was in Compostela by the time this letter was written (July 15, 1539), the friar's sending of interim messages means that this may well not have been the case. Marcos may not have reached Compostela until a week or so after Vázquez de Coronado dispatched his letter to the king. Bolton, 38; William K. Hartmann and Richard Flint, "Before the Coronado Expedition: Who Knew What and When Did They Know It?" in Flint and Flint, *From the Distance of 460 Years*, 31.

20. "The excellent method" referred to is that the reconnaissance is being performed by unarmed friars. See the introduction to Document 4.

21. This comment about spotty Christianization of Indians repeats Vázquez de Coronado's findings at the mines of Nuestra Señora de la Concepción, reported to the king in December 1538. See Document 1, fol. 2r.

22. For Spaniards of the day, masonry architecture was one of the hallmarks of civilization, which was one of the reasons that later reports of stone buildings at Cíbola so fired the imaginations of residents of Nueva España with visions of sophisticated and affluent people. An excerpt from the royal *cédula* referred to here is transcribed in Tello, 321–22.

23. The first administrative body created for the New World, on January 20,

1503, was designed to warehouse goods going to and coming from the Indies. Its location was the Room of the Admirals in the Alcázares Reales in Sevilla, where it remained until 1717, when it was moved to Cádiz. Four officials (a *factor*, a treasurer, and two *contadores*) were assigned to the Casa de la Contratación and were to be knowledgeable about merchandise, commerce, shipping, and navigation. Additionally, this body handed down rules for handling gold from the Indies, mining, and the treatment of Indians, and it dispensed licenses to travel to the New World. See also Appendix 1, Consejo Real de Indias. Carmen Galbis Díez, "La Casa de la Contratación," in *Archivo General de Indias*, ed. Pedro González García (Madrid: Lunwerg Editores y Ministerio de Educación y Cultura, 1995), 131–68.

24. Just such an accounting later resulted in the copying of the records dealing with the estate of expedition member Juan Jiménez, which are published in this volume as Document 27. Both records of indebtedness and public auction of the goods of the deceased were typical of Spanish testamentary procedures in the sixteenth century and for centuries before and after. See Partida 6 in *Siete Partidas*, 5:1175–1302, and Della M. Flusche, "The Tribunal of Posthumous Estates in Colonial Chile, 1540–1769," *Colonial Latin American Historical Review* 9 (2000), 1:1–66, 2:243–98, 3:379–428, 4:509–44. H&R, 48, gratuitously insert "or," rendering this phrase "were sold at public auctions or on credit."

25. This closing is written in Vázquez de Coronado's hand and bears his signature, although the body of the letter is in an *escribano*'s hand. See the introduction to this document.

26. "Nueva Galicia" is written in a more modern hand, different from the others on the document.

27. The notes "Answered" and "To His Majesty from Francisco Vázquez de Coronado, 15 July 1539" are in the same sixteenth-century hand, distinct from others appearing on this document. It is the same hand responsible for the similar notation on Document 1.

28. As with the corresponding report from Vázquez de Coronado in 1538 (Document 1), the notes "Reviewed" and "thank him for the attention he is paying to it," from an unidentified official of the Consejo de Indias, express full approval of the governor's activities. They are in the same hand as marginalia on Document 1.

29. Hobo = *hubo*.

30. Meter. *DRAE*, 1365: "poner o colocar en un lugar una persona."

31. Esperar. *DRAE*, 894: "creer que ha de suceder alguna cosa, especialmente si es favorable."

32. The absence of the personal "a" before "los naturales" here and in other places throughout the documents may indicate an attitude that the Indians were not "persons" deserving of that standard grammatical construction.

33. Andar = *obrar*. *DRAE*, 138.

34. Doctrina = *teaching*. *DRAE*, 770.

35. Por bien = *bien a bien* = *de buen grado* = voluntarily. *DRAE*, 289, 290, 1051.

36. Posibilidades. *DRAE*, 1646, "medios disponibles."

Document 4. Letter of the Viceroy to the King, 1539

1. Fray Marcos's official report is published here as Document 6.

2. Bartolomé de las Casas, *Del Único modo de atraer a todos los pueblos a la verdadera religión* (México, DF: Fondo de Cultura Económica, 1942).

3. AGI, México, 1088, L.3, "Royal *cédula*, Valladolid, Nov. 22, 1538," fols. 1r–1v.

4. Lewis Hanke, *The Spanish Struggle for Justice in the Conquest of America* (Boston: Little, Brown, 1965), 77–81, 95.

5. Fol. 355r.

6. Fol. 355v.

7. Ibid.

8. The five ecclesiastics were fray Marcos de Niza, fray Juan de Padilla, fray Antonio de Castilblanco, fray Daniel, and fray Luis de Úbeda. An incorrect reading of the seventeenth-century cleric Antonio Tello has led to the inclusion of an additional name among those friars who participated in the expedition, Juan de la Cruz. None of the contemporary documents mention any such person, and Tello specifically states that fray Juan de Padilla left a fray Juan de la Cruz at Tuchpan when he, Padilla, departed for Cíbola. In 1968 Angélico Chávez made a confused and unconvincing argument for fray Juan's presence on the expedition. Chávez's fanciful reconstruction rested entirely on a misreading of the statement of Tello. Tello, 406;

fray Angélico Chávez, *Coronado's Friars* (Washington, DC: Academy of American Franciscan History, 1968), 32–36.

9. For a full discussion of these charges and the subsequent formal investigation of the expedition's treatment of Native Americans, see Flint, *Great Cruelties*.

10. Giovanni Battista Ramusio, *Terzo volume delle navigationi et viaggi* (Venice: La Stamperia de Giunti, 1556), fols. 355r–355v.

11. For a fuller discussion of the reliability of Ramusio's translations, see the introduction to Document 2.

12. Hakluyt, *Principal Navigations*, 9:121–24; Henri Ternaux-Compans, trans. and ed., "Mendoza to Carlos V [by the last ships]," in *Voyages, relations et memoires*, 9:285–90.

13. H&R, 50–53.

14. For biographical information about Antonio de Mendoza and fray Marcos, see Appendix 1. For geographical information on San Miguel de Culiacán, see Appendix 2.

15. Reference here is to Carlos I (Emperor Carlos V) and his mother, Juana, who from 1506 until her death in 1555 served as Queen Proprietress of Castile, a monarch in name alone. John H. Elliott, *Imperial Spain, 1469–1716* (London: Penguin, 1990), 139.

16. This is almost certainly a misreading of the surname in the original document. The man mentioned is probably Miguel de Hoznayo, an *hidalgo* from Guadalajara in Spain who had arrived in Nueva España in the viceroy's entourage in 1535. He was apparently a companion and neighbor of the Coronado expeditionary Gaspar de Saldaña; the two applied for licenses to travel to the New World on the same day and appear adjacent to each other in the register. Mendoza may have sent Hoznayo back to Spain as a courier with messages. Hakluyt jumped to the conclusion that "Usnago" was admiral of the fleet. Boyd-Bowman, 2: no. 4650; *Pasajeros*, 2: no. 1263; Hakluyt, *Principal Navigations*, 9:121.

17. These two ecclesiastics were fray Marcos de Niza and fray Onorato. See Document 6, fol. 2r.

18. H&R, 50, mistranslate this as "across the mountains."

19. This is probably not an exaggeration. It is an indication of how common it was for Spanish-led expeditions of the day to be composed in large measure of native warriors from relatively recently conquered areas. For a fuller discussion, see the introduction to Document 13. See the entry on Nuño Beltrán de Guzmán in Appendix 1 for biographical information.

20. The death of many of the allies participating in the *entrada* of Nuño de Guzmán during the first years of the 1530s is confirmed in García del Pilar, "Circa 1532: García del Pilar on the Expedition of Nuño de Guzman to Michoacan and New Galicia," in Parry and Keith, *Central America and Mexico*, vol. 3, 554.

21. For geographical information, see the entry for Nueva Galicia in Appendix 2.

22. The little fleet was under the overall command of Diego Hurtado de Mendoza, a cousin of Hernán Cortés's. It was composed of the *San Miguel* and *San Marcos* and departed from Acapulco at the end of June 1532. Cortés ignored this voyage in his 1540 recital of those he had sent into the Gulf of California. Francisco López de Gómara, *Cortés: The Life of the Conqueror by His Secretary*, trans. and ed. Lesley Byrd Simpson (Berkeley: University of California Press, 1964), 397. See Document 18, fol. 4r. For brief biographical information about Hernán Cortés, see the introduction to Document 18.

23. The pilot in question was Fortún Jiménez and the captain was Diego Becerra. Many details of this mutinous voyage of 1533 are provided in López de Gómara, *Cortés*, 398. Tello, 161, gives the place of origin of both men. Jiménez was a *vizcaino* and Diego Becerra de Mendoza was from Mérida. Their ship was *La Concepción*. The other ship was the *San Lázaro*, with Hernando Grijalva, a native of Cuellar, as captain and Martín de Acosta, a native of Oporto, Portugal, as pilot.

24. At the time of this expedition in 1535, the bishop of Santo Domingo was *licenciado* Sebastián Ramírez de Fuenleal. He had been appointed bishop in February 1527 and was named president of the first Audiencia de México in 1530, a post he held until the arrival of Viceroy Antonio de Mendoza in 1535. Schäfer, *Consejo Real* 2:599.

25. The voyage began from Chiametla during the final days of 1535. The three *navíos* were the *Santa Agueda*, the *San Lázaro*, and the *Santo Tomás*. López de Gómara, *Cortés*, 399.

26. For biographical information, see the entries for Andrés Dorantes and Pánfilo de Narváez in Appendix 1.

27. Fray Antonio de Ciudad Rodrigo was the second provincial of the Fran-

ciscan Province of the Holy Gospel in Nueva España from 1537 until 1540, when he was succeeded by Marcos de Niza. Fray Angélico Chávez, trans. and ed., *The Oroz Codex* (Washington, DC: Academy of American Franciscan History, 1972), 92 n. 112.

28. By way of Compostela, the straight-line map distance from the Ciudad de México to Culiacán is approximately 660 miles. This yields 3.3 miles to the league and suggests that Mendoza was using the *legua común*. The viceroy's origin in strongly moorish Granada, where this longer league was in common use, may explain this. Chardon, "Linear League," 136, 144.

29. These were Indians who had come to Nueva España with Cabeza de Vaca and Dorantes. According to Vázquez de Coronado, they also included Indian slaves made during Guzmán's tenure, who had been freed by the viceroy. See Document 6, fol. 1r, and Document 3, fols. 1v–2r.

30. This is an indication of the sorts of goods included in the trade and gift kit of the subsequent expedition to Tierra Nueva.

31. At least some of that information had come by way of Vázquez de Coronado's letter of March 8, 1539, Document 2. For geographical information, see the entry for Topira in Appendix 2.

32. According to Álvar Núñez Cabeza de Vaca, "through it [Corazones] is the entrance to many provinces that lie toward the South Sea. And if those who should go searching for it do not pass through here, they will perish." This statement and the arrangement referred to here—for Marcos and Vázquez de Coronado to meet at Corazones—make it unlikely that Marcos did not pass through that community, even though he did not mention it by name in his *relación*. Adorno and Pautz, *Núñez Cabeza de Vaca*, 1:234–35. The anonymous author of the "Relación del Suceso" gives the distance instead as 150 leagues. Document 29, fol. 1r. See also the introduction to Document 29. For geographical information, see the entry for Los Corazones in Appendix 2.

33. In other words, Guzmán, Cortés, and Vázquez de Coronado have all been frustrated in their efforts to penetrate the north, whereas fray Marcos's *entrada* seems to be proceeding smoothly. It was common for those of Christian faith of the time to see direct divine intervention in human affairs. Use of the description "mendicant friar" refers to the fact that the Franciscans were founded as a mendicant order, meaning that they had to solicit alms for their support.

34. There is no explicit statement in the written instructions given to fray Marcos requiring him to correspond directly with the king, although Mendoza does state that the friar is to make note of many things "so that His Majesty can be informed about everything." Document 6, fol. 1v.

35. Dette = *diede*.

36. (Di)scontento. As is often the case in Ramusio translations, at this point the translator opts for a slightly corrupted version of a Spanish word (*descontento*), rather than supplying the Italian equivalent (*scontento*).

37. Praticai. This use of "praticai" is almost certainly an instance of the translator's attaching an Italian verb ending to a Spanish verb (*platicar/praticar*) and is evidence of his unfamiliarity with the Italian equivalent (*conversare*).

38. Se(c)greto. Again the translator uses a Spanish word (*secreto*) rather that its Italian cognate (*segreto*).

39. Danari = *denari*.

40. Co(n)- / scien(ti)za. Yet again the translator chooses to Italianize a Spanish word (*conciencia*) rather than use the Italian form (*coscienza*).

41. Daria. Here the translator uses the conditional form of the Spanish verb *dar* and is seemingly unfamiliar with the corresponding Italian *darebbe*.

Document 5. Decree of the King Appointing Vázquez de Coronado Governor of Nueva Galicia, April 18, 1539

1. Donald E. Chipman, *Nuño de Guzmán and the Province of Pánuco in New Spain, 1518–1533* (Glendale, CA: Arthur H. Clark, 1967), 249.

2. Vázquez de Coronado was evidently appointed governor provisionally in August 1538. Bolton, 21. See also Document 1, fol. 1r.

3. Tello, 299–302.

4. Compare, for example, the *cédula* naming Hernán Cortés governor and captain general of Nueva España in 1522. José Luis Martínez, ed., *Documentos Cortesianos*, 4 vols. (México, DF: Universidad Nacional Autónoma de México, 1992), 1:250–53.

5. Juan López, "Reconocimiento y homenaje," in Tello, 111. Also see Alfredo

Corona Ibarra, "Introduction," in *Crónica miscelánea de la sancta provincia de Xalisco, libro segundo*, by fray Antonio Tello, 2 vols. (Guadalajara: Gobierno del Estado de Jalisco and Universidad de Guadalajara, 1968), 1:xvii–xxiv.

6. A *guardián* was the local superior of a group of Franciscan friars. One *guardián* was required for each six friars. *Convento* applies to both male and female communities of religious living under the rules of their orders.

7. José Cornejo Franco, "Introducción," in *Crónica miscelánea de la sancta provincia de Xalisco, libro tercero*, by fray Antonio Tello (Guadalajara: Editorial Font, 1942), xi–xviii.

8. The *convento* at Zacoalco (also spelled Zacualco) was founded in 1550 near the lake of the same name south of Guadalajara and about 15 miles west of Lake Chapala in the modern state of Jalisco, Mexico. Peter Gerhard, *A Guide to the Historical Geography of New Spain*, rev. ed. (Norman: University of Oklahoma Press, 1993), 240–41; López, "Reconocimiento," 115; Cornejo Franco, "Introducción"; Corona Ibarra, "Introduction," xix.

9. Tello's transcript of the entry erroneously states that it is for January 1539. See notes 12 and 13, this document.

10. The Tovar papers were evidently still together during the first half of the eighteenth century when Matías de la Mota y Padilla used them in writing his *Historia de la conquista del reino de la Nueva Galicia*. Presumably Mota y Padilla found these in the collection left by Tello. A. Grove Day, "Mota Padilla on the Coronado Expedition," *Hispanic American Historical Review* 20, no. 1 (1940): 89, 109.

11. Tello.

12. This marginal note, or *postila*, appears to be in Tello's own hand, but it is in error because the document he was copying was evidently also in error. The year was actually 1540. See note 13.

13. The year was actually 1540, which had begun on December 25. The *escribano* of the *cabildo* here makes a mistake equally common among modern check writers and bill payers in the early days of each January. Out of year-long habit, he enters the previous year's number, 1539. His error is demonstrated by the fact that the *cédula* copied into the *cabildo* minutes for this month was not drafted and sent until April 1539. For the beginning date of the Spanish year, see Russell J. Barber and Frances F. Berdan, *The Emperor's Mirror: Understanding Cultures through Primary Sources* (Tucson: University of Arizona Press, 1998), 87.

14. On January 28, 1541, Santiago de Aguirre y de Recalde was granted a coat of arms. He came to Nueva España in 1528 and served with Guzmán in the expedition to Nueva Galicia and later was appointed *alcalde* and *regidor* of the *provincia*. La Sociedad de Bibliófos Españoles, *Nobiliario de conquistadores de Indias* (Madrid: M. Tello, 1892), 301–2.

15. Diego Fernández de Proaño was *encomendero* of Xalpa in Nueva Galicia from about 1540 until perhaps as late as 1570. Gerhard, *North Frontier*, 101. Toribio de Bolaños was said to have led the conquest of the Tequila area of Nueva Galicia in the 1530s. He was a miner in the area of Bolaños in Nueva Galicia after 1541 and was *encomendero* of Tlaltenango in Nueva Galicia from the 1530s until around 1558. Gerhard, *North Frontier*, 71, 146, 149. Juan del Camino was *encomendero* of Tototlán, about 40 miles east of Guadalajara, in the 1530s. Until the 1540s he was also *encomendero* of Ocotique and Huehuetitlán, north of Guadalajara. Gerhard, *North Frontier*, 69, 79, 122. Regarding Pedro de (Plaza) Plasencia, at this point in the document the name is mistakenly written as Plaza, but it is corrected by Tello or the original *escribano* on fol. 407v. A native of Sevilla, Pedro de Plasencia came to Nueva España with Guzmán in 1527 and was with him in Nueva Galicia in 1530. He became both a *vecino* of Guadalajara and the *encomendero* of Contla and Xala in the jurisdiction of Cuquío. Robert Himmerich y Valencia, *The Encomenderos of New Spain, 1521–1555* (Austin: University of Texas Press, 1991), 217; Gerhard, *North Frontier*, 79. In the 1530s Miguel de Ybarra was *encomendero* of Nochistlán, one of the foci of the Mixtón War, during which Ybarra served as a captain. In the late 1520s he had been co-owner of a *caravel* (a three-masted, generally lateen-rigged vessel of about 70 feet) with Lope de Saavedra. Gerhard, *North Frontier*, 101; Baltasar de Obregón, *Historia de los descubrimientos antiguos y modernos de la Nueva España, escrita por el conquistador en el año de 1584*, ed. Mariano Cuevas (México, DF: Editorial Porrúa, 1988), 33; Himmerich y Valencia, *Encomenderos*, 232. Regarding Hernán Flores, on fol. 407v the name is rendered as Hernando López. An Hernando Flores was *encomendero* of Suchipila in Nueva Galicia from 1541–48. Gerhard, *North Frontier*, 101. As Document 32 attests, Hernán Flores was in Guadalajara in 1551 testifying for his brother-in-law, Melchior Pérez. He had married a sister of Pérez's. It seems convincing that this is the same *regidor* Flores in the present document. He was a native of Salamanca who

arrived in Nueva España in 1528. He served as *alférez* with Guzmán in Nueva Galicia in 1530 and became a *vecino* of Guadalajara. Boyd-Bowman, 2: no. 7454. Francisco de la Mota was *encomendero* of Copala and Quilitlán north of Guadalajara until his death during the Mixtón War. Gerhard, *North Frontier,* 122.

16. This list summarizes a mini-history of the conquest of the Iberian Peninsula through time. The Christian sovereigns Fernando and Isabel, Carlos V's grandparents, held Castilla, León, Aragón, Galicia, Navarra, Vizcaya, Molina, and Barcelona by inheritance. That domain had already been expanded with the fitful dispossession of the Moors in the southern portion of the peninsula. Sevilla, the Mallorcas, Córdoba, Murcia, Jaén, the Algarves (southern Portugal), Algeciras, Gibraltar, Toledo, and Valencia had all been added during the thirteenth century. Then, under the Catholic sovereigns, Granada was annexed in 1492. Thereafter, Pope Alexander VI's donation of 1493, confirmed by conquests and discoveries in the New World, enlarged the Spanish realm with the Indies and all lands in the Ocean Sea. By inheritance through his father, Archduke Philip of Burgundy, Carlos was the count of Flanders, Tyrol, etc. Richard Fletcher, *Moorish Spain* (Berkeley: University of California Press, 1992); Elliott, *Imperial Spain,* 46–53, 77–86, 135–44.

Meanwhile, Neopatria had been created in the fourteenth century on the Grecian peninsula to the south of Thessaly. In association with the Duchy of Athens, it became a dependent of Aragón in 1377 as a result of an expedition led by Roger de Flor. It was still claimed by Carlos V and his mother, Juana, the current occupants of the throne of Aragón in 1539, although it was in the hands of the Florentine Acciaiuoli family after 1390 and had been taken by the Ottoman Turks in 1460. Antoni Maria Alcover et al., *Diccionari Català-Valencià-Balear,* 10 vols. (Palma de Mallorca: Editorial Moll, 1956–68), 7:737. The Catalans had become masters of Sardinia and the Sicilys in the fourteenth century. These areas in what is now Italy were subsequently incorporated into the *reino* of Aragón in 1409. Elliott, *Imperial Spain,* 27. Pope Clement VI granted the Canaries to Castilla in 1344. In 1431 Portugal attempted unsuccessfully to take possession of the islands. Nearly 70 years later, in 1479, Fernando and Isabel definitively reasserted their hold on the Canaries. José Suárez Acosta, Félix Rodríguez Lorenzo, and Carmelo L. Quintero Padrón, *Conquista y colonización,* in *Historia popular de Canarias,* vol. 2 (Santa Cruz de Tenerife: Centro de la Cultura Popular Canaria, 1988), 24, 38, 40. As to the island of Corsica, it had been seized by Alfonso V of Aragón in 1420. *Enciclopedia universal ilustrada europeo-americana,* 70 vols. (Barcelona: Hijos de J. Espasa, 1907–30), 15:509.

The monarchs of Aragón had long included sovereignty of Jerusalem among their titles. The crusaders of 1095 simply declared Jerusalem a Christian kingdom, and Balduíno was declared king. He reigned in name only from 1100 to 1118. However, in 1492, as in 1539, it was in the possession of the Ottoman Turks. Peggy K. Liss, *Isabel, The Queen: Life and Times* (New York: Oxford University Press, 1992), 240; *Enciclopedia universal,* 28:2698. Conspicuously absent from the list is España, or Spain. The country as we know it today had only finally been united under a single hereditary monarchy by King Carlos in 1516. Throughout his reign as king and then emperor, in official documents he continued to refer to the individual *reinos* that made up the country and empire.

17. An *escudero* was an attendant of a *caballero,* usually a boy or young man, often of *hidalgo* status. Among his functions was to carry the *caballero's* shield when he was not using it, but an *escudero's* duties were extremely varied. Covarrubias, 497. An *hombre bueno* was a member of the community of *vecinos* that made up a town, excluding the nobles, clergy, and military. *DRAE,* 1117, 905.

18. "Delay," *larga. DRAE,* 1231.

19. See Document 1, note 52.

20. A *pragmatica* was a law emanating from a competent authority; it was differentiated from a royal decree and a general ordinance in the formula of its publication.

21. This salary of 1,500 *ducados* was to be paid beginning April 18, 1539. Because Vázquez de Coronado had already been serving as governor since late 1538, the king also authorized another payment to him of 1,000 *ducados* to cover the period prior to the official appointment that is being made by the present document. The same base salary of 1,500 *ducados* was stipulated for Hernando de Soto in his governorship and captaincy general of Cuba and La Florida, although he was granted an additional 500 *ducados* gratuity. Lawrence A. Clayton, Vernon James Knight, Jr., and Edward C. Moore, eds., *The De Soto Chronicles: The Expedition of Hernando de Soto to North America in 1539–1543,* 2 vols. (Tuscaloosa: University of Alabama Press, 1993), 1:360.

22. "Issued in the *ciudad* of Toledo . . .": At this period the royal court was peripatetic, that is, moving from city to city. On this date, although the king himself

was abroad, the royal family was residing in Toledo. In fact, just weeks after this *cédula* was issued, Queen Isabel died there. Henry Kamen, *Philip of Spain* (New Haven, CT: Yale University Press, 1997), 6.

23. Juan de Sámano served as secretary, or chief *escribano,* of the Consejo de Indias from 1524 to 1558. Schäfer, *Consejo Real,* 1:369.

24. Recibir. *DRAE,* 1740: "admitir uno a otro en su compañia o comunidad."

25. Por bien = *bien a bien = sin contradicción. DRAE,* 289, 290.

26. Alguaçiladgos = *alguacilazgos. DRAE,* 99.

27. Entender en. *DRAE,* 847: "tener una autoridad, facultad o jurisdicción para conocer de materia determinada."

28. Favor y ayuda, aid and assistance. This is an instance of the common sixteenth-century rhetorical practice of using paired synonyms or near synonyms. See the general introduction.

29. Embargo, obstruction. *DRAE,* 801: "dificultad, impedimento, obstáculo."

30. "Que les sean." The López Portillo y Rojas edition omits "les." Tello, 314.

Document 6. The Viceroy's Instructions to Fray Marcos de Niza, November 1538; Narrative Account by Fray Marcos de Niza, August 26, 1539

1. AGI, Patronato, 184, R.27, "Letter to the King," fol. 14v.

2. Lewis Hanke, "Pope Paul III and the American Indians," *Harvard Theological Review* 30 (1937):65–102.

3. Hanke, *Spanish Struggle for Justice,* 76.

4. The friars may actually have been accompanied by armed horsemen for at least part of their journey. That is suggested by a comment made by Juan de Cuevas at the end of the February 1540 muster roll: "The horsemen total two hundred and thirty-odd [226] besides and in addition to those who are going ahead in the company of the religious." Document 12, fol. 9v.

5. Little is known with certainty about Marcos's early years. That his first language was French is inferred from a 1539 statement of Gerónimo Ximénez de San Esteban. Father Charles Polzer has estimated that Marcos must have been in his forties in 1539. More recently, the French researcher Michel Nallino has suggested that the friar was born about 1495, which would have made him 44 in 1539. The late-sixteenth-century Franciscan historian fray Pedro Oroz informs us that Marcos was a native of Nice in the Duchy of Savoy, which Nallino points out was in the Franciscan province of Aquitaine. Henry R. Wagner, "Fr. Marcos de Niza," *New Mexico Historical Review* 9 (April 1934):184–85; William K. Hartmann, "Pathfinder for Coronado: Reevaluating the Mysterious Journey of Marcos de Niza," in *The Coronado Expedition to Tierra Nueva: The 1540–1542 Route Across the Southwest,* eds. Richard Flint and Shirley Cushing Flint (Niwot, CO: University Press of Colorado, 1997), 85; Michel Nallino, "Fray Marcos de Niza: In Pursuit of Franciscan Utopia in the Americas," paper presented at the conference "Contemporary Vantage on the Coronado Expedition through Documents and Artifacts" (Las Vegas, NM, 2000), 4, 5; Chávez, *Oroz Codex,* 130–31 n. 274.

6. Las Casas, *Devastation of the Indies,* 115–18.

7. Chávez, *Coronado's Friars,* 10; Chávez, *Oroz Codex,* 131. Wagner, in "Fr. Marcos de Niza," 186, earlier claimed that Marcos did not reach Peru until 1534.

8. Fray Marcos de Niza, "Testimony, Santiago de Guatemala, Sept. 25, 1536," in Wagner, "Fr. Marcos de Niza," 194–98.

9. Juan de Zumárraga, "Letter to an unknown religious from Juan de Zumárraga, México, April 4, 1537," in Wagner, "Fr. Marcos de Niza," 198–99.

10. Juan de Velasco, *Historia del reino de Quito en la América Meridional: Historia antigua* (Quito: Editorial Benjamín Carrión, 1996). The Velasco manuscript, written about 1790, is discussed at length in Nallino, "Fray Marcos de Niza."

11. Marcos de Niza, "Testimony," in Wagner, "Fr. Marcos de Niza," 194–98.

12. Zumárraga, "Letter," in Wagner, "Fr. Marcos de Niza," 198–99.

13. Fol. 2r.

14. Document 28, fol. 16r.

15. Document 8, fol. 69r.

16. For more complete information on investments in the expedition, see Shirley Cushing Flint, "The Financing and Provisioning of the Coronado Expedition," in Flint and Flint, *From the Distance of 460 Years,* 42–56.

17. The idea that Marcos might have lied in his *relación* in order to further some scheme of the viceroy's has been advanced by A. Grove Day and others. Day, *Coronado's Quest,* 331–33 n. 22.

18. Chávez, *Oroz Codex*, 131.

19. As the members of the expedition themselves reckoned the date, it was near the end of the first week in July. To coordinate European time under the Julian calendar then in force with the solar calendar observed by the native people the expedition encountered, we have converted the time of the arrival at Cíbola into the modern, Gregorian calendar.

20. This is according to Pedro de Castañeda de Nájera. Document 28, fol. 31r.

21. Document 19, fol. 361r.

22. Document 19, fol. 360r.

23. Cleve Hallenbeck, *The Journey of Fray Marcos de Niza* (Dallas, TX: Southern Methodist University Press, 1949; reprint with introduction by David J. Weber, 1987); Carl O. Sauer, "The Discovery of New Mexico Reconsidered," *New Mexico Historical Review* 12, no. 3 (1937):270–87; Wagner, "Fr. Marcos de Niza," 184–227.

24. Hartmann, "Pathfinder for Coronado," 73–101.

25. Flint, *Great Cruelties*, 396, 403.

26. Ibid., 396, 403.

27. Ibid., 364, 385. To be fair, Marcos made no claim to have seen these places. Rather, he reported only what he had been told about them by natives of Sonora.

28. Document 28, fol. 34v.

29. Ibid.

30. Pedro de Castañeda de Nájera explicitly stated that Marcos turned around and headed south as soon as he met Esteban's fleeing companions: "they returned from there without examining the land more than [hearing] what the Indians told them." Document 28, fol. 14v.

31. The ostracism apparently did not begin immediately upon Marcos's return to the Ciudad de México. The viceroy consulted him and took him to Jalisco during the final campaign of the Mixtón War in late 1541 and early 1542, as if relations between the two were unstrained. Chávez, *Coronado's Friars*, 76; Tello, 462.

32. For the legal prohibition against a person serving as a witness "who has been proved to have given false evidence," see *Siete Partidas*, 3:668.

33. Fol. 7r.

34. Ibid.

35. Hallenbeck, *Journey of Fray Marcos*, 69.

36. Fol. 7v.

37. Madaleine Rodack agrees, even going so far as to write that "it is most likely that he [Marcos] *was* seen. The Indians surely were on the lookout after Estevan's arrival." Madaleine Turrell Rodack, "Cíbola, from fray Marcos to Coronado," in Flint and Flint, *Tierra Nueva*, 111.

38. Carl Sauer made a similar observation in 1941. Carl O. Sauer, "The Credibility of the Fray Marcos Account," *New Mexico Historical Review* 16 (April 1941):242–43.

39. David Weber has admirably surveyed modern arguments over Marcos's truthfulness. David J. Weber, "Fray Marcos de Niza and the Historians," in Weber, *Myth and the History of the Hispanic Southwest* (Albuquerque: University of New Mexico Press, 1988), 19–32.

40. Sauer, "Credibility," 233–43; Lansing B. Bloom, "Was Fray Marcos a Liar?" *New Mexico Historical Review* 16 (April 1941):244.

41. George J. Undreiner, "Fray Marcos de Niza and His Journey to Cibola," *The Americas* 3 (April 1947):470.

42. Daniel T. Reff, "Anthropological Analysis of Exploration Texts: Cultural Discourse and the Ethnological Import of Fray Marcos de Niza's Journey to Cíbola," *American Anthropologist* 93 (1991):639–40.

43. Hartmann and Flint, "Before the Coronado Expedition," 37.

44. Chávez, *Coronado's Friars*, 11.

45. Both copies may have been collected by the sixteenth-century historian Juan Páez de Castro. See Document 30, note 38.

46. For Craddock's dismissal of marginal marks, see Jerry R. Craddock, "Fray Marcos de Niza, *Relación* (1539): Edition and Commentary," *Romance Philology* 53 (Fall 1999):69–11870.

47. These three instances of highlighting occur on fols. 4v, 6v, and 4v, respectively. The remaining eight occurrences are these: (1) that Marcos is to send back samples, fol. 1v; (2) that the Indians of Sinaloa and Sonora are more skilled in hiding than in planting, fol. 2v; (3) the distance to an island in the Gulf of California, fol. 2v; (4) the existence of a second island, fol. 2v; (5) that Esteban was to send a large cross as an indication of marvelous things ahead, fol. 3r; (6) that messengers from Esteban brought a cross as large as a man, fol. 3r; (7) that the

people of Sonora repeatedly touched Marcos's clothing, fol. 4r; and (8) that there were many turquoises and bison hides in Sonora, fol. 4r.

48. Craddock, "Fray Marcos," 69–118.

49. *CDI*, 3:325–51.

50. Hallenbeck, *Journey of Fray Marcos*, li–lxxi.

51. Ramusio, *Terzo volume*, 356r–359v.

52. Fols. 3r and 5r.

53. Ramusio, *Terzo volume*, fol. 359r.

54. Translation by the authors.

55. The added passage bears a striking resemblance to a portion of Vázquez de Coronado's letter to the viceroy of March 8, 1539, which Ramusio also published. Especially interesting is the mention of emeralds and the use of golden dishes. The Ramusio passage, however, refers to houses decorated with gold rather than turquoise. See Document 2, fol. 354v.

56. Henri Ternaux-Compans, trans. and ed. "Instruction donnée par don Antonio de Mendoza" and "Relation de frère Marcos de Niza," in *Voyages, relations et memoires*, 9:251–84.

57. Hakluyt, *Principal Navigations*, 9:125–44.

58. Álvar Núñez Cabeza de Vaca, *The Journey of Alvar Nuñez Cabeza de Vaca and His Companions from Florida to the Pacific, 1528–1536*, trans. Fanny R. Bandelier, ed. Adolph F. Bandelier (New York: A. S. Barnes, 1905; reprint, Chicago: Rio Grande Press, 1964), 195, 197–231 (page citations are to the reprint edition).

59. Percy M. Baldwin, trans. and ed., *Discovery of the Seven Cities of Cibola by the Father Fray Marcos de Niza*, Historical Society of New Mexico, Publications in History, vol. 1 (Albuquerque: El Palacio Press, 1926).

60. Bonaventure Oblasser, ed. and trans., *Arizona Discovered, 1539: The Story of the Discovery of the Seven Cities by Fray Marcos de Niza* (Topowa, AZ: n.p., 1939). Oblasser's assumption that an inscription found near Phoenix, Arizona, was a genuine mark left by fray Marcos (on which depended much of his interpretation of the friar's route) was subsequently shown to be mistaken; the inscription was a nineteenth-century fake. Katharine Bartlett and Harold S. Colton, "A Note on the Marcos de Niza Inscription near Phoenix, Arizona," *Plateau* 12 (April 1940):53–59.

61. H&R, 63–82.

62. Hallenbeck, *Journey of Fray Marcos*.

63. For geographical information, see the entry for Culiacán in Appendix 2.

64. This is the common use of the future subjunctive. Mendoza often uses the future subjunctive in this directive, indicating that he is dealing with events he considers unlikely to occur in the future but for which he makes provision nonetheless.

65. This is one of many indications that the crown was distressed that the conquest and establishment of *encomiendas* in the New World were resulting in injury to native people more often than not.

66. For biographical information, see the entry for Esteban in Appendix 1.

67. Consistently, the first aim of *entradas* of this period was to learn the sizes of native communities, because eventual tribute collection was an important goal.

68. A mark of scribal highlighting usually denotes a point of interest and often was made in the Consejo de Indias by either an advisor or the councilor himself.

69. During both the "solo" reconnaissance of fray Marcos and the full Coronado expedition, samples of precious metals were taken, though not samples of ores, for the expedition was seeking people who already had knowledge of metalworking and were producing precious finished commodities. See also fol. 2v.

70. For geographical information, see the entry for Mar del Sur in Appendix 2.

71. Marking conspicuous trees was standard procedure for expeditions of the period. Later, when the Coronado expedition agreed to leave crosses for Pedro de Tovar to follow, they, too, would certainly have been placed conspicuously at prominent locations. See Document 28, fol. 76v, and Richard Flint and Shirley Cushing Flint, "Coronado's Crosses: Route Markers Used by the Coronado Expedition," *Journal of the Southwest* 35, no. 2 (1993):207–16.

72. In other words, as William Hartmann has been at pains to point out, as he progressed northward Marcos was to send interim reports back to the viceroy by means of Indian couriers. Hartmann and Flint, "Before the Coronado Expedition," 29–32.

73. This is a scribal rendition rather than Mendoza's actual signature.

74. Marcos was an Observant Franciscan, meaning he fully adhered to Saint Francis's admonition to live in poverty, without worldly goods.

75. Tonalá was a civil jurisdiction extending from the city limits of Guadalajara south and east to the Río Grande de Santiago. Today it is in central Jalisco, forming

the suburbs of Guadalajara. Nuño de Guzmán conquered the female ruler of Tonalá in 1530 and placed the area within the jurisdiction of the new *villa* of Espíritu Santo (see Compostela in Appendix 2). The native people were Coca-speaking Tecuexes. Gerhard, *North Frontier,* 153–56.

76. This is a scribal rendition rather than Marcos's actual signature.

77. The Order of [Friars] Minor is the Franciscan Order. Fray Antonio was a native of Ciudad Rodrigo in what is now the *comunidad* of Castilla-León in Spain. He was among the original 12 friars, Los Doce, sent to Nueva España in 1524. He was elected the second provincial. He had returned to Spain in 1527 to plead before Carlos V for better treatment of the Indians. Fray Antonio was elected bishop of Nueva Galicia but declined the office. He returned to Spain a second time in 1529 and brought the friars Bernardino de Sahagún, Alonso Rengel, Juan de San Francisco, and perhaps Juan de Padilla with him on his return to Nueva España. He died in 1553. Chávez, *Oroz Codex,* 92–95. From 1524 until 1565 the province of the Santo Evangelio, or Province of the Holy Gospel, headquartered in the Ciudad de México, was the chief administrative unit of the Franciscan Order in Nueva España, including Michoacán, Colima, and Nueva Galicia. John L. Kessell, *Kiva, Cross, and Crown,* 2nd ed. (Albuquerque: University of New Mexico Press, 1987), 74.

78. Marcos provides little evidence of his knowledge of cosmography in the *relación,* except that he evidently took a reading of latitude at the place he understood was due east of the head of the Gulf of California. That measurement was off by about 3 degrees, a sizable error. That same year Francisco de Ulloa determined the latitude of the head of the Gulf as 34 degrees, also in error by about 2 degrees. Francisco López de Gómara, writing in the 1550s and apparently using the measurement reported by Hernando de Alarcón, stated more correctly that the head of the Gulf was at "32° N. Lat., or a little higher." Henry R. Wagner, *Spanish Voyages to the Northwest Coast of America in the Sixteenth Century* (San Francisco: California Historical Society, 1929), 19; López de Gómara, *Cortés,* 403.

79. The Franciscan lay friar (that is, not ordained as a priest) named Onorato had come to the New World during the summer of 1533 in the same group that included fray Juan de Padilla. He was in his late thirties to around 40 when he set off with fray Marcos. In 1544 he was in Guadalajara and was able to sign his name. According to Antonio Tello, Onorato was also with the Ibarra *entrada* in 1563. AGI, Contratación, 4675, L.5, "Casa de Contratación, Account book for 1530–1537," fols. 335r–336r; AGI, Justicia, 339, N.1, R.1, "Residencia;" Tello, 590.

80. For information about Vázquez de Coronado's appointment, see Document 5, note 2.

81. Included here is a scribal rendition rather than fray Antonio's actual signature.

82. For geographical information, see the entry for Petatlán in Appendix 2.

83. William Hartmann has suggested that this may refer not to a period of 72 hours but rather to some portion of three periods of daylight. Thus, for instance, the period from a Monday afternoon through a Wednesday morning might well be covered by Marcos's "three days."

84. Hernán Cortés, the Marqués del Valle, and his associates had visited more than one island, as well as the Baja California peninsula, which for a time was thought to be an island.

85. A recent study of nineteenth- and twentieth-century Seris on Isla San Esteban indicates considerable continuity with regard to raft transportation: "The reedgrass balsa was crucial to the existence of San Esteban islanders . . . [and] gave them contact with other Seris. . . . The San Esteban people depended on the balsa as an item of daily necessity, and each man owned one." Thomas Bowen, *Unknown Island: Seri Indians, Europeans, and San Esteban Island in the Gulf of California* (Albuquerque: University of New Mexico Press, 2000), 21–22.

86. This distance is grossly inaccurate, if Marcos is referring here to the peninsula of Baja California, which had been thought to be an island and to which Cortés had dispatched several sea expeditions beginning in 1533, going there himself in 1536. On the other hand, Marcos may be speaking here about one of several islands lying just off the southwestern coast of modern Sonora, such as Isla Huivuili and Isla Lobos, which were probably visited in 1539 by Francisco de Ulloa under orders from Cortés.

87. This may well have been Isla Tiburón. Francisco de Ulloa would become the first European known to have visited it, at Hernán Cortés's behest, while Marcos was on his reconnaissance. Several Seri bands occupied Tiburón and nearby San Esteban islands. López de Gómara, *Cortés,* 398–99; Thomas Bowen, "Seri," in *Handbook of North American Indians,* vol. 10, *Southwest,* edited by Alfonso Ortiz (Washington, DC: Smithsonian Institution Press, 1983), 231–32; Bowen, *Unknown Island.*

88. An archipelago of at least 19 islands, known as the Midriff Islands, stretches across the Gulf of California in the latitude of Isla Tiburón, including Tiburón, Alcatraz, Dátil, Patos, San Esteban, San Pedro Mártir, San Lorenzo, San Lorenzo Norte, Salsipuedes, Rasa, Partida, and Ángel de la Guarda. In addition, a string of 16 more small islands lies along the southeastern coast of Baja California Sur from Tortuga in the north to Isla Cerralvo southeast of Bahía de la Paz. It is certainly these 35 islands to which the friar refers here. Bowen, *Unknown Island,* xxix; Undreiner, "Fray Marcos," 431.

89. In this case, Marcos is careful to distinguish what he was told from what he himself saw.

90. Pointing to the lack of any linguistic or major cultural division, Carl Sauer insisted that such ignorance of Spaniards would have been unlikely for any native group in this region at the time. Sauer, "Credibility," 240–41.

91. About the word *sayota,* Craddock has written recently, "I am unaware of any successful linguistic analysis of the term." Craddock, "Fray Marcos," 105. It is interesting, however, that a town called Sayopa exists on the middle Yaqui River. The similarity of that name and *sayota* may be more than coincidence. Sayopa is in the San Andrés de la Sierra region, which was occupied at contact by Acaxees and Xiximes (Taracahitan speakers, Ópata perhaps). See Gerhard, *North Frontier,* 227, 280; Thomas B. Hinton, "Southern Periphery: West," in Ortiz, *Southwest,* vol. 10, 316–17; Hartmann, "Pathfinder for Coronado," 94; and Daniel T. Reff, "The Relevance of Ethnology to the Routing of the Coronado Expedition in Sonora," in Flint and Flint, *Tierra Nueva,* 168.

92. This, too, was the goal of the lay Spaniards. One of the characteristics of "civilization," in the sixteenth-century Spanish view, was production of valuable commodities.

93. "Wide, level valley," *abra. DRAE,* 10, "abertura ancha y despejada entre dos montañas." The only other instance of this uncommon term in the Coronado expedition documents occurs in Juan Jaramillo's narrative, Document 30, fol. 1r: "Una Abra que las sierras hazian A mano derecha del camino." Presumably, both uses refer to the same wide valley. An interim report of gold in this *abra* may have been conflated with the final report on Cíbola to trigger some of the rumors that later developed about Cíbola. See Hartmann and Flint, "Before the Coronado Expedition," 33. "Tillable land," *tierra. DRAE,* 1976, "terreno dedicado a cultivo o propio para ello."

94. Marcos showed metal samples as he had been instructed. It is curious that he did not report having used this procedure as he neared Cíbola. See also fol. 1v.

95. This instruction is not among those recorded in Viceroy Mendoza's formal directive copied at the beginning of this document. Thus, the written list of instructions appears to be incomplete and may represent only instructions relative to the treatment of native people and some other issues.

96. If the location of Vacapa suggested in note 97 is approximately correct, these people would have been Ópatas. Hinton, "Southern Periphery: West," 316.

97. It was thus three days' travel from the place Marcos called Sayota (the Soyopa area?) to Vacapa (Mátape?) and three days from there to where the people had firsthand knowledge of Cíbola (Ures/Corazones?). Marcos states that it was some 40 leagues (about 100 miles) from Vacapa to the sea. This matches Mátape very well (maps 1 and 2). Adolph Bandelier, too, believed that Vacapa was in the vicinity of Mátape. Adolph F. Bandelier, "Fray Marcos of Nizza," *Contributions to the History of the Southwestern Portion of the United States,* Part 4, Papers of the Archaeological Institute of America, American Series 5 (Cambridge, MA, 1890; reprint, New York: AMS Press, 1976), 122–25 (page citation is to the reprint edition). Castañeda de Nájera also referred to Vacapa/Vacapan, indicating that up to at least this point the expedition probably followed the same route that Marcos had. Document 28, fol. 39v. Craddock, "Fray Marcos," 106, summarizes the many and disparate conclusions scholars have reached over the years about the location of Vacapa.

98. Dominica de Pasión was celebrated on the Sunday two weeks before Easter, or Pascua. In 1539 Dominica de Pasión was March 23, and Easter was April 6, in the Julian calendar. *OED,* 2093, defines Passion Sunday as the fifth Sunday in Lent and cites a passage from Richard Torkington's 1517 "Pilgrimage to Jerusalem": "Passion Sunday, the xxix Day of Marche [Easter Sunday was 12 April]." Domingo de Pasión, *DRAE,* 773, "quinto domingo de cuaresma [Lent]." Pascua, *DRAE,* 1540, "fiesta solemne de la Resurrección del Señor, que se celebre el domingo siguiente al plenilunio posterior al 20 de marzo." Because there has been considerable discussion of late about the dates in Marcos's *relación,* we have left the original language, though it is clear that the friar is referring here to the fifth Sunday in

Lent, the Sunday preceding Palm Sunday. For the date of Easter Sunday, see Alonso de Chaves, *Quatri partitu en cosmografía práctica, y por otro nombre Espejo de navegantes*, eds. Paulino Castañeda Delgado, Mariano Cuesta Domingo, and Pilar Hernández Aparicio (Madrid: Instituto de Historia y Cultura Naval, 1983), 95–97. Domínica = *domingo* in ecclesiastical usage. *DRAE*, 773.

99. The code of crosses established between Marcos and Esteban strongly suggests that Esteban was illiterate, something not at all unusual for a slave.

100. For geographical information, see the entry for Cíbola in Appendix 2.

101. "One story," *sobrado*. *DRAE*, 1890, "cada uno de los altos o pisos de una casa."

102. "Discussion," *demandas y respuestas*. *DRAE*, 677, "altercados y disputas que ocurren en un asunto." The instance referred to here, however, seems less confrontational than the *DRAE* suggests.

103. Pascua de Flores, Pascua Florida, Pascua de la Resurrección, and Pascua alone all refer to Easter Sunday. *DRAE*, 1540. In 1539 Easter fell on April 6. See the perpetual calendar and table of movable feasts provided by *piloto mayor* (chief pilot) Alonso de Cháves in the late 1530s. Chaves, *Espejo de navegantes*, 79–99.

104. Because *frente*, translated here as "forehead," can also mean "face," this could refer to the Seri practice of piercing the nasal septum and inserting a shell, as reported by the seventeenth-century Jesuit missionary Adamo Gilg. *DRAE*, 995; Charles C. Di Peso and Daniel S. Matson, eds. and trans., "The Seri Indians in 1692 as Described by Adamo Gilg, S.J.," *Arizona and the West* 7 (1965):33–56.

105. This document is not known to exist.

106. This probably refers to the *carrizo* reed boat or raft formerly used by the Seri. Bowen, "Seri," 239, 241.

107. *Pintado* probably refers to a type of tattooing in which a series of dots, rather than solid markings, forms the design. *DRAE*, 1606: *pintado* = *pintojo* = "que tiene pintas o manchas." The Suma and Jumano peoples at this time occupied territories to the northeast of the Ópata that would have reached almost to the Pueblo region along the Rio Grande in what is now New Mexico. Both groups practiced tattooing, as did a number of their neighbors. William B. Griffen, "Southern Periphery: East," in Ortiz, *Southwest*, vol. 10, 333.

108. This may record a sweeping arm gesture made by the *indios pintados* to indicate an extensive territory across which they made seasonal rounds. *CDI*, 3:334, erroneously has "en cerco." Craddock, "Fray Marcos," 107, is in essential agreement with our reading. Hallenbeck, *Journey of Fray Marcos*, 20, and Baldwin, *Discovery of the Seven Cities*, 16, ignore the term "arco." H&R, 67, have "their settlements form a circle."

109. Y así = consequently. *DRAE*, 210.

110. Second day of Pascua = Easter Monday.

111. Three days' travel from Vacapa/Mátape would have put Marcos in the vicinity of Ures/Corazones. Certainly his description here would fit a major population center such as Corazones, though Marcos omits the name (see map 2).

112. For geographical information, see the entries for Marata, Acus, and Totonteac in Appendix 2.

113. Individuals or groups seasonally traveling long distances to labor for pay present a markedly different picture of regional interaction among protohistoric native peoples of the region from that which is commonly accepted. It is also possible that Marcos misunderstood his informants on this point and that he was actually being told about long-distance trade in exotic raw materials or finished commodities.

114. A number of the older kachina/koko figures at Zuni, such as Sayatasha and the Kokkothlanna of the Newekwe, wear long, loose, white cotton shirts. These may recall dress that was once more general among the Zunis. Mathilda Coxe Stevenson, *The Zuñi Indians, Their Mythology, Esoteric Fraternities, and Ceremonies*, Twenty-Third Annual Report of the Bureau of American Ethnology, 1901–1902 (Washington, DC: U.S. Government Printing Office, 1904; reprint, Glorieta, NM: Rio Grande Press, 1984), 435 and color plate 63 (page citations are to the reprint edition). Carroll Riley has pointed out that accounts of the Chamuscado-Rodríguez and Espejo *entradas* of the 1580s, both of which visited Zuni, "make it clear that the inhabitants of Zuni did not grow cotton (or, at best, only a little) but traded with the Mohose [Hopi] people for raw cotton." Carroll L. Riley, *The Frontier People: The Greater Southwest in the Protohistoric Period*, rev. ed. (Albuquerque: University of New Mexico Press, 1987), 185.

115. This is behavior reminiscent of what Cabeza de Vaca and his party had experienced in this general region three years earlier. See, for instance, Adorno and Pautz, *Núñez Cabeza de Vaca*, 1:230–31.

116. Evidently this was another of the many Ópata settlements in the Sonora Valley.

117. Crecia, *crecer* = was growing more favorable. This use of *crecer* is similar to *DRAE*, 593, "tomar alguien mayor autoridad, importancia o atrevimiento."

118. Reference here is to the unsettled region, four days' journey in expanse, between the upper waters of the Río Sonora and the San Pedro River that is reported later, on fol. 4r (map 2).

119. Although certainly not as voluminous as the documents prepared and witnessed on the occasion of the assumption of formal possession of New Mexico by Juan de Oñate on April 30, 1598, the elements of what Marcos recorded and certified in writing were certainly the same: a statement of his authority to take possession in the name of King Carlos I, a statement of the peoples and territories being brought under royal dominion, and a signed statement about when and where possession was taken. Drafting of this document ordinarily followed the erection of a cross, just as Marcos reports he did later at other places, including near Cíbola and at the *abra*, or wide valley. For a record of the elaborate ritual and ceremony—including delivery of a lengthy speech and presentation of a play—employed by Oñate, see Gaspar Pérez de Villagrá, *Historia de la Nueva México, 1610*, eds. and trans. Miguel Encinias, Alfred Rodríguez, and Joseph P. Sánchez (Albuquerque: University of New Mexico Press, 1992), 131–38, fols. 5v, 7r, and 7v. See also Hammond and Rey, *Oñate*, 1:329–36.

120. "They persisted in telling me," *cargandome la mano*. Cargar la mano, *DRAE*, 1312, "insistir con empeño o eficacia sobre una cosa." Unjustifiably, H&R, 69, make Esteban the subject of this sentence, "He always persisted in telling me. . . ."

121. Marcos was still in the Sonora Valley at this point. This is evidently the four-day *despoblado* (unsettled area) between Ispa (Arispe) and the Río Nexpa/San Pedro River referred to by Jaramillo (map 2). Document 30, fol. 1v.

122. Presumably this irrigated *pueblo* was in the extreme upper Sonora River Valley (map 2).

123. "With turquoise ornaments which hang from their noses and ears," *encaconados con turquesas*. According to Rubén Cobos, *A Dictionary of New Mexico and Southern Colorado Spanish* (Santa Fe: Museum of New Mexico Press, 1983), 60, this comes from the Zuni word *cacona* and means "wearing turquoise ornaments on noses and ears." Formation of the verb follows a common Spanish formula of converting a noun into a verb by prefixing it with *en-* and adding the *-ar* verb endings. *Cacona* may a derivative of the Zunian word *kuchuna*, meaning "multicolored object." Stanley Newman, *Zuni Dictionary* (Albuquerque: n.p., 1956), 1:31. Craddock, "Fray Marcos," 109, states that "the source of *cacona* . . . has not been identified."

124. Probably this is *pinole* rather than *piñon*, as H&R, 70, and Craddock, "Fray Marcos," 88, incorrectly interpret it. The tilde included in H&R's rendition is in fact the dotting of the i. *Pinole* is toasted corn flour, sometimes sweetened and mixed with chocolate, cinnamon, or anise.

125. "Gourd bowls," *xicara* = *jícara*. Cobos, *Dictionary*, 91, "a drinking vessel made from a gourd shell cut in half."

126. "Muslim Zaragosa was noted as a center for dressing furs." Ruth Mathilda Anderson, *Hispanic Costume, 1480–1530* (New York: Hispanic Society of America, 1979), 117. Zaragoza may be the fabric referred to as "chamelote, camlet" in Document 7, fol. 23r. María del Carmen Martínez Meléndez, *Los Nombres de tejidos en castellano medieval* (Granada, Spain: Universidad de Granada, 1989), 170–1, regarding the textile industry in the Corona de Aragón: "desarrollo continuó a lo largo del siglo XIV extendiéndose la industria textil por todo el reino, los principales núcleos fueron: . . . Zaragosa." The information Marcos gives here about cloth made from animal hair at Totonteac is similar to that obtained later by Melchior Díaz and reported by the viceroy. See Document 17, fol. 2r.

127. Greyhound, *galgo* = *lebrel*. John Grier Varner and Jeannette Johnson Varner, *Dogs of the Conquest* (Norman: University of Oklahoma Press, 1983), 196.

128. We have supposed that this was the San Pedro Valley in extreme southern Arizona, but recent archaeology has revealed that the upper (southern) San Pedro Valley was largely unsettled during the sixteenth century (map 2). Email from the archaeologist William Doelle, March 28, 2003: "The archaeological evidence that we have currently indicates that during the 1400s there was apparent decline of the former large villages that had platform mounds and substantial masonry architecture—along with lots of polychrome pottery. The latest sites are concentrated in the area around Aravaipa Creek north to the Gila, and ceramic evidence indicates occupation to around 1450. After that, our ability to identify archaeological sites drops away altogether, and we don't see any other sites until the late 1600s—the

Kino period of the 1690s provides both documentary evidence and some archaeological sites that appear to match well with the documents. . . . Thus we find the hypothesis that the river was abandoned increasingly attractive. One caveat in responding to your specific question about 'the upper San Pedro' is that the research has been less intensive from Benson south to the headwaters than it has been from Benson north. Still, the same hypothesis seems pretty attractive for the entire river." Much the same statement appears in Jeffery J. Clark and Patrick D. Lyons, "Mounds and Migrants in the Classic Period," *Archaeology Southwest* 17, no. 3 (2003):10.

129. "Things of civilization" would have been a red flag for Mendoza and Vázquez de Coronado, reinforcing the notion that the people of Cíbola were like Europeans. The notion of long-distance travel to labor for pay is unexpected with reference to the protohistoric peoples of the region. See note 113, this document.

130. "Penetrating the land," *meter* = "entrarse por la tierra." *DRAE*, 1366.

131. Over the years there has been much discussion about whether this phrase, "I understood clearly," should be taken literally and that therefore Marcos saw the turn of the coast *visually* and *personally*. The extended sense of the verb *ver*, meaning "to understand," is common and seems more appropriate here, given the friar's great distance from the gulf. It seems likely that after walking westward for several days, it became obvious to Marcos that it was still several more days to the coast, indicating that the coast had, indeed, turned to the west. For this usage of *ver*, see *DRAE*, 2075. The sharp bend near the head of the Gulf of California is at about 31.5 degrees. Marcos had to have taken this reading using either a cross-staff or an astrolabe. Both were notoriously error–prone. An error of similar magnitude is recorded in the "Relación del Suceso," Document 29, fol. 2r. As one more contemporary example, Juan Rodríguez Cabrillo was off by two degrees in his 1542 measurement of the latitude of San Diego Bay. And as Antonio de Mendoza wrote in October 1541, "all the data concerning this Mar del Sur are incorrect because the pilots' books [necessary for making calculations from cross-staff or astrolabe observations] were prepared in España." Jerry MacMullen, "It's a Wonder that They Ever Got Home," in *Cabrillo's World: A Commemorative Edition of Cabrillo Festival Historic Seminar Papers* (San Diego, CA: Cabrillo Historical Association, 1991), 38–39. See also note 78, this document; Document 25, notes 35 and 36; Document 29, note 50; Document 25, fol. 459r.

132. Craddock, "Fray Marcos," 110, citing Giovanni Battista Ramusio, *Navigazioni e viaggi*, ed. Marica Millanesi, 6 vols. (Turin: Einaudi, 1978–88), 6:599 n. 4, provides a plausible explanation for Marcos's joy about the westward bend of the coast: namely, that it fit with notions that the land of Cíbola adjoined and was contiguous with Asia, still the acknowledged goal of much European exploration.

133. "Like an evergreen garden," *vergel*. Covarrubias, 960, "dijose vergel a vivore, porque se procura que todo el año esté verde."

134. The construction of this sentence leaves it open to question whether the natives of this valley were actually in the habit of traveling to Cíbola annually to labor there, for it only compares their reports to those of people who do go to Cíbola and does not explicitly state that they themselves do. Baldwin, *Discovery of the Seven Cities*, 21, even inserts the word "would" (as people would who went there each year), rendering the statement not at all a declaration that the people travel to Cíbola.

135. Marcos must have misunderstood his informant, because there is no other evidence from this time period that any individual governed one of the *pueblos* of Cíbola or that any *pueblo* had authority over the others. See, for example, Castañeda de Nájera, Document 28, fol. 106r. Ahacus is Hawikku. See, for example, Jesse Green, ed., *Cushing at Zuni: The Correspondence and Journals of Frank Hamilton Cushing, 1879–1884* (Albuquerque: University of New Mexico Press, 1990), 114.

136. There is no evidence, either documentary or archaeological, that buildings at Hawikku or any other of the ancestral Zuni towns reached this height. Frederick Hodge estimated that the five roomblocks in Hawikku had been from one to three stories high. Watson Smith, Richard B. Woodbury, and Nathalie F. S. Woodbury, *The Excavation of Hawikuh by Frederick Webb Hodge: Report of the Hendricks-Hodge Expedition, 1917–1923*, Contributions from the Museum of the American Indian–Heye Foundation, vol. 20 (New York: Museum of the American Indian–Heye Foundation, 1966), 11.

137. This may refer to the practice, still followed at Zuni, of decorating the interiors of rooms used during ceremonies such as Shalako with strings of turquoise, often draped around the stuffed and mounted heads of game animals, particularly deer.

138. "It still rules itself," *sobre*. *DRAE*, 1890, "con dominio y superioridad."

139. The Spanish word is *ueste*, or west, and several early translators rendered it accordingly: Hakluyt, *Principal Navigations*, 9:136; Ternaux-Compans, "Relation de Frère Marcos de Niza," 270; Ramusio, *Terzo volume*, fol. 358r. Beginning with Pacheco and Cárdenas in the 1860s, however, the word was rendered erroneously as *sueste*, or southeast. *CDI*, 3:340; Baldwin, *Discovery of the Seven Cities*, 22; Oblasser, *Arizona Discovered*, 18; Hallenbeck, *Journey of Fray Marcos*, 26; H&R, 72; Mora, 154. More recently, Craddock, "Fray Marcos," 89, rendered the word correctly again as "ueste."

140. Making things even more confusing is the modern spelling of the Keresan name of Acoma used by the people of that pueblo, Haaku. See, for instance, the tribe's official seal.

141. Judging from what is probably a misinterpretation of a native's description of the horn of this animal, it may have been a large desert bighorn. The horns of the bighorn arise, as Marcos's informant states, from a massive bony process at the top of the forehead. Charles D. Hansen, "Physical Characteristics," in Gale Monson and Lowell Sumner, eds., *The Desert Bighorn: Its Life History, Ecology, and Management* (Tucson: University of Arizona Press, 1980), 56–58.

142. This may be a tacit admission on Marcos's part that he had not seen some of the things Esteban saw and was only trusting what Esteban told him through messengers. It certainly would be a rationalization for stating as facts things he might not have seen—perhaps Cíbola, for example.

143. Hallenbeck, *Journey of Fray Marcos*, 28, incorrectly has "and the numbers of them."

144. Regarding documents of possession, see note 119, this document.

145. As in legal proceedings of the day, leading questions may have dominated Marcos's inquiry, which must also have been conducted through one or more interpreters.

146. May 9, 1539, is one of the few dates Marcos supplies in his *relación*. At this point it has thus been 63 days since the friar left Culiacán, on many of which—at least 16—he has not traveled. With 15 days of travel ahead of him before he can reach Cíbola, it seems likely that Esteban is already there and may already be dead.

147. This is one of several indications that Marcos followed well-established trails on his way from Culiacán toward Cíbola and is suggestive of the extensive trade and other communication that existed throughout the region during protohistoric times. See Carroll L. Riley, "The Road to Hawikuh: Trade and Trade Routes to Cíbola-Zuni during Late Prehistoric and Early Historic Times," *Kiva* 41 (1975):137–59.

148. One would have expected Marcos to have met Esteban's companions fleeing southward considerably before having traveled 12 of the final 15 days toward Cíbola. Rather than being three days from Cíbola, one might expect him to be only three days into the *despoblado* (unsettled area), because Marcos was probably at least 16 days behind Esteban, unless the Moor had slowed his travel drastically. Castañeda de Nájera specifically states that Esteban "got so far ahead of the friars that when they reached Chichilticale, which is [at] the beginning of the unsettled land, he was already in Cíbola." This is a further indication that Marcos probably did not get as close to Cíbola as he later claimed. Document 28, fol. 12v. Still a popular meat bird in Spain, the *perdiz*, or common/gray partridge (*Perdix cinerea*), is abundant throughout the Iberian Peninsula. *Enciclopedia universal*, 43:570.

149. Craddock, "Fray Marcos," 112–13, suggests "covered with sweat, with his face and body scraped and bruised," although there is absolutely no indication that this man was anything more than frightened and exhausted. He had not been attacked by the people of Cíbola himself. Compare *aquejar* = *fatigar*, *DRAE*, 176.

150. Esteban had been given this gourd at least three years earlier, somewhere in what is now Tamaulipas. At that point he and the other Narváez expedition survivors "began to carry gourds with us, and we added to our authority this ceremony." Adorno and Pautz, *Núñez Cabeza de Vaca*, 1:205.

151. See note 135, this document.

152. This conceivably could have been a fairly large "unit-type," Chaco-era building known as Hawikku West, which lies in the plain some 700 yards immediately west of Hawikku. It would have been a ruin in 1539. Frederick W. Hodge, *Circular Kivas near Hawikuh, New Mexico*, Contributions of the Museum of the American Indian–Heye Foundation, vol. 7, no. 1 (New York: Museum of the American Indian–Heye Foundation, 1923).

153. This is the Zuni River, which runs just over two miles west of Hawikku. The pueblo would have been visible from there, as would the intervening plain (see map 3).

154. Again Marcos's times seem not to jibe with how far behind Esteban he must have been.

155. This is in stark contrast to the report given less than a year later to Vázquez de Coronado at Hawikku, according to Castañeda de Nájera, that no one other than Esteban had been killed. This exaggeration cannot be laid at Marcos's feet. Evidently his informants were mistaken. See Document 28, fol. 14r.

156. Hallenbeck, *Journey of Fray Marcos*, 75, says, "Several times in his narrative Marcos quotes Indians verbatim and at considerable length: such conversations of course never took place." Marcos did, however, have a number of interpreters with him and he could have been told what had been said, though the quality of translation may have been poor.

157. Hallenbeck, *Journey of Fray Marcos*, 31, fails to translate "tristes" (melancholy). H&R, 77, have "went back very dejectedly."

158. "He was intent on going there," *querer* = *tener determinación*. *DRAE*, 1706.

159. This story is almost exactly a repetition of what the first fleeing Indian had told Marcos. See fol. 6r.

160. Craddock, "Fray Marcos," 113, like others before him, suggested that this was a kiva, or ceremonial chamber. That seems unlikely, given modern rules among Pueblo groups about who can and cannot enter kivas. Instead, see note 152, this document.

161. This is an interesting shift to the first person, as if Marcos is quoting the report of an Indian who had been with Esteban.

162. Hallenbeck, *Journey of Fray Marcos*, 32, scrambles this phrase and the preceding one as, "I confess it seemed to me I was at fault." H&R, 78, are somewhat closer with their free translation: "I must confess that I did not know what to do."

163. This suggests that Marcos had personal slaves or servants with him, in addition to the free Indians who accompanied him en masse from Culiacán.

164. This may also refer to those who went with Esteban, reinforcing the claim that they are probably all dead.

165. This sentence has usually been interpreted as meaning that Cíbola was larger than the Ciudad de México, a patent falsehood. We think the comparison is more likely to Cíbola's finer or more impressive appearance. *Mayor, DRAE*, 1340, "que excede a una cosa en cantidad *o calidad*" [emphasis added].

166. "I had rendered," *ofrecer* = *presentar y dar. DRAE*, 1468.

167. "The excellence," *disposición* = *gallardía. DRAE*, 764.

168. Assigning a name to the land was part of the formula of taking formal possession for the king, as was erecting a cross. See note 119, this document.

169. "At that place": According to Castañeda de Nájera, this was the area of Chichilticale, which was near the southern end of the *despoblado* (unsettled area). Document 28, fol. 12v.

170. This is the *abra*, or wide valley, mentioned on fol. 2v. See note 93, this document.

171. "Failing," *dejar* = *faltar. DRAE*, 674.

172. In the Coronado expedition documents, seven seems to occur with unusual frequency in referring to the numbers of settlements. Besides Cíbola, four other *provincias* are said to have seven towns: Tusayán, Quirix, Jemez, and the unnamed group "on the other side of the snowy mountains" from Tiguex (see maps 3 and 5). Document 28, 115r.

173. By this Marcos indicates the existence of many houses. This interpretation is reinforced by the fact that the plural of *humo* can mean "homes or houses." *DRAE*, 1133. It is at least interesting, if not evidence of lying, that Marcos made no similar observation at Cíbola.

174. Stretching the verb *tratar*, H&R, 80, have "the natives make it into vessels and jewels." Hallenbeck, *Journey of Fray Marcos*, 35, and Baldwin, *Discovery of the Seven Cities*, 30, are in essential agreement with our reading. *Tratar en* = *comerciar géneros. DRAE*, 2018.

175. This pointed elliptical Franciscan *comisario* seal bears the image of the Cross of Calvary and the crossed arms of Christ and Francis of Assisi. The legend surrounding the image reads "Generalis Comisarius Omnium Indiarum Maris Occidentalis." Craddock, "Fray Marcos," 115. *Comisario, DRAE*, 518: "En la Orden de San Francisco, religioso a cuyo cargo estaba el gobierno de sus provincias en Indias."

176. The date is in the Julian calendar.

177. For geographical information, see the entry for Mar Océano in Appendix 2.

178. Ceynos had been appointed *audiencia* judge (*oidor*) in 1558. He was still serving in that capacity in 1565 when Jerónimo Valderrama, *visitador* in Nueva España, declared that he was not fit to be a judge due to his age. Vigil, *Alonso de Zorita*, 179, 192, 226.

179. Both Herrera and Turcios inscribed their rubrics at the bottom of each page of the *relación*, and both signed to authenticate the document at the end. Juan Baeza de Herrera was a native of Baeza in what is now the *comunidad* of Andalucía in Spain, and a son of Ruy Díaz de Baeza, a *criado* of the royal household. Baeza de Herrera served a lengthy term at court as *aposentador* (chamberlain) of the empress. He accompanied Mendoza to Nueva España in 1535 and became secretary and chief *escribano* of the royal *audiencia*. He was married to Inés de Vargas and had died by 1547. Boyd-Bowman, 2: no. 5508; Himmerich y Valencia, *Encomenderos*, 193. For biographical information about Antonio de Turcios, see Appendix 1.

180. *Comissaría* = commissariat.

181. Hallenbeck, *Journey of Fray Marcos*, 37, and Baldwin, *Discovery of the Seven Cities*, 33, both incorrectly have "signed with our signatures." H&R, 82, make no improvement with "signed with our names." It was, in fact, the registered symbol assigned to each of the *escribanos* that served to authenticate a document, in addition to their signatures.

182. For biographical information, see the entry for Antonio de Almaguer in Appendix 1. Fray Martín de Ojacastro was a Franciscan. In 1548 fray Martín Sarmiento de Ojacastro became bishop of Tlaxcala-Puebla. He died in October 1557. María Justina Sarabia Viejo, *Don Luis de Velasco, virrey de Nueva España, 1550–1564* (Sevilla: Escuela de Estudios Hispano-Americanos, 1978), 138; Schäfer, *Consejo Real*, 2:600.

183. All these heading notes were written by one or more *escribanos*, probably in the sixteenth century, but not the same *escribano* who wrote the body of the *relación*. The body of the *relación* is in the hand of an unidentified *escribano* probably from the *audiencia* staff. Despite fray Marcos's not having been a native speaker of Castellano, the *relación* is quite well written. It is possible that is the doing of the *escribano*.

184. Ys = *vais*. See Craddock, "Fray Marcos," 101, B2 1r1; the manuscript B2 has, "ys a."

185. (A) que. B2 omits the *a*. We have removed it here also, because it is superfluous.

186. B2 has "dexaran libres."

187. *Der* is supplied by B2. The bottom right corner of fol. 1r in B1 has flaked away from being repeatedly touched.

188. Aviso = *cuidado. DRAE*, 239.

189. Craddock alters this to "hace." Craddock, "Fray Marcos," 82. However, this is parallel construction with the "dexar" several lines earlier.

190. H&R, 60, have "particularly."

191. The phrase "que se pudiese" is absent from B2.

192. Autos = *actos. DRAE*, 232. H&R, 60, translate this passage as though "senales" refers to marking boundaries and "autos" refers to preparing a document.

193. Recado = *regalo, presente. DRAE*, 1737.

194. Esecutto = *ejecutó*.

195. B2 lacks the heading "Relaçion."

196. Supplied by B2. The bottom right corner of fol. 2r in B1 has flaked away from being repeatedly touched.

197. B2 has "quieren dezir" without "ser."

198. B2 has "truxesen gentte."

199. In both B1 and B2 (as well as the later Vienna copy of the *relación*) the *m* is missing from "palmo," although it is clear that the common unit of measurement of the day is intended.

200. De aya = *de alla*. Craddock, "Fray Marcos," 85, in his transcription of B2, has "de ay a."

201. Supplied by B2. The bottom right corner of fol. 3r in B1 has flaked away from being repeatedly touched.

202. B2 has "dezianme," changing from preterite to imperfect, a not uncommon difference between contemporary versions of the same document. See Flint, *Great Cruelties*, "The Texts," 20.

203. Demas de = *además de*.

204. Supplied by B2. The right margin of fol. 4r in B1 has flaked away from being repeatedly touched.

205. B2 has "con esteban."

206. Supplied by B2. The bottom right corner of fol. 4r in B1 has flaked away from being repeatedly touched.

207. B2 has only "de ellos."

208. The *escribano* of B1 wrote "hallo," apparently slipping into the third person, in which documents of the period were most commonly written. The *escribano* of B2 wrote "halle," which we have accepted.

209. Turar = *durar*. Covarrubias, 941. B2 has "me turo."

210. B2 has "commo subian."

211. Supplied by B2. The upper right corner of fol. 5r in B1 has flaked away from being repeatedly touched.

212. Supplied by B2. The upper right corner of fol. 5r in B1 has flaked away from being repeatedly touched.

213. Supplied by B2. The upper right corner of fol. 5r in B1 has flaked away from being repeatedly touched.

214. Supplied by B2. The upper right corner of fol. 5r in B1 has flaked away from being repeatedly touched.

215. Supplied by B2. The upper right corner of fol. 5r in B1 has flaked away from being repeatedly touched.

216. Supplied by B2. The upper right corner of fol. 5r in B1 has flaked away from being repeatedly touched.

217. Supplied by B2. The upper right corner of fol. 5r in B1 has flaked away from being repeatedly touched.

218. B2 has "persona que el senor tiene alli en cibola puesta." Differences such as this one between B1 and B2 suggest the possibility that they were not both copied from the same original.

219. Supplied by B2. The lower right corner of fol. 5r in B1 has flaked away from being repeatedly touched.

220. Supplied by B2. The lower right corner of fol. 5r in B1 has flaked away from being repeatedly touched.

221. Supplied by B2. The lower right corner of fol. 5r in B1 has flaked away from being repeatedly touched.

222. Supplied by B2. The lower right corner of fol. 5r in B1 has flaked away from being repeatedly touched.

223. Supplied by B2. The lower right corner of fol. 5r in B1 has flaked away from being repeatedly touched.

224. B2 has "ya que hasta alli."

225. *CDI*, 3:342, erroneously has "los naturales de esta villa." H&R, 74; Mora, 155; and Hallenbeck, *Journey of Fray Marcos*, 28, all copied this error, clearly without checking the manuscripts; both B1 and B2 have "valle." Craddock, "Fray Marcos," 90.

226. Supplied by B2. The upper right corner of fol. 6r in B1 has flaked away from being repeatedly touched.

227. Supplied by B2. The upper right corner of fol. 6r in B1 has flaked away from being repeatedly touched.

228. Supplied by B2. The upper right corner of fol. 6r in B1 has flaked away from being repeatedly touched.

229. Supplied by B2. The upper right corner of fol. 6r in B1 has flaked away from being repeatedly touched.

230. Supplied by B2. The upper right corner of fol. 6r in B1 has flaked away from being repeatedly touched.

231. Supplied by B2. The upper right corner of fol. 6r in B1 has flaked away from being repeatedly touched.

232. Supplied by B2. The upper right corner of fol. 6r in B1 has flaked away from being repeatedly touched.

233. Allegar = *llegar*. DRAE, 120.

234. Llegar = *tocar*. DRAE, 1281.

235. Supplied by B2. The lower right corner of fol. 6r in B1 has flaked away from being repeatedly touched.

236. Supplied by B2. The lower right corner of fol. 6r in B1 has flaked away from being repeatedly touched.

237. Supplied by B2. The lower right corner of fol. 6r in B1 has flaked away from being repeatedly touched.

238. Supplied by B2. The lower right corner of fol. 6r in B1 has flaked away from being repeatedly touched.

239. It is clear that the conditional and not the imperfect tense of the verb is appropriate here, because the reception was still in the future at this point.

240. B2 has "no escaparon mas de nosotros." Craddock, "Fray Marcos," 92.

241. Supplied by B2. The upper right corner of fol. 7r in B1 has flaked away from being repeatedly touched.

242. *Sus pa* is supplied by B2. The upper right corner of fol. 7r in B1 has flaked away from being repeatedly touched. The *a* is superfluous and may indicate Marcos's lack of full command of Castellano. Or it may simply be a slip by Marcos or the *escribano*.

243. Supplied by B2. The upper right corner of fol. 7r in B1 has flaked away from being repeatedly touched.

244. Once again it is clear that the conditional and not the imperfect tense of the verb is appropriate here.

245. B2 has "para ver."

246. Supplied by B2. The lower right corner of fol. 7r in B1 has flaked away from being repeatedly touched.

247. Supplied by B2. The lower right corner of fol. 7r in B1 has flaked away from being repeatedly touched.

248. B2 has "a poblar y señorear estotra."

249. The certification beginning with "En la gran ciudad" is in the hand of Antonio de Turcios.

Document 7. Letters from Antonio de Mendoza and Rodrigo de Albornoz, October 18, 1539

1. AGI, Patronato, 57, N.2, R.1, "Méritos y servicios de Antonio de Mendoza, March 1545"; Himmerich y Valencia, *Encomenderos*, 116; Aiton, *Mendoza*, 11. For an outline of the revolt and its suppression, see Elliott, *Imperial Spain*, 151–59.

2. Carlos V, "Carta de Carlos V a Hernán Cortés, Valladolid, October 1522," in Martínez, *Documentos Cortesianos*, 1:255.

3. Himmerich y Valencia, *Encomenderos*, 14.

4. AGI, México, 1064, L.1\1, "Informes de los conquistadores y pobladores de México y otros lugares en Nueva España, en el año 1644 [1547]," compiled by Gil Gonzalez Dávila.

5. AGI, Patronato, 87, N.1, R.5, "Méritos y servicios de García Rodríguez y biznieto, 1617."

6. Aiton, *Mendoza*, 11–12. For more complete biographical information, see the entry for Antonio de Mendoza in Appendix 1.

7. Alonso de la Torre was named royal treasurer for Santo Domingo in July 1535, because of the death of his predecessor in the office. He was married to doña María de Cogollos. He died in August 1544 in Santo Domingo while in jail as a result of irregularities in his accounts that were uncovered during his *residencia*. Fray Cipriano de Utrera, *Noticias Históricas de Santo Domingo*, ed. Emilio Rodríguez Demorizi, 6 vols. (Santo Domingo, Dominican Republic: Editora Taller, 1978–83), 2:12, 4:85, 6:146.

8. Fol. 22v.

9. Fols. 22v and 23r.

10. Fol. 22r.

11. Pérez de Tudela Bueso, "Vida y escritos," cxviii.

12. Document 25, fols. 457v and 458r.

13. Pérez de Tudela Bueso, "Vida y escritos," x, xxxiii, xl, xlviii, cxix.

14. Adorno and Pautz, *Núñez Cabeza de Vaca*, 3:6; Pérez de Tudela Bueso, "Vida y escritos," cxl.

15. Sources vary on the year of Oviedo's death, giving dates of 1556, 1557, and 1558. Adorno and Pautz, *Núñez Cabeza de Vaca*, 3:6; Pérez de Tudela Bueso, "Vida y escritos," clxvi; *The National Union Catalog, Pre-1956 Imprints*, 754 vols. (London: Mansell Information/Publishing and American Library Association, 1976), 435:698, 436:1–3. The first complete publication of the *Historia* was Gonzalo Fernández de Oviedo y Valdés, *Historia general y natural de las Indias*, ed. José Amador de los Rios, 4 vols. (Madrid: Real Academia de la Historia, 1851–55).

16. Adorno and Pautz, *Núñez Cabeza de Vaca*, 3:17–18; Demetrio Ramos, *Ximénez de Quesada en su relación con los cronistas y el epítome de la conquista del Nuevo Reino de Granada* (Sevilla: Escuela de Estudios Hispano-Americanos, 1972).

17. Fols. 22v and 23r.

18. The two extant manuscripts that together make up Oviedo's *Historia* were penned by two different, sixteenth-century hands. The larger of the two manuscripts, which comprises Parts 1 and 2 of the *Historia*, seems to be a copy of an earlier example, judging from the corrected date in Document 25, fol. 459v. This leaves the possibility that Part 3 (which includes the excerpt published here) is in Oviedo's own hand.

19. Only Part 3 of the *Historia* is conserved at the Biblioteca Real. The first two parts are found in the Real Academia de la Historia in Madrid. See the introduction to Document 25 for more complete information on those two parts.

20. In order to press his case with the king and Consejo de Indias, the Marqués del Valle, Hernán Cortés, returned to Spain in 1540, where he died seven years

later, still in hope of recovering his lost prerogatives. López de Gómara, *Cortés*, 407–8. Francisco López de Gómara, Cortés's secretary, reported: "Cortés and don Antonio de Mendoza quarreled bitterly over the expedition to Cíbola." López de Gómara, *Cortés*, 407. For a concise statement of Cortés's position in the dispute, see Document 18. Theirs was not the only dispute over the right to mount such an expedition. Also involved were Hernando de Soto, Nuño de Guzmán, and Pedro de Alvarado, all powerful forces in the Indies. The legal action before the Consejo de Indias that resulted from the dispute was not definitively settled in favor of Mendoza until 1541, more than a year after the expedition to Tierra Nueva had been launched. A transcription of the final stages of the legal case is "Proceso del Marqués del Valle y Nuño de Guzmán y los Adelantados Soto y Alvarado, sobre el Descubrimiento de la Tierra Nueva, 1541," in *CDI*, 15:300–408. For the formal resolution of differences on this subject between Alvarado and Mendoza, see Document 20.

21. In the English-speaking world, the name Española is more commonly written Hispaniola. This Caribbean island now comprises the countries of Haiti and the Dominican Republic. Santo Domingo, on its southern coast, was, from 1511, the seat of the only royal court, or *audiencia*, in the Indies until the establishment of the Audiencia de México in 1527. In 1540 Santo Domingo still held onto some pretension as the premier representative of the king's authority. Schäfer, *Consejo Real*, 2:443, 451. Temistitán = Tenochtitlan, the ruins on which Mexico City was built.

22. Mendoza, showing his age and formality, wrote in an older style and used out-of-date terms and constructions more frequently than was usual at this time.

23. These Franciscan friars were Marcos de Niza and Onorato. See Document 6, fol. 2r. For geographical information about the Mar del Sur, see Appendix 2.

24. Marcos's formal report is Document 6 in this volume.

25. Reference here is to the small fleet led by Hernando de Alarcón. His formal report of that trip is Document 15 in this volume. The two *navíos* were the *San Pedro* and the *Santa Catarina*. Document 15, fol. 363r. The muster roll of the expedition lists just 25 arquebusiers and 19 crossbowmen. Document 12.

26. Thus Oviedo claims that the excerpt is copied verbatim. Excluding inadvertent copying errors, there seems to be little reason to doubt his assertion. Oviedo reinforces his claim on fol. 23r, where he writes that "what is stated [here] I extracted verbatim [*a la letra*]." For a discussion of Oviedo's reliability as a copyist, see the introduction to this document and Adorno and Pautz, *Núñez Cabeza de Vaca*, 3:15–18.

27. For biographical information, see the entry about Nuño Beltrán de Guzmán in Appendix 1.

28. As Francisco de Ulloa was about to report, this supposed island was actually a peninsula, what we now know as Baja California. For a brief account of these voyages between 1532 and 1539, see López de Gómara, *Cortés*, 396–404.

29. These are fray Marcos and Esteban de Dorantes. Document 6, fol. 1r. For biographical information, see the entry about Pánfilo de Narváez in Appendix 1.

30. "Going to travel until," *parar* = go as far as. *DRAE*, 1528, "llegar al fin."

31. These seven *ciudades* made up Cíbola. For more complete geographical information, see the entry for Cíbola in Appendix 2. See also Document 6.

32. See the introduction to Document 6 for a discussion of whether fray Marcos's claim to have seen Cíbola can be taken as true.

33. For suggestions about the identity and location of Marate, see the entry for Marata in Appendix 2.

34. There is no mention of such Old World animals in Marcos's report. But expectations that such beasts would be encountered in the New World, still thought to be linked to Asia, were prevalent at the time. As Susan Milbrath has written: "Long after the early explorers, fanciful images connecting America and Asia persisted." Susan Milbrath, "Old World Meets New: Views across the Atlantic," in Jerald T. Milanich and Susan Milbrath, eds., *First Encounters: Spanish Explorations in the Caribbean and the United States, 1492–1570* (Gainesville: University of Florida Press, 1989), 186. See also note 35 below.

35. These same animals seem to be described by fray Marcos in his report. Document 6, fol. 5v.

36. These long articles of clothing are reminiscent of the *albornozes* (hooded capes) referred to by the witnesses in Habana a month or so later. Document 8, fols. 68r and 69r. The notion that there were camels in the Americas during protohistoric times may have originated from Marcos's use of the designation "Zaragoza" to describe fabric woven at Totonteac. Rodrigo de Albornoz apparently interprets that to mean *chamelote*, or "camlet," a luxurious, water–repellant fabric once made from

a combination of silk and camel's hair. Covarrubias, 244: "la tela de la lana del camello, despide el agua que no la cala." Martínez Meléndez, *Nombres de tejidos*, 472: "Despues de la Edad Media, parecer ser que el *camelote* más conocido era el elaborado con pelo de camello y se utilizaba para protegerse de la lluvia." *OED*, 2:323. See also Document 6, fol. 4v. "In Moorish style" evidently refers to Marcos's use of the phrase "a Bohemian outfit." Document 6, fol 4r.

37. "[Who] says it pertains to him," *pertenecer*. *DRAE*, 1584, "serle debida; ser una cosa del cargo, ministerio u obligación de uno."

38. Thus, as early as October 1539 Vázquez de Coronado had been designated to lead the expedition. This throws into doubt Herbert Bolton's suggestion that the viceroy himself had planned to lead the *entrada*, which he based on the relatively late date of the captain general's formal appointment. Bolton, 53–54. See Documents 9 and 10 for Vázquez de Coronado's formal appointment. The current count of men-at-arms of Old World origin or ancestry who participated in the Coronado expedition is 353. See Appendix 3 for the full current list. "To make an extensive report," *tomar larga relación*. *DRAE*, 1991, "con ciertos nombres verbales significa lo mismo que los verbos de donde tales nombres se derivan."

39. In fact, only five friars accompanied the *entrada*: Marcos de Niza, Juan de Padilla, Luis de Úbeda, Antonio de Castilblanco, and Daniel. Chávez, *Coronado's Friars*. See also Document 4, note 8.

40. That is, departure was evidently scheduled for the first days of December 1539. It appears that most people left the Ciudad de México no later than then. Some may have left earlier. Viceroy Mendoza himself was in Michoacán by no later than December 31. Fintan B. Warren, *Vasco de Quiroga and his Pueblo-Hospitals of Santa Fe* (Washington, DC: Academy of American Franciscan History, 1963), 99.

41. "The return of the Tierra Firme and New Spain fleets always included a landfall in Havana." Although this statement applies to the period of the regular *flotas*, or fleets, beginning in the 1560s, it describes equally the less regulated sailings before then. Pablo E. Pérez-Mallaína, *Spain's Men of the Sea: Daily Life on the Indies Fleets in the Sixteenth Century*, trans. Carla Rahn Phillips (Baltimore, MD: Johns Hopkins University Press, 1998), 14.

42. Aquesta tierra ysla. PTBOviedo, 4:350, incorrectly has "aquesta rica ysla."

43. Aun = *también*. *DRAE*, 230.

44. Sabido. PTBOviedo, 4:350, has "sabiendo."

45. Da nueVas. PTBOviedo, 4:350, incorrectly has "daba."

46. Dizque. PTBOviedo, 4:350, modernizes this as "dice que."

47. Uincornios = *unicornios*.

48. Suelo. PTBOviedo, 4:350, incorrectly has "cuello."

49. Se concluye. PTBOviedo, 4:350, incorrectly has "se conosce."

Document 8. *Testimony of Witnesses in Habana regarding Fray Marcos's Discoveries, November 1539*

1. Documents 18, 20, and 21.

2. Their formal agreement is Document 20.

3. It remains an open question how the two resulting expeditions might have behaved had they met each other somewhere in the southern Great Plains. It is conceivable that, in continuation of their leaders' rivalry, they might have fought, with the idea of defending the territory over which each thought it held exclusive right to establish control. This happened with other expeditions in places such as Peru and Nueva Granada during the sixteenth century.

4. *CDI*, 15:304.

5. Clayton, Knight, and Moore, *De Soto Chronicles*, 1:360.

6. David J. Weber, *The Spanish Frontier in North America* (New Haven, CT: Yale University Press, 1992), 36.

7. The Río de las Palmas is now identified as the Río Soto la Marina, which empties into the Gulf of Mexico about midway along the coast of the modern Mexican state of Tamaulipas. Robert S. Weddle, "Coastal Exploration and Mapping: A Concomitant to the Entradas," in *The Mapping of the Entradas into the Greater Southwest*, eds. Dennis Reinhartz and Gerald D. Saxon (Norman: University of Oklahoma Press, 1998), 114.

8. The same document that conceded to Soto the right to mount an expedition also conferred on him "the government of the said Island of Cuba." Clayton, Knight, and Moore, *De Soto Chronicles*, 1:361.

9. Fol. 67v.

10. Fol. 69v.

11. Day, *Coronado's Quest*, 66.

12. Fol. 68v.

13. Fol. 69r.

14. Charles Hudson, *Knights of Spain, Warriors of the Sun: Hernando de Soto and the South's Ancient Chiefdoms* (Athens: University of Georgia Press, 1997), 62, 119.

15. Fol. 67v.

16. Hartmann and Flint, "Before the Coronado Expedition," 34.

17. The following contemporaries of Marcos explicitly accused him of lying about Cíbola: Diego López, Pedro de Castañeda de Nájera, Vázquez de Coronado, and Lorenzo Álvarez. Flint, *Great Cruelties*, 364, 396; Document 28, fols. 20v and 34v; Document 19, fol. 360r. See also the introduction to Document 6.

18. In this matter the great historian relied completely on information provided by the seventeenth-century historian fray Antonio Tello and the eighteenth-century historian Matías de la Mota y Padilla. Bolton, 53. See, for instance, Tello, 326, which describes Mendoza as "wanting to go in person on this reconnaissance and expedition."

19. Fol. 68r.

20. The king's formal appointment was made in June 1540; see Document 10.

21. *CDI*, 15:376–79. This is the only known claim that the king expended funds to support fray Marcos's trip. The validity of that claim has not been confirmed.

22. Soto would actually never have heard the name Cíbola, for his final contact with the world outside La Florida took place before fray Marcos's return from the north. He was, however, well aware of and heavily influenced by the earlier reports of Álvar Núñez Cabeza de Vaca and his companions. Hudson, *Knights of Spain*, 349, 407.

23. Nancy Adele Kenmotsu, James E. Bruseth, and James E. Corbin, "Moscoso and the Route in Texas: A Reconstruction," in *The Expedition of Hernando de Soto West of the Mississippi, 1541–1543*, eds. Gloria A. Young and Michael P. Hoffman (Fayetteville: University of Arkansas Press, 1993), 122–23.

24. Cíbola as reported by Marcos de Niza.

25. Juan de Barrutia represented Hernando de Soto's interests before the Consejo de Indias during 1540 and 1541 in its effort to sort out which person or persons had a legitimate right to mount an expedition to Cíbola. The contending parties were, besides Soto, Hernán Cortés, Pedro de Alvarado, Nuño Beltrán de Guzmán, and Antonio de Mendoza. *CDI*, 15:300–408. Barrutia was a native of Mondragón in the modern *provincia* of Guipúzcoa in the País Vasco. When he left Spain in 1538, it was with the Soto expedition bound for La Florida. Boyd-Bowman, 2: no. 4815; *Pasajeros*, 2: no. 4133. Known today simply as Habana, Cuba, in 1539 San Cristóbal de Habana was in its modern location on the island's northwest coast. It had been transferred there from the south coast in late 1518 and early 1519. Said to have the best port in Spanish America, it became a regular stopping point for ships returning from the Indies to Spain. Hugh Thomas, *Conquest: Montezuma, Cortés, and the Fall of Old Mexico* (New York: Simon and Schuster, 1995), 147; Pérez-Mallaína, *Spain's Men of the Sea*, 14.

26. According to the testimony of Pero Núñez and others, Mendoza's order actually was that none of the ships he was sending to Spain was to land in Cuba at all. Fol. 67v.

27. It was either in these ships or others dispatched at about the same time that Mendoza sent fray Marcos's *relación* to the king and Consejo de Indias, as well as his own letter of October 16, 1539, to the royal treasurer in Santo Domingo. The *relación* is Document 6, and the letter is published in Document 7 in this volume.

28. This is the statement of an unidentified official of the Consejo de Indias and appears in his hand.

29. The Consejo de Indias, like the rest of the king's councils at this time, was peripatetic: it moved around as the king did and had no permanent seat. In December 1540, Prince Felipe, nominally ruler during one of his father's many absences (this time in Flanders), and therefore the court and the councils, was in residence in Madrid. In part this was to attend the wedding of the daughter of the king's secretary, Francisco de los Cobos, which was also attended by Hernán Cortés. Hayward Keniston, *Francisco de los Cobos, Secretary of the Emperor Charles V* (Pittsburgh: University of Pittsburgh Press, 1959), 232–33. For general information about the Consejo de la Indias, see Appendix 1.

30. The island now known as Cuba was given the name Fernandina in honor of the king of Aragón on October 15, 1492, by Cristóbal Colón. Oliver Dunn and James E. Kelley, Jr., trans. and eds., *The Diario of Christopher Columbus's First Voyage to America, 1492–1493* (Norman: University of Oklahoma Press, 1989), 84, 85.

31. Like all other dates in this document, this one is according to the Julian calendar.

32. This could be a man from Burgos who went to the Indies in 1513. Boyd-Bowman, 1: no. 668.

33. A native of Cuellar in the *provincia* of Segovia in the modern Spanish *comunidad* of Castilla y León, the hidalgo Juan de Rojas reached Habana with his brother Manrique no later than 1524. There he served as an *alcalde* and as Hernando de Soto's lieutenant governor. Boyd-Bowman, 2: no. 7883.

34. The addressee, although unnamed, is undoubtedly Juan de Rojas.

35. "Trade for gold," *rescatar*. *DRAE*, 1779: "cambiar o trocar oro u otros objetos preciosos por mercaderías ordinarias." Ayala's claim here is that a principal purpose of Marcos's trip was to secure gold through trade, something not specifically mentioned in the viceroy's formal instructions to the friar. However, Marcos's own statement in Document 6, fol. 6r, about "clothing and trade items I was taking along, which until then I had not touched or given anything of to anyone," lends some credence to Juan de Ayala's claim. This suggests there were other, unwritten instructions Marcos received from the viceroy.

36. For a summary of the *marqués's* complaints against Mendoza, see Document 18.

37. This would have been mid-August 1539. Fray Marcos arrived in the Ciudad de México during the final days of August. Document 6, fol. 7v.

38. All of the Habana witnesses place Cíbola between 400 and 500 leagues from the Ciudad de México. At 2.63 miles to the league, this would be 1,000 to 1,300 miles. The actual shortest straight-line distance to Zuni (by way of Tepíc [old Compostela] and the Sonora Valley) is closer to 1,400 miles (see map 1).

39. Río de Palmas: see note 7, this document.

40. This refers to the voyage undertaken by Francisco de Ulloa at Cortés's instance in the summer of 1539. Bolton, 46. For brief biographical information about Hernán Cortés, see the introduction to Document 18.

41. This would have been early to mid-October 1539.

42. This is an accurate description of the Zuni pueblos. Compare, for instance, Frank Hamilton Cushing's description from 1879. Jesse Green, ed., *Zuñi: Selected Writings of Frank Hamilton Cushing* (Lincoln: University of Nebraska Press, 1979), 48.

43. What is being referred to here is unclear. The protohistoric Zunis/Cíbolans are not known to have used standard measures of weight or length. This rumor was probably taken as an indication that Cíbolans had precious metals, which in Europe were associated with the need for accurate and consistent measurement.

44. The use of the term "hooded cloaks" is one of many examples of depictions of the natives of North America as close relatives of Arabs, which conformed to prevalent European geographical conceptions of the day. Anderson, *Hispanic Costume*, 97: "the burnoose (*albornoz*), a hooded cape." See also note 70, this document. Because none of the protohistoric peoples of what is today the southwestern United States and northwestern Mexico were equestrians, the reference to people traveling about "mounted on animals" is sheer fantasy.

45. "In order to raise a troop," *hacer gente*. *DRAE*, 1082: "juntar, convocar."

46. This incomplete statement of the leadership of the Coronado expedition is correct as far as it goes. See, for instance, Document 28, fols. 16v–19r. For biographical information about Hernando de Alarcón, see Document 15, note 6. For biographical information on Pedro de Tovar, see Document 28, note 102.

47. "Master [of the ship]," *maestre*. *DRAE*, 1290: "persona a quien después del capitán correspondía antiguamente el gobierno económico de las naves mercantes." "[The master's] mission was easy to define but difficult to carry out: to see that the ship had all the material and human resources necessary to arrive at its destination and that the passengers and cargo were delivered in perfect condition, after having paid all their taxes." Pérez-Mallaína, *Spain's Men of the Sea*, 87.

48. Then as now, Matanzas was a town on the north coast of Cuba, approximately 50 miles east of Habana.

49. Again, this would have been mid-October 1539.

50. This is erroneous, a rumor given credence by wishful thinking and mistaken conceptions of geography.

51. This apparently refers to Nahuatl. In this the witness is mistaken. Zuni is not a Uto-Aztecan language, as Nahuatl is. What shared origins it has with other languages are unclear, although it has been suggested that Zuni is related to Penutian. Fred Eggan, "Pueblos: Introduction," in *Handbook of North American Indians*, vol. 9, edited by Alfonso Ortiz (Washington, DC: Smithsonian Institution Press, 1979), 226.

52. The suggestion here that Cíbola was distant from any coast was certainly accurate (map 1).

53. The Vera Cruz founded by Hernán Cortés in 1519 as la Villa Rica de la Vera Cruz is now generally known as Vera Cruz Vieja, or La Antigua, in order to distinguish it from the nearby modern town of the same name. The town, at its various locations on the Gulf of Mexico coast, has been throughout its history the principal east-coast port of Nueva España and Mexico. In the sixteenth century all ships legally departing from Nueva España for Spain embarked from there. Pérez-Mallaína, *Spain's Men of the Sea*, 11–12.

54. Indeed, part of the land located by Marcos extended along the sea coast. However, that did not include the region specifically reported as wealthy. As Pero Sánchez had testified earlier, Cíbola was at a considerable distance from the coast.

55. Spanish settlements were first established on the island of Puerto Rico in 1508 by Juan Ponce de León. Throughout the sixteenth century ships bound from Spain to Veracruz regularly stopped at Puerto Rico for firewood and drinking water. Peter Bakewell, *A History of Latin America* (Oxford: Blackwell, 1997), 73; Pérez-Mallaína, *Spain's Men of the Sea*, 11.

56. Hernando de Sotomayor was from Medina del Campo in the modern *provincia* of Valladolid in the *comunidad* of Castilla y León in Spain. He traveled to the Indies in 1511 and again in 1514. Boyd-Bowman, 1: no. 4538.

57. For geographical information, see the entry for Puebla de los Angeles in Appendix 2.

58. For biographical information, see the entries for Andrés Dorantes, Álvar Núñez Cabeza de Vaca, and Pánfilo de Narváez in Appendix 1.

59. Mendoza had at least two secretaries at the time. One was Juan de León and a second was Antonio de Almaguer. AGI, Patronato, 64, R.1, "Juan de Aguilar." For biographical information about Almaguer, see Appendix 1.

60. A relative of Hernán Cortés, Francisco de Villegas was a native of the modern *comunidad* of Extremadura in Spain. He was in the Ciudad de México by 1521 and was a *vecino* there in 1525. He went with Nuño de Guzmán to Nueva Galicia in 1530 and became the *alcalde* of Compostela. He was still alive in 1547. He was also the *encomendero* of Uruapan. In January 1530 he accused the Cazonzi (principal native leader) in Michoacán of murdering Spaniards. Adorno and Pautz, *Núñez Cabeza de Vaca*, 3:348; Boyd-Bowman, 1: no. 5115a; Icaza, 1: no. 368. See also Document 25, note 19.

61. Estate administrator," *hacedor.* Covarrubias, 619: "el agente que tiene a su cargo el beneficiar la hacienda del señor."

62. This is the most detailed information about precious metals in Cíbola attributed to fray Marcos. See the introduction to this document. "Necklace," *sarta.* Covarrubias, 885: "collar o gargantilla."

63. "Blacksmith's forge," *herrería.* This could also refer to ironworks, including foundries. Covarrubias, 631: "donde . . . el hierro . . . se purifica y se pone en barras para los herreros."

64. Hernando Florencio surrounded Rojas's signature with his attestation.

65. *Ad perpetuam rei memoriam.* DRAE, 1164: "que se hace judicialmente y a prevención, para que conste en lo sucesivo una cosa." "For the perpetual remembrance of the matter." Eugene Ehrlich, *Amo, Amas, Amat and More* (New York: Harper and Row, 1985).

66. The body of this document is written in the hand of Hernando Florencio, with his rubric at the bottom of each page. All of fol. 66r is a later addition, probably in the hand of an *escribano* of the Consejo de Indias (A). On fol. 66v, "el Adelantado soto" and "en madrid / A xxiij de diziembre de jUdxL" are in the hand of another scribe of the Consejo (B), while the Consejo's decision, "que se ponga en el pro- / ceso," is in the hand of yet another scribe of the Consejo (C). On fol. 67r, the heading that begins "en madrid . . ." is in the hand of scribe B.

67. The *escribano* slips into the third person here and writes "su parte" rather than "mi parte."

68. *En*bargante que en toCar. CDI, 15:396, incorrectly has "que no toca."

69. Pasaba. CDI, 15:397, mistakenly has "estaba," having read that word from the line immediately above.

70. Alvornyos. There is no such word as "alvornyos." The *escribano* was clearly unfamiliar with what he was copying. *Albañil* = master mason, DRAE, 81; *albornía* = a large, glazed vessel, DRAE, 84; *albornozes* = hooded cloaks, DRAE, 84. Marcos's *relación* mentions both *albornozes* and ceramic vessels. García Navarro (fol. 68r) specifically mentions *albornozes* in his testimony. Therefore it remains unclear what is intended here. CDI, 15:397, is of no help. Pacheco and Cárdenas transcribed the word as "albarnios," an unknown word with no good candidate for its intended significance.

Document 9. The Viceroy's Appointment of Vázquez de Coronado to Lead the Expedition, January 6, 1540

1. The text of this *cédula* is incorporated into the letter of appointment, fols. 23 right–24 left.

2. Fols. 24 left–24 right.

3. Fol. 25 right.

4. See Document 10.

5. See Document 8.

6. Nearly a century later, Matías de la Mota y Padilla wrote the same thing. Writing in 1949, Herbert Bolton accepted Tello's and Mota y Padilla's statements as fact. Tello, 326; Matías de la Mota y Padilla, *Historia de la conquista del reino de la Nueva Galicia*, ed. José Ireneo Gutiérrez (Guadalajara: Talleres Gráficos de Gallardo y Álvarez del Castillo, 1920), 149; see also Day, "Mota Padilla," 91; Bolton, 53.

7. Aiton, *Mendoza*, 46.

8. See the introduction to Document 20.

9. Arthur S. Aiton, "Documents: Coronado's Commission as Captain-General," *Hispanic American Historical Review* 20, no. 1 (1940):83.

10. That *cédula* is included in this volume as Document 5.

11. Fol. 25 left.

12. Fol. 25 right.

13. For discussion of this suit and its outcome, see the introduction to Document 34.

14. The annotations specify in detail the differences that exist between the copy in AGI, Justicia, 336, N.1, "sobre ciertos yndios," and the copy in AGI, Justicia, 339, N.1, R.1, "Residencia." For the sake of space, similar comparisons with the copies in AGI, Justicia, 339, N.1, R.2, "Residencia, August 1544," and AGI, Justicia, 1021, N.2, Pieza 1, "Acusación," have been omitted.

15. For biographical information, see the entry for Diego de Almaguer in Appendix 1.

16. Balbuena's given name is provided by Document 11, fol. 68r.

17. For biographical information about Antonio de Turcios, see Appendix 1.

18. Aiton, "Documents," 83–87.

19. H&R, 83–86.

20. Agapito Rey, transcriber, "La acusación contra Don García López de Cárdenas por ciertas crueldades, AGI, Justicia, 1021, Pieza 1," Bolton Papers, no. 401, Bancroft Library, University of California, Berkeley, 106–12.

21. This is one of three excerpts from AGI, Justicia, 336, N.1, that appear in this volume. The other two are Documents 11 and 34.

22. This portion of AGI, Justicia, 336, N.1, "sobre ciertos yndios," uses a relatively uncommon folio numbering system in which facing sheets bear the same number, rather than the more usual "recto-verso" designation of the two sides of a single sheet.

23. This is the standard preamble to a royal *cédula* of the period. See Document 5, note 16.

24. For geographical information, see the entry for Culiacán and San Miguel de Culiacán in Appendix 2.

25. Servirse, would likely be of service. DRAE, 1872: "valerse de una cosa para el uso propio de ella."

26. For biographical information about fray Marcos, see the introduction to Document 6.

27. "Even *reinos.*" An *escribano* called attention to this with marginal highlighting.

28. The friar's formal, written report is published here as Document 6.

29. One of the harmful effects of delay, from fray Marcos's viewpoint, would have been that Indians would die unconverted and therefore would be deprived of the possibility of attaining paradise. A second and extremely negative effect for a millenarian Franciscan like Marcos would have been that delay in conversion would also delay the second coming of Christ, which was thought to be imminent but dependent on making Christianity known to all the peoples of the world. For many followers of Saint Francis of Assisi in the early 1500s, the missionary enterprise had this special urgency. Delno C. West, "Medieval Ideas of Apocalyptic Mission and the Early Franciscans in Mexico," *The Americas* 45 (Jan. 1989):293–313.

30. "Convert," *reduzyr.* "Reducir" could presumably entail force, whereas AGI, Justicia, 339, N.1, R.1, "Residencia," fol. 1v, has "resçibir," welcome, a much more benign concept.

31. Although Viceroy Mendoza here presents the Coronado expedition as existing primarily in order to safeguard missionary friars, the evidence is overwhelming that lay members of the expedition and most other Europeans in Nueva España at the time did not view the undertaking in the same way. Two years after the expedition, for instance, the investigation judge and *oidor* of the *audiencia* Lorenzo de Tejada consistently characterized the purpose of the expedition as "to reconnoiter and subjugate the province of Cíbola, Cicuique, and Tiguex." See also, for example, the testimony of Francisca de Hozes in Flint, *Great Cruelties*, 58.

32. This refers to the five friars who accompanied the land component of the Coronado expedition and the unknown friars who sailed with Hernando de Alarcón. In all likelihood Alarcón's voyage of 1540 included one or more priests, as his proposed second voyage was slated to. See Document 16, fol. 1r, and Chávez, *Coronado's Friars*, 1–2.

33. For brief biographical information about Hernán Cortés, see the introduction to Document 18.

34. King Carlos left Spain from Barcelona in April 1535 for an expedition against Tunis. Kamen, *Philip of Spain*, 4; Otto von Habsburg, *Charles V*, trans. Michael Ross (New York: Praeger, 1969), 239.

35. H&R, 83, omit everything preceding "I, the King" from their translation of this document.

36. This is Francisco de los Cobos, who was *comendador mayor* (the highest administrator and *caballero* in one of the religious-military orders) of León from August 1, 1524, until May 5, 1547. From late 1503 until his death in mid-1547 he served in the royal government, first as royal scribe, then as chief accountant, and finally as secretary and advisor to Carlos V. A native of Úbeda in the *provincia* of Jaén in Andalucía, Cobos was born about 1477. He married María de Mendoza y Pimental (more than 20 years his junior) in 1522. Schäfer, *Consejo Real*, 1:369; Keniston, *Francisco de los Cobos*. Following Cobos's title, AGI, Justicia, 339, N.1, R.1., "Residencia," fol. 2r, has a rare mark of punctuation, "/," indicating the end of a section of the document.

37. For geographical information, see the entries for Acus and Cíbola in Appendix 2. The name Matata is rendered the same way in both AGI, Justicia, 339, N.1, R.1, "Residencia," and AGI, Justicia, 339, N.1, R.2, "Residencia, August 1544," although it generally appears as Marata in other Coronado expedition documents. The difference here is most likely a product of the scribal process. For geographical information, see the entry for Marata in Appendix 2. "Totinteac" is an uncommon spelling and is probably a scribal error. Both AGI, Justicia, 339, N.1, R.1., "Residencia," fol. 2v, and AGI, Justicia, 339, N.1, R.2, "Residencia, August 1544," have the more usual spelling, "Totonteac." For geographical information, see the entry for Totonteac in Appendix 2.

38. "Effort," *industria*. Covarrubias, 666.

39. "As our captain general," *del capitan. De = por* = as. DRAE, 663–64.

40. Although this provision appears to grant Vázquez de Coronado sole authority to appoint captains, he testified in 1544 that "in consultation with the viceroy, [Vázquez de Coronado] named the rest of the captains." Flint, *Great Cruelties*, 277.

41. "May be approved," *bien visto*. DRAE, 2098: "se juzga bien."

42. "You can judge and may judge," *conocer de causa*. DRAE, 544: "entender en un asunto con facultad legitima para ello."

43. The directive referred to here must have included a provision requiring use of the *requerimiento*, which since 1513 was to be given to and employed by all expeditions of reconnaissance and conquest and which the leaders of the Coronado expedition routinely read to native people they encountered. The full directive does not accompany the copy of Vázquez de Coronado's appointment that has been preserved. Nevertheless, it probably included many of the specific provisions of the then-current regulations governing conquests, including the requirement that the leader of any such enterprise render a full report to the *audiencia*. See Hanke, *Spanish Struggle for Justice*, 30–36. See also Angel de Altoaguirre y Duvale, ed., "Título IX," in *Governación espiritual y temporal de las Indias: Códice publicado en virtud de acuerdo de la Real Academia de la Historia*, vol. 20, *Colección de Documentos Inéditos de Ultramar*, 2nd series (Madrid: n.p., 1927), 306–22. See Appendix 4 for a version of the *requerimiento* from the period.

44. "Word for word," *al pie de la letra*. DRAE, 1596, 1248.

45. This is a formulaic phrase that appears routinely in royal appointments, indicating the granting of all power and authority requisite to the office.

46. For geographical information, see the entry for Tierra Nueva in Appendix 2.

47. Vázquez de Coronado's salary as governor was 1,500 *ducados*, or 572,000 *maravedís*. See Document 5.

48. "Has jurisdiction," *pertenecer*. DRAE, 1584: "ser una cosa del cargo, ministerio u obligación de uno."

49. For biographical information, see the entry for Antonio de Almaguer in Appendix 1.

50. There is disagreement over the surname of Diego Agundes. Aiton transcribed the name as Aguidez, whereas Agapito Rey settled on Agundez, the latter name matching our own reading. We have been unable to locate information about him under either name. In agreement with the two copies of the 1540 letter in AGI, Justicia, 339, the name of the *chanciller* (chancellor) should be Gaspar de Castilla. This is probably *licenciado* Gaspar de Montoya, who previously had been a judge in the Chancillería de Valladolid. He joined the Consejo de Indias in December 1528 and was then named *consejero* (counselor) of Castilla in March 1529. Aiton, "Coronado's Commission," 87; Rey, "La acusación," 112; Schäfer, *Consejo Real*, 1:354.

51. For biographical information about Antonio de Turcios, see Appendix 1.

52. Two decades later Simón de Coca was an *escribano* in Guadalajara. Tello, 579.

53. Nuestro. This appears as a scribal emendation in both AGI, Justicia, 336, N.1, "sobre ciertos yndios," and AGI, Justicia, 339, N.1, R.1, "Residencia."

54. Fuese. AGI, Justicia, 339, N.1, R.1, "Residencia," fol. 1r, has "tuviese" instead.

55. "Determinación" is supplied by AGI, Justicia, 339, N.1, R.1, "Residencia," fol. 1r. AGI, Justicia, 336, N.1, "sobre ciertos yndios," mistakenly has "termynaçion."

56. El dicho. This is missing from AGI, Justicia, 339, N.1, R.1, "Residencia," fol. 5r, and AGI, Justicia, 339, N.1, R.2, "Residencia, August 1544."

57. Que por. AGI, Justicia, 339, N.1, R.1, "Residencia," fol. 1v, has "que porque."

58. Lo que *en* las di*c*has tierras *h*Ay podria suçeder ynconVinyentes. This entire phrase is omitted from AGI, Justicia, 339, N.1, R.1, "Residencia," fol. 1v.

59. E aqu(e)i. AGI, Justicia, 339, N.1, R.1, "Residencia," fol. 1v, has "y q*u*e."

60. Don hernando. AGI, Justicia, 339, N.1, R.1, "Residencia," fol 2r, erroneously has "donde hernando."

61. Dier(o)en. Although AGI, Justicia, 336, N.1, "sobre ciertos yndios," has "dieron," the imperfect subjective, "dieren," is called for in this situation. Indeed, that is what appears in AGI, Justicia, 339, N.1, R.1, "Residencia," fol. 2r.

62. Cosas. AGI, Justicia, 339, N.1, R.1., "Residencia," fol. 2r, has "casos." AGI, Justicia, 339, N.1, R.2, "Residencia, August 1544," agrees with AGI, Justicia, 336, N.1, "sobre ciertos yndios."

63. Nos paresca. AGI, Justicia, 339, N.1, R.1., "Residencia," fol. 2r, erroneously has "a nos p*er*tenesca."

64. Treynta y ÇinCo anos. AGI, Justicia, 339, N.1, R.1., "Residencia," fol. 2r, omits "años."

65. Fuere *en*Comendado y Cometido. AGI, Justicia, 339, N.1, R.1., "Residencia," fol. 2r, has "mandado y encomendado."

66. Que alla hallaredes. AGI, Justicia, 339, N.1, R.1., "Residencia," fol. 2r, omits "alla."

67. De las tierras y proVinçias. AGI, Justicia, 339, N.1, R.1., "Residencia," fol. 2r, has instead "de las otras proVyncias."

68. Vos de nuestra parte. AGI, Justicia, 339, N.1, R.1., "Residencia," fol. 2v, omits "Vos."

69. ProVeer. AGI, Justicia, 339, N.1, R.1., "Residencia," fol. 2v, has "poner."

70. Aponer. AGI, Justicia, 339, N.1, R.1., "Residencia," fol. 2v, omits "a."

71. Quanto. AGI, Justicia, 339, N.1, R.1., "Residencia," fol. 2v, has "quando."

72. Mandado dar y dada. AGI, Justicia, 339, N.1, R.1., "Residencia," fol. 3r, has instead "manda dar y da."

73. Ynstruyçion. AGI, Justicia, 339, N.1, R.1., "Residencia," fol. 3r, erroneously has "just*ic*ia."

74. Hagan dar. AGI, Justicia, 339, N.1, R.1., "Residencia," fol. 3r, erroneously has "hagan guardar."

75. Vays. AGI, Justicia, 339, N.1, R.1., "Residencia," fol. 3r, mistakenly has "Aveys."

76. PareÇiere. AGI, Justicia, 339, N.1, R.1., "Residencia," fol. 3r, mistakenly has "partesÇiere."

77. *H*abidos. AGI, Justicia, 339, N.1, R.1.,"Residencia," fol. 3r, mistakenly has "ellos."

78. Uso. AGI, Justicia, 339, N.1, R.1., "Residencia," fol. 3v, mistakenly has "os."

79. En tyenpo alguno. Absent from AGI, Justicia, 339, N.1, R.1., "Residencia," fol. 3v.

80. ViRey de la nueVa espana. AGI, Justicia, 339, N.1, R.1., "Residencia," fol. 3v, adds "y governador."

81. The certification is naturally different in the four versions; those from AGI, Justicia, 339, were made in 1544.

82. Fiz = fize = hize. Lloyd, *Latin to Spanish*, 365.

83. Because this is a copy of Turcios's copy, his mark does not appear.

Document 10. The King's Confirmation of Vázquez de Coronado's Appointment, June 11, 1540

1. Bolton, 472–75.

2. Ibid., 474.

3. *Catalog* (New York: Christie's, 1995), 47.

4. The definitive statement of the viceroy's claim appears in a document filed in support of that claim by *licenciado* Juan de Villalobos in his capacity as *fiscal* of the Consejo de Indias on May 25, 1540. "Proceso del Marqués del Valle," in *CDI*, 15:300–408.

5. Fol. 1r.

6. It is clear that messengers made regularly scheduled, if infrequent, trips between the expedition and the viceregal capital. For instance, in his letter of October 6, 1541, Mendoza states that he is expecting a letter from Vázquez de Coronado within days: "This coming month of November I am expecting the detailed report about all of this." From the other end of the line, Castañeda de Nájera reports that at Tiguex in the fall of 1541 "with don Pedro de Tovar came letters from Nueva España, both from the viceroy don Antonio de Mendoza and from private individuals." Document 25, fol. 458v; Document 28, fol. 127r.

7. This also suggests that the two versions of the letter might have been in the custody of descendants of Vázquez de Coronado's and that it was from them that they came into the collectors' market at some undetermined time in the past.

8. Because "40" also appears on the Madrid original, that number probably indicates the letter's position in the packet dispatched to Nueva España in a 1540 fleet bound for the Indies. Turcios simply copied the number from the original to his copy and then struck it out and inscribed a new number, 4, perhaps recording its position in the *legajo* (bundle) dispatched to Tierra Nueva. It is tempting to imagine that the three folios in front of it were a letter from the viceroy to the captain general.

9. Antonio de Turcios has corrected the *provincia*'s name in this copy; it appears as simply Galicia in the original Madrid letter. Vázquez de Coronado was appointed its governor in 1538, at age 27. For a fuller description of Nueva Galicia, see the entry under that heading in Appendix 2. For the appointment as governor, see Document 5. And for biographical information about Antonio de Turcios, see the entry under his name in Appendix 1.

10. The letter referred to here makes up Document 3 in this volume. Incorrectly written as 1540 in the original, the date was corrected to 1539 by Turcios. This is the kind of scribal error that occurs frequently, and Turcios's change exemplifies the sorts of unnoted "corrections" that *escribanos* routinely made when copying documents.

11. For biographical information about Marcos de Niza, see the introduction to Document 6.

12. A marginal note made in Spain on Vázquez de Coronado's July 15, 1539, letter instructs that such a directive be sent to the viceroy. Document 3, fol. 4v.

13. The Dominican friar García de Loaysa was not only a member of the college of cardinals but also served as president of the Consejo de Indias from 1524 until 1546, when he was succeeded by Antonio de Mendoza's brother Luis Hurtado de Mendoza. During the sixteenth century, and before and after, ecclesiastics often held governmental positions in Spain and its empire. Schäfer, *Consejo Real*, 1:351. For biographical information about Juan de Sámano, see Document 5, note 23.

14. Turcios likely made one or more copies of the king's letter to dispatch to Vázquez de Coronado in the north, since he had already reached northern Sonora or southern Arizona by the time the letter was signed in Madrid. AGI, Justicia, 258, Pieza 1, "Testimony of Antonio de Turcios," in "Visita hecha al virrey . . . por Francisco Tello de Sandoval, November 3, 1545," fol. 108v; Bernardo Pérez Fernández del Castillo, *Historia de la escribanía en la Nueva España y del notariado en México*

(México, DF: Editorial Porrúa, 1994), 99; Agustín Millares Carlo and J. I. Mantecón, *Índice y extractos de los Protocolos del Archivo de Notarías de México, DF*, 2 vols. (México, DF: Colegio de México, 1945), 2:195.

Document 11. Testimony of Juan Bermejo and of Vázquez de Coronado's Purchasing Agent, Juan Fernández Verdejo, 1552

1. Flint, "Financing and Provisioning," 44–46.

2. Fol. 73v.

3. AGI, Justicia, 339, N.1, R.1, "Residencia."

4. Fernández Verdejo was a native of Cuema or Cuerna de Guese or Guete, a place presumably in Spain that we have been unable to locate. He was able to sign his name. Although he was intimately involved in the provisioning of the expedition, he did not participate in the actual trek. AGI, Justicia, 268, N.1, "Visita hecha a Gonzalo Cerezo, alguacil mayor de la audiencia, December 18, 1546."

5. Fol. 43r.

6. It is possible, though certainly not proven, that Juan Bermejo was a relative of fellow expeditionaries and cousins Juan Martín Bermejo and Hernando Martín Bermejo (the captain general's secretary). Some credence is lent to this possibility by the fact that all three are listed fairly close together on the February 1540 muster roll. Only five names separate Juan Bermejo and Juan Martín Bermejo, who were both crossbowmen, while another 16 names separate Juan Martín Bermejo from his more illustrious cousin Hernando, a horseman. See Document 12, fols. 7v–8v.

7. This count of horses taken by Vázquez de Coronado jibes with the "twenty-two or twenty-three horses" reported at the time of the muster. Document 12, fol. 1r.

8. Bermejo came from Torrelaguna in the *provincia* of Madrid. He was probably of very modest social rank, since his education was scant enough that he did not know how to sign his name. He would have been about 20 when the expedition to Tierra Nueva departed from Compostela in 1540. AGI, Justicia, 339, N.1, R.1, "Residencia."

9. For further discussion of this lawsuit, see the introductions to Documents 9 and 34.

10. AGI, Justicia, 336, N.1, "Probança."

11. Fols. 42v and 43v.

12. The other two make up Documents 9 and 34.

13. The answers made to this question reveal that the persons referred to are Vázquez de Coronado and the *fiscal*, Juan Rodríguez. The *encomienda pueblos* in question are one-half of Aguacatlán and Xala, with their *estancias* and *sujetos;* one-half of the *estancias* of Mezquitlán and Guaxacatlán, in the valley of Guaxacatlán, which had been entrusted to Francisco de Villegas; one-half of the *pueblos* and *estancias* of Tepujuacán, Misquitlán, Amaxaque, and Amatlán, with their *sujetos,* which formerly were held by Álvaro de Bracamonte; and Quinsique with the Chichimecas Otomis, with their *estancias* and *sujetos.* AGI, Justicia, 336, N.1, "Recovery of Encomiendas," fol. 3r. See also Document 34 regarding this petition to recover *encomiendas.*

14. For geographical information, see the entry for Nueva Galicia in Appendix 2.

15. For geographical information, see the entry for Mar del Norte in Appendix 2.

16. Vázquez de Coronado's appointment reads, "It is our will and desire that each year you are to obtain and receive one thousand five hundred *ducados,* which amount to five hundred seventy-two thousand *maravedís.*" See Document 5, fol. 407r.

17. "Taken charge," *tomar. DRAE,* 1991: "recibir una cosa y hacerse cargo de ella."

18. The New Laws, or "Leyes y Ordenanzas nuevamente hechas por su Magestad para la Gobernación de las Indias y buen Tratamiento y Conservación de los Indios," were formally issued on November 20, 1542. The 40 articles in the New Laws covered a wide range of topics dealing with the New World. They provided procedures governing operation of the Consejo de Indias and established additional *audiencias* in the New World. They severely restricted the holding of *encomiendas.* Their major thrust, however, was to insist that natives of the New World be treated as benevolently as possible. Indian slavery and forced labor were forbidden. *Audiencias* throughout the Indies were enjoined to energetically seek out and prosecute people who abused Indians. The provisions on *encomiendas* were especially distasteful to many European residents of the Indies, and widespread unrest was threatened as a result. Open revolt erupted in Peru. Viceroy Mendoza averted a similar catastrophe in Nueva España by suspending implementation of the New Laws. Stevens and Lucas, *New Laws of the Indies.*

19. For brief biographical information about Hernán Cortés, see the introduction to Document 18. For biographical information on Guzmán, see the entry for Nuño Beltrán de Guzmán in Appendix 1.

20. For biographical information, see the entry for Hernando Martín Bermejo in Appendix 1.

21. For geographical information, see the entry for Tierra Nueva in Appendix 2. The text of the two documents making up the royal commission composes Documents 9 and 10 in this volume.

22. The reference here is to King Fernando and Queen Isabel, the grandparents of Carlos I and the unifiers of Spain.

23. Many elements in this *interrogatorio* are typical of such questionnaires of the period. This question about suffering was common. "Danger," *necesidad. DRAE,* 1431: "especial riesgo o peligro."

24. For Vázquez de Coronado's own account of the wounds he received at Cíbola, see Document 19, fol. 361r.

25. "No means was found," *no se hallo disposiçion. Disposición, DRAE,* 764: "cualquiera de los medios que se emplean para ejecutar un propósito."

26. For geographical information, see the entries for Cíbola and Quivira in Appendix 2.

27. This is one of the clearest statements of the economic motives of the expedition.

28. *Licenciado* Hernando Caballero was a native of Sanlúcar de Barrameda in the *provincia* of Cádiz in Spain. He arrived in Nueva España in 1536. He married doña Inés de Obregón, daughter of Rodrigo de Baeza. Caballero served in a number of posts over the years, including those of *abogado* (attorney) in the Audiencia de México; *pesquisidor* (investigating judge) in Oaxaca and the mines of Mixteca; *visitador* in Chiapas; and *residencia* judge and *justicia mayor* in Puebla. Icaza, 2: no. 545.

29. This attesting signature is not recorded in the March 2 copy of the *interrogatorio.* Balbuena was secretary of the Audiencia de Nueva Galicia (Guadalajara).

30. This is a scribal copying error. The date should be March 2. In the original document the month must have been recorded as "m°," which is a standard abbreviation for both *marzo* and *mayo.* The copyist, probably working in the month of May, naturally misinterpreted the abbreviation. The error is apparent from the fact that the testimony of Fernández Verdejo, with an ostensible May date, appears in the *legajo,* or bundle of documents, before testimony that was recorded in April.

31. Vázquez de Coronado's attorney, Pedro Ruiz de Haro, was born in Peñaranda de Duero in the jurisdiction of Burgos, Spain, in about 1515 and arrived in Nueva España in 1526. He participated in the conquest of Nueva Galicia with Nuño de Guzmán. From at least the early 1540s to the early 1550s he served as Vázquez de Coronado's attorney. He was a public *escribano* at Compostela from 1533 or earlier until as late as 1552 and also served as *escribano* of the *cabildo* there. Still alive in 1570, he had been *encomendero* of the *pueblo* of Otomistlán in the jurisdiction of Tepíc since about 1548. Boyd-Bowman, 2: no. 2539; Icaza, 2: no. 1177; AGI, Patronato, 61, N.2, R.9, "Méritos y servicios de Alonso Alvarez de Espinosa, Compostela, 1551"; AGI, Justicia, 339, N.1, R.1, "Residencia"; AGI, Justicia, 336, N.1, R.3, "Concerning certain pueblos"; AGI, Guadalajara, 30, N.1, "Letter from the *cabildo* of Compostela to the king, Compostela, February 19, 1533"; Gerhard, *North Frontier,* 141. The *licenciado* de la Marcha was Hernán Martínez de la Marcha, *oidor* of the Audiencia de Guadalajara. He served there from 1547 to 1553 and died in 1560. AGI, México, 216, N.28, "Informaciones, Francisco Martínez de la Marcha, primer poblador de Nueva España, 1582"; AGI, Justicia, 303, "Residencias, Guadalajara, 1556–1560"; Schäfer, *Consejo Real,* 2:494.

32. For biographical information, see the entry for *licenciado* Lorenzo de Tejada in Appendix 1.

33. This is one of the few references to the expedition's having taken pigs among its livestock. Pigs were not at all rare on sixteenth-century Spanish expeditions, despite the seeming difficulty of herding pigs over long distances. For instance, the contemporary Soto expedition relied heavily on domestic pigs for meat. See Rodrigo Rangel, "Account of the Northern Conquest and Discovery of Hernando de Soto," trans. and ed. John E. Worth, in Clayton, Knight, and Moore, *De Soto Chronicles,* 1:259, 274, 275.

34. This claim contrasts significantly with the testimony of witnesses in the 1544 investigation of the expedition's treatment of native people. During that testimony, numerous witnesses said that thievery of food and other goods by the expedition precipitated native uprisings. Flint, *Great Cruelties,* passim.

35. This refers to Vázquez de Coronado's period of unconsciousness at Cíbola in

July 1540. Compare Castañeda de Nájera's account and others. Most other accounts report Vázquez de Coronado's gravest injury as having resulted from his being struck with a stone slab. Document 19, fol. 361r; Document 28, fol. 32r.

36. The referent for "it," "la," is extremely unclear. The two most likely possibilities are the "jornada," or expedition, and the "tierra," or land, both being feminine and both appearing in relative proximity. In any case, the statement sounds like a threat of mutiny.

37. "Occur[red]," *pasa.* The *escribano's* use of the present tense is curious here. We assume it is in error.

38. For biographical information about Juan Fernández Verdejo, see the introduction to this document.

39. AGI, Justicia, 336, N.1, "Probança," fol. 41r, gives the name of the *fiscal* as Juan Rodríguez.

40. "Seen them," *visto.* This seems to imply familiarity with documents but could also refer to his having heard them mentioned. *DRAE,* 2075: "por extención, percibir algo con cualquier sentido."

41. Direct quotations are rare in records of testimony of the day. Why the *escribano* chose to quote this particular statement is unknown.

42. "Separated," *desviada. DRAE,* 736: "apartar, alejar, separar."

43. Tierra Firme was the name given to Panamá and South America.

44. For information about the Consejo de las Indias, see the entry in Appendix 1.

45. Castañeda says that the *ciudad* of Jalisco became Compostela. However, Gerhard, *North Frontier,* 139, shows on a map that Espírtu Santo was first settled and then moved to Compostela and that Xalisco was one league south of Tepic and therefore not at all the same place. There is still a Jalisco in Nayarit in the same location as Xalisco.

46. Doña Beatriz, born in Nueva España in 1524 or 1525, was the first of the children of Marina Gutiérrez Flores de la Caballería and Alonso de Estrada to be born in the New World. She was their fifth daughter and the seventh of eight children known to have been born to the couple. Her father had been assigned to Nueva España as the royal treasurer in late 1522. Beatriz married Vázquez de Coronado at the age of 12 (considered to be a legal age to marry), probably in late 1536 or early 1537, a year after his arrival in Nueva España. Her dowry included a one-half share in the *encomienda* of Tlapa. AGI, Justicia, 213, N.4, "Lawsuit regarding Teocaluyacan and Cayuca, 1551"; Francisco Fernández de Bethencourt, *Historia Genealógica y heráldica de la monarquía española casa real y grandes de España* (Madrid: Jaime Ratés, 1912), 9:498; Francisco Fernández del Castillo, "Alonso de Estrada: Su familia," in *Memorias de la Academia Mexicana de la Historia* 1 (1942):424a.

47. Unfortunately, this ledger is not known to exist today.

48. There is reference to a Gabriel de Aguilera, who was a relative of Alonso de Zorita's and *encomendero* of Guazalingo in the archbishopric of México. He had arrived in Nueva España in 1527 and became a *vecino* of the Ciudad de México. He was also said to hold three other *encomiendas:* Cipotecas, Sochicoatlan, and Huexutla. Vigil, *Alonso de Zorita,* 39, 334, 214; Himmerich y Valencia, *Encomenderos,* 115; Boyd-Bowman, 2: no. 5732; Gerhard, *Historical Geography,* 144, 243.

49. For biographical information about Juan de Zaragosa, see Document 27, note 28.

50. Distinta. This is a scribal error for *distante.* The March 2 copy of the *interrogatorio,* on fol. 35 right, has the correct word.

51. Mag*est*ad *en* los pueblos. "En" is supplied from fol. 35 left in the March 2 copy of the *interrogatorio.*

52. Los qu*ales* son *los.* "Los" is supplied from fol. 36 right in the March 2 copy of the *interrogatorio.*

53. Yr *a* la di*c*ha jornada. "A" is supplied from fol. 36 right in the March 2 copy of the *interrogatorio.*

54. Tierras *e* en esp*eci*al. "E" is supplied from fol. 37 right in the March 2 copy of the *interrogatorio.*

55. (Cumplir) *ampliar.* "Cumplir" is clearly a scribal copying error for "ampliar," in repetition of the phrase in the previous line. The word is written correctly on fol. 38 left of the March 2 copy of the *interrogatorio.*

56. Distinto. This is a scribal copying error for *distante.*

57. There is a change of *escribano* beginning with this folio.

58. The remainder of the excerpt is in the hand of the same *escribano* who had been making the copy before fol. 43r.

Document 12. Muster Roll of the Expedition, Compostela, February 22, 1540

1. For full geographical information, see the entries for Compostela and Nueva Galicia in Appendix 2.

2. Juan de Cuevas not only served as principal *escribano* for the muster roll but also sent several unnamed persons on the expedition and paid for their outfitting. Icaza 1: no. 386.

3. One of these men, named Cepeda, actually did not make the trip. See note 60, this document.

4. Compare, for example, the muster "of the notable people" Hernando de Alarcón was ordered to make before embarking on his proposed second voyage in 1541. Document 16, fol. 1r. For discussion of another, though somewhat different list, this one recording the conquistadores who earned shares of Atahuallpa's ransom in Peru in 1533, see James Lockhart, *The Men of Cajamarca: A Social and Biographical Study of the First Conquerors of Peru* (Austin: University of Texas Press, 1972), 90–102.

5. Fol. 1r.

6. Aiton, "Muster Roll," 556–70.

7. Ibid., 557.

8. H&R, 87–108. Hammond and Rey frequently adhere to Arthur Aiton's transcriptions, even when he is incorrect.

9. Mora, 199–211.

10. For a fuller discussion of the roles and identities of the *indios amigos,* see the introduction to Document 13. For the small amount of information that is available about individual natives, see Appendix 3.

11. Flint, *Great Cruelties,* 280.

12. See, for instance, ibid., 258.

13. Document 28, fols. 135v–135r.

14. For the names of the five friars, see Document 4, note 8.

15. See H&R, 104–8. Hammond and Rey do not indicate that the names they list under the heading "Additions to Muster Roll" are their own additions and not Juan de Cuevas's. There are a number of errors among the names Hammond and Rey appended. For the most complete and current roster of named individuals known to have participated in the Coronado expedition on the basis of contemporary documentary sources (including the muster roll), see Appendix 3. Notes to that appendix also discuss the erroneous additions made by Hammond and Rey.

16. Fol. 9v.

17. See Document 14.

18. AGI, Patronato, 60, N.5, R.4, "Probanza de los méritos y servicios de Juan de Zaldívar, [1566]."

19. AGI, Justicia, 339, N.1, R.1, "Residencia," fol. 288v.

20. AGI, Patronato, 63, R.5, "Juan de Paladinas [*sic*]"; AGI, México, 1064, L.1\1, "Informes de los conquistadores," fol. 228r; Flint, *Great Cruelties,* 58–62; AGI, Mexico, 168.

21. Document 28, fol. 149v.

22. Fol. 3v.

23. Flint, *Great Cruelties,* 253, 282.

24. Fols. 1r–2v.

25. For sixteenth-century Spanish observations on the war organization of various central Mexican native groups, see, for instance, Diego Durán, *The History of the Indies of New Spain,* trans. and ed. Doris Heyden (Norman: University of Oklahoma Press, 1994), 278–82; and Bernal Díaz del Castillo, *Historia verdadera de la conquista de la Nueva España,* ed. Carmelo Sáenz de Santa María (México, DF: Alianza Editorial, 1991), 161.

26. Recently, independent documentary evidence has come to light that further illuminates the subject of armor worn by members of the expedition. See the inventory of Juan Jiménez's goods in Document 27, fols. 7r–8r. For more on native arms and armor, see Richard Flint, "Armas de la Tierra: The Mexican Indian Component of Coronado Expedition Material Culture," in Flint and Flint, *Tierra Nueva,* 62.

27. Combined with given names, place names were commonly used both as surnames and to identify place of origin in the sixteenth century. Which usage is employed in any given case cannot be determined without further information about the person in question.

28. Fol. 5v.

29. H&R, 97.

30. Diego Gutiérrez de la Caballería may never have made the long trip to Cíbola. He appears to have died in Jalisco in February 1542, killed by natives, several months before the Coronado expedition as a whole abandoned its mission and returned south. It is possible, therefore, that Diego Gutiérrez de la Caballería never left Compostela, did not go beyond Culiacán, or was one of the founders of the expedition's supply and communication base at San Gerónimo de los Corazones in Sonora (maps 1 and 2). A daughter of his married one Alonso Pérez, who also went on the expedition. And a son, also named Diego, went to Costa Rica with Juan Vázquez de Coronado, nephew of Francisco, in the 1560s and was killed there. AGN, Civiles, vol. 1276, "Defensa del Tesorero Alonso de Estrada, (n.d.)"; Icaza, 1: no. 244; Ricardo Fernández Guardia, *Cartas de Juan Vázquez de Coronado, conquistador de Costa Rica* (Barcelona: la viuda de Luis Tusso, 1908), 55, 61.

31. Fol. 3r. See H&R, 91.

32. The document begins in the hand of Juan de Cuevas himself, and his rubric appears at the bottom of the folios he wrote. He continued to record the muster through fol. 4v.

33. Juan de Cuevas was a native of Aranda de Duero in the modern *provincia* of Burgos in the *comunidad* of Castilla y León in Spain. He was married to Francisca de Guevara, the daughter of Diego de Guevara (an expedition member) and Isabel de Barrios. AGI, México, 73, R.2, N.24, "Méritos y servicios, Juan de Cuevas y Guevara, May 17, 1610"; AGI, Justicia, 258, Pieza 1, "Testimony of Antonio de Turcios."

34. For information on Antonio de Mendoza, Cristóbal de Oñate, Peralmindez Cherino, and *licenciado* Alonso Maldonado, see Appendix 1. For biographical information on fray Marcos de Niza, see the introduction to Document 6. Gonzalo de Salazar, a native of Granada in the modern *comunidad* of Andalucía, was the son of doctor Guadalupe Salazar and doña Catalina de Salazar, *criados* of the Catholic Monarchs and among the first *vecinos* of Granada. Gonzalo was a page for the Catholic Sovereigns. He was not among the initial royal officials named, but in 1523 he was sent to Nueva España to be the royal *factor.* He became a *vecino* and *regidor* of the Ciudad de México and *encomendero* of Taximaroa and Tepetlavzcuco and other *pueblos* in Michoacán. All of these were eventually taken from him. He often sided with *veedor* Cherino against two other officials, Estrada and Albornoz, resulting in prolonged bitterness and contention within the government. Salazar's widowed daughter, doña Catalina, married Cristóbal de Oñate. His son, Hernando de Salazar, was appointed *factor* when Salazar returned to Spain in 1529, but Hernando died the following year. Icaza, 1: no. 369. See also the entry for Pero Almíldez Cherino in Appendix 1 and Himmerich y Valencia, *Encomenderos,* 234.

35. For selected information about the individuals listed in the muster roll, see Appendix 3.

36. This and other numbers in the left margin of the document refer to the number of horses taken on the expedition by the person in question.

37. Exactly what these armored horse trappings included in Vázquez de Coronado's case is not specified. Pieces of horse armor, or *bardas,* could have included frontal (head armor), crinet (neck armor), peytral (breastplate), flanchard (flank armor), crupper (rump armor), tail guard, and rein guard, or any selection from these. Charles Ffoulkes, *The Armourer and His Craft from the Eleventh to the Sixteenth Century* (London: Methuen, 1912; reprint, Mineola, NY: Dover, 1988), 8. The terms long and short stirrups refer to two riding styles and methods of harnessing a horse in use in the sixteenth century: European style, with heavy saddle and long stirrup straps (*brida*), and Moorish style, with light saddle and short stirrup straps (*gineta*).

38. Castañeda de Nájera has Urrea, but *Pasajeros,* 2: no. 3806 and no. 3805, read the same as the muster roll. H&R, 88, and Aiton, "Muster Roll," both have Gurrea. Document 28, fol. 19r. For biographical information, see Document 28, note 106.

39. This repetition of "native arms and armor" is probably a scribal error.

40. Castañeda de Nájera supplies the complete surname, Manrique de Lara. Document 28, fol. 19r.

41. The surname is Santillana in AGI, Patronato, 79, N.3, R.2, "Méritos y servicios de Francisco de Santillana, Mérida, 1594."

42. H&R, 89, have "do Campo."

43. The final *s* is supplied by AGI, México, 1064, L.1\1, "Informes de los conquistadores," fol. 199r.

44. If physical placement of names on the page is significant in this case, then it is curious that the names Velasco and Sotomayor are closer to the margin than

others. There is no other evidence that Sotomayor was leader of the men listed under him, though he was a man of some stature, being the expedition's official chronicler. Document 28, fol. 47v. The Spanish phrase "dos pares," translated here as "two sets," could also mean "two pairs." It is uncertain which is intended. "Set" could refer to an entire outfit of arms and armor, including a headpiece, a round shield, shoes, a *macana* (a native weapon similar to a sword, consisting of a flattened piece of wood whose edges are studded with prismatic obsidian blades), and a tunic. A "pair," on the other hand, could refer to only a "body suit and headpiece" of the standard warrior armor. See Frances F. Berdan and Patricia Rieff Anawalt, eds., *The Essential Codex Mendoza* (Berkeley: University of California Press, 1997), 45.

45. H&R, 90, leave this as Xuarez, as in the Spanish original.

46. A sallet is a helmet with a wide rear brim, and a beaver is a chin and throat guard commonly used with a sallet. Ffoulkes, *The Armourer and His Craft*, 155 and 165.

47. This is the subtotal of the number of horses.

48. A corselet is a suit of light half-armor—an armored jerkin—usually made of leather. *DRAE*, 586.

49. This may refer to front and back pieces of torso armor.

50. The subtotal of the number of horses is incorrect. Those recorded on this folio bring the running total to 160.

51. Aiton, "Muster Roll," 562, omits the first name. See the introduction to this document for further information about this man.

52. *Zaragüelles* are wide chain-mail breeches. For a description of cloth *zaragüelles*, see Anderson, *Hispanic Costume*, 73.

53. This apparent surname may in reality refer to his place of origin, Ciudad Real. "Villareal" is often used interchangeably with "Ciudad Real." Villareal may have been a relative of or had another close relationship with the captain of this company, since the Gutiérrez de la Caballería family was from Almagro, very near Ciudad Real.

54. Gerónimo de Estrada may also be a relative of the captain of this company, since Diego Gutiérrez de la Caballería was brother-in-law of Alonso de Estrada, father of Vázquez de Coronado's wife.

55. H&R, 92, and Aiton, "Muster Roll," 562, incorrectly transcribe "G°" as "Gerónimo." The abbreviation is, rather, that for "Gonzalo." See Galende, *Diccionario de abreviaturas*, 106.

56. The subtotal of horses is actually 206. At the top of fol. 3v, "6" is struck out, again leaving the incorrect subtotal of 201.

57. Covarrubias, 954: in Sevilla, Córdoba, and other places in Andalucía this designation was used for *regidores*, since there were 24 *regidores* in each *ciudad*'s *cabildo*.

58. Nofre was an unusual, but occasionally used, equivalent of Onofre.

59. Graviel was a not uncommon given name at this period. H&R, 92, have Gabriel.

60. Juan de Cepeda left the expedition at Culiacán because of illness. AGI, México, 1064, L.1\1, "Informes de los conquistadores," fol. 273r. See note 3, this document.

61. A *bastidor* is a pack frame. Covarrubias, 171: "dos perchas con sus hembras en que se embastan las orillas de lo que se ha de bordar." In this case the term may refer to the native backpack common in Mesoamerica at the time. For a description of this type of pack, see Ross Hassig, *Trade, Tribute, and Transportation: The Sixteenth-Century Political Economy of the Valley of Mexico* (Norman: University of Oklahoma Press, 1993), 28. For an illustration, see Bernardino de Sahagún, *Florentine Codex: General History of the Things of New Spain*, book 12, *The Conquest of Mexico*, eds. and trans. Arthur J. O. Anderson and Charles E. Dibble (Salt Lake City: University of Utah Press, 1955), plate 77.

62. The subtotal of horses is actually 251.

63. It is unclear whether *criados* in this case refers to the members of Arellano's company or to his personal retinue. Most of the high-status members of the expedition, such as Arellano, were accompanied by such retinues.

64. H&R, 93, and Aiton, "Muster Roll," 563, mistakenly render this name "Jorge Páez." This was the Jorge Báez who, still a member of Arellano's company in February 1541, was appointed one of the executors of the estate of fellow expedition member Juan Jiménez. See Document 27.

65. "Skirts," *faldas*. *DRAE*, 947: "en la armadura, parte que cuelga desde la cintura abajo."

66. This is Pedro de Castañeda de Nájera, the author of Document 28. For biographical information, see the introduction to Document 28.

67. A gorget is a collar of armor for protecting the throat. Ffoulkes, *The Armourer and his Craft*, 161.

68. The subtotal of horses is actually 298.

69. Since González is listed as an *alférez*, another company may begin here, although the captain is apparently not listed. He could, however, be a second *alférez* under Guevara. In this regard, it is also curious that González's name begins a new folio as well.

70. H&R, 94, incorrectly have "Ponares," while Aiton, "Muster Roll," 564, is also mistaken with "Portales." Castañeda de Nájera confirms our reading as "Pobares." Document 28, fol. 67r.

71. According to fray Antonio Tello, Paniagua was shot in the eyelid with an arrow, but his *capirote* of iron (chain mail hood) and beaver saved him. Neither the *capirote* nor the beaver is listed in the muster. Tello, 423.

72. Aiton, "Muster Roll," 564, incorrectly has Pedro Gomes.

73. Aiton, "Muster Roll," 564, mistakenly has Gomes.

74. Aiton, "Muster Roll," 564, incorrectly has Gomes.

75. The *escribano* continues to make errors in addition. The number of horses listed on this folio brings the running total to 341.

76. The *escribano* changes beginning with this folio. The replacement continues to record the muster through fol. 8v. The identity of this second *escribano* is unknown.

77. At this point, the new *escribano* stops using the word *armas* for headgear and switches to *armaduras*.

78. Ramírez de Vargas was a *caballero* and the royal *contador* for the expedition. Document 28, fol. 19r; AGI, México, 206, N.35, "Investigation of Cristóbal de Escobar, February 7, 1561"; AGI, Patronato, 68, N.2, R.4\1, "Méritos y servicios de Juan de Céspedes, 1568," fol. 16r.

79. Since Ovando was a captain, his name may begin the listing for his company.

80. Aiton, "Muster Roll," 564, mistakenly has Gomes.

81. This is the Juan Jaramillo who authored Document 30.

82. H&R, 96, render "bent head [armor]" incorrectly as "head armor, double thickness."

83. This is Rodrigo de Paz Maldonado. AGI, Patronato, 112, R.2\1, "Méritos y servicios de Rodrigo de Paz Maldonado, Santa Marta, 1564."

84. This is the second of two people with the same name. The earlier one is listed on fol. 2v.

85. The actual running total of horses is 391.

86. This man's surname, written as Ribera in the document, was actually Ribero. AGI, México, 204, N.33\2, "Méritos y servicios de Pedro de Benavides, February 14, 1551," fol. 2r.

87. The full surname is López de Urrea. AGI, Patronato, 56, N.3, R.2, "Méritos y servicios de Pedro Jerónimo, November 21, 1542." Both H&R, 97, and Aiton, "Muster Roll," 565, mistakenly have Urrel.

88. H&R, 97, and Aiton, "Muster Roll," 565, both include Dávila in the surname. However, see the introduction to this document.

89. Aiton, "Muster Roll," 565, incorrectly has Ramíres.

90. Statements in Castañeda de Nájera's *relación* suggest that this man's surname was Cervantes. See H&R, 105 n. 94, and Document 28, fol. 75v. It seems likely, however, that Castañeda de Nájera was recalling the name incorrectly (he certainly could not recall the man's first name) after the 20–year gap and that the scribe wrote down the correct name. There is also a town in the *provincia* of Palencia called Cervatos de la Cueza.

91. H&R, 97, and Aiton, "Muster Roll," 565, incorrectly have Garavel. Mora, 205, has Garivel.

92. The actual running total of horses is 435.

93. Although H&R, 98 n. 62, agree that Juan Rodríguez was a native of Alanje, they continue to include "de Alanje" as part of his name. However, his name is given elsewhere without the place-name addition. AGI, México, 1064, L.1\1, "Informes de los conquistadores," fol. 262r.

94. Gaztaca = Gastaca. See *Pasajeros*, 2: no. 3585.

95. H&R, 98, include "del Barco Dávila" in the surname. Given the existence of the town El Barco de Ávila in the *provincia* of Ávila, this element probably serves only to distinguish a man with a common name by adding his place of origin.

96. H&R, 98, include "Sayago" as part of the surname. However, Juan López de la Rosa was his name, and he was from Sayago. AGI, México, 1064, L.1\1, "Informes de los conquistadores," fol. 229r.

97. As H&R, 99 n. 66, point out, this man's more complete name was Diego de Madrid Avendaño.

98. Baltasar de Obregón gives this man's surname as Ureña. Mora, 206, has "Garuena." Aiton, "Muster Roll," 566, has "Garueña." And H&R, 99, have "Garbena." See Obregón, *Historia,* 153.

99. The actual running total of horses is 477.

100. This is the man who died at Tiguex in February 1541, the disposal of whose estate is the subject of Document 27.

101. H&R, 99, have "de Fromista" as part of the surname. But see Document 27, fol. 9r, where he is listed simply as Diego Sánchez.

102. H&R, 99, and Aiton, "Muster Roll," 566, have Mathín. Machín, however, was a rarely used Basque given name and is consistent with the paleography of the document.

103. H&R, 100, include "de la Fuente del Maestre" as part of the surname. However, see *Pasajeros,* 3: no. 236, where his name is given simply as Juan Martín, originating from the town of Fuente del Maestre.

104. The actual running total of horses is 511.

105. H&R, 100, use Ciudad Real as part of the surname. This man may well be the person listed simply as Pedro López, a native of Ciudad Real, in *Pasajeros,* 2: no. 2578.

106. Gómez served as an *escribano* in the *provincia* of Culiacán following the expedition. Flint, *Great Cruelties,* 346, 424, 551.

107. Aiton, "Muster Roll," 567, has Pedro, which matches AGI, Patronato, 56, N.3, R.2, "Pedro Jerónimo."

108. H&R, 100, include "de Encinasola" a part of the surname. This may be the man referred to simply as Andrés Hernández, without place of origin, in *Pasajeros,* 3: no. 407. There are at least two places with the name Encinasola in Spain, one in the *provincia* of Salamanca and the other in the *provincia* of Sevilla.

109. The actual running total of horses is 536.

110. Mora, 207, omits this entire folio side.

111. H&R, 100, have "Aorta, a Portuguese." However, both Homem and Horta are common Portuguese surnames. On the other hand, *home* is an archaic version of *hombre.* It is thus impossible to tell what this man's name was without further evidence. It was almost certainly misunderstood by Cuevas. See Maria Helena Ochi Flechor, *Manuscritos dos séculos XVI ao XIX* (São Paulo: Edições Arquivo do Estado, 1991), 297; *DRAE,* 1119.

112. Vázquez de Coronado's secretary's full name was Hernando Martín Bermejo. See, for instance, *Pasajeros,* 2: no. 2201.

113. Aiton, "Muster Roll," 567, incorrectly has Girones.

114. The running total of horses is omitted.

115. H&R, 106, add a Juan de Cuevas from Aranda de Duero to the muster. However, it seems to us that the *escribano* of this document, Juan de Cuevas (also a native of Aranda de Duero), perhaps did not wish to confuse his name with the Juan de Cuevas (a possible relative) who went on the expedition and thus recorded his name as Juan de Duero. Icaza, 1: no. 386; AGI, Justicia, 258, Pieza 1, "Testimony of Antonio de Turcios."

116. H&R, 101, include "de Santo Domingo" in the surname. However, Boyd-Bowman, 1: no. 3370, lists a Diego Díaz, who may be this man's father, who arrived at Santo Domingo in 1509 and later participated in the conquest of Tenochtitlan. This suggests that the place name was simply appended to the younger man's name to distinguish him from his father.

117. Aiton, "Muster Roll," 568, mistakenly has Gómez.

118. This man is listed in *Pasajeros,* 2: no. 2211, as Juan Martín Bermejo, whose parents were *vecinos* of Fuente de Arco.

119. H&R, 101, include "de Zafra" in the surname. This appears unlikely, since this man later signed his name simply as Rodrigo Álvarez. AGI, Justicia, 339, N.1, R.2, "Residencia, August 1544," fol. 32v. Also, there is a listing for Rodrigo Álvarez whose parents were *vecinos* of Zafra in *Pasajeros,* 2: no. 4298.

120. H&R, 102, include "de Ribadeo" in the surname. Given the location of the town of Ribadeo in the *provincia* of Lugo in Galicia, it is also possible that the place name is simply appended as an additional identifier. Which is correct is impossible to determine without further evidence.

121. The running total of horses is omitted here.

122. The hand of Cuevas resumes here. He adds his rubric to the foot of each folio from here to the end of the document.

123. This highly unusual surname suggests a scribal error. The correct name may have been either Jérez or Goiríz, the latter of which is a place near Villalba in Galicia.

124. This man is the Juanes de Guernica referred to in Document 27, fol. 6v. The duplication of "sword" is likely a scribal error.

125. The running total of horses is omitted here.

126. H&R, 103, incorrectly have Gabriel.

127. The final tally of horses is actually 558.

128. The listed individuals actually total 226, including the two sons mentioned in their fathers' entries.

129. This mode of travel, the religious members ahead of the main expedition, is not alluded to elsewhere in documents deriving from the expedition, unless this is a reference to men-at-arms who might have accompanied fray Marcos at least as far as Culiacán and then remained there.

130. If the absent Pablo de Melgosa is included, the total is 63 footmen.

131. Fray Francisco de Vitoria (or Victoria) left Spain in the summer of 1538 along with fray Antonio de Castilblanco, a participant in the expedition. Upon their arrival they were both sent to Jalisco. Chávez, *Coronado's Friars,* 9.

132. This scribal correction and several others in the roster suggest that the signed manuscript is a copy of an earlier draft.

133. The *escribano* incorrectly wrote this as "cosete." Mora, 201, misreads this as "copete." Aiton, "Muster Roll," 561, has "corsete," a word we are unable to locate. Meanwhile, H&R, 90, translate the word correctly as "corselet." Another instance of *coselete* (corselet) in the muster roll, this time spelled correctly, is on fol. 3r, in the entry for Juan de Villareal.

134. Platas. This is a scribal error for *placas* = plate armor. Mora, 203, and Aiton, "Muster Roll," 563, fail to correct the error.

135. Mandar = *legar. DRAE,* 1304.

Document 13. Record of Mexican Indians Participating in the Expedition, 1576

1. For a full discussion of the fleeting appearance of Indian allies in Spanish-authored documents deriving from the Coronado expedition, see Richard Flint, "What's Missing from This Picture? The *Alarde* or Muster Roll of the Coronado Expedition," in Flint and Flint, *From the Distance of 460 Years,* 57–80.

2. Document 28, fols. 16r–16v.

3. See Appendix 3 for a complete listing of the known non-Indian members of the expedition.

4. Serving as a witness on behalf of Viceroy Mendoza in 1547, Vázquez de Coronado agreed with what was stated in the two-hundredth question of his patron's *interrogatorio,* that 1,300 Indian allies had accompanied him on the expedition to Cíbola. Arthur S. Aiton and Agapito Rey, "Coronado's Testimony in the Viceroy Mendoza *Residencia,*" *New Mexico Historical Review* 12 (July 1937): 314.

5. Document 28, fol. 27v.

6. Flint, *Great Cruelties,* 278.

7. Ibid., 286.

8. Document 28, fol. 39r.

9. Document 28, fols. 60v–61r.

10. Document 28, fol. 62r.

11. Document 28, fol. 41r.

12. Rudolfo Hernández and José Francisco Román, "Presencia tlaxcalteca en Nueva Galicia," in *Constructores de la nación: La Migración tlaxcalteca en el norte de la Nueva España,* ed. María Isabel Monroy Castillo (San Luis Potosí: Colegio de San Luis and Gobierno del Estado de Tlaxcala, 1999), 19.

13. Donald Robertson, *Mexican Manuscript Painting of the Early Colonial Period: The Metropolitan Schools* (Norman: University of Oklahoma Press, 1994), 38.

14. Fol. 47r.

15. Chávez, *Oroz Codex,* 314.

16. Lewis Hanke, *Los Virreyes españoles en América durante el gobierno de la Casa de Austria, México,* 5 vols., in *Biblioteca de autores españoles desde la formación del lenguaje hasta nuestros dias,* vols. 273–77 (Madrid: Ediciones Atlas, 1976), 1:70.

17. Document 30, fol.5v.

18. Testimony of Francisco Troche and padre Juan Vanegas, in AGI, Justicia, 263, Pieza 1, "Probanza hecha en nombre de don Antonio de Mendoza, Zacatula, 1546–1547."

19. Tello, 485.

20. Diego Pérez de Luxán, "Diego Pérez de Luxán's Account of the Antonio de Espejo Expedition into New Mexico, 1582," in Hammond and Rey, *Rediscovery of New Mexico,* 184.

21. Antonio de Espejo, "Report of Antonio de Espejo," in Hammond and Rey, *Rediscovery of New Mexico*, 225.

22. Document 30, fol. 5v. The Zapotlán referred to here is probably the place of that name later held in *encomienda* by members of the Oñate and Zaldívar families, located less than 10 leagues east of Guadalajara. Gerhard, *North Frontier*, 135–37.

23. Obregón, *Historia*, 71, 74–75.

24. Robert H. Barlow, *Tlatelolco, fuentes e historia: Obras de Robert H. Barlow*, vol. 2 (México, DF: Instituto Nacional de Antrolopología e Historia, 1989), 262. The only church of San José depicted in the 1550 plan of the Valley of Mexico preserved in the library of the University of Uppsala is shown as one "block" south and two long "blocks" west of the *zócalo* in S. Linné, *El Valle de la Ciudad de México en 1550*, New Series, Publication no. 9 (Stockholm: Statens Etnografiska Museum, 1948), map 6.

25. *Codex Aubin*, "Chronicle of Mexican History to 1576, continued to 1607," Add MSS 31219 (London: Library of the British Museum), fol. 48v.

26. *Codex Aubin*, fols. 68r–69r.

27. Eloise Quiñones Keber, *Codex Telleriano-Remensis: Ritual, Divination, and History in a Pictorial Aztec Manuscript* (Austin: University of Texas Press, 1995), 195.

28. Fol. 46v.

29. Ross Hassig, *Time, History, and Belief in Aztec and Colonial Mexico* (Austin: University of Texas Press, 2001), 111.

30. Fol. 47r.

31. *Codex Aubin*, fol. 1r.

32. For a thorough explanation of the various Mesoamerican calendars, see Hassig, *Time, History, and Belief*, 7–17. A much more abbreviated account is in Michael D. Coe, *Mexico*, 3rd ed. (New York: Thames and Hudson, 1984), 160–61.

33. For a similar opinion, see James Lockhart, *The Nahuas after the Conquest: A Social and Cultural History of the Indians of Central Mexico, Sixteenth through Eighteenth Centuries* (Stanford, CA: Stanford University Press, 1992), 357.

34. Quiñones Keber, *Codex Telleriano-Remensis*, x.

35. Barlow, *Tlatelolco*, 261–305; Charles E. Dibble, *Historia de la nación mexicana: Codice de 1576 (Codice Aubin)* (Madrid: Ediciones José Porrúa Turanzas, 1963).

36. Walter Lehmann, Gerdt Kutscher, and Günter Vollmer, *Geschichte der Azteken: Codex Aubin und verwandte Dokumente* (Berlin: Gebr. Mann, 1981).

37. Diego Panitzin, also known as Diego Huanitzin, was a brother of Montezuma and former ruler at Ecatepec. This codex entry commemorates his having been selected as what was actually the fifteenth *tlatoani*, or state/community ruler, of Tenochtitlan, counting from Acamapichtli in 1372, rather than the twelfth as stated here. He was recognized among the Spaniards by the title "governor." As the entry for 1540 relates, he was succeeded in that year by his uncle's grandson, Diego Tehuetzqui. Charles Gibson, *The Aztecs under Spanish Rule: A History of the Indians of the Valley of Mexico, 1519–1810* (Stanford, CA: Stanford University Press, 1964), 169; Hassig, *Time, History, and Belief*, 21.

38. The minutes of the city council of the Ciudad de México record that in the last days of August 1535 the *cabildo* was rushing to prepare for the new viceroy's imminent arrival in the city. It was not until November 14, 1535, however, that the viceroy was officially received in the city. He attended his first meeting of the *cabildo* three days later. *Actas de Cabildo*, 4:121–23, 129, 131.

39. "[Gun]boat," *acalco*. "Acalco" has previously been assumed to have been a place, though Molina's 1571 *Vocabulario* indicates that it means simply a boat or canoe. Certainly a rendering as "boat" is consistent with the graphic element that accompanies this entry, which depicts a nautical vessel from which a cannon is being fired. Barlow, *Tlatelolco*, 268; Dibble, *(Codice Aubin)*, 64; Molina, *Vocabulario*, 1r. An *estancia* associated with the town of Yautepec southeast of Cuernavaca went by the similar name Guacalco (also spelled Oacalco). It is thus possible that the entry refers to the flight of Tenochca to that place, although in that case the associated pictorial element seems incongruous. Gerhard, *Historical Geography*, 97. The name Tenochca refers to the residents of Tenochtitlan, or Mexica Indians. Thomas, *Conquest*, xix.

40. It has become conventional to date the beginning of the Coronado expedition from its official muster, conducted at Compostela in February 1540. In fact the expedition began for specific persons and groups at different times and different places. The earliest northward travel that can legitimately be placed under the rubric of the Coronado expedition began when fray Marcos de Niza and Francisco Vázquez de Coronado departed from the Ciudad de México late in 1538. It can also be argued that March 7, 1539, should be taken as the beginning of the expedition's activity, the date when Marcos and fray Onorato set out northward from Culiacán on their own (accompanied by a large contingent of Mexican Indians).

This entry in the *Codex Aubin*, however, memorializes the late 1539 departure of the bulk of the expedition, both the large indigenous component and the smaller European component, from the Ciudad de México. For all practical purposes the expedition was fully under way no later than this time, although some members continued to join the force as late as Eastertime 1540 in the *provincia* of Culiacán.

41. Diego Tehuetzqui was a grandson of Montezuma's uncle, Tizoc. He was actually the sixteenth ruler of the Tenochca, rather than the thirteenth as this entry states. Gibson, *Aztecs*, 169; Hassig, *Time, History, and Belief*, 21.

42. Reference here is to the native people of Nueva Galicia who were defeated at Juchipila in 1541 by a large force including Indians from Tenochtitlan led by Viceroy Mendoza. This marked the end of the Mixtón War.

43. A royal mint had been established in the Ciudad de México in 1536. Beginning in 1542, it produced copper coins in denominations of one, two, and four *maravedís* for a period of about 18 years. Bakewell, *History*, 203; Kathleen Deagan, *Artifacts of the Spanish Colonies of Florida and the Caribbean, 1500–1800*, vol. 2, *Portable Personal Possessions* (Washington, DC: Smithsonian Institution Press, 2002), 245. Presumably the *villa* referred to here is Cíbola/Hawikku. Most of the occurrences of "via" throughout the Codex Aubin are in the context of geographical locations. This probably indicates a confusion on the part of the Nahua annalist in setting down the Spanish word *villa*.

44. Apparently, the contingent of Tenochca that had fought in the Mixtón War remained in Nueva Galicia until the Coronado expedition returned from the north.

45. The reference here is to drought, a delayed onset of the rainy season, which was recorded many times in later years in the Ciudad de México and which with some regularity resulted in poor harvests and famine. See Gibson, *Aztecs*, 315, 452–59.

46. Two indigenous communities are known to have gone by the name of Atempan, both about equidistant from Tenochtitlan, one to the northeast and the other more directly east. Both lay on the eastern slopes of the Sierra Madre Oriental. One is in the modern state of Hidalgo, the other in Puebla. Gerhard, *Historical Geography*, 244, 257–58.

47. Although contemporaneous descriptions of the disease referred to here as *cocoliztli* are vague, it is most commonly identified as typhus. Hans Prem, however, has recently suggested caution in this identification. Whatever the responsible infectious agent, the epidemic of 1545 was "probably the most disastrous ever to hit central Mexico," resulting in a death rate among native people of 60 to 90 percent. Hans Prem, "Disease Outbreaks in Central Mexico during the Sixteenth Century," in Nobel David Cook and W. George Lovell, eds, *"Secret Judgments of God": Old World Disease in Colonial Spanish America* (Norman: University of Oklahoma Press, 1992), 31–34, 40–42.

48. This market was held near the site of the church of San Hipólito, which today stands on the site of its sixteenth-century predecessor, one block northwest of the Alameda not far from the center of modern Ciudad de México. *Eyewitness Travel Guides' Mexico* (New York: DK Publishing, 1999), 85. The tradition of approximately weekly markets antedated the Spanish conquest throughout central Mexico.

49. Motlatocatlalli. Rémi Siméon, *Diccionario de la lengua nahuatl o mexicana*, trans. Josefina Oliva de Coll (México, DF: Siglo Ventiuno Editores, 1977), 709: *tocatlalia* = "registrar, inscribir el nombre de alguien"; 281: *mo* = third-person reflexive pronoun; 615: *tlan* = preposition "con, después, de, cerca, en, debajo, entre."

50. Motlatique. *Motlatiqui* = *escondido*. Siméon, *Diccionario*, 293.

51. Acalco. Siméon, *Diccionario*, 6: *acalco*, "cf. acalli"; 7: *acalli* = "barco, chalupa, embarcación."

52. Ompeuhque. *Nompeua* = *salir*. Siméon, *Diccionario*, 381.

53. Tlacoxiuhtica. Siméon, *Diccionario*, 571: *tlaco* = *mediano*; 770: *xiuhuitl* = *año*.

54. Momiquilico. *Momiqilico* = he died. Siméon, *Diccionario*, 278.

55. Mayanalloc. This is probably a scribal error for "mayanaloc." *Mayanaloc* = *hubo escasez*. Siméon, *Diccionario*, 249.

56. Tzatzic. *Tzatzi* = *gritar*. Siméon, *Diccionario*, 727.

Document 14. Hearing on Depopulation Charges, February 26, 1540

1. Document 28, fol. 16r–16v.

2. Fray Antonio Tello reported the first serious uprising following Guzmán's conquest of Nueva Galicia in 1530–32 as having occurred near Guadalajara in

1536. Beginning in 1538 there were intermittent uprisings that culminated in the Mixtón War. Tello, 233–37; José López-Portillo y Weber, *La Rebelión de Nueva Galicia* (México, DF: n.p., 1939), 397.

3. AGI, Justicia, 259, Pieza 2, "Visita a Antonio de Mendoza, 1543," fol. 1v.

4. Document 18, fol. 5r.

5. This refers to the company sent out with Melchior Díaz and Juan de Zaldívar in November 1539. The assertion that all the men died is erroneous. Ibid.

6. Although there had been significant, intermittent hostility in Nueva Galicia since 1538, the opening conflicts of the Mixtón War are usually dated to the final four months of 1540. López-Portillo y Weber, *Rebelión de Nueva Galicia*, 397.

7. See *descargo* 35 in AGI, Justicia, 259, Pieza 3, "Visita a Antonio de Mendoza, 1546," fol. 1r.

8. Ibid.

9. Flint, *Great Cruelties*, 437–38.

10. Fol. 5r.

11. See, for instance, fol. 2v.

12. Fol. 3r.

13. See the introduction to Document 12.

14. Included are all 10 captains, plus Diego de Alcaraz, Tomás Blaque, Juan Carlos de Bonilla, Juan Gómez de Paradinas, Juan Jaramillo, Pedro López de Urrea, Cristóbal de Mayorga, Gerónimo Méndez Sotomayor, Francisco Muñoz, Pedro Nieto, Fernán Páez, Juan de Peñas, Melchior Pérez, Diego de Puelles, Luis Ramírez de Vargas, Gaspar de Saldaña, Rodrigo Sánchez, Rodrigo Simón, Rodrigo de Tamarán, Francisco Temiño, Juan Xuárez de Ávila, and Rodrigo de Ysla.

15. Fol. 1r.

16. See Flint, *Great Cruelties*, 509–10; Chipman, *Nuño de Guzmán*, 259.

17. *CDI*, 14:373–84; H&R, 109–16.

18. For geographical information, see the entries for Compostela and Nueva Galicia in Appendix 2.

19. Dates in this document are in the Julian calendar.

20. For biographical information, see the entry for Antonio de Mendoza in Appendix 1.

21. León was still Viceroy Mendoza's secretary and an *escribano* of the Real Audiencia de Nueva España in 1543. At the time of the Mixtón War, he was a member of an unsuccessful diplomatic delegation sent to the *peñol* (a steep, rocky butte or headland) of Mixtón. After the return of Juan Rodríguez Cabrillo's fleet from California in 1543, León took testimony from the survivors, which he condensed into a summary report. A person of this name from Medina del Campo received license to travel to Nueva España in 1538. Whether this was the viceroy's secretary is unknown. Harry Kelsey, *Juan Rodríguez Cabrillo* (San Marino, CA: Huntington Library, 1998), 72, 113; Aiton, *Mendoza*, 146; *Pasajeros*, 2: no. 5055.

22. For biographical information about Francisco Vázquez de Coronado, see the introduction to Document 1. For biographical information on Marcos de Niza, see the introduction to Document 6.

23. The names of the complainants are unknown, although they probably included Hernán Cortés, Pedro de Alvarado, and their *criados* and partisans. Because they were hoping to mount northward expeditions themselves, they tried many means to stymie the viceroy's plans. Cortés specifically made such a complaint four months later. See Document 18, fol. 5r.

24. Indeed, hardly had the Coronado expedition departed from Compostela when the first incidents in what became a widespread native uprising in the *provincia* occurred. Eventually known as the Mixtón War, the uprising may have been triggered or aggravated by the departure of the expedition. Tello, 338–40.

25. For biographical information, see the entry for Pero Almíldez Cherino in Appendix 1, and, regarding, Gonzalo de Salazar, Document 12, note 34.

26. For biographical information, see the entries for Alonso Maldonado and Cristóbal de Oñate in Appendix 1. Hernán Pérez de Bocanegra y Córdoba was a native of Córdoba in the modern Spanish *comunidad* of Andalucía. He came to Nueva España from Cuba in 1526 with *licenciado* Luis Ponce de León, a relative. Pérez de Bocanegra y Córdoba was a *vecino* of the Ciudad de México by the mid-1530s, *alcalde ordinario* of the *ciudad* in 1537 and 1543, *alcalde de mesta* (governor over the cattle breeders) in 1538, *regidor* of the Ciudad de México in 1540, and, by 1544, an *encomendero*. He married doña Beatriz Pacheco of Trujillo, a native of Extremadura and a lady-in-waiting to Juana of Portugal. Three of their sons married three of Vázquez de Coronado's daughters: Bernardino Pacheco de Bocanegra y Córdova married Isabel de Luján; Nuño de Cháves Pacheco de Córdova y Bocanegra married Marina Vázquez de Coronado; and Luis Ponce de

León married Luisa de Estrada. Pérez de Bocanegra y Córdoba died in 1567. Boyd-Bowman, 2: no. 4004; Himmerich y Valencia, *Encomenderos*, 215.

Juan de Xaso is probably Juan de Jaso, "el viejo," who was a native of San Juan del Pié del Puerto in Navarra in Spain. He had come to Nueva España in 1523 with Francisco de Montejo. Jaso participated in Cortés's expedition to Honduras and had become a *vecino* of the Ciudad de México by 1527. He was *encomendero* of Guachinango. He went to California with Cortés and served with the viceroy in putting down the Mixtón War. Icaza, 2: no. 536.

Antonio Serrano de Cardona, a native of Medina de Rioseco in the *provincia* of Valladolid in the modern *comunidad* of Castilla y León in Spain, went by the name Antonio de Villarroel until 1528, when he adopted the surname Serrano de Cardona. He was with Cortés during the conquest of Tenochtitlan. By 1525 he was a *vecino*, *alguacil mayor*, and *regidor* of the Ciudad de México. He died early in 1546. Himmerich y Valencia, *Encomenderos*, 263.

In the body of the document, Sebastián Béjarano's name is given as Serván Béjarano. See fols. 4r and 4v. Serván was a native of Benalcázar in Córdoba *provincia* in the modern Spanish *comunidad* of Andalucía. He arrived in Nueva España from Jamaica in 1520 with Diego de Camargo and participated in the conquest of Tenochtitlan. He became a *vecino* of the Ciudad de México. He was a *criado* of Gonzalo Salazar's and also an *encomendero*. He had died by 1547. Himmerich y Valencia, *Encomenderos*, 127–28; C. Harvey Gardiner, *The Constant Captain: Gonzalo de Sandoval* (Carbondale: Southern Illinois University Press, 1961), 153.

The Diego Ordóñez referred to here may have been a relative of Sancho Ordóñez, a member of the Coronado expedition who was also a *vecino* and one of the first settlers of Puebla de los Ángeles. Sancho Ordóñez was a native of Alhanje in the modern *comunidad* of Extremadura in Spain. He had come to Nueva España in 1523 and went to Baja California with Cortés. Icaza, 2: no. 949; AGI, Justicia, 265, Pieza 2, "Probanza hecha en nombre de don Antonio de Mendoza, Puebla de los Ángeles, 1546–1547"; Document 12, fol. 7r.

Juan Fernández is probably Juan Fernández de Híjar/Ijar, a first settler, *vecino*, *teniente de capitán* (undercaptain), and *alcalde mayor* of the *villa* of Purificación. Before the start of the expedition he gave Vázquez de Coronado a horse. That gift later became an issue during the captain general's *residencia*. Fernández de Híjar, called a *caballero*, came from Zaragosa in the *reino* of Aragón in Spain. He was still living at Purificación at least as late as 1543. AGI, Justicia, 339, N.1, R.2, "Residencia, August 1544"; Tello, 253, 505. The community of Purificación is located in the modern Mexican state of Jalisco, in the Río Purificación valley, about 100 miles southwest of Guadalajara. Juan Fernández de Híjar was an *encomendero* there. Gerhard, *North Frontier*, 117–21.

27. Sunday was the twenty-second of February, as reported in Document 12, fol. 1r, and confirmed by Cháves, *Espejo de navegantes*, 82, 94.

28. For biographical information about Domingo Martín, see Document 33, note 41.

29. Alonso Sánchez and his wife, Francisca de Hozes, were later among 60 or more disgruntled members of the expedition who petitioned to stay in Tierra Nueva. Natives of Ciudad Real in the *provincia* of the same name in the *comunidad* of Castilla–La Mancha in Spain, the two were early settlers of the Ciudad de México, having come from Spain in 1522 with at least some of their children. Alonso had served the crown during the Comunero Revolt and in Italy. Prior to the expedition, he worked as a shoemaker in the Ciudad de México. It was said that indebtedness had led the couple, likely in their forties, to expend what they had to take a chance on Tierra Nueva. Accompanying them to the north was a son old enough to be listed among the men-at-arms. Boyd-Bowman, 2: no. 3672 and no. 3726. For further biographical details, see Flint, *Great Cruelties*, 54–57.

30. Twenty-four years old at the time of the muster of the Coronado expedition and a son of *bachiller* Alonso Pérez, Alonso Pérez de Bocanegra had just recently arrived in the New World from Vázquez de Coronado's place of origin, Salamanca, in the *provincia* of the same name in the modern *comunidad* of Castilla y León in Spain. This suggests that he might have been attending the university there. He subsequently married a daughter of Diego Gutiérrez de la Caballería's, another member of expedition and an in-law of Vázquez de Coronado's. By 1578 he was a *regidor* of the Ciudad de México. AGI, Patronato, 78A, N.1, R.6, "Méritos y servicios de Jorge Báez, 1585"; AGI, México, 97, R.1, "Méritos y servicios de Tristán de Luna y Arellano, 1559"; AGI, México, 1064, L.1\1, "Informes de los conquistadores," fol. 114v; AGI, Patronato, 87, N.1, R.5, "García Rodríguez y biznieto."

31. "Journeymen," *oficiales*. *DRAE*, 1467: "el que en un oficio manual ha terminado el aprendizaje y no es maestro todavía."

32. For biographical information, see the entry for Lope de Samaniego in Appendix 1.

33. "Who holds a benefice," *beneficiado*. H&R, 113, omit this word. A benefice is an ecclesiastical office funded by a donor or patron and held for life by a priest. The term "benefice" applied to "the obligation to discharge an ecclesiastical office, ... the right to enjoy the fruits attached to the office, ... and the fruits themselves." John Frederick Schwaller, *The Church and Clergy in Sixteenth-Century Mexico* (Albuquerque: University of New Mexico Press, 1987), 83–84.

34. "Very short of funds," *muy alcançado*. *Estar alcanzado*, Covarrubias, 49: "no tener hacienda que pueda ajustar con lo que ha menester, conforme a su estado."

35. At least seven expeditionaries were or had been *vecinos* of Guadalajara in 1540: Juan Hernández, Diego López, Esteban Martín, Francisco Martín, Melchior Pérez, Pedro de Tovar, and Juan de Zaldívar. Tello, 135, 167, 171, 223; Biblioteca del Escorial, Códice &-II-7, Doc. LXXVIII, "Pobladores sin yndios, [late 1540s]." For geographical information about Guadalajara, see the entry in Appendix 2.

36. In the context of early colonial Nueva España, "the means by which to sustain oneself" probably referred to an *encomienda* or to rents of some form.

37. For biographical information, see the entry for Antonio de Almaguer in Appendix 1.

38. Notificado. *CDI*, 14:375, mistakenly has "ordenado."

39. Dixero*n* lo syguy*ente* secreta e apa*r*tadame*n*te. *CDI*, 14:375, in error records "dijo" instead of "dixeron" and omits "secreta."

40. *Vido* is an obsolete preterite form of *ver*. Lloyd, *Latin to Spanish*, 306.

Document 15. *Narrative of Alarcón's Voyage, 1540*

1. This is as stated in the viceroy's instructions to Hernando de Alarcón in 1541. Document 16, fol. 2r.

2. Document 6, fol. 1v.

3. Document 6, fol. 2v.

4. Document 6, fol. 3r.

5. Document 8, fol. 68v.

6. Such expectations explain Rodrigo Maldonado's 1540 trip downriver (probably the Río Senora) from Señora to the seacoast in search of a port. Later that year Vázquez de Coronado expressed misgivings about information from fray Marcos concerning what he called the port of Chichilticale. Such information must have been provided orally or in a document not known to have survived, because there is no mention of Chichilticale by name or of a port associated with such a place in Marcos's formal report. Document 28, fol. 33r; Document 19, fol. 360r; Document 6. There is conflicting information about Alarcón's place of origin. A modern museum exhibit in Trujillo in Extremadura claimed him as a native son there. Meanwhile, sixteenth-century passenger license lists show that his parents, at least, were *vecinos* of Granada. This latter may help to explain Alarcón's association with Viceroy Mendoza, who was also a *granadino* (someone from the *provincia* of Granada). The future captain arrived in the New World in 1535, already in Mendoza's entourage. Display, Convento de la Coria, Trujillo, Extremadura, Spain, May 1997; *Pasajeros*, 2: no. 1261. AGI, Justicia, 259, Pieza 2, "Visita, 1543," lists Alarcón as an *escudero de a caballo*, or mounted *escudero* (see Document 5, note 17), in Mendoza's personal guard in January, June, and September 1538; January, May, and September 1539; and January 1540.

7. "This is the main reason for which we are sending you." Document 16, fol. 1r.

8. Document 28, fol. 20v.

9. Díaz del Castillo, *Historia verdadera*, xiv, 830–31.

10. See fol. 367r.

11. Pérez-Mallaína, *Spain's Men of the Sea*, 92.

12. Weddle, "Coastal Exploration and Mapping," 123–24.

13. For biographical information on Ramusio and how he might have come into possession of the documents he published, see the introduction to Document 2.

14. Fols. 369v and 370r.

15. Fols. 363r–370v.

16. "The modern languages that contributed most to Italian vocabulary in the sixteenth-century were Spanish and French. . . . Sometimes Italian syntax was affected." Bruno Migliorini, *The Italian Language*, trans. T. Gwynfor Griffith (London: Faber and Faber, 1966), 253–54. The Italian of the day was in the process

of being unified and standardized. Still prominent was a series of regional dialects, including one from Venice and its hinterland. One of the characteristics of that Venetian dialect was the frequent dropping of final vowels. But the irregular, frequent dropping of final *o* and *e* from verb forms throughout the Ramusio translations appears to go well beyond that regional quirk. Giacomo Devoto, *The Languages of Italy*, trans. V. Louise Katainen (Chicago: University of Chicago Press, 1978), 233.

17. Antonio de Herrera y Tordesillos, *Historia general de los hechos de los castellanos en las islas y tierra-firme de el Mar Oceano*, ed. J. Natalicio González (Buenos Aires: Editorial Guaranía, 1946), 8:178–86.

18. See notes 71, 102, and 104, this document.

19. Henri Ternaux-Compans, trans. and ed., "Relation de la navigation et de la découverte faite par le capitaine Fernando Alarcon," in *Voyages, relations et memoires*, 9:299–348. Hakluyt, *Principal Navigations*, 9:279–318; H&R, 124–55.

20. For biographical information, see the entry for Antonio de Mendoza in Appendix 1. For geographical information, see the entry on Colima in Appendix 2.

21. The lengthy title of the document given here and the summary headings scattered throughout the document were added by Ramusio or his translator.

22. This was probably at the modern Bahía de Santiago, just up the Pacific coast from Manzanillo, Colima, Mexico.

23. This is evidently the anchorage at the mouth of the Río Guayabal, some 17 leagues from Culiacán. López de Gómara, *Cortés*, 400. Guayaval, a long island on the west coast, north of San Miguel de Culiacán, between Río de Pascua and Río de Nuestra Señora, is depicted on the Mapa de la Audiencia de Nueva Galicia, from Antonio de Herrera y Tordesillas's *Décadas* (Madrid, 1601–15), in *Mapas de América en los libros españoles de los siglos XVI al XVIII*, Francisco Vindel (Madrid: Góngora, 1955). It seems to correspond to the similarly shaped island now called Isla de Altamura that fronts the Bahía Santa María.

24. This indicates that Alarcón was familiar with Ulloa's report or had on board one or more persons who had been with Ulloa the year before. Certainly Domingo del Castillo participated in both voyages. It is possible also that fray Antonio de Meno and fray Reymundo, who had been with Ulloa, also accompanied Alarcón. See note 27, this document. See also Document 16, fol. 1r. For biographical information on Francisco de Ulloa, Document 18, note 20.

25. As mentioned in the introduction, Alarcón was not himself a seaman or navigator. As captain, he was in command of the fleet but not the direction of individual ships. Nor would he necessarily have had the knowledge or skill to pilot one. For a description of the role of the captain in sixteenth-century ocean travel, see Pérez-Mallaína, *Spain's Men of the Sea*, 92. The expression of the opinions of the men here is an indication that a council was convened to determine the advisability of proceeding.

26. "Secret of that gulf": that is, whether it was a gulf or a strait. That question had been all but settled the previous year when Ulloa had reached the same shoals at the mouth of the Colorado River.

27. Castillo, who had also been on Francisco de Ulloa's voyage the previous year, later prepared a map of the Gulf of California on the basis of information obtained during this voyage. He was evidently scheduled to be chief pilot on Alarcón's second voyage. Weddle, "Coastal Exploration and Mapping," 123; Kelsey, *Cabrillo*, 104–5. Nicolás Zamorano, *señor* (a minor noble) de Ocuila, is probably the person of that name from Porcuna, Jaén, who was in Cuba in 1518 and a conqueror of Tenochtitlan in 1519. Boyd-Bowman, 1: no. 2152.

28. The Italian has the singular here, although there were evidently two boats with two pilots.

29. Reference here is to the tidal bore that is usual at the mouth of the Colorado River. According to the Baja California boatman Ray Cannon, as the tide rises "immense pressure is built up at the narrow mouth of the Rio Colorado, and a wall of water goes racing upstream." Ray Cannon, *The Sea of Cortez* (Menlo Park, CA: Lane Magazine and Book Co., 1966), 36. The term used by Antonio de Herrera y Tordesillos, which may have had its origin in Alarcón's original report, is *marea*, or "tide." Herrera y Tordesillos, *Historia general*, 8:178. For a thorough description and explanation of the bore, see Steve Nelson, "In Search of El Burro: The Tidal Bore on the Río Colorado Delta," in Richard S. Felger and Bill Broyles, eds., *Dry Borders: Great Natural Areas of the Gran Desierto and Upper Gulf of California* (Salt Lake City: University of Utah Press, 2005).

30. This Rodrigo Maldonado is not to be confused with two members of the ground expedition, don Rodrigo Maldonado and Rodrigo Paz Maldonado.

31. This date, like all those in Alarcón's report, is according to the Julian calendar. By this time the advance guard of the expedition had been in Cíbola for a month

and a half, having reached Cíbola, according to the "Traslado de las Nuevas," on July 7. See Document 22, fol. 1r.

32. These people were likely ancestors of the tribal group known today as Cocopa, who still inhabit the area around the mouth of the Colorado River. Anita Álvarez de Williams, "Cocopa," in Ortiz, *Southwest*, vol. 10, 99–112. The Italian word (*capanne*) that is translated here as "rude shelters" was possibly a translation of the original Spanish word *chozas* (see Document 28, note 159).

33. The reference here is to the insignias affixed to the backs of Mexica and other Mesoamerican warriors, both prehistorically and in early colonial times. For contemporary indigenous images of such banners, see, for example, Berdan and Anawalt, *Essential Codex Mendoza*, 139.

34. H&R, 127, mistakenly have "the stern of the boat."

35. At first Alarcón says that his interpreter and the Indians could not understand each other, yet he continues to report as if the Indians understood him and his wishes for them to move to a hill and approach him only 10 at a time. The vagaries of communication between Europeans and Native Americans are certainly being glossed over.

36. A description of this type of "bread" from among the Quechan, a lower Colorado River Yuman tribe, is in Robert L. Bee, "Quechan," in Ortiz, *Southwest*, vol. 10, 87.

37. H&R, 129, unaccountably have "masks."

38. "Like a helmet," *à guisa di cimiero*. Antonio de Herrera y Tordesillos confirms this translation. The word he uses, perhaps taken directly from Alarcón's original report, is *celada*. Herrera y Tordesillos, *Historia General*, 8:179.

39. This reference to sweat scraping is similar to that made by Marcos de Niza about people of a town in Sonora. It may indicate either ritual sweating or more mundane sweat removal during the hot, humid summer of the Colorado River delta. Document 6, fol. 2v.

40. The cane tubes referred to here may have been used as tobacco pipes or, as mentioned by Felger and Moser, as containers for various powders. Richard S. Felger and Mary Beck Moser, *People of the Desert and Sea: Ethnobotany of the Seri Indians* (Tucson: University of Arizona Press, 1985), 311. Recently, Felger has pointed out that a number of seeds, especially those of Gulf of California salt grass (*Distichlis palmeri*), were used to make a gruel-like drink by natives of the Colorado River delta. Richard S. Felger, *Flora of the Gran Desierto and Río Colorado of Northwestern Mexico* (Tucson: University of Arizona Press, 2000), 529.

41. "Wrapper or covering," *rinvolto = involto*. H&R, 130, mistakenly have "bunch."

42. This has reference to the genital area and corresponds to the earlier statement on fol. 364r about the men wearing a loincloth "in front."

43. Herrera y Tordesillos provides information about items included among the trade goods—information that might have come directly from Alarcón's original report: "cuentas de colores" (colored beads), "sartales" (strings of beads), and "cuentecillas de vidrio de colores" (colored glass beads). Herrera y Tordesillos, *Historia general*, 8:179, 180.

44. To say that they came from the sun was a common device of conquistadores and even missionaries of the day. They often elicited the title "son of the sun" from New World natives, as is later the case with Alarcón. See note 46, this document.

45. H&R, 131, inexplicably have "They did not refuse anything that I requested of them."

46. Although calling themselves sons of the sun would have been considered heretical by many Spaniards of the day, it was nevertheless a common device employed by conquistadores and missionaries in the New World in an effort to identify the Christian God with what they interpreted as the chief supernatural being throughout the Native American world. Hernán Cortés, Álvar Núñez Cabeza de Vaca, and Francisco de Ibarra, for example, all elicited the designation "sons of the sun" from indigenous groups they encountered. The appearance of the same designation here on the Lower Colorado River was almost certainly not spontaneous but rather coached or suggested by the Spaniards themselves. Such was the case elsewhere. As Fernando Cervantes has written: "In early Franciscan plays, the Indian leaders are made to recognize the Spaniards as the 'children of the Sun.'" Hernán Cortés, "Tercera carta-relación—15 de Mayo de 1522," in *Cartas de Relación*, Hernán Cortés (México, DF: Editorial Porrúa, 1993), 158; Adorno and Pautz, *Núñez Cabeza de Vaca*, 1:165, 203; Obregón, *Historia*, 180; Fernando Cervantes, *The Devil in the New World: The Impact of Diabolism in New Spain* (New Haven, CT: Yale University Press, 1994), 13.

47. This is the record of a remarkable mediated conversation between Alarcón

and a skeptical leader of this indigenous group. But it begs the question of how such a conversation, dealing with abstract concepts including "friendship, war, choice, lord, brother, God, and peace," was possible, given the major linguistic and cultural divide between the parties.

48. The alacrity with which this leader offers submission to Alarcón and his small party renders this entire conversation suspect. For one thing, by law Alarcón was required to read the official *requerimiento*, not to extemporize a fanciful speech about being sent by the sun. It is possible, of course, that this particular native band foresaw some immediate pragmatic advantage in cooperating with the expeditionary party. But such ready acceptance of Spanish overlordship is all but unheard of in the documentary record of the period.

49. This phrase follows the common sixteenth-century Spanish rhetorical method of using two near synonyms in succession to emphasize a point, in this case the verbs *andare*, to go, and *partire*, to leave. This usage suggests, at the least, that the speech of the native leader is not literally a translated quotation.

50. This report could refer to personnel from one or more of the voyages sponsored by Cortés, including that of Ulloa just the previous year, to *entradas* made years before from the south by Guzmán's forces and residents of Culiacán, or to the land units of the Coronado expedition on their way to Cíbola.

51. Presumably Alarcón is referring here to the place called Totontec in other documents. This and another instance on fol. 367v are the only known documentary instances of mention of a river with that name. See Document 6, fols. 3v, 4v, 5r, 5v, and 7r; Document 19, fol. 362r. See also the entry under Totonteac in Appendix 2.

52. Ethnographic reports of the Quechan people of the lower Colorado River indicate that among them "war was probably incessant but usually not very costly in lives." Bee, "Quechan," 93.

53. The practice of ritual cannibalism was not recorded later among the Quechan and Cocopa, leading to the possibility that this is a fanciful addition by either Alarcón or Ramusio. Cannibalism was widely viewed as "unnatural" in Europe and as a sufficient reason to wage war. Francisco de Vitoria, one of the great Spanish scholars of the day and often an upholder of Indian rights, nevertheless argued in the mid-1530s that "there are some sins against nature . . . such as cannibalism . . . that any Christian prince can compel them not to do." Bee, "Quechan," 93; Álvarez de Williams, "Cocopa," 107; Francisco de Vitoria, "On the Evangelization of Unbelievers," in *Colonial Latin America: A Documentary History*, eds. Kenneth Mills, William B. Taylor, and Sandra Lauderdale Graham (Wilmington, DE: Scholarly Resources, 2002), 74.

54. This would have been a matter of a few days at most.

55. H&R, 136, treat "Naguachato" as a proper name, translating this phrase as "called Naguachato." The word, though, is a form of the Nahuatl "nauatlato or nahuatato [translator or interpreter]." The term was widely applied by sixteenth-century Spaniards outside the Nahuatl-speaking region. Molina, *Vocabulario*, fol. 63v.

56. H&R, 136, instead have "some small gourds." However, both the Quechan and Cocopa also cultivated cushaw squash (*Cucurbita mixta*). Álvarez de Williams, "Cocopa," 104; Edward F. Castetter and Willis H. Bell, *Yuman Indian Agriculture* (Albuquerque: University of New Mexico Press, 1951), 113.

57. H&R, 136, have instead "he offered" and "he had." Because the singular noun "la gente" (the people) is the closest referent, it seems more appropriate to use the third-person plural in English.

58. This repetition of behavior seen earlier suggests the speed with which news traveled among the peoples of the lower Colorado River, much as it did throughout Tierra Nueva more generally.

59. This indicates that a linguistic boundary had been passed, probably between areas in which distinct Yuman languages were spoken. The divide here may have been between Cocopa and Quechan speakers. Kenneth M. Stewart, "Yumans: Introduction," in Ortiz, *Southwest*, vol. 10, 1.

60. Kenneth Stewart lists 15 tribal groups living along or near the Colorado River in the nineteenth century that spoke Yuman languages. He also indicates that there was "persistent warfare between the tribes [which] precipitated numerous population shifts and amalgamations." Stewart, "Yumans: Introduction," 1–3.

61. This report of stone masonry architecture suggests that these mountain people might have been ancestral Yavapais of what is now west-central Arizona. Their descendants in the nineteenth century were still using some stone masonry, though they had abandoned sedentary lives. Sigrid Khera and Patricia S. Mariella, "Yavapai," in Ortiz, *Southwest*, vol. 10, 38–40, 49.

62. This annual round, as Richard Felger has pointed out, included planting after the late spring river floods receded and retreating to higher, cooler terrain during the hot summer to gather luxury items such as sweet agave and piñon nuts. Return to the river would come after the spring-planted crops matured. Felger, personal communication, Feb. 8, 2004.

63. This description suggests the account of shelters seen by the party of Melchior Díaz several weeks later along the Colorado River. They were said to be "excavated into the ground in the same way pig pens [are]." Document 28, fol. 35v. See also Document 28, note 159. An illustration of a similar structure, "a Cocopah traditional winter dwelling of posts, poles and thatch banked with earth for insulation," is in Anita Álvarez de Williams, *The Cocopah People* (Phoenix, AZ: Indian Tribal Series, 1974), 13.

64. H&R, 139, have "moved to another nation," which seems to be a drastic change of residence not required by *paesi*, the term in the Italian original.

65. Among the Cocopa, "cremation is the custom of the people and is still practiced formally by the American Cocopa." Álvarez de Williams, "Cocopa," 110.

66. Álvarez de Williams, "Cocopa," 110, writes that the Cocopa in the twentieth century believed that "the soul leaves the body at the time of cremation and goes to live . . . in a spirit land of plenty and festivity in an area of salt flats near the mouth of the Colorado River."

67. There were a number of epidemics in early colonial Mexico that involved copious bleeding from the nose and mouth. Although the disease has not been positively identified, "there is general agreement that [such an] epidemic of 1578–80, like the ones preceding and following it, was an outbreak of typhus." Prem, "Disease Outbreaks," 40.

68. This may refer to the locality in Oaxaca known as Taviche. Gerhard, *Historical Geography*, 73.

69. This seed was probably panic grass (*Panicum hirticaule*), which the Cocopa and neighboring Yuman groups grew and used extensively to make "cakes, gruel or mush." One piece of evidence for protohistoric use of panic grass seed is a woven bag of seeds dating to about the time of the Alarcón trip that was collected archaeologically near the lower Colorado River. Besides a large amount of panic grass seed, it also contained seeds of tepary beans and green-striped cushaw squash. Gary Paul Nabhan, *Gathering the Desert* (Tucson: University of Arizona Press, 1985), 151–52; Felger, *Flora of the Gran Desierto*, 544–45.

70. This point evidently marked a territorial boundary that may have coincided with a linguistic change, perhaps to another branch of the Yuman language family. The specific boundary being crossed is all but impossible to ascertain on the basis of much later ethnographic information, especially since territories and affiliations were very fluid in the lower Colorado River region. Martha B. Kendall, "Yuman Languages," in Ortiz, *Southwest*, vol. 10, 4.

71. There is a discontinuity in the dialogue here. Either Alarcón or Ramusio has omitted part of the conversation or else the Indian informant's reply is simply a non sequitur. As the dialogue is presented, the Indian man seems spontaneously to bring up a subject that he knows will be of interest to Alarcón. It seems more reasonable to suppose that again part of the conversation has been omitted, namely, a question from Alarcón that elicited this response.

72. This long garment seems similar to the "long cotton shirts" that Marcos de Niza reported he was told the people of Cíbola wore. Document 6, fol. 4r.

73. Presumably the notes from which this report was prepared also included the date, which unfortunately is omitted here, as it is throughout this portion of the report. Whether this omission is Alarcón's or Ramusio's is unclear.

74. The reference here is clearly to Esteban de Dorantes, his greyhound, and the green-glazed European ceramics he took with him to Cíbola in 1539.

75. The gender of the past participles "chiamato" and "chiamata" makes it clear that these are the names of the places rather than the lords themselves. In Italian, *ch* is pronounced like English *k* and Spanish *qu*, making "Chicama" a phonetic match for "Quicama," which appears in Document 16, fol. 2r. The people of Quicama and Coama have been identified with the Yuman-speaking Maricopa groups now known as the Halyikwamai and Kahwan, respectively. In the sixteenth century they may have occupied a territory along the lower Gila River in what is now southwestern Arizona, much as they did in the eighteenth century. Henry O. Harwell and Marsha C. S. Kelly, "Maricopa," in Ortiz, *Southwest*, vol. 10, 72, 84.

76. This is the same man who was called a *nagauchato* on fol. 365v. At that time he and the people with him were unarmed.

77. The same word, *yuca*, is applied to both yucca and cassava. Although the lower Colorado River is outside the known range of cultivated cassava, several species of plants with tuberous roots are native there and might have seemed similar enough to cassava to warrant the use of the name. As Richard Felger points out, however (personal communication, Feb. 8, 2004), this "might be *Yucca baccata* fruits—they keep well, people did trade, they did make expeditions, the green/ripe fruits might keep for a week even in summer if shielded from the sun." See also Felger, *Flora of the Gran Desierto*, 472.

78. The nonsense word "bessuchi" in the Italian manuscript, which we have translated as "reeds," resulted from a misreading by the Italian translator of the Spanish word *bejucos*. Antonio de Herrera y Tordesillos, who evidently had access to the original Alarcón report or a copy of it, includes the phrase "corteças de bejucos" in his summary of the voyage. *J* and *z* were often difficult to distinguish in sixteenth-century written Spanish; hence the translator's error of converting what he thought was a *z* to *ss*. Herrera y Tordesillos, *Historia general*, 8:185. What is referred to here as the "inner bark of reeds" was probably the inner bark of willows, which Quechan and Cocopa people used to make fabric even during recent historic times. Bee, "Quechan," 89; Álvarez de Williams, "Cocopa," 107.

79. This would have been an opportunity for Alarcón to show the lord samples of silver and gold, but it appears that he did not.

80. H&R, 144, omit the phrase "si sol*l*eva," "[the sun] should get itself up."

81. The addressee of Alarcón's report is Viceroy Mendoza.

82. The reference here is to Esteban de Dorantes, whom Marcos de Niza had sent ahead of him from Vacapa at Eastertime 1539. Document 6, fol. 3r.

83. This phrase is highly ambiguous. The reference could be either to the name of the woman or to the name of the place. Guatuzaca sounds very Mesoamerican, as though it came to Alarcón through an interpreter of Nahua origin.

84. At least on the basis of apparent population size, this would have made what Alarcón was reporting very enticing to potential conquistadores and missionaries.

85. This is certainly the bison of the American Great Plains. These measurements from top of head to chin and across the widest part of the face reflect the large size of the adult male bison's head. A span is the distance between the tip of the thumb and the tip of the extended little finger. *OED*, 2938. "The rear feet and forefeet [are] more than [two] palmos [in width]" is clearly either an error or a gross exaggeration here. H&R, 146, assume that the measurement is correct but the body part is not. Thus, they have "Its forelegs and hind legs were more than seven spans long." We suggest, rather, that less violence is done to the original text by assuming that the scribe or compositor mistakenly picked up "sette," or "seven," from the phrase describing the length of the bison's face two lines above. Because the remainder of the description of the bison is accurate, the number in the original manuscript was probably "dui," or "two."

86. Although when the elder left the *barca* there was only one other man reported on shore (fol. 368r), in this and several other instances the verb forms are plural. Thus it seems that there may have been more men on shore. There is no indication in any of the known documents of who these men might have been or where the sighting might have occurred

87. H&R, 147, interpret the phrase "doing his work" in a sexual way, although that is not explicit in the Italian. They have "a son of his dressed as a woman and used as such."

88. H&R, 148, ignore the phrase "if it [is] all right with them" and omit it from their translation.

89. H&R, 148, ignore the word *pane*, bread, and translate this as "what goods has he taken from you?"

90. These are some of the thousands of Old World domestic cattle and sheep that were taken along on the Coronado expedition. A count of them is provided in Document 28, fol. 149v.

91. What seems to be described here is the arrival at Cíbola of the advance guard of the Coronado expedition in July 1540. The description suggests that the expeditionaries were strung out over a considerable distance and did not travel in a single large mass. It also suggests that the contingent of Indian allies accompanying the advance guard was very large, perhaps comprising "most of the [native] allies," as Castañeda de Nájera reported. Document 28, fol. 27v.

92. This suggests that small cloaks or capes were among the trade and gift goods carried by the Coronado expedition.

93. Cumana formerly has been thought to be synonymous with the Coana and Coano mentioned earlier. More recently the name has been identified with the Yuman people known as the Kahwan. See notes 75 and 106, this document. Because the Maricopa/Kahwan probably occupied part of the lower Gila River at this time, Alarcón and his party were, at this point in the narrative, probably not far

upstream, if at all, from the confluence of the Gila and Colorado Rivers (maps 1 and 2).

94. This marks a dramatic change in relations between Alarcón and this Indian elder.

95. "To visit the navíos." H&R, 149, have "to inspect the ships," which is a possibility.

96. Evidently Alarcón is referring here to either the Colorado River or the Gila, either of which could lead to Cíbola (map 2). The Gila appears the more likely, because of the virtual impassability of the Grand Canyon of the Colorado, particularly proceeding upstream.

97. H&R, 150, ignoring the word "perche," render this sentence as "I ordered all the boats that were not needed in the ships to be made ready."

98. Mendoza's coat of arms was surmounted by an eight-pointed star, or compass rose, and the legend "Buena Guía," which had been added by his father, Iñigo López de Mendoza. Aiton, *Mendoza*, 8 n. 14.

99. Camorano = Çamorano = Zamorano.

100. Like the few other dates in this document, this is a date in the Julian calendrical system. Alarcón had now been on the river just under three weeks, since August 26. Fol. 363v.

101. The reference here is almost certainly to tropical macaw feathers, which were highly prized and widely traded among native peoples of the region during the protohistoric period. Riley, *Frontier People*, 13.

102. There is another discontinuity in the narrative here, evidence that, as Alarcón himself says shortly, this report is made up of excerpts from a longer work, "a book of mine which I am carrying." This book has not yet come to light.

103. For biographical information about Agustín Guerrero, see Document 16, note 56.

104. Here again there appears to be a discontinuity in the narrative. The gap between Alarcón's conversation with his first interpreter and his arrival at Quicama must have amounted to several days and many leagues.

105. Neither Alarcón's having reached Coana during his first ascent of the river nor his having left a Spaniard there is mentioned earlier in Ramusio's version of his report. It is possible that this earlier information was edited out by the Italian publisher or even before that by Alarcón. See fol. 367r and note 93, this document, where the place name is spelled Coama.

106. Alarcón has referred earlier (fol. 369r) to "a lord of Cumana" who was threatening to attack downstream natives. The anthropologists Harwell and Kelly incorrectly conflated Cumana and Coana. Harwell and Kelly, "Maricopa," 84.

107. Because the men from Cumana clearly had not persuaded the elder to attack Alarcón, a phrase must be missing from the Italian version of the report.

108. This wording is strikingly similar to that of the *requerimiento* mandated by the king to be read to newly encountered peoples in the New World. See Appendix 4.

109. This suggests the possibility that Alarcón had a painter with him, as Vázquez de Coronado did on his land expedition. Two painters are known to have participated in the land expedition: Cristóbal de Quesada and Bartolomé Sánchez. AGI, México, 1064, L.1\1,"Informes de los conquistadores," fol. 270r; AGI, Contratación, 199, N.23, "Bienes de difuntos de Bartolomé Sánchez, 1561."

110. Assuming that Alarcón was on the modern Gila River in southwestern Arizona (see notes 75, 93, and 96, this document), this may describe the point at which the river rounds the northern end of the Gila Mountains near today's Kinter Siding, Arizona, between Yuma and Dome Valley, traversing a narrow pass between the Gila Mountains and the Laguna Mountains. For the distance of about four miles the two mountain ranges (really a single formation geologically) are separated only by the river's floodplain, which averages about one mile in width. Within that pass, at the location of the McPhaul Bridge on old U.S. Highway 80, the channel of the Gila River is hemmed in by two unnamed prominences that rise about 300 feet above the elevation of the river itself and are each within 20 yards of it. The bridge site may thus be the exact location of the narrows referred to here. A corresponding candidate narrowing of the Colorado River is located between the north end of the Laguna Mountains and the south end of the Chocolate Mountains, north of modern Yuma. These two ranges, however, never approach closer than a mile, so that the description "very narrow" seems not to apply. Herbert Bolton, having in mind some rather minor cutbanks along the Colorado River downstream from its confluence with the Gila, wrote: "The captain was now apparently at Yuma, where the Colorado River runs for a mile, more or less, through a narrow channel, with high, cliff-like banks on either side." That location, however, lacks the proximity of *sierras*, or high mountains. U.S. Department of the Interior, Geologic

Survey (USGS), 7.5 Minute Topographic Quadrangle, "Laguna Dam, Arizona, California," 1979 ed.; Bolton, 166.

111. As reported by Castañeda de Nájera, Melchior Díaz some days or weeks later found this tree, which bore the inscription, "Alarcón reached this point. At the foot of this tree there are letters." Document 28, fol. 37r.

112. In indicating why he came to this conclusion, Alarcón is less forthcoming than he has been up until now. Were there, for example, threats from the people of Cumana? Was navigation becoming too toilsome?

113. "The Spaniard": see fol. 369v.

114. Computing on the basis of the *legua legal*, this would have been close to 80 miles and would place the point of Alarcón's farthest penetration in the vicinity of the north end of the modern Gila Mountains. This matches exactly the possible location on the narrow, straight run of the Gila River near Kinter, Arizona, discussed in note 110.

115. Although we do not have Alarcón's figure for comparison, Ulloa reported a latitude reading at the head of the Gulf of California of 34 degrees, which is in fact slightly more than 2 degrees greater than the modern value of approximately 31 degrees 40 minutes. Wagner, *Spanish Voyages*, 20. For a discussion of widespread errors in latitude measurements during the sixteenth century, see Document 29, note 50.

116. This number seems to be in error, unless it is the total of Alarcón's travel on the river, adding the two upstream journeys and the two downstream. Compare the figure of 30 leagues earlier on this folio. Both Arthur Aiton and Herbert Bolton were of the opinion that Alarcón's farthest penetration inland was to the general region of modern Yuma, Arizona, rather than 130 miles or so farther upstream, as the 85-league figure would suggest. On the basis of Domingo del Castillo's resulting map, Robert Weddle asserted that Alarcón did not reach even the confluence of the Colorado and Gila Rivers. Bolton, 167; Aiton, *Mendoza*, 129; Weddle, "Coastal Exploration and Mapping," 124. Because Alarcón spent much of his time in the lower Colorado and Gila River drainages on land questioning indigenous informants, rather than having his boats towed upstream, his daily rate of travel is impossible to estimate. Indeed, it probably varied widely from day to day, but it seems to have been very slow.

117. Reference here is to Viceroy Mendoza.

118. For biographical information, see the entry for Luis de Castilla in Appendix 1. "Ghenero" is an Italian translator's misreading of "Guerrero," which would convert to Italian as Guerriero.

119. This is the *galera* referred to in Document 21, fol. 23v.

120. This gives some indication of how serious the rivalry was between Viceroy Antonio de Mendoza and Adelantado Pedro de Alvarado and how close to the edge of violence affairs were at this time before the signing of the formal agreement between the two parties in November 1540, just a few weeks after this. See Document 20.

121. For an account of the movements of Alvarado's fleet, see Documents 20 and 21.

122. "Alvise" is a copying error for "Luis" (Luigi in Italian), which is correctly read above.

123. Alzana = *alzaia*.

124. Busi = *buci*.

125. Dessero = *dettero*.

126. Si gittavano = *si gettavano*.

127. "Avrebbono" is probably a copying error for *avrebbero*, the present conditional form of the auxiliary verb *avere*, to have, being used here to form the conditional perfect of *fare*, to do.

128. Figliuolo = *figliolo*.

129. (H)avea mandato. This is probably a copying or typesetting error for the pluperfect form *aveva mandato*.

130. Vieni. This is a use of the formal second-person singular present of *venire*.

131. Several instances of "però" on this folio appear to be typographical errors for *perciò*, "therefore."

132. Anco = *ancora*.

133. Dicea = *diceva*.

134. Diceano = *dicevano*.

135. Volsi = *vòlli*, the first-person preterit indicative of *volere*, to want.

136. Perchio = *perciò*.

137. Abbrusciare = *bruciare*.

138. Dessi = detti = *diedi*.

139. (O)*ufficio*. The compositor or scribe suggests here, with his use of "officio" instead of "ufficio," that he may not have been a native speaker of Italian but rather of Spanish. This possibility is further reinforced by his preference for verb infinitives ending in *r* (as in Spanish) instead of *re* (as in Italian). The 1565 edition of the *Navigationi e viaggi* changes many of these "hispanisms." See the introduction to this document.

140. Desisterio must be an error for *desiderio*.

141. So- / spitione. Sospitione = *sospetto*.

142. Dieronmi. *Dieron = dièdero*. This is another example of the tendency to use Spanish elements in this otherwise Italian document—in this case, substituting *dieron*, the third-person preterit of the Spanish verb *dar*, for the equivalent form of the Italian verb *dare*.

143. Concertaron = *concertarono*. *Concertaron*, the third-person plural preterit of the Spanish verb *concertar*, is substituted to the corresponding form of the Italian verb *concertare*. This is another example of the tendency to use Spanish elements in this otherwise Italian document.

144. "Schincho" must be an error for *stinco*.

145. Coda torta. As in many sixteenth-century manuscripts, probably including the one from which the scribe or Ramusio was copying, lowercase *c* and *t* are often indistinguishable. So the scribe read "torta," or "twisted," instead of "corta," or "short," which would be an accurate description. H&R, 146, share our conclusion.

146. Affirmarono. *Afirmaron*, the third-person plural preterit of the Spanish verb *afirmar*, is substituted for the corresponding form of the Italian verb *affinrmare*. This is another example of the tendency to use Spanish elements in this otherwise Italian document.

147. Maravigliosa. Once again this suggests someone perhaps more comfortable in Spanish than Italian. The use of "maravi-" is reminiscent of the Spanish word *maravillosa*, whereas the corresponding Italian term has an *e* in the first syllable.

148. Ir. Here the translator left the Spanish verb *ir* instead of translating it with the Italian equivalent *andare*.

149. Dierono. Here the translator simply Italianized the Spanish verb *dieron* by adding an *o* to the end, rather than translating it into the appropriate Italian form, *dièdero*.

150. Veneria. Once again the Spanish-speaking translator modifies an Italian verb with a Spanish ending, in this case the conditional ending -*ía*, rather than using the corresponding Italian form, *verrebbe*.

151. Ve(ni)rremo. Yet again the translator follows Spanish practice, more or less, rather than Italian, attempting to form the future tense by adding a suffix to the infinitive.

152. Rob(b)a. This is probably the translator's erroneous rendition of *ropa*, or clothing.

153. Disviato. *Disviare = traviare*.

154. Anzana. This must be a copying error; both Spanish and Italian have the term *amarra*, meaning "cable or hawser," which may have been intended here. Another possibility is *alzàia*, "towrope." A similar error appears on fol. 363v.

155. Presuppos(i)to. The insertion of an *i* here is yet another example of the translator's tendency to slide toward Spanish forms.

Document 16. The Viceroy's Instructions to Hernando Alarcón, May 31, 1541

1. For information on the life and career of Alarcón and his relationship to the viceroy, see the introduction to Document 15.

2. Mendoza writes that "it is all the same [undertaking]." Fol. 2r.

3. Fol. 2v.

4. Fols. 1v and 3r.

5. Fol. 2v.

6. Fol. 1r.

7. Fol. 1v; Document 15, fol. 369r.

8. Fol. 2r.

9. Ibid.

10. García López de Cárdenas once granted his power of attorney jointly to don Luis de Castilla and Vázquez de Coronado. AGI, Justicia, 263, Pieza 1, "Probanza de Mendoza, Zacatula"; AGI, Justicia, 1021, N.2, Pieza 5, "Probanza fecha a pedimiento de don García López de Cárdenas, Guadalajara, 1546, and México, 1547–1548."

11. Relying on the 1560 testimony of a sailor (who did not claim to have participated in the voyage) and the 1546 testimony of don Luis de Castilla, Harry Kelsey has suggested that Alarcón's second voyage did indeed take place. Kelsey's argument is weak. Both don Luis and the sailor, Francisco de Vargas, said they had seen Alarcón sail out of the port of La Navidad on September 8, 1541, bound up the coast. Don Luis further reports that he tried to stop the three ships and was able to bring two back to port. At this late date Viceroy Mendoza would already have known, from at least one letter from Vázquez de Coronado dispatched from Tiguex in April 1541, that the expedition was hundreds of leagues from the Río de la Buena Guía, that it planned to trek hundreds of leagues farther to the east that year, and that the captain general had no plans to send another unit to the Buena Guía, as he had in 1540. All this would have meant that the chief purpose of a second Alarcón voyage (locating and making contact with the expedition) was hopeless of success. If in fact Alarcón sailed from La Navidad in 1541, as Vargas and don Luis de Castilla reported, it might well have been to retrieve iron goods from Culiacán, as Mendoza had originally instructed him. That iron would have been sorely needed as the Mixtón War continued to rage. Kelsey, *Cabrillo*, 85, 104, 212 n. 129–33.

12. Aiton, *Mendoza*, 130; Gerhard, *Historical Geography*, 58–61.

13. Following Alvarado's death during the Mixtón War, Mendoza dispatched part of the 13-ship fleet up the California coast. Rather than sailing under Alarcón, the fleet was now led by Juan Rodríguez Cabrillo, a close associate of Alvarado's. Additionally, part of the fleet headed across the Pacific Ocean under Ruy López de Villalobos. With some modification, this was the earlier Mendoza-Alvarado plan. Aiton, *Mendoza*, 131. See also the introduction to Document 20.

14. See note 19, this document.

15. Thomas Buckingham Smith, ed., *Colección de Varios Documentos para la Historia de la Florida y Tierras Adyacentes* (London: Trübner [1857]), 1–6; H&R, 117–23.

16. This is the Gulf of California, or Sea of Cortés.

17. Now in the Mexican state of Jalisco, the Pacific Ocean port of La Navidad was established at the bay of the same name late in 1540. It was first located by Juan Rodríguez Cabrillo, operating under instructions from Pedro de Alvarado and Viceroy Mendoza. For a month or two it was known as the port of Colima. A busy shipyard was functioning there by 1541. Gerhard, *Historical Geography*, 58–61; Kelsey, *Cabrillo*, 82.

18. "Take charge," *recibir*. DRAE, 1740: "hacerse cargo uno de lo que le dan."

19. The identity of the ship is omitted in the signed original of the instructions. On fol. 391 of the draft version (Doc. no. LXVI), however, a marginal notation in the hand of Antonio de Mendoza provides this information about the ship: "de luys de castilla," or "belonging to Luis de Castilla." Manuel Fraile Miguélez pointed out that the note was written by Mendoza, as were those on two other draft instructions from the same year pertaining to voyages along the coast of the Mar del Sur, which are included in the same codex of documents in the Escorial. Manuel Fraile Miguélez, *Catálogo de los códices españoles de la Biblioteca del Escorial, 1: Relaciones históricas* (Madrid: Imprenta Helénica, 1917), 240–41.

20. Because a *barca* was a fairly small vessel, Mendoza is here indicating one of larger than normal size. H&R, 117 n. 2, incorrectly assume that the ships to be taken on the second voyage were the same two taken the previous year. H&R, 117, omit "which is ready to sail" from their translation.

21. "Master," *maestre*. DRAE, 1290: "persona a quien después del capitán correspondía antiguamente el gobierno económico de las naves mercantes."

22. "Copy," *tanto*. DRAE, 1940. For biographical information, see the entry on Luis de Castilla in Appendix 1.

23. "List," *copia*. For examples of this usage, see Boyd-Bowman, *Léxico*, 224.

24. "With care," *a punto*. DRAE, 1697: "con la prevención y disposición necesarias para que una cosa pueda servir al fin a que se destina."

25. In other words, this roster was not intended to be exhaustive. Clearly excluded would be persons of low rank, most women, servants, slaves, and Indian allies among them. In this respect Alarcón's muster roll was to be similar to the one prepared for the land expedition at Compostela in February 1540. See Document 12.

26. This seems to imply that Alarcón himself would be financing the provisioning of the *barca*.

27. This entry did not appear in the draft version (Doc. no. LXVI). However, a marginal note on fol. 391 in that version (in this case in a scribal hand and not Mendoza's) directed that such a paragraph be added. The note reads, "aquí entra el Capítulo de los Religiosos que el lleVa conforme a el que estaba en la de francisco

Vazqu*ez* [insert here the paragraph concerning the religious he is taking, in conformance with the (instructions) for Francisco Vázquez]."

28. These same two friars were with Ulloa in 1539 and early 1540 and returned to Nueva España ahead of their captain, shortly before Alarcón's departure on his first voyage into the gulf. It is possible, therefore, that they accompanied Alarcón in 1539 as well. Wagner, *Spanish Voyages*, 12.

29. The sense of this clause requires the negative, although it is missing in the manuscript.

30. This is an indication of the shortage of iron that existed in Nueva España, which was exacerbated by the Mixtón War, then raging.

31. H&R, 118, omit "The other half [of the iron] you shall leave in the town for what might be necessary [there]" entirely, although Amador de los Rios, whose transcription they were following, included the sentence, as is correct.

32. For geographical information about San Miguel de Culiacán, see the entry in Appendix 2.

33. In September 1539 the small fleet commanded by Francisco de Ulloa located and named Puerto de los Puertos, a deep, sandy-bottomed anchorage that included many coves capable of accommodating ships. Hence the name, meaning "Port with [many] Ports." Ulloa wrote that "this harbor has two entrance channels, formed by an island at the mouth of it." According to Ulloa, Puerto de los Puertos was located 104 leagues from the head of the Gulf of California on its eastern shore. Converting this distance using the *legua geográfica* yields a distance of about 410 miles. This would place Puerto de los Puertos on the Sonoran coast west of modern Ciudad Obregón at the site of today's Estero de Lobos, which does, in fact, have multiple coves and is enclosed by an island forming two entrances, one an east-west channel and the other a north-south channel. In 1929 Henry Wagner suggested, instead, that Puerto de los Puertos was the nearby Puerto de Guaymas, which does not match the documentary description nearly as well as Estero de Lobos. Wagner, *Spanish Voyages*, 19, 20, 306 n. 40; Chardon, "Linear League," 140, 144.

34. At this date Viceroy Mendoza was still unaware that Díaz had died late in 1540 during his effort to rendezvous with Alarcón. Díaz had departed from the *villa* of Señora in September or October 1540 and must have reached the Colorado River the following month, by which time Alarcón was en route back to the port of Navidad (still called the port of Colima then). Document 28, fols. 33v and 35r. For biographical information, see the entry for Melchior Díaz in Appendix 1, and for geographical information, the entry for Los Corazones in Appendix 2.

35. Alarcón had bestowed the name Buena Guía on what is now the Colorado River the previous year. Document 15, fol. 369r.

36. This passage is typical of documents of the era in that it is replete with pronouns, often totally lacking referents.

37. "Suitable," *convenible = conveniente. DRAE*, 563.

38. For geographical information, see the entry for Cíbola in Appendix 2.

39. This must refer to Vázquez de Coronado's letter to the viceroy dated August 3, 1540; see Document 19.

40. H&R, 119, garble this with "his people appreciate you." The instructions apparently refer here to Alarcón's amicable encounters with native people along the Río de Buena Guía the previous year. See Document 15.

41. "Information," *lengua. DRAE*, 1242: "noticia que se desea o procura para un fin."

42. Designated by the Spanish king to be the *contador* of the islands of the Far East, Diego López de Zúñiga was to captain the small fleet that, in 1541, was to follow the coast of California to Asia. This was one of the two elements of the joint Mendoza-Alvarado enterprise agreed to in November 1540. Before the trip could be launched, the Mixtón War erupted, and López de Zúñiga was sent with a company of men-at-arms to control the indigenous community of Izatlán, west of Guadalajara. When the voyage finally took place, in 1542, Juan Rodríguez Cabrillo, rather than López de Zúñiga, served as captain. Kelsey, *Cabrillo*, 83, 84, 105. See Document 20 and Gerhard, *Historical Geography*, 156–58.

43. This is a reference to the voyage to the Lequios (Ryukyu) Islands that was an element in the joint Mendoza-Alvarado enterprise. Given their projected course to the west, hearing word of these ships either in the Gulf of California or along the California coast would have been unlikely except in the event of mutiny, storm, or shipwreck. See Document 25, fol. 459r.

44. The reference here is either to a contingent of Indian allies whom Alarcón was to take with him or to those few natives of the lower Colorado River whom he had taken south with him at the conclusion of his first voyage and who might now have been planning to return to their home territories. An indigenous contingent

was part of almost every expedition of conquest and reconnaissance during the sixteenth century. See the introductions to Documents 12 and 13.

45. "Suffer," *reciban. DRAE*, 1740: "padecer uno el daño que otro le hace."

46. "Companionship," conver*Sacion* = *compañía. DRAE*, 563.

47. In the Italian version of Alarcón's report of his 1540 voyage, these place names are rendered as Chicama (phonetically equivalent to Quicama in Spanish) and Coama. For tentative identification of these places, see Document 15, note 75. See also Document 15, fol. 367r, and Document 15, note 93.

48. This may be a mild rebuke for Alarcón's earlier frequent reference to himself as a "son of the sun." Document 15, passim.

49. "Deliver," *convenir = importar. DRAE*, 563.

50. "The aforesaid," *tal. DRAE*, 1934: "úsase a veces como pronombre demostrativo."

51. This is evidently the same Francisco Pilo who exercised Vázquez de Coronado's power of attorney to call and question *de parte* witnesses during Lorenzo de Tejada's investigation, which indicates a close connection with both captain general and viceroy. Flint, *Great Cruelties*, 344–46. Francisco Pilo was the son of *licenciado* Pilón, *alcalde mayor* of Sevilla in Spain. He was in Nueva España by at least 1539, when a royal *cédula* was issued authorizing that he be assigned a *corregimiento*. He was an *estante* in Culiacán when, in 1544, he was given Vázquez de Coronado's power of attorney in order to have testimony taken there on his behalf. By the late 1540s he was a resident of Guadalajara and *encomendero* of Tequila, northwest of that town. He held Tequila in *encomienda* until his death about 1550. AGI, Mexico, 1088, L.3, "Royal *cédula*"; Biblioteca del Escorial, Códice &-II-7, Doc. no. LXXIX, "Memoria de las personas, conquistadores y pobladores de la nueva galizia (no date)"; Gerhard, *North Frontier*, 147.

52. These documents would be of the type that were in the possession of Juan Jiménez at the time of his death in Tiguex in 1542. See Document 27, fols. 17r–18r.

53. "Arms and armor supplied to men-at-arms," *armas de municion. DRAE*, 1417: "dicese de lo que el Estado suministra por contrata a la tropa." H&R, 122, misinterpret this as "arms and munitions" and hence miss the point of the sentence.

54. The distinction here is one of class between those who have invested in the expedition and are thus due a share of its proceeds, rather than a salary, and those who are serving as employees. The latter might or might not also receive a share of proceeds as part of that salary.

55. "Legal arrangement," *cuenta. DRAE*, 616: "cuidado, incumbencia, cargo, obligación, deber."

56. This is the only mention in the Coronado expedition documents of a pivotal figure in the viceroyalty of Nueva España, Agustín Guerrero. A native of Alcaraz in the modern *provincia* of Albacete in the Spanish *comunidad* of Castilla–La Mancha, he had arrived in Nueva España in 1535 in the company of the new viceroy, his friend don Antonio de Mendoza. He served Mendoza as both his *mayordomo* and the captain of his personal guard, one member of which was Hernando de Alarcón. Together with don Luis de Castilla, Guerrero negotiated the 1540 settlement between the viceroy and Pedro de Alvarado (Document 20), which ended a potentially dangerous dispute between the two over the right to mount expeditions of conquest and reconnaissance. When, in 1541, Mendoza determined personally to lead a large armed force to Jalisco to quell the native uprising there known as the Mixtón War, it was Guerrero who went as his principal lieutenant. Aiton, *Mendoza*, 48, 123, 152; *Pasajeros*, 2: no. 1271.

57. For biographical information about Beatriz de Estrada, see Document 11, note 46.

58. H&R, 123, mistakenly turn these individuals into those who are sending the goods, instead of those who are taking care of them en route.

59. For biographical information, see the entry for Antonio de Almaguer in Appendix 1.

60. At the conclusion of an eighteenth-century transcription of the instructions now in the collection of the Gilcrease Institute is a note by the copyist that there is a statement in the viceroy's hand "en la vuelta del original [on the verso of the original manuscript]." That statement, according to the note, specifies that measurements (presumably of latitude) are to be taken along the whole coast, and a plot of the coast is to be drafted showing each degree of latitude. That instruction is not included in the signed copy of the directive to Alarcón (Biblioteca del Escorial, Códice &-II-7, Doc. no. LXVII), nor did we find it on the draft that bears other notes in the viceroy's hand (Biblioteca del Escorial, Códice &-II-7, Doc. no. LXVI). Nevertheless, Domingo del Castillo, one of Alarcón's pilots, did subsequently prepare just such a map of the Gulf of California and much of the Baja

California peninsula, which lays out the degrees of latitude. It is curious, however, that Castillo evidently used the latitude measurements made by Francisco de Ulloa, ignoring Alarcón's correct pronouncement that they were in error by two degrees. Antonio de Mendoza, "Instructions to Alarcón," Gilcrease Institute of American History and Art, HD 131-4. See fig. 15.1.

61. This should be "recaudo," as it is on fol. 391 of the draft version (Doc. no. LXVI).

62. (H)a de ser. This phrase is related to "¡como ha de ser!" *DRAE*, 1868.

Document 17. The Viceroy's Letter to the King, Jacona, April 17, 1540

1. Álvar Núñez Cabeza de Vaca, *Naufragios y comentarios con dos cartas*, 9th ed. (México, DF: Espasa-Calpe Mexicana, 1985), 92; PTBOviedo, 4:307.

2. Document 4, fol. 355r.

3. Document 6, fol. 3v.

4. Castañeda de Nájera gives the size of the party as 14. Document 28, fol. 24v.

5. Fol. 1r.

6. Tello, 407–11; Document 28, fols. 35v–39r, 70v–72r.

7. AGI, Patronato, 60, N.5, R.4, "Juan de Zaldívar."

8. Tello, 303.

9. AGI, Justicia, 336, N.2, "Suit concerning distribution of Indians to Diego de Colio, Guadalajara, 1565; el fiscal con Diego de Colio sobre repartimiento de yndios, 1565."

10. Fols. 1r–1v.

11. Document 28, fol. 24v; Flint, *Great Cruelties*, 253–54.

12. Flint, *Great Cruelties*, 254, and fols. 1v–2v.

13. Document 28, fol. 24v; Flint, *Great Cruelties*, 396.

14. Document 28, fols. 24v–25r.

15. Fol. 1v.

16. Ibid.

17. Flint, *Great Cruelties*, 254.

18. See Document 19, fol. 360r, and Document 28, fol. 27v.

19. Document 19.

20. Henri Ternaux-Compans, trans. and ed., "Mendoza to Carlos V, April 17, 1540," in *Voyages, relations et memoires*, 9:290–98.

21. *CDI*, 2:356–62.

22. Winship, 311–17.

23. H&R, 156–61.

24. A vertical line calls attention to the first section of the letter. It was probably added by staff of the Consejo de Indias.

25. For geographical information, see the entry for Compostela in Appendix 2.

26. This would have been February 28, 1540, exactly one week after the muster of the expedition had been conducted. During that week the bissextus, or leap year day, occurred, repeating the date of the twenty-fourth. According to Castañeda de Nájera, on the second day after the muster, February 24, the expedition departed from Compostela, accompanied by the viceroy for the first two days. Apparently, Mendoza left the expedition on the twenty-sixth and was back in Compostela by the evening of the twenty-seventh, the same day Juan de Cuevas drew up the muster roll of the expedition. See Document 28, fol. 22v; Document 12, fols. 1r and 10v; and *OED*, 220.

27. To establish settlement implies the founding of at least one Spanish-style community (a *villa, pueblo*, or *ciudad*) that would incorporate a church and a building for the governing *cabildo*. See, for instance, James Lockhart and Stuart B. Schwartz, *Early Latin America: A History of Colonial Spanish America and Brazil* (Cambridge: Cambridge University Press, 1983), 66–67.

28. For biographical information, see the entry for Lope de Samaniego in Appendix 1.

29. For geographical information, see the entries for Culiacán and Chiametla in Appendix 2.

30. Further detail is provided in Document 28, fol. 23v.

31. The reference to the "fortress" here is to sheds built in the Ciudad de México to house and protect boats used on Lake Texcoco. *Bergantines* were shallow-drafted, oared sailing boats used for military purposes and supplying the Ciudad de México since the time of the conquest. *DRAE*, 284; López de Gómara, *Cortés*, 411.

32. Lake Texcoco was the largest of the five interconnecting lakes that occupied the lowest elevations in the Basin of Mexico in the sixteenth century. It surrounded the indigenous island cities of Tenochtitlan and Tlatelolco and their successor, the Spanish Ciudad de México. According to fray Toribio de Benavente, Lake Texcoco began to dry up as early as 1524. It continued to shrink until a disastrous flood in 1555. Gibson, *Aztecs*, 303–5.

33. This whole section is badly garbled by Winship, 311.

34. For biographical information, see the entry for Melchior Díaz in Appendix 1. See also the introduction to this document. For biographical information about fray Marcos, see the introduction to Document 6.

35. Juan de Zaldívar, the son of Cristóbal de Oñate's sister, doña María Pérez de Oñate, and Ruy Díaz de Zaldívar, was born in Vitoria in the Basque *provincia* of Álava in Spain in 1514 or 1515. He arrived in Nueva España in 1529 and went to Nueva Galicia with Guzmán in 1530. By 1540 he was a *vecino* of Culiacán. In addition to participating in the Coronado expedition, he also later offered to lead an expedition to the Philippine Islands. He was a founding *vecino* of Zacatecas and was married to doña María de Mendoza, daughter of Capitán Luis Marín and doña María de Mendoza. He was a wealthy man, an *encomendero*, and an owner of mines, grain fields, farms, slaves, *estancias*, and and other agricultural land. He died sometime before 1580. Donald E. Chipman, "The Oñate-Moctezuma-Zaldívar Families of Northern New Spain," *New Mexico Historical Review* 52, no. 4 (1977):297–310; Tello, 268; AGI, Justicia, 336, N.2, "Diego de Colio"; AGI, Justicia, 339, N.1, R.1, "Residencia"; Boyd-Bowman, 2: no. 13623; AGI, Patronato, 76, N.1, R.5, "Méritos y servicios by Francisco de Zaldívar, March 29, 1580"; AGI, Patronato, 60, N.5, R.4 , "Juan de Zaldívar."

36. For geographical information, see the entry for Río de Petatlán in Appendix 2.

37. These Indians were natives of lands farther south, perhaps even central Mexico, who were unprepared for such cold weather. Their presence is further evidence that every known component of the Coronado expedition was accompanied by American natives.

38. This mark, resembling a cursive *p*, is one of the rare instances of scribal punctuation in any of the Coronado expedition documents. It occurs five more times in this document.

39. This report has not been located.

40. For geographical information, see the entry for Cíbola in Appendix 2.

41. A *pie* is a length equal to approximately 11 inches, based upon the length of a human foot.

42. The Spanish for this sentence is "por labrar las mas casas se mandan por las açoteas con sus esCaleras a las calles." Ignoring "por labrar," H&R, 158, incorrectly have, "Most of the houses are entered from the terraces, with ladders to the streets." Winship, 312, does nearly the same.

43. It is interesting that Díaz felt he had to explain that by "first" he meant "ground floor." That is contrary to modern Spanish usage, in which the first floor is the one above the ground floor.

44. "They make use of," *servirse de. DRAE*, 1872: "valerse de una cosa para uso propio de ella."

45. For a discussion of cannibalism as an "unnatural" practice justifying war, see Document 15, note 53.

46. "Large Castilian bird dogs," *grandes podencos de caStilla. Podenco*, Covarrubias, 827, and *DRAE*, 1582: "de cuerpo algo menor, pero mas robusto que el de lebrel."

47. "Colored wigs/falls," *cabelleras de colores. Cabellera*, Covarrubias, 222: "el cabello postizo por toda la cabeza." Evidently such samples as this, and others sent later to the viceroy by Vázquez de Coronado, have disappeared over the years. What hairpieces are described here is unclear. They could have been wigs such as are still worn by some of the koko/kachina impersonators at Zuni, such as the Towa Chakwaina. Or perhaps this is a reference to enemy scalps. See Barton Wright, *Kachinas of the Zuni* (Flagstaff, AZ: Northland Press, 1985), 89; Green, *Zuñi*, 153–56.

48. This report of using hair in clothing manufacture seems very similar to the one fray Marcos was given regarding Tusayán. See Document 6, fol. 4v.

49. "Be good-tempered," *estar de buen gesto. DRAE*, 1038. H&R, 158, and Winship, 313, have "of good appearance."

50. A chemise was a long, unfitted female garment. See Anderson, *Hispanic Costume*, 183–91, for descriptions of sixteenth-century European versions.

51. This is apparently the squash-blossom hairdo that is still used on some ceremonial occasions among the Hopi and which appears on a number of Zuni and Hopi kachinas. The description is ambiguous enough, though, that it could also refer to braids. See Document 23, note 35.

52. For biographical information, see the entries for Álvar Núñez Cabeza de Vaca and Andrés Dorantes in Appendix 1.

53. Again, this seems similar to the Zuni practice continued by some men to this day, especially on ceremonial occasions. *Toca*, Covarrubias, 923: "en algunas partes de España no traen los hombres caperuzas ni sombreros, y usan de unas tocas revueltas en la cabeza."

54. See Anderson, *Hispanic Costume*, 78–80, for descriptions and illustrations showing sixteenth-century Spanish buskins (soft boots, *borceguíes*).

55. These were very likely quartz crystals (*cristal de roca*). *DRAE*, 597.

56. "The cloth," "la rropa." *DRAE*, 1811: "todo género de tela que . . . sirve para el uso o adorno de las personas."

57. This is Zuni Salt Lake. Stevenson, "Zuñi Indians," 354–61, provides a lengthy description of a salt gathering trip to the lake in the late 1800s or early 1900s. The lake lies 42 miles south-southeast of modern Zuni.

58. "Their holes, where they place their fingers, yield many tunes," "sus puntos do ponen sus dedos hazen muchos sones." H&R, 159, divide the sentences differently and render this as "some flutes which have holes for the fingers. They make many tunes. . . ."

59. For biographical information, see the entry for Esteban in Appendix 1.

60. Totonteac, or the Hohokam area of the Salt River Valley, is confused here with Tusayán, the Hopi country, which is what Díaz seems to be referring to. For geographical information, see the entry for Totonteac in Appendix 2.

61. Mathilda Coxe Stevenson mentioned the cultivation of amaranth and "a variety of herbs" at Zuni in the late eighteenth and early nineteenth centuries. Perhaps it is some of these that are referred to here. Stevenson, "Zuñi Indians," 353.

62. These animals may have been mountain goats. See Document 19, note 79.

63. A squiggly vertical line in the left margin calls attention to the statement on the size of the seven *lugares*. It was probably added by staff of the Consejo de Indias.

64. Naturally, the length of a crossbow shot may vary. The maximum range of a group of fifteenth-century military crossbows test-fired in the late nineteenth century was 390 yards, though their deadly range was less than 20 percent of that. This lower figure of 65 to 70 yards might well be intended here. Three such lengths (about 200 yards) is at least on the same order of magnitude as the long axis of Hawikku (about 350 feet, or 120 yards). Ralph Payne-Gallwey, *The Crossbow, Mediaeval and Modern, Military and Sporting: Its Construction, History, and Management*, 2nd edition (London: Holland Press, 1995), 20; Smith, Woodbury, and Woodbury, *Excavation of Hawikuh*, fig. 37.

65. There is no known protohistoric, non-Zuni/Cíbolan pueblo only a day's journey from Hawikku. It is possible that this reference is to Acoma, about two days distant, with which the Zunis' had occasional conflicts over the centuries. See map 3.

66. Here Melchior Díaz offers his explanation of why the Spaniards heard about the Pueblo people from such a great distance. He could just as well have added "and not because they have gold."

67. This is the place from where Díaz was writing, evidently somewhere in the vicinity of Chichilticale. See Document 28, fol. 24v.

68. H&R, 160, mistakenly reverse the roles of the people of Chichilticale and those of Cíbola. For geographical information about Chichilticale, see the entry in Appendix 2.

69. This is the Senora/Señora Valley. The distance from Culiacán to the valley (see map 1) matches that reported in other contemporary documents, including the "Relación del Suceso." Document 29, fol. 1r.

70. Winship, 317, misinterprets this as "houses with lofts."

71. In other words, *encomiendas* among these people would not be profitable because they produced no valuable commodities.

72. This seems to be a sincere statement of regret on Mendoza's part over abuse of the natives of the Americas.

73. "May you supply ecclesiastics, considering both that [fact] and what [must be done] from now on," "provea de Religiosos asy para aquello como para lo de aqui." H&R, 161, stretch the meaning of *aquello* and *lo* to render this as "may you provide friars both for those regions and for these." Winship, 317, reads the sentence in a third way, as "nor priests provided, either for that country or this."

74. An arc in the left margin was apparently incorporated by the original *escribano* to draw attention to this passage concerning ecclesiastics.

75. Mendoza had been in Colima when Zaldívar reached him with the report from Díaz. Flint, *Great Cruelties*, 254. For geographical information, see the entry for Colima in Appendix 2.

76. Jacona is in the modern Mexican state of Michoacán, west of Morelia and southeast of Lake Chapala.

77. This date is in the Julian calendar.

78. This passage is written in the viceroy's own hand. Like Vázquez de Coronado in Documents 1 and 3, Mendoza does not append a rubric to his signature here.

79. Two other documents evidently accompanied this letter in transmission to the king. Doctor Bernal is doctor Juan Bernal Díaz de Luco, a *consejero* (counselor) in the Consejo de Indias from January 1531 until May 1545. He had been the *provisor* (diocesan judge) of the Archbishopric of Toledo and served as bishop of Calahorra. Schäfer, *Consejo Real*, 1:355. For information about the Consejo de las Indias, see the entry in Appendix 1.

80. Evidently *había* was intended.

81. Decir = *opinar*. *DRAE*, 666.

82. Ya que. *CDI*, 2:358, has "y á que."

83. Maderar = *enmaderar*. *DRAE*, 1288.

84. Hartas = *hartura*.

85. *Aunque* makes no sense here.

86. Conversar = *comunicar*. *DRAE*, 563.

Document 18. Hernán Cortés's Brief to Carlos V concerning the Injuries Done to Him by the Viceroy of Nueva España, June 25, 1540

1. López de Gómara, *Cortés*, 7, 19, 54.

2. Martínez, *Documentos Cortesianos*, 3:49–54.

3. Ibid., 3:78.

4. López de Gómara, *Cortés*, 397–404.

5. Fol. 4v.

6. See *CDI*, 15:376–79. See also the introduction to Document 20.

7. López de Gómara, *Cortés*, 408.

8. Martínez, *Documentos Cortesianos*, 4:210–15. Other modern editions in Spanish include Martín Fernández de Navarrete, Miguel Salvá, and Pedro Sáinz de Baranda, *Colección de documentos inéditos para la historia de España*, 112 vols. (Madrid: n.p., 1842–95), 4:209–17; Hernán Cortés, *Escritos sueltos de Hernán Cortés* (México, DF: Biblioteca Histórica de La Iberia, 1871), no. 12; and Hernán Cortés, *Cartas y documentos* (México, DF: Editorial Porrúa, 1963), 405–11.

9. This entry is in the hand of an unidentified official of the Consejo de Indias. It represents part of the standard procedure for logging and filing documents presented before the *consejo*.

10. The reference here is to the *cédula* referred to in the introduction to this document. See also Martínez, *Documentos Cortesianos*, 3:49–54. For general information, see the entry under Consejo de las Indias and Antonio de Mendoza in Appendix 1.

11. For biographical information on fray Marcos de Niza, see the introduction to Document 6.

12. The voyage referred to began in 1535. On several occasions it nearly ended in disaster from mishaps at sea. López de Gómara, *Cortés*, 399–402.

13. The bulk of the *cédula* of 1529 conceding to Cortés the right to mount reconnaissance missions into the Mar del Sur is taken up with generic royal instructions for such enterprises regarding the benevolent treatment of native peoples. Martínez, *Documentos Cortesianos*, 3:79–84.

14. Evidently not a close relative of Viceroy Antonio de Mendoza's, Diego Hurtado de Mendoza arrived in Nueva España in about 1528. He became a *vecino* of Guadalajara and died around 1570. His parents were Rodrigo Hurtado and Inés de Tapia. Himmerich y Valencia, *Encomenderos*, 176.

15. For geographical information, see the entry for Mar del Sur in Appendix 2.

16. In April 1535 Cortés established a colony at Bahía de la Santa Cruz (now Bahía Pichilingue) in modern Baja California Sur, which was abandoned by late 1536 or early 1537. Gerhard, *North Frontier*, 289.

17. At least five of these people subsequently died from hunger. Others died from overeating when Cortés finally returned with provisions. López de Gómara, *Cortés*, 401.

18. The reference here is to fray Marcos's 1539 report about Cíbola and the subsequent stir it caused. See Document 6.

19. This is the first known public assertion that Marcos had a habit of stretching

the truth. After the Coronado expedition reached Cíbola in July 1540, many others came to share that opinion, though with regard to points other than those that are Cortés's concern here. The documentary evidence is too skimpy to allow confident conclusions to be drawn about Cortés's specific charges.

20. Francisco de Ulloa arrived in Nueva España in 1528 and was with Cortés in Mexico in 1535. He was a *vecino* of Mérida in the modern *provincia* of Badajoz in Extremadura and a *criado* of Cortés's. He was evidently granted the *encomienda* of Guachinango in Nueva Galicia by Nuño de Guzmán. The *marqués* continued to make use of Ulloa after the conquest, leaving him in charge at Santa Cruz in Baja California in 1536. A year earlier Ulloa had been one of the witnesses to the act of possession executed there by Cortés. He went to Perú and lived there illicitly with Ana Palla, a native of Cuzco. He died in 1553 or sometime before. Constanza Sarmiento, probably Ulloa's legal wife, served as *encomendera* of Guachinango from 1539 until 1544. Boyd-Bowman, 2: no. 1644; Martínez, *Documentos Cortesianos*, 4:147, 153 n. 1, 246; Tello, 252; Gerhard, *North Frontier*, 87. During the 1539 voyage that Ulloa commanded, he followed the Pacific coast north of Culiacán in three ships. He reconnoitered the Gulf of California all the way to the bay at its head and followed the coast of Baja California, rounding the peninsula and sailing north to the latitude of the bay on the gulf side. López de Gómara, *Cortés*, 401–3.

21. For geographical information about Santiago de Buena Esperanza, see Document 15, note 22. For geographical information about Colima, see the entry in Appendix 2.

22. Maldonado later served as a captain during the Coronado expedition. For biographical information, see the entry for Rodrigo Maldonado in Appendix 1.

23. The application of torture was a common and legally sanctioned method of interrogation at that time, even though information obtained solely by means of torture was not legally valid. See Partida 3, Título 13, Law 5, in *Siete Partidas*, 3:650.

24. The port of Guatulco is on the Pacific coast of the modern state of Oaxaca in Mexico on the margins of the Golfo de Tehuantepec. The modern spelling of the associated nearby inland town is Huatulco. The bay was used as a terminal for Spanish shipping from Central America as early as the late 1530s. Gerhard, *Historical Geography*, 123–26.

25. "Prohibiting," *defendio*. DRAE, 671: "vedar, prohibir."

26. Guamelula is a town in southern Oaxaca, northeast of the port of Guatulco (see note 24, this document), between that place and Tehuantepec. Gerhard, *Historical Geography*, 123–26. Tecoantepeque = Tehuantepec. As it was in the mid-sixteenth century, Tehuantepec, in southeastern Oaxaca, is still a major population center of the region. Cortés reserved the extensive *encomienda* of Tehuantepec for himself in 1524. The 1529 *cédula* delineating the territory of the *marquesado* (holdings belonging to a *marqués*) del Valle de Oaxaca includes specific reference to Tehuantepec. Beginning in the late 1520s, the nearby shipyard, located since about 1535 at the mouth of the Río Tehuantepec, was the focus of Cortés's Pacific maritime activity. Gerhard, *Historical Geography*, 264–67; Martínez, *Documentos Cortesianos*, 3:50.

27. "Were in charge of," *entendian en*. Entender en, be in charge of, DRAE, 847: "tener una autoridad, facultad o jurisdicción."

28. "Are more intelligent and clever," *de mas entendimiento e saber*. DRAE, 848: "muy inteligente"; DRAE, 1822: "tener habilidad para una cosa."

29. Indeed, a serious native uprising broke out in late 1540 in the wake of departure of the Coronado expedition, which escalated into what has come to be called the Mixtón War. It was not quelled until 1542. For a thorough account of the Mixtón War, see Tello, 343–407, 442–73.

30. Cortés evidently refers here to the party led northward late in 1539 by Melchior Díaz and Juan de Zaldívar in an attempt to verify fray Marcos's reports. Castañeda de Nájera agrees that they took 12 horsemen with them. All, however, seem to have survived, so Cortés's informant was incorrect. See Document 28, fol. 24v.

31. "Request," *digo*. DRAE, 666: "pedir, rogar."

32. Instead, the case before the Consejo de Indias was concluded, as the *consejo*'s *fiscal* had recommended, in favor of the viceroy, and Cortés's claim was specifically invalidated. See CDI, 15:376–79.

33. "Requested again," *repetido*. DRAE, 1773: "pedir muchas vezes."

34. "Contract in which pledge money has been paid," *contrato oneroso*. DRAE, 561: "que implica alguna contrapestación."

35. "May be preserved," *vel*. From *velar*, DRAE, 2068: "cuidar solicitamente de una cosa."

36. "Informal hearing," *pleito ordinario*. DRAE, 1624: *pleito* "que se dilata o se hace común y muy frecuente, cediendo del rigor con que comenzó."

37. "Judicial examination," *tela de juicio*. DRAE, 1952: "examen, disputa o controversia para dilucidar algo."

38. "Exercise," *administrar*. DRAE, 44: "ejercer la autoridad o el mando sobre un territorio."

39. Martínez, *Documentos Cortesianos*, 4:210, incorrectly has this address in the singular.

40. This note, probably by a functionary at the Consejo de Indias, is omitted by Martínez, *Documentos Cortesianos*, 4:210.

41. Porque. Martínez, *Documentos Cortesianos*, 4:211, mistakenly has "pero."

42. Limitado. Martínez, *Documentos Cortesianos*, 4:211, mistakenly has "otorgado."

43. (^Tre)^dozientos. The *escribano* originally wrote "trezientos" but wrote over that, amending it to "dozientos." Martínez, *Documentos Cortesianos*, 4:211, mistakenly retains "trescientos," although the *escribano*'s intent is confirmed by his entering "dozientos" without correction later on fol. 5v.

44. Llego alli. Martínez, *Documentos Cortesianos*, 4:211, mistakenly has "aqui."

45. Yo ya. Martínez, *Documentos Cortesianos*, 4:211, omits "ya."

46. "A vista" is inserted by the *escribano*.

47. Reseferiendo = *refiriendose*. Martínez, *Documentos Cortesianos*, 4:212, omits "se."

48. Escrive (^va de) la nueva, "escriueva de la nueva." The *escribano* was evidently copying from an earlier version and lost his place, which was not an unusual scribal error, in this case aggravated by the identity of "u" and "v" in sixteenth-century scripts.

49. (^?). The *escribano* struck something out, which is now illegible.

50. *Ha* s(e)ido proveydo. Martínez, *Documentos Cortesianos*, 4:213, mistakenly has "he seido proveido."

51. Dozientos. Because of the decision he had made earlier on fol. 4r, Martínez, *Documentos Cortesianos*, 4:214, mistakenly "corrects" this to "trescientos," although the original document is unequivocal at this point.

52. AUtos. Martínez, *Documentos Cortesianos*, 4:214, mistakenly has "actos."

53. (^Y) sin dar. This is another indication that the *escribano* was copying from an earlier version. The same phrase but with the "y" appears in the very next line, which he picked up here in copying and then corrected himself.

54. *Estar* mandado. We have inserted "estar" because the construction demands an auxiliary verb, although none was recorded by the *escribano*.

Document 19. Vázquez de Coronado's Letter to the Viceroy, August 3, 1540

1. For biographical information about Giovanni Battista Ramusio, see the introduction to Document 2.

2. These four are Documents 2, 4, 15, and 19.

3. Missing from the excerpt are, at least, the address, salutation, and name of the author of the letter, all of which would ordinarily have appeared at the beginning. In addition, the text that survives opens much more abruptly than do most letters of the period, suggesting that Ramusio has omitted some introductory material. That may have included text which the Venetian considered not germane to the strongly linear, narrative report that makes up the portion he chose to publish. So our gratitude to Ramusio is tempered slightly by the suspicion that information not of interest and therefore suppressed by him might well be of interest to us today. Although lamentation over the incompleteness of the excerpt is not particularly productive, awareness of that incompleteness is important.

4. Fol. 360r. In six other places the captain general repeats essentially the same message: a second time on fol. 360r, once each on fols. 359v and 361r, and three times on 362r.

5. Fol. 361r.

6. Fol. 362v.

7. Document 29, fol. 1r.

8. Document 28, fol. 24v.

9. Flint, *Great Cruelties*, 396.

10. Fol. 359v.

11. Document 6, fol. 2v.

12. Fol. 359v.

13. Fol. 363r.

14. Fol. 361v.

15. Fol. 361v.

16. Fol. 362v.

17. Document 22, fols. 1r–1v.

18. See especially the introduction to Document 15.

19. Hakluyt, *Principal Navigations*, 9:145–63.

20. Winship, 318–35; H&R, 162–78. The Hammond and Rey version relies heavily on Winship's text, often following him word for word, even in cases when he has made errors. Theirs cannot be regarded as an independent translation. H&R, 162 n. 1, state that Henri Ternaux-Compans published a French translation of the August 1540 letter in volume 9 of his *Voyages, relations et memoires sur la dècouverte de la Amérique*. That is incorrect. Hammond and Rey confuse this letter with Vázquez de Coronado's October 1541 letter to Carlos V, Document 26 in this volume.

21. Ramusio, *Navigazioni e viaggi*, 6:611–25.

22. All dates included in this letter are in the Julian calendar. As H&R, 162 n. 3, also point out, Winship, 318, erroneously reads this as "to Culiacán." For geographical information about Culiacán, Los Corazones, and Señora, see the entries under those headings in Appendix 2.

23. This is the same period for which the advance guard was provisioned, according to the anonymous author of the "Traslado de las Nuevas." Meanwhile, the anonymous author of the "Relación Postrera de Cíbola" writes that the advance guard reached Cíbola "on the seventy-third [day]." Document 22, fol. 1r; Document 29, fol. 1r. For geographical information about Cíbola, see Appendix 2.

24. Very close to the modern U.S. pound, the *libra* was one-twenty-fifth of an *arroba*. Thomas G. Barnes, Thomas H. Naylor, and Charles W. Polzer, *Northern New Spain: A Research Guide* (Tucson: University of Arizona Press, 1981), 73.

25. With no knowledge that a painter, one Cristóbal de Quesada, had been sent on the expedition by the viceroy specifically "to paint the things of the land," both Winship, 319, and H&R, 163, attempted to make what sense they could of this statement. They both ambiguously turned the painting into "a drawing of this route." On the basis of these translations, Herbert Bolton imagined this painting as a "drawing of [the] route to Cíbola," which suggests a map of the entire route. The syntax of the Italian text, however, strongly points to a painting of the rugged mountains and rivers. AGI, México, 1064, L.1\1, "Informes de los conquistadores," fol. 270r; Bolton, 474.

26. Presumably the reference here is to "the land four or five days' journey inland," about which fray Marcos had a great deal to say regarding populousness and wealth. According to Castañeda de Nájera, Vázquez de Coronado had also previously sent Díaz ahead from Culiacán six months before. On that scouting trip he, Juan de Zaldívar, and a company of 12 had reached Chichilticale. On their return they rendezvoused with the full-fledged expedition at Chiametla and revealed discouraging news about Cíbola. From where Díaz's second scouting trip, which is referred to here, departed is not explicitly stated, though it must have been south of the Laquimí/Yaquimí River. Perhaps the best guess is that it was 30 leagues south of the wide, fertile valley reported by fray Marcos as four or five days inland. In the equivalent of eight days of normal travel (four days at double speed) Díaz could probably have gone no farther than 65 leagues in all, or about 170 miles. This would have gotten him somewhere on an arc ranging from modern southern Sonora to southern Chihuahua in the Sierra Madre Occidental. Document 6, fol. 2v; Document 28, fol. 24v. For biographical information about fray Marcos, see the introduction to Document 6. For biographical information about Melchior Díaz, see Appendix 1.

27. If the location of these settlements was in southern Sonora or southeastern Chihuahua, as suggested in note 26, then these probably were Tarahumara *rancherías*. Susan M. Deeds, *Defiance and Deference in Mexico's Colonial North: Indians under Spanish Rule in Nueva Vizcaya* (Austin: University of Texas Press, 2003), 42, 49–50.

28. H&R, 163, following Winship, 319, incorrectly and unfortunately render the first-person preterit indicative *diedi* as third person and grossly alter the meaning of this clause as "the whole company felt displeased at this."

29. This side trip would have been into the *abra*, or wide, level valley, that Marcos reported. Document 6, fol. 2v.

30. Italian *ch* = Spanish *qu*. Charles Di Peso identified the Río Lachimí or Río Yaquimí as the modern Río Mayo in extreme southern Sonora. This matches the area where it would have been necessary to enter and traverse a long stretch of mountainous terrain before arriving in the Río Sonora Valley. Hammond and Rey, as well as Bolton, assert that this was the modern Yaqui River, somewhat farther north in Sonora (maps 1 and 2). Di Peso, Rinaldo, and Fenner, *Casas Grandes*, 4:90,

103; H&R, 164 n. 4, 296 n. 5; Bolton, 101. Compare the distance from the Río Petatlán to the Río Yaquimí reported by Jaramillo. Document 30, fol. 1r.

31. Winship, 319, and H&R, 164, who uncritically followed him, all misinterpreted *balza* as "toil" rather than "cliff."

32. Following Winship, 319, exactly, H&R, 164, mistranslate this as "although they did not travel more than two leagues daily."

33. Continuing to follow Winship, 319, H&R, 164, incorrectly transfer the clause "and rested there for several days" to this sentence from the previous one.

34. These people were surely slaves. The enslavement of Muslims from North Africa and from residual enclaves in Spain, such as the refugee settlements of the Alpujarras, was not unusual at this time. See, for example, Miguel F. Gómez Vozmediano, *Mudéjares y moriscos en el campo de Calatrava* (Ciudad Real: Área de Cultura, Diputación Provincial, 2000), 63–66.

35. The Mar del Oeste is the Pacific Ocean, more commonly known at this time as the Mar del Sur. Five days' travel would represent 30 to 35 leagues, or between 75 and 87 miles. The most likely candidate for Los Corazones—the Ures, Sonora, area (map 2)—is nearly 110 miles from the coast. Charles Di Peso's hypothesized location for Corazones, near modern Rosario, Sonora, on the other hand, is about 74 miles from the coast. See the entry for Mar del Sur in Appendix 2 and Di Peso, Rinaldo, and Fenner, *Casas Grandes*, 4:90.

36. There is no record of any Portuguese fleet or single ship entering the Gulf of California at this time. Presumably this was one of Hernando de Alarcón's northbound ships. See Document 15.

37. For geographical information, see the entry about Chichilticale in Appendix 2.

38. The name of the river probably indicates the presence of wild flax. There are some six native species of *Linum* in Arizona, most growing at elevations of 2,000 to 9,000 feet. One or more of these species also grows in Sonora. Thirty leagues, or nearly 70 miles, from the Ures area could place this river (or stretch of the same river) in the vicinity of modern Arispe, Sonora, like Ures on the Río Sonora (map 2). This may mean that the vanguard of the expedition purposely avoided traveling within the heavily populated and cultivated Sonora Valley. In contrast, Juan Jaramillo, who was with Vázquez de Coronado in the advance guard, specifically mentions the settlement of Señora, presumably between Corazones and the Río del Lino. Anne Orth Epple, *A Field Guide to the Plants of Arizona* (Guilford, CT: Globe Pequot Press, 1995), 130. Compare Document 30, fol. 1v.

39. This again seems to confirm the Ures area as the site of Corazones (map 2). Due west of Ures on the coast is Cabo Tepopa, the only significant westward-trending peninsula on the eastern Gulf of California coast between Guaymas and the head of the gulf. The length of the cape, however, is only about 16 miles, or roughly 6 leagues, rather than the 10 or 12 reported here. It must be remembered that members of the expedition did not actually see this westward turn. Instead, the distance figure cited here represents an interpretation of information provided by native informants.

40. There is no mention of such a port in fray Marcos's formal report. This is one of many indications that the friar provided much additional informal and oral information to the viceroy, Vázquez de Coronado, and probably others. See Document 6.

41. Following immediately the captain general's statement about Marcos's questionable information, this sentence implies that any mishap the fleet might have encountered would have been the result of the friar's misguidance.

42. Reference to a delay implies that Vázquez de Coronado's own plans were being frustrated because of the failure to rendezvous with Alarcón's fleet. This may be explained in the very next sentence—namely, that Vázquez de Coronado had expected resupply from the fleet and now was required to go ahead without proper rest because that resupply did not occur.

43. This is the same ten-day *despoblado* (unsettled area) between Chichilticale and Cíbola reported by other expeditionaries. The feast day referred to here is June 24, the commemoration of the birth of San Juan Bautista. The eve of the feast would have been 64 days after the advance guard's departure from Culiacán. See Document 6, fol. 5v, and Document 28, fol. 30r. Chaves, *Espejo de navegantes*, 86.

44. Read literally, this phrase can be taken only as sarcasm, because this was no relief at all, but rather reinforced the previous difficulties. We assume that the Italian translator omitted a negative particle from the original document. Winship, 323, and H&R, 166, following him word for word, render the phrase literally "for a change from our past labors."

45. This is Francisco de Espinosa, who mustered into the expedition as an arquebusier serving under Captain Melgosa. The same incident was recounted more

than 20 years later by Juan Jaramillo. Document 12, fol. 8r; Document 30, fol. 2r; Document 33, fol. 4v.

46. For biographical information, see the entry on García López de Cárdenas in Appendix 1.

47. Also called *perruna* or *zarza de perro* in the sixteenth century, this was the white-flowered dog rose, an Old World rose, *Rosa canina*. Technically, the name applied to the fruit or "hip" of this rose. Covarrubias, 489–90.

48. These trees were most likely the Arizona walnut, *Juglans major*, which is found "along streams and in canyons in upper desert," generally at elevations between 3,500 and 7,000 feet, and the Texas or Mexican mulberry, *Morus microphylla*, the only native mulberry species in Arizona (in which state, or extreme western New Mexico, the advance guard likely was at this point), usually found at elevations between 2,000 and 6,000 feet. Epple, *Plants of Arizona*, 41, 49.

49. For biographical information about Fernando/Hernando Alvarado, see the introduction to Document 24.

50. This evidently refers to the same sort of conch trumpet that is mentioned by Castañeda de Nájera. Document 28, fol. 114r.

51. A *mina* was a variable measure of dry volume, usually between 110 and 120 liters, or slightly more than 3 bushels. Ramusio, *Navigazioni e viaggi*, 6:616 n. 7.

52. Vázquez de Coronado later recounted a very similar version of the approach to and capture of Hawikku. Flint, *Great Cruelties*, 280–81. For biographical information, see the entries for fray Luis de Úbeda and Hernando Martín Bermejo in Appendix 1. Fray Daniel, an Italian lay brother and resident of the church's province of Santiago, may have arrived in Nueva España as early as 1525. He was fluent in Nahuatl; he was a famous embroiderer; and his penitential behavior was renowned among his confreres. Before leaving for Tierra Nueva, fray Daniel was in residence at Tuxpán. He returned to Nueva España after the capture of Cíbola. He died about 1567 at Guadalajara. Chávez, *Coronado's Friars*, 37–39, 78–81; Tello, 406. As specified in the *requerimiento* itself, its having been read three times was to be attested in writing by an *escribano* and other witnesses. Bermejo, the captain general's secretary, fulfilled the capacity of *escribano*, or notary, in this case. Charles Gibson, ed., *The Spanish Tradition in America* (Columbia: University of South Carolina, 1968), 60. See also Appendix 4.

53. The subtitle of this book, *They Were Not Familiar with His Majesty, nor Did They Wish to Be His Subjects*, is a paraphrase of the reaction of people at Tiguex to a reading of the *requerimiento* several months after the one being recounted here. The paraphrase was given in an *interrogatorio* prepared by Vázquez de Coronado and his attorney in 1544. See Flint, *Great Cruelties*, 353.

54. The person referred to here is probably don Diego de los Cobos, the Marqués de Camarasa, who was the king's *gran canciller*, or high chancellor, for the Indies from 1532 to 1575. It is not, as H&R, 168 n. 7, suggest, a copyist's error. Schäfer, *Consejo Real*, 1:353.

55. Another account of the captain general's injuries is told from a different perspective in Document 22, fol. 1v. The anonymous author of that document states unequivocally that Vázquez de Coronado "got out on his own [two] feet." Also compare the account of Pedro de Castañeda de Nájera, who was not an eyewitness to these events, in Document 28, fol. 32r, and that included in Document 29, fol. 1v.

56. The plural in the Italian may be incorrect here. According to the muster roll, Melgosa was the sole captain of footmen. However, on this occasion all four of these captains may have been assigned companies of footmen. See Document 12, fol. 7v. For biographical information about don Pedro de Tovar, (Gómez) Suárez, and Pablo de Melgosa, see Document 28, notes 102, 106, and 107.

57. Of the three men named Torres known to have been on the Coronado expedition, only Francisco was a *vecino* of Pánuco, although *estante* was likely the word in the Spanish original that was translated as *abitore*. He was a native of Trujillo in the modern *provincia* of Cáceres in Extremadura, Spain. He came to Nueva España in 1529 and later served as *corregidor* in Guasteca. AGI, México, 1064, L.1\1, "Informes de los conquistadores," fol. 155v.

58. It must be remembered that there was little metal armor, gilded or not, on the expedition, so anyone in such armor would have stood out. See the introduction to Document 12.

59. The only man with the surname Villegas known to have been on the expedition was Juan de Villegas, brother of one of the *regidores* of the Ciudad de México. Flint, *Great Cruelties*, 112; Document 12, fol. 5r. See also Document 28, note 246. For biographical information about don Alonso Manrique de Lara, see Document 28, note 106.

60. The Italian translator has chosen *turchino*, turquoise blue (the color), rather than *turchese*, turquoise (the stone), here. Nevertheless, from a parallel usage on fol. 361v it is clear that the stone is intended.

61. This is a description of the subterranean ceremonial and male residence chambers known today as kivas, which are still in use among the Pueblos. Compare a similar description in Document 28, fols. 105v–106r.

62. For identification of these seven communities, see the entry for Cíbola in Appendix 2.

63. Compare the corresponding distances cited in three contemporaneous documents: four leagues in Document 22, fol. 1v; five leagues in Document 23, fol. 124v; and six leagues in Document 30, fol. 2r.

64. Document 22, fol. 1r, amplifies the statement "there is some similarity about it" by specifying the similarity: "it looks like the Albaicín." Granada's relationship with the viceroy stems from the fact that since 1492 the Mendoza family had been closely associated with the formerly Moorish capital in Spain. The viceroy's brother Luis Hurtado de Mendoza had been captain general of Granada since 1512. Aiton, *Mendoza*, 9.

65. The author of the "Relación Postrera de Cíbola" agrees exactly. Document 23, fol. 123v. The word "wall" in both Spanish and Italian, *muro*, refers here not to a free-standing wall, or *tapia*, but rather to *muralla*, the blank, defensive, exterior face of a medieval Spanish town, often incorporating the walls of houses or other buildings.

66. Like the painting mentioned earlier, these were presumably prepared by Cristóbal de Quesada. See note 25, this document.

67. The size of the native population was a key factor in determining the viability of a Spanish settlement, because there would have to be enough people to provide *encomiendas* to all the expeditionaries who merited them. Much less interesting to conquistadores of the day would have been the body size of natives, as H&R, 171, render this.

68. Beginning with Hakluyt, *Principal Navigations*, 9:155, English translators have ignored the phrase "because it would seem to me," so that the result is, "I do not think that they have the judgment and intelligence needed to be able to build these houses." H&R, 171; see also Winship, 326. This is another of the many cases in which earlier translations have clearly influenced later ones.

69. Lack of clothing was taken as a sign of inferior intelligence and absence of civilization.

70. Exactly how we are to imagine this hair arrangement is unclear. That is because there seems not to have been a single style among native men of the Valley of Mexico. The *Codex Mendoza*, for instance, depicts three distinct styles. See Berdan and Anawalt, *Essential Codex Mendoza*, 133–41.

71. As they do consistently elsewhere, H&R, 171, interpret this assessment as referring to physical appearance. We see it, on the other hand, as a positive assessment of attitude and behavior that portrays the native people as suitable for missionizing and incorporating into Spanish society. Our view is buttressed by the archaic equivalence of *crear* and *criar*, meaning "to raise or bring up." DRAE, 593.

72. Because the protohistoric Pueblos did not make or use paper, the circumstance of this discovery suggests that the gemstone flakes referred to here originated with some member of the expedition or perhaps even a year earlier with Esteban. Vázquez de Coronado reports a similar occurrence later when the expedition is on the Great Plains. Regarding that, he writes, "I have not seen any other metal in these places except that [piece], some small copper bells which I sent to him, and a very small [piece] of metal that appears [to be] gold. I have not found out where the latter comes from, although I think that the Indians who gave it to me obtained it from those whom I brought here as servants." Document 26, fol. 2r.

73. Indeed, the modern summer weather regime in New Mexico is very similar to that of the Valley of Mexico, featuring high temperatures and the prevalence of thunderstorms, just as Vázquez de Coronado points out here.

74. Vázquez de Coronado's conclusions about the winter weather were borne out later by the expedition's experience in Tiguex, where the winter of 1540–41 was especially snowy and cold. See Document 28, fols. 56v–57r and 63v.

75. Reference here is to Zuni Salt Lake. See Document 17, note 57.

76. Reference here is to the increasing width of the North American continent as one moves north. H&R, 172, completely miss the point with, "Your Lordship may thus see how extensive this country is." Winship, 327, is much closer. For geographical information about the Mar del Norte, see Appendix 2.

77. The reference here is to jaguars and mountain lions. Jaguars have been present in Sonora throughout historic times and still make solitary forays into

southern New Mexico and Arizona. The most recent confirmed sighting was in 1996, and nearly 60 have been seen since 1900. While the northern limit of the jaguar's range probably lay across central Utah, Colorado, and Kansas as recently as 10,000 years ago, that range has shrunk drastically in the last couple of centuries, now being confined to the Sierra Madre Occidental and its foothills in southeastern Sonora. The principal wild prey of northern jaguars is thought to be the small Coues white-tailed deer and the javelina, and the ranges of jaguars and javelinas are often coextensive. David E. Brown and Carlos A. López González, *Borderland Jaguars: Tigres de la Frontera* (Salt Lake City: University of Utah Press, 2001), 6–9, maps 1 and 2, 30–31, 51, 55. More credence is given to our rendering of "leones pardos" as "jaguars" here by the facts that the scientific name for leopard is *Panthera pardus* and that the common name derives from the Greek elements *leonto* and *pardos*. Application of the name for leopard to the jaguar would have been natural for Spaniards of the sixteenth century, the leopard being the great Old World spotted cat and the jaguar being the great New World spotted cat.

78. The sheep referred to here are desert bighorns. "Both sexes of mountain sheep possess horns that serve several functions (for example, they are both shields and weapons). Females of the desert races of mountain sheep have longer horns than other North American mountain sheep. Their horns are nearly twice as long as those of female Rocky Mountain sheep, and more widely flared. The thermoregulatory function of these horns in the desert may explain their larger size compared with the horns of their northern cousins in cooler climates." Paul R. Krausman, "The Exit of the Last Wild Mountain Sheep," in *Counting Sheep: Twenty Ways of Seeing Desert Bighorn*, ed. Gary Paul Nabhan (Tucson: University of Arizona Press, 1993), 244–45.

79. These may have been mountain goats, although their native range today is much farther north, in the high mountains from Montana to Alaska. It is perhaps more likely that what members of the Coronado expedition called goats were immature bighorns. Olaus J. Murie, *A Field Guide to Animal Tracks*, 2nd ed. (Boston: Houghton Mifflin, 1974), 305–7.

80. These "wild boars" were peccaries, or javelinas. Related to domestic pigs, they range today over much of Mexico and into the southern parts of Arizona and New Mexico. Murie, *Animal Tracks*, 294.

81. Like the tigers mentioned earlier, these "leopards" were probably jaguars. See note 77, this document. The "very large deer" may have been elk.

82. This mention of travel must refer to members of the party who were led toward the east at about this time by Hernando de Alvarado. For accounts of this foray, see Document 24 and Document 28, fols. 48r–51v.

83. For geographical information about Totonteac, Marata, and Acus, see their respective entries in Appendix 2.

84. In the Spanish original this must have appeared as "Tuçan," which corresponds to "Tuzan" in Document 29, fol. 2r. In other contemporary documents this name is usually rendered as Tusayán. See Document 28, fol. 42r, and Document 30, fol. 2r. For geographical information, see the entry for Tusayán in Appendix 2. This probable use of "Tuçan" here suggests again that Documents 19 and 29 were both written by persons very close to Vázquez de Coronado or even that the preparers of the two documents were the same person, given that they share the same unusual pronunciation. See the introduction to Document 29.

85. *Paño* is the word inferred to have been in the Spanish original; it would signify that coarse woolen cloth was made at Totonteac. Covarrubias, 802: "la tela de lana de que nos vestimos." See also Document 6, fol. 4v.

86. Vázquez de Coronado makes it clear that all three names—Totonteac, Marata, and Acus—are foreign to the people of Cíbola. In order to satisfy their questioners, they turn Totonteac into a hot lake, say Marata does not exist, and go on a linguistic fishing expedition to identify Acus as Acoma.

87. These are the pueblos on the Río de Tiguex/Rio Grande in what is now central New Mexico (see map 5). They are more fully described by Pedro de Castañeda de Nájera in Document 28, fols. 107r–110r. H&R, 174, have, instead, "a river, which I have seen, and of which the Indians have told me." However, there is no evidence that Vázquez de Coronado had personally been to the Rio Grande within the first month after the capture of Cíbola, so the sentence requires a different rendering.

88. Winship, 331, and H&R, 174, inadvertently omit the phrase "and on our horses." Hakluyt, *Principal Navigations*, 9:159, on the other hand, includes the phrase. This is again an indication that Hammond and Rey were essentially following Winship's translation and not the original document in preparing their own translation.

89. Following Hakluyt, *Principal Navigations*, 9:159, and Winship, 331, H&R, 174, mistranslate "across cliffs" as "over hills."

90. "Food," *sostanze*. Probably the corresponding word in the Spanish original was *sustento*.

91. According to Castañeda de Nájera, this was Mats'a:kya, near Dowa Yalanne, the mesa that overlooks Zuni Pueblo from the southeast. Document 28, fol. 105r.

92. This information from Indian informants contrasts sharply with Castañeda de Nájera's statement that "in that land there is not any [cotton]." But it agrees with the report from the "Relación del Suceso" that "[Indians of Tuzan] harvest cotton." Document 28, fol. 44r; Document 29, fol. 2r. For a discussion of protohistoric cultivation of cotton in the American Southwest, see Document 30, note 86.

93. When Tovar did return, he evidently provided a written report, which is not known to exist. See Document 28, fol. 45r.

94. This foreshadows the captain general's decision less than two years later to give up the expedition. It may even hint that he is already contemplating such an eventuality.

95. This is a measure of volume or weight, in Sicily formerly equal to about 6.6 grams. Salvatorre Battaglia, *Grande dizionario della lingua italiana*, 21 vols. (Torino: Unione Tipografico-Editrice Torinese, 1961–2002), 15:76.

96. J. J. Brody has identified the period from 1300 to 1700 as "the florescence" of Pueblo painting. He writes that "as in the past, both interior and exterior walls of many pueblos were painted," and that murals dating from the period have been revealed archaeologically "from rooms and kivas." Since the discovery of elaborate kiva murals at Kuaua in the 1930s, such decoration has become well known. Less well known but also not uncommon was paint decoration of living rooms. As but one example, excavation of Mound 7 at Las Humanas Pueblo (Gran Quivira) in the 1960s revealed six domestic rooms "decorated in color." J. J. Brody, "The Florescence of Painting: A.D. 1300–1700, in his *Anasazi and Pueblo Painting* (Albuquerque: University of New Mexico Press, 1991), 86, 102; Alden Hayes, Jon Nathan Young, and A. Helene Warren, *The Excavation of Mound 7, Gran Quivira National Monument, New Mexico* (Washington, DC: National Park Service, 1981), 37.

97. This evidently refers to men known as "first conquerors," who, prior to the Coronado expedition, had participated in the subjugation of Tenochtitlan, Michoacán, Nueva Galicia, or other areas.

98. This seems to be contradicted by Vázquez de Coronado's own statement later: "In this place some gold and silver have been found." Fol. 363r. Another reading, which reconciles the two statements, would have the captain general reporting that some precious metals have been found, but there seems to be no possibility of obtaining any in quantity.

99. This should not be construed to mean that members of the Coronado expedition were prospecting for precious metals. Among the known inventory of the expedition's equipment, no items can be identified as pertaining specifically to prospecting, mining, assaying, smelting, or working gold, silver, or other precious metals. Aside from a few multipurpose digging bars, there is a complete lack of items such as picks, milling tools, scales, cupels, crucibles, and blow pipes, which are specifically mentioned in documents for the later expeditions of Francisco de Ibarra and Juan de Oñate. Richard Flint, "The Pattern of Coronado Expedition Material Culture" (M.A. thesis, New Mexico Highlands University, 1992), 145–47. Although items made from precious metals were, without doubt, high on the list of goods desired by the expeditionaries, they hoped to locate such items being fabricated by technologically sophisticated peoples. The Coronado expedition member Pedro de Castañeda de Nájera, looking back after 20 years and more, thought that in the mountains of what is now northern New Mexico "there were sources of silver, *if they had been looked for*" (emphasis added). This statement implies that no prospecting went on. Document 28, fol. 91v.

100. This is likely a reference to the "woman's black dress fastened over both shoulders with the opening down the front in the oldest style of the Zuni woman's dress," still worn today by the Chakwaina Okya kachina. Wright, *Kachinas of the Zuni*, 24–25.

101. H&R, 177 n. 18, refer to unnamed archaeologists who have suggested that these mantas were embroidered rather than painted.

102. This seems to contradict Vázquez de Coronado's own earlier statement of uncertainty about the existence of gold and silver there. He writes on folio 362v, "if it exists here." This marked inconsistency within the document may mean that the different statements were written at different times, between which a small amount of precious metals was shown to the expeditionaries by Indians. Since none was subsequently located in the area, it could be that the

pieces of gold or silver mentioned here actually originated with members of the expedition who were carrying them as samples. Such was apparently the case later in Quivira. Document 26, fol. 2r. On the other hand, the apparently contradictory statements raise the possibility that one statement or the other does not derive from the original letter but was added by Ramusio or his translator. Given Ramusio's practice elsewhere of exaggerating the presence of precious metals, if either of the statements is an editorial intrusion, it is likely this one. See the introduction to Document 6. For another reading that could reconcile the two statements, see note 98, this document.

103. Who these persons may have been and whether they truly had experience in mining and identifying ores is unknown. This is the only reference in surviving Coronado expedition documents to the presence of people with such skills. No one identified as a miner, assayer, or gold worker is known to have been on the expedition. Further, there is no known reference to prospecting or assaying having been conducted by members of the expedition. It seems unlikely that anyone with significant prospecting or mining experience was present. The expedition traversed numerous areas where metal ores are now known to be located, without noting their presence or even making any attempt to locate ores. For example, the expedition (or units of it) passed many times within several miles of the lead and turquoise mines that the Pueblo people themselves were then actively exploiting in the Cerrillos Hills of modern central New Mexico, without knowing of its presence. In the same area, simple placer prospecting would likely have revealed the presence of gold in the nearby Ortiz Mountains.

104. (H)avessi esaminato. Both Winship, 319, and H&R, 163, incorrectly turn this first-person singular compound verb into the third person, applying it therefore to Díaz, when it rightly applies to Vázquez de Coronado.

105. Rindrizzare. From *drizzare*, to straighten. Melzi, *Italian Dictionary*, 141.

106. Seno*n*. This seems to be an abbreviation of the Italian conjunctive phrase *se non ché*, or *senonché*, meaning "but."

107. Uscendo. This use of the gerund is probably in error. The syntax requires the preterit indicative, *uscirono*.

108. Fussino. This is an erroneous verb form. It is *furono*, the preterit indicative of *essere*, to be, that would be appropriate. Errors of this sort tend to confirm the suggestion made in the introduction to Document 15 that the sixteenth-century Italian translator of the documents Ramusio published may not have been a native speaker and occasionally exhibited his less than complete knowledge of the language.

109. Car(r)icavono. *Caricare* (Italian) = *atacar* (Spanish). *Diccionario Universal, Italiano* (Barcelona: Oceano Langenscheidt Ediciones, 1999), 41.

110. Scaloni. Evidently this is a copyist's or compositor's error for *scalini*, steps or rungs.

111. Terre. *Terra = città*. Battaglia, *Grande Dizionario*, 20:942.

112. Abbruciarne. *Abbruciare = bruciare*, to burn. Battaglia, *Grande Dizionario*, 1:35.

113. À bastanza. *A bastanza = abbastanza, averne abbastanza, esserne stanco*. Battaglia, *Grande Dizionario*, 1:18, 2:95.

114. C*ampagne* is supplied by the 1565 edition, fol. 361v. The 1556 edition has *cèpagne*.

115. (H)averiano. This represents an error by the Italian translator for *avrebbero*, the present conditional, *potencial simple*, of *avere*, to have. Evidently the translator did not know how to form this mood in Italian and therefore followed Spanish usage by adding *ian* to the infinitive. He then Italianized the result by adding an *o* at the end.

116. Terracci(a)*o*. *Terraccio = terrìccio*. Battaglia, *Grande Dizionario*, 20:946.

117. Esterminio = *danno gravissimo, disastro, rovina*. Battaglia, *Grande Dizionario*, 5:441. Presumably the word in the Spanish original was *extremidad* or *extrema*, but either the Italian translator was not familiar with the equivalent word in that language or his translation was garbled by the compositor.

118. Lavorata. Given the subsequent reference to use of a needle, the word in the Spanish original was likely *labrada*, embroidered.

119. Coroglie. This word is probably *coróllo* or *corólla*, a small crown. Battaglia, *Grande Dizionario*, 3:796.

120. Anco = *anche*. Battaglia, *Grande Dizionario*, 1:446.

121. Dierono. Evidently the Italian translator did not know how to form the preterit indicative of *dare*, to give. Instead, he Italianized the corresponding form of Spanish *dar*, the result being *dierono*.

Document 20. Formation of a Company between Mendoza and Pedro de Alvarado, Tiripitío, November 29, 1540

1. Much the same was true of territorial expansion during the long Reconquista of the Iberian Peninsula from the 700s to 1492. Among the better known episodes of freelance reconquest are the seizure of Valencia by Rodrigo Díaz de Vivar, El Cid, in 1094, and the capture of Córdoba by a group of soldiers of fortune in 1236. For a concise account of these reconquest events, see Fletcher, *Moorish Spain*, 101–2, 128.

2. For a brief summary of the grants Carlos V originally made to Cortés after the conquest of Tenochtitlan and Cortés's later efforts to regain some of those grants after they were rescinded, see López de Gómara, *Cortés*, 390–91, 407–8.

3. See Document 25, note 27.

4. For Oviedo's account of the killing of Balboa, see PTBOviedo, 3:252–56. For a nearly contemporary report of the fighting between Cortés and Narváez, see López de Gómara, *Cortés*, 201–4.

5. Himmerich y Valencia, *Encomenderos*, 120.

6. PTBOviedo, 4:160–61, 183.

7. Christopher H. Lutz, *Santiago de Guatemala, 1541–1773: City, Caste, and the Colonial Experience* (Norman: University of Oklahoma Press, 1994), 3–6.

8. Kelsey, *Cabrillo*, 47, 51, 62, 70; Aiton, *Mendoza*, 122; Bolton, 43.

9. See, for example, note 17, this document.

10. Kelsey, *Cabrillo*, 81–82.

11. See *CDI*, 15:300–408.

12. Fol. 5r.

13. "Who may see," *vieren*. This is the future subjunctive. As was common in legal documents of the time, this one is peppered with the future subjunctive, to cover even remote possibilities.

14. For biographical information, see the entry for Antonio de Mendoza in Appendix 1.

15. Tiripitío was a native settlement east of Pátzcuaro in Michoacán. It had originally been an *encomienda* of Hernán Cortés's. At this time it was held by Juan de Alvarado. Since 1538 it had been the site of an Augustinian mission. Gerhard, *Historical Geography*, 345, 348. After Pedro de Alvarado died, his body was interred in the Guadalajara church; it was then moved to the Augustinian convent of Tiripitío and thence to the *convento* (see Document 5, note 6) of Santo Domingo in the Ciudad de México. Finally, his bones were transported to Guatemala. Tello, 371.

16. For biographical information about Juan de León, see Document 8, note 59, and Document 14, note 21. Diego de Robledo was the official *escribano* for Alvarado's fleet. A native of Valladolid in the modern Spanish *comunidad* of Castilla y León, he had come to the New World with the *adelantado* in 1538. Kelsey, *Cabrillo*, 78; *Pasajeros*, 2: no. 5463.

17. See AGN, Hospital de Jesús, 123, Expediente 31, "Cédula of July 10, 1540," published in Martínez, *Documentos Cortesianos*, 4:216–19.

18. For geographical information, see the entry for Mar del Sur in Appendix 2.

19. "Written compact," *capitulación*. The same written compact and stipulation is referred to in a *cédula* from Carlos V. See note 17, this document.

20. Regarding Santiago de Buena Esperanza in Colima, see Document 15, note 22.

21. The port of Acapulco had been in existence in the 1520s. It was perhaps first seen by Rodrigo Álvarez Chico in late 1521 and was the location of a shipyard from about 1528. The port of Guatulco in Oaxaca was in the early years preferred to Acapulco by ships trading with Central America and Peru. Later, Acapulco was the terminus for the trans-Pacific trade. Gerhard, *Historical Geography*, 27–28, 39–41. A *fragata* was a very small vessel that a *galera* commonly carried and used to travel to land or to other vessels. A *fusta* was a small, swift *galera* with oars and one or two masts, used frequently for coastal exploration.

22. Probably a 200-ton *galeón*, the *Santiago* later made the voyage to the Moluccas as Ruy López de Villalobos's flagship. Kelsey, *Cabrillo*, 75. The *Diosdado*, owned by Antonio Diosdado, may have made the voyage to the Moluccas. Kelsey, *Cabrillo*, 68, 76. The ship *Juan Rodríguez* was so called because its original owner and builder was Juan Rodríguez Cabrillo. It bore the official name *San Salvador* and eventually made a voyage to the peninsula of Baja California as the flagship of Francisco de Bolaños. Kelsey, *Cabrillo*, 76, 85, 105. The ship *Álvar Núñez* was co-owned by a man of that name and Pedro de Alvarado. Kelsey, *Cabrillo*, 69. Like a

number of other ships in the fleet, the *Antón Hernández* was named after its owner, Antón Hernández. Kelsey, *Cabrillo*, 69. The ship *Figueroa*, too, was named after one of its three owners, who were Santos de Figueroa, Álvaro de Paz (Alvarado's *mayordomo*), and a man named Cisneros. Kelsey, *Cabrillo*, 56, 69–70.

23. The 1541 report of Bernardo Molina (Document 21) says there were by then 13 ships. Harry Kelsey lists all their names in Kelsey, *Cabrillo*, 76. See also Document 21, note 16.

24. How many people were with Alarcón is unknown, but with three ships, it would not have been at all unusual to have had a combined crew of more than 60. Presumably there were also passengers, including men-at-arms, likely to have amounted to another 180 to 200 persons. Pérez-Mallaína, *Spain's Men of the Sea*, 130–31. For geographical information on Nueva Galicia, see that entry in Appendix 2. For biographical information on fray Marcos de Niza, see the introduction to Document 6. For biographical information about Hernando de Alarcón, see the introduction to Document 15.

25. There is no information that such a grant was made, and in fact no information about Alarcón's subsequent activities and fate.

26. For geographical information, see the entry for Tierra Nueva in Appendix 2.

27. Port[s] of Coliman = La Navidad. See Document 16, note 17.

28. There has been scholarly debate about how voluntary Alvarado's participation in the partnership was. Hubert Howe Bancroft, on one hand, insisted that Alvarado was forcibly compelled by Mendoza's embargo of his fleet. Arthur Aiton, the viceroy's biographer, on the other hand, portrayed Alvarado as eager to accept a lucrative deal. Aiton, *Mendoza*, 123 n. 14.

29. Presumably such a long term was established for the partnership as part of the viceroy's effort to ensure years of stability for his jurisdiction.

30. Xirabaltique = Girabaltique. Girabaltique was Alvarado's Guatemalan shipyard near the mouth of the Río Michatoya, just upriver from Iztapa. Kelsey, *Cabrillo*, 65–66.

31. Under this umbrella would have to be included the great codification of Castilian law, the *Siete Partidas*, prepared in the 1200s under the direction of King Alfonso X. That voluminous compilation dealt with virtually every aspect of life, though it was never uniformly or completely applied to all Spanish jurisdictions. See Joseph F. O'Callaghan, "Alfonso X and the Partidas," in *Siete Partidas*, 1:xxxviii–xl. The distinction between "special [or] general" is equivalent to the one between private and ordinary legislation in the modern U.S. Congress.

32. The Order of Santiago was one of three great religious-military orders established in Castilla in the twelfth century. The other two orders were those of Alcántara and Calatrava. Membership in the orders was restricted to very high-status persons. Elliott, *Imperial Spain*, 32, 88–89.

33. This was a standard oath of the time.

34. For biographical information, see the entry for don Luis de Castilla in Appendix 1.

35. Marroquín was the *provisor* (diocesan judge) of the Ciudad de México. Advised of his appointment as bishop on August 8, 1523, he did not assume his post until February 16, 1536. He served as bishop until his death on April 18, 1563. Schäfer, *Consejo Real*, 2:577. For biographical information, see the entries for Alonso Maldonado and Peralmindez Cherino in Appendix 1. Gonzalo López is a common name, but it seems highly likely that this person was the man from Sevilla who was the *maestre de campo* for Guzmán. This López led a 1530 expedition north and east from modern-day Río San Lorenzo on the Pacific coast to the eastern portion of Durango or western Coahuila. He reported on the conquest of Nueva Galicia and explored the Culiacán-Humaya-Tamazula river system. Boyd-Bowman, 2: no. 9512; Adorno and Pautz, *Núñez Cabeza de Vaca*, 2:221, 3:328, 365. For biographical information on Hernán Pérez de Bocanegra, see Document 14, note 26.

36. *Numero segundo*. This is not written by the same *escribano* as the one who wrote the body of the document. It appears to be in a more modern hand.

37. Presydente en el aUdienÇia. Unaccountably, *CDI*, 3:352, slightly alters this phrase as "presidente de la su audiencia."

38. Asyento Y capitulaÇion. *CDI*, 3:352, gratuitously adds "y concierto y capítulos."

39. La capitana santiago. *CDI*, 3:353, inserts "nombrada," so that the phrase reads "la capitana nombrada santiago."

40. *CDI*, 3:353, omits this line from its transcription.

41. Del dicho descubrimyento. *CDI*, 3:353, omits "dicho."

42. Que su magestad. *CDI*, 3:353, gratuitously inserts "con."

43. Descubrimiento en que ha gastado. *CDI*, 3:353, erroneously adds "que en nombre de S.M. hizo."

44. Sy no. *CDI*, 3:353, mistakenly combines these into "sino."

45. La quarta Parte de todos. *CDI*, 3:354, mistakenly reads "quinta Parte."

46. Quarta parte. Again *CDI*, 3:354, mistakenly reads "quinta Parte."

47. Otro qualquyer capitan. *CDI*, 3:354, erroneously omits "qualquyer."

48. De esta carta. *CDI*, 3:355, omits "carta."

49. Le fizo. *CDI*, 3:356, incorrectly has "le hace."

50. O con los / naVios de ella o de fuera de ella que el dicho señor Adelantado. *CDI*, 3:356, omits this entire phrase by mistake.

51. ConÇierto. *CDI*, 3:357, mistakenly has "condición."

52. Que hizo con la gente que enVyo por tierra como. *CDI*, 3:357, omits this entire phrase in error.

53. Adelantado hA fecho en fazer. *CDI*, 3:357, incorrectly omits "ha fecho."

54. Pida nynguna cosa. *CDI*, 3:358, omits "ninguna" and adds instead "alguna." From this point on a different person seems to be making the transcript, because the rate of errors falls off radically.

55. "Botaraen" is clearly a word the *escribano* was unfamiliar with and could not read clearly in the original document. The intended word could be either *botavante* (boarding pike) or *botavara* (grappling hook). In either case, the *escribano*'s transcription includes the common error (among both sixteenth-century scribes and modern paleographers) of mistaking a *v* for an *r*.

56. This is the Latin negative, often employed in legal contexts.

57. De la su casa. Probably this should have been "las de su casa."

58. Por sentencia. *CDI*, 3:361, incorrectly has "como por sentencia."

59. Dom(e)iÇilio = domiciliario. *DRAE*, 773.

60. Pleyto homenaje = homenaje de fidelidad al rey. *DRAE*, 1624.

61. Alonso maldonado. *CDI*, 3:362, gratuitously adds "oidor de la Audiencia Real de S.M."

62. Gonzalo lopez. *CDI*, 3:362, incorrectly has "Gregorio López."

63. The *escribano* incorrectly renders the ecclesiastical Latin place name for Guatemala, which derives from the Maya "Tecpam-Quauhtemalan." *Enciclopedia universal*, 26:1636.

64. Por / testigo el licenÇiado maldonado. *CDI*, 3:362, adds Maldonado's first name, Alonso.

65. The text on this folio side is in the hand of a sixteenth-century *escribano*, but someone other than the *escribano* who copied the body of the document.

Document 21. Account of Pedro de Alvarado's Armada, 1541

1. For information on the career and work of Oviedo, see the introduction to Document 7. That the *criado*'s name was Bernardo de Molina is revealed by Oviedo in Libro 41, Capítulo 2, of his *Historia general y natural de las Indias*, 4:354.

2. For information about the port of Colima, see Document 16, note 17.

3. A brief summary of this 1538 contract appears in *CDI*, 15:303. The contract was entered into while Alvarado was in Spain, during the trip he made there during 1536–39. Kelsey, *Cabrillo*, 70; Bolton, 43. This was one of a series of conflicting contracts that rendered the rivalry among a group of conquistadores (Alvarado, Mendoza, Cortés, Guzmán, and Soto) very complicated and messy. See the introductions to Documents 18 and 20.

4. Document 20.

5. Libro 41, Capítulo 3, in PTBOviedo, 4:356.

6. Ibid.

7. Document 7, fol. 22r.

8. Fol. 23v.

9. Fol. 24r.

10. Ibid.

11. See the introduction to Document 7 for a fuller discussion of the authorship of the various manuscripts comprising Oviedo's *Historia*.

12. "Readied," *ordenar* = *poner en orden*. *DRAE*, 1484. *Poner*, *DRAE*, 1638: "con la preposición en y algunos nombres, ejercer la acción de los verbos a que los nombres corresponden."

13. For biographical information about Pedro de Alvarado, see the introduction to Document 20. For geographical information about the Mar del Sur, see Appendix 2. Tierra Firme was the name given to Panamá and South America.

14. For information about the Consejo de las Indias, see Appendix 1.

15. Istapa = Iztapa, Guatemala. Iztapa, 14 leagues south of Santiago de Guatemala on the Río Michatoya near its mouth, was Guatemala's principal port. Alvarado's shipyard, at Girabaltique, was just upriver from there. Acaxucla = Acajutla. The transformation of this name is another instance of misreading *x* for *j* and *c* for *t*, both common errors for sixteenth-century *escribanos* and modern paleographers. Acajutla, on the Pacific coast in what is now El Salvador, was the seaport for Trinidad and San Salvador. Kelsey, *Cabrillo*, 65–66. For identification of the seven *ciudades*, see the entry for Cíbola in Appendix 2.

16. Juan Rodríguez Cabrillo's *galeón San Salvador* was among these 13, as were the *galeónes Santiago* and *Diosdado*. The remaining 10 ships were *San Cristóbal, San Martín, San Miguel, San Jorge, San Antonio, San Francisco, San Juan de Letrán, Figueroa, Antón Hernández,* and *Álvar Núñez*. Kelsey, *Cabrillo*, 72, 75–76.

17. A *galeón* was a large, strong, heavy sailing vessel used as a fighting or merchant ship and was both square- and lateen-rigged. About the *fusta*, see Document 20, note 21. A *tonelada* was a unit of weight or capacity used to calculate the displacement of ships; it was approximately equal to the weight of 20 *quintales*, or 2,000 pounds (see also Document 28, note 161). A small barrel was a *tonel*, and by extension, the provision for so many *toneles* in a *navío* indicated its size.

18. The term "Indies" would now include the Western Hemisphere plus Spain's possessions in the Far East and the Philippines.

19. The *criado*'s name was Berna(l)rdo de Molina. Interestingly, there was also at the time a Francisca de Molina in the household of Beatriz de la Cueva, Pedro de Alvarado's wife. It is possible that she was a relative, maybe even the wife, of Bernardo de Molina. PTBOviedo, 4:357. *César* = the emperor. Carlos V was the Holy Roman Emperor, heir to the Caesars.

20. Unfortunately, this painting, made on cloth, is not known to exist today. PTBOviedo, 4:354.

21. Cumplir. PTBOviedo, 4:351, incorrectly has "ampliar."

22. Los *dichos* navios. PTBOviedo, 4:351, incorrectly has "los ocho navios."

23. Que le en*Vio*. PTBOviedo, 4:351, incorrectly has "que el envió."

24. Dexo. PTBOviedo, 4:351, incorrectly has "dijo."

Document 22. *Traslado de las Nuevas (Anonymous Narrative), 1540*

1. See the introduction to Document 30.

2. Castañeda, *Journey of Coronado*, 100 n. 1.

3. Fol. 1v; Flint, *Great Cruelties*, 167, 236, 281.

4. Document 28, fol. 32r: "García López de Cárdenas and Hernando de Alvarado, who threw themselves over him and took him away [while themselves] receiving blows from stones."

5. Fol. 1v. Other possibilities for the author are the expedition's official chronicler, Pedro Méndez de Sotomayor, and Hernando Bermejo, Vázquez de Coronado's personal secretary.

6. Fol. 1v.

7. *CDI*, 19:529–32.

8. Mora, 171–72.

9. Winship, 336–39; H&R, 179–81.

10. The date 1531, added by the copyist or another, later *escribano*, is incorrect. The correct year is of course 1540.

11. For geographical information, see the entries for Cíbola, Tierra Nueva, and Culiacán in Appendix 2.

12. The original of this report was thus written at Cíbola in the summer of 1540.

13. "More than," *largas*. DRAE, 1231: "aplicado a una cantidad, que pasa de lo que realmente se dice." H&R, 179, with a too-literal translation, have "long leagues," as does Winship, 336.

14. The problem of food scarcity was thus one not of a lack of agriculture but of the maturity of the crops along the way. The corn would have been too young until the end of May. This information is echoed in Document 29, fol. 1r: "Because the planted crops were [still] young, there was no corn on the entire route." See also Document 29, note 35. The same document also reports that Arellano was to depart from Culiacán "twenty days after he [did]," which would be about May 12. Document 29, fol. 1r.

15. This implies that the count of 75 men in the advance guard includes only the persons of a certain status. However, each of them would have taken *criados*.

16. The reference to locating and breaking trails is probably an exaggeration, because documents from the Guzmán *entradas* of the 1530s as well as those from the Coronado expedition consistently indicate that the groups followed well-known native trade routes virtually everywhere they went. This does, however, reinforce Vázquez de Coronado's statement in Document 19, fol. 360r, that "we all cheerfully traveled along a very difficult trail that could not be traversed without either [ourselves] preparing one or restraightening the track that was there." It is possible that what is being referred to in both instances is that the trails had to be widened. See Riley, *Frontier People*, 76.

17. An old Castilian unit of dry measure, one *celemín* was equivalent to four *cuartillos*, or about one-eighth of a U.S. bushel. *DRAE*, 451; Barnes, Naylor, and Polzer, *Northern New Spain*, 69.

18. Jaramillo confirms that Espinosa died en route to Cíbola but adds that he died from eating a poisonous herb. Document 30, fol. 2r; Document 19, note 45.

19. Both H&R, 180, and Winship, 336, attach this phrase to the preceding sentence, making for an awkward and confusing construction.

20. The Albaicín was at that time the Moorish quarter of Granada, on the north bank of the Río Darro and opposite the Alhambra. The streets are narrow and winding, and the white houses stair-step up the hill. Thus, one can imagine the accurate comparison with the multistoried pueblo of Hawikku. Another element that probably figured in the choice of the name Granada was that the city of that name in Spain had been the last Islamic state to fall in the Christian reconquest of the Iberian Peninsula only 50 years before the expedition. It would have been appropriate to assign that name to another recently conquered "heathen" polity, this time in the New World. Further, association of Cíbola with Granada would tend to magnify the advance guard's accomplishment, putting it on a par with Fernando and Isabel's capture of the great Moorish city.

21. If this actually happened, then the supposition of Edmund Ladd and others that a ceremonial event was in progress at Cíbola/Hawikku when the advance guard arrived is unlikely. Edmund J. Ladd, "Zuni on the Day the Men in Metal Arrived," in Flint and Flint, *Tierra Nueva*, 225–33.

22. Vázquez de Coronado reported in August 1540 that he sent two friars, Luis and Daniel, ahead to deliver the *requerimiento*, which was required by royal mandate from 1512 to 1573. Expedition member Domingo Martín later testified that it was fray Juan de Padilla and fray Marcos de Niza who were dispatched to read the formal demand for submission. Other witnesses before Lorenzo de Tejada in 1544 testified that fray Juan had delivered the summons. Vázquez de Coronado himself, testifying in 1544, continued to say that he had sent fray Luis to read the *requerimiento*. Melchior Pérez, who claimed to have been among the group sent forward to the deliver the summons, testified that the message was delivered through a native interpreter who knew the language of Cíbola. Document 19, fol. 360v; Flint, *Great Cruelties*, 93, 110, 129, 146, 167, 210, 280. For an English translation of the formal summons itself, see Appendix 4.

23. For biographical information, see the entry for Hernando Bermejo in Appendix 1.

24. The reference here is to fray Juan de Zumárraga. See the entry for Luis de Úbeda in Appendix 1.

25. Most deaths at this point probably resulted from wounds inflicted by mounted lancers. There is no evidence that either arquebuses or crossbows saw action until later.

26. "Wall like a city wall," *casamuro*, a defensive wall formed by the buildings. *DRAE*, 430. During Frederick Hodge's excavation of Hawikku, the presumed location of this *ciudad* of Cíbola, between 1917 and 1923, no evidence of such a wall was noted, though the Cíbolans could have created the appearance of a walled town by erecting short segments of wall between roomblocks in preparation for defense. If this were the case, it would imply that the approach of the advance guard was known well ahead of its actual arrival and that the Cíbolans anticipated having to fend off an attack. Smith, Woodbury, and Woodbury, *Excavation of Hawikuh*, fig. 1, following page 336.

27. "Determined," *acordo*. *DRAE*, 31: "determinar o resolver deliberadamente una sola persona."

28. In his August 3, 1540, letter to the viceroy, Vázquez de Coronado explained that "my armor was gilded and shiny." Document 19, fol. 361r.

29. "With errant stone[s]," *a piedra perdida*. H&R, 181, ignore the word *perdida*, rendering the phrase simply as "by stones." Winship, 339, on the other hand, is very close to our translation, with "by chance stones."

30. See notes 3 and 4 and the introduction to this document. Vázquez de Coro-

nado's own account of the circumstances of his wounding is in Document 19, fol. 361r. Herbert Bolton, relying on Hammond and Rey's and Winship's questionable translations of Document 22 at this point, put it this way: "By Don García and the soldiers Coronado was carried as dead to a tent." Bolton, 125; H&R, 169; Winship, 325.

31. H&R, 181, suggest that the Traslado was addressed to Viceroy Mendoza and that this sentence implies a message is to be forwarded to the king. The suggestion regarding the king seems questionable, because reference to the king would ordinarily have been to "su Magestad," rather than to "mi señor." For discussion of the letter's addressee, see the introduction to the document.

32. "Steep, rugged hill of rock," *piñol = peñol.* This is probably Dowa Yalanne, the isolated mesa southeast of modern Zuni that has repeatedly been used as a refuge by the Zuni people. Dowa Yalanne is almost exactly the four leagues (10.5 to 12 miles) from Hawikku stated here. T. J. Ferguson and E. Richard Hart, *A Zuni Atlas* (Norman: University of Oklahoma Press, 1985), 35.

33. In all likelihood, "mi señora" (my lady) refers either to Beatriz de Estrada, Vázquez de Coronado's wife, or to the wife of "my lord" (Mendoza), referred to earlier. See note 31, this document.

34. This was salt from Zuni Salt Lake, which the Cíbolans/Zunis used themselves and likely traded to other native groups. Riley, *Frontier People*, 194–95.

35. Tuvo nueva. *CDI*, 19:529, misreads this as "tuvo que va."

36. Cosyeron. *CDI*, 19:531, mistakenly has "cogieron."

37. Traya. *CDI*, 19:531, misreads this as "tenia."

38. Porque el dia / que aqui llegamos no creo que habia que comer para otro dia. *CDI*, 19:531, completely omits this entire phrase.

39. Plazo, "it pleased." *CDI*, 19:532, misreads this as *pongo*. Mora, 172, who uncritically accepts *CDI*'s transcription, has the same. Winship, 339, renders the word in English as "praised be," and H&R, 181, again trying to make sense of *CDI*'s error, have "is my witness."

40. Mi señora, "my lady." *CDI*, 19:532, mistakenly reads this as "mi señoria." Mora, 172, followed this without consulting the original document. Likewise, H&R, 181, did not check the original but followed *CDI*, rendering this as "my Lord," which confuses the sense of the text.

41. Mi señora. *CDI*, 19:532, completely omits *mi señora* in this case. Thus, so do Mora, 172, and H&R, 181. Winship, 339, on the other hand, did notice the words but apparently misread them as *mi señoria*.

Document 23. La Relación Postrera de Cíbola (Fray Toribio Benavente's Narrative), 1540s

1. Molina, *Vocabulario*, fol. 60v.

2. Nancy Joe Dyer, "Introducción," in fray Toribio de Benavente Motolinía, *Memoriales*, ed. Nancy Joe Dyer (México, DF: Colegio de México, 1996), 23.

3. Nancy Joe Dyer, "'La Relación Postrera de Siuola' (Motolinía): Género, estilo, síntesis cultural hispanoamericana," *Nueva Revista de Filología Hispánica* 39, no. 2 (1991):884–85.

4. Ibid., 890.

5. However, a battle that took place in October of that year is mentioned in the body of the text, as are the death of Pedro de Alvarado in July 1541 and the disaster in Guatemala that September. Benavente Motolinía, *Memoriales*, 399–400.

6. "Y en esta sazón an llegado cartas como an hallado prinçipios de grandes pueblos y de mucha gente. La primera çiudad se dize Çibola, en la qual quedauan los españoles; créese ser gran puerta para adelante." Benavente Motolinía, *Memoriales*, 122.

7. Ibid., 553–56.

8. Dyer, "Introducción," 31, 33.

9. Ibid., 69–72.

10. Georges Baudot, cited in Dyer, "Relación Postrera," 889.

11. Fol. 123v.

12. Document 6, fols. 4r and 5r.

13. Document 28, fol. 101v; Document 29, fol. 1r.

14. Fol. 123v.

15. See note 27, this document.

16. See note 41, this document.

17. Fol. 124v.

18. Dyer, "Introducción," 31–36.

19. Nancy Joe Dyer, "*Libro de Oro*: El Manuscrito," in Benavente Motolinía, *Memoriales*, 93.

20. Dyer, "*Libro de Oro*," 110.

21. Ibid., 93–96; fray Toribio de Benavente Motolinía, *Memoriales de Fray Toribio de Motolinía: Manuscrito de la colección del señor don Joaquín García Icazbalceta*, ed. Luis García Pimentel (México, DF: Casa del Editor, 1903); fray Toribio de Benavente Motolinía, *Memoriales: Libro de las cosas de la Nueva España de los naturales de ella*, ed. Edmundo O'Gorman (México, DF: UNAM, Instituto de Investigaciones Históricas, 1971); Benavente Motolinía, *Memoriales*.

22. An 1893 transcript by Joaquín García Icazbalceta was published in Winship, 340–42, in 1896, and was republished by Mora, 177–79.

23. Winship, 342–49; H&R, 308–12.

24. The text is annotated with marginal notes that are in a post-sixteenth-century hand; all except one highlight place names.

25. For geographical information, see the entries for Culiacán and Cíbola in Appendix 2.

26. On the matter of population density, see the introduction to this document.

27. The apparent lack of agricultural produce was the result of the season's having been too early for crop maturity. As the author of the Relación del Suceso wrote, "Because the planted crops were [still] young, there was no corn on the entire route." The previous year Marcos de Niza received "much game (deer, rabbits, and quail) and corn and *pinol*, all in great abundance." Juan Jaramillo's account seems to jibe with the friar's: "For their food, which I think never fails them, they have corn, beans, and squash." Document 29, fol. 1r; Document 6, fol. 4v; Document 30, fol. 1v.

28. "The houses are round and small, [so] that a standing man hardly fits inside." According to the Relación del Suceso, "their houses are all made of cane mats and some among them [have] low, flat roofs." Juan Jaramillo described the construction of such shelters in this way: "After setting up poles very much in the manner of ovens, though much larger, they cover them with mats." Document 29, fol. 1r; Document 30, fol. 1v.

29. Vázquez de Coronado agrees exactly. Document 19, fol. 361v.

30. Photographs of Frederick Hodge's 1917–23 excavation of Hawikku correspond well to this description, although the walls are principally of stone laid in adobe mortar. See especially Smith, Woodbury, and Woodbury, *Excavation of Hawikuh*, plates 14 and 15.

31. "Hatchways," *escotillones*. The reference to hatchways here implies that the rooms were entered through their roofs, which is consistent with the archaeology of Hawikku.

32. Unsupported by the Spanish, H&R, 308, have "The houses are built compact and adjoining one another."

33. The use of "maguey" probably refers to woven yucca fiber.

34. The combination of deerskin moccasins and knee-high leggings of the same material was observed at Zuni in the 1890s by Mathilda Coxe Stevenson, as were rabbit-skin blankets. Stevenson, "Zuñi Indians," 370.

35. Hair whorls are now usually associated with unmarried Hopi women. At Zuni today they are mostly confined to kachina/koko impersonations, such as Santo Domingo Kokokshi Girl and Hopi Harvest Kachina Girl. Wright, *Kachinas of the Zuni*, 87, 114. However, see also Document 28, note 426. See fig. 17.1.

36. These were still the staple crops of the Zunis in the early twentieth century. Stevenson, "Zuñi Indians," 350–51.

37. For identification of the seven towns, see the entry for Cíbola in Appendix 2. The distance between Hawikku and Mats'a:kya, the two Zuni pueblos that are farthest apart, is about 13 miles, almost exactly five leagues (*leguas legales*).

38. Converting on the basis of the *legua legal*, 60 leagues is about 158 miles, and 40 leagues, about 105 miles. By modern road the shortest distance from Hawikku to the Rio Grande at Albuquerque is about 155 miles, and from Hawikku to Acoma is about 110 miles, both remarkably close to the author's figures (see map 3). For geographical information, see the entries for Tiguex and Acuco in Appendix 2.

39. The two unrelated languages referred to here are Zuni at Zuni and Keresan at Acoma. Edward P. Dozier, *The Pueblo Indians of North America* (New York: Holt, Rinehart, and Winston, 1970; reprint, Prospect Heights, IL: Waveland Press, 1983), 122, 181–82 (page citations are to the reprint edition).

40. Both rivers are extremely variable in width, depending on rainfall and snowmelt, but they are of the same order of magnitude. Interestingly, if coincidentally, Guadalquivir, the name of the river at Sevilla, means "big river," as does Rio Grande, the modern name of the Río de Tiguex.

41. This is clearly an intrusion of fray Toribio's into the text, which raises the issue of where else he might have inserted words or phrases of his own without announcing them in any way. Twelve pueblos along the Río de Tiguex agrees with Castañeda de Nájera's count. Document 28, fol. 107r. If the refuge pueblo of Moho is included in this count, then the 12 might have been those stretching from the area of the confluence of the Jemez River and the Rio Grande on the north to Piedras Marcadas on the south (see map 5). There is much disagreement about the number and location of the pueblos of Tiguex in the 1540s. For other possible configurations, see Appendix 2.

42. Juan Jaramillo, for instance, says there were 15 pueblos. Document 30, fol. 2v.

43. This echoes the earlier statement about walls at Cíbola. The thinness seem excessive and is not borne out archaeologically.

44. In other words, the expeditionaries improved a ford.

45. This hypothetical statement about wagons is another confirmation that there were no wheeled vehicles on the Coronado expedition.

46. For information on cultivation of cotton along the middle Rio Grande, see Document 30, note 86.

47. Juan Jaramillo concurs in this distance from Tiguex to Cicique/Pecos, but Castañeda de Nájera has "five days' travel." See map 3. Document 30, fol. 2v; Document 28, fol. 51r.

48. This spelling, Cicuic, also appears in Castañeda de Nájera's *relación* and is apparently related to the spelling "Cicuique," which appears in the Jaramillo narrative and the 1544 investigation documents. Document 28; Document 30; Flint, *Great Cruelties*, passim. For geographical information, see the entry for Cicuique in Appendix 2.

49. This seems to be a gross underestimate of the size of Cicuique. Castañeda de Nájera, for instance, says it was "a pueblo of as many as five hundred fighting men," which is hardly consistent with only 50 households. Document 28, fol. 112r.

50. This evidently refers to the party's reaching the Río de Cicuique/Pecos River, beyond which the terrain indeed becomes less broken, as Castañeda de Nájera records, although the extremely level Llano Estacado was not reached for about two weeks after the river was crossed. See maps 1 and 4. Flint, "Reconciling the Calendars," 155.

51. This same comparison of bison hair to merino wool appears in Castañeda de Nájera's *relación*. Document 28, fol. 150v.

52. This description of *Bison bison* is quite accurate. Compare Jerry N. McDonald, *North American Bison: Their Classification and Evolution* (Berkeley: University of California Press, 1981), and Document 28, fols. 150–151rv.

53. Navaja. Molina, *Vocabulario*, fol. 38r: "itztli," a sharp blade of obsidian or other similar material.

54. These are the people called Teyas in the Castañeda de Nájera *relación*. The author omits mention here of their neighbors, the Querechos. See Document 28, fols. 78r, 81r, and 83v.

55. "This land" is Nueva España.

56. These packsaddles were used in addition to the dragged litter, or travois, mentioned immediately following.

57. This sounds slightly different from the dragged litter, or travois, familiar in Plains Indian use with horses in later centuries. Apparently no load was carried on the poles dragged by the dogs.

58. For biographical information, see the entry for Juan de Padilla in Appendix 2.

59. This comment, probably an interjection by fray Toribio, means that the document or documents the friar collates here were written before September 1541 and may have been dispatched while the captain general was still absent from Tiguex. There may have been a regularly scheduled departure date for a courier during the month of August, given that the previous year the captain general had also dispatched a letter to the viceroy in August (see Document 19).

60. Beginning here, the remainder of the document consists of remarks made by fray Toribio.

61. In describing a region called Rudbar in modern Iran, Marco Polo and his co-author, Rustichello, mentioned large, white oxen with "a round hump, fully two palms in height," between their shoulders. The easy equation Toribio de Benavente makes here between animals of the Americas and those of the Middle East is indicative of the belief, still widely held in the 1530s and 1540s, that the northern American land mass was an extension of Asia. Polo's book was still very popular in Spain in the sixteenth century. Marco Polo, *The Travels of Marco Polo*, trans. and ed.

Ronald Latham (Harmondsworth, UK: Penguin Books, 1958), 64; and see the introduction to Document 28.

62. Edmundo O'Gorman has identified this man as Nicolo di Conti, a Venetian who flourished between about 1419 and 1444. Pope Eugene IV (a Venetian himself who was pope from 1431 to 1447) directed him to report on his travels to Giovanni Poggio Bracciolini, who at that time was papal secretary. Cited in Dyer, "Relación Postrera," 894 n. 15, and *Encyclopedia Americana*, 1956 edition, 30 vols. (New York: Americana Corporation, 1956), 10:566.

63. *Micer* = my lord. *DRAE*, 1368: "título antiguo honorifico de la corona de Aragón." This is Giovanni Francesco Poggio Bracciolini, an Italian humanist of the fifteenth century. He was papal secretary and later chancellor of Florence from 1453 to 1458. A Spanish edition of Poggio Bracciolini's work, together with Marco Polo's *Travels*, had been published in Sevilla in 1503. *Encyclopedia Americana*, 22:279; Dyer, "Introducción," 59.

64. A *codo* was a length of approximately 0.4 meter, or 16.5 inches. It was also referred to as a cubit, the distance from the elbow to the tip of the extended fingers

65. Cántaro. *DRAE*, 390: a large pitcher. This was a liquid measure of wine equal to approximately three gallons, though it varied from region to region in Spain. The term also applied to the container, a large vessel of clay or metal, narrow at the mouth, wide through the belly, narrow at the foot, and commonly with one or two handles. Among modern archaeologists it is commonly called an olive jar.

66. Polo, *Travels*, 330.

67. Postrera = *última = más recién*. Covarrubias, 2044.

68. P(r)esada. The *r* was probably added by assimilation from "tierra."

69. TigUex. H&R, 309, and Mora, 177, all read this as "Tibex." But because this would be the only instance of this spelling among the known Coronado expedition documents, and because *U* and *b* are all but indistinguishable in sixteenth-century Spanish script, it makes more sense to ascribe this variant to a copying error in which the *g* was omitted.

70. Y el asentando el rio. H&R, 309, say "the river freezes so hard." They evidently followed Pacheco and Cárdenas without checking the original manuscript, which is very clear. Likewise, Mora, 178, accepts *CDI*'s faulty transcription, "y hiélase tanto el río."

71. Curar de = *cuidar de*. *DRAE*, 628.

72. Llamanse. Mora, 178, drops the *n:* "llamase."

73. Alesna = *lesna*. *DRAE*, 94.

74. Andan(^d) donde andan (^V). This kind of scribal correction confirms that the scribe was copying from an existing manuscript and not, for instance, recording dictation.

75. HA visto. Mora, 179, and H&R, 311, agree that the *escribano* omitted "visto" from the manuscript.

76. Canes. Can, Covarrubias, 248: "no es nombre castellano, sino tomado del nombre latino *canis*, perro."

Document 24. Hernando de Alvarado's Narrative, 1540

1. Flint, *Great Cruelties*, 315.

2. Vázquez de Coronado's August 3, 1540, letter mentions that he is "sending don Pedro de Tovar to see [Tusayán] with his company and some other horsemen" and that Tovar will not be back for "at least thirty days." According to Pedro de Castañeda de Nájera, Tovar "returned from there and gave this report to the general. Promptly, [Vázquez de Coronado] dispatched don Garci López de Cárdenas there, with about twelve companions, to reconnoiter this river [the Tizón]." As recorded by the "Relación del Suceso," it was only four days after that Alvarado and Padilla were sent east. Document 19, fol. 362v; Document 28, fol. 45r; Document 29, fol. 2v.

3. Document 28, fol. 48r.

4. Document 28, fol. 48v.

5. Fol. 1r. Castañeda de Nájera and Melchior Pérez, who was one of the horsemen who accompanied Alvarado, agree that the party consisted of 20 horsemen. Juan Troyano, however, who was also a member of the Alvarado party, states explicitly that "Hernando de Alvarado and twenty-three other men" made the reconnaissance. Document 28, fol. 49r; Flint, *Great Cruelties*, 168, 211, 282.

6. Flint, *Great Cruelties*, 211.

7. Document 28, fol. 50v.

8. Fol. 1r.

9. Flint, *Great Cruelties*, 194.

10. Document 29, fol. 3v; Document 28, fol. 50v.

11. Document 28, fols. 51r and 51v–52r.

12. Fol. 1r.

13. Flint, *Great Cruelties*, 277; Document 28, fols. 54v–55r; Victor M. Álvarez, *Diccionario de conquistadores* (México, DF: Instituto Nacional de Antropología y Historia, 1975), 1:25; AGI, Justicia, 1021, N.2, Pieza 6, "Probanza del fiscal Villalobos, México, January 10, 1547"; AGI, Justicia, 1021, N.2, Pieza 5, "Probanza de López de Cárdenas"; AGI, México, 1064, L.1\1, "Informes de los conquistadores," fol. 261r.

14. Fol. 1r.

15. Smith, *Colección de varios documentos*, 65.

16. *CDI*, 3:511–13.

17. Winship, 384–85.

18. H&R, 182–84.

19. Mora, 197–98.

20. That this document is labeled "Mar del Sur" gives an idea of the poor state of precise geographical knowledge in Spain in 1540. Alvarado and Padilla went east from Cíbola, not west toward the Mar del Sur, or Pacific Ocean. This heading was certainly added by someone who was not with the Alvarado-Padilla party, most likely an *escribano* in either the Audiencia de México or the Consejo de Indias. For geographical information, see the entry for Mar del Sur in Appendix 2.

21. For biographical information, see the entry for Juan de Padilla in Appendix 1.

22. For Vázquez de Coronado's renaming of the first *ciudad* of Cíbola as Granada, see Document 19, fol. 361r. For a suggestion that Alvarado's departure was not from Hawikku/Granada but rather from the area of Dowa Yalanne, see Carroll L. Riley and Joni L. Manson, "The Cíbola-Tiguex Route: Continuity and Change in the Southwest, *New Mexico Historical Review* 58, no. 4 (1983):355. Documentary support for the Riley-Manson view comes from Juan Jaramillo, who was a member of the Alvarado-Padilla party. He wrote: "From this first pueblo of Cíbola we went, as I have said, to another one of them, which is probably about one short day's journey." Document 30, fol. 2r. On the other hand, about 70 years ago Frederick Webb Hodge asserted that Alvarado traveled east from Hawikku "by way of the Ojo Caliente valley directly to Acoma." This seems unlikely. While a more southerly route such as Hodge's is geographically conceivable for persons bound for Acoma, it would make no sense for a route to Chia/Zia, which Alvarado states diverges from the one he followed. See map 3. Frederick W. Hodge, *History of Hawikuh, New Mexico, One of the So-Called Cities of Cíbola* (Los Angeles: Southwest Museum, 1937), 42, and fol. 1r of this document. As it is today, the feast of the beheading of San Juan was celebrated in 1540 on August 29. Cháves, *Espejo de navegantes*, 88. For geographical information, see the entries for Cíbola and Acuco in Appendix 2.

23. If, as Riley and Manson have suggested (see note 22, this document), the Alvarado party made its departure from Mats'a:kya, then the party's travel eastward would certainly have been by way of the Zuni River and the Pescado Valley to the area of modern Ramah, New Mexico. En route the group would have passed a number of ruins estimated archaeologically to have been abandoned in the thirteenth and fourteenth centuries. The very large *ciudad* mentioned by Alvarado here may correspond to the site known as Heshotauthla (LA 15605). It and "a very large cluster of earlier pueblos" identified in its vicinity by Keith Kintigh and his associates could have seemed "exceedingly large." Keith Kintigh, *Settlement, Subsistence, and Society in Late Zuni Prehistory* (Tucson: University of Arizona Press, 1985), 22, 56; Keith Kintigh, personal communication, Aug. 7, 2003. Before reaching Heshotauthla, Alvarado would have passed two known smaller sites, Yellowhouse (Zuni Archeology Program site NM:J3:99) and Spier 81 (Zuni Archeology Program site NM:12:J3:147). These could have been two of the fortresslike buildings Alvarado refers to. The third would remain unlocated at this time. Kintigh, *Settlement, Subsistence, and Society*, 22, 25, 44.

24. *Piedras berroqueñas*, or granite stones, probably refer to basalt building stones, because that is the only masonry material other than sandstone found in the archaeological ruins of the region. The next large ruin (actually cluster of ruins) east of Heshotauthla, following the Río Pescado fork of the Zuni River, comprises three ruins surrounding Pescado Springs. They are Pescado West (Zuni Archeology Program site NM:I3:4), Lower Pescado (Zuni Archeology Program site NM:12:I3:6), and Upper Pescado (LA 9108). At least one of these ruins (Lower Pescado) includes basalt building stones. Together, the three sites may total about

1,000 rooms—certainly a place of *ciudad* size. This same sequence of ruins was noted by Lt. James H. Simpson in 1849. Kintigh, *Settlement, Subsistence, and Society*, 22, 50, 55; James H. Simpson, *Navaho Expedition: Journal of a Military Reconnaissance from Santa Fe, New Mexico, to the Navaho Country, Made in 1849*, ed. Frank McNitt (Norman: University of Oklahoma Press, 1964), 120–24. Although there are a number of other ruins of equal age farther east in El Morro Valley, along the route to Acoma, Alvarado does not mention them. We suggest that is because he is only ticking off the ruins between Mats'a:kya and the point where the routes to Chia and Acoma divide, as a guide for those who want to travel to one place or the other. In other words, he may not have been interested in the ruins per se but rather as route indicators.

25. Riley and Manson discuss a number of route possibilities in this region and conclude that this fork was "in the Ramah area." They also suggest that Alvarado was mistaken about the destinations of the two routes. If, however, the identification of the *ciudad* with granite/basalt stones suggested in note 24 is correct, then the route division would have to be some five miles or so west of the Riley-Manson suggestion—that is, not far from Pescado Springs. Indeed, nineteenth-century maps reveal just such a route division near Pescado. One fork heads northeast, crossing the Zuni Mountains by way of a prominent defile, then skirting the western and northern margins of Mount Taylor and arriving at Zia Pueblo. The other continues east, swings around the north end of the Malpais lava flows, and then dips southward to Acoma. Riley and Manson, "Cíbola-Tiguex Route," 355; Kintigh, *Settlement, Subsistence, and Society*, 22; "Map Showing Location of the Pueblos of Arizona and New Mexico," in James Stevenson, "Illustrated Catalogue of the Collections Obtained from the Indians of New Mexico and Arizona in 1879," in *Second Annual Report of the Bureau of Ethnology to the Secretary of the Smithsonian Institution, 1880–1881* (Washington, DC: Government Printing Office, 1883), facing page 319. Chia, or Zia, has been identified with Old Zia Pueblo, the ruins of which lie along the lower Jemez River in Sandoval County, New Mexico (map 3). The expedition to Tierra Nueva did not visit or make note of any other pueblos along the Jemez River affiliated with Chia. Conspicuous by its absence is any mention of the pueblo later known as Santa Ana. Indeed, it seems likely that Santa Ana did not come into existence until after the departure of the expedition to Tierra Nueva. Albert H. Schroeder, "Pueblos Abandoned in Historic Times," in Ortiz, *Southwest*, vol. 9, 244.

26. This description applies equally well to many of the houses in Acoma today, particularly those along the northernmost street.

27. The reference here is most likely to the area around modern Laguna Pueblo, New Mexico. H&R, 183 n. 5, agree with Hodge in this identification, as do Riley and Manson, "Cíbola-Tiguex Route," 357.

28. Río de Nuestra Señora = Río de Tiguex, or modern Rio Grande. For geographical information, see the entry for Río de Tiguex in Appendix 2. As it still is today, in 1540, September 8 was celebrated in the Roman Catholic Church as the birth date of the Virgin Mary. Cháves, *Espejo de navegantes*, 89.

29. "Terraced stories," *terrados*. *Terrado* contrasts with *alto*, a more generic term, in that it refers to stories of a building that are stepped back from the perimeter, forming a usable space or terrace on the roof of the story below. Covarrubias, 917: "por otro nombre dicho azutea, porque el suelo es terrizo."

30. This is evidently a reference to the same towns in or near the Galisteo Basin in New Mexico (map 3) that are mentioned by Castañeda de Nájera as having been destroyed by the Teyas. See Document 28, fol. 113v. "Destroyed by," *destruido de*. De, DRAE, 663: "se usa en ciertas construcciones con el agente de la pasiva." H&R, 183, misconstrue "de" in this case as a simple preposition of possession. "Dyed yellow," *enbijados*: *en* (to become) + *bija* (annatto, a yellow dye) + verbal ending.

31. This seems to refer to the people of Quivira and suggests a possible close relationship between the Teyas and the Quivirans.

32. "Offer me their friendship," *darme la paz*. DRAE, 1553: "saludarle besándole en el rostro en señal de amistad."

33. Presumably this refers to the oral account made by the guides.

34. The "Relación del Suceso" mentions Yuraba (Taos) as having 18 sections. Reference here is evidently to the same pueblo. Document 29, fol. 3r.

35. The reference is to feather-decorated prayer sticks and pollen or cornmeal, all of which continue to have ceremonial uses among the Pueblos today. See, for instance, Charles H. Lange, *Cochiti: A New Mexico Pueblo, Past and Present* (Albuquerque: University of New Mexico Press, 1990), 229, 258; and Green, *Zuñi*, 254.

36. A number of members of the rose family are native to the Pueblo areas of New Mexico, including Apache plume (*Fallugia paradoxa*) and cliffrose (*Cowania*

mexicana), both of which could have been in bloom at this time of year (early to mid-September). Pauline M. Patraw, *Flowers of the Southwest Mesas*, 6th ed. (Globe, AZ: Southwest Parks and Monuments Association, 1977), 26–27.

37. The three entries on the document's cover are in the hands of three separate *escribanos*.

38. Albanares = *albañales*.

39. A sus casas. *CDI*, 3:512, omits the phrase "a sus casas," as of course do Mora, 197, and H&R, 183. Surprisingly, Winship 384, also omits it.

40. Entre Unas rriVeras. This seems to be a scribal error for "en unas riberas."

41. De madera y estos Dan Vuelta A todo el barrio A la rredonda. *CDI*, 3:513, omits this entire passage, as do Mora, 198, H&R, 184, and Winship, 385.

Document 25. Letter from Viceroy Mendoza to Fernández de Oviedo, October 6, 1541

1. Fol. 457v.

2. Gerbi, *Nature in the New World*, 169, 171, 172; Helen Nader, *The Mendoza Family in the Spanish Renaissance, 1350 to 1550* (New Brunswick, NJ: Rutgers University Press, 1979), 199. See the introduction to Document 2 for fuller information about Ramusio and his links to Oviedo and Diego Hurtado de Mendoza, the viceroy's brother.

3. Fol. 457v.

4. Fol. 458v.

5. Ibid.

6. Vázquez de Coronado refers to this April 20, 1541, letter in another letter he wrote to the viceroy after returning from Quivira. Unfortunately, the whereabouts of that April letter is unknown. See Document 26, fol. 1r.

7. Fol. 458v.

8. Ibid. Mendoza is referring to the letter dated October 20, 1541, which probably did not reach the Ciudad de México before late December of that year. Document 26.

9. See Document 7, introduction and note 15.

10. For biographical information about Antonio de Mendoza, see the entry in Appendix 1.

11. The reference here is to Gonzalo Fernández de Oviedo y Valdés himself, on the island of Hispaniola. See the introduction to this document for more information about the chronicler.

12. Española = Hispaniola. For geographical information about Hispaniola, see Document 7, note 21. Founded by Bartolomé de Colón in 1496, Santo Domingo was the third Spanish settlement in the New World. From the time of its founding, it served as the capital of the island of Hispaniola. Bakewell, *History of Latin America*, 72.

13. The term *mexicanos*, seen here in its original sense, refers to the Nahuatl-speaking inhabitants of the Valley of Mexico, the Mexica.

14. The region of Guazacalco (Guazacualco) comprised what is in Mexico today the easternmost part of Veracruz and western Tabasco states. The region was named for the river that flows through it. Gerhard, *Historical Geography*, 137–41.

15. According to indigenous Mexican traditions reconstructed by Wigberto Jiménez Moreno, a tenth-century Toltec ruler and priest named Topiltzin established his seat of authority at Tula, north of Mexico City, but was later exiled. He was active in and afterward identified with the penitent cult of Quetzalcoatl, the Feathered Serpent, which was widespread in Mesoamerica. The memory of this historical personage became conflated with traditions of the deity he worshiped. In that half-human, half-supernatural guise, Topiltzin/Quetzalcoatl figures in many stories tracing the trajectory of Nahua migrations. Coe, *Mexico*, 124–25.

16. For the definition of a *pie*, see Document 17, note 41.

17. This distribution of parts seems to match contemporaneous accounts of ritual killing of enemy warriors by Nahuas and the distribution of their body parts for consumption and preservation as trophies. See, for instance, Inga Clendinnen, *Aztecs: An Interpretation* (Cambridge: Cambridge University Press, 1991).

18. Montezuma Xocoyotl was the tenth ruler of the Mexica state, from 1502 to 1520. The splendor of his person and the empire he controlled, as described in the letters of Hernán Cortés and other contemporary reports, fired European imaginations for decades. See particularly Cortés's second letter. Hassig, *Time, History, and Belief*, 21; Hernán Cortés, "Segunda carta-relación—30 de octubre de 1520," in Cortés, *Cartas de Relación*, 30–100. The name México, now applied to the vast

Estados Unidos de México, in the sixteenth century pertained only to the Ciudad de México (the prehistoric island metropolis of Tenochtitlan and Tlatelolco) and its subject environs. Gerhard, *Historical Geography*, 180.

19. "Cazonzi" was the title of the principal leader of the protohistoric Purépecha people (popularly known as Tarascans) of what is now the Mexican state of Michoacán. The Cazonzi was said to possess large quantities of gold, silver, and jewels. Eugene R. Craine and Reginald C. Reindorp, trans. and eds., *The Chronicles of Michoacán* (Norman: University of Oklahoma Press, 1970), vii–xvi, 78–79.

20. "Recognize . . . as their overlord," *reconoçian*. *DRAE*, 1743: "confesar con cierta publicidad la dependencia, subordinación o vasallaje en que se está respecto de otro."

21. Although gambling may have been forbidden, it is unlikely that the ban was strictly observed. It has been written about similar claims concerning sixteenth-century sailors that "everyone played games of chance on board ships, and everyone knew it was prohibited by royal ordinances." Pérez-Mallaína, *Spain's Men of the Sea*, 154.

22. The clause "up to the present they [those engaged in reconnaissance] have found [them] in abundance" is ambiguous. It could mean that all the items in question had been found in abundance or that only the last named item, food, had been.

23. The reference here is to the Coronado expedition's going to Quivira.

24. "By," *en*. *DRAE*, 815: "con verbos de percepción . . . seguida de un substantivo, por."

25. For biographical information about Pedro de Alvarado, see the introduction to Document 20. For geographical information about the Mar del Sur, see the entry in Appendix 2.

26. This concession to Mendoza is mentioned in Document 20, fols. 1v and 2v.

27. Mendoza refers here to the protracted civil war that broke out in Peru among rival conquistadores in 1537. It resulted in the deaths of both of the principal collaborators in the conquest of Peru, Francisco Pizarro and Diego de Almagro, and was not brought to a definitive end until 1548. Bakewell, *History of Latin America*, 109–11.

28. The agreement between Alvarado and Mendoza had been formally concluded in November 1540 with the signing of a contract between the two. Document 20.

29. According to a map published by Antonio de Herrera y Tordesillas in 1601, the archipelagos of Lequio Mayor and Lequio Menor lay off the coast of China (Catayo, Catay, Cathay), north of the Tropic of Cancer and between the Philippines and Japan. The Lequios are the two clusters of islands now known as the Ryukyu Islands, which include Okinawa. "Lequio" is a variant pronunciation of "Ryukyu" resulting from metathesis of *r* and *l*. *Enciclopedia universal*, 23:1349; Lloyd, *Latin to Spanish*, 347–48.

30. Alvarado went at Mendoza's request to assist Nueva Galicia's acting governor, Cristóbal de Oñate, in putting an end to the native uprising known as the Mixtón War. Oviedo himself tells this story in more detail later in his *Historia*. PTBOviedo, 4:356. For geographical information about Nueva Galicia and Guadalajara, see the entries in Appendix 2.

31. In the event, Mendoza mounted a large force of Europeans and Indian allies and departed from the Ciudad de México during the first days of January 1542. He joined forces with Cristóbal de Oñate and succeeded in quelling the uprising. Tello, 442–73.

32. "To be improving," *ir en aumento*. *DRAE*, 230.

33. "Latitudes," *alturas*. Reference here is to "alturas del ecuador," or angular distance of a location from the equator. *DRAE*, 117. See also note 36, this document.

34. During the period from November 1535 to October 1541, only two total eclipses of the moon were visible from both Toledo and the Ciudad de México, one on the night of November 16–17, 1537, and the other on the night of March 11–12, 1541. Fred Espenak, "Catalog of Lunar Eclipses: Lunar Eclipses, 1501 to 1600," (NASA/Goddard Space Flight Center, 1999), 6, http://sunearth.gsfc.nasa.gov/eclipse/LEcat.

35. This longitudinal distance converts to 120 degrees 38 minutes 30 seconds. With Toledo at 4 degrees 1 minute west and the Ciudad de México at 99 degrees 9 minutes west, the currently accepted figure is 95 degrees 8 minutes of longitude between the two. Mendoza's number is thus grossly inaccurate, his difficulty being the lack of accurate and consistent timekeeping devices and an unwarranted supposition of simultaneity of observation. See Dava Sobel, *Longitude: The True Story of a Lone Genius Who Solved the Greatest Scientific Problem of His Time* (London: Fourth Estate, 1996).

36. This "incorrectness" of the existing pilots' books may help explain the errors in the contemporary latitude measurements provided by fray Marcos de Niza, the author of the "Relación del Suceso," Juan Rodríguez Cabrillo, and many others. See Document 6, fol. 5r; Document 29, fol. 2r; Document 6, notes 78 and 131; and Document 29, notes 50 and 107. "Pilots' books," *regim(i)entos. DRAE*, 1755: "libro en que se daban a los pilotos las reglas y preceptos de su facultad."

37. Francisca Pacheco had married Iñigo López de Mendoza, the second Conde de Tendilla, in 1480. She died in 1507. Nader, *Mendoza Family*, 152, 270. Juan Pacheco, the first Marqués de Villena, had led a coup against King Enrique IV, eventually supporting Isabel to succeed Enrique to the Castilian throne. Meanwhile, the Mendozas were of the opposing faction. But in 1473 the issue was resolved, and the two families (Pacheco and Mendoza) reconciled. Juan Pacheco died in 1474. An element of the continuing reconciliation was the marriage of his daughter Francisca to Iñigo López de Mendoza. Nader, *Mendoza Family*, 22, 51–54, 270. *Maestre* in this case refers to a high official in one of the military orders.

38. Truxo = *trajo*. Lloyd, *Latin to Spanish*, 365.

39. Desorden = *exceso. DRAE*, 723.

40. El dia de *hoy*. PTBOviedo, 4:252, interpolates "en el dia de hoy."

41. *En que* yo toviesse parte. We have inserted "en" because the construction ordinarily requires it.

42. A la fin. Although now a masculine noun, "fin" was formerly ambiguous in gender. *DRAE*, 970.

43. Caudal. PTBOviedo, 4:253, incorrectly has "calidad."

44. (^1542). This correction of the date by the *escribano* suggests that the manuscript is a second-generation copy rather than Oviedo's original. The incorrect date of 1542 was probably picked up when the copyist's eye strayed forward to the beginning of the next chapter, which consists of a transcript of a later letter to Oviedo from Mendoza that refers to 1542 in its opening lines.

Document 26. Vázquez de Coronado's Letter to the King, October 20, 1541

1. This volume includes copies of two other signed letters from Vázquez de Coronado, Documents 1 and 3. Document 19, also from the captain general, is at a farther remove from his own words. It doubtless went through the same scribal filter described here but in addition was then translated into Italian and edited by a contemporary collector and publisher of documents. See the introduction to Document 19. See also Document 1, note 16.

2. Fol. 1r.

3. Ibid.

4. Fol. 1v.

5. Ibid.

6. Ibid.

7. Ibid.

8. Fol. 2r.

9. Ibid.

10. Fol. 2v.

11. *CDI*, 3:363–69.

12. Ibid., 13:261–68.

13. Winship, 364–69.

14. H&R, 185–90.

15. Mora, 173–76.

16. The reference here is to the king's letter confirming Vázquez de Coronado's appointment to lead the expedition, a copy of which is published in this volume as Document 10. Modern research by us and others (Bolton, 474) has not located the original of this April 1541 letter. For geographical information, see the entry for Tiguex in Appendix 2.

17. "Detailed," *particular*; similar to *particularizar. DRAE*, 1536: "expresar una cosa con todas sus circunstancias y particularidades."

18. "Has probably ordered reviewed from my letters," "lo *h*abra mandado Ver por mis cartas." This may point toward Vázquez de Coronado's familiarity with Consejo and court procedures in which officials would draw each other's attention to particular portions of messages and suggest that they be given special review. H&R, 185, ignore the word *mandado* and render this as "must have noted by my letters." Winship, 364, on the other hand, did not ignore *mandado* but interpreted *ver* oddly, with this result: "ordered me to relate in my letters."

Certainly this is a clumsy and unclear passage; it may indicate an error on the part of the *escribano*.

19. Here the expedition is once again revealed as in pursuit of "civilized" peoples who produced valuable commodities.

20. The captain general seems skeptical, as indeed he had every right to be, having already been disappointed by the reports of fray Marcos, as well as by the natives of Tierra Nueva. Indeed, as Diego López testified in 1545, even before the expedition left Chiametla there was "no hope that they would come across anything [worthwhile]." Flint, *Great Cruelties*, 396.

21. All dates cited in this letter are in the Julian calendar. To coordinate them with dates provided by other documents reporting the same events, it is easiest to convert these dates to the Gregorian calendar, which can be done by adding 10 days. That would render the date of departure from Tiguex as May 3, 1541, in the modern calendar. See Flint, "Reconciling the Calendars," 151–63.

22. Vázquez de Coronado is evidently referring to the generally level land east of the Pecos River in the Canadian River drainage of east-central New Mexico and on the southern Great Plains, including the Llano Estacado (maps 1 and 4). Juan Jaramillo also considered the plains to begin east of the Pecos. Document 30, fol. 2v. See also Flint, "Reconciling the Calendars," 151–63. The "Relación del Suceso" is in essential agreement, giving the distance traveled on the plains as "three hundred and thirty leagues." Document 29, fol. 5r.

23. For discussion of the possible archaeological identification of these nomadic peoples, see the entry for Querechos in Appendix 1.

24. "Pavilion-like tents," *pabellones*. This reference is to tepees. See Document 29, note 110. "Dressed and greased" is an abbreviated description of the Querechos' process of converting hides to pliable, water-resistant leather. "Have their privacy," *se meten. Meter = encerrar* = retire from the world. *DRAE*, 823, 1365.

25. See also Document 29, note 111.

26. "Best disposed," *mas bien dispuesto*. This phrase is extremely ambiguous. It could refer to the Querechos' physical appearance, as H&R, 186, and Winship, 367, interpreted it. It could also refer to their tractability or even their bravery. Without contextual support one way or another, we have chosen to retain the ambiguity.

27. This inability "to give me a report" is ambiguous. It could indicate either translation difficulties or ignorance of the subject. But in light of the apparent ease of communication described later, on fol. 1v, between the guides and the Teyas (possibly both Caddoan speakers), mutual unintelligibility between the guides and the Querechos (Athapaskan speakers) seems the most likely possibility.

28. "Some plains so without landmarks," *unos llanos tan sin seña*. This statement marks the arrival of the expedition on the Llano Estacado of the Texas Panhandle. See maps 1 and 4.

29. "Became confused," *desatinaron*. A word is missing in the original document, either *se*, which would convert the verb to the passive voice, or *nos*, which would render the phrase as an active undertaking of the guides: "they confused us." Either interpretation seems possible. If we are to take El Turco's later confession at face value, perhaps the active voice is preferable. Nevertheless, we have used the passive construction, as did H&R, 186, and Winship, 367.

30. For identification of the Teyas, see Appendix 1.

31. "Decorated," *labrados*. This could be either tattooed or painted, though the use of distinctive facial painting seems to have been most common among these people. See Nancy Parrott Hickerson, *The Jumanos: Hunters and Traders of the South Plains* (Austin: University of Texas Press, 1994), 116–17, 212.

32. Obtaining this report implies that the expedition's guides were able to speak with the Teyas but not the Querechos and so may have spoken a language related to that of the Teyas. Compare the difficulty of communication with the Querechos mentioned on fol. 1r.

33. This could refer to either the Teyas or the guides making Vázquez de Coronado understand. There is no way to decide.

34. By his own assertion on fol. 1v, the captain was already skeptical of the reports of Quivira before his departure from Tiguex. The reference to muddy water indicates that the bison were so numerous that they had been drinking from and wading in most of the playa lakes that the expedition came across.

35. The danger Vázquez de Coronado refers to here was probably from constipation. According to Sophie and Michael Coe, because of "the chronic constipation with which the invaders were afflicted, through diet which was almost all meat and lard, with few if any fruits and vegetables, the conquistadores searched for native Mexican laxatives as avidly as they did for aphrodisiacs." Sophie D. Coe and Michael D. Coe, *The True History of Chocolate* (London: Thames and Hudson, 2000), 95.

36. For biographical information, see the entry for Tristán de Luna y Arellano in Appendix 1.

37. The "Relación del Suceso" states that "after thirty days' journey we found the Río de Quivira," a statement with which Juan Jaramillo agrees. According to both of these sources, it was six or seven days' travel from there to Quivira and 25 leagues (perhaps five days) farther on to the most distant point they reached. This totals 40 or 41 days, extremely close to the captain general's count here. Document 29, fol. 4v; Document 30, fols. 3v and 4r.

38. Using dung as fuel was a common practice for hundreds of years among people who lived on or crossed the Great Plains.

39. For geographical information, see the entry for Quivira in Appendix 2.

40. Under the rubric "other *provincias*," Vázquez de Coronado would likely have included the Querecho *rancherías*, the Teya settlements, Taraque, and Arahey.

41. The rendering of obedience would have consisted of not demonstrably objecting to the reading of the *requerimiento*. In addition, a cross was erected and formal possession was declared, although, according to Juan Jaramillo, this was done not in the natives' presence but at a place away from the settlements of Quivira. Document 30, fol. 4v. For an example of a *requerimiento*, see Appendix 4.

42. "Well-proportioned," *de buena disposiçion*. In this case *disposición* seems to refer to the women's physical appearance, because further physical description follows. For contrast, see note 26, this document.

43. Although "Moorish women" appears to be a neutral descriptive statement, there is likely a disparaging component as well, given the climate in Christian Spain at the time, in which Moors were commonly viewed as enemies and infidels. Gómez Vozmediano, *Mudéjares y moriscos*, 43–70.

44. This gift of a piece of copper agrees with the accounts in the "Relación del Suceso" and Castañeda de Nájera's *relación*. Document 29, fol. 5r; Document 28, fol. 88r.

45. "Small copper bells," *caxcabeles*. By means of comparative analysis, Victoria Vargas has determined that all pre-*entrada* copper bells in what is now the American Southwest and northwest Mexico were produced in western Mexico and traded north. Victoria D. Vargas, *Copper Bell Trade Patterns in the Prehistoric U.S. Southwest and Northwest Mexico* (Tucson: Arizona State Museum, University of Arizona, 1995).

46. Vázquez de Coronado reported what may have been a similar incident earlier at Cíbola, concerning small gemstone fragments. See Document 19, fol. 361v. Indian allies and servants originating from central Mexico might well have possessed small utensils and items of adornment made of gold. On the other hand, Vázquez de Coronado may be referring to Moorish or European slaves, who might have owned or pilfered golden objects from their owners.

47. "I am unable to discover the truth about its source from the previously mentioned individual," *de otra parte yo no le puedo hallar el nasçimiento*. *Hallar*, *DRAE*, 1086: "descubrir la verdad de algo." If the expedition's practice in regard to El Turco is any guide, this suggests that the native who had the piece of possible gold might have been subjected to torture in an attempt to extract information from him about its origin. The "previously mentioned individual" is evidently the *prinçipal* who wore the piece of copper.

48. This is one of the few references in the Coronado expedition documents to problems in communication with native people, something that must have been a frequent difficulty.

49. "Whether there might be some place," *habria donde*. H&R, 188, and Winship, 368, ignore the explicit reference to place and instead make the focus of the phrase "anything." This exhibits a subtle though fundamental misunderstanding on the part of these excellent scholars about the targets of subjugation and conquest, which were first and foremost places—populous and wealthy places over which conquistadores could exercise jurisdiction for the crown and be recompensed through tribute.

50. Converting from *leguas legales*, this would be about 2,370 miles, which closely matches a straight-line map distance (by way of Compostela, the Río Sonora Valley, Zuni, Pecos, and the Caprock Canyons) of approximately 2,290 miles. See maps 1 and 2.

51. If, as is generally thought, Quivira was a group of ancestral Wichita towns in Rice, McPherson, Butler, and Cowley Counties, Kansas (maps 1 and 4), then modern latitude measurements put the reading at about 38.5 degrees. See Waldo R. Wedel, *Archaeological Remains in Central Kansas and Their Possible Bearing on the Location of Quivira*, Smithsonian Miscellaneous Collections 101, no. 7 (Washington, DC: Smithsonian Institution, 1942), and Waldo R. Wedel, "Coronado,

Quivira, and Kansas: An Archeologist's View," lecture delivered Nov. 3, 1990, at the Coronado-Quivira Museum, Lyons, Kansas. See also the introduction to this document for further discussion of the latitude of Quivira. For a general discussion of the inaccuracy of latitude measurements during early modern times, see Document 29, note 50.

52. "Walnuts," *nueces*. Most likely the reference here is to black walnuts, rather than pecans, the native distribution of which in Kansas is confined to the eastern portion. Charles Sprague Sargent, *Manual of the Trees of North America*, 2 vols. (Boston: Houghton Mifflin, 1922; reprint, New York: Dover, 1965, 1:172, 178–79; page citations are to the reprint edition). "Mulberries," *moras*. It is not altogether certain which fruit is being referred to here, because both mulberries and blackberries would have been known to Europeans of the day and both are native to central Kansas. Sargent, *Manual of the Trees*, 1:330. *Mora* and *moral*, Covarrubias, 762: "la fruta del moral"; 763: "árbol conocido." The Covarrubias definitions indicate the use of *mora* for the fruit of a tree (therefore mulberry) rather than of a bramble (blackberry).

53. This is an interesting statement in that the letter makes no mention of the garroting of El Turco, on the basis of which the captain general was later accused of abuse of Indians. Flint, *Great Cruelties*, passim.

54. "Whether there was," *si habia*. Either Vázquez de Coronado or his *escribano* seems unfamiliar with the subjunctive, which would have been appropriate here. Nevertheless, just a few words later the subjunctive *pudiese* appears.

55. This reference to disappointment over the absence of precious metals and populous places is another indication of the goals of the expedition.

56. "Grass straw," *cañas*. As *DRAE*, 393, states, *cañas* could refer to the stems of many gramineous plants, from grasses to pond reeds. Archaeological and ethnographic evidence, though, strongly suggests that Quiviran houses and other buildings were thatched with bundles of tall, stout grass. Tom Witty, "The Tobias Archeological Site/Museum of the Quivira Indian," unpublished paper, 1990, in possession of the editors. See fig. 28.8.

57. "Thus," *por manera que = de suerte que*. *DRAE*, 1306.

58. "I believe," *creyendo*. We have translated the present participle here as present indicative. This sentence and those that immediately follow make the most sense when Vázquez de Coronado is made the subject of *creyendo* (although no subject is specified in the document). H&R, 189, and Winship, 369, however, made the Indian guides the subject. "Que por ser" and "que por consejo" are parallel constructions, a fact that H&R and Winship ignored.

59. Vázquez de Coronado is certainly not speaking here about Quivira, which he has just described as well watered. Instead, he must be referring to the Llano Estacado, where, he said earlier, the water was poor and largely stagnant.

60. Testimony of Juan de Zaldívar in 1544 claimed that El Turco had been ordered to act as he did by Bigotes and the *cacique* from Ciuique. Flint, *Great Cruelties*, 260.

61. "Look after the safety," *a poner recaudo*. *A recaudo*, *DRAE*, 1738: "bien custodiado, con seguridad, ú[sase] m[as] con verbos *estar, poner,* etc."

62. This statement is a summary of the entire letter and the message most important for the king to receive.

63. That is, the Río de Tiguex boasted the largest, most "civilized" population. In contrast, Juan Jaramillo insisted 20 years later that Quivira was the most promising land, because European motivations had shifted somewhat over that period. See the introduction to Document 30.

64. For geographical information, see the entries for Cíbola, Mar del Sur, and Mar del Norte in Appendix 2.

65. This is a reference to the *maestre de campo*'s imminent return to Spain to assume the title vacated by the death of his brother. See Document 28, fol. 127r, and Document 29, fol. 5v. For biographical information, see the entry for García López de Cárdenas in Appendix 1.

66. Again, this is according to the Julian calendar.

67. All of this closing is in Vázquez de Coronado's own hand.

68. Los ojos. Mora 173 mistakenly has "mis ojos."

69. De ylla a Ver. *CDI*, 13:262, mistakenly truncates this to "de ir a ver."

70. Me quisieron guiar. *CDI*, 13:262, has "me quisieran guiar."

71. Yo los anduVe. *CDI*, 13:262, omits "los."

72. Les halle. Mora, 173, incorrectly copies "los halle."

73. Los llaman querechos. *CDI*, 13:262, has instead "les llaman querechos."

74. Se Viste. Mora, 173, omits "se."

75. Mudandose con ellas. *CDI*, 13:263, mistakenly has "mudandose con ellos."

76. Que yo hasta *hoy* he Visto. *CDI*, 13:263, omits "hasta hoy."

77. Las guias. Mora, 174, mistakenly has "los guias," an error repeated throughout her transcription.

78. De buena yerva. *CDI*, 13:263, mistakenly has "de buenas yerbas."

79. Las casas de paja. *CDI*, 13:263, mistakenly has "la casa de paja."

80. Harta pena. Mora, 174, omits "harta."

81. Hartos la bebi. Mora, 174, gratuitously inserts "veces" and converts the phrase into "hartas veces la bebi." *CDI*, 13:263, mistakenly has "harto la bebi."

82. Nos acabo. Mora, 174, incorrectly has "les acabo."

83. Hubo de aguas. Mora, 174, incorrectly has "que habian de aguas."

84. VentaJa. *CDI*, 13:265, mistakenly has "bentajas."

85. Para alla. *CDI*, 13:265, mistakenly has "para ella."

86. Le enVie. *CDI*, 13:265, mistakenly has "le envió."

87. Ni se de donde. *CDI*, 13:265, mistakenly omits "se."

88. Muy buenas aguas. *CDI*, 13:266, erroneously has "muy buenas ganas."

89. Halle çiruelas como las de españa. Mora, 175, inadvertently skips back a line to render this as "halle las cosas de españa."

90. Por ser el Camino. Mora, 175, omits "ser."

91. Lo *h*abian hecho. *CDI*, 13:266, mistakenly has "le habina hecho."

92. Don garçi lopez de cardenas. Mora, 176, erroneously has "don Gonzalo Pérez de Cárdenas."

Document 27. Disposal of the Juan Jiménez Estate, 1542 (Copy, 1550)

1. Affidavit of testimony on behalf of Francisco Vázquez de Coronado, Culiacán, 1545, in AGI, Patronato, 216, N.2, "Affidavit of testimony on behalf of Francisco Vázquez de Coronado, Culiacán, 1545, in a legal action concerning Nuño de Cháves, Mexico City, 1566"; Flint, *Great Cruelties*, 358.

2. *Pasajeros*, 2: no. 2332; Document 12, fol. 6v.

3. Fols. 6r–7r.

4. Jorge Báez died between Tiguex and Cíbola during the expedition's return march. AGI, Patronato, 78A, N.l, R.6, "Jorge Báez."

5. This *cédula* is referred to on folio 32r.

6. We published a selection from AGI, Contratación, 5575, N.24, "Bienes de difuntos, Juan Jiménez, 1550 copy of August 13, 1545, original" in *New Mexico Historical Review*. Editor Durwood Ball kindly permitted re-publication of portions of that article here. Richard Flint and Shirley Cushing Flint, "A Death in Tiguex, 1542," *New Mexico Historical Review* 74, no. 3 (1999):247–70.

7. The previously known strictly contemporaneous documents are the muster roll from February 1540 (Document 12); the "Traslado de las Nuevas," probably August 1540 (Document 22); Vázquez de Coronado's letter to the viceroy from Cíbola, August 1540 (Document 19); a report presumed to be by Hernando de Alvarado, fall 1540 (Document 24); Vázquez de Coronado's letter to the king from Tiguex, October 1541 (Document 26); and the "Relación Postrera de Cíbola," a secondhand account, probably late 1541 (Document 23). The documents from 1541 and 1542 copied into AGI, Contratación, 5575, N.24, "Juan Jiménez," are these: a petition by Antón Negrín, Mexico City, September 1542; an *auto* (decision) by Antón Negrín and Jorge Báez, Coafor, February 1542; a record of the auction of Jiménez's goods, Coafor, March 1542; an inventory of Jiménez's goods, Coafor, February 1542; the record of delivery of Jiménez's goods to Negrín, Coafor, March 1542; an *auto* (judicial decree) denying Negrín's right to dispose of the goods, Mexico City, September 1542; a decision of the Audiencia de Nueva España reversing the previous decision, September 1542; and an *obligación* (liability) from Juan Jiménez to Juan Barragán, Tiguex, April 1541.

8. Nothing is known with certainty about Juan Barragán. However, a document in the Archivo Historico del Municipio de Colima, Protocolos, 1536–68, refers to the death of a person by that name on June 26, 1547. Hernando de Alvarado served as executor in this case. Mathes, "New Research in Mexico."

9. Flint, "Material Culture."

10. Indeed, more than 90 percent of all of the European members of the expedition who passed muster in Compostela in February 1540 declared that they had with them native arms and armor. In contrast, the amount of European metal armor was scant. Apart from the dozen or so most elite members of the expedition, most expedition members were said to have had none. See Document 12.

11. Fol. 9r.

12. Fol. 12r.

13. For comparison, Jiménez's tunic (*sayo*), jerkin (*jubón*), headgear (*caperusa*), shoes, and sandals, plus a breast band for a horse and two sacks, sold at auction in 1542 for 7 *pesos*. Fol. 6v.

14. For Jiménez's inability to sign his name, see fol. 22v.

15. The exact number of Europeans who participated in the Coronado expedition is unknown. From various documents we now know by name 358 European members of the expedition, including the eight newly revealed members. There is, however, the possibility of duplication of individuals in all the existing lists, owing to variations in the spelling of names. Nevertheless, the current number comes very close to the figure of 300 horsemen and 70 or 80 footmen provided in the 1546 testimony of Francisco Gorbalán. The February 1540 muster roll, on the other hand, lists only 224 horsemen and 62 footmen, a decided undercount. To the muster roll number, George Hammond and Agapito Rey added 48 names that appear in other documents, bringing their total to 334. We know by name only one black member of the expedition, Pedro, the *pregonero* (crier), revealed by the Jiménez document. Blacks are mentioned in the extant documents very infrequently; many European members reported that they took black slaves with them but did not indicate numbers. Thus, we cannot even begin to guess the number of black people who participated in the expedition. The largest component of the expedition was made up of Indians from central and west Mexico. Estimates of their numbers range from 1,000 to 1,500. Of these, we know only 11 by name and place of origin. Though persons of color made up the overwhelming bulk of the expedition, information about them and their activities still eludes us for the most part. It is not at all difficult to suppose the total population of the expedition to have been 2,000 or more. See the introduction to Document 12 and Appendix 3. See also AGI, Justicia, 1021, N.2, Pieza 5, "Probanza de López de Cárdenas"; Document 12; and H&R, 104–8.

16. Pedro de Castañeda de Nájera wrote that in 1541–42 the Pueblo world comprised 66 pueblos with a total of 20,000 inhabitants. The pueblo of Cicique (Pecos) might have had 2,000 residents (judging from Castañeda's estimate of 500 warriors), but all the others were much smaller. Document 28, fols. 112r and 115v–116r.

17. Document 28, fols. 75v and 127v.

18. Flint, *Great Cruelties*, 358.

19. Document 28, fol. 138r.

20. Document 28, fol. 135v; AGI, Patronato, 78A, N.l, R.6, "Jorge Báez."

21. By the spring of 1542 this must have been a familiar leg of travel for some members of the expedition, because of movement between the settlement of San Gerónimo in Sonora and the New Mexico Pueblo world. See map 2; Document 30, fol. 2v.

22. Fol. 11r.

23. Many of the testamentary protocols are spelled out in a royal *cédula* of February 17, 1531, which is transcribed in Tello, 152–56. A much more extensive compilation of the legal requirements incident to property of the deceased, dating from the thirteenth century but in widespread use for centuries, is in the *Siete Partidas*. See specifically "The Sixth Partida," in *Siete Partidas*, 5:1175–1302.

24. The letters *r* and *x* are often indistinguishable in this *escribano*'s hand. In conformance with the various spellings of the name of this pueblo in other documents, all of which end in *r*, we have rendered it "Coafor." Flint, *Great Cruelties*, 284, 358. For geographical information about Tiguex, see the entry in Appendix 2.

25. Despite his pivotal role in the affairs of Juan Jiménez, all that is known about Antón Negrín comes from this document. For biographical information about Hernando Caballero, see Document 11, note 28. Largely at the instigation of Hernán Cortés and his supporters, royal *cédulas* of May and June 1543 directed *licenciado* Francisco Tello de Sandoval, a member of the Consejo de Indias, to conduct a *visita* of all the royal officials in Nueva España. Tello de Sandoval was canon of the cathedral in Sevilla, Spain, and a member of the Consejo de Indias from 1543 until 1558, when he became president of that body. In Nueva España his investigations from 1544 through 1546 raised the ire of many and, according to Lorenzo de Tejada, split the viceroyalty into rancorous factions. The *visitador* eventually brought charges against the president and three *oidores* of the *audiencia*, as well as numerous lesser functionaries. In 1546 the king recalled Tello de Sandoval to Spain under pressure from the viceroy's brother Luis Hurtado de Mendoza, who had become president of the Consejo de Indias. Two years later the Consejo absolved the viceroy and chastised the former *visitador*. Ernesto Schäfer, *Las Rúbricas del Consejo Real y Supremo de las Indias desde la fundación del consejo en 1524*

hasta la terminación del reinado de los Austrias (Sevilla: Universidad de Sevilla, 1934; reprint, Nendeln, Liechtenstein: Klaus Reprint, 1975, 4; page citation is to reprint edition); Arthur Aiton, "The Secret Visita against Viceroy Mendoza," in *New Spain and the Anglo-American West: Historical Contributions Presented to Herbert Eugene Bolton,* vol. 1 (Los Angeles: privately printed, 1932), 1–7; AGI, Indiferente, 1093, R.2, N.16, "Letter, Tello de Sandoval to the king, San Lucar de Barrameda, November 3, 1543"; AGI, Mexico, 68, R.13, N.38, "Carta de Lorenzo de Tejada a Marqués de Mondejar, presidente del Consejo de Indias, April 24, 1547"; Pilar Arregui Zamorano, "Quejas sobre Incumplimiento de Oficio," in *La Audiencia de México según los visitadores (siglos XVI y XVII)* (México, DF: Universidad Nacional Autónoma de México, 1981), 111–60. Sebastián Vázquez was a native of Granada in the modern *comunidad* of Andalucía in Spain. He arrived in Nueva España in 1538. Two uncles of his served as *alcalde* of the court and secretary of the *audiencia,* respectively. Sebastián was married to Ana de Terrazas, daughter of Francisco de Terrazas. He held the office of *receptor* (a tribunal *escribano* in charge of taking proofs, making collections, and other judicial acts) until 1544. He emigrated to Perú in 1545 for lack of means to sustain himself in Nueva España. Icaza, 1: no. 278; Boyd-Bowman, 2: no. 4537.

26. The royal *escribano* Melchior Gómez is probably the native of Sevilla by that name who arrived in Nueva España in 1522 and was one of the first settlers of Puebla de los Ángeles. Icaza, 2: no. 700; Boyd-Bowman, 2: no. 9307. Andrés de Herrera had arrived in Nueva España with his wife in about 1529. He was one of the first settlers of Puebla de los Ángeles in 1532 and was a *vecino* there at least as late as 1549. Boyd-Bowman, 2: no. 9383.

27. Clearly, Negrín and other members of the Coronado expedition must have reached the Ciudad de México on their return trip by sometime in August or very early September 1542.

28. Gerónimo Ruiz de la Mota was a native of Burgos in the modern Spanish *comunidad* of Castilla y León. He arrived in Nueva España in 1521 in time for the final conquest of Tenochtitlan. He became a *vecino* of the Ciudad de México and then *alcalde ordinario* and *regidor* of the city. He married a daughter of Francisco de Orduña's (see note 83, this document). He held *encomiendas* in Chiapas. Icaza, 1: no. 125. Juan de Zaragosa was an *escribano* in the Ciudad de México and a *vecino* of Tenuxtitán. Son of Miguel de Zaragosa and Beatriz de la Fuente, Juan was a native of the *reino* of Aragon (possibly of the city of Zaragosa). He joined his father in Nueva España in 1523. On February 13, 1548, he received a coat of arms, primarily on the basis of his father's deeds. Icaza, 1: no. 185; Boyd-Bowman, 2: no. 12868; Sociedad de Bibliófos Españoles, *Nobiliario de conquistadores,* 232–33.

29. For geographical information, see the entry on Tierra Nueva in Appendix 2.

30. "There was none in that pueblo": no one there was licensed to practice as an *escribano* and notary.

31. Jorge Báez arrived in Nueva España with Narváez and served with Cortés in the conquest of Tenochtitlan. At the time of the Coronado expedition he was residing in Puebla de los Ángeles. Many years later his two daughters, Ana and María, stated that he was married to doña Luisa Báez. As this document shows, however, he also had a son, Rodrigo de Trujillo, with the native woman Luisa. The "surname" given to this son suggests the possibility that Báez himself was from Trujillo in the modern *provinicia* of Cáceres in the *comunidad* of Extremadura. AGI, Patronato, 78A, N.1, R.6, "Jorge Báez."

32. Báez died during the first ten days of April 1542, somewhere in what is now west-central New Mexico, perhaps along the Río San José or crossing the Zuni Mountains, as the expedition began its return trek from Tierra Nueva. AGI, Patronato, 78A, N.1, R.6, "Jorge Báez."

33. "Accepting," *oya. DRAE,* 1469: "admitir la autoridad petitiones, razonamientos o pruebas de las partes antes de resolver."

34. "Expeditionary force," *ejército. DRAE,* 795: "collectividad numerosa organizada para la realización de un fin."

35. For biographical information about Tristán de Luna y Arellano and Hernando Bermejo, see the entries in Appendix 1.

36. At the beginning of the expedition to Tierra Nueva, 15-year-old Alonso Álvarez del Valle was standard bearer for Vázquez de Coronado. Sometime during the winter of 1540–41 he lost or resigned his post. He had arrived in the New World on the same ship as Cristóbal de Escobar in 1537 or 1538. On the 1540 muster roll he is listed in Melgosa's infantry company. AGI, Patronato, 74, N.2, R.2, "Méritos y servicios, Alonso Rodríguez Para y de su hijo Juan que fueron descubridores y conquistadores de la provincia de Cíbola, November 9, 1575"; Flint, *Great Cruelties,* 312; Document 33, fol. 17v; Document 12.

37. "One night . . . while he was walking about on watch": This passage is ambiguous. It could mean either "on watch one night" or "on the first of the three overnight watches," that known as *de la noche.* The other two watches were traditionally designated *modorra* and *de la alba.* Cháves, *Espejo de navegantes,* 231.

38. This indicates that at least two pueblos that had been abandoned by the Tiguex were taken as residences by the expedition, at least one on one side of the Río de Tiguex/Rio Grande and at least one more on the opposite bank.

39. Antón Pérez Buscavida was a native of Conil de la Frontera, which was held by the Duque de Medina Sidonia in the sixteenth century and now is in the *provincia* of Cádiz in the Spanish *comunidad* of Andalucía. He had arrived in Nueva España in 1535. AGI, México, 1064, L.1\1\, "Informes de los conquistadores," fol. 251r.

40. "Obtain," *lleguen = alleguen. DRAE,* 120, 1281.

41. Possibly a native of Mondragón in the Basque *provincia* of Guipúzcoa, Juan Pérez de Vergara was Vázquez de Coronado's *mayordomo. Pasajeros,* 4: no. 407; AGI, Justicia, 339, N.1, R.1, "Residencia," pliego 9, fol. 30r. Jaque (or Jaco) de Brujas was most likely a Fleming from Bruges in what is now Belgium and may have served in Arellano's company. Document 12. Diego Gallego is an unidentified person who does not appear on the muster roll.

42. A *notario* was a paralegal functionary authorized to certify contracts, wills, and other extrajudicial acts. In antiquity he wrote very fast, using many abbreviations.

43. Because the surviving document is a copy of a copy, the registered mark is not included.

44. Rodrigo de Trujillo, the mestizo son of Jorge Báez, was a native of Veracruz in Nueva España. During the expedition to Tierra Nueva he may have served under Tristán de Luna y Arellano.

45. "From [today's] date," *de la hecha. Hecha = fecha.*

46. Garnica = Guernica. This is the Basque town made infamous by Nazi bombing in 1937 during the Spanish Civil War and made graphic by Pablo Picasso's painting of the event. Juanes de Guernica is listed on the muster roll as Juan Vizcaíno. He served as a footman under Pablo de Melgosa. He was a native of Guernica y Luno (Gernika-Lumo) in Vizcaya in the modern País Vasco. In 1538 he was a member of Viceroy Mendoza's personal guard. Document 12; AGI, Justicia, 259, Pieza 2, "Visita, 1543."

47. Diego de Mata served as a footman under Pablo de Melgosa. Document 12.

48. "Native tunic" refers to the quilted cotton armor widely used in central Mexico during protohistoric times. Writing in the seventeenth century about the expedition to Tierra Nueva, fray Antonio Tello mentioned specifically the expeditionaries' use of this garment. In Nahuatl the quilted cotton tunic was called *ichcahuipil.* Tello, 327. For illustrations, see *Lienzo de Tlaxcalla* (México, DF: Alfredo Chavero; reprint, *Artes de México* 11, nos. 51–52 [1964]), 14, 15, 18, and passim. A *caperuza* was a pointed hood or cap. The term was applied to a piece of indigenous American head armor, probably of the tall, pointed type depicted on numerous folios of the *Codex Mendoza,* which was painted in the 1540s at the request of the viceroy of Nueva España. *Colección de Mendoza, o Códice Mendocino: Documento mexicano del siglo XVI que se conserva en la Biblioteca Bodleiana de Oxford, Inglaterra,* ed. Jesus Galindo y Villa (México, DF: Editorial Innovación, 1980).

49. Cristóbal Pérez was a native of Ávila in the modern Spanish *comunidad* of Castilla y León. He was over 21 when he joined the expedition to Tierra Nueva. It is not known in which company he served. AGI, Justicia, 339, N.1, R.1, "Residencia," fol. 20v; Document 12.

50. "Bison or cowhide," *cuera de vaca.* This may have been either a cowhide or a bison hide, because at the time the Spanish word *vaca* was applied to both animals, and both were available to the Tierra Nueva expeditionaries. For a definition of a *tomín de oro de minas,* see the glossary.

51. "The color of blood sausage, bluish-black, *morzillo. DRAE,* 1401.

52. Items for sleeping, eating, and hunting are not included in the inventory. This raises the possibility that such equipment and utensils were held communally, at least among humble footmen.

53. Melchior Pérez de la Torre was a native of Villa de la Torre (Torremejía) in the modern *provincia* of Badajoz in Extremadura. He was 26 years old at the time the expedition began. His father was *licenciado* Diego Pérez de la Torre, interim governor and *residencia* judge for Nueva Galicia. Melchior later became father-in-law to Pedro de Ledesma, another member of the expedition to Tierra Nueva. He had arrived in Nueva España with don Luis de Castilla in early 1530. He served as *alguacil mayor* and *aposentador* (billeting officer) for the expedition. He was in the company commanded by Juan de Zaldívar. Document 32; AGI, Patronato, 60, N.5,

R.4, "Juan de Zaldívar." Because there were three men on the expedition who bore the name Miguel Sánchez, it may be that the suffix "de Plasencia" in this case simply indicates this particular Miguel Sánchez's place of origin (Plasencia in the *provincia* of Cáceres in Extremadura), to distinguish him from his two namesakes. It is quite possible that he did not append this element to his name in other circumstances. He served in the company commanded by Tristán de Luna y Arellano. Document 12.

54. Because the surviving document is a copy of a copy, the registered mark is not included.

55. This inventory was made one month and one day prior to the auction recorded above, leaving open the possibility that the following items not sold at auction were appropriated by one of the executors or someone else in the interim: cowhide with hair, hat, lance point, packsaddle, and spurs. Or, as suggested in the introduction, perhaps no one was interested in these items.

56. Two men named Alonso González participated in the Coronado expedition. One was the brother and the other a nephew of the Ciudad de México *regidor* Ruy González. Both were probably from Villanueva de Fresno in the modern *provincia* of Badajoz in the Spanish *comunidad* of Extremadura, also Ruy González's place of origin. It is likely that the Alonso González mentioned here was the son or nephew of *alférez* Alonso González. He probably served in Tristán de Luna y Arellano's company. AGI, Patronato, 61, N.2, R.7\1, "Méritos y servicios de Rui González, May 25, 1558." Two men named Miguel Torres are listed on the muster roll. The man mentioned here could have been either of them. Document 12.

57. A native of Benavente in the modern *provincia* of Zamora in the Spanish *comunidad* of Castilla y León, Pedro de Benavides arrived in Nueva España around 1531. He was a cousin to expedition member Cristóbal Mayorga and probably related to Juan de Benavides and Pedro de Benavente, both also members of the expedition. AGI, México, 204, N.33\2, "Pedro de Benavides."

58. Alonso López served in Diego Gutiérrez de la Caballería's company and, like Jiménez, may have been a native of Guadalcanal in modern Sevilla in the *provincia* in Andalucía. Document 12; *Pasajeros*, 2: no. 1058.

59. Juan Francés is listed on the muster roll as a footman in Pablo de Melgosa's company. Document 12.

60. Although he did not state where he hailed from, this may be the Alonso Jiménez who, like Juan Jiménez, was a native of Guadalcanal. He may also have been related to Juan. Alonso is listed on the muster roll as a footman under Pablo de Melgosa. AGI, México, 1064, L.1\1, "Informes de los conquistadores," fol. 246v; *Pasajeros*, 1: no. 3071; Document 12.

61. Juan Galleas's surname appears elsewhere in the Coronado expedition documents as Galeras, Galleas, Gallas, and Galeasso. He was a native of Almendralejo in the *provincia* of Badajoz in the modern Spanish *comunidad* of Extremadura. He was about 23 years old at the time the expedition began. Like Melchior Pérez, he served as *alguacil mayor* and *aposentador* (billeting officer) of the expedition. He may have been in López de Cardenas's company, since he went with that captain to the Grand Canyon and seems to have been under his orders. AGI, Justicia, 1021, N.2, Pieza 5, "Probanza de López de Cárdenas"; AGI, Justicia, 336, N.1, "Probança"; Document 32.

62. The machete, hammer, pliers, and hoof parer do not appear among the list of auctioned items and indeed were subsequently declared not to have sold at auction. Fol. 17r.

63. However, five additional worn horseshoes and a sword belt are included in the list of items that were later auctioned, although they are not inventoried here. Whether the inventory list is in fact complete, even with those additions, is open to question. Certainly the clothing Jiménez was wearing and the bedding he was using at the time of his death are not included here. We cannot say whether pilfering went on before the inventory was made or even while Jiménez was still alive. Fol. 6v.

64. Velasco de Barrionuevo, a captain from Granada in the modern Spanish *comunidad* of Andalucía, was left as *maestre de campo* in Culiacán under Tristán de Luna y Arellano. His brother Rodrigo also participated in the expedition. Velasco was present during the siege of the Pueblo del Cerco. During the summer of 1541, Luna y Arellano sent a Francisco de Barrionuevo (probably Velasco, since there is no other mention of Francisco among Coronado expedition documents) north from Tiguex to Jemez, Yuque-Yunque (map 1), and Brava to get supplies. From September 1537 until at least the end of 1539 Velasco had served in Viceroy Mendoza's personal guard. Document 12; Bolton, 208; Document 28, fol. 18v; Flint, *Great Cruelties*, 278, 548.

65. Báez may not have known how to sign his name but used a mark or flourish instead. James Lockhart provides a brief summary of the levels of literacy in sixteenth-century Spain that mentions "the misshapen, awkward scrawls or empty rubrics of those who learned to sign [their names] as adults." Perhaps Báez was one of these. Lockhart, *Men of Cajamarca*, 35.

66. Only a Diego Sánchez de Fromista is listed in the muster roll. This strongly suggests that this is the person referred to here and that he was a native of Fromista in the modern *provincia* of Palencia in the *comunidad* of Castilla y León. The latter is rendered more likely because he uses Sánchez alone as his surname in this document. See also Document 12.

67. Because the surviving document is a copy of a copy, the registered mark is not included.

68. The petition, which appears on fols. 1v and 2r, was, as Negrín states on fol. 9v, "that I asked [the *alcalde*] to permit me and grant me authority so I could prepare a will in the name of Juan Jiménez." "Was denied," *no haber lugar. DRAE*, 1274: "expresión con que se declara que no se accede a lo que se pide."

69. "The stipulations," *solemnidad. DRAE*, 1898: "conjunto de requisitos legales para la validez de los otorgamientos testamentarios." Many of the legal requirements then in force were included in the 1505 codification of the 83 Leyes de Toro. Most of those dealt with testamentary issues. See particularly Laws 31–39. *Compendio de los comentarios extendidos por el maestro Antonio Gómez, a las ochenta y tres Leyes de Toro* [1785], facsimile ed. (Valladolid: Editorial Lex Nova, 1981), 127–41.

70. "Without merit," *ninguno. DRAE*, 1440: "nulo y sin valor."

71. "Show," *esiba. Escibir = exhibir*. Boyd-Bowman, *Lexico*, 367. The present subjunctive is *esciba*.

72. Both Sancho López de Agurto and Alonso Sánchez (not the man of this name who was a member of the Coronado expedition) were *escribanos* in the Ciudad de México. AGI, Justicia, 21, "Relación de los escribanos del Cabildo de México, June 10, 1546." Document 31, fol. 2r, gives López de Agurto's surname as López de Agurto de Murcia, which suggests that he was from Murcia. Nevertheless, other documentary evidence shows that he was a native of Bilbao in the *provincia* of Vizcaya in the modern País Vasco in Spain. Born about 1504, he was a son of Pedro Martín de Agurto and María Ochoa de Aguirre. He had been in Nueva España since about 1525 and was serving as an *escribano* as early as 1531. He was still earning his living that way until at least 1572. AGI, México, 1064, L.1\1, "Informes de los conquistadores," fol. 175r.

73. "Judgment," *oficio. DRAE*, 1468: "auto de oficio."

74. This is in accordance with Law 32 of the Leyes de Toro. *Compendio*, 130.

75. It is not known to whom Zaragosa is referring here.

76. It is unclear which bequests are referred to here. No bequests of this small size were stipulated by law. Wills of the period, however, did ordinarily make provision for a donation to the parish church where masses were to be said for the deceased. This *donación* was for the purpose of purchasing "ornaments," meaning things such as candles and incense. Given the small size of the bequests, only one *tomín*, it may be that they are for such support of a church. For an example of a generic will that includes just such a bequest, see fray Alonso de Molina's 1569 model testament. Sarah Cline, "Fray Alonso de Molina's Model Testament and Antecedents to Indigenous Wills in Spanish America," in *Dead Giveaways: Indigenous Testaments of Colonial Mesoamerica and the Andes*, eds. Susan Kellogg and Matthew Restall (Salt Lake City: University of Utah Press, 1998), 28–30. For a concise statement of the general restraints on bequests under Spanish law of the period, see Flusche, "Posthumous Estates, Part 1," 7. For the form of wills prescribed by law, see *Siete Partidas*, 3:746–47.

77. "Bull of indulgence as a participant in a holy crusade," *bula de la santa cruzada*. Reference here is to the expedition to Tierra Nueva, which is portrayed as a holy crusade against infidels. See *DRAE*, 332.

78. The text of this promissory note is on fols. 21v and 22r. Juan Barragán was a native of Llerena in the modern *provincia* of Badajoz in the Spanish *comunidad* of Extremadura. He may have been with Juan Jiménez in Tristán de Luna y Arellano's company.

79. Negrín presented no note or other document substantiating this debt. It is possible that García was from Sevilla and that Cristóbal García, another expedition member, was his brother. He may have served under *alférez* Alonso González.

80. Negrín presented no note or other document substantiating this debt. Cordero was between the ages of 25 and 30 at the time the expedition got under way. He served alongside Juan Troyano, so he may have served in the company led by Hernando de Alvarado. Document 31, fol. 1r.

81. "It is waived," *se lo suelta. Soltar, DRAE,* 1900: "perdonar o remitir a uno el todo o parte de lo que debe."

82. A native of Moguer in the modern *provincia* of Huelva in Andalucía, Spain, Alonso Grande arrived in Nueva España in 1529. He married an Indian woman and was one of the original settlers of Puebla de los Ángeles in 1532. He was still a *vecino* of Puebla as least as late as 1547. Boyd-Bowman, 2: no. 5211. As his name suggests, Gregorio Genovés was a native of Rense, just three leagues from Geneva, or Genovés, Switzerland. He had arrived in Nueva España with Luis Ponce in 1526. He had married in 1534 and, as this document indicates, was a *vecino* of Puebla de los Ángeles. Boyd-Bowman, 2: no. 13281.

83. A *vecino* and *regidor* of Puebla de los Ángeles, Francisco de Orduña was a native of Orduña in the modern *provincia* of Burgos in the Spanish *comunidad* of Castilla y León. He arrived in Nueva España with Cortés in 1521 and participated in many conquests. He served as *visitador* of Nueva España and *residencia* judge in Guatemala. He held the *encomienda* of Tezalco. Icaza, 1: no. 129. Pedro de Villanueva received a coat of arms in 1559. He was a *vecino* and *regidor* of Puebla de los Ángeles. He participated in several conquests—with Cortés in the conquest of Tenochtitlan and Pánuco and with Guzmán in Xalisco. Sociedad de Bibliófos Españoles, *Nobiliario de conquistadores,* 19–20.

84. Fols. 13r–16r comprise a second nearly identical copy of the petition, decision, and will already recorded on fols. 9v–12v. We therefore have not included a second transcription and translation here. The transcript and translation resume on fol. 16r. The second copy of this section is in the hand of the same *escribano* as the first, although the ink of the second copy is blue rather than the more usual rust brown. Fols. 14v and 15r show many examples of simple scribal errors, probably the result of fatigue or boredom.

85. Ordinarily, one was either a *vecino* or an *estante* of a given town, not both at the same time. So we presume that the *escribano* erroneously wrote *estantes,* plural, in the copy (see transcription) and have translated it in the singular here.

86. Diego de Ordás was a *vecino* of Puebla and a native of Castroverde de Campos in the modern Spanish *comunidad* of Castilla y León. He was the son of Hernando de Villagómez and Francisca de Ordás and a nephew of Diego de Ordás, conqueror of Cuba. In 1558, Diego Ordás de León received a coat of arms for the deeds of his father, Juan González de León, in the conquest of Tenochtitlan. Sociedad de Bibliófos Españoles, *Nobiliario de conquistadores,* 206–07; Icaza, 1: no. 404.

87. By law the executor of a will was to complete his duties within one year if, at the time of his appointment, he had been outside the Spanish kingdoms and absent from the town where the deceased had resided. In this case, however, three and a half years had elapsed. Law 33 of the Leyes de Toro. *Compendio,* 132.

88. *Tepuzque,* derivative from *tepuztli,* a Nahuatl word for iron or copper, was a designation for a low-quality monetary unit. A *peso de tepuzque* was a coin lessened in value by having base metal added to its silver.

89. "Ledger adjustment," *descargo. DRAE,* 699, "data o salida que en las cuentas se contrapone al cargo o entrada."

90. This was quite likely the Hernando Gómez de la Peña who was *escribano* at Nuestra Señora de los Remedios in 1545 and recorded *de parte* testimony for Vázquez de Coronado. He was a native of Ledesma in the *provincia* of Salamanca in the modern Spanish *comunidad* of Castilla y León. He arrived in Nueva España in 1539 and was a settler of San Miguel de Culiacán. He was a son of Fernando Gómez and Mencia Suárez. Flint, *Great Cruelties,* 346; Boyd-Bowman, 2: no. 7312.

91. Indeed, as shown later, Negrín did not collect on any of the promissory notes held by Jiménez at the time of his death, which suggests that he may have made no extraordinary effort to do so.

92. Negrín, then, had been unable to recover the purchase price of the horse from his friend Jorge Báez's son Rodrigo Trujillo, again suggesting a lack of either luck or effort on the *albacea's* (executor's) part.

93. "Is owed," *alcança,* similar to *alcance. DRAE,* 87: "en materia de cuentas, saldo que, según ellas, está debiendose." Negrín declares adjustments that exceed the total he is responsible for.

94. This Diego Ramírez was probably the man who was a native of Soria and a *vecino* of the Ciudad de México who arrived in Nueva España in 1534. At that time he brought with him a royal *cédula* of appointment for office. He also served as *visitador* in Hidalgo, and in 1553 he was in Pánuco in the same capacity. Interestingly, he was the father-in-law of Agustín de las Casas, the nephew of Bartolomé de las Casas. Icaza, 2: no. 540; Boyd-Bowman, 2: no. 10575a; Adorno and Pautz, *Núñez Cabeza de Vaca,* 2:411; Vigil, *Alonso de Zorita,* 178, 214. A *juez visitador de agravios y bienes de difuntos* was an investigating judge assigned to conduct a review of the disposition of the property of the deceased. Flusche, "Posthumous Estates, Part 1," 1.

95. Cristóbal de Heredia was a public *escribano* and *escribano* of the court in Puebla de los Ángeles. A native of Portillo, an unidentified location in Spain, he arrived in Nueva España in 1537. He married a daughter of fellow *escribano* Sancho López de Agurto. Icaza, 2: no. 737.

96. Evidently the copyist skipped over the names of the witnesses, although they may well have been Gaspar de Arana and Diego (de Padilla) (see fol. 23v), as in the preceding entry.

97. The statement "I received [the goods]" seems to be contradicted only a few words later by "which at the present time has not occurred."

98. One of the laws referred to here is probably Law 33 of Title 18 of the Third Partida of Renaissance Spain's fundamental law code, the *Siete Partidas,* which deals with extension of the time limit for repayment of debts. *Siete Partidas,* 3:706.

99. A fuller version of this title or opening phrase (*sid convenerit juresdicione anium judicium*) appears on fol. 24v. The correct Latin is *si convenerit jurisdictione.*

100. This probably has reference to Laws 5 and 6 of Title 13 of the Fifth Partida. These two laws deal with property that can and cannot be pledged as surety. *Siete Partidas,* 4:1127–28.

101. Diego Hernández was the *alférez* for Diego de Guevara's company and was most likely the son of Ruy González. González reported that he had sent four men along with his brother to Cíbola. This would make Diego a relative of both men named Alonso González who were on the expedition. If this is he, then he was a native of Frenegal in the *provincia* of Badajoz in the modern *comunidad* of Extremadura in Spain, and he arrived in Nueva España in the company of don Juan Infante in 1539. Document 12; *Pasajeros,* 3: no. 101. There were two men named Lope de la Cadena on the expedition. The person referred to here most likely served directly under Vázquez de Coronado. That would have placed him in a situation similar to that of Diego Hernández. Document 12.

102. Because the surviving document is a copy, the mark is not present.

103. This point on the Río Frío is no more than five days' travel (75–88 miles) along the route from Cíbola to Chichilticale. That distance points to the modern San Francisco River in west-central New Mexico. H&R, 298 n. 12, state that Hodge thought it was the Colorado Chiquito. Pedro de Castañeda de Nájera writes that the returning expedition reached Cíbola on the tenth or eleventh of April 1542, yet Trujillo states here that it was already beyond Cíbola on the ninth. Compare Document 28, fols. 135v and 138r.

104. Rodrigo de Ysla was over 22 years old when the expedition started. He served in the company of *maestre de campo* García López de Cardenas. AGI, Patronato, 63, R.5, "Juan de Paladinas [*sic*]"; Document 12. Francisco de Parada served under Captain Diego Gutiérrez de la Caballería. Document 12.

105. Because the surviving document is a copy, the mark is not reproduced.

106. This Diego González was most likely the man listed as a *vecino* of Puebla de los Ángeles and a trial attorney there who had died by 1547. That man was a native of Parra in the old *condado* (holdings belonging to a *conde*) de Fría in Spain (perhaps Parral de Villovela near Segovia). He had arrived in Nueva España with Cortés and had received *encomiendas* that were later taken from him. Icaza, 1: no. 44.

107. This begins the process of repossessing the horse that Trujillo had purchased from Jiménez's estate. The repossession has already been referred to on fols. 20r and 20v.

108. "Oaths of no malice and stipulation," *juramentos de calumnia y decisorio. DRAE,* 1214.

109. Payment had been due no later than September 9, 1542, making the payment nearly three years overdue at this point. See fol. 24v.

110. The Laws of Toledo referred to here were probably the *Fuero Real* or its companion code, the *Espéculo,* both of which were promulgated by King Alfonso X during the Cortes of Toledo in March 1254. *Siete Partidas,* 1:xxxiii.

111. Rodrigo de Coria was a native of Utrera in the modern *provincia* of Sevilla in Andalucía. He arrived in Nueva España in 1544 and became *alguacil mayor* of Puebla de los Ángeles. He went to Oaxaca with an Arévalo. Icaza, 1: no. 1317.

112. This Luisa may have been a native of the Veracruz area, since her son Rodrigo de Trujillo indicates that he is a native of that place. She possibly was not married to Rodrigo's father, Jorge Báez, although the situation is unclear. Báez's wife, reportedly the daughter of a conquistador, was also named Luisa. Whether these are two Luisas or one cannot be determined. The Indian Luisa probably gave birth to Rodrigo in the late 1520s, which makes it all but impossible that she was the daughter of a conquistador of Tenochtitlan. Both the date of her son's birth and

her own parentage could, nevertheless, be reconciled if she was a native of the Caribbean region. See fol. 23v and note 31, this document.

113. Antón Martín Breva (also spelled Brena) was a native of Coria in the modern *provincia* of Cáceres in Extremadura. Breva was a *vecino* of Puebla de los Ángeles. He had arrived in Nueva España in 1523 and was assigned the *encomienda* of Mycasto. Icaza, 2: no. 524; Boyd-Bowman, 2: no. 2875.

114. A native of Ciudad Rodrigo in the modern *provincia* of Salamanca in the *comunidad* of Castilla y León, Andrés Núñez was *alguacil mayor* in Puebla de los Ángeles. This may have been the *escudero* (shield bearer) of that name who came to the Indies in 1510 and was a conqueror of Tenochtitlan in 1519 and who also captained of one of Cortés's *bergantines* (for definition, see Document 17, note 31). Boyd-Bowman, 1: no. 2599.

115. "Handle," *pasar. DRAE*, 1540: "ser tratado o manejado por uno un asunto; se usa hablando de los escribanos y notarios ante quienes se otorgan los instrumentos."

116. "Booming voice," *voz. DRAE*, 2107: "grito, voz esforzada y levantada."

117. It is conceivable, though not proven, that this Pedro was the same *pregonero* (crier) as the one named Pedro who was on the Coronado expedition and who conducted the original auction of Jiménez's property, including this horse, in 1542. Fol. 7r. However, there was evidently no shortage of black *pregoneros* in Nueva España at the time. For instance, another such person is recorded in the Archivo de la Villa de Colima, Registros, 1535–83, who was active there in 1556. Mathes, "New Research in Mexico."

118. Pedro de Meneses was a native of Talavera in the modern *provincia* of Toledo in the Spanish *comunidad* of Castilla–La Mancha. He arrived in Nueva España with Narváez at the age of 20. He served as *visitador* and *juez de términos* (district judge). By 1547 he had been married 21 years and had eight children. He purchased half of the *encomiendas* Çicoac and Çultepeque and also held title to Coyuca. Icaza, 1: no. 65. Alberto de Cáceres, residing in Puebla de los Ángeles in 1547, was a native of Coria in the modern *provincia* of Cáceres in Extremadura. He had served in the Gran Canaria before arriving in the New World in 1524. He participated in expeditions to La Florida, the Isla de las Perlas, and Yucatán. Icaza, 2: no. 964; Boyd-Bowman, 2: no. 2837.

119. Always previously Puebla de los Ángeles has been referred to as a *ciudad*, as indeed it was. This is probably a scribal error.

120. This Juan de Sotomayor may have been the *caballero* who was on the expedition to Tierra Nueva and served under Vázquez de Coronado's banner. Document 28, fol. 19r.

121. In November 1547 Alonso Valiente, a *vecino* of Puebla de los Ángeles, was awarded a coat of arms. He was a native of Medina de las Torres in the old *maestrazgo* (holdings belonging to a *maestre*, or high official of one of the military orders) of Santiago. He had come to Nueva España in 1521 with his wife and family. He participated in the discovery and settlement of the *provincia* of Michoacán and served as *alguacil mayor* there. He also was with Cortés during the pacification of Pánuco and Honduras. Sociedad de Bibliófos Españoles, *Nobiliario de conquistadores*, 124–26; Icaza, 1: no. 947.

122. This net amount appears to be incorrect; it results from adding the fees to the auction price instead of deducting them. *Grano* is literally a "grain" of gold or silver valued at almost 3 *maravedís*.

123. Tenancingo = Tenantzinco. Tenancingo was an Indian settlement southwest of the Ciudad de México held in *encomienda* at this time by Juan de Salcedo. Why the copy was being made there is unknown. Gerhard, *Historical Geography*, 170–71.

124. This section at the end of the document represents standard sixteenth-century scribal procedure. To lessen the possibility of tampering with documents, the *escribano* certifies the corrections, deletions, and emendations he has made in the process of preparing the copy. Any others would then be considered illegitimate. The first correction referred to in this section—"It is corrected where it says 'had discussed' [in 14r]"—was actually not made.

125. The lines at the top of the page are by perhaps four *escribanos* other than López de Legazpí. Jiménez's name and the date are in the hand of one *escribano*, probably from the mid-sixteenth century, the same hand as that which appears in most of the *legajo* (bundle). "No 15" is written in what appears to be brown pencil and seems to be part of the Archive's system for numbering the documents within the *legajo*.

126. Començado. This is apparently a scribal error for *comunicado*.

127. *De* is the third-person singular preterit of *dar*, a holdover from the Latin *ded*. Lloyd, *Latin to Spanish*, 302.

128. Ri(e)*ndieren. Rendir* = *restituir. DRAE*, 1769.

129. The date "17 Febrero" is in the hand of a different *escribano*.

130. "HuerVe" is most likely a scribal error for "Huelva.'

131. Çerca de = *acerca de. DRAE*, 461.

132. Por Razon de = *a razón de. DRAE*, 1731.

133. Constringan = *constriñan*. The *g* is a holdover from the Latin root, *constringere*. Lloyd, *Latin to Spanish*, 291.

134. Bien a(n)si = *así también. DRAE*, 289.

135. Home = *hombre. DRAE*, 1119.

136. Fincar = *quedar. DRAE*, 970.

137. This section constitutes a change of *escribano*. The hand of this same *escribano* also appears on fol. 1r: "Juan ximenez di*funto* natural de GuadalCanal."

138. Çierto Con. This is a scribal error for *concertado*.

139. In this section the *escribano* changes to López de Legazpí.

140. The *escribano* who wrote this label was the one who labeled all the documents in AGI, Contratación, 5575, N.24, "Juan Jiménez." He was probably an archive functionary, but possibly the person who earlier assembled the *legajo* (bundle).

Document 28. *The Relación de la Jornada de Cíbola, Pedro de Castañeda de Nájera's Narrative, 1560s (copy, 1596)*

1. AGI, Guadalajara, 46, N.8, "Información de oficio y parte, cabildo de San Miguel de Culiacán, 1566."

2. Apparently deducing from the evidence of his name and accepting the statement in a heading on folio 95r of the *relación* (which states flatly that the chronicler is a "*vecino* of Naxara"), both Frederick W. Hodge and A. Grove Day concluded that Pedro de Castañeda was a native of the town of Nájera in Spain. There is, however, no documentary evidence to refute Antonio Tello's seventeenth-century claim that Baeza was his hometown. The heading on folio 95r quite possibly represents a conclusion drawn by *licenciado* Niño Velásques while preparing the 1596 copy of the *relación* (also based on the chronicler's name). Frederick W. Hodge, "Introduction," in *Spanish Explorers in the Southern United States, 1528–1543*, eds. Frederick W. Hodge and Theodore H. Lewis (New York: Barnes and Noble, 1907; reprint, Austin: Texas State Historical Association, 1990), 276; Day, *Coronado's Quest*, 383; Tello, 135.

3. AGI, Guadalajara, 46, N.8, "Cabildo de San Miguel de Culiacán."

4. See, for example, fols. 40r, 56r, 57r, and 57v.

5. For instance, Diego de Guevara and his company, presumably including Pedro de Nájera, were at the siege of Pueblo del Cerco and participated in the lancing of its fleeing inhabitants. Fol. 69v.

6. Fol. 5r.

7. Fol. 3v.

8. Fol. 131r.

9. Fols. 143r–143v.

10. Because Tello uses none of the terms *conquistador, fundador,* or *primero poblador* in referring to Pedro de Nájera, there is no implication that the chronicler was among the members of Nuño Beltrán de Guzmán's expedition when Culiacán was founded in 1532, as some have interpreted Tello's statement. His arrival in Culiacán some years after its founding jibes with the chronicler's own testimony in 1566, when he stated that he had lived in Culiacán about 24 years—that is, only since the return of the Coronado expedition. Tello, 135; Hodge, "Introduction," 276; AGI, Guadalajara, 46, N.8, "Cabildo de San Miguel de Culiacán."

11. Fol. 148v.

12. Fol. 5v.

13. Fol. 6r.

14. It is clear, however, that the chronicler Pedro de Castañeda de Nájera did not participate in the Francisco de Ibarra *entrada* to Paquimé and die there in 1565, as Day claims, for he was alive in Culiacán in 1566. Day, *Coronado's Quest*, 383; AGI, Guadalajara, 46, N.8, "Cabildo de San Miguel de Culiacán." Hodge claims and Day repeats that Pedro de Castañeda's wife has been identified as María de Acosta, with whom he had nine children. This seems to be a mistaken interpretation of a transcribed document containing an entry relative to the children of one Pedro Franco, a conquistador of Nueva España in 1520–21, most of whose children bore the surname Castañeda. Hodge, "Introduction," 276; Day, *Coronado's Quest*, 383; *CDI*, 14:206.

15. Fol. 148v.

16. Fol. 2r.

17. AGI, Guadalajara, 46, N.8, "Cabildo de San Miguel de Culiacán."

18. Fol. 1r.

19. Fol. 4v.

20. The proposal was not approved before Zorita fell ill and then returned to Spain in 1566. AGI, Justicia, 1029, N.7, R.1, "Méritos y servicios de Alonso de Zorita, 1560s"; AHN, Diversos-Colecciones, 24, N.45, "Memorial de licenciado Zorita sobre la Florida y Nuevo Méjico, 1560–1561."

21. AGI, México, 204, N.36, "Méritos y servicios, Juan Gallego, 1551, 1554, 1556"; AGI, México, 97, R.1, "Luna y Arellano"; Document 31.

22. Lucas had fled south from Quivira after the martyrdom of fray Juan in 1542. Chávez, *Oroz Codex*, 275 n. 7, 316.

23. AHN, Diversos-Colecciones, 24, N.51, "fray Cyndos to the king, July 20, 1561."

24. A similar procedure had been adopted by Viceroy Luis de Velasco earlier in the 1550s before commissioning Luis Cortés to reconnoiter toward the north. Then, about 10 years later, Velasco granted to Francisco de Ibarra the right to lead an *entrada* north. That expedition departed in April 1564 from the mines of San Martín. Obregón, *Historia*, 40–45.

25. It has been suggested that the "exalted person" to whom the *relación* is addressed could have been Francisco de Ibarra, who was governor of the new and rival *provincia* of Nueva Vizcaya and who mounted an expedition to the north between 1564 and 1566. However, considerable animosity existed between Ibarra and the residents of Culiacán at the time. In 1566 the *cabildo* of Culiacán took testimony in support of its formal complaints against Ibarra, who was accused of luring away residents of Culiacán. The most vociferous witness during that testimony was Pedro de Nájera. Considering his clear rancor toward Ibarra, it seems unlikely that he would have so cordially supplied information about the expedition to Tierra Nueva to Ibarra. Obregón, *Historia*, 45–238; AGI, Guadalajara, 46, N.8, "Cabildo de San Miguel de Culiacán."

26. AGI, Justicia, 1029, N.7, R.1, "Alonso de Zorita."

27. Fols. 153r–153v.

28. Fol. 4v.

29. Hodge, "Introduction," 276; Day, *Coronado's Quest*, 382.

30. See, for instance, Carmen de Mora, "Códigos culturales en la *Relación de la Jornada de Cíbola* de Pedro Castañeda Nájera," *Nueva Revista Filología Hispánica* (1991):901–12; Maureen Ahern, "*La Relación de la Jornada de Cíbola*: Los Espacios orales y culturales," in *Conquista y contraconquista: La Escritura del Nuevo Mundo* (México, DF: Colegio de México and Brown University, 1994), 187–99; and Maureen Ahern, "Mapping, Measuring, and Naming Cultural Spaces in Castañeda's *Relación de la Jornada de Cíbola* (1563)," in Flint and Flint, *From the Distance of 460 Years*, 265–89.

31. Fol. 3v.

32. Fols. 95v–96r.

33. Ahern, "Mapping, Measuring, and Naming," 282.

34. Fol. 143v.

35. As, for instance, on fols. 39r, 48r, 71r, 74r, and 132r–135r.

36. On fols. 55r and 74r, for example.

37. As on fols 131v and 138v.

38. Fols. 78r, 82r, 83r, 102v, and 120v.

39. Marco Polo, *The Travels of Marco Polo* (New York: Orion Press, 1958); also, Polo, *The Travels of Marco Polo*, trans. and ed. Ronald Latham (Harmondsworth, UK: Penguin Books, 1958).

40. Fol. 83r; Polo, *Travels* (Latham), 35, 46–47.

41. Fol. 130v.

42. Fol. 117v.

43. This has made the *relación* and other reports of the expedition extremely valuable for ethnologists and other anthropologists.

44. See Hartmann and Flint, "Before the Coronado Expedition," 20–41.

45. Fol. 96r.

46. Fol. 116v.

47. Fol. 144r.

48. Fol. 140r.

49. Fol. 34v.

50. Fol. 19r.

51. AGI, Guadalajara, 46, N.8, "Cabildo de San Miguel de Culiacán."

52. This is in marked contrast with the stark recital of days of travel in much of Juan Jaramillo's narrative, for instance.

53. This is a fact that must give historians pause about uncritically accepting what Pedro de Nájera writes, especially since much of what he reports also comes secondhand. In our notes to the *relación* we have made every effort to point out instances in which the chronicler's work is at variance with other, contemporary reports.

54. Fol. 4v.

55. Fol. 2v.

56. The *conde*, whose family seat was in the *provincia* of Jaén, in which Pedro de Nájera's hometown of Baeza lies, may therefore have had special interest in the work of a fellow Jiniense. A. Grove Day calls the copyist an "unknown clerk." He, like all previous analysts of the *relación*, apparently failed to read the first three folios of the manuscript, which clearly identify Niño Velásques. Gonzalo Argote de Molina, *Nobleza de Andalucía* (Sevilla: Fernando Díaz, 1588), 116v–118v; Day, *Coronado's Quest*, 382.

57. Angélico Chávez cites a June 6, 1562, letter from Francisco de Ibarra to Diego de Ibarra in John Lloyd Mecham's *Francisco de Ibarra and Nueva Vizcaya* (Durham, NC: Duke University Press, 1927), 80–81, saying, "Fray Jacinto and another friar accompanied Francisco de Ibarra in the discovery of Copala." Chávez, *Oroz Codex*, 275 n. 5.

58. Ternaux-Compans, a German-educated French diplomat and well-known collector of manuscripts and rare books, was a nephew of the French statesman Baron Guillaume Louis Ternaux. Henri also published the great Spanish bibliography "Bibliothèque Américaine." In 1844 he sold his collection of Spanish American documents to the American bookseller Obadiah Rich. Ternaux-Compans died in 1864. José de Onís, "Alcedo's *Biblioteca americana*," *Hispanic American Historical Review* 31, no. 3 (1951):537; Edwin Blake Brownrigg, "Introduction," in *Colonial Latin American Manuscripts and Transcripts in the Obadiah Rich Collection: An Inventory and Index*, ed. Edwin Blake Brownrigg (New York: New York Public Library and Readex Books, 1978), xiii–xv.

59. Uguina was a close friend of the Spanish royal historian Juan Bautista Muñoz. Uguina's collection included many documents that Muñoz had located in preparation for writing his *Historia del nuevo mundo*, among them the *relación* of Pedro de Nájera. Only the first of three planned volumes of the *Historia*, dealing with the period up to 1500, was ever finished. Onís, "Alcedo's *Biblioteca americana*," 536–37; Brownrigg, "Introduction," x–xiii.

60. George Parker Winship, "Bibliographic note," in Winship, 107.

61. Paris: A. Bertrand, 1838, 9:1–246.

62. Onís, "Alcedo's *Biblioteca americana*," 536–41; Brownrigg, *Colonial Latin American Manuscripts*, 62.

63. Jerry R. Craddock, "Pedro de Castañeda y Nájera, *Relación de la Jornada de Cíbola*: Acotaciones gramaticales y léxicas" (unpublished material in possession of the editors).

64. Most of the *postilas* (marginal notes) to this copy of the *relación* appear to be in the same hand as the body of the text.

65. Ternaux-Compans, Winship, Hammond and Rey, and Mora all failed to transcribe and translate the first three folios of the original document, which provide the only available information about who made this 1596 copy and where the document from which the copy was made came from. The first three folios, like all the rest of the copy, are in the hand of a *licenciado* Bartolomé Niño Velásques. Either the copy was being made for the *conde* Fernando González (de Castilla) or the document being copied came from the *conde's* collection. Men of González's lineage had held the title of Conde de Castilla since the 900s. Argote de Molina, *Nobleza de Andalucía*, 116v–118v. For geographical information, see the entry for Cíbola in Appendix 2.

66. For geographical information about Tierra Nueva, see the entry in Appendix 2. For biographical information about Antonio de Mendoza, see the entry in Appendix 1.

67. Castañeda de Nájera refers here to the lack of lengthy, detailed reports about the expedition. The situation likely would have been different had the expedition's official chronicler, Pedro Méndez de Sotomayor, not died shortly after the conclusion of the expedition. Testimony of doña Catalina de Sotomayor, in AGI, Justicia, 263, Pieza 3, "Probanza hecha en nombre de don Antonio de Mendoza, Michoacán, 1546."

68. For further discussion of Cortés's expeditions to Baja California, see Document 18 and also its introduction for information on Cortés himself.

69. "[I] pray," *plega*. *Plega* is similar to *plegaría*, prayer or supplication; *DRAE*, 1645. *Pregar = suplicar*; Alonso, *Enciclopedia del Idioma*, 3:3379.

70. "Highest seats," *talanquera*. Covarrubias, 909: "lugar levantado en alto en las orillas de las plazas, dende el cual se ven correr los torros y otras fiestas de plaza."

71. For biographical information, see the entry for Nuño Beltrán de Guzmán in Appendix 1.

72. Oxitipar, also spelled Oxitipa and Oxitipan, was in the colonial jurisdiction of Valles, now in the eastern part of the Mexican state of San Luis Potosí. It was claimed by Cortés and in 1527 reassigned to Guzmán, and thereafter to his kinsman Pedro de Guzmán. In 1533 Nuño de Guzmán founded the *villa* of Santiago de los Valles de Oxitipa. The area had a dense Huaxtecan- and Náhuatl-speaking population. Huaxtecan is in the Mayan language group. The *Codex Mendoza* lists Oxitipan as a distant tributary of the Aztecs/Mexica. Because Tejo was a native of Oxitipar, he was most likely a Huaxtecan. Gerhard, *Historical Geography*, 5, 354; Berdan and Anawalt, *Essential Codex Mendoza*, 140–41.

73. Such long-distance trade linked the major markets throughout Mesoamerica for several centuries during prehistoric times. See, for example, Hassig, *Trade, Tribute, and Transportation*, 149. Certainly these "sumptuous feathers" would have included plumage of the tropical scarlet macaw (*Ara macao*), for which there is abundant evidence of trade during the protohistoric period into modern northern Mexico and the American Southwest. The manifestation of that trade on the northwestern fringe of Mesoamerica has been called the Greater Aztatlán Mercantile System. See, for example, Paul R. Fish and Suzanne K. Fish, "Reflections on the Casas Grandes Regional System from the Northwestern Periphery," in *The Casas Grandes World*, eds. Curtis F. Schaafsma and Carroll L. Riley (Salt Lake City: University of Utah Press, 1999), 39. See also Michael S. Foster, "The Aztatlán Tradition of West and Northwest Mexico and Casas Grandes," in Schaafsma and Riley, *Casas Grandes World*, 160.

74. "*Pueblos* so grand," *grandes pueblos*. *Grande* has usually been interpreted to refer to the size of the towns, but the significance of the Spanish word is much broader than that. *DRAE*, 1054: "Que supera en tamaño, importancia, dotes, intensidad, etc., a lo común y regular." Although it is our opinion that in this case *grande* refers to magnificence rather than physical size, we have sought to retain its inherent ambiguity by translating it as "grand."

75. That the pueblos were seven in number had special significance for Spaniards of the day. Iberian popular lore included a story of seven Portuguese bishops who fled the Moorish invasion of the peninsula in the early 700s. They reportedly founded seven new cities far to the west of Europe. Those cities had supposedly become very prosperous, but their exact location was unknown. By the sixteenth century those seven cities of Antillia were eagerly sought by Spanish conquistadores. Hartmann and Flint, "Before the Coronado Expedition," 22.

76. A similar description of the Great Plains is on fol. 119v. A *jeme* was a length equal to the distance between the outstretched thumb and forefinger, approximately 0.17 meters, or 6.7 inches. One *jeme* equaled two *palmos*. Covarrubias, 680.

77. These few sentences provide a capsule summary of the conquest of Nueva Galicia and *entradas* toward the north carried out by a force under Nuño Beltrán de Guzmán between 1529 and 1533. The direction of Guzmán's march reported here may refer to travel from the Pátzcuaro/Tzintzuntzán area northeast to Cuitzeo before swinging northwest to Tonalá, Nochistlán, and Jalisco. Pilar, "Circa 1532," in Parry and Keith, *Central America and Mexico*, 3:550–51. For geographical information about the Mar del Norte, see the entry in Appendix 2.

78. For geographical information about Culiacán and Nueva Galicia, see the entries in Appendix 2.

79. Although no mountains actually reach the sea in the region of Culiacán, this reference may be generally to the Sierra Madre Occidental or a particular range within it, such as the Sierra Espinazo del Diablo (devil's backbone) northeast of Culiacán.

80. For geographical information about Compostela, see Appendix 2. For Jalisco, see Document 11, note 45. For Tonalá, see Document 6, note 75.

81. For the Cabeza de Vaca report, see Adorno and Pautz, *Núñez Cabeza de Vaca*, 1:14–279, and Oviedo, *Historia*, 287–315. For biographical information, see the entry for Álvar Núñez Cabeza de Vaca in Appendix 1.

82. For biographical information, see the entry for Diego de la Torre in Appendix 1.

83. For biographical information about doña Beatriz de Estrada, see Document 11, note 46.

84. For biographical information about Andrés Dorantes and Pánfilo de Narváez, see the entries in Appendix 1.

85. "Storied," *doblados*. That the word *doblados* refers here to stories of a building is clear, although the *DRAE*, Covarrubias, and other sources do not include such a meaning. *Doblado* is used in the same sense again on fol. 112r. Craddock, "Castañeda y Nájera," 15, speculates that the word may have been equivalent to *esquina*, although this makes little sense in either of its occurrences in the *relación*.

86. See Document 3, note 17, and AGI, Patronato, 184, R.27, "Letter to the King," fol. 14v.

87. Compare Document 6, fol. 2r, where only two friars are mentioned, Niza himself and Onorato. Castañeda de Nájera is evidently in error in referring to a fray Antonio de Santa María here. No such person is known to have participated in the Coronado *entrada*. He may, instead, mean fray Antonio Castilblanco. Chávez, *Coronado's Friars*, 47n. For biographical information about fray Marcos de Niza, see the introduction to Document 6.

88. For biographical information about Pedro de Alvarado, see the introduction to Document 20. For fray Daniel, see Document 19, note 52. For Esteban de Dorantes, see Appendix 1.

89. Castañeda de Nájera seems to employ the *legua legal*. At this rate, the distance from Chichilticale to Cíbola would be about 210 miles, placing Chichilticale at the latitude of Eagle Pass, near modern Willcox, Arizona, or Apache Pass, at the north end of the Chiricahua Mountains, also in modern southeastern Arizona. Chardon, "Linear League," 145. See also note 123, this document. For geographical information about Chichilticale, see its entry in Appendix 2.

90. For a discussion of Zuni political organization, see Edmund J. Ladd, "Zuni Social and Political Organization," in Ortiz, *Southwest*, vol. 9, 482–91.

91. Presumably Castañeda de Nájera refers here to fray Marcos and fray Onorato. Document 6, fol. 2r.

92. This statement is in direct contradiction to Marcos's *relación*, in which the friar claims that 300 Indians who accompanied Esteban were killed. Document 6, fol. 6v.

93. Again using the *legua legal*, this point would have been about 158 miles from the Zuni pueblos. This is at the latitude of modern Virden, New Mexico, or Thatcher, Arizona.

94. Castañeda de Nájera explicitly states that Marcos was 60 leagues from Cíbola when he turned back. He implies the same thing later, saying of the advance guard's arrival at Chichilticale that "there was no one who had seen it [the marvelous place that lay ahead] except the Indians who had gone with the Black." Fol. 30r. On the other hand, Marcos himself claims that he was 12 days into the 15-day unsettled region when he met Esteban's fleeing companions. From there Marcos supposedly proceeded to within sight of Cíbola. Document 6, fols. 6r and 7r.

95. For geographical information, see the entry for Topira in Appendix 2. Vázquez de Coronado reports this expedition to Topira in Document 2, fol. 354v.

96. This confirms that Guzmán, Vázquez de Coronado, and Marcos were all accompanied by native allies, as were most *entradas* of the day.

97. The chronicler continues to insist that there was more than one friar. See note 87, this document.

98. For geographical information about the Mar del Sur, see the entry in Appendix 2.

99. In addition to these 800 natives of Nueva España, the expedition evidently included at least 500 more Indians from what is now western Mexico. This makes the total of 1,300 that Vázquez de Coronado reports later. See Document 13, note 4. How Native American allies were recruited for the Coronado and other contemporary expeditions has hardly been studied. Two intriguing possibilities come from "Memorial of the Indians concerning Their Services, c. 1563," in *Nombre de Dios, Durango: Two Documents in Náhuatl concerning Its Foundation*, Robert H. Barlow and George T. Smisor, eds. and trans. (Sacramento: House of Tlaloc, 1943), 3, 31. In one case an *alcalde mayor* threatened to impose a fine if the "Mexicanos" would not go to "help put down the Chichimecs," and in another case Mexican Indians were promised that they would be allowed to keep prisoners they took while serving as auxiliaries. A further possibility is suggested from this example in Sinaloa in 1612: "the captain . . . drafted two thousand Indian warriors from several Christian and allied gentile nations. In exchange for their service the latter asked to be allowed to take enemy scalps with which to dance. . . . The captain agreed to their request." Andrés Pérez de Ribas, *History of the Triumphs of Our Holy Faith amongst the Most Barbarous and Fierce Peoples of the New World*, trans. and eds. Daniel T. Reff, Maureen Ahern, and Richard K. Danford (Tucson: University of Arizona Press, 1999), 104, 238.

100. "Would likely give more attention." H&R, 200, have "he *should* have paid

more attention" (emphasis added), making this a more judgmental statement than is warranted by the language of the sentence alone.

101. This income would have been his salary as governor and the tribute from his *encomiendas*. See Documents 5 and 34.

102. Pedro de Tovar was a *caballero* and a son of don Fernando de Tovar. He hailed from Villamartín in the modern *provincia* of León in the Spanish *comunidad* of Castilla y León. Pedro was in the Ciudad de México by 1529 and accompanied Guzmán to Nueva Galicia. He was one of first settlers of Guadalajara in 1531 and one of the founders of San Miguel de Culiacán. His wife, doña Francisca de Guzmán, was a daughter of the governor of Cuba. He was 22 years old at the time of the expedition. His brother was don Sancho de Tovar, *regidor* of Sahagún. He may also have been a nephew of Antonio de Mendoza's. Boyd-Bowman, 2: no. 6017; AGI, Patronato, 216, N.2, "Affidavit of testimony"; Tello, 125; Gerhard, *North Frontier*, 258. Juana died in April 1555. Kamen, *Philip of Spain*, 12. *Alférez general* = chief lieutenant. A *mayordomo mayor* was the principal boss (*jefe*) of the palace, whose responsibility was the care and management of the king's house.

103. The building of these fortified dockyards had been undertaken at the direction of Hernán Cortés. Hernán Cortés, "Cuarta carta-relación—15 de octubre de 1524," in Cortés, *Cartas de Relación*, 197. For biographical information about Lope de Samaniego, see Appendix 1.

104. For biographical information about Tristán de Arellano, García López de Cárdenas, and don Rodrigo Maldonado, see Appendix 1. Pedro de Guevara is an error for Diego de Guevara. In 1539 the king directed Viceroy Mendoza to provide Guevara a position as *corregidor*. Guevara, appointed *alcalde mayor* of Nueva Galicia in 1547, was a son of the Conde de Oñate, don Juan de Guevara, and was married to doña Isabel de Barrios. Upon his father-in-law's death in 1548, Guevara became *encomendero* of half of Meztitlán, north of Mexico City. The other half of Meztitlán was held for a time by fellow expeditionary Rodrigo Maldonado. AGI, Justicia, 259, Pieza 2, "Visita, 1543"; AGI, Mexico, 97, "Letter, Francisco Morales to the king, Mexico City, May 19, 1563"; Tello, 531; Gerhard, *Historical Geography*, 184; Luis de Velasco, *Relación de las encomiendas de indios hechas en Nueva España a los conquistadores y pobladores de ella, año de 1564*, publicados por France V. Scholes y Eleanor B. Adams (México, DF: Jose Porrúa e hijos, 1955), 34–35.

Diego López, one of the 24 *regidores* of his native Sevilla, was about 25 when the expedition started. He had arrived in Nueva España in 1538. By 1545 he was an *estante* in the mines of Nuestra Señora de los Remedios in the *provincia* of Culiacán. He was the *encomendero* of the *pueblo* of Guachimeto and halves of two others. In 1567, López was dead, and his son Gonzalo held 19 *pueblos* in the *provincia* of Culiacán once held by his father. Patronato, 216, N.2, "Affidavit of testimony"; *Pasajeros*, 2: no. 4804; Biblioteca del Escorial, Códice &-2-7, Doc. no. LXXX, "Memoria de los vecinos de culiacán para lo del repartimiento," n.d.; Charles Wilson Hackett, *Historical Documents Relating to New Mexico, Nueva Vizcaya, and Approaches Thereto* (Washington, DC: Carnegie Institution of Washington, 1923), 1:95.

"Twenty-four councilmen of Sevilla," *veinte quatro de Sevilla*. Covarrubias, 954: "En Sevilla y en Córdoba, y en otros lugares del Andalucía, vale lo mesmo que en Castilla regidor, por ser veinte y cuatro regidores en número."

Gutiérrez de la Caballería was probably a native of Almagro in the modern *provincia* of Ciudad Real in the Spanish *comunidad* of Castilla–La Mancha. He was an uncle by marriage of Vázquez de Coronado's. Shirley Cushing Flint, "*La Sangre Limpiada* of Marina Flores Gutiérrez de la Caballería," *Colonial Latin American Historical Review* 11, no. 1 (2002):48. For further biographical information, see the introduction to Document 12 and Document 12, note 30.

105. Castañeda de Nájera is mistaken in his recollection here. There were two Barrionuevo brothers on the expedition to Tierra Nueva, Rodrigo and Velasco. The chronicler likely confused Francisco with Velasco. For biographical information about Velasco de Barrionuevo, see Document 27, note 64. For biographical information about Juan de Zaldívar, see Document 17, note 35. A Juan Gallego, *vecino* of the *villa* of Purificación, testified on Vázquez de Coronado's behalf during his *residencia* in 1544. He had known the governor and captain general since 1538 and claimed to know that Vázquez de Coronado had spent more than 20,000 pesos from his own funds in support of Nueva Galicia. This Gallego was 60 years old at the time of his testimony, which places him in his middle to late fifties during the expedition to Tierra Nueva. Such an age seems to argue against his having performed the strenuous feats narrated later by Castañeda de Nájera. If this is not the Juan Gallego mentioned here, then his life both before and after the expedition is unknown. AGI, Justicia, 339, N.1, R.1, "Residencia," fols. 147v–151v. Melchior versus Melchor: for a discussion of the popularity in Spain at this time of the

French spelling, Melchior, see Document 32, note 36. For biographical information about Melchior Díaz, see the note in Appendix 1.

106. Don Alonso Manrique, an *hidalgo*, hailed from Valladolid in the modern *comunidad* of Castilla y León in Spain. He sailed in the expedition of Pedro de Mendoza to the Río de la Plata in 1535. By 1536 he was in Nueva Galicia. Following the expedition to Tierra Nueva, Manrique went with Ruy López de Villalobos to the Philippines and returned afterward to Nueva España. There he was *alcalde mayor* of Coatzacoalco and Tabasco in 1550. AGI, México, 1064, L.1\1, "Informes de los conquistadores," fol. 279v; Boyd-Bowman, 2: no. 12150.

The muster roll (Document 12) spells the surname Urrea "Gurrea," as does the entry for don Lope in *Pasajeros*, 2: no. 3804. Although he was clearly a person of high status, little is known about Urrea or Gurrea. His rank is attested by the five horses he took on the expedition. He was a *vecino* of Zaragosa in Spain and was reputedly bound for Tierra Firme in September 1537. Before arriving there he heard of the expedition to Tierra Nueva and proceeded to Nueva España. Document 12, fol. 1v; *Pasajeros*, 2: no. 3804.

Gómez Suárez de Figueroa mustered into the expedition to Tierra Nueva as a horseman in a group including Melchior Pérez and Domingo Martín, each of whom had three to five horses. He was wounded by an arrow at Cíbola. According to Juan de Contreras, Gómez Suárez repeatedly urged Vázquez de Coronado to have Turco killed. Document 12, fol. 2r; Document 19, fol. 361r; Flint, *Great Cruelties*,, 115.

The 21-year-old *contador* of the expedition to Tierra Nueva, Luis Ramírez de Vargas, was a native of Madrid in Spain. In 1555 he was serving as *residencia* judge and *justicia mayor* in the *provincias* of Xilotepeque. AGI, México, 206, N.35, "Cristóbal de Escobar"; AGI, México, 1064, L.1\1, "Informes de los conquistadores," fol. 277v; AGI, México, 205, N.12, "Información de Luis de Quesada, México, July 29, 1555."

Juan de Sotomayor may be the person of that name who years later participated in the auction of expeditionary Rodrigo de Trujillo's repossessed horse in Puebla de los Ángeles. Document 27, fol. 30v. Francisco Gorbalán served under López de Cardenas and was 29 at the time the expedition to Tierra Nueva began. See AGI, Justicia, 1021, N.2, Pieza 5, "Probanza de López de Cárdenas." Antonio de Ribero was a native of Medina del Campo in the modern *provincia* of Valladolid in the Spanish *comunidad* of Castilla y León. He was a *criado* of Mendoza's who arrived in Nueva España with him in 1535 and was a member of the viceroy's personal guard. Ribero was over 18 when he departed with the expedition as its *factor*. Castañeda de Nájera misspells his surname, rendering it Riberos. *Pasajeros*, 2: no. 1262; AGI, México, 204, N.33\2, "Pedro de Benavides."

107. Pablo de Melgosa was born in Burgos in the modern *comunidad* of Castilla y León in Spain about 1516. He had returned there from Nueva España after the expedition to Tierra Nueva when, as a *vecino* of Burgos, he testified on behalf of García López de Cárdenas in October 1546. During the expedition Melgosa was captain of the footmen. He served under López de Cárdenas during both the march to Tusayán in the summer of 1540 and the siege of Pueblo del Arenal that winter. AGI, Justicia, 1021, N.2, Pieza 5, "Probanza de López de Cárdenas"; Document 12, fol. 7v. For biographical information about Hernando de Alvarado, see the introduction to Document 24.

108. This is contrary to Mendoza's own later testimony during the *visita* of Tello de Sandoval. AGI, Patronato, 57, N.2, R.1, "Antonio de Mendoza."

109. To avoid such provocation, Viceroy Mendoza arranged for several people to travel ahead of the expedition, at least between the Ciudad de México and Compostela, to purchase food at native settlements. Luis de León Romano was one of those. He was dispatched to the town of Ocareo to purchase provisions for the expeditionaries who would be passing there. AGI, Justicia, 263, Pieza 1, "Probanza de Mendoza, Zacatula."

110. When Castañeda de Nájera reports that "there is nothing to report that occurred during this trip [to Compostela]," he implies that he heard no reports from those who departed from the Ciudad de México, since he himself did not make that leg of the journey. His own statement in 1566 reveals that he was living on the outskirts of Guadalajara at the time the expedition assembled at Compostela. See the introduction to this document.

111. Tuesday of Carnival was February 10, 1540, according to the Julian calendar. Cháves, *Espejo de navegantes*, 79–97. "Year [one thousand five hundred and forty {1540}]," *del año de quarenta (y / {1541} Uno)*. Castañeda is in error here; the year was 1540.

112. The document itself gives "Pedro de alarcon" (see transcript), but that given

name is incorrect; it should be Hernando. For biographical information about Alarcón, see the introduction to document 15. For geographical information on the port of Navidad on the Costa del Sur, see the entry for Navidad in Appendix 2. See also Document 16, note 17. The port of Jalisco was also known as Santa Cruz. Gerhard, *North Frontier,* 142.

113. "[One thousand five hundred and forty]," *el año nueVo de qua-/renta (y uno).* Again Castañeda de Nájera is in error here. The year was 1540. At this time throughout the Spanish Empire the new year began on December 25. See Document 5, note 13. It was evidently at this point that the expedition added to its number a group of natives of Pátzcuaro of unknown size, led by their *principal,* known as don Alonso. AGI, Justicia, 263, Pieza 1, "Probanza de Mendoza, Zacatula."

114. For biographical information, see the entry for Cristóbal de Oñate in Appendix 1.

115. See Document 12.

116. This is one of several statements in the documents published here of the principal motives for the expedition to Tierra Nueva.

117. For geographical information, see the entry for Chiametla in Appendix 2.

118. In actuality, most of the gear was probably carried by mules rather than horses, although many horses also served as pack animals. The presence of mules is attested in several places. See, for example, Document 29, fol. 3v.

119. "Wide and fat." It was in the sixteenth century and remains today a common element of Spanish rhetoric to employ two or more synonyms together, like *gordo* and *holgado* in this case, both referring to corpulence or excessive girth. This results in a redundancy that seems superfluous in modern English. But we have tried to adhere to the Spanish style whenever it occurs in the documents (and it does frequently). Other examples of this rhetorical trait are "a la ligera y por la posta," both meaning "rapidly," on fol. 86r, and "haber Visto y entendido," both meaning "to have understood," on fol. 95v. Craddock, "Castañeda y Nájera," 5, interprets *holgados* as "rested," although *DRAE,* 1116, also has "ancho."

120. "Brain." Craddock, "Castañeda y Nájera," 5: *celebro = cerebro.* Also *DRAE,* 451.

121. As a captain under Nuño de Guzman, Lope de Samaniego had earlier led the brutal conquest of Chiametla. His death at this early stage in the Coronado expedition was possibly an act of revenge on the part of natives of that area. Also see an account of this event in Document 17, fol. 1r.

122. This is the opening episode of violence between the expedition and native people. It was to prove typical of the expedition.

123. Converting to the *legua legal,* the distance from Culiacán to Chichilticale would be about 580 miles, again placing Chichilticale at the latitude of Eagle Pass and Apache Pass in modern southeastern Arizona. Not only does this seem to confirm that Chilchilticale must have been at that latitude, but it also demonstrates that Castañeda uses the *legua legal.* Use of a larger league, such as the *legua común,* would mean that the measurements from Culiacán to Chichilticale and Cíbola to Chichilticale would not coincide at the same latitude. See note 89, this document.

124. In 1544 Diego López reported Díaz's news as similarly disheartening. Flint, *Great Cruelties,* 396. For a written version of Melchior Díaz's report of what he and Zaldívar had learned about Cíbola, see Document 17.

125. The implication is that Marcos was referring to Cíbola, but there is no way to verify that from the context.

126. *Tierra de guerra* was any region of hostile natives not yet pacified by the Spaniards.

127. "Evening before" and "day after Easter." The evening before and day after Easter were March 27 and March 29, 1540, respectively. Cháves, *Espejo de navegantes,* 79–97. Delay of the welcoming celebration was necessary because it was not permitted on the holy day of Easter.

128. The injured artilleryman was Francisco Muñoz. AGI, México, 1064, L.1\1, "Informes de los conquistadores," fol. 116r.

129. That "rich dress" is not apparent in the February 1540 muster roll or in any other known contemporary document. See Document 12.

130. Fernandarias de Saavedra was a native of Sevilla in the modern Spanish *comunidad* of Andalucía and son of Hernán Darias de Saavedra, Conde de Castellar, and doña Catalina de Guzmán. Castañeda de Nájera, referring to Fernandarias as the uncle rather than the son on the *conde,* might have had in mind a subsequent holder of that title. He was in Nueva España by 1530. He went with Cortés to the Isla de California. Afterward, he was a captain and lieutenant governor at Culiacán, where he helped provide for the expedition to Tierra Nueva. Icaza, 1: no. 1264.

131. This large number of allies helps explain the later ease with which this otherwise seemingly small unit overran Cíbola.

132. "Charming," *donoso.* The word is used in an ironic sense here.

133. The man left in Culiacán was likely Pedro de Trujillo and not Rodrigo de Trujillo, who later bought Juan Jiménez's horse at auction. See Document 27, fol. 6r.

134. This is the only mention of a friar by the name Antonio Vitoria in the Coronado expedition documents. There is no other evidence that this friar participated in the *entrada.* Rather, the reference here is probably to Antonio de Castilblanco. Fray Antonio de Castilblanco and fray Francisco de Vitoria were together in Nueva Galicia when the expedition got under way, which may account for the confusion here. The two men remained closely connected all their lives. In 1544, however, Vázquez de Coronado himself identified the friar in question at this point as Castilblanco. Fray Antonio de Castilblanco arrived in Nueva España in 1538, coming from the Franciscan province of Los Ángeles in Castile. He was assigned to northern Nueva Galicia, where he developed a close relationship with the new governor, Francisco Vázquez de Coronado, becoming his personal confessor. Following his two years with the expedition to Tierra Nueva, fray Antonio became *guardian* at Xochimilco, where fray Marcos de Niza was in residence. After a sojourn of several years in Peru, fray Antonio returned to the Ciudad de México area, where he died before 1559. H&R, 9; Chávez, *Coronado's Friars,* 9, 30–31, 76–77; Flint, *Great Cruelties,* 290.

135. Castañeda de Nájera here implies again that fray Marcos did not reach Cíbola before July 1540.

136. This appears to confirm the suggestion that the expedition was receiving old stories and legends as if they reflected the contemporary state of affairs. See Document 19, note 86.

137. There is archaeological evidence to support the notion that some structures in modern southeastern Arizona, where Chichilticale presumably was, were built and inhabited by people of "northern" (Anasazi) traditions. William K. Hartmann and Richard Flint, "Migrations in Late Anasazi Prehistory: 'Eyewitness' Testimony," *Kiva* 66, no. 3 (2001):375–85. Castañeda de Nájera later claims that Chichilticale was built by people who "split off from Cíbola," fol. 104r.

138. The chronicler, both before and after this, states that the breadth of the unsettled area between Chichilticale and Cíbola was "eighty leagues," which took 15 days to cross. Fols. 12v and 104v; Document 6, fol. 5v. The Río Bermejo is the Little Colorado River (see map 2).

139. "Whiskered carp," *barbos = barbel. OED,* 947: "a large European freshwater fish of the carp family." *DRAE,* 265, adds the description that this fish has four whiskers.

140. The chronicler, who was not present at these events, omits recounting the division of the advance guard into two units, as told by Vázquez de Coronado. Document 19, fol. 360v.

141. *DRAE,* 199: *arriscar* = plunge over a cliff. *DRAE,* 165: *apeñuscar = agrupar* = to heap or pile on. At variance with these senses, H&R, 208, have, "It is a small, rocky pueblo, all crumpled up," and Winship, 203, has, "It is a little, unattractive village, looking as if it had been crumpled all up together."

142. This description is consistent with the site plan of Hawikku prepared as a result of its excavation by Frederick Hodge between 1917 and 1923. The description would, however, also fit many other contemporaneous pueblos. Smith, Woodbury, and Woodbury, *Excavation of Hawikuh,* fig. 37.

143. Edmund Ladd has suggested that the reported presence of residents of other pueblos at Cíbola at this time was occasioned by a ceremonial event associated with the summer solstice. Such an event, including a pilgrimage to the sacred lake of Ko:thluwala:wa, was described in detail by the nineteenth-century observer Mathilda Coxe Stevenson. Ladd, "Zuni on the Day the Men in Metal Arrived," in Flint and Flint, *Tierra Nueva,* 225–33; Stevenson, *Zuni Indians,* 148–62.

144. Vázquez de Coronado must have shouted, "Santiago!" This was the standard war cry, invoking St. James, patron saint of Spain and champion against the infidels. *DRAE,* 1843.

145. This again fits the archaeological plan of Hawikku, especially the passageway at the northeastern corner of the pueblo. Smith, Woodbury, and Woodbury, *Excavation of Hawikuh,* fig. 37.

146. Certainly the hundreds of native allies of the expedition who were present and fighting had something to do with the speed of the town's capture, although the chronicler fails to mention them or ascribe any assistance to them at this point. Compare this whole account of the capture of Cíbola with Vázquez de Coronado's letter of August 1540 (Document 19, fols. 360v–361r). Neither of the two principal

accounts of the fighting at Cíbola (this one and the October 1540 letter) was written by an eyewitness to the pueblo's capture. Castañeda de Nájera was with the main body of the expedition at San Gerónimo, and the captain general was unconscious as a result of a severe head wound. See Flint, *Great Cruelties*, for testimony of a number of eyewitnesses to the fighting. See also Document 22, fol. 1v. All the surviving European accounts agree that the conflict was intense but brief.

147. See Flint, *Great Cruelties*, 60, for Arellano's being called "the general."

148. Cabeza de Vaca's own account of his time in Corazones is in Adorno and Pautz, *Núñez Cabeza de Vaca*, 1:234–35. For geographical information about Corazones, see the entry in Appendix 2.

149. Regarding Niño Velasques's use of the phrase "I mean Senora" (*digo Senora*), see note 598, this document. For geographical information about Señora/Senora/Sonora, see the entry in Appendix 2. A similar relation between Corazones and Senora/Sonora to that expressed here seems to be reflected in Pérez de Ribas's account of Ures and Sonora. This supports the suggestion made by several researchers that Ures and Corazones were one and the same place. Pérez de Ribas, *Triumphs*, 389; Richard A. Pailes, "An Archaeological Perspective on the Sonoran Entrada," in Flint and Flint, *Tierra Nueva*, 186.

150. "The reported gigantic stature practically identifies the Indians ... with the Seri [Comcáac]." "The mean stature of the adult Seri may be estimated at about 6 feet (1.825 meters) for males." William John McGee, "The Seri Indians," in *Seventeenth Annual Report of the Bureau of American Ethnology to the Secretary of the Smithsonian Institution, 1895–96*, Part 1 (Washington, DC: Smithsonian Institution, 1898), 53, 136.

151. The Río del Tizón is the modern Colorado River between Arizona and California. Tello, 505, gives the name as Río del Tizontzico.

152. The large amount of information Castañeda de Nájera provides about Señora suggests that he was with the rear guard that stayed behind with Tristán de Arellano. Later, on fol. 40r, his presence with the main body of the expedition is confirmed when he includes in his account of the main body's northward march the statement that "the guards saw a herd of rams pass by. I saw them and followed them." This point is further demonstrated with the chronicler's consistent use of the third person when referring to the advance guard, as on fol. 30v.

153. Gallego was one of several men who served as couriers between the expedition and points south. Others included Juan de Cepeda and Luis de Figueredo. AGI, México, 1064, L.1\1, "Informes de los conquistadores," fol. 273r; Flint, *Great Cruelties*, 406.

154. Castañeda de Nájera, with this reference to brocades that failed to materialize, continues to express his opinion that fray Marcos, and therefore other friars and priests, had not told the truth about what he saw during his 1539 trek north.

155. H&R, 210, mistakenly have "Don Tristán de Arellano remained," overlooking the evident omission of Díaz (or anyone else) as the subject of "quedó."

156. Prior to the expedition to Tierra Nueva, Diego de Alcaraz and his brother Juan had both been residents of Culiacán. In 1536, while captain of a slaving patrol, probably in modern northern Sinaloa, he had met and treated roughly the survivors of the Narváez expedition to La Florida and their large following of indigenous people. Tello, 184.

157. For a reconstruction of the route followed by Melchior Díaz and his party from San Gerónimo to the lower Colorado River, see Ronald L. Ives, "The Grave of Melchior Díaz: A Problem in Historical Sleuting," *Kiva* 25, no. 1 (1959):31–40. Ives's route departs from Ures, Sonora, and heads northwest to Magdalena, Caborca, and Sonoita before turning more to the west-northwest. It skirts the northern fringe of the lava field associated with the Sierra Pinacate, crosses into what is now the United States, and visits the reliable water at Tinajas Altas. It then joins the Gila River near Wellton, Arizona, and follows the Gila downstream to its junction with the Colorado (see map 2). Only in its western reaches does Ives's routfe differ from and improve upon Herbert Bolton's. Bolton, 169–75.

158. One hundred fifty *leguas legales* would place this encounter nearly 400 miles from Ures/Corazones, along the lower Colorado River. The large people described here must have been some group of Yuman speakers. Kendall, "Yuman Languages," 8.

159. The term *choza* possibly derives from Arabic, meaning a hut for shepherds, or a rude shelter. When a house was poor and in ruins it might also be called a *choza*. Covarrubias, 392. "Pig pens" = *sahurdas* = *zahurdas*. This may describe thatch-covered shelters similar to those commonly used in the past by the Pima neighbors of the Yuman speakers in extreme northwestern Sonora, and perhaps also by the Yumans themselves. See an illustration in Robert A. Hackenberg, "Pima

and Papago Ecological Adaptations," in Ortiz, *Southwest*, vol. 10, 173. See also Document 15, note 63.

160. H&R, 210, ignore the age implication of "chicos y grandes" and use "large and small."

161. A *quintal* was a unit of weight equal to approximately 100 pounds. However, the unit varied throughout Spain and cannot with certainty be equated to 100 pounds in today's world.

162. According to Covarrubias, 639, *hogaza* was a coarse bread also baked in ashes. *DRAE*, 1115: "pan grande que pesa más de dos libras."

163. Cool nights in November, when Díaz was in the region of the lower Colorado River, could certainly qualify as "cold" in a relative sense but would not have begun to compare with the snow and subfreezing temperatures the main body of the expedition was soon to experience in Tiguex during the winter of 1540–41. See fols. 56r–57r.

164. H&R, 211, and Winship, 205, mistakenly read this as "more than two leagues across at the mouth. At that place [unspecified] it was half a league across."

165. The items placed at the foot of the tree could also have included maps, since *carta* can refer to both letters and maps.

166. This is the Baja California peninsula, thought to be an island until Francisco de Ulloa and Hernando de Alarcón demonstrated that it was part of the continental land mass in 1539 and 1540. This information was apparently unavailable to many subsequent cartographers until the eighteenth century. For many examples of maps showing California as an island, see Katherine R. Goodwin, "Entrada, The First Century of Mapping the Greater Southwest: An Exhibition," in *The Mapping of the Entradas into the Greater Southwest*, eds. Dennis Reinhartz and Gerald D. Saxon (Norman: University of Oklahoma Press, 1998), 152–206.

167. In modern usage, *soldado* is usually rendered as "soldier," but we have chosen "man-at-arms" in order to call attention to the fact that the men of the Coronado and other contemporary, quasi-military enterprises were not what we would recognize as soldiers today. They were private citizens who almost all pursued nonmilitary occupations. Few were in the employ of the viceroy or the captain general, and certainly not of the king. Because many were from the lowest ranks of the nobility, they had martial training as part of their education as young men and were expected to be able to engage in combat when necessary. And they lived in a time when that often came about.

168. The use of torture as a tool of legal investigation was common throughout Europe during this period and would have been altogether standard procedure in a case such as this. The Coronado expedition performed interrogation under torture a number of times, including of Bigotes and the *cacique* from Cicuique and of El Turco at Quivira. Flint, *Great Cruelties*, passim. For the prevailing legal basis for application of torture in investigations, see *Siete Partidas*, 3:650.

169. "Manpower," *cuerpos y fuerzas*. This represents another case of the use of synonyms together, referring here to large military units such as corps and legions. H&R, 212, ignore the military allusion and the fact that both nouns are plural and have "as they had power and strength."

170. Mora, 80, finds this "un poco extraña" and thinks that the sense is "siendo balseadores unas veces los amigos y otras los españoles."

171. "At the same time," *a la par. DRAE*, 1524.

172. The use of such literary devices indicates Castañeda de Nájera's familiarity with books and the writing profession.

173. The sequence of the *relación* suggests that Vacapan is north of Señora. If true, this Vacapan is apparently a different place from the Vacapa visited earlier by Marcos de Niza, which seems to have been no more than 30 leagues north of Petatlán, far south of Señora. See Document 6, fol. 3r; also Document 6, notes 96 and 97. Riley, *Frontier People*, 126, has suggested that Vacapan was "somewhere in the Gila drainage, probably south of the Gila." This may well be correct. At any rate, Vacapan seems to have lain between Señora and Chichilticale.

174. The Spanish appends the term "natural," which may indicate that only daylight hours were counted, as in "dia natural." *DRAE*, 740: "tiempo que dura la luz del Sol."

175. This first-person statement demonstrates that the chronicler was among the main body of the expedition under Arellano and thus did not witness the fighting at Cíbola or the first arrivals at Tiguex.

176. The fifteen-day unsettled area began at Chichilticale and ended at Cíbola. Therefore, the "very deep canyon" mentioned here would have been three days' travel from Chichilticale (no more than about 55 miles). If Chichilticale was near

Eagle Pass, then the canyon would have been located north of the Gila River on what is now the San Carlos Apache Reservation. If, on the other hand, it was near Apache Pass, then the canyon would have been one of the canyons north or northeast of Virden, New Mexico. See Document 30, note 61. Bolton identifies the "very deep canyon" with the Gila River itself beyond Eagle Pass, which would be a poor match for the physical description. Bolton, 195.

177. If this was a contemporary horn and not a fossil from a much earlier time, it was certainly the horn of a desert bighorn. In modern times the size of the horns of bighorns is determined by "length," meaning the distance from the base to the tip measured "along the outside of the curl," combined with circumference. Examples are known that have measured nearly four feet in "length" and 17 inches in basal circumference. Hansen, "Physical Characteristics," 56–58. A *braza* was a unit of length equal to approximately 1.7 meter, or 5.5 feet, the distance of outstretched arms. Two *varas* equaled one *braza*.

178. "Features," *faicion = facción. DRAE*, 943: "Figura y disposición con que una cosa se distingue de otra."

179. Vázquez de Coronado reveals in his letter of August 1540 that this was a wary peace at Cíbola. Only a relative few residents returned to Cíbola while the expedition was in residence. Document 19, fols. 361v and 362r.

180. Juan Jaramillo gives the distance as that which could be covered in five days' travel, about 80 miles. This is somewhat farther than the 25 leagues (approximately 66 miles) stated here. See Document 30, note 78. For geographical information about Tusayán (map 1), mistakenly called Tutahaco, see the entry in Appendix 2.

181. Chávez, *Coronado's Friars*, 21, refers to Padilla's quick temper. As Chávez also pointed out (47 n. 11), the translation of this phrase by Winship, 208, and H&R, 214 (followed by Bolton, 76)—"who in his youth had been a military man"—is simply incorrect. We are in full agreement with Chávez on this point. For biographical information about fray Juan de Padilla, see the entry in Appendix 1.

182. This description of the Hopis as stay-at-homes is at variance with their known protohistoric involvement in trade, hunting, and ceremonial activities that frequently meant absence from their homes. In addition, there is abundant evidence of frequent contacts between Tusayán/Hopi and Cíbola/Zuni. See, for instance, Riley, *Frontier People*, 167, 190–98; and fol. 42r.

183. This eastern Hopi pueblo might well have been Awatovi, now a ruin situated on Antelope Mesa overlooking Jeddito Wash. Ross Gordon Montgomery, Watson Smith, and John Otis Brew, *Franciscan Awatovi: Reports of the Awatovi Expedition, Report no. 3* (Cambridge, MA: Peabody Museum, Harvard University, 1949), 3, 5 n. 7.

184. Once again, contact between the expedition and natives is indirect. Presumably the interpreters were from Cíbola.

185. This gives an unflattering view of Juan de Padilla, in which he seems uninterested in conversion of native peoples, but it seems consistent with Castañeda de Nájera's styling him "combative." Fol. 42v.

186. A *real* was a large tent or complex of texts, a pavilion, and an encampment of an army. It was especially the place where the tent of the king or general was located.

187. Because there was at the time no comprehensive government among the Hopis, such a political submission by one pueblo on behalf of all the others seems unlikely. A similar situation existed in the Tiguex pueblos, as Vázquez de Coronado was informed by the *principal* Juan Alemán. Fols. 58v–59r.

188. This statement contrasts sharply with what Vázquez de Coronado wrote in August 1540: "much cotton is harvested among them," Document 19, fol. 362v. For a discussion of protohistoric cultivation of cotton in the American Southwest, see Document 30, note 86.

189. *Pinole* (and on fol. 50v). Clevy Lloyd Strout, "A Linguistic Study of the Journals of the Coronado Expedition" (Ph.D. dissertation, University of Colorado, 1958), 538, has "piñol" and erroneously derives the word from "piñon." H&R, 215 and 218, follow the same reasoning, translating the word as "piñon nuts." For a definition, see Document 6, note 124.

190. "Gave," *dieron, dar. DRAE*, 661, "Sujetar, someter alguien alguna cosa a la obediencia de otro."

191. See note 90, this document.

192. This may be an error picked up from the preceding sentence. The Grand Canyon is not as far as twenty days' travel from Hopi. Twenty leagues would be more appropriate. This may represent another case of mistaken substitution of "days" for "leagues," as happens on fol. 77r.

193. The North Rim of the Grand Canyon, at an elevation of more than 8,000 feet, is cool to cold all year. Even in the warmest season, daily low temperatures average a chilly 43 degrees F. When López de Cárdenas was at the canyon, in very late August, the passage of an early cold front would also have been possible.

194. Modern mapping shows the Colorado River from Marble Canyon through the Grand Canyon to be no more than about one eighth mile (about one-twentieth league) in width.

195. For biographical information about Juan Galeras, see Document 27, note 61.

196. "Because of the height," "que el Viso." Mora, 83, has "quel biso" and, citing the *Diccionario de autoridades*, 83 n. 66, insists that "viso" is "Voz anticuada equivalente a 'vista.'" However, *DRAE*, 2097, has viso = "altura o eminencia, sitio o lugar alto, desde donde se ve y descubre mucho terreno." In the context of this passage, the *DRAE* meaning seems more fitting.

197. Although portable clocks existed in the 1540s, there is no indication that any were included in the equipment of the expedition to Tierra Nueva. Hourglasses, however, certainly accompanied the expedition. Even lacking such devices, means were known by which the hour could be determined, such as the one described in Cháves, *Espejo de navegantes*, 207. For mid-sixteenth-century clocks, see Dava Sobel and William J. H. Andrewes, *The Illustrated Longitude* (New York: Walker, 1998), 44.

198. Reference here is to the cathedral tower, the Giralda, although it was not called this until the 1570s. See Magdalena Valor Piechotta, "La Torre y la catedral de Sevilla entre 1248 y 1560," in *VIII Centenario de la Giralda, 1198–1998*, ed. Teodor Falcón Márquez (Sevilla: Caja Sur Publicaciones, 1998), 59–82. During the first half of the sixteenth century the tower of the cathedral in Sevilla (a former minaret) stood at a height of approximately 248 feet, or 76.3 meters. It did not reach its modern height of 298 feet, or 91.6 meters, until remodeling was completed in 1568, at which time the structure that houses the bells and supports the famous weathervane was added. Miguel Ángel Tabales, Ana Salud Romo, and Enrique García, "Nuevos avances en el estudio del Alminar (La Giralda)," in Falcón Márquez, *VIII Centenario*, Lamina 4, 122; J. L. Justo Alpañes, "El Comportamiento de la Giralda durante los movimientos sísmicos de Sevilla," in Falcón Márquez, *VIII Centenario*, fig. 2, 162.

199. Throughout the New World, sixteenth-century Europeans commented on the remarkably long distances the pedestrian natives were capable of walking, routinely outdistancing their European counterparts.

200. "Crystal breasts," "s(i)enos de christal." Both Craddock, "Castañeda y Nájera," 7, and Mora, 84, leave this unchanged as "sinos." Craddock asserts that stalactites are intended, but he admits that "no tengo ejemplos de sino con este significado." *Descolgadero* = something falling like beads on a string. *DRAE*, 701, *descolgar*: "Bajar odejar caer poco a poco una cosa pendiente de cuerda, cadena o cinta." Strout, "Linguistic Study," 811, has simply "waterfall."

201. Pedro Méndez de Sotomayor was the official chronicler of the expedition. Unfortunately, neither this report of the trip to the Colorado River nor any more extensive report by him is known to have survived. Bolton lists the report in his compilation of "lost documents." Nothing else is known for certain about Sotomayor except that he was married to doña Catalina de Sotomayor, a *vecina* of Michoacán, and that she was widowed by 1546. That the chronicler died so soon after the return of the expedition might account for the disappearance of his chronicle or, possibly, its nonexistence. It is possible that he took notes but never got around to writing a complete account. Bolton, 474; AGI, Justicia, 263, Pieza 3, "Probanza de Mendoza, Michoacán."

202. Using the *legua legal*, the distance given here would be about 184 miles (using the *legua común*, it would be about 240 miles). Actual modern road mileage between Zuni/Cíbola and Pecos Pueblo/Cicuique is approximately 212 miles, almost exactly halfway between Castañeda de Nájera's values using the equivalents for the *legua legal* and *legua común*. The "Relación del Suceso" gives the aggregate distance from Cíbola to Cicuique as 75 leagues (*leguas legales*), about 197 miles. See maps 1 and 3; Document 29, fols. 2v and 3r. For geographical information about Cicuyc, see the entry in Appendix 2. Mora, 84; H&R, 217; and Winship, 210, all consistently use the spelling "Cicuye," which in the document is actually quite rare, perhaps being a mistake for "Cicuyc" (the equivalent of "Cicuique").

203. Bigotes was one of a party of three or four Indians from the pueblo of Cicuique who arrived at Cíbola in July 1540, shortly after its capture by the expedition to Tierra Nueva. His mustaches, being unusual among the Pueblos, attracted attention and occasioned the Spaniards' application of the sobriquet Bigotes. What

he was called in his own community is unknown. Though a young man, he was apparently an important person, said by the Spaniards to be both a captain and a *cacique*. He might have been a war chief or society chief, and the party he was with might have been a trading party, though it is also possible that its mission was primarily diplomatic. El Turco, a guide provided by Bigotes to Hernando de Alvarado, claimed that Bigotes had a gold bracelet and other jewelry of his. As a result, Bigotes was seized and kept prisoner for six months in the expedition's camp at Tiguex. He was tortured by dog attack in order to extract information but was allowed to return to his home at Cicuique in the spring of 1541 and was not seen by the Spaniards thereafter. Following his return, the people of Cicuique were openly hostile toward the expedition. See Flint, *Great Cruelties*, passim; Carroll L. Riley, "Pecos and Trade," in *Across the Chichimec Sea: Papers in Honor of J. Charles Kelley*, eds. Carroll L. Riley and Basil C. Hedrick (Carbondale: Southern Illinois University Press, 1978), 55; and Carroll L. Riley, *Rio del Norte: People of the Upper Rio Grande from Earliest Times to the Pueblo Revolt* (Salt Lake City: University of Utah Press, 1995), 163–64.

204. The referents are thoroughly ambiguous here. "They" and "them" refer to the two groups, but which is which is not at all clear.

205. "Head armor" = helmets = *capaçetes*. DRAE, 396.

206. A general discussion and list of trade and gift items used by the Coronado expedition is in Flint, "Material Culture," 170–82. Other trade or gift items referred to in the documents published in this volume are glass beads, knives, clothing, and cloaks. Document 4, fol. 355v; Document 15, fols. 364v and 369r. *Margarita* (see transcript, fol. 48v) was at the time a term for glass beads in general. Marvin T. Smith, *Archaeology of Aboriginal Culture Change in the Interior Southeast: Depopulation during the Early Historic Period* (Gainesville: University of Florida Press, 1987), 45–46; Flint, "Material Culture," 180. *Cascabeles* = hawksbells. Flint, "Material Culture," 181.

207. "Body," *en las carnes*. The use of the plural is curious here and may be an error. DRAE, 418, refers specifically to the muscular part of the body; hence, this could refer to biceps or pectorals, for example.

208. Without apparent justification, H&R, 217, have "the hair was so wooly and tangled." Craddock, "Castañeda y Nájera," 7, provides the solution: "mala lectura" "que parece ser derivado de *buriel*." DRAE, 334.

209. For geographical information, see the entry for Acuco in Appendix 2.

210. "Cavities," *agujeros*. These are hand and toe holds.

211. Despite this claim of invulnerability, Vicente de Zaldívar led a successful assault on Acoma in 1599. Hammond and Rey, *Oñate*, 1:460–62.

212. In the 1920s three sizable natural rock reservoirs were still in use at Acoma. Mrs. William T. Sedgwick, *Acoma, the Sky City: A Study in Pueblo Indian History and Civilization* (Cambridge, MA: Harvard University Press, 1927), 25.

213. This does not jibe with the account of the "Relación del Suceso," in which the author (who was with Alvarado) states that the people of Acuco "came out to us in peace." Document 29, fol. 3r.

214. This appears very similar to the procedure followed at Cíbola and Tusayán. On the supposition that the people of Hawikku were in the midst of a ceremony related to summer solstice at the time the advance guard arrived, Ed Ladd suggested that the meaning of the lines was something like, "Do not enter right now; we're having a ceremony." The similar action at Tusayán has not, however, been linked to a ceremonial event. Flint, *Great Cruelties*, 236; Ladd, "Zuni on the Day the Men in Metal Arrived," 232.

215. As at Cíbola and Tusayán, fighting at Acoma was of very short duration.

216. Triguex = Tiguex. This is the only known occurrence of this spelling, which is evidently an error. For geographical information, see the entry for Tiguex in Appendix 2.

217. Slavery of adult males was unusual among the Pueblos. As James Brooks recently put it, "here is an indigenous pattern:" men would die, "while their spouses and children were assimilated through marriage and adoption into victorious Indian families." This suggests that El Turco's status might have been more complicated than the term used here conveys. James F. Brooks, *Captives and Cousins: Slavery, Kinship, and Community in the Southwest Borderlands* (Chapel Hill: University of North Carolina Press, 2002), 54.

218. For biographical information on don Fernando de Soto, see the introduction to Document 8.

219. "This [man]" = *este*. H&R, 219, insert here the fact that he was called El Turco, moving that phrase from 12 lines later in the manuscript.

220. In 1611 Covarrubias, 866, wrote that in his day "riches" had come to be restricted to "dinero y hacienda [money and real property]."

221. For biographical information about Turco, see Appendix 1.

222. This is the first use of García instead of Garci in this document.

223. Several accounts from the 1544 investigation of the expedition generally imply that relinquishment of the pueblo was voluntary, perhaps even initiated by the Tiguex people themselves. In contrast, Gaspar Saldaña testified that "the *maestre de campo* asked the Indians to provide quarters for him." Flint, *Great Cruelties*, 94, 111, 168, 194, 440.

224. "Toward the north," *debajo del norte*. Craddock, "Castañeda y Nájera," 8, interprets this as "hacía el norte," as do H&R, 220, and Winship, 216, translating the phrase as "toward the north."

225. The chronicler here reveals his geographical conceptions, implying that Greater India (modern eastern Asia) would have been reached by traveling toward the north.

226. This also marks the point at which Castañeda de Nájera reached Cíbola. Thus, the chronicler has recounted most of the material in the preceding two chapters from secondhand information.

227. Tutahaco was a region, or *provincia*, as sixteenth-century Spaniards put it, of Pueblo settlements, comprising eight or nine towns situated along the Rio Grande roughly between its junction with the Rio Puerco and what is now Albuquerque, New Mexico (see map 3). Elinore M. Barrett, *Conquest and Catastrophe: Changing Rio Grande Pueblo Settlement Patterns in the Sixteenth and Seventeenth Centuries* (Albuquerque: University of New Mexico Press, 2002), 24–26.

228. Members of the contemporary Soto expedition saw such canoes on the Mississippi River—for instance, "a canoe that carried 80 Indian warriors." Luys Hernández de Biedma, "Relation of the Island of Florida," trans. and ed. John E. Worth, in Clayton, Knight, and Moore, *De Soto Chronicles*, 1:245. Carroll Riley earlier pointed out the similarity of this description with the Mississippi. Carroll L. Riley, "Early Spanish-Indian Communication in the Greater Southwest," *New Mexico Historical Review* 46, no. 4 (1971):304–6.

229. The governor mentioned here is evidently the man called *cacique* elsewhere. The title is an Arawak word meaning "headman." It was applied by the Spaniards of the expedition to Tierra Nueva to an elderly and important man from the pueblo of Cicuique. He may have been with Bigotes in the trading-diplomatic party that arrived at Cíbola in July 1540 and offered alliance with the Spaniards. He may also have been a leader of that party and an important person among the religious-political hierarchy of Cicuique. It is possible that he was what has since become known as Elder Brother Bow Priest among some of the Pueblos. Riley, *Rio del Norte*, 163, 176; Bolton, 200. The tents in use on expeditions of the period were circular and conical-topped. One example of such a tent is known to survive. It is curated in the Museo del Ejército in Madrid and was made for the Portuguese governor of Cambala, India, between 1542 and 1545. Antonio Fernández Puertas and Cristina Partearroyo, "Military Tent, Generally Known as Charles V's Tent, 1542–1545," in *Art and Culture around 1492*, ed. Joan Sureda i Pons (Sevilla: Sociedad Estatal para la Exposición Universal Sevilla 92, 1992), 82–83.

230. This use of the editorial "we" and another on fol. 74r are further evidence of Castañeda de Nájera's ease with a literary style.

231. Tigues = Tiguex.

232. As the chronicler informs us on fol. 105r, this was the pueblo of Mats'a:kya.

233. Although the layouts of all the protohistoric Zuni pueblos have not been exposed archaeologically, the plan of Hawikku and surface indications at Binna:wa, Chalo:wa, and Kechiba:wa indicate the prevalence of roomblocks completely enclosing plazas, with few or no ground-level "streets" or "alleys." Kintigh, *Settlement, Subsistence, and Society*, 58–70.

234. Use of the first person here again shows that the chronicler himself was with the main unit under Arellano.

235. It is possible that members of the expedition were allowed or forced themselves onto the roofs of the pueblo; otherwise it is difficult to explain their taking shelter under balconies. Such covered, open-air spaces are not known to have been used on the ground floors of protohistoric pueblos. Certainly the excavation of Hawikku revealed no such features.

236. This is the first mention of snowfall during the winter of 1540–41, which was a exceptionally wet period, according to modern reconstructions of precipitation. See Henri D. Grissino-Mayer, "A 2129-Year Reconstruction of Precipitation for Northwestern New Mexico, USA," in *Tree Rings, Environment, and Humanity*, eds. Jeffrey S. Dean, D. M. Meko, and T. W. Swetman (Tucson: *Radiocarbon* [Department of Geosciences, University of Arizona], 1996), 191–204. For temperature and precipitation reconstruction, see Carla R. Van West and Henri D.

Grissino-Mayer, "Dendroclimatic Reconstruction," in *Archaeological Data Recovery in the New Mexico Transportation Corridor and First Five-Year Permit Area, Fence Lake Coal Mine Project, Catron County, New Mexico*, vol. 2, Part 1, *Draft Report* (Tucson, AZ: Statistical Research, 2004). *Codo:* see Document 23, note 64.

237. "Bed[roll]s," *lechos portatiles.* It is unlikely that many, if any, of the members of the expedition were transporting pieces of furniture even as bulky as cots.

238. Interpolating a different referent for what was not being touched, H&R, 223, have "they do not seem to touch the walls with their hands." Because the hand and toe holds at the top of the ascent would have required the use of hands, it seems much more likely that Castañeda de Nájera is commenting here on the ability of the Acoma people to carry their loads without touching them.

239. Already by early December 1540, before arrival of the van of the expedition, the imposition of the Europeans and their allies was insupportable.

240. This pueblo was the one called Arenal. See fol. 63v. For geographical information, see the entry for Coofor in Appendix 2.

241. H&R, 223, and Winship, 218, render this phrase as "without any one of them being to blame" and "without being to blame for it," respectively. Both of these translations seem to stretch and misinterpret the text. The information contained in chapter 15 of the *relación* is secondhand, because the events narrated there happened before the chronicler arrived in Tiguex.

242. This is the first instance of the spelling Cicuye. Prior to this the name has been spelled with a terminal *c*, Cicuyc. See, for instance, fol. 48r. Bolton consistently used the Cicuye spelling. In the past we have followed his lead. It now seems quite likely, however, that "Cicuye" is a scribal artifact and that the final syllable of the name reproduced in the documents included a hard *k* sound. In the documents, *c* and *e* are often difficult to distinguish. This may explain an *escribano*'s miscopying "Cicuye" for "Cicuyc."

243. Tello, 420, renders this surname variously as Román, Lomán, and Lamán. Jumena, Juan Eman, or Juan Alemán was a *principal* at the Tiguex pueblo of Coofor. He was thoroughly disenchanted with the members of the expedition to Tierra Nueva. It has been suggested that his Tiwa name was Xauian. Months after the abandonment of Coofor by its residents, he took part in an attempt at Pueblo del Cerco, or Moho (map 5), to kill *maestre de campo* García López de Cárdenas. Riley, *Rio del Norte*, 176; fols. 64r–64v. The Juan Alemán in the Ciudad de México whom Jumena was said to resemble was Juan Henche, a merchant doing business in the viceregal capital who also had mining interests in Sultepec. Ida Altman, "Spanish Society in Mexico City after the Conquest," *Hispanic American Historical Review* 71, no. 3 (1991):427.

244. For a discussion of the identity of these pueblos, see the entry for Tiguex in Appendix 2.

245. Castañeda de Nájera gives an account of the requisitioning of clothing that is very sympathetic to the Pueblos. That seems not to have been unusual among expedition members. See, for instance, Flint, *Great Cruelties*, 80, 143, 149, 238, 317.

246. This possible rapist is identified elsewhere as Juan de Villegas. See Flint, *Great Cruelties*, 171, 214, 317. Juan de Villegas was a native of Zafra in the modern *provincia* of Badajoz in the *comunidad* of Extremadura in Spain. He joined the expedition to Tierra Nueva as a horseman, taking three horses with him. He had arrived in Nueva España in 1538. Juan de Contreras, however, testified during Tejada's 1544 investigation that Villegas was not punished because his brother, Pedro de Villegas, was a *regidor* of the Ciudad de México. As such, Pedro served on the *cabildo* with Vázquez de Coronado. The rape doubtless contributed to friction between the people of Tiguex and the expeditionaries. *Pasajeros*, 2: no. 4946; Document 12; Flint, *Great Cruelties*, 112.

247. Juan de Contreras and other expedition members conceded that Vázquez de Coronado was aware that Villegas had committed the rape but did nothing to punish him. Flint, *Great Cruelties*, 112.

248. H&R, 225, alter the meaning of "viendo" and append this sentence to the previous one, making it part of the Spaniard's denial.

249. "Fighting the horses," *corriendo los cavallos. Correr, DRAE*, 579: "lidiar los toros."

250. This is Pueblo del Arenal. See Flint, *Great Cruelties*, 441, 442, 451, 452, 515.

251. "General" is being used in the generic sense of "leader" here, referring in this case to López de Cárdenas.

252. "Started large, smoky fires," *daban humazos. DRAE*, 1132: "Hacer de modo que se retire del lugar adonde solia concurrir incomodando."

253. "Ground-floor rooms," *sotanos.* Ordinarily *sótano* would refer to a basement or cellar, but because the ground-floor rooms of a Rio Grande pueblo occupied a

similar position relative to the inhabited rooms (second floor and up), it is fittingly applied to them here.

254. "Gave themselves up without submitting to [the Spaniards'] will," *se dieron a merced. Darse a merced, DRAE*, 1359: "darse a discreción" = "Entregarse sin capitulación al arbitrio del vencedor" (759) = "surrender without submitting to the will of the victor." H&R, 226, have "surrendered at their mercy," and Winship, 30, has "received pardon." The rendering we have used is more consistent with the rest of the passage.

255. "Surrendering involuntarily." If the Indians had surrendered voluntarily, then the terms of peace would have applied. If they were taken by force, then the Spaniards would not have considered themselves bound by any conditions. Thus, our use of "involuntarily" in translation here reflects our inference that the word *contra* is missing from the Spanish text, which should have read "contra su Voluntad" instead of "de su Voluntad."

256. The use of "general" here is ambiguous. It could refer to either López de Cárdenas or Vázquez de Coronado, although no other known contemporary documents mention Vázquez de Coronado's having given such an order.

257. The chronicler seems to excuse López de Cárdenas here, although the official investigation of this event in 1544 resulted in his punishment. Flint, *Great Cruelties*, 336–41.

258. The large number of persons referred to is an indication that this was a *real*, or very large tented complex.

259. This is the most detailed surviving account of the attack on the Pueblo prisoners. Castañeda de Nájera's version indicates that the result was nearly wholesale slaughter of the male residents of Arenal. There is no evidence that the chronicler was himself present.

260. This is an ambiguous sentence. The unfortunate occurrence could be either the killing of the Indians or the spreading of the news of the Spaniard's treachery.

261. The arrival of the main body of the expedition has already been referred to on fol. 58r.

262. This reference to excessive snowfall is another indication of the exceptional wetness of the year, which probably resulted in extraordinary snowpack in the mountains. See note 236, this document.

263. Reference to the pueblo of Tiguex must be in error here. The pueblo in question is evidently Pueblo del Cerco. The expedition itself was apparently housed in Tiguex. The same error appears on fol. 65v.

264. Just a few lines earlier Juan Alemán seemed to have only one companion.

265. This pueblo, like so many of the Tiguex pueblos, has not been identified with certainty. We suggest that it is one of the long-abandoned pueblos on Santa Ana Mesa, nearly overlooking modern San Felipe Pueblo. One possible candidate is the archaeological ruin designated as LA 2049.

266. Again, the name appears to be an error, since the expedition was evidently lodged in the pueblo of Tiguex. The same error appears on fol. 64r.

267. A hundred seems like an extraordinarily high number of casualties. See Tello, 264; he names the following as having been killed: so-and-so Benítez (possibly Martín, see Appendix 3), (Francisco) Carabajal, brother of Hernando de Trejo (who was lieutenant governor for Francisco de Ibarra in Chiametla), and a *vizcaíno* (someone from the *provincia* of Vizcaya), Alonso de Castañeda (Machín Castañeda; see "H&R Incorrect Additions" in Appendix 3).

268. This period of 50 days is in approximate agreement with the account from the "Relación del Suceso," which states that the siege lasted "two months." Document 29, fol. 4r.

269. "Well," *poso.* If this *pozo* was a water well, then its great depth indicates that Pueblo del Cerco was not in the immediate floodplain of the Rio Grande. As indicated by *DRAE*, 1651, *pozo* can also refer to an "Hoyo profundo, aunque esté seco." Thus, it could have been a cistern or even a quarry for rock, which the Spaniards interpreted as a water well.

270. A Francisco de Ovando de Saavedra, the son of Diego de Ovando and Beatriz de Cháves, *vecinos* of Cáceres in the modern Spanish *comunidad* of Extremadura, had received a license in April 1535 to travel to Santo Domingo. Boyd-Bowman, 2: no. 2774; *Pasajeros*, 2: no. 495. A Francisco de Pobares, son of Francisco de Pobares and Quíteria de Vera, *vecinos* of Sabiote in the modern *provincia* of Jaén in the Spanish *comunidad* of Andalucía, arrived in Nueva España in 1536. *Pasajeros*, 2: no. 2673.

271. The quarter called "la modorra" is the middle of the three night watches. For information on the watches, see Cháves, *Espejo de navegantes*, 231, and Document 27, note 37.

272. "Camp," *cuartel. DRAE*, 609: "Cada uno de los puestos o sitios en que se reparte o acuartela el ejército cuando está en campaña."

273. "Made a stand," *se recibieron. Recibirse: DRAE*, 1740, "cuadrarse," said usually of bulls.

274. Because Pedro de Nájera was in Guevara's company, the chronicler himself would be expected to have been involved in the siege of this nearby pueblo, which seems to be confirmed by the detailed account that follows of the ploy used to lure defenders from that pueblo. See Document 12, fol. 4r.

275. These women and children were evidently distributed as servants to members of the expedition, as had been done earlier with the survivors of the flight from Moho. Fol. 69v.

276. The year must have been in error on the copy from which Niño Velásques was working. The year was actually 1541. This may mean that the copy Niño Velásques had was already a second-generation copy containing this error made by an earlier copyist. On the other hand, Niño Velásques may have been copying from the original, in which case the error was made by Castañeda de Nájera himself.

277. Diego de Alarcón, as the manuscript has it (see transcript, fol. 71r), is an error for Diego de Alcaraz.

278. This is an accurate description of the overall trend of the west shore of the Gulf of California.

279. "Caverns," *lagos. Lago* can apply to a cave. See *DRAE*, 1224: "lago de leones. Lugar subterráneo o cueva en que los encerraban."

280. Castañeda de Nájera's descriptions here match well the geothermal area in extreme northern Baja California known today as the Cerro Prieto. Ives, "Grave of Melchior Díaz," 32–33. H&R, 231, have "beds of burning lava," which is off the mark, although it too could describe the Cerro Prieto.

281. This is a fighting lance [*lanza de encuentro*], as opposed to a tournament lance [*lanza de torneo*].

282. Speculation about the location of Díaz's death and burial is the subject of Ives, "Grave of Melchior Díaz." In that article he argues that the captain died in the vicinity of modern Caborca, Sonora (see map 2).

283. These messages to the viceroy may have included the letter Vázquez de Coronado wrote in April 1541, to which he refers in his letter of October that year. The April letter is not known to have survived. Document 26, fol. 1r.

284. In keeping with centuries-old Spanish practice, in short order fighting men from newly subjugated Los Corazones were enlisted or impressed into service against their recalcitrant neighbors.

285. Pérez de Ribas referred to the use of the same poison 85 years later. Pérez de Ribas, *Triumphs*, 90, 395 n. 24: "Apparently the famed *yerba de flecha*—made from species of Euphorbiaceae . . . , small trees that grow at higher elevations on the slopes of the sierras. The trees produce a sticky substance or *goma* that was used for arrow points as well as fish stupefaction." Pennington identifies the poison as the white sap from a species of Euphorbiaceae, *Sebastiana appendiculatum*, called *yerba de la flecha*. Campbell W. Pennington, *The Material Culture: The Pima Bajo of Central Sonora, Mexico*, vol. 1 (Salt Lake City: University of Utah Press, 1980), 218. In the 1560s Baltasar de Obregón had firsthand experience with *yerba de flecha* in the vicinity of Oera, Sonora, reporting that he was told it produced a painful death and describing the trees from which the sap came. Obregón, *Historia*, 147, 148. The antidote for the poison was reported to be quince juice. See fol. 140v.

286. Suya, sometimes incorrectly spelled Fuya (there was no *f* phoneme in the now extinct Ópata language), was the site for the final outpost of the expedition, to be called San Gerónimo, some 40 leagues, or about 100 miles, from the Señora Valley (see map 2). To the members of the expedition the people at Suya seemed culturally and physically the same as those at Señora. This is in agreement with current understandings of the ancestral Ópata culture area that occupied much of what is now central Sonora at the time. Like their neighbors to the south, the Lower Pimas, the Ópatas were devastated by European diseases in the century following the expedition to Tierra Nueva. It is unclear exactly where Suya was, although Carroll Riley has suggested it was in extreme northern modern Sonora, perhaps along the headwaters of the Río San Pedro. More recently, Daniel Reff has said flatly that it was in the area of Bacoachi in northern Sonora, but still on the Río Sonora. Reff offers several possibilities, including especially a large ruin called San José near modern Baviácora, Sonora, and another called Las Delicias near Banámichi. Information from the "Relación del Suceso" is consistent with Señora's having been located in the vicinity of Baviácora. Campbell W. Pennington, "Bosquejo grammática y vocabulario de la lengua ópata, sacada de un obra de Natal Lombardo, S.J., que sirve dentro los Ópatas de Sonora durante las últimas décadas

del siglo diecisiete" (unpublished manuscript, Library, Laboratory of Anthropology, Museum of New Mexico, Santa Fe, n.d.); Hinton, "Southern Periphery," 317; Daniel T. Reff, *Disease, Depopulation, and Culture Change in Northwestern New Spain, 1518–1764* (Salt Lake City: University of Utah Press, 1991), 245; Riley, *Frontier People*, 72; Reff, "Relevance of Ethnology," 171–72.

287. Quisvira. The interpolation of an *s* is probably a scribal error, since it is the only known occurrence of this spelling.

288. Chia = Zia. For geographical information, see Document 24, note 25.

289. Throughout the period of fighting in Tiguex the people of Chia/Zia maintained a status as ostensible allies of the expedition. These artillery pieces were likely four of the six *versillos* (see note 589, this document) of which Juan Troyano was in charge, under the overall command of Hernando de Alvarado. Document 31.

290. Quirix = Keres. See map 5. For geographical information, see the entry for Tiguex in Appendix 2.

291. This lack of resettlement suggests the devastation of the Tiguex people that had occurred during the winter fighting and the animosity they harbored toward the expedition.

292. The unusual occurrence and duration of ice covering the river is another indication of the severity of the winter of 1540–41, which saw extreme cold and unusually high precipitation. See also notes 236 and 262, this document. That the Río de Tiguex/Rio Grande was fordable contrasts with the situation at the Río de Cicuique, which only days later had to be bridged because it was running so deep. See fols. 77v–78r.

293. It has been suggested that the Guas, Guaes, Guaches, Guales, or Guaces were a tribal people living north and east of Quivira, perhaps to the west of the great bend of the Missouri River. Bolton, 233. For geographical information about Arehe, see the entry in Appendix 2.

294. We have suggested that this surname should actually be Cervatos or Cerbatos. See Document 12, note 90.

295. The record of this second muster, conducted at Tiguex, is not known to have survived.

296. "Entrusted them with the good treatment of the Spaniards." H&R, 234, reverse the subject and object of this clause, which results in their erroneous translation, "ordered that they be well treated by the Spaniards."

297. The erection of crosses was a common practice of Spanish expeditions of the period and of the Coronado expedition in particular. We have previously suggested that crosses were placed on elevations and that each likely was visible from its immediately preceding neighbor. See Flint and Flint, "Coronado's Crosses," 207–16.

298. This is probably the Old Style (Julian) date of April 23 reported by Vázquez de Coronado (in Document 26), corrected by Niño Velásques for the change to the Gregorian calendar, which had taken place in 1582. See Document 26, fol. 1r; Flint, "Reconciling the Calendars," 151–63; and Harry Kelsey, "The Gregorian Calendar in New Spain: A Problem in Sixteenth-Century Chronology," *New Mexico Historical Review* 58 (July 1983):239–51.

299. One implication of this statement may be that Bigotes and the governor continued to insist that El Turco was lying. This would run counter to the notion of a conspiracy between El Turco and the people of Cicuique. Such a conspiracy was later "admitted to" by El Turco. See fols. 87r–87v. See also note 343, this document. Whether Xabe was this boy's name in his native tongue is unknown. The Spaniards, however, commonly assigned names of their own to native people they dealt with, and a number of Arabic borrowings were current in sixteenth-century Spanish that had "xabe" as a major element. These had to do with nets and catching with nets. Covarrubias, 675.

300. None of the rivers of east-central New Mexico would ordinarily be characterized as swift and deep. This suggests a set of unusual circumstances that from time to time cause the Pecos River (and others of the region) to run with such a flow for relatively short periods. In late spring, as the season is here, high water and flooding are typically caused by rapid snowmelt in the Sangre de Cristo Mountains (map 3), perhaps augmented or accelerated by rainfall.

301. The Río de Cicuyc is the modern Pecos River. For a discussion of the identity of the Río de Cicuyc and the route from Cicuyc to the site where the bridge was constructed, see Richard Flint and Shirley Cushing Flint, "The Coronado Expedition: Cicúye to the Río de Cicúye Bridge," in Flint and Flint, *Tierra Nueva*, 262–77. This is the only bridge reported as having been built by the expedition. For a discussion of the type of bridge built, see Richard Flint, "Who Designed Coronado's Bridge across the Pecos River?" *Kiva* 57, no. 4 (1992):331–42.

302. Arab-like, *alárabe*. Use of the adjective "Arab-like" may refer to the Querechos' mode of living, in tents and on the move. On the other hand, it may be used in a derrogatory sense, implying brutishness. For information about the Querechos, see the entry in Appendix 1.

303. The Coronado expedition seems generally to have had success in communicating with native people by means of hand signs. That medium, though, has severe limitations, especially when attempts are made to convey foreign concepts and abstract ideas.

304. This reference to a downstream direction indicates that at this point the expedition was still in the broad valley of the Canadian River (maps 1 and 4).

305. A. Grove Day, following Frederick Webb Hodge, suggested that Haxa was a Caddoan community in East Texas, though it may instead have been Arahe, east of Quivira. Day, *Coronado's Quest*, 356 n. 19.

306. Many have suggested that the reference here is to the lower Mississippi River and the sophisticated native peoples who lived along it in protohistoric times. This certainly seems to be the case. Riley, "Early Spanish-Indian Communication," 305–6; Mildred Mott Wedel, "The Indian They Called Turco," in *Pathways to Plains Prehistory: Anthropological Perspectives of Plains Natives and Their Pasts*, eds. Don G. Wyckoff and Jack L. Hofman (Duncan, OK: Cross Timbers Press, 1982), 154–55; Donald J. Blakeslee, Richard Flint, and Jack T. Hughes, "Una Barranca Grande: Recent Archeological Evidence and a Discussion of Its Place in the Coronado Route," in Flint and Flint, *Tierra Nueva*, 379–80.

307. "For two days," *desde a dos dias*. H&R, 236, render this as "two days later," whereas Winship, 236, shares our reading, "for two days." The latter reading implies that the northeasterly course was of short duration. For a full discussion of the route in this region, see Flint, "Reconciling the Calendars," 151–63.

308. "Settled land" evidently refers to the pueblos along the Rio Grande in New Mexico.

309. It appears that the expedition met Querechos in this year and at this season only northwest of the Llano Estacado (map 4), and not on the great plain itself. See Flint, "Reconciling the Calendars," 156–58.

310. Descriptions here and elsewhere among the documents relating to the expedition indicate that the landform encountered at this point was the Llano Estacado of eastern New Mexico and the Texas Panhandle (maps 1 and 4).

311. Haya = Haxa. *Y* and *x* are often indistinguishable in sixteenth-century texts.

312. This is a rare mention of a loss of equipment and animals by the expedition.

313. This episode has been analyzed recently by the social geographer John Morris. He contends that the small river (*pequeño río*) mentioned here was Running Water Draw, west of modern Plainview, Texas, and that the course followed by López's company was precisely 61.5 degrees east-northeast. John Miller Morris, *El Llano Estacado: Exploration and Imagination on the High Plains of Texas and New Mexico, 1536–1860* (Austin: Texas State Historical Association, 1997), 49–55. Morris's precision is probably unwarranted, especially since the phrase "toward where the sun rose" (*haçia adonde salia el sol*) applied broadly to the east and not to the actual current spot on the horizon where the sun rose. "Toward where the sun rose" (fol. 79v) is an example of the use of this phrase to refer to a generally easterly direction, rather than a precise compass point. "At the ingresses to and egresses from the river," *en las entradas o las salidas del rio*. The bare, muddy ground at such crossings would naturally have testified to the passage of horses. H&R, 236–37, misconstrue this passage as "at the source and mouth of the river." Bolton, 252, followed Hammond and Rey and concluded from their poor rendering that "Coronado was obviously still close to the Canadian River, most of whose branches here are short, run north and south, and would thus cut across the path of López returning from the east."

314. Again, these are some of the Indian allies who formed the bulk of the expedition.

315. "Twenty leagues." Because López and his company were traveling with unusual speed for two days, this provides a reasonable upper limit for the daily rate of travel by the expedition or its subunits of 10 leagues per day.

316. "Tattooed," *pintado*. Literally, *pintado* implies "dotted," which suggests a type of tattooing in which a series of shallow punctures in the skin are filled with pigment to form the design.

317. The very name the Europeans assigned to this man implies that he was a teller of tales. Ysopete is equivalent to Aesop in Spanish. Aesop was, of course, the best-known fable teller of classical Greece. This suggests that the name was not given to this Plains Indian man until he informed expedition members about marvelous places to the east. See Jane MacLaren Walsh, "Myth and Imagination in

the American Story: The Coronado Expedition, 1540–1542" (Ph.D. dissertation, Catholic University of America, 1993). Isopete, Ysopete, or Sopete was a native of Quivira, perhaps a member of a Wichita band, who in 1540 was at the town of Cicuique. By modern historians he is often said to have been a slave of Bigotes and the *cacique* of Cicuique, who had captured him on the buffalo plains. As in the case of El Turco, "slave" may be an inappropriate term in its modern usage. H&R, 237 n. 4; Riley, *Rio del Norte*, 169; Bolton, 188; Walsh, "Myth and Imagination," 202. For a discussion of slavery among the Pueblos, see note 217, this document.

318. This reference to Colima implies that Castañeda de Nájera was familiar with that area in western Nueva España. Michael Mathes has recently offered the observation that a series of *barrancas* in what was the sixteenth-century *provincia* of Colima closely resembles the southern Caprock Canyons on the eastern margin of modern Texas's South Plains, particularly Blanco Canyon in Floyd and Crosby Counties (map 4). Specifically, he points out a congruence in scale (not extremely large) and coloration (whitish) and suggests that two series of canyons are those the chronicler is comparing here. A campsite of the Coronado expedition has been located archaeologically in Blanco Canyon. Known as the Jimmy Owens Site, it is under continued archaeological investigation by Donald J. Blakeslee and his students from Wichita State University. Gerhard, *Historical Geography*, 79; W. Michael Mathes, "A Large Canyon Like Those of Colima," in Flint and Flint, *Tierra Nueva*, 365–69; Blakeslee, Flint, and Hughes, "Una Barranca Grande," 370–83.

319. Álvar Núñez Cabeza de Vaca and Andrés Dorantes, along with Alonso del Castillo Maldonado and Dorantes's slave Esteban, survived the disastrous expedition to La Florida led by Pánfilo de Narváez. During the early to middle 1530s they made their way on foot from Galveston Bay to the Spanish settlement of Culiacán. According to modern reconstructions of the route followed by these shipwreck survivors, they did not travel far enough north to have entered even the southernmost of Texas's Caprock Canyons. While the chronicler's statement is thus not literally true, it is quite possible that Cabeza de Vaca met this Teya band somewhere farther south in its seasonal, seminomadic round, to which Castañeda de Nájera later refers. The expedition member Juan Jaramillo recorded that the encounter had happened "closer to Nueva España." Jaramillo's version of events jibes well with what is now known about the territory of the Teyas. They seem to have ranged over a wide area of West Texas and extreme northern Mexico, moving seasonally in pursuit of natural resources and trading opportunities. In particular, some Teya bands are now thought to have spent part of the year in the vicinity of the junction of the Rio Grande and the Río Conchos (map 1), known as La Junta. The ethnohistorian Carroll Riley has maintained for years that Cabeza de Vaca met the Teyas, whom Vázquez de Coronado later encountered in Blanco Canyon, at or near La Junta. As it happens, that proposal puts the meeting between Teyas and the Cabeza de Vaca party squarely on what is now considered Cabeza de Vaca's most likely route. Donald E. Chipman, "In Search of Cabeza de Vaca's Route across Texas: An Historiographical Survey," *Southwestern Historical Quarterly* 91, no. 2 (1987):127–48; Riley, *Rio del Norte*, 150–51; Document 30, fol. 3r; Adorno and Pautz, *Núñez Cabeza de Vaca*, 1:93–199.

320. "Heap," *montón*. The Spanish term *montón* in this context implies items considered booty to be distributed by shares to those who had invested in the expedition. The disorderly looting of the pile described later was all but mutiny. For the *montón* tradition in the sixteenth century, see Pérez-Mallaína, *Spain's Men of the Sea*, 99.

321. "Stole," *dan sacomano*. Covarrubias, 875, defines *dar sacomano* as *robar*, or "to steal."

322. During Cabeza de Vaca's trek, a procedure evolved in which the host Indians gave their goods to Cabeza de Vaca and the others, who then blessed them and distributed them to the Indian guides who accompanied them. Those people who had thus lost their goods were recompensed at the next native settlement. One instance of blessing food distributed to their guides was recorded this way: "Each one came to us with the portion assigned to him so that we might blow on it and make the sign of the cross over it because otherwise they would not dare to eat of it. And many times we brought with us three or four thousand people. And our labor was so great because we had to blow on and make the sign of the cross over what each of them was to eat and drink." Adorno and Pautz, *Núñez Cabeza de Vaca*, 1:197, 213.

323. This is not a neutral comparison. As elsewhere in the *relación*, the chronicler here equates American natives with Christian Spaniards' long-time enemies, the Moors.

324. "[And] they accent their eyes with kohl," *alcoholan*. Although both George Winship and Carmen de Mora transcribe the word as "ahogolan," the second letter of the word is in fact an *l*. Comparison with other instances of *h* and *l* elsewhere in the text shows that the word is indeed *alcogolan* or, in modern spelling, *alcoholan*. Mora herself notes that *alcoholan* was the word intended by the *escribano*. Winship, 144; Mora, 102 n. 119. *Alcoholan* derives from the Arabic *kohol*, meaning "antimony." On fol. 82r Castañeda de Nájera makes it clear that the women used antimony to decorate their eyes, in the manner of eyeliner. Winship, 236, has simply "they decorate their eyes." See Mora, 102 n. 119.

325. This describes a late spring–early summer thunderstorm such as is typical of West Texas. These are often accompanied by hail and storm winds. The devastation this particular storm wrought may explain the large number of objects associated with the expedition that have been excavated from the Jimmy Owens Site in Blanco Canyon near Floydada, Texas. Obregón, reporting this storm 44 years afterward, wrote: "sobrevino una grande y cargada nube de cantidad de agua y granizo de el tamaño de gruesas naranjas" (a large amount of rain fell suddenly from an enormous and ponderous cloud, as well as hail the size of plump oranges). Obregón, *Historia*, 23. For a fine modern description of such a storm, see Dan Flores, *Caprock Canyonlands: Journeys into the Heart of the Southern Plains* (Austin: University of Texas Press, 1990), 52.

326. This is one of the rare mentions of black people in the Coronado expedition documents and is important evidence of the unknown number of black slaves and servants who accompanied the expedition. See the introduction to Document 12.

327. As expedition members understood it, the Teyas produced no pottery of their own. This is at variance with what is known archaeologically about the Teyas (people of the Garza Complex). See David Snow, "'Por allí no hay losa ni se hace': Gilded Men and Glazed Pottery on the Southern Plains," in Flint and Flint, *Tierra Nueva*, 344–64; and Judith Habicht-Mauche, "Striated Utility Ware from the Southwest and Southern Plains," chapter 5 in *Pottery, Food, Hides, and Women: Labor, Production, and Exchange across the Protohistoric Plains-Pueblo Frontier* (book in preparation).

328. This is undoubtedly an overstatement. Forty years later Hernán Gallegos, of the Rodríguez-Chamuscado *entrada*, reported of Plains nomads that they "ate nothing but buffalo meat during the winter" and that "during the rainy season they would go to the areas of the prickly pear and yucca," evidently to harvest those wild vegetable foods. Hernán Gallegos, "Gallegos' Relation of the Chamuscado-Rodríguez Expedition," in Hammond and Rey, *Rediscovery of New Mexico*, 87. Habicht-Mauche even leaves open the possibility that the Teyas might have done some farming. Habicht-Mauche, *Pottery, Food, Hides, and Women*.

329. "Resembling those of Bedouins," *a manera de alixares*. *Alijares*, Covarrubias, 65: spacious lands outside of a town to which people go to relax and enjoy themselves. *Alijar*, "acaso de *disar*, casa de campo," Alonso, *Enciclopedia del idioma*, 1:257. *Alijar*, *Simon and Schuster's International Dictionary*, 922: a Bedouin camp or settlement. Most likely this is a comparison of Teya settlements to temporary camps of pavilions, or *casetas*. In addition to being descriptive, this characterization again links American natives with those of North Africa, the Moors and other enemies of the Roman Catholic Church. A later reader of this passage tried to clarify the word by writing "alixeres" in the margin, but no clarification was necessary according to our reading. H&R, 239, avoid the problem of interpretation with "other rancherías resembling *alixares*." Winship, 237, omits the phrase from his translation, adding the footnote that "the word means threshing floor." There seems to be no justification for that translation, although a number of modern researchers have followed Winship on this.

330. The beans referred to here were probably mesquite beans. Another use of *frijol* to signify the mesquite bean (*Prosopis* var.) occurs in Pérez de Ribas, *Triumphs*, 87. John Morris and others maintain that the beans mentioned here were *Phaselous vulgaris*, the common cultivated bean. Morris identifies the plums as Chickasaw sand plums (*Prunus angustifolia*). Morris, *Llano Estacado*, 80.

331. The exact location and extent of Cona is unknown. The identification of the Jimmy Owens Site in the 1990s strongly suggests that it was along the southeastern margin of the Llano Estacado, as portrayed by John Morris, *Llano Estacado*, map, p. 101.

332. The narrative here returns to the body of the expedition, still in the *barranca* like those of Colima, the first *barranca* encountered.

333. The second *barranca* has not been identified, though it was probably four day's travel (perhaps 25 leagues, or about 65 miles) or so from Blanco Canyon, in Castañeda de Nájera's telling. It seems possible that the realization that Quivira was

toward the north came only at the second *barranca*, but compare Jaramillo's version of these same events in Document 30, fol. 3v. There, it seems apparent that a determination about the direction to Quivira was made at the first *barranca*. If the latter was the case, then it seems improbable that the direction of travel from the first to the second *barranca* would have been other than at least generally northerly. It is also clear that the second *barranca* was outside of territory occupied by the Teyas (certainly at least that year). See maps 1 and 4. John Morris prefers to think that the expedition moved southeastward from the first *barranca* to the second, in the face of a postulated need for vegetable food in an area whose season was slightly more advanced. Morris, *Llano Estacado*, 76. For general information about the Teyas, see the entry in Appendix 1.

334. "Rosebushes," *rrosales*. Donald Blakeslee has argued that a scribal error for "grosilles" has masked a reference to gooseberries here. John Morris, on the other hand, writes, "*Rosales* could refer to any of several berries found in Blanco Canyon, such as squawbush or bison currants." In any case, the array of flora listed here is not distinctive enough to allow discrimination among the various Caprock Canyons. Donald J. Blakeslee, "Which Barrancas? Narrowing the Possibilities," in Flint and Flint, *Tierra Nueva*, 304–5; Morris, *Llano Estacado*, 81.

335. "Walnuts," *nueses*. Because there has been recent discussion about Castañeda de Nájera's meaning here, it is worth quoting briefly from Covarrubias: "Nogal. Árbol conocido, *latine nux*, que significa el árbol nogal [walnut], 2. y la nuez su fruta," and "Nuez. Fruta conocida, *latine* NUX, *juglans*." The fruit of no other nut tree is included in the 1611 definitions of *nuez*. One variety of walnut, the little walnut (*Juglans microcarpa*), is native to West Texas. Consistent with sixteenth-century usage, Clevy Lloyd Strout translated *nuez* as "walnut." Nevertheless, most students of Spanish *entradas* that traversed Texas have translated *nuez* as "pecan." The pecan, an American hickory (*Carya illinoensis*) all but unknown to Europeans in the early 1540s, is native to the eastern two-thirds of Texas as well as much of the lower Mississippi basin. The nut and leaves of the pecan broadly resemble those of various walnut varieties. It is understandable that sixteenth-century European observers might have applied the word *nuez* to both walnut and pecan. At the time Covarrubias prepared his dictionary, the existence of a separate hickory species was not recognized. Indeed, even today the Spanish terms for hickory and pecan are, respectively, *nogal americana* and *nogal pacanero*. Covarrubias, 779, 781; Strout, "Linguistic Study," 852; J. W. Williams, "Coronado: From the Rio Grande to the Concho," *West Texas Historical Association Yearbook* 35 (1959):66–98; Álvar Núñez Cabeza de Vaca, *The Account: Álvar Núñez Cabeza de Vaca's Relación*, eds. and trans. Martin A. Favata and José B. Fernández (Houston: Arte Público Press, 1993), 66, 131 n. 17; Morris, *Llano Estacado*, 81.

336. "Small hair shirts of penitents with fringe on them that reaches to mid-thigh. [They are worn] over the tunics," *faldellín* and *sanbenitillos*. According to Covarrubias, 535, a *faldellín* was a long shawl typically worn with the ends crossed, over a blouse. Castañeda de Nájera later compares some of them to *sambenetillos*, garments covering the chests and shoulders of penitents. *Fadellín* can also mean "a short skirt." That is the meaning Winship, 237, and H&R, 239, use in their translations. Their choice is reinforced by the chronicler's similar description of the dress of women at Petatlán. There he says that they wore "[e]naguas," or skirts, and "sanbenitillos," or tunics. A possible resolution is to consider the *faldellín* an over-the-head skirted garment like a *huipil* of sixteenth-century central Mexico or a modern tunic.

337. This rate seems to be a fairly accurate figure for the expedition's overall average daily travel. It also agrees with the figure implicit in the narrative of Juan Jaramillo, who was in the advance guard from Culiacán to Cíbola. See Document 30, note 61.

338. This measurement probably was made from Coofor, the expedition's winter quarters on the Rio Grande. The travel time accounted for by Castañeda de Nájera amounts to 24 days from Coofor to the first *barranca* and perhaps as many as 8 days from the first *barranca* to the last, for a total of 32 at most. If one adds the 4 days spent building the bridge over the Río de Cicuique, the total is 36, very close to the 37 reported here. Both Vázquez de Coronado and Juan Jaramillo recorded similar travel times from Coofor to the last *barranca*: Vázquez de Coronado 35 days, and Jaramillo 36. Documents 26 and 30; Flint, "Reconciling the Calendars."

339. The calling of such conclaves was standard procedure on Spanish expeditions of the period. Consultation among the investors, leaders, and royal officials on all major decisions was the rule. Ordinarily a captain general did not and would not act unilaterally.

340. This seems to imply that Diego López and the messengers from Arellano did not cross paths.

341. "He was welcomed peacefully because of the guides he took. He asked El Turco why he had lied." H&R, 241, place the phrase "por las guias" with the thought that follows it. The result is, incorrectly, "They asked the Turk through the guides why he had lied." "Asked" definitely understates the case and glosses over the likelihood that torture was applied to El Turco.

342. A similar story was told by several other members of the expedition. This confession must not be taken at face value. It was extorted under torture. Furthermore, El Turco spoke no more than a smattering of Spanish gained during his year as a prisoner with the expedition, nor did the Spaniards speak more than a few words of his language. The possibility of Lockhart's "double mistaken identity" is everywhere throughout the accounts of the expedition, but especially at this point. Stories of deceit by Indian guides are common in the narratives of sixteenth-century expeditions throughout the Americas. Similar stories were part of the canon of chivalric romances of the day. One must ask, then, to what extent El Turco's confession was a product of Spanish expectation and projection. Flint, *Great Cruelties*, 260.

343. In 1544 several former members of the expedition testified that El Turco had been plotting with people from Quivira to attack Vázquez de Coronado's detachment from the expedition and that this was why he was executed. Flint, *Great Cruelties*, 81, 132, 151, 217, 240, 260, 292–93.

344. "Lord," *señor*. The Spaniards were quick to attribute their own hierarchical social system to peoples they met. In this case, "lord" must refer to an important man in Quivira who was seen to exercise some authority. He may have been a headman of a band. Francisco López de Gómara, secretary to Hernán Cortés, writing in the 1540s or early 1550s and relying on unknown sources, called this man a king and recorded his name as Tartarrax. Francisco López de Gómara, *Historia general de las Indias: Edición facsimilar* (Lima, Peru: Comisión Nacional del V Centenario del Descubrimiento de América, 1993), fol. 95r.

345. This piece of copper was the only metal encountered during the entire expedition. Its source may have been the copper deposits in the area of Lake Superior, which were mined prehistorically. Again ascribing the name Tartarrax to this man, López de Gómara provided otherwise the same information regarding the pendant of sheet copper. López de Gómara, *Historia general*, fols. 95r and 95v.

346. This statement indicates that the last *barranca* was outside of the territory of Teya occupation.

347. Numerous researchers over the years have suggested that this more direct route was by way of the Portales Valley to the Pecos River in the vicinity of modern Fort Sumner/Bosque Redondo and thence up the Pecos River to Cicuique (map 4). David Donoghue, "The Route of the Coronado Expedition in Texas," *New Mexico Historical Review* 4, no. 1 (1929):77–90; William C. Holden, "Coronado's Route across the Staked Plains," *West Texas Historical Association Yearbook* 20 (1944):3–20; Bolton, 272–75, 412; Waldo R. Wedel, "Coronado's Route to Quivira," *Plains Anthropologist* 15, no. 49 (1970):161–68; Morris, *Llano Estacado*, 101; Blakeslee, Flint, and Hughes, "Una Barranca Grande," 382.

348. This was evidently a procedure the chronicler himself witnessed, although the method seems unnecessary except perhaps at midday or under heavy overcast, when the sun could not reliably serve as a guide.

349. These are often identified as a series of some 40 salty lakes south of the dune field that crosses Lamb and Bailey Counties in West Texas. Morris, *Llano Estacado*, 100–102.

350. These squirrel-like animals were probably prairie dogs. Morris, *Llano Estacado*, 100.

351. "Below it," *por baxo de ella*. Because the third-person singular pronoun is in the feminine gender here, it seems most likely that an *escribano* lost his place and began copying "ellas," referring to the prairie dogs several lines earlier, and not, as H&R, 243, render it, "below the town," which would have required a masculine pronoun. Using the *legua legal*, 30 leagues is about 80 miles. Assuming that the bridge was built near the junction of the Pecos and Gallinas Rivers, as we have suggested (or even in the Anton Chico area, as some others have claimed), the point at which the main body of the expedition intersected the Pecos River would have been located in the general area of modern Fort Sumner/Bosque Redondo, New Mexico, or slightly south of there (map 4). Bolton, 273–74; Chardon, "Linear League," 145.

352. Although Castañeda de Nájera does not name this plant, it might well have been a "mora," or member of the blackberry family, such as Strout concludes the chronicler refers to elsewhere. Blackberry leaves, however, do not much resemble parsley. Clevy Lloyd Strout, "Flora and Fauna Mentioned in the Journals of the Coronado Expedition," *Great Plains Journal* 11, no. 1 (1971):16.

353. Strout suggests that the grapes in question might have been *Vitis arizonica*, and he identifies the "oregano" as wild marjoram. Whatever the precise plant, the "oregano" must have been a member of the *Labiatae*, or mint, family with a square stem. Strout, "Flora and Fauna," 22, 23.

354. The distance from Fort Sumner, New Mexico, to the junction of the Rio Grande and the Pecos River along the modern Texas-Mexico border is something over 400 miles, which, at a travel rate of 15 miles per day for the expedition, would represent about 27 days' travel, a remarkable degree of congruence.

355. The Mississippi was then called the Río del Espíritu Santo by Europeans. The conjecture offered here that the Rio Grande and Mississippi united is incorrect. It was nearly two more centuries before Europeans delineated the full course of the Rio Grande/Río de Tiguex, though the Native American geography was extremely precise long before that.

356. Again, the term *slave* is used here advisedly. Recently, James Brooks has shown that female captives were frequently incorporated into Pueblo families by marriage or adoption and became part of the free social group. Brooks, *Captives and Cousins*, 54. This woman's subsequent capture by members of the Soto expedition at the Indian community of Naçacahoz in what is now in East Texas is related by expedition member the *hidalgo* of Elvas. "The Account by a Gentleman from Elvas," trans. and ed. James Alexander Robertson, in Clayton, Knight, and Moore, *De Soto Chronicles*, 1:146. For the possible location of Naçacahoz, see illustrations 24 and 25 in Gloria A. Young and Michael P. Hoffmann, eds., *The Expedition of Hernando de Soto West of the Mississippi, 1541–1543* (Fayetteville: University of Arkansas Press, 1993).

357. The survivors of the Soto expedition made their way to the Ciudad de México during the fall of 1543. There, Viceroy Antonio de Mendoza received them cordially and recorded information about their travels. Garcilaso de la Vega, "La Florida by the Inca," trans. Charmion Shelby, ed. David Bost, in Clayton, Knight, and Moore, *De Soto Chronicles*, 2:546–49. There was either miscommunication with the Indian woman or a copying error about the length of time in the manuscript somewhere along the line. The time period of her flight and freedom must have actually been in excess of one year, since she fled from Zaldívar in May 1541 and was captured by Soto expedition survivors in what is now East Texas in late summer 1542. This is another instance of the dates in the *relación* being off by one year. See "Account by a Gentleman of Elvas," 1:146.

358. The reabandonment of pueblos is an indication of the disruptions in the Pueblo world caused by the presence of the expedition, even when there were no active hostilities.

359. The Spanish reads "1542," but once again the year is incorrect. It should be 1541.

360. Hemes = Jemez. Yuque Yunque (map 1) was one of the ancestral San Juan pueblos. If this represents only one trip, the report provides no indication of what route was taken from the Jemez pueblos to San Juan Pueblo. Two possibilities present themselves: downstream along the Jemez River, then upstream along the Rio Grande, or northward along the western flank of the Jemez Mountains, then downstream along the Chama River. Without further description of the "seven towns" it is impossible to identify exactly which of the apparently nine ancestral Jemez pueblos that were inhabited into the sixteenth century are intended here. Barrett, *Conquest and Catastrophe*, 43.

361. These strong towns may have been four protohistoric Tewa pueblos in the lower Chama River drainage whose ruins are now known by the names Te'ewi, Tsama, Hupobi, and Ponsipa. Ann F. Ramenofsky and C. David Vaughan, "Jars Full of Shiny Metal: Analyzing Barrionuevo's Visit to Yuque-Yunque," in Flint and Flint, *From the Distance of 460 Years*, 116–39. "Rugged," *aspera*. Covarrubias, 131: "todo aquello que es insuaue al sentido, sea gusto, tacto o oído."

362. Most likely this shiny metal was galena, or lead sulfide, which Pueblo peoples of the Rio Grande area used throughout late prehistory and the early historic period as a flux in glaze paint for decorating ceramics. Ramenofsky and Vaughan, "Jars Full of Shiny Metal," 127. Castañeda's wry remark that sources of silver were nearby "if they had been looked for" is one of several indications in the documents that the Coronado expedition did little if any prospecting for precious metals and was, in fact, seeking only ready-made wealth. The *cronista* repeats his reference to "silvery metal" later on fol. 117v. Forty-four years later, Obregón, having talked with veterans of the Coronado expedition and having read the "escrituras y relaciones," concluded that "es ciertísimo estar en aquella gran serranía y sus ramos de ellas la mayor gruesa de metales de todas las Indias" (it is most certain that there is in the great mountain range and its branches in that [land] the greatest

body of metal in all the Indies). Tello, on the other hand, reported that Vázquez de Coronado, upon his return to Compostela in 1542, spoke of the "miserias y pobreza que había en la tierra de adonde venía" (deficiencies and poverty there were in the land from which he had come). Obregón, *Historia*, 28; Tello, 486.

363. For geographical information, see the entry for Brava in Appendix 2.

364. Castañeda de Nájera, who must not have seen the pueblo himself, misinterpreted reports of Pueblo Creek, which runs through Taos Pueblo, as referring to the Rio Grande (which Barrionuevo had been following northward).

365. In this case the chronicler seems to be describing the Rio Grande, which flows in a deep gorge approximately 10 miles west of Taos Pueblo.

366. These pueblos south of Tutahaco were certainly some of the nine Piro pueblos whose ruins are located along the Rio Grande within and adjacent to the Socorro basin, including the ruins now known as Senecú, Sevilleta, Alamillo, and Qualacú. Barrett, *Conquest and Catastrophe*, 19–20.

367. This marginal note, "{a river that vanishes}," is not in Niño Velásques's hand. Reference is still to the Rio Grande, which, during some years in the past, has occasionally ceased to flow on the surface in the area of modern Elephant Butte Lake and Caballo Reservoir. The distance of 80 leagues (about 210 miles) from Tiguex to the point of no surface flow given here very nearly coincides with this area. The Río Guadiana runs through Mérida and Badajoz in Extremadura.

368. News received in advance of Vázquez de Coronado suggests either a unit preceding the party that had gone to Quivira or, as may be more likely, word coming from Pecos/Cicuique Indians who had been visiting, hunting, trading, or on some other business to the east.

369. The pass in question is what is today known as Glorieta Pass.

370. Xabe had evidently returned west with the bulk of the expedition when the decision was made to send it back to Tiguex from the second *barranca*.

371. Reference to the relative weakness of Vázquez de Coronado's party at this point suggests that the force that went to Quivira did not include a large contingent of *indios amigos*.

372. The name of a town and also an element in the chronicler's surname was written as "Naçera" on fols. ir and iiir. The modern name is Nájera, which, both here and earlier, was misinterpreted by one or more *escribanos*. The sequence of spellings was probably this: Naxera (equivalent to Najera) became Nazera (because *x* and *z* are often extremely difficult to distinguish in sixteenth-century orthography), which became Naçera (because *z* and *ç* were equivalent). This probably means that none of the *escribanos* involved was familiar with the small northern Spanish town of Nájera.

373. This is probably a reference to fray Marcos's report or the stories it spawned.

374. *Bacallao* is the Spanish word for codfish. There are several islands off Newfoundland with this name. See Samuel Eliot Morison, *The European Discovery of America: The Northern Voyages, 1492–1616* (New York: Oxford University Press, 1971), 203. Castañeda de Nájera is clearly indicating the northern reaches of North America and understands that there is a continuous coastline from Florida to Canada.

375. This peninsula, Baja California, Castañeda de Nájera characterizes as similar and symmetrical to La Florida. *Debaxo del sur* = toward the south. See Craddock, "Castañeda y Nájera," 12.

376. The absence of snakes is certainly inaccurate. The members of the expedition may have seen no snakes because they spent so much of their time in proximity to large bison herds, which would have kept snakes in hiding.

377. "(As opposed to [the barbarity] of brutish men)," *bestia*. Covarrubias, 185: "llamamos al hombre que sabe poco."

378. Members of the Coronado expedition who were first settlers of Culiacán were don Pedro de Tovar, Diego López, and Esteban Martín. Tello incorrectly implies that Castañeda de Nájera was also a first settler of Culiacán. Tello, 136.

379. "Not counting several others to which [the natives] of [the *provincia*] respond," *sin otras variables que de ella responden*. Winship, 251, renders this as "besides other related dialects have." H&R, 247–48, have "in addition to other dialects derived from them." This phrase is rendered more complex by the apparent scribal omission of letters or words. Hence, like Winship and Hammond and Rey, we have had to ignore gaps and fill in the blanks in order to make sense of the phrase.

380. Tahue, long extinct, is thought to have been a Cahitan dialect of a Uto-Aztecan language. The people at Petatlán seem to have shared the language of the Tahues. Wick R. Miller, "Uto-Aztecan Languages," in Ortiz, *Southwest*, vol. 10, 122.

381. These "offerings to the devil" were offerings to non-Christian deities.

382. The eating of human flesh was particularly abhorrent to most sixteenth-century Spaniards and was specifically targeted by royal provision to be eradicated among American natives. The November 1526 ordinances on discoveries and good treatment of the Indians directed conquistadores to "dissuade them [Indian people] from vices such as the practice of eating human flesh." Hanke, *Spanish Struggle for Justice*, 111.

383. Homosexual behavior was of great interest to members of Spanish expeditions, one reason being that its practice could render warfare against the natives justifiable. See Federico Garza Carvajal, *Butterflies Will Burn: Prosecuting Sodomites in Early Modern Spain and Mexico* (Austin: University of Texas Press, 2003), especially the discussion of the 1497 royal *pragmática* on sodomy on pages 40–43.

384. *Areito. DRAE*, 184: from the Taíno language of the Caribbean islands. This application of a Caribbean word to areas far removed from there hints at the Spanish (and in a broader sense, European) penchant for seeing all American natives as exemplifying a single, widespread culture and overlooking the enormous differences among the hundreds of distinct cultures present in the Americas at the time of European colonization.

385. A *rancho* can be a temporary shelter or one made from impermanent materials; see *ranchería* in the glossary and note 159, this document.

386. "Sometimes," *a sus tiempos. DRAE*, 1975: "a veces."

387. The Pacaxes probably were related to the Acaxees, if indeed they were a distinct group. See note 388, this document.

388. Acaxee, long extinct, is thought to have been a Cahitan dialect of a Uto-Aztecan language. The Acaxee-Xixime people of the mountains of the Sinaloa-Durango border are now thought to have been agriculturalists who engaged in "frequent intertribal warfare." Miller, "Uto-Aztecan Languages," 22; Hinton, "Southern Periphery: West," 316; Deeds, *Defiance and Deference*, 45.

389. "Although not intended as a means of acquiring calories, ritual cannibalism usually followed battles as a part of victory celebrations." Deeds, *Defiance and Deference*, 45.

390. According to Susan Deeds, after a coastal epidemic in 1536, "most Xiximes and Acaxees remained in the mountains but at warmer, lower elevations in canyons and valleys. These sites were separated by steep canyon walls and high summits, which made communication difficult and hazardous but provided protection from enemies." Deeds, *Defiance and Deference*, 43.

391. Culiacán is, in fact, approximately at the latitude of the southern extremity of the Gulf of California (map 1), and the Sierra Madre Occidental does make its closest approach to the west Mexican coast in this stretch. Converting to miles using the *legua legal* yields a distance across the lower gulf of about 80 miles. Actual airline mileage is closer to 120 miles. La California was the name used at this time for the entirety of the Baja California peninsula.

392. "Size [length]," *es ancho, anchura. DRAE*, 137: "Amplitud, extensión o capacidad grandes." The long dimension of the gulf is clearly what Castañeda de Nájera is referring to here, since in fact the Gulf of California is somewhat over five times longer than it is wide, exactly the ratio of the distances in this sentence and the one preceding it. One hundred fifty leagues is about 400 miles. The actual length of the gulf is 696 miles. H&R, 249, are incorrect in rendering the sentence as, "They say the gulf is 150 leagues wide from shore to shore."

393. As before, characterizations such as this one of the marginality of the natives' humanity served to justify conquest and missionization of the native population.

394. For geographical information, see the entry for Petatlán in Appendix 2.

395. Although "congregated" is not the formal missionary usage of *congregación*, it was important to note dense, aggregated populations, which were generally more easily missionized and administered than were dispersed settlements. Further, they promised viable *encomiendas*.

396. This river is probably the modern Río Sinaloa (map 1). As Dan Reff has pointed out, in 1533 the *entrada* led by Diego de Guzmán visited the town called Petatlán on that river, some 32 leagues north of the modern Río Culiacán (which in turn is 10 leagues or so north of the site of San Miguel de Culiacán). Reff, *Disease, Depopulation, and Culture Change*, 31–32.

397. "Of the same social level and habits," *de la calidad y rritos*. In similar circumstances, Baltasar de Obregón, writing in 1584, used the phrase "modo de vivir." Obregón, *Historia*, 157.

398. Tahues = Tahus on fol. 97v.

399. Esteban de Dorantes's native companion from Petatlán, called Bartolomé,

evidently spoke Nahuatl and Ópata as well as his native Cahitan language. Flint, *Great Cruelties*, 571.

400. Boyomo was probably the place called Mayomo on the Arroyo de los Cedros, a tributary of the Río Mayo, that was attacked by Diego de Guzmán. Hedrick and Riley suggest it was located in the vicinity of modern Camoa, Sonora. Reff, *Disease, Depopulation, and Culture Change*, 31, 34; Basil C. Hedrick and Carroll L. Riley, *Documenta Ancilary to the Vaca Journey*, University Studies 5 (Carbondale: Southern Illinois University Museum, 1976), 29. On the basis of information from Diego de Guzmán's *entrada*, Reff locates a town called Teocomo on today's Arroyo Alamos in extreme northern Sinaloa. Reff, *Disease, Depopulation, and Culture Change*, 31, 33. For geographical information about the Río Yaquimí, see Document 19, note 30. The Río Sinaloa is the river of the same name today, which flows west out of the Sierra Madre Occidental to the Gulf of California within the modern Mexican state of Sinaloa (maps 1 and 2).

401. "Base," *caudal. DRAE*, 442: "Capital o fondo."

402. Reff has marshalled strong evidence in support of the contention that Senora/Señora was in the modern middle Sonora River valley (maps 1 and 2). In addition to citing archaeological evidence, he points out that Andrés Pérez de Ribas (Pérez de Ribas, *Triumphs*, 419) and Cristóbal de Cañas, missionaries in the region during the seventeenth and eighteenth centuries, came to the same conclusion. Reff, "Relevance of Ethnology," 173–74. "Heavily populated by very intelligent people." H&R, 250, instead have "thickly settled with comely people." The difference in translation hinges on the word *dispuesto*, which can mean either "good looking" or "intelligent." In this case, "intelligent" seems the better rendering, given the context of the sentence. To wit, the sentence that follows deals with the clothing of the women of Señora. The wearing of clothing was generally seen as an indication of civilization and intelligence. Thus this sentence makes a general statement that is followed by the evidence that supports it.

403. *Naguas* = petticoat-like skirts made of cured deerskin. *DRAE*, 1424: "Saya interior de tela blanca." Indeed, it may have been the whiteness of the skirts that was reminiscent of *naguas*. It was certainly not their being worn beneath other skirts. A *sambenito* was a garment covering the chest and shoulders like a tunic. It became associated with penitents under penalty imposed by the Inquisition.

404. Reff reports the archaeological discovery of small (two-meter-wide) earthen platform structures at several sites in the Sonora River valley that may correspond to the chronicler's description here. Reff, "Relevance of Ethnology," 172.

405. "[The bristles of] a hedgehog," *erizo*. With the word *erizo* Castañeda de Nájera could be making reference to the bristly exterior of either the hedgehog or the chestnut. Covarrubias, 485, 486: like [the bristles of] a hedgehog.

406. This series of place names has been rendered very differently by different scholars. See, for example, H&R, 250, and Winship, 253. Riley reads the list as "Comupa, Trico, Mochila, Guayarispa, and Vallecillo." He then identifies Comupa and Guayarispa with the places Obregón called Cumupa and Guaraspi. Riley, *Frontier People*, 71–72. "Patrico," on the other hand, may be a scribal error for "patuco" (a simple and not uncommon error of the period in transcribing *ri* for *u*). Reff has identified this place as Batuco. He also identifies Comu as Cumupas and Arispa as Arispe, all towns in the Sonora River valley. Reff, "Relevance of Ethnology," 173. No mention of Batuco was made in accounts of the northbound journey, giving rise to the possibility that, if Reff's reading is correct, the return route of the expedition was somewhat different. Of the two settlements named Batuco in modern Sonora, it was probably the one on the Río Moctezuma that the expedition visited in 1542. Jerry Gurulé, "Francisco Vázquez de Coronado's Northward Trek through Sonora," in Flint and Flint, *Tierra Nueva*, 160.

407. As with Patuco and Petatlán, the copyist seems unsure about the spelling of this name. At 40 *leguas legales* from Señora, Suya would be about 105 miles. The placement of Suya/Fuya hinges of the location of the principal town of Señora, which was most likely in the vicinity of modern Baviácora, Sonora. On the modern map, this would place Suya just below the present U.S.-Mexico border on the upper waters of either the Río Sonora or the San Pedro River (maps 1 and 2). See note 286, this document.

408. The *pitahaya*, or *pitahaya dulce* (*Lemaireocereus thurberi*), is the organ pipe cactus, which is plentiful in western Sonora. In the nineteenth century, Ópatas in this same area of Sonora continued to prepare an alcoholic drink by fermenting *pitahaya* fruits. Edward F. Castetter and Willis H. Bell, "The Aboriginal Utilization of the Tall Cacti in the American Southwest," *University of New Mexico Bulletin, Biological Series* 5, no. 1 (1937):27–35.

409. Melons are of Asian origin and usually are considered to have been intro-

duced to the Americas by Europeans in the sixteenth century. Obregón, for instance, states that the melons of Sonora were grown from seeds "left when Alcaraz was killed." Given Castañeda de Nájera's account here, Obregón's suggestion must be incorrect. Nevertheless, the melons he refers to may have come from European seeds that were obtained in trade with other native groups to the south before actual Spanish contact. Riley has pointed to this fact as strong evidence for southern trade. Riley, *Frontier People*, 62, 63; Obregón, *Historia*, 149.

410. Interpreting this statement—"the lords keep them for their magnificence"—very broadly, H&R, 251, render the sentence as, "The native dignitaries have them as an emblem of power." Reff refers to a 1619 instance of a group of *caciques* along the Río Yaqui bearing a gift of three eagles, which may be an echo of Castañeda de Nájera's statement here. Reff, *Disease, Depopulation, Culture Change*, 63.

411. Again, reference to European flora and fauna in the area prior to the Coronado expedition seems to be evidence of trade from the south, but it is then difficult to account for the lack of European fowl in the Señora Valley and Corazones. Riley, *Frontier People*, 63.

412. These rams and goats were probably desert bighorns. See Document 19, note 78.

413. This boundary is between the Lower Sonoran life zone, characterized by the large cacti, creosote bush, mesquite, paloverde, and other spiny plants and generally located below 4,500 feet in elevation, and the Upper Sonoran life zone, where piñon, juniper, and oak are typical. Epple, *Plants of Arizona*, 5.

414. This assertion that Chichilticale is at the latitude of the head of the Gulf of California is evidently an error on the chronicler's part. All of his other reports of distance would place Chichilticale in what is now south-central or southeastern Arizona, somewhere around latitude 33 degrees north. The head of the Gulf of California, on the other hand, is at less than 32 degrees. This suggests that the chronicler is relying here on latitude measurements taken by Marcos de Niza, which, like many such measurements of the time, were consistently too high by one to two degrees. See Document 6, notes 78 and 131.

415. Mention of friars is a reference to fray Marcos's 1539 trip. The name Chichilticale, therefore, may have been given by speakers of Nahuatl who accompanied Marcos. It is usually considered to be a Nahuatl compound comprising the elements *chichiltic* and *calli*, meaning "red house." However, as Riley points out, Albert Schroeder held that the name might instead have Apachean or Yavapai roots. Molina, *Vocabulario*, fols. 11v and 19v; Riley, *Frontier People*, 126–27. "Inhabited by people who split off from Cíbola": see note 137, this document.

416. The distinction is made here and elsewhere between areas with permanent towns and those with short-term *rancherías*.

417. This probably means that no permanent architecture was seen.

418. This is a nearly classic description of the larger vegetation in a piñon-juniper forest typical of the foothill or montane areas of western New Mexico and eastern Arizona, with piñons reaching a height of as much as 15 to 18 feet (three *estados*). Castañeda de Nájera's description thus places the expedition at a relatively lower elevation than that of the route reconstructed by some modern historians, who have envisioned it passing through Arizona's White Mountains and over the Mogollon Rim (map 2), where the dominant large vegetation is the much taller ponderosa pine. Stewart L. Udall, *To the Inland Empire: Coronado and Our Spanish Legacy* (Garden City, NY: Doubleday, 1987), 94; Bolton, 108.

419. "Juniper trees," *sav(o)inas*. Mora, 115, transcribes this as a nonsense word, "fanonas." The fruit of these trees is described here as looking like dry coriander candy—in other words, like large BBs. Covarrubias, 382, provides instructions for making the candy: "Perpárarse remojándola en vinagre fuerte, y despues de seca le dan una camisilla de azúcar." Castañeda de Nájera also says this fruit was very sweet, which would seem not to fit juniper berries.

420. Pennyroyal (*poleo*) and oregano are two members of the mint family. Strout offers the possibility that *poleo* refers here to false pennyroyal (*Hedeoma drummondii*), while he is unable to identify the plant called oregano (which is an Old World native). Strout, "Flora and Fauna," 23.

421. "Leopards [jaguars]," *leones pardos*. This refers to *leopardos*, or leopards/jaguars. *DRAE*, 1245; *OED*, 1604. Strout, 872, in contrast, says, "I believe the animal referred to is most likely the mountain lion or cougar." See also Document 19, note 77.

422. This would put the distance between Chichilticale and Cíbola at about 210 miles. In a straight line (ignoring the wandering of an actual on-the-ground route) this would place Chilchilticale no farther from Hawikku than the area of Cochise, Arizona. See notes 89 and 123, this document.

423. This characterization indicates that the general direction of travel was slightly east of north. It is not an accurate description of the direction of travel over the entire route from Culiacán to Cíbola (see map 1), but it would certainly apply from at least Los Corazones to Cíbola. Castañeda de Nájera may therefore have intended "Corazones" rather than "Culiacán" in this passage. The chronicler's rather imprecise statement here raises the question of the whereabouts, at this point, of the sea compass that the expedition has earlier in the narrative been reported as having. Fol. 79v.

424. For the identity of the seven pueblos, see the entry for Cíbola in Appendix 2.

425. "The women are dressed in *mantas* which they tie or tie together over the left shoulder," *que las atan o añudan sobre el honbro izquierdo.* H&R, 252, erroneously interpret the phrase "que las atan" as "wrapped tightly around their bodies," ignoring the conjunction "o" that follows, which makes the phrase *que las atan* the equivalent of *añudan,* "they tie together."

426. "Buns of a [Spanish] hairdo," *papos. DRAE,* 1523: "Moda de tocado que usaron las mugeres, con unos huecos o bollos que cubrían las orejas." This appears to be a description of the hair whorls worn by young unmarried Hopi women, as illustrated in John C. Connelly, "Hopi Social Organization," in Ortiz, *Southwest,* vol. 9, 546. A similar hairstyle was evidently in use among the Cibolans/Zunis in the sixteenth century. Slightly more than 40 years after the Coronado expedition, Diego Pérez de Luxán reported Zuni women wearing their hair "done up in large puffs." Pérez de Luxán, "Luxán's Account," 184. For a sixteenth-century example of the corresponding Spanish hairstyle, see Anderson, *Hispanic Costume,* 206, fig. 475.

427. This description matches well the Zuni River valley from the area of modern Zuni eastward.

428. This description of planting refers to the Zunis' use of the digging stick to poke holes in the soil for planting corn. For a nineteenth-century account of Zuni corn planting, see Frank Hamilton Cushing, "Corn Raising: The Decay of the Seed," in Green, *Zuñi,* 257–69.

429. This large yield per ear seems to argue for precolumbian selection to improve the strain of corn among the Zunis and tends to confirm Paul Mangelsdorf's 1974 assertion that "at some stage in the development of Indian agriculture . . . the practice of artificial selection began and has persisted to this day." Paul C. Mangelsdorf, *Corn: Its Origin, Evolution, and Improvement* (Cambridge, MA: Harvard University Press, 1974), 208. The corn, or maize, referred to here was undoubtedly a descendant of Maíz de Ocho, or eight-rowed corn, and teosinte-introgressed Chapalote corn. Mangelsdorf, *Corn,* 113–14; Linda S. Cordell, *Prehistory of the Southwest* (San Diego, CA: Academic Press, 1984), 171.

430. "Lions, and short-tailed cats," *leones gatos cervales.* Whether these lions were mountain lions or jaguars or both is unclear. The short-tailed cats were either lynxes or bobcats, both of which had historic ranges in New Mexico. Charles Yocom et al., *Wildlife of the Southern Rocky Mountains,* rev. ed. (Healdsburg, CA: Naturegraph Company, 1969), 81. *Lobo cerval,* lynx, *DRAE,* 1267. *Gato cerval, DRAE,* 1029: "Especie de gato [en España] cuya cola llega a 35 centímetros."

431. The Coronado expedition documents served as a major data source in Carroll Riley's elaboration of the notion that the Zuni/Cíbola pueblos were the western entrepôt of Pueblo trade with peoples to the south and west, including the peoples of Sonora. In addition to turquoise, significant quantities of bison hides, saltwater shells, cotton, and exotic bird feathers were elements in the trade passing through Cíbola during the protohistoric period. Riley, *Frontier People,* 190–198.

432. There seems to have been significant continuity in political organization at Zuni since the 1540s and earlier. In sketching that long-lived system, Ed Ladd wrote that "the whole political system revolved around the religious leaders, who acted as a unit rather than as individuals." This priestly council was not elected as are the members of the modern tribal council. Ladd also told of the probable existence of a "supreme council" for external affairs, which existed even "when [the Zunis] lived in segregated towns [that is, until the 1690s]." Ladd, "Zuni Social and Political Organization," 488–89.

433. This statement about the absence of homosexuality among the Zunis is contradicted by abundant ethnographic evidence, suggestive rock art evidence, and the existence of a berdache kachina/koko among the Zunis' supernaturals. Ethnographic data from the nineteenth century include reports of a berdache who "formed a relationship with a young Zuni man and the couple set up housekeeping." Will Roscoe, *The Zuni Man-Woman* (Albuquerque: University of New Mexico Press, 1991), 22–23, 24–28, 148–49. For a photograph of a modern Zuni berdache, see figure 17.1.

434. This distance and direction would be about 53 miles at the rate of 2.63

miles per league. In fact, it is about 100 straight-line miles from modern Zuni to First Mesa on the Hopi Reservation/Tusayán. This is one of the rare instances in the *relación* in which the distances provided by the chronicler seem, on the basis of the modern identification of places, to be grossly inaccurate. Even the 25 leagues reported by Castañeda de Nájera earlier on fol. 42r would be much too few, unless a league is considered equal 4 miles, a figure inconsistent with other distances reported in the *relación.* On the basis of the chronicler's statement of distance to Tusayán as 20 or 25 leagues, Henry Dobyns argued that in 1540 the settled area of Tusayán extended as far east as the Little Colorado River (maps 1 and 2). Henry F. Dobyns, "Sixteenth-Century Tusayán," *American Indian Quarterly* 15, no. 2 (1991):187–200. Obregón, *Historia,* 24, informs us that Tusayán was the same group of settlements that Antonio de Espejo called Mohoce.

435. For discussion of the identity of the pueblos of Tusayán, see the entry for Tusayán in Appendix 2.

436. At the rate of the *legua legal,* this would be just over 105 miles. In fact the distance from modern Zuni to Albuquerque is about 160 miles. Using the *legua común* would give a Zuni-to-Albuquerque distance of about 138 miles, considerably closer to the actual travel distance. Presumably the "northern" route ran up the Zuni River valley, through El Morro Valley, and then by way of Capulín and Zuni Canyons (east and north of El Morro) to the vicinity of modern Milan, New Mexico. From there the route eastward skirted the northern edge of the Malpais lava flows through the McCarty's narrows until reaching the Río San José. It was then necessary to diverge from the river valley, possibly in the area of modern McCarty's, in order to reach Acoma. From Acoma the route probably rejoined the Río San José, continuing eastward to its junction with the Río Puerco, where the route struck off northeastward to the southernmost Tiguex pueblos on the western terrace above the Río Grande, within modern Albuquerque (map 3). Carroll L. Riley, "Coronado in the Southwest," in *Archaeology, Art, and Anthropology: Collected Papers in Honor of J. J. Brody,* Meliha S. Duran and David T. Kirkpatrick, eds., Papers of the Archaeological Society of New Mexico, no. 18 (Albuquerque: Archaeological Society of New Mexico), 151; Riley and Manson, "Cíbola-Tiguex Route," 347–67. For an even more northerly route, by way of Zia Pueblo, see Document 24, note 25.

437. For discussion of the identity of these 12 pueblos, see the entry for Tiguex in Appendix 2. This is a description of the Rio Grande Valley and adjacent Sandia Mountains in the vicinity of modern Albuquerque that is still easily recognizable. See maps 3 and 5.

438. Schroeder offers no positive identification of these seven pueblos on the eastern flank of the Sandia Mountains, though he does give them collectively the name Ubates. Barrett identifies four ruined pueblos as candidates for inclusion in the chronicler's group of seven: Tonque, Paa-ko, San Antonio, and the Silva Site. The seven may have been among the nine or ten pueblos listed 60 years later by Juan de Oñate as "near the mines of Anunciación." Schroeder, "Pueblos Abandoned," 248–50; Elinore M. Barrett, *The Geography of the Rio Grande Pueblos Revealed by Spanish Explorers,* Research Paper Series, no. 30 (Albuquerque: Latin American Institute, University of New Mexico, 1997), 14–16, 42.

439. At 2.63 miles per league, this would be about 18 miles. From Santiago/Coofor to Santo Domingo (the largest of the modern Keres pueblos) is just over 20 miles, which jibes with Castañeda de Nájera's figure here.

440. "To the northwest." The document itself reads "a el nordeste," but it should be "a el noroeste," northwest. At some point in the copying process an *o* must have been mistaken for a *d.* Jemez Pueblo is indeed to the northwest of the Tiguex area. The distance of 40 leagues, however, is in error. Fourteen would be more accurate. This difficulty of mistaking *o* for *d* may help explain sixteenth-century European mapmakers' consistent misplacement of Cicuique and Quivira to the west of Cíbola, rather than to the east. See, for example, Abraham Ortelius, *Americae Sive Novi Orbis, Nova Descriptio* (Amsterdam, 1570), and Gerhardus Mercator, *Nova et Aucta Orbis Terrae Descriptio ad Usum Navigantium Emendate Accommodata* (Duisberg, 1569).

441. Acha may apply to the ruin now known as Tonque Pueblo. The actual straight-line distance between the ruins of Santiago and Tonque is about 15 miles (rather than the approximately 10.5 given here by Castañeda de Nájera), though the direction is northeast, as the chronicler reports. Acha is inexplicably not included in his tabular list of pueblos on fol. 115r.

442. For Tutahaco, see note 227, this document. Castañeda de Nájera's directional reference of southeast here is slightly inconsistent with what he reports earlier, on fol. 53r.

443. Presumably Castañeda de Nájera's reference here is to a European game rather than the indigenous ball game of Mesoamerica and what became the American Southwest and northwestern Mexico. The European game consisted in throwing an iron ball with the hand, either while remaining motionless or while running. The player who, at the end of the game, had moved his ball farthest was the winner. *DRAE*, 305.

444. This indicates a misunderstanding of indigenous use of cornfield stubble, which was harvested throughout the winter as needed for use as fuel. See Flint, *Great Cruelties*, 525–26.

445. Such large harvests were certainly not the case every year. Indeed, the chronicler's report here probably reflects the extraordinary wetness of the years 1540–42 in the Pueblo world. See note 236, this document.

446. "Ravens," *cuervos*. The Spanish word *cuervo* refers to both ravens and crows without discrimination. "Robins," *tordos*. *Tordo* could refer to any member of the family *Turdidae*, which includes thrushes and bluebirds in addition to robins, although given modern distributions and populations, robins seem most likely. Chandler S. Robbins, Bertel Brun, and Herbert S. Zim, *A Field Guide to Field Identification: Birds of North America* (New York: Golden Press, 1966), 230–33.

447. "Small secluded room," *retrete*. Covarrubias, 864: "El aposento pequeño y recogido en la parte más secreta de la casa y más apartada."

448. This arrangement of three grinding stones (*metates*) was still in daily use in many New Mexico pueblos in the first half of the twentieth century. The following description is from Cochití Pueblo: "Modern Cochití recognize three grades of *metate* (*ya'ni*), called, from the roughest to the smoothest, *osh'kolina*, *po'trañi*, and *o'pañiwan*." Lange, *Cochití*, 116.

449. "Breaks the grain," *frangolla*. *DRAE*, 992: "quebrantar los granos de cereales o legumbres."

450. This statement about the absence of nuts and fruits is certainly an exaggeration. Archaeologists have identified a number of other wild and cultivated fruits from Pueblo ruins of the Rio Grande region, including sunflower seeds, squash, beans, prickly pear tunas, wild onions, serviceberries, juniper berries, acorns, and yucca fruits. Riley, *Frontier People*, 261; Cordell, *Prehistory of the Southwest*, 31.

451. Regarding the death of Francisco de Ovando, see fol. 67r.

452. Presumably this captivity occurred from the winter of 1540–41 to the winter of 1541–42.

453. "Pottery glazed with lead," *alcohol* = *galena*. *DRAE*, 89. These are the ceramic types known archaeologically as Rio Grande glaze-paint wares or glaze wares. The glaze elements on these ceramics consist of geometric designs in dark (red-brown to black to greenish brown) paint made from mineral oxides, especially lead oxides, that vitrified on firing. The designs stand out dramatically against a red- or white-slipped matte background. This use of lead glaze paint among the Pueblos of the American Southwest from the 1300s to about 1700 was unique in the Americas (with the possible exception of plumbate wares from Mesoamerica), though it never achieved an all-over sealing of the pots. Glaze-paint wares were common throughout the Rio Grande Pueblo region, except among the Tewa pueblos of the lower Chama River and adjacent Rio Grande. Kenneth Honea, *Revised Sequence of Rio Grande Glaze Pottery*, Texas Tech Archaeological Survey, Bulletin 1 (Lubbock: Texas Tech University, Department of Sociology and Anthropology, 1967); Prudence M. Rice, *Pottery Analysis: A Sourcebook* (Chicago: University of Chicago Press, 1987), 20; A. Helene Warren, "The Glaze Paint Wares of the Upper Middle Rio Grande Valley," in *Adaptive Change in the Northern Rio Grande Valley*, vol. 4, eds. Jan V. Biella and Richard C. Chapman, Archeological Investigations in Cochití Reservoir, New Mexico (Albuquerque: University of New Mexico, Office of Contract Archeology, 1979), 187–216.

454. As determined archaeologically, the plan of the north pueblo at Cicuique/Pecos (its oldest part) is a rectangle rather than a square, although the remainder of Castañeda de Nájera's description matches Pecos very well. Obregón, almost certainly basing his excellent description on information from veterans of the Coronado, Rodríquez-Chamuscado, and Espejo expeditions, later wrote that Cicuique/Cicuic was situated "en una loma alta y angosta y cercado de entrambos lados de dos arroyos de agua y mucha arboleda" (on a high, narrow hill surrounded on both sides by flowing arroyos and thick forest). Obregón, *Historia*, 21.

455. See note 85, this document. H&R, 257, interpret this phrase incorrectly as "The second terrace is all surrounded," whereas Winship, 273, is more accurate in translating the phrase as "There are corridors going all around it at the first two stories." Following Spanish usage, this excludes the ground floor.

456. Remains of that wall are still visible along the eastern side of Pecos ruins.

457. Ximena, Jimena, was probably Galisteo Pueblo (LA26), the ruins of which lie east of modern Galisteo, New Mexico (map 5). Barrett, *Conquest and Catastrophe*, 40.

458. *Silos, DRAE*, 1880: "lugar subterraneo y seco donde se guarda el trigo u otros granos, semillas or forrajes." These were probably the same sorts of underground storage pits as those referred to by the Nahuatl-derived term "coscomates" 160 years later in the Diego de Vargas journals. See especially John L. Kessell, Rick Hendricks, and Meredith Dodge, eds., *Blood on the Boulders: The Journals of don Diego de Vargas, New Mexico, 1694–1697* (Albuquerque: University of New Mexico Press, 1998), 460 n. 157. Barrett has identified this pueblo as the ruins now known as San Lázaro, south of Galisteo Creek and east of the modern town of Cerrillos, New Mexico. Riley suggests, instead, that it was Galisteo Pueblo, just northeast of the modern town of the same name. See map 5. Barrett, *Conquest and Catastrophe*, 40; Riley, *Rio del Norte*, 184.

459. Barrett and Riley agree that this pueblo was San Cristóbal, the ruins of which stand along San Cristóbal Arroyo east of the modern town of Galisteo, New Mexico (map 5). Barrett, *Conquest and Catastrophe*, 40; Riley, *Rio del Norte*, 184–85. The presence, however, of numerous large, naturally occurring, spherical stone concretions that are weathering out of exposed sandstone bedrock at and near San Lázaro Pueblo in the Galisteo Basin some 10 miles west of San Cristóbal suggests strongly that it is the site described here. Forrest Fenn, *The Secrets of San Lazaro Pueblo* (Santa Fe, NM: One Horse Land and Cattle Co., 2004), 258–59.

460. *Arroba* can refer to either a dry measure (weight) or a liquid measure (volume). The latter is intended here. The ceramic vessel (*botija*) referred to here as a jug is what is now known among American archaeologists as an olive jar. "Old-style" olive jars, in use from about 1500 to 1570, were nearly spherical. A one-*arroba*, "old-style" olive jar has a diameter of about 34.25 centimeters, or 13.5 inches. John L. Kessell et al., eds., *That Disturbances Cease: The Journals of don Diego de Vargas, New Mexico, 1697–1700* (Albuquerque: University of New Mexico Press, 2000), 445; Kathleen Deagan, *Artifacts of the Spanish Colonies of Florida and the Caribbean, 1500–1800*, vol. 1, *Ceramics, Glassware, and Beads* (Washington, DC: Smithsonian Institution Press, 1987), 30–33.

461. "War machine," *ingenio*. H&R, 257, go too far in translating the term *ingenios* as "guns." Winship, 274, is closer with "engines." The reference is certainly to siege engines, devices then being used in Europe for hurling heavy projectiles. These would have included constructions such as the giant *ballesta*, or crossbow, sketched by Leonardo da Vinci during the last decades of the 1400s. Ladislao Reti, ed., *The Unknown Leonardo* (New York: McGraw-Hill, 1974), 176–77.

462. The same episode, in about 1525, may also have resulted in the destruction and abandonment of three other pueblos in the Galisteo Basin (map 3): Blanco, Colorado, and Shé. Riley, *Rio del Norte*, 184.

463. "Teules," superhumans. *Teules* is a hispanicized version of the Nahuatl word *teutl*, meaning "god." Gerhard attests this early use of the term: "The rulers of Etzatlan and Ahuacatlan in 1525 described the people north of the (Coanos?) as 'Teules chichimecas, who are like beasts.'" Molina, *Vocabulario*, fol. 112r; Gerhard, *North Frontier*, 40. Náhuas of central Mexico called all the northerners beyond civilized life "Chichimeca," a name meaning something like "lineage of the dog." Nomadic hunters using bows and arrows and not cultivating the land inhabited the inner plateau of northern Mexico between the two Sierra Madre ranges. Coe, *Mexico*, 122–23.

464. This mention of a conch shell is one of many indications of trade between Cicuique and other pueblos of the Rio Grande region and peoples with access to marine shells from the coasts of the Gulf of Mexico and the Pacific Ocean.

465. These are the seven towns referred to earlier on folio 107r. See note 438, this document.

466. This is Pueblo (or Glorieta) Creek, which flows along the western base of the eminence on which the ruins of Pecos Pueblo stand.

467. The group of pueblos here called Aguas Calientes probably comprised the ruins known as Unshagi (LA123), Nanishagi (LA541) and Guisewa (LA679), on the western side of the Jemez River in the vicinity of today's Jemez Springs, New Mexico. The inhabitants of these pueblos could have been what Vargas later called the San Juan Jemez, who lived on San Juan Mesa in the Vallecitos drainage east of the Jemez River (map 3). H&R, 259 n. 1; Barrett, *Conquest and Catastrophe*, 7, 43, 98, and Table 9.

468. Evidently this group included the pueblos to which the people of Yuque Yunque fled. See fols. 91r–91v.

469. In fact the chronicler's numbers total 71.

470. At 2.63 miles per league, this would be between 315 and 370 miles. Using the lower of these figures and measuring downstream from Valladolid/Taos, this would place the likely southern limit of Pueblo settlement along the Rio Grande in 1540 at about modern Radium Springs, New Mexico, not far downstream from Hatch, where the Rio Grande makes a dramatic bend to the east, possibly the "turn to the east" just mentioned by Castañeda de Nájera. This is considerably farther downstream than the Milligan Gulch (Socorro County) limit recognized by Elinore Barrett. Barrett, *Geography of the Rio Grande Pueblos*, 4, 39. Carroll Riley has suggested that these southernmost pueblos might have pertained to native peoples later called Mansos. Riley, *Rio del Norte*, 166.

471. This statement about population is a key element in the chronicler's assessment of the unsuitability of the Pueblo region for Spanish colonization. As he writes later, a population of this size was insufficient to constitute *encomiendas* for more than a few people. Fol. 130v.

472. This statement and another on fol. 116v show that even in the 1560s, when Castañeda de Nájera composed the *relación*, he still was convinced of the proximity of Greater India to the area the expedition had traversed. Similarly, López de Gómara, writing in the 1540s or early 1550s, stated that "many persons think that the land is linked from there to China." López de Gómara, *Historia general*, fol. 94v.

473. Río de Tiguex. For geographical information, see the entry for Tiguex in Appendix 2.

474. This northeasterly direction seems to be at odds with Castañeda de Nájera's surmise on the previous folio side that the Pueblos originated to the west. Or the Spanish original may actually have been "noroeste," representing another confusion of handwritten *o* and *d*. See note 440, this document.

475. Ruy López de Villalobos, nephew of Viceroy Antonio de Mendoza, led a sea expedition of six ships across the Pacific Ocean in 1542. Samuel Eliot Morison, *The European Discovery of America: The Southern Voyages, 1492–1616* (New York: Oxford University Press, 1974), 492–93. Mar de Poniente = Mar del Sur = Pacific Ocean.

476. "Across," *en el ancho*. *Anchura*, DRAE, 137: "En una superficie, su dimensión considerada de derecha a izquierda o de izquierda a derecha en contraposición a la considerada de arriba abajo o de abajo arriba."

477. Again the chronicler expresses the expeditionaries' disappointment over the lack of potential for supporting themselves as *encomenderos* among the Rio Grande pueblos.

478. As earlier on fol. 91v, the chronicler here holds out the tantalizing possibility of silver deposits in the Pueblo region.

479. The two ranges the chronicler is referring to here are the Rocky Mountain system and the Appalachian Mountain system. He was, of course, unaware of other *cordilleras* (mountain chains) in North America, such as the Sierra Nevada and Coastal Ranges.

480. For discussion of the distance between Cíbola and Cicuique, see note 202, this document.

481. From Pecos Pueblo this would be about 80 miles (using the rate of 2.63 miles per league). Following the Rowe Mesa–Cañon Blanco route we have suggested, this would place the beginning of the plains just east of the Pecos River bridge crossing. This jibes with Juan Jaramillo's statement that the expedition began to enter the plains just after crossing the river. Document 30, fol. 2v.

482. This is the Gulf of California.

483. "Unsettled" means "without permanent, fixed habitations." Such uninhabited areas were of almost no interest to the expeditionaries, because they were devoid of potential tribute payers.

484. Many researchers have commented on the accuracy of this description of the Llano Estacado in the Texas counties of Parmer, Castro, Swisher, Lamb, Hale, Floyd, Lubbock, and Crosby—what is known as the South Plains. Some 25,000 intermittent, small playa lakes are sprinkled across the southern and eastern Llano. Morris, *Llano Estacado*, 121–25; Blakeslee, "Which Barrancas?" 311.

485. The native cover of the Llano Estacado is dominated by short grasses such as buffalo grass, blue gramma, sideoats gramma, and little bluestem. Flores, *Caprock Canyonlands*, 45. *Jeme:* see note 76, this document.

486. "Barren earth," *tierra muerta*. Compare *arena muerta*, DRAE, 185: "La que por estar pura y sin mezcla de tierra, no sirve para el cultivo."

487. "Across these plains," *por estos llanos*. This phrase could be attached to either the thought that precedes it (as Mora, 127, has it) or to the succeeding thought (which we think makes better sense). Several times in this chapter and the preceding one we have disagreed with the way Mora breaks the Spanish up into

sentences. So also does Craddock, "Castañeda y Nájera," 16. However, we do not always agree with Craddock either.

488. This evidently left the Llano Estacado and its margins without human presence during the winter months and is also an indication of the extensive trade network operated by the Teyas/Jumanos, which Nancy Hickerson has outlined in detail. Hickerson, *Jumanos*, 215–19.

489. "According to what was understood from these people": our translation here relies on the figurative sense of *ver*, meaning "to understand" rather than literally "to see." H&R, 261, render the phrase too literally as "from what was seen of these natives." Their translation then leads them to have the chronicler state (contrary to his own report) that the Querechos and Teyas were more numerous than the Pueblos. Our translation avoids this difficulty.

490. Thus, had this larger population been fact, the Plains region would have been much more attractive to Spanish settlement of the type envisioned by most members of the Coronado expedition, settlement founded on the extraction of tribute from native peoples.

491. Once again Native Americans are compared to Arabs and Turks. See note 302, this document.

492. "Giving a cutting edge to them [the flints] on [the bison's] own teeth," *dandoles los filos en sus propios dientes*. H&R, 262, render this phrase improbably as "they sharpen the flints on their own teeth." Winship, 280, says essentially the same. What makes much more sense is that the bison skinners would use the large, hard teeth of the bison as flaking tools. They were of essentially the same bonelike material as antler, which was the most common such tool. Besides, flaking a flint blade in one's own mouth would be extremely dangerous—it would be all but impossible to do without slicing one's lips, tongue, and cheeks, and the resulting sharp microflakes could do great damage if held in one's mouth or swallowed.

493. This is probably a reference to coyotes, which, over the centuries, were frequently portrayed as trailing the bison herds of the Great Plains.

494. "[Northeast,]" *a el poniente*. The chronicler's westerly direction here is at variance with other contemporary accounts of the route followed from the Teya settlements to Quivira, which place Quivira north-northeast of the canyons (maps 1 and 4). It should be remembered that Castañeda de Nájera was not among those who made the trip from the *barrancas* to Quivira. The chronicler also contradicts his own earlier report (fol. 83v) that Quivira was to the north. Compare also, for instance, Document 30, fol. 3v.

495. That is, the natives of the plains do not spin and weave flax.

496. The reference here is evidently to residential structures in western Nueva España. Obregón, for example, refers to the houses at Ocoroni (not far from Petatlán) as "de lanas y esteras, de ellas son tumbadas y redondas" (made of woven cloth and straw mats; [they are] made arched and rounded out of [those materials]). Prehistoric ceramic images of thatched-roof dwellings are plentiful from the Mexican state of Nayarit. Obregón, *Historia*, 75; Ignacio Bernal, *The Mexican National Museum of Anthropology*, rev. ed. (México, DF: Ediciones Lara, 1970), 165.

497. When Castañeda de Nájera wrote in the 1560s, Portugal and Spain were separate kingdoms, although that was to change in less than 20 years. The turn of phrase used here may then represent an emendation by Niño Velásques, rather than being the chronicler's own characterization. As Castañeda de Nájera says at the end of this paragraph, the Portuguese man's name was Campo. There were two Campos on the muster roll, but from Antonio Tello's *Historia* it is known that the man referred to here was Andrés de Campo. Elliott, *Imperial Spain*, 271–73; Document 12, fols. 2r and 4v; Tello, 485. On unknown authority, Francisco López de Gómara provides the information that Andrés de Campo was the *hortelano*, or orchardman, of a Francisco de Solís. López de Gómara, *Historia general*, fol. 95v.

498. His sources unknown, López de Gómara, writing in the 1540s or early 1550s, adds that Padilla also took with him 12 Indians from Michoacán. López de Gómara, *Historia general*, fol. 95v. One community called Zapotlán was in the jurisdiction of Pachuca in the modern Mexican state of Hidalgo, just northeast of Mexico City. Another was in the jurisdiction of Tuspan in what is now Jalisco. Gerhard, *Historical Geography*, 209–11, 338–40. Pánuco was the first Spanish political enclave to be established on the northern frontier of Nueva España. The jurisdiction of Pánuco comprised an area along the Gulf of Mexico coast from Tampico indefinitely northward. Nuño de Guzmán was recognized as its governor from 1527 to 1533. By 1534 Pánuco had ceased to exist as an independent political entity, having been subsumed under Nueva España. Gerhard, *North Frontier*, 10.

499. Arache, as understood through reports of members of the Soto expedition,

is here evidently equated with Arahe or Harahey, a land supposedly to the east of Quivira.

500. This description fits well the Missouri-Mississippi river system.

501. Hispalis was the Roman name for the city that eventually became Sevilla in Spain's modern *comunidad* of Andalucía.

502. "Abundant," *larga*. *DRAE*, 1231.

503. This is an unequivocal statement that the expedition was seeking populated places, rather than empty land in which to settle or prospect for precious metals.

504. This reference to the arrival of letters is one of a number of indications in the contemporary documents that there was regular, if infrequent, communication between the expedition and people in Nueva España. There exist also, for example, the viceroy's statement in October 1541 that he was expecting a message from Vázquez de Coronado, the captain general's October 1541 reference to having dispatched at least one letter to the king, and Luis de Figueredo's statement that he had been sent to Señora with dispatches. Document 25, fol. 458v; Document 26, fol. 1r; Flint, *Great Cruelties*, 409.

505. This statement indicates that hostilities may have continued between the expeditionaries and at least some of the Pueblos during the winter of 1541–42.

506. "Very poorly dressed," *desnudo*. This is a figurative use of *desnudo*. *DRAE*, 722. At this stage in the expedition, most of the European clothing was probably threadbare and in tatters.

507. "Obviously," *de si*. In other words, the members of the expedition needed new clothes without lice, so they wanted to burn the old ones.

508. Writing a hundred years later, fray Antonio Tello said the general "cayó dando un gran golpe con la boca en el suelo" (fell, severely banging his mouth on the ground), leaving him with a "gran chinchón [chichón] que despues le abrieron" (very large swelling, which later they opened up). With such detail, this description gives every appearance of having derived ultimately from an eyewitness. Tello, 440. On the basis of Castañeda de Nájera's description of this injury and its aftermath, trauma coordinator and epidemiologist Daniel G. Judkins, of University Medical Center, Tucson, recently assessed the probable nature of the captain general's wound. Rejecting the possibilities of subdural hematoma, epidural hematoma, concussion, and diffuse axonal shear injury, he concluded that Vázquez de Coronado likely suffered "a moderate frontal lobe cerebral contusion." Judkins went on to explain: "He did recover enough to be able to decide to return to Mexico and to travel back there and to go about usual daily functions. He likely had some personality change or mild cognitive deficit, and if so, this would imply that the most likely injury was a frontal contusion. Contusion to the frontal lobe often is associated with a 'flat' personality affect, other behavior changes, etc. Coronado seems to have lost his ambition for the project, and his enthusiasm declined. This fits very well with frontal lobe injury." Judkins, personal communication, March 4, 2004.

509. Because his fall happened after winter was over, and the expedition turned about and departed from Tiguex about April 1, the captain general's convalescence probably lasted no more than a month, if that.

510. The sequence of events related here indicates that the occurrence most decisive in determining the expedition's return to Nueva España was the uprising at Suya, rather than the captain general's fall, as both Castañeda de Nájera and Herbert Bolton maintain. Bolton, 331.

511. "Astrologer," *matematico* = *antiguo astrólogo*. *DRAE*, 1336. Astrology was at the time a respected study. Covarrubias, 132, calls *astrología* "ciencia que trata de los astros y los efectos que de ellos proceden . . . que por otro nombre dicen astronomía."

512. Such a physician specialized in treatment of wounds and injuries. Covarrubias, 317: "el médico que cura de heridas o llagas." Of such "practical surgeons" James Lockhart writes that often they fell "completely out of the professional class and into the class of artisans through their collateral trade of barbering." Certainly the surgeon in this case was of this lower level, since he evidently did not bear even the lowest academic title of *bachiller*. James Lockhart, *Spanish Peru, 1532–1560* (Madison: University of Wisconsin Press, 1968), 50.

513. This is another reference to the standard Spanish practice of the day of deliberating on major decisions in a council of the highest-status individuals in the group. See also Document 15, fol. 369v, and Document 30, fol. 4v.

514. This is among the most succinct statements revealing the principal motivations of lay members of the Coronado and other contemporary expeditions: access to wealth through the *encomienda* system.

515. "Trunk," *cofre*. This *cofre* was probably a "caja de tres llaves," a strongbox that required keys held by three separate officials to open. Such a depository was the common means of securing money and important papers. A sixteenth-century example of such a strongbox is depicted in González García, *Archivo general de Indias*, 137.

516. "Mattress," *colchón*. *DRAE*, 505: "pieza cuadrilonga, rellena de lana u otro material blando u elástico." With or without the support of a bedstead, such cloth bags stuffed with soft material were undoubtedly in wide use as camp beds.

517. This group of 70 evidently was to include Francisca de Hozes and her husband, Alonso Sánchez. Flint, *Great Cruelties*, 61, 69.

518. There is no known documentary evidence to support this charge.

519. Obregón, writing more than 40 years later, reported that Alcaraz had 100 or a hundred-odd people with him at San Gerónimo 3 (see map 2). Obregón, *Historia*, 19, 151. For geographical information about San Gerónimo, see the entry for Los Corazones in Appendix 2.

520. Hernán Darias de Saavedra was a brother of Luis de Saavedra, who married Marina de Estrada (Vázquez de Coronado's sister-in-law) in 1528. Luis died in 1537, followed by Marina in 1540. Fernández de Bethencourt, *Historia genealogia*, 9:499.

521. Castañeda de Nájera's report about Alcaraz is much more sympathetic than that provided, for example, during the 1544 testimony concerning the expedition's conduct, in which all the blame for the debacle at San Gerónimo was laid at his feet. Flint, *Great Cruelties*, 61, 65, 92, 110, 133, 145, 192, 210, 235, 255.

522. For information about this poison, see note 285, this document.

523. More extended accounts of the reasons behind the uprising at San Gerónimo are offered by the witnesses in Flint, *Great Cruelties*, passim. Obregón provides a far more detailed account of the attack on San Gerónimo and the death of Alcaraz, apparently obtained from survivors. Obregón, *Historia*, 151–54.

524. This was most likely the upper waters of the Río Sonora in extreme northern Sonora. The area, called Suya by Castañeda de Nájera, is identified by Riley as Ispa or Guaraspi. Riley, *Frontier People*, 53, 72. See note 286, this document.

525. Whether these servants were Indians, Blacks, Europeans, or a combination of the three is unknown.

526. Obregón reported in 1584, on the basis of conversation with one of the survivors, that "los que escaparon fué un clérigo e cinco soldados" (those who escaped were a priest and five men-at-arms). He also reported that his informant was a man named Ureña, a name not otherwise associated with any of the priests who accompanied the expedition. Obregón, *Historia*, 153.

527. If this characterization of the people of Corazones as having been consistently friendly to the expedition is accurate, they would have been unusual among the native groups encountered in Tierra Nueva. One possibility is that hostility between the people of Suya and those from Corazones might have contributed to the latter town's kind treatment of enemies of Suya.

528. It is unclear whether it was El Turco's physical appearance or his behavior that resulted in his being called a Turk.

529. "Beginning," *entrado*. *DRAE*, 850: "referido a una estación o a un período de tiempo, que y no está en su comienzo pero tampoco ha llegado aún a su mitad."

530. The dates in the manuscript are consistently off by one year. In this instance, a marginal note, perhaps in Niño Velásques's hand, should read "1542."

531. Order of (Friars) Minor = Franciscans.

532. For biographical information, see the entry for fray Luis de Úbeda in Appendix 1.

533. This is Andrés de Campo.

534. This black man is not identified, but Jaramillo reported that he was an interpreter and later became a Franciscan friar. As Angélico Chávez pointed out, a black man could not have been admitted to the Order of Friars Minor at this time. Document 30, fol. 5v; Chávez, *Coronado's Friars*, 60.

535. "Indians from Nueva España." See fol. 123r.

536. This description of the people of Cicuique as "not the least bit violent" does not match the chronicler's own account of their behavior toward Tristán de Arellano's company the preceding fall. See fol. 93r.

537. Presumably this refers to political damage the captain general would suffer if he allowed Indians to be removed from Tierra Nueva. H&R, 271, are more cautious, rendering this phrase as "fearing that the taking of natives from that land to New Spain might result in harm." In doing so, they ignore the indirect object of *dañase* by simply not translating it and thereby not specifying to whom or what the harm might accrue. Winship, 294, on the other hand, has "fearing that they might be injured if people were carried away from that country to New Spain." At least

he attempted, however mistakenly, to deal with the problem of the indirect object.

538. This attitude of "better mistreated than heathen" was common among the expeditionaries who testified during Lorenzo de Tejada's investigation of the expedition's treatment of Indians in 1544. See Flint, *Great Cruelties*, passim.

539. Departure took place around April 1, 1542. Document 27 reports that the expedition was on the Río Frío, five days' travel from Cíbola toward Chichiltcale, on April 9. The April 9 date indicates that at least part of the expedition must have left Tiguex several days before April 1.

540. The cause of the horses' deaths may have been disease or poisoning, since the deaths were spread over a number of days and occurred at different locations.

541. Carroll Riley has suggested that as many as 200 Indian allies of the expedition may have stayed behind at Cíbola and elsewhere in the Pueblo world when the expedition returned south. Carroll L. Riley, "Mesoamerican Indians in the Early Southwest," *Ethnohistory* 21 (Winter 1974):25–36.

542. "Astern," *por popa.* This is another example of a nautical literary device employed by Castañeda de Nájera. See also his use of "set their prow" (*puesto la proa*) on fol. 131v.

543. H&R, 272, stretch the meaning of *enojar,* rendering the phrase as, "However, it is believed that it was not to harm them."

544. Gallego had been sent south with a message for the viceroy after Cíbola was captured in 1540. See fol. 34v.

545. In other words, Gallego did not mask his disappointment that the expedition was returning.

546. Such continuous hostility is reminiscent of the experience of the Soto expedition in the Southeast. The expedition was now passing back through the region where Gallego had just cut a bloody swath.

547. "Shrieks," *gritas.* H&R, 273, misinterpret *gritas* and render this phrase as, "At some places there were outbreaks by the Indians, and some horses wounded and killed." Somewhere between these two readings is that of Winship, 295, who is a little closer to the sense of the phrase with, "In several places yells were heard and Indians seen, and some of the horses were wounded and killed."

548. This was Antonio Mesa. AGI, Patronato, 56, N.3, R.2, "Pedro Jerónimo."

549. This apparently exceptional period without rest suggests that ordinarily the expedition would lay by for rest days, although none is referred to in any of the known documents except here.

550. This statement implies that the people of the entire region from Suya south to Petatlán, a distance of some 225 leagues (nearly 600 miles) had risen up against the expedition.

551. This again testifies to Castañeda's residence in the *provincia* of Culiacán, perhaps even specifically at Petatlán, following the expedition. See also note 573, this document.

552. The date of the feast of Saints Juan and Pablo is June 26, which is approximately the beginning of the summer rainy season typical of much of Mexico. Chaves, *Espejo de navegantes,* 86.

553. "Crocodile," *lagarto.* Of the two classes of crocodilians in the Western Hemisphere, the alligator and the American crocodile (*Crocodylus acutus*), only the American crocodile exists in western and southwestern Mexico. This crocodile is found in southern Mexico, Central America, and most of warmer South America. The American alligator, on the other hand, ranges from the southeastern United States to the Rio Grande in Texas. Felger and Broyles, *Dry Borders.*

554. Presumably this was a written report. It is not known to have survived, although Bolton did not include it in his list of "missing documents." Bolton, 472–75.

555. Although Vázquez de Coronado did lose the governorship of Nueva Galicia, he remained a *regidor* of the *cabildo* of the Ciudad de México until his death in 1554, serving several times as that body's legal agent and official representative. *Actas de Cabildo,* 5:15, 32, 78, 165–66.

556. An *audiencia* for Nueva Galicia was authorized to be established in Compostela in 1548. The *audiencia* did not actually convene until January 1549. Tello, 534; Gerhard, *North Frontier,* 45.

557. The reference to East India here is an interesting statement of the goal of the *entrada* and clearly indicates what were still common geographical conceptions even as late as the 1560s.

558. Such books earned great popularity during the first half of the sixteenth century. They included *Cuatro libros de Amadís de Gaula* (1508), *Las Sergas de Esplandián* (1510), *Florisando* (1510), *Palmerín de Oliva* (1511), and *Amadís de*

Grecia (1530). Irving A. Leonard, *Books of the Brave: Being an Account of Books and of Men in the Spanish Conquest and Settlement of the Sixteenth-Century New World* (Berkeley: University of California Press, 1992), 16–18.

559. A book called *Historia de Carlo Magno y de los doce Pares* appeared in print sometime before 1525. It narrated the chivalric deeds of the paladins, or twelve knightly companions, of the ninth-century Frankish king Charlemagne. Leonard, *Books of the Brave,* 55.

560. "Arms and armor," *armas.* The term *armas* comprehends both arms and armor. Covarrubias, 118: "arma puede ser ofensiva, como la espalda, la lanza, etc . . . y defensiva como la cota, el casco, la rodela, el coselete, etc."

561. "Jackrabbits," *liebres. Liebres* are large rabbits, probably jackrabbits.

562. Like most Spanish accounts of the day, this brief mention grossly misstates the size of Cortés's force by failing to count the tens of thousands of Tlaxcalan, Cholulan, and other native allies who accompanied and fought along with the Europeans. See, for example, López de Gómara, *Cortés,* 233, 246, 251, 256, 264, 280, 284. For brief biographical information about Hernán Cortés, see the introduction to Document 18.

563. Here, Tenochtitlan is described as the "riñon," or heart, of the land, meaning its geographic, or possibly demographic, center, just as Tiguex had been described earlier. See, fol. 115v, this document. At this period, "México" referred to both the prehistoric city of Tenochtitlan and the Spanish and Indian city that was founded on its rubble. It did not apply to territory outside the urban area. Many documents of the period from 1520 to about 1550 use both names in tandem, calling the city México Tenochtitlan.

564. All these expeditions of conquest were also dominated by corps of native allies. See, for example, Robert S. Chamberlain, *The Conquest and Pacification of Yucatán, 1517–1550,* Carnegie Institution of Washington, Publication 582 (Washington, DC: Carnegie Institution of Washington, 1948); Lutz, *Santiago de Guatemala,* 3–6; and José Ignacio Avellaneda, *The Conquerors of the New Kingdom of Granada* (Albuquerque: University of New Mexico Press, 1995), 30. Tierra Firme was the name given to Panamá and South America. For biographical information about Pedro de Alvarado, see the introduction to Document 20. Francisco de Montejo was a native of Salamanca in the modern Spanish *comunidad* of Castilla y León. At the age of about 44 he was one of the captains of the Grijalva expedition along the Mexican Gulf Coast. He joined Cortés's *entrada* and became an *encomendero.* He became *adelantado* and governor and captain general of Yucatán in 1526. Himmerich y Valencia, *Encomenderos,* 198; *Diccionario Porrua: Historia, biografía y geografía de Mexico,* 5th ed., 3 vols. (México: Editorial Porrúa, 1986), 2:1951.

565. This statement of obligation may imply that the addressee of the *relación* had requested its preparation, since the chronicler does not use the reflexive form of the verb (*obligarse*), which would imply that the necessity was self-imposed.

566. San Gerónimo was moved from Los Corazones to Señora, to Fuya/Suya (map 2). The three Indian towns/regions were fixed locales, but the Spaniards moved their people. According to Obregón, writing in 1584, it was 200 leagues from Suya to Culiacán. Converting to miles using the *legua legal,* the distance would be approximately 526 miles. This would again place Suya at about the modern U.S.-Mexican border. Obregón, *Historia,* 153. Compare note 286, this document.

567. H&R, 277, mistakenly attribute the 200 leagues to the *tierra de guerra* (for definition, see note 126, this document).

568. These people included those from Petatlán to Suya, that is, all the sedentary, agricultural people of Sinaloa and Sonora.

569. Gallego was a veteran of the Guzmán *entrada.* His use of preemptive violence might have been a habit from that experience or might have derived only from the perceived urgency of this later mission.

570. The men-at-arms on the expedition to Tierra Nueva identified as having been shot in the eyelid or eye were Juan de Paniagua (at Tiguex) and Juan de Orduña (geographical location unknown). Probably the man referred to here was Orduña. Tello, 423; AGI, México, 1064, L.1\1, "Informes de los conquistadores," fol. 279.

571. "Quince juice." See also fol. 140v.

572. "They considered [the Spaniards' deeds] more as a divine thing than a human [one]," *los tenian mas por cosa divina que humana.* H&R, 278, interpret the antecedent of *los* as being "the Spaniards" rather than "the Spaniards' deeds," as we do.

573. This statement provides additional evidence of the chronicler's residence in Culiacán. See also note 551, this document.

574. This number of allies and servants (1,500) may be close to the truth and would put the total number of people on the expedition at around 2,000.

575. That the rear guard was out of sight of the nearest unit of the expedition is further evidence that the expedition traveled as discrete units, probably companies, and was thus spread out over a considerable distance.

576. See Edwin L. Kiser, "The Reexamination of Pedro de Castañeda's Bone Bed by Geological Investigations," *Bulletin of the Texas Archaeological Society* 49 (1978):331–39, for a plausible identification of this "windrow" of bison bones as a large deposit of pleistocene-age bison bone known as the Silver Lake Bison Site in Hockley County, Texas (map 4).

577. Many bison with split ears must have been simply a coincidence. A famous woodcut of a bison roughly matching this description appeared in the 1554 edition of Francisco López de Gómara's *Historia general de las Indias*. It is possible that López de Gómara's artist based his illustration on an image made by one of the two artists who accompanied the Coronado expedition, Cristóbal de Quesada and Bartolomé Sánchez, though none of their work has been located. AGI, México, 1064, L.1\1, "Informes de los conquistadores," fol. 270r; AGI, Contratación, 199, N.23, "Bartolomé Sánchez."

578. The reference to exceptionally level land here is to the Llano Estacado of eastern New Mexico and the Texas Panhandle, where, indeed, the phenomenon of seeing sky between the legs of distant livestock is still noted.

579. Feather-decorated "prayer sticks" are still features of traditional Pueblo shrines. For examples of late-nineteenth-century Zuni shrines that incorporate plumed sticks, see Stevenson, *Zuñi Indians*, plates 21, 108, and 128. For a Zuni shrine including an object incorporating a cruciform element, see Stevenson, *Zuñi Indians*, plate 137. For Puebloan rock art from the Galisteo Basin that includes crosslike elements, see Polly Schaafsma, *Warrior, Shield, and Star: Imagery and Ideology of Pueblo Warfare* (Santa Fe: Western Edge Press, 2000), 35, 67. Schaafsma interprets such prehistoric Pueblo images as representing Venus, an icon of war.

580. This statement about previous knowledge of the Christian cross is reminiscent of the convictions of some early Franciscan missionaries in Nueva España who believed that the Indians had been miraculously evangelized by one of Christ's apostle's centuries before Columbus's landfall. Others held that the Indians were a lost tribe of Jews or that they instinctively practiced many Christian virtues. John Leddy Phelan, *The Millennial Kingdom of the Franciscans in the New World*, 2nd ed. (Berkeley: University of California Press, 1970), 24–26, 59.

581. In September 1546 native guides led Spaniards to silver at a location that soon became Zacatecas. Not until further discoveries of silver were made in the area in 1548, however, did a European population move there that was of sufficient size to ensure Spanish sovereignty. Bakewell, *Silver Mining*, 4, 15.

582. Living at the time of the Guzmán *entrada* in what is now northeastern Jalisco, the Guachichiles were hunters and gatherers evidently speaking a Uto-Aztecan language. They migrated northward following the Chichimec War of the 1590s. Gerhard, *North Frontier*, 42, 49, 63, 104.

583. This sentence is poorly rendered by H&R, 281, as "and not if following the round-about way taken by the army of Francisco Vázquez Coronado." Winship, 307, is much closer to our translation, giving "for the army of Francisco Vázquez Coronado went the very farthest way round to get there."

584. Once again the direction given in the document seems incorrect and ought to be "noroeste." See note 440, this document.

585. The distances listed in the manuscript at this point total only 460 leagues. This would have gotten the expedition only as far as Cíbola. The remaining 390 are not accounted for here, but most of that distance would have been entailed in travel from Cíbola to Quivira. See map 1.

586. According to Winship, "The dictionary of Dominguez says 'Isla de negros o isla del Almirantazgo, en el grande océano equinoccial; grande isla de la América del Norte, sobre la costa oeste.' Apparently the location of this island gradually drifted westward with the increase of geographical knowledge, until it was finally located in the Philippines." Winship, 307 n. 4.

587. "Who could be civilized," *que tengan aquella policía*. H&R, 282, completely ignore this important phrase and render it as "the people of Tiguex . . . and other similar peoples." Winship, 307, handles the passage much as do Hammond and Rey.

588. Winship, 308, skips this phrase, indicating an ellipsis. H&R, 282, on the other hand, stretch the meaning of the Spanish considerably to render it as "make the Indians respect the leaders of the army."

589. That the expedition took along only very light swivel guns is confirmed by the 1560 testimony of Rodrigo Maldonado. Document 31, fol. 1r. A *versillo* was a light swivel gun with a bore of less than two inches, most commonly mounted with a pin on the gunnel of a ship.

590. This rubric appears under the headings of nearly each page and at the ends of paragraphs. It may have been used to take up space and prevent any unauthorized insertions.

591. Hallava. Mora, 64, and Winship, 111, have "hallaría."

592. Juntar. Both Winship, 114, and Mora, 68, have "portar."

593. Dudo. Ink bleeding through from the recto of this folio makes the word appear to be "dado."

594. This could be read as either "y aquel" or "ya que el," either of which would render the sentence intelligible. Both Winship, 114, and Mora, 69, have "ya que el." We concur.

595. Puesto que = *aunque. DRAE*, 1691.

596. A uso de guerra. Mora, 73, has "en son." Winship, 121, has "anso."

597. Esp*eraron*. An ink blot obscures most of this word.

598. The word *digo* and the phrase *por mejor decir* are used, altogether, 12 times in this copy of the *relación* as Niño Velasques corrects his own errors (fols. 33r, 44r, 50r, 52r, 56r, 77r, 82v, 86r, 89r, 91v, 139v, 146v, and 148r). This was standard scribal procedure of the day, done to guard against falsification.

599. Buscar. The word is blotted out in the text, but the *escribano* himself supplies it in the margin.

600. Bre y tan alto que *el* hom-. This is an inadvertent repetition of part of the immediately preceding line

601. Paso el cam- / po y la villa señora. Craddock, "Castañeda y Nájera," 6, has "pasaje confuso, parece que hay que entender 'pasó el campo a la villa de Señora.'"

602. Pesga = *pesa. DRAE*, 1586.

603. Piadad = *piedad.*

604. Confuçion. Winship, 126 has "con frision."

605. Porte = *aparte.*

606. Armas del freno. Craddock, "Castañeda y Nájera," 7, has "camas del freno."

607. Alli se ha- / llaron. This is a copying error. The *escribano* picked this phrase up from several words earlier and then corrected his mistake.

608. A el b(a)ordo. Winship, 127, and Mora, 83, leave the word as "bado," though what that would mean is a mystery. Indeed, Winship's translation of this whole passage (following Ternaux) is garbled. If we accept *bordo* as the intended word, miscopied by an *escribano* as "bado," then the phrase becomes clear. Winship, 209. *DRAE*, 313: *bordo = borde = extremo.*

609. Braçada is an archaic form of *braza. DRAE*, 322.

610. *Curar = cuidar* = "Poner diligencia, atención y solicitud en la ejecución de una cosa." *DRAE*, 622.

611. Comunicanse. Mora, 89, and Winship, 135, have "comunes anse."

612. Dicho sea. Craddock, "Castañeda y Nájera," 8, has "Más bien, 'dicho se ha' eso es 'ya se ha dicho.'"

613. Mandado = *noticia. DRAE*, 1304.

614. Priesa = *prisa.*

615. Dar batería = *combatir. DRAE*, 275.

616. "Primera" is repeated by error on the recto here, instead of "parte."

617. Esentamente = *exentamente.*

618. Rrenpugaban = *rempuxaban* or *repujaban*. It is to make this clarification that the *xa* is inserted in the margin.

619. The passage beginning with "hallavan" is extremely obscure. The most likely possibility is that it represents a scribal error, a slip of three lines.

620. A recaudo en cadena. Winship, 145, erroneously has "arrecando en cadena." H&R, 240, simply ignore "a recaudo." Mora, 103, has the correct transcription.

621. Hogaredas = *hogueras.*

622. Cayda = *declinación. DRAE*, 355. *Declinación, DRAE*, 668: "Ángulo que forma . . . una alineación, con el meridiano del lugar."

623. Apparently by analogy, "desrrumbar" = *desviar*. "Desrumbar" does not appear in the *DRAE*.

624. Corrido = *avergonzado. DRAE*, 580.

625. Enarco. This is the third-person singular preterite of *enarcar,* not, as in Mora, 109, and Winship, 155, "en arco."

626. A el lue*n*go. *DRAE*, 1274: "a lo largo."

627. Petlatlan. The copyist seems unsure of the spelling of this name and has written over and "corrected" several instances, including this one.

628. En su torno. This is related to "en torno a." *DRAE*, 1998: "alrededor de."

629. Fayçion = *faicion = facción. DRAE*, 943: "Figura y disposición con que una cosa se distingue de otra."

630. Gordor = *gordura.*

631. Se precia. Mora, 122, has "se precian," evidently interpreting a dot above the *a* as a sign that an *n* was omitted. However, no *n* is needed. We read that dot as one of many stray dots of ink bleed-through that pepper the manuscript.

632. Venediços = *advenedizos.* DRAE, 2971.

633. Tras = *detras de.* DRAE, 2013.

634. Harto mas gente. Mora, 127, renders this incorrectly as "harto mas grande."

635. Como y en que se trata. The phrase *como y* seems to represent a false start either by the copyist or by Castañeda de Nájera. It does not fit with the remainder of the heading.

636. "La esperanca de la Vuelta que se *havia* de hacer" is the verbatim repetition of a phrase just three lines earlier and probably represents a copying error.

637. Sufrir. Mistakenly, Mora, 133, and Winship, 172, have "su fin."

638. Volvería = *devolvería.* DRAE, 2105.

639. Negoçios = *pretensiones.* DRAE, 1433.

640. Compaña = *compañía.* DRAE, 520.

641. Patlatlan. This is a scribal error for Petlatlán (Petatlán), which exhibits the kind of vowel transformation known to linguists as assimilation.

642. (^E)asentar. Craddock, "Castañeda y Nájera," 20, has "'a esentar' . . . ; *exentar* 'dejar exento.'" Craddock seems to be wrong here.

643. O(b)cupacion. Winship, 176, has "obenpación," a nonsense word. Meanwhile, Mora, 138, has "obcupación," also an unknown word.

644. Sierto = *cierto* = *sabedor.* DRAE, 473.

645. The copyist fails to repeat "nuestros" in the beginning of fol. 145r.

646. Parpalo = *párpado.*

647. Viviendo en p(r)obreça. Winship, 178, and Mora, 140, have "viniendo en pobreza." Indeed, *v* and *n* are often indistinguishable in sixteenth-century written Spanish.

648. Façion = *facción.* See note 629, this document. Craddock, "Castañeda y Nájera," 21, reads this word as "faición." Strout, "Linguistic Study," 287, is in agreement with our reading.

649. Ser. Mora, 140, and Winship, 178, both have "sin." The *escribano* wrote over this word, so it is very unclear, but in its final form the word appears to end in an *r* rather than an *n.*

650. De esto. This is a scribal error, a nonsense phrase. One would expect "de altura" or "de alto," parallel with the earlier "de largo" and the following "en ancho."

651. Sinta = *cinta* = *cintura.* DRAE, 478.

652. Raspante. Because no recorded sense of *raspar* or *raspante* seems to fit here, Craddock, "Castañeda y Nájera," 21, suggests that the intended word was *rampante.* His suggestion seems reasonable. The beginning portion of Chapter 8 contains a number of what appear to be scribal errors, as though the *escribano* was tiring or losing concentration as the end of the long manuscript approached. This may be one of those. Verbs are frequently omitted in this section, as though a series of abbreviated notes was being copied into the text without expansion.

653. Jumetria = *geometría.*

654. Lumbre = *noticia.* DRAE, 1275.

655. Hase = *se ha.*

Document 29. The Relación del Suceso (Anonymous Narrative), 1540s

1. Fols. 1r–1v, 3r, and 5r.

2. Fol. 1r.

3. Fols. 2r and 5r. See note 49, this document.

4. Fols. 2r and 3v.

5. Because the distance values the author gives are never more precise than to the nearest 5 to 10 leagues, their margin of error must be in this range.

6. Fol. 4r.

7. For the location of the Jimmy Owens Site and its identification, see Donald J. Blakeslee and Jay C. Blaine, "The Jimmy Owens Site: New Perspectives on the Coronado Expedition," in Flint and Flint, *From the Distance of 460 Years,* 205.

8. Fol. 3r.

9. Document 28, fol. 84v.

10. See also the introduction to Document 30.

11. Fol. 2r.

12. Document 28, fol. 104v; Document 6, fol. 5v; Document 30, fol. 1v.

13. What makes "1" and "4" so easy to confuse is the long left-hand flag or serif at the top of "1," which makes it look very much like a "4" with the horizontal member omitted or very faint.

14. Fol. 2r.

15. Fols. 2r and 5r.

16. For examples of sixteenth-century *derroteros,* see Pedro González García, general ed., *Archivo General de Indias* (Madrid: Lunwerg Editores y Ministerio de Educación y Cultura, 1995), 170, 180.

17. For the Pisan romancer Rustichello's role in writing *The Travels,* see Ronald Latham, "Introduction," in Marco Polo, *The Travels of Marco Polo,* trans. and ed. Ronald Latham (Hammondsworth, UK: Penguin, 1958), 16–17.

18. Fol. 2r.

19. Stevenson, "Zuñi Indians," 110–12. See note 48, this document.

20. Fol. 5r.

21. *CDI,* 20:318–29.

22. Mora, 181–87.

23. Winship, 350–63.

24. H&R, 284–94.

25. This suggests, as does Diego López's 1544 testimony, that even before the expedition departed from Culiacán at least some members, including the captain general, had concluded that Cíbola was not what they had come to expect from the report of fray Marcos. Flint, *Great Cruelties,* 396. For geographical information about Cíbola and Culiacán, see the entries in Appendix 2.

26. For biographical information, see the entry for Melchior Díaz in Appendix 1.

27. In contrast, the "Traslado de las Nuevas," Document 22, fol. 1r, has "seventy-five companions on horseback and thirty footmen." Jaramillo's narrative, Document 30, fol. 1r, indicates only that 60 horsemen accompanied the captain general, and Pedro de Nájera's *relación,* Document 28, fol. 27v, reports "fifty horsemen and a few footmen."

28. The scheduled departure would have been about May 12. This is at variance with the "Traslado de las Nuevas," which reports that Arellano was to leave Culiacán "at the end of May." Document 22, fol. 1r. For biographical information, see the entry for Tristán de Arellano in Appendix 1.

29. For geographical information, see the entry for Corazones in Appendix 2.

30. This second wait would have put the main body of the expedition 20 days, plus an unknown additional time, behind the captain general and the advance guard.

31. See the introduction to this document.

32. Juan Jaramillo, however, reports a second, four-day unsettled area (that is, without permanent habitations) between Corazones and Cíbola, from Ispa (Arispe) to the Río Nexpa/San Pedro River (map 2). This same unsettled area appears also to have been reported by fray Marcos. Document 30, fol. 1v; Document 6, fol. 4r.

33. Converting the distance between Señora and Corazones provided here on the basis of the *legua legal* would place the two about 26 miles apart. If Corazones was in the immediate vicinity of Ures, Sonora (map 2), then Señora would have been very near or at the modern town of Baviácora, Sonora. For geographical information, see the entry for Señora in Appendix 2.

34. H&R, 285, ignore the partition "E" between this sentence and the following one and erroneously run the two together. Winship, 350, does the same, turning the first sentence into an independent clause.

35. The food shortage problem, therefore, was one not of a lack of agriculture but of the maturity of the crops along the way. The corn would have been too young until the end of May. This information is echoed in Document 22, fol. 1r: "was supposed to depart at the end of May . . . until then they would find no food of any sort along the whole route." This is the most definitive statement among the Coronado expedition documents concerning the reason for lack of corn in this otherwise productive and fertile region.

36. "[The members of the expedition] got," *sacaron. Sacar* is an ambiguous word that could cover the range from "stole" to "obtained." DRAE, 1824.

37. The captain general himself, writing in August 1540, says that the trip took "eighty days of travel." Document 19, fol. 359v.

38. The loss of packhorses implies also the loss of food supplies, which helps explain why the advance guard arrived at Cíbola in such desperate need of food. See, for instance, Document 22, fols. 1r and 1v.

39. This use of the first person indicates that the author was with the advance guard and present at the battle at Cíbola.

40. This account, combined with those in other documents in this volume, indicates that the attack on Cíbola had three phases. An initial mounted lance attack was followed by an attack on foot, culminating in an attempt to scale the walls. When that attack was repulsed, the light artillery, including probably arquebuses and crossbows, was brought into play from a greater distance. It was evidently during that third onslaught that the Cíbolan defenders decided to abandon the pueblo. Document 19, fols. 360v and 361r; Document 22, fol. 1v; Document 28, fols. 31v and 32r.

41. "I am even sure he would have died there," *quedar = acabar = morir. DRAE*, 16, 1704. H&R, 285, and Winship, 351, ignore the extended meaning of *quedar* and have "I am sure that he would have been there yet."

42. For biographical information about García López de Cárdenas, see the entry in Appendix 1.

43. For biographical information about fray Marcos, see the introduction to Document 6.

44. Modern estimates of the 1540 population of Cíbola based on archaeological evidence from the six ancestral Zuni towns generally agreed to have been inhabited at the time (Hawikku, Kechiba:wa, Kwa'kin'a, Halona:wa, Mats'a:kya, and Kyaki:ma) total about 4,109 persons. Roger Anyon, "The Late Prehistoric and Early Historic Periods in the Zuni-Cíbola Area, A.D. 1400–1600," in *Current Research on the Late Prehistory and Early History of New Mexico*, ed. Bradley J. Vierra (Albuquerque: New Mexico Archaeological Council, 1992), 81. Newer evidence indicates the possibility that as many as three more ancestral Zuni towns—Chalo:wa, Binna:wa, and Ah:kya:ya—were occupied in 1540, which would augment that population estimate. Keith W. Kintigh, "Introduction," in *Hemenway Southwestern Archaeological Expedition*, vol. 6, *Selected Correspondence, June 1, 1888, through 1889*, ed. David Wilcox (in preparation).

45. In general this description is compatible with the report of Frederick Hodge's excavation of the ruins of Hawikku from 1917 to 1923. Smith, Woodbury, and Woodbury, *Excavation of Hawikuh*, 11–97.

46. For most Spaniards of the day, to consider a people to be civilized, it was necessary that they exhibit a series of attributes including dwelling in permanent (preferably stone) houses, being fully clothed in public, possessing a written language, forbidding multiple spouses, practicing a religion, and being ruled by a formal government. Only on the criterion of written language did the Cíbolans not match the Spanish prescription. See John H. Parry, *The Age of Reconnaissance* (Cleveland, OH: World Publishing Co., 1963), 305–14.

47. Rather than the fiber of true henequen (*Agave fourcroydes*) of the tropics, what is probably being referred to here is fiber of one of the species of the somewhat similar-looking yucca (*Yucca* var.).

48. These little painted sticks were *te'likinawe*, or prayer sticks/plumes, similar to those still in use at Zuni. For a description from the nineteenth century, see Stevenson, "Zuñi Indians," 110–12; for a color illustration, plates 25 and 128. The yellow powder referred to here is either crushed, dried flowers or pollen, both of which are still used ceremonially at Zuni and other pueblos. Elsie Clews Parsons, "Isleta, New Mexico," in *Forty-seventh Annual Report of the Bureau of American Ethnology* (Washington, DC: Government Printing Office, 1932), 275–337 and passim.

49. "This is as far as thirty-four and a half degrees [north latitude]. And from there to Cíbola, [it is] to the northeast." Compare Juan Jaramillo's statement that from Culiacán the route "turns and goes approximately to the northwest." Jaramillo's direction is the more accurate, because the expedition's travel northward from Culiacán to the dogleg on the San Pedro River incorporated a significant westward component (map 1). The 1540 location of Culiacán (on the Río San Lorenzo) lies at about 107 degrees west longitude, whereas the middle Sonora River valley (Sonora) and the San Pedro River valley (Sonora and Arizona) are at approximately 110 degrees. With regard to travel distance, see the introduction to this document.

50. In fact, Zuni is at a little less than 35 degrees north latitude. Like many of the expedition's latitude measurements (including those of fray Marcos de Niza earlier), the figure given here is too high (2.0 degrees here, 3.5 for Marcos). Latitude measurements of the era have generally been found to be one to two degrees too high. One possibility for this is that consistent error resulted from sighting the bottom "limb," or edge, of the solar disc when using an astrolabe or cross-staff, rather than the upper "limb," or edge. This may explain why, for instance, Juan Rodríguez Cabrillo's 1542 determination of the latitude of San Diego harbor was also about two degrees too far north. Another, and perhaps more likely, explanation

is that the *regimento*, or astrolabe table, then in use was itself in error or was incorrectly used in conjunction with readings of the sun's altitude as it crossed the meridian based on magnetic north rather than geographic north. This latter possibility is given weight by Antonio de Mendoza's October 1541 assertion that "all the data concerning this Mar del Sur are incorrect because the pilots' books [*regimentos* necessary for making calculations from cross-staff or astrolabe observations] were prepared in Spain." Cabrillo National Memorial Foundation, *An Account of the Voyage of Juan Rodríguez Cabrillo* (San Diego, CA: Cabrillo National Memorial Foundation, 1999), 64. See also MacMullen, "It's a Wonder that They Ever Got Home," 37–41; Patricia Seed, "The Astrolabe," in *Ceremonies of Possession in Europe's Conquest of the New World, 1492–1640* (Cambridge: Cambridge University Press, 1995), 120–28; Document 25, fol. 459r; and Document 25, notes 34 and 35.

51. A plausible reconstruction of the route Tovar followed to reach Tuzan/Tusayán—the Hopi pueblos—was offered by Katharine Bartlett in 1940. She assumed that the party followed existing Indian trails as delineated by Edmund Nequatewa, a modern Hopi informant. Katharine Bartlett, "How don Pedro de Tovar Discovered the Hopi and don Garcia Lopez de Cardenas Saw the Grand Canyon, with Notes upon their Probable Route," *Plateau* 12 (Jan. 1940):37–45. For biographical information about Pedro de Tovar, see Document 28, note 102. For geographical information about Tuzan, see the entry for Tusayán in Appendix 2.

52. Assuming use of the *legua legal*, this would be about 92 miles. The actual straight-line map distance from Hawikku to Awatovi is remarkably close, approximately 94 miles. The direction given here, though, is to the northwest rather than west.

53. "A little better." This could also be "a little bigger."

54. Diego Pérez de Luxán reported having seen large fields of cotton growing at the Hopi pueblos/Tuzan in 1583. Pérez de Luxán, "Luxán's Account," 192.

55. The report referred to here was Vázquez de Coronado's letter to the viceroy, August 3, 1540. Document 19.

56. This settlement was the second location of the *villa* of San Gerónimo (map 2). See Document 28, fol. 33r.

57. For information on the route Díaz followed to the Colorado River (Buena Guía), see Document 28, note 157. For biographical information about Hernando de Alarcón, see the introduction to Document 15.

58. These people are thought to have been antecedents of the Yuman-speaking Cocopas who lived along the lower reaches of the Colorado River and combined corn-bean-squash agriculture with harvesting of wild foods. During the colder months they lived in "rectangular structure[s] with excavated floor[s]." Alvarez de Williams, "Cocopa," 99–112.

59. Alarcón himself reported that he traveled 85 leagues up the river. Document 15, fol. 370r.

60. An expanded version of Díaz's death is reported by Castañeda de Nájera. Document 28, fol. 72r.

61. For two routes Cárdenas might have followed, based on known Indian trails, see Bartlett, "How don Pedro de Tovar Discovered the Hopi."

62. The *legua legal* would put López de Cárdenas's westernmost advance about 132 miles west of the Hopi pueblos. Straight-line map measurement west-northwest from Oraibi places this point on the Colorado River in the vicinity of Supai, Arizona—then, as now, the center of Havasupai settlement. Such a destination would have been consistent with the expedition's dominant goal, to locate populous places. Katharine Bartlett's route reconstruction, cited in the previous note, relies only on Castañeda de Nájera's narrative and takes the López de Cárdenas party no farther west than modern Grand Canyon Village, more than 40 miles short of Supai. Bartlett, "How don Pedro de Tovar Discovered the Hopi," 44.

63. The gorge referred to here is the Grand Canyon formed by the Colorado River.

64. This river is the Guadalquivir. Its width where it passed through Sevilla in the sixteenth century was very similar to that of the modern channel, given that sixteenth-century structures or their remains still stand on the modern bank as they did 500 years ago. It therefore would have been slightly less than a quarter of a mile wide.

65. Castañeda de Nájera, in reporting this episode, implies a stay at the canyon of at least three days. Document 28, fol. 45v.

66. This description fits the course of the Colorado River over the 60 miles or so downstream from Supai. It would also match the stretch of river from the Green River junction in Utah to the confluence of the Little Colorado River in Arizona. It could also be a macro-description of the course of the entire Colorado River from

its source to the Gulf of California. In any case, this is undoubtedly information gleaned from the native guides rather than obtained from direct observation by López de Cárdenas's party.

67. The routes by which the Alvarado party and later the main body of the expedition traveled from Cíbola to Tiguex have been reconstructed on the basis of Indian trails by Carroll Riley and Joni Manson. Their routes cross the Zuni Mountains (map 3) and skirt the north end of the Malpais lava flow. Riley and Manson, "The Cíbola-Tiguex Route," 347–67. For a more recent reconstruction, see Document 24, notes 23, 24, and 25. For biographical information about Hernando de Alvarado, see the introduction to Document 24.

68. This would be about 79 miles. Acoma Pueblo, presumably the place that goes by the name Acuco in the "Relación del Suceso," lies about 81 straight-line map miles from Hawikku/Cíbola (see map 3). For geographical information about Acuco, see the entry in Appendix 2.

69. "They well could have refused to do it." This statement implies that, as at other native towns, the Spaniards read the *requerimiento,* to which the natives of Acus appeared to acquiesce. The rendering by H&R, 288, is "could have spared themselves the trouble," which obscures this likelihood. Winship, 355, has "it would have been easy to decline to do this," which is closer to our rendition.

70. For discussion of the distance between Acoma and the Tiguex River/Rio Grande, see the introduction to this document and map 3.

71. This compares with 71 pueblos listed by Castañeda de Nájera. The latter count includes both towns along the Río de Tiguex and those away from it, such as Cíbola and Tusayán. Document 28, fols. 115r–115v.

72. For discussion of protohistoric cotton cultivation along the middle Rio Grande, see Document 30, note 86.

73. "Tiánguez" refers to the great, well-organized markets that were customary in central Mexico. The word is a Nahuatl term. See, for instance, Gibson, *Aztecs,* 352.

74. Using the *legua legal,* this represents an area of about 132 miles from north to south and 92 miles east to west. The longitudinal figure varies greatly from Castañeda de Nájera's estimate of the extent of Pueblo settlement: 130 leagues north to south along the Río de Tiguex (about 342 miles). Document 28, fol. 115v; Document 28, note 470. "And off to the sides fifteen or twenty leagues." H&R, 288, misconstrue this as "some pueblos being fifteen or twenty leagues apart." Although it is confusing, Winship's, 355, translation seems similar to ours: "some villages are 15 or 20 leagues distant, in one direction and the other."

75. It seems that the author of the "Relación del Suceso" has mistakenly taken Pueblo Creek at Taos Pueblo, New Mexico, to be the headwaters of the Rio Grande/Río de Tiguex. Instead, it rises considerably farther north, in modern Hinsdale County, Colorado.

76. This population figure for Taos Pueblo/Yuraba is undoubtedly many times inflated. Castañeda de Nájera estimated the total population of the 71 pueblos he listed as only 20,000. A 1912 estimate of Taos Pueblo's population in 1680 was 2,000. Even that figure may be high. Document 28, fol. 116r; Dozier, *Pueblo Indians,* 122. For geographical information about Yuraba, see the entry for Brava in Appendix 2.

77. For geographical information, see the entry for Cicuique in Appendix 2.

78. As suggested in the introduction, the author's knowledge of when a message was sent to the captain general raises the possibility that the *escribano* who drafted the message and the author of the "Relación del Suceso" were one and the same person.

79. Presumably this is the modern Pecos River in New Mexico. Considering only the portion north of the Canadian Escarpment, this could, however, also refer to today's Canadian River, which would fit better with the full expedition's travel, presumably over the same route, the following spring. See maps 1 and 4.

80. Conversion from *leguas legales* yields some 260 miles. This distance must be incorrect, for it would have taken Alvarado's party either far down the Pecos River or into extreme western Oklahoma along the Canadian River, neither of which matches other versions of Alvarado's trip or the full expedition's trek about eight months later. Castañeda de Nájera reports, instead, that the men with Alvarado "did not diligently pursue the search for [bison] beyond seeing a few" and turned around quickly to report stories told by one of their guides. Document 28, fol. 51v. For geographical information about Quivira and the Río de Quivira, see the entry for Quivira in Appendix 2.

81. This use of the first person implies that the author was with the Alvarado party during the first foray onto the plains.

82. Being in the midst of large bison herds suggests several difficulties faced in trying to cross the plains while keeping one's bearings. The dust raised, the lack of visible landmarks, and the spooking of horses and other livestock would have been challenging.

83. According to Castañeda de Nájera, the main body of the expedition arrived in Tiguex in early December. Document 28, fol. 56v. For geographical information about Tiguex and the Río de Tiguex, see the entry for Tiguex in Appendix 2.

84. In 1544 Juan Gómez de Paradinas and Juan de Contreras testified that "fifty or sixty" horses were killed. During the same investigation Rodrigo Ximón and Pedro de Ledesma stated that the number was 30 or 40, Juan Troyano said it was more than 40, and the captain general himself said it was "about thirty-five." Flint, *Great Cruelties,* 80, 113, 131, 171, 238, 289.

85. The punishment referred to here is the notorious incident of burning prisoners alive, which later earned López de Cárdenas the imposition of a fine and enforced service to the king at his own expense. Flint, *Great Cruelties,* 336–39. H&R, 290, have "executed," while Winship, 356, reads "executed justice." These earlier translations show the range of possibilities inherent in the Spanish. Hammond and Rey, apparently relying on Castañeda de Nájera's *relación,* certainly exceed what is being stated here by the author of the "Relación del Suceso." Winship, on the other hand, may be close to the prevailing attitude among members of the expedition—namely, that any injury inflicted on the Tiguex people was deserved because they had broken an agreement with the Spaniards.

86. This "strongest" pueblo was Pueblo del Cerco, so called by Lorenzo Álvarez, Rodrigo de Frías, and Pedro de Tovar during the 1544 investigation of the expedition's treatment of Indians and also called Moha (Moho) by Vázquez de Coronado. Flint, *Great Cruelties,* 196, 290, 362, 420. "At which the expedition spent two months." Again, H&R, 290, bring in information from other documents to render this as "which the army besieged for two months." The author of the "Relación del Suceso" seems instead to be purposely euphemizing or temporizing, suggesting that the siege lasted only a portion of that two months. Castañeda de Nájera reports that the siege of this town took 50 days. Document 28, fol. 66v.

87. Again, use of the first person suggests that the author was present at the siege of Moho.

88. Here the author jumps back several months to pick up the results of Alvarado's reconnaissance to the east the previous summer.

89. H&R, 290, and Winship, 356, both have "Harale." *CDI,* 14:325, in contrast, has "Harall." These various transcriptions nearly cover the gamut of possibilities. In sixteenth-century Spanish scripts, *l* and *e* are often indistinguishable. There is nothing in the manuscript in this case, however, to justify the presence of *l.* The *escribano* himself may well have been guessing about the spelling. For geographical information about Arae/Haraee, see the entry in Appendix 2. For the Indies, see Document 21, note 18. This sentence is the only explicit statement about the origin of El Turco in existing Coronado expedition documents. For biographical information on Turco, see the entry in Appendix 1.

90. The author paints the captain general in an unfavorable light here, with a hint of criticism, which he does once more later. See fol. 5v.

91. For discussion of this distance, see the introduction to this document.

92. The other expeditionary documents all indicate that there was only one other guide besides El Turco, a man called Ysopete or Sopete. See, for instance, Document 28, fol. 80v, and Document 30, fol. 3v.

93. The reference here is to the calling of a council of captains and other leading men, which was standard practice in deciding crucial issues on expeditions of the era. For other examples, see Document 15, fol. 369r; Document 28, fols. 130r–130v; and Document 30, fols. 3v and 4v.

94. This information is probably correct and is to be accepted over the implication in Castañeda de Nájera's *relación* that the *maestre de campo*'s accident had occurred days earlier at the second Querecho camp. Document 28, fol. 79r. For the rationale for accepting this version, see Flint, "Reconciling the Calendars."

95. "Following the compass ourselves," *seguiendonos por Aguja.* H&R, 291, have "traveling by the needle." At this point no direction is either stated or implied.

96. Using the *legua legal,* this would be about 79 miles. Assuming that the Río de Quivira is the modern Arkansas River in Kansas and that Quivira itself was in Rice County (both of which assumptions are widely accepted), straight-line map mileage from the western boundary of the county where it crosses the Arkansas River would place the point at which Vázquez de Coronado and his companions reached the river almost exactly at Ford, Kansas (which is also generally accepted). See map 4. Wedel, *Archeological Remains in Central Kansas;* Bolton, 285.

97. H&R, 291, gratuitously insert "many," so that they have "we met many natives." Winship, 359, translates the phrase exactly as we do.

98. Regarding sixteenth-century Spanish conceptions of civilization, see note 46, this document.

99. There are a number of native representations of sixteenth-century, thatched-roof, Tarascan/Purépechan dwellings in sketches that accompany the "Relación de las ceremonias y ritos y población y gobernación de los indios de la provincia de Mechuacán," Códice C-IV-5 in the Real Biblioteca del Escorial. Craine and Reindorp, *Chronicles of Michoacán*; see especially plate 34. For comparison, see a nineteenth-century photograph of a Wichita thatched dwelling in Wedel, *Archeological Remains in Central Kansas*, 25. See also fig. 28.8.

100. The reference here is to tortillas, which were a staple of the central Mexican diet.

101. This would be about 66 miles. In which direction is not indicated here or in other expeditionary documents, although it is usually assumed to have been generally eastward.

102. This may have been the place called Teucarea by Jaramillo. Document 30, fol. 4r. Hodge thought the people of Tareque were also Wichitas. Bolton wondered whether it was just another name for Harahey. Bolton, 395. For Teucarea, see Document 30, note 107.

103. Castañeda de Nájera reports that this was a "copper medallion" worn by a native leader. Such a find was certainly a tantalizing hint that somewhere farther ahead lived people who produced valuable commodities, the sort of people among whom profitable *encomiendas* might be granted. Document 28, fol. 88r.

104. Use of the first person indicates that the author participated in the trip to Quivira and was thus one of the chosen thirty.

105. The outbound journey would thus have been about 870 miles, the terminus of which would have been 180 leagues (close to 475 miles) from the *barranca* where the expedition split up. If the figure provided here by the "Relación del Suceso" is approximately correct, it could place that farthest point a little east of modern Emporia, Kansas.

106. This distance would convert to about 526 miles. This number may be incorrect, because 526 straight-line map miles from the Emporia, Kansas, area would reach only to about the Pecos River/Río de Cicuique, some 100 miles short of the Tiguex pueblos in the area of modern Bernalillo, New Mexico. On the other hand, the counting of the return trip's distance might not have begun at the most extreme point, but rather on the western edge of Quivira. In that case the mileage about fits. See map 1.

107. If Quivira was located in the area of modern Rice County, Kansas, as is generally thought, then the latitude reading here is badly off. Rice County lies at about 38 degrees. Latitude measurements of the era, taken with astrolabe or crossstaff, were notoriously poor. As Pablo Pérez-Mallaína writes, "in general, one can detect in the documentation a certain lack of confidence on the part of contemporaries about the precision of the positions calculated by the pilots." Pérez-Mallaína, *Spain's Men of the Sea*, 86. See also note 52, this document. For discussion of the identity and latitude of this river, see the introduction to this document.

108. Castañeda de Nájera also reports this disappearance. Document 28, fol. 79r.

109. For discussion of the possible archaeological identification of these nomadic peoples, see Appendix 1.

110. A sixteenth-century *pabellón* was a large, pyramidal or conical campaign tent, supported inside with a hefty pole driven into the ground and secured to the land around the base with ropes and stakes. This shape would have been familiar to members of the expedition, since it was the most common field accommodation of the day. The expedition itself doubtless used a number of *pabellones*. See also Document 28, note 229.

111. This is a reference to the dog travois widely used on the Great Plains before the reestablishment of the horse into North America, probably at the end of the sixteenth century.

112. This single statement about native religion seems out of place, a stray thought not much connected to the rest of the "Relación del Suceso."

113. This trade in bison products between nomads of the Plains and the sedentary Rio Grande Pueblos has often been commented on by historians and anthropologists. See, for example, Kessell, *Kiva, Cross, and Crown*, 137, and Riley, *Rio del Norte*, 130.

114. López de Cárdenas's inheritance of a title in Spain is also related by Castañeda de Nájera. Document 28, fol. 127r.

115. For geographical information about San Gerónimo, see map 2 and the entry in Appendix 2.

116. Castañeda de Nájera reports, instead, "three Spaniards, many servants, and more than twenty horses dead." Document 28, fol. 134v.

117. This decision, like almost all other major decisions during the expedition, was actually made in agreement with a council of captains and other leaders. This council is hinted at by Castañeda de Nájera in his reporting of the captain general's collecting signatures of assent from the captains and *caballeros*. Document 28, fols. 130r and 130v.

118. "He was more motivated than anyone [else]," "tenya mas Gana que nadie." H&R, 293, misinterpret "nadie" and have "he longed for this more than anything else." Once again they seem to have relied on *CDI*, 14:328, which misreads the word as "nada."

119. This disintegration of the expedition is also related by Castañeda de Nájera. Document 28, fol. 142r.

120. As earlier, on folio 4r, the author shows Vázquez de Coronado in a less than flattering light, again with the hint of criticism.

121. For biographical information, see the entries on fray Luis de Úbeda and fray Juan de Padilla in Appendix 1.

122. This would have been a remarkable cold spell. The National Oceanic and Atmospheric Administration reports, for instance, that for the period 1941 to 1970 the monthly mean temperature at Bernalillo, New Mexico, never fell below 34 degrees F. U.S. Department of Commerce, National Oceanic and Atmospheric Administration, *Monthly Normals of Temperature, Precipitation, and Heating and Cooling Days, 1941–70: New Mexico* (Asheville, NC: Environmental Data Service, 1973).

123. In this the author of the "Relación del Suceso" is in agreement with Juan Jaramillo. See the introduction to Document 30.

124. Sementera = *cosa sembrada*. DRAE, 1860.

125. Doblaronsenos. *CDI*, 14:319, omits "nos."

126. Mas mayor. *CDI*, 14:322, has "mucho mayor." In the manuscript the word is abbreviated, either "mˢ," as we read it, or "mº," as *CDI* reads it. According to Galende, *Abreviaturas españolas*, 146 and 150, "mˢ" is a common abbreviation for *mas*, whereas "mº" is not listed at all as an abbreviation for *mucho*. In addition, the character in question resembles the *s* in this *escribano*'s hand much more closely than his *o*.

127. Por manera que = *de manera que*. DRAE, 1306.

128. Ensangostar = *angostar*.

129. Ya que = *una vez que*. DRAE, 2113.

130. Las çinquenta Al sueste. *CDI*, 14:325, erroneously has "las cinquenta al Sur." H&R, 291, and Winship, 359, repeated this error, evidently without consulting the original document, which clearly reads "sueste."

131. El mundo = a multitude. DRAE, 1417.

132. Cabe = *cerca de*. DRAE, 341.

133. Ni Apartarse. Probably "si apartarse" was intended.

134. Hyncadas, *hincadas*. *CDI*, 14:328, inadvertently omits this word.

135. Y t(r)asajos secos al soL. *CDI*, 14:328, omits this phrase. Whoever among the *CDI* team was doing the transcription must have been rushed or tired, because several errors of omission and misreading were made in the last two folio sides.

136. Rrescatan. *CDI*, 14:328, misreads this as "recatan," although to be fair, the first *a* is also missing from the original.

137. There is a change of *escribano* nearly at bottom fol. 5r (line 26).

138. Harta Ventura. *CDI*, 14:328, grossly misreads this as "fray Ventura."

139. Desimulaba. *CDI*, 14:329, misreads this as "disumulada."

Document 30. Juan Jaramillo's Narrative, 1560s

1. As an example of the confusion of persons with this name, in his list of microfilmed documents related to the Coronado expedition curated by the Panhandle-Plains Historical Museum at West Texas A&M University in Canyon, Texas, Douglas Inglis lists a *probanza* for the Cortés-era Captain Juan Jaramillo. In the same microfilm collection is a *probanza* for that earlier Jaramillo's wife, the well-known interpreter and guide for Cortés, Marina/Malintzin. Hammond and Rey imply incorrectly that an investigation into the *encomienda* of Juan Jaramillo was focused on the chronicler of the Coronado expedition by that name. The problem of multiple persons with the same name is one that confronts all historians of colonial Spanish America, because the repertoire of names in circulation was relatively small and the modern conventions for their use were still solidifying. Douglas

Inglis, "A Guide to the History of the Spanish Southwest Collection in the Panhandle-Plains Historical Museum Research Center," in *Coronado and the Myth of Quivira*, ed. Dianna Everett (Canyon, TX: Panhandle-Plains Historical Society, 1985), 72; AGI, Patronato, 54, N.8, R.6, "Ynformacion de los servicios de Juan Jaramillo conquistador de Nueva Espana con Hernan Cortés, México, 1532"; AGI, Patronato, 56, N.3, R.4, "Probanza de los buenos servicios y fidelidad con que sirvio en la conquista de Nueva Espana la famosa dona Marina, india, Mexico, 1542"; H&R, 295 n. 1. See also Day, *Coronado's Quest*, 337 n. 29.

2. Two recorded statements by Jaramillo provide ambiguous information about his birth. In his 1547 testimony on behalf of *fiscal* Villalobos, Jaramillo reported that he was then more than 30 years old. More than 30 years later, in 1578, he identified himself as being more than 68 years old. Although these two statements are not necessarily inconsistent, neither one positively confirms the other. AGI, Justicia, 1021, N.2, Pieza 6, "Probanza del fiscal Villalobos"; "Probanza, December 1578," in AGI, Patronato, 87, N.1, R.5, "García Rodríguez y biznieto."

3. Fol. 4v; AGI, México, 1064, L.1\1, "Informes de los conquistadores," fol. 213v.

4. *Pasajeros*, 2: nos. 3191 and 3193. See also Appendix 3.

5. AGI, México, 1064, L.1\1, "Informes de los conquistadores," fol. 213v.

6. See fols. 5r and 5v and Document 12, fol. 5r.

7. Fols. 1r, 2r, 3v, and 4r.

8. Fol. 5r.

9. AGI, México, 1064, L.1\1, "Informes de los conquistadores," fol. 213v; AGI, Patronato, 87, N.1, R.5, "García Rodríguez y biznieto."

10. Fol. 1r.

11. Fol. 5v.

12. Without an explicit internal statement about when Jaramillo's narrative was composed or the copy made, we are left with only a single hint in the document itself. In recounting travel between watercourses in what is probably now southeastern Arizona, Jaramillo writes that "it has been so long since we crossed that [river] that I could be mistaken about some days' travel." He also refers to two men, Gonzalo Solís de Meras and Isidro de Solís, who were apparently prominent in the Ciudad de México at the time of the writing and known to the recipient of the report. To date we have been unable to identify them further or pin down the period of their residence in the Ciudad de México. If that could be done, the *relación* might be more confidently dated. Because of similarities in the purposes of the *relaciónes* and in addressees, we suggest that it was written about the same time Castañeda de Nájera wrote his, in the early 1560s, and in response to the same call for reports from veterans of the Coronado expedition. Fols. 1v and 5v. See the introduction to Document 28 for the full rationale behind the assertion that the addressee of both Jaramillo's narrative and Castañeda de Nájera's "Relación" was an *oidor* of the Audiencia de Nueva España, doctor Alonso de Zorita, who intended to lead an expedition back toward Tierra Nueva in the early 1560s.

13. Fols. 2r, 2v, and 4r–5r.

14. Don Fadrique Enríquez de Ribera was Marqués de Tarifa and *adelantado* of Andalucía, as well as a councilman of Sevilla—as was his contemporary Diego López of the Coronado expedition. He died in 1539. Manuel González Jiménez, "La Biografía de don Fadrique Enríquez de Ribera," in *Paisajes de la tierra prometida: El Viaje a Jerusalén de don Fadrique Enríquez de Ribera*, Pedro García Martín et al. (Madrid: Miraguano Ediciones, 2001), 79, 95.

15. The first of several editions of don Fadrique's travelogue had appeared in 1521. Vicenç Beltran, "Los Manuscritos del *Viaje a Jerusalén*," in García Martín et al., *Paisajes*, 113–68; María del Carmen Álvarez Márquez, ed. "Manuscrito 9.355 de la Biblioteca Nacional de Madrid," in García Martín et al., *Paisajes*, 153–54, 183.

16. Fols. 3v and 4v.

17. Fol. 2r.

18. Ibid.

19. Vicente de Zaldívar, "An Account of Sergeant Major Vicente de Zaldívar's Expedition to the Buffalo Herds, September 15 to November 8, 1598," in *Zaldívar and the Cattle of Cíbola: Vicente de Zaldívar's Expedition to the Buffalo Plains in 1598. The Spanish Texts*, Jerry R. Craddock, ed.; John H. R. Polt, trans. (Dallas: William P. Clements Center for Southwest Studies, Southern Methodist University, 1999), 33.

20. Habicht-Mauche, *Pottery, Food, Hides, and Women*, 4–25.

21. Fol. 2v.

22. Fol. 5v.

23. Ibid.

24. Such uses of the subjunctive appear throughout the document, but see, for instance, the use of "viesemos," "durara," and "habra" on fol. 1r.

25. See, for example, fols. 1v and 3r, "a mi paresçer" and "creo"; fol. 2r, "paresçieron ser"; fols. 2r, 2v, 3r, and 4v, "no se si" and "no se como"; and fols. 2v, 4r, and 4v, "si bien me acuerdo."

26. These seven instances are three times during the stretch from the Río Nexpa/San Pedro River to the Río Bermejo/Little Colorado River and once each in specifying the direction from Tiguex to Cicuique/Pecos, from Cicuique to the Río de Cicuique/Pecos River, onward from the Río de Cicuique, and along the Río de San Pedro y San Pablo/Arkansas River.

27. Fol. 2r: "facing the northeast or not quite."

28. In an effort to find literal sense in the phrase "beyond northeast" ("mas que al nordeste"), one could argue that southeast is farther clockwise around the compass from northeast (in other words, "beyond"). But this seems to push the bounds of interpretation. Fol. 2v.

29. For a full discussion of the course of this portion of the expedition's route, see Flint and Flint, "Cicúye to the Río de Cicúye Bridge."

30. The discovery and identification of a campsite of the expedition at the Jimmy Owens Site in Floyd County, Texas, has convincingly demonstrated that the navigation record provided by Jaramillo concerning this part of the expedition's route is far off the mark. See Blakeslee and Blaine, "Jimmy Owens Site."

31. See Document 28, note 418.

32. See Document 28, fols. 107r and 154v, and note 474.

33. Fols. 5r–5v.

34. *CDI*, 14:304–17.

35. Mora, 189–96. As H&R, 295 n. 1, put it, the Pacheco and Cárdenas text "has numerous bad readings."

36. Winship, 370–83; H&R, 295–307.

37. See note 38, this document.

38. Having discharged the functions of the office without holding the title for some time, Juan Páez de Castro was named King Carlos I's official chronicler in 1555. It is thanks to his work of collecting documents for a history of the king's reign that this copy of Juan Jaramillo's *relación* was preserved. Páez de Castro's history, unfortunately, was never completed, but the chronicler's copy of Jaramillo's *relación* is now curated in AGI, Patronato, 20, N.5, R.8, along with copies of two other documents published in this edition that were collected by Páez or prepared at his request: the "Traslado de las Nuevas" (Document 22) and the "Relación del Suceso" (Document 29). Also included in AGI, Patronato, 20, N.5, is Andrés de Urdaneta's copy of Juan León's account of the 1542–43 voyage of Juan Rodríguez Cabrillo, which bears the same notation, "de Juan Páez," in the same hand as that which appears here on fol. 1r. The two existing copies of fray Marcos de Niza's *relación* (Document 6) are also curated in AGI, Patronato, 20, N.5, but in R.10. While the Marcos documents bear no notations that definitively link them with Páez, they might well derive from his collection. Miguélez, *Catálogo de los códices españoles*, 142; Kelsey, *Cabrillo*, 114, 207 n. 51; *Enciclopedia universal*, 40:1455–56; James D. Nauman, "Preface to the Account," in *An Account of the Voyage of Juan Rodríguez Cabrillo* (San Diego, CA: Cabrillo National Monument Foundation, 1999), 36–38.

39. For geographical information about Quivira and Cíbola, see the entries in Appendix 2.

40. Jaramillo was not a captain while on the Coronado expedition but apparently achieved that status later. For geographical information about Tierra Nueva, see the entry in Appendix 2.

41. The straight-line map distance from the Ciudad de México to Tepíc/Compostela is about 390 miles, and the distance would be appreciably farther by road. This suggests that Jaramillo is using the longest of the Spanish land leagues, the *legua común*. Chardon, "Linear League," 145. For geographical information about Compostela, see the entry in Appendix 2.

42. The actual airline distance is about 244 miles, again suggesting Jaramillo's use of the *legua común*. For geographical information about Culiacán, see the entry in Appendix 2.

43. "Repartimiento" refers here to the distribution of Indians of the area in *encomienda* to residents of the *villa* by Núno de Guzmán in 1531. Gerhard, *North Frontier*, 257.

44. Although this statement may seem confusingly out of place, Jaramillo is evidently referring to the significant change in course at Compostela. The bearing of rhumb lines from Compostela to Culiacán and from Culiacán to Corazones/Ures is identical for practical purposes and is, as Jaramillo states, to the northwest. At any rate, there would have been no significant change in direction at Culiacán. See map 1.

45. Castañeda de Nájera amplified on the size of the advance guard by writing, "fifty horsemen and a few footmen, as well as most of the [native] allies," making this a much larger unit than Jaramillo's account indicates. Document 28, fol. 27v. Winship, 370, incorrectly has "70 horsemen."

46. This opening is evidently the *abra*, or wide, level valley, mentioned by fray Marcos de Niza in his report to the viceroy. Document 6, fol. 2v.

47. For geographical information about Chichilticale and Petatlán, see the entries in Appendix 2. For the Río Sinaloa, see Document 28, note 396. For the Río Yaquimí, see Document 19, note 30. According to Herbert Bolton, Arroyo de los Cedros is the modern stream of that name that joins the Río Mayo at Conicari, Sonora. The junction is now under the waters of Presa Macuzari. Peter Gerhard is in essential agreement, writing, "all the early recorded expeditions (Cabeza de Vaca, Marcos, Coronado, Ibarra) followed the route between Conicari and Onavas," up the Arroyo Cedro. Bolton, 99; Gerhard, *North Frontier*, 265.

48. "Stream," *arroyo* = "agua corriente, pero no con caudal que se pueda llamar río." Covarrubias, 124.

49. For Cabeza de Vaca's own account, see Adorno and Pautz, *Núñez Cabeza de Vaca*, 1:235. For biographical information about Álvar Núñez Cabeza de Vaca, Andrés Dorantes, and Estebanillo/Estebanico, see the entries in Appendix 1. Castillo is Alonso del Castillo Maldonado. For geographical information about Los Corazones, see the entry in Appendix 2.

50. Two days' journey would probably have been about 32 miles.

51. See Document 28, note 285.

52. If Corazones was located at the site of modern Ures (see Appendix 1), then the reference here is probably to Ures Gorge (or, as Daniel Reff calls it, the *barranca* below Mazocahui) in central Sonora, and the river is the Río Sonora (map 2). Reff, "Relevance of Ethnology," 168.

53. Beginning with the Ures Valley on the south, there are four distinct, lengthy widenings of the Río Sonora valley as one heads north, or upstream, each closed off from its neighbors by significant gorges, or *barrancas*. There are also several much smaller pockets of arable land along the valley. It is the larger discreet segments where agriculture is possible and where significant indigenous populations were established that Jaramillo and others refer to as separate valleys. "Ures-H12D32," "La Puente del Sol-H12D33," "Baviácora-H12D23," "Aconchi-H12D13," "Banamichi-H12B83," "Arizpe-H12B73," and "Bacoachi-H12B64," in Comisión de Estudios del Territorio Nacional, *Carta topográfica* (México, DF: CETENAL, 1975).

54. The reference to denser population here seems to indicate that Señora was the most heavily populated of the three Sonoran *provincias*.

55. Jaramillo evidently used the *legua común*. Using this conversion rate, six or seven leagues would be 21 to 25 miles. See notes 41 and 42, this document. Baltasar de Obregón, a member of the Ibarra expeditions of the 1560s, saw and described the valleys of Corazones and Señora similarly: "dos hermosos valles de cinco y seis leguas." This length matches well the extent of the Ures/Corazones Valley but is much too short for the Baviácora-Banamichi/Señora Valley, which is more than 64 miles long. Obregón, *Historia*, 147; "Baviácora-H12D23," "Aconchi-H12D13," and "Banamichi-H12B83," in Comisión de Estudios del Territorio Nacional, *Carta topográfica*.

56. From Jaramillo's description and location of Ispa, Carroll Riley identifies Ispa, or Guaraspi (modern Arizpe, Sonora), as Suya. See map 2. Riley, *Frontier People*, 53, 72. See also Document 28, note 286.

57. Four days of travel equals around 64 miles, which is approximately the distance between the upper waters of the Río Sonora near Cananea, Sonora, and the middle reaches of the Nexpa/San Pedro River at St. David, Arizona (maps 1 and 2). This is evidently the four-day unsettled region also referred to by Marcos de Niza. Document 6, fol. 4r. The San Pedro is a north-flowing river with its headwaters just east of Cananea in the modern Mexican state of Sonora. It flows to the east of Benson, Arizona, and intersects the Gila River east of Florence, Arizona. There is also a Río Nexpa in Michoacán. Bolton, 105.

58. "Maguey stalks," *pencas de mahuey*. *DRAE*, 1566: "tallo en forma de hoja, craso o carnoso, de algunas plantas, como el nopal y la pita." Centuries later in this same area of southeastern Arizona the Chiricahua Apaches similarly ate the roasted young flower stalk of the agave, or maguey, as well as the crown at the base of the leaves. Morris E. Opler, "Chiricahua Apache," in Ortiz, *Southwest*, 10:413. For a discussion of *pitahaya*, see Document 28, note 408.

59. A number of researchers, most notably Herbert Bolton, have placed Chichilticale near Eagle Pass, between the Pinaleno and Santa Teresa Mountains just south of the Gila River in south-central Arizona. The Eagle Pass location,

though, is evidently closer than two days' travel from the San Pedro River and also much too far north. A location that much better fits Jaramillo's description is Apache Pass, about 50 miles southeast of Eagle Pass, at the north end of the Chiricahua Mountains. Furthermore, there are prehistoric ruins along the west and northwest sides of the Chiricahua Mountains that have not been well studied and are candidates for Chichilticale. One in particular that deserves investigation is the Pinery Canyon Site, which is associated with ceramics "suggesting Hawikuh ware." Bolton, 106; Carl Sauer and Donald Brand, "Pueblo Sites in Southeastern Arizona," *University of California Publications in Geography* 3 (Aug. 1930):439. See the entry for Chichilticale in Appendix 2 for a more complete discussion.

60. Bolton identified this feature as the Gila River, which, being in a wide, flat valley, fails utterly to match Jaramillo's description. If, instead, it was Apache Pass the advance unit was now traversing, there is immediately below its summit the dependable and still flowing Apache Spring, located in a narrow defile between steep, high slopes—that is, in a *cañada*. Apache Spring was later utilized by the Butterfield Stage route and determined the location of adjacent Fort Bowie. As Albert J. Fountain, a participant in a battle between a U.S. Army unit and Apache Indians there in 1862, remembered, the spring is "between two steep hills 300 feet high." Another participant in that battle, Captain John C. Cremony, later wrote that "immediately commanding the springs are two hills, both high and difficult of ascent," and he called the vicinity of the spring a "battlemented gorge." Bolton, 108–9; Allan Radbourne, ed., *The Battle for Apache Pass: Reports of the California Volunteers* (London: English Westerners' Society, 2002), 24; John C. Cremony, *Life among the Apaches* (San Francisco: A. Roman and Co., 1868), 161, 163.

61. The date of the feast of San Juan Bautista is June 24. Chaves, *Espejo de navegantes*, 86. This river seems most likely to have been the Gila in the vicinity of Virden, New Mexico, which is about 48 miles (three days' travel) northeast of Apache Pass. Bolton thought it was the Salt River near the junction with the Black River. Bolton, 197; Document 28, fol. 12v. The daily rate of travel used here and throughout the notes dealing with the segment of the expedition's route from Chichilticale to Cíbola is based on dividing the total distance as reported by Castañeda de Nájera (80 leagues using the *legua legal*) by the number of days required for its crossing according to Jaramillo (13), which yields 16.2 miles per day.

62. "We went more toward the north through land [that is] somewhat broken to another river we called [Río] de las Balsas," *fuimos a otro rrio por tierra Algo doblada y mas hazia El norte Al rrio que llamamos de las balsas.* H&R, 298, insert the phrase "and from there," thus turning this into a reference to two rivers, we think unjustifiably: "we went over somewhat hilly country to another river, and from there more to the north to the river we named Las Balsas." Winship, 374, on the other hand, agrees more closely with our translation, writing, "we went to another river, through somewhat rough country, more toward the north, to a river we called The Rafts." Two full days' travel (38 miles) north from Virden, New Mexico, brings the expedition to the San Francisco River downstream from Pleasanton, New Mexico. This is a stream fully capable of requiring rafts for crossing when the water is high, as after heavy summer rain—it was now about the end of June, with adjustment for the change to the Gregorian or modern calendar. See also Riley, "Coronado in the Southwest," 150. Bolton, on the other hand, thought this was the White River, at Fort Apache. Bolton, 109.

63. Arroyo de la Barranca was, according to Bolton, Post Office Canyon, north of White River, Arizona. We suggest instead that the number of days' travel, translated into a rough number of miles (31 miles), would bring the expedition into Leggett Canyon south of Rancho Grande Estates, Catron County, New Mexico, north-northeast from the San Francisco River crossing. Leggett Canyon is an impressive, steep-walled, rocky *barranca* and a major tributary of the San Francisco River. Bolton, 110.

64. Eighteen miles of travel (one day) north-northwest from Leggett Canyon—Jaramillo does not specify the direction—would have brought the expedition to another crossing of the wandering San Francisco River near Luna, New Mexico. Now much higher in elevation—approximately 7,000 feet—and nearer its source, its water would have been decidedly colder. See Document 27, note 103, for a possible location of the Río Frío.

65. Thirty-two miles of travel through ponderosa pine and piñon forest (definitely more than one day) to the northwest—no direction specified by Jaramillo—would have brought the expedition to Coyote Creek, a major tributary of the Little Colorado River east of modern Springerville, Arizona. It is possible, of course, that Jaramillo's memory failed him regarding the number of days of travel in this stretch, as his use of "probably" warns us.

66. See Document 19, note 45.

67. "The same [general] course, but rather to the north[west]," "la mysma derrota menos *que* nel nordeste." H&R, 298, translate this as "in the same direction, but not so much to the northeast." There is no major problem with this rendition so long as the direction intended by Jaramillo is in fact northeast. However, as we pointed out in regard to Castañeda de Nájera's *relación* (Document 28, notes 440 and 474), the similar orthography of *o* and *d* in some sixteenth-century Spanish scripts led not infrequently to copying errors by scribes in which "noroeste" (northwest) was transformed into "nordeste" (northeast), and vice versa. If such is the case here, then the sense of the phrase might best be rendered as "on the same [general] course, but rather to the north[west]." On this assumption, two days of travel (32 miles) north-northwest would have brought the expedition to the Bermejo/Little Colorado River near Volcanic Mountain, just northwest of modern St. Johns, Arizona. At this point our proposed routing and that of Bolton and others rejoin.

68. Castañeda de Nájera agrees that the first Indians from Cíbola were seen at the Río Bermejo. Document 28, fol. 30v.

69. Adorno and Pautz, *Núñez Cabeza de Vaca*, 2:422, maintain that Esteban died not at one of the Zuni pueblos but somewhere in southern Arizona. They thus ignore virtually all reports by members of the Coronado expedition, including Jaramillo, Castañeda de Nájera, and Vázquez de Coronado, who all confirmed Esteban's death at Cíbola/Zuni. Adorno and Pautz's reasoning is faulty on this point.

70. Excavation of Hawikku from 1917 to 1923 confirmed stone masonry construction using mud mortar throughout the pueblo. "With very few exceptions, all [walls] were built of sandstone blocks . . . in abundant mortar . . . 'stiff red adobe.'" Smith, Woodbury, and Woodbury, *Excavation of Hawikuh*, 15–16.

71. For biographical information about fray Marcos de Niza, see the introduction to Document 6.

72. In contrast, Castañeda de Nájera says that "Cíbola comprises seven pueblos," as do other contemporary accounts. Document 28, fols. 105r and 115r. See also the entry for Cíbola in Appendix 2 for discussion of the identity of the pueblos of Cíbola.

73. The pueblos thought to have made up Cíbola in the sixteenth century, from Hawikku on the southwest to Kiaki:ma on the northeast, occupied a rough oval of territory in the Zuni River drainage with a long axis of about 20 miles, which is approximately equal to Jaramillo's statement here of six leagues (18 miles) as the length of the route connecting the pueblos. Vázquez de Coronado, however, writing to the viceroy in August 1540, said that the seven pueblos of Cíbola were spread over a distance of only four leagues. Document 19, fol. 361r.

74. Jaramillo is referring here to the sparse grass of the Zuni area, which, as in piñon-juniper forests throughout the region, does not ordinarily form a sod but rather grows in sometimes widely separated clumps.

75. *Bernia = capa larga a modo de manto.* Covarrubias, 182. This is a long cape in the style of a mantle or student's gown, with a sash. It takes its name from Ibernia (Ireland).

76. "Encircled," *çenydas = ceñidas*, from "ceñir, cerrar o rodear una cosa a otra." *DRAE*, 459. The style of Zuni women's dress was still similar when Matilda Coxe Stevenson observed and reported on it in the late nineteenth century: "The gown is of black diagonal cloth . . . draping gracefully over the right shoulder . . . while the gown is carried under the left arm. A long belt of Zuni or Hopi manufacture is wrapped several times around the waist." Stevenson, "Zuñi Indians," 370.

77. This use of northeast (geographic) as an orienting direction may indicate an awareness that magnetic north is—and was in the 1500s—east of geographic north in the western part of North America. If so, the expedition was familiar with the magnetic declination at Cíbola.

78. Five days' journey would be about 80 miles, according to Jaramillo's usual rate of travel, much closer to the actual distance to the Hopi pueblos (Tusayán) than is Castañeda de Nájera's estimate of 53 miles. Document 28, fol. 106v. See Document 28, note 434, for a discussion of Castañeda de Nájera's short reported distance.

79. Jaramillo is referring here to what is now known as the continental divide, which runs north to south between Zuni and Acoma approximately 40 miles east of Zuni. For geographical information, see the entries for Mar del Norte and Mar del Sur in Appendix 2.

80. The reference here is probably to Mats'a:kya, the largest of the pueblos of Cíbola—as reported by Castañeda de Nájera—and one of the easternmost, near Dowa Yalanne, or Corn Mountain. Document 28, fol. 105r.

81. The most direct distance from the ruins of Mats'a:kya to the Río de Tiguex/Rio Grande at modern Albuquerque by modern highways (NM Highway 53 and Interstate 40) is approximately 147 miles, which is extremely close to Jaramillo's figure of nine days at 16.2 miles per day (a total of 145.8 miles). For geographical information on Tihuex, see the entry for Tiguex in Appendix 2.

82. Jaramillo misapplies the name Tutahaco to Acoma here. Acoma, on its stone-walled mesa, is about 70 airline miles from Mats'a:kya, corresponding well to Jaramillo's location of it.

83. Jaramillo's distance of 20 leagues (about 60 miles, using the *legua común*, which was Jaramillo's habit) corresponds to a good part of what Elinore Barrett has called the Middle Rio Grande Subregion of protohistoric–early historic Pueblo settlement. The Middle Rio Grande Subregion stretches from the confluence of the Jemez River and Rio Grande south to the Rio Grande's junction with the Rio Puerco (of the east), a distance of about 87 miles (map 5). It includes the ruins of some 19 pueblos that were evidently inhabited for at least part of the sixteenth century. Barrett, *Conquest and Catastrophe*, 25; Barrett, *Geography of the Rio Grande Pueblos*, 41.

84. Archaeology has confirmed that, unlike the towns of Cíbola and Acoma, the towns of Tiguex and Tutahaco of the middle Rio Grande were built of earth, generally puddled adobe and not the more modern "bricks." Typical is this archaeological description of Piedras Marcadas Pueblo (LA 290), on a terrace above the west bank of the Rio Grande: "four major adobe-walled apartments." United States Department of the Interior, National Park Service, National Register of Historic Places, Inventory-Nomination Form, n.d., 5.

85. The names Uraba and Brava are both retained in the translation because there is no independent means of verifying which was intended, and the orthography of the Spanish permits both transcriptions. Chia, Brava, and Cicuique correspond to the locations now called Zia Pueblo, Taos Pueblo, and Pecos Pueblo, respectively. See map 3. For geographical information, see the entries in Appendix 2.

86. "Cotton," *alhodon = algodon*. Cotton was evidently grown prehistorically in the central and southern Rio Grande Valley of New Mexico. Members of the Espejo expedition of the early 1580s observed that "a great deal of cotton is grown in these settlements." Florence Hawley Ellis reported that cotton was being grown at Isleta Pueblo as late as the nineteenth century. Carroll Riley, in agreement with Kate Peck Kent's seminal study on prehistoric cotton cultivation, maintains that the cotton being grown throughout what became the American Southwest during prehistoric and protohistoric times was Hopi cotton, *Gossypium hopi*. Kate Peck Kent, *The Cultivation and Weaving of Cotton in the Prehistoric Southwestern United States*, Transactions of the American Philosophical Society 47 (1957):465–67; Riley, *Rio del Norte*, 122; Lange, *Cochití*, 95; Hammond and Rey, *Rediscovery of New Mexico*, 142; Florence Hawley Ellis, "Isleta Pueblo," in Ortiz, *Southwest*, vol. 9, 355; Riley, *Frontier People*, 60.

87. These pueblos were probably two of the three Galisteo Basin pueblos mentioned by Castañeda de Nájera, Ximena and Los Silos. Document 28, fol. 113r. For geographical information about Ximena and Los Silos, see Document 28, notes 457 and 458. Four days of travel at Jaramillo's usual rate of 16.2 miles per day would have been about 65 miles, very close to the estimated trail mileage from Santiago Pueblo to Pecos Pueblo. See maps 3 and 5. Flint and Flint, "Cicúye to the Río de Cicúye Bridge," 271.

88. This would have been nearly 50 miles. Castañeda de Nájera, however, states that travel from Cicuique/Pecos to the site of the bridge across the Río de Cicuique occupied four days, in which a distance of about 65 miles would have been covered. We have accepted Castañeda de Nájera's figure because Jaramillo twice indicates uncertainty at this point and is certainly incorrect in his memory of the direction of travel to the bridge site, which he states was northeast, when it was southeast instead. Document 28, fol. 77v; Flint and Flint, "Cicúye to the Río de Cicúye Bridge."

89. This four or five days' travel translates into 65 to 80 miles, which would put at least the vanguard of the expedition's first contact with bison in the general vicinity of modern Tucumcari, New Mexico. This seems approximately to match the area where Vicente de Zaldívar and his company first encountered large herds of bison in September 1598, 10 days, or 35 leagues, from Pecos Pueblo—somewhere between modern Montoya and just east of Tucumcari, depending on which league (*legal* or *común*) is used. Craddock and Polt, *Zaldívar and the Cattle of Cíbola*, 8–13. Detailed analysis and comparison of this document with Documents 26 and 28 strongly suggest that at this point the expedition's rate of travel dropped considerably. That was probably due in part to diversion by first-time experience with bison. Almost without exception, historic groups encountering bison for the first time seem to have spent much time observing, chasing, and hunting the impressive

animals. That such was the case for the Coronado expedition is suggested by Francisco López de Gómara's contemporary statement that during the first day's encounter with bison the expeditionaries killed 80 of them. Though this statement lacks attribution to any eyewitness source, clearly López de Gómara relied on one or more such sources in writing his brief account of the expedition. Only a little farther along, the expeditionaries were also distracted by bison-hunting nomads, the Querechos. So until the expedition reached the Llano Estacado, it slowed to a comparative crawl. See Flint, "Reconciling the Calendars." For information about the Querechos, see the entry in Appendix 1.

90. "Vacas" in this context seems at first ambiguous; it could refer either to bison generally or to female bison specifically. However, the preceding sentences suggest that "bison cows" is the intended meaning, and Jaramillo's statement jibes better with Castañeda de Nájera's account of the same events if that meaning is taken. This location then also determines where the first Querechos were encountered, according to Jaramillo, which would likely have been between modern Tucumcari, New Mexico, and Adrian, Texas—not yet on the Llano Estacado but rather within the broad Canadian River valley (map 4). Flint, "Reconciling the Calendars"; Document 28, fol. 78r.

91. The tipi as described here remained in use among nomadic Indians of the Great Plains and adjacent regions until well into the nineteenth century.

92. "Who was guiding us," *que nos guiava*. This whole passage is full of incomplete sentences that we have rearranged somewhat in translation to make the sense more obvious. H&R, 301, have "From here the Indian guided us. . . ." Obviously following *CDI,* 14:310, without consulting the actual document, they ignore a "que" that turns the phrase about guiding into a qualifying phrase and not the main thrust of the passage.

93. El Turco seems to have been leading the expedition straight for the Teyas, which would have made good sense if they, like he, were Caddos. What Turco may have been doing was avoiding his people's Querecho/Apachean enemies to reach the safety of fellow Caddoans (the Teyas).

94. For geographical information, see the entry for Arahey, Harahey in Appendix 2. For biographical information about El Turco, see the entry in Appendix 1.

95. It must be remembered that this statement of Turco's motivation derives from a confession extorted under intense pressure, probably including torture, which was a not unusual interrogatory procedure of the day. That confession may have had more to do with Spanish preconceptions and expectations than with Turco's true intentions. For instance, the lying or deceiving guide was a stock character in the chivalric romances of the day, which were so wildly popular and such an influential part of Spanish cultural nurturing in that time that they have to be considered a key filtering element heavily influencing the way expeditionaries saw the exotic world around them. See, as one of countless examples, the case of two boatmen who trick the hero Esplandián and his companion Sargil at the very beginning of their adventures. Garci Rodríguez de Montalvo, *Las Sergas de Esplandián* (Zaragosa: Simon de Portonariis, 1586; reprint, Madrid: Ediciones Doce Calles,1998), fol. 4v.

96. It is this disagreement between the two guides, rather than being lost, as is often said, that was the dilemma for the expedition at this point. The portrayal of the Coronado expedition as lost on the Llano is mostly a myth generated by the readings of modern historians. A close examination of the documents shows that rather than wandering aimlessly, the expedition beelined for what is now the Texas South Plains. They traveled straight and at a steady rate into the South Plains. There was no time for wandering. See Flint, "Reconciling the Calendars." For biographical information about the second guide, Ysopete, see Document 28, note 317.

97. In fact, the three documents that report this portion of the expedition's travel indicate that only 8 days elapsed from the time the expedition reached the Llano Estacado (that is, when El Turco began leading the expedition in the direction of La Florida) until it arrived at the first *barranca* (at which point direction was changed toward the north for the small contingent that continued on to Quivira), not the 20 days that Jaramillo refers to here. See Flint, "Reconciling the Calendars."

98. Castañeda de Nájera, too, recounts this report of Álvar Núñez Cabeza de Vaca, Andrés Dorantes, Alonso del Castillo Maldonado, and Dorantes's slave, Esteban, having been seen by people of this Teya settlement at least five years before. Jaramillo, by adding the information that this occurred "closer to Nueva España," makes this comprehensible, because the Cabeza de Vaca party is not thought to have gotten anywhere near the South Plains of Texas, which is where the Teya settlement was at this time. Document 28, fol. 82r; Chipman, "In Search

of Cabeza de Vaca's Route," 127–48. See Document 28, note 319, for a fuller discussion of the encounter of Teyas with the Cabeza de Vaca party.

99. Castañeda de Nájera also reports this council. That major decisions were reached by such councils was standard practice on Spanish-led expeditions of the period. Ordinarily a council would include all of the persons of leadership and high social rank, including at least some priests. See Document 28, fol. 85r. Evidently Jaramillo was among the higher-status persons who were invited to councils, although he is not known to have held a captaincy at this time.

100. This was the second and final great *barranca*.

101. With this use of the first person Jaramillo indicates that he was among the chosen 30 who made the trip to Quivira. His use of "north" is ambiguous here, since on at least one occasion he seems to distinguish between geographic north and magnetic north (east of north). The "Relación del Suceso" states that the chosen 30 traveled guided by a compass, though without specifying the direction taken. Bolton, assuming that the direction was due north, provides information about the magnetic declination in Palo Duro Canyon (his second *barranca*) and then traces the select 30 to what is now Ford, Kansas (map 4). Bolton, 284–86, 412.

102. Most modern researchers have identified this river as the modern Arkansas (maps 1 and 4). From Blanco Canyon in Floyd County, Texas (possibly the first *barranca*), to Ford, Kansas (traditionally considered to have been where Vázquez de Coronado's party reached the Arkansas), is about 260 airline miles, or only slightly over 8.5 miles per day, which would truly be, as Jaramillo states here, "not long days of travel." We use Blanco Canyon as the starting point for this portion of the route, even though it surely was not, only because the location of the second *barranca* is unknown, nor is there even agreement about what direction it was from the first *barranca*. Wherever the second *barranca* was, though, it would not dramatically change the length of daily journeys, or *jornadas,* made during the northward trip. Bolton, 288; H&R, 303 n. 21. The date of celebration of the feast of San Pedro and San Pablo in 1541, as today, was June 29 (though in the Julian Calendar). Chaves, *Espejo de navegantes,* 86.

103. The statement "having arrived below Quivira" is in error, because the point at which the advance guard reached the river was both upstream from and at a higher elevation than Quivira, so travel from there was downstream to Quivira, as Jaramillo himself writes immediately afterward. The place where the river was struck was presumably at a more southerly latitude than Quivira and below it in that sense, but the sense of south as "below" was not intuitive in sixteenth-century Spain; map conventions of the day had not yet firmly settled on north being toward the top of the page. Neither Winship, 379, nor H&R, 303, point out or attempt to explain this error.

104. "Three or four days of our travel," *tres U quatro hornadas de las nuestras.* H&R, 303, have "which was about three or four days from us, farther down," ignoring the fact that the word is the possessive "nuestras."

105. As unlikely as the presence of a Christian seems, many Europeans from the Narváez expedition of 1528 who are presumed to have died are in fact unaccounted for. This anticipation of a Christian leader ahead could also represent a misunderstanding of communication by means of signs or imperfect translation. On the other hand, it may have been only an inference made by the Coronado expedition members, as Jaramillo suggests afterward.

106. "It is to be understood," *que se Entiende.* H&R, 304, ignore the tense of the verb and write "since it was understood."

107. Bolton suggests that "Teucarea" is a "mistranscription of *taováias*—that is, Taováias or Towásh," the name of a much later Wichita group. Bolton's view has been supported recently by William Newcomb and Douglas Parks. They equate "Teucarea" with "Tawakoni." Depicting Wichita territory in the late sixteenth to early eighteenth centuries, they show Tawakoni villages downstream from present-day Tulsa, Oklahoma, and at other locations farther south. The Quivirans may have been referring here to the group on the Arkansas, since it was closer to them than the other sites. Bolton, 293; William W. Newcomb, Jr., "Wichita," in *Handbook of North American Indians,* vol. 13, part 1, *Plains,* ed. Raymond J. DeMallie (Washington, DC: Smithsonian Institution, 2001), 548–66. This may be the place called Tareque in the "Relación del Suceso." Document 29, fol. 5r.

108. This is another example of the convening of a council in order to decide the expedition's course of action. For other examples, see fols. 3r–3v, this document, as well as Document 15, fol. 369r, and Document 28, fols. 85r, 130r, and 130v.

109. This is past the middle of August in the Julian calendar. According to the modern, or Gregorian, calendar this would have been around the end of August or the first days of September.

110. "To plow it," *aralla*. This is the only known reference in documents contemporary with the Coronado expedition that suggests an intent and preparation to put in crops. There is, however, no mention, either here or elsewhere, that the expedition carried seeds or the equipment for plowing and harvesting. This statement may indicate that such items were expected to be supplied to the expedition later. Flint, "Material Culture," 79.

111. For more complete accounts of the execution of El Turco, see Flint, *Great Cruelties*, passim.

112. This is the only known reference to the acquisition of corn in Quivira by the Coronado expedition. Whether this was through purchase, trade, or extortion is unknown.

113. Erection of such a cross was part of the formal act of taking possession for the Spanish crown. In addition, the expedition followed the procedure of setting up crosses as route markers. See Document 28, fol. 76v, and Flint and Flint, "Coronado's Crosses."

114. The statement beginning with "This land has a very beautiful appearance" is clearly Jaramillo's opinion and must not be construed as part of the inscription on the cross, as Waldo Wedel evidently did. Wedel, *Archeological Remains in Central Kansas*, 13. As Bolton, 297, puts it, "he [Jaramillo] among these first Europeans was loudest in his praise."

115. These plums were *Prunus arkansana*, found throughout the central and southern Great Plains, where the purple-red fruit generally ripens in August and September. Wild plum pits have been recovered archaeologically from protohistoric aboriginal (Great Bend Aspect) sites in central Kansas, generally thought to be the location of Quivira. The captain general also specifically mentions the existence of plums in Quivira. Sargent, *Manual of the Trees*, 2:565–66; Wedel, *Archeological Remains in Central Kansas*, 3; Document 26, fol. 2r.

116. This was *Linum lewisii*, wild blue flax, which grows in clumps up to two feet tall throughout the West. Yocom et al., *Wildlife and Plants*, 21.

117. For more than a hundred years researchers have identified the dwelling type described here as that of ancestral Wichita bands. Wedel, *Archeological Remains in Central Kansas*, 10. For photographs of modern examples of such structures, see Jones, *Coronado and Quivira*, 68, 79. See also fig. 28.8.

118. This comparison evidently refers to the straw houses in the area where Jaramillo was writing in the 1560s, the Ciudad de México or its immediate environs.

119. The reference here is to the area of the Querecho *ranchería* from which El Turco led the expedition onto the Llano Estacado. See fol. 3r.

120. At least two more complete accounts of this fall exist. Castañeda de Nájera reports that Vázquez de Coronado was hit in the head by the horse's hoof. Fray Antonio Tello, however, writes that he hit his mouth on the ground. Document 28, fol. 129r; Document 28, note 508. H&R, 306, put a negative slant on the phrase "from which he showed signs of poor health," translating it as "he showed a mean disposition and plotted the return."

121. Jaramillo here reveals that he was among those who did not want to leave Tierra Nueva.

122. For biographical information, see the entry on Juan de Padilla in Appendix 1. The man here called fray Luis de Escalona was fray Luis de Úbeda. Angélico Chávez asserted that Jaramillo used the Escalona surname in error and that the name was not connected with this fray Luis in any way. Chávez, *Coronado's Friars*, 29 n. 3. See also the entry for fray Luis de Úbeda in Appendix 1. The provincial who authorized their remaining in Tierra Nueva at this time was fray Marcos de Niza.

123. This is one of the rare instances in the Coronado expedition documents in which slaves of members of the expedition are mentioned. Personal slaves were undoubtedly common among the expeditionaries. Flint, "What's Missing from this Picture?" 66–67.

124. Jaramillo seems to refer to two separate servants or slaves named Sebastián, one an Indian, the other a Black. See also note 130, this document. For biographical information about Melchior Pérez, see the introduction to Document 32.

125. This is the only reference among contemporary documents of the expedition to wives and children of servants and slaves being present on the expedition, although this surely was not the only such case.

126. Presumably it was this same Andrés who, along with another Indian called Gaspar, was found still living at the Zuni pueblo of Halona in 1583. Pérez de Luxán, "Luxán's Account," 186; Espejo, "Report," 225. This is a rare mention of the Indian allies of the expedition and provides evidence about where at least some of them were from.

127. A *ladino* is a person who is culturally and linguistically Hispanic, though of other ethnic origin.

128. Again, this provides rare information about the origins of Indians from central Mexico who participated in the expedition. One of these men is evidently the Indian *donado* (lay brother) named Lucas who in 1559 made a trip to Zacatecas with fray Jacinto de San Francisco, Alonso de Zorita's partner in a proposed expedition to the north. See the introduction to Document 28. For geographical information about Zapotlán, see Document 28, note 498.

129. Like Castañeda de Nájera, Jaramillo addresses his report to an illustrious person, very likely Alonso de Zorita.

130. Jaramillo seems to refer to two separate servants or slaves named Sebastián, one an Indian, the other a Black. This reference to Sebastián indicates that both *donados*, he and Lucas, who went to Quivira with fray Juan de Padilla survived the trip, despite the friar's murder. See also note 124, this document.

131. Dereçera = *derechera*. *DRAE*, 683. *CDI*, 14:304, unjustifiably substitutes "derrota."

132. Sin comidas. *CDI*, 14:304, and therefore Mora, 189, mistakenly have "sin comodidad."

133. Dexarlas. *CDI*, 14:305, and therefore Mora, 189, have "dexar luz." Close inspection of the document, though, shows the vowel to be closed.

134. A la qual pusimos nonbre. H&R, 295, make the phrase "pusimos nombre en," incorrectly applying the name to the pass rather than to the mountain chain. *CDI*, 14:305, incorrectly has "a la que."

135. Vase, "he went." The document uses the present tense here. *CDI*, 14:305, erroneously has "pase."

136. Por Una Abra. *CDI*, 14:305, incorrectly has "por una obra."

137. Jaramillo makes frequent use of the imperfect subjunctive, as in "viesemos" here.

138. Y detras. *CDI*, 14:305, incorrectly has "y otras."

139. Y se Va por. *CDI*, 14:305, incorrectly has "sa baja."

140. Y segun(d). *CDI*, 14:306, incorrectly has "y seguro."

141. E nasç(i)e. *CDI*, 14:306, incorrectly has the nonsense "en cuasci."

142. Que El mysmo arroyo haze. *CDI*, 14:306, erroneously has "del mismo arroyo sale."

143. Turara = *durara*.

144. Que mas pudieron. *CDI*, 14:306, incorrectly has "que nos pudieron."

145. (^La p) ^*isp*a que. *CDI*, 14:306, simply omits these words, as it often does with passages that are especially difficult to decipher.

146. No *ver* de. *CDI*, 14:307, seems unfamiliar with the common scribal symbol for "ver," instead rendering it as "y."

147. Camino de tihues. *CDI*, 14:309, mistakenly renders this as "Tihueq."

148. *H*aY. *CDI*, 14:309, incorrectly has "á."

149. En Un puesto. *CDI*, 14:309, mistakenly renders this as "en un puerto."

150. *H*ay fuera de el. *CDI*, 14:309, mistakenly renders this as "y fuera dél."

151. Çicuyque. *CDI*, 14:309, distorts this into "Tienique."

152. Ralo = *raro* = excellent. *DRAE*, 1721.

153. Del qual. *CDI*, 14:309, mistakenly has "despues."

154. Çicuyque. *CDI*, 14:309, mistakenly renders this as "Ticuique." Minuscule *c* is often difficult to distinguish from *t* in sixteenth-century Spanish scripts.

155. (H)era. *CDI*, 14:309, erroneously has "sera," an easy but still sloppy mistake.

156. Lo tienen de las Vacas. *CDI*, 14:310, unaccountably has "es de las vacas."

157. Arahey ser tierra. *CDI*, 14:310, renders these words poorly as "Arache, y ser tierra" and confuses things further by inserting a comma.

158. Vivienda. *CDI*'s lack of effort to make sense of difficult words and passages, as here on 14:311, is surprising. It turns the word into the nonsense "brenda."

159. {El Yndio Ciego / Con q*ue h*a dias}. This marginal note seems to be incomplete.

160. Ve(^x)^gas. *CDI*, 14:312, fails to decipher the *escribano*'s correction of his own error and so renders this word as "bejas."

161. En tihuex. *CDI*, 14:312, omits this phrase.

162. Cosas q*ue* por. Once again, *CDI*, 14:312, fails to recognize the scribal contraction of "que."

163. Llamamos. *CDI*, 14:312, interpolates an *a*, erroneously transforming this word into "allamos."

164. Y parados. *CDI*, 14:313, omits the "y" and then mistakenly renders the rest as "pasados."

165. En rret(r)aguardia. *CDI*, 14:313, incorrectly renders this as "entre nuestra guardia."

166. Seis U (seis) = *seis U siete.*

167. Para signyficarnoslo teucarea. *CDI,* 14:313, omits these three words.

168. Rresidir. *CDI,* 14:314, erroneously has "recibir."

169. Y sabella. *CDI,*14: 314, distorts this into "Isabella."

170. El ma(h)iz. *CDI,* 14:314, mistakenly has "en maiz."

171. En este puesto alço (^f). This appears to be a correction of a copying error. The *escribano* had probably jumped ahead two lines to "fran*cisco.*"

172. Tanta quant*i*a. *CDI,* 14:315, incorrectly has "tanta cuanto."

173. "Hebrezitas" derives from "hebra" or *hierba. CDI,* 14:315, incorrectly has "e brecitas."

174. Çumaque. *CDI,* 14:315, unaccountably omits this word.

175. El fray luis. *CDI,* 14:316, incorrectly has only "el fraile."

176. QuyVira y arahe. *CDI,* 14:317, omits "y arahe."

177. {Lo / los muy / los muy Yll*ustr*es}. These three lines seem to indicate that an *escribano* used this folio to get the ink flowing from his pen. These are words that apparently have nothing to do with Jaramillo's *relación.*

178. The date is clearly in error. Who wrote this on the document is unknown, although it was quite possibly done in the sixteenth century.

179. This notation suggests that the document bundle now designated as AGI, Patronato, 20, N.5, R.8, was previously number 46 in Juan Páez de Castro's collection.

Document 31. Juan Troyano's Proof of Service, 1560

1. Document 28, fol. 130v.

2. Adorno and Pautz, *Núñez Cabeza de Vaca,* 1:296. Besides Juan Troyano, at least 16 other members of the Coronado expedition (or their relatives on their behalf) are known to have had testimony taken to prove their *méritos y servicios,* based in part on their service in Tierra Nueva. They were Jorge Báez (AGI, Patronato, 78A, N.1, R.6, "Jorge Báez"), Juan de Céspedes (AGI, Patronato, 68, N.2, R.4\1, "Juan de Cespedes"), Cristóbal de Escobar (Document 33; AGI, México, 206, N.35, "Cristóbal de Escobar"), Juan Gómez de Paradinas (AGI, Patronato, 63, R.5, "Juan de Paladinas [*sic*]"), Pedro Jerónimo (AGI, Patronato, 56, N.3, R.2, "Pedro Jeronimo"), Tristán de Luna y Arellano (AGI, México, 97, R.1, "Luna y Arellano"; AGI, Patronato, 74, N.1, R.11\1, "Méritos y servicios, Tristán de Arellano, Nueva España, 1575"), Diego Madrid Avendaño (AGI, Patronato, 87, N.2, R.2, "Méritos y servicios, Diego Madrid Avendaño, México, García, 1618"), Rodrigo de Paz Maldonado (AGI, Patronato, 112, R.2\1, "Rodrigo de Paz Maldonado"; AGI, Patronato, 117, R.5, "Méritos y servicios de Rodrigo de Paz Maldonado, 1571"), Melchior Pérez (Document 32; AGI, México, 207, N.39, "Méritos y servicios, Melchor Pérez, 1563"), García Rodríguez (AGI, Patronato, 87, N.1, R.5, "García Rodríguez y biznieto"), Alonso Rodríguez Para (AGI, Patronato, 74, N.2, R.2, "Alonso Rodríguez Para"), Gaspar de Saldaña (AGI, Patronato, 110, R.7\1, "Méritos y servicios de Gaspar de Saldaña, Nueva España y Perú, 1563"), Francisco Santillana (AGI, Patronato, 79, N.3, R.2, "Francisco Santillana"), Alonso de Saavedra (AGI, Patronato, 127, N.1, R.10, "Méritos y servicios de Alonso de Saavedra, 1583"), Francisco Vázquez de Coronado (AGI, México, 124, R.5, "Pedimiento de Francisco Pacheco de Córdova y Bocanegra, México, 1605"), and Juan de Zaldívar (AGI, Patronato, 60, N.5, R.4, "Juan de Zaldívar"; AGI, Patronato, 76, N.1, R.5, "Francisco de Zaldívar"). As Murdo MacLeod has put it, it was common "to think of merits and services as capital and to use them openly to 'buy' a better position from the king or the viceroy." Murdo J. MacLeod, "Self-Promotion: The *Relaciones de méritos y servicios* and Their Historical and Political Interpretation," *Colonial Latin American Historical Review* 7, no. 1 (1998):28.

3. Fol. 2v.

4. Fol. 1r. Troyano was a native of Medina de Ríoseco in the *provincia* of one of the royal seats of the day, Valladolid, in what is now the *comunidad* of Castilla y León in Spain. His parents were Antonio Clavijo and Catalina de Villagarcía. Troyano was not present at the muster of the expedition to Tierra Nueva on February 22, 1540. AGI, México, 168, "Letter from Juan Troyano to the king, December 20, 1568"; Document 12. For further biographical information, see Flint, *Great Cruelties,* 161–64.

5. After his return from Tierra Nueva, Troyano, now 46, evidently gave up his military career.

6. Fol. 1r.

7. Ibid.

8. AGI, México, 168, "Letter from Troyano, 1568."

9. Fol. 1v.

10. AGI, México, 168, "Letter from Troyano, 1568."

11. AGI, México, 98, N.33, "Informaciones contra Juan Troyano, 1569."

12. AGI, México, 98, N.33e, "Letter from Troyano to the viceroy, 1569." For definition of a *bergantín,* see Document 17, note 31.

13. Fol. 2r.

14. Fol. 2v.

15. AGI, México, 98, N.33k, "Letter from Troyano to the king, [post-1568]."

16. AGI, México, 98, N.33, "Informaciones contra Juan Troyano." Luis Velasco was the second viceroy of Nueva España, succeeding Antonio de Mendoza, who was transferred to the viceroyalty of Peru in 1550. Schäfer, *Consejo Real,* 2:439, 441.

17. Flint, *Great Cruelties,* 165–88.

18. AGI, México, 98, N.33, "Informaciones contra Juan Troyano."

19. AGI, México, 168, "Letter from Troyano, 1568."

20. This date and all others in this document are in the Julian calendar.

21. "Proof," *ynformaçion. DRAE,* 1164: "pruebas que se hacen de la calidad y circunstancias necesarias en un sujeto para un empleo u honor."

22. As opposed to *de parte* testimony, which in this case is lacking.

23. Pedro Villalobos had served in the Audiencia de Panamá since March 22, 1539. He was named to the Audiencia de Nueva España on December 18, 1556, and held that office from 1557 to 1572. In April 1572 he was named president of the Audiencia de Guatemala, and in 1577, president of the Audiencia de Charcas. He declined this last post, possibly because of ill health or age. Sarabia Viejo, *Luis de Velasco,* 47; Schäfer, *Consejo Real,* 2:452, 467, 505. For biographical information on Rodrigo Maldonado, see the entry in Appendix 1.

24. This is in reference to the full case file, within which the record of *de parte* testimony would have been placed before the *de oficio* testimony. Troyano was undoubtedly referred to a number of times prior to what appears to be the first instance of his name here.

25. In other words, since the time of the Coronado expedition.

26. For biographical information, see the entry for Antonio de Mendoza in Appendix 1.

27. For geographical information, see the entry for Cíbola in Appendix 2.

28. By and large, members of the expedition who were not personally sent by the viceroy claimed to have received no financial assistance for outfitting and subsistence from him or the king. Domingo Martín testified in 1543 that he "did not see [such pay] given to any person who went to the war." See, for instance, Document 32 and Document 33, especially fol. 15r.

29. For geographical information, see the entry for Tierra Nueva in Appendix 2.

30. "Responsible man," *hombre de bien. DRAE,* 1117: "el que cumple puntualmente sus obligaciones."

31. It is thus possible that Troyano helped design and build the bridge erected by the expedition across the Río de Cicuique in 1541, although Cristóbal de Escobar also claimed credit for devising the structure. Maldonado would have had knowledge of this activity, since he was present. See Documents 28, fol. 78r, and 33, fol. 1r.

32. For biographical information about Hernando de Alvarado, see the introduction to Document 24.

33. *Versillos* were small, lightweight swivel guns. See Document 28, notes 289 and 589. "Supplied by the viceroy," *de muniçion. DRAE,* 1417: "lo que el Estado suministra por contrata a la tropa . . . a diferencia de lo que el soldado compra de su bolsillo."

34. For geographical information, see the entry for Culiacán in Appendix 2.

35. "The general did not take with him [all] those he selected," *no escogio el general los que llevo consigo.* This is a rare instance among these documents in which we have had to alter radically the sequence of phrases in a sentence to make sense out of what otherwise seems to be a hopeless muddle. We are at a loss to explain how the *escribano* came to jumble this so badly, unless the similarity in appearance of "consigo" and "escogio" led to miscopying.

36. López de Cárdenas's given name is sometimes recorded as "Garci" and sometimes as "García." For biographical information about him, see the entry for García López de Cárdenas in Appendix 1.

37. These were questions concerning the witness's relationship to the petitioner—whether, for instance, they were close relatives or enemies, both of which would have disqualified the witness's testimony. *Siete Partidas,* 3:668–74.

38. Because the existing document is a copy, the signatures are not affixed here.

39. For biographical information about Juan Cordero, see Document 27, note 80.

40. This is, of course, an underestimate, since 20 years before, in 1540, as Cordero himself testifies, Troyano and Cordero were sent to Cíbola together. Folio 1v, this document.

41. *Casa poblada* literally means "populated house." It refers to a fully functional household, including physical structures, family, retainers, servants, and slaves, as well as appurtenances. The assertion that one maintained a *casa poblada* shows intention to remain as a *vecino* of a particular locale. Such an establishment was expected to be maintained by an *encomendero*.

42. This is a formulaic statement typical of *probanzas* of *méritos* (worthiness) and *servicios* (services) such as this and is in direct contradiction to Rodrigo Maldonado's earlier testimony. The statement may have been inserted by the *escribano* rather than made by Cordero. See fol. 1r, this document.

43. This is again a formulaic statement and should not be trusted, for instance, as evidence that Troyano took slaves with him. His apparent humble status would probably have precluded his ownership of slaves. As suggested in note 42, this statement might have been inserted unthinkingly by the *escribano*.

44. The reference here is to the advance unit Vázquez de Coronado took with him from Culiacán to Cíbola. Castañeda de Nájera writes that this group consisted of "fifty horsemen and a few footmen." Document 28, fol. 27v.

45. This story is told elsewhere. Document 28, fols. 79r–79v: "Also, a Spaniard was lost when he went out hunting and did not find his way back to the *real* because the land was very flat." This man was most likely Bartolomé del Campo (Document 12, fol. 4v) and not Andrés de Campo, the Portuguese who remained with fray Juan de Padilla at Quivira. It is unclear whether Bartolomé survived being lost on the plains, although Document 24 seems to imply that he never returned to camp.

46. "Notable," *gentil. DRAE,* 1035.

47. Because the existing document is a copy, the signatures are not affixed here.

48. For biographical information, see the entry on Antonio de Turcios in Appendix 1. For biographical information about López de Agurto, see Document 27, note 72.

49. The members of the *audiencia* might have been fooled by Troyano's "surname," which they took as an indication of his place of origin (Troy). He was, however, a native of Medina de Rioseco in Spain. For additional biographical information, see the sketch in Flint, *Great Cruelties,* 161–64.

50. "Built a *bergantín*." Compare AGI, México, 98, N.33e, "Letter from Troyano, 1569." For a definition, see Document 17, note 31.

51. *Licenciado* Alonso de Zorita was an *oidor* in the *audiencia* in Santo Domingo from 1547 to 1553 and in the *audiencia* in Guatemala from 1553 to 1555. He was named to the Audiencia de México on September 8, 1555. For more complete biographical information, see the introduction to Document 28 and Schäfer, *Consejo Real,* 2:444, 473. Jerónimo de Orozco was first a *licenciado* and later a doctor. He was appointed an *oidor* of the Audiencia de México on December 29, 1557, and served until April 30, 1572, when he was named first president of the Audiencia de Guadalajara. He served there from July 30, 1572, until his death in December 1580. During his tenure at Guadalajara, Orozco also served as governor of Nueva Galicia. Schäfer, *Consejo Real,* 2:452, 492; Tello, 479. Vasco de Puga was first a *licenciado* and later a doctor. He was appointed an *oidor* of the Audiencia de México on the same day as doctor Orozco. He served until 1575, suffering two suspensions during that time. Schäfer, *Consejo Real,* 2:452.

52. The *escribano* changes at the beginning of this line.

53. The *escribano* changes again at the beginning of this line.

54. The letter to the king is in the hand of the *escribano* who prepared folios 1r–2r.

55. Here the hand changes to that of an unknown *escribano*.

Document 32. Melchior Pérez's Petition for Preferment, 1551

1. In addition to the case of Melchior Pérez recorded in the present document, there are seven other known instances of children or more remote descendants making application to the king for reward on the basis of their forebears' service in the expedition to Cíbola. They were Jorge Báez (AGI, Patronato, 78A, N.1, R.6, "Jorge Báez"), Tristán de Luna y Arellano (AGI, Patronato, 74, N.1, R.11\1, "Tristan de Arellano"), Diego Madrid Avendaño (AGI, Patronato, 87, N.2, R.2, "Diego Madrid Avendaño"), García Rodríguez (AGI, Patronato, 87, N.1, R.5,

"García Rodríguez y biznieto"), Francisco Santillana (AGI, Patronato, 79, N.3, R.2, "Francisco Santillana"), Francisco Vázquez de Coronado (AGI, México, 124, R.5, "Francisco Pacheco de Córdova y Bocanegra"), and Juan de Zaldívar (AGI, Patronato, 76, N.1, R.5, "Francisco de Zaldívar").

2. Diego Flores de la Torre was a descendant of a sister of Melchior Pérez's and her husband, Hernán Flores, one of the *de parte* witnesses whose testimony is recorded in the document that follows. Flores de la Torre was the first Jesuit priest at the church in Compostela before becoming archdeacon at Guadalajara. Tello, 219.

3. For a discussion of *méritos,* see the introduction to Document 31.

4. AGI, México, 1064, L.1\1, "Informes de los conquistadores," fol. 237r.

5. Fol. 4v.

6. Document 1, fol. 1r.

7. Document 1, fol. 3r.

8. Fol. 8r; Gerhard, *North Frontier,* 123.

9. Document 12, fol. 2v.

10. AGI, Patronato, 60, N.5, R.4, "Juan de Zaldívar."

11. See, for example, Flint, *Great Cruelties,* 206–49.

12. Fol. 8r. Pérez himself claims in this document to have spent 3,000 *pesos de minas* (fol. 3v). Four years earlier the number he gave was 2,000 *castellanos.* AGI, México, 1064, L.1\1, "Informes de los conquistadores," fol. 237r.

13. Fol. 3v.

14. Ibid.

15. Ibid. *Ladino:* see Document 30, note 127.

16. The distinction between an *encomienda* and a *corregimiento* was principally one of authority. In an *encomienda,* authority over a native community was conceded to a private individual, whereas in a *corregimiento* it remained in the hands of the monarch and was exercised through a salaried royal official. For further discussion, see the glossary.

17. Fol. 8v.

18. Gerhard, *North Frontier,* 133; AGI, México, 1064, L.1\1, "Informes de los conquistadores," fol. 154v.

19. As Enrique Semo writes about this period, "prices reflected a steady upward trend." Enrique Semo, *The History of Capitalism in Mexico: Its Origins, 1521–1763,* trans. Lidia Lozano (Austin: University of Texas Press, 1993), 40.

20. Prem, "Disease Outbreaks," 31–34.

21. Elliot, *Imperial Spain,* 199–200.

22. AGI, México, 207, N. 39, "Melchor Pérez."

23. Biblioteca del Escorial, Codíce &-2-7, Doc. no. LXXIX, "Memoria de las personas, conquistadores y pobladores de la nueva galizia, sin fecha"; AGI, México, 1064, L.1\1, "Informes de los conquistadores," fols. 154v and 237r; AGI, México, 207, N. 39, "Melchor Pérez."

24. AGI, México, 207, N. 39, "Melchor Pérez"; Gerhard, *Historical Geography,* 332–33.

25. AGI, Justicia, 336, N.1, R.3, "Concerning certain pueblos"; AGI, Patronato, 60, N.5, R.4, "Juan de Zaldívar."

26. This is in contradistinction to Document 31, which includes only *de oficio* testimony. Document 33, like Document 32, incorporates only *de parte* testimony.

27. "Copy," *tanto. DRAE,* 1940: "copia o ejemplar que se dar de un escrito trasladado de su original."

28. "Certified copy," *testimonio. DRAE,* 1971: "instrumento autorizado por escribano o notario, e que se da fe de un hecho, se traslada total o parcialmente un documento."

29. "Proof of status," *información.* See Document 31, note 2.

30. For biographical information about Flores de la Torre, see note 2, this document. The *arcediano,* or archdeacon, was the second highest-ranking member of the cathedral chapter, or governing body of a cathedral. "His duties included examining all candidates for the holy orders and assisting the bishop in their ordination." In the absence of the bishop, the archdeacon could take over his administrative duties. Schwaller, *Church and Clergy,* 15–16.

31. "Forebears," *mayores. DRAE,* 1340: "abuelos y demás progenitores de una persona."

32. For geographical information, see the entry on Guadalajara in Appendix 2.

33. For geographical information, see the entry on Nueva Galicia in Appendix 2.

34. This date is in the Gregorian calendar, but the dates in the incorporated copy of Melchior Pérez's 1551 petition are in the Julian calendar.

35. Juan de Bolívar y Cruz served as *relator* (court reporter or secretary) in the

Audiencia de México, then as *fiscal* (1650–58) and *oidor* (1658–59) in the Audiencia de Manila. From there he was transferred to the Audiencia de Guadalajara as *oidor*, where he died in office. Schäfer, *Consejo Real*, 2:496, 521, 523.

36. For biographical information about Melchior Pérez de la Torre, see the introduction to this document and Document 27, note 53. In all earlier documents (including those contemporary with Pérez's life) his given name is spelled "Melchior," evidence of the widespread adoption of French forms that were in vogue in Spain for several generations.

37. For biographical information, see the entry for Diego Pérez de la Torre in Appendix 1. Because this document is a copy of the original, Pérez de la Torre's signature is not affixed here. The same holds true for the other signature lines in this document.

38. Archdeacon Diego Flores de la Torre evidently traced his relationship to Melchior Pérez as a descendant of Hernán Flores and Ángela de Velarde, the sister of Melchior Pérez de la Torre. We infer that Jacinto de Pineda y Ledesma, the owner of the papers the archdeacon is seeking to use, was a descendant of Pedro de Ledesma and Catalina Mejía, the daughter of Melchior Pérez de la Torre. This makes Pineda y Ledesma and Flores de la Torre distant cousins. Pineda y Ledesma had a stronger claim to Melchior Pérez's proofs of service and their use in furthering his own cause than did the archdeacon, who was related only collaterally as a relative no closer than a great-great-nephew (his exact degree of relation is unknown). Fols. 6v, 8r, and 9r.

39. "Authenticated," *autorizados*. *DRAE*, 234: " dar fe el escribano o notario en un documento."

40. "For it, etc.," *para ello etcetera*. This abbreviated statement is a certification in accordance with the provision in Ley 10, Título 19, of Partida 3 of the Siete Partidas that copying of a document is permissible only if "no injury can result to the other party" as a result. *Siete Partidas*, 3:763–64.

41. "Responses," *recados*. *DRAE*, 1737: "mensaje o respuesta que de palabra se da."

42. Until 1966, Orendáin was a separate community in the modern Spanish *comunidad* of Guipúzcoa; thereafter, it was subsumed into the community of Iruerrieta. *Diccionario enciclopédico Espasa*, 11th ed., 12 vols. (Madrid: Espasa-Calpe, 1989), 7:6118. This place name might well have become a true surname in the case of don Tomás.

43. "Exercise," *interponga*. *DRAE*, 1181: "utilizar en favor de otro."

44. This date and the others that appear in the inserted copy are in the Julian calendar.

45. Cornejo, himself a former member of the expedition to Tierra Nueva, had been a *vecino* of Guadalajara since at least 1547. He was born about 1514 at Salamanca in the modern *comunidad* of Castilla y León in Spain, the son of Álvaro Cornejo and Ana Maldonado. He had been in Nueva España since about 1527 and participated in Nuño de Guzmán's conquest of Jalisco. AGI, México, 1064, L.1\1, "Informes de los conquistadores," fol. 156v.

46. Montoya had arrived in the New World with Pedro de Alvarado's armada in 1538 and spent time in the *adelantado's* jurisdiction of Guatemala. He was a *vecino* of Burgos in the modern *comunidad* of Castilla y León in Spain. As early as November 1531 he had been designated an *escribano* for the Indies. *Pasajeros*, 2: no. 5215.

47. Juan Galeasso was evidently the former expeditionary Juan Galeras. His surname is spelled several ways in the Coronado expedition documents: Galeras, Galleas, Gallas, and Galeasso. Document 12, fol. 4v. For biographical information, see Document 27, note 61. Alonso de la Vera evidently never actually testified on Pérez's behalf. Who this individual was is unclear. A Rodrigo de Vera, perhaps a relative, participated in the Coronado expedition. A likely candidate for this Alonso de la Vera is a native of Llerena in the modern *provincia* of Badajoz in Extremadura, Spain, who arrived at the Ciudad de México in 1529 and went with Hernán Cortés to Baja California in the 1530s. Boyd-Bowman, 2: no. 1455; Icaza, 2: no. 1348.

48. Francisco de Olivares, 26 years old in 1540, served in Captain Diego de Guevara's company during the expedition to Tierra Nueva. He was a native of Béjar del Castañar in Salamanca *provincia* in the modern Spanish *comunidad* of Castilla y León. AGI, Justicia, 339, N.1, R.1, "Residencia"; AGI, México, 1064, L.1\1, "Informes de los conquistadores," fol. 258v; Document 12, fol. 4r. Andrés de Villanueva was a *vecino* of Guadalajara by 1547. He had been with Nuño de Guzmán in the conquest of Nueva Galicia and was an *encomendero*, holding the right to collect tribute from the native communities of Guacel and Huehuetitlan in the colonial jurisdiction of San Cristóbal de la Barranca, as well as from Ocotique, Cuquío, Coinan-Tototlan, La Barca, and Teteuque, all in Nueva Galicia. He hailed

from Logroño, in the modern *comunidad* of La Rioja in Spain. Icaza, 2: no. 1169; Gerhard, *North Frontier*, 79, 101, 122. Diego de Colio, a native of Cabrales in the modern Spanish *comunidad* of Asturias, was on the island of Cuba by 1518. He served under Hernán Cortés during the conquest of Tenochtitlan and made *entradas* in Jalisco and Guatemala. He became a *vecino* of the Ciudad de México. AGI, Justicia, 336, N.2, "Diego de Colio"; Himmerich y Valencia, *Encomenderos*, 143. Hernán Flores was serving as a *regidor* in Guadalajara in 1539. He married a sister of Melchior Pérez's. For additional biographical information, see Document 5, note 11. Melchior Pérez's son-in-law and fellow expeditionary, Pedro de Ledesma, was 24 years old in 1540. He was a native of Zamora in the modern *comunidad* of Castilla y León in Spain. At the time of the expedition to Tierra Nueva he was a *criado* of Vázquez de Coronado's. He later became a *regidor* of Guadalajara. AGI, Justicia, 339, N.1, R.2, "Residencia, August 1544"; AGI, Justicia, 336, N.2, "Diego de Colio." See also Flint, *Great Cruelties*, 230–32.

49. For geographical information, see the entries for Cíbola and Tierra Nueva in Appendix 2.

50. The presence of pigs on the expedition is to be noted, because previously published sources have made no reference to them. For another reference to pigs on the expedition, see Document 11, fol. 43r.

51. This is one of numerous indications in the documents that many more people were on the Coronado expedition than has previously been appreciated. Many of the men listed on the muster roll, for instance, were accompanied by retinues similar to this one that Pérez took. *Ladino:* see Document 30, note 127.

52. For biographical information, see the entry for García López de Cárdenas in Appendix 1.

53. For geographical information, see the entry for Culiacán in Appendix 2.

54. As in Document 28, a *tierra de guerra* was any region of hostile natives not yet pacified by the Spaniards.

55. For biographical information, see the entry for Lorenzo de Tejada in Appendix 1.

56. A *fanega* was a dry measure equal to approximately 50 quarts, or 1.5 bushels. Barnes, Naylor, and Polzer, *Northern New Spain*, 69.

57. For the legal requirements concerning the giving of dowries to minor relatives of whom one has guardianship, see *Siete Partidas*, 4:934.

58. For a brief discussion of such questions, see Document 31, note 37.

59. At the instance of Hernán Cortés and with the approval of the Audiencia de México, don Luis de Castilla led an *entrada* into Nueva Galicia in 1536, in order to enforce a pair of royal *cédulas* concerning *encomiendas* granted by Nuño de Guzmán. It was with this *entrada* that Melchior Pérez and Francisco de Olivares first arrived in Nueva Galicia. Tello, 238–48. For additional biographical information about Luis de Castilla, see the entry under his name in Appendix 1.

60. "Since," *despues que*. *DRAE*, 731: "seguido de *que* solia equivaler a *desde*."

61. Bartolomé de Coca was a son of *vecinos* of Reoyo, an *arrabal* (suburb or outskirts) of Portillo in the *provincia* of Valladolid in the modern *comunidad* of Castilla y León in Spain. He arrived in Nueva España in 1537 or 1538. By 1547 he had become a *vecino* of Guadalajara. *Pasajeros*, 2: no. 5122; Icaza, 2: no. 1120.

62. At this point in the copy is inserted a list of words and characters that had been struck out in the original. The copyist excluded the strike-outs from the 1671 copy, thus correcting it in accordance with the original *escribano's* intent. No mention is made of the strike-outs that occur in the 1671 copy itself, such as "porque este *que*" on folio 5r.

63. (Fran*cis*Co) *Juan* Gal(l)e*asso*. "Francisco" is a scribal copying error.

64. Vei = *vi*. This represents a conjugation of an older form of *ver*, of which the infinitive was *veer* and therefore the first-person singular preterit was *vei*. Lloyd, *Latin to Spanish*, 320.

65. Esxri(p)to. This is a correction produced by the *escribano*/copyist's writing over an earlier word, which is now impossible to make out.

Document 33. Cristóbal de Escobar's Proof of Service, 1543

1. Fols. 4r and 6r; AGI, México, 206, N.51, "Información de Francisco Muñoz, 1561." Escobar had arrived in Nueva España in 1538 with his wife, Isabel Ortiz, and probably at least one black slave. A native of Aracena in the *provincia* of Huelva in the modern *comunidad* of Andalucía, Spain, he became a *vecino* of the Ciudad de México in 1546. *Pasajeros*, 2: no. 4370; AGI, Indiferente, 423, Libro 18, fol. 65r, "Permission to Cristóbal de Escobar to transport one black slave to the Indies,

December 30, 1537"; AGI, México, 1064, L.1\1, "Informes de los conquistadores," fol. 185r.

2. Document 12, fol. 6r.

3. Fol. 4r; Document 12, fol. 6r.

4. Flint, *Great Cruelties*, 591, ch. 4, n. 5.

5. Fol. 4v.

6. Fol 5v; Document 32, fol. 3v.

7. Fols. 1r and 5r; Flint, *Great Cruelties*, 146. An account of the building of the bridge is in Document 28, fol. 78r. Juan Troyano may also have participated in this bridge construction. Document 31, fol. 1r.

8. Flint, *Great Cruelties*, 141–60.

9. AGI, México, 206, N.35, "Cristóbal de Escobar."

10. Fol. 1r.

11. Fols. 8v, 9r, 11r, and 11v.

12. Fol. 20r.

13. Sociedad de Bibliófilos Españoles, *Nobiliario de Conquistadores*, 112–13.

14. The orthography is ambiguous in the key document. There were three communities with the name Xilotepeque and one called Xicotepeque in Nueva España in the sixteenth century. In terms of modern political geography, the locations of the four places range from eastern Oaxaca to central Veracruz and northeastern México state. The most likely candidate for Escobar's *corregimiento* seems to be Xicotepeque, which had been converted from *encomienda* to *corregimiento* status in 1531. AGI, México, 206, N.35, "Cristóbal de Escobar"; Gerhard, *Historical Geography*, 116–18, 195–99, 373–77, 383–86.

15. The jurisdiction of Guachinango, northeast of the Ciudad de México, included the community of Xicotepeque, increasing the likelihood that this was Escobar's *corregimiento*.

16. AGI, México, 206, N.35, "Cristóbal de Escobar."

17. For discussion of the distinction between *de parte* and *de oficio* testimony, see the introduction to Document 31 and the glossary.

18. Fol. 20v.

19. *Casa poblada*, "populated house." See Document 31, note 41.

20. For geographical information, see the entry for Tierra Nueva in Appendix 2.

21. Escobar is claiming credit for designing the bridge the expeditionaries built across the Pecos River in New Mexico in May 1541, thereby providing a possible answer to the question we asked years ago in Flint, "Who Designed Coronado's Bridge?" There is also the possibility that Juan Troyano was involved in designing and/or building the bridge. Document 31, fol. 1r. For an account of the building of the bridge, see Document 28, fol. 78r.

22. "Heraldic banners," *reposteros*. *DRAE*, 1775: "paño cuadrado o rectangular, con emblemas heráldicos."

23. It was customary practice for a petitioner to submit a design of the proposed coat of arms. That drawing is missing from the document, but see figure 33.1.

24. This is apparently addressed to someone at the Consejo de Indias. At the time, the only member of the Consejo with that title was doctor Juan Bernal Díaz de Luco. He served as a member of the Consejo from 1531 until 1545. Schäfer, *Consejo Real*, 1:354.

25. For the basis of this translation of *ad perpetuam Rey memoriam*, see Document 8, note 65.

26. During the sixteenth century, several variant spellings of Tenuxtitan were current, Temixtitan being another. In modern usage it is Tenochtitlan. For geographical information on the Indies of the Ocean Sea, see the entry for Mar Océano in Appendix 2. A *justicia ordinaria* was a judge who had primary jurisdiction in the locality where he resided.

27. Antonio de la Cadena was an *hidalgo* from Sevilla in Spain. He had been in Nueva España since 1523 and had held a variety of minor offices. He was married to doña Francisca, daughter of *bachiller* Pedro Díaz de Sotomayor. Himmerich y Valencia, *Encomenderos*, 246. For biographical information about Sancho López de Agurto, see Document 27, note 72.

28. "Since," *despues que*. *DRAE*, 731: "seguido de *que* solia equivaler a *desde*."

29. Escobar's servant is another example of a person who participated in the Coronado expedition who does not appear on the muster roll. Indeed, the only known mention of him occurs in the present document. See the introduction to Document 12.

30. "Took part in," *anduve en*. *DRAE*, 138: "tomar parte . . . en algo."

31. "For the whole time," *muy cumplidamente*. Compare "soldado cumplido," *DRAE*, 1897: "el que ha servido todo el tiempo a que estaba obligado."

32. What formal titled position of authority, if any, Escobar might have held is unknown. As Miguel Entrambasaguas testified, "[Escobar's] captain commonly assigned *entradas* to him." Fol. 11v.

33. The Coronado expedition documents are all consistent with a distance between Cíbola and Los Corazones of 150 leagues. See, for example, Document 29, fol. 1r, and Document 28, fol. 101r. For geographical information, see the entries for Cíbola and Los Corazones in Appendix 2.

34. This question presents a much starker picture of the march of the advance guard to Cíbola than is offered elsewhere. For instance, Vázquez de Coronado, in Document 19, fol. 360v, writes that "some of my Indian allies died as well as a Spaniard named Espinosa and two Moors." And Juan Jaramillo, in Document 30, fol. 2r, has "a Spaniard called Espinosa and two other persons died from poisonous herbs." Escobar's question here also indicates that a large number of the Indian allies must have accompanied the advance guard, as we have maintained elsewhere. Flint, "What's Missing from This Picture?" 63.

35. For geographical information, see the entry for Mar del Sur in Appendix 2.

36. The reference here is probably to the crossing of the Gran Desierto and Pinacate region in the extreme northwest of the modern Mexican state of Sonora (map 2) by the party led by Melchior Díaz. See Document 28, fol. 35v and note 157.

37. Like Melchior Pérez, Escobar evidently took livestock with him in order to sell to other expeditionaries.

38. "Is commonly held to be true," *publiCa Voz y fama*. *DRAE*, 2107: "expresión con que se da a entender que un cosa se tiene corrientemente por cierta y verdadera."

39. "Was delegating," *cometia*. *DRAE*, 517: "ceder alguien sus funciones a otra persona."

40. For the scant biographical information available about Lope de Cadena, see Document 27, note 101. A native of Madrid, Lope de Madrid immigrated to Nueva España with his wife and parents in 1533. Boyd-Bowman, 2: no. 6324.

41. Miguel de Entrambasaguas was about 23 years old when the Coronado expedition began. He took a slave with him on the *entrada*. Arriving from his hometown of Burgos in the *provincia* of the same name in the modern Spanish *comunidad* of Castilla y León, he reached Nueva España in 1537. Forty years later he was a *vecino* of San Francisco in Quito, in what is now Ecuador. There he had married doña Isabel Pizarro, daughter of Pedro Pizarro. AGI, Patronato, 121, R.8, "Méritos y servicios de Miguel de Entrambasaguas, Dec. 11, 1577"; *Pasajeros*, 2: no. 3628; AGI, Patronato, 127, N.1, R.10, "Alonso de Saavedra." Domingo Martín, 38 when the expedition to Tierra Nueva began, was a native of Las Brozas in the *provincia* of Cáceres in the modern Spanish *comunidad* of Extremadura. He had been on the voyage made by Juan de Grijalva in 1518. In November 1526 Martín was granted the *encomienda* of Yagualicán and its *sujeto* in the *provincia* of Pánuco, but it was later taken away by Nuño de Guzmán. He was recognized as a *vecino* of the Ciudad de México in 1540 but did not have a house there. He claimed always to have been personally with Vázquez de Coronado during the expedition. Document 14, fol. 3r; AGI, Justicia, 1021, N.2, Pieza 6, "Probanza del fiscal Villalobos"; AGI, México, 1064, L.1\1, "Informes de los conquistadores," fol. 67v; AGI, Justicia, 124, N.2, "Domingo Martín vecino de México con Gómez Nieto vecino de la villa de Santistevan sobre el derecho a el pueblo de Yagualican, 1536"; Flint, *Great Cruelties*, 91.

42. There are two men of this name on the muster roll of the Coronado expedition, a Juan López and a Juan López de Sayago (later referred to as Juan López de la Rosa). The first served under García López de Cárdenas; the second was from Sayago in the *provincia* of Zamora in the *comunidad* of Castilla y León and was a *vecino* of Puebla in 1547. Document 12, fols. 3r and 6r; AGI, México, 1064, L.1\1, "Informes de los conquistadores," fol. 229r.

43. Álvarez arrived in the New World on the same ship that brought Escobar. Fol. 17v. For additional biographical information about Álvarez, see Document 27, note 36. Because Gutiérrez said that he was acquainted with Escobar's parents, he, like they, might have been from Aracena. That has not been independently verified, however.

44. Thus, Escobar was in Melchior Díaz's company.

45. For biographical information, see the entry on Tristán de Luna y Arellano in Appendix 1.

46. For geographical information, see the entry on Tiguex in Appendix 2.

47. For information on inflation in Nueva España during this period, see the introduction to Document 32.

48. In the wake of the just-ended Mixtón War, Nueva Galicia saw several uprisings of native peoples, including one of Tecoxquines shortly after Vázquez de Coronado's return to Compostela. Within a matter of weeks the captain general led a force to put down that uprising. AGI, Patronato, 60, N.5, R.4, "Juan de Zaldívar." For geographical information, see the entries for Culiacán and Compostela in Appendix 2.

49. "Suffered," *reçibio. DRAE,* 1740: "padecer uno el daño que otro le hace o casualmente le sucede."

50. "Had accoutered," *lleVo . . . adereçada. Llevar, DRAE,* 1282: "con el participio de ciertos verbos transitivos, haber realizado . . . lo que el participio denota."

51. Occasionally witnesses were called to respond only to certain specific questions from *interrogatorios,* as in the case of Hernando Gutiérrez.

52. The license Escobar received to make passage to the Indies shows that he arrived in 1538, not 1536 as Gutiérrez's figure would have it. *Pasajeros,* 2: no. 4370.

53. Fols. 1r and 1v were prepared by two scribes other than Antonio de la Cadena, who drafted the remainder of the document.

54. *Con muy* poca gente [. . .] *pasando a.* The original document has disintegrated, leaving two holes here. One or more words are missing from this line and cannot be reconstructed with any certainty.

55. (^A la) is a copying error. This scribal correction shows that this document is a copy and not the "original."

56. The *escribano* stops numbering folios with fol. 12r, as was standard practice halfway through a *signatura* (catalog number), since because of the folding of folios, there could be no further confusion in the event the folios were shuffled.

57. Despoblados de gran poblaçion. This statement as written is self-contradictory and likely represents a scribal copying error. The intended sense seems clear: "both unsettled areas and dense settlements."

58. The *escribano* changes here. The remainder of the document is in the hand of López de Agurto. La Cadena signs first; then López de Agurto adds his certification, surrounding la Cadena's signature.

Document 34. Vázquez de Coronado's Petition for Recovery of Encomiendas, 1553

1. See, for instance, Documents 31, 32, and 33.

2. For biographical information on Ruiz de Haro, see Document 11, note 31.

3. Arthur S. Aiton, "Report on the Residencia of the Coronado Government in New Galicia," *Panhandle-Plains Historical Review* 13 (1940):17. In the same year H&R, 383, offered a variant translation.

4. Published as Document 11 in this volume are the testimonies of Juan Fernández Verdejo and Juan Bermejo, who gave evidence in April and May 1552 about the level of Vázquez de Coronado's expenses in mounting the expedition.

5. H&R, 292 n. 2.

6. This folio is in the hand of an unidentified *escribano.*

7. For geographical information, see the entry for Guadalajara in Appendix 2.

8. The text of this document was prepared by Antonio de Turcios, chief *escribano* of the *audiencia* in the Ciudad de México. However, the first two lines of this folio are in the hand of an unknown *escribano* in Spain. For biographical information, see the entry for Antonio de Turcios in Appendix 1.

9. This year, 1554, was the year of Vázquez de Coronado's death. The exact date is unknown, but it occurred in September. *Actas de Cabildo,* 5:152. Valladolid was one of several cities in Spain that was from time to time the seat of the peripatetic royal court and its councils, including the Consejo de Indias, to which this case was referred. Since 1543 King Carlos had been out of the country, leaving his son Felipe as regent. After a trip to northern Europe himself in 1548–51, Felipe returned to Valladolid in September 1551. He and the court remained in nearly continuous residence there until he sailed for England and his marriage to Queen Mary in July 1554. Kamen, *Philip of Spain,* 26, 49, 56. "Sealed envelope," *pliego. DRAE,* 1625: "carta, oficio o documento de cualquier clase que cerrado se envia de una parte a otra."

10. For geographical information, see the entries for Compostela and Nueva Galicia in Appendix 2.

11. An *audiencia* had been established in Nueva Galicia in February 1548. Schäfer, *Consejo Real,* 2:492. For biographical information about Pedro Ruiz de Haro, see Document 11, note 31.

12. One of Vázquez de Coronado's difficulties in supporting his household was the high transportation costs for European goods sold in Nueva Galicia. All such items had to be brought overland from Veracruz or the Ciudad de México by pack train or native load bearers, *tamemes.* Transportation cost was mentioned as a key factor in total expenditure by men who had purchased supplies for the expedition. See, for instance, Document 11, fol. 72r. For information on the various modes of transportation and their costs in early colonial Nueva España, see Hassig, *Trade, Tribute, and Transportation,* 187–93, 211–19. Included in the property Vázquez de Coronado held in Nueva España was one-half of the *encomienda* of Tlapa, which he had received as dowry upon his marriage in 1536/37 to Beatriz de Estrada. AGI, Justicia, 259, Pieza 4, "Certification of suit concerning Tlapa." Vázquez de Coronado's annual salary as governor was set at "one thousand five hundred *ducados*" by the letter of his appointment. Document 5, fol. 407r.

13. Assigning *encomiendas* to themselves was a common practice among governors of the period. Aguacatlán and Xala: Ahuacatlán and Jala are located in the modern Mexican state of Nayarit, northwest of Guadalajara, near the Volcán Ceboruco. Peter Gerhard gives the number of tribute payers in this *encomienda* as between 2,200 and 2,800 at this time. Gerhard, *North Frontier,* 60–62. Mezquitlán and Guaxacatlán were former settlements in the colonial jurisdiction of Hostotipaquillo, now in the modern Mexican state of Jalisco. As Gerhard points out, the native people of the region, the Coanos, were "primitive farmers living in dispersed rancherías." Vázquez de Coronado shared this *encomienda* with Álvaro de Bracamonte. It is not clear that either of them ever received tribute from the *encomienda.* Gerhard, *North Frontier,* 94–97.

14. For biographical information on Villegas, see Document 8, note 60.

15. Amaxaque, Tepujuacán (Tepuzuacán), Amatlán (Amatlán de las Cañas), and Mezquitlán were four communities in the colonial jurisdiction of Guachinango. Today the area is in the Mexican state of Nayarit. As with Mezquitlán and Guaxacatlán, Vázquez de Coronado shared this *encomienda* with Álvaro de Bracamonte. Again, the indigenous population comprised "relatively primitive farmers." It is doubtful that tribute from this *encomienda* amounted to much, if anything, at this time. Gerhard, *North Frontier,* 86–89. Álvaro de Bracamonte evidently participated with Guzmán in the conquest of Nueva Galicia in the early 1530s, since he was granted *encomiendas* by him. A native of Paladinas de Ávila in Spain, he had come to Nueva España with the first *audiencia* in 1529. He was one of the founders of Compostela. In 1547 he was still a *vecino* of Nueva Galicia. Icaza, 1: no. 407; Boyd-Bowman, 2: no. 529.

16. The identity of the native community of Quinsique is uncertain. It could have been Iztinstique or Chistique, both in the region of Amatlán, which Vázquez de Coronado and Álvaro de Bracamonte jointly held in *encomienda.* Gerhard, *North Frontier,* 86–89. To the list given in this document, Robert Himmerich y Valencia adds Xalcingo and Cacluta as communities held by Vázquez de Coronado in this same area. Himmerich y Valencia, *Encomenderos,* 257. For information on who the Chichimeca Otomí were, see Document 28, note 463.

17. For biographical information about Bermejo, see the introduction to Document 1.

18. For geographical information, see the entry on Tierra Nueva in Appendix 2. For biographical information about fray Marcos, see the introduction to Document 6.

19. The text of this royal commission makes up Document 9 in this volume.

20. The exact statement in the commission reads, "[we order that] the Indians who are given to you in *encomienda* and placed in your keeping by us in our royal name are not be to removed from you or taken away at any time." Document 9, fol. 25 right.

21. There is no such explicit offer of reward and grants in either the original commission issued in January 1540 or the king's confirmation of it in June 1540. Documents 9 and 10.

22. This huge investment (equivalent to 71,000 silver *pesos*) was somewhat smaller than the 85,000 *pesos* invested by the viceroy. Only Pedro de Alvarado's late in-kind investment of approximately 90,000 *pesos* in value was of a comparable size among those who financed the expedition. Flint, "Financing and Provisioning," 46. In 1544 Vázquez de Coronado claimed to be "more than ten thousand gold *pesos de minas*" in debt as a result of the expedition. Flint, *Great Cruelties,* 359.

23. The reference here is to the wounds Vázquez de Coronado received at Cíbola in July 1540. See, for instance, Document 19, fol. 361r. Key to the concept of "just conquest" was the reading of the *requerimiento* and the "refusal" of people of Cíbola and other communities of Tierra Nueva to submit as a result. Because Vázquez de Coronado had been conscientious in having the *requerimiento* read

before engaging in battle, he could feel confident in calling the conquest "just." Hanke, *Spanish Struggle for Justice*, 33–35.

24. In 1544 Tejada was dispatched to Nueva Galicia to investigate charges of abuse of native peoples by the Coronado expedition and, simultaneously, to take the *residencia* of Vázquez de Coronado and the other royal officials of the *provincia*. See Flint, *Great Cruelties*, 29–38. For biographical information, see the entry on Lorenzo de Tejada in Appendix 1.

25. For general information on the New Laws, see Document 11, note 18.

26. *Licenciado* Cristóbal de Benavente had come to Nueva España from his native Zamora in Spain by 1529. He was appointed the temporary *fiscal* for the *audiencia* in the Ciudad de México in 1535, which post was made permanent as of July 2, 1540. He served as *fiscal* until 1550, when he returned to Spain. Schäfer, *Consejo Real*, 2:463. See also Flint, *Great Cruelties*, 325–26.

27. For the text of this decision, see Flint, *Great Cruelties*, 457–501.

28. In the years after 1544, several of the jurisdictions included within the *encomiendas* in question, Guaxacatlán in particular, became mining districts and thus could have yielded significant tribute. Gerhard, *North Frontier*, 95.

29. This is *licenciado* Hernando Caballero. For biographical information, see Document 11, note 28.

30. (Es)tuVe. This appears to be a scribal error; "tuve" seems intended rather than "estuve."

31. Se me rrepresentaron. *Representar = presentar. DRAE*, 1776.

32. Guardar = *cumplir. DRAE*, 1067.

33. VenÇido. *Vencer = prevalecer. DRAE*, 2070.

34. Ex a*b*rruptamente. *Ex abrupto, DRAE*, 928: "arrebatadamente, sin guarder el orden establecido."

35. Executoria. *DRAE*, 794: "sentencia que alcanzó la firmeza de cosa juzgada."

Appendix 4. Requerimiento

1. A native of Cuenca, Alonso de Ojeda was a member of Columbus's second and third voyages to the New World. It was an expedition Ojeda led into the Vega Real of Española that discovered the first gold on that island. He led Europeans in the first mass battle against New World natives in March 1495. He subsequently led several voyages to the northern coast of South America in 1499, 1501, 1504, and 1508. He died at Santo Domingo on Española in 1515. Morison, *European Discovery*, 2:118, 136, 153, 185, 190–94.

2. Between "tuvieredes" and "como lo han," the Altoaguirre y Duvale copy of the *requerimineto* inserts "y no vos compelerá a que os tornéis cristianos salvo si vosotros informados de la verdad os quisiereis convertir a la santa fe católica" ([Becoming Christians] will not be forced upon you. However, if you are informed of the truth, [then] you would want to convert to the Holy Catholic Faith). Altoaguirre y Duvale, *Gobernación espiritual*, 313.

Glossary

adelantado. Government: a person authorized by the Crown to settle a new territory and be its perpetual governor, with both military and civil authority. The office was assumed to be heritable.

alcaide. Government: a warden or commander of a fortress. When campaigning, an *alcaide* holds the rank of captain.

alcalde. Government: the title derives from the Arabic for a person who governs a locale; a judge-administrator. There were *alcaldes* at many levels of government, from the royal court to *aldeas*, or hamlets.

alcalde mayor. Government: a royally appointed official who had administrative and judicial jurisdiction over a community or group of communities and was subordinate to a governor. See also *corregidor*.

alcalde ordinario. Government: a judge who had primary (first instance) jurisdiction; a member of a *cabildo*.

alférez. Government: the person entrusted with a company's banner. The title derives from the Arabic for a "caballero."

alguacil. Government: a law enforcement officer, constable. The word comes from the Arabic for the person charged with arresting and bringing to justice those ordered to be apprehended by the king's court or his judges.

alguacil mayor. Government: chief law enforcement officer, a constable who could be a *regidor*.

armada. Nautical and military: an armed fleet of ships; sometimes also applied to a land-based armed force.

arroba. Weights and measures: as a liquid measurement, about 4.25 US gallons; as a dry weight, about 25 pounds. The word derives from the Arabic for "one-fourth" of a *quintal*.

audiencia. Government: the governing body of a *provincia*- or *reino*-sized jurisdiction in the Spanish Empire. In conjunction with a viceroy or president, the *audiencia* exercised both legislative and judicial authority. It was the highest regional appellate court and heard appeals from the courts of the *corregidores* as well as from municipal judges.

bachiller. Education: an academic title roughly equivalent to the modern university level of bachelor's degree, but held much more rarely than today.

barca. Watercraft: a small vessel for fishing, moving along seacoasts, crossing rivers, or taking merchandise and passengers from *navíos* to land.

barranca. Geography: a canyon or ravine; gorge.

caballero. Society: an *hidalgo* of proven nobility. The designation derives from a Roman term for those in the equestrian order who were granted special privileges and status.

cabildo. Government: the governing council of an urban area and its surroundings. In the largest *ciudades*, the *cabildo* was composed of 24 members, including *regidores* and *alcaldes*. A *cabildo* exercised administrative, legislative, and judicial authority and was responsible for granting *vecino* status and for distributing land to *vecinos*.

cacique. Government: an Arawak word meaning "headman," widely used in Spanish America. This was usually a native ruler with vassals or someone whom the Spaniards understood to have such status.

castellano, castellano de minas. Monetary unit: the most common form of gold coinage in Spain. In the Spanish colonies it came to be called a *peso de oro*, or "weight of gold," and was valued between 450 and 480 *maravedís*.

cédula. Government: a written order, often from the king or the royal court.

chancillería. Government: a tribunal in which appeals to royal justice were reviewed and adjudicated according to the laws. The name derives from the judges' practice of sitting behind screens, or "canceles."

ciudad. Geography: a status conferred on a settlement by the king, indicating its relatively large size and great importance and usually accompanied by the concession of a coat of arms, escutcheon, and honorific titles. Use of the word *ciudad* throughout the Coronado expedition documents is significant. In Spanish usage of the day, the term was applied only to communities of the highest political and social rank, ordinarily administrative and commercial centers; in Nueva España in 1540 the term was applied only to the Ciudad de México and Puebla de los Ángeles. Its use in relation to Cíbola is a continuing indication of the expectations Europeans held concerning the wealth, size, and sophistication of Tierra Nueva.

comunidad. A modern Spanish geopolitical designation: a semiautonomous region in many ways equivalent to a "state" in the United States or Mexico.

conde. Society: a title of nobility. A person with this title had lower status than a *duque*. The title was often conferred in peacetime.

conquistador. Society: a conqueror, especially of Mexico, Peru, or another area of the New World.

consejo. Government: a council. Among the documents of the Coronado expedition, *consejo* most often refers to the king's royal councils, such as the Consejo de Indias, but sometimes applies to municipal councils.

contador. Government: an accountant. The office of *contador* was one of the four standard royal offices established in each overseas colony, the other three being *veedor, factor,* and *tesorero* (treasurer).

corregidor. Government: a royally appointed official who administered an *encomienda* held directly by the Crown and governed the native community. See also *alcalde mayor*.

corregimiento. Government: an *encomienda* or other jurisdiction held directly by the Crown and also, on occasion, the office of a *corregidor*.

criado. Society: literally a servant, but more often a henchman or retainer. A *criado* was a full-time employee or dependent who might function in a variety of capacities, including tradesman, artisan, or apprentice. The term often referred to a poor or orphaned relative and was equivalent to and cognate with the archaic English usage of "creature," meaning a retainer.

de oficio. Judicial: a modifier applied to testimony or exhibits initiated at the request of the court in the course of a legal case, often for purposes of verifying information provided by private parties. It also applied to what today would be called prosecution testimony.

de parte. Judicial: a modifier applied to testimony or exhibits initiated at the request and on behalf of a private party to a legal case—for instance, testimony offered to support a party's claim or to refute that of another party or a charge leveled by the *fiscal*, or investigating judge.

ducado. Monetary unit: a silver coin valued between 375 and 385 *maravedís*.

duque. Society: a title of nobility. A person bearing this title was of the highest status after the royal family, often a commander who was elevated to the title for especially outstanding services during war.

encomendero. Government: a person holding and exercising an *encomienda*.

encomienda. Government and geography: a grant of the right to collect tribute, labor, or both from an indigenous community, usually granted by the king as reward for service. Limited to a specific native polity, the grant also entailed responsibility for providing defense and religious instruction to the community. See also *repartimiento*.

entrada. Society: an expedition penetrating new territory.

escribano. Government: a combination secretary, scribe, and notary. *Escribano* could be either a governmental or a private position and was the most abundant class of bureaucratic functionaries.

estado. Weights and measures: a length equal to approximately 1.7 meter, or 5.5 feet, and therefore equivalent to a *braza*, or the distance of outstretched arms. There were an *estado común* and a somewhat longer *estado real*.

estancia. Geography: a term applied to a native community that was subordinate to another community, or *cabecera*. The latter was usually larger and was the seat of political, economic, and ceremonial power of a district that often conformed in boundaries to a preconquest native polity. An *estancia* could also be a stock ranch.

estante. Government and society: a resident of a community without full political rights. See also *vecino*.

estufa. Housing: the word members of the Coronado expedition and later *entradas* applied to separate, sometimes subterranean ceremonial chambers found in the pueblos of New Mexico and Arizona, usually known today as kivas. The members of the expedition interpreted them as "sweating rooms." The heat of such chambers, sometimes crowded with ceremonial performers and superheated by smoky fires, inspired the Spaniards' application of the word *estufa*, or "oven."

factor. Government: a royal official charged with collecting tribute owed to the king; also an agent for the king who reported on the results of an expedition. This was one of the four standard royal offices, the others being *contador*, *veedor*, and *tesorero* (treasurer).

fiscal. Government: court official roughly equivalent to a prosecuting attorney.

galera. Watercraft: a type of oar-propelled, sail-aided *navío* used mainly for coastal and occasionally seagoing voyages.

hidalgo, hijodalgo. Society: a man of the lower nobility in Spain. The word derives directly from the Latin *a fide* and *algo*: a good, loyal, and noble man who keeps the faith and his word. In Roman times such a person was a *caballero* who had property worth at least 400,000 sesterces (a silver coin).

indios amigos. Society: native warriors and other persons serving as allies of the Spaniards. Such allies were often only recently subjugated themselves but were assumed to be nominally Christian.

interrogatorio. Government: written questionnaire for examining witnesses in a legal action.

justicia. Government: minister of justice; a judge or panel of judges.

justicia mayor. Government: chief judicial officer and deputy of an *alcalde mayor*.

legua común. Weights and measures: a league equal to 3.46 miles.

legua geográfica. Weights and measures: a sixteenth-century Spanish league equal to 3.95 miles. This was the common nautical chart league of the day.

legua legal. Weights and measures: Burgos league, equal to 2.63 miles.

licenciado. Education: a university graduate, roughly the equivalent to a modern master's level.

lugar. Geography: status conferred on a settlement by the king, indicating its small size. A *lugar* was a hamlet, smaller than a *villa*.

maestre de campo, maese de campo. Government: field commander; the second in command after the general.

manta. Clothing: a shawl-like article of indigenous clothing common during and before the Spanish colonial period.

maravedí. Monetary unit: an archaic basic unit of Spanish currency. In the sixteenth century it was not a physical coin but a term used in counting.

marqués. Society: a title of nobility with status inferior to that of a *duque* and superior to that of a *conde*.

mayordomo. Government: a foreman or custodian of public or private property.

mestizo. Society: in Latin America, a person of racially mixed ancestry, Native American and European.

navío, nao. Watercraft: an ocean-going, high-sided, square-rigged, three-masted sailing vessel of around 100 *toneladas* in capacity, manned by a crew of 20 or more.

oidor. Government: judge-legislator who is a member of an *audiencia*.

palmo. Weights and measures: a unit of length equal to approximately 0.07 meter, or 2.75 inches. The measurement derived from the concept that the width of four fingers made a palm, or *palmo*. There was also a *palmo mayor*, which equaled 8.25 inches.

peso. Monetary unit: a denomination of both gold and silver coinage; often the metal is not specified in documents. A silver *peso* (or "weight of silver") was valued at 275 *maravedís*. For the gold *peso*, see *castellano*.

peso común, peso de oro que corre. Monetary unit: an unminted, low-quality gold coin valued at 272 *maravedís*, approximately equal in value to the silver *peso*. Such coins were the most common ones in circulation in Nueva España in the sixteenth century.

peso de minas. Monetary unit: a high-quality gold coin with a standard value of 450 *maravedís*. See also *castellano*.

principal. Government: an indigenous leader.

probanza. Government: generically, an affidavit of testimony; specifically, often refers to a proof of a person's antecedents (*méritos*) and worthy deeds (*servicios*).

procurador. Judicial: a legal representative or agent.

provincia. Geography: a political division of a *reino* administered by a governor; if the same official commanded the provincial military, he was styled "captain general." When the term was applied in indigenous contexts, a similar hierarchy was assumed.

pueblo. Geography: a status conferred on a settlement and its hinterland by the king, indicating its intermediate size and importance. When applied to indigenous settlements, a similar hierarchical relation was assumed. See also *villa* and the General Introduction.

ranchería. Geography: a transitory settlement; a congregation of *ranchos* (temporary shelters), *chozas* (rude shelters), tents, or other shelters.

regidor. Government: an elected member of the *cabildo* of a municipality (*ciudad, pueblo,* or *villa*). Upon leaving office, the *regidor* often nominated his replacement, with the approval of the governor.

reino. Geography: a semiautonomous region subject to the Spanish monarchs. When applied to an indigenous political unit, an analogous authority was assumed to exist.

relación. Literature: an example of a literary genre consisting of narrative accounts of exotic places and peoples, usually written by a firsthand observer though often also incorporating journalistic elements.

repartimiento. Government and geography: literally a "distribution"; often, in the sixteenth century, a synonym for *encomienda*.

requerimiento. Government: a formal summons to submit to the authority of the king of Spain. A text specified by law was in use from 1513 until 1573, although increasingly infrequently as time passed. For an example of the full text, see Appendix 4.

residencia. Government: judicial review of the performance of a royal official held at the end of his term in office and sometimes conducted by his successor. It was so called because the outgoing official usually was present or in residence during the review.

sujeto. Geography: see *estancia*.

tomín. Monetary unit: one-eighth of a gold *peso*.

tomín de oro común, tomín de oro que corre. Monetary unit: one-eighth of a low-quality gold *peso*, valued at about 34 *maravedís*.

tomín de oro de minas. Monetary unit: one-eighth of a high-quality gold *peso*, valued at about 56 *maravedís*.

vara. Government: an emblematic staff of office; also a unit of length equal to approximately 0.84 meter, or 33 inches. Two *varas* equaled one *braza*.

vecino. Government and society: a person with full political rights in a municipality. Such rights were not automatic but were granted by the *cabildo* after the person paid a fee and pledged to establish and maintain a residence for a certain length of time. Residents without full political rights were *estantes*.

veedor. Government: an inspector with responsibility for judging conformance with the laws, especially with regard to the supply of provisions. This was one of the four standard royal officials, the others being *contador, factor,* and *tesorero* (treasurer).

villa. Geography: a status conferred on a settlement and its hinterland by the king, indicating its inferior size and importance. A *villa* was smaller than both a *ciudad* and a *pueblo*. Often in the Coronado expedition documents *villa* is used to distinguish a small Spanish community from an indigenous one of similar size and importance (a *pueblo*).

visita. Government: an extraordinary judicial review of the performance of officials.

visitador general. Government: a special investigator dispatched to make an inspection of the entirety of a *reino* or *provincia*. He was often sent to resolve some particular problem or complaint that had arisen.

Bibliography

Archival Material

AGI, Contratación, 199, N.23. "Bienes de difuntos, Bartolomé Sánchez, 1561."

AGI, Contratación, 490, N.1, R.2. "Bienes de Pedro de Benavides, que murió en Antequera del valle de Oaxaca; albacea, su hermano Juan de Benavides, 1596."

AGI, Contratación, 707, N.1. "Información hecha a pedimento de Juan Bautista de San Vitores sobre la venta de un negro, June 14, 1537."

AGI, Contratación, 4675, L.5. "Casa de Contratación, account book for 1530–1537."

AGI, Contratación, 5575, N.24. "Bienes de difuntos, Juan Jiménez, 1550 copy of August 13, 1545 original."

AGI, Guadalajara, 5, R.1, N.5. "Letter from Vázquez de Coronado to the king, Compostela, December 15, 1538."

AGI, Guadalajara, 5, R.1, N.6. "Letter of Vázquez de Coronado to the king, Compostela, July 15, 1539."

AGI, Guadalajara, 5, R.1, N.7. "Muster Roll of the Expedition, Compostela, February 22, 1540."

AGI, Guadalajara, 30, N.1. "Letter from the *cabildo* of Compostela to the king, Compostela, February 19, 1533."

AGI, Guadalajara, 46, N.8 "Información de oficio y parte, cabildo de San Miguel de Culiacán, 1566."

AGI, Indiferente, 127, N.51\1. "Méritos, Alonso Pérez de Bocanegra, September 28, 1679."

AGI, Indiferente, 423, Libro 18, fol. 65r. "Permission to Cristóbal de Escobar to transport one black slave to the Indies, December 30, 1537."

AGI, Indiferente, 1093, R.2, N.16. "Letter, Tello de Sandoval to the king, San Lucar de Barrameda, November 3, 1543."

AGI, Justicia, 21. "Relación de los escribanos del Cabildo de México, June 10, 1546."

AGI, Justicia, 124, N.2. "Domingo Martín vecino de México con Gómez Nieto vecino de la villa de Santistevan sobre el derecho a el pueblo de Yagualican, 1536."

AGI, Justicia, 127, N.2. "Investigation of treatment of Indians at Sultepec, February and March 1537."

AGI, Justicia, 144, N.1. "Tristán de Arellano e Isabel de Rojas, vecinos de la ciudad de Antequera de Oaxaca, contra Gabriel Bosque, sobre . . . el pueblo de Tlacotepec, 1546–1550."

AGI, Justicia, 198, N.3. "Jorge Carrillo vs. el fiscal sobre pueblos de indios, 1543."

AGI, Justicia, 213, N.4. "Lawsuit regarding Teocaluyacan and Cayuca, 1551."

AGI, Justicia, 258, Pieza 1. "Testimony of Antonio de Turcios." In "Visita hecha al virrey . . . por Francisco Tello de Sandoval, November 3, 1545."

AGI, Justicia, 259, Pieza 2. "Visita a don Antonio de Mendoza, 1543."

AGI, Justicia, 259, Pieza 3. "Visita a don Antonio de Mendoza, 1546."

AGI, Justicia, 259, Pieza 4. "Certification of suit concerning Tlapa, Mexico City, 1544."

AGI, Justicia, 260, Pieza 1. "Cargos y descargos, visita contra Tejada, 1546."

AGI, Justicia, 260, Pieza 4. "Visita contra Benavente, 1546, 1547."

AGI, Justicia, 262, N.1. "Visita hecha por Francisco Tello de Sandoval, 1545–1547."

AGI, Justicia, 263, Pieza 1. "Probanza hecha en nombre de don Antonio de Mendoza, Zacatula, 1546–1547."

AGI, Justicia, 263, Pieza 2. "Probanza hecha en nombre de don Antonio de Mendoza, Colima, 1547."

AGI, Justicia, 263, Pieza 3. "Probanza hecha en nombre de don Antonio de Mendoza, Michoacán, 1546."

AGI, Justicia, 265, Pieza 2. "Probanza hecha en nombre de don Antonio de Mendoza, Puebla de los Ángeles, 1546–1547."

AGI, Justicia, 267, N.3. "Proceso de Francisco Vázquez, Mexico City, March 1547."

AGI, Justicia, 268, N.1. "Visita hecha a Gonzalo Cerezo, alguacil mayor de la audiencia, December 18, 1546."

AGI, Justicia, 268, N.2, Pieza 2. "Gabriel de Castellanos vs. Juan de Sámano, alguacil major de México, 1544."

AGI, Justicia, 268, N.2, Pieza 3. "Visita hecha a Diego de Puelles, teniente de alguacil major de México, 1544."

AGI, Justicia, 303. "Residencias, Guadalajara, 1556–1560."

AGI, Justicia, 336, N.1. "Probança de Francisco Vázquez hecha en Compostela, March and April, 1552."

AGI, Justicia, 336, N.1. "Francisco Vázquez Coronado, vecino y regidor de la Ciudad de México con el fiscal de su magestad sobre ciertos yndios, Guadalajara, 1553."

AGI, Justicia, 336, N.1. "Vázquez de Coronado's Petition for Recovery of Encomiendas, 1553."

AGI, Justicia, 336, N.1, R.3. "Testimony concerning certain pueblos, Compostela, spring 1552."

AGI, Justicia, 336, N.2. "Suit concerning distribution of Indians to Diego de Colio, Guadalajara, 1565; el fiscal con Diego de Colio sobre repartimiento de yndios, 1565."

AGI, Justicia, 339, N.1, R.1. "Residencia que el licenciado Lorenzo de Tejada, oidor de la Audiencia Real de Nueva España, tomo a Francisco Vázquez de Coronado, Guadalajara, December 1544 and January 1545."

AGI, Justicia, 339, N.1, R.2. "Residencia of Francisco Vázquez de Coronado, August 1544."

AGI, Justicia, 339, N.1, R.3. "Regarding the pueblo of Tepic, September 1544."

AGI, Justicia, 1021, N.2, Pieza 1. "Acusación e información contra García Ramírez de Cárdenas, Madrid, 1546–1547."

AGI, Justicia, 1021, N.2, Pieza 2. "Report extracted from the affidavit prepared for don García Ramírez de Cárdenas, n.d."

AGI, Justicia, 1021, N.2, Pieza 5. "Probanza fecha a pedimiento de don García López de Cárdenas, Guadalajara, May 1546, and México, 1547–1548."

AGI, Justicia, 1021, N.2, Pieza 6. "Probanza del fiscal Villalobos, México, January 10, 1547."

AGI, Justicia, 1029, N.7, R.1. "Méritos y servicios de Alonso de Zorita, 1560s."

AGI, México, 68, R.13, N.38. "Carta de Lorenzo de Tejada a Marqués de Mondejar, presidente del Consejo de Indias, April 24, 1547."

AGI, México, 73, R.2, N.24. "Méritos y servicios, Juan de Cuevas y Guevara, May 17, 1610."

AGI, México, 97. "Letter, Francisco Morales to the king, Mexico City, May 19, 1563."

AGI, México, 97, R.1. "Méritos y servicios de Tristán de Luna y Arellano, 1559."

AGI, México, 98, N.33. "Informaciones contra Juan Troyano, 1569."

AGI, México, 98, N.33e. "Letter from Troyano to the viceroy, 1569."

AGI, México, 98, N.33k. "Letter from Troyano to the king, [post-1568]."

AGI, México, 124, R.5. "Pedimiento de Francisco Pacheco de Córdova y Bocanegra, México, 1605."

AGI, México, 168. "Letter from Juan Troyano to the king, December 20, 1568."

AGI, México, 203, N.13. "Report concerning Lope de Samaniego, Mexico City, 1531."

AGI, México, 204, N.14. "Méritos y servicios de Cristóbal de Escobar, 1543."

AGI, México, 204, N.33\2. "Méritos y servicios de Pedro de Benavides, February 14, 1551, México."

AGI, México 204, N.36. "Méritos y servicios, Juan Gallego, 1551, 1554, 1556."

AGI, México, 205, N.12. "Información, Luis de Quesada, México, July 29, 1555."

AGI, México, 206, N.12. "Méritos y servicios de Juan de Troyano, 1560."

AGI, México, 206, N.35. "Investigation of Cristóbal de Escobar, February 7, 1561–1562."

AGI, México, 206, N.51. "Información de Francisco Muñoz, 1561."

AGI, México, 207, N.39. "Méritos y servicios, Melchor Pérez, 1563."

AGI, México, 216, N.28. "Informaciones, Francisco Martínez de la Marcha, primer poblador de Nueva España, 1582."

AGI, México, 228, N.23\1. "Informaciones for Diego Gutiérrez de Bocanegra, 1608."

AGI, México, 1064, L.1\1. "Informes de los conquistadores y pobladores de México y otros lugares en Nueva España, en el año 1644 [1547]." Compiled by Gil González Dávila.

AGI, México, 1088, L.1. "Royal *cédula*, Madrid, November 9, 1529."

AGI, México, 1088, L.3. "Royal *cédula*, Valladolid, November 22, 1538."

AGI, Patronato, 20, N.5, R.8. "Juan de Jaramillo's Narrative, 1560s."

AGI, Patronato, 20, N.5, R.8. "Relación del Suceso (Anonymous Narrative), 1540."

AGI, Patronato, 20, N.5, R.8. "Traslado de las Nuevas (Anonymous Narrative), 1540."

AGI, Patronato, 20, N.5, R10. "The Viceroy's Instructions to fray Marcos de Niza, November 1538," and "Narrative Account by fray Marcos de Niza, August 26, 1539."

AGI, Patronato, 21, N.2, R.3. "Ynfformacion que ynvia el muy illustre senor visorrey de la nueva espana para ante su magestad sobre la gente que va a servir a su magestad a la tierra nueva . . ., February 21–27, 1540."

AGI, Patronato, 21, N.2, R.4. "Proceso del Marqués del Valle y Nuño de Guzmán y los adelantados Soto y Alvarado, sobre el descubrimiento de la tierra nueva, 1540–1541." Also in *Colección de documentos inéditos relativos al descubrimiento, conquista y organización de las antiguas posesiones españoles de América y Oceania*, series 1, 42 vols., edited by Joaquín F. Pacheco, Francisco de Cárdenas, and Luis Torres de Mendoza, 300–408. Madrid: José María Pérez, 1864–84.

AGI, Patronato, 21, N.2, R.4\2. "Memorial de Hernán Cortés a Carlos V acerca de los Agravios que le hizo el virrey de la NS, June 25, 1540."

AGI, Patronato, 21, N.3, R.2. "Formation of a Partnership between Antonio de Mendoza and Pedro de Alvarado, Tiripitío, November 29, 1540."

AGI, Patronato, 22, R.13\9. "Traslado de los ensayos que se *ho*bieron de las minas de mohoque."

AGI, Patronato, 26, R.23. "Hernando de Alvarado's and fray Juan de Padilla's Narrative, 1540."

AGI, Patronato, 54, N.8, R.6. "Ynformacion de los servicios de Juan Jaramillo conquistador de Nueva Espana con Hernan Cortés, México, 1532."

AGI, Patronato, 56, N.3, R.2. "Méritos y servicios de Pedro Jerónimo, November 21, 1542."

AGI, Patronato, 56, N.3, R.4. "Probanza de los buenos servicios y fidelidad con que sirvio en la conquista de Nueva Espana la famosa dona Marina, india, Mexico, 1542."

AGI, Patronato, 57, N.2, R.1. "Méritos y servicios de Antonio de Mendoza, March 1545."

AGI, Patronato, 60, N.5, R.4. "Probanza de los méritos y servicios de Juan de Zaldívar, [1566]."

AGI, Patronato, 61, N.2, R.7\1. "Méritos y servicios de Rui González, May 25, 1558."

AGI, Patronato, 61, N.2, R.9. "Méritos y servicios de Alonso Alvarez de Espinosa, Compostela, 1551."

AGI, Patronato, 63, R.5. "Méritos y servicios de Juan de Paladinas [*sic*], June 6, 1560."

AGI, Patronato, 63, R.23\1. "Méritos y servicios, Cristóbal Méndez, November 7, 1559."

AGI, Patronato, 64, R.1. "Méritos y servicios, Juan de Aguilar, Santiago de Guatemala, December 7, 1564."

AGI, Patronato, 68, N.2, R.4\1. "Méritos y servicios de Juan de Céspedes, 1568."

AGI, Patronato, 74, N.1, R.11\1. "Méritos y servicios, Tristán de Arellano, Nueva España, 1575."

AGI, Patronato, 74, N.2, R.2. "Méritos y servicios, Alonso Rodríguez Para y de su hijo Juan que fueron descubridores y conquistadores de la provincia de Cíbola, November 9, 1575."

AGI, Patronato, 76, N.1, R.5. "Méritos y servicios by Francisco de Zaldívar, March 29, 1580."

AGI, Patronato, 78A, N.l, R.6. "Méritos y servicios de Jorge Báez, Mexico City, 1585."

AGI, Patronato, 79, N.1, R.2. "Méritos y servicios, Diego y Hernando (C)Santillana, conquistadores de Nueva España, 1586."

AGI, Patronato, 79, N.3, R.2. "Méritos y servicios de Francisco de Santillana, Mérida, 1594."

AGI, Patronato, 87, N.1, R.5. "Méritos y servicios de García Rodríguez y biznieto, 1617."

AGI, Patronato, 87, N.2, R.2. "Méritos y servicios, Diego Madrid Avendaño, México, Cíbola, 1618."

AGI, Patronato, 110, R.7\1. "Méritos y servicios de Gaspar de Saldaña, Nueva España y Perú, 1563."

AGI, Patronato, 112, R.2\1. "Méritos y servicios de Rodrigo de Paz Maldonado, Santa Marta, 1564."

AGI, Patronato, 112, R.2\2. "Méritos y servicios, Rodrigo de Paz Maldonado, Quito, 1564."

AGI, Patronato, 117, R.5. "Méritos y servicios de Rodrigo de Paz Maldonado, 1571."

AGI, Patronato, 121, R.8. "Méritos y servicios de Miguel de Entrambasaguas, December 11, 1577."

AGI, Patronato, 127, N.1, R.10. "Méritos y servicios de Alonso de Saavedra, 1583."

AGI, Patronato, 184, R.27. "Antonio de Mendoza, letter to the king, Mexico City, December 10, 1537."

AGI, Patronato, 184, R.31. "Antonio de Mendoza, letter to the king, Jacona, April 17, 1540."

AGI, Patronato 184, R.34. "Vázquez de Coronado's letter to the king, Tiguex, October 20, 1541."

AGI, Patronato, 205, R.1\2. "Consejo Indias: sumaria contra culpados: rebelión Nueva España, 1566–67."

AGI, Patronato 216, N.2. "Affidavit of testimony on behalf of Francisco Vázquez de Coronado, Culiacán, 1545, in a legal action concerning Nuño de Cháves, Mexico City, 1566."

AGI, Patronato, 277, N.4, R.36. "Appointment of López de Cárdenas, Mexico City, April 8, 1538."

AGI, Patronato, 281, N.1, R.34. "Carta ejecutoría, Ramírez de Cárdenas, September 1551."

AGI, Patronato, 291, R.37. "Emplazamiento a don Rodrigo Maldonado, vecino de México, y doña Isabel de Aux, su mujer, en pleito con doña Isabel de Barrios, February 21, 1566."

AGN, Civiles, volume 1276 (n.d.). "Defensa del Tesorero Alonso de Estrada."

AGN, Hospital de Jesús, 123, Expediente 31. "Cédula of July 10, 1540." In *Documentos Cortesianos*, vol. 4, edited by José Luis Martínez, 216–19. México, DF: Universidad Nacional Autónoma de México y Fondo de Cultura Económica, 1990.

AGnot, 1, Diego de Isla, IV. "Distribution of inheritance from Alonso Sánchez, Mexico City, 1553."

AGS, Camara de Castilla, 121–46. "Petition of Juan Vázquez de Coronado, Granada, December 5, 1516."

AHN, Diversos-Colecciones, 24, N.45. "Memorial de licenciado Zorita sobre la Florida y Nuevo Méjico, 1560–1561."

AHN, Diversos-Colecciones, 24, N.51. "Fray Cyndos to the king, July 20, 1561."

AHN, Órdenes Militares, 304, Expillo. 13408. "Order of San Juan to Juan Vázquez de Coronado." n.p., n.d.

Archeological Records Management System (ARMS). "Site files for LA 187, Kuaua Pueblo; LA 288, Corrales Pueblo; LA 289, Calabacillas Pueblo; LA 290, Piedras Marcadas Pueblo; LA 294, Sandia Pueblo; LA 326, Santiago Pueblo; LA 421, Alameda Pueblo; LA 677, Watche Pueblo; LA 716; LA 717, Maigua Pueblo; and LA 22765, Chamisal Pueblo." Unpublished files. Laboratory of Anthropology, Museum of New Mexico, Santa Fe.

Benavente Motolinía, fray Toribio de. "Narrative, Relación Postrera de Cíbola, 1540s." JGI 31 XVI C, fols. 123v–124v. Austin: University of Texas, Nettie Lee Benson Latin American Collection.

Biblioteca del Escorial. Códice &-II-7, Doc no. LXVI. "The Viceroy's Instructions to Hernando Alarcón, May 31, 1541, Draft."

———. Códice &-II-7, Doc no. LXVII. "The Viceroy's Instructions to Hernando Alarcón, May 31, 1541."

———. Códice &-II-7. Doc. no. LXXVIII. "Pobladores sin yndios [late 1540s]."

———. Códice &-II-7, Doc. no. LXXIX. "Memoria de las personas, conquistadores y pobladores de la nueva galizia (sin fecha)."

———. Códice &-II-7, Doc. no. LXXX, "Memoria de los vecinos de culiacán para lo del repartimiento (no date)."

Castañeda de Nácera, Pedro de. "Relación de la jornada de Cíbola compuesta por Pedro de Castañeda de Nácera donde se trata de todos aquellos poblados y ritos, y costumbres la qual fue el año de 1540 [1563]." Case 12, Rich Collection 63, Nuevo Mexico. Sevilla, 1596. 157 11, quarto bound. New York Public Library, Rare Books and Manuscripts Division.

Codex Aubin. "Chronicle of Mexican History to 1576, continued to 1607." Add MSS 31219, London, Library of the British Museum.

Fernández de Oviedo y Valdés, Gonzalo. *Historia general y natural de las Indias,* Segunda Parte, Libro XXXIII, Capítulo LII, 1547, fols. 457v–459v. Academia Real de la Historia, Madrid, Colección Salazar y Castro, 9/555 (H-32).

———. *Historia general y natural de las Indias.* Tercera Parte, Libro XL, Capítulos I and II, 1547, fols. 22r–24r. Biblioteca Real, Madrid, II/3042.

Flores de la Torre, Diego. "Proof of status of Diego Flores de la Torre, Archdeacon of the Church of Guadalajara, 1671." M-M 1714. Bancroft Library, University of California, Berkeley.

Mendoza, Antonio de. "Instructions to Alarcón." Gilcrease Institute of American History and Art, HD 131-4.

Rey, Agapito, transcriber. "La acusación contra don García López de Cárdenas por ciertas crueldades, AGI, Justicia, 1021, Pieza 1." Bolton Papers, no. 401. Bancroft Library, University of California, Berkeley.

Tello, fray Antonio. "Decree of the king, appointing Vázquez de Coronado governor of Nueva Galicia." In "Libro Segundo de la Cronica Miscelanea y conquista Espiritual y temporal de la sancta Provinica de Xalisco en el nuevo Reyno de la Galiçia y nueva Vizcaya y descubrimiento del nuevo Mexico," fols. 406r–407v. John Carter Brown Library, Brown University, Providence, Rhode Island.

Published Material

"The Account by a Gentleman from Elvas." Translated and edited by James Alexander Robertson. In *The De Soto Chronicles: The Expedition of Hernando de Soto to North America in 1539–1543,* vol.

1, edited by Lawrence A. Clayton, Vernon James Knight, Jr., and Edward C. Moore, 33–219. Tuscaloosa: University of Alabama Press, 1993.

Actas de Cabildo. Compiled by Ignacio Bejarano. 64 vols. México, DF: Aguilar e Hijos, 1889–.

Adorno, Rolena, and Patrick Charles Pautz. *Álvar Núñez Cabeza de Vaca: His Account, His Life, and the Expedition of Pánfilo de Narváez.* 3 vols. Lincoln: University of Nebraska Press, 1999.

Ahern, Maureen. "Mapping, Measuring, and Naming Cultural Spaces in Castañeda's *Relación de la Jornada de Cíbola.*" In *The Coronado Expedition from the Distance of 460 Years,* edited by Richard Flint and Shirley Cushing Flint, 265–89. Albuquerque: University of New Mexico Press, 2003.

———. "La *Relación de la Jornada de Cíbola:* Los Espacios orales y culturales." In *Conquista y contraconquista: La Escritura del Nuevo Mundo,* 187–99. México, DF: Colegio de México and Brown University, 1994.

Aiton, Arthur Scott. *Antonio de Mendoza: First Viceroy of New Spain.* Durham, NC: Duke University Press, 1927.

———. "Coronado's First Report on the Government of New Galicia." *Hispanic American Historical Review* 19, no. 3 (1939):306–13.

———. "Documents: Coronado's Commission as Captain-General." *Hispanic American Historical Review* 20, no. 1 (1940):83–87.

———. "Muster Roll." *American Historical Review* 64, no. 3 (1939):556–70.

———. "Report on the Residencia of the Coronado Government in New Galicia." *Panhandle-Plains Historical Review* 13 (1940):12–20.

———. "The Secret Visita against Viceroy Mendoza." In *New Spain and the Anglo-American West: Historical Contributions Presented to Herbert Eugene Bolton,* vol. 1, 1–22. Los Angeles: privately printed, 1932.

Aiton, Arthur S., and Agapito Rey. "Coronado's Testimony in the Viceroy Mendoza *Residencia.*" *New Mexico Historical Review* 12 (July 1937):288–329.

Alcover, Antoni Maria, et. al. *Diccionari Català-Valencià-Balear.* 10 vols. Palma de Mallorca: Editorial Moll, 1956–68.

Alonso, Martín. *Enciclopedia del idioma.* 3 vols. Madrid: Aguilar, 1958.

Alpañes, J. L. Justo. "El Comportamiento de la Giralda durante los movimientos sísmicos de Sevilla." In *VIII Centenario de la Giralda, 1198–1998,* edited by Teodor Falcón Márquez, 159–68. Sevilla: Caja Sur Publicaciones, 1998.

Altman, Ida. "Spanish Society in Mexico City after the Conquest." *Hispanic American Historical Review* 71, no. 3(1991):413–45.

Altoaguirre y Duvale, Ángel de, ed. "Título IX." In *Governación espiritual y temporal de las Indias: Códice publicado en virtud de acuerdo de la Real Academia de la Historia,* vol. 20, *Colección de Documentos Inéditos de Ultramar.* 2nd series. Madrid: n.p., 1927.

Álvarez, Victor M. *Diccionario de conquistadores.* México, DF: Instituto Nacional de Antropología y Historia, 1975.

Álvarez de Williams, Anita. "Cocopa." In *Handbook of North American Indians,* vol. 10, *Southwest,* edited by Alfonso Ortiz, 99–112. Washington, DC: Smithsonian Institution Press, 1983.

———. *The Cocopah People.* Phoenix, AZ: Indian Tribal Series, 1974.

Álvarez Márquez, María del Carmen, ed. "Manuscrito 9.355 de la Biblioteca Nacional de Madrid." In *Paisajes de la tierra prometida: El Viaje a Jerusalén de don Fadrique Enríquez de Ribera,* edited by Pedro García Martín et al., 171–347. Madrid: Miraguano Ediciones, 2001.

Anderson, Clinton P. "Foreword." In *The Entrada of Coronado: A Spectacular Historic Drama,* by Thomas Wood Stevens. Albuquerque: Coronado Cuarto Centennial Commission, 1940.

Anderson, Ruth Mathilda. *Hispanic Costume, 1480–1530.* New York: Hispanic Society of America, 1979.

Anonymous. "The Coronado Entrada Will Be Presented." In *The Coronado Magazine: The Official Program of the Coronado Cuarto Centennial in New Mexico,* n.p. Albuquerque: Coronado Cuarto Centennial Commission, 1940.

———. "Cuarta relación anónima de la jornada de Nuño de Guzmán." In *Colección de documentos para la historia de México.* 2nd facsimile ed. Edited by Joaquín García Icazbalceta. México, DF: Editorial Porrúa, 1980.

———. "Publications of the Coronado Cuarto Centennial Commission." In *The Entrada of Coronado: A Spectacular Historic Drama,* by Thomas Wood Stevens. Albuquerque: Coronado Cuarto Centennial Commission, 1940.

Anyon, Roger. "The Late Prehistoric and Early Historic Periods in the Zuni-Cíbola Area, 1400–1680." In *Current Research on the Late Prehistory and Early History of New Mexico,* edited by Bradley J. Vierra, 75–83. Albuquerque: New Mexico Archaeological Council, 1992.

Argote de Molina, Gonzalo. *Nobleza de Andalucía.* Sevilla: Fernando Díaz, 1588.

Arregui Zamorano, Pilar. "Quejas sobre Incumplimiento de Oficio." In *La Audiencia de México según los visitadores (siglos XVI y XVII).* México, DF: Universidad Nacional Autónoma de México, 1981.

Avellaneda, José Ignacio. *The Conquerors of the New Kingdom of Granada.* Albuquerque: University of New Mexico Press, 1995.

Bakewell, Peter. *A History of Latin America.* Oxford: Blackwell, 1997.

———. *Silver Mining and Society in Colonial Mexico: Zacatecas, 1546–1700.* Cambridge: Cambridge University Press, 1971.

Baldwin, Percy M., trans. and ed. *Discovery of the Seven Cities of Cíbola by the Father Fray Marcos de Niza.* Historical Society of New Mexico, Publications in History, vol. 1. Albuquerque: El Palacio Press, 1926.

Bandelier, Adolph F. "Fray Marcos of Nizza." *Contributions to the History of the Southwestern Portion of the United States,* Part 4. Papers of the Archaeological Institute of America, American Series 5. Cambridge, MA, 1890. Reprint, New York: AMS Press, 1976.

Barber, Russell J., and Frances F. Berdan. *The Emperor's Mirror: Understanding Cultures through Primary Sources.* Tucson: University of Arizona Press, 1998.

Barlow, Robert H. *Tlatelolco, fuentes e historia: Obras de Robert H. Barlow,* vol. 2. México, DF: Instituto Nacional de Antropología e Historia, 1989.

Barlow, Robert H., and George T. Smisor, eds. and trans. "Memorial of the Indians concerning Their Services, c. 1563." In *Nombre de Dios, Durango: Two Documents in Náhuatl concerning Its Foundation.* Sacramento: House of Tlaloc, 1943.

Barnes, Thomas G., Thomas H. Naylor, and Charles W. Polzer. *Northern New Spain: A Research Guide.* Tucson: University of Arizona Press, 1981.

Barrett, Elinore M. *Conquest and Catastrophe: Changing Rio Grande Pueblo Settlement Patterns in the Sixteenth and Seventeenth Centuries.* Albuquerque: University of New Mexico Press, 2002.

———. *The Geography of the Rio Grande Pueblos Revealed by Spanish*

Explorers. Research Paper Series no. 30. Albuquerque: Latin American Institute, University of New Mexico, 1997.

Bartlett, Katharine. "How don Pedro de Tovar Discovered the Hopi and don Garcia Lopez de Cardenas Saw the Grand Canyon, with Notes upon Their Probable Route." *Plateau* 12 (Jan. 1940):37–45.

Bartlett, Katharine, and Harold S. Colton. "A Note on the Marcos de Niza Inscription near Phoenix, Arizona." *Plateau* 12 (April 1940):53–59.

Battaglia, Salvatorre. *Grande dizionario della lingua italiana*. 21 vols. Torino: Unione Tipografico-Editrice Torinese, 1961–2002.

Bee, Robert L. "Quechan." In *Handbook of North American Indians*, vol. 10, *Southwest*, edited by Alfonso Ortiz, 86–98. Washington, DC: Smithsonian Institution Press, 1983.

Beltran, Vicenç. "Los Manuscritos del *Viaje a Jerusalén*." In *Paisajes de la tierra prometida: El Viaje a Jerusalén de don Fadrique Enríquez de Ribera*, edited by Pedro García Martín, et al., 113–68. Madrid: Miraguano Ediciones, 2001.

Benavente Motolinía, fray Toribio de. *Memoriales*. Edited by Nancy Joe Dyer. México, DF: Colegio de México, 1996.

———. *Memoriales: Libro de las cosas de la Nueva España de los naturales de ella*. Edited by Edmundo O'Gorman. México, DF: UNAM, Instituto de Investigaciones Históricas, 1971.

———. *Memoriales de Fray Toribio de Motolinía: Manuscrito de la colección del señor don Joaquín García Icazbalceta*. Edited by Luis García Pimentel. México, DF: Casa del Editor, 1903.

Berdan, Frances F., and Patricia Rieff Anawalt, eds. *The Essential Codex Mendoza*. Berkeley: University of California Press, 1997.

Bermúdez Plata, Cristóbal. *Catálogo de pasajeros a Indias durante los siglos XVI, XVII, y XVIII*. 3 vols. Sevilla: Editorial de la Gavidia, 1940, 1942.

Bernal, Ignacio. *The Mexican National Museum of Anthropology*. Rev. ed. México, DF: Ediciones Lara, 1970.

Blakeslee, Donald J. "Which Barrancas? Narrowing the Possibilities." In *The Coronado Expedition to Tierra Nueva: The 1540–1542 Route Across the Southwest*, edited by Richard Flint and Shirley Cushing Flint, 302–19. Niwot, CO: University Press of Colorado, 1997.

Blakeslee, Donald J., and Jay C. Blaine. "The Jimmy Owens Site: New Perspectives on the Coronado Expedition." In *The Coronado Expedition from the Distance of 460 Years*, edited by Richard Flint and Shirley Cushing Flint, 203–18. Albuquerque: University of New Mexico Press, 2003.

Blakeslee, Donald J., Douglas K. Boyd, Richard Flint, Judith Habicht-Mauche, Nancy P. Hickerson, Jack T. Hughes, and Carroll L. Riley. "Bison Hunters of the Llano in 1541: A Panel Discussion." In *The Coronado Expedition from the Distance of 460 Years*, edited by Richard Flint and Shirley Cushing Flint, 164–86. Albuquerque: University of New Mexico Press, 2003.

Blakeslee, Donald J., Richard Flint, and Jack T. Hughes. "Una Barranca Grande: Recent Archeological Evidence and a Discussion of Its Place in the Coronado Route." In *The Coronado Expedition to Tierra Nueva: The 1540–1542 Route Across the Southwest*, edited by Richard Flint and Shirley Cushing Flint, 370–83. Niwot, CO: University Press of Colorado, 1997.

Blanco-González, Bernardo. "Introducción, biográfica y crítica." In *Guerra de Granada*, Diego Hurtado de Mendoza, 7–69. Madrid: Editorial Castalia, 1970.

Bloom, Lansing B. "Was Fray Marcos a Liar?" *New Mexico Historical Review* 16 (April 1941):244–46.

Bolton, Herbert E. *Coronado on the Turquoise Trail: Knight of Pueblos and Plains*. Albuquerque: University of New Mexico Press, 1949.

Bowen, Thomas. "Seri." In *Handbook of North American Indians*, vol. 10, *Southwest*, edited by Alfonso Ortiz, 230–49. Washington, DC: Smithsonian Institution Press, 1983.

———. *Unknown Island: Seri Indians, Europeans, and San Esteban Island in the Gulf of California*. Albuquerque: University of New Mexico Press, 2000.

Boyd-Bowman, Peter. *Indice geobiográfico de cuarenta mil pobladores españoles de América en el siglo XVI*. 2 vols. Bogotá, Columbia: Instituto Caro y Cuervo, 1964, and México, DF: Editorial Jus, 1968.

———. *Lexico hispanoamericano del siglo XVI*. London: Tamesis Books, 1971.

Brand, Donald D. "Erroneous Location of Two Sixteenth-Century Spanish Settlements in Western Nueva España." In *Across the Chichimec Sea: Papers in Honor of J. Charles Kelley*, edited by Carroll L. Riley and Basil C. Hedrick, 193–201. Carbondale: Southern Illinois University Press, 1978.

Brew, John O. "Hopi Prehistory and History to 1850." In *Handbook of North American Indians*, vol. 9, *Southwest*, edited by Alfonso Ortiz, 514–23. Washington, DC: Smithsonian Institution Press, 1979.

Brody, J. J. "The Florescence of Painting: A.D. 1300–1700." In *Anasazi and Pueblo Painting*, J. J. Brody, 81–113. Albuquerque: University of New Mexico Press, 1991.

Brooks, James F. *Captives and Cousins: Slavery, Kinship, and Community in the Southwest Borderlands*. Chapel Hill: University of North Carolina Press, 2002.

Brown, David E., and Carlos A. López González. *Borderland Jaguars: Tigres de la Frontera*. Salt Lake City: University of Utah Press, 2001.

Brownrigg, Edwin Blake. "Introduction." In *Colonial Latin American Manuscripts and Transcripts in the Obadiah Rich Collection: An Inventory and Index*, edited by Edwin Blake Brownrigg, vii–xx. New York: New York Public Library and Readex Books, 1978.

Brownrigg, Edwin Blake, ed. *Colonial Latin American Manuscripts and Transcripts in the Obadiah Rich Collection: An Inventory and Index*. New York: New York Public Library and Readex Books, 1978.

Cabrillo National Memorial Foundation. *An Account of the Voyage of Juan Rodríguez Cabrillo*. San Diego, CA: Cabrillo National Memorial Foundation, 1999.

Calvo, Thomas, Eustaquio Celestino, Magdalena Gómez, Jean Meyer, and Ricardo Xochitemol. *Xalisco: La Voz de un pueblo en el siglo XVI*. México, DF: Centro de Investigaciones y Estudios Superiores en Antropología Social and Centro de Estudios Mexicanos y Centroamericanos, 1993.

Cannon, Ray. *The Sea of Cortez*. Menlo Park, CA: Lane Magazine and Book Co., 1966.

Carlos V. "Carta de Carlos V a Hernán Cortés, Valladolid, October 1522." In *Documentos Cortesianos*, vol. 1, edited by José Luis Martínez, 254–56. México, DF: Universidad Nacional Autónoma de México y Fondo de Cultura Económica, 1990.

Castañeda de Nájera, Pedro de. *The Journey of Coronado, 1540–1542*. Translated and edited by George Parker Winship. Introduction by Donald C. Cutter. Golden, CO: Fulcrum Publishers, c. 1990.

————. *Narrative of the Coronado Expedition.* Edited by John Miller Morris. Chicago: R. R. Donnelley, 2002.

Castañeda, Pedro de, et al. *The Journey of Coronado.* Translated and edited by George Parker Winship. San Francisco: Grabhorn Press, 1933. Reprint, New York: Dover, 1990.

Castetter, Edward F., and Willis H. Bell. "The Aboriginal Utilization of the Tall Cacti in the American Southwest." *University of New Mexico Bulletin, Biological Series* 5, no. 1 (1937):27–35.

————. *Yuman Indian Agriculture.* Albuquerque: University of New Mexico Press, 1951.

Catalog. New York: Christie's, 1995.

Cervantes, Fernando. *The Devil in the New World: The Impact of Diabolism in New Spain.* New Haven, CT: Yale University Press, 1994.

Chamberlain, Robert S. *The Conquest and Pacification of Yucatán, 1517–1550.* Carnegie Institution of Washington, Publication 582. Washington, DC: Carnegie Institution of Washington, 1948.

Chardon, Roland. "The Linear League in North America." *Annals of the Association of American Geographers* 70, no. 2 (1980):129–53.

Chaves, Alonso de. *Quatri partitu en cosmografía práctica, y por otro nombre Espejo de navegantes.* Edited by Paulino Castañeda Delgado, Mariano Cuesta Domingo, and Pilar Hernández Aparicio. Madrid: Instituto de Historia y Cultura Naval, 1983.

Chávez, Fray Angélico. *Coronado's Friars.* Washington, DC: Academy of American Franciscan History, 1968.

Chávez, Fray Angélico, trans. and ed. *The Oroz Codex.* Washington, DC: Academy of American Franciscan History, 1972.

Chipman, Donald E. "In Search of Cabeza de Vaca's Route across Texas: An Historiographical Survey." *Southwestern Historical Quaterly* 91, no. 2 (1987):127–48.

————. *Nuño de Guzmán and the Province of Pánuco in New Spain, 1518–1533.* Glendale, CA: Arthur H. Clark, 1967.

————. "The Oñate-Moctezuma-Zaldívar Families of Northern New Spain." *New Mexico Historical Review* 52, no. 4 (1977):297–310.

Clark, Jeffery J., and Patrick D. Lyons. "Mounds and Migrants in the Classic Period." *Archaeology Southwest* 17, no. 3 (2003):7–10.

Clayton, Lawrence A., Vernon James Knight, Jr., and Edward C. Moore, eds. *The De Soto Chronicles: The Expedition of Hernando de Soto to North America in 1539–1543.* 2 vols. Tuscaloosa: University of Alabama Press, 1993.

Clendinnen, Inga. *Aztecs: An Interpretation.* Cambridge: Cambridge University Press, 1991.

Cline, Sarah. "Fray Alonso de Molina's Model Testament and Antecedents to Indigenous Wills in Spanish America." In *Dead Giveaways: Indigenous Testaments of Colonial Mesoamerica and the Andes,* edited by Susan Kellogg and Matthew Restall, 13–33. Salt Lake City: University of Utah Press, 1998.

Cobos, Rubén. *A Dictionary of New Mexico and Southern Colorado Spanish.* Santa Fe: Museum of New Mexico Press, 1983.

Coe, Michael D. *Mexico.* 3rd ed. New York: Thames and Hudson, 1984.

Coe, Sophie D., and Michael D. Coe. *The True History of Chocolate.* London: Thames and Hudson, 2000.

Colección de documentos inéditos relativos al descubrimiento, conquista y organización de las antiguas posesiones españolas de América y Oceania. Series 1. Edited by Joaquín F. Pacheco, Francisco de Cárdenas, and Luis Torres de Mendoza. 42 vols. Madrid: José María Pérez, 1864–84.

Colección de Mendoza, o Códice Mendocino: Documento mexicano del siglo XVI que se conserva en la Biblioteca Bodleiana de Oxford, Inglaterra. Edited by Jesus Galindo y Villa. Mexico City: Editorial Innovación, 1980.

Comisón de Estudios del Territorio Nacional. "Ures-H12D32," "La Puente del Sol-H12D33," "Baviácora-H12D23," "Aconchi-H12D13," "Banamichi-H12B83," "Arizpe-H12B73," "Bacoachi-H12B64." In *Carta Topográfica.* México, DF: CETENAL, 1975.

The Compact Edition of the Oxford English Dictionary. 2 vols. New York: Oxford University Press, 1971.

Compendio de los comentarios extendidos por el maestro Antonio Gómez, a las ochenta y tres Leyes de Toro [1785]. Facsimile edition. Valladolid: Editorial Lex Nova, 1981.

Connelly, John C. "Hopi Social Organization." In *Handbook of North American Indians,* vol. 9, *Southwest,* edited by Alfonso Ortiz, 539–53. Washington, DC: Smithsonian Institution Press, 1979.

Convento de la Coria. Display. Trujillo, Extremadura, Spain, May 1997.

Cordell, Linda S. *Prehistory of the Southwest.* San Diego, CA: Academic Press, 1984.

Cornejo Franco, José. "Introducción." In *Crónica miscelánea de la sancta provincia de Xalisco, libro tercero,* fray Antonio Tello, xi–xviii. Guadalajara: Editorial Font, 1942.

Corona Ibarra, Alfredo. "Introduction." In *Crónica miscelánea de la sancta provincia de Xalisco, libro segundo,* fray Antonio Tello, vol. 1, xvii–xxiv. Guadalajara: Gobierno del Estado de Jalisco and Universidad de Guadalajara, 1968.

Cortés, Hernán. *Cartas de relación.* México, DF: Editorial Porrúa, 1993.

————. *Cartas y documentos.* México, DF: Editorial Porrúa, 1963.

————. "Cuarta carta-relación—15 de octubre de 1524." In *Cartas de relación,* Hernán Cortés, 173–206. México, DF: Editorial Porrúa, 1993.

————. *Escritos sueltos de Hernán Cortés.* México, DF: Biblioteca Histórica de La Iberia, 1871.

————. "Segunda carta-relación—30 de octubre de 1520." In *Cartas de Relación,* Hernán Cortés, 30–100. México, DF: Editorial Porrúa, 1993.

————. "Tercera carta-relación—15 de Mayo de 1522." In *Cartas de relación,* Hernán Cortés, 101–72. México, DF: Editorial Porrúa, 1993.

Covarrubias Orozco, Sebastián de. *Tesoro de la lengua castellana o española.* Edited by Felipe C. R. Maldonado. 2nd ed. Madrid: Editorial Castalia, 1995. Originally published Madrid: Luis Sánchez, 1611.

Craddock, Jerry R. "Fray Marcos de Niza, *Relación* (1539): Edition and Commentary." *Romance Philology* 53 (Fall 1999):69–118.

————. "Pedro de Castañeda y Nájera, *Relación de la Jornada de Cíbola:* Acotaciones gramaticales y léxicas." Unpublished material in possession of the editors.

Craine, Eugene R., and Reginald C. Reindorp, trans. and eds. *The Chronicles of Michoacán.* Norman: University of Oklahoma Press, 1970.

Cremony, John C. *Life among the Apaches.* San Francisco: A. Roman and Co., 1868.

Cushing, Frank Hamilton. "Corn Raising: The Decay of the Seed." In *Zuñi: Selected Writings of Frank Hamilton Cushing,* edited by Jesse Green, 257–69. Lincoln: University of Nebraska Press, 1979.

————. "A Lesson in History." In *Zuñi: Selected Writings of Frank Hamilton Cushing,* edited by Jesse Green, 172–75. Lincoln: University of Nebraska Press, 1979.

Day, A. Grove. *Coronado's Quest: The Discovery of the Southwestern States.* Berkeley: University of California Press, 1940.

———. "Mota Padilla on the Coronado Expedition." *Hispanic American Historical Review* 20, no. 1 (1940), 88–110.

Deagan, Kathleen. *Artifacts of the Spanish Colonies of Florida and the Caribbean, 1500–1800,* vol. 1, *Ceramics, Glassware, and Beads.* Washington, DC: Smithsonian Institution Press, 1987.

Deeds, Susan M. *Defiance and Deference in Mexico's Colonial North: Indians under Spanish Rule in Nueva Vizcaya.* Austin: University of Texas Press, 2003.

Devoto, Giacomo. *The Languages of Italy.* Translated by V. Louise Katainen. Chicago: University of Chicago Press, 1978.

Díaz del Castillo, Bernal. *Historia verdadera de la conquista de la Nueva España.* Edited by Carmelo Sáenz de Santa María. México, DF: Alianza Editorial, 1991.

Dibble, Charles E. *Historia de la nación mexicana: Codice de 1576 (Codice Aubin).* Madrid: Ediciones José Porrúa Turanzas, 1963.

Diccionario de autoridades. Biblioteca Románica Hispánica, V. *Diccionarios.* 3 vols. 1726–37. Facsimile ed. Madrid: Gredos, 1979.

Diccionario enciclopédico Espasa. 11th ed. 12 vols. Madrid: Espasa-Calpe, 1989.

Diccionario Porrua: Historia, biografía y geografía de Mexico. 5th ed. 3 vols. México: Editorial Porrúa, 1986.

Diccionario universal, italiano. Barcelona: Oceano Langenscheidt Ediciones, 1999.

Di Peso, Charles C., and Daniel S. Matson, eds. and trans. "The Seri Indians in 1692 as Described by Adamo Gilg, S.J." *Arizona and the West* 7 (1965):33–56.

Di Peso, Charles C., John B. Rinaldo, and Gloria J. Fenner. *Casas Grandes: A Fallen Trading Center of the Gran Chichimeca.* 8 vols. Dragoon, AZ: Amerind Foundation, 1974.

Dobyns, Henry F. "Sixteenth-Century Tusayán." *American Indian Quarterly* 15, no. 2 (1991):187–200.

Donoghue, David. "The Route of the Coronado Expedition in Texas." *New Mexico Historical Review* 4, no. 1 (1929):77–90.

Dozier, Edward P. *The Pueblo Indians of North America.* New York: Holt, Rinehart, and Winston, 1970. Reprint, Prospect Heights, IL: Waveland Press, 1983.

Duffen, William A., and William K. Hartmann. "The 76 Ranch Ruin and the Location of Chichilticale." In *The Coronado Expedition to Tierra Nueva: The 1540–1542 Route Across the Southwest,* edited by Richard Flint and Shirley Cushing Flint, 190–211. Niwot, CO: University Press of Colorado, 1997.

Dunn, Oliver, and James E. Kelley, Jr., trans. and eds. *The Diario of Christopher Columbus's First Voyage to America, 1492–1493.* Norman: University of Oklahoma Press, 1989.

Dunnigan, Timothy. "Lower Pima." In *Handbook of North American Indians,* vol. 10, *Southwest,* edited by Alfonso Ortiz, 217–29. Washington, DC: Smithsonian Institution Press, 1983.

Durán, Diego. *The History of the Indies of New Spain.* Translated and edited by Doris Heyden. Norman: University of Oklahoma Press, 1994.

Dyer, Nancy Joe. "Introducción." In *Memoriales,* fray Toribio de Benavente Motolinía, edited by Nancy Joe Dyer, 19–91. México, DF: Colegio de México, 1996.

———. "*Libro de Oro:* El Manuscrito." In *Memoriales,* fray Toribio de Benavente Motolinía, edited by Nancy Joe Dyer, 93–114. México, DF: Colegio de México, 1996.

———. "'La Relación Postrera de Siuola' (Motolinía): Género, estilo, síntesis cultural hispanoamericana." *Nueva Revista de Filología Hispánica* 39, no. 2 (1991):883–900.

Eggan, Fred. "Pueblos: Introduction." In *Handbook of North American Indians,* vol. 9, *Southwest,* edited by Alfonso Ortiz, 224–35. Washington, DC: Smithsonian Institution Press, 1979.

Ehrlich, Eugene. *Amo, Amas, Amat and More.* New York: Harper and Row, 1985.

Elliott, John H. *Imperial Spain, 1469–1716.* London: Penguin, 1990.

Ellis, Florence Hawley. "Isleta Pueblo." In *Handbook of North American Indians,* vol. 9, *Southwest,* edited by Alfonso Ortiz, 351–65. Washington, DC: Smithsonian Institution Press, 1979.

Enciclopedia universal ilustrada europeo-americana. 70 vols. Barcelona: Hijos de J. Espasa: 1907–1930.

Encyclopedia Americana. 1956 edition. 30 vols. New York: Americana Corporation, 1956.

Epple, Anne Orth. *A Field Guide to the Plants of Arizona.* Guilford, CT: Globe Pequot Press, 1995.

Espejo, Antonio de. "Report of Antonio de Espejo." In *The Rediscovery of New Mexico, 1580–1594: The Explorations of Chamuscado, Espejo, Castaño de Sosa, Morlete, and Leyva de Bonilla and Humaña,* edited by George P. Hammond and Agapito Rey, 213–31. Albuquerque: University of New Mexico Press, 1966.

Espenak, Fred. "Catalog of Lunar Eclipses: Lunar Eclipses, 1501 to 1600." (NASA/Goddard Space Flight Center, 1999), 6, http://sun-earth.gsfc.nasa.gov/eclipse/LEcat.

Espinosa, J. Manuel. *The First Expedition of Vargas into New Mexico, 1692.* Albuquerque: University of New Mexico Press, 1940.

Eyewitness Travel Guides' Mexico. New York: DK Publishing, 1999.

Falcón Márquez, Teodor, ed. *VIII Centenario de la Giralda, 1198–1998.* Sevilla: Caja Sur Publicaciones, 1998.

Felger, Richard S. *Flora of the Gran Desierto and Río Colorado of Northwestern Mexico.* Tucson: University of Arizona Press, 2000.

Felger, Richard S., and Mary Beck Moser. *People of the Desert and Sea: Ethnobotany of the Seri Indians.* Tucson: University of Arizona Press, 1985.

Fenn, Forrest. *The Secrets of San Lazaro Pueblo.* Santa Fe, NM: One Horse Land and Cattle Co., 2004.

Ferguson, T. J., and E. Richard Hart. *A Zuni Atlas.* Norman: University of Oklahoma Press, 1985.

Fernández de Bethencourt, Francisco. *Historia genealógica y heráldica de la monarquía española casa real y grandes de España,* vol. 9. Madrid: Jaime Ratés, 1912.

Fernández de Navarrete, Martín, Miguel Salvá, and Pedro Sáinz de Baranda. *Colección de documentos inéditos para la historia de España.* 112 vols. Madrid: n.p., 1842–95.

Fernández de Oviedo y Valdés, Gonzalo. *Historia general y natural de las Indias.* Edited by José Amador de los Rios. 4 vols. Madrid: Real Academia de la Historia, 1851–55.

———. *Historia general y natural de las Indias.* Edited by Juan Pérez de Tudela Bueso. 5 vols. Madrid: Ediciones Atlas, 1992.

Fernández del Castillo, Francisco. "Alonso de Estrada: Su familia." In *Memorias de la Academia Mexicana de la Historia* 1 (1942):398–431.

Fernández Guardia, Ricardo. *Cartas de Juan Vázquez de Coronado, conquistador de Costa Rica.* Barcelona: la viuda de Luis Tusso, 1908.

Fernández Puertas, Antonio, and Cristina Partearroyo. "Military Tent, Generally Known as Charles V's Tent, 1542–1545." In *Art and Culture around 1492,* edited by Joan Sureda i Pons, 82–83. Sevilla: Sociedad Estatal para la Exposición Universal Sevilla 92, 1992.

Ffoulkes, Charles. *The Armourer and His Craft from the Eleventh to the Sixteenth Century.* London: Methuen, 1912. Reprint, Mineola, NY: Dover, 1988.

Fish, Paul R., and Suzanne K. Fish. "Reflections on the Casas Grandes Regional System from the Northwestern Periphery." In *The Casas Grandes World,* edited by Curtis F. Schaafsma and Carroll L. Riley, 27–42. Salt Lake City: University of Utah Press, 1999.

Fletcher, Richard. *Moorish Spain.* Berkeley: University of California Press, 1992.

Flint, Richard. "Armas de la Tierra: The Mexican Indian Component of Coronado Expedition Material Culture." In *The Coronado Expedition to Tierra Nueva: The 1540–1542 Route Across the Southwest,* edited by Richard Flint and Shirley Cushing Flint, 57–70. Niwot, CO: University Press of Colorado, 1997.

———. *Great Cruelties Have Been Reported: The 1544 Investigation of the Coronado Expedition.* Dallas, TX: Southern Methodist University Press, 2002.

———. "The Pattern of Coronado Expedition Material Culture." M.A. thesis, New Mexico Highlands University, 1992.

———. "Reconciling the Calendars of the Coronado Expedition, Tiguex to the Second Barranca, April and May 1541." In *The Coronado Expedition from the Distance of 460 Years,* edited by Richard Flint and Shirley Cushing Flint, 151–163. Albuquerque: University of New Mexico Press, 2003.

———. "What's Missing from this Picture? The *Alarde,* or Muster Roll, of the Coronado Expedition." In *The Coronado Expedition from the Distance of 460 Years,* edited by Richard Flint and Shirley Cushing Flint, 57–80. Albuquerque: University of New Mexico Press, 2003.

———. "Who Designed Coronado's Bridge across the Pecos River?" *Kiva* 57, no. 4 (1992):331–42.

Flint, Richard, and Shirley Cushing Flint. "The Coronado Expedition: Cicúye to the Río de Cicúye Bridge." In *The Coronado Expedition to Tierra Nueva: The 1540–1542 Route Across the Southwest,* edited by Richard Flint and Shirley Cushing Flint, 262–77. Niwot, CO: University Press of Colorado, 1997.

———. "Coronado's Crosses: Route Markers Used by the Coronado Expedition." *Journal of the Southwest* 35, no. 2 (1993):207–16.

———. "A Death in Tiguex, 1542." *New Mexico Historical Review* 74, no. 3 (1999):247–70.

Flint, Richard, and Shirley Cushing Flint, eds. *The Coronado Expedition from the Distance of 460 Years.* Albuquerque: University of New Mexico Press, 2003.

Flint, Shirley Cushing. "The Financing and Provisioning of the Coronado Expedition." In *The Coronado Expedition from the Distance of 460 Years,* edited by Richard Flint and Shirley Cushing Flint, 42–56. Albuquerque: University of New Mexico Press, 2003.

———. "*La Sangre Limpiada* of Marina Flores Gutiérrez de la Caballería." *Colonial Latin American Historical Review* 11, no. 1 (2002):35–54.

Flores, Dan. *Caprock Canyonlands: Journeys into the Heart of the Southern Plains.* Austin: University of Texas Press, 1990.

Flusche, Della M. "The Tribunal of Posthumous Estates in Colonial Chile, 1540–1796." *Colonial Latin American Historical Review* 9 (2000), 1:1–66, 2:243–98, 3:379–428, 4:509–44.

Foster, Michael S. "The Aztatlán Tradition of West and Northwest Mexico and Casas Grandes." In *The Casas Grandes World,* edited by Curtis F. Schaafsma and Carroll L. Riley, 149–63. Salt Lake City: University of Utah Press, 1999.

Galbis Díez, Carmen. "La Casa de la Contratación." In *Archivo General de Indias,* general editor Pedro González García, 131–68. Madrid: Lunwerg Editores y Ministerio de Educación y Cultura, 1995.

Galende, Juan Carlos. *Diccionario general de abreviaturas españolas.* Madrid: Editorial Verbum, 1997.

Gallegos, Hernán. "Gallegos' Relation of the Chamuscado-Rodríguez Expedition." In *The Rediscovery of New Mexico, 1580–1594: The Explorations of Chamuscado, Espejo, Castaño de Sosa, Morlete, and Leyva de Bonilla and Humaña,* edited by George P. Hammond and Agapito Rey, 67–114. Albuquerque: University of New Mexico Press, 1966.

García-Mason, Velma. "Acoma Pueblo." In *Handbook of North American Indians,* vol. 9, *Southwest,* edited by Alfonso Ortiz, 450–66. Washington, DC: Smithsonian Institution Press, 1979.

Gardiner, C. Harvey. *The Constant Captain: Gonzalo de Sandoval.* Carbondale: Southern Illinois University Press, 1961.

Garza Carvajal, Federico. *Butterflies Will Burn: Prosecuting Sodomites in Early Modern Spain and Mexico.* Austin: University of Texas Press, 2003.

Gerbi, Antonello. *Nature in the New World: From Christopher Columbus to Gonzalo Fernández de Oviedo.* Translated by Jeremy Moyle. Pittsburgh: University of Pittsburgh Press, 1985.

Gerhard, Peter. *A Guide to the Historical Geography of New Spain.* Rev. ed. Norman: University of Oklahoma Press, 1993.

———. *The North Frontier of New Spain.* Rev. ed. Norman: University of Oklahoma Press, 1993.

Gibson, Charles. *The Aztecs under Spanish Rule: A History of the Indians of the Valley of Mexico, 1519–1810.* Stanford, CA: Stanford University Press, 1964.

Gibson, Charles, ed. *The Spanish Tradition in America.* Columbia: University of South Carolina Press, 1968.

Gómez Vozmediano, Miguel F. *Mudéjares y moriscos en el campo de Calatrava.* Ciudad Real: Área de Cultura, Diputación Provincial, 2000.

González García, Pedro, gen. ed. *Archivo General de Indias.* Madrid: Lunwerg Editores y Ministerio de Educación y Cultura, 1995.

González Jiménez, Manuel. "La biografía de don Fadrique Enríquez de Ribera." In *Paisajes de la tierra prometida: El Viaje a Jerusalén de don Fadrique Enríquez de Ribera,* edited by Pedro García Martín et al., 77–98. Madrid: Miraguano Ediciones, 2001.

Goodwin, Katherine R. "Entrada, The First Century of Mapping the Greater Southwest: An Exhibition." In *The Mapping of the Entradas into the Greater Southwest,* edited by Dennis Reinhartz and Gerald D. Saxon, 152–206. Norman: University of Oklahoma Press, 1998.

Green, Jesse, ed. *Cushing at Zuni: The Correspondence and Journals of Frank*

Hamilton Cushing, 1879–1884. Albuquerque: University of New Mexico Press, 1990.

———. *Zuñi: Selected Writings of Frank Hamilton Cushing.* Lincoln: University of Nebraska Press, 1979.

Griffen, William B. "Southern Periphery: East." In *Handbook of North American Indians,* vol. 10, *Southwest,* edited by Alfonso Ortiz, 329–42. Washington, DC: Smithsonian Institution Press, 1983.

Grissino-Mayer, Henri D. "A 2129-Year Reconstruction of Precipitation for Northwestern New Mexico, USA." In *Tree Rings, Environment, and Humanity,* edited by Jeffrey S. Dean, D. M. Meko, and T. W. Swetman, 191–204. Tucson: *Radiocarbon* (Dept. of Geosciences, University of Arizona), 1996.

Gurulé, Jerry. "Francisco Vázquez de Coronado's Northward Trek through Sonora." In *The Coronado Expedition to Tierra Nueva: The 1540–1542 Route Across the Southwest,* edited by Richard Flint and Shirley Cushing Flint, 149–64. Niwot, CO: University Press of Colorado, 1997.

Habicht-Mauche, Judith A. "Coronado's Querechos and Teyas in the Archaeological Record of the Texas Panhandle." *Plains Anthropologist* 140 (1992):247–59.

———. "Striated Utility Ware from the Southwest and Southern Plains." Chapter 5 in *Pottery, Food, Hides, and Women: Labor, Production, and Exchange across the Protohistoric Plains-Pueblo Frontier,* by Judith A. Habicht-Mauche. In preparation.

Hackenberg, Robert A. "Pima and Papago Ecological Adaptations." In *Handbook of North American Indians,* vol. 10, *Southwest,* edited by Alfonso Ortiz, 161–77. Washington, DC: Smithsonian Institution Press, 1983.

Hackett, Charles Wilson. *Historical Documents Relating to New Mexico, Nueva Vizcaya, and Approaches Thereto.* 2 vols. Washington, DC: Carnegie Institution of Washington, 1923.

Hackett, Charles W., and Charmion C. Shelby. *Revolt of the Pueblo Indians of New Mexico and Otermín's Attempted Reconquest, 1680–1682.* 2 vols. Albuquerque: University of New Mexico Press, 1942.

Hakluyt, Richard, ed. and trans. *The Principal Navigations, Traffiques, and Discoveries of the English Nation Made by Sea or Over-land to the Remote and Farthest Distant Quarters of the Earth at any Time within the Compasse of these 1600 Yeeres.* 12 vols. Glasgow: James MacLehose and Sons, 1903–4.

Hallenbeck, Cleve. *The Journey of Fray Marcos de Niza.* Dallas, TX: Southern Methodist University Press, 1949. Reprint with introduction by David J. Weber, 1987.

Hammond, George P., and Agapito Rey, eds. and trans. *Don Juan de Oñate: Colonizer of New Mexico.* 2 vols. Albuquerque: University of New Mexico Press, 1953.

———. *Narratives of the Coronado Expedition, 1540–1542.* Albuquerque: University of New Mexico Press, 1940.

———. *The Rediscovery of New Mexico, 1580–1594: The Explorations of Chamuscado, Espejo, Castaño de Sosa, Morlete, and Leyva de Bonilla and Humaña.* Albuquerque: University of New Mexico Press, 1966.

Hanke, Lewis. "Pope Paul III and the American Indians." *Harvard Theological Review* 30 (1937):65–102.

———. *The Spanish Struggle for Justice in the Conquest of America.* Boston: Little, Brown, 1965.

———. *Los Virreyes españoles en América durante el gobierno de la Casa de Austria, México.* 5 vols. In *Biblioteca de autores españoles desde la forma-*

ción del lenguaje hasta nuestros días, vols. 273–77. Madrid: Ediciones Atlas, 1976.

Hansen, Charles D. "Physical Characteristics." In *The Desert Bighorn: Its Life History, Ecology, and Management,* edited by Gale Monson and Lowell Sumner, 52–63. Tucson: University of Arizona Press, 1980.

Hartmann, William K. "Pathfinder for Coronado: Reevaluating the Mysterious Journey of Marcos de Niza." In *The Coronado Expedition to Tierra Nueva: The 1540–1542 Route Across the Southwest,* edited by Richard Flint and Shirley Cushing Flint, 73–101. Niwot, CO: University Press of Colorado, 1997.

Hartmann, William K., and Richard Flint. "Before the Coronado Expedition: Who Knew What and When Did They Know It?" In *The Coronado Expedition from the Distance of 460 Years,* edited by Richard Flint and Shirley Cushing Flint, 20–41. Albuquerque: University of New Mexico Press, 2003.

———. "Migrations in Late Anasazi Prehistory: 'Eyewitness' Testimony." *Kiva* 66, no. 3 (2001):375–85.

Harwell, Henry O., and Marsha C. S. Kelly. "Maricopa." In *Handbook of North American Indians,* vol. 10, *Southwest,* edited by Alfonso Ortiz, 71–85. Washington, DC: Smithsonian Institution Press, 1983.

Hassig, Ross. *Time, History, and Belief in Aztec and Colonial Mexico.* Austin: University of Texas Press, 2001.

———. *Trade, Tribute, and Transportation: The Sixteenth-Century Political Economy of the Valley of Mexico.* Norman: University of Oklahoma Press, 1993.

Hayes, Alden, Jon Nathan Young, and A. Helene Warren. *The Excavation of Mound 7, Gran Quivira National Monument, New Mexico.* Washington, DC: National Park Service, 1981.

Hedrick, Basil C., and Carroll L. Riley. *Documents Ancilary to the Vaca Journey.* University Studies 5. Carbondale: Southern Illinois University Museum, 1976.

Hernández, Rudolfo, and José Francisco Román. "Presencia tlaxcalteca en Nueva Galicia." In *Constructores de la nación: La Migración tlaxcalteca en el norte de la Nueva España,* edited by María Isabel Monroy Castillo, 17–33. San Luis Potosí: Colegio de San Luis and Gobierno del Estado de Tlaxcala, 1999.

Hernández de Biedma, Luys. "Relation of the Island of Florida." Translated and edited by John E. Worth. In *The De Soto Chronicles: The Expedition of Hernando de Soto to North America in 1539–1543,* vol. 1, edited by Lawrence A. Clayton, Vernon James Knight, Jr., and Edward C. Moore, 225–46. Tuscaloosa: University of Alabama Press, 1993.

Herrera y Tordesillos, Antonio de. *Décadas* (Madrid, 1601–15). In *Mapas de América en los libros españoles de los siglos XVI al XVIII,* Francisco Vindel. Madrid: Góngora, 1955.

———. *Descripción de las Indias occidentales.* Década I, Libro VII. Madrid: Nicolás Rodríguez Franco, 1725.

———. *Historia general de los hechos de los castellanos en las islas y tierra-firme de el Mar Oceano.* Edited by J. Natalicio González. Buenos Aires: Editorial Guaranía, 1946.

Hickerson, Nancy Parrott. *The Jumanos: Hunters and Traders of the South Plains.* Austin: University of Texas Press, 1994.

Himmerich y Valencia, Robert. *The Encomenderos of New Spain, 1521–1555.* Austin: University of Texas Press, 1991.

Hinton, Thomas B. "Southern Periphery: West." In *Handbook of North American Indians,* vol. 10, *Southwest,* edited by Alfonso Ortiz, 315–28. Washington, DC: Smithsonian Institution Press, 1983.

Hodge, Frederick W. *Circular Kivas near Hawikuh, New Mexico.* Contributions of the Museum of the American Indian–Heye Foundation 7, no. 1 (1923).

———. *History of Hawikuh, New Mexico, One of the So-Called Cities of Cíbola.* Los Angeles: Southwest Museum, 1937.

———. "Introduction." In *Spanish Explorers in the Southern United States, 1528–1543,* edited by Frederick W. Hodge and Theodore H. Lewis, 275–80. New York: Barnes and Noble, 1907. Reprint, Austin: Texas State Historical Association, 1990.

Hodge, Frederick W., George Hammond, and Agapito Rey. *The Revised Memorial of Fray Alonso de Benavides, 1634.* Albuquerque: University of New Mexico Press, 1945.

Holden, William C. "Coronado's Route across the Staked Plains." *West Texas Historical Association Yearbook* 20 (1944):3–20.

Honea, Kenneth. *Revised Sequence of Rio Grande Glaze Pottery.* Texas Tech Archaeological Survey, Bulletin 1. Lubbock: Texas Tech University, Department of Sociology and Anthropology, 1967.

Howard, David A. *Conquistador in Chains: Cabeza de Vaca and the Indians of the Americas.* Tuscaloosa: University of Alabama Press, 1997.

Hudson, Charles. *Knights of Spain, Warriors of the Sun: Hernando de Soto and the South's Ancient Chiefdoms.* Athens: University of Georgia Press, 1997.

Icaza, Francisco A. de. *Conquistadores y pobladores de Nueva España: Diccionario autobiográfico sacado de los textos originales.* 2 vols. Madrid: Adelantado de Segovia, 1923.

Inglis, Douglas. "A Guide to the History of the Spanish Southwest Collection in the Panhandle-Plains Historical Museum Research Center." In *Coronado and the Myth of Quivira,* edited by Dianna Everett, 71–80. Canyon, TX: Panhandle-Plains Historical Society, 1985.

Ives, Ronald L. "The Grave of Melchior Díaz: A Problem in Historical Sleuthing." *Kiva* 25, no. 2 (1959):31–40.

Jones, Paul A. *Coronado and Quivira.* Lyons, KS: Lyons Publishing Company, 1937.

Julyan, Robert. *The Place Names of New Mexico.* Albuquerque: University of New Mexico Press, 1996.

Kamen, Henry. *Philip of Spain.* New Haven, CT: Yale University Press, 1997.

Kelly, Isabel. *Excavations at Chametla, Sinaloa.* Ibero-Americana 14. Berkeley: University of California Press, 1938.

Kelsey, Harry. *Juan Rodríguez Cabrillo.* San Marino, CA: Huntington Library, 1998.

———. "The Gregorian Calendar in New Spain: A Problem in Sixteenth-Century Chronology." *New Mexico Historical Review* 58 (July 1983):239–51.

Kendall, Martha B. "Yuman Languages." In *Handbook of North American Indians,* vol. 10, *Southwest,* edited by Alfonso Ortiz, 4–12. Washington, DC: Smithsonian Institution Press, 1983.

Keniston, Hayward. *Francisco de los Cobos, Secretary of the Emperor Charles V.* Pittsburgh: University of Pittsburgh Press, 1959.

Kenmotsu, Nancy Adele, James E. Bruseth, and James E. Corbin. "Moscoso and the Route in Texas: A Reconstruction." In *The Expedition of Hernando de Soto West of the Mississippi, 1541–1543,* edited by Gloria A. Young and Michael P. Hoffman, 106–31. Fayetteville: University of Arkansas Press, 1993.

Kent, Kate Peck. *The Cultivation and Weaving of Cotton in the Prehistoric Southwestern United States.* Transactions of the American Philosophical Society 47 (1957):465–67.

Kessell, John L. *Kiva, Cross, and Crown.* 2nd edition. Albuquerque: University of New Mexico Press, 1987.

Kessell, John L., Rick Hendricks, and Meredith Dodge, eds. *Blood on the Boulders: The Journals of don Diego de Vargas, New Mexico, 1694–1697.* Albuquerque: University of New Mexico Press, 1998.

Kessell, John L., Rick Hendricks, Meredith Dodge, and Larry D. Miller, eds. *That Disturbances Cease: The Journals of don Diego de Vargas, New Mexico, 1697–1700.* Albuquerque: University of New Mexico Press, 2000.

Khera, Sigrid, and Patricia S. Mariella. "Yavapai." In *Handbook of North American Indians,* vol. 10, *Southwest,* edited by Alfonso Ortiz, 38–54. Washington, DC: Smithsonian Institution Press, 1983.

Kintigh, Keith. "Introduction." In *Hemenway Southwestern Archaeological Expedition,* vol. 6, *Selected Correspondence, June 1, 1888, through 1889,* ed. David Wilcox. In preparation.

———. *Settlement, Subsistence, and Society in Late Zuni Prehistory.* Tucson: University of Arizona Press, 1985.

Kiser, Edwin L. "The Re-examination of Pedro de Castañeda's Bone Bed by Geological Investigations." *Bulletin of the Texas Archeological Society* 49 (1978):331–39.

Krausman, Paul R. "The Exit of the Last Wild Mountain Sheep." In *Counting Sheep: Twenty Ways of Seeing Desert Bighorn,* edited by Gary Paul Nabhan, 242–50. Tucson: University of Arizona Press, 1993.

Krieger, Alex D. *We Came Naked and Barefoot: The Journey of Cabeza de Vaca across North America.* Austin: University of Texas Press, 2002.

Ladd, Doris M. *The Mexican Nobility at Independence, 1780–1826.* Austin: Institute of Latin American Studies, University of Texas, Austin, 1976.

Ladd, Edmund J. "Zuni on the Day the Men in Metal Arrived." In *The Coronado Expedition to Tierra Nueva: The 1540–1542 Route Across the Southwest,* edited by Richard Flint and Shirley Cushing Flint, 225–33. Niwot, CO: University Press of Colorado, 1997.

———. "Zuni Social and Political Organization." In *Handbook of North American Indians,* vol. 9, *Southwest,* edited by Alfonso Ortiz, 482–91. Washington, DC: Smithsonian Institution Press, 1979.

Lange, Charles H. *Cochití: A New Mexico Pueblo, Past and Present.* Albuquerque: University of New Mexico Press, 1990.

Lapesa, Rafael. *Historia de la lengua española.* 9th ed. Madrid: Editorial Gredos, 1981.

las Casas, Bartolomé de. *Del Único modo de atraer a todos los pueblos a la verdadera religión.* México, DF: Fondo de Cultura Económica, 1942.

———. *The Devastation of the Indies: A Brief Account.* Translated by Herma Briffault. Baltimore, MD: Johns Hopkins University Press, 1992.

Latham, Ronald. "Introduction." In *The Travels of Marco Polo,* edited and translated by Ronald Latham, 7–29. Hammondsworth, UK: Penguin, 1958.

la Vega, Garcilaso de. "La Florida by the Inca." Translated by Charmion Shelby; edited by David Bost. In *The De Soto Chronicles: The Expedition of Hernando de Soto to North America in 1539–1543,* vol. 2, edited by Lawrence A. Clayton, Vernon James Knight, Jr., and Edward C. Moore, 25–559. Tuscaloosa: University of Alabama Press, 1993.

Lehmann, Walter, Gerdt Kutscher, and Günter Vollmer. *Geschichte der*

Azteken: Codex Aubin und verwandte Dokumente. Berlin: Gebr. Mann, 1981.

Leonard, Irving A. *Books of the Brave: Being an Account of Books and of Men in the Spanish Conquest and Settlement of the Sixteenth-Century New World.* Berkeley: University of California Press, 1992.

Leyes y ordenanças nuevamente hechas por Su Magestad para la governación de las Indias. In *The New Laws of the Indies,* edited and translated by Henry Stevens and Fred W. Lucas. London: Chiswick Press, 1893. Reprint, Amsterdam: N. Isreal, 1968.

Lienzo de Tlaxcala. México, DF: Alfredo Chavero. Reprint, *Artes de México* 11, nos. 51–52 (1964):1–82.

Linné, S. *El Valle de la Ciudad de México en 1550.* New series, publication no. 9. Stockholm: Statens Etnografiska Museum, 1948.

Liss, Peggy K. *Isabel, the Queen: Life and Times.* New York: Oxford University Press, 1992.

Lloyd, Paul M. *From Latin to Spanish,* vol. 1, *Historical Phonology and Morphology of the Spanish Language.* Memoirs of the American Philosophical Society, vol. 173. Philadelphia: American Philosophical Society, 1987.

Lockhart, James. *The Men of Cajamarca: A Social and Biographical Study of the First Conquerors of Peru.* Austin: University of Texas Press, 1972.

———. *The Nahuas after the Conquest: A Social and Cultural History of the Indians of Central Mexico, Sixteenth through Eighteenth Centuries.* Stanford, CA: Stanford University Press, 1992.

———. *Spanish Peru, 1532–1560.* Madison: University of Wisconsin Press, 1968.

Lockhart, James, and Stuart B. Schwartz. *Early Latin America: A History of Colonial Spanish America and Brazil.* Cambridge: Cambridge University Press, 1983.

López, Juan. "Reconocimiento y homenaje." In *Libro segundo de la Crónica miscelánea, en que se trata de la conquista espiritual y temporal de la santa provincia de Xalisco en el Nuevo Reino de la Galicia y Nueva Vizcaya y descubrimiento del Nuevo México,* fray Antonio Tello. Guadalajara, México: Republica Literaria, 1891. Reprint, México, DF: Editorial Porrúa, 1997.

López de Gómara, Francisco. *Cortés: The Life of the Conqueror by His Secretary.* Translated and edited by Lesley Byrd Simpson. Berkeley: University of California Press, 1964.

———. *Historia general de las Indias: Edición facsimilar.* Lima, Peru: Comisión Nacional del V Centenario del Descubrimiento de América, 1993.

López-Portillo y Weber, José. *La Rebelión de Nueva Galicia.* México, DF: n.p., 1939.

Lorenzana, Francisco Antonio. *Historia de Nueva España escripta por su esclarecido conquistador Hernán Cortés: Aumentada con otros documentos y notas.* México, DF: Imprenta del Superior Gobierno, 1770.

Luna y Arellano, don Tristán de. *The Luna Papers: Documents Relating to the Expedition of don Tristán de Luna y Arellano for the Conquest of La Florida in 1559–1561.* 2 vols. Translated and edited by Herbert Ingram Priestley. Freeport, NY: Books for Libraries Press, 1971.

Lutz, Christopher H. *Santiago de Guatemala, 1541–1773: City, Caste, and the Colonial Experience.* Norman: University of Oklahoma Press, 1994.

MacLeod, Murdo J. "Self-Promotion: The *Relaciones de méritos y servicios* and Their Historical and Political Interpretation." *Colonial Latin American Historical Review* 7, no. 1 (1998):25–42.

MacMullen, Jerry. "It's a Wonder that They Ever Got Home." In *Cabrillo's World: A Commemorative Edition of Cabrillo Festival Historic Seminar Papers,* 37–41. San Diego, CA: Cabrillo Historical Association, 1991.

Mangelsdorf, Paul C. *Corn: Its Origin, Evolution, and Improvement.* Cambridge, MA: Harvard University Press, 1974.

Marcos de Niza, fray. "Testimony, Santiago de Guatemala, September 25, 1536," translated by Henry R. Wagner. In "Fr. Marcos de Niza," Henry R. Wagner, *New Mexico Historical Review* 9 (April 1934):184–227.

Martínez, José Luis, ed. *Documentos Cortesianos.* 4 vols. México, DF: Universidad Nacional Autónoma de México, 1992.

Martínez Meléndez, María del Carmen. *Los Nombres de tejidos en castellano medieval.* Granada, Spain: Universidad de Granada, 1989.

Mathes, W. Michael. "A Large Canyon Like Those of Colima." In *The Coronado Expedition to Tierra Nueva: The 1540–1542 Route Across the Southwest,* edited by Richard Flint and Shirley Cushing Flint, 365–69. Niwot, CO: University Press of Colorado, 1997.

———. "New Research in Mexico regarding Francisco Vázquez de Coronado." Paper presented at the conference "Contemporary Vantage on the Coronado Expedition through Documents and Artifacts." Las Vegas, NM, 2000.

McDonald, Jerry N. *North American Bison: Their Classification and Evolution.* Berkeley: University of California Press, 1981.

McGee, William John. "The Seri Indians." In *Seventeenth Annual Report of the Bureau of American Ethnology to the Secretary of the Smithsonian Institution, 1895–96,* Part 1, 9–344. Washington, DC: Smithsonian Institution, 1898.

Mecham, John Lloyd. *Francisco de Ibarra and Nueva Vizcaya.* Durham, NC: Duke University Press, 1927.

Medina Encina, Purificación. "El Consejo de Indias." In *Archivo General de Indias,* general editor Pedro González García, 169–247. Madrid: Lunwerg Editores y Ministerio de Educación y Cultura, 1995.

Melzi, R. C. *Langenscheidt's Standard Italian Dictionary.* Berlin: Langenscheidt, 1990.

Mendoza, Antonio de. "Letter of the Viceroy to the King, 1539." In *Terzo volume delle navigationi et viaggi,* Giovanni Battista Ramusio, fols. 355r–355v. Venice: Stamperia de Giunti, 1556.

Mercator, Gerhardus. *Nova et Aucta Orbis Terrae Descriptio ad Usum Navigantium Emendate Accommodata.* Duisberg, 1569.

Migliorini, Bruno. *The Italian Language.* Translated by T. Gwynfor Griffith. London: Faber and Faber, 1966.

Miguélez, Manuel Fraile. *Catálogo de los códices españoles de la Biblioteca del Escorial, 1: Relaciones históricas.* Madrid: Imprenta Helénica, 1917.

Milbrath, Susan. "Old World Meets New: Views across the Atlantic." In *First Encounters: Spanish Explorations in the Caribbean and the United States, 1492–1570,* edited by Jerald T. Milanich and Susan Milbrath, 183–210. Gainesville: University of Florida Press, 1989.

Millares Carlo, Agustín, and J. I. Mantecón. *Índice y extractos de los Protocolos del Archivo de Notarías de México, DF.* 2 vols. México, DF: Colegio de México, 1945.

Miller, Wick R. "Uto-Aztecan Languages." In *Handbook of North American Indians,* vol. 10, *Southwest,* edited by Alfonso Ortiz, 113–24. Washington, DC: Smithsonian Institution Press, 1983.

Molina, Alonso de. *Vocabulario en lengua mexicana y castellana.* México, DF: Antonio de Spinosa, 1571. Reprint, Madrid: Ediciones de Cultura Hispánica, 2001.

Montgomery, Ross Gordon, Watson Smith, and John Otis Brew. *Franciscan Awatovi: Reports of the Awatovi Expedition, Report no. 3.* Cambridge, MA: Peabody Museum, Harvard University, 1949.

Mora, Carmen de. "Códigos culturales en la *Relación de la Jornada de Cíbola* de Pedro Castañeda Nájera." *Nueva Revista Filología Hispánica* (1991):901–12.

———. *Las Siete Ciudades de Cíbola: Textos y testimonios sobre la expedición de Vázquez Coronado.* Sevilla: Ediciones Alfar, 1992.

Morison, Samuel Eliot. *The European Discovery of America: The Northern Voyages, 1492–1616.* New York: Oxford University Press, 1971.

———. *The European Discovery of America: The Southern Voyages, 1492–1616.* New York: Oxford University Press, 1974.

Morris, John Miller. *El Llano Estacado: Exploration and Imagination on the High Plains of Texas and New Mexico, 1536–1860.* Austin: Texas State Historical Association, 1997.

Mota y Padilla, Matías de la. *Historia de la conquista del reino de la Nueva Galicia.* Edited by José Ireneo Gutiérrez. Guadalajara: Talleres Gráficos de Gallardo y Álvarez del Castillo, 1920.

Murie, Olaus J. *A Field Guide to Animal Tracks.* 2nd ed. Boston: Houghton Mifflin, 1974.

Myers, Harry C. "The Mystery of Coronado's Route from the Pecos River to the Llano Estacado." In *The Coronado Expedition from the Distance of 460 Years,* edited by Richard Flint and Shirley Cushing Flint, 140–50. Albuquerque: University of New Mexico Press, 2003.

Nabhan, Gary Paul. *Gathering the Desert.* Tucson: University of Arizona Press, 1985.

Nader, Helen. *The Mendoza Family in the Spanish Renaissance, 1350 to 1550.* New Brunswick, NJ: Rutgers University Press, 1979.

Nallino, Michel. "Fray Marcos de Niza: In Pursuit of Franciscan Utopia in the Americas." Paper presented at the conference "Contemporary Vantage on the Coronado Expedition through Documents and Artifacts." Las Vegas, NM, 2000.

The National Union Catalog, pre-1956 Imprints. 754 vols. London: Mansell Information/Publishing and American Library Association, 1976.

Nauman, James D. "Preface to the Account." In *An Account of the Voyage of Juan Rodríguez Cabrillo,* 35–42. San Diego, CA: Cabrillo National Monument Foundation, 1999.

Nelson, Steve. "In Search of El Burro: The Tidal Bore on the Río Colorado Delta." In *Dry Borders: Great Natural Areas of the Gran Desierto and Upper Gulf of California,* edited by Richard S. Felger and Bill Broyles. Salt Lake City: University of Utah Press, 2005.

Newcomb, William W., Jr. "Wichita." In *Handbook of North American Indians,* vol. 13, part 1, *Plains,* edited by Raymond J. DeMallie, 548–66. Washington, DC: Smithsonian Institution Press, 2001.

Newman, Stanley. *Zuni Dictionary.* 2 vols. Albuquerque: n.p., 1956.

Núñez Cabeza de Vaca, Álvar. *The Account: Álvar Núñez Cabeza de Vaca's Relación.* Edited and translated by Martin A. Favata and José B. Fernández. Houston: Arte Público Press, 1993.

———. *The Journey of Alvar Nuñez Cabeza de Vaca and His Companions from Florida to the Pacific, 1528–1536.* Translated by Fanny R. Bandelier; edited by Adolph F. Bandelier. New York: A. S. Barnes, 1905. Reprint, Chicago: Rio Grande Press, 1964.

———. *Naufragios y comentarios con dos cartas.* 9th ed. México, DF: Espasa-Calpe Mexicana, 1985.

Oblasser, Bonaventure, ed. and trans. *Arizona Discovered, 1539: The Story of the Discovery of the Seven Cities by fray Marcos de Niza.* Topowa, AZ: n.p., 1939.

Obregón, Baltasar de. *Historia de los descubrimientos antiguos y modernos de la Nueva España, escrita por el conquistador en el año de 1584.* Edited by Mariano Cuevas. México, DF: Editorial Porrúa, 1988.

O'Callaghan, Joseph F. "Alfonso X and the Partidas." In *Las Siete Partidas,* translated by Samuel Parsons Scott and edited by Robert I. Burns, vol. 1, xxx–xl. Philadelphia: University of Pennsylvania Press, 2001.

Ochi Flechor, Maria Helena. *Manuscritos dos séculos XVI ao XIX.* São Paulo: Edições Arquivo do Estado, 1991.

Onís, José de. "Alcedo's *Biblioteca americana.*" *Hispanic American Historical Review* 31, no. 3 (1951):537.

Opler, Morris E. "Chiricahua Apache." In *Handbook of North American Indians,* vol. 10, *Southwest,* edited by Alfonso Ortiz, 401–18. Washington, DC: Smithsonian Institution Press, 1983.

Ortelius, Abraham. *Americae Sive Novi Orbis, Nova Descriptio.* Amsterdam, 1570.

Pailes, Richard A. "An Archaeological Perspective on the Sonoran Entrada." In *The Coronado Expedition to Tierra Nueva: The 1540–1542 Route Across the Southwest,* edited by Richard Flint and Shirley Cushing Flint, 177–89. Niwot, CO: University Press of Colorado, 1997.

Parry, John H. *The Age of Reconnaissance.* Cleveland, OH: World Publishing, 1963.

Parry, John H., and Robert G. Keith, eds. *New Iberian World.* 5 vols. New York: Times Books, 1984.

Parsons, Elsie Clews. "Isleta, New Mexico." In *Forty-Seventh Annual Report of the Bureau of American Ethnology,* 193–466. Washington, DC: Government Printing Office, 1932.

Patraw, Pauline M. *Flowers of the Southwest Mesas.* 6th ed. Globe, AZ: Southwest Parks and Monuments Association, 1977.

Payne-Gallwey, Ralph. *The Crossbow, Mediaeval and Modern, Military and Sporting: Its Construction, History, and Management.* 2nd ed. London: Holland Press, 1995.

Pennington, Campbell W. "Bosquejo grammática y vocabulario de la lengua ópata, sacada de un obra de Natal Lombardo, S.J., que sirve dentro los Ópatas de Sonora durante las últimas décadas del siglo diecisiete." Unpublished manuscript. Library, Laboratory of Anthropology, Museum of New Mexico, Santa Fe, n.d..

———. *The Material Culture: The Pima Bajo of Central Sonora, Mexico,* vol. 1. Salt Lake City: University of Utah Press, 1980.

Pérez de Luxán, Diego. "Diego Pérez de Luxán's Account of the Antonio de Espejo Expedition into New Mexico, 1582." In *The Rediscovery of New Mexico, 1580–1594: The Explorations of Chamuscado, Espejo, Castaño de Sosa, Morlete, and Leyva de Bonilla and Humaña,* edited by George P. Hammond and Agapito Rey, 153–212. Albuquerque: University of New Mexico Press, 1966.

Pérez de Ribas, Andrés. *History of the Triumphs of Our Holy Faith amongst the Most Barbarous and Fierce Peoples of the New World.* Edited and translated by Daniel T. Reff, Maureen Ahern, and Richard K. Danford. Tucson: University of Arizona Press, 1999.

Pérez de Tudela Bueso, Juan. "Vida y escritos de Gonzalo Fernández de Oviedo." In *Historia general y natural de las Indias,* Gonzalo Fernández de Oviedo y Valdés, edited by Juan Pérez de Tudela Bueso, vol. 1, vii–clxxv. Madrid: Ediciones Atlas, 1992.

Pérez de Villagrá, Gaspar. *Historia de la Nueva México, 1610.* Edited and translated by Miguel Encinias, Alfred Rodríguez, and Joseph P. Sánchez. Albuquerque: University of New Mexico Press, 1992.

Pérez Fernández del Castillo, Bernardo. *Historia de la escribanía en la Nueva España y del notariado en México*. México, DF: Editorial Porrúa, 1994.

Pérez-Mallaína, Pablo E. *Spain's Men of the Sea: Daily Life on the Indies Fleets in the Sixteenth Century*. Translated by Carla Rahn Phillips. Baltimore, MD: Johns Hopkins University Press, 1998.

Phelan, John Leddy. *The Millennial Kingdom of the Franciscans in the New World*. 2nd ed. Berkeley: University of California Press, 1970.

Piechotta, Magdalena Valor. "La Torre y la catedral de Sevilla entre 1248 y 1560." In *VIII Centenario de la Giralda, 1198–1998*, edited by Teodor Falcón Márquez, 59–82. Sevilla: Caja Sur Publicaciones, 1998.

Pilar, García del. "Circa 1532: García del Pilar on the Expedition of Nuño de Guzman to Michoacan and New Galicia." In *New Iberian World*, vol. 3, *Central America and Mexico*, edited by John H. Parry and Robert G. Keith, 549–55. New York: Times Books, 1984.

Polo, Marco. *The Travels of Marco Polo*. New York: Orion Press, 1958.

———. *The Travels of Marco Polo*. Translated and edited by Ronald Latham. Harmondsworth, UK: Penguin, 1958.

Prem, Hanns J. "Disease Outbreaks in Central Mexico during the Sixteenth Century." In *"Secret Judgments of God": Old World Disease in Colonial Spanish America*, edited by Noble David Cook and W. George Lovell, 20–48. Norman: University of Oklahoma Press, 1992.

Primera y segunda relaciónes anónimas de la jornada que hizo Nuño de Guzmán a la Nueva Galicia. México, DF: Chimalistac, 1952.

Ptolemy, Claudius. *The Geography*. Translated and edited by Edward Luther Stevenson. New York: Dover, 1991.

Quiñones Keber, Eloise. *Codex Telleriano-Remensis: Ritual, Divination, and History in a Pictorial Aztec Manuscript*. Austin: University of Texas Press, 1995.

Radbourne, Allan, ed. *The Battle for Apache Pass: Reports of the California Volunteers*. London: English Westerners' Society, 2002.

Ramenofsky, Ann F., and C. David Vaughan. "Jars Full of Shiny Metal: Analyzing Barrionuevo's Visit to Yuque Yunque." In *The Coronado Expedition from the Distance of 460 Years*, edited by Richard Flint and Shirley Cushing Flint, 116–39. Albuquerque: University of New Mexico Press, 2003.

Ramos, Demetrio. *Ximénez de Quesada en su relación con los cronistas y el epítome de la conquista del Nuevo Reino de Granada*. Sevilla: Escuela de Estudios Hispano-Americanos, 1972.

Ramusio, Giovanni Battista. *Navigazioni e viaggi*. Edited by Marica Milanesi. 6 vols. Turin: Einaudi, 1978–88.

———. *Terzo volume delle navigationi et viaggi*. Venice: Stamperia de Giunti, 1556.

Rangel, Rodrigo. "Account of the Northern Conquest and Discovery of Hernando de Soto." Translated and edited by John E. Worth. In *The De Soto Chronicles: The Expedition of Hernando de Soto to North America in 1539–1543*, vol. 1, edited by Lawrence A. Clayton, Vernon James Knight, Jr., and Edward C. Moore, 251–306. Tuscaloosa: University of Alabama Press, 1993.

Real Academia Española. *Diccionario de la lengua española*. 21st. ed., 2 vols. Madrid: Editorial Espasa Calpe, S.A., 1992.

Reff, Daniel T. "Anthropological Analysis of Exploration Texts: Cultural Discourse and the Ethnological Import of Fray Marcos de Niza's Journey to Cíbola." *American Anthropologist* 93 (1991):636–55.

———. *Disease, Depopulation, and Culture Change in Northwestern New Spain, 1518–1764*. Salt Lake City: University of Utah Press, 1991.

———. "The Relevance of Ethnology to the Routing of the Coronado Expedition in Sonora." In *The Coronado Expedition to Tierra Nueva: The 1540–1542 Route Across the Southwest*, edited by Richard Flint and Shirley Cushing Flint, 165–76. Niwot, CO: University Press of Colorado, 1997.

Reti, Ladislao, ed. *The Unknown Leonardo*. New York: McGraw-Hill, 1974.

Rice, Prudence M. *Pottery Analysis: A Sourcebook*. Chicago: University of Chicago Press, 1987.

Riley, Carroll L. "Coronado in the Southwest." In *Archaeology, Art, and Anthropology: Collected Papers in Honor of J. J. Brody*, edited by Meliha S. Duran and David T. Kirkpatrick, 147–56. Papers of the Archaeological Society of New Mexico, no. 18. Albuquerque: Archaeological Society of New Mexico, 1992.

———. "Early Spanish-Indian Communication in the Greater Southwest." *New Mexico Historical Review* 46, no. 4 (1971):285–314.

———. *The Frontier People: The Greater Southwest in the Protohistoric Period*. Rev. ed. Albuquerque: University of New Mexico Press, 1987.

———. "Marata and Its Neighbors." In *The Gran Chichimeca: Essays on the Archaeology and Ethnohistory of Northern Mesoamerica*, edited by Jonathan E. Reyman, 208–23. Aldershot, UK: Avebury, 1995.

———. "Mesoamerican Indians in the Early Southwest." *Ethnohistory* 21 (Winter 1974):25–36.

———. "Pecos and Trade." In *Across the Chichimec Sea: Papers in Honor of J. Charles Kelley*, edited by Carroll L. Riley and Basil C. Hedrick, 53–64. Carbondale: Southern Illinois University Press, 1978.

———. *Rio del Norte: People of the Upper Rio Grande from Earliest Times to the Pueblo Revolt*. Salt Lake City: University of Utah Press, 1995.

———. "The Road to Hawikuh: Trade and Trade Routes to Cíbola-Zuni during Late Prehistoric and Early Historic Times." *Kiva* 41 (1975):137–59.

———. "The Teya Indians of the Southwestern Plains." In *The Coronado Expedition to Tierra Nueva: The 1540–1542 Route Across the Southwest*, edited by Richard Flint and Shirley Cushing Flint, 320–43. Niwot, CO: University Press of Colorado, 1997.

Riley, Carroll L., and Joni L. Manson. "The Cíbola-Tiguex Route: Continuity and Change in the Southwest." *New Mexico Historical Review* 58, no. 4 (1983):347–67.

Robbins, Chandler S., Bertel Brun, and Herbert S. Zim. *A Field Guide to Field Identification: Birds of North America*. New York: Golden Press, 1966.

Robertson, Donald. *Mexican Manuscript Painting of the Early Colonial Period: The Metropolitan Schools*. Norman: University of Oklahoma Press, 1994.

Rodack, Madeleine Turrell. "Cíbola, from fray Marcos to Coronado." In *The Coronado Expedition to Tierra Nueva: The 1540–1542 Route Across the Southwest*, edited by Richard Flint and Shirley Cushing Flint, 102–15. Niwot, CO: University Press of Colorado, 1997.

Rodríguez de Montalvo, Garci. *Las Sergas de Esplandián*. Estudio introductorio de Salvador Bernabéu Albert. Zaragosa: Simon de Portonariis, 1586. Reprint, Madrid: Ediciones Doce Calles, 1998.

Romera Iruela, Luis, and María del Carmen Galbis Díez. *Catálogo de pasajeros a Indias durante los siglos XVI, XVII y XVIII*, vols. 4 and 5. Sevilla: Ministerio de Cultura, 1980.

Roscoe, Will. *The Zuni Man-Woman*. Albuquerque: University of New Mexico Press, 1991.

Ruiz Medrano, Ethelia. "La Política del Virrey Mendoza." In *Gobierno y sociedad en Nueva España: Segunda audiencia y Antonio de Mendoza*, 162–205. Michoacán: Colegio de Michoacán, 1991.

Sahagún, Bernardino de. *Florentine Codex: General History of the Things of New Spain*, book 12, *The Conquest of Mexico*. Edited and translated by Arthur J. O. Anderson and Charles E. Dibble. Salt Lake City: University of Utah Press, 1955.

Sarabia Viejo, María Justina. *Don Luis de Velasco, virrey de Nueva España, 1550–1564*. Sevilla: Escuela de Estudios Hispano-Americanos, 1978.

Sargent, Charles Sprague. *Manual of the Trees of North America*. 2 vols. Boston: Houghton Mifflin, 1922. Reprint, New York: Dover, 1965.

Sauer, Carl O. "The Credibility of the Fray Marcos Account." *New Mexico Historical Review* 16 (April 1941):233–43.

———. "The Discovery of New Mexico Reconsidered." *New Mexico Historical Review* 12, no. 3 (July 1937):270–87.

Sauer, Carl, and Donald Brand. "Pueblo Sites in Southeastern Arizona." *University of California Publications in Geography* 3 (Aug. 1930):415–58.

Schaafsma, Polly. *Warrior, Shield, and Star: Imagery and Ideology of Pueblo Warfare*. Santa Fe, NM: Western Edge Press, 2000.

Schäfer, Ernesto. *El Consejo Real y Supremo de las Indias: Su historia, organización y labor administrativa hasta la terminación de la Casa de Austria*. 2 vols. Sevilla: Universidad de Sevilla, 1935.

———. *Las Rúbricas del Consejo Real y Supremo de las Indias desde la fundación del consejo en 1524 hasta la terminación del reinado de los Austrias*. Sevilla: Universidad de Sevilla, 1934. Reprint, Nendeln, Liechtenstein: Klaus Reprint, 1975.

Schroeder, Albert H. "Pueblos Abandoned in Historic Times." In *Handbook of North American Indians*, vol. 9, *Southwest*, edited by Alfonso Ortiz, 236–54. Washington, DC: Smithsonian Institution Press, 1979.

———. "Vásquez de Coronado and the Southern Tiwa Pueblos." In *Archaeology, Art, and Anthropology: Collected Papers in Honor of J. J. Brody*, edited by Meliha S. Duran and David T. Kirkpatrick, 185–91. Papers of the Archaeological Society of New Mexico, no. 18. Albuquerque: Archaeological Society of New Mexico, 1992.

Schwaller, John Frederick. *The Church and Clergy in Sixteenth-Century Mexico*. Albuquerque: University of New Mexico Press, 1987.

Scott, Samuel Parsons, trans., and Robert I. Burns, ed. *Las Siete Partidas*. 5 vols. Philadelphia: University of Pennsylvania Press, 2001.

Sedgwick, Mrs. William T. *Acoma, the Sky City: A Study in Pueblo Indian History and Civilization*. Cambridge, MA: Harvard University Press, 1927.

Seed, Patricia. "The Astrolabe." In *Ceremonies of Possession in Europe's Conquest of the New World, 1492–1640*, by Patricia Seed, 120–28. Cambridge: Cambridge University Press, 1995.

Semo, Enrique. *The History of Capitalism in Mexico: Its Origins, 1521–1763*. Translated by Lidia Lozano. Austin: University of Texas Press, 1993.

Siméon, Rémi. *Diccionario de la lengua nahuatl o mexicana*. Translated by Josefina Oliva de Coll. México, DF: Siglo Ventiuno Editores, 1977.

Simmons, Marc. "History of Pueblo-Spanish Relations to 1821." In *Handbook of North American Indians*, vol. 9, *Southwest*, edited by Alfonso Ortiz, 178–93. Washington, DC: Smithsonian Institution Press, 1979.

———. *The Last Conquistador: Juan de Oñate and the Settling of the Far Southwest*. Norman: University of Oklahoma Press, 1991.

Simon and Schuster's International Dictionary, English/Spanish, Spanish/English. Edited by Tana de Gámez. New York: Macmillan, 1973.

Simpson, James H. "Coronado's March in Search of the 'Seven Cities of Cibola' and Discussion of Their Probable Location." *Annual Report of the Board of Regents of the Smithsonian Institution for 1869*, 309–40. Washington, DC: n.p., 1872.

———. *Navaho Expedition: Journal of a Military Reconnaissance from Santa Fe, New Mexico, to the Navaho Country, Made in 1849*. Edited by Frank McNitt. Norman: University of Oklahoma Press, 1964.

Simpson, Lesley Byrd. *The Encomienda in New Spain: The Beginning of Spanish Mexico*. Rev. ed. Berkeley: University of California Press, 1982.

Smith, Marvin T. *Archaeology of Aboriginal Culture Change in the Interior Southeast: Depopulation during the Early Historic Period*. Gainesville: University of Florida Press, 1987.

Smith, Thomas Buckingham, ed. *Colección de varios documentos para la historia de la Florida y tierras adyacentes*. London: Trübner [1857].

Smith, Watson, Richard B. Woodbury, and Nathalie F. S. Woodbury. *The Excavation of Hawikuh by Frederick Webb Hodge: Report of the Hendricks-Hodge Expedition, 1917–1923*. Contributions from the Museum of the American Indian–Heye Foundation, vol. 20. New York: Museum of the American Indian–Heye Foundation, 1966.

Snow, David. "'Por allí no hay losa ni se hace': Gilded Men and Glazed Pottery on the Southern Plains." In *The Coronado Expedition to Tierra Nueva: The 1540–1542 Route Across the Southwest*, edited by Richard Flint and Shirley Cushing Flint, 344–64. Niwot, CO: University Press of Colorado, 1997.

Sobel, Dava. *Longitude: The True Story of a Lone Genius Who Solved the Greatest Scientific Problem of His Time*. London: Fourth Estate, 1996.

Sobel, Dava, and William J. H. Andrewes. *The Illustrated Longitude*. New York: Walker, 1998.

La Sociedad de Bibliófilos Españoles. *Nobiliario de conquistadores de Indias*. Madrid: M. Tello, 1892.

Stevens, Henry, and Fred W. Lucas, trans. and eds. *The New Laws of the Indies for the Good Treatment and Preservation of the Indians*. London: Chiswick Press, 1893. Reprint, Amsterdam: N. Isreal, 1968.

Stevens, Thomas Wood. *The Entrada of Coronado: A Spectacular Historic Drama*. Albuquerque: Coronado Cuarto Centennial Commission, 1940.

Stevenson, James. "Illustrated Catalogue of the Collections Obtained from the Indians of New Mexico and Arizona in 1879." In *Second Annual Report of the Bureau of Ethnology to the Secretary of the Smithsonian Institution, 1880–1881*, 307–422. Washington. DC: Government Printing Office, 1883.

Stevenson, Mathilda Coxe. *The Zuñi Indians: Their Mythology, Esoteric Fraternities, and Ceremonies*. Twenty-third Annual Report of the Bureau of American Ethnology, 1901–2, 3–634. Washington, DC: Government Printing Office, 1904. Reprint, Glorieta, NM: Rio Grande Press, 1984.

Stewart, Kenneth M. "Yumans: Introduction." In *Handbook of North American Indians*, vol. 10, *Southwest*, edited by Alfonso Ortiz, 1–3. Washington, DC: Smithsonian Institution Press, 1983.

Strout, Clevy Lloyd. "Flora and Fauna Mentioned in the Journals of the Coronado Expedition." *Great Plains Journal* 11, no. 1 (1971):5–40.

———. "A Linguistic Study of the Journals of the Coronado Expedition," Ph.D. diss., University of Colorado, 1958.

Suárez Acosta, José, Félix Rodríguez Lorenzo, and Carmelo L. Quintero Padrón. *Conquista y colonización*. In *Historia popular de Canarias*, vol. 2. Santa Cruz de Tenerife: Centro de la Cultura Popular Canaria, 1988.

Tabales, Miguel Ángel, Ana Salud Romo, and Enrique García. "Nuevos avances en e estudio del Alminar (La Giralda)." In *VIII Centenario de la Giralda, 1198–1998*, edited by Teodor Falcón Márquez, 109–27. Sevilla: Caja Sur Publicaciones, 1998.

Tello, fray Antonio. *Crónica miscelánea de la sancta provincia de Xalisco, libro segundo*. 2 vols. Guadalajara: Gobierno del Estado de Jalisco and Universidad de Guadalajara, 1968.

———. *Crónica miscelánea de la sancta provincia de Xaliso, libro tercero*. Guadalajara: Editorial Font, 1942.

———. *Libro segundo de la Crónica miscelánea, en que se trata de la conquista espiritual y temporal de la santa provincia de Xalisco en el Nuevo Reino de la Galicia y Nueva Vizcaya y descubrimiento del Nuevo México*. Guadalajara, México: Republica Literaria, 1891. Reprint, México, DF: Editorial Porrúa, 1997.

Ternaux-Compans, Henri, trans. and ed. "Instruction donnée par don Antonio de Mendoza." In *Voyages, relations et memoires originaux pour servir a l'histoire de la decouverte de l'Amerique*, vol. 9, 256–84. Paris: A. Bertrand, 1838.

———. "Mendoza to Carlos V [by the last ships]." In *Voyages, relations et memoires originaux pour servir a l'histoire de la decouverte de l'Amerique*, vol. 9, 285–90. Paris: A. Bertrand, 1838.

———. "Mendoza to Carlos V, April 17, 1540." In *Voyages, relations et memoires originaux pour servir a l'histoire de la decouverte de l'Amerique*, vol. 9, 290–98. Paris: A. Bertrand, 1838.

———. "Relation de Frère Marcos de Niza." In *Voyages, relations et memoires originaux pour servir a l'histoire de la decouverte de l'Amerique*, vol. 9, 256–84. Paris: A. Bertrand, 1838.

———. "Relation de la navigation et de la découverte faite par le capitaine Fernando Alarcon." In *Voyages, relations et memoires originaux pour servir a l'histoire de la decouverte de l'Amerique*, vol. 9, 299–348. Paris: A. Bertrand, 1838.

Thomas, Hugh. *Conquest: Montezuma, Cortés, and the Fall of Old Mexico*. New York: Simon and Schuster, 1995.

Udall, Stewart L. *To the Inland Empire: Coronado and Our Spanish Legacy*. Garden City, NY: Doubleday, 1987.

Undreiner, George J. "Fray Marcos de Niza and His Journey to Cibola." *The Americas* 3 (April 1947):415–86.

U.S. Department of Commerce, National Oceanic and Atmospheric Administration. *Monthly Normals of Temperature, Precipitation, and Heating and Cooling Days, 1941–1970: New Mexico*. Asheville, NC: Environmental Data Service, 1973.

U.S. Department of the Interior. Geologic Survey. 7.5-Minute Topographic Quadrangle. "Laguna Dam, Arizona, California." 1979 ed.

———. National Park Service. National Register of Historic Places. Inventory-Nomination Form, n.d., 5.

Utrera, fray Cipriano de. *Noticias históricas de Santo Domingo*. Edited by Emilio Rodríguez Demorizi. 6 vols. Santo Domingo, Dominican Republic: Editora Taller, 1978–83.

Van West, Carla R., and Henri D. Grissino-Mayer. "Dendroclimatic Reconstruction." In *Archaeological Data Recovery in the New Mexico Transportation Corridor and First Five-Year Permit Area, Fence Lake Coal Mine Project, Catron County, New Mexico*, vol. 2, Part 1, *Draft Report*. Tucson, AZ: Statistical Research, 2004.

Vargas, Victoria D. *Copper Bell Trade Patterns in the Prehistoric U.S. Southwest and Northwest Mexico*. Tucson: Arizona State Museum, University of Arizona, 1995.

Varner, John Grier, and Jeannette Johnson Varner. *Dogs of the Conquest*. Norman: University of Oklahoma Press, 1983.

Vázquez de Coronado, Francisco. "Letter from Vázquez de Coronado to Mendoza, San Miguel de Culiacán, March 8, 1539." In *Terzo Volume delle navigationi et viaggi*, Giovanni Battista Ramusio, fols. 354v–355r. Venice: Stamperia de Giunti, 1556.

Velasco, Juan de. *Historia del reino de Quito en la América meridional: Historia antigua*. Quito: Editorial Benjamín Carrión, 1996.

Velasco, Luis de. *Relación de las encomiendas de indios hechas en Nueva España a los conquistadores y pobladores de ella, año de 1564*. Publicados por France V. Scholes y Eleanor B. Adams. México, DF: Jose Porrúa e hijos, 1955.

Vierra, Bradley J. *A Sixteenth-Century Spanish Campsite in the Tiguex Province*. Laboratory of Anthropology Notes 475. Santa Fe: Museum of New Mexico, Research Section, 1989.

Vierra, Bradley J., and Stanley M. Hordes. "Let the Dust Settle: A Review of the Coronado Campsite in the Tiguex Province." In *The Coronado Expedition to Tierra Nueva: The 1540–1542 Route Across the Southwest*, edited by Richard Flint and Shirley Cushing Flint, 249–61. Niwot, CO: University Press of Colorado, 1997.

Vigil, Ralph H. *Alonso de Zorita: Royal Judge and Christian Humanist, 1512–1585*. Norman: University of Oklahoma Press, 1987.

Vitoria, Francisco de. "On the Evangelization of Unbelievers." In *Colonial Latin America: A Documentary History*, edited by Kenneth Mills, William B. Taylor, and Sandra Lauderdale Graham, 65–77. Wilmington, DE: Scholarly Resources, 2002.

von Habsburg, Otto. *Charles V*. Translated by Michael Ross. New York: Praeger, 1969.

Wagner, Henry R. "Fr. Marcos de Niza." *New Mexico Historical Review* 9 (April 1934):184–227.

———. *Spanish Voyages to the Northwest Coast of America in the Sixteenth Century*. San Francisco: California Historical Society, 1929.

Walsh, Jane MacLaren. "Myth and Imagination in the American Story: The Coronado Expedition, 1540–1542." Ph.D. diss., Catholic University of America, 1993.

Warren, A. Helene. "The Glaze Paint Wares of the Upper Middle Rio Grande Valley." In *Adaptive Change in the Northern Rio Grande Valley*, vol. 4, edited by Jan V. Biella and Richard C. Chapman, 187–216. Archeological Investigations in Cochiti Reservoir, New Mexico. Albuquerque: University of New Mexico, Office of Contract Archeology, 1979.

Warren, Fintan B. *Vasco de Quiroga and His Pueblo-Hospitals of Santa Fe*. Washington, DC: Academy of American Franciscan History, 1963.

Weber, David J. "Fray Marcos de Niza and the Historians." In *Myth and the History of the Hispanic Southwest*, David J. Weber, 19–32. Albuquerque: University of New Mexico Press, 1988.

———. *The Spanish Frontier in North America*. New Haven, CT: Yale University Press, 1992.

Weddle, Robert S. "Coastal Exploration and Mapping: A Concomitant to the Entradas." In *The Mapping of the Entradas into the Greater Southwest*, edited by Dennis Reinhartz and Gerald D. Saxon, 107–31. Norman: University of Oklahoma Press, 1998.

Wedel, Mildred Mott. "The Indian They Called Turco." In *Pathways to Plains Prehistory: Anthropological Perspectives of Plains Natives and Their Pasts*, edited by Don G. Wyckoff and Jack L. Hofman, 153–62. Duncan, OK: Cross Timbers Press, 1982.

Wedel, Waldo R. *Archeological Remains in Central Kansas and Their Possible Bearing on the Location of Quivira*. Smithsonian Miscellaneous Collections, 101, no. 7. Washington, DC: Smithsonian Institution, 1942.

———. "Coronado, Quivira, and Kansas: An Archeologist's View." Lecture delivered at the Coronado-Quivira Museum, Lyons, Kansas, Nov. 3, 1990.

———. "Coronado's Route to Quivira." *Plains Anthropologist* 15, no. 49 (1970):161–68.

West, Delno C. "Medieval Ideas of Apocalyptic Mission and the Early Franciscans in Mexico." *The Americas* 45 (Jan. 1989):293–313.

Williams, J. W. "Coronado: From the Rio Grande to the Concho." *West Texas Historical Association Yearbook* 35 (1959):66–98.

Winship, George Parker. "Bibliographic Note." In *The Coronado Expedition, 1540–1542*, edited and translated by George Parker Winship, *Fourteenth Annual Report of the Bureau of American Ethnology of the Smithsonian Institution, 1892–1893*, Part 1, 107–8.

Washington, DC: Government Printing Office, 1896. Reprint, Chicago: Rio Grande Press, 1964.

Winship, George Parker, ed. and trans. *The Coronado Expedition, 1540–1542*. In *Fourteenth Annual Report of the Bureau of American Ethnology of the Smithsonian Institution for 1892–1893*, Part 1, 329–613. Washington, DC: Government Printing Office, 1896. Reprint, Chicago: Rio Grande Press, 1964.

Witty, Tom. "The Tobias Archeological Site/Museum of the Quivira Indian." Unpublished paper, 1990, in possession of the editors.

Wright, Barton. *Kachinas of the Zuni*. Flagstaff, AZ: Northland Press, 1985.

Yocom, Charles, William Weber, Richard Beidleman, and Donald Malick. *Wildlife of the Southern Rocky Mountains*. Rev. ed. Healdsburg, CA: Naturegraph, 1969.

Young, Gloria A., and Michael P. Hoffmann, eds. *The Expedition of Hernando de Soto West of the Mississippi, 1541–1543*. Fayetteville: University of Arkansas Press, 1993.

Zaldívar, Vicente de. "An Account of Sergeant Major Vicente de Zaldívar's Expedition to the Buffalo Herds, September 15 to November 8, 1598." In *Zaldívar and the Cattle of Cíbola: Vicente de Zaldívar's Expedition to the Buffalo Plains in 1598. The Spanish Texts*, edited by Jerry R. Craddock; translated by John H. R. Polt, 32–36. Dallas, TX: William P. Clements Center for Southwest Studies, Southern Methodist University, 1999.

Zavala, Silvio A. *La encomienda indiana*. 2nd ed. México, DF: Editorial Porrúa, 1973.

Zumárraga, Juan de. "Letter to an Unknown Religious from Juan de Zumárraga, México, April 4, 1537," translated by Henry R. Wagner. In "Fray Marcos de Niza," Henry R. Wagner, *New Mexico Historical Review* 9 (April 1934):184–227.

Index

Guzmán, Nuño Beltrán de (former governor of Nueva Galicia): 1, 91, 93, 120, 123, 128, 131, 389, 440; at Culiacán, 386, 437; bio., 387, 415, 438, 470, 594; conflict with Cortés, 387, 438; dispute with Mendoza, 95, 106, 272; *encomiendas* in Nueva Galicia, 23, 27, 41, 44; expedition of, 47, 49; failed to find Seven Ciudades, 45-46, 47, 49; reconnoitered Nueva Galicia, 386-87, 437-38; report from Tejo, 386, 437

Habana, San Cristóbal de (Cuba): 92, 94, 96, 98, 101, 102, 105, 633doc7n41; geo. data, 634doc8n25

Habicht-Mauche, Judith (anthropologist): 509

Hacus: see **Acuco**

Hakluyt, Richard (publisher): 32, 46, 64, 187, 253

Hallenbeck, Cleve (author): 61, 63, 64

Hammond, George P. and Agapito Rey (authors): 5, 6, 7, 8, 10, 64, 107, 135, 136, 138, 187, 224, 234, 253, 290, 304, 318, 383, 511

Haraee: see **Arahey**

Hartmann, William K. (author): 61, 62

Hassig, Ross (anthropologist): 167

Hawikku (NM): 72, 84, 495; arrival of expedition at, 2; death of Esteban at, 513, 520; distance to Dowa Yalanne, 293, 295; map, 18

Haxa, Haya (on Mississippi River): 408, 463, 679doc28n305

Hemes: see **Jemez**

Heredia, Cristóbal de (*escribano*): 345-77, passim; bio, 668doc27n95

Hermosillo (SON, Mexico): map, 17

Hernández, Alonso (expedition member): 150, 162; bio., 608

Hernández, Andrés (expedition member): 147, 159; bio., 608, 641doc12n108

Hernández, Bartolomé: witness, 348, 373

Hernández, Diego (*alférez*): 143, 155; 346, 371; bio, 608, 668doc27n101

Hernández, Gonzalo (expedition member): 141, 154; bio., 608

Hernández, Graviel (expedition member): 150, 162; bio., 608

Hernández, Juan (expedition member): bio., 608

Hernández, Luis (expedition member): 143, 155; bio., 608

Hernández, Manuel (expedition member): 143, 156; bio., 608

Hernández, Martín (expedition member): 143, 156; bio., 608

Hernández, Martín (expedition member): 142, 154; bio., 608

Hernández, Miguel (expedition member): 149, 161; bio., 608

Hernández, Nofre (Onofre) (expedition member): 142, 154; bio., 608

Hernández, Pero (expedition member): 142, 154; bio., 608

Hernández, Pero (expedition member): 143, 156; bio., 608

Hernández Calvo, Pero (expedition member): 147, 159; bio., 608

Hernández Chillón, Martín (expedition member): 149, 161; bio., 608

Hernández de Arriba, Francisco (expedition member): bio., 608

Hernández de Guadalajara, Pero (expedition member): 149, 161; bio., 608

Hernández Moreno, Cristóbal (expedition member): 147, 159; bio., 608

Herrera, Andrés de (*escribano*): 330, 337, 339, 343, 354, 361, 363, 368

Herrera y Tordesillos, Antonio (historian): 186

Hispaniola, Española: 285, 311, 314; geo. data, 633doc7n21

Hodge, Frederick W. (anthropologist): 6, 289

Homem, Horta (expedition member): 147, 159, 641doc12n111; bio., 609

Honduras: 274, 280, 285, 287, 288

Horses and mules: 201, 218, 235, 239, 245, 248, 260, 268, 292, 294, 335, 338, 349, 351, 352, 358, 362, 374, 375, 376, 517, 524, 537, 538, 540, 542, 547, 548, 549, 551, 552, 554, 556, 557, 559, 561, 564, 565, 569, 570, 572, 573, 576, 577; as pack animals, 291, 294, 392, 444; auction of, 334, 358; death and wounding of, 255, 256, 258, 264, 265, 266, 292, 294, 320, 324, 329, 405, 409, 427, 428, 429, 460, 465, 484, 486, 487, 500, 501-02, 506, 507, 558, 562, 565, 566, 571, 575, 578, 579, 688doc28n540, 692doc29n84; loss of, 255, 264, 408, 464, 497, 503, 561, 563, 564, 574, 575, 577, 690doc29n38; necessary for conquest, 434, 493; number of, 135, 138, 139-50, 152-62, 432, 490; stolen, 403, 457; worn out, 256, 265, 558, 561, 570, 574

Hoz, Cristóbal de la (expedition member): 140, 153; bio., 609

Hozes, Francisca de (expedition member): 175, 177, 178, 181, 183, 184; bio., 609, 643doc14n29; wife of Alonso Sánchez, 136

Huelva (Huerve), Pedro de (expedition member): 327; bio., 609; witness, 335, 341, 359, 366

Huerta, García de (expedition member): bio., 609

Hurtado de Mendoza, Diego (lt. and captain general): bio., 651doc18n14; fleet of, 624doc4n22; reconnaissance of Mar del Sur, 244, 248

Hurtado de Mendoza, Diego (brother of viceroy Mendoza): Spanish ambassador to Venice, 31, 309

Hurtado de Mendoza, Luis (captain general of Granada): 21, 637doc10n13

Ibarra, Francisco de (governor of Nueva Vizcaya): 382, 670doc28n25

Illness: 165, 169, 170, 196, 213, 238, 241, 326, 329, 332, 356, 642doc13n47, 646doc15n67

Indian allies: 255, 264, 564, 576, 650doc17n37, 688doc28n564; casualties of, 3, 165, 235, 239, 256, 265, 291, 294, 403, 457, 497, 501-02, 503, 507, 557, 558, 562, 566, 570, 575, 578, 624doc4n20; fled, 255, 264; illus., frontispiece and 166; impact on conquest, 165; majority of expedition, 2, 165; missing from official record, 164; number of, 389, 392, 432, 440, 444, 490, 558, 570, 641doc13n4, 671doc28n99, 688doc28n574; names of, 166; origin of, 165-66; 406, 427, 429, 461, 485, 487; organization of, 137; preceded advance guard, 135, 164, 165; present as warriors, 135, 164, 403, 457, 673doc28n146; record of, 1576, 169, 170; remained in Tierra Nueva, 3, 135; 428, 486; roles of, 164, 165; sent ahead of Marcos de Niza, 48, 50; slaves and servants of, 164; sufferings of, 257, 265, 395, 449; with Nuño de Guzmán, 47, 49; with units of expedition, 48, 50, 65, 78, 135, 303, 392, 431, 444, 490, 649doc16n44; wives of, 164

Indian rights movement: 107; see also Bartolomé de las Casas

Iñigo, Francisco (*vecino*): 53, 56

Interpreters: 39, 42; inability of, 191, 192, 195, 209, 210, 213; lack of, 244, 248, 321, 324; use of 189, 190, 192, 193, 194, 197, 198, 200, 203, 207, 208, 210, 211, 212, 214, 215, 217, 220, 257, 262, 265, 270, 387, 393, 394, 399, 403, 438, 446, 448, 453, 457, 498, 504

Photo by Julia C. Breyer

RICHARD FLINT and SHIRLEY CUSHING FLINT, historians and Spanish paleographers, are among the foremost authorities on the Coronado expedition. They have researched in Mexico, Spain, and the United States and have directed two conferences on the expedition. Separately and in collaboration, the Flints have published many articles as well as three books, including *Great Cruelties Have Been Reported: The 1544 Investigation of the Coronado Expedition* (SMU, 2002).